TECHNICAL PROGAM PLANNING COMMITTEE

WALTER G. REUTER
E.G.&G. Idaho, Inc.
Idaho Falls, ID
Chairman

JONATHAN D. ROGERS
Sandia National Labs
Albuquerque, NM
Vice-Chairman

JONATHAN S. EPSTEIN
E.G.&G. Idaho, Inc.
Idaho Falls, ID
Vice-Chairman

WEI-YANG LU
University of Kentucky
Lexington, KY
Education

HENRY R. BUSBY
Ohio State University
Columbus, OH
Research

MARK E. TUTTLE
University of Washington
Seattle, WA
Technical Divisions Council

ALBERT S. KOBAYASHI
University of Washington
Seattle, WA
Intersociety Liaison

KENNETH A. GALIONE
SEM, Inc.
Bethel, CT
Managing Director

KATHERINE M. RAMSAY
SEM, Inc.
Bethel, CT
Conference Manager

EXECUTIVE BOARD 1991-1992

WILLIAM L. FOURNEY
University of Maryland
College Park, MD
President 1991-1992

KENNETH A. GALIONE
SEM, Inc.
Bethel, CT
Secretary 1991-1992

MARK E. TUTTLE
University of Washington
Seattle, WA
Member 1990-1992

FRANK D. ADAMS
Wright Laboratory
Wright Patterson AFB, OH
President-Elect 1991-1992

ALBERT S. KOBAYASHI
University of Washington
Seattle, WA
Past President 1989-1990

ELIZABETH A. FUCHS
Sandia National Labs
Livermore, CA
Member 1991-1993

GARY CLOUD
Michigan State University
East Lansing, MI
Vice-President 1991-1992

ROBERT F. SULLIVAN
IBM Corporation
San Jose, CA
Past President 1990-1991

ROBERT T. REESE
Sandia National Labs
Albuquerque, NM
Member 1991-1993

SUSAN K. FOSS
Deere & Co. Tech. Ctr.
Moline, IL
Treasurer 1991-1992

JOHN HALL
Micro Engineering II, Inc.
Upland, CA
Member 1990-1992

ABOUT SEM - The Society for Experimental Mechanics, Inc. (formerly) the Society for Experimental Stress Analysis (SESA) was founded in 1943 as a non-profit scientific and educational organization. Its objective is to "promote and encourage the furtherance of knowledge pertaining to experimental mechanics".

The members of SEM represent a unique network of leaders in experimental mechanics in the U.S. and abroad. They are active in academia, government and industrial research and development and include scientists, engineers, manufacturers, consultants, users and venders of plant equipment, services and systems. SEM also maintains close contact with other professional groups throughout the world with cooperative meetings and joint membership options.

Proceedings of the

VII International Congress

on Experimental Mechanics

COSPONSORED BY:

- SOCIETY FOR EXPERIMENTAL
  MECHANICS, INC.

- AMERICAN SOCIETY FOR
  NONDESTRUCTIVE TESTING

- BRITISH SOCIETY FOR STRAIN
  MEASUREMENT

- EUROPEAN PERMANENT
  COMMITTEE FOR EXPERIMENTAL
  MECHANICS

- IMEKO-TC 3 AND

- ITALIAN ASSOCIATION FOR
  STRESS ANALYSIS

- JAPAN SOCIETY OF MECHANICAL ENGINEERS

- KOREAN SOCIETY OF MECHANICAL ENGINEERS

- SEM REPUBLIC OF CHINA SECTION -TAIWAN

- SHOCK AND VIBRATION
  INFORMATION ANALYSIS CENTER

- SOUTH AFRICAN SOCIETY FOR
  EXPERIMENTAL MECHANICS

- SESA SECTION OF SOUTH AFRICA

- STRUCTURAL ...

VOLUME I

THE SOCIETY FOR EXPERIMENTAL MECHANICS, INC.
7 School Street
Bethel, Connecticut 06801 USA
(203) 79)-6373; FAX: (203) 790-4472

ISSN # 1046-672X
ISBN # 0-912053-38-0

TABLE OF CONTENTS

SESSION 17   APPLICATION TO DYNAMICS

SESSION 18   OPTICAL METHODS II-APPLICATIONS IN ELECTRONICS AND MATERIAL SCIENCE

SESSION 19   PERFORMANCE EVALUATION OF CIVIL STRUCTURES I

SESSION 20   PHOTOELASTICITY II

SESSION 25   FATIGUE FRACTURE II

SESSION 26   OPTICAL METHODS III

SESSION 27   STRAIN GAGES

SESSION 46   TECHNICAL COMMITTEE ON STRAIN GAGES II

See Session 41 for papers presented in this session

SESSION 47   TRANSDUCERS AND SENSORS I

SESSION 48   TESTING OF CIVIL ENGINEERING STRUCTURES

SESSION 49   FATIGUE FRACTURE III

SESSION 50   BRITTLE MATERIALS AND CRACK PROPAGATION

SESSION 51   COMPOSITES V

SESSION 56   FIBER OPTICS AND EXPERIMENTAL MECHANICS

SESSION 57   AUTOMOTIVE APPLICATIONS OF DYNAMICS

SESSION 58   COMPOSITES VI

SESSION 59   FRACTURE III

SESSION 60   FUNDAMENTALS OF ACOUSTICS AND NOISE CONTROL

SESSION 61   RESIDUAL STRESS III

SESSION 62   DIGITAL IMAGE CORRELATION AND FRINGE ANALYSIS TECHNIQUE

SESSION 68   COMPOSITES VIII – DELAMINATION AND CRACKS

Papers from this session were placed in other sessions as follows:

Strain Rate Effect on Crack Growth Behavior in a Composite Polymeric Material (moved to Session 51, page 1205)

Crack Growth Behavior and Fracture Surface Characteristics of Viscoelastic Expoxy Resin (moved to Session 58, page 1396)

SESSION 69   FRACTURE V

PAPERS OUT OF ORDER

A VISUAL APPROACH TO STRUCTURAL DESIGN IN ARCHITECTURE

G. Matsui

FOREWORD

The visualisation of stresses and deformations is extremely useful in structural engineering as a tool for research, design, and education. This paper is an abstract of the author's achievements in this field over several decades.

INTRODUCTION

In photoelasticity, stresses on free boundaries can be determined easily. As an example, stresses in the vicinity of the Pharaoh's Chamber, in Giza's famous Cheops Pyramid will be shown. This structure is 150 m high and 240x240 m wide at its base. At first the overall state of stresses was examined by using a finite element analysis. A homogenous material was assumed with a Young's modulus of 500.0 ton/cm^2, a Poisson ratio of 0.24, and a specific weight of 2.6 ton/m^3. At the Chamber, which is located roughly in the centre of the Pyramid (both plan-wise and height-wise), the compressive stresses in the directions of the vertical and horizontal axes of the Pyramid were determined as 8.5 kg/cm^2 and 1.6 kg/cm^2 respectively. That is, the ratio of horizontal and vertical compressive stresses was approximately 20 percent.

Right above the Pharaoh's Chamber, five beams are stacked on spacer stones, as shown, in Fig.1. This part is often referred to as the "load distribution room". Photoelastic experiments were carried out both without, and with, the consideration of that part; Figures. 2 to 4, and 5 to 7 show the models, photos, and stress distributions, respectively. No significant differences could be monitored in the stress distribution between the two cases. Furthermore, after transforming the stresses measured on the models to the real structure, a maximum compressive stress of only approximately 18.0 kg/cm^2 was found; that is less than 10 percent of the compressive strength (300 to 400 kg/cm^2) of stone. One may conclude that the "stress distribution room" was actually not required, as far as the statics of the Pyramid is concerned.

Much speculation has been aired by archeologists on the possibility of the existence of some other void, in the Pyramid, not far from the Pharaoh's Chamber. In addition, according to survey reports, extensive cracks have been found on the beams of the "load distribution room" mentioned before. In order to consider a large void being at one side of the Pharaoh's Chamber, the experiment was repeated in a similar arrangement to that shown in Fig.5, but with no horizontal loading at the left side of the model. Figures 8 and 9 show the results; high tensile stresses were measured at the beam ends that would correspond to approximately 30.0 kg/cm^2 on the real structure. It could be an explanation to the cracking of the stone.

G. Matsui is professor emeritus of structural engineering in the Department of Architecture, University of Waseda, Tokyo, Japan, and member of the board in The Japan Society for Photoelasticity, Tokyo, Japan.

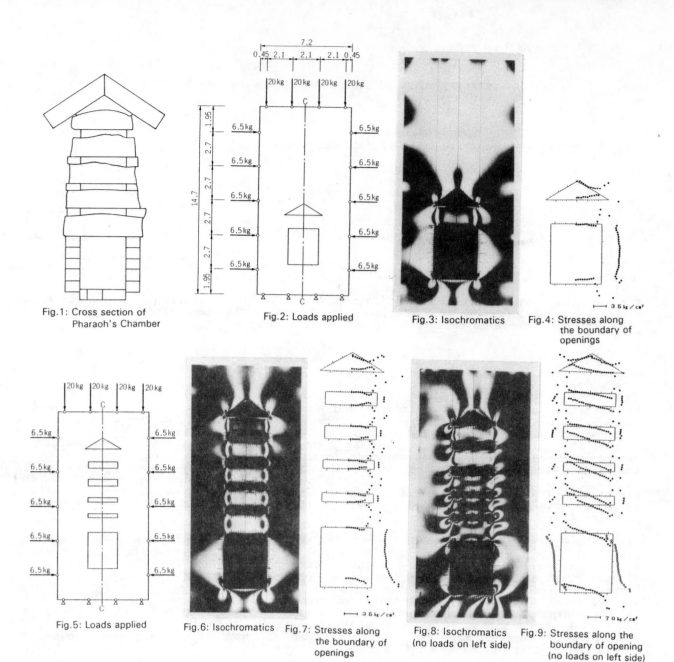

Fig.1: Cross section of Pharaoh's Chamber

Fig.2: Loads applied

Fig.3: Isochromatics

Fig.4: Stresses along the boundary of openings

Fig.5: Loads applied

Fig.6: Isochromatics

Fig.7: Stresses along the boundary of openings

Fig.8: Isochromatics (no loads on left side)

Fig.9: Stresses along the boundary of opening (no loads on left side)

As a further example for determining stresses on free boundaries, arched openings will be dealt with. Arches have long been used in architecture, mostly in stone and brick construction. In the experiments to be introduced hereinafter, the rib of, and the infill construction around, the arch were assumed to be a homogenous continuum. It was also assumed that the openings are regularly placed in an infinitely long wall. A typical test piece and arrangement is shown, in Fig.10. (Note that arches are always compressed in reality; tensile loading was however applied in testing for convenience.) Horizontal and vertical tensile loads were applied simultaneously, whereas their ratio P_y/P_x was in correspondence with the Poisson ratio (ν)

Five different types of opening (see Fig.11) were investigated by three different Poisson ratios (ν = 0.00, 0.16, and 0.24). A collection of the test photos, and the corresponding stress diagrams are shown, in Figures 12, and 13, respectively. The continuous lines in the stress diagrams indicate the results obtained through the theory of elasticity by applying conformal transformations of the approximated shapes of arches on to the infinite plane.

It is well known that significant tensile stresses can be harmful by causing cracks around the crown of an arch; judging from this point of view, a round arch, for example, is less favourable than a pointed one.

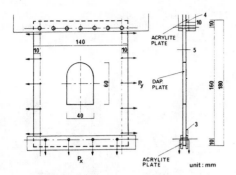

Fig.10: Photoelastic experiment

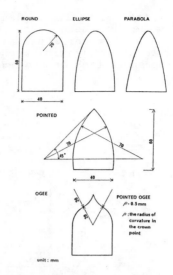

Fig.11: Arched openings

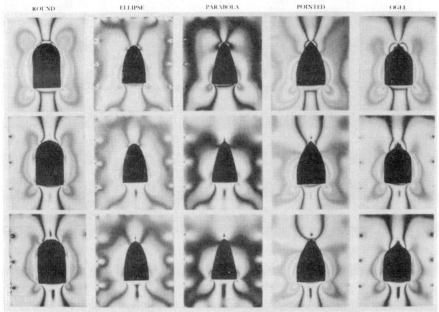

Fig.12: Isochromatics around arched openings

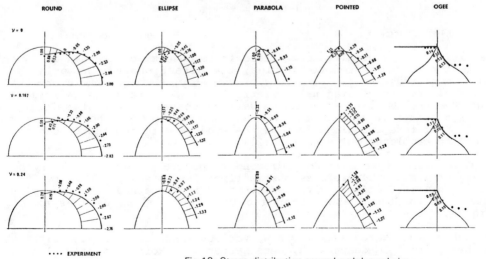

•••• EXPERIMENT
——— THEORY

Fig.13: Stress distribution around arch boundaries

As a third example of free boundaries, plane frames will be shown. In slender structural members, bending stresses can usually be assumed as being of a triangular distribution along the height of a member while normal stresses as being constant. Hence, bending moments and axial forces in structural members can be calculated from the axial stresses measured along the top and bottom of the member. Figures 14 to 18 show such a case.

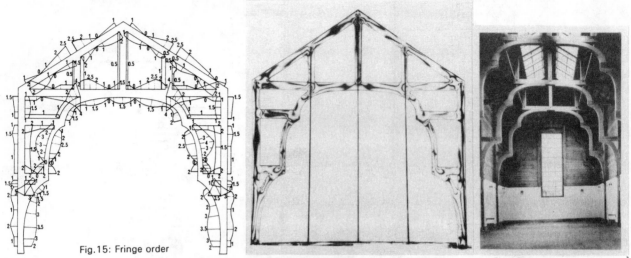

Fig.15: Fringe order

Fig.14: Isochromatics for vertical loads, Community Hall, Higashino

Fig.18: Interior photo of Community Hall, on completion

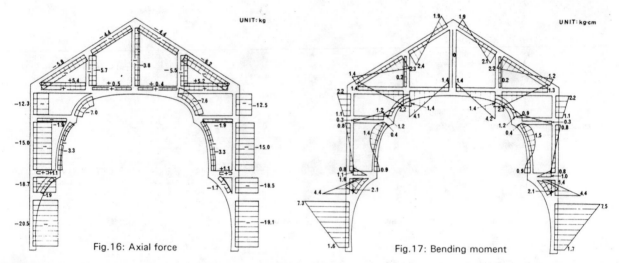

Fig.16: Axial force

Fig.17: Bending moment

In photoelasticity, it is usually more difficult to determine stresses in interior points since, unlike the case of free boundaries, the directions of the principal stresses should also be measured. In special points of symmetry, however, the aforementioned angle is known: e.g., in points of diagonal symmetry it is 45 degrees. As an example of application, Fig.19 shows the test of a shear wall which was to resist seismic forces. The shear stresses measured in the central axes of the junction of the four windows (Fig.20) were too high. Therefore the dimensions of the windows were reduced as can be seen on the photograph of the completed building (Fig.21).

When bracing is required at a window, diamond shape braces would normally be preferable to cross shape ones as these are less obstructive. It was easily shown by photoelasticity that as far as their effectiveness to resist shear is concerned, the two types are equivalent (Figures 22 to 25). Diamond shaped braces can even be used as an architectural feature (Fig.26).

Leaving the subject of photoelasticity now, various kinds of analogies with the deflected shape of membranes will be dealt with, hereinafter; the Moire method will be used for the visualisation of contour lines of membranes.

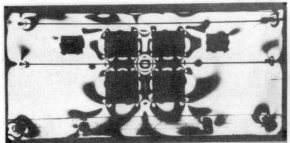

Fig.19: Isochromatics, junction of four windows, Town Hall, Mano

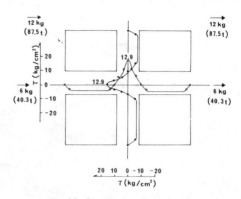

Fig.20: Shear stress in centre lines

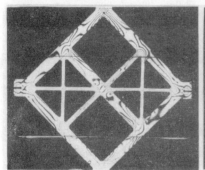

Fig.21: Elevation of Town Hall, on completion

Fig.22: Isochromatics, cross braces   Fig.24: Isochromatics, diamond braces

Fig.26: Elevation of building, Faculty of Engineering, Univ. Waseda

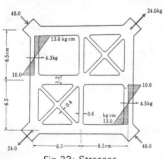

Fig.23: Stresses

Fig.25: Stresses

At first, streamline curved beams will be introduced. By denoting the directions of the principal beams α, and that of the secondary beams β, so that $\beta = \alpha + 90°$, the resulting curved beam grid is considered as a field of orthogonal trajectories. Shear forces in the primary beams are denoted as Q_α; those in the secondary beams denoted as Q_β are assumed to vanish on the entire field investigated. The state of equilibrium in a differentially small portion of this field is depicted, in Fig.27. In case of uniformly distributed loading, the load differential is zero, and the equation of equilibrium takes the following form:

$$\frac{\partial^2 Q\alpha}{\partial x^2} + \frac{\partial^2 Q\alpha}{\partial y^2} = 0$$

This is the Laplace equation which equally applies to the potential of fluids and to the deflection of non-loaded membranes.
A few examples of application of this analogy are shown, in Figures 28 to 39.

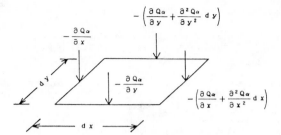

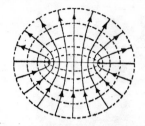

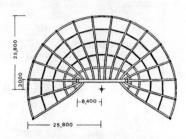

Fig.27: Equilibrium of differential portion

Fig.29: Speed potential and streamlines

Fig.30: Beam plan of roof

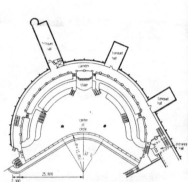

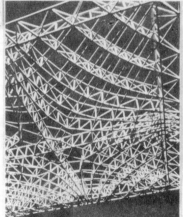

Fig.31: Photo of roof during construction

Fig.32: Interior photo, on completion

Fig.28: Plan of restaurant, Hotel New Akao, Atami

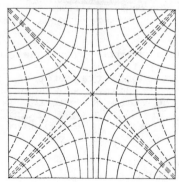

Fig.33: Membrane model for square plans

Fig.34: Moire fringe pattern

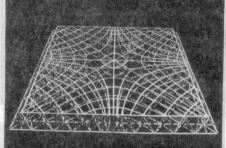

Fig.36: Model of Sports Hall, Hong Kong

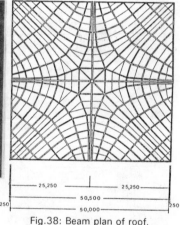

Fig.38: Beam plan of roof,
High School, Shioda

Fig.35: Streamline curved beam system   Fig.37: Same as Fig.36, view from below

Fig.39: Interior photo, on completion,
High School, Shioda

Fig.28 shows the plan of a semi-circular building. The associated streamlines, and the actually designed beam plan are seen, on Figures 29, and 30; whereas, the principal beams conform to the streamlines, while the secondary beams follow the potential lines. (A bird's-eye view photo taken during the construction of the building, and another one showing the interior on completion, can be seen in Figures 31, and 32, respectively.)

The next examples are roofs on square plans. Shear forces vanish along the diagonals of the squares, and take maximum values at the centre points of the sides. From membrane tests (Fig.33), the contour lines (Fig.34) were visualised, and the corresponding curved beam system (Fig.35) was designed for a 100 x 100 m span roof of a gymnasium. (Photos of its model can be seen, in Figures 36, and 37.) The same idea was also applied to another gymnasium of 50 x 50 m span. (The beam plan and an interior photo of the completed building can be seen, in Figures 38, and 39, respectively.)

Next, the torsion of solid, straight struts of orthotropical material properties will be discussed. The analogy which exists between the stress functions of torsion and the deflections of uniformly loaded membranes has long been known, and applied in experiments, as far as isotropic material properties are concerned. In the case of wood, however, the moduli of shear rigidity in the direction of the annual rings (G_θ), and across the grain (G_r) are different. By denoting their ratio as $k = G_\theta / G_r$, the angle of distortion as ω, the stress function as Ψ, and further assuming that the centre of the annual rings is in the torsional centre of the strut, the following equation is obtained:

$$\frac{\partial^2 \Psi}{\partial r^2} + \frac{1}{r}\frac{\partial \Psi}{\partial r} + k\frac{1}{r^2}\frac{\partial^2 \Psi}{\partial \theta^2} = -2G_\theta\,\omega$$

With the transformation of variables:

$$\theta = \theta'\sqrt{k} \qquad \frac{\partial^2 \Psi}{\partial r^2} + \frac{1}{r}\frac{\partial \Psi}{\partial r} + \frac{1}{r^2}\frac{\partial^2 \Psi}{\partial \theta'^2} = -2G_\theta\,\omega$$

parameter k can be eliminated from the above equation, that is the analogy with the deflection of membranes still exists. Figures 40 to 45 show contour lines of membranes all being in analogy with the torsion of a strut of square cross section, for different values of k. Maximum shear stresses occurring at the centre points of the sides of the square, and determined from the angle of inclination of membranes thereof, are plotted, in Fig.46.

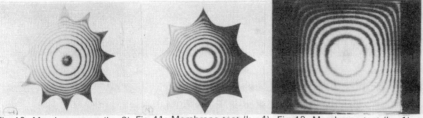

Fig.40: Membrane test (k = 9) Fig.41: Membrane test (k = 4) Fig.42: Membrane test (k = 1)

Fig.43: Membrane test (k = 9/16)   Fig.44: Membrane test (k = 4/16)   Fig.45: Membrane test (k = 1/16)

Fig.46: Maximum shear stress in square struts

An example of application of another classical analogy with respect to transversally loaded plates will now be introduced: since the sum of bending moments in two perpendicular directions is analogous with the deflection of uniformly loaded membranes, shear forces, that are derivatives of the aforesaid sum, can be determined from the corresponding angle of inclination of membranes. Shear forces of flat slabs were visualised by using this analogy, for various shapes of supporting drop panels(Figures 47 to 50). It was found that the maximum shear force occurring at the corners of square drop panels is threefold that occurring in the case of round drop panels.

Fig.47: Membrane test, square drop panel

7

Fig.48: Membrane test, hexagonal drop panel   Fig.49: Membrane test, octagonal drop panel   Fig.50: Membrane test, round drop panel

Though it may be of less practical importance, it is worth mentioning the analogies between transversally loaded plates and some problems of plane elasticity: the same biharmonic equation describes the deflection of the former, and the displacement of the latter; appropriate consideration of boundary conditions is also required. As an example of application of this analogy, the shear rigidity of a wall with an opening will be determined from a test on a transversally loaded plate. In Fig.51, the photoelastic test piece subject to pure shear (compressed in the vertical and tensed in the horizontal direction) is shown. The corresponding stresses along one side of the opening are plotted, in Fig.52; it is almost a linear distribution except in the vicinity of the corners. The analogous test piece, a square plate lifted at its diagonal corners, is depicted, in Fig.53. The Moire fringes of its transversal displacements can be seen, in Fig.54. The declining rigidities against the increasing size of opening is plotted, in Fig.55.

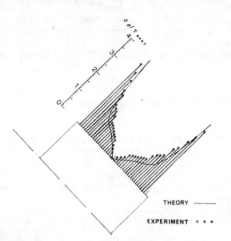

Fig.52: Stress distribution along one side of opening

Fig.51: Isochromatics around square opening, pure shear

Fig.54: Moire fringe patterns of of distorted plates

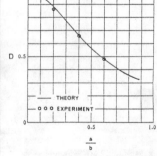

Fig.55: Reduction of shear rigidity versus sizes of opening

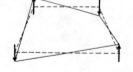

Fig.53: Distortion test of plate

ON NONLINEAR VISCOELASTIC CONSTITUTIVE EQUATIONS
FOR COMPOSITE MATERIALS

R. A. Schapery [1]

ABSTRACT

Constitutive equations for deformation behavior of fiber-reinforced plastics are discussed. The primary source of nonlinear and time-dependent behavior of structural composites is the resin matrix, and therefore we consider first models based on the physics of glassy polymers. Then some aspects of the nonlinear viscoelastic behavior of composite materials are reviewed in order to motivate the subsequent discussion on constitutive equations. The influences of stress state and stress history are characterized using currently available models, and certain important needs in these models and experimental results are discussed.

INTRODUCTION

There is an increasing need for better understanding and improved mathematical models of the nonlinear viscoelastic behavior of fiber-reinforced plastics. This is brought about, in part, by the growing use of composites with tough resin matrices. This toughening has been achieved in part by adding toughening agents, such as rubber particles, to normally brittle thermoset (crosslinked) resins or by using thermoplastic (non-crosslinked) resins [1], which often results in greater nonlinearity and time or strain rate dependence as compared to untoughened thermosets. Thermoplastic composites may offer significantly reduced production costs and time through well-designed forming processes, which, in turn, require good understanding of nonlinear viscoelastic behavior at process temperatures [2]. Increased use of thick laminates and high compressive loading, such as in marine applications, similarly places a greater demand on our understanding of resin-sensitive mechanical behavior of thermoplastic and thermoset composites. It should be noted that thermoplastics are often said to exhibit "viscoplasticity"; in this paper we consider this behavior to be a type of nonlinear viscoelasticity.

First, we discuss two different nonlinear constitutive models for the resin matrix which are based on the physics of polymeric solids. While encouraging, physically based models of resin behavior apparently have not yet been used to predict fiber composite material behavior. At this time, existing nonlinear viscoelastic constitutive equations for composite materials are essentially a blend of composite experimental data, thermodynamic and mathematical principles, as well as simplifications motivated by observed behavior and elementary composite micromechanics. In the remainder of this paper we discuss composite material behavior and constitutive equations.

Experimental results from tests of two different composites made of continuous carbon fiber-reinforced plastics are used to motivate the discussion on constitutive equations. One composite is Hexcel's T2C145/F155 material which has a rubber-toughened, epoxy matrix. The other is ICI's composite with the thermoplastic matrix Peek; here, these *composites* will be abbreviated as F155 and Peek, respectively.

PHYSICALLY-BASED MODELS FOR THE RESIN MATRIX

Significant effects of temperature, solvent concentration and strain (or stress) histories on viscoelastic behavior of glassy and rubbery polymeric materials, whether crosslinked or non-crosslinked, have been related semi-quantitatively to the molecular structure through the amount of so-called free volume (voids associated with molecular packing irregularities) [3]. The instantaneous amount of free volume is believed to have a profound influence on the molecular mobility in polymers near and below their glass-transition temperature

[1]R. A. Schapery is Cockrell Family Regents Chair Professor in Engineering, Department of Aerospace Engineering and Engineering Mechanics, The University of Texas at Austin, Austin, TX, 78712.

T_g, and thus on their viscoelastic behavior. The well-documented physical aging of glassy polymers has been attributed to the gradual time-dependent reduction in free volume when a polymer is held at a fixed temperature below T_g, after cooling from a temperature above T_g [4]. Recognizing the importance of free volume to viscoelastic behavior of glassy polymers, Knauss and Emri [5,6] and Losi and Knauss [7] accounted for it in their nonlinear viscoelastic constitutive equations for small strain, three-dimensional behavior of isotropic polymers; these equations are identical to those for linear viscoelastic behavior except for the effect of dilatation on the material's time-scale for mechanical response. In place of physical time t in the relaxation moduli or creep compliances, *reduced time ψ* , is used,

$$\psi = \int_0^t \frac{du}{\Phi} \tag{1}$$

where Φ is a time-scale factor which gives the dependence of viscosity or relaxation times on the fractional free volume, f. The Doolittle equation is used for Φ,

$$\log_{10} \Phi = \frac{b}{2.303} \left(\frac{1}{f} - \frac{1}{f_0} \right) \tag{2}$$

where f was given by Knauss et al. as,

$$f = f_0 + A\{\alpha dT\} + B\epsilon_{kk} \tag{3}$$

in which f_o is a reference constant ($\Phi(f_o) = 1$) and A, B, and b are experimentally determined constants; ϵ_{kk} is the macroscopic dilatation or volume strain. Also, the braces denote a convolution integral in reduced time; specifically, for a generic pair of time-dependent functions, g and h, we use throughout this paper the following shorthand notation

$$\{gdh\} \equiv \int_{-\infty}^{\psi} g\left(\psi - \psi'\right) \frac{dh}{d\psi'} d\psi' \tag{4}$$

According to equation (1), $d\psi = dt/\Phi$, and therefore we may also write,

$$\{gdh\} = \int_{-\infty}^{t} g(\psi - \psi') \frac{dh}{dt'} dt' \tag{5}$$

where $\psi' = \psi(t')$. When using equation (5) in (3), $g(\psi)$ is the function for thermal volume expansion $\alpha(\psi)$, and $h(t')$ is the temperature, $T(t)$. Inasmuch as the dummy time variable of integration in equation (1) is u, the quantities t and $\psi(t)$ in equation (5) should be replaced by u and $\psi(u)$ when f is substituted into (1). Figure 1 shows, for uniaxial tensile stressing, a prediction of the free volume-based model and experimental data for poly(vinyl acetate) [6]; curve A is for linear viscoelastic behavior.

Shay and Caruthers [8] proposed a similar model, but allowed for large strains and used a fractional free volume which depends on the current values of pressure, dilatation and temperature. Much earlier, Schapery [9,10] used irreversible thermodynamic principles to develop strain-based constitutive equations which contain the free volume-based models described above; but explicit dependence of the time-scale factor on free volume was not given or assumed. Augl [11] investigated nonlinear effects of physical aging in an epoxy, and characterized this aging behavior using a modified form of Schapery's model in which stresses, rather than strains, are the independent variables [10, 12]. Sternstein et al. [13, 14] argue that mechanically-induced changes in physical aging (and thus in nonlinear viscoelastic behavior) are shear, rather than dilatation, driven. This conclusion was based in part on observations that mechanically enhanced aging is about the same under uniaxial tensile and compressive stresses. In view of this finding it is likely that macroscopic shearing influences the molecular packing or distribution of voids which, in turn, affects the rate of change of thermally-induced free volume.

Constitutive equations for thermoplastics which are distinctly different from the free volume-based model were developed and applied by Boyce et al [15]. Figure 2 shows schematically the type of stress-strain behavior which was modeled. The initial peak stress and subsequent stress decrease are associated with overcoming intermolecular resistance to segment rotation. The increase in stress at the highest strains is attributed to molecular alignment. Molecular entanglements, rather than chemical crosslinks, tie the long chains together. Emphasis was on large strain behavior, and the model was applied to elevated temperature behavior of PMMA. It is not known how well the model will work in the nonlinear, low strain range of glassy polymers. Free volume changes were not included, although physical aging was discussed for future applications. It is also of interest to observe that Knauss and Emri [6] predicted a local maximum in the stress for constant applied axial strain rate under some conditions. In the Boyce et al. model the initial nonlinearity and stress decay is shear stress driven, while in the Knauss et al. model it is dilatation driven. Considering previous comments, it is likely that both drivers are needed in a model that is to have broad applicability.

In order to make a further comparison of the Boyce et al. and Knauss et al. constitutive models it will be helpful to use the mechanical analog in Fig. 3. For a uniaxial stress state, the Knauss et al. constitutive equation may be represented by the generalized Voigt model in which there are an arbitrary number of Voigt units, N. The springs have constant moduli E_i, while the dashpot viscosities are all proportional to Φ, as given by equation (2). This type of model applies to shear and dilatational behavior in which $\eta_m = \infty$ for dilatation, but η_m may be finite for shear. In contrast, $N = 1$ and $\eta_m = \infty$ for the Boyce et al. model. With large strains, this three element spring and dashpot assembly cannot depict all details of the constitutive model. Nevertheless, we can think of the η_1-dashpot strain as their plastic strain and the dashpot stress as their T^*, the driving stress for inelastic processes; η_1 is a function of the dashpot strain history. The E_1-spring stress is their backstress B, and our σ is their applied stress T, thus giving the equation $T^* = T - B$ shown in Fig. 2. For a three-dimensional state of stress, T^* is the equivalent shear stress. The increasing slope of the stress curve at high strains in Fig. 2 is due to the effect of molecular alignment on the backstress.

One final, related observation is that the type of stress-strain behavior exhibited by the Boyce et al. model for thermoplastics, was recently found for partially constrained shearing of an epoxy thermoset by Liechti and Liang [16]. Consequently, the latter model may have some applicability to thermosets, although it was originally developed for thermoplastics.

BEHAVIOR OF COMPOSITES

Under certain conditions, the nonlinear viscoelastic behavior of fiber-reinforced plastics exhibits considerable simplicity in behavior, in contrast to what one might expect from the apparently complex behavior of the matrix. Important elements of this simplicity and their implications for constitutive equations will be discussed here. Figure 4 shows the uniaxial stress-strain curve for a carbon/Peek composite tested under constant strain rate conditions, with loading, unloading and reloading segments [17]. For the 45° angle-ply layup, the shear stress that is tangent to the fibers in each unidirectional ply is equal to $\sigma/2$ (apart from edge effects) while the associated shearing strain is $(1 + \nu)\epsilon$, where σ, and ϵ and ν are the overall, axial stress, axial strain and Poisson's ratio of the laminate; the ply stress normal to the fibers is relatively small because of the high fiber modulus. Thus, the stress-strain behavior in Fig. 4 is essentially that for simple shearing in the principal material directions of a ply, apart from the aforementioned scale factors. When the composite is strained monotonically to failure, the stress-strain curve is practically that in Fig. 4 without the unloading branches. For matrix-dominated behavior, the writer has never seen a decrease in stress for constant strain rate loading (cf. Fig. 2) in this or other fiber composites, unless it is due to matrix cracking or delamination. Moreover, the strain rate ($\dot{\epsilon}$) dependence is often quite simple; for the laminate of Fig. 4, over a three-decade range $5 \times 10^{-6} \le \dot{\epsilon} \le 5 \times 10^{-3}(s^{-1})$, we found $\sigma \sim \dot{\epsilon}^n$ at all strains, where $n \simeq 0.033$.

The shape of the shear stress-strain curves of an untoughened carbon/epoxy composite, with ramp unloading and reloading segments, is essentially the same as in Fig. 4 [18]. Even the unloading-reloading stress loops have about the same proportions. One significant difference is that the strain for zero stress, at the bottom of the unloading ramp, is significantly higher for the Peek composite, as compared to the untoughened composite. For a metal, the unloading line has an essentially constant slope equal to the initial loading modulus; the dashed line in Fig. 4 shows such behavior. If we use ϵ_p to denote the strain at which this straight line intersects the strain axis, then it may be seen in Fig. 4 that the actual strain at zero stress is approximately

$0.6\epsilon_p$. In contrast, the strain at zero stress for the untoughened composite is on the average $0.3\epsilon_p$ for shear dominated behavior [18].

Next, we shall discuss a relatively simple type of behavior exhibited by specimens of the F155 composite under rather complex multiaxial loading, as reported by Lamborn and Schapery [19] and Lamborn [20]. In one set of tests, rectangular composite bars with an angle-ply layup (alternating fiber angle, $\theta = \pm 35^0$, with respect to the axial direction) were subjected simultaneously to various axial and torsional deformations through controlled movement of the end-grips. The different deformation paths are identified in Fig. 5 by number; for example, the bottom line type is used for axial history 1 during the first loading period and axial history 6 during unloading, while the corresponding torsional histories are 2 and 5. The "nominal" shear stress and shear and axial strains are quantities which are proportional to the torque, twist, and axial displacement, respectively; the proportionality coefficients depend only on the specimen dimensions, and are introduced to minimize the effect of specimen-to-specimen size differences; if the material were linear and isotropic, these nominal quantities would be the maximum values in the specimen, apart from end-effects. The axial stress is only weakly dependent on torsion, exhibits behavior similar to that in Fig. 4 for Peek, and therefore is not shown.

At the end of the first loading period the applied strains are equal; the five different strain paths are seen to result in practically the same stress (Fig. 5) and have been found to require the same total work input from both axial and torsional loading. The same behavior holds for the unloading and reloading segments. In contrast, unreinforced aluminum bars of a comparable width/thickness ratio exhibit significant path-dependence [19]; we do not know if fiber-reinforced aluminum would exhibit less path-dependence.

Unloading and reloading behavior of the F155 composite under pure axial or torsional straining is similar to that shown in Fig. 5; there is significant hysteresis and the average slope of the loop decreases with increasing strain at the first strain reversal point. The stress during loading does not usually exhibit a maximum prior to fracture, in contrast to that in Fig. 5. Significant edge delaminations have been found at the highest stresses for deformation histories like those in Fig. 5. Yet the overall behavior is quite simple, as described above.

The primary effects of deformation history on the composite appear to be associated with the sign of (nominal) strain rate and the strain magnitude when the sign last changed. There is a small effect of strain rate at the common strain points. The small differences in stress at these points in Fig. 5 reflects at most the extent of the rate dependence found in other tests for the same 5:1 ratio of strain rates as in the dual-rate tests of Fig. 5 [20]. In order to minimize effects of viscoelasticity, we selected the common strain points so that they occurred at the same test time. Behavior similar to that of the F155 composite was found for Hercules' AS4/3502, an untoughened carbon/epoxy composite [20]; but the degree of nonlinearity and hysteresis was somewhat less for this brittle-resin system.

The local stresses and strains (as opposed to the "nominal"quantities in Fig. 5) are distributed very nonuniformly throughout the specimens used in these axial-torsional tests, and thus the results cannot be used directly in a basic material characterization of the composite. However, it is unlikely that the specimens' overall behavior would exhibit the path-independence described above if the ply-level constitutive equations did not have this type of behavior. The specimen width-to-thickness ratio is small enough that there are strong three-dimensional effects; indeed, wider specimens were also used and they exhibited less nonlinearity and hysteresis.

Guided by the path-independence of nominal stress and work observed during loading of the toughened and untoughened composites, as well as theoretical considerations of the effect of damage growth and other changes in the microstructure [21], a detailed material characterization was done for in-plane loading. The results for AS4/3502 and F155 are reported in [18] and [22], respectively for unidirectional and angle-ply laminates. Time/rate effects were neglected in the former study, while constant load (creep), constant load rate and constant crosshead rate were used in the latter study to investigate viscoelastic effects. Also, the constitutive model in [22] was extended to a three-dimensional state of stress to be able to analyze bonded composite joints [23]. With both materials, path-independence of isochronal stress-strain behavior was found to be satisfied reasonably well. Thus, for loading (over a range of proportional and nonproportional strain paths), the nonlinear constitutive behavior for both materials may be expressed approximately in terms of a work function using time and strains as independent variables or a complementary work function using time and stresses as independent variables. Let us now discuss this simple type of behavior in specific terms.

The unidirectional ply behavior of F155 was characterized using complementary work, which will be described here. The stresses σ_i and strains $\varepsilon_i (i = 1, 2, ..., 6)$ are referred to the principal material coordinates $x_i (i = 1, 2, 3)$; the x_1 axis is parallel to the fibers while the x_3 axis is normal to the ply plane (cf. Fig. 6). In this discussion it will be convenient to use this single index notation. As is customary, $i = 4, 5, 6$ for the shearing variables, and the relationship between single and double indexed tensor components is

$$\sigma_{11} = \sigma_1, \quad \sigma_{22} = \sigma_2, \quad \sigma_{33} = \sigma_3, \quad \sigma_{23} = \sigma_4, \quad \sigma_{13} = \sigma_5, \quad \sigma_{12} = \sigma_6, \tag{6}$$

$$\varepsilon_{11} = \varepsilon_1, \quad \varepsilon_{22} = \varepsilon_2, \quad \varepsilon_{33} = \varepsilon_3, \quad \varepsilon_{23} = \varepsilon_4, \quad 2\varepsilon_{23} = \varepsilon_4, \quad 2\varepsilon_{13} = \varepsilon_5, \quad 2\varepsilon_{12} = \varepsilon_6$$

The constitutive equation has the quasi-elastic form,

$$\in_i = \partial W_c / \partial \sigma_i \tag{7}$$

where $W_c = W_c(\sigma_i, t)$ is the complementary work function. For F155 a good approximation for W_c is

$$W_c = W_0 + W_1 t^q \tag{8}$$

where $q = 0.05$ and

$$W_0 = \frac{1}{2} S_{ij}^0 \sigma_i \sigma_j, \qquad W_1 = A \tau_s^r \tag{9}$$

The summation convention for repeated indices is used. The quantity W_0 is the complementary work for a linear elastic composite and A and r are constants; the S_{ij}^0 are the linear elastic compliances. Also, $\tau_s = \tau_s(\sigma_i)$ is a quadratic function of the stresses. The start of the nonlinear range is defined by a particular value of τ_s. When $\tau_s \leq \tau_c$, then $r = 1$, while $r = 1.7$ when $\tau_s > \tau_c$. The value of A is of course different for the linear and nonlinear ranges. In order to account for differences between stress-strain behavior for unloading and loading we would have to use different forms of W_c. One thermodynamically-consistent approach to doing this is to introduce internal state variables in the work potential or complementary work potential [18, 24]; a natural loading parameter is τ_s, so that loading (including neutral loading) is defined by the condition $\dot{\tau}_s \geq 0$ whenever $\tau_s = \tau_s(\text{maximum})$.

Motivation for selection of a single quadratic function of stress τ_s to characterize the nonlinear behavior came from the much earlier work of Lou and Schapery [25]. It was found that such a function accounted for the primary effect of stress state on the functions used to characterize nonlinear viscoelastic behavior of a unidirectional glass/epoxy composite. The form of this parameter was based on the observation that the octahedral shear stress τ_{oct} normally can be used to correlate multiaxial yielding of plastics if the mean stress is not relatively large. As a simplification, the matrix was viewed as a uniformly stressed layer of material sandwiched between layers of rigid fiber material; i.e.,the lines in Fig. 6 at the angle θ were imagined to define layers rather than fibers. The square of this shear stress, for plane stress, is proportional to τ_s ,

$$\tau_s \equiv \sigma_2^2 + c\sigma_6^2 \tag{10}$$

where c was considered to be a free constant. However, c was also related to the ratio ν_e of axial (x_1)-to-transverse (x_2) stress in the matrix to obtain

$$c = 3/(1 - \nu_e + \nu_e^2) \tag{11}$$

13

For a linearly elastic, isotropic matrix, ν_e is the Poisson's ratio, and for a linearly elastic or rigid-plastic incompressible matrix, $\nu_e = 0.5$. As reported in [25], a finite element analysis of a linear elastic composite with a square array of fibers was made to predict the average octahedral shear stress in the matrix. Apart from a numerical factor (which can be absorbed in the function W_1), equation (10) with $\nu_e = 0.35$ was found to be a fairly good approximation to this average. (Introduction of the effect of axial fiber strain in τ_{oct} did not appreciably influence the simple result in equation (10) [25]. For a three-dimensional state of stress in a transversely isotropic material, τ_{oct}^2 is proportional to

$$\tau_s = \sigma_2^2 + \sigma_3^2 + 2c_1\sigma_2\sigma_3 + c_2\sigma_4^2 + c\left(\sigma_5^2 + \sigma_6^2\right) \tag{12}$$

where the c_i are constants. If the simple layer model is used to derive these constants, then $c_1 = 1 - c/2$ and $c_2 = c$; however, there is no point in restricting τ_s in this way. In fact, if one assumes only that W_1 is a function of a quadratic function of the stresses, and uses the conditions of transverse isotropy and independence of σ_1, equation (12) results, where the c_i are arbitrary constants.

The quadratic function of stress in equation (10) was successfully used to correlate nonlinear behavior of a unidirectional laminate or ply by Sun et al. in studies of time-independent behavior of a carbon/epoxy composite (c = 2.5) and of a boron/aluminum composite (c = 4), both from off-axis tensile loading [26]; later carbon/Peek in compression was studied, to obtain c = 3.4 [27]. Concepts from plasticity theory were used, in which the plastic potential was assumed to be a function of only a quadratic function of the applied stresses. The stress σ_1 was omitted because of the insensitivity of the plastic strains to loading in the fiber direction. Then, using an associated flow rule, they developed expressions for plastic strains due to proportional loading for plane stress (off-axis, uniaxial loading of unidirectional composites). For this case of proportional loading, the resulting plasticity constitutive equation for strains is equivalent to equation (7), in which $W_c = W_c(\tau_s)$. However, we have found that even with strongly non-proportional loading, a work potential is applicable [18, 19]. Sun et al. [28, 29] extended the formulation to viscoplastic behavior of a Peek composite by using a so-called "overstress" viscoplasticity model, introduced originally for metals. While good agreement between theory and experiment was reported, including good correlation of nonlinear behavior based on a power law in τ_s, characterization for different types of strain histories required different values of material parameters.

It is not always possible to characterize nonlinear composite behavior in terms of τ_s, whether using a power law or not. For the carbon/epoxy in [18], we found τ_s^r provided only a crude representation. Instead, correlation of nonlinear multiaxial behavior was achieved using the difference between total work and stored strain energy. The resulting constitutive equation exhibited path-independence for loading and for unloading.

VISCOELASTIC CONSTITUTIVE EQUATIONS FOR COMPOSITES

Under sufficiently restrictive stress or strain histories, a simple constitutive equation may be applicable, such as the quasi-elastic representation, equation (7), and specializations of the complementary work potential, like equation (8). Of course, for even a linear viscoelastic material under a general stress or strain history, one needs to use convolution integrals like equation (4) (or their differential equation equivalents),

$$\sigma = \{Ed\epsilon\} \qquad \text{or} \qquad \epsilon = \{Dd\sigma\} \tag{13}$$

where E is the relaxation modulus and D is the creep compliance. At this time there does not appear to be any one generally accepted method of modeling nonlinear viscoelastic behavior for complex loading histories. Existing models for resin behavior, when incorporated into a micromechanical model for predicting composite behavior, may provide some guidance; but they are of uncertain generality at this time. The overstress method adapted to composites [28, 29] has about the same status. In this section we shall briefly revisit a thermodynamically-based constitutive theory [30]. Special versions [12] have met with some success for moderately complex loadings on thermosets [e.g. 31, 32] and fiber-reinforced thermosets [e.g. 25, 33], and have been used for the resin model to predict composite material behavior by means of a numerical micromechanical analysis, with experimental verification [34]. In reference [33] an accelerated

14

characterization procedure based on time-temperature superposition is reviewed, and the importance of edge effects in laminate creep behavior is emphasized; also, it is shown that in creep of laminates the ply stresses are not necesarily monotonic functions of time. Here, we shall discuss the stress-based constitutive theory in [30] with a view toward modeling time-dependent, multiaxial loading of composites with either thermoset or thermoplastic matrices. (The strain-based theory in [9] provides an analogous constitutive model.) Omitting here for notational simplicity effects of temperature, a relatively general version of the constitutive equation for anisotropic media is

$$\epsilon_i = \frac{\partial W_o}{\partial \sigma_i} + \frac{\partial \hat{\sigma}_j}{\partial \sigma_i}\{\Delta S_{jk} d(\hat{\sigma}_k/a_g)\} \tag{14}$$

where the notation of equation (4) or (5) is used, and the time scale factor Φ in reduced time (1) is completely arbitrary at this point. The quantities $\hat{\sigma}_j = \hat{\sigma}_j(\sigma_i)$ are material functions of stress and $\Delta S_{jk} = \Delta S_{jk}(\psi) = \Delta S_{kj}$ are transient components of the *linear* viscoelastic creep compliances. The initial linear or nonlinear elastic response is represented by the complementary work function W_o (which is not necessarily quadratic in the stresses). For a uniaxial state of stress, equation (14) may be written in the form,

$$\epsilon = g_0 S_0 \sigma + g_1 \{\Delta S d(g_2 \sigma)\} \tag{15}$$

where g_0, g_1 and g_2 are functions of stress which are unity when $\sigma = 0$; it is this equation, together with the assumption that Φ is a function of the instantaneous stress (and temperature), that has been used in much of the resin and composite modeling work cited previously. For a creep test, starting at $t = 0$, and assuming $\Phi = \Phi(\sigma)$, equation (15) reduces to

$$\epsilon = g_0 S_0 \sigma + g_1 g_2 \Delta S(t/\Phi)\sigma \tag{16}$$

Let us now suppose that in equation (14),

$$\hat{\sigma}_i = \partial F/\partial \sigma_i \tag{17}$$

where

$$F = \frac{1}{2} A_{ij} \sigma_i \sigma_j \tag{18}$$

and the A_{ij} are constants; note that τ_s , equation (10) or (12), is a special case of F . Without loss in generality we may assume $A_{ij} = A_{ji}$ because the anti-symmetric components have no effect on F .

A normally very good approximation for high modulus fiber composites and their resin matrices is

$$\Delta S_{ij} = k_{ij} \Delta S \tag{19}$$

where $\Delta S = \Delta S(\psi)$ and the k_{ij} are constants. Substitution of equations (17) - (19) into (14) yields,

$$\epsilon_i = \frac{\partial W_o}{\partial \sigma_i} + \left\{ \Delta S d\left(\frac{\partial W_G}{\partial \sigma_i}\right)\right\} \tag{20}$$

where $W_G = W_G(G)$ is an arbitrary function of G, in which

$$G \equiv \frac{1}{2} b_{ij} \sigma_i \sigma_j \tag{21}$$

and b_{ij} is a constant, symmetric matrix; a_G was absorbed into W_G. For constant stresses applied at $t = 0$, and if $\Phi = \Phi(G)$, then

$$\epsilon_i = \frac{\partial W_0}{\partial \sigma_i} + \frac{\partial W_G}{\partial \sigma_i} \Delta S(t/\Phi) \tag{22}$$

With further specialization, in which $G = \tau_s$ and $\Delta S = \psi^q$, the present model reduces to equations (7) and (8) if we select W_1 as

15

$$W_1 = \int_0^{\tau_s} \Phi^{-q} \frac{dW_G}{d\tau'_s} d\tau'_s \tag{23}$$

Use of power laws in τ_s for Φ and W_G produces the special form of W_1 in equation (9). We may thus consider equation (20) to be a thermodynamically-consistent generalization of equation (7) for more general stress histories than used experimentally in developing (7).

Equation (20) does not have stress-dependent factors outside of the braces. However, they may be needed to account for a possible difference between elastic strain due to a stress which is suddenly applied and one which is suddenly removed [25]. A matrix of such factors appears in equation (14). If, for example, we had used the form

$$\hat{\sigma}_i = \partial \hat{F}/\partial \sigma_i \tag{24}$$

where $\hat{F} = \hat{F}(F)$, instead of equation (17), the factors appear (such as g_1 in equation (15)). When, for example, the plane-stress viscoelastic behavior of a unidirectional off-axis composite under uniaxial stress $\sigma \equiv \sigma_x$ is to be characterized in terms of $(\sigma_1, \sigma_2, \sigma_6)$ by means of equation (14), then the $\hat{\sigma}_i$ functions in (24) give rise to a factor outside of the braces in equation (15) which cannot be expressed entirely in terms of τ_s ; individual stress components appear explicitly besides τ_s. Past use of equation (15) [25] did not account for this complexity in g_1.

The one-dimensional constitutive equation (15) can be represented by the generalized Voigt model in Fig. 3 [30], where $E_m = 1/g_o S_0$, and the second term in (15) is to be identified with strains in the remaining elements of the mechanical model, using as many Voigt units as necessary. On the basis of findings for the thermoplastic PEEK composite [35], the strain response after load removal cannot be characterized by equation (15), assuming $\Phi = \Phi(\tau_s)$. However, the recoverable part of the creep strain was consistent with equation (15) in which $g_1 g_2 = 1$. One way of generalizing equation (15), or its three-dimensional version, equation (14), which may be sufficient to account for the nonrecoverable strain (and possibly the time dependence of the strain following partial or total unloading) is to add an additional term to (14) which is associated with the nonrecoverable component, and for which $\Delta S_{jk} \sim \psi$. In terms of the model in Fig. 3, this amounts to adding a free dashpot whose nonlinear behavior is independent of the rest of the model. More generally, we may, if necessary, use additional terms like the second one in (14), each with a different set of nonlinear functions, such as $\hat{\sigma}_j$, and creep compliances.

A different approach to characterizing behavior during unloading and reloading has been employed by Sun et al. [28, 29] using the overstress model, and by Schapery [18] in which, apart from viscoelastic effects, a linear stress-strain curve is used corresponding to the average slope of each loop in Fig. 4.

Another type of generalization that may be needed is related to changes in free volume (and possibly chain-segment rotation), discussed previously for the resin. Physical aging, generally associated with free volume changes, is exhibited to varying degrees by thermoset and thermoplastic resins and their composites below the glass-transition temperature [e.g. 11, 36], and has been characterized through changes in the time-scale factor, Φ. In the Knauss et al. work discussed earlier, all nonlinear effects in the resin were expressed in terms of the influence of macroscopic dilatation ϵ_{kk} on Φ , equation (3). The discussion in this section on composites lead us to the use of shearing effects (as expressed by τ_s or its strain counterpart) in Φ. Although the stresses are distributed nonuniformly throughout the matrix phase in a composite, one approach that combines the Knauss et al. model with findings on nonlinear behavior of composites is to use, for the composite, a time scale factor that depends on both ϵ_{kk} and τ_s (besides $\{\alpha dT\}$) , where ϵ_{kk} is the average dilatation of the matrix phase. Here, the simple layer model that lead to equation (12) might be adequate; in this case the composite dilatation is $\epsilon_{kk}^c = v_m \epsilon_{kk}$, where v_m is the matrix volume fraction.

CONCLUDING REMARKS

Presently, there does not appear to be any generally accepted nonlinear viscoelastic constitutive model for glassy polymers, with or without fiber reinforcement. There are, however, some relatively general models that appear to be valid for at least limited stress states and histories. The influence of stresses or strains on the time scale for basic material response, such as in creep or relaxation, clearly exists but is presently not well understood. One manifestation of this influence is stress-enhanced physical aging. It is believed that a major need at this time is experiments which are designed to assess the range of validity of existing models for resins and composites and to provide guidelines for improvements in them or in the development of new models. Loading, unloading and reloading with and without rest periods should be used. One important question is what are the drivers for changes in the time scale factor Φ that determines the material's time scale. Are they temperature, dilatation *and* octahedral (or effective) shear stress or shear strain? Are their histories needed? Although experimental studies of nonlinear viscoelastic behavior are time-consuming and may require a high degree of precision in measurement, they really are needed if we are to make progress in understanding time-dependent mechanical behavior of composites.

Computational mechanics appears to be sufficiently advanced to predict nonlinear composite material behavior from constituent behavior. Existing and future resin models can be used in this numerical modeling of composite behavior to assess, through comparison with experiment, their validity for the complex micro-stress state in composites. Such comparisons already have been made, but only to a very limited degree.

Acknowledgment - Sponsorship of this work by the Office of Naval Research under Grant No. N00014-91-J-4091 is gratefully acknowledged.

REFERENCES

1. Johnston, N. J., Toughened Composites, STP 937, American Society for Testing and Materials (ASTM), Philadelphia, 1987.

2. Sun, C. T. and Wang, C., "Characterization of APC-2 Thermoplastic Composite under Forming Temperatures," Proc. 36th International SAMPE Symposium, San Diego, April, 1991.

3. Ferry J. D., Viscoelastic Properties of Polymers, John Wiley & Sons, Inc., Third Ed., New York, 1980.

4. Struik, L. C. E., Physical Aging in Amorphous Polymers and Other Materials, Elsevier Sci. Pub. Co., Amsterdam, 1978.

5. Knauss, W. G. and Emri, I. J., "Non-Linear Viscoelasticity Based on Free Volume Considerations," Computers & Structures, 13, pp. 123-128, 1981.

6. Knauss, W. G. and Emri, I., "Volume Change and the Non-Linearly Thermo-Viscoelastic Constitution of Polymers," Polymer Eng'g. Sci., 27, pp. 86-100, 1987.

7. Losi, G. V. and Knauss, W. G., "Free Volume Theory and Non-linear Thermoviscoelasticity," to appear, Polymer Eng'g. Sci., April, 1992.

8. Shay, R. M. Jr. and Caruthers, J. M., "A New Nonlinear Viscoelastic Constitutive Equation for Predicting Yield in Amorphous Solid Polymers," J. Rheology, 30, pp. 781-827, 1986.

9. Schapery, R. A., "A Theory of Non-Linear Thermoviscoelasticity Based on Irreversible Thermodynamics," Proc. 5th U.S. Nat. Cong. Appl. Mech., ASME, pp. 511-530.

10. Schapery, R. A., "On a Thermodynamic Constitutive Theory and its Application to Various Nonlinear Materials," Thermoinelasticity, IUTAM Symposium 1968, East Kilbride, Springer-Verlag, New York, pp. 259-285, 1970.

11. Augl, J. M., "Nonlinear Creep Effects of Physical Aging, Temperature and Moisture of an Epoxy Resin," J. Rheology, 31, pp. 1-36, 1987.

12. Schapery, R. A., "On the Characterization of Nonlinear Viscoelastic Materials," J. Polymer Eng. Sci., 9, pp. 295-310, 1969.

13. Sternstein, S. S., "Homogeneous and Inhomogeneous Properties of Glassy Polymers," Polymer Preprints, 17, p. 136-141, 1976.

14. Myers, F. A., Cama, F. C., and Sternstein, S. S., "Mechanically Enhanced Aging of Glassy Polymers," Annals of the New York Academy of Sciences, 279, p. 94-99, 1976.

15. Boyce, M. C., Parks, D. M. and Argon, A. S., "Large Inelastic Deformation of Glassy Polymers. Part I. Rate Dependent Constitutive Model," Mechanics of Materials, 7, pp. 15-33, 1988.

16. Liechti, K. M. and Liang, Y. M., "Shear Banding in a Crosslinked Epoxy," to appear, Proc. International Congress of Applied Mechanics, Haifa, August, 1992.

17. Harbert, B. C. and Schapery, R. A., unpublished research.

18. Schapery, R. A., "Mechanical Characterization and Analysis of Inelastic Composite Laminates with Growing Damage," Mechanics of Composite Materials and Structures, AMD-Vol. 100, American Society of Mechanical Engineering, pp. 1-9, 1989.

19. Lamborn, M.J. and Schapery, R. A., "An Investigation of Deformation Path-Independence of Mechanical Work in Fiber-Reinforced Plastics," Proc. 4th Japan-U.S. Conference on Composite Materials, Technomic, pp. 991-997, 1988.

20. Lamborn, M. J., "Deformation and Delamination of Inelastic Laminates under Tensile and Torsional Loading," Ph.D. Dissertation, Dept. of Civil Engineering, Texas A&M University, College Station, Texas, Dec. 1989.

21. Schapery, R. A., "A Theory of Mechanical Behavior of Elastic Media with Growing Damage and Other Changes in Structure," J. Mech. Phys. Solids, 38, pp. 215-253, 1990.

22. Mignery, L. A., "Viscoelastic Adherend Effects in Adhesively Bonded Composite-to-Composite Joints, Ph.D. Dissertation, Dept. of Aerospace Engineering, Texas A&M University, College Station, Texas, Dec. 1988.

23. Mignery, L. A. and Schapery, R. A., "Viscoelastic and Nonlinear Adherend Effects in Bonded Composite Joints," J. Adhesion, 34, pp. 17-40, 1991.

24. Schapery, R. A., "A Method for Mechanical State Characterization of Inelastic Composites with Damage," Advances in Fracture Research, Proc. 7th Int. Conf. on Fracture, 3, pp. 2177-2189, 1989.

25. Lou, Y. C. and Schapery, R. A., "Viscoelastic Characterization of a Nonlinear Fiber-Reinforced Plastic," J. Comp. Mat., 5, pp. 208-234, 1971.

26. Sun, C. T. and Chen, J. L. "A Simple Flow Rule for Characterizing Nonlinear Behavior of Fiber Composites," J. Comp. Mat., 23, pp. 1009-1020, 1989.

27. Sun, C. T. and Rui, Y., "Orthotropic Elasto-Plastic Behavior of AS4/PEEK Thermoplastic Composite in Compression," Mechanics of Materials, 10 pp. 117-125, 1990.

28. Yoon, K. J. and Sun, C. T., "Characterization of Elastic-Viscoplastic Properties of an AS4/PEEK Thermoplastic Composite," J. Comp. Mat., 25, pp. 1277-1296, 1991.

29. Gates, T. S. and Sun, C. T., "Elastic/Viscoplastic Constitutive Model for Fiber Reinforced Thermoplastic Composites," AIAA J., 29, pp. 457-463, 1991.

30. Schapery, R. A., "Further Development of a Thermodynamic Constitutive Theory: Stress Formulation," Purdue Univ. Report No. AA&ES 69-2, February, 1969.

31. Peretz, D. and Weitsman, Y., "Nonlinear Viscoelastic Characterization of FM-73 Adhesive," J. Rheology, 26, pp. 245-261, 1982.

32. Augl, J. M. "Creep Prediction of the HBRF 241 Epoxy Resin Under Multi-Step Loading," Naval Surface Weapons Center, NSWC TR 87-140, 1987.

33. Dillard, D. A., Gramoll, K. C. and Brinson, H. F., "The Implications of the Fiber Truss Concept for Creep Properties of Laminated Composites," Composite Structures, 11, pp. 85-100, 1989.

34. Mohan, R. and Adams, D. F., "Nonlinear Creep-Recovery of a Polymer Matrix and its Composites," Experimental Mechanics, pp. 262-271, 1985.

35. Xiao, X., "Studies of the Viscoelastic Behavior of a Thermoplastic Resin Composite," Comp. Sci. Technol., 34, pp. 163-182, 1989.

36. Sullivan, J. L., "Creep and Physical Aging of Composites," Comp. Sci. Technol., 39, pp. 207-232, 1990.

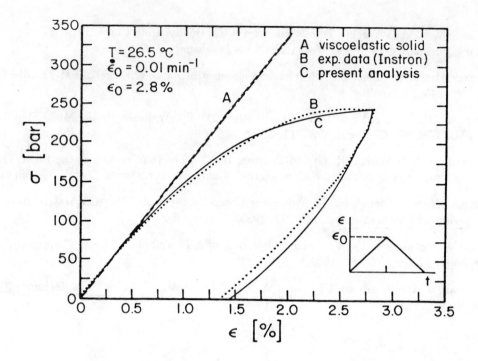

FIGURE 1. Example of nonlinear viscoelastic response modeled in Ref. (6).

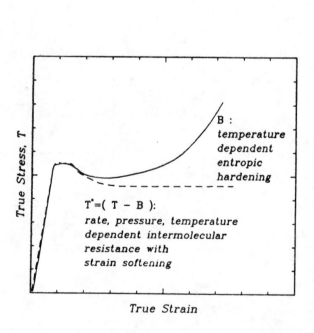

FIGURE 2. Schematic of the model for the stress-strain behavior of a glassy polymer. From Ref. (15).

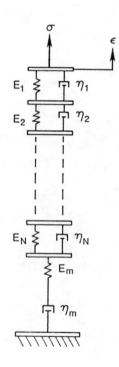

FIGURE 3. Generalized Voigt model.

20

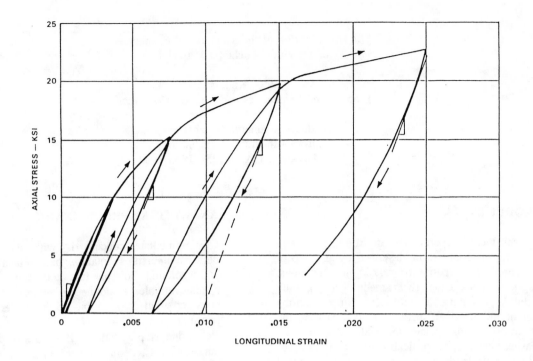

FIGURE 4. Complex strain tests of carbon/Peek
composite $(\pm 45)_{2S}$ at 75°F. From Ref. (17).

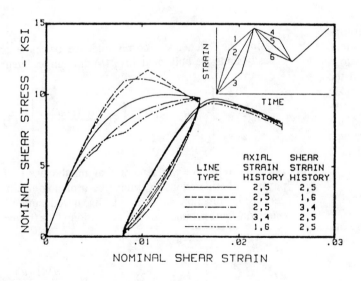

FIGURE 5. Shear stress-strain curves for
proportional and nonproportional
straining of an angle-ply laminate
at 75°F. Hexcel T2C145/F155
carbon/epoxy $(\pm 35)_{6s}$; 0.15" thick
X 0.5" wide X 8.75" long.
From Ref. (19).

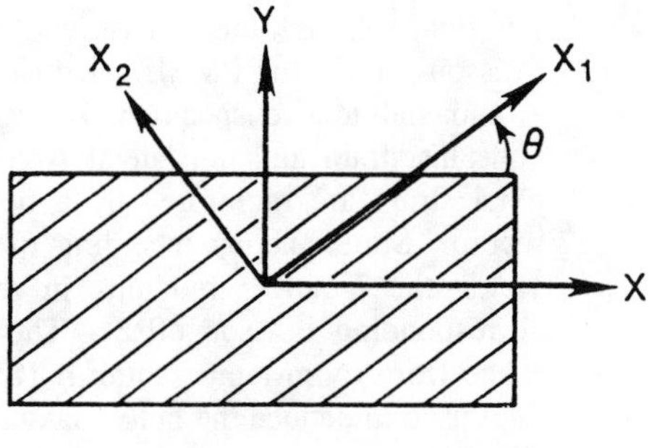

FIGURE 6. Unidirectional ply
and coordinates.

21

The Investigation of the Mechanical Properties of Thermoviscoelastic Material

W.G. Knauss
Professor of Aeronautics and Applied Mechanics

Graduate Aeronautical Laboratory
California Institute of Technology
Pasadena, CA 91125 USA

INTRODUCTION

The mechanical properties of an isotropic linearly viscoelastic material can be described by any two of the four time-dependent relaxation functions: Young's modulus $E(t)$, shear modulus $G(t)$, bulk modulus $k(t)$ or Poisson's ratio $v(t)$. Since, with the advent of more refined methods of computation the need arises to manipulate material behavior with increasing degree of sophistication, it becomes important to be able to determine more than the standard engineering properties. To date, few data or even methods have been reported for a full characterization. For example, few reliable records of the time dependent Poisson effect exist, estimates ranging between 0.3 and 0.44 for PMMA. The understanding difficulties derive from the viscoelastic character of the materials, their temperature sensitivities, and the fact that both large and small deformations are involved.

An Image Moire method is employed to determine Poisson's ratio for PMMA at different temperatures. A uniaxial tensile specimen is strained axially to a constant strain and the lateral strain as well and the axial strain are monitored by a period photographic record. Simultaneous recording of the tensile stress yields the Young's mudulus in relaxation and the corresponding Poisson effect. The test temperatures range from room temperature to 125^oC. This data is then used to deduce the bulk relaxation moduli.

Several investigators have contributed to the relaxation characterization of PMMA, with some estimation of Poisson behavior. For resons of brevity we only list the appropriate references and forego any detailed review or discussion at this point. [1-9][1]

---

1. This paper is a summary of reference 1.

ANALYTICAL PRELIMINARIES

Our immediate concern is with the interrelation between uniaxial relaxation, bulk relaxation and the corresponding Poisson function. Let x,y,t be the spatial variables as defined in figure 1 and time and consider small deformations so that under an imposed (step) strain $\varepsilon_{yy}(t) = \varepsilon_{yo}H(t)$ with $H(t)$ denoting the Heaviside step function. If $\tau_{yy}(t)$ is the resulting uniaxial stress, defined on the undeformed specimen dimensions and decreasing monotonically with time, the Young's relaxation modulus is

$$E(t) = \frac{\tau_{yy}(t)}{\varepsilon_{yo}} \qquad (1)$$

Correspodingly, the Poisson function under relaxation $v(t)$ is defined as

$$v(t) = -\frac{\varepsilon_{xx}(t)}{\varepsilon_{yo}} \qquad (2)$$

Using the viscoelastic correspondence principle one easily finds the bulk modulus $k(t)$ through an integral equation

$$E(t) = 3\left\{ (1-2v_g)k(t) + 2\int_{o,t}^{t} k(t)\frac{d\gamma(t-u)}{du}du \right\} \quad (3)$$

For later reference we remark that on the basis of physical considerations $k(t)$ must be a monotonically decreasing function of time. Upon introducing N (non-constant) subintervals of integration ($t_o \equiv 0$) one has

$$E(t_N) = 3\left\{ (1-2v_g k)(t_n) + 2\sum_{n=1}^{N}\int_{t_{n-1}}^{t_n} k(u)\left[\frac{dv(t-u)}{d(t-u)}\right]du \right\}$$

and replacing the integrands by their interval midvalues for sufficiently small intervals one obtains, after some manipulation [see e.g., 10] the bulk modulus at discrete times as

$$k(t_n) = \left\{ \frac{1}{3}E(t_n) + k_g\left[v(t_n) - v(t_n - t_{n-1})\right] \quad + (4) \right.$$

$$\sum_{i=1}^{i=n-1} k(t_i)\left[v(t_n - t_{i-1}) - v(t_n - t_{i+1})\right] \biggr\} \bullet$$

$$\bullet\left\{1 - v_g - v(t_n - t_{n-1})\right\}^{-1}$$

with

$$k(t_1) = \frac{E(t_1)/3 = k_g[v(t_1) - v_g]}{1 - v_g - v(t_1)}$$

$$\text{and } k_g = \frac{E_g}{3(1 - 2v_g)}, \quad E_g = E(o), \quad v_g = v(o)$$

MATERIAL AND SPECIMEN PREPARATION

The model material was commercial PMMA (Rohm & Hass, nominally 3/16" thick, $T_g = 105^o C$), which was annealed for two hours at $120^o C$ and cooled (slowly) at $5^o C/hr$ to room temperature. This annealing process was necessary because the as-received material contained residual strains as a result of the rapid cooling in the production process: while there exists a mild anisotropy in the material prior to annealing, that material feature disappeared within experimental error after annealing.

The specimen, shown in figure 1, has its ends reinforced with aluminum tabs to reduce creep in that portion of the specimen during testing, and as a result, very stable strains were obtained as monitored photographically during the whole test period, using moire grating with 40 lines per millimeter, finer gratings developed resolution problems derived from multiple reflections as the light beam passed through the (multi-pane) window of the environmental chamber.

TEST ARRANGEMENT AND DATA PROCESSING

A schematic of the test set-up is given in figure 2. The lens system is adjusted to provide an initial, small mismatch between the grating on the specimen and its screen image to enhance the sensitivity of the measurements. The temperature was continuously monitored close to the specimen and was always within $\pm 0.2^o C$; the room humidity remained at about 50%. The load cell on the MTS tester was calibrated to within 0.1% of full scale and allowed easy

resolution of maximally $\pm 0.5N$. Straining was accomplished by ramp deformation to less than 0.5% strain with a typical rise time of 1/3 sec. This small strain (usually only 0.2%) was desirable to stay away from possible nonlinear effects [11].

Photographs taken of the fringes indicative of the strain in the axial and transverse directions were photgraphed periodically, and enlarged photographs were passed through a digitizer to obtain an average scan of the gray level distribution. After calibrating this data reduction method with an interferometrically generated fringe pattern of known frequency, the strains were determined (analysis not shown) to render Poisson behavior with an accuracy of ±10%. Dimension and load levels were such as to allow the relaxation modulus to be determined with an accuracy of ±4%.

RESULTS AND DISCUSSION

Figure 3 shows the relaxation data at various temperatures, with the "standard" entropic correction multiplication T_o/T (absolute temperatures) included; figure 4 shows the corresponding Poisson data. The "standard" time-temperature shifting of this data does not produce a master curve that is smooth in terms of the measurement errors. Although there is no common understanding or agreement that such shifting in the glassy region is valid, it has been observed to hold for several materials (e.g., see for PVAC, ref. (11) and an epoxy, ref. (12)) To illustrate this point, figure 5 shows a selected number of curve segments from figure 3, which indicate clearly that the slopes of these segments are not commensurate. We note that the data in reference (2) contains the same features, which were, however, apparently overlooked or suppressed. The appearance of the mastercurve is significantly improved, if one allows also for a vertical (temperature dependent) shift along the ordinate; this process affects, of course, also the size of the shift along the abscissa. The net result of this process for the relaxation modulus and for the poisson data (shifted consistently) is shown in figures 6 and 7, with the coresponding shift functions shown in figures 8 and 9.

Using this data in equations (4) one obtains the bulk modulus as rendered in figure 10. In this context one must note that using simply some average of the Poisson data in figure 7 can (and did) induce a non-monotonically varying bulk function, which behavior is, of course, physically not expected. Enforcing this monotonicity required the use of the solid-line-function in figure 7, which is obviously admissible because it falls well within the scatter band of the data.

There remains the question as to whether the uncommon "vertical shift" introduced here has any physical implication. The fact that under more common circumstances such a shift is not introduced implies that the relaxation spectrum is not affected by the time-temperature trade-off. That situation does not seem to be the case here with the data indicating that at the lower tempertures the material becomes stiffer, which could only come from the (unlikely) introduction of additional stiff deformation mechanisms or from the conversion of some of the more compliant molecular deformation mechanisms to stiffer ones. It will be part of further discussion to illuminate this possibility, as well as potential results of nonlinearly viscoelastic behavior applied to this phenomenon.

ACKNOWLEDGEMENTS

This work was supported by the Program on Advanced Technologies (PAT) at Caltech under the sponsorship of Aerojet General, General Motors and TRW and by NASA under Grant #NSG 1483, with Dr. Tom Gates as the technical associate.

REFERENCES

1. X. Zhang and W.G. Knauss, "Poisson and Bulk Relaxation Properties of Polymethylmethacrylate", CALTECH GALCIT SM Report 91-9.

2. J.R. McLoughlin and A.V. Tobolsky, J. Colloid Sci., 7, 555 (1952)

3. A.V. Tobolsky and J.R. McLoughlin, J. Polymer Sci., 5, 543 (1952)

4. D. McCammond and S. Turner, Polymer Eng. and Sci., Vol. 13, 187-193 (1973)

5. I. Wilson, A. Conningham and I.M. Ward, J. Materials Sci., 11, 2181-2188 (1976)

6. I. Wilson, N.M. Ladizesky and I.M. Ward, J. Materials Sci., 11, 2177-2180 (1976)

7. M.M. Khan and R.I. Tanner, Xth International Congress on Rheology, Sidney (1988)

8. T.W. Gilmore, A. Trainor and R.N. Haward, J. App. Polym. Sci., 23, 3129 (1979)

9. I. Gilmour, A. Trainor and R.N. Haward, J. Polymer Sci., Polymer Physics Edition, Vol. 12 (1974)

10. N.W. Tschoegl, "A Research Program on the Effect of Pressure on the Mechanical Properties of Polymers" Final report, Part II, Oct. 1984

11. I.J. Emri and W.G. Knauss, Computers and Structures, Vol. 13, 123-128, (1981)

12. S. Matsukawa, W. McDonough and D.L. Hunston, "Mech. Properties of Toughened Epoxies" Proc. of the 15th Annual Meeting of the Adhesion Society, Library of Congress number 92-70209.

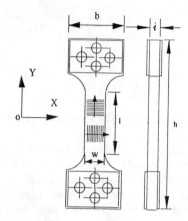

Fig. 1: Specimen geometry and grid location $h = 140mm$, $b = l = 50mm$, $w = 20mm$, $i = 4mm$.

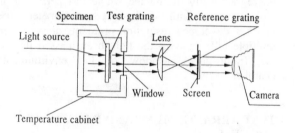

Fig. 2: Test and recording arrangement.

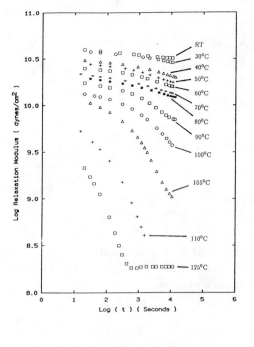

Fig. 3: Relaxation modulus data.

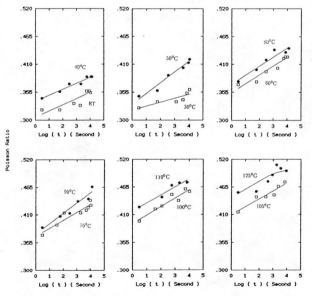

Fig. 4: Poisson data.

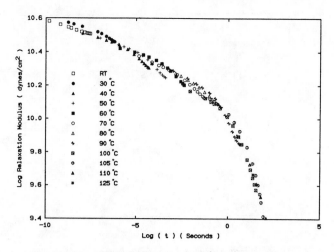

Fig. 5: "Standard" shift of data in figure 3 along the log time axis.

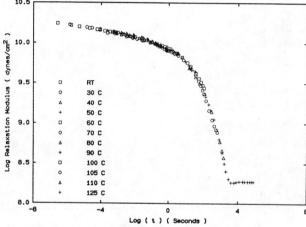

Fig. 6: Master curve with shift along ordinate and abscissa.

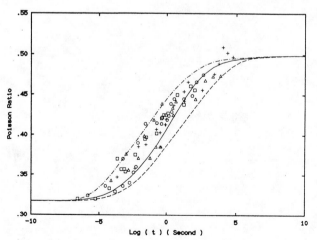

Fig. 7: Poisson data consistent with fig. 6.

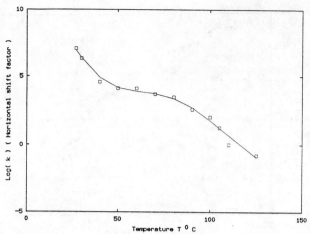

Fig. 8: Time-temperature shift factor for figures 6 and 7.

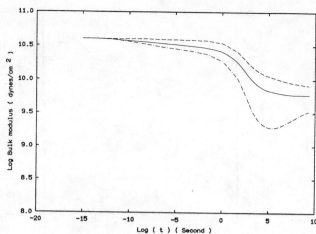

Fig. 10: Bulk relaxation modulus corresponding to figures 6 and 7; dashed curves corresponds to bounds in fig. 7.

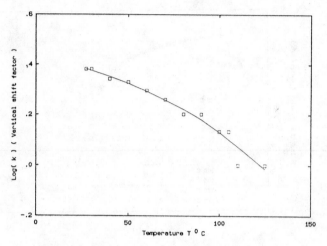

Fig. 9: Ordinate (modulus) shift factor for figure 6.

ESTIMATION OF TIME DEPENDENT MECHANICAL BEHAVIOR OF COMPOSITES FROM FREQUENCY DOMAIN VIBRATION TEST DATA

S. J. Hwang and R. F. Gibson
Advanced Composites Research Laboratory
Mechanical Engineering Department
Wayne State University
Detroit, Michigan, USA

ABSTRACT

This paper summarizes two frequency domain techniques for the estimation of time dependent creep behavior of structural polymer composites. The first technique requires measurements of complex modulus in a suitable frequency range by using the hysteresis loop method. The measured complex modulus data were converted to the time domain creep compliance by using the Inverse Fast Fourier Transform. The second technique involves measurements of complex moduli in a higher frequency range using an impulsive excitation method. The resulting complex moduli were then used in a Standard Linear Solid viscoelastic model for quick estimation of the short term creep response. This method provides a rapid screening test for creep susceptibility of composites. Applications of the two techniques to the analysis of creep behavior of typical polymer composites are presented, along with a discussion of the relative merits of the two techniques.

INTRODUCTION

Polymer matrix fiber reinforced composite materials are known to exhibit time-dependent creep or relaxation response because of the viscoelastic behavior of the polymer matrix materials. The time-dependent creep response is generally magnified by environmental conditions such as elevated temperature and/or humidity, and this is a major concern in the design of aerospace and automotive structures. This paper addresses the characterization of creep behavior of polymer composites used in such structures.

Difficulties have always been encountered in the measurement of long term creep response because of the time consuming nature of the actual creep tests. Thus, alternative procedures such as the time-temperature superposition (TTS) method have been used for accelerated determination of creep response. The TTS method involves measurements of creep for relatively short time periods at a number of different elevated temperatures and then shifting this data to form a master curve at a reference temperature [1-3]. However, because of the extreme temperatures introduced in the TTS method, material nonlinearities may result, and the resulting master curve may not reflect the true isothermal linear viscoelastic behavior of the material at the reference temperature. In addition to the effects of elevated temperature, recent work by Sullivan [4] has shown that the TTS method is only valid for momentary creep results (where the time duration of a creep test is much less than the aging time of the specimen), and is not suitable for determining long term creep response. Thus, there is a need for the development of alternative techniques in the determination of the long term creep response.

The development of analytical models and experimental techniques for the determination of creep behavior of polymer composites has been the subject of many previous publications [1-9]. The work presented here involves the development of analytical models and experimental techniques. The first method is concerned with the use of the Fourier Transform to convert the measured-frequency domain complex moduli of polymer composite materials to time domain creep compliance [10]. Secondly, the use of a Standard Linear Solid (SLS) viscoelastic model, along with measurements of frequency domain complex moduli obtained from a impulsive excitation method, for rapid estimation of creep response is described [11].

FREQUENCY-TIME TRANSFORMATIONS

The first technique introduced here involves the use of Fourier transformations to convert the frequency domain complex moduli to time domain creep compliance. The technique had been previously used to describe the behavior of isotropic linear viscoelastic solids [12]. Our work, however, has been concerned with the behavior of anisotropic linear viscoelastic fiber reinforced polymer composites. As will be shown later, beam specimens of polymer composites were subjected to uniaxial cyclic loading to measure the frequency domain complex modulus. The transformation equation used for characterizing the creep response under such a uniaxial loading situation was derived on the basis of the derivative theorem for Fourier transforms [13], "If $c(t)$ has the Fourier Transform $C(f)$, then $dc(t)/dt$ has the Fourier transform $i2\pi fC(f)$." Thus, for a uniaxial creep compliance $c(t)$,

$$F\left[\frac{dc(t)}{dt}\right] = (i2\pi f)F[c(t)] = C^*(f) \tag{1}$$

and $\quad F^{-1}[C^*(f)] = \dfrac{dc(t)}{dt}$ $\qquad\qquad\qquad\qquad\qquad\qquad\qquad\qquad$ (2)

where
$\quad i = \sqrt{-1}$
$\quad t$ = time
$\quad f$ = frequency
$\quad c(t)$ = time domain creep compliance
$\quad C(f)$ = Fourier transform of $c(t)$ = $F[c(t)]$
$\quad C^*(f)$ = frequency domain complex compliance = $(i2\pi f)[C(f)]$ = $(i2\pi f)F[c(t)]$
$\quad F$ = Fourier transform operator
$\quad F^{-1}$ = inverse Fourier transform operator

The creep compliance is then

$$c(t) = \int_0^t \{F^{-1}[C^*(f)]\}dt + c(0) \qquad\qquad\qquad\qquad (3)$$

where $c(0)$ = initial creep compliance at $t = 0$. A similar derivation leading to the corresponding relationships between the time domain relaxation modulus and the frequency domain complex modulus has been reported in [10]. It should be mentioned that

$$C^*(f) = \frac{1}{E^*(f)} \qquad\qquad \text{for all frequencies, } f \qquad\qquad (4)$$

where
$\quad E^*(f)$ = complex modulus = $E'(f) + iE''(f)$ = $E'(f)[1 + i\eta(f)]$
$\quad E'(f)$ = storage modulus
$\quad E''(f)$ = loss modulus
$\quad \eta(f)$ = loss factor = $E''(f)/E'(f)$

but $\quad c(t) \neq \dfrac{1}{e(t)} \qquad\qquad$ except when $t = 0$ or $t = \infty$ [9]

where $e(t)$ = time domain relaxation modulus

Equation (4) along with the integral of Equation (3) provides a transformation to convert the frequency domain complex modulus to time domain creep compliance. Similar equations for the general three-dimensional case are given in [10]. The first step in the analysis is to measure the complex moduli over a suitable frequency range. In order to obtain long term creep response, measurements of complex moduli over a low frequency range was required. This is because the frequency interval for the inverse Fourier transform is the reciprocal of the total time record length (i.e. the time range over which the creep response is desired). The hysteresis loop method was therefore used for such low frequency measurements

HYSTERESIS LOOP MEASUREMENTS

Complex modulus data at each tested frequency were calculated from the uniaxial hysteresis loop as shown in Figure 1. The calculated complex modulus $E^*(f)$ was used to find the corresponding complex compliance $C^*(f)$ by using Eqn. (4), then the creep compliance was found from Eqn. (3). Details are given in [10].

Figures 2 and 3 present the variation of the resulting complex modulus with respect to frequency for specimens made of Celion 6000/PMR-15 graphite/polyimide [+45/-45] 16-ply symmetric laminate [10]. The resulting regression curves were discretized to provide input to the inverse fast Fourier transform (IFFT) and a numerical integration using Eqn. (3).

Figure 4 shows the resulting creep curve obtained from the frequency-time transformation. It should be mentioned that the resulting creep curve obtained from the IFFT technique is only valid in a time range up to 10^4 seconds, which corresponds to measured frequency domain complex moduli over 0.001-1 Hz. Creep data beyond 10^4 seconds were generated by extrapolation. The results were compared with TTS results from tests of the same materials conducted at Boeing [10]. The curves in Figure 4 differ only in the initial compliance values. If the frequency-time transformation results are recalculated using the initial compliance from the Boeing TTS data, it appears that the agreement is excellent.

MOISTURE EFFECTS

The frequency-time transformation technique has also been used to determine the effects of moisture absorption on the creep response of glass/PPS composites in two fiber reinforcement configurations: (1) random fiber mat, and (2) symmetric [+45/-45] 16-ply continuous fiber laminate. Data was generated for the two material configurations at room temperature in both the as-fabricated "dry" condition and in the fully moisture-saturated "wet" condition. Figures 5 and 6 show the resulting storage modulus and loss factor with respect to frequency. The symmetric [+45/-45] continuous fiber laminate in the wet condition exhibits very high damping.

Figure 7 shows the resulting creep curves for the two material configurations in both dry and wet conditions. The shapes of the creep curves are consistent with expected behavior that the creep compliance increases with increasing time. The effects of moisture on both the initial creep compliance and the creep rate of symmetric [+45/-45] continuous fiber laminate were found to be significant. Such effects can also be clearly observed from the resulting frequency domain complex modulus curves. The moisture absorption tends to increase the material loss factor (Figure 6), while decreasing the storage modulus of the material (Figure 5). For the case of random fiber mat composites, the moisture absorption does not have such a drastic effect on the initial creep compliance and the creep rate. In addition, random fiber mat composites exhibit higher creep compliance than that of symmetric [+45/-45] laminates. The exception was for the case of [+45/-45] laminates in the wet condition, which exhibited a drastic increase in both the initial creep compliance and the creep rate. Such an unexpected increase in creep is to be due to improper fiber surface treatments, and resulting degradation of the fiber/matrix interface by moisture.

COMPRESSIVE CREEP BEHAVIOR

Further research on the work of creep response of glass/PPS composites has led to the conclusion that degradation of the fiber/matrix interface was the cause for the high damping exhibited in the "wet" [+45/-45] laminate. Two solutions for the problem of degradation in the "wet" [+45/-45] glass/PPS laminates were proposed; (1) modify the layup to include some 0° plies without changing the fiber/matrix interface, and (2) develop improved fiber surface treatments so that the original layup could be used. Further, it was decided that, since the materials were to be used in a compressive loading environment, the compressive creep behavior should be investigated. The work reported here is concerned with compressive creep of a new layup including some 0° plies with the original fiber surface treatment. The compression specimens tested here were made of 24-ply symmetric glass/PPS composite laminates. The reinforcement configuration was [RF/RF/0/0/+45/RF/-45/0/0/+45/RF/-45]$_s$, where RF denotes a random fiber fabric ply. By comparison, the previously tested tensile specimens consisted of symmetric ±45° layups.

A special fixture was developed for compressive loading [14]. Both dry and wet specimens were tested over a frequency range of 0.001-1 Hz, which corresponds to a time range up to 10^4 seconds. Obvious differences between the dry and wet specimens can be seen from the resulting creep curves, as shown in Figure 8. It should be mentioned that the creep curves beyond 10^4 seconds were based on extrapolation, and that only the creep compliance data in the range of 0-10^4 seconds were obtained based on frequency-time transformation. The resulting creep curves are consistent with expected behavior, in that the creep compliance increases with increasing time. The moisture absorption causes a significant increase in the initial creep compliance. However, the time rate of change of the creep compliance is very low for both dry and wet specimens, and is not significantly affected by moisture. By comparison, both the initial compliance and the creep rate were significantly affected by moisture in the previous tensile creep tests. Since the layups were different in tensile and compressive tests, however, it is not possible to distinguish between the effects of layup and the effects of the sign of the applied stress. The creep results for the wet specimens were compared with experimental creep test results generated at Boeing (Figure 9), and the only significant difference is found only in the amount of the initial creep compliance. If the same initial creep compliance was used in the two creep curves, excellent agreement would be obtained.

RAPID SCREENING TEST

Rapid estimation of creep susceptibility is particularly important in the selection of structural polymer composites which exhibit viscoelastic behavior. While the previously described frequency-time transformation technique provides a viable alternative to other creep test methods, it is not particularly fast. We have recently developed a rapid screening technique for estimating the creep response based on a viscoelastic model involving both time and frequency domain behavior [11]. In order to accomplish a rapid estimation of the creep response, a so-called impulse-frequency response vibration technique was used for quick determination of the frequency domain complex modulus. The measured complex moduli were then rapidly converted to time domain creep compliance by using the Standard Linear Solid (SLS) viscoelastic model.

The SLS model shown in Figure 10 consists of two elastic spring elements and a viscous dashpot which adequately describes the creep behavior of polymers in the linear viscoelastic range [2]. The expressions for storage modulus and loss modulus (i.e. $E'(\omega)$ and $E''(\omega)$, respectively) of the model are [11]

$$E'(\omega) = \frac{k_1 k_2^2 + \omega^2 \mu^2 (k_1 + k_2)}{k_2^2 + \mu^2 \omega^2} \tag{5}$$

$$E''(\omega) = E'(\omega)\eta(\omega) = \frac{\omega \mu k_2^2}{k_2^2 + \mu^2 \omega^2} \tag{6}$$

where $\eta(\omega)$ = loss factor, k_1 and k_2 are elastic moduli, μ is the dashpot viscosity [2], and

    ω = circular frequency of harmonic oscillation = $2\pi f$
    f = frequency in Hz

Two sets of complex modulus data (i.e. $E'(\omega)$ and $\eta(\omega)$) at two frequencies ω_1 and ω_2 (i.e. first and second modes of the specimen), respectively, were then measured by using the impulsive excitation method which is described in detail in References [11] and [15]. These values of complex modulus and frequencies were substituted into Eqn. (6) to generate two independent equations, and the two unknown parameters k_2 and μ were solved simultaneously. The calculated values of k_2 and μ were used, along with the measured storage modulus at one frequency ω, in Eqn. (5) to find k_1. The creep compliance, $c(t)$, was then found by substituting the values of k_1, k_2 and μ into the creep compliance expression for the Standard Linear Solid given by Eqn. (7):

$$c(t) = \frac{1}{k_1} \left[1 - \frac{k_2}{k_1 + k_2} \exp\left(- \frac{k_1 k_2}{(k_1 + k_2)\mu} t\right) \right] \tag{7}$$

The basic premise of the impulsive vibration method is that the frequency domain complex modulus data at various frequencies can be quickly obtained to determine the three creep parameters such as k_1, k_2 and μ, which in turn provides a rapid screening technique for the estimation of creep response by using the Standard Linear Solid viscoelastic model.

The rapid screening test was evaluated by testing unidirectional E-glass/vinylester (Derekane 470-36) composites having fiber orientations of 0° and 90°. First, the specimens were subjected to a flexural vibration test by using the impulsive vibration method. The resulting complex moduli at two resonant frequencies were used to predict the creep response by the SLS model. The predicted results obtained from the current method were compared with experimental creep results by Sullivan [16], as shown in Figures 11 and 12 for 0° and 90° unidirectional E-glass/vinylester composites, respectively. It is seen that the creep curve obtained by the rapid screening test agrees closely with the actual creep curve for the 0° case. For the 90° case, the two curves agrees closely for short times, but the difference between the two curves increases with increasing time. The 0° and 90° orientations were selected in order to establish limiting cases, with the 90° representing the maximum viscoelastic response and the 0° case representing the minimum viscoelastic response. Clearly, the rapid screening test works best for short times (i.e. 90°) and when the creep compliance does not change much with time (i.e. 0°). This rapid screening technique has also been successfully applied to predict creep response of E-glass/polyester SMC-R25 composite specimens in both dry and wet conditions [11].

CONCLUSIONS

The frequency-time transformation technique based on Fourier transform relationships between frequency domain and time domain viscoelastic behavior has been successfully applied to composite materials. The method has also used to characterize the effects of moisture absorption on creep of polymer composites.

It has been demonstrated that the impulsive vibration response technique, along with the Standard Linear Solid viscoelastic model, provides a quick estimation of the creep susceptibility of polymer composite materials. At this time, the method can produce creep curves which are in good agreement with short term creep test results for a unidirectional composite with 0° fiber orientation and reasonably good agreement for a unidirectional composite having 90° fiber orientation. On the whole, the method described here has significant potential for rapid screening of creep susceptibility in the selection of structural plastics and plastic composites. Further work on the evaluation of improved viscoelastic models to extend the time range for creep predictions is required in order to make the technique more practical.

ACKNOWLEDGEMENT

The authors would like to acknowledge the support of a research grant from the Ford Motor Company.

REFERENCES

1. Ferry, J. S. "Viscoelastic Properties of Polymers". 3rd Edition, New York, Wiley, 1980.
2. Ward, I. M. "Mechanical Properties of Solid Polymers". 2nd Edition, New York, Wiley, 1983.
3. Nielsen, L. E. "Mechanical Properties of Polymers and Composites". Vols. 1 and 2, New York, Marcel Dekker, 1974.
4. Sullivan, J. L. "Creep and Physical Aging of Composites". Composites Science and Technology, 39, 207-232, 1990.
5. Brinson, H. F., Griffith, W. I. and Morris, D. H. "Creep Rupture of Polymer matrix Composites". Experimental Mechanics, 21, 329-335, 1981.
6. Cartner, J. S., Griffith, W. I. and Brinson, H. F. "The Viscoelastic Behavior of Composite Materials for Automotive Applications". Composite Materials in the Automobile Industry, S. V. Kulkarni, Ed., American Society of Mechanical Engineers, New York, 159-169, 1978.
7. Schapery, R. A. "Mechanics of Composite Materials". Vol. 2, G. Sendeckyj, Ed., New York, Academic Press, 85-168, 1974.
8. Findley, W. N., Lai, J. S. and Onaran, K. "Creep and Relaxation of Nonlinear Viscoelastic Materials". New York, North-Holland, 1976.
9. Christensen, R. M. "Theory of Viscoelasticity: An Introduction". 2nd Edition, New York, Academic Press, 1982.
10. Gibson, R. F., Hwang, S. J. and Sheppard, C. H. "Characterization of Creep in Polymer Composites by the Use of Frequency-Time Transformations". J. Composite Materials, 24, 441-453, 1990.
11. Gibson, R. F. and Kathawate, G. R. "Rapid Screening of Creep Susceptibility of Structural Polymer Composites". Plastics and Plastic Composites: Material Properties, Part Performance and Process Simulation, Edited by V.J. Stokes, ASME MD 29, 161-171, American Society of Mechanical Engineers, New York, 1991.
12. Gottengerg, W. G. and Christensen, R. M. "An Experiment for Determination of the Mechanical Property in Shear for a Linear Isotropic Viscoelastic Solid". Int. J. of Engineering Science, 2, 45-57, 1964.
13. Bracewell, R. N. "The Fourier Transform and Its Applications". 2nd Edition, New York, McGraw-Hill, 1978.
14. Gibson, R. F., Hwang, S. J., Kathawate, G. R. and Sheppard, C. H. "Measurements of Compressive Creep Behavior of Glass/PPS Composites Using the Frequency-Time Transformation Method". Proc. of the 23rd Int. SAMPE Technical Conference, Kiamesha Lake, New York, 208-218, Oct. 21-24, 1991.
15. Suarez, S. A. and Gibson, R. F. "Improved Impulse-Frequency Response Techniques for Measurement of Dynamic Mechanical Properties of Composite Materials". J. Testing and Evaluation, 15, 114-121, 1987.

16. Sullivan, J. L., Ford Motor Company, Dearborn, Michigan, Personal Communication, 1991.

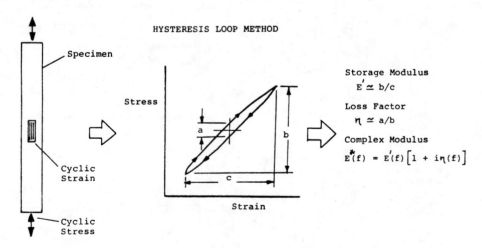

Fig. 1. Hysteresis loop method for measurement of storage modulus and loss factor of a structural material under cyclic loading.

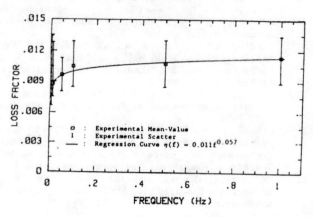

Fig. 2. Variation of storage modulus in low frequency range for Celion 6000/PMR-15 [+45/-45] 16-ply symmetric laminate.

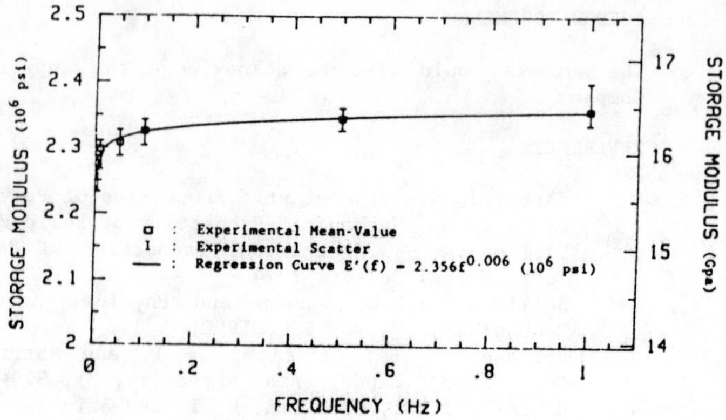

Fig. 3. Variation of loss factor in low frequency range for Celion 6000/PMR-15 [+45/-45] 16-ply symmetric laminate.

Fig. 4. Comparison of creep compliance from frequency-time transformation with time-temperature superposition data for Celion 6000/PMR-15 [+45/-45] 16-ply symmetric laminate.

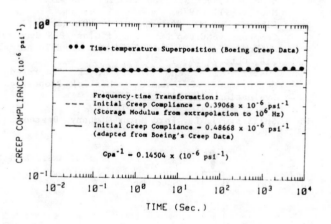

Fig. 5. Variation of storage modulus with frequency for glass/PPS composites from hysteresis loop tests.

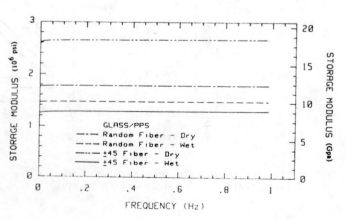

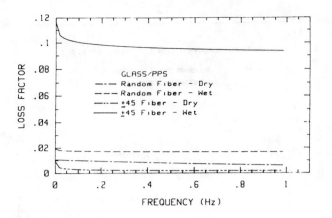

Fig. 6. Variation of loss factor with frequency for glass/PPS composites from hysteresis loop tests.

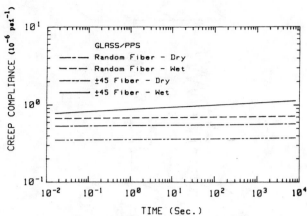

Fig. 7. Variation of creep compliance with time for glass/PPS composites from frequency-time transformations.

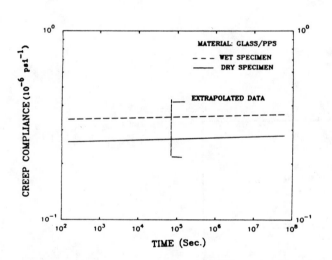

Fig. 8. Variation of compressive creep compliance with time for glass/PPS specimens from frequency-time transformations.

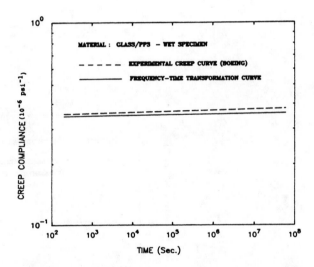

Fig. 9. Comparison of compressive creep compliance from frequency-time transformations with the experimental creep data for wet glass/PPS specimens.

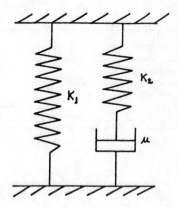

Fig. 10. Standard Linear Solid viscoelastic model.

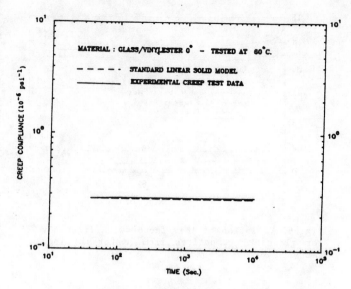

Fig. 11. Comparison of actual experimental creep curve with predicted creep curve from rapid screening test (Standard Linear Solid) for unidirectional 0° glass/vinylester composite.

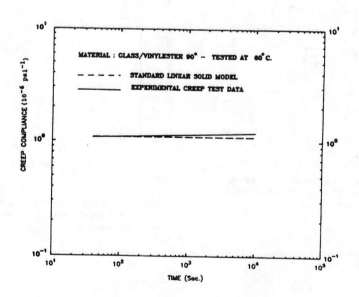

Fig. 12. Comparison of actual experimental creep curve with predicted creep curve from rapid screening test (Standard Linear Solid) for unidirectional 90° glass/vinylester composite.

THE NONLINEAR VISCOELASTIC/VISCOPLASTIC BEHAVIOR OF IM6/5260 GRAPHITE/BISMALEIMIDE

by:

A. Pasricha, Research Assistant
P. Van Duser, Research Assistant
M. E. Tuttle, Associate Professor
A. F. Emery, Professor
Department of Mechanical Engineering, FU-10
University of Washington
Seattle, WA 98195

INTRODUCTION

Modern fiber-reinforced plastics offer several advantages over their metallic counterparts, primarily due to their very high strength-to-weight and stiffness-to-weight ratios. In addition they offer improved fatigue resistance and their properties can be tailored to meet the strength, stiffness, or thermal expansion characteristics required for a specific design application. For these reasons, fiber-reinforced plastics have emerged as a major class of structural materials and are currently being used in many weight-critical components in the aerospace, automotive, and other industries. Nevertheless, concerns remain regarding their long term durability because of their time-dependent behavior. The principal source of this behavior is the polymeric matrix, although for composites in which an organic fiber is used (e.g., Kevlar), the fiber is also a contributing factor. Many mechanisms contribute towards the time-dependent nature of the polymeric matrix, and for the present discussion it is convenient to classify them into the three broad categories shown in Figure 1:

- Nonlinear Viscoelastic-Viscoplastic Behavior[1]: All polymers are viscoelastic to some extent, and many polymers (especially thermoplastics) are also viscoplastic. The viscoelastic-viscoplastic response typically becomes more pronounced and more highly nonlinear at high temperatures and/or high stress levels.

- Chemical Degradation: Included in this category are "physical aging" effects, usually associated with the loss of free volume, and "chemical aging" effects, which are caused by a wide array of phenomena, including oxidation, moisture sorption-desorption, outgassing, ultraviolet or gamma radiation, etc.

- Mechanical Degradation: Included in this category are physical defects which develop under load with time, which can include include matrix cracking, delaminations, fiber-matrix interfacial bond failures, etc.

Note that although these mechanisms are presented in separate categories, they are in reality all highly coupled. There is a widely-recognized need to develop a methodology which can be used to predict the long-term durability of composites based solely on short-term tests. Such a prediction must account for the coupled effects of all of the factors noted above and unfortunately is well beyond the current state-of-the-art. In order to advance the state-of-the-art it is necessary to select for study only one or two of the many variables which can impact the long-term durability and to simultaneously attempt to minimize or hold constant the impact of all other factors.

In the present study the nonlinear viscoelastic-viscoplastic behavior of IM6/52560 graphite-bismaleimide is being studied. The effects of chemical degradation are not being considered directly, although they are likely negligible for the time durations and conditions considered during this study. Mechanical degradation is being considered indirectly, in the sense that any irrecoverable strains which develop during testing are treated as "viscoplastic" strains. The overall study involves 10-hr creep/creep-recovery tests at temperatures of 93, 121, and 149°C (200, 250, and

---

[1] In this paper the phrase "viscoelastic strains" refers to strains which do not occur instantaneously upon application of a stress but rather develop with the passage of time, and which can be completely recovered if all stresses are relieved and sufficient time passes. The phrase "viscoplastic strains" also refers to strains which do not occur instantaneously upon application of a stress but rather develop with the passage of time. However viscoplastic strains are permanent and irrecoverable, even if all stresses are removed for long times.

300°F). As of the date of this report only the 93°C tests have been completed, however, and so only this data will be described herein. Measurements at the additional test temperatures will be reported in later publications.

The data being collected are interpreted using the nonlinear viscoelastic/viscoplastic model developed by Schapery[1,2]. The Schapery model has been successfully applied to a variety of materials, including, for example, glass-epoxy[3,4], graphite-epoxy[4,5,6], FM-73 epoxy [7], and Kevlar/epoxy[8]. To the authors' knowledge this is the first time the Schapery model has been applied to a graphite-bismaleimide system.

EXPERIMENTAL DETAILS

TESTING FACILITY

All the creep/creep-recovery tests were performed using a seven station lever-arm creep frame designed and built in-house during the present study. Each of the seven lever arms has a fixed load ratio of 15.1:1, and is designed to apply a maximum load of 20,000 lbf per arm. Loads can be independently applied to each lever arm by raising or lowering a weight trolley car, which is computer-controlled using a stepper motor. All tests stations are equipped with an environmental chamber. The internal cavity of each chamber is nominally 24" x 15" x 12" in, and each chamber is insulated using 3" thick temperlite brand insulation. All chambers are interconnected using a 4" dia insulted duct, which also connects them to a high temperature blower and to two heater boxes containing resistive heaters. Heat is introduced in each chamber by an air-flow created using the blower, and heated by the resistive heaters. Temperatures are sensed using a K-series thermocouple in each chamber. The temperature in an individual chamber can be maintained to within about ±3.6°C (±2°F).

SPECIMENS

All specimens tested were provided by the Boeing Commercial Airplane Co. Nominal specimen width and length was 38 and 305 mm (1.5- and 12-in), respectively. Two-inch long fiberglass end tabs were adhesively bonded to both ends of the specimen, so the nominal gage length (defined by the tab-to-tab distance) was 203 mm (8 in).

Nominal specimen thickness was 3.43 mm (0.135 in), except for the 0-deg specimens which had a nominal thickness of 1.71 mm (0.0675 in). The specimens were fabricated several months prior to testing. They were stored at room temperature in chambers filled with dessicant, which maintained a relative humidity of 30-35%. The specimens were removed from these chambers only to be strain gaged, and/or just prior to testing.

The specimens were instrumented with Micro-Measurement CEA-06-125UT-350 ohm gages, mounted back-to-back and wired in series. This arrangement provided high gage resistance and also electrically averaged any effects due to specimen bending. Thermal compensation of the strain gage signal was accomplished using the dummy gage technique. The gages were mounted to the specimens using M-Bond 610 adhesive and cured at 110C for 4 hours.

DATA ACQUISITION

Strains were measured using a Measurements Group Series 2100 multi-channel signal conditioner/amplifier. The analog voltages representing strain and temperature were monitored using a Macintosh IIci computer equipped with a National Instruments NB-MIO-16X multifunction board and AMUX-64 analog multiplexer. An automatic data acquisition and temperature control program was written in-house using the National Instruments LabView-2 programming language.

THE SCHAPERY THEORY

For the case of uniaxial loading at a constant temperature, the Schapery theory reduces to the following single-integral expression.

$$\varepsilon(t) = g_0^t A_0 \sigma^t + g_1^t \int_{0^-}^{t} \Delta A(\psi - \psi') \frac{d(g_2^\tau \sigma^\tau)}{d\tau} d\tau \qquad (1)$$

where

$$\psi = \int_{0^-}^{t} \frac{dt}{a_\sigma} \quad \text{and} \quad \psi' = \int_{0^-}^{\tau} \frac{d\tau}{a_\sigma}$$

In equation (1), $\varepsilon(t)$ represents uniaxial kinematic strain at current time t, A_0 is the instantaneous elastic compliance and ΔA is the linear creep compliance function.

g_0, g_1, g_2, and a_σ are stress-dependent nonlinearizing parameters. The specific mathematical form of the linear creep compliance is not specified by the theory. In the present study the following creep compliance was used, as suggested by Schapery [12]:

$$\Delta A = \sum_r A_r[1 - e^{-\lambda_r \psi}] + D_f \psi \qquad (2)$$

The terms A_r, λ_r, and D_f are all material constants. The exponential terms can be interpreted as representing a series of kelvin elements and therefore represent viscoelastic behavior, while $D_f \psi$ represents a steady flow component which results in an irrecoverable strain upon load removal and therefore represents viscoplastic behavior.

Substituting equation (2) into equation(1) results in

$$\varepsilon(t) = g_0^t A_0 \sigma^t + g_1^t \int_{0^-}^{t} \{\sum_r A_r[1 - e^{-\lambda_r(\psi - \psi')}]\} \frac{d(g_2^\tau \sigma^\tau)}{d\tau} d\tau$$
$$+ g_1^t \int_{0^-}^{t} D_f(\psi - \psi') \frac{d(g_2^\tau \sigma^\tau)}{d\tau} d\tau$$

$$(3)$$

A recursive relationship which represents the above integral, but without the viscoplastic component $D_f \psi$, was obtained by Henriksen[9] and was subsequently implemented by Roy and Reddy[10] and Ha and Springer[6]. A similar derivation of the Henriksen recursive algorithm, but which includes the $D_f \psi$ term, was obtained during the present study and is described in the appendix. The recursive relationship is:

$$\varepsilon(t) = (g_0^t A_0 + g_1^t g_2^t \sum_r A_r - g_1^t g_2^t \sum_r A_r \beta_r^t) \sigma^t$$
$$+ g_1^t \{\sum_r A_r[g_2^{t-\Delta t} \beta_r^{t-\Delta t} \sigma^{t-\Delta t} - e^{-\lambda_r \Delta \psi^t} q_r^{t-\Delta t}]\} \qquad (4)$$
$$+ g_1^t D_f[p^{t-\Delta t} + 0.5(\psi^t - \psi^{t-\Delta t})(g_2^t \sigma^t + g_2^{t-\Delta t} \sigma^{t-\Delta t})]$$

Calculation of Viscoelastic Parameters

All of the material parameters in equation(4) can be obtained through a series of creep/creep-recovery tests . The stress history applied during such tests is shown in Figure 2. During the creep time (i.e., for time $0 < t < t_1$),

equation(4) reduces to the following expression for creep:

$$\varepsilon_{creep}(t) = (g_0^t A_0 + g_1^t g_2^t \sum_r A_r[1 - e^{-\lambda_r t/a_\sigma^t}]) \sigma_0$$
$$+ (g_1^t g_2^t D_f t / a_\sigma) \sigma_0 \qquad (5)$$

Note that the value for g_0, g_1, g_2, and a_σ are dependent upon the applied constant creep stress level σ_0. At times (t $> t_1$), the creep-recovery response is given by:

$$\varepsilon_{recovery}(t) = g_2^t \sigma_0 \sum_r A_r[e^{-\lambda_r(t - t_1)} (1 - e^{-\lambda_r t_1/a_\sigma^t})]$$
$$+ D_f g_2^t \sigma_0 \frac{t_1}{a_\sigma^t} \qquad (6)$$

Linear viscoelastic behavior is usually observed at relatively low stress levels, hence at these levels $g_0 = g_1 = g_2 = a_\sigma = 1$. Using these values the creep equation (5) reduces to

$$\varepsilon_{creep}(t) = (A_0 + \sum_r A_r[1 - e^{-\lambda_r t}]) \sigma_0 + (D_f t) \sigma_0 \qquad (7)$$

and the recovery equation(6) reduces to

$$\varepsilon_{recovery}(t) = \sigma_0 \sum_r A_r[e^{-\lambda_r(t - t_1)} (1 - e^{-\lambda_r t_1})]$$
$$+ D_f \sigma_0 t_1 \qquad (8)$$

Nonlinear behavior is usually initiated at relatively high stress levels. In general at these higher stress levels $g_0 \neq g_1 \neq g_2 \neq a_\sigma \neq 1$. To obtain all the material parameters, creep/creep-recovery tests are carried out at linear and nonlinear stress levels. By numerical curve fitting equation(8) to the recovery data obtained from tests at linear stress levels, the material constants A_r, λ_r, and D_f can be obtained. Subsequently by curve fitting equation(7) to the creep data from tests using linear stress levels, the instantaneous compliance A_0 can be obtained. The nonlinearizing parameters are obtained by using the data obtained from creep/creep-recovery tests conducted at relatively high stress levels where it is assumed that A_0, A_r, λ_r, and D_f are already known. Parameters g_2 and a_σ are obtained by using the recovery data from the nonlinear stress level tests and the parameters g_0 and g_1 are obtained by using the creep data of the same tests.

Test of 0 degree Specimen

Tensile tests with the 0-deg specimen were conducted to determine E_{11} and ν_{12}. The 0-deg specimens exhibited no time dependency for either E_{11} or ν_{12} at 93C. These values were therefore treated as linear-elastic properties. The results obtained were:

$$E_{11} = 158 \text{ GPa} \qquad \text{and} \qquad \nu_{12} = 0.32$$

These values can be favorably compared to the following values obtained by Gates [11] : At 70 C, E_{11}= 161.7 GPa and at 125 C, E_{11}= 156.5 GPa. The value of Poisson's ratio ν_{12} obtained by Gates was: at 70C, ν_{12}=0.31 and at 125C, ν_{12}= 0.36.

Test of 90 degree Specimen

The 90 degree specimens were used to determine the time dependency of E_{22}.Strain data were obtained at seven different stress levels ranging from 11.5 to 38.5 MPa. An automatic data acquisition was used to record the strains during the tests. A sample of a complete data set is shown in Figure 3. Isochronous stress-strain curves, obtained using strain data from 1 minute and 470 minutes after loading, is presented in Figure 4. A slight nonlinearity is observed at stresses above 23.12 GPa. The data obtained at stress levels at 23.12 GPa or below were treated as linear whereas data obtained at higher stress levels were treated as nonlinear data. As stated earlier, an exponential series plus a flow term was used for the linear viscoelastic/viscoplastic compliance. The material constants A_0, A_r, λ_r, and D_f were determined by curve fitting the strain data from tests at linear stress levels. In the series expansion of the linear viscoelastic compliance up to four pairs of A_r, λ_r were used. The average values for these linear parameters are:

$$A_0 = 0.1086 \text{ E-10}$$

$A_1 = 1.556\text{E-12}$	$\lambda_1 = 0.0162$
$A_2 = 0.678\text{E-12}$	$\lambda_2 = 0.1412$
$A_3 = 0.129\text{E-12}$	$\lambda_3 = 0.1426$
$A_4 = 0.710\text{E-12}$	$\lambda_4 = 0.544$
$D_f = 1.901\text{E-15}$	

A_i are given in units of Pa^{-1}, λ_i are in units of min^{-1}, and D_f has units of $(\text{min}-\text{Pa})^{-1}$.The parameter A_0 is the inverse of E_2, so $E_2 = 9.21$ GPa. The values of E_2 reported by Gates are: at 70C, $E_2 = 9.2$ GPa, and at 125C, $E_2 = 8.8$ GPa

By curve fitting the creep/creep-recovery data at nonlinear stress parameters, it was found that in the transverse direction the material was nonlinearly elastic but linearly viscoelastic. That is, only g_0 deviates away from a value of 1.0 at nonlinear stress levels, all other nonlinearizing parameters (g_1, g_2, and a_σ) were found to be equal to 1.0 at all stress levels.. Figure 7 shows the variation of g_0 with stress and the curve fit to that data. Peretz and Weitsman[7] have assumed an exponential form for the nonlinearizing parameters $g_0(\sigma)$, $g_1(\sigma)$, $g_2(\sigma)$, and $a_\sigma(\sigma)$. The expression obtained for $g_0(\sigma)$ by curve fitting is:

$$g_0(\sigma) = 1 + 1.0553 \text{ E-5} \exp(\frac{\sigma}{5.134})$$

Figures 8 and 9 show sample creep/creep-recovery curves for the 90 degree specimens at linear and nonlinear stress levels, along with the curve fits using the values given above.

Test of 45 degree Specimen

The 45 degree specimen was used to determine the time dependency of the matrix dominated modulus G_{12}.A biaxial rosette was used to monitor axial and transverse strains in the 45 degree specimen. Tests were conducted at shear stress levels ranging from 5.6 MPa to 113 MPa. A sample of a complete data set is shown in Figure 4. An isochronous stress-strain curve, obtained using strain data from 1 minute and 470 minute after loading is presented in Figure 5. From the isochronous curve it is seen that the strain response is linear for stress levels below about 13.7 MPa. As before, the parameters used in the linear compliance were determined from strain data obtained at linear stress levels. The average values of these parameters are:

$$A_0 = 1.7665\text{E-10}$$

$A_1 = 2.885\text{E-12}$	$\lambda_1 = 0.0137$
$A_2 = 1.119\text{E-13}$	$\lambda_2 = 0.0157$
$A_3 = 1.372\text{E-12}$	$\lambda_3 = 0.090$
$A_4 = 1.451\text{E-12}$	$\lambda_4 = 0.279$
$D_f = 6.489\text{E-15}$	$A_0 = 1.7665\text{E-10}$

A_i are given in units of Pa^{-1}, λ_i are in units of min^{-1}, and D_f has units of $(\text{min}-\text{Pa})^{-1}$. For the 45 degree specimen, A_0, is the inverse of the shear modulus G_{12}. Therefore $G_{12} = 5.66$ GPa. The values obtained by Gates for G_{12} are: at 70C, $G_{12} = 5.7$ GPa, and at 125C, $G_{12} = 5.3$ GPa.

The 45 degree specimen was both nonlinearly elastic as well as nonlinearly viscoelastic. The expressions obtained for $g_0(\sigma)$, $g_1(\sigma)$, $g_2(\sigma)$, and $a_\sigma(\sigma)$ by curve fitting the creep/creep-recovery data at nonlinear stress levels are given below.

$$g_0(\sigma) = 1 + 0.00996 \exp(\frac{\sigma}{14.06})$$

$$g_1(\sigma) = 1 + 0.02914 \exp(\frac{\sigma}{24.10})$$

$$g_2(\sigma) = 1 + 0.1335 \exp(\frac{\sigma}{72.63})$$

$$a_\sigma = \exp(-0.0208\sigma)$$

Summary and Conclusions

Schapery's theory has been used to characterize the viscoelastic and viscoplastic response of IM6-5260 material. at 93C. An exponential series along with a flow term was used for the viscoelastic compliance. The flow component used in the viscoelastic compliance results in an irrecoverable strain upon load removal and therefore represents the viscoplastic strain. 0, 90, and 45 degree specimens were used to derive the material properties. Tests at higher temperatures (121 and 149°C) are currently underway.

APPENDIX

Evaluation of Viscoelastic Strains using the Schapery integral

As previously discussed, a recursive algorithm based on an exponential series expansion of the linear viscoelastic compliance and a flow term representing linear viscoplastic response was developed during this study. The derivation of the algorithm is briefly described in this appendix. Similar results have been obtained by Kennedy [12].

Viscoelastic strains are calculated using the Schapery nonlinear hereditary integral. The Schapery integral can be derived from fundamental principles using the concept of irreversible thermodynamics. However, the theory does not indicate the specific mathematical form of the linear viscoelastic compliance, $\Delta A(\psi)$. The linear viscoelastic used here is as suggested by Schapery.

$$\Delta A = \sum_r A_r[1 - e^{-\lambda_r \psi}] + D_f \psi \qquad (1a)$$

where A_r, λ_r, and D_f are material constants.

Schapery integral for the case of uniaxial loading at constant temperature, after substituting for the linear creep compliance becomes:

$$\varepsilon(t) = g_0^t A_0 \sigma^t + g_1^t \int_{0^-}^t \{\sum_r A_r[1 - e^{-\lambda_r(\psi - \psi')}]\} \frac{d(g_2^\tau \sigma^\tau)}{d\tau} d\tau$$
$$+ g_1^t \int_{0^-}^t D_f(\psi - \psi') \frac{d(g_2^\tau \sigma^\tau)}{d\tau} \qquad (2a)$$

Integration of the first two terms of equation (2a) has been carried out by Henriksen[9], but is presented here for completeness. By referring to the first two terms of equation (2a) as $\varepsilon_{ve}(t)$, and last term of the above equation as $\varepsilon_{pl}(t)$, we can write

$$\varepsilon(t) = \varepsilon_{ve}(t) + \varepsilon_{pl}(t) \qquad (3a)$$

Evaluating $\varepsilon_{ve}(t)$ first, by letting $G^\tau = (g_2^\tau \sigma_2^\tau)$ we can rewrite $\varepsilon_{ve}(t)$ as

$$\varepsilon_{ve}(t) = g_0^t \sigma^t A_0 + g_1^t \sum_r A_r \int_0^t \frac{dG^\tau}{d\tau} d\tau$$
$$- g_1^t \sum_r A_r \int_0^t e^{-\lambda_r(\psi - \psi')} \frac{dG^\tau}{d\tau} d\tau \qquad (4a)$$

The integral embedded within the third term on the right hand side of equation(4a) is now separated into two parts, the first part with limits from zero to $(t - \Delta t)$ and the second part from with time limits covering only the current time step, i.e. from $(t - \Delta t)$ to t. Hence:

$$\int_0^t e^{-\lambda_r(\psi - \psi')} \frac{dG^\tau}{d\tau} d\tau = \int_0^{t - \Delta t} e^{-\lambda_r(\psi - \psi')} \frac{dG^\tau}{d\tau} d\tau$$
$$+ \int_{t - \Delta t}^t e^{-\lambda_r(\psi - \psi')} \frac{dG^\tau}{d\tau} d\tau \qquad (5a)$$

The first term on the right hand side of equation (5a) can be rewritten as

$$\int_0^{t - \Delta t} e^{-\lambda_r(\psi - \psi')} \frac{dG^\tau}{d\tau} d\tau = \left\{ e^{-\lambda_r \Delta \psi^t} \right\} \left\{ q_r^{t - \Delta t} \right\} \qquad (6a)$$

where

$$\Delta \psi^t = \psi^t - \psi^{t - \Delta t} \qquad (7a)$$

$$q_r^{t - \Delta t} = \int_0^{t - \Delta t} e^{-\lambda_r(\psi^{t - \Delta t} - \psi^\tau)} \frac{dG^\tau}{d\tau} d\tau \qquad (8a)$$

The second integral on the right hand side of equation (5a) is now integrated by parts. In order to carry out the integration, it is assumed that G^t varies linearly with time and hence its second derivative is zero. Since G^t has been assumed linear function over the current load step, we can write

$$\frac{dG^t}{dt} = \frac{G^t - G^{t-\Delta t}}{\Delta\psi^t} \qquad (9a)$$

Substitution of equation (9a) into the second integral in equation (5a) gives

$$\int_{t-\Delta t}^{t} e^{-\lambda_r(\psi^t-\psi^\tau)}\frac{dG^\tau}{d\tau}d\tau = \left[G^t - G^{t-\Delta t}\right]\beta_r^t \qquad (10a)$$

where

$$\beta_r^t = \frac{1 - e^{-\lambda_r\Delta\psi^t}}{\lambda_r\Delta\psi^t} \qquad (11a)$$

Substituting equations (8a) and (10a) back into (4a), and writing $G^t = g^t\sigma^t$, one obtains

$$\varepsilon_{ve}(t) = \left[g_0^t A_0 + g_1^t g_2^t \sum_r A_r - g_1^t g_2^t \sum_r A_r\beta_r^t\right]\sigma^t$$
$$+ g_1^t\left\{\sum_r A_r\left[g_2^{t-\Delta t}\beta_r^t\sigma^{t-\Delta t} - e^{-\lambda_r\Delta\psi^t}q_r^{t-\Delta t}\right]\right\} \qquad (12a)$$

Defining instantaneous compliance A_I^t as the compliance term multiplying the instantaneous stress σ^t, and the remaining terms in equation (12a) as hereditary strains E_t, we can write

$$\varepsilon_{ve}(t) = A_I^t\sigma^t + E^t = F(\sigma) \qquad (13a)$$

where

$$A_I^t = g_1^t\left\{\sum_r A_r\left[g_2^{t-\Delta t}\beta_r^t\sigma^{t-\Delta t} - e^{-\lambda_r\Delta\psi^t}q_r^{t-\Delta t}\right]\right\} \qquad (14a)$$

$$E^t = g_1^t\left\{\sum_r A_r\left[g_2^{t-\Delta t}\beta_r^t\sigma^{t-\Delta t} - e^{-\lambda_r\Delta\psi^t}q_r^{t-\Delta t}\right]\right\} \qquad (15a)$$

Equation (13a) expresses Schapery's single integral constitutive law in terms of a stress operator that includes instantaneous compliance and hereditary strains. The term $q_r^{t-\Delta t}$ in equation (15a) is the rth component of the hereditary integral series at the end of the previous load step (i.e. at times $(t-\Delta t)$). Thus, the expression for the hereditary integral at the end of the current load step (i.e. at time t) can be derived in the form of a recurrence formula. From equation (8a) we can write

$$q_r^t = \int_0^t e^{-\lambda_r(\psi^t-\psi^\tau)}\frac{dG^\tau}{d\tau}d\tau = \int_0^{t-\Delta t} e^{-\lambda_r(\psi^t-\psi^\tau)}\frac{dG^\tau}{d\tau}d\tau$$
$$+ \int_{t-\Delta t}^{t} e^{-\lambda_r(\psi^t-\psi^\tau)}\frac{dG^\tau}{d\tau}d\tau \qquad (16a)$$

Using the result from equations (8a) and (11a), the above equation can be reduced to

$$q_r^t = e^{-\lambda_r\Delta\psi^t}q_r^{t-\Delta t} + \left[g_2^t\sigma^t - g_2^{t-\Delta t}\sigma^{t-\Delta t}\right]\beta_r^t \qquad (17a)$$

where β_r^t is defined by equation (11a). Now evaluating $\varepsilon_{pl}(t)$, where

$$\varepsilon_{pl}(t) = g_1^t\int_0^t\left[D_f(\psi^t - \psi^\tau)\right]\frac{dG^\tau}{d\tau}d\tau \qquad (18a)$$

A recursive equation can now be developed for $\varepsilon_{pl}(t)$, by proceeding in similar way as used for evaluating $\varepsilon_{ve}(t)$. The integral in equation (18a) is now separated into two parts, with the first part with limits from zero to $(t - \Delta t)$ and the second part with limits covering only the current time step, i.e., from $(t - \Delta t)$ to t. Then,

$$\varepsilon_{pl}(t) = g_1^t\left\{\int_0^{t-\Delta t}\left[D_f(\psi^t - \psi^\tau)\right]\frac{dG^\tau}{d\tau}d\tau + \int_{t-\Delta t}^{t}\left[D_f(\psi^t - \psi^\tau)\right]\frac{dG^\tau}{d\tau}d\tau\right\} \qquad (19a)$$

The first part of the integral in equation (19a), with limits from zero to $(t - \Delta t)$, can be written as $p^{t-\Delta t}$, where

$$p^{t-\Delta t} = \int_0^{t-\Delta t}\left[D_f(\psi^t - \psi^\tau)\right]\frac{dG^\tau}{d\tau}d\tau \qquad (20a)$$

The second term of the equation can be easily evaluated by parts, by using the approximations

$$\frac{dG^t}{dt} = \frac{G^t - G^{t-\Delta t}}{\Delta t} \qquad (21a)$$

and

$$\int_{t-\Delta t}^{t}\psi^t = \frac{(\psi^t + \psi^{t-\Delta t})}{2}\Delta t \qquad (22a)$$

and by observing that G^t has been assumed linear over the current time step, thus its second derivative is zero. By carrying out the integration of equation (19a), we finally obtain:

$$\varepsilon_{pl}(t) = p^{t-\Delta t} + 0.5(\psi^t - \psi^{t-\Delta t})(G^t + G^{t-\Delta t}) \qquad (23a)$$

where $p^{t-\Delta t}$ in equation (23a), is the recursive term which can be evaluated by

$$p^t = p^{t-\Delta t} + 0.5(\psi^t - \psi^{t-\Delta t})(G^t + G^{t-\Delta t}) \qquad (24a)$$

Now by substituting the results of equation (12a) and (23a) into equation (3a), we finally obtain:

$$\varepsilon_{pl}(t) = g_1^t \varepsilon(t) = (g_0^t A_0 + g_1^t g_2^t \sum_r A_r - g_1^t g_2^t \sum_r A_r \beta_r^t)\, \sigma^t$$

$$+ g_1^t \{ \sum_r A_r [g_2^{t-\Delta t} \beta_r^t \sigma^{t-\Delta t} - e^{-\lambda_r \Delta \psi^t} q_r^{t-\Delta t}] \} \qquad (25a)$$

$$+ g_1^t\, D_f [p^{t-\Delta t} + 0.5(\psi^t - \psi^{t-\Delta t})(g_2^t \sigma^t + g_2^{t-\Delta t} \sigma^{t-\Delta t})]$$

Acknowledgements

This work is sponsored by a grant from the Boeing Commercial Airplane. This financial support as well as the many helpful discussions with Mr. Ramesh Khanna of the Boeing Co. are gratefully acknowledged.

References

1. Schapery, R.A., "A Theory of Non-linear Thermoviscoelasticity Based on Irreversible Thermodynamics", PROC 5th US National Congress Appl Mech, ASME(1966).

2. Schapery, R.A., "Further Developments of a Thermodynamic Constitutive Theory: Stress Formulation", Purdue Univ Report, AA&ES 69-2, (February 1969).

3. Lou, Y.C., and Schapery, R.A., "Viscoelastic Characterization of a Nonlinear Fiber-Reinforced Plastic", J. Composite Materials, Vol 5, pp 208-234 (April 1971).

4. Mohan, R., and Adams, D.F., "Nonlinear Creep-Recovery Response of a Polymer Matrix and its Composites", Experimental Mechanics, Vol 25 (3), pp 262-271 (September 1985).

5. Tuttle, M.E., and Brinson, H.F., "Prediction of the Long-Term Creep Compliance of General Composite Laminates", Experimental Mechanics, Vol 26 (1), pp 89-102 (March 1986)

6. Ha, S.K., and Springer, G.S., "Time Dependent Behavior of Laminated Composites at Elevated Temperatures", J. Composite Materials, Vol 23, pp 1159-1197 (November 1989).

7. Peretz, D., and Weitsman Y., "Nonlinear Viscoelastic Characterization of FM-73 Adhesive", J. of Rheology, Vol 26(3), pp 245-261 (1982)

8. Walrath, D.E., "Viscoelastic Response of a Unidirectional Composite Containing Two Viscoelastic Constituents", Experimental Mechanics, Vol 31(2), pp 111-117 (June 1991)

9. Henriksen, M., "Nonlinear Viscoelastic Stress Analysis - A Finite Element Approach," Computers and Structures, Vol 18(1), pp 133-139 (1984)

10. Roy, S., and Reddy, J.N., "A Finite Element Analysis of Adhesively Bonded Composite Joints With Moisture Diffusion and Delayed Failure," Composites and Structures, Vol. 29, No. 6, pp 1011-1031, (1988).

11. Gates, T.S., "Effects of Elevated Temperature on The Viscoplastic Modeling of Graphite/Polymeric Composites", NASA Technical Memorandum 104160, October 1991.

12. Schapery, R.A., "On the Characterization of Nonlinear Viscoelastic Materials," Polymer Engineering and Science, Vol 9, 1969, pp 295-310.

13. Personal communication, Prof. T. Kennedy, Mechanical Engineering Department, Oregon State University, Corvallis, Oregon.

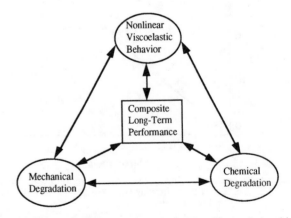

Figure 1: A pictorial representation showing a relationship between different factors effecting the long term Composite performance

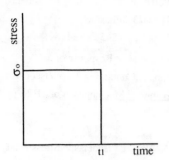

Figure 2: Stress profile used for creep/creep-recovery tests

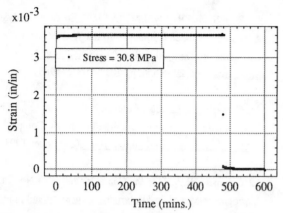

Figure 3: A complete creep/creep-recovery test using a 90 degree specimen.

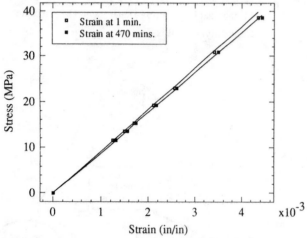

Figure 4 : Isochronous Stress/Strain curve for the 90 deg. specimen showing strains at 1 min. and 470 mins after loading.

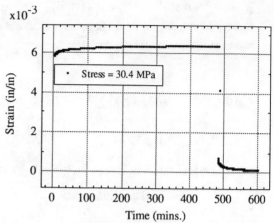

Figure 5: A complete creep/creep-recovery test using a 45 degree specimen.

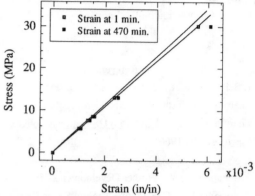

Figure 6: Isochronous Stress/Strain curve for the 45 deg. specimen showing strains at 1 min and 470 mins after loading.

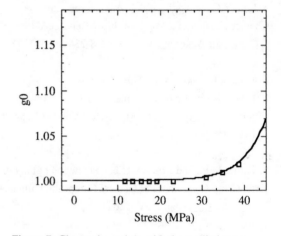

Figure 7: Change in $g_0(\sigma)$ with the applied stress.

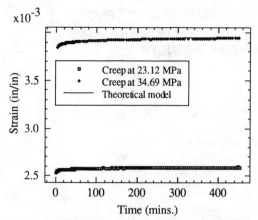

Figure 8 : Creep response of the 90 degree specimen at
23.12 MPa and 34.69 MPa

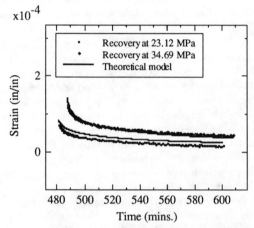

Figure 9:   Recovery of the 90 degree specimen after 8 hr.
creep load of 23.12 MPa and 34.69 MPa

FATIGUE FRACTURE IN THIN PLATES SUBJECTED TO TENSILE AND SHEARING LOADS: CRACK TIP FIELDS, J INTEGRAL AND PRELIMINARY EXPERIMENTAL RESULTS

by

ALAN T. ZEHNDER[1], MARK J. VIZ[2], and ANTHONY R. INGRAFFEA[3]
Cornell University
Ithaca, NY 14853 (607)255-9181

ABSTRACT

In one scenario of a crack in an airplane fuselage, the crack is subjected to cyclic tensile and out of plane shearing loads. To predict the fatigue crack growth in such a situation, experiments are being performed to measure the crack growth rate in laboratory specimens subjected to similar loadings. The mechanics of this problem are reviewed, the energy release rate is calculated and designs for an experiment are discussed along with some preliminary experimental observations.

INTRODUCTION

A common location for crack initiation in aircraft fuselages is the rivet holes of lap joints in the fuselage skin. Over time, cracks originating from the rivet holes link up to form a large crack as sketched in Fig. 1. In most cases these cracks are observed to grow from the top row of rivets, leaving a large crack just above the lap joint. Due to the larger amount of material below the crack than above and due to stiffeners (stringers) along the lap joint, material above the crack line is less stiff than that below the crack line. When the fuselage is pressurized, air pressure causes the fuselage to bulge out along the crack. The top half, which is less stiff, bulges out more, resulting in a relative out of plane displacement at the crack tip.

The fracture mode due to bulging out is similar to Mode-III, but not the same as a Mode-III crack in a thick material, since the aircraft skin is actually a thin shell. Let us call this loading "nominal Mode-III". In addition to the nominal Mode-III loading, there is tension in the skin, resulting in a Mode-I stress intensity factor at the crack tip. Most existing experimental work on fatigue crack growth is for Mode-I conditions. There is very little data for cracks under Mode-III loading, and

no data for cracks in thin shells growing under nominal Mode-III loading. However these are the data that are needed to predict crack growth in cracked fuselage structures. We have begun an experimental program to measure the fatigue crack growth rate in thin plate specimens under in plane Mode-I and out of plane, nominal Mode-III loadings.

The experiments will be performed on single edge cracked samples loaded in tension and torsion, see Fig. 2. To correlate the crack growth rate the relevant stress intensity factors must be identified and calculated. For the in plane tension loading this has already been done; there are hundreds of stress intensity factor solutions available[1]. For torsional loading of a finite plate, analytical solutions are available only for linear plate theory[2], which will be violated in the experiments since the displacements are several times larger than the plate thickness. To compute stress intensity factors for plate deflections beyond the linear range, simulations of the test specimen using the finite element method (FEM) are needed. Methods for extracting the stress intensity factor from FEM results are being investigated. The asymptotic crack tip fields based on classical and Reissner plate theories will be discussed first. Calculation of the J integral based on classical plate theory is outlined and then the experiments are described.

CRACK TIP FIELDS

The asymptotic crack tip fields for plates under bending, twisting and shearing loads are discussed here. All of the results are given with respect to a coordinate system centered at the crack tip as illustrated in Fig. 3. A cracked plate subject to three different loads in shown in Figure 4. Bending parallel to the crack line produces tensile and compressive stresses on the line ahead of the crack tip. Twisting or shearing produce shear stresses on the line ahead of the crack tip. Both the Reissner and classical plate theories predict such stresses, however the details of the stress fields differ in the two theories.

---

[1] Assistant Professor, Department of Theoretical and Applied Mechanics.

[2] Graduate Student, Department of Theoretical and Applied Mechanics.

[3] Professor, Department of Civil and Environmental Engineering.

Classical Theory. Classical (or Kirchoff) plate theory assumes that the deflection of the plate is less than its thickness and that lines originally perpendicular to the plate remain perpendicular to the plate when it is bent. This is equivalent to the plane sections remain plane assumption of beam theory and results in no shear strains through the thickness of the plate, although shear stresses are present. This restrictive kinematic assumption results in being able to specify only two boundary conditions in a problem. For the free edge along the crack the boundary conditions are $M_\theta = 0$, and $V_\theta - \frac{\partial M_{r\theta}}{\partial r} = 0$, where M_θ is the bending moment, $M_{r\theta}$ is the twisting moment and V_θ is the shear force. In general it is not possible to satisfy exactly the stress free boundary conditions of a crack. Violation of the exact boundary conditions causes the plate theory results to deviate from elasticity results in a boundary layer near the edge of the plate.

The asymptotic deflection of a plate at the crack tip is[3].

$$w(r,\theta) = b_1 r^{3/2} \left[-\cos(3\theta/2) + \frac{3(1-\nu)}{(7+\nu)} \cos(\theta/2) \right]$$
$$+ b_2 r^{3/2} \left[\sin(3\theta/2) - \frac{3(1-\nu)}{(5+3\nu)} \sin(\theta/2) \right].$$
(1)

Complete expressions for the asymptotic stress fields are given in [1,3,4]. The stresses on a line just ahead of the crack ($\theta = 0$) are

$$\sigma_{\theta\theta} = \frac{k_1}{\sqrt{2r}} \left(\frac{2z}{h} \right),$$
$$\sigma_{r\theta} = \frac{k_2}{\sqrt{2r}} \left(\frac{1+\nu}{3+\nu} \right) \left(\frac{2z}{h} \right),$$
(2)
$$\sigma_{\theta z} = \frac{-k_2}{(2r)^{3/2}} \frac{(h/2)^2}{3+\nu} \left[1 - \left(\frac{2z}{h} \right)^2 \right].$$

Note that the out of plane shear stress $\sigma_{\theta z}$ is singular as $r^{-3/2}$, while the other stress components are singular as $r^{-1/2}$, which is the singularity calculated using elasticity theory. The higher order singularity in the out of plane shear stresses arises mathematically because the out of plane shear is one order higher derivative that the in plane stresses, and arises physically because the stress free crack face boundary conditions are not satisfied exactly.

The stress intensity factors k_1 and k_2 are related to b_1 and b_2 by [4],

$$k_1 = \frac{-3\sqrt{2}(3+\nu)Ehb_1}{2(7+\nu)(1+\nu)},$$
$$k_2 = \frac{-3\sqrt{2}(3+\nu)Ehb_2}{2(5+3\nu)(1+\nu)}.$$
(3)

The stress intensity factors are defined in the above form so that solutions for the stress intensity factors for various geometries will have a simple form. Figure 4 gives k_1 and k_2 for loadings of an infinite plate containing a finite crack.

Reissner Theory. The Reissner plate theory also assumes small deflections of the plate, but allows lines originally perpendicular to the plate surface to rotate relative to the surface. This extra degree of freedom allows for shearing strains in the plate and allows one to satisfy exactly the stress free boundary conditions on the face of a crack.

The stresses ahead of the crack ($\theta = 0$) all have an $r^{-1/2}$ singularity and are given by Refs. [5-7] (the equations below are slightly modified to make them consistent with classical theory as much as possible).

$$\sigma_{\theta\theta} = \frac{K_1}{\sqrt{2r}} \left(\frac{2z}{h} \right)$$
$$\sigma_{r\theta} = \frac{K_2}{\sqrt{2r}} \left(\frac{2z}{h} \right)$$
(4)
$$\sigma_{\theta z} = \frac{K_3}{\sqrt{2r}} \frac{3}{2h} \left[1 - \left(\frac{2z}{h} \right)^2 \right],$$

where K_1, K_2, and K_3 are the stress intensity factors. The complete stress fields are given in [6,7]. The order of singularity and the angular distribution agree exactly with the fields calculated using elasticity theory, indicating that the Reissner theory is a very close approximation to elasticity theory, at least for crack problems in plates. Available analytical solutions for stress intensity factors based on the Reissner theory are for cracks in infinite plates[1]. The results show that if a K_3 component is present a K_2 component is always present. For thin plates K_3 and K_2 appear to be approximately equal. Thus the K_2 and K_3 stress intensity factors can be thought of as a single quantity. This is consistent with the classical theory results where the shear stress components are both characterized by a single quantity, k_2.

Let us make a direct comparison between a classical theory and a Reissner theory result. For a thin plate subject to bending parallel to the crack line, (thin means that the crack length is long compared to the plate thickness)

$$k_1 = \frac{6M_0\sqrt{a}}{h^2},$$
$$K_1 = \frac{F_1 6M_0\sqrt{a}}{h^2},$$

where F_1 ranges from $.577 - .655$ for $0 < \nu < 1/2$[8]. Thus the classical theory over estimates the crack tip stresses.

Boundary Layer. Many authors have pointed out that the classical and Reissner theories differ only in a boundary layer of size h, where h is the plate thickness. For the ranges of in plane stress intensity factor anticipated in the tests being planned $K_I \approx 20 MPa\sqrt{m}$, and the yield stress $\sigma_0 \approx 400MPa$, thus the plastic zone size $r_p \approx \frac{1}{\pi}\left(\frac{K_I}{\sigma_0}\right)^2 = .79mm$ (.03 in.), which is about one third of the plate thickness for the test specimens and very close to the plate thickness for aircraft fuselage skins.

A model (or cartoon) for the stress fields near the crack in a thin plate is sketched in Fig. 5. Very near the crack tip (some fraction of the plate thickness) the stress fields would be given by the Reissner theory if the material deformed linearly elastic. In an annular region with inner radius approximately equal to the plate thickness and outer radius approximately 10% of the crack length, the stress field is given by the classical plate theory results. The classical theory results can be thought of as far field boundary conditions for the Reissner theory fields.

Stress Intensity Factors for Correlating Crack Growth. Use of stress intensity factors or of energy release rates based on three dimensional elasticity, Reissner theory or classical theory are being considered for correlating the crack growth data. The quantity chosen must be both descriptive of the crack tip failure process and must be easily calculable. Stress intensity factors or energy release rate based on 3D elasticity theory can be calculated accurately using finite elements[9]. These calculations are however, somewhat expensive to perform due to the typically large problem size. Stress intensity factors based on the Reissner theory can possibly be calculated numerically using two dimensional plate theory if elements that capture the kinematics of the theory are used. To our knowledge such calculations have not been reported. Stress intensity factors based on the classical plate theory have been tabulated for a number of practical test geometries and are readily available to experimenters[1]. However, when applying the results, numerical calculations of the stress intensity factor will be needed since there are no existing tabulations of results for cracked, pressurized fuselage skins. Thus a method for calculating the stress intensity factors based on two dimensional finite elements with linear plate elements is needed. We feel that such calculations will be possible, using procedures analagous to those developed for plane strain problems.

In the spirit of small scale yielding, a consistent approach for correlating crack growth in metal plates subject to bending and twisting is to use the stress intensity factors predicted by the classical plate theory. Since the nonlinearities at the crack tip will eliminate the Reissner theory fields, whatever stress and strains are present at the crack tip are completely determined by the classical plate stress intensity factors as long as the region of dominance of the classical theory asymptotic solution is larger than the plastic zone.

J INTEGRAL

As pointed out in Ref. [10], the energy release rate based on linear and Reissner plate theories differ by a factor which is on the order of $(h/a)ln(h/a)$, where h is the plate thickness and a is the crack length. In the planned experiments, this factor is less than .05. Thus calculation of the energy release rate using linear theory provides an accurate measure of the crack tip driving force. It may also provide a method for relating the energy release rate (which can be accurately calculated using finite elements) to the stress intensity factor, when extracting stress intensity factors from finite element results.

For linear elastic materials, and for cracks that grow straight ahead the J integral is equal to the energy release rate, and is given as an integral over a surface surrounding the crack tip. For a plate the integral is

$$J = \int_\Gamma \int_{-h/2}^{h/2} (Wn_x - \vec{t}\cdot\vec{u}_{,x})dzd\Gamma, \qquad (5)$$

where Γ is a contour around the crack tip, W is the strain energy density, $\vec{t}$ is the traction vector, $\vec{u}_{,x}$ is the derivative of the displacement vector with respect to x, and n_x is the x component of the unit outward normal vector to Γ. For a circular contour around the crack tip, using polar coordinates,

$$\vec{t}\cdot\vec{u}_{,x} = (\sigma_{rr}\hat{e}_r + \sigma_{r\theta}\hat{e}_\theta + \sigma_{rz}\hat{e}_z)\cdot$$
$$((u_r\hat{e}_r)_{,x} + (u_\theta\hat{e}_\theta)_{,x} + w_{,x}\hat{e}_z), \qquad (6)$$

where $\hat{e}_r, \hat{e}_\theta,$ and $\hat{e}_z$ are unit vectors in the r, θ, z directions, $u_r = -zw_{,r}$ and $u_\theta = (-z/r)w_{,\theta}$. Substituting for u_r and u_θ and integrating through the thickness

$$\int_{-h/2}^{h/2} \vec{t}\cdot\vec{u}_x dz = (M_{rr}\hat{e}_r + M_{r\theta}\hat{e}_\theta + Q_r\hat{e}_z)\cdot$$
$$(-(w_{,r}\hat{e}_r)_{,x} - ((w_{,\theta}/r)\hat{e}_\theta)_{,x} + w_{,x}\hat{e}_z), \qquad (7)$$

where M_r, $M_{r\theta}$ and Q_r are respectively the resultant bending moment, twisting moment and shear force given in Ref.[11], pp. 283-284 in terms of derivatives of w. The through the thickness integral of W is given in Ref. [11], p. 346 in terms of derivatives of w as well.

Substituting in the above for w given by eqns.(1,3) and integrating over a circular contour

$$J = \frac{k_1^2 h\pi(1+\nu)}{3E(3+\nu)}$$
$$+ \frac{k_2^2 h\pi(1+\nu)}{3E(3+\nu)} \qquad (8)$$

Note that J for a plate differs in dimension from that for two dimensional elasticity since we have integrated through the thickness. To maintain the usual dimensions of work/length^2 one can divide the above by the plate thickness h.

EXPERIMENTS

Here we will describe the plan of the experiments and will discuss results from a preliminary set of experiments on fatigue crack growth in thin plates with out of plane loading.

Planned Experiments. The application of the results of the current study is for predicting fatigue crack growth in aircraft fuselage skins. In such cases the crack will be subject to in plane, Mode-I loading and to out of plane, "nominal Mode-III" loading. To simulate the loading in the intended application, our experiments will load the crack with a combination of in plane and out of plane loads.

The test specimen chosen for the experiments is a 2024-T3 aluminum single edge notched specimen loaded in tension and torsion, (Fig.2). Approximate specimen dimensions are 15cm (6in.) long, 7.5cm. (3in.) wide, 2.5cm (1in.) initial crack length, and .23cm. (.090in.) thickness. Torsion provides the out of plane loading, leading to K_2 and K_3 (or k_2 in classical theory) stress intensity factors. The following fatigue crack growth rate tests are planned: (1) Tension and torsion in phase, with $R = 0.7$ for tension load and $R = 0$ for the torsion, where $R \equiv P_{min}/P_{max}$. The ratio of in plane to torsional load will be varied about a value representative of the stress state in the aircraft fuselage. (2) Tension and torsion in phase, with $R = 0.7$ for tension and $R = -1.0$ for torsion. (3) Constant tension with cyclic torsion, $R = 0$. Further tests will be performed as the research evolves.

Preliminary Experiments. The preliminary experiments were performed with loads applied to the specimen perpendicular to the plate, and in such a way as to produce no bending moment about the crack line, eliminating Mode-I bending stresses at the crack A photograph of the specimen and loading fixture is shown in Fig. 6. The fixture, loaned to us by Prof. Daniel Swenson of Kansas State University, is essentially a universal joint connection between the testing machine and the specimen. Such a connection is needed because the points where the specimen is bolted onto the fixture rotate about axes perpendicular to and parallel to the plate. Different types of starter cracks were used, including saw cut, .13mm (.005 in.) wire EDM cut and cracks prefatigued in Mode-I.

To determine the upper bound to the Mode-III toughness, tearing tests will be performed. In our preliminary tests we found that Mode-III cracks can be torn in a sheet of aluminum and that the cracks grow straight. Tearing can be initiated from either a sawcut or prefatigued crack. The only change is the load for initiating crack growth. It was observed that at the tearing load, the deflection of the plate was very large (1 inch or more) and that the plate acquired a permanent bend due to plastic deformations. There is a significant amount of plasticity involved in the tearing of plates, meaning that elastic, asymptotic stress fields (i.e. stress intensity factor) will most likely be insufficient for correlating tearing test data.

To obtain some experience with fatigue crack growth in Mode-III loading of plates, we performed a number of exploratory experiments, varying the load levels. Two central results emerged. At "low" loads the crack did not grow straight ahead. Instead it grew off at an angle to the initial crack tip. At loads on the order of 80% of the tearing load the crack grew straight ahead for a small distance before it kinked and grew at an angle.

For example, crack growth results from two tests on .63mm thick samples of 2024-T3 aluminum are shown in Figure 7. In both of these tests the crack was started from a sawcut notch. After only a few hundred cycles, a fatigue crack began to form straight ahead of the initial notch. This crack grew straight ahead at a rate on the order of 10^{-6} m/cycle for a short distance. In the case of sample N10, loaded from 13-133N (3-30lbs.), the crack grew to 1.3cm (0.5in.) and then slowed down greatly and began to kink. The final crack path was very irregular. Sample N11, loaded at a lower load of 13-120N (3-27 lbs.) grew only .46cm (.18in) before beginning to kink. During these tests a great deal of crack face contact occurred. This could be seen clearly by the black, ground up aluminum emitted from the crack during the test and could be heard as the crack faces ground each other down. Very similar results were observed on samples of a 2.29mm thick material.

At low loads, about 4.5-45N (1-10 lbs.) for the .63mm specimens, the crack did not grow straight ahead, but grew perpendicular to the main crack. In this direction the new fracture surface is perpendicular to the tensile stresses due to bending.

That the cracks, even at the higher loads, begin to kink after a small amount of crack growth is consistent with the behavior of the cracks at low loads. After the crack has grown for some distance, the crack face contact becomes so great that the stress intensity at the crack tip is greatly reduced. The stresses at the crack tip are then dominated by the tensile and compressive bending moments acting on a line perpendicular to the crack line.

The implication of this result to future work is clear. It is not practical to measure fatigue crack growth under conditions of pure Mode-III loading, due to the crack face contact. One might get around this complication by programming a testing machine to increase the load as the crack grows in order to maintain a constant crack tip stress intensity factor. However this requires a solution for the effects of crack contact on the Mode-III stress intensity factor. Experiments will have to be performed with enough Mode-I loading to eliminate crack closure.

It is feasible to perform tearing tests under pure Mode-III loadings. The cracks grow stably and straight. All that one needs to record are the load, displacement and crack length. However the analysis of the test will require geometric and material nonlinear calculations. The crack tip plasticity may require us to correlate the tearing data with the J integral or similar quantity rather than the stress intensity factor.

ACKNOWLEDGEMENTS

This work was performed with support from NASA Langley Research Center, contract NAG-1-1311. The authors are grateful to Prof. C.Y. Hui, Dr. Wawrzynek, Mr. David Potyondy and Mr. Will Riddell of Cornell and to Dr. James Newman of NASA for their many helpful discussions of this work and to Prof. Daniel Swenson of Kansas State University for loaning us a test fixture and specimens. Use of the facilities of the Materials Science Center at Cornell, NSF/MSC-DMR-8818558 is gratefully acknowledged as well.

REFERENCES

[1] Murakami, Y, (ed.), *Stress Intensity Factors Handbook - Vol. 2*, Pergammon Press, Elmsford, N.Y., (1987).

[2] Hasebe, N., Matsura, S., and Kondo, N., "Stress Analysis of a Strip with a Step and a Crack," *Engineering Fracture Mechanics, Vol. 20* pp. 447-462, (1984).

[3] Williams, M.L., "The Bending Stress Distribution at the Base of a Stationary Crack," *Journal of Applied Mechanics*, pp. 78-82, (March 1961).

[4] Sih, G.C., Paris, P.C., and Erdogan, F., "Crack Tip Stress- Intensity Factors for Plane Extension and Plate Bending Problems," *Journal of Applied Mechanics*, pp. 306-312, (1962).

[5] Knowles, J.K., and Wang, N.M., "On the Bending of an Elastic Plate Containing a Crack," *Journal of Mathematics and Physics, Vol. 39*, pp. 223-236, (1960).

[6] Wang, N.M., "Twisting of an Elastic Plate Containing a Crack," *International Journal of Fracture Mechanics, Vol 6*, pp. 367-378, (1970).

[7] Tamate, O., "A Theory of Dislocations in the Plate under Flexure with Applications to Crack Problems," *Technology Reports, Tohoku University, Vol. 40*, pp. 67-88, (1975).

[8] Joseph, P., and Erdogan, F., "Bending of a Thin Reissner Plate with a Through Crack," *Journal of Applied Mechanics, Vol. 58*, pp. 842-846, (1991).

[9] Banks-Sills, L., "Use of Three Dimensional Finite Elements in Linear Elastic Fracture Mechanics," in *Analytical, Numerical and Experimental Aspects of Three Dimensional Fracture Processes, ASME AMD-Vol. 91*, Rosakis et al. (eds.), (1988).

[10] Simmonds, J.G., and Duva, J., "Thickness effects are Minor in the Energy-Release Rate Integral for Bent Plates Containing Elliptic Holes or Cracks," *Journal of Applied Mechanics, Vol 48*, pp. 320-326, (1981).

[11] Timoshenko, S., and Woinowsky-Krieger, S., "Theory of Plates and Shells," McGraw-Hill Publishing Company, (1959).

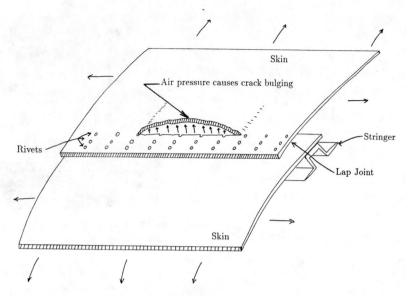

Figure 1. Lap joint in fuselage with a fatigue crack that spans several rivets.

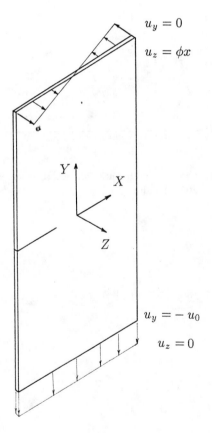

Figure 2. Proposed single edge cracked specimen loaded in tension and torsion.

$u_y = 0$

$u_z = \phi x$

$u_y = -u_0$

$u_z = 0$

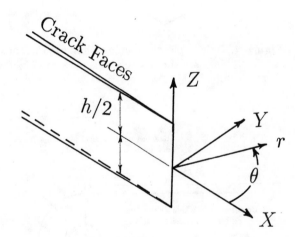

Figure 3. Coordinate system for a crack in a plate.

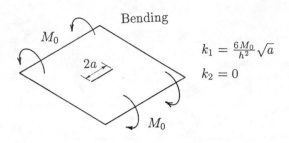

Bending

$$k_1 = \frac{6M_0}{h^2}\sqrt{a}$$
$$k_2 = 0$$

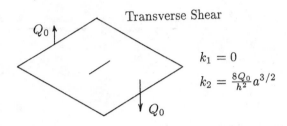

Transverse Shear

$$k_1 = 0$$
$$k_2 = \frac{8Q_0}{h^2}a^{3/2}$$

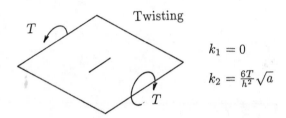

Twisting

$$k_1 = 0$$
$$k_2 = \frac{6T}{h^2}\sqrt{a}$$

Figure 4. Infinite plate containing a finite crack. Three loadings are shown. Solutions for k_1 and k_2 are from Ref.[4].

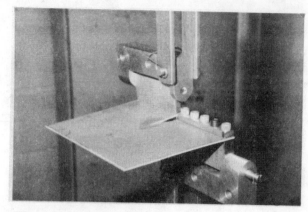

Figure 6. Test specimen and fixture for preliminary experiments.

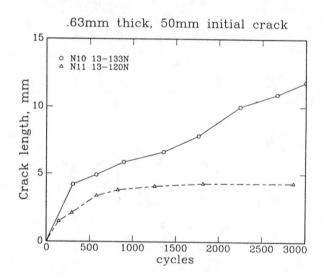

Figure 7. Crack growth data for two tests on .63mm thick 2024-T3 aluminum.

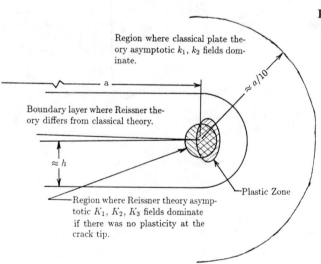

Figure 5. Hypothesized model of the stress fields at the tip of a crack in a thin plate of an elastic-plastic material.

EFFECT OF MECHANICAL STRESS-RELIEVING ON DEFORMATION NEAR A CRACK IN WELDMENT

I. Oda, H. Sakamoto and M. Yamamoto

ABSTRACT

An as welded plate and a welded plate stress-relieved mechanically are dealt with. Each of them has a through-thickness center crack perpendicular to the welding bead. The crack initiates after welding or after stress-relieving. A uniform tensile load perpendicular to the crack is applied to the plate. Stress, strain, plastic zone near a crack and crack opening displacement are examined by elasto-plastic finite element analysis as well as experiment. The residual stresses due to welding and those after stress-relieving are nondestructively measured by means of the ultrasonic technique. The residual stress is considered in the analysis. The effect of stress-relieving on the deformation near a crack are revealed. The tensile residual stress around a crack tip contributes to the increase of stress, strain, plastic zone size near the crack and crack opening displacement. The stress-relieving contributes to the increase of fracture strength of welded plate.

INTRODUCTION

The welding residual stress affects the failure of machines and structures by contributing to buckling and brittle fracture when those failures occur at low applied stress levels. In addition, residual stress may contribute to fatigue or corrosion failures. Considerable papers[1,2] which experimentally examined the effect of residual stress on the brittle fracture strength of weldment have been published. The effect of stress-relieving on the brittle fracture strength has been experimentally examined too[3]. The effect of welding residual stress on the stress intensity factor in a weldment was also reported[4]. There have been, however, few analytical works concerned with stress and strain near a crack in the welding residual stress field. In the above mentioned papers, the residual stress distributions were measured by the stress-relaxation method[1], assumed as a simple curve[2] and represented by a simple function[4].

In the present study an as-welded cracked plate and a welded cracked plate stress-relieved mechanically are dealt with. It is very useful from an engineering viewpoint to estimate residual stress nondestructively, for it can be applied to practical machines and structures. In the present study, residual stresses caused by welding and those after mechanical stress-relieving were measured by the ultrasonic technique based on the acoustoelasticity. The effectiveness of the acoustoelastic method for the nondestructive evaluation of residual stresses are examined. And then, the effect of stress-relieving on the deformation of the cracked welded plate are also examined by an elasto-plastic finite element analysis as well as experiment. The residual stresses are considered in the analysis.

EXPERIMENT

The material supplied is mild steel, SS41 in JIS. Figure 1 shows the shape and dimensions of a test specimen(type SR or type T) used in the experiment. The longest axis of the specimen is parallel to the roll direction of raw plate. Three types of specimen were used. They are type N, type T and type SR. Each type of specimen has a through-thickness center crack of the same length perpendicular to the longest axis of specimen. Type N is not welded. A V-groove without root gap was prepared by cutting on both surfaces, in parallel to the major axis(y axis), in type T and type SR. In type T, the pre-crack was prepared after the arc welding beads were laid on the grooves under the conventional welding condition. In type SR, the residual stress was relieved mechanically by prestraining. A uniform tensile stress was applied in the direction of weld line and then released. The ratio of applied net stress to yield stress of raw plate was 0.80. The pre-crack was prepared after the mechanical stress-relieving in type SR. Both tips of the pre-crack are electrospark machined with a wire of 0.03 mm diameter.

A uniform tensile load was applied to each specimen in parallel to the y axis. Strains in x and y directions as well as the crack opening displacement were measured during loading. The strains were measured by means of the two-dimensional strain gauges with 2 mm gauge length glued to both specimen surfaces along the x axis.

I. Oda is Professor, H. Sakamoto is Lecturer, and M. Yamamoto is Technical Official, Department of Mechanical Engineering, Kumamoto University,
Kurokami 2-39-1, Kumamoto 860, JAPAN.

ANALYSIS

The deformation near the tip of a crack in a plane stress field, which is uniaxial tension in the y direction, was analyzed. An elasto–plastic finite element analysis with an incremental theory of plasticity[5] was used. Three types of specimen model shown in Fig. 2 were used in the analysis, which correspond to those in the experiment. The material was assumed to harden according to the following power low relation between stress and strain suggested by Swift.

$$\bar{\sigma} = c(\alpha + \bar{\varepsilon})^n \qquad (1)$$

where $\bar{\sigma}$(MPa) is the equivalent stress and $\bar{\varepsilon}$ is the equivalent plastic strain. Table 1 shows material constants used in the analysis. Material constants for the weld metal and HAZ differ from those for the base metal. These constants were used based on the result of hardness test and the relation between strength and hardness. The shortest length of the side of a triangular element used in the analysis was 0.05 mm.

For type T and type SR, the residual stresses redistributed after pre– cracking were considered in the analysis. The distributions of the residual stress were nondestructively measured by the acousto–elastic method[6]. An weakly anisotropic solid plate subjected to a plane stress state was assumed in the acousto–elastic measurements. The acousto–elastic constants for the supplied material were measured before welding. The velocities of the shear and the longitudinal wave were measured at several points along the x axis of specimen. Both waves were propagated in the through– thickness direction. The directions of two perpendicular polarizations of the shear waves almost coincided with the principal inplane residual–stress directions, that is, x and y directions. The wave velocities were measured by the pulse–echo–overlap method before welding and after pre–cracking. A ceramics transducer of 7 mm diameter was used at a nominal 5 MHz operating frequency.

Figure 3 shows distributions of $\sigma_{ry} - \sigma_{rx}$ along the x axis, obtained by the acousto–elastic birefringence using only shear wave velocities[7]. Stress σ_{ry} and σ_{rx} are the longitudinal and transverse welding residual stress respectively. In Fig.3, the result for as–welded plate and that obtained after mechanical stress–relieving and precracking are compared. It is obvious from the figure that the welding residual stress is significantly relieved by prestraining. In order to evaluate the effect of residual stresses on the deformation of the plate, stresses should be determined absolutely. Besides the acousto–elastic birefringence, the ratio of longitudinal wave velocity to shear wave velocity was measured for type T. Combining those results, the absolute values of stress σ_{ry} and σ_{rx} were obtained[8]. Figure 4 shows the distributions of the absolute values of σ_{ry} and σ_{rx} along x axis for type T. The dashed lines and the solid lines show the distributions caused by welding and those after precracking respectively. The redistributions of stresses caused by preparing a precrack are obvious from the figure. The acousto–elastic method is found to be effective for the nondestructive evaluation of residual stresses. For type T, the residual stresses redistributed after precracking were considered in the analysis. In type SR, the absolute values of σ_{rx} are estimated to be significantly low[6]. It is somewhat difficult to accurately measure the low stress value by the present procedure[6]. Therefore, it is assumed in the present study that σ_{rx} for type SR is equal to zero. And then, the distribution shown by the solid line in Fig. 3 is considered in the analysis, for approximation, as the distribution of stress σ_{ry}.

RESULTS AND DISCUSSION

The analyzed distributions of stress σ_y, the stress in the direction of the applied tensile load, on the prolongation of the crack are shown in Fig. 5. In the figure, the stress σ_y includes the residual stress and shows the stress value in the case where the ratio of applied net stress to yield strength of the base metal is 0.4. The deformation behaviors at the same stress ratio are shown hereinafter. As shown in Fig. 5, the high stress concentration is found at the crack tip in all the specimen types. The absolute value of the stress σ_y near the crack tip is influenced by the residual stress distribution and becomes higher in the order, for type N, type SR, type T. In type SR, the value of stress σ_y near the crack tip is remarkably influenced by the mechanical stress–relieving and is much lower than that for type T.

Figure 6 shows the distributions of stress σ_y on the x axis obtained by subtracting the residual stress σ_{ry} from the value shown in Fig. 5. That is to say, Fig. 6 shows the increase of stress σ_y due to the applied uniform tension. There is also the stress concentration at the crack tip in all the specimen types. In type T, however, the increase of stress σ_y caused by the external load is considerably small near the crack tip. Because, in type T, the large plastic zone spreads near the crack tip, as detailed later in Fig. 9, even when the low external load is applied. That arises from the residual tensile stress in that region which is as high as the yield strength as shown in Fig.4. In type SR, the increase of stress σ_y caused by the external load is also smaller than that for type N in the vicinity of the crack tip because of the same reason as in type T. But, in the other region than the close vicinity to the crack tip, the increase of stress σ_y for type SR is almost the same as that for type N. The experimental stress values are also shown in Fig. 6, which are obtained by the theory of elasticity for plane stress using biaxial strain measurements. The experimental values agree well with the analytical results.

Figure 7 shows the analyzed distributions of strain ε_y, the strain in the direction of the applied tensile load, on the prolongation of the crack. In the figure, the strain ε_y includes the residual strain. For type T, the value of strain ε_y is much higher in the vicinity of the crack tip when compared with that for type N, because the high tensile residual strain is superimposed on the strain concentration in that region. The ε_y value near the crack tip for type SR is much lower than that for type T, influenced by the stress–relieving, and lies in general between those of type T and type N.

Figure 8 shows the distributions of the increase of strain ε_y on the x axis caused by the applied tension, which is obtained by subtracting the residual strain from the value shown in Fig. 7. The increase of ε_y in type T is much higher than those in other two types, because the large plastic zone spreads near the crack tip even at the low applied stress level in this type. For type SR, the increase of ε_y is much lower than that for type T influenced by the stress–relieving and is almost the same as that for type N except in the close vicinity to the crack tip. The analytical results agree well with the experimental values as shown in the figure.

The plastic zones for three specimen types at the same stress level are compared in Fig. 9. In type T, the plastic deformation, whose zone is shown as " Initial" in the figure, near the crack tip already occurs before the external tension is applied because of the high tensile residual stress. When the external tensile load is applied, the plastic zone spreads extremely wide including the " Initial" region. The plastic zone size for type T is remarkably larger than that for type N. Though the plastic zone size for type SR is larger than that of type N, it is considerably smaller, influenced by the stress–relieving, than that for type T. The plastic zone size near the crack tip for type SR lies between those for type T and type N when compared at the same applied–stress level.

Figure 10 shows the relationship between crack opening displacement V_g at 4 mm inside from the tip and applied gross stress σ. The relation is normalized by dividing V_g and σ by the semi–crack–length a and yield strength σ_{ys}, respectively. Although there is a little difference between the analytical results and the experimental ones because of the finite element mesh and some other assumptions in the analysis, both results show the same tendency. The crack opening displacement becomes larger in the order, type N, type SR, type T when compared at the same stress level. This phenomenon can be explained by the plastic zone sizes mentioned above. It is obvious from the figure that the stress–relieving as in type SR can restrain the marked increase of the opening displacement of crack in the welding tensile residual stress field like in type T.

If there are no considerable differences in fracture toughness among these specimen types, based on the so–called COD criterion, the stress–relieving can contributes to the increase of fracture strength of welded plate in the low applied stress level. This phenomenon can explain the effect of the mechanical stress–relieving on the brittle fracture strength of welded plate, which was reported already[9].

CONCLUSIONS

The following conclusions may be drawn:

(1) Although the high stress concentration occurs at the crack tip in all the specimen types, the distributions of stress σ_y, the stress in the direction of the applied tensile load, are influenced remarkably by the welding residual stresses and the stress–relieving. The σ_y value near the crack tip for type SR(which is a plate stress–relieved mechanically after welding) lies between those of type T(which is an as–welded plate) and type N(which is not welded).

(2) The value of strain ε_y near the crack tip for type SR is much lower than that for type T, influenced by the stress–relieving, and lies between those of type T and type N.

(3) The plastic zone size near the crack tip for type SR becomes considerably smaller, influenced by the stress–relieving, than that for type T and lies between those for type T and type N when compared at the same applied–stress level.

(4) The crack opening displacement for type SR lies between those for type T and type N when compared at the same applied–stress level. The stress–relieving can restrain the marked increase of the opening displacement of crack in the welding tensile residual stress field.

(5) The effect of the stress–relieving on the deformation of a welded plate can be sufficiently estimated by combining the nondestructive stress measurement technique with the finite element analysis.

REFERENCES

1. Kihara, H. and Masubuchi, K., " Effect of Residual Stress on Brittle Fracture", Welding Journal, 38(4), 159s–168s(1959).
2. Akita, Y., Yada, T. and Sakai, K., " Effect of Residual Stress on Brittle Fracture in Steel Structure", Journal Soc. Nav. Archit. Jpn., 125, 227–235(1969)(in Japanese).
3. American Welding Society, Welding Handbook, 7th Ed., 1, AWS, 231– 234(1976).
4. Tada, H. and Paris, P.C., " The Stress Intensity Factor for A Crack Perpendicular to the Welding Bead", Int. J. of Fracture, 21, 279–284(1983).
5. Yamada, Y., Plasticity. Visco-elasticity, Baifukan, Tokyo, (1972)(in Japanese).
6. Oda, I., Iwasaki, S. and Gyotoku, H., " Nondestructive Evaluation of Residual Weld Stress and Mechanical Stress Relieving by Acoustoelasticity", Q. J. Jpn. Weld. Soc., 9(2), 299–304(1991)(in Japanese).
7. Oda, I., " Estimation of Residual Weld Stress and Mechanical Stress Relieving from Ultrasonic Measurements", Proc. 5th Int. Symp. JWS, Tokyo, 995–1000(1990).
8. Toda, H., Fukuoka,H. and Aoki, Y., " R–Value Acoustoelastic Analysis of Residual Stress in A Seam Welded Plate", Jpn. J. Appl. Phys., Supplement 23(1), 86–88(1984).
9. Kihara, H., Masubuchi, K., Iida, K. and Oba, H., " Effect of Stress Relieving on Brittle Fracture Strength of Welded Steel Plate",

IIW Document,X–218–59(1959).

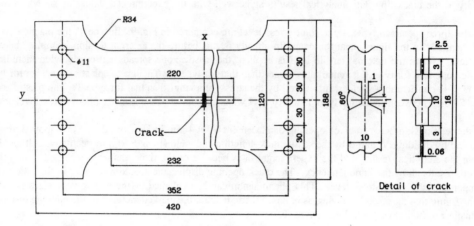

Fig.1 Specimen used in experiment

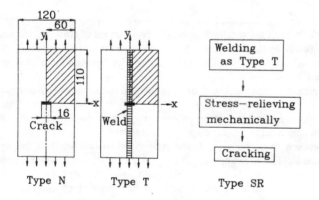

Fig.2 Models for FEM analysis

Table 1 Mechanical properties of material used

	E (MPa)	ν	σ_{ys} (MPa)	σ_u (MPa)	α	c (MPa)	n
Base metal	20·58×10⁴	0·3	304	441	0.013	721	0·2
Weld metal + HAZ			421	541	0.026	873	

E : Young's modulus
ν : Poisson's ratio
σ_{ys} : Yield strength
σ_u : Ultimate strength

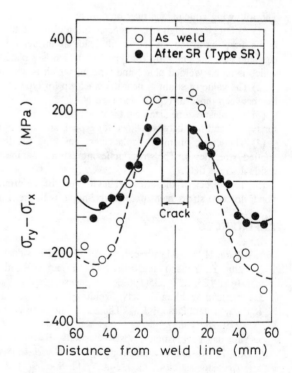

Fig.3 Effect of stress-relieving on residual stress distribution

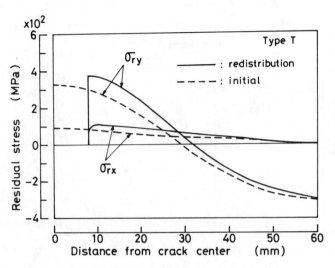

Fig.4 Distributions of residual stresses
on the prolongation of crack(type T)

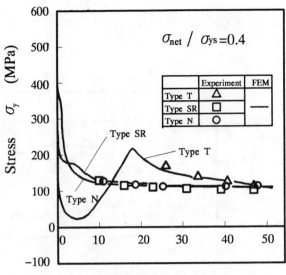

Fig.6 Increase of stress σ_y caused
by external load

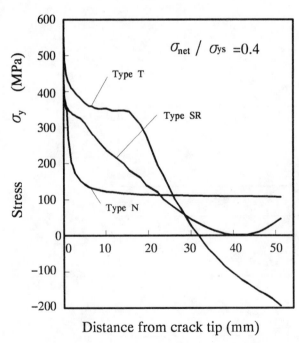

Fig.5 Distributions of stress σ_y on
the prolongation of crack

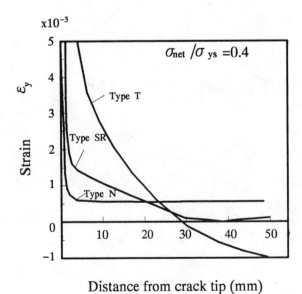

Fig.7 Distributions of strain ε_y on the
prolongation of crack

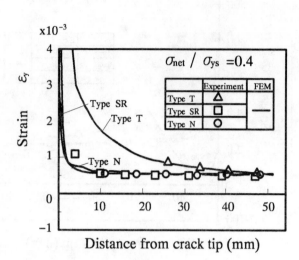

Fig.8 Increase of strain ε_y caused by external load

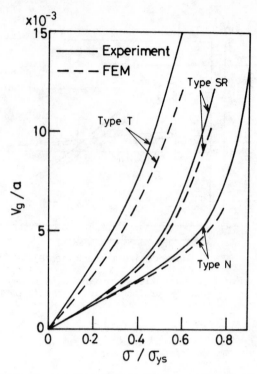

Fig.10 Relationships between crack opening displacement and applied stress

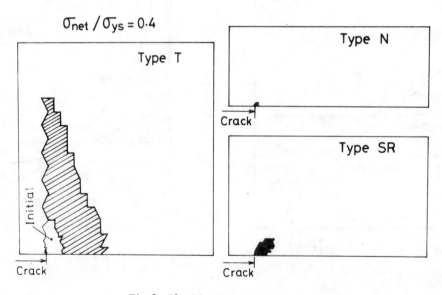

Fig.9 Plastic zones

LOCAL STRAIN BEHAVIOR NEAR CRACK TIP DURING FATIGUE CRACK INITIATION AND PROPAGATION IN POLYCARBONATE AND ITS LIFE EVALUATION

Akira Shimamoto, Eisaku Umezaki and Yasubumi Furuya

ABSTRACT

Polymers have been applied to various industrial fields and used as machine parts and structural members with the swift advance of industry, the usage conditions of polymers have been variously changed, and then the problems of fatigue fracture and of environmental fracture have been intensified. Therefore, the experiment for low cycle fatigue fracture of polycarbonate have been done in this research. Local strain in the vicinity of the notch root and crack tip was measured in real time by using fine grid method. The relationships among the local strain, crack initiation from the notch root and crack propagation of the crack tip have been studied, and the method for the more precise life estimation was suggested in this paper.

INTRODUCTION

Recently, polymers with a high elastic modulus and strength are widely used as machine parts and structural members in cooperation with the rapid development of industry, and demands for scaling up of and making lighter machines and structures, and speeding up of working. As they are used under severer conditions, complex fracture phenomena are found in them. Therefore, understand of deformation and fracture phenomena characteristic to polymers is important for making better reliability of machines and structures, and preventing any accidents caused by their fracture. However, in comparison to metallic materials, there have been not many studies made on the fracture mechanics of polymers, especially on the relations among their deformation behavior and fracture, fracture by fatigue, and failure due to environmental causes. Although initiation and propagation of fatigue cracks have a very important significance for the strength to fatigue fracture which accounts for most of fracture in polymers, the process of fatigue fracture is not well known yet because it occurs in the small zone of crack tip. Polymer, especially polycarbonate has a different fatigue fracture phase compared with that in metals at some levels of stress. To understand it, the relation between local strain behavior and fracture mechanism at the root of notch and the tip of crack has to be known.

The authors[1] have reported a fundamental study on fracture by low cycle fatigue of polymers using the fine grid method. In this study, local strain at the root of notch during process of crack initiation and local strain at the tip of crack during process of crack propagation were measured in real time under low cycle fatigue tests by using the fine grid method, and the relations between local strain and crack initiation and crack propagation were investigated. In addition, a life evaluation method for fatigue crack initiation, and the possibility of unifying the two processes of fatigue crack initiation and propagation were discussed.

SPECIMENS AND EXPERIMENTAL METHOD

Specimens used were polycarbonate (Lexan9030) on the market. Its mechanical properties are shown in Table 1, and dimensions of specimen, in Fig.1. Round notch with a depth of 1.5mm and a radius of 0.4mm was provided at its one side by machining. In order to measure local strain at the root of notch and the tip of crack, fine-dot grids ($25.4\mu m$ pitch and $4\mu m$ diameter) were printed on the surface of specimen using photographic printing technique, as shown in Fig.2. The depth of photo-printed grids was approximately $2\mu m$.

The specimens were naturally dried keeping them in a thermostatic room having conditions of temperature $20°C$ and humidity around 65% for sufficiently long period of time before use, and fatigue tests were conducted in the same room. Fatigue tests were carried out using a hydraulic servo-controlled uniaxial-tension-compression type fatigue machine of 9807N capacity with a digital servo-controller under the condition of a constant load-amplitude at a stress ratio, $R = \sigma_{min}/\sigma_{max}$ of 0, 0.2, 0.3, 0.5, 0.6, 0.65, 0.7, 0.75 and 0.8. Cyclic frequency was 0.02Hz with a sine waveform. In these fatigue tests, K-increasing method was used which implies increase in ΔK with crack propagation. The length of fatigue crack was measured on one side of

A. Shimamoto is associate professor of Department of Mechanical Engineering, Saitama Institute of Technology, Okabe, Osato, Saitama 369-02, Japan.
E. Umezaki is associate professor of Department of Mechanical Engineering, Nippon Institute of Technology, Miyashiro, Saitama 345, Japan.
Y. Furuya is research associate of Department of Materials Processing, Tohoku University, Aoba, Aramaki, Sendai 980, Japan.

specimen by using a X-Y stage with a accuracy of 0.001mm.

Photographs were taken of grids in the area of root of notch and local zone of crack tip using a camera equipped with automatic exposure and automatic film advancing functions through a relay lens and an optical microscope of 100 magnification, at regular intervals of the repetition.

Strain at the notch root and crack tip was obtained by measuring the deformation of grids on the negative film with reference to the grids in the pretested state through a enlarging profile projector with a photosensor. For strain calculation, the gauge length used was 76.2μm (three grids long). Figure 2(a) shows the local region settled for measuring the notch-root and crack-tip strain. In addition, to analyze the crack propagation process, the change and history of local strain at the small fatigued element ahead of the crack tip as shown in Fig.2(b) were investigated until it was broken by advancing of the crack tip, in the similar manner as measurement of strain at the notch root and crack tip.

The crack initiation cycle (Nc) was determined by two methods. One was the confirmation of initiated small crack propagation (crack length=5-10μm) from the notch root by microscopic observation, and the other used the crooked point on the curve of maximum strain ($\varepsilon_{l(max)}$) at the first-line grid from the notch root vs number of cycles, as shown in Fig.4.

RESULTS AND DISCUSSIONS

Fatigue crack initiation from notch root

Low cycle fatigue tests was carried out at a nominal maximum stress, σ_{max} of 32.86MPa and a nominal minimum stress, σ_{min} of 0(R=0), 6.572MPa (R=0.2), 9.858MPa(R=0.3), 16.43MPa(R=0.5), 19.716MPa(R=0.6), 21.359MPa(R=0.65), 23.002MPa (R=0.7), 24.645MPa(R=0.75), and 25.288MPa (R=0.8) in the parallel part of specimen. Presented in Figs.3 and 4 are the relationships between crack length (a)(i.e. notch depth was replaced by crack length) and number of load cycles (N), and local strain range (ε_l) at the notch root and number of load cycles (N) during the process of crack initiation, respectively. As shown in Fig.3, increasing stress ratio (R) caused an increase in fatigue crack initiation cycle (Nc), and decreased the slope of curve of crack length (a) to number of load cycles (N) during crack propagation. However, regardless of stress ratio (R), for example, as shown in Fig.4, $\varepsilon_{l(max)}$ decreased at once after starting fatigue test, became about a constant after the decrease, and increased gradually with an increase in the number of load cycles. When $\varepsilon_{l(max)}$ was approximately consistent with its initial value, crack initiation occurred. $\varepsilon_{l(min)}$ was about a constant through load cycles. It was also found that only at the local zone at which crack initiated, local strain range ($\Delta\varepsilon_l(=\varepsilon_{l(max)}-\varepsilon_{l(min)})$) increased, and there was not very much change in local strain at adjacent zones of the crack. From this fact, it was confirmed that fatigue crack propagation occurred at an extreme local zone[2]-[4].

For metals, fatigue crack initiation was controlled by local-strain damage accumulation was indicated, and for a quantitative expression

of cumulative fatigue damage, mean local strain range ($\Delta\overline{\varepsilon}_l$) was proposed as follows[5].

$$\Delta\overline{\varepsilon}_l = \frac{1}{Nc} \int_0^{Nc} \Delta\varepsilon_l \, dN \qquad (1)$$

Then, the relationships between mean local strain range ($\Delta\overline{\varepsilon}_l$) and crack initiation cycle (Nc) at different stress ratios (R) are shown in Fig.5. Each data point was arranged on a certain line very well whose slope was -0.38 in a log-log coordinate graph, regardless of the values of stress ratio (R). Therefore, the linear cumulative damage law[6] based on local strain range was almost confirmed for fatigue crack initiation in polycarbonate. In Fig.6, mean local strain range ($\Delta\overline{\varepsilon}_l$) is plotted against stress ratio (R). Each data point was arranged on a certain line very well whose slope was -0.15 in a semi-logarithmic graph. This fact also showed that mean local strain range ($\Delta\overline{\varepsilon}_l$) was affected by stress ratio (R).

Evaluation of crack initiation Life

For the investigation of the crack initiation life by parameter $\Delta\varepsilon_{Nc}$ (local strain range) at crack initiation cycle (Nc), it was attempted statiscally to standardize the curves showing the relationship between ε_l and N, for example, such as Fig.4 into one approximated curve and to present it by an equation using only two dimensionless parameters which can be expressed as

$$y(x)=(\Delta\varepsilon_N - \Delta\varepsilon_{Nc})/\Delta\varepsilon_{Nc} \qquad (2)$$
$$x=N/Nc$$

where $\Delta\varepsilon_N$ is the value of local strain range at arbitrary cycle number (N). The standardized approximate curve shown in Fig.7 can be expressed as

$$y(x)=1.101x^3-0.8406x^2-0.1785x-0.0544 \qquad (3)$$

Using $y(N1/Nc)$, $y(N2/Nc)$ and $y(N3/Nc)$ obtained from eq (2), the relation between $y(N1/Nc)-y(N2/Nc)$ and $y(N2/Nc)-y(N3/Nc)$ become as the equation

$$y(N1/Nc)-y(N2/Nc) = \beta[y(N2/Nc)-y(N3/Nc)] \qquad (4)$$

where

$$\beta=(\Delta\varepsilon_{N_1}-\Delta\varepsilon_{N_2})/(\Delta\varepsilon_{N_2}-\Delta\varepsilon_{N_3})$$

and $\Delta\varepsilon_{N_1}$, $\Delta\varepsilon_{N_2}$ and $\Delta\varepsilon_{N_3}$ are the local strain ranges at the notch root measured for the cycle numbers, N1, N2 and N3, respectively. The crack initiation cycle (Nc) is hence determined from ($\Delta\varepsilon_{N_1}$, $\Delta\varepsilon_{N_2}$ and $\Delta\varepsilon_{N_3}$) at N1, N2 and N3), eqs (3) and (4)[7],[8].

The correlation between local strain (ε_l) and cyclic number (N) estimated from this evaluation method is shown in Fig.8. In this figure, the alternate long and short dashed lines represent the approximate curve obtained experimentally, with three cycle numbers used in eq (4), and three open circles represent observed points. The crack initiation cycle (Nc') estimated from eq (4) are in good agreement with the observed crack initiation point (Nc). In consequence, the validity of this method for estimating fatigue crack initiation life was confirmed.

Relation of crack propagation rate to stress intensity range and local strain at crack tip

The relation between crack propagation rate (da/dN) and stress intensity range (ΔK) used generally for small fatigue crack initiated from the notch root is presented at different stress ratios in Fig.9. ΔK was calculated from the equation[9]

$$\Delta K = y \Delta \sigma \sqrt{a} \qquad (5)$$

where y is expressed as

$$y = 1.99 - 0.41(a/W) + 18.70(a/W)^2 \\ -38.48(a/W)^3 + 53.85(a/W)^4 \qquad (6)$$

As shown in Fig.9, ΔK was about a constant, which depends on the values of stress ratio (R), until fatigue cracks initiated. After fatigue cracks initiated, da/dN increased, regardless of R. Therefore, initiated fatigue crack propagation behaviors were thought to be strongly affected by the states of plastic deformations near the notch root. However, the relation between da/dN and ΔK at the range of da/dN values from 1×10^{-4} to 1×10^{-2} mm/cycle was expressed with a certain line whose slope was 4 in a log-log coordinate graph, showing Paris' 4th power law in polymer. Therefore, it was confirmed that da/dN for low cycle fatigue can not be expressed linearly with ΔK, in other words, both small and large crack propagation behaviors for low cycle fatigue can not be evaluated uniformly with ΔK. This is because the small yielding condition used in linear fracture mechanics is not almost satisfied as small crack propagates with the local plastic zone due to fatigue crack containing in the plastic zone formed by a stress concentration at the notch root[10].

In Fig.10, the relation between crack propagation rate (da/dN) and local strain range at the crack tip ($\Delta \varepsilon_l^T (= \varepsilon_l^T (\max) - \varepsilon_l^T (\min))$) is presented. As shown in Fig.10, each data point was arranged on a line very well whose slope was 5 in a log-log coordinate graph. They did not show dependence on R as has been experienced with plotting against ΔK, showing effectiveness thereof in the evaluation of crack propagation rate.

Correlation between local-strain damage accumulation curves for crack initiation and propagation

To analyze the crack propagation process, the change and history of local strain at the small fatigued (cyclically strained) element, A (10th grid element ahead of the crack tip, see Fig.2(b)) were investigated until it was broken by advancing of the crack tip. Figure 11 shows an example of the change of $\Delta \varepsilon_l^T$ until the number of Ne.f.=4500. The distance from the location of the crack tip to point A (i.e., Ne.f. point) is also shown in the horizontal axis below the cycle number (N). As shown in this figure, the value of $\Delta \varepsilon_l^T$ at point A increased rapidly as the access of the crack tip. To discuss whether some correlation would exist between crack initiation and propagation processes from the viewpoint of local strain value, mean local-strain accumulation value, $\Delta \overline{\varepsilon}_l^T$ was also calculated in the similar manner as $\Delta \overline{\varepsilon}_l$ value. Next, the curve of $\Delta \overline{\varepsilon}_l^T$ ver-

sus Ne.f. in crack propagation was compared with $\Delta \overline{\varepsilon}_l$ versus Nc curve in crack initiation.

As a result, very similar relationships between two lines were obtained, as shown in Fig.12. From this similarity, it was though that fatigue crack might also propagate under the failure condition or mechanism similar to crack initiation process.

CONCLUSIONS

Fatigue crack initiation from the notch root and fatigue crack propagation in polycarbonate, a polymer were investigated varying the stress ratio (R) using the real-time fine grid method. Resultant findings were as follow.
(1) Local strain ($\varepsilon_{l(\max)}$) at the notch root decreased at once after starting fatigue, and increased with an increase in the number of load cycles, crack initiation occurred when $\varepsilon_{l(\max)}$ is approximately consistent with its initial value.
(2) The relation between mean local strain range ($\Delta \overline{\varepsilon}_l$) and crack initiation cycle number (Nc) was expressed by a line whose slope was -0.38 in a logarithmic graph as well as mean local-strain damage accumulation value ($\Delta \overline{\varepsilon}_l^T$) and cycle number (Ne.f.) that 10th element ahead of the crack tip was broken by the crack tip advancing. In addition, local-strain damage accumulation law in the fatigue crack initiation stage of polymers was effective, too.
(3) The relation between $\Delta \varepsilon_l$ and N was statistically standardized with two dimensionless parameters, $(\Delta \varepsilon_N - \Delta \varepsilon_{N_c})/\Delta \varepsilon_{N_c}$ and N/Nc, and the standardized curve was used to estimate the crack initiation cycle number (Nc). In consequence, the method was effective.
(4) The relation between crack propagation rate (da/dN) and stress intensity range (ΔK) at the range of da/dN values from 1×10^{-4} to 1×10^{-2} mm/cycle was expressed by a line whose slop was 4 in a logarithmic graph, showing Paris' 4th power law and depended on stress ratios (R).
(5) The relation between crack propagation rate (da/dN) and local strain range at the crack tip ($\Delta \varepsilon_l^T$) was expressed by a line whose slop was 5 in a logarithmic graph without showing dependency on stress ratios (R).
(6) The possibility that the condition or mechanism of fatigue crack initiation process might be similar to that of fatigue crack propagation process was shown.

REFERENCES

1.Shimamoto, A., Takahashi, S. and Yokota, A., "Fundamental study on rupture by low-cycle fatigue of polymers applying the fine-grid method", Exp. Mech., 31(1), 65-69(1991).
2.Shimamoto, A., Yokota, A. and Takahashi, S., "Analysis on the crack initiation and strain in the vicinity of notch root under the low cycle by fine grid method"(in Japanese), J. of Japan NDI, 37-9A, 849-850(1988).
3.Shimamoto, A., Umezaki, E. and Takahashi, S.,"A fundamental study on rupture by low-cycle fatigue of polymers employing the fine-grid method"(in Japanese), J. of Japan NDI,38(12),1101-1106(1989).
4.Sato, T., Shimada, H. and Furuya, Y., "Relation between local-strain and fatigue cyclic number of crack initiation from notch-root under low cycle fatigue"(in Japanese), Trans. of Japan SME,

51(466), A, 1534-1540(1985).

5.Shimada, H. and Furuya, Y., "Local crack-tip strain concept for fatigue crack initiation and propagation", Trans. of ASME, Engng Mater. Tech., 109(4), 101-106(1987).

6.Kikukawa, M., "Damage accumulation in fatigue process"(in Japanese), Preprint of 15th Symposium on Material Strength and Fracture, 71-78(1970).

7.Sato, T. and Shimada, H., "Evaluation of fatigue crack initiation life from a notch", Int. J. of Fracture, 10(4), 243-247(1988).

8.Sato, T., Kimura, K. and Iguchi, H., "Local strain behavior at the notch-root and the crack-tip on corrosion fatigue"(in Japanese), Preprint of 22nd Symposium on Stress and Strain Measurement, 143-148(1990).

9.Srawley, J. E., Fracture, 4, edited by Liebowitz, IV., Academic Press, 64(1969).

10.Hudak, S. J., "Small crack behavior and the prediction of fatigue life", Trans. of ASME, Engng Mater. Tech., 103(1), 26-35(1981).

Table 1 Mechanical properties of polycarbonate

Tensile strength	(MPa)	60.80
Elastic limit	(MPa)	40.21
Modulus of longitudinal elasticity	(MPa)	2099
Photoelastic sensitivity	(mm/ N)	0.146

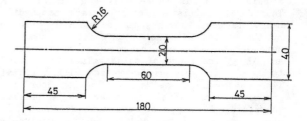

Fig.1 Shape and dimensions of specimen

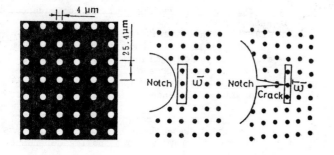

Fig.2(a) Fine dot grid and schematic view of local strain measurement area

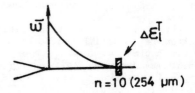

Fig.2(b) Fatigue crack-tip element

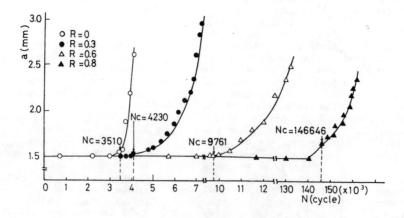

Fig.3 Relation between crack length (a) and number of load cycles (N)

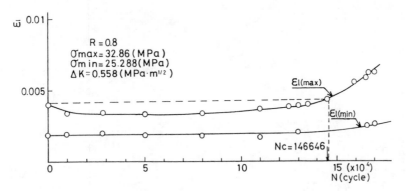

Fig.4 Relation between local strain at the notch root (ε_l)
and number of load cycles (N)

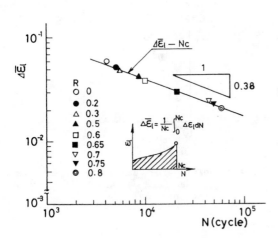

Fig.5 Relation between mean local strain range
($\Delta\bar{\varepsilon}_l$) and number of crack initiation
cycles (Nc)

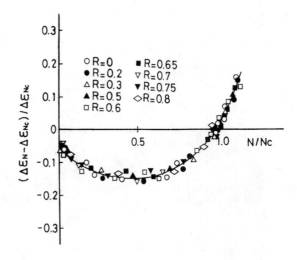

Fig.7 Approximate curve standardized with two
dimensionless parameters

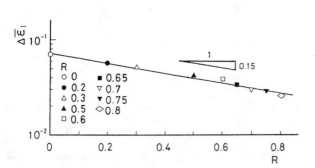

Fig.6 Relation between mean local strain range
($\Delta\bar{\varepsilon}_l$) and stress ratio (R)

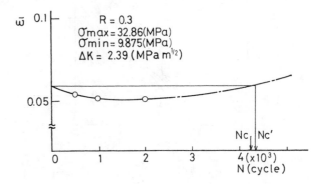

Fig.8 Relation between local strain at the notch
root (ε_l) and number of load cycles (N)
calculated

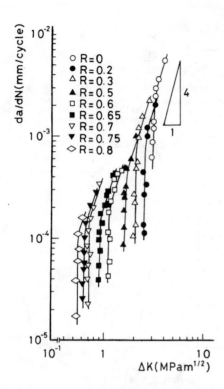

Fig.9 Relation between crack propagation rate (da/dN) and stress intensity factor range (ΔK)

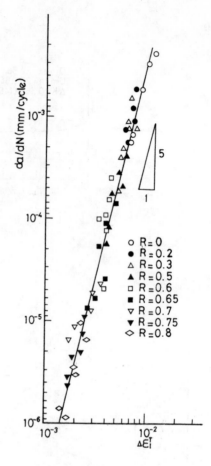

Fig.10 Relation between crack propagation rate (da/dN) and local strain range at the crack tip ($\Delta\varepsilon_l^T$)

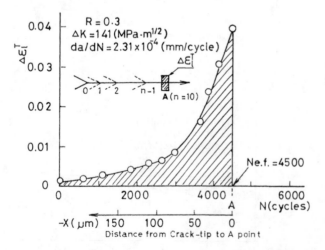

Fig.11 Changes of $\Delta\varepsilon_l^T$ at point A as crack tip advances

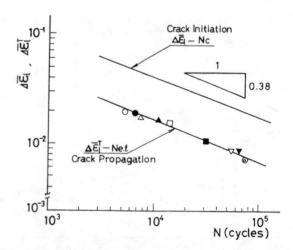

Fig.12 Correlation between local-strain damage accumulation curve ($\Delta\bar{\varepsilon}_l$ versus Nc) and crack-tip strain damage accumulation curve ($\Delta\bar{\varepsilon}_l^T$ versus Ne.f.) on crack propagation

Characteristic Fatigue Crack Extension
Behavior and Fractography in Policarbonate

Shunji Nagasaka

Abstract

A fatigue crack extends discontinuously leaving striationlike patterns. Theae pattern forming mechanism and discontinuous extension behaviour has been illustriated using the craze breaking model, but these observation lack the fatigue crack tip opening behaviour. The objective of this investigation is to explore the micromechanism of fatigue crack propagation and the fatigue pattern forming from the observation of crack tip opening behaviour during one loading cycle.

1. Introduction

There has been a considerable amount of published date on fatigue crack extention polymers described by the well known Paris equation.Fatigue crack extend discontinuously leaving a striation like pattern on the fracture surface. These pattern forming mechanism and discontinuous extension behaviour has been illustrated using the craze breaking model. These observations lack a appropriate explanation on the discontinuous extension behavoiur and the fatigue pattern formation mechanism. The objective of this investigation was to explore the micromechanism of fatigue crack propagation and the fatigue pattern forming mechanism.

2 Experimental procedure

Commercially prepared polycarbonate material (IUPILON: manufactured by Mitsubishi Gas Chemical Company Inc.) was used for the eexperiments. Single-edge notch cramped loaded specimens (Fig.1) were utilized for a fatigue testing An Shimazu electro-hydraulic closed loop test machine was used for fatigue testing. Operating frequency was 5Hz.Testing environment was not controlled; relative humidity was measured to be between 40 and 60 percent.
The crack growth was measured by a ✕ 100 travelling microscope with a resolution of 0.01 mm. The crack length was measured at the midthickness without stopping the system.
A white-length was to illuminate the specimen from behind which alowed wiewing the crack tip at the mid-thickness and at the surface. The crack length was measured at the mid-thickness without stopping the system. Fatigue crack propagation testing was carried out under constant load.

3 Result and discussion

3.1 Crack extension behaviour

The fatigue crack extension behaviour in log-log relationship between dl/dN and ΔK is shown in Fig.2 for positive and negative stress ratio.

(1) Crack Extension Behaviour for $R \leqq 0$
The charactaristic figure fatigue crack extension curve is shown in Fig.3 ;
The crack growth behaviour is constructed from the three rection,that is,the stage I,the stage II and the stage III,and the stage II is classified into the three kinds of extension behaviour having the equal m value at the stage II_d and the stage II_c ,and the m value distributed over the range of $3.0 \sim 6.0$ at the stage II_m ,which indicate unstable crack extension behaviour in the stage.These behaviour different from the other preceding papers.

(2) Crack Extension behaviour for $R > 0$
Fig.4 shows the extension behaviour for $R > 0$. The extension behaviour is indicate in a bilinear relation with a short range of the stage II_m .

These fatigue crack extension behaviour different from the other preceding papers , which has been indicated in a straight line.

3.2 Interrelation between fatigue crack grwing behaviour and feature of fracture surface

In the crack extension behaviour with negative sign, the stage II_d following the stage I has the same fracture pattern Sd to the stage I. This pattern vanish at the stage II_m apearing no pattern, and after, the crack extends in the stage III having a S_{s1} and a S_{s2} pattern. The fracture patterns appeared in the stage II_c are mingled with the S_c pattern in the brittle fracture surface. These fracture patterns are made up of discontinuous crack extension behaviour after several repeated loading cysles. The formula (1) is applicable to the stage I and the stage II different from the stage III. In the stage III, the fatigue crack extension patterns correspond to each loading cycle different from the another patterns appeared at the stage I and the stage II. In this stage, the relation between dl/dN and ΔK does not indicate the stright line (Fig.3), the point B, beginning point of the crack extension to the stage III, is the starting point of unstable fracture. The value K_{max} at this point is equal to the value of brittle fracture K_{Ic} (=9.8 kgf/mm). The K value for the beginning of the stage II crack extension declines and the mirror surface appears at the point near the T point .

The photograph to each patterns are shown in Fig.5 .
The Fig.6 indicate the charactaristic feature to each pattern. In the range of $R < 0$, the fracture pattern arranges in order of indicating in Fig.6. In the range of $R > 0$, the pattern S_c appeared nearby the crack initiation district and changes from S_{s1} to S_{s2} according to increasing in the R value. The same pattern arrangement lacking of S_d pattern appeared in the negative R pattern.

3.3 Fatigue crack growth mechanism

3.3.1 State of prastic zone at fatigue crack tip

According to the photoelastic experiment for the observation of fatigue crack tip opening behaviour,a compressive stress arises at the cracked surface ;the photoelastic fringe order changes from decreasing to increasing at the crack tip approaching the lower end of the loading cycle, it revealed that the crack tip was in positive stress state at the load zero;the crack tip has a positive stress at the lower terminal of one loading cycle.
The deformation mesurment at the crack tip by the microgrid method indicated these

phenomena at the crack tip also,coinside with the photoelastic observation. therefore, it is concluded that the crack tip opening behaviour during the loading cycle is as follows:① the stress decreasing accompanied by unloading turn into increasing caused by the compressive stress arised at cracked surface,② the plastic zone increased in its volume will be compressed into the volume decreasing by elastic recovery of elastic zone around the prastic zone. ③ the stress balance at the applied load is zero.The variation of the stress distribution during one loading cycle is shown in Fig.7(2).
From the loading condition,stated above, there are two kinds of plastic zone, which is a plastic zone(r_c) accepted three times loading cycles and a monotonic plastic zone r_p accepted the same loading cycle to applied loading cycle. These plastic zones can be seen in Fig.8. The plastic zone size can be given by the Irwin's formula with effective stress intensity factor Up Kmax

$$r_z = \frac{1}{\pi} \left(\frac{K_{eff}}{\sigma_{ys}} \right)^2 = \frac{1}{\pi} \left(\frac{U_z K_{max}}{\sigma_{ys}} \right)^2$$

$$= \frac{0.62}{\pi} \left(\frac{K_{max}}{\sigma_{ys}} \right)^2 \quad (1)$$

$$r_z = \frac{0.21}{\pi} \left(\frac{K_{max}}{\sigma_{ys}} \right)^2 \quad (2)$$

Up: coefficient of effected stress intensity factor for polycarbonate given by the auther.
σ_{ys}: static yield stress

3.3 Fatigue crack extinsion mechanism

(1) Extensionmechanism in the stage II$_d$
The interval of the pattern of Sd type (D.G.B) is equal to the plastic zone size produced at the fatigue tip which indicate that the fatigue crack tip plastic zone is the same as the spacing of the s$_d$ type pattern interval as shown in Fig.9. The area of repeated plastid zone(r$_p$) is the area having such damage as the breaking of molecular chain and growing many microvoids. As stated preceeding section, the fatigue crack tip plastic zone consist of the two phase, the monotonic plastic zone (r$_p$) and the repeated plastic zone r$_c$, which accept three times repeated loading cycles compared by the monotonic plastic zone. It can be observed jigjag pattern along the boundary from r$_c$ zone to r$_p$ zone. This pattern denote that the fatigue crack extended at one cycle loading after scores cyclic loading through the both plastic zone. The forming mechanism of the mirror zone following the s$_d$ pattern is not definite. The plastic zone with the stress whitening is shown in Fig.10. According to the observation by a microscope, the fatigue crack extends such behaviour that the shear band ,AB,come into forming at an angle of 45° degrees to the direction of the crack extension with the stress whitening between the both shear band and the fatigue crack extends through the whitening area at a time after receiveing the scores times of repeated loading.

(2) Extension mechanism in stage II$_c$
The pattern finded at the fracture surface in stage II$_c$ are the mixed phase of the S$_c$ pattern and a brittle fracture phase. The S$_c$ pattern is the same to the pattern appeared at the repeated plastic zone (r$_c$) and a length of δ$_{sc}$ of the pattern can be expressed using the formula (3) experimentaly(Fig.10.).

$$\delta S_c = (0.21/\pi)(K_{max}/\sigma_{ys})^2 + C_d \qquad (3)$$

In this stage with the higher K$_{max}$, the crack tip plastic zone spread from the point A in Fig.9(2) rapidly, and after, the whitening zone spread solwely over the plastic zone, but in this stge, the crack extends within the plastic zone without extending through the plastic zone. The surface patterns of this stage are the pattern with many of S$_c$ pattern the length of δ$_{sc}$ equal to the plastic zone size r$_c$ with a constant C$_d$. Therefore, it is concluded that the fatigue crack extends through the plastic zone r$_c$ having many of microvoids as the unit of the extension length in this stage.
From the above observation, the formation mechanism for the band δ$_{sc}$ which has many of microvoids would be considered as following. The fatigue crack is stying in the plastic zone and the interval δ$_{sc}$ is expressed in the Fig.(3). The interrelation between r$_c$ and r$_p$ is

$$r_p \fallingdotseq 3r_c \qquad (4)$$

Therefore, if the crack extension length δ$_{sc}$ equals to r$_p$/3 ,the state of the fatigue crack tip plastic zone should be expressed should be expressed as Fig.11 schematically. When the crack tip is located at the point C, the area inside of the plastic zone A-① -① belong to the crack tip C will be overlapped with the each plastic zone belong to the crack tip A' and A". Then, the plastic zone should be constructed from the area which accepted the different number of repeated cycles over the each length of r$_p$/3 ; the r$_p$/3 plastic zone located just at the crack tip become the area having a good many microvoids and damage caused by three times repeated load compared to the another area.
Then, the crack grows by the r$_p$/3 plastic zone length. The charactaristic figure is shown in Fig.11. with D.G.B. pattern

(3) Crack extension mechanism in stage III
The stage III begin at the K$_{max}$ = 9.8 kgf/mm . The fatigue crack extension behaviour in this stage can not arrange by the linear fracture mechanics. The fatigue crack extend by the each cycle and the stress whitening area vanish in this area.

4. Conclusion

(1) The fatigue crack extension behaviour of poly carbonate is constructed from the three different behaviour indicating the different fracture pattern.

(2) It was revealed that the fatigue pattern formation mechanism is affected by the crack tip opening behaviour.

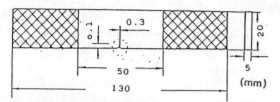

Fig.1 Specimen

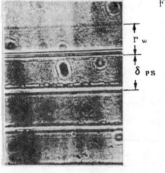

Fig.8 Fatigue crack tip whitening zone and δ_{ps}

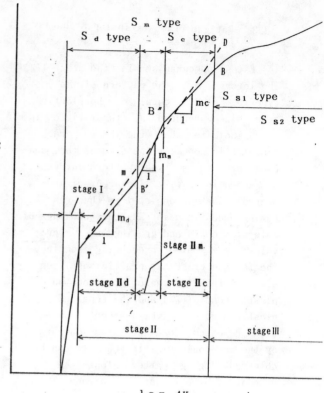

Fig.3 Characteristic behaviour of fatigue crack extension ($R \leqq 0$)

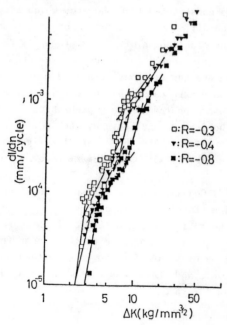

$\square$:R=-0.3
$\blacktriangledown$:R=-0.4
$\blacksquare$:R=-0.8

Fig.2 Fatigue crack extention behaviour (R<0)

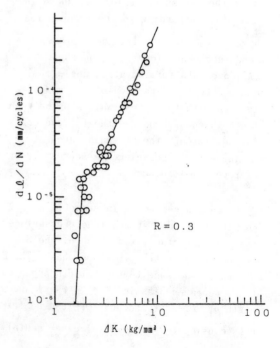

R = 0.3

Fig.4 Fatigue crack extention behaviour (R>0)

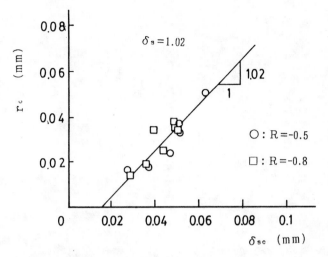

Fig.10 Interrelation between repeated
plastic zone r_c and spacing δ_{sc}

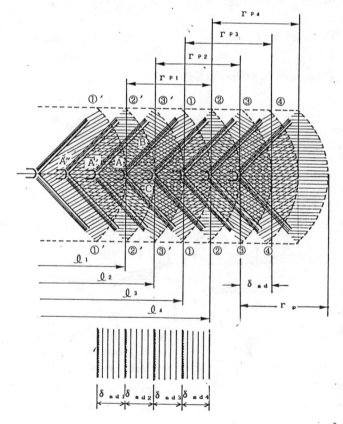

Fig.11 Fatigue crack pattern Sc at stage IIc

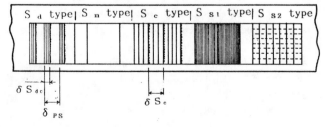

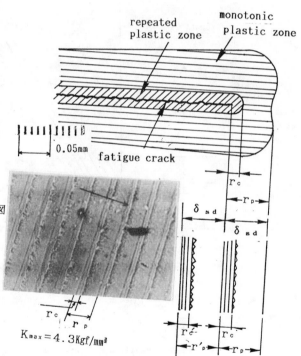

fatigue crack   shear band

plastic zone

stress
whitening zone

r_c

r_p

δ_{PS}

(1) S$_d$ type

shear band

fatigue crack

plastic zone

stress
whitening zone

δ_{sc}

r_p

(2) S$_c$ type

Fig.9 Stress whitening at fatigue
crack tip plastic zone.

repeated
plastic zone

monotonic
plastic zone

0.05mm   fatigue crack

$K_{max}=4.3 Kgf/mm^2$

Fig.6 Characteristic figurs for fatigue
pattern in polycarbonate

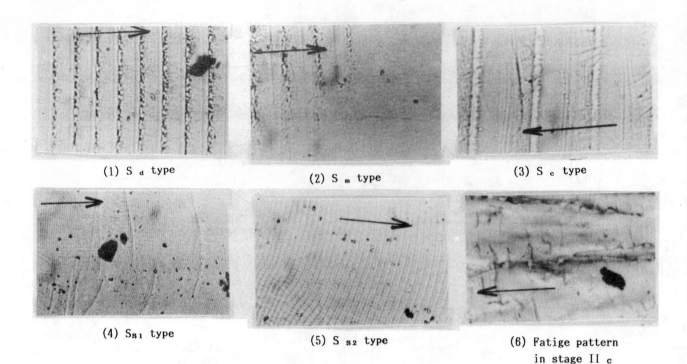

(1) S$_d$ type   (2) S$_m$ type   (3) S$_c$ type

(4) S$_{s1}$ type   (5) S$_{s2}$ type   (6) Fatige pattern in stage II$_c$

Fig.5 Photograph of fatigue pattern (R$\leqq$0)

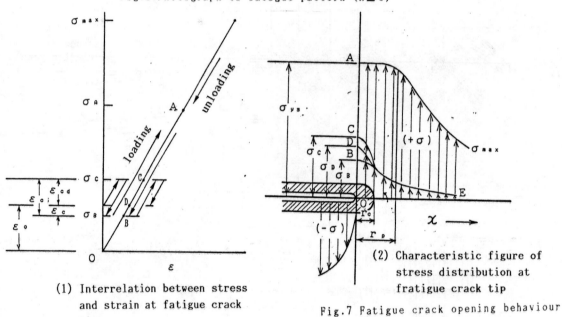

(1) Interrelation between stress and strain at fatigue crack tip

(2) Characteristic figure of stress distribution at fratigue crack tip

Fig.7 Fatigue crack opening behaviour during load cycles

REFERENCES

1) M.E.Macky,T.G.Teng,J.M.Schulty,J.Master,Sci.,14,pp.221,(1979)

2) M.D.Skibo,R.W.Hertzberg,J.A.Manson,S.L.Kim,J.Master.Sci.,12,pp.531(1977)

3) R.W.Hertzberg,M.D.Skibo,J.A.Manson,Fatigue Mechanism(Ed.:J.T.Fong), A.S.T.M.,(1979)

4) S.Nagasaka,Proc.19th Stress-Strain Sympo.pp.57,(1987)(in Japanese)

5) M.D.ettenmaier,Polymer Fracture,Springer Verlagl,pp.354,(1986)

6) S.Nagasaka.Proc.7th Japan Photoelastic.,(1985)

7) M.T.Takemori,R,P.Kambour,J.Mater,Sci.,16,pp.1108,(1981)

A Study on Low Cycle Fatigue Behavior of Polycarbonate Material
(The Relation Between Fatigue Life and Cyclic Relaxation)

Hiroshi UNO* and Akira SHIMAMOTO** and Susumu TAKAHASHI***

1. Introduction

In the recent industrial world, metallic materials are increasingly replaced with new generation materials along with the trend for energy saving and use of lighter materials. Among those, engineering plastics are widely used not only for parts of auxiliary machines but also for structural members. Importance is placed more and more on the fatigue life design applied under the environment where cycle stress is imposed. Althongh many studies are made on the fatigue evaluation and testing methods using these materials,"Fatigue Crack Initiation and Propagation in Smooth Specimens of Polycarbonate" by Hyakutake and Yamamoto[1], for example, they are mostly related to practical aspects. Evaluation technology necessary for design on site has not been established yet.

Material testing technology has been developed for many years mostly in relation to metallic materials, but they are not necessarily applicable to polymers, characteristics of polymers being different from those of metallic materials. Area of hysteresis loop generated between stress and strain as a paramenter for fatigue evaluation is approximately proportional to the plastic amplitude generated at the average position of stress amplitude in the case of metallic materials, but in the case of polycarbonate plastic amplitude and loop area are not in a simple and proportional relationship, and value of plastic strain is too small to be observed, either.

Results of strain restricted repeated fatigue tests attendant with mean stress indicate a remarkable cyclec stress relaxation phenomenon derived from area distribution. It was found that there was a specific relationship between the stress relaxation phenomenon and amount of fatigue damage.

2. Test Specimen and Test Method

Material used for the present test is polycarbonate commercially available in the form of extruded round bar(manufactured by Toyo Plastic Seimitsu INC). Shape and dimensions of test specimens are shown in Figure 1. Test specimens were naturally dried for a long period of time in a constant temperature chamber under the conditions of temperature 21°C and humidity 65%.

Before use for experiments, confirmation was made that the temperature rise of specimens during fatigue processes was neglegibly small. The fatigue tester used was an electohydraulic servo-type uniaxial tention compression fatigue tester (manufactured by Saginomiya INC) controlled by a computer of 9.8kN capacity. To eliminate the effect of creep, tests were conducted at the strain velocity of 0.3~5% /sec, using triangular wave of a constant strain amplitude. Three types of strain ratios were applied, strain ratio $R=(Emin/Emax)= -1$ and $R = 0$, $R=\infty$.

In the case of polycarbonate material used in the present experiments, the upper limit of total strain amplitude in the low cycle fatigue tests was 8%. Beyond 8%, material changes its quality rapidly and does not provide stable data, so that the range exceeding 8% was excluded from the subject of examination.

*   Saginomiya Seisakushiyo, Inc.   535 Sasai, Saitama-City,Saitama 350-13,JAPAN
** Saitama Institute of Technology   1690 Fusaiji,Okabe,Osato,Sitama 340,   JAPAN
*** Kanto Gaguin University   4834, Mutuura,Kanagawa,Yokohama,221,   JAPAN

3. Experimental Results and Discussion

3-1) Behavior of Strain-Stress Hysteresis Loop

To see the hysteresis loop behavior of poliymer, incremental step tests were conducted. Result are indicated in Figure 2. In the top left, a chart for a typical metallic material (copper)in also shown for comparison purpose. As can be seen in Figure 2, hysteresis loops of metallic material for every strain amplitude show an approximately straight line for the portion of load release from the point of maximum stress to the point of stress zero. The slope indicates modulus of longitudinal elasticity, and the width of plastic strain which is determined by the position of mean stress is nearly proportional to the loop area.

This relationship is not maintained in the case of polycarbonate material. In this case, the plastic width is approximately proportional to the squre of loop area, and the residual stress generated at strain zero was found to be small regardless of a large loop area.

3-2) Fatigue Lives for Completely Reverses Strain[2] and Half Reverses Strain Tests.

To investigate the peculiar relation between the stress-strain hysteresis characteristics and fatigue life of polycarbonate, completely reverse strain test of mean stress and strain zero, strain ratio R=-1, and cyclic strain test with a mean stress existing, strain ratio R=0, =∞ under strain control were conducted.

3-2-1 Completely Reversed Strain Test and Fatigue Life.

In the completely reversed strain test, stress amplitude, young's modulus, and area of hysteresis loop resulting in the breakage in the constant strain amplitude were examined. Relation of stress amplitude and number of cycles obtained as a result of above is shawn in Figure 3. As can been seen from Figure 3, nearly constant stress amplitude was maintained for every repetal strain until immediately before the breakage, so that no cyclic hardening, cyclic softning, nor stress relaxation were recognized from changes in stress amplitude.

Hysteresis loop area until breakage occurs for each strain amplitude is indicated in Figure 4. As seen from Figure 4, for the case of strain amplitude 6% and more, areas were changing until they were close to the point of breakage.

Indicated of Figure 5 is the relationship between the modulus of longitudinal elasticity and number of cycles. The modulus of longitudinal elasiticity indicate here is the mean value obtained by averaging the value given from the tension side and the value given from the compression side. As can been seen from Figure 5, it was confirmed that the modulus of longitudinal elasticity was maintained almost constant until it was close to the point of breakage.

Indicate by mark (○) in Figure 6 is the fatigue life curve expressed by strain amplitude and number of cycle to breakage of completely reversed, R=-1, strain tests. While the relation between the strain amplitude and number of cycles to breakage Nf, in a low cycle fatigue region (10^4 cycles or less) for metal is expressed by curves on a double-logarithmic graph, it was found that a linear relationship was maintained in the case of policarbonate.

3-2-2 Relation between Mean Stress and Stress Relaxation.

Relaxation behavior of the tension side(R=0) and the compression side(R=∞) are shown in Figure 7a. Figure 7a is for the case of a constant strain amplitude and the solid line indicates at the start of the test and dots line indicates same cycle before breakage in the test with strain ratio R=0 and strain ratio R=∞. As can been seen from Figure 7a, cyclic stress relaxation was small recognized in the case of compression stress(R=∞), on the other hand, cyclic relaxation was large recognized in the case of tension stress(R=0).

In Figure 7b is shown the reason of cyclic relaxation for the case of a constant strain amplitude. As can been seen from Figure 7b, it was found that plastic residual stress $\triangle S$ is generated at the point of minimum stress. so that the cyclic relaxation phenomenon is caused by this $\triangle S$.

Indicated of Figure 8 is the relationship between the maximum-minimum stress amplitude and number of cycles. As can been seen from Figure 8, it was recognized that the amplitude which difference between maximam and minimum was changed remarkable increase until it was close to the point of breakage. From Figure 8 and Figure 7a, it is shown that stress amplitude was increased along with the stress relaxation and inclination was converged on the line determined by the modulus of longitudinal elasticity.

In the case of polycarbonate imposed with mean stress R=0, cyclic stress relaxation take place due to uneven area of hysteresis loop, and the mean stress is tranfered towards the direction of uniform loop area. It was found that, as a result of above loop area was also decreased so that damage to the material also decreased with repeated cycles.

Indicated of Figure 8 is the relationship between the maximum-minimum stress amplitude and number of cycles. As can been seen from Figure 8, it was recognized that the amplitude which difference between maximam and minimum was changed remarkable increase until it was close to the point of breakage. From Figure 8 and Figure 7b, it is shown that stress amplitude was increased along with the stress relaxation and inclination was converged on the line determined by the modulus of longitudinal elasticity.

In the case of polycarbonate imposed with mean stress R=0, cyclic stress relaxation take place due to uneven area of hysteresis loop, and the mean stress is tranfered towards the direction of uniform loop area. It was found that, as a result of above loop area was also decreased so that damage to the material also decreased with repeated cycles.

3-2-3 Fatigue Life in Cyclic Half Stress Test

Marked (x) in the Figure 6 are the results of R=0 cyclic constant strain fatigue life tests. Tests made for the condition of number of cycles to breakage to be 2×10^4 or less. Slope marked(x) has small value. Thus, it was found difficult to evaluate the effect of mean stress on the life as generaly performed for many kinds of matallic material.

3-3 Relation between Fatigue Damage and Stress Relaxation

Conceivable parameters which indicate whether or not the given material has received damage in the past include the modulus of longitudinal elasticity, hysteresis area, stress amplitude, and width of strain plasiticity. In the stress relaxation phenomenon generated in the constant strain R=0 test, hysteresis loop area transferred towards the direction of decreased area . In this respect, Figure 9 indicates the result of experiments in terms of relationship between the area and number of cycles.

As seen from Figure 9, areas are decreased as number of cycles increased for each strain amplitude excluding the vicinity of breakage. In figure 9, in which different inclination are seen between those marked(x) and those marked(o), resulting of half cycle stress relaxation test conducted on the material which was given in advance fatigue damage by the completely reversed (R=-1) strain test are shown.

As can be seen from Figure 9, rate of area reduction due to stress relaxation differs according to whether or not there was fatigue damage in the past. It was found that the material which was given damage in advance showed faster stress relaxation velocity by repeated cycles, so that area was decreased more rapidly.

Since the velocity of strain relaxation is affected by whether or not there has been damage, it is considered that information concerning whether or not there has been damage should be included in the data of very first cycle of the stress relaxation test with mean stress given. As seen from Figure 9, early stage characteristics of material are refrected on the changes in area during several initial cycles. In this aspect, study was made on rate of area change in relation to the fatigue damage and stress relaxation.

In Figure 9, the solid line indicates the rate of area decrease θ, obtained from data during 1~5 cycles by the method of least squares. As a result of tests using multiple specimens for each strain amplitude, relation between the rate θ of area reduction and the area at 1 cycle was obtained. Result is shown in Figure 10.

As seen from Fatigue 10, the smaller the strain amplitude and area, the larger is the inclination θ indicating the rate of area decrease, and in the elasitic region in the vicinity of area =0, inclination is apploximately -0.1. As a result, it was found that the range of incrination is approximately -0.1 or larger. To investigate the change in the incrination θ while fatigue damage proceeds, fatigue was given by conducted 50 cycles of completely reversed strain test with strain ratio R=-1, and strain 6%.

In succession, with the purpose to measure damage, 5 cycles of stress relaxation test of 3% strain was conducted with mean stress given at the strain ratio R=0, and inclination θ was measured.
Constituting a unit block in combination of these two stages of stress ratio, blockes were repeated until breakage occurred, and changes in inclination θ due to proceeding fatigue were investigated. Indicated in Figure 11 is the experimental wave pattern. Relation between θ obtained from each block and the hysteresis area constituted by the first of each block of stress relaxation test is shown in Figure 12. It was identified that θ was increased as fatigue preceeded, in the case of strain ratio R=-1, as can been seen from Figure 12. Also confirmed was the fact that when θ became -0.1 or less, there existed fatigue damage.

4   Conclusion

(1) It was found in the case of polycarbonate material that, when mean stress is existed at tension side and strain ratio R=0~1, stress relaxation phenomenon takes place which shows significant dependence on repeated cycles derived from the area distribution of stress-strain curve.

(2) It was found that, when mean stress is existed at compression side and strain ratio R=1~∞, stress relaxation phenomenon is small recognized.

(3) It was grasped that the rate of area decrease of hysteresis loop having mean stress is affected by the historical damage given to the material in advance.

References
(1) H.H yakutake,T.yamamoto. Jounal of the Japan Society of Mechanical Engineering. Vol .56
No.529(Sept.1990)
(2) H.Uno, A.Shimamoto, S.Takahashi. The Japan Society of Mechanical Strength No.508

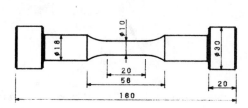

Fig.1　Dimensions of the specimen

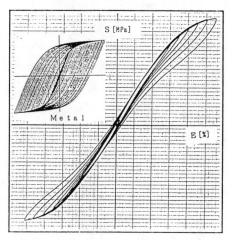

Fig.2　Stress-strain response of incremental
step strain test

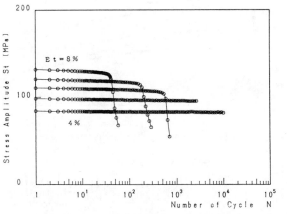

Fig.3　Stress amplitude-cycles showing stress
response of polycarbonate

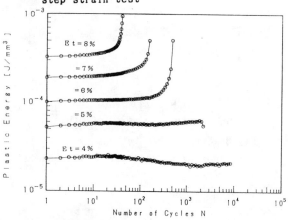

Fig.4　Hysteresis area-cycles showing area
response of polycarbonate

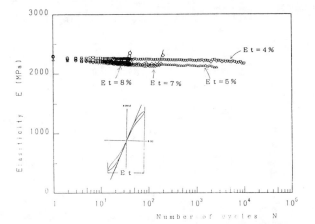

Fig.5　Longitudinal elasticity-cycles showing
response of polycarbonate

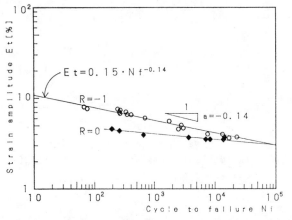

Fig.6　Strain range-cycles to failure curve

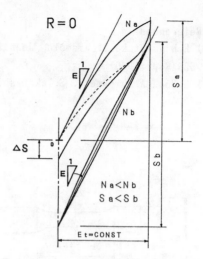

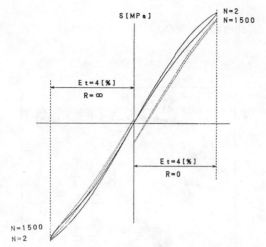

Fig.7a Relaxation behaivor of two specimens under condition of R=∞ and R=0.

Fig.7b Relationship between relaxation and residual stress △S.

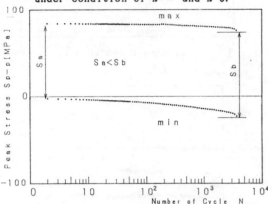

Fig.8 Stress peak to peak range-cycles showing response of polycarbonate

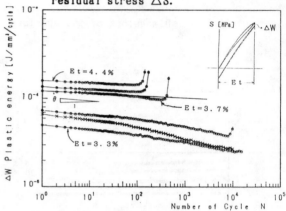

Fig.9 Area-cycles behaivor

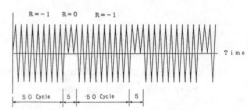

Fig.11 Wave of damage test (R=-1,R=0)

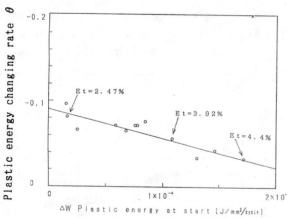

Fig.10 Plastic energy change rate-plastic energy at fist cycles. (non-damaged material)

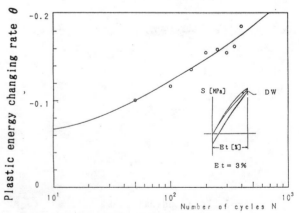

Fig.12 Energy changing rate under damaging

APPLICATION OF AN AUTOMATIC GRATING TECHNIQUE FOR THE
STRUCTURAL ANALYSIS OF COMPOSITE MATERIALS

F. Ginesu, F. Bertolino and W.M. Sun

ABSTRACT

A phase grating technique has been used in conjunction with microscope observation for analysing the strain behaviour of composite materials. Both moiré-interferometry and electrical extensometer measurements validate the experimental data. The results of some tests performed on composite laminates of graphite fibre-peek (polyetheretherketone) matrix are reported.

INTRODUCTION

Composites behave very differently to metals as they are simply a heterogeneous medium which may have multiple defects and where various types of failures can occur.

As opposed to metals, the direct measurement of fatigue limit is difficult for these materials. Repeated loading cycles can cause failure and the composites do not seem to show an endurance limit. For metals, the two stages of initiation and propagation of fracture are basic to an understanding of the phenomenon. For composites, the nature of crack growth is quite different. Their polymeric matrix contains stiff and strong fibres. The material is anisotropic and cracks propagate easily throughout the matrix. Damage is caused by the accumulation of random fibre ruptures and these are the source of small cracks in the matrix along the fibres. More and more cracks develop as loading is repeated until some of these coalesce to produce catastrophic failures. Usually, after the first loading cycle the general material properties can be assessed such that its subsequent behaviour under further loading can be predicted.

Angle-ply laminates, in particular, show highly nonlinear stress-strain tensile behaviour, mainly due to the presence of transverse matrix cracking and delaminations. After unloading, which essentially follows a linear law, the composites show large permanent strain. The strain field observable on the lateral surface of the specimen during the loading cycle is generally nonuniform because of the presence of cracks and of the different behaviour of the layers.

It is important therefore to use experimental techniques that can both detect faults in and characterize such materials. The knowledge of the microstructural behaviour of composite laminates is required to predict the influence of defects on the overall strength of the material. Recently, the authors have used different experimental and numerical techniques for analysing fracture growth and propagation in composite laminates /1/.

A grating technique /2,3/ has recently been proposed for observing the strain field on the lateral surface of a specimen subjected mainly to static but also to fatigue loading. The technique is based on observations with an optical microscope and subsequently monitoring a phase grating printed on the lateral surface of the composite specimen /4/. The in-plane displacements and strains can be calculated from the pitch variation measurements. Here the technique is extensively applied to several angle-ply laminates subjected to static loading. An automated procedure for depicting and computing displacements and strains, based on image processing, is presented. A series of results related to strains in the nonlinear stress-strain field is analysed. The presence of transversal matrix cracks and their influence on the strain field is also discussed.

To check the results, the moiré-interferometry technique /5/ was also used at different stages of load. The same image processing procedures were then applied, in this case achieving 3D reconstruction of the strain fields comparable with those of the grating technique. A further comparison was provided by electrical strain gauge measurements which gave a mean value over the field studied with optical techniques.

F. Ginesu is Professor of Machine Element Design and F. Bertolino a researcher at the Department of Mechanical Engineering, University of Cagliari, Italy. W.M. Sun is a researcher at the Ninxia Institute of Technology, Yinchuan, China.

EXPERIMENTAL TECHNIQUES

The optical technique consists of a simple phase grating bonded onto the specimen, which is observed under a microscope of average magnification, mounted in front of the specimen, tensionally loaded by a test machine. The experiment is performed out of the holographic bench. The grating manufacture is described in detail elsewhere /6/: here frequencies of 250-300 lines/mm have been adopted.

By comparing the grid spacing before and after a load step, or after a fatigue cycle, it is possible to measure deformation in every point of the surface. It is also possible to get a moiré effect by simply superposing the undeformed and deformed grid pictures. Strains up to 0.1% can be detected and measured. Transverse matrix cracking and interlaminar debonding can also be evidenced.

The usefulness of the high precision and sensitivity of optical interferometric methods combined with the high speed of computer analysis is highlighted.

Here both loaded and unloaded gratings are independently recorded to avoid any possible decorrelation due to vibrations of the test machine. To enhance and analyse grid patterns, the digital image techniques previously adopted /7/ have been implemented here and improved on a new software code suitable for Apollo-Hewlett Packard and IRIS (Silicon Graphics) work-stations. This new code, written completely in standard Fortran language, allows both the analysis and the enhancement of the grid patterns.

One of the main features is the automatic treatment of gratings, which is performed by reading in sequential fashion, line by line and storing the information on the pixels position. The high power of the work-stations allows to create data matrices where additional information on the single pixels is stored and this avoids the nesting of a single byte for each pixel, required by previous programs.

The new feature is the spatial representation of displacement functions and their derivatives, which gives either graphical or numerical values of engineering parameters over the whole model. A first release of this program has been successfully used for the structural analysis of reinforced circular discs /8/.

The grating technique is particularly useful during loading on the test machine because it is little affected by vibrations and noise, but on the other hand it is not very sensitive to the displacements themselves. Besides the grating-microscope approach, an optical interferometric technique, suitable only on the holographic bench, has been used to observe the strain field in greater detail. This technique is known as moiré-interferometry /5/ and consists in superimposing two phase gratings, the first replicated on the lateral surface of the test model and the second given by the interference of two laser beams. This method is easy to apply on a holographic bench and the superposition of the two gratings gives a fringe pattern system representing the pitch changes and thus the displacements of the loaded specimen. The fringe pattern was studied in real time and here it was recorded with a CCD camera, digitized, and converted using the usual procedure into a 3D reconstruction model. A grating of 1000 lines/mm was used and such a great sensitivity restricted the use of the method to the holographic bench. The tests consisted in the following stages: a fringe pattern of the unloaded specimen was first recorded; after a loading fatigue cycle on a test machine, the specimen was checked again on the holographic bench and a new fringe pattern was recorded.

NUMERICAL PROCEDURE

The whole procedure is schematically represented by the flow-chart in Fig. 1. The first step is achieved by the optical methods mentioned above. For the second, a CCD camera and a personal computer with digital image features are used. The third and last step is realized by powerful work-stations.

As mentioned above, a phase grating was replicated onto the lateral surface of graphite-peek laminates to evidence the behaviour of the different layers under fatigue load cycle. A gold coating allowed good reflection efficiency of the grating replica and its observation, by means of a binocular microscope, proved satisfactory. The different loading steps were recorded and digitized by a CCD camera and converted into a numerical array of 480 rows and 512 columns using an IBM personal computer. The images were sent to an HP-DN400 work-station where a software code (DIP) converted the initial data into 3D representation of the displacements and deformations of the tested specimens. In particular, the initial numerical array was first enhanced by means of algorithms commonly used in image processing analysis: first the look-up table was changed, then a Prewitt filter was used twice, taking into account the grating frequency. At this point an interactive algorithm was used, capable of recognizing the grating lines: it looks for the brightest pixels (both centre and maximum of the single lines) and follows the different paths so as to define, line by line, the whole picture. The algorithm requires the assistance of the operator and requests it at the beginning when the search of the different lines starts and when a noisy area is present. A general purpose approach was used, which does not require prior knowledge of the nature of the fringes /9,10/. At the end of this process a certain number of points describes the lines and a triangular frame is then provided automatically /11/. This frame behaves like a finite element model: the shape of the elements are optimized and the values of the displacements can be readily calculated over the whole model by simple interpolations. The displacement data can now be reconstructed by a three-dimensional model of the frame or, using shading algorithms, such as Gouraud's and Phong's, a clearer 3D reconstruction can be achieved. The representation of displacements was in our case very poor because the parameters involved are global parameters and are unable to evidence the significant differences between the layers of composite laminates of this type. But it was easy to obtain strains from displacements simply calculating a numerical derivative of the 3D frame described above. A 3D reconstruction of the derivative of both the frame and the shading can again be made. More details of the complete procedure can be found in /5/.

TEST ANALYSIS AND COMPARISON

The DIP computer code is able to process and display data in different ways. 3D reconstructions of loaded fields are easily obtained using different points of view to evidence strain gradient. Some new routines provide orthographic projections of the field, evidencing by a scale of colours the regions of equal deformation (either displacement or strain).

A phase grating of 0.005 mm pitch was replicated onto the lateral surface of a graphite-peek angle-ply $[45/-45]_{4s}$ laminate. Figure 2a shows the microscopic scheme of the layers and a picture of the specimen. In the same figure the diagram (b) represents the cycle load and it was continuously recorded with an electrical strain gauge supplied by the same manufacturers as the test machine, M.T.S. In the diagram two characteristic points are highlighted. Figs. (c) and (d) give an isometric view and an orthographic equal-strain region respectively for points 1 and 2.

Figure 3 shows the different results obtained with the moiré-interferometry technique. On the opposite surface of the same specimen a phase grating of 0.001 mm pitch in longitudinal direction was replicated. This grating allowed to analyse the permanent displacement by reading the moiré-interferometric fringe pattern after unloading the specimen.

Figure 3(a) shows both an initial fringe pattern system and the triangularized frame of the unloaded model. Figs.3(b) and (c) depict the fringe pattern obtained after unloading the specimen with a permanent strain of 0.008 m/m. Both pictures with respective histograms represent the fringe pattern before and after equalization treatment. Lastly, Figs. 3(d) and (e) are the isometric view and orthographic projection respectively at equal-strain regions on the deformed specimen. The nonuniform behaviour throughout the thickness clearly emerges. The average value of 0.008 m/m was in good agreement with the strain gauge data.

Summing up, from the displacements, represented by the initial fringe pattern, obtained here with moiré-interferometry, a spatial representation of the deformed model has been achieved. In this way information on the points can be extracted over the whole field examined.

Comparison of the results obtained with the different techniques shows that the data are in fairly good agreement.

CLOSURE

The main advantages of optical techniques, such as moiré-interferometry and the grating one used here, are their great sensitivity and whole field measurements. However, these features are sometimes of no benefit because of both the tedium of manual data extraction and the subjective element introduced by human operation. The procedure presented here permits fringe patterns to be immediately converted into 3D visions and a friendly analysis of the data. Consequently, it is possible to read the measurements point by point and data can even be transformed using numerical procedures. In brief, stress can be calculated from the displacements fringe pattern.

So far the different samples tested and the comparisons made seem to point to the general advantage of this approach. The results reported here refer only to a few specimens but the same procedure has been successfully adopted in a number of other applications.

Further work aimed at improving the program code will provide an automatic comparison, point by point, between field results for different load conditions. This feature will avoid tedious computations and difficult correlations between images.

ACKNOWLEDGEMENTS

The present research work was carried out with the financial support of the C.N.R. (National Research Council) and the M.P.I. (Italian Ministry of Education).

REFERENCES

1. Aymerich, F., Ginesu, F., Priolo,P, Advanced materials characterization by means of moiré techniques. Proceedings of the SPIE Second International Conference on Photomechanics and Speckle Metrology, Vol.1554B, pp.304-314, San Diego (CA), July 1991.

2. Parks, V.J., Strain measurements using grids. Optical Engineering, Vol.21, No.4, July/August 1982.

3. SEM Ed., Handbook on Experimental Mechanics, Chap.6, pp.313, by Vincent J. Parks, Prentice-Hall, Inc., Englewood CLiffs, New Jersey 07632.

4. Aymerich, F., Ginesu, F., Priolo, P. and Sun, W.M., Static and fatigue progression in graphite fibre reinforced peek. Proceedings of the Joint FEFG/ICF International Conference on Fracture of Engineering Materials and Structures, Singapore, pp. 209-214, Aug. 1991.

5. SEM Ed., Handbook on Experimental Mechanics, Chap.7, pp.314-387 by Daniel Post, Prentice-Hall, Inc., Englewood Cliffs, New Jersey 07632.

6. Ginesu,F., Rossi,R., Characterization of composite materials by means of a reflection moiré-holographic technique. 9th International Congress on Experimental Mechanics, Copenhagen, Aug. 1990.

7. Ginesu, F. and Rossi, R., Structural analysis of reinforced discs by numerical processing of fringe patterns. SEM Spring Conference on Experimental Mechanics, Boston, 1989.

8. Ginesu, F. and Bertolino, F., Numerical analysis of fringe patterns for structural engineering problems. Proceedings of the SPIE Laster Interferometry IV: Computer-Aided Interferometry, Vol. 1553, pp.313-324, San Diego (CA), 1991.

9. Reid, G.T., Automatic fringe pattern analysis: a review. Optics and Lasers in Engineering, 7 pp. 37-68, (1986/87).

10. Krishnaswamy, S., Algorithm for computer tracing of interferometric fringes. Applied Optics, Vol.30, No.13, May 1991.

11. Bertolino, F., Design, determination and representation of surfaces by points triangularization. Il Progettista Industriale, March 1991 (in Italian).

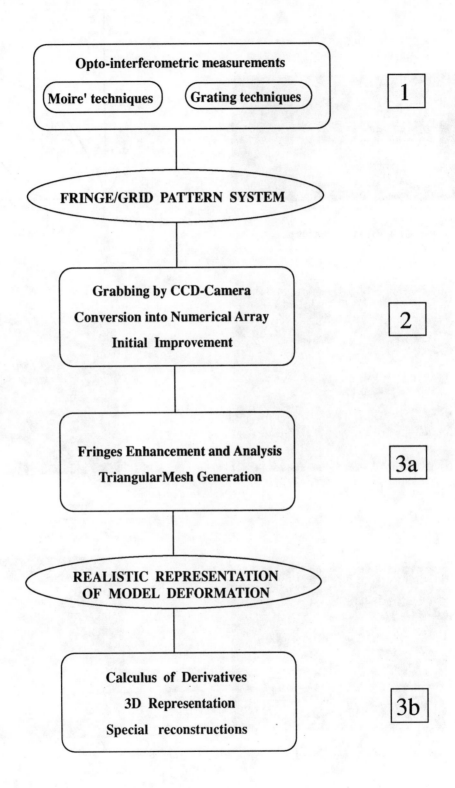

Fig. 1 – Flow-chart of the whole procedure

a) Laminate structure

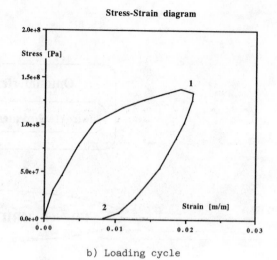

b) Loading cycle

c) Results for point 1

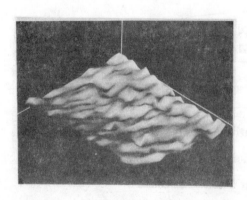

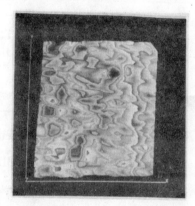

d) Results for point 2

Figure 2 - Grating-microscope technique

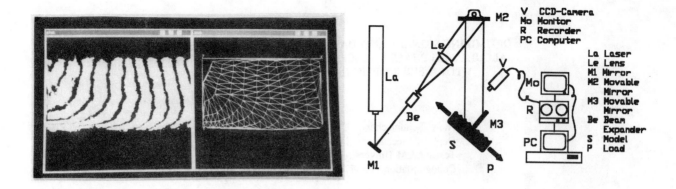

a) Unloaded model and experimental set-up

b) Fringe pattern after unloading

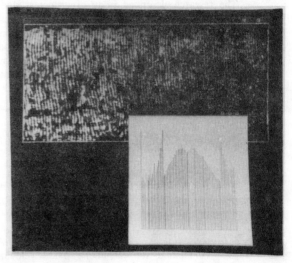

c) The same as b) after equalization

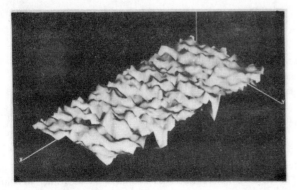

d) Isometric view of the field

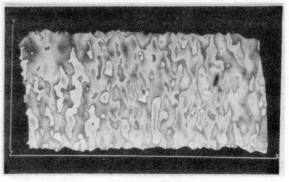

e) Orthographic projection of the field

Fig. 3 - Moiré-interferometry technique

OPTIMIZING SIGNALS AND DATA ANALYSIS TECHNIQUES FOR CALCULATING PHASE VELOCITIES OF LAMB WAVES DETECTED WITH A FIBER OPTIC INTERFEROMETER SYSTEM

N. A. Schumacher
Dept. of Mechanical Eng.
Texas A&M University
College Station, TX 77843

C. P. Burger
Dept. of Mechanical Eng.
Texas A&M University
College Station, TX 77843

ABSTRACT

The research described is an experimental study of the effects of windowing on calculating the phase velocities of transient Lamb waves. In particular, time domain signals that contain reflections or do not decay are investigated. Square windows and modified Hamming windows are compared. It is shown that the phase information from the low frequency components of the waves studied are greatly affected by the placement of the windows in the time domain.

INTRODUCTION

Lamb waves have numerous applications as a tools for NDE. An example is the Lamb wave's sensitivity to the material's geometrical and elastic properties.[1,2] The material's properties (both geometrical and elastic) can be deduced by measuring the Lamb wave's phase velocity characteristics. Therefore, to extract accurate properties it is necessary to extract accurate phase velocities. A method for calculating phase velocities from transient signals, developed by Sachse[3], can be applied to Lamb waves. Sachse's method involves using the phase information from FFT's of time domain signals to calculate the corresponding phase velocity as a function of frequency. The expression can be written as:

$$V(f) = \frac{2\pi f d}{-(\phi_2 - \phi_1)}$$

where f is the frequency, d is the geometric separation between two points on a surface where the time domain signals are detected, ϕ_1 is the phase as a function of frequency at a reference position, and ϕ_2 is the phase as a function of frequency at a distance d from the reference location. For the experimental data described, the transient Lamb waves were generated with a pulsed ND:Yag laser and then detected with a fiber optic interferometer system. Details of the experiment are described elsewhere.[4] The interferometers were used to record the time displacement histories at two locations on the surface of a 0.92 mm thick steel plate. The advantage of using interferometers is that they are totally non-invasive detectors so that accurate phase comparisons can be derived from sequentially detecting the same pulse as it propagated through a distance, d, between two interferometers.

ANALYSIS

Figure 1 displays the time histories of the lowest order antisymmetric Lamb wave (a_0) as detected by the two fiber tip interferometers, FTI 1 and FTI 2.[4] Both of the signals shown in Figure 1 contain reflections after approximately 26 microseconds. Also, neither signal appears to decay in the time frame shown. Therefore, some windowing must be done to these signals to perform FFTs. Figure 1 shows five possible choices for square windows all starting at 15μs and proceeding to time T1b (22.5μs), T1a (24.5μs) for FTI 1 and to time T2c (24.0μs), T2b (25.8μs), and T2a (27.5μs) for FTI 2. The cut-off points for these windows coincide with zero crossings of the FTI signals. The signals were truncated at the desired window end points and then zero padded to extend the arrays to 256 points for computing the FFTs.

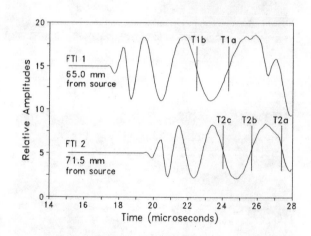

Figure 1 - Time displacement histories of transient Lamb waves (zero order anti-symmetric mode) on a 0.92 mm thick steel plate. The regions indicated show the limits in the time domain for various square windows. All windows start at 15μs.

The a_0 wave has well defined dispersive group (energy) velocity characteristics.[5] For this mode, the velocity increases with frequency and asymptotes at the Rayleigh wave speed.

Because of their dispersive nature, windowing time domain signals containing Lamb waves will effect the frequency components calculated for the signal through an FFT. To investigate this, FFTs were computed for each of the five time domain regions shown in Figure 1. Figure 2 shows that all five FFTs have different center frequencies, i.e. the maximum relative amplitudes occur at different frequencies. However, there are two pairs of magnitudes in Figure 2 that have similar center frequencies. The windows T1a and T2a were chosen because they were found to contain approximately the same frequency content. Also, windows T1b and T2b were chosen because they were found to have similar center frequencies. The window T2c was chosen as a comparison. As shown in Figure 2, it contains predominately higher frequencies.

Since phase velocity calculations use only the phase information from the FFT and not the magnitude information, the effect of the time window on the phase of the signal will be studied. Shown in Figure 3 are the corresponding phase plots as a function of frequency for each of the square windows. Notice in Figure 3 that beyond approximately 0.4 MHz the phase values, for the different windows of FTI 1 and FTI 2 respectively, converge. This is shown more clearly in Figure 4 which is an expanded view of the first 0.6 MHz from Figure 3. The phases plotted show a clear variance in phase for the low frequency components of each successively smaller window.

A plot of change in phase versus frequency is also relevant. Figure 5 shows the change in phase as a function of frequency for three combinations of windows for FTI 1 and FTI 2. The change in phase is defined as $-(\phi_2 - \phi_1)$ at a given frequency. The minus sign is used to make the difference positive. The three delta ϕ's shown in Figure 5 include two combinations that have similar center frequencies, T1a & T2a along with T1b & T2b, and one combination from FFTs with different center frequencies, T1a & T2c. As shown in Figure 5, there is a high degree of correlation between combinations from windows of similar center frequencies. This suggests that, in order to compare the signals and phase information from two FTI's from square windows on time domain signals, the windows must be chosen to yield FFTs that have approximately the same center frequencies. If it is not possible to window the data with similar center frequencies, several window choices should be used in order to see over which range of frequency information the data is valid. It can be concluded that, even for the largest difference between center frequencies of the windows chosen (T1a and T2c ref. Figures 1 and 2), the change in phase information is still valid beyond 0.4 MHz. Beyond this point, there is very little scatter in the data for any of the square window combinations.

An alternative way of time windowing the signals is to multiply a functional window to the signal causing a gradual decay in amplitude. Examples are Hanning and Hamming windows. These windows are typically applied over the entire wave envelope in that both the beginning and ending of the signals are functionally decayed to zero amplitude. For the waves shown in Figure 1, the functional window was applied over a short time domain on the end part of the signals. In particular, a half-Hamming (weighted cosine function whose amplitude varies from 1 to near 0 over the specified time span) was applied to the signals causing a decay in amplitude over approximately 3 microseconds. These waves are shown in Figure 6. Two different windows were chosen for FTI 1. One applied approximately 2 microseconds earlier in time. The waves shown with "Hamming 1" for FTI 1 and FTI 2 w

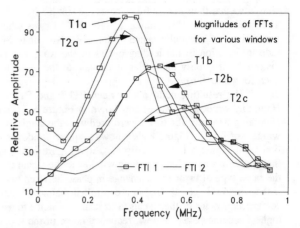

Figure 2 - Magnitudes of FFTs for each of the time domain regions indicated in Figure 1. Each FFT was calculated with a square window in the time domain.

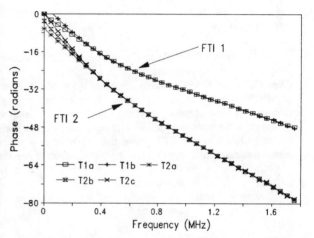

Figure 3 - Phase as a function of frequency for each of the square windows indicated in Figure 1. The phases also correspond to the magnitudes shown in Figure 2.

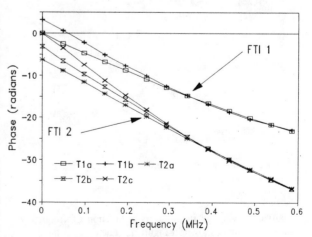

Figure 4 - An expanded view of the phase as a function of frequency from zero to 0.6 MHz in Figure 3.

chosen so that their center frequencies are similar (ref. Figure 7). The wave labeled "Hamming 2" for FTI 1 was chosen for comparison of dissimilar center frequency. Note that the amplitude information in the leading cycles of the wave has not been distorted. It is only the cycles at the tale of the wave that have been forced to zero.

The resulting delta ϕ's between FTI 1 and FTI 2 for the Hamming windowed waves are shown in Figure 8. Both of the Hamming windows for FTI 1 were used with the single Hamming window of FTI 2. Figure 8 also shows a square window combination from Figure 5 for comparison. From Figure 8 it is apparent that applying a modified Hamming window to the signal can create the same type of error in the change in phase between two signals if the window is not applied in a controlled manner. That is, the center frequencies of the signals must nearly coincide to assure the highest accuracy over the low frequency range of the signal. The square window combination shows excellent agreement with the modified Hamming window combination (if both combinations are chosen with similar center frequencies).

CONCLUSIONS

For both of the windowing techniques used, square and modified Hamming windows, there is a variation in phase for a given FTI signal based on the placement of the window in the time domain. This variation in phase is most evident in the low frequency portion of the signal for the a_0 mode of the Lamb wave. However, if the windows for both FTI signals are chosen such that the magnitudes of the FFTs have the approximately the same center frequency and shape, there is little variation in the change in phase between possible window combinations. If it is not possible to chose a window combination with similar center frequencies and shape, then several windows should be examined to see the region of convergence for the change in phase between signals.

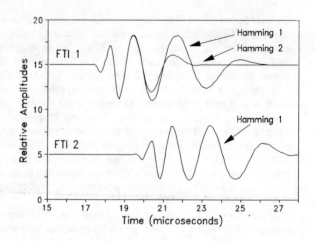

Figure 6 - Time histories of Figure 1 with Hamming windows applied to the end of the signals.

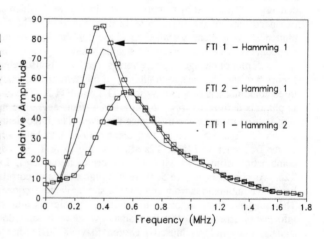

Figure 7 - Magnitudes of FFTs for waves shown in Figure 6.

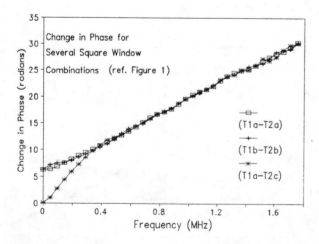

Figure 5 - Change in phase as a function of frequency for the square windows shown in Figure 1. Each plot is the difference of two plots shown in Figure 2.

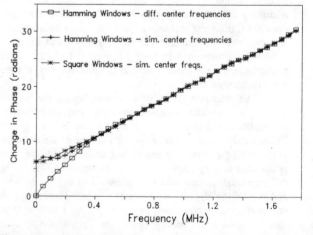

Figure 8 - Change in phase as a function of frequency for the phase information from the FFTs of the waves shown in Figure 6. As a comparison, the change in phase for one of the square window combinations (Figure 5) is also shown.

ACKNOWLEDGEMENTS

This research was sponsored by the National Science Foundation under project number MSS-9114533.

REFERENCES

1.   Bresse, L.F., Hutchins, D.A., and Lundgren, K., "Elastic Constant Determination using Generation by Pulsed Lasers," *J. Acoust. Soc. Am.*, **84**(5), 1751-1757 (1987).

2.   Hutchins, D.A., Lundgren, K., and Palmer, S.B., " A Laser Study of Transient Lamb Waves in Thin Materials," *J. Acoust. Soc. Am.*, **85**(4), 1441-1448 (1989).

3.   Sachse, W. and Pao, Y.H, "On the Determination of Phase and Group Velocities of Dispersive Waves in Solids," *J. Appl. Phys.*, **49**(8), 4320-4327 (1978).

4.   Schumacher, N.A., Burger, C.P, and Gien, P.H., "Analysis of Transient Lamb Waves in Metal Plates, Composite Panels and Curved Members via Laser and Fiber Optic Methods," *Review of Progress in Quantitative Non-Destructive Evaluation*, Bowdoin College, Brunswick, Maine, (1991).

5.   Viktorov, I.A., *Rayleigh and Lamb Waves*, Plenum Press, New York, N.Y., (1967).

CHARACTERISTICS OF CAUSTICS FORMED AT INNER FACES OF A LAMINATED PLATE---IN CASE OF UNIFORMLY INDUCED DISPLACEMENTS ACROSS WHOLE THICKNESS OF PLATE

K.Isogimi

ABSTRACT

Characteristics of caustics formed in a laminated plate composed of two sheets with different elastic properties are investigated to obtain basic data used in applying the experimental caustic method to semi three dimensional stress analysis. Subjected loads are the concentrated and distributing ones which induce approximately uniform deformation across the thickness of the plate. The following are clarified through this research. The caustic curves calculated by simplified optical theory conform with the practical caustics accurately enough. Some characteristic changes appear depending on the arrangement of the materials.

INTRODUCTION

The experimental caustic method has been applied to simple two dimensional problems only, especialy contact problems and others which determine the stress intensity factor for cracks. The author has been investigating the characteristics of caustics in detail in case of a half plane and a wedge-shaped plane with external forces and has shown that we can estimate the edge values of external loads and the coefficients which characterize their distributions. It seems, however, that it is very useful to develop this method and apply it to various three dimensional problems. In the foregoing papers[1],[2], a homogenuous plate with a discontinuously distibuting load across it was chosen as the research object.

In this paper, caustics formed by the reflected light rays at the inside of a laminated plate composed of two sheets with different kinds of properties (E_1, ν_1, E_2, ν_2) are obtained, and the relationships between characteristics of caustics and the reflecting positions and the arrangement of materials are clarified.

The research is performed under a discontinuously distributing load across the plate, whose intensity changes at the interface of the two materials, and which induces approximately uniform deformation to any material. The experimental caustics are investigated and compared with those calculated based on simplified optical theory.

THEORETICAL CAUSTIC EUATIONS

The change in the optical path length in an isotropic and homogenuous object caused by the external load is derived in the aforementioned paper[1]. Therefore the procedure to derive the caustic equations is shown only under the condition of inducing approximately uniform deformations to any material. To simplify the calculations, the following assumptions are introduced.

(1) The position of the middle plane does not shift under load.
(2) The stresses in a laminated plate are under the plane stress condition, and the stresses in one region do not affect those in another region beyond the bonded interface.

Calculations should be performed in the following two cases, respectively.

[A] Light reflects at the interface of both materials.

As shown in Fig.1, consider a plate of total thickness d and that the interface of both materials at distance $k_1 d$ from the front surface coincides with the reflecting plane of light rays. The plate is subjected to distributing loads $P_1 \sigma$ and $P_2 \sigma$ (σ :standard value of external force, P_1 and P_2:load intensity coefficients at each region). If the front surface under loading is taken as the basic position, change ΔS in optical path length can be obtained as follows.

$$\Delta S = 2d \left\{ k A_1 - (n_1 - 1) \frac{\nu_1 k P_1}{E_1} - \frac{\nu_2 (1/2 - k) P_2}{E_2} \right\} (\sigma_1 + \sigma_2) \quad : 0 \leq k \leq 0.5 \qquad (1)$$

$$\Delta S = 2d \left\{ A_1 k P + \frac{(1/2 - n_1 k) P_1 \nu_1}{E_1} \right\} (\sigma_1 + \sigma_2) \quad : 0.5 \leq k \leq 1 \qquad (2)$$

where A is the optical constant of the materials.

K.Isogimi is Professor of Mechanical Engineering in the Faculty of Engineering, Mie University, Kamihama-cho, Tsu 514, Japan.

[B] Light always reflects at the front surface.
Change ΔS can be obtained similarly,

$$\Delta S = 2\,d\left\{\frac{\nu_1\,k\,P_1}{E_1}+\frac{\nu_2\,(1/2-k_1)P_2}{E_2}\right\}(\sigma_1+\sigma_2) \qquad : 0\le k \le 0.5 \tag{3}$$

$$\Delta S = 2\,d\;(\nu_1 P_1 / 2E_1)\;(\sigma_1+\sigma_2) \qquad : 0.5 \le k \le 1 \tag{4}$$

The deviation of the reflecting light rays from any point on the reflecting plane is generally given by eq.(5) on the screen[3].

$$\vec{W} = z_r \operatorname{grad}\Delta S \tag{5}$$

where z_r is the distance from the middle plane to the screen. The equations of caustic curves are obtained from above eq.(5).

$$x = -\lambda\left\{r\cos\theta \pm \frac{C_g K}{2\,r_1\,r_2}\sin(\theta_1+\theta_2)\right\} \tag{6}$$

$$y = \lambda\left\{r\sin\theta \pm \frac{C_g K}{2\,r_1\,r_2}\cos(\theta_1+\theta_2)\right\} \tag{7}$$

and the conditional equation is

$$r^4 - 2\,a^2\,r^2\cos 2\theta - C_g\,|K|\,r + a^4 = 0 \tag{8}$$

where

$$C_g = 16\,\sigma\,a\,d / \pi\,\lambda \tag{9}$$

$$K = 2\,z_r\,d\;(A\,k+\nu_1\,k/E_1) \tag{10}$$

$$\theta_1 = \tan^{-1}\left\{\frac{r\sin\theta}{r\cos\theta - a}\right\} \tag{11}$$

$$\theta_2 = \tan^{-1}\left\{\frac{r\sin\theta}{r\cos\theta + a}\right\} \tag{12}$$

$$r_1 = (r^2 - 2\,r\,a\cos\theta + a^2)^{1/2} \tag{13}$$

$$r_2 = (r^2 + 2\,r\,a\cos\theta + a^2)^{1/2} \tag{14}$$

and values r_1, r_2, θ_1 and θ_2 are shown in Fig.2.

EXPERIMENTAL PROCEDURES

The loading equipment and the optical layout are similar to those employed in the previous paper[1]. Optical dimensional values $\lambda=0.4$ and $z_r=260\text{mm}$ are constant throughout the experiment. The whole thickness of the specimens is kept at about 3mm by combining two kinds of acrylate resin plates whose properties are shown in Table 1. The reflecting plane is created by means of vacuum deposition of Aluminium. In order to induce approximately uniform deformation across the plate thickness, the value of ratio P_1/P_2 euals to that of Young's modulus E_1/E_2.

RESULTS AND DISCUSSIONS

Figure 3 shows, as an example, the caustics formed at the front surface of the plates composed by the two different kinds of arrangements subjected to the concentrated load on the backward one third region. The caustics coincide well with one another. Therefore it can be concluded that no problem will arise during bonding.

[A]Case of coincidence of reflecting face and material interface
Figure 4(a),(b) show the caustics created in case of different arrangements of both materials. Both computational and practical caustics correspond well to the same reflecting position coefficient k. When k=0, they are the front type, but when k=0.33, they convert to the rear type, and they enlarge gradually with the increase of k. The difference between the caustics created in each arrangement can be mentioned as follows. If a plate is made one body, almost similar caustic is created regardless of materials. However, when the forward material has bigger elastic constants, caustics created are somewhat larger than those in the inverse case. It can be concluded from these results that, in spite of the calculation assumptions, loadings affect one another beyond the boundary and those by backward material with bigger Young's modulus are stronger.
Figure 5(a),(b) show the relationships between k and caustic dimensions. When k $\geqq 0.5$, the dimensions depend upon the forward material, and when k<0.33, upon the backward one. Critical position coefficient k_{cr} where the configuration of caustic changes from the front type to the rear one are

$$k_{cr} = 0.27 \qquad : E_1 / E_2 = 2/1$$
$$k_{cr} = 0.28 \qquad : E_1 / E_2 = 1/2 \tag{15}$$

[B]Case of fixed reflecting face at front surface

The caustics obtained from different arrangement of materials are shown in Fig.6(a),(b), and the relationship between k and maximum height H_D is shown in Fig.7. The feature of dimension changing is vise versa with values E_1/E_2.

CONCLUSIONS

1. Though the specimens are fabricated by means of bonding appropriate materials, the influence of bonding on created caustics is negligible small.
2. The characteristics of caustics for uniform deformation across the whole thickness are similar to those under uniform load.
3. The critical position coefficients where caustics exchange from the front type to the rear one are obtained as eq.(15).

REFERENCE

1. Kiyoshi Isogimi,"Characteristics of Caustics Formed at Inner Faces of a Plate," Proc. 9th Int. Conf. on Exp. Mech., Copenhagen, 5, 1916-1920, 1990.
2. Kiyoshi Isogimi,"Characteristics of Caustics Formed at Inner Faces of a Laminated Plate," Proc. of Japan Soc. of Mech. Engrs. (in Japanese), No.910-62, A, 46-48, 1991.
3. P.S.Theocaris, "Stress-singularities at Concentrated Load," Exp. Mech., 511-518, 1973-12.

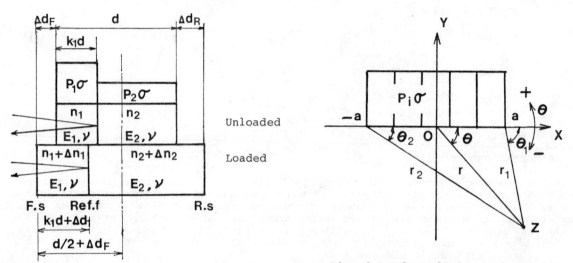

Fig. 1 Change of optical path length

Fig. 2 Load condition and notations

Table 1 Optical properties of employed materials

Optical constant	A	-0.55×10^{-10} m/N
Refractive index	n_1	1.491
	n_2	1.491
Young's modulus	E_1	3.25×10^3 MPa
	E_2	1.6×10^3 MPa
Poisson ratio	ν_1	0.355
	ν_2	0.399

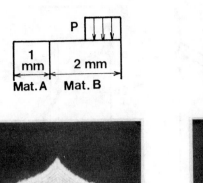
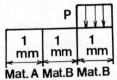

(a) Specimen A   (b) Specimen B

Fig. 3 Influences of bonding on created caustics

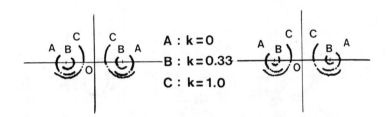

A : k=0
B : k=0.33
C : k=1.0

(a) Computational caustic curves.

Practical caustics created in $E_1:E_2=2:1$

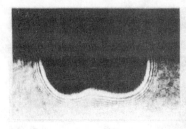
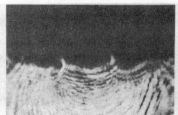

Practical caustics created in $E_1:E_2=1:2$

(b) Practical caustic patterns

Fig. 4 Caustics in case [A]

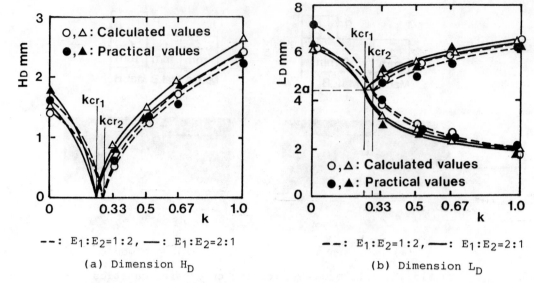

(a) Dimension H_D (b) Dimension L_D

Fig. 5 Relationships between position ratio k and caustic dimensions.

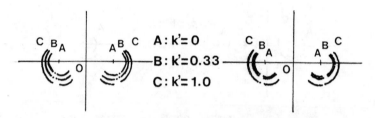

(a) Computational caustic curves.

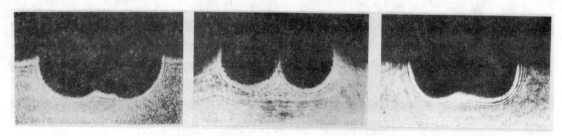

Practical caustics created in $E_1:E_2=2:1$

Practical caustics created in $E_1:E_2=1:2$

(b) Practical caustic patterns.

Fig. 6   Caustics in case [B]

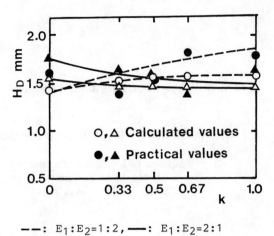

--: $E_1:E_2=1:2$, —: $E_1:E_2=2:1$

Fig. 7 Relationships between k and caustic dimensions

A NONLINEAR STUDY OF LASER HEATING FOR NDE

R.S. MACHIRAJU, P.H. GIEN, AND C.P. BURGER

Department of Mechanical Engineering
Texas A&M University
College Station, Texas 77843

ABSTRACT

Recent advances in laser induced thermal shock waves for use in ultrasonic NDE have shown that there is a need for modelling the absorption of laser light into common structures. Ready's equation for studying the temperature-time histories generated by the absorption of a very short pulse of high power laser light at the surface of a semi-infinite solid is predominantly linear, with the thermophysical properties of the target medium assumed to be constant. The maximum values for the predicted surface temperatures were unreasonably high. To address this deficiency, temperature dependent thermophysical properties were introduced, and the resulting nonlinear equation was reformulated as a differential equation and solved numerically. Using this approach, the predicted peak temperatures were substantially lower.

A computer program was written to model the absorption of laser light coming out of a fiber-optic bundle, onto the surface of a semi-infinite solid, using linear superposition of the nonlinear solution developed for the absorption of a single spot of laser radiation at the surface of a semi-infinite solid. The thermal heating patterns corresponded well with the geometric configuration of the individual fibers in the fiber-otic bundle.

A nonlinear scanning laser heating model was developed to study the absorption of a scanning laser beam, at the surface of a semi-infinite solid. It was found that there exists a critical velocity, which acts as a borderline between the laser heating pattern going from symmetric to asymmetric.

INTRODUCTION

The absorption of high-power laser light at an opaque surface has to be fully understood in order to understand the application of lasers in the area of ultrasonic NDE. The task of studying the absorption of laser radiation at opaque surfaces has been an area of ongoing research for many years. There are several models available to study the absorption of laser light at a target surface. All of these models assume constant thermophysical properties. Consequently, the surface temperatures predicted by these models are erroneous, since, for most materials, the thermophysical properties, such as the coefficient of thermal conductivity and the coefficient of thermal diffusivity vary with the temperature of the target surface.[1,2,3,4,5]

This research is concerned with the development of nonlinear models to predict the temperature profiles generated by the absorption of high power laser radiation at the surface of a semi-infinite solid. These nonlinear models include, a single laser spot incident on an absorbing surface, a fiber-optic bundle of laser sources arranged in an arbitrary geometric arrangement, and finally a laser source scanning across a surface producing a particular kind of temperature wavefront as it scans a predetermined path.

NONLINEAR PROPERTIES OF THE ABSORBING MEDIUM

It is important to understand the nonlinear properties of the absorbing medium, in order to fully appreciate the necessity for including them in their nonlinear form in laser heating models.

Table 1 lists the most common variables that appear in most laser absorption models. The variation of thermal conductivities of some typical solids with temperature are shown in Figure 1[1,2,4,5]. The variation of thermal diffusivities of some typical solids with temperature are shown in Figure 2[1,2,3,5]. Due to absorption of high power laser radiation at their surfaces, most materials exhibit dramatic changes in these properties due to the steep temperature changes as a consequence of laser absorption.

The last two nonlinear variables listed in Table 1, are correlated, in that, the reflectivity gives a measure of the absorption efficiency of the surface and hence leads to the total absorbed power. The absorption efficiency or absorptivity α is $(1 - R)$.

Table 1 -Nonlinear Variables

Variable	Definition of the variable
K	Thermal conductivity
κ	Thermal diffusivity
F	Total absorbed power
R	Reflectivity

Reflectivity is dependent on several factors, such as; wavelength of the incident radiation, temperature of the absorbing surface, and it is also highly dependent on the finish and type of coating (oxide or corrosion layer) present on the surface of the absorbing medium. The dependence of reflectivity on all these parameters is shown in Figures 3 and 4 for titanium[6] as a representative case. Although reflectivity exhibits a highly nonlinear behavior, it is kept as a constant in this research, due to the lack of experimental data for reflectivity of common materials and oxide coatings.

ABSORPTION OF SINGLE SPOT PULSED LASER LIGHT

Ready's equation for computing the temperature at depth z and radial distance r from the center of a focussed laser spot as a function of time t is[7]:

$$T(r,z,t) = \frac{F_{max}d^2}{K}\left(\frac{\kappa}{\pi}\right)^{1/2}$$
$$\times \int_0^t \frac{p(t-t')'}{t'^{1/2}(4\kappa t' + d^2)} e^{\left[-\frac{z^2}{4\kappa t'} - \frac{r^2}{4\kappa t' + d^2}\right]} dt' \qquad (1)$$

With, $p(t)$ being the normalized laser pulse profile, d being the laser spot size, and F_{max} being the maximum absorbed flux density.

The procedure followed to include temperature dependent properties in Equation 1, is to make the thermophysical properties (the conductivity and diffusivity) functions of temperature, and the resulting nonlinear equation is reformulated as a differential equation. Using a Runge-Kutta algorithm allows one to solve the nonlinear problem numerically. In order to make the thermophysical properties a function of temperature, a least-square polynomial is fitted to the property data obtained[1,2,3,4,5]. The order of the polynomial was chosen on a trial basis until a smooth fit was obtained. Two solutions to Equation 1 were produced, the first with constant thermophysical properties, and the second, with nonlinear temperature dependent polynomial representations of these properties. The Nd-YAG laser beam parameters used for this analysis were; τ, the pulse duration = 36 nanoseconds, and E the total energy delivered by the beam is = 300 millijoules[8]. The laser spot size had a radius of 2.5 mm.

Figure 5 shows the curve fitted temperature dependent thermophysical properties for pure titanium, with diffusivity fitted to a polynomial of order 4 and conductivity data fitted to a polynomial of order 5. The results of the analysis for titanium are presented in Figure 6, with the dotted line showing the result of the linear constant property model, and the solid line showing the nonlinear model's results. The results in Figure 6 illustrate that the linear model is approximately 158% in error compared to the nonlinear model.

MULTIPLE LASER SOURCES IN A FIBER-OPTIC BUNDLE

A computer program has been written in ANSI C, as a part of this research, for multiple laser sources (fiber-optic bundle) arranged in an arbitrary geometric pattern. The code, based on linear superposition of temperatures due to randomly placed laser sources, prompts the user for the number of laser sources, and the coordinates of the center of the focussed spot with reference to a reference coordinate system. The program assumes that, the

energy sent into the fiber bundle is distributed evenly between each individual fiber, each fiber maintained the circular Gaussian nature of the laser beam, and the crystal structure of the target material is isotropic. This analysis was done, by applying the nonlinear Ready's equation, and solving it, for multiple laser sources. This was accomplished by simple linear superposition of the individual nonlinear solutions, i.e., the laser light coming out of each fiber is considered as an independent laser spot and nonlinear formulated Ready's equation is applied, and all such independent nonlinear solutions are added. This procedure of linear superposition of nonlinear solutions yields correct results, as long as the laser spots do not overlap. Figure 7 shows a semi-circular arc fiber input of energy into the target surface and its corresponding results are shown in Figure 8. The resultant surface temperature map shown in Figure 8 appears to be consistent with the input pattern.

A NONLINEAR STUDY OF SCANNING LASER BEAM HEATING

An interesting way of generating spatially conditioned waves is the use of a scanning laser source instead of the traditional stationery source.

The governing equation for obtaining the temperature at (x,y,z) due the absorption of a scanning laser beam, scanning at a constant velocity v, in metals is[9]:

Where, P is the power, C_p is the heat capacity per unit volume, and R is the laser spot size.

$$T = \frac{P}{C_p} \int_0^\infty \frac{e^{\left[-\left\{\frac{[(x+vt')^2+y^2]}{2R^2+4\kappa t'} + \frac{z^2}{4\kappa t'}\right\}\right]}}{(\pi^3\kappa t')^{1/2}(2R^2+4\kappa t')} dt' \qquad (2)$$

The next step is to extend the predominantly linear analysis of Equation 2 to take into account nonlinear properties. The approach that will be followed is similar to the one that was used before, that is, to reformulate Equation 2 as a differential equation and making the thermophysical properties a function of temperature. Using a Runge-Kutta algorithm allows one to solve the nonlinear problem numerically.

The first results which will be looked at are, the variation of the temperature along the x-axis when the laser is being scanned with a constant velocity, v, in the x-axis direction. Both the linear and the nonlinear solutions have been worked out in order to prove the advantage of considering nonlinear thermophysical properties in laser heating models. The results of this analysis for titanium are presented in Figures 9 and 10. In Figures 9 and 10, the origin of the coordinate system is attached to the moving laser. The plots show that the linear model is approximately 112% in error.

Chen and Lee[10] have found that there exists a critical velocity v_o (the ratio of the thermal diffusivity, κ, to the Gaussian ($1/e$) radius, ω, of the laser beam) below which the effect of scanning is negligible and above which a true scanning heating pattern appears, with the temperature in the wake of the scanning laser being higher than in front of it. In other words, the peak temperature occurs at the origin for scan velocities less than the critical velocity, and the temperature peak is offset from the origin for scan velocities greater than the critical velocity.

The next result presented is an attempt at extending this concept of critical velocity into the realm of the nonlinear model. Figure 11 shows the results for titanium with $v_o = 7.505$cm/sec as the critical velocity. The result for $v=0.01*v_o=0.07505$ cm/sec. is depicted in the first curve, the second curve depicts the results for $v=0.1*v_o=0.7505$ cm/sec., and the lowest curve depicts the results for $v=0.3*v_o=2.2515$ cm/sec. The gradual degradation from symmetry to asymmetry can be clearly seen in Figure 11. An important conclusion that can been drawn, as a result of the introduction of nonlinear thermophysical properties into Equation 2 is that the critical velocity is lowered considerably when compared to the linear, constant property critical velocity value.

CONCLUSIONS

The incorporation of nonlinear temperature dependent thermophysical properties into the predominantly linear Ready's equation for predicting the temperature profiles generated by a single Gaussian laser beam incident on a target with an opaque surface, produced improved results, when compared with earlier models that assumed that thermal properties do not change with temperature.

Spatially conditioned thermal waves and subsequently spatially conditioned elastic waves can be generated by impingement of multiple laser sources arranged in an arbitrary geometric pattern in a fiber-optic bundle.

Scanning velocity is a very strong function of material thermophysical properties and the laser beam spot size. The introduction of temperature dependent properties into scanning heating models, brings down the critical scan velocity. Increasing scan speed decreases the peak temperatures with the power remaining the same.

REFERENCES

1. Touloukian, Y.S., Powell, R.W., Ho, C.Y., and Klemens, P.G., "Thermal Conductivity: Metallic Elements and Alloys," *Thermophysical Properties of Matter: The TPRC Data Series*, **Vol.1**, IFI/Plenum Press, New York (1970).

2. Holman, J.P., *Heat Transfer*, 4th ed., McGraw-Hill Kogakusha, Ltd., Tokyo, 1-22 (1976).

3. Touloukian, Y.S., Powell, R.W., Ho, C.Y., and Nicolaou, M.C., "Thermal Diffusivity", *Thermophysical Properties of Matter: The TPRC Data Series*, **Vol. 10**, IFI/Plenum Press, New York (1973).

4. Touloukian, Y.S., *Thermophysical Properties of High Temperature Solid Materials*, **Vol. 2: Nonferrous Alloys**, The Macmillan Co., New York (1966).

5. Myers, G.E., *Analytical Methods in Conduction Heat Transfer*, McGraw-Hill, New York, Appendix K (1971).

6. Goldsmith, A., Waterman, T.E., and Hirschhorn, H.J., *Handbook of Thermophysical Properties of Solid Materials*, **Vol. 1: Elements**, The Macmillan Co., New York (1961).

7. Ready, John F., *Effects of High-Power Laser Radiation*, 1st ed., Academic Press, New York (1971).

8. Duffer, Charles E., *Use of Fiber-Optic Guided, Laser Induced Acoustic Waves for NDE*, M.S. Thesis, Texas A&M University (1990).

9. Cline, H.E. and Anthony, T.R., "Heat Treating and Melting Material with a Scanning Laser or Electron Beam", *Journal of Applied Physics*, **48**(9), 3895-3900 (1977).

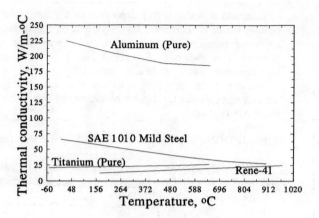

Fig. 1 - Variation of Conductivity with temperature.

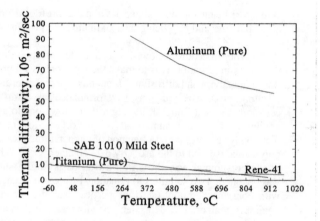

Fig. 2 - Variation of diffusivity with temperature.

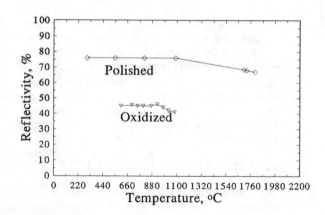

Fig. 3 - Reflectivity vs. temperature for titanium (Wavelength = 0.665 μm).

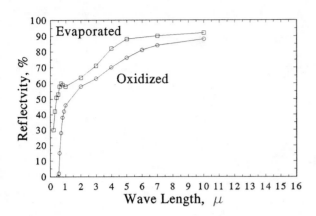

Fig. 4 -Reflectivity vs. wavelength for titanium (Room temperature).

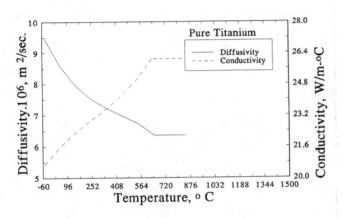

Fig. 5 -Diffusivity and conductivity vs. temperature, for titanium

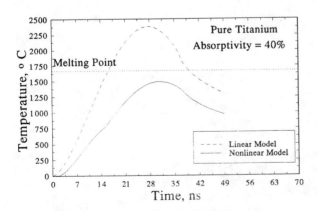

Fig. 6 -Temperature time history (r=0, z=0), for titanium

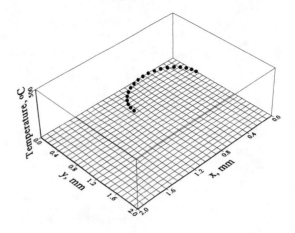

Fig. 7 -Semi-circular arrangement of individual fibers in the fiber bundle

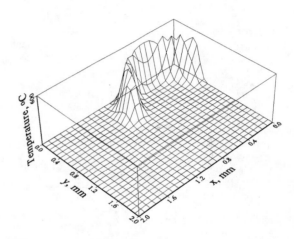

Fig. 8 -Surface temperature map for aluminum t=28 ns, for semi-circular input

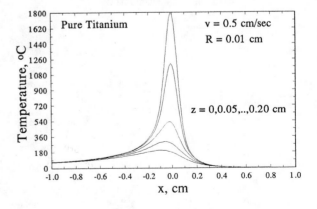

Fig. 9 -Temperature along the x-axis, for titanium (linear model)

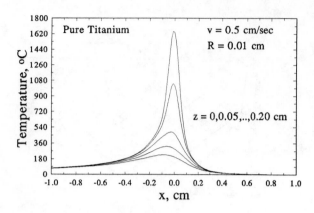

Fig. 10 -Temperature along the x-axis, for titanium (nonlinear model)

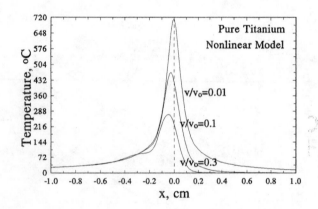

Fig. 11 -Temperature along the x-axis, for different scan velocities, for titanium

IMPROVEMENT OF POSSIBILITY AND IMPORTANCE OF EXPERIMENTAL SOLID MECHANICS BY HYBRID METHODS.

Prof. Dr.-Ing.Dr.-Ing.E.h. Karl-Hans Laermann
Bergische Universität - GH Wuppertal
Fachbereich 11
Pauluskirchstr. 7
D - 5600 Wuppertal 1

ABSTRACT

The considerable achievements in measurement techniques combined with computer technique enables application of experimental analysis to solve a large variety of solid mechanic problems in design, optimisation, damage analysis, quality- and system-control, screening of numerical analysis as well as in inspection of production processes. Advanced experimental techniques and advanced perceptions of theory to describe and to model real events consequently lead towards a combination of mathematical and experimental methods, towards "hybrid" techniques in order to improve reliability and accuracy of the results. This will be proved by some characteristic examples.

INTRODUCTION

The ongoing developments in measuring devices, the modern concepts of measurement configurations and the increasing tendencies towards automatisation of the whole measuring and evaluation processes are obviously leading to ever extending application in research and - more important - in industrial practice. New possibilities are given to investigate mechanical problems, which couldn't be analyzed as yet. Furthermore, methods of measurement and experimental mechanics are used in quality and safety control. They are necessary to minimize technical risks in a world, in which the living conditions are more and more determined by technique and technical achievements; they have to contribute in environment protection as well as to overcome the unacceptable differences in the economical and ecological situation between the industrialized and the less developed countries. Experimental mechanic has to face up to the international challenge towards a better world!

MODELLING AND HYBRID TECHNIQUES

To analyze any "event" mathematically "heuristic" models must be designed. The real "events" must be translated into a mathematical language, i.e. they must be described by algorithms. For that purpose suppositions and simplifications are to introduce despite the possibility of comprehensive computer simulation techniques nowadays. This leads to an approach of the real events only. The reliability of thus obtained results is often unknown or hardly to estimate unless they are proved by the reality, i.e. mainly by measurement.

By "iconic" models, however, the events can be reproduced quite more realistically. Those "iconic" models may be prototypes of products and structures or scaled-down replicas or even analogies. Now it might be argued such iconic modelling considering prototypes especially to be too expensive, time-consuming and sometimes too risky. Therefore, computer-simulation should be given preference. However, in order to develop such "simulation"-models and to prove their reference to reality it is necessary to introduce "experience" and to introduce at least numerous sets of data, which must be obtained by measurements, i.e. by experiments in the broadest sense.

The recent developments in methods as well as in equipment and in complex measuring systems warrant high resolution of the data to be measured. Simultaneously, the amount of data to be handled increases rapidly. Therefore, controlling the measuring system and the measuring process itself, data acquisition and their evaluation requires powerful computer equipment too. On-line procedures, i.e. the connexion of the experiment and the measuring system with the computer has become necessary and inalienable. It must be regarded also, that generally the observed phenomena are not identical with the finally wanted information. In modern experimental analysis therefore, proper theories and advanced mathematical models of the experimental methods as well as of the "event" to be investigated must be introduced. The statement of J.T.PINDERA, the well known senior in experimental mechanics, is remarkable: "There is no experiment without a proper theory behind it!"

These considerations consequently lead towards the philosophy of "hybrid techniques" [1] [2] [3] [4], the combination of "heuristic" and "iconic" models, i.e. the combination of mathematical and experimental analysis.

It must be pointed out, that it is of outmost importance to look at the whole analysing process as a cybernetic process. Because in modern engineering the results of any analysis are to feed back and to relate always to the real event considered, no matter whether these results are taken by mathematical/numerical, experimental/numerical or "hybrid" analysis. (Fig. 1)

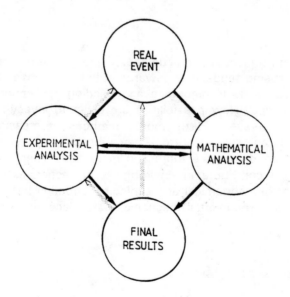

Fig. 1

The combination of theory and experiment, i.e. the symbiosis of "heuristic" and "iconic" models only yields more accurate and reliable knowledge on the reactions in structures and structural systems with regard to the increasing economical and ecological requirements and safety demands. Different stages of combining mathematical and experimental pathes of analyzing a given solid mechanics problem are possible depending on different parameters like for instance the problem itself, the purpose of the investigation, wanted results, demanded accuracy, availability of experimental equipment and computer capacity. (Fig. 2)

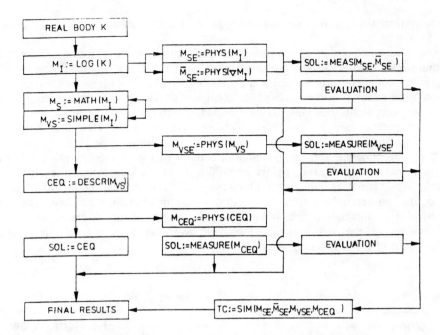

Fig. 2

Because of the thus given possibilities towards a more realistic modelling now much more complex problems can be analyzed. And especially in solid mechanics new fields of application are accessible. Beside statically and/or dynamically loaded structures, impact loading and wave propagation, beside problems of stability, fracture mechanics and fatigue also geometrical and physical non-linear problems as well as those of large displacements can be taken into consideration. Moreover, the influence of elastic-plastic, time-depending, viscoelastic, viscoplastic as well as non-isotropic and inhomogeneous response of material including composites on the state of displacements and strain in structures and their components and in structural systems can be investigated.

The principle of such "hybrid techniques" shall be demonstrated by some characteristic examples.

1) As an example of nonlinear-geometric problems plates-in-bending under large deflection are considered [5] "Heuristic" modelling of the birefringence effects in photoelasticity taking into account the rotation of the principal directions in the superimposed membrane and bending stress state yields the relations between the data to be measured, i.e. the retardation and the characteristic directions, and the difference of the principal stresses of both these stress states as well as the principal directions of the membrane stress state. The bending stress state only is analyzed by Ligtenberg-moiré-method (Fig. 3).

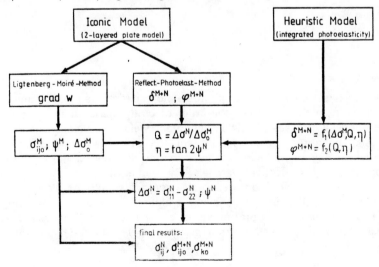

Fig. 3

The numerical evaluation of the experimental data can be performed only be using a PC.

2) An effective combination of mathematical and experimental methods will be demonstrated by the stress analysis of thick plates-in-bending [6]. Based on the theory of elasticity the differential equations are derived and solved by means of Bessel- and hyperbolic functions expanded in series of k terms. Depending on the load as well as on the boundary conditions the unknown coefficients must be determined. On the other hand analyzing the stress state merely experimentally by the "frozen-stress" technique of photoelasticity is quite time consuming and yields results of considerable uncertainty only. However, measuring the order of birefringence and the principal directions of the secondary principal stresses in an arbitrary number of discrete points $m > 2k$ in few slices along axes of symmetry and introducing these data into the mathematical solution the as yet unknown coefficients $\tilde{C}_k$ and $\tilde{\psi}_k$ can be determined easily by solving a system of linear equations. The results will be improved by considering the redundancy of determination because of $m > 2k$. The components of the stress tensor then are given as functions of the coordinates and independent of the measuring points m (Fig. 4).

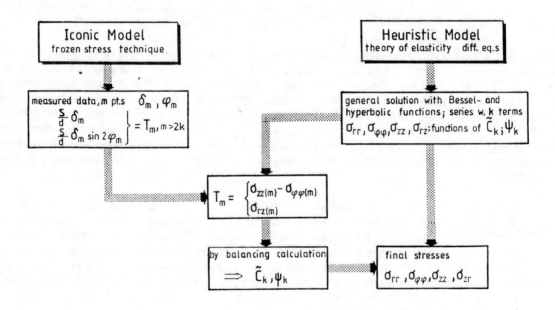

Fig. 4

3) To analyse the stress state by means of photoelastic experiments in two-dimensional objects consisting of different model materials the order of birefringence may be measured only to determine the principal stresses [7]. The experiment yields the values of the sum S^r of the principal stresses along the outer boundary of the object and the difference Δ of the principal stresses in any point M inside the different domains Ω_r taking into account the different response of the respective materials. By means of the boundary element method the trace S_M will be determined considering the contact conditions along the contact lines between the domains Ω_r (Fig. 5). After having evaluated the isochromatic fringe pattern by digital image processing the determination of the principal stresses is performed automatically as the whole process if formulated in proper computer programs.

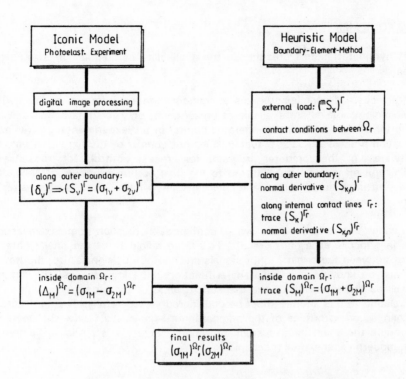

Fig. 5

4) According to the theory of elasticity and based on Green's formula the internal state of displacements in three dimensional objects can be descibed depending on the displacement u^Γ and their derivatives respectively on the object surface Γ [8]. The displacements u^Γ are determined by means of holographic interferometry (multiple hologram analysis) and introduced into an algorithm for discrete numerical evaluation, a reduction process, which can be performed meaningful computeroriented only (Fig. 6).

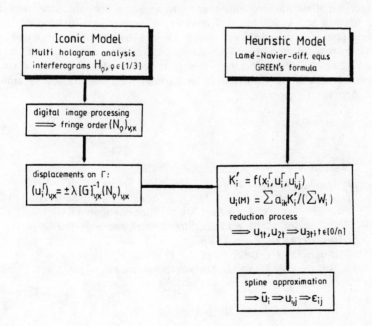

Fig. 6

TRENDS IN MEASURING EQUIPMENT

All these applications of hybrid techniques presuppose the availability of complex measuring and on-line processing systems.

Multiposition measuring devices and complex systems to transform optical information directly into digital data on a high technological level are available at present, not only for data acquisition and data processing, but also for automatic computer-operated control of the experimental as well as of the measuring and evaluation processes. Such a system does not consist of the hardware only but has to include the software e.g. the computer programs for process control, for transmission, converting and processing the measured input data up to the final output information. Nowadays the software is of increasing importance, the operational capability of the whole system strongly depends on the software.

It is of substantial importance not to look at the whole configuration of such complex measuring and evaluation systems in principle as a "black box". To assure reliability of the finally obtained informations the relations between the original input signals and the output signals, i.e. the flow of energy in the system must be known. The real transfer-functions, the impedances, the different signal-noise ratios as well as the extension of the measuring range of the single elements in the configuration and their relation to one another must be considered very carefully. This is necessary to avoid uncontrolled changes or distortions of the original input-signals. To follow the course of signal transmission through the measuring system thoroughly step by step is an extremely important supposition in modern experimental mechanics.

APPLICABILITY IN PRACTICE

Many a one may think that the recent and probably the future developments in measuring techniques and in experimental processes, the tendencies towards ever increasing complexity of the experimental systems, the such highly sophisticated configurations may not fit to practical applications. One may be afraid that these more or less "academic orchids" will withdraw themselves from the needs in practice. This possibility really exists, that is undeniable! However, it is a challenge to all who are engaged in the field of experimental mechanics: they must try to make scientific knowledge and new experimental procedure easy to manage for practical application, otherwise this knowledge is useless and superfluous. Therefore, scientists and researchers have to cooperate closely with practitioners in the different fields, in which methods of experimental mechanics contribute in solving practical problems. This statement includes the request to intensify the activities in education and training. Considering the national as well as the international situation one cannot but drawing the conclusion that education in experimental mechanics is still quite "under-exposed" despite the increasing importance!

REFERENCES

[1]	Laermann, K.H.:	Messen + Prüfen, Automatik April 1983
[2]	Laermann, K.H.:	Akad. d. Wissenschaften d. DDR, FMC-Series No. 37, 1988
[3]	Laermann, K.H.:	Proc. VIth Int. Conf. Exp. Mech., Vol II, SEM, Portland/Oreg. 1988
[4]	Laermann, K.H.:	Proc. 9th Int. Conf. on Exp. Mech., Copenhagen 1990
[5]	Laermann, K.H.:	Proc. 7th Int. Conf. on Exp. Stress Analysis, Haifa 1982
[6]	Laermann, K.H.:	VDI-Berichte Nr. 679, 1988
[7]	Laermann, K.H.:	VDI-Berichte Nr. 882, 1991
[8]	Laermann, K.H.:	J. Struct. Eng., Vol. 16, No. 4 (1990), India

Computer-Controlled Elastic-Plastic Fatigue Crack Growth Testing Using Multi-Task Programming

Shinsuke SAKAI, Takeshi ASAKAWA and Hiroyuki OKAMURA
Dept. Mechano-Informatics, the University of Tokyo,
7-3-1 Hongo, Bunkyo-ku, Tokyo 113, Japan

Abstract

This paper describes a method for computer-controlled elastic-plastic fatigue crack growth testing using multi-task programming technique. The developed system has been utilized to measure the elastic-plastic crack growth rates in JIS SM41B steel under constant ΔJ control on compact tension specimens. The results show that there is an excellent linear correlation between the number of cycles and the crack length and this confirms the efectiveness of ΔJ in elastic-plastic crack growth. The crack closure behavior was also analysed and it was shown that the crack closure loads were always compressive and increased with crack length.

1 INTRODUCTION

It has been widely acknowledged that the propagation rate of a elastic-plastic fatigue crack is expressible as the power function of the cyclic J, since Dowling and Begley [2] first applied the J-integral method to fatigue crack propagation under elastic-plastic conditions. They found that there is a correlation with J-integral values estimated from load versus deflection hysteresis loops. This Paris law type correlation between propagation rate and the cyclic J has been confirmed for many materials:ASTM A516 steel[4], AISI 316 steel[3], 304 stainless steel and HY100[5], JIS SM41B[6] and A533B steel[2]. To clarify the fact that the fatigue crack growth rates are unique function of the effective J-integral range (ΔJ), the constant ΔJ tests would be a most powerful way. Joyce and Sutton[1] developed an automated computer-controlled testing system to perform low-cycle fatigue crack growth tests including constant ΔJ tests. This system had real-time control of the ΔJ and real time calculations of closure load and crack length. They used a Z80 microprocessor in addition to a minicomputer controller to perform the J-control tests because of the limited processor speed. The additional microprocessor was utilized to measure the specimen compliance over a specified load range and to transfer the value to the main controller when requested. Two computer system, however, would make the test sytem rather complicated. Jablonski[5] also developed a direct J-controll test sytem. The software control program had four possible control modes including constant ΔJ test.He showed the validity of ΔJ by performing fatigue crack growth tests under conditions of increasing, decreasing, and constant ΔJ range. The crack closrue loads under these test conditions were also measured.

The objective of this paper is to show the effectiveness of multi-task system in J-controlled fatigue crack growth tests. It is shown that the complicated process of controlling ΔJ can be made far easier if the software system is devided into several tasks and the task priorities are appropriately allocated to them. This automated system has been utilized to measure the elastic-plastic crack growth rates in JIS SM41B steel under constant ΔJ control on compact tension specimens. The results show that there is an excellent linear correlation between the number of cycles and the crack length and this confirms the effectiveness of ΔJ in elastic-plastic crack growth. The crack closure behavior was also analysed and it was shown that the crack closure loads were always compressive and increased with crack length.

2 EXPERIMENTAL PROCEDURE

2.1 Materials and Specimen Geometry

The material used in this investigation was JIS SM41B. Plate supplied in 25 mm thickness was used for all tests. The chemical compositions and mechanical properties of the plate are presented in Tables 1 and 2, respectively. The specimens used in these tests were compact specimens of 24 mm thickness as shown in Fig. 1. Side grooves were provided for 4 specimens machined in the L-T orientation to ensure straight crack front shape. The specimen was notched to allow the measurement of crack opening displacement(COD) on the load line. Specimens were machined from two orientations, T-L and L-T, as outlined in Table 3 along with test conditions.

2.2 J-Integral Analysis and Calculations

The J-integral for a compact specimen can be calculated using the analysis of Merkle and Corten[7] from the expression

$$J = \frac{\beta A}{Bb}$$ (1)

$$\beta = 2[(1 + \alpha)/(1 + \alpha)]^2 \tag{2}$$

$$\alpha = \sqrt{\left(\frac{2a}{b}\right)^2 + 2\left(\frac{a}{b}\right) + 2} \tag{3}$$

$$b = W - a \tag{4}$$

where

a = crack length,

W = speciment width,

A = area under load-displacement curve, and

b = uncracked ligament.

The β is obtained from a modified form of the Merkle-Corten analysis by Clarke and Landes[8]. A is the area under the load-displacement curve that is above the crack closure load as represented by the hatched area in Fig. 2.

An accurate determination of the crack closure load is greatly important in the calculation of ΔJ. Therefore, the highest priority in the multi tasks is given to this procedure so that the accurate ΔJ-controlled test can be achieved as shown in the subsequent section. The crack closure load is determined by locating the point on the loading slide of the cycle at which the slope of the load-displacement curve falls to the value of the slope found over the elastic unloading slope of the previous cycle, labelled C in Fig. 2. Dowling and Begley[2] found that the relation between the rate of growth of cracks and ΔJ can be represented by the Paris law type form as

$$\frac{da}{dN} = C\Delta J^n \tag{5}$$

where

N=cycles, and

C and n=material dependent constants.

In this paper, constant ΔJ tests are performed and the linear correlations between a and N are expected.

2.3 System Hardware

The fatigue test sytem consists of the following hardware components as shown in Fig. 3:

• serve-hydraulic fatigue test systems
• personal computer and associated peripherals.

The loading system is a servo-hydraulic test machine of 5t capacity. A NEC 9801UV personal computer was used for this investigation. This computer has 16bit CPU of V30 which is compatible to 8086 along with the numerical co-processor 8087. Computer interface consisted of 12-bit analog-to-digital converter(A/D), and a 12-bit analog-to-digital converter(D/A).

2.4 System Software

The automated elastic-plastic fatigue crack testing system was run under the real-time operating system PC-TRON which was designed by Micronix Corp. for multitasking and multiprogramming environments on micro-computers. All programs are written in C-language. There are eleven independent tasks included in the automated system along with main proram. The priorities of the execution are given to the individual task as tabulated in Table 4. The part of the software for the ΔJ-controlled fatigue test consists of four tasks(Task2-5) to which high priorities are given as shown in Table 4. By using multi-task programming, the important tasks for controlling ΔJ are kept from being interrupted by low priority tasks, such as the task for storing data(Task 6), monitoring errors in the system(Task 7), handling manual interuptions(Task 8), changing experimental conditions in real-time(Task 9), handling the termination of the experiment(Task 10) and drawing a-N diagram(Task 11). The Task 1 includes the following procedures:

• get sizes of the specimen,
• get the experimental parameters including ΔJ value and the termination condition,
• relate the analog signals of the testing machine to the physical units in the application program,
• activate all tasks.

Thus, the Task 1 must be run at the beginning of the experiment. Flow diagrams for Task 2- Task 5 are shown in Fig. 4(a)-(d), respectively. The independence of the individual task as shown in Fig. 4 makes the software system far easier to administrate. The procedure for calculating ΔJ is as follows:First, the elastic unloading compliance is determined by a least square analysis and is input into the following equation to calculate the crack length(Task 4).

$$a/w = c_0 + c_1 F + c_2 F^2 + c_3 F^3 + c_4 F^4 + c_5 F^5 \tag{6}$$

where F is a transfer function defined as follows:

$$F = \frac{1}{(BE'\lambda)^{1/2} + 1} \tag{7}$$

The Task 4 sends values of the evaluated compliance λ_u and crack length a to Task 5 through mail-box. The Task 5 is run by receiving thse data and decreases the load level until the load-line displacement reaches the displacement value under the unloading condition. The value of the minimum load P_{min} along with a λ_u are sent to Task 2 through mail-box, which run the Task 2. In Task 2, a slope is fit to the first N loading data points by a linear regression analysis and the loading compliance λ_l is evaluated at the midpoint of the fit(that is, at N/2). If this λ_l is equal to the unloading compliance λ_u, then the closure load P_{cl} is defined as the load at the midpoint of the fit. If λ_l is not equal to λ_u, the loading data is incremented by one data interval and the compliance is reevaluated for points 2 to N+1. This incremental complicance evaluation is continued until the condition, $\lambda_u = \lambda_l$, is satisfied. If this condition is not satisfied within the specific number of incremental evaluation, the closure load P_{cl} is defined as the minimum load P_{min}. After the Task 2 sends a, P_{cl}, and P_{min} to the Task 3, the Task 3 increases the load and calculates ΔJ by continuously integrating the load-displacement data during loading. The load direction is reversed when the evaluated value of ΔJ reaches the target one. Thus, ΔJ-control in real-time can be achieved. After sending the data necessary for storing on the disk to the Task 6, the Task 4 is run and the cycle is repeated until the termination condition is satisfied.

3 RESULTS AND DISCUSSION

3.1 Crack growth rate

It was expected that the relation between the crack length and the number of cycles would be linear and thus the crack growth rate would be constant because the value of ΔJ was kept constant. The crack length versus cycle count output data for a specimen controlled at three magnitudes of ΔJ value are shown in Fig. 5 and the linear relations are observed. Fig. 6 shows the relations between the cycle counts and the load values of P_{max}, P_{cl} and P_{min} for a specimen controlled at a constant ΔJ $= 2.0 \times 10^6 Pa \cdot m$(specimen no.LTSG3). The change in slope at N=2000 cycles which is shown by arrow in Fig. 5 is found to correspond to the cycle at which the load-displacement record developes a slope-definable crack closure which is shown by also the arrow in Fig. 6. This shows the difficulty in definning the closure load by the slope method described above during the early cycles of constant ΔJ tests. The region A in Fig. 6 corresponds to the cycles where the crack closure can not be detected. In the region B, the closure loads are not clear and are ambiguous. The region C corresponds to the cycles where the load-displacement record developes a slope-definable crack closure. The relation between da/dN and ΔJ obtained for the three magnitudes of ΔJ is shown in Fig. 7 along with the solid line crack grwoth rates evaluated from all experimental results. Though some of the open marks corresponding to early cycles of experiments deviate from the solid line, those data approach to the solid line as shown by solid marks by reevaluating the ΔJ using the virtual closure loads as shown by the dotted line in Fig. 6. The virtual closure loads are extrapolated to the region A from region B and C. This shows the necessity of the precise determination of the closure loads in the early cycles of experiments. The authors will leave this problem in the further study.

The relation between da/dN and ΔJ for all experimental results is shown in Fig. 8 along with the solid line which presents Eq.(5). The results are close to those obtaned by Tanaka[6] et.al. for the same material which is shown by the dotted line in the figure. The crack growth rate is calculated according to the seven-point polynominal method specified in the ASTM Test Method for Constant-Load-Amplitude Fatigue Crack Growth Rates Above 10^{-8}m/Cycle(E647-83). Good agreement is observed between the crack growth rates and Eq.(5) independent of the experimental conditions and this confirms the applicability of ΔJ evaluated using distinctly definable closure load.

3.2 Crack Closure Behavior

The crack closure loads were measured every cycle in real time. Fig. 9 shows plots of the closure load versus crack length. The closure loads are always compressive and increased with crack length. The closure behavior is a function of the magnitude of ΔJ. It becomes more compressive when ΔJ is increased. The relations between the effective fraction U of the applied load and the cycle count are investigated. Two definitions of the effective fraction, U_1, U_2, are used here:

$$U_1 = P_{cl}/P_{max} \tag{8}$$

$$U_2 = (P_{max} - P_{cl})/(P_{max} - P_{min}) \tag{9}$$

The relations between $U_1 - N$ and $U_2 - N$ are shown in Fig. 10 and Fig. 11, respectively. The U_1 decreases with increasing a/w over the first $0.65 \sim 0.75$ of growth, and then increases, whereas the U_2 decreases monotonically with increasing a/w as shwon in Fig. 11. This tendency is contrary to the results obtained under load-controlled test conditions as shown by Tanaka et. al.[6]. It seems that the U_2-a/w relation is independent of the magnitude of ΔJ. This implies the possible master curve for the U_2-a/w relation which is independent of the magnitude of ΔJ. Further study is required to confirm this.

4 Conclusions

The automated test system for computer-controlled low-cycle fatigue crack growth can be achived using multi-task programming. The results of constant ΔJ test show the degree of success achieved with this system. This automated system integrates ΔJ range in real time and controlls it. It was shown that the task priorities in multi-task system gave great efficiency in developing the automated elastic-plastic fatigue crack growth system. The test system described herein was used to produce results of the constant ΔJ test for the material of JIS SM41B. The crack growth rates remained constant for many constant ΔJ tests as expected. In these elastic-plastic crack growth rate experiments, the closure load was always compressive and was a function of both the magnitude of ΔJ and crack length. The closure loads increased with crack length.

References

[1] Joyce, J.A. and Sutton, G.E. *"An Automated Method of Computer-Controlled Low-Cycle Fatigue Crack Growth Testing Using the Elastic-Plastic Parameter Cyclic J,"* Automated Test Methods for Fracture and Fatigue Crack Growth, ASTM STP 877, 227-247 ,1985.

[2] Dowling, N.E. and Begley, J.A. *"Fatigue Crack Growth During Gross Plasticity and the J-Integral,"* Mechanics of Crack Growth, ASTM STP 590, 82-103, 1976.

[3] Lambert, Y., Saillard, P. and Bathias, C. *"Application of the J Concept to Fatigue Crack Growth in Large-Scale Yielding,"* Fracture Mechanics: Nineteenth Symposium, ASTM STP 969, 218-329, 1988.

[4] El Haddad, M.H. and Mukherjee, B. *"Elastic-Plastic Fracture Mechanics Analysis of Fatigue Crack Growth",* Elastic-Plastic Fracture:Second Symposium, Vol.II-Fracture Resistance Curves and Engineering Applications. ASTM STP 803, II-689-II-707, 1983.

[5] Jablonski, D.A., *"An Experimental Study of the Validity of a Delta J Criterion for Fatigue Crack Growth,"* Nonlinear Fracture Mechanics:Vol. I-Time-Dependent Fracture, ASTM STP 995, 361-387, 1989.

[6] Tanaka, T., Hoshide, T. and Nakata, M., *"Elastic-Plastic Crack Propagation Under High Cyclic Stress,"* Elastic-Plastic Fracture:Second Symposium, Vol.II, Fracture Curves and Engineering Applications, ASTM STP 803 II-708-II-722 1983.

[7] Merkle, J.G. and Corten, H.T., *"A J-Integral Analysis for the compact Specimen Considering Axial Force as Well as Bending Effects,"* Journal of Pressure Vessel Technology, Trans. ASME, 286-292, Nov. 1974.

[8] Clarke, G.A. and Landes, J.D., *"Evaluation of J for the Compact Specimen,"* Journal of Testing and Evaluation, Vol. 7, No.5, 264-269, Sept. 1979.

Table. 1 Chemical composition of SM41B

Material	C	Si	Mn	P	S
SM41B	0.16	0.33	1.2	0.014	0.002

Material	Yield Point (MPa)	Tensile Strength (MPa)	Elongation (%)
SM41B	352.8	509.6	29

Table. 3 ΔJ control tests summary

Specimens	Specimen Orientiation	Side groove,%	ΔJ (x10^4 Pa·m)	Time sec/cycle
LTSG2	L-T	16.7	3	17 - 36
LTSG1	L-T	16.7	5	22 - 34
LTSG3	L-T	16.7	2	15 - 40
LT2	L-T	0	3	28 - 59
LT3	L-T	0	2	19 - 28
LT1	L-T	0	5	15 - 52
TLSG2	T-L	16.7	2	20 - 35
TLSG1	T-L	16.7	5	25 - 50
TL2	T-L	0	3	19 - 36
TL1	T-L	0	5	22 - 54
TL3	T-L	0	2	18 - 32
TLSSY1	T-L	0	(6×10^3)	27 - 34
TLSSY2	T-L	0	($\Delta P = 4900$ N)	

Table. 4 Task functions and priorties

		Function of Tasks	Priority
	Task 1	Initialize system and get test parameters	140
	Task 2	Decision of crack closure point	50
	Task 3	Calculate ΔJ and ajiust ΔJ levels	60
	Task 4	Calculate crack length	70
	Task 5	Unloading	80
	Task 6	Store data in disk	100
	Task 7	Keep watch for error and detect end of test condition	110
	Task 8	Manage man-machine interface	120
	Task 9	Change test conditions	125
	Task 10	Stop test and terminate real	240
	Task 11	Draw crack length vs. cycle graph	150
		MS-DOS Shell	127

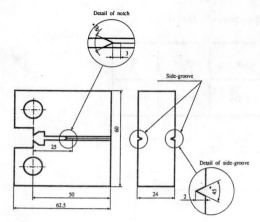

Fig.1 Specimen geometry

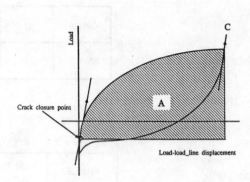

Fig.2 Schematic showing area of load-displacement curve used to calculate the applied ΔJ and definition of the crack closure load

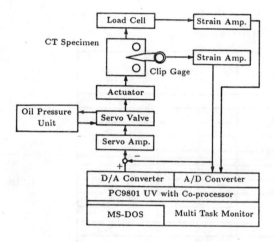

Fig.3 Schematic of automated elastic-plastic fatigue crack growth rate test system

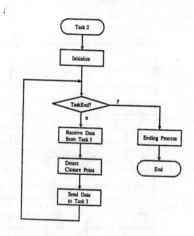

(a) Task2

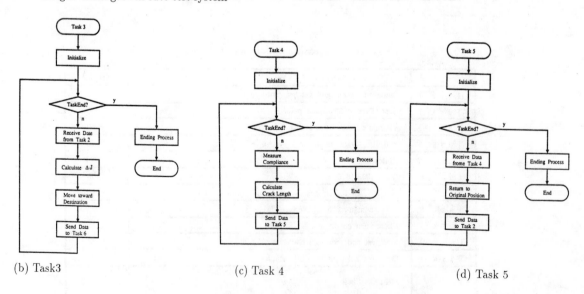

(b) Task3　　　　　　(c) Task 4　　　　　　(d) Task 5

Fig. 4 Flow charts of Task2-Task5

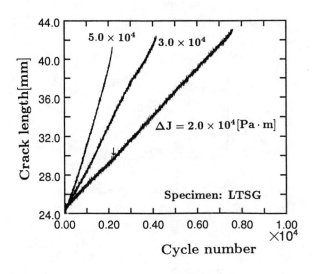

Fig.5 Record of crack length versus cycles

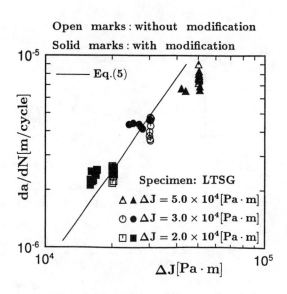

Fig.7 Crack grwoth rate data at three constant magnitudes of ΔJ

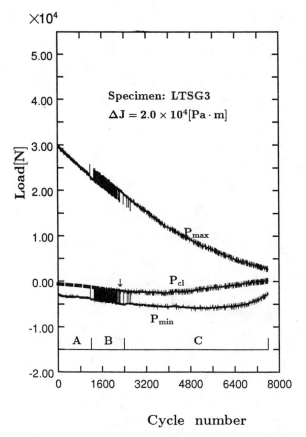

Fig.6 Record of load versus cycles at $\Delta J = 2.0 \times 10^4 Pa \cdot m$

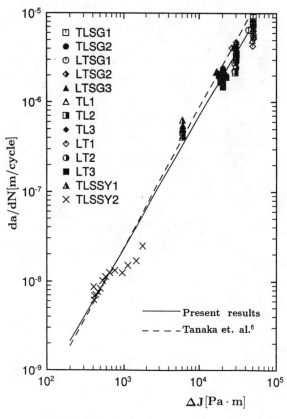

Fig.8 Relation between crack grwoth rate and ΔJ

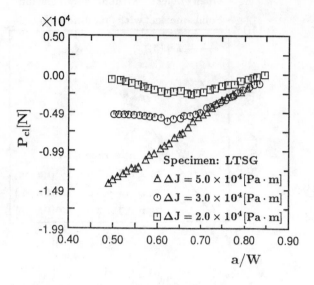

Fig.9 Crack closure load versus crack length

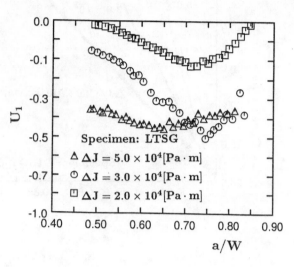

Fig.10 Effective fraction U_1 versus crack length

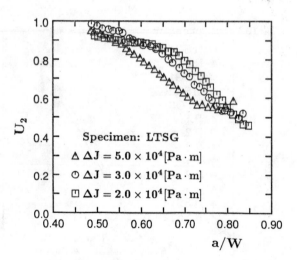

Fig.11 Effective fraction U_2 versus crack length

HYBRID ANALYSIS OF DEFORMATION USING INTERFEROMETRIC MEASUREMENTS

S-Y. Lin, M.Y. Tsai, D. Peters, R. Czarnek and J. Morton

NSF Center for High Performance Polymeric Adhesives and Composites

Virginia Polytechnic Institute and State University

ABSTRACT

Two hybrid methods of deformation analysis combining moiré interferometry and finite element techniques are introduced. The hybrid methods are applied to determine the strain fields in the test section of a composite cruciform specimen in order to evaluate the uniformity of the shear strain field. Both methods show that there are significant shear strain gradients in the specimen test section. One of the hybrid methods - the full-field analysis using the random-node mesh generator - detects the presence of material property nonuniformity which is assumed uniform in the boundary-node method.

INTRODUCTION

Moiré interferometry [1, 2] provides abundant whole-field displacement data in the form of pairs of fringe patterns for the two components of in-plane surface deformation. Usually the displacement data must be processed or reduced to provide strain and/or stress distributions for engineering application. Unless the region of interest is very limited and the strain gradients are very small the determination of the strain fields from the moiré fringe patterns can become extremely tedious and inaccurate. To overcome the limitations of manual data reduction a number of methods have been developed [3,4,5]. In the present study two hybrid methods of deformation analysis will be illustrated through the application of moiré interferometry in the determination of the strain distributions in a composite cruciform specimen [6].

MOIRÉ INTERFEROMETRY

Moiré interferometry is an optical method which provides whole-field information of in-plane surface displacements [1,2]. It is based on two-beam interference. To begin, a high-frequency diffraction grating is replicated on the specimen surface and deforms together with it. The specimen grating is illuminated by two mutually coherent collimated beams of laser light, as illustrated in Figure 1. Their +1 and -1 diffraction orders carry information about the deformation of the specimen grating. The diffracted beams interfere, producing an interference fringe pattern. This fringe pattern is a contour map of in-plane displacements in the direction perpendicular to the grating lines. Consequently, in the x-y plane, the grating lines parallel to the x-axis yield a displacement pattern in the y-direction, V, and similarly those parallel to the y-axis produce an x-displacement component, U. In practice a two-directional moiré interferometer is used, providing two orthogonal components of in-plane displacements simultaneously. Figure 2 shows a diagram of the interferometer used in this work [7].

The governing equations for U and V are

$$U = \frac{\lambda}{2 \sin \theta} N_x \qquad \text{and} \qquad V = \frac{\lambda}{2 \sin \theta} N_y \qquad (1)$$

where N_x and N_y are the fringe orders of the U and V fringe patterns, respectively, λ is the wavelength of the used light, and 2θ is the angle of intersection of the two illuminating beams. A fringe order is defined as a number assigned to a fringe and is equal to the measured parameter divided by a contour interval.

The sensitivity of the measurements is $l/(2 \sin\theta)$ and, with the standard configuration, is equal to 0.417 μm per fringe order.

Problems of data reduction

Typically high-sensitivity moiré interferometry, because of its full-field nature, provides a tremendous amount of data. However, the extraction of this data can be very tedious and time consuming. Because of that very often only a small fraction of the information contained in the fringe patterns is utilized.

As was mentioned earlier, a moiré fringe pattern is a contour map of displacements. Most often the information needed is strain; thus the derivatives of the displacement field must be taken. Many different methods have been employed in this process. In the most primitive approach, an increment of displacement is measured over an increment of a given coordinate and their ratio is used as average strain, in a more elaborate approach a surface is fitted into the experimental data and its derivatives are calculated. In both cases the more data points that are used the more severe the errors that are encountered. This is because the resolution of moiré interferometry stays the same, regardless of the gauge length (the strain error equals the displacement resolution divided by the gauge length).

Traditional data-interpretation techniques can be practical only in a qualitative analysis of measurements performed on relatively large specimens subjected to significantly high strain levels. New structural materials and measurements of deformation on small fields of view require new, more sophisticated methods of analysis.

HYBRID METHODS

Hybrid methods of analysis of deformation of solid bodies combine full-field experimental techniques with numerical methods of processing the experimental data. In principle, many different numerical and experimental techniques could be used in hybrid methods. In practice the finite element method appears to be the most convenient for the task. In the present work two variations of the hybrid technique of combining moiré interferometry data with the finite element method were investigated and their respective advantages and limitations evaluated.

Boundary-node method

The boundary-node method is a two-dimensional strain (or stress) data reduction of a moiré fringe pattern by imposing the assumption of material homogeneity in the analyzed region [4,5]. In the application of the boundary-node method to the cruciform specimen (see below) a rectangular mesh consisting of 528 constant-strain four-node rectangular elements was used in the specimen test section (region of interest). The displacement components (U,V) at each node around the boundary of the region of interest were determined by linear interpolation of the moiré data which generally did not coincide with the nodes of the finite element mesh. The experimentally determined displacement data were then used as the input data in the finite element calculation which also required the appropriate orthotropic material properties. The finite element implementation provided the strain and stress fields in the specimen test section.

The boundary-node method provides an effective and efficient data reduction process for the plane problem. A knowledge of the material constitutive laws is required although generally the accuracy of the calculated strains is not very sensitive to the values of the material property data. Another limitation of the boundary-node method is the two-dimensional formulation. This limitation can be used to advantage by applying the method as a check for the presence of three-dimensional effects in the experimental moiré data [4,5].

Full-field analysis using a random-node mesh generator

In this approach a finite element model of an elastic plate is used to interpolate the function describing the distribution of displacements on the surface of the specimen [8]. The data are collected from the whole field of interest with a digitizing tablet. Only high-quality data are collected along the center lines of the fringes, following the high-resolution data reduction technique [3]. In this case, however, the density of the collected data points varies with the importance of the analyzed region. For example, in zones of higher gradients the density of the data points is high and in the far field where strains are close to uniform the density is low. This approach allows much quicker data collection and more efficient processing than was the case in the earlier work where a grid of data points had to correspond to a rectangular matrix of coordinates. As before, however, the density of the fringes can be increased, if necessary, by a low-frequency carrier pattern.

When using this hybrid method, three sets of data points are collected. The first one defines the boundary of the region of interest, the second one represents the displacements in the direction of the x-axis and the last one corresponds to the displacements in the y-direction. The collected data are fed into the specially developed mesh generator that builds an FEM mesh using the randomly collected data points as nodes of the mesh and connecting them into triangular elements [9]. This mesh is then modified by the addition of spring elements, which are used to force the model to deform. The displacements measured with interferometry are used as boundary conditions at the ends of these springs opposite to the nodes of the original mesh.

Two variations of the method have been considered. In the first one the mesh represents an elastic plate loaded with springs perpendicular to its surface [8]. The deflection of the plate due to the forces applied by the springs corresponds to the component of displacement under consideration. In this approach each displacement component is analyzed separately and the slopes corresponding to the derivatives of the displacement field are calculated. These slopes represent either normal strains or cross-derivatives used to calculate the shear strains.

In the second variation the model deforms in its plane. This model must be built out of special elements that satisfy not only the displacement continuity condition but also the continuity of all four derivatives. In this case both components of in-plane displacement field can and should be analyzed together.

COMPOSITE CRUCIFORM SPECIMEN

The cruciform specimen was designed with a view to determining the shear strength of composite materials. The general concept is illustrated in Fig. 3(a) in which a cross-ply composite cruciform specimen is subjected to equal tensile and compressive loads. The fiber directions are at $+45°$ to the load axes so that a state of pure shear is developed in the material (1-2) directions, Fig. 3(a). Under ideal conditions the shear strain field produced in the specimen should be uniform as well as pure throughout the specimen test section. Moiré interferometry provides a unique method of assessing the extent to which the ideal conditions are achieved in practice.

The production of the equal tensile and compressive loads in the cruciform specimen is achieved using the fixture shown in Fig. 3(b). The straps (steel bars of rectangular cross-section) of the fixture must be stiff compared to the extensional stiffness of the composite specimen for the required loading condition to be achieved. These straps limited the optical access to the specimen test section which was instrumented with a 1200 lines/mm cross-line grating on one side and a three-gage strain gage rosette on the other.

The specimen was loaded in a convenient screw-driven test machine and interrogated in a two directional, achromatic inteferometer [7]. At predetermined loads the fringe patterns viewed in the interferometry were recorded photographically.

RESULTS

A typical pair of fringe patterns is shown in Fig. 4. It is clear from the fringe patterns in Fig. 4 that the deformations produced in the specimen test section are not uniform. It is also apparent that the fringes are not perfectly smooth. The corresponding strain fields obtained using the boundary-node method are presented in Fig. 5(a-c). The normal strain distributions ε_x and ε_y are similar in form but not exactly equal and opposite, indicating that the desired loading mode of biaxial tension and compression loads of P/2 and -P/2 are not achieved in the experiment. The difference in the magnitude of the normal strains from the average, estimated using the boundary-node method, is about 5%. Except at the boundaries of the region in which the data are processed the strain countours are smooth. The strain data obtained from the full-field analysis using the random-node mesh generator are shown in Fig. 6. The general form of the strain distributions and the values of the strains at equivalent positions are similar for both methods of data reduction. However, the distributions obtained using the full-field analysis using the random-node mesh generator appear to be less smooth than the distributions from the boundary-node method. An approximate method of producing normal strain distributions from the moiré fringe patters is the differentiation technique based on mechanical shifting of two identical displacement patterns [10]. When this method is applied to the fringe patterns in Fig. 4, the patterns shown in Fig. 7 are obtained. These mechanically produced strain distributions are also similar in from to those from the hybrid methods of data reduction. Close inspection of the strain contours shows that the mechanically produced strain contours and those from the full-field analysis using the random-node mesh generator share some of the same local strain non-uniformity.

A comparison of the strain fields obtained by the various methods of data reduction is presented in Fig. 8 in which the normal strain ε_x from manual differentiation is also shown. It is apparent that the two hybrid techniques provide very similar distributions along the horizontal centerline of the specimen test section (x-axis), except, as observed also above, at the edge of the data reduction region. The manually reduced strain distribution is much less smooth and, in places, has strain values significantly different from the other distributions.

DISCUSSION

The achromatic interferometer used in the experiment produced high quality, high contrast moire fringes over the test section of the cruciform specimen, despite the limited access caused by the loading fixture. The fringe patterns, Fig. 4, for the horizontal (U) and vertical (V) displacement fields were similar in form but rotated through 90° relative to each other, as would be expected from the specimen and the desired loading condition. The fringe patterns contain clear evidence that the strains in the specimen are not uniform in a global sense but that the magnitudes of the normal strains at the center of the specimen test section are significantly larger than at the edges of the data zone.

Both hybrid data reduction techniques provided very similar strain distributions. However, the full-field analysis using the random-node mesh generator appeared to resolve some global non uniform deformation which does not appear in the data obtained from the boundary-node method. The nonuniformity is though to be related to the fiber distribution in the cross-ply composite specimen, as has been observed previously. This is equivalent to non uniform material properties. The boundary-node method is based on the assumption of uniform material properties within the data reduction region so that any effects due to inhomogeneity cannot be resolved.

It has been observed that the strain distributions obtained with the two hybrid techniques are extremely close, Fig. 8, except near the boundary of the data reduction region. The difference in the boundary region is caused by a sensitivity of the boundary-node method to errors in the interpolation of the input displacement data in order to obtain the displacement components at the boundary nodes of the regular mesh used in this approach.

For homogeneous materials both hybrid methods of data reduction should give identical strain fields from the same fringe patterns. The difference in the techniques can be used to detect the presence of nonuniformity of the material such as in the present case of the cross-ply composite, or in the case of woven fabric composites, to detect the presence of three-dimensional effects in the deformation field [11].

CONCLUSIONS

The achromatic interferometry provided direct measurement of the surface deformation of the test section of the composite cruciform specimen. Two methods of hybrid moiré data reduction gave similar results which illustrated that the strain fields produced were not uniform as had been desired in the specimen design. The full-field analysis using the random-node mesh generator indicated the presence of some non uniform material properties in the specimen test section.

ACKNOWLEDGMENTS

The authors gratefully acknowledge the support of the NSF Science & Technology Center for High Performance Polymeric Adhesives and Composites at VPI&SU and NASA Langley Research Center.

REFERENCES

[1]   J. Guild, "The Interference Systems of Crossed Diffraction Gratings; Theory of Moiré Fringes," Oxford at the Clardendon Press, (1956).

[2]   J. Guild, "Diffraction gratings as measuring scales," Oxford University Press, New York, (1960).

[3]   Robert Czarnek, Joosik Lee and Tom Rantis, "Moiré interferometry with enhanced resolution," *Experimental Techniques*, Vol. 14, No. 4, July/August 1990.

[4]   Tsai, M. Y., " Application of Localized Hybrid Methods of Stress Analysis to Some Problems in the Mechanics of Composites," *Ph.D. Dissertation,* Virginia Polytechnic Institute and State University, Blacksburg, (Nov. 1990).

[5]   Tsai, M. Y. and Morton, J., "New Developments in the Localized Hybrid Method of Stress Analysis," *Experimental Mechanics.* 31(4), pp. 298-305, (1991)

[6]   Farley, G. L., Baker, D. J., "In-plane Shear Test of Thin Panels", *Experimental Mechanics*, V. 23, no. 1, 1983, pp. 81-88

[7]   Czarnek, R., "High-sensitivity Moire Interferometry with Compact Achromatic Interferometer", *Optics and Lasers in Engineering*, pp. 99-115, 13, 1990.

[8]   Lin, S. Y., Lee, J, Czarnek, R., "Intergration and Processing of Moire Interferometry Data", Proceedings of 1991 SEM Spring Conference on Experimental Mechanics, pp. 513-518, Milwaukee, Wisconsin, July 1991.

[9]   Lee, J., "High Resolution Interferometric Measurements of Residual Strains in Composites", Ph.D. Dissertation, Engineering Science & Mechanics Department, Virginia Polytechnic Institute & State University, December 1990.

[10]   "An experimental method for recording curvature contours in flexed elastic plates," J.P. Duncan and P.G. Sabin, *Experimental Mechanics*, Vol. 5, No. 1. pp. 22-28, January 1965.

[11]   H. Ho, M.Y. Tsai, J. Morton and G.L. Farley, "In-Plane Iosipescu Shear Properties of Graphite Woven Fabric Composites," to be submitted to *Experimental Mechanics*..

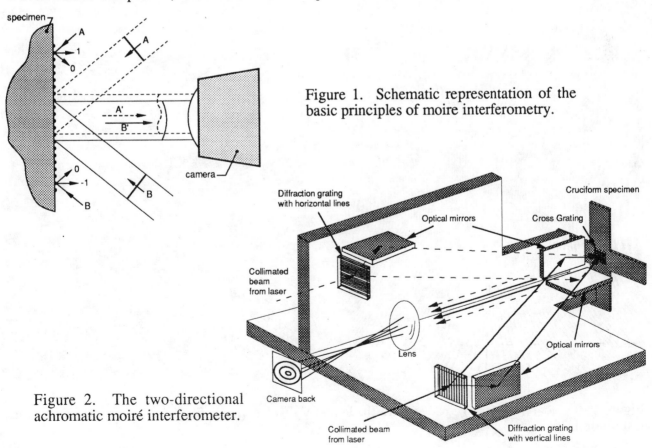

Figure 1.   Schematic representation of the basic principles of moire interferometry.

Figure 2.   The two-directional achromatic moiré interferometer.

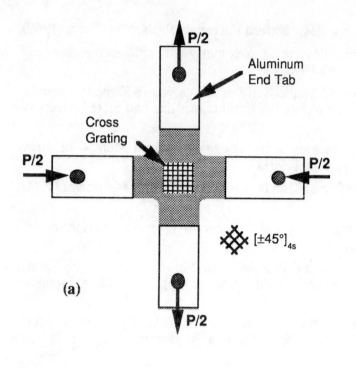

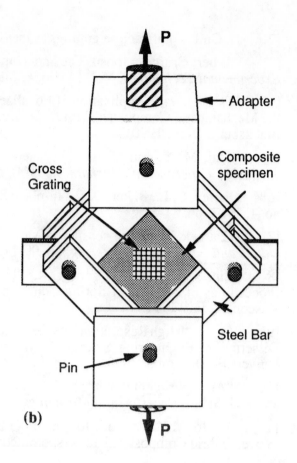

Figure 3.
(a)The cruciform composite shear test specimen.
(b)The cruciform test specimen and loading fixture.

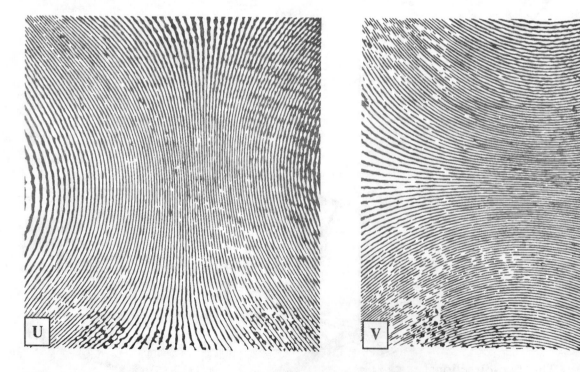

Figure 4. Typical moiré fringe patterns for the U and V displacements fields in the cruciform specimen test section.

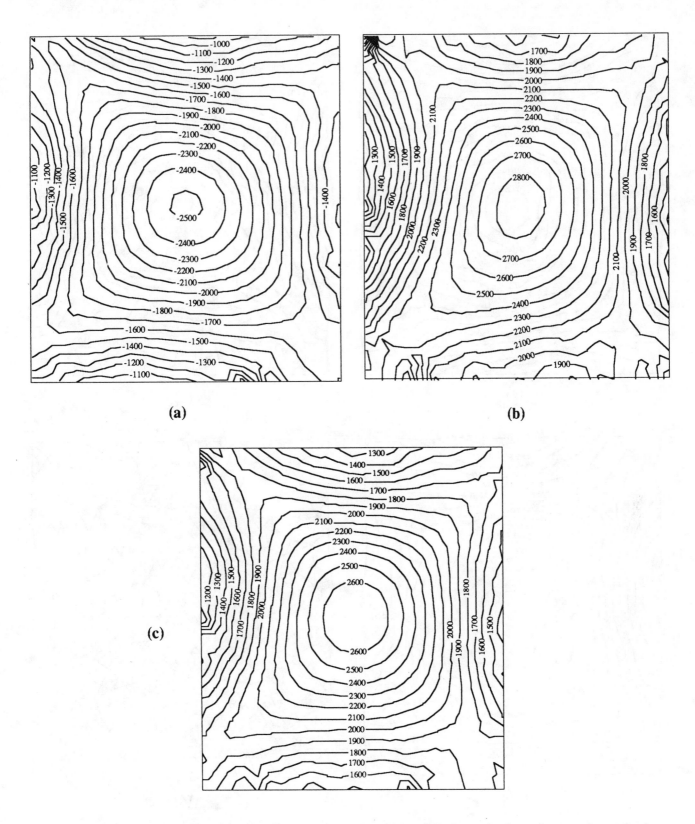

Figure 5. Contour maps of (a) ε_x, (b) ε_y and (c) shear $(\varepsilon_y-\varepsilon_x)/2$ from the boundary-node method.

Figure 6. Contour maps of (a) ε_x, (b) ε_y and (c) shear $(\varepsilon_y-\varepsilon_x)/2$ from the full-field analysis using the random-node mesh generator. Figure (d) illustrates the generated mesh.

118

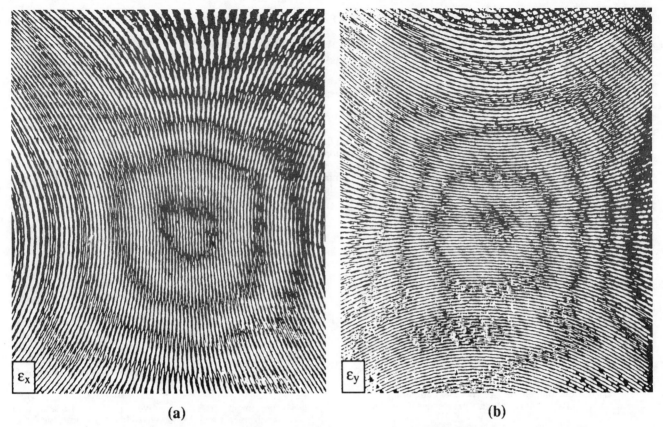

(a) **(b)**

Figure 7. Contour maps of (a) ε_x, and (b) ε_y produced by mechanical differentiation.

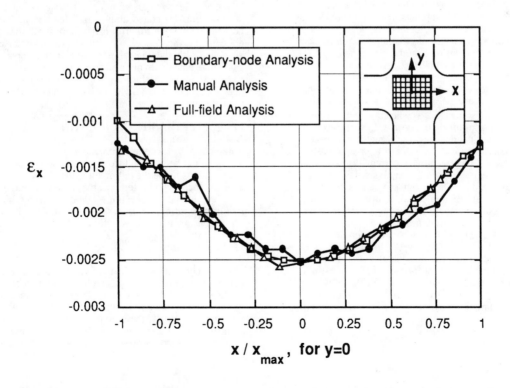

Figure 8. Comparison of the distribution of strain ε_x along the horizontal centerline obtained using the hybrid and manual data reduction techniques.

A CONCEPT OF HYBRID THEORETICAL AND EXPERIMENTAL STRESS ANALYSIS USING PHOTOELASTIC IMAGE DATA

Shizuo MAWATARI, Masahisa TAKASHI and Takeshi KUNIO

Abstract

The aim of this paper is placed on development of a new hybrid method for stress and displacement analysis that can find efficiently out accurate solutions of the governing equations without troubles in the current numerical stress analysis, involving a self-compatible method for error estimation, by use of photoelastic image data. The five basic concepts, i.e., the distribution element, the canomical boundary, the compatible, the three part and the morphological error estimation methods, are derived from comparison and examination of algorithms in computational mechanics.

I. INTRODUCTION

During the past decade, considerable attention has been directed toward developing numerical methods for stress analysis, e.g., the finite element , the boundary element and the difference methods. The recent growth of these methods have prevailed on the scientific field of computational mechanics, and produced excellent results in analysis of actual phenomena and in rational design, etc. The computational mechanics includes three process, such as the pre-, main- and post-processing, thus it requires unavoidably a lot of time. For the purpose of saving time, efficient methods for stress analysis, such as parallel processing with a super computer, fuzzy processing, application of neutral network have been suggested. Development of super parallel computing in next generation will affect the computational mechanics in future.

In spite of these brilliant successes of computer mechanics, the numerical stress analysis have at least two important problems to be solved. The first problem is the procedure for discretization. History of development in computational mechanics indicates that the current techniques and algorithms depend excessively on capacity of computer. Even in case that numerical stress analysis on a model is available, the accumulation of theoretical or numerical error in various steps of analysis such as discretization and computation within finite digits deteriorates the accuracy of numerical solutions, particularly, in the case of a large scale computation. Furthermore, there are some cases[1] where a direct computational modeling is prohibitively expensive. In such case, the combination of numerical and theoretical methods is necessary for an efficient stress analysis. One of the major reasons for these problems will be placed in the current discretization technique by which the domain for analysis devided into small geometrical regions. The second problem is the procedures in error analysis of numerical solution. Notwithstanding the necessity of severe estimation of errors in numerical analysis, the appropriateness and accuracy of the method are usually evaluated in comparison with the corresponding theoretical solution. This type of error analysis will obviously be inadequate for problems that the exact solutions are not known. Although several formulae for error estimation are proposed, it seems still impossible to know the bound of absolute or relative error. In other words, the usual method for error estimation can only give a rough measure of accuracy.

A typical way for the accuracy of estimation of computed values is to compare numerical solutions with the corresponding experimental results. Experimental stress analysis is, to be sure, powerful in cases that theoretical solution is not obtainable and that propriety of theoretical or numerical solutions obtained has to be examined. This method requires often , however, not only expensive laboratory equipments but also high level skill and elaboration. Also it is not always simple to put into practice and to find efficient and accurate solutions suitable for the purpose. In this point of view, several recent papers[2] emphasizes the necessity of development of hybrid experimental and theoretical stress analysis. Thus, the analysis of errors in large scale numerical analysis is getting more and more difficult.

The present authors' effort involves a simultaneous settlement of two problems mentioned above. In other words, the major aims of this paper is placed on the development of a new hybrid method for stress analysis that will be able to find efficiently out accurate solutions of the governing equation without troubles stated above, and that can include a self-compatible method for error estimation synthesizing knowledge in the theoretical,experimental and numerical stress analysis. Although the basic concepts in this paper are applicable to problems involving various types of partial differential equation, discussions will be concentrated only on stress analysis problems in a framework of linear elasticity in two or three dimension.

II. FIVE BASIC CONCEPTS

Some clues for accomplishment of the purpose mentioned above would be obtained from comparison and examination of algorithms in the prevailing methods of computational mechanics, such as the difference, the finite element, the boundary element and the spectral methods. Taking the situation into consideration, let us discuss the following five concepts for establishment of a new hybrid method for stress analysis.

II-1. Distribution Element Method

The first concepts is on the procedure of discretization. The kernel of discretization is placed in both construction of a basis function and determination of unknown parameters in an approximation function for the object solution. In the current numerical methods, the domain of variable is divided into geometrically small partitions. Then, the unknown piecewise functions on each partition are presented and composed into

Shizuo Mawatari is Associate Professor of Industry and System Engineering and Masahisa Takashi is professor of Mechanical Engineering, Aoyama Gakuin University, 6-16-1, Chitosedai, Setagaya-ku, Tokyo, Japan, Takeshi Kunio is professor of Mechanical Engineering, Kanto Gakuin University, 4834 Mutuura-cho, Kanazawa-ku, Yokohama, Japan

useful relationships between unknown parameters on the basis of governing equations. And the parameters are determined with the collocation, the weighted residuals or the projective approximation method etc.. However, partition carried out with these methods is not always suitable, also judgment whether it is adequate or not to the object has to rely on intuition. Even if the partition could be adequate, each partition has to be sufficiently fine to meet the accuracy required. For this reason, a great deal of time is necessarily consumed for computation. Taking propagation and proliferation of various errors into account, in general, the accuracy of computed results becomes increasingly worse with increase of the scale of computation. On the other hand, in the spectral method an approximation of unknown object function is performed with a procedure as follows. The object function is described in the form of an infinite series of proper function which satisfies the boundary conditions. Truncating the expanded series into a finite number of terms, algebraic equations constructed on the basis of governing equation is solved with respect to the parameters. This method requires selection of proper functions satisfying boundary conditions, but it is not always easy to construct such a function suitable to the object. In addition , several difficulties exist in finding a truncation rule for finite sum with satisfactory accuracy regardless to the geometry of domain contour. After all, so far discretization is concerned, the partition of analytic domain and simple truncation of expanded series of the proper function turns out full of issues.

In order to solve this kind of problems, as discussed later, it will be much appropriate to use a polyharmonic distribution as a coordinate function. This distribution possesses a good and favorable properties for stress analysis. We represent an object approximation function by a linear combination of these distributions satisfying the other necessary conditions. We will call this type of discretization the distribution element method, hereafter.

II-2 Canonical Boundary Method

The second concept is on the procedure for adaptability to the government equations. There are many methods for construction of the approximation function. They are grouped into three classes according to the stages where the government equations are satisfied. The interior method is the one that satisfies exactly the boundary condition, but approximately the differential equation inside of the analytic domain. The boundary method is the one that satisfy exactly the differential equations, but only approximately the boundary condition. The mixed method is the one that satisfy only approximately both conditions. The examples of the interior, boundary and mixed methods are the spectral, the boundary element and the finite element methods respectively.

Let us consider first conformation to differential equation. In addition to difficulties in adequate division of analytic domain, the finite element method, however, commits to the so called variational crime, and does not always satisfy the equilibrium and the compatibility equations. In the boundary element method, an approximation function is constructed using shape function on the boundary, and unknown coefficients is determined by solving linear algebraic equations. Since some elements in the coefficient matrix of the linear equations often encounters singular integral, accuracy is not always satisfactory. This method, however, has an excellent property that the dimension of problem is reduced by one. Secondly, we will discuss adaptability to boundary conditions. In the case that the boundary of domain is not included in a segment parallel to the coordinate axis, the difference method can not always satisfy the boundary conditions on arbitrary geometries, even if the Thompson's method[3] for

numerical grid generation is applicable. Since the finite element and the boundary element methods can put always vertices of some elements on boundary, the degree of conformity to boundary condition is much higher than that of the difference method. This is the most important reason why the finite element method has rapidly developed, covering up the weak point of the difference method. Although the boundary element and the spectral methods have been contrived so as to satisfy boundary condition, serious difficulties still exist as mentioned above.

It would be obvious from the above discussion that the boundary method is going ahead of the other two methods in respect to the scale of computation and discretization technique. Paying our attention to these points, the present article proposes a new boundary method involving discretization technique and determination of unknown coefficient in which the approximation procedure for conformation to the boundary conditions can be accomplished by the canonical numerical computation method, e.g. the usual method of least-square, without troubles in the boundary element method. Now, let us call this method a canonical boundary method.

II-3 Compatible Method

The third concept is related to the substance represented by approximation function. In many cases of stress analysis, both stress and displacement are required to be analyzed. Numerical stress analysis methods are classified into three types, i.e. the displacement method, the force method and the mixed method. In the displacement method,the compatibility equations and boundary conditions are formulated in terms of unknown displacement functions. Then, the equilibrium equations are transformed into a form written by displacement components using the relations between stress and strain. Constructing equations for discretization on the basis of the principle of virtual work, unknown coefficients are determined by solving linear algebraic equations. The force method is proceeded as follows. Taking stress as approximate unknown function, the equilibrium equations and boundary conditions in terms of stress are derived.This method translates the compatibility equations into a form written by stress components and constructs equations for discretization using the principle of complementary virtual work, in order to determine unknown coefficients by linear algebraic equations. The mixed method is the combination of the two. It would be inappropriate in a general sense that translation from one side to the other often increases errors. Thereby, when both stress and displacement are necessary, the mixed method might be convenient in practice. Since close relations exist between stress and displacement, determination of one hand could be equivalent to that of the other. The present paper inquire into an algorithm from this point of view. Hereafter, we call this algorithm a compatible method.

II-4 Three Part Method

The fourth concept regards to representation of approximation function. There are two kinds of coordinate function, i.e. a global or local coordinate function, according to the area of the support. The usual coordinate function for expansion into infinite series, e.g. orthogonal series, Fourier series and etc., is one of the global coordinate functions since the supports are equal to the whole area of the domain analyzed. The coordinate function used in the finite element method and the boundary element method is, on the other hand, the local coordinate functions where the supports are limited to a small subset of the domain analyzed. A global coordinate function is available for representation of approximation function in which the domain is described by a simple convex set. But the global form is not always available for such cases where the domain is not convex type and its boundary has various shape in geometry. In such circumstances, it is necessary to use the local coordinate function. However, it is generally difficult to construct a smooth and computable local coordinate function of multivariable. The finite element method has got this difficulty around by constructing a piecewise polynomial as a local coordinate function using a support on small partitions. However, this procedure depends strongly on the style of geometrical division, causing many troubles mentioned before.

Furthermore, it is necessary to discuss representation of stress distribution. The conformability of numerical analysis to boundary condition was already discussed in the previous section. Smaller mesh is inevitable to improve the accuracy of numerical analysis particularly in the neighborhood of singular or stress concentration point, while as larger mesh as possible is desirable to save computation time. The current numerical analysis requires the prior selection of element shape and mesh fineness for the domain analyzed taking the existence of singularity or stress concentration into account. Since the prior determination of these conditions is so difficult, the preprocessing in numerical stress analysis need a great effort and a lot of computation time. Meanwhile, the theoretical stress analysis is capable to analyze stress and displacement in the neighborhood of singular and concentrated point to some extent. In addition, geometrical shape and detailed conditions about the boundary can be known beforehand.

In the present article, the authors discuss on the representative functions of object solutions dividing the whole domain into three different parts, i.e. the singular part, the boundary part and the other part. Determining the form of representative function at each part, an approximation analytic solution suitable for our purpose is derived. On the basis of theoretical stress analysis, this function can also express various state of stress and displacement avoiding many difficulties in the domain partition problem often encountered in the other methods. Then, we call this procedure the three part method, while the usual numerical stress analysis could be named as the one part method.

II-5 Morphological Estimation of Error

The fifth concept is related to treatment of error estimation. Formulae for error estimation in the difference, the finite element and the boundary element methods are already known theoretically, in which the order of accuracy regarding truncation error has to be in a range of certain values in some norm. However, since the formulae involve inevitably unknown constants, it is impossible to compute the actual values of error based on these formulae. Furthermore, since all the recent digital computation are carried out in a fixed finite number of significant digits, extremely inaccurate result often come out from cancelation, loss of information and the proliferation of errors, in addition to the ordinary computational errors. The extremely large scale recent computation is accelerating this tendency. In other words serious error involved in computational models and algorithms necessarily have to be taken into consideration for the evaluation of numerical solutions. It is, thus, a matter of vital importance in the application of computed result, because the accuracy of the final numerical solutions is unspecified, when the exact solution is not known. Several recent studies on the finite element method have proposed a treatment for error estimation that minimizes the energy norm representing the magnitude of error. However, the treatment have not resolved the difficulties because the norm itself is computed using the numerical method, namely it falls in a trap set by itself. In addition, Kulish, U. et al.[4] have proposed a numerical method with the guaranteed accuracy which is self-validating numerics to

scientific computation. Although this method is drawing attention in the recent scientific computation, it seems yet difficult to obtain numerical solution of partial differential equation because the computing procedure is not only extensive but also complicated. The best way for estimation of the error in numerical solution is to compare it with corresponding experimental results. However this way is not easy to carry out, as mentioned before. The next best policy is to compare morphologically a graph constructed from numerical solution with that from experiment, synthesizing knowledge both on theoretical treatment and experimental data. In this point of view, the present article describes a method for estimation of error by comparing a map generated from the numerical solution with a fringe pattern obtained from photoelastic experiment. Here after, this method for estimation of error is referred to as a morphological method.

As seen up to this point, the basic concepts for our purpose have been stated. Namely, a new hybrid method for stress analysis which can hopefully overcome serious difficulties in the usual numerical stress analysis is proposed.The feature of the method is summarized in the following procedures.

1) Representing unknown function regarding object solution from viewpoints of both the compatible and the three part method.
2) Discreting it with the distribution element method.
3) Finding the values of stress and displacement components determining the indeterminate coefficients by use of the canonical boundary method.
4) Estimating error of the approximation analytic solution using algorithms with the morphological error estimation method.

III. THEORETICAL STRESS TREATMENT AND APPROXIMATE ANALYTICAL SOLUTION

For convenience, let us discuss only on linear theory of isotropic elastic body within small deformation. It is a matter of course that the method proposed is not restricted only in such a case, and is applicable to analysis of two and three dimensional stress analysis problem in the same framework. Theoretical stress analysis derive the representative functions of stress and displacement components using the stress functions, the displacement functions and the potential functions etc. It is however difficult to construct computable analytic solutions satisfying all governing equations exactly and simultaneously. The method proposed can successfully construct an approximation analytic solution with the concepts mentioned above starting from one of those functions. Let us show first some aspects of a framework of Galerkin vector.

III-1 Assumption on Boundary and Body Force

We suppose that the boundary and the body force hold the following properties for the strict mathematical treatment.

(1) Interior of the domain under analysis is not empty, and the boundary is a continuous surface that is piecewisely the C^2-class.

(2) Components of body force, almost everywhere, is continuous on the boundary and real analytic inside the domain. Furthermore the singular support is empty or compact.

III-2 Major Relation in Compatible Method

Let f_α a body force in the equilibrium equation of stress, then we define a particular solution of the equation (1) as the function (2).

$$\Delta^2 Q_\alpha = -\frac{1}{1-\nu} \int f_\alpha \, d\alpha \qquad (\alpha = x, y, z) \qquad (1)$$

$$Q_\alpha = E_2 * \left(-\frac{1}{1-\nu} \int f_\alpha \, d\alpha \right) \qquad (2)$$

where E_2 is the fundamental solution of the equation : $\Delta^2 E = \delta$ with the usual Laplace operator Δ and the Dirac function δ. Using this particular solution and 3-harmonic functions P_x, P_y, P_z, (the construction method of them will be shown later), we define the function :

$$G_\alpha = \frac{\partial}{\partial\alpha}(P_\alpha + Q_\alpha) \qquad (\alpha = x, y, z) \qquad (3)$$

Furthermore, we define the following symbol with a vector $P = (P_x, P_y, P_z)$:

$$del\, P = \sum_{\alpha=x}^{z} \frac{\partial^2}{\partial\alpha^2} P_\alpha \qquad (4)$$

Then, we can establish the following propositions using the vector P, $Q = (Q_x, Q_y, Q_z)$, $G = (G_x, G_y, G_z,)$:

Proposition 1

G is the Galerkin vector satisfying the relation :

$$\Delta^2 G = -\frac{1}{1-\nu} f \qquad (5)$$

if and only if the following conditions are satisfied :

$$\frac{\partial}{\partial\alpha} \Delta^2 P_\alpha = 0 \qquad (\alpha = x, y, z) \qquad (6)$$

Proposition 2

Under the conditions (6), each component of the displacement u_α, strain $\varepsilon_{\alpha\beta}$ and stress $\sigma_{\alpha\beta}$ is represented as follows :

$$u_\alpha = \frac{1+\nu}{E} \frac{\partial}{\partial\alpha} \left[2(1-\nu)\{\Delta(P_\alpha + Q_\alpha)\} - del(P+Q) \right] \qquad (7)$$

$$\varepsilon_{\alpha\beta} = \frac{1+\nu}{E} \frac{\partial^2}{\partial\alpha\partial\beta} \left[(1-\nu)\{\Delta(P_\alpha + P_\beta + Q_\alpha + Q_\beta)\} \right.$$
$$\left. - del(P+Q) \right] \qquad (\alpha, \beta = x, y, z) \qquad (8)$$

$$\sigma_{\alpha\alpha} = \frac{\partial^2}{\partial\alpha^2} \left[2(1-\nu)\{\Delta(P_\alpha + Q_\alpha)\} - del(P+Q) \right]$$
$$(\alpha = x, y, z) \qquad (9)$$

$$\sigma_{\alpha\beta} = \frac{\partial^2}{\partial x \partial y} \left[(1-\nu)\{\Delta(P_\alpha + P_\beta + Q_\alpha + Q_\beta)\} - del(P+Q) \right]$$
$$(\alpha, \beta = x, y, z; \quad \alpha \neq \beta) \qquad (10)$$

We define the above $P, Q, P+Q$ etc. so as to be elastic vectors, and the components of those vectors to be elastic functions. The expressions (7)-(10) indicate that if components of either stress or displacement have been determined, the other components are also determined simultaneously. In other words, the above method is one of the compatible method mentioned already.

III-3 Discretization and Boundary Condition

The following aspects are important for discretization in order to construct an approximation solution.

(1) Computation of indefinite integral Q_α for body force

Since body force function f_α is already known and calm as supposed above, it is easy to compute the integral (2), using approximation function in the next chapter, if necessary

(2) Computation for conformation to boundary condition
Elastic functions defined for the object solution satisfy all governing equations except the boundary conditions. In order to conform the functions to the boundary condition, the approximation function, is constructed in the form of linear combination of them with the coordinate function adopted in the next chapter. The indeterminate coefficients in it are determined by using the canonical boundary method, e.g. the collocation least-square method on the boundary.

IV   COORDINATE FUNCTION AND POLYHARMONIC FUNCTION

In advance of construction of an approximation function , it is necessary to clarify the desirable property for coordinate functions.

IV-1 Mathematical Condition for Approximation Function

(1) Adjustability to boundary condition
The first condition for our treatment is that the approximation analytic solution, have to be adjustable to the boundary condition in a high accuracy, regardless to geometrical shape of the boundary.

(2) Local dependence of function values
The second is that the value of approximation function at a point is desirable to be dependent mainly on the function values in the neighborhood of itself and little on other points far apart. Since the usual global coordinate function does not hold this property, it is difficult to construct an accurate approximation function where the domain under analysis involve non convex or singular point. Adopting the coordinate function vanishing at infinity as mentioned later, this condition could be satisfied.

(3) Determinability of the number of monomials
The third condition is that the number of monomials in the approximation function must be determinable with a well-grounded argument. Many functions can be represented in a form of infinite series, e.g. Taylor series, Fourier series, or eigenfunction series. However, since it is difficult to estimate the truncation error regarding finite sum made by simple truncation of these infinite series. Such a finite sum does not meet the needs in our treatment.

(4) Desirable mathematical property
The fourth condition is that an approximation function must hold similar mathematical property with object exact solution. For example, when the exact solution is biharmonic, it is desirable that the approximation function is also biharmonic.

IV-2   Polyharmonic Spline Function

The general approximation functions holding all of the above four properties are not known. The partial sums of Laurent series, Puiseux series and etc. often satisfy those conditions if the domain is a simple convex region such as a disk or a rectangle. However it is necessary to construct a new different coordinate function for the domain having other complex shapes. The most suitable function must be polyharmonic cardinal spline function constructed by Madych et. al.[5,6].

(1) Definition of polyharmonic cardinal spline function
A k-harmonic cardinal spline is a tempered distribution u on R^n which satisfies the following two conditions :

(i) $u \in C^{2k-n-1}$, and (ii) $\Delta^k u = 0$ on $R^n \setminus Z^n$.
Here Δ is the usual Laplace operator and, if k is greater than unity, Δ^k denotes its kth iterate. Of course $\Delta^1 = \Delta$ and Z^n denotes the lattice of points in R^n whose coordinates are integers. We say that the function or distribution is a polyharmonic cardinal spline if it is one of the k-harmonic cardinal spline.

(2) Major property of the polyharmonic spline function[5,6]

i) Given a sequence $\{a_j\}$, j in Z^n, of polynomial growth and an integer k satisfying 2k≥n+1 there is a unique k-harmonic spline f such that f(j)=a_j for all j in Z^n.

ii) Every k-harmonic spline f holds the representation

$$f(x) = \sum_{j \in Z^n} f(j) L_k(x-j) \tag{11}$$

where the series converges absolutely and uniformly on compact subsets of R^n. For more details, see [5,6].

iii) There are positive constants A and a, depending on n and k but independent of x, such that for all x in R^n;

$$|L_k(x)| \le A \exp(-a|x|)$$

iv) Let $L^2_k(R^n)$ the linear space defined as the class of those tempered distributions on R^n all of whose kth order derivatives are square integrable. Then the cardinal interpolation on $L^2_k(R^n)$ is an orthogonal projection.

(3) Application of polyharmonic spline
The condition iii) indicates that the polyharmonic cardinal function holds a desirable property about the coordinate function as mentioned before. Using the polyharmonic spline (11), we construct a approximation function for stress analysis treatment. Then all the above difficulties are ironed out.

V. EXPRESSION OF APPROXIMATION ANALYTIC FUNCTION

Using polyharmonic function and the concept of three part method, the proposed analytic approximation function are constructed as follows.

V-1 Expression of Singular Part

The expression of singular stress or displacement field will be performed in the procedures as follows.

(1) There are some cases in which the biharmonic function $\tilde{p}_\alpha$ for expression of singular field can be constructed in a framework of theoretical analysis. In such a case expression of the elastic function by indefinite integral of the biharmonic function as follows :

$$\tilde{P}_\alpha = \int \tilde{p}_\alpha \, d\alpha \quad (\alpha = x, y, z) \tag{12}$$

(2) In other cases, let us pay attention to the fact that the singular stress field is similar to a body force field in the form of governing equations. Hence, expression of singular stress field are similar to that of body force as the expression (2).

V-2 Expression of Regular Part

The remaining part except the region of both singularity and boundary part in the domain under analysis will be named as the regular part. This part is represented in a form of polyharmonic function as follows :

$$\hat{P}_\alpha = \int \left\{ \sum_{j \in Z^n} a_{\alpha j} L_k(x-j) \right\} \quad (\alpha = x, y, z) \tag{13}$$

V-3 Expression of Boundary Part

The boundary under consideration can be regarded as parametrized surface by introducing Gauss's parametric representation. Then, a net consisted of a family of parametric curve could be preferably constructed on it. Each intersection in this net is named the lattice point on boundary. Treating the lattice points on boundary similarly in the case of regular part, a polyharmonic spline function can be also constructed. The representation of boundary part would be, then, obtained in a form of spline function:

$$\check{P}_\alpha = \int \left\{ \sum a_{\alpha j} L_k(x-j) \right\} \quad (\alpha = x, y, z) \tag{14}$$

Summarizing the above discussions, an approximation analytic solution can be represented by the summation:

$$P_\alpha = \check{P}_\alpha + \hat{P}_\alpha + \tilde{P}_\alpha \tag{15}$$

of the three part of the singular , regular and boundary part. The unknown coefficients is, moreover, easily determined by the collocation least-square method.

VI. MORPHOLOGICAL ESTIMATION OF ERROR

Now let us consider the morphological estimation of error, which compares a map generated from numerical solution with the fringe pattern obtained from a photoelastic experiment. The procedures and merits of this method for error estimation are describe as follows.

VI-1 Procedure of Morphological Estimation of Error

(1) A numerical solution is obtained with the algorithm stated above, then secondary principal stresses on an arbitrary section are computed from the solution.

(2) Using the representative equation of fringe pattern in photoelastic data, a map of isochromatics, isoclinics, isostatics, isopachics etc. are generated with the computer graphics technique.

(3) The difference between patterns of the map and fringe from photoelastic experiment is investigated precisely.

(4) According to degree of the difference, the accuracy of numerical solution can be estimated.

VI-2 Bases for Morphological Estimation of Error

(1) Photoelastic effect in a state of three dimensional stress equals to the case where the secondary principal stresses on a normal plane in the direction of incident light could be regarded as the principal stresses in the ordinary two dimensional photoelastic experiment.

(2) Values of two principal stresses in the two dimensional photoelastic experiment correspond univalently to both the difference and direction of those stresses.

VI-3 Advantage of Morphological Estimation of Error

(1) A plane considered corresponds to a plate specimen sliced in the stress freezing method. In cases that several nondestructive techniques in three-dimensional photoelasticity

can be successfully applicable, the plane under consideration could be interpreted as an optical slice.

(2) Utilizing the knowledge of photoelasticity and the object stress state, the method proposed for error estimation is applicable even if actual photoelastic experimental data can not be obtained

VII. APPLICATION TO THE TIMOSHENKO'S PROBLEM

There are very few cases where theoretical stress analysis can find out an exact solution in a computable form. For example, the exact theoretical solution for the problem of a ring under a pair of diametral compression (Fig.1) can not be found in a computable form. Timoshenko[7] solved the problem with the superposition method and constructed a computable approximation analytic representation of stress. Detinko[8] examined theoretically a part of the Timoshenko's results later. Now let us apply the algorithm proposed to this problem to construct another representation.

(1) Three parts of stress function
At first, an object representation with a stress function will be constructed. Since the boundary of a ring under consideration is a subset of line parallel to the axis in a polar coordinate, the boundary part in our three part method can be omitted. Then, a stress function χ is expressed as the sum $\chi = \chi_1 + \chi_2$ of the singular part χ_1 and the regular part χ_2

(2) Expression of the singular part
Let the ring $D=\{(x,y):R_1^2 \leq x^2+y^2 \leq R_2^2\}$ in the Cartesian coordinates. The theoretical stress analysis with the Airy's stress function on the singular part χ_1 gives the following expression of a biharmonic function as,

$$\chi_1 = \frac{P}{\pi} x \left\{ \tan^{-1}\left(\frac{y-R_2}{x}\right) - \tan^{-1}\left(\frac{y+R_2}{x}\right) \right\} \quad (16)$$

(3) Expression of the regular part
Let the ring $D=\{(r,\theta):R_1 \leq r \leq R_2, 0 \leq \theta \leq 2\pi\}$ in the Polar coordinates. Except the neighborhood of the singular point, the regular part χ_2 is described as follows:

$$\chi_2 = a_0(r) + \sum_{k=1}^{N} a_{2k}(r)\cos 2k\theta \quad (17)$$

where

$$a_0(r) = a_{00} + a_{01}\log R + a_{02}R^2 + a_{03}R^2 \log R \quad (18)$$

$$a_n(r) = a_{n0}R^{-n} + a_{n1}R^{-n+2} + a_{n2}R^n + a_{n3}R^{n+2} \ (n \geq 2) \quad (19)$$

$$R \equiv \frac{r}{R_2} \quad (20)$$

(4) Expression of stress components
Since $x=r\cos\theta$, $y=r\sin\theta$, the stress components σ_{rr}, $\sigma_{\sigma\sigma}$ and $\sigma_{r\theta}$ inside the ring are represented as follows:

$$\sigma_{rr} = \cos^2\theta \frac{\partial^2\chi}{\partial y^2} + \sin^2\theta \frac{\partial^2\chi}{\partial x^2} - \sin 2\theta \frac{\partial^2\chi}{\partial x \partial y} \quad (21)$$

$$\sigma_{\theta\theta} = \sin^2\theta \frac{\partial^2\chi}{\partial y^2} + \cos^2\theta \frac{\partial^2\chi}{\partial x^2} + \sin 2\theta \frac{\partial^2\chi}{\partial x \partial y} \quad (22)$$

$$\sigma_{r\theta} = \frac{1}{2}\sin 2\theta \left(\frac{\partial^2\chi}{\partial x^2} - \frac{\partial^2\chi}{\partial y^2}\right) - \cos 2\theta \left(\frac{\partial^2\chi}{\partial x \partial y}\right) \quad (23)$$

(5) Boundary conditions
Boundary conditions are written as:
$$\sigma_{rr}=0, \ \sigma_{r\theta}=0 \quad (24)$$

(6) Determination of the unknown coefficients
On the boundary of the ring :

$$B = \left\{ (r,\theta): \ r = R_1 \text{ or } R_2, \ \ 0 < \theta < \frac{\pi}{2} \right\},$$

we select some sampling point (r, θ_m) as follows:
$$r=R_1 \text{ or } r=R_2 \quad (25)$$
$$\theta_m = \frac{m\pi}{4(N+2)}, \quad m = 1, 2, \cdots, 2(N+1) \quad (26)$$

The unknown coefficients are determined with the ordinary least-square method so that the boundary conditions are satisfied on all of these sampling points. This method is one of the canonical boundary method as stated before.

(7) Computed results and error estimation
The examples of unknown coefficients computed with the algorithm proposed are shown in Table 1. Graphic expressions of the results and the experimental data of photoelastic fringe pattern and its gray level are show in Fig.2, Fig.3 and Fig.4. The computed patterns show good agreement with the experimental ones. Furthermore, the graphic expression of the computed stress components σ_{rr}, $\sigma_{\theta\theta}$, $\sigma_{r\theta}$ are also show in Fig. 5. These patterns are consistent with the knowledge both from the theoretical stress analysis and the photoelastic experiment. As we have seen, the approximation analytic solution obtained from the algorithm proves to be highly accurate.

VIII. CONCLUDING REMARKS

A hybrid stress analysis method has been developed for application to the general two- and three-dimensional problems of stress and displacement analysis. The method is formulated in the form of an approximation analytic solution standing upon the five basic concepts and requirement only on the canonical boundary discretization. Furthermore, this method holds, in itself, a new error estimation method which is always available even if the exact solution is not known. These are particularly attractive for stress and displacement analysis, since this methods may overcome the main difficulties in the current methods of stress analysis. One simple example of the approximation analytic solution is shown to validate this new formulation. However, since the method is only under way, several refinements will be necessary to foster this hybrid stress analysis method to general applications.

REFERENCES

1. Rajiyah, H. and Atiuri, S.N., "Analysis of Embedded and Surface Elliptical Flaws in Transversely Isotropic Bodies by the Finite Element Alternating Method", Journal of Applied Mechanics, 58, 435-443, 1991.
2. Huang, Y.M. Lin, C.H. Suhling and Rowlands,R.E., "Determining the Three Individual Stress Components from Measured Isochromatic Fringe", Experimental Mechanics, 31, 310-318, 1991
3. Thompson, J.F., "Numerical Grid Generation", Elsevier, 1982.
4. Kulisch, U. and Miranker, W.L., "The Arithmetic of the Digital Computer: A New Approach", SIAM Review, 28, 1-40, 1986.
5. Madych, H.R. and Nelson S.A., "Polyharmonic Cardinal Splines", Journal of Approximation Theory, 60, 141-156, 1990.
6. Madych, H.R. and Nelson S.A., "Polyharmonic Cardinal Splines: A Minimization Property", Journal of Approximation Theory, 63, 303-320, 1990.
7. Timoshenko, S.P., Phil. Mag., 44, 1014-1018, 1922.
8. Detinko, F. M., Int. J. Eng. Sci., 27, 1001-1006, 1989.

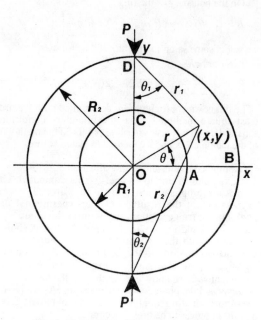

Fig.1 Coordinate System for Circular
Ring under Diametral Compression

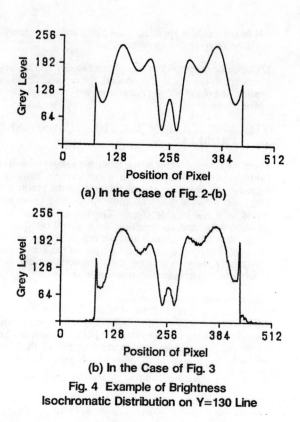

(a) In the Case of Fig. 2-(b)

(b) In the Case of Fig. 3

Fig. 4 Example of Brightness
Isochromatic Distribution on Y=130 Line

Table 1 Typical Examples of Coefficient a_{nj} in Approximation Regular Part Function (17)

(a) $R_1=100$, $R_2=200$, $P=1$, $N=7$

n\j	0	1	2	3
0	0.0	-3.46331×10^1	0.0	-2.90289×10^1
2	1.02172×10^1	-8.72390×10^1	1.43826×10^2	-6.68046×10^1
4	-2.33370×10^{-1}	1.26492×10^0	-3.89283×10^0	2.86128×10^0
6	1.24631×10^{-2}	-6.02771×10^{-2}	2.74422×10^{-1}	-2.26608×10^{-1}
8	-7.56656×10^{-4}	3.47413×10^{-3}	-2.09844×10^{-2}	1.82668×10^{-2}
10	4.68888×10^{-5}	-2.08992×10^{-4}	1.57268×10^{-3}	-1.41067×10^{-3}
12	-2.89435×10^{-6}	1.26475×10^{-5}	-1.15218×10^{-4}	1.05377×10^{-4}
14	1.80142×10^{-7}	-7.76697×10^{-7}	8.38093×10^{-6}	-7.76057×10^{-6}

(b) $R_1=150$, $R_2=200$, $P=1$, $N=7$

n\j	0	1	2	3
0	0.0	-7.30214×10^1	0.0	9.35954×10^0
2	2.82200×10^2	-1.21610×10^3	1.58561×10^3	-6.51704×10^2
4	-1.25174×10^1	3.15524×10^1	-6.36226×10^1	4.45876×10^1
6	1.85391×10^0	-4.06576×10^0	1.14172×10^1	-9.20535×10^0
8	-4.05043×10^{-1}	8.34439×10^{-1}	-3.03014×10^0	2.60074×10^0
10	1.07927×10^{-1}	-2.14951×10^{-1}	9.62312×10^{-1}	-8.55288×10^{-1}
12	-3.02016×10^{-2}	5.87170×10^{-2}	-3.11985×10^{-1}	2.83469×10^{-1}
14	9.11681×10^{-3}	-1.74676×10^{-2}	1.07789×10^{-1}	-9.94387×10^{-2}

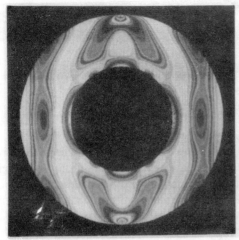

(a) Timoshenko's Method

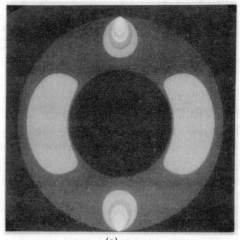

(a) σ_{rr}

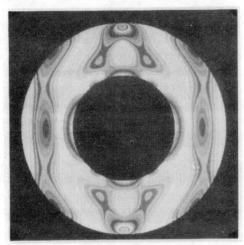

(b) The MEthod Proposed
Fig.2 Calculated Isochromatic
$R_1=100$, $R_2=200$, $P=300$

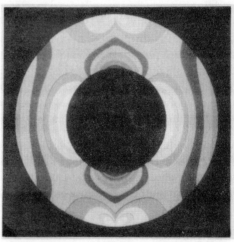

(b) $\sigma_{\theta\theta}$

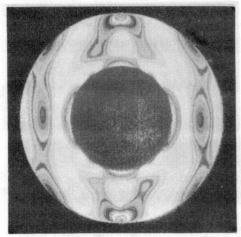

Fig.3 Experimental Isochromatics

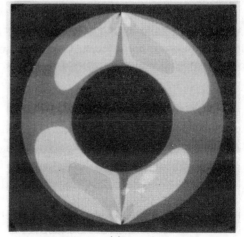

(c) $\sigma_{r\theta}$
Fig.4 Typical Results of Stress Calculated
$R_1=100$, $R_2=200$, $P=300$

Hybrid Experimental/Numerical Techniques for NonLinear Material Behavior

G. C. Kirby[1], P. Matic[1], V.G. DeGiorgi[1], D.P. Harvey[1], A.J. Kee[2] and A. K. Wong[3]

ABSTRACT

Two hybrid methods used to study nonlinear material behavior are presented. The first method is traditional in approach since experimental measurements of temperature are incorporated into a finite difference scheme to derive the full temperature field and the heat generated during an uniaxial fatigue test. The method utilizes a least squares procedure coupled with Lagrange multipliers. The solution obtained is the best fit to the measured data subject to the constraints of the governing equations. The second method uses experimental measurements of load, displacement and specimen geometry to iterate on the solution for a material's constitutive parameters. In this respect it is nontraditional since full experimental field quantities are not utilized in the conventional manner nor does the numerical model aid in the differentiation of experimental data.

INTRODUCTION

Traditionally, a hybrid methodology uses experimental data as input on the boundaries or the region of a model of a physical phenomena (1-5). The computational portion of the method is then used to either analyze the experimental data over the region modelled or obtain derivatives of the experimental data over the region. The technique has advantages over both purely experimental techniques and purely numerical techniques. Advantages over purely experimental techniques are analysis of the measured full field quantities and differentiation of data which is sensitive to experimental error. Examples are separation of principle stresses in photoelasticity (4) and determination of strains from displacements in moiré (3). Advantages over purely numerical techniques are the use of measured boundary conditions and modelling limited regions which result in a savings in computational cost (5).

A more generalized view of the hybrid technique is any method that uses experimental data to guide the computational solution. Such a procedure may be iterative in nature as follows: 1) Make experimental measurements ; 2) Perform a numerical simulation; 3) Compare results from the numerical simulation with experimental data; 4) Revise the model or its parameters if the differences are significant; 5) Repeat steps 2 - 4 until suitable agreement between experimental data and the numerical solution is obtained.

This paper discusses the application of the hybrid methodology to two specific areas of research at the Naval Research Laboratory. The first application is the determination of heat generation during low cycle fatigue and uses a traditional technique. The second application is the determination of constitutive parameters for ductile metal alloys and a iterative approach.

APPLICATION TO LOW CYCLE FATIGUE

It has been proposed (6-8) that fatigue failure may be predicted through thermodynamic means. Specifically, the change in the internal energy state may be viewed as a "damage" energy and failure occurs when the accumulated damage energy reaches a critical value. Phase changes, development of residual stresses, translations of dislocations and the creation and/or enlargement of internal surfaces such as voids are examples of damage that occurs during the deformation process. Consideration of the first law of thermodynamics quickly leads to the fact that if $\dot{W}$ is the applied work rate and $\dot{Q}$ the heat dissipation rate, then for negligible kinetic effects, the rate at which damage energy $\dot{U}$ is being accumulated within the material is given by

$$\dot{U} = \dot{W} - \dot{Q}. \qquad (1)$$

While $\dot{W}$ may be easily and accurately determined from load-displacement data, accurate measurements of $\dot{Q}$ are much more difficult to achieve. Most experimental methods are based either on the use of an electrically heated calibration

---

1. Research Engineer, Mechanics of Materials Branch, Naval Research Laboratory, Washington D.C.
2. Mechanical Engineer, Geo-Centers, Fort Washington, MD.
3. Research Scientist, Aeronautical Research Laboratory, Melbourne, Victoria 3001 Australia.

specimen (7), or by direct calibration of the heat passing out of the specimen from temperature measurements either on or outside of the specimen gage length(6). Both of these techniques require elaborate experimental setups and do not account for transient effects.

A generalized hybrid method may be applied to determine $\dot{Q}$ if the equation governing the temperature field is coupled with experimental temperature measurements. The one-dimensional heat diffusion equation

$$\frac{\partial \theta}{\partial t} - \alpha \frac{\partial^2 \theta}{\partial x^2} = \frac{\dot{Q}}{\rho C} \tag{2}$$

may be written in finite difference form as

$$\theta_{i-1} - A\theta_i + \theta_{i+1} = Bq + C_i, \tag{3}$$

in which $A = -2\left(1 + \frac{\Delta x^2}{\alpha \Delta t}\right)$, $B = -2\frac{\Delta x^2}{\alpha}\rho C$, $C_i = -\theta_{i-1}^{t-1} + 2\left(1 - \frac{\Delta x^2}{\alpha \Delta t}\right)\theta_i^{t-1} - \theta_{i+1}^{t-1}$ and where θ is the average

temperature measured over one cycle, t and x are the respective independent temporal and spatial variables, α is the coefficient of diffusivity, ρC is the specific heat per unit mass and q is the time averaged value of the heat dissipation rate over one cycle. For convenience the default superscript t has been omitted.

A direct procedure for determining q is to define an objective function for which q may be solved given some measured temperature data. An obvious choice is a least squares criterion between the measured temperature T_i and the computed temperature θ_i. The solution q is one which minimizes

$$S = \sum_i (T_i - \theta_i)^2. \tag{4}$$

Once boundary conditions are specified, a straightforward approach would be to solve equations 3 and 4 iteratively by adjusting q until the error is minimized. However, this procedure is relatively inefficient. Furthermore, specification of the exact boundary conditions is at best difficult. For example, isothermal boundary conditions would seem appropriate for massive hydraulic wedge grips. However, consider a bar of 6061-T6 aluminum mounted in such grips. After 100 seconds the temperature profile was obtained as shown in figure1. Extrapolating the temperature field to the grips in-

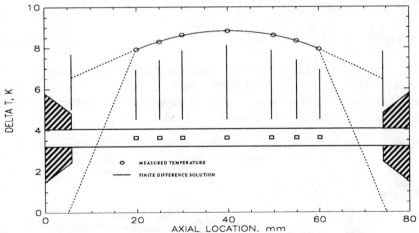

Figure 1. Linear Extrapolation of Temperature to Boundaries.

dicates that the assumption of isothermal boundary conditions was not appropriate. Another method would be to measure the temperature at the boundary and assign this value as the boundary conditions. However, this forces the solution to pass through these points and implies that the temperature measurements at the boundaries are more accurate than the temperature measured elsewhere by the same method. The above problems may be overcome by the use of Lagrange multipliers (8).

Treating eq. 3 as the constraints to the minimization of eq. 4, an objective function X is written as

$$X = \sum_i [(T_i - \theta_i)^2 \delta_i + \lambda_i (\theta_{i-1} - A\theta_i + \theta_{i+1} - Bq - C_i)], \tag{5}$$

where λ_i are the Lagrange multipliers. In general the finite difference discretization of the problem will result in more computed temperature nodes than measurements. Therefore, the notation of $\delta_i = 1$ at nodes where temperature measurements exist and $\delta_i = 0$ for nodes where temperature measurements do not exist is used. For the solution to exist, we require

$$\frac{\partial X}{\partial \lambda_i} = 0 \qquad i = 2, ..., N-1; \tag{6a}$$

$$\frac{\partial X}{\partial \theta_i} = 0 \qquad i = 1, ..., N; \tag{6b}$$

$$\frac{\partial X}{\partial q} = 0. \tag{6c}$$

The expansion of eq. 6 results in a linear set of equations which may be solved for the temperature field and heat source term q.

Figure 2 shows the results for applying this method to a numerical simulation. The exact solution for the one dimen-

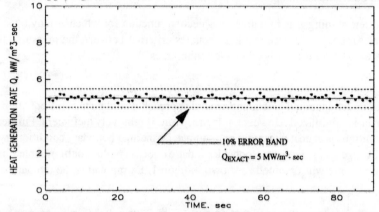

Figure 2. Heat Generation Error Due to ±0.01 K Random Temperature Error.

sional heat diffusion equation with a constant heat source term was obtained (9). The temperature at several nodes was determined and then a random error between ±0.01 K was added to simulate errors in the measurement process. The accuracy of the method may be shown by demonstrating that it is able to accurately determine the heat source term and the temperature field. The error in the reproduction of q was less than 10%.

Figure 3 shows the temperature solution when the numerical scheme was applied to actual measured data. The data

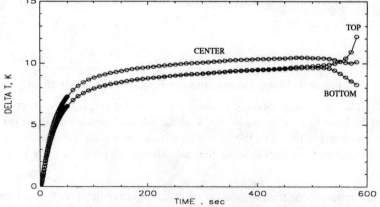

Figure 3. Temperature History for 6061-T6 Aluminum, $\varepsilon = \pm 0.52\%$.

were obtained from a 6061-T6 aluminum round bar cycling between ±0.52%strain. The agreement between experiment and computation is excellent. Note at approximately 150 cycles before failure the temperature between the top and bottom temperature measurements begin to diverge. For all specimens the "hotter" end invariably was the fractured end. Thus, it is conjectured that crack initiation occurred at this point. and thus the temperature data may be used to determine crack initiation. Figure 4 shows the work-heat conversion efficiency for the same test. For most of the test

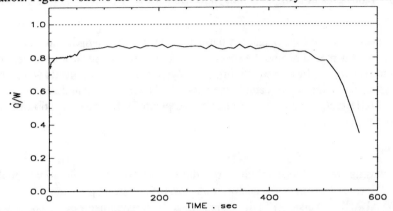

Figure 4. Work-Heat Efficiency for 6061-T6 Aluminum, ε= ±0.52%.

approximately 85% of the irreversible work was dissipated in the form of heat. However, for the first 5 cycles a considerable portion of the irreversible energy is dissipated as damage.

APPLICATION TO CONSTITUTIVE PARAMETERIZATION OF DUCTILE MATERIALS

Accurate knowledge of large deformation ductile material behavior is required for many design and analysis applications. Two equally important issues make the continuum characterization of inelastic materials in general nontrivial. These issues are 1) the rational development of stress, strain and constitutive formulations for a wide class of materials and 2) the determination of material constitutive parameters from material test specimen response for use in a particular constitutive formulation. Solutions to the second issue require quantitative determination of a material's uniaxial continuum stress versus strain response, valid over its full range of deformation from zero to final fracture.

In the case of ductile metals, the uniaxial tensile test specimen is used to obtain global load-displacement data. In principle, this data can be easily normalized to uniaxial material stress-strain data. From a practical point of view, the necking phenomenon in ductile material specimens has been a formidable barrier to accurate and complete constitutive characterization. As a result, constitutive parameters are usually determined from data obtained prior to necking over the deformation range where purely uniaxial and homogenous deformations are assumed to exist. The resulting material description is strictly valid only in applications for which the effective stress and strain measures do not exceed the bounds of the uniaxial data. For ductile engineering alloys presently in use, the specimen uniaxial data obtained prior to necking only describe a small portion of the full strain range experienced by the material from zero deformation to fracture initiation at the center of the neck. However, the combined interaction between specimen geometry, applied load and material behavior, which in combination produce specimen necking, can be used to effectively solve for the material constitutive response. Such a solution combines numerical analysis with experimental observations and therefore by definition is a hybrid method.

Several researchers (10-13) have used hybrid analysis to establish an uniaxial stress-strain response for different ductile metals. Such procedures treat the uniaxial stress-strain response as the unknown to be solved in an iterative fashion. For each iteration a candidate stress-strain response is used in a numerical simulation of the tensile specimen. Iteration continued until suitable agreement is obtained between the numerical simulation and experimental observations. Matic et al (12) have refined the procedure for iteration of the material response curve for HSLA 80 and is subsequently described.

Description of Experiments

The first step in the constitutive parameter solution procedure was performing tensile tests on two different specimen geometries with length to diameter (L/D) ratios 1.0 and 2.0. For low L/D ratios the extent of the necking phenomenon occurs throughout the entire gage length. Thus, the measured response is composed primarily of material undergoing large deformations. For higher L/D ratios both extensive deformation within the neck volume and moderate deformation in the specimen volume outside the neck occur within the gage length. Therefore, the measured specimen response is dependent upon the relative balance of constitutive parameters simultaneously governing deformation in both regions. However, for L/D ratios greater than 3.0 an unsymmetric neck may develop as was observed for HY100 steel (11).

Round bar tensile test specimens were spray painted flat black and the gage length was defined by two white gage marks. A white background was placed behind the specimen. The resulting contrast was sufficient to define the specimen profile and strain measurements by subsequent image analysis. Load measurements were synchronized with the video recording of the specimen image at 10 second time intervals. The horizontal and vertical resolution provided by the image analysis was 0.0318 cm/pixel and 0.0178 cm/pixel respectively for the L/D ratio of 2 and 0.0127 cm/pixel and 0.0076 cm/pixel for the L/D ratio of 1.

Description of Numerical Simulation

The second step in the constitutive parameter solution procedure was iterative computational simulation of the laboratory tensile specimens. The candidate uniaxial Cauchy stress- logarithmic strain pairs in multilinear form were used as the formal input into the ABAQUS (Version 4.5) finite element code. Axisymmetry of the specimen required that only one quarter of the specimen be modelled. Type CAX8H axisymmetric continuum elements with an independent hydrostatic pressure variable were used. All analysis were performed with full geometric nonlinearity to account for large strains and large rotations. Displacement boundary conditions were prescribed to simulate the physical loading of the laboratory tests. The material constitutive behavior was modelled using an incremental rate independent plasticity theory (14).

Description of Comparison Software

The third step in the solution procedure, performed iteratively in conjunction with each computational simulation of the specimens, was comparison of laboratory and computational simulation data. Seven points on the laboratory and the computational specimen profile were used to define subgage volumes and lengths within the specimen gage length. A methodology was developed that facilitated the iteration process by comparing subgage deformation data between numerical and experimental results. Laboratory and computational subgage axial stretch ratios were compared to identify the locations of relative differences and agreement between predicted and observed subgage responses. Differences between computational predictions and laboratory measurements of subgage axial stretch ratios guided the modification of the Cauchy stress-log strain pairs beyond the largest pair accepted as the material constitutive solution curve. Satisfactory agreement was taken to be less than five percent difference between engineering stress values over the entire engineering strain range for both specimen geometries.

Six subgages were used over half the specimen length. Subgage axial stretch ratios λ were defined from experimental and computational displacement data z by

$$
{}^t_e\lambda_i = \frac{{}^t_e z_{i+1} - {}^t_e z_i}{{}^0_e z_{i+1} - {}^0_e z_i} \qquad {}^t_c\lambda_i = \frac{{}^t_c z_{i+1} - {}^t_c z_i}{{}^0_c z_{i+1} - {}^0_c z_i} \tag{7}
$$

where the subscripts c and e indicate computational or experimental values for subgage i at time t. The ratio of these two quantities

$$
{}^t R_i = \frac{{}^t_c\lambda_i}{{}^t_e\lambda_i} \tag{8}
$$

was used to identify subgage surface displacement errors at the onset of global specimen response errors. As anticipated, the subgage responses nearest to the neck contraction were influenced by the largest material deformations within the specimen gage volume.

Effective plastic strain values at each quadrature point for a given load were used to create a histogram of the specimen constitutive response. The histogram of the computational simulation, at the load corresponding to the departure from laboratory experiment, identified the range of constitutive parameter values which did not accurately represent the material response.

The specimen with the lowest L/D ratio was modelled first because of the wide range of nonlinearity due to the neck volume dominating the gage section volume. This geometry establishes the general trend of the material stress strain response. As a starting point for the iteration, a power law fit through the experimental data at small strains was used and extrapolated to higher strains. As evident from figure 5, the simulation using the initial guess does not provide suit-

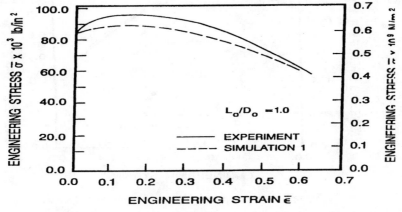

Figure 5. Computational Solution 1 using Specimen #1.

able agreement with experiment. However, after five iterations and modifications to the constitutive parameters according to the procedure described above, the simulation is in good agreement with experimental observations as shown by figure 6. At this point it is necessary to test the adequacy of the constitutive parameters at predicting load displace-

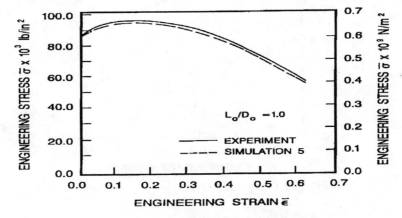

Figure 6. Computational Solution 5 using Specimen #1.

ment response for another geometry and modify the parameters accordingly. The second specimen geometry was used as a check and to fine tune the constitutive parameters. This geometry provides a fully developed neck material undergoing unloading in the gage section. However, as can be seen from figure 7,, the constitutive parameters obtained from

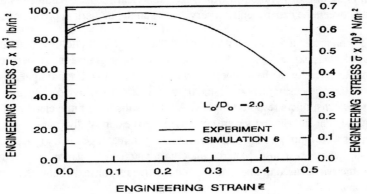

Figure 7. Computational Solution 6 using Specimen #2.

133

the previous geometry were not sufficient in predicting the global response for the second geometry. Once again the comparison algorithm was performed for three iterations until suitable agreement between the predicted and the observed load displacement is obtained as shown in figure 8. As a check on the suitability of the constitutive parameters

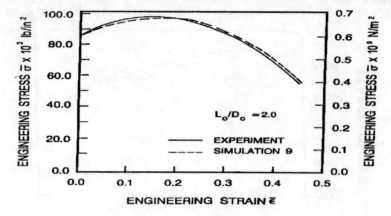

Figure 8. Computational Solution 9 using Specimen #2.

the load displacement response for the first geometry is obtained using the modified constitutive parameters from the second geometry. As seen from figure 9 satisfactory results are obtained.

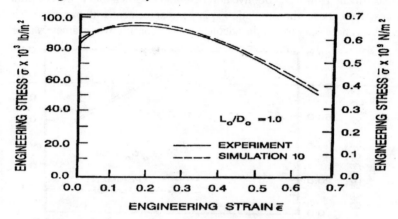

Figure 9. Computational Solution 10 using Specimen #1.

SUMMARY

Hybrid methods are techniques in which experimental observations guide the numerical solution of a physical problem. The traditional implementation of a hybrid method uses measured field quantities as the boundary conditions of a numerical model or uses a numerical model to perform differentiation of experimental data. A general, but nontraditional implementation is the use of iteration in which the numerical model's parameters are adjusted until suitable agreement is obtained between the experimental observations and the numerical predictions.

Two applications have been presented as demonstrations of the hybrid methodology to nonlinear material behavior. The first application used a least squares method in conjunction with Lagrange multipliers to formulate a constrained minimization procedure to solve for the heat generated during uniaxial low cycle fatigue. Use of this procedure does not require the specification or measurement of boundary conditions. The second application used a general hybrid procedure to solve for the constitutive response for HSLA 80. Results from finite element models and measurements of specimen load, displacement and geometry were compared and the constitutive parameters were adjusted iteratively. Two specimen geometries were employed to ensure constitutive parameter geometry independence. The first geometry was used to establish the general response. Material undergoing large deformation was predominate within the gage length. The second geometry was used to fine tune the constitutive response. A balance of material undergoing both moderate deformation and necking was present within the gage length.

REFERENCES

1. Sirkis, J.S. and Taylor, C.E. "Displacement Pattern Matching and Boundary-element Methods for Elastic-plastic Stress Analysis.", Exp. Mech., 30, 26-33, 1990.

2. Balas, J., Sladek,J. and Drzik,M. "Stress-Analysis by Combination of Holographic Interferometry and Boundary Integral Method.", Exp. Mech., 23, 196-202, 1983.

3. Morton, J., Post, D., Han, B. and Tsai, H.Y. "A Localized Hybrid Method of Stress Analysis: A Combination of Moiré Interferometry and FEM.", Exp. Mech., 30, 195-200, 1990.

4. Mahfuz H., Case, R.O. and Wong, T.L. "Hybrid Stress Analysis by Digitized Photoelastic Data and Numerical Methods.", Exp. Mech., 30, 190-194, 1990.

5. Gilbert, J.A., Dudderar, T.D., Matthys, D.R., Johnson, H.S. and Franzel, R.A. "Two-Dimensional Stress Analysis Combining High-Frequency Moiré Measurements with Finite-Element Modeling.", Exp. Tech., 24-28, Mar, 1987.

6. Gurevich, S.E. and Gaevoi, A.P. "Method of Experimentally Determining Rupture Energy in Cyclical (fatigue) Loading.", Zavodskaya Laboratoriya, 39, 1110-1114, 1973.

7. Romashov, R.V. and Fedorov, V.V "Method of Experimentally Checking Thermodynamic Ideas on the Failure of a Solid Body During a Fatigue Test.", Zavodskaya Laboratoriya, 41, 229-232, 1975.

8. Wong, A.K. and Kirby, G.C. "A Hybrid Numerical/Experimental Technique for Determining the Heat Dissipated During Low Cycle Fatigue." Eng. Frac. Mech., 37 (3), 493-504, 1990.

9. Hildebrand, F.B., Advanced Calculus for Applications, 2nd ed., Prentice Hall, 1976, 484-490.

10. Norris, D.M., Moran, B., Scudder J.K. and Quinones, D.F. "A Computer Simulation of the Tensile Test.", J. Mech. Phys. Solids, 26, 1-19, 1978.

11. Matic, P., Kirby, G.C. and Jolles, M.I. "The Relation of Tensile Specimen Size and Geometry Effects to Unique Constitutive Parameters for Ductile Materials.", Proc. R. Soc. Lond., A417, 309-333, 1988.

12. Matic, P., Father, P., Kirby, G.C. and Jolles, M.I. "Ductile Alloy Constitutive Response by Correlation of Iterative Finite Element Simulation with Laboratory Video Images.", Eng. Frac. Mech., 40 (2), 395-419, 1991.

13. Wong, A.K., Matic, P. and Kirby, G.C. "An Inverse Experimental/Computational Scheme for Determining Stress/ Strain Data Under Large Strains.",Proc. of 6th Intl Conf in Australia on Finite Element Methods, Univ of Sydney, NSW, Australia, July 8-10, Vol 2, 550-557,1991.

14. Hibbit, H.D., Karlsson, B.I. and Sorensen, E.P., 1984, ABAQUS User's Manual, Hibbitt, Karlsson, and Sorensen, Inc., Providence, RI.

PHOTOELASTIC DETERMINATION OF STRESS CONCENTRATIONS ASSOCIATED WITH UNICORTICAL DEFECTS IN BONE UNDER TORSIONAL LOADING

Michael R. Harms (Graduate Student)
Mohammad Mahinfalah (Assistant Professor)
Mechanical Engineering and Applied Mechanics
North Dakota State University, Fargo ND

INTRODUCTION

The stress concentration due to circular holes through one wall of a tubular torsional model are not completely understood. This knowledge is particularly important to the medical community in the development of guidelines for creating cortical defects in long bone. The objectives of this study were to determine the effects of hole size on the stress concentration factor (Ktg) and the location of the maximum stress. The torsional model used is a femur of an adult sheep. What makes this study unique is the use of bone as a torsional model and the use of the Photoelastic coating technique as the experimental method.

BACKGROUND

Wang (1946) developed the theoretical Ktg for an infinite elastic isotropic plate containing a circular hole, subjected to pure shear in the plane of the hole. This theory predicts a stress concentration factor of 4.0 for the hole, with the location of the maximum tensile and compressive stresses being 45 degrees from the horizontal or vertical axis of the hole.

Jessop (1958) used the "frozen stress" technique of photoelasticity to determine the stress concentration factors associated with holes through both sides of a tubular model. It was assumed that the stress pattern in the tube with the hole was similar to that of the stress pattern around a hole in an infinite plate, subject to shear. To determine the maximum stress, based on this assumption, slices were taken at 45 degrees from the tube axis. Tube geometries studied included: a/D from 5% to 40% and d/D from 0% to 90%, where a is the hole diameter, D is the outer diameter of the tube, and d is the inner diameter of the tube. The study found the maximum stress to occur at the bore of the hole just below the surface.

Kuo (1989) used an acrylic tubular model (d/D=0.6) with a hole through the thickness of one wall which was subjected to a high rotational rate. The fracture initiation line was found to rotate from the 45 degree incline clockwise through an angle $\Delta\theta$, which was dependant on the defect ratio a/D. The following linear relationship was reported:

$\Delta\theta = -6.28 + 55(a/D)$.

Bartlett (1989) used the finite element method to model tubes with holes through one wall and tubes with holes through both walls and found no discernible differences in Ktg for small holes (a/D< .2). The stress concentration factor was also found to be insensitive to material properties.

MATERIALS AND METHODS

In this study a single femur from an adult sheep was used as the torsional model. The bone ends were machined flat and two 6.35 mm (0.25 inch) holes were drilled in the end portions of the bone 152.4 mm (6.0 inches) apart on center with the bone's longitudinal axis. Two 6.35 mm (0.25 inch) pins were used to align the axis of the bone with the loading brackets designed to apply the torsional load (Figure 1). The torsional load was applied to the flat portions of the bone ends through the use of steel plates which fit between the brackets and the bone. The bone's surface was sealed with a thin layer of the reflective cement, PC 1, to assure a good bond to the coating. The bone was coated with a 2.54 mm (0.100 inch) thick transparent, high sensitivity, PL 1 photoelastic material and cemented to the already sealed bone with a thin layer of PC 1. Six holes with diameters ranging from approximately 10% to 60% of the bone's medial diameter were concentrically machined through the posterior cortex, the thinnest and most stress sensitive side of the eccentric bone (Figure 2). For the femur used the ratio of the inner diameter to the outer diameter, d/D was 0.76.

The slowly applied torque was between 7.9N-m and 11.3N-m, (70-100 in-Lb) for all six cases. This low torque was necessary to avoid fracture of the bone. Small and large field reflective polariscopes and a linear compensator were used to analyze the system.

Using normal incidence readings, the fringe orders represent the difference in principal strains ($\epsilon_1-\epsilon_2$). When readings are made at free boundaries, such as holes, the fringe order represents the stress tangent to the free surface, since the stress perpendicular to the edge is known to be zero. The gross stress concentration factor (Ktg) is defined as the stress at the edge of the hole divided by the nominal principal stress, away from the hole. For a circular cylinder subjected to torsion the maximum principal strain is equal and opposite to the minimum principal strain ($\epsilon_1 = -\epsilon_2$), in regions away from a defect. The directions of the principal strains occur at 45 degrees from the longitudinal axis.

To confirm this assumption for the femoral sheep bone, a torsional experiment using the specially designed loading brackets was performed on a separate sheep femur with no defect. Six strain gages (gage type WA-06-060WR-120), three mounted 45 degrees apart on the posterior side and three mounted 45 degrees apart on the anterior side were used to record strains as the bone was torqued in increments of 1.13 N-M (10 in-lb). The principal strains on the posterior determined experimentally were within 10% of each other and occurred at 45 ± 3 degrees. The maximum strain on the posterior side was 40% higher than the maximum strain on the anterior side of the femur, confirming the stress sensitivity of the posterior. The bone fractured at a torque of 22.6 N-M (200 in-lb) forming a 45 degree spiral fracture line. The relationship between strain and torque is linear (Figure 3). The discrepancy between the magnitudes of principal strains and their deviance from the expected 45 degree location was most likely due to a slight misalignment of the bone axis causing some bending. A second strain gage experiment was performed on a second sheep femur in which three strain gages were mounted 45 degrees apart on the anterior side. In this experiment the principal strains occurred at 45 degrees with virtually no difference in magnitude.

Although bone is a viscoelastic, anisotropic, nonhomogeneous material, the stress is proportional to the strain in the elastic region. Thus, the stress concentration factor determined from the photoelastic model can be written as:

$$Ktg = (\sigma_1)_{hole} / (\sigma_1)_{nominal} \qquad (1)$$

Using normal incidence measurements, the data obtained is the difference in principal stresses or maximum shear stress, thus the ratio between the shear stress at the hole to the shear stress away from the hole is:

$$\text{shear ratio} = (\sigma_1 - \sigma_2)_{hole} / (\sigma_1 - \sigma_2)_{nominal} \qquad (2)$$

However, $\sigma_2 = 0$ at the free surface around the hole and $\sigma_1 - \sigma_2 = 2\sigma_1$ nominally, thus:

$$\text{shear ratio} = (\sigma_1)_{hole} / (2\sigma_1)_{nominal} \qquad (3)$$

The shear ratio (eq. 3) is one-half the magnitude of the stress concentration factor (eq.1), thus the stress concentration can be defined in terms of the shear ratio as:

$$Ktg = 2(\text{shear ratio}) \qquad (4)$$

The relationship between the fringe order and the difference in stress is:

$$\sigma_1 - \sigma_2 = N\lambda / 2 t_c K C x (E_b /1+\upsilon_b) \qquad (5)$$

where: N - the fringe order (normal incidence) determined experimentally
λ - wave length of white light, 5.77E-4mm (22.7E-6 inches)
t_c - thickness of the birefringent coating
K - strain optical constant of the coating, (0.091 determined experimentally)
C - reinforcement correction factor
E_b - modulus of elasticity of the bone
υ_b - poisson ratio of the bone

Using the photoelastic relationship (eq. 5) and the relationship between shear stresses (eq. 4), the stress concentration factor is:

$$Ktg = 2(N\lambda /2t_c KC)_{hole} x (E_b /1+\upsilon_b)$$
$$/(N\lambda /2t_c KC)_{nominal} x (E_b /1+\upsilon_b) \qquad (6)$$

Making the assumption that the strain optical constant, reinforcement factor, modulus of elasticity, and poisson ratio are constant across the surface of the bone, the above equation can be simplified to:

$$Ktg = 2(N)_{hole} (t_c)_{nominal} / (N)_{nominal} (t_c)_{hole} \qquad (7)$$

If the coating thickness at the hole is the same as the nominal thickness the stress concentration is simply:

$$Ktg = 2N_{hole} / N_{nominal} \qquad (8)$$

RESULTS

The location of the maximum strains in the bone at the boundary of the hole were found to rotate through an angle, $\Delta\theta$ from the 45 degree location and is a function of defect ratio a/D (Figure 4). The shift occurs for both the tensile and compressive concentrations, i.e., the concentrations shift toward the midsection of the tube. The shift appears to be linear, with the best fit line: $\Delta\theta = 36.59(a/D)-4.85$, Rsq = 0.94. Accuracy in the measurements of the strain locations is estimated at ± 3 degrees. The stress distribution around the hole is symmetric about the center axis of the hole. Figure 5 shows a sketch of the isochromatic fringe pattern traced from a photograph of a 55.5% defect in the d/D = 0.76 femur. The stress concentration factors are listed in Table 1, their estimated accuracy is $\pm 5\%$.

Table 1 - Stress concentration factors (d/D = 0.75)

Defect (a/D)	S.C.F	Shift $\Delta\theta$
0.104	3.78	0
0.209	4.00	0
0.322	4.84	10
0.444	5.85	10
0.555	6.55	15
0.664	7.62	20

Figure 6 shows the stress concentration factor (Ktg) versus the defect ratio (hole diameter/bone outer diameter). The relationship appears to be second order for defects up to 30% and linear for defects from 30% to 66%.

DISCUSSION and CONCLUSIONS

The stress concentrations around circular defects in bone were found to shift from the predicted 45 degree location. The location and magnitude of the stress concentration factor is dependant upon two factors, the hole's radius of curvature and the net reduction in material from the midsection of the bone. As the curvature of the hole increases, Ktg is expected to decrease, much like the stress concentration decrease seen by increasing the radius of a fillet in a stressed region. However, as the hole curvature increases the hole diameter increases and the remaining material in the region of the hole is decreased. This causes an increase in the stress concentration and a shift in the location of the maximum stress toward the midsection of the bone. This finding is consistent with Kuo's acrylic fracture model, of which the inner to outer diameter was 0.6. It is difficult to directly compare the stress concentration factors in the bone to the previous photoelastic, finite element, or fracture models because of the eccentric cross section of the bone. However, using the hole diameter divided by the medial/lateral diameter as a/D, seems logical because this is the diameter perpendicular to the direction of the defect. The stress concentration factors for defects from 10% to 30% in the bone compare well with interpolated values from Jessop's photoelastic results with a/D=0.75. However, Jessop's Ktg for a 40% defect is 11% higher than an interpolated Ktg from this study. This discrepancy is due to the two-sided hole present in Jessop's study in which the removal of material is large. Because Jessop took slices at 45 degrees from the tube axis while this study would predict a maximum stress location closer to 35 degrees, the actual Ktg would be expected to be higher than Jessop's reported value. No data is available from Jessop to compare 50% and 60% defects.

REFERENCES

1. Savin, G.N. (1961) Stress Concentrations Around Holes New York: Pergamon Press. P.234-300.

2. Jessop, H.T., Snell, C. & Allison, I.M. (1959), "Stress Concentration Factors in Cylindrical Tubes with Transverse Circular Holes" Aeronautical Quarterly P. 326-344.

3. Kuo, R.F. (1989), "Stress Concentration and Torsional Strength Of Tubular Structure with Circular Defect" Orthopaedic Research

4. Bartlett, J.P. (1989) "Finite Element Modeling Of Circular Cortical Defects In Bone" MS Thesis North Dakota State University, Fargo, ND

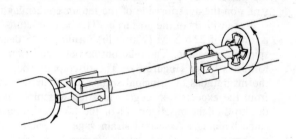

Figure 1 - Loading fixture and setup

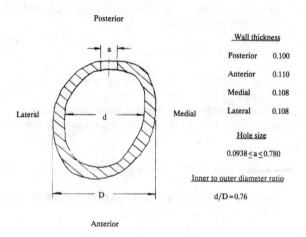

Figure 2 - Sheep femur cross section

Wall thickness	
Posterior	0.100
Anterior	0.110
Medial	0.108
Lateral	0.108

Hole size

$0.0938 \leq a \leq 0.780$

Inner to outer diameter ratio

$d/D = 0.76$

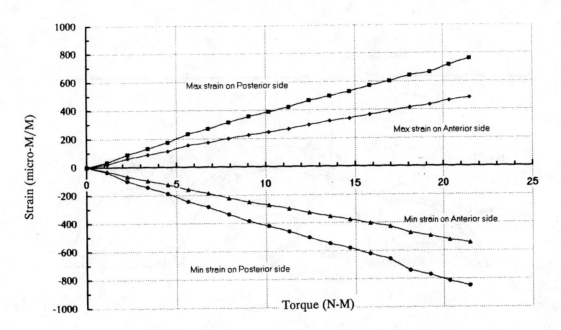

Figure 3 - Strain gage experiment, Principal strains vs. Torque

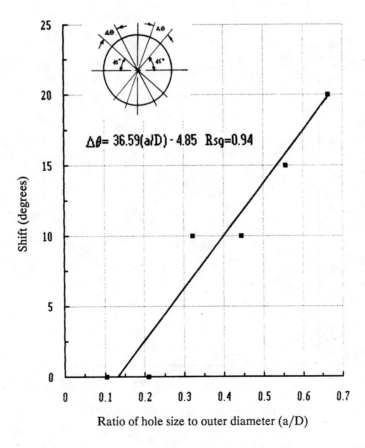

$$\Delta\theta = 36.59(a/D) - 4.85 \quad R_{sq} = 0.94$$

Figure 4 - Shift in maximum stress location

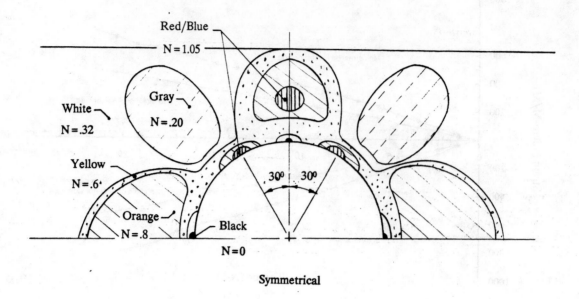

Symmetrical

$$S.C.F = 2(N_{hole}/N_{nominal}) = 2(1.05/.32) = 6.55$$

Figure 5 - Isochromatic fringe pattern for 55.5% defect (a/D=0.555)

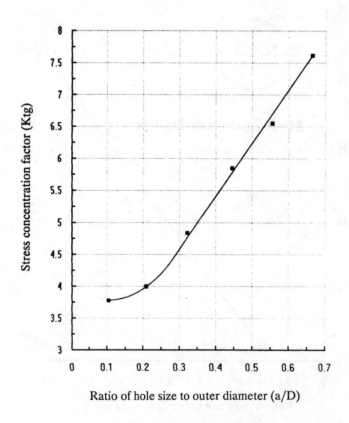

Ratio of hole size to outer diameter (a/D)

Figure 6 - Stress concentration factor vs. defect ratio (a/D)

FRACTIONAL FRINGE MOIRE' INTERFEROMETRY ON

BOVINE CORTICAL BONE COMPACT TENSION SPECIMENS

J. P. Bartlett, G. R. Gessel, A. S. Voloshin, and P-H. Tsao

ABSTRACT

Fractional fringe moire' interferometry was used to obtain displacement data on the surface of bovine cortical bone compact tension specimens. Stress intensities and strain concentrations were measured.

INTRODUCTION

The frequency of accidental bone fracture and the demand for reliable bone and joint prostheses have resulted in a need for cortical bone stress-intensity values. If cortical bone micro-strain characteristics were more fully understood, optimizing prosthesis design would be easier.

Bone fracture characteristics are dependent on age, sex, diet, exercise and the presence of any degenerative diseases. At a microscopic level, fracture in bone is dependent on osteon volume fraction, osteon orientation, material anisotropy, intrinsic flaw size, crack propagation rate, porosity, density and crack orientation.

To gain a better understanding of cortical bone stress intensity factors and micro-strain concentrations fractional fringe moire' interferometry (FFMI) was used to locate and measure strain concentrations in bovine cortical femoral bone. Stress-intensity factors were obtained from FFMI displacements and compared to same values obtained using load-displacement curves. Prior to this work, moire' interferometry had not been used to study bone.

BACKGROUND

The structural unit of compact bone is the osteon. Although bone is anisotropic, under controlled conditions cortical bone can be modeled as linear, orthotropic, and elastic (Cowin & Hart, 1990). Orthotropic elastic properties were available in the literature (Cowin, 1989) and were used for all stress intensity calculations.

J. P. Bartlett is Graduate Teaching Fellow, G. R. Gessel is Associate Professor, Department of Mechanical Engineering and Applied Mechanics, North Dakota State University, Fargo, ND, USA. A. S. Voloshin is Associate Professor, P-H. Tsao is Graduate Research Assistant, Department of Mechanical Engineering and Mechanics, Lehigh University, Bethlehem, PA, USA.

The compact tension (CT) fracture test allowed for the smallest specimen and was the most suitable for studying cortical bone. The CT bone specimens are detailed in Figure 1, together with the seven sizes used in this work. In Figure 1, "a" is the crack length, and "W" is the specimen width, as prescribed in ASTM Standard E399-83. The loading holes and crack tip root were each 0.79 mm (1/32 inch) in diameter. "B" is the specimen width. Notch width was 0.508 mm (0.020 inch) for all specimens. The crack tip and notch were centered between the top and bottom edges of the specimen.

According to Piekarski (1970), bone can be classified as a composite material. He concluded that bone fractures as a brittle material at high strain rates and the failure mechanism depends on strain rate. Consequently, this work used a crosshead speed appropriate for linear elastic fracture mechanics (8.4 x 10^{-6} m/sec from Bonfield, Grynpas, & Young, 1978).

Bonfield and Behiri (1989, p. 618) stated: "Circumscribing the outermost concentric lamella of the Haversian system is a narrow zone known as the cement line, which contains calcified mucopolysaccharides and is devoid of collagen. It is 1-2 μm thick and is the weakest constituent of bone." Piekarski (1970) observed osteon pull-out at the cement lines during slow crack propagation. These observations prompted the expectation that strain concentrations would be observed at osteon intersections (i.e., cement lines).

The small plastic zone size of Robertson, Robertson, and Barrett (1978) indicated linear elastic fracture. To determine K_I from FFMI displacement data, equation 1 was evaluated (Hellan, 1984). The critical value (K_{IC}) was found by calculating K_I at fracture.

$$K_I = C_{1n} (2 \pi)^{1/2} \tag{1}$$

To determine C_{1n} the Cartesian components of the displacements were measured experimentally, and expressed in polar coordinates using equation 2.

$$U = U_r \cos \theta - U_\theta \sin \theta \tag{2}$$

Finally, the C_{1n} term was calculated using equations 3 and 4.

$$U_r = \sum_{n=1,3\ldots}^{\inf} r^{n/2}\, c_{1n} \left(\frac{1}{2G(1+v)}\right) \left[\frac{(2(3-4v)-n)(1+v)}{2}\cos\frac{n-2}{2}\theta\right.$$

$$\left. +\frac{(n-2)(1+v)}{2}\cos\frac{n+2}{2}\theta\right] +$$

$$\sum_{n=2,4\ldots}^{\inf} r^{n/2}\, c_{1n} \left(\frac{1}{2G(1+v)}\right) \left[\frac{(2(3-4v)-n)(1+v)}{2}\cos\frac{n-2}{2}\theta\right.$$

$$\left. +\frac{(n+2)(1+v)}{2}\cos\frac{n+2}{2}\theta\right] \qquad (3)$$

$$U_\theta = \sum_{n=1,3\ldots}^{\inf} r^{n/2}\, c_{1n} \left(\frac{1}{2G(1+v)}\right) \left[\frac{(1+v)(n+2(3-4v))}{2}\sin\frac{n-2}{2}\theta\right.$$

$$\left. -\frac{(n-2)(1+v)}{2}\sin\frac{n+2}{2}\theta\right] +$$

$$\sum_{n=2,4\ldots}^{\inf} r^{n/2}\, c_{1n} \left(\frac{1}{2G(1+v)}\right) \left[\frac{(1+v)(n+2(3-4v))}{2}\sin\frac{n-2}{2}\theta\right.$$

$$\left. -\frac{(n+2)(1+v)}{2}\sin\frac{n+2}{2}\theta\right] \qquad (4)$$

where: r represents the radial distance from the crack tip to the point of interest.

θ is the angle from the crack plane measured clockwise to the r vector.

G is the shear modulus.

v is Poisson's ratio.

n represents the term number in the series.

Displacement data for the calculation of stress intensity factors has been determined using moire' interferometry (Bastawros & Voloshin, 1990). In FFMI, digital image analysis is used to enhance the moire' fringe patterns (Post, 1987).

FFMI with its 0.417 μm per fringe order resolution is suitable for studying bone fracture morphology and determining fracture toughness of bone. The Haversian canals in cortical bone range in size from 22 to 110 μm and are surrounded by concentric lamellae forming osteons that range from 34 to 250 μm in diameter (Bonfield & Behiri, 1989).

METHODOLOGY

Bovine bone was chosen because it was available and had widely published mechanical and fracture properties. Bone from seven to eight year old (adult) Holstein cows was used for this study. Each CT specimen was extracted from a bovine femora at mid-diaphysis (mid-shaft) posterior. Using specimens from this single location minimized structural variations and maximized osteon content. Maximum osteon content was desirable because human bone is primarily osteon bone. Five identical specimens were used in order to determine scatter in the critical stress intensity values. Crack orientations longitudinal to the bone axis have been reported to be most physiologic (Bonfield, Grynpas, & Young, 1978), see Figure 2.

Immediately following slaughter, the femora used in this study were kept in ice 30 minutes prior to being rough cut with a band saw. When not undergoing either preparation or moire' testing operations each specimen was wrapped in a saline soaked cloth, placed into an air tight, resealable plastic bag and frozen. Dry ice was used to keep specimens frozen during transportation. All testing was completed within four weeks of slaughter in accordance with Sedlin and Hirsch (1966).

Figure 3 is a photograph of the motorized mechanical crosshead unit. This unit was attached to a rotating plate fixed perpendicular to a rotating table. The rotating plate and rotating table were used to obtain degrees of freedom necessary for laser alignment. A load cell was fabricated using one tee rosette strain gage (Micro-Measurements, EA-13-100TG-350) on each side of a 1.59 mm (1/16 inch) thick aluminum beam.

Upper and lower clevis units were used to transfer crosshead displacement and fixation to the CT bone specimens using loading pins. The clevis configuration that resulted from several design iterations is illustrated in Figure 4. This Figure shows both upper and lower clevis units. Each CT specimen was mounted on the front of the clevis units and retained with loading pins. This forward specimen position was needed to prevent interference with the laser beams.

Millivolt analog output from a Micro-Measurements P-3500 required amplification to work with the data aquisition system. This data aquisition system was a model DAS-16 card with Streamer software (both from MetraByte Inc.). A two stage instrumentation amplifier with total gain of 477 was constructed.

Immediately prior to the moire' submaster to bone replication, each bone specimen was thawed and dried using compressed air. Using surgical tweezers, each specimen was placed into a 0.01 ml pool of optical cement (NOA 61 UV manufactured by Norland Products, Inc.). One edge of the specimen was lowered first followed by the opposite edge to minimize air entrapment. Specimen movement was minimized following the placement of the bone specimen onto the silicone rubber submaster. Specimen movement after this placement caused air entrapment, decreased reflectivity, and reduced the grating to bone adhesion area. Using a 1.0 ml syringe, optical cement was dropped onto the submaster at the desired specimen location. The specimen's weight was used to seat it against the alignment bar by holding the submaster at a slight incline for ten seconds while the bone specimen slid toward the alignment bar in the pool of uncured optical cement. Additional weights were delicately placed onto each specimen. These weights applied 10 to 30 KPa to the optical cement to produce a 25 μm thick grating. This grating thickness both minimized the effect on deformation loads, and provided enough cement to complete the grating replication. Excess optical cement was removed using tissue paper.

Following placement on the submaster, the specimen and submaster were exposed to ultraviolet light for 20 minutes to cure the cement. Subsequently, the specimen was pried free from the submaster using a razor blade. This left a reflective aluminum grating on the bone surface. The small amount of optical cement which cured in specimen notch was considered insignificant. Prior to mounting each specimen into the test system, cured optical cement was cleaned from the load pin holes using a 0.794 mm (1/32 inch) drill. Total air exposure time, including moire' testing, for each bone specimen was less than one hour.

Following application of the reflective grating, the specimen was mounted into the test system clevis units. All specimens were oriented such that the moire' U-field was parallel with the principal displacement direction of the CT specimen geometry. Clevis pins were then inserted and the specimen was pushed against the parallel backing plates in order to minimize both twisting and bending. Once the specimen was in test system, all mirrors and the laser beam were adjusted to bring the fixed virtual grating and the displaceable specimen grating into coincidence on the specimen surface.

Next, a U field fringe pattern was observed on the television screen, video recording commenced, and the test system was switched on. The crosshead moved at a constant rate of 8.4 x 10^{-6} m/sec until specimen failure while the data aquisition system recorded ten load values per second. Following fracture, the video camera and data aquisition system were switched off. Once the fringe patterns were recorded on VHS video tape, only displacement field analysis remained to be completed.

Dynamic moire' fringe patterns were captured at the rate of 30 frames per second. The first seven seconds of loading history provided the clearest fringe patterns for determining strain concentrations. Both visual fringe counting methods and fractional fringe image processing were used to extract normal strain concentrations.

Visual Fringe Counting

Counting the moire' fringes visually was most

efficient and adequate. This was done by viewing one video frame at a time. Strain concentration regions were identified by a three step process. First, the location of the zero displacement fringes were identified in regions where they would occur for the specimen geometry and loading. Second, all dark and light fringes were scanned to identify regions of fringe concentration. Finally, fringe concentration regions were checked for air pockets and grating defects. Air pockets appeared as black areas with smooth perimeters. Haversian canals, Volkmann canals, and grating defects also appeared as black areas but had their respective outlines. Air pocket and grating defect conditions occasionally caused a strain concentration. A strain concentration was considered valid and measured if it was found free from air pockets and grating defects.

To measure a strain concentration, a line was drawn perpendicular to the CT starter notch and extended through the region of highest fringe concentration. A second line was drawn parallel to the first through the nearest region of nominal fringe separation. A dark fringe bounding the concentrated region was taken as the datum fringe. The distance across this concentrated region and the distance across the same number of fringes in the nominal region were measured using a metric engineering scale. The number of millimeters in the nominal region divided by the number of millimeters in the concentrated region defined the strain concentration, equation 5. The displacement of the bone surface between fringe centers was 1/2400 millimeters.

$$K = \frac{\text{mm Across Nominal Region Fringes}}{\text{mm Across Concentrated Region Fringes}} \quad (5)$$

Fractional Fringe Methodology

A PC-based digital image processing system was used to grab video frames and analyze their respective fringe patterns pixel by pixel. The host computer was a Zenith ZBF-2526 work station running at 12 Mhz with a 80287 math coprocessor.

Following the recording of moire' fringe patterns, the VHS data video was played back to monitor each frame simultaneously on a black and white television screen and the PC monitor. Video frames were grabbed at desired times. Time was measured from the start of the crosshead movement and was easily tracked by a time display overlaying each image. Once a frame was grabbed, lines of displacement were chosen with either a mouse or keypad. Each line was composed of pixels for which displacements were calculated based on the light intensity. The calculated displacements were all U directed, as dictated by the moire' field selection. The pixel lines were chosen to minimize the influence of air pockets, bone structure shadows, and grating defects. The clearest contrast between dark and light fringes was desired.

Surface displacements were then calculated and saved to file. A QuickBasic program was written to subtract the null field from the final displacement field and convert the resulting net displacements into X and Y coordinates measured from the crack tip. The program's input parameters included the screen vertical pixel to horizontal pixel aspect ratio, the beginning pixel coordinate of the selected line, the crack tip pixel coordinates, the full scale horizontal length across the crack tip diameter, and the pixel horizontal length across the displayed crack tip diameter. This program wrote a file containing x, y coordinates and net displacement data of selected points. This file was used as input to a FORTRAN program used to calculate stress intensity values.

RESULTS

Effects of Optical Cement on Fracture Toughness

Five specimens, with the size three dimensions given in Figure 1, were used to study the effect of the optical cement on K_{IC}. Three specimens had no cement and two were coated liberally with optical cement before grating transfer. This application of excess optical cement resulted in loads three pounds higher than those without cement and resulted in a 0.3 MPa $M^{1/2}$ increase in K_{IC}. This effect was mostly caused by optical cement in the notch. Most of the cement in the notch was removed from each of the 35 test specimens before ultra violet curing. Consequently, the loads induced by the remaining optical cement was considered insignificant.

Cement Line Micro-Strain Concentrations

Study of normal strain concentrations (K) near the crack tip revealed from one to five obvious sites within 3 mm^2 area on each CT specimen. K values ranged from 1 to 5.

Figure 5 is a single video frame taken of the moire' fringe pattern observed on a size three CT specimen. Five strain concentrations are identified with their respective values. K values were obtained from video frames about one second after load application. The normal strain concentrations remained constant during the first seven seconds of loading. Prior to seven seconds, fringes remained low in number and clear in contrast. The orientation, location, and size of the strain concentrations correlated to the cement lines which surround osteons.

Stress Intensity Values

Mode I critical stress intensity factors (K_{IC}) were evaluated using two methods. For benchmarking purposes, load versus deflection curves were used as described in the Standard Test Method for Plane Strain Fracture Toughness of Metallic Materials, ASTM E399-83. Table 1 lists the compact tension specimen sizes, dimensions as detailed in Figure 1, K_{IC} values, and K_{IC} standard deviations (σ). All of the K_{IC} values in Table 1 were accurate to 0.2 MPa $m^{1/2}$.

Table 1 Average Compact Tension Specimen Critical Stress Intensities

Size	Dimensions (mm)			K_{IC} (MPa m$^{1/2}$)	σ
	a	W	B		
1	4.50	9.00	5.11	3.5	1.4
2	3.99	7.98	5.11	6.5	0.8
3	3.51	6.93	5.11	2.9	0.9
4	3.00	5.82	5.08	3.6	0.2
5	2.49	5.03	4.60	3.8	0.6
6	2.01	3.91	4.14	3.7	1.1
7	1.50	2.97	4.11	4.6	0.4

The second method of evaluating critical stress intensity values required the moire' displacement field data and used the FORTRAN coded form of equations 1 through 4. The K_{IC} results obtained using this method were within 1 Mpa m$^{1/2}$ of those obtained using the load verses deflection curves (See Table 1). This method required subtraction of rotational displacements, precise location of a point relative to the crack tip, and extrapolation of stress intensities measured at early times (one to seven seconds) to the critical time.

The average K_{IC} determined for the crosshead speed of 8.4×10^{-6} m/sec was 3.7 MPa $M^{1/2}$. Bonfield, Grynpas, & Young (1978) found K_{IC} to be 3.4 MPa $M^{1}/^{2}$ for the same crosshead speed. Nine percent difference between the two studies was considered acceptable in view of biological variations.

In-Plane Rigid-Body Rotational Fringes

In-plane rigid-body rotation was apparent in the moire' fringe patterns. This rotational component was inherent to the small CT bone specimens and tended to multiply the number of moire' fringes. Net surface displacements were obtained by subtracting the rotational components. Fringes attributed to rotation increased linearly to fracture. At fracture, these rotational fringes corresponded to a 0.02 mm displacement in the moire' surface plane perpendicular to the crack tip and at a distance one millimeter away from the crack tip.

DISCUSSION

For the present analysis, a visual fringe counting technique for the determination of normal strain concentrations was more expedient than fractional fringe methods. This was because the CT specimen geometry gave rise to relatively large displacements, and resulted in a large number of fringes per unit length. The fractional fringe computing time and the visual pixel by pixel analysis that was required by the fractional fringe software proved tedious. However, using the fractional fringe displacement data as input to a FORTRAN stress intensity (K_I) code was an efficient method for determining stress intensity values.

Aligning the moire' U-field along the principal strain direction of the CT specimens produced the greatest number of fringes per unit length.

In retrospect, fewer fringes per unit length would be preferred. Therefore, a specimen orientation with the U moire' displacement field perpendicular to a principal displacement direction would be preferable. Reduced fringe densities would allow recording of clear fringe patterns at later times. The recording of both U and V fields would be even more desirable because transverse shear strains could be determined (Post, 1987).

Clinical Relevance

This work represented the first measurement of strain concentrations in bone. Strain concentrations are a topic of considerable interest in bone biomechanics (D. Fyhrie, Director, Henry Ford Hospital, Bone and Joint Center, personal communication, July 30, 1991). For example, bone strain concentrations are needed by finite element models that are being used to study remodeling processing in human cortical bone. These models use Wolf's law and bone strain concentrations to predict bone growth.

This study was the first to use moire' interferometry on bone. This successful application of moire' interferometry and fractional fringe moire' interferometry to cortical bone should encourage further use of moire' interferometry on animal and human bone.

Strain concentrations at cement lines was evidence that micro-fractures may begin along cement lines. Computed tomography can identify three dimensional cement lines in cortical bone. Finite element models could then identify the highest strain concentration sites.

CONCLUSIONS

Moire' interferometry and fractional fringe moire' interferometry were used for the first time on bone. Optical cement was sufficient to adhere displacable moire' gratings to bovine cortical bone CT specimen polished surfaces.

The application of a grating with optical cement increased fracture loads by three pounds. This corresponded to a 0.3 MPa m$^{1/2}$ increase in fracture toughness (K_{IC}) and was mostly caused by optical cement in the notch. The loads induced by the optical cement were insignificant.

The study of normal strains near the crack tip revealed three to five obvious sites of strain concentration within an area 3 mm^2. Strain concentration values ranged from 1 to 5. The structure to which these concentrations corresponded were cement lines. Normal strain concentrations were not induced at Haversian canals.

No correlation was found between the number or magnitude of surface strain concentrations to K_{IC}.

In-plane rigid-body rotation was apparent from the moire' fringe patterns. This rotational component, inherent to the geometry of small CT specimens and the micro-structure of cortical bone, multiplied the number of moire' fringes. This rigid-body rotation did not effect normal strain values.

REFERENCES

ASTM Standard E399-83. (1983). Annual Book of ASTM Standards, 681-705.

Bastawros, A. F., & Voloshin, A. S. (1990). Mixed Mode Stress-Intensity Factors By Fractional Fringe Moire' Interferometry. Proceedings of the 1990 SEM Spring Conference on Experimental Mechanics, 69-75.

Bonfield, W., & Behiri, J. C. (1989). Fracture Toughness of Natural Composites with Reference to Cortical Bone. In K. Friedrich (Ed.), Application of Fracture Mechanics to Composite Materials (pp. 615-627). Elsevier Science Publishers.

Bonfield, W., Grynpas, M. D., & Young, R. J. (1978). Crack Velocity and the Fracture of Bone. Journal of Biomechanics, 11, 473-479.

Cowin, S. C. (1989). Bone Mechanics. Boca Raton: CRC Press.

Cowin, S. C., & Hart, R. T. (1990). Technical Note: Errors in the Orientation of the Principal Stress Axes if Bone Tissue is Modeled as Isotropic. Journal of Biomechanics, 23(4), 349-352.

Hellan, J. K. (1984). The Stationary Crack under Static Loading. Introduction to Fracture Mechanics (pp. 7-14). New York: McGraw-Hill.

Piekarski, K. (1970). Fracture of Bone. Journal of Applied Physics, 41(1), 215-223.

Post, D. (1987). Moire' Interferometry. In A. S. Kobayashi, (Ed.), Handbook of Experimental Mechanics (pp. 314-487). Englewood Cliffs, NJ: Prentice Hall.

Robertson, D. M., Robertson, D., & Barrett, C. R. (1978). Fracture Toughness, Critical Crack Length and Plastic Zone Size in Bone. Journal of Biomechanics, 11, 359-364.

Sedlin, E. D., & Hirsch, C. (1966). Factors Affecting the Determination of the Physical Properties of Femoral Cortical Bone. Acta Orthop. Scand., 37, 29-48.

Adult Cow Femora Compact
Tension Specimen Dimensions

Size	Dimensions (mm)		
	a	W	B
1	4.50	9.00	5.11
2	3.99	7.98	5.11
3	3.51	6.93	5.11
4	3.00	5.82	5.08
5	2.49	5.03	4.60
6	2.01	3.91	4.14
7	1.50	2.97	4.11

ASTM Standard

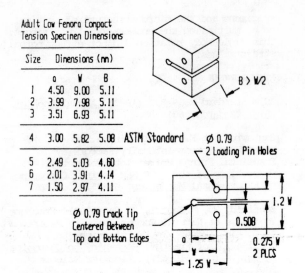

B > W/2

Ø 0.79
2 Loading Pin Holes

Ø 0.79 Crack Tip
Centered Between
Top and Bottom Edges

1.2 W

0.508

a

W

1.25 W

0.275 W
2 PLCS

Figure 1. Detail of Compact tension Bone Specimen.

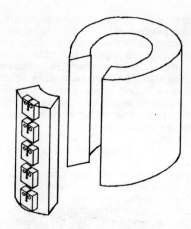

Figure 2. Compact Tension Specimens in Bovine Cortical Bone Illustrating Crack Orientation in Posterior Section.

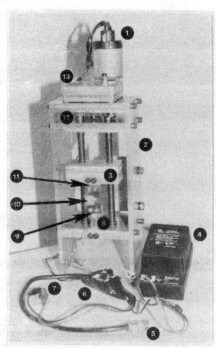

Figure 3. Motorized Mechanical Crosshead Unit.
(1) Permanent magnet DC gearmotor, 0.3 amp, 12 volt, 2410:1, 50 inch-lb. (2) Loading Frame. (3) Crosshead. (4) Universal ac/dc adapter with off/on and polarity switch for up/down. (5) Connector from P-3500 mv strain output. (6) Motor and load cell remote switches. (7) Clips to connect with amplifier. (8) Aluminum beam load cell, tee-rosette strain gages, and wiring. (9) Lower clevis unit. (10) Fractured compact tension bone specimen with grating. (11) Upper clevis unit. (12) Precision spur gears. (13) 15 turn, 100 Ohm potentiometer.

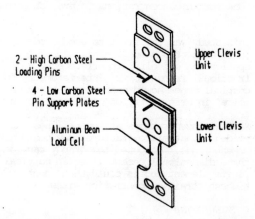

2 - High Carbon Steel
Loading Pins

4 - Low Carbon Steel
Pin Support Plates

Aluminum Beam
Load Cell

Upper Clevis
Unit

Lower Clevis
Unit

Figure 4. Upper and lower Clevis Units Used to Load Compact Tension Bone Specimens.

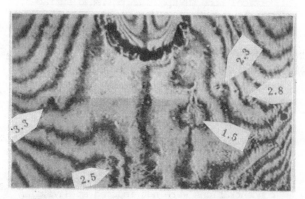

Figure 5. Normal Strain Concentrations at Osteon Intersections on Compact Tension Specimen Surface.

ULTRASONIC MEASUREMENT OF THICKNESSES OF BONE AND BONE MARROW

WITHIN FEMUR INSERTED WITH A METAL STEM

Yoshihisa MINAKUCHI, Takatoshi IDE, Kenji TACHI,
Hajime MURABAYASHI and Noriya AKAMATSU

ABSTRACT

The thicknesses of bone and bone marrow within a pig femur inserted with a metal stem are investigated non-destructively by means of an ultrasonic technique. These results are compared with those of a vernier calipers, and both results are graphically presented. The utility of the proposed method is also discussed.

1. INTRODUCTION

Non-destructive measurement in thicknesses of bone and bone marrow within femur inserted with a prosthesis stem of the total hip replacement system is important to study stress-related bone structure, load transfer in bone-prosthesis stem interface and to predict the onset of advanced osteoporosis. Especially, the postoperative loosening between the prosthesis stem and the bone is related to the geometrical factors of the prosthesis and the bone structure. Thus, an accurate measurement of the bone thickness within femur inserted with a prosthesis stem is very important clinically. The measurement of the bone thickness within femur has mostly been reported based on the roentgenography [1][2] as well as CT scans. Recently, an ultrasonic method is used to measure the bone thickness within femur. The thicknesses of bone and bone marrow within femur inserted with the prosthesis stem can not exactly measure by using the roentgenography and CT scans because of halation caused by the prosthesis stem. In this problem, the ultrasonic method is considered to be most effective. But, this study seems to have been done yet [3].

The thicknesses of bone and bone marrow within a pig femur inserted with a metal stem are investigated non-destructively by means of the ultrasonic method. First, the wave velocities of bone and bone marrow are determined using the ultrasonic pulse echo technique and thereby observing the time intervals between the first and the second echoes in these specimens. Next, an ultrasonic wave is emitted toward the femur inserted with the metal stem which is immersed in the water tank, and the distances from a normal probe to the boundary surfaces of the bone and the metal stem are measured by using the linear scanning and circular scanning methods. Subsequently, the real thicknesses of the bone and the bone marrow are measured by using a vernier calipers. The measured results of the ultrasonic wave and the vernier calipers are graphically presented and are compared. The utility of the proposed ultrasonic method is investigated.

2. MEASUREMENT PRINCIPLE OF ULTRASONIC PULSE ECHO TECHNIQUE

When an ultrasonic wave arrives perpendicularly at a boundary surface between dissimilar media, a part of the wave is reflected and the other part is transmitted. Then the relation between the sound pressure of reflection wave P_r and incident wave P_1 are given as follows:

$$R_p = \frac{P_r}{P_1} = \frac{Z_2 - Z_1}{Z_1 + Z_2}$$
$$= \frac{\rho_2 C_2 - \rho_1 C_1}{\rho_1 C_1 + \rho_2 C_2} \qquad (1)$$

Where R_p is the reflection coefficient. Z_1 and Z_2 are acoustic impedances in the

Y. Minakuchi is Associate Professor in the Faculty of Engineering, Yamanashi University, 4-3-11, Takeda, Kofu-shi, Yamanashi Pref. 400, Japan.
T. Ide is Assistant in the Department of Orthopaedic Surgery, Yamanashi Medical College, 1110, Shimokato, Tamaho-cho, Nakakoma-gun, Yamanashi Pref. 409-38, Japan.
K. Tachi is a Graduate Student in the Faculty of Engineering, Yamanashi University.
H. Murabayashi is an Engineer, Kyocera Corporation, 46-1, Takehana-donomae-cho Yamashina-ku, Kyoto 607, Japan.
N. Akamatsu is Professor in the Department of Orthopaedic Surgery, Yamanashi Medical College.

media 1 and 2, respectively. These are expressed as the product of density ρ_i (i=1,2) and wave velocity C_i (i=1,2) in these media.

Figure 1 is a measurement principle of ultrasonic pulse echo technique by an immersion testing. It is shown the situation that the ultrasonic pulse emitted from a normal probe propagates through the living body which is immersed in the water tank. Then, the relation between the echo height and the time is shown. From this figure, the distance l_i between each boundary surface is given as follows:

$$l_i = v_i \times \frac{t_i}{2} \quad (i=1,2,3,\cdots) \qquad (2)$$

where v_i is the wave velocity and t_i is the round trip propagation time. Accordingly, if v_i is a known value, l_i is obtained by measuring t_i.

3. WAVE VELOCITY MEASUREMENT OF BONE

3.1 Experimental method

In order to measure the thickness of a bone by using the ultrasonic wave, the wave velocity through the bone needs to be previously selected.

Two femurs of pigs as shown in Fig.2 are used. The bone chips of about thickness 2mm are prepared from the parts of ①~⑤ of the center of the bone. After glycerin is painted on each bone chip as a coupling medium, the normal probe (frequency:5MHz, diameter of transducer:6mm) is attached on each bone chip and is pressed with a load of 2.3N. Next, the wave velocity through the bone is selected so that the thickness of the bone chip and the distance on a CRT display of the ultrasonic device agree. A gain set up to 30dB. Furthermore, the normal probe will be used even each experiment after this.

3.2 Measured results

Table 1, 2 show the measured results of the thickness and the wave velocity through the bone chips which is 2520 ~3000m/s. This value changes to depend on the organization condition of the bone. Therefore, the wave velocity adopts the mean value of 2775m/s.

4. WAVE VELOCITY MEASUREMENT OF BONE MARROW

4.1 Experimental method

In order to measure the thickness of a bone marrow, the wave velocity through the bone marrow at the living body temperature needs to be previously selected.

The bone marrow taken out from a femur is tightly sealed in an aluminum container as shown in Fig.3. The bone marrow is warmed up until temperature becomes 38℃. A normal probe is attached to the upper part of the aluminum container in this condition.

Then, the wave velocity of the bone marrow is selected so that the thickness of the bone marrow and the distance on a CRT display of the ultrasonic device agree. A gain set up to 40dB.

4.2 Measured results

The wave velocity in the bone marrow is 1410m/s at 38℃. Furthermore, the bone marrow mixes with liquid and jelly at the living body temperature.

5. EXPERIMENTAL METHOD OF THE THICKNESS WITHIN FEMUR INSERTED WITH A METAL STEM

5.1 Production method of measurement specimen

In order to measure the thickness through the bone inserted with the metal stem, ultrasonic pulse echo technique by the immersion testing is used. The femur is cut in round pieces about length 30mm from parts of ①, ②, ③ in Fig.2. The square metal stem of 12mm, or the circular metal stem of diameter 12mm is inserted inner these specimens. Then, the rubber plate of thickness 3mm is bonded to the one side of the bone. Furthermore, the other side of the bone tightly seals by using a thin and transparent plastic.

Figure 4 shows the femur specimen inserted with the square and circular metal stems. This section is observed from a condyle side. Furthermore, the sides of A, B, C and D is determined every 90°. The metal stem is inserted so as to become as parallel as possible.

5.2 Measuring method of thickness inside bone by linear scanning
5.2.1 Bone inserted with a square metal stem

The femur specimen is putted in the water at 38℃ in Fig.4. First, the thickness inside the bone is measured by the linear scanning method. Fig.4(a) shows the situation that the bone inserted with the square metal stem of 12mm is fixed to the position about 19mm apart from the normal probe. When the normal probe moves a straight line at the upper surface in the water every 1~2mm toward z´ axis, an echo position reflected from the boundary surface is measured. At this time, the wave velocity of the ultrasonic device set up to 1410m/s which is the wave velocity of bone marrow. Also, a gain set up to 60dB. Furthermore, the thickness inside the bone is measured in 4 sides of A~D as shown in Fig.4.

In order to check a fundamental echo characteristic reflected from the metal stem by the linear scanning method, only the square metal stem of 12mm is fixed to the position of 19mm apart from the normal probe in Fig.4(a). And, an echo position reflected from the stem is measured when the normal probe is moved every 1 mm toward z´ axis. At this time, the wave velocity of the ultrasonic device set up to 1500m/s which is the wave velocity of water. Also, a gain set up to 50dB.

5.2.2 Bone inserted with a circular metal stem

Figure 5(b) shows the situation that the thickness inside the bone inserted with a circular metal stem of diameter 12mm is measured by the linear scanning method. an experiment is carried out in the same way as section 5.2.1.

In order to check a fundamental echo characteristic reflected from metal stem by the linear scanning method, the experiment that the only circular metal stem of diameter 12mm in Fig.4(b) is used is carried out in the same way as section 5.2.1.

5.3 Measuring method of thickness inside bone by circular scanning

5.3.1 Bone inserted with a square metal stem

The thickness inside the bone is measured by the circular scanning method in Fig.4. In this case, Fig.4(a) shows the situation that the bone inserted with the square metal stem of 12mm is the position about 19mm apart from the normal probe. The normal probe is fixed at the upper surface of the water. When the specimen is rotated with $\alpha=0°$, 90°, 180° and 270°, an echo position reflected from the boundary surface is measured. At this time, the wave velocity of the ultrasonic device set up to 1410m/s which is the wave velocity of the bone marrow. Also, a gain set up to 60dB.

5.3.2 Bone inserted with a circular metal stem

Figure 4(b) shows the situation that the thickness inside the bone inserted with a circular metal stem of diameter 12mm is measured by the circular scanning method. The bone specimen is rotated with 30°, 60°,..., 330°. The experiment is carried out in the same way as section 5.3.1.

6. EXPERIMENTAL RESULTS

6.1 Measured results in the thickness inside bone
6.1.1 Fundamental echo characteristics

Figure 5 shows the experimental results which is done section 5.2.1 by the linear scanning method. The mark ■ in the figure indicate the distance from the normal probe to the square metal stem surface of 12mm. If the position of the normal probe is $|z'|\leqq 8mm$, the measured result is the same distance as a real measured value. The point of $|z'|=8mm$ is in the measured limit position. The range of a sound wave from the the metal stem plane is only 1mm as the transducer diameter is 6mm.

Figure 6 shows the measured results

obtained by the linear scanning method which is done section 5.2.2. The mark ■ in the figure shows the distance from the normal probe to the metal stem surface of a diameter 12mm. In this case, the echo reflected from the metal stem surface is able to measure in $|z'|\leqq 6mm$. The result of the section form is fairly bigger than that of diameter 12mm. The cause is conceivable in the following manner.

Figure 7 shows the shortest propagation process PQR of the sound wave which is reflected from the metal stem surface and is propagated with the angle of beam spread θ. At this time, the echo obtained on a CRT display is indicated the place where the time is in the shortest. In other words, when the normal probe is in point P, the echo position received from the metal stem is not the distance of PS but is the half of process PQR.

6.1.2 Bone inserted with a square metal stem

Figure 8 shows the measured results by the linear scanning method which is done section 5.2.1. These indicates the results obtained at C face in the bone inserted with a square metal stem of 12mm. The marks ●, ○ and ■ show the distances from the normal probe to the outside of the bone, the inside of the bone and the metal stem surface. In this figure, the wave velocity of the ultrasonic device set up to $v_m=1410m/s$ which is the wave velocity of the bone marrow. The wave velocities of the bone and the water are $v_b=2775m/s$ and $v_w=1500m/s$, respectively. These differ from the wave velocity of the bone marrow. Accordingly, the distances apart of the bone and the water is not obtained directly from the position indicated on a CRT display. Therefore, these distances are modified by the following manner.

The wave velocity set up to the wave velocity v_m of the bone marrow. If the distances of apart of the bone and the water indicated on a CRT display are l_b' and l_w', respectively, the real distances of l_b and l_w are given by the following equations.

$$l_b = l_b' \times \frac{v_b}{v_m} \qquad (3)$$

$$l_w = l_w' \times \frac{v_w}{v_w} \qquad (4)$$

Now, the measured results in Fig.8 are indicated the only point that the echo is able to measure in the echoes reflected from the bone and the metal stem. Because, the echoes become unable to be measured When the distance between the metal stem and the inside of the bone are small, and the echoes from those boundary surfaces overlap each other or overlap with the delayed echoes. From these reasons, the measured point from the metal stem plane is not the same number with the right and left to z' axis in Fig.8.

Figure 9(a)~(c) show the echo wave forms when the normal probe is in the position of z' =0, 3, 5mm at C side of the specimen. 1st, 2nd and 3rd wave forms from the left side in Fig.9(a) show the echo heights reflected from the outside of the bone, the inside of the bone and the metal stem surface. The 2nd and 3rd echo heights in Fig.9(b) are fairly smaller than the echo heights in Fig.9(a). Also, the 2nd echo height in Fig.9(c) is almost the same as that in Fig.9(b). However, the 3rd echo height is fairly smaller. The echo height becomes small as the measured point separates from position of z' =0, and the echo position becomes unable to measure.

Figure 10 shows the distances from the metal stem surface to the echo positions of outside and inside of the bone on the basis of the result of Fig.10. The experimental results in the figure indicate the marks ● and ○. A solid line is the section form of the bone measured with a vernier calipers. From the figure, the distance from the center of the specimen to the inside of the bone is able to measure with fairly accuracy in the position within 6mm. However, a little measurement error is observed in the outside of the bone. For this cause, the inside and the outside of the bone is a complicated curved surface. Then, as measured point separates from the center of the specimen, the sound wave emitted to the curved bone surfaces becomes difficult to able to receive. Moreover, the echo position becomes unable to indicate the section form of the bone precisely.

6.1.3 Bone inserted with a circular metal stem

Figure 11 shows the measured results by the linear scan method which is done section 5.2.2. These indicate result obtained at C side in the bone inserted with a circular metal stem of diameter 12mm. The marks ●, ○ and ■ show the distances from the normal probe to outside of the bone, inside of the bone and the metal stem surface. In this figure, if the measured point is |z'| ≤ 3mm, the echo position does not change very much and is the result close to a straight line fairly. Furthermore, the distances of the part of the bone and the water indicate the results modified in the same way as section 6.1.2. In this case, it is considered that these wave velocities are v_b=2775m/s and v_w=1500m/s, respectively. Also, the echo results is shown the only measured position.

Figure 12 shows the distances from the metal stem surface to the echo position of the outside and the inside of the bone on the basis of the result of Fig.5. Also, the experimental results in the figure indicate the marks ● and ○.

A solid line is the section form of the bone measured with a vernier calipers. From this figure, when the normal probe is on the center of the specimen, the distance from the center of the specimen to the inside and the outside of the bone is able to measure with fairly accuracy. However, when the measured point separates from the center of the specimen, the measurement accuracy becomes bad.

6.2 Measurement results in the thickness inside bone by circular scanning method

6.2.1 Bone inserted with a square metal stem

Figure 13 shows the measured results by the circular scanning method which is done section 5.3.1. In this case, the specimen is rotated at α=0°, 90°, 180° and 270°. The marks ●, ○ and ■ show the distances from the normal probe to the outside of the bone, the inside of the bone and the metal stem surface. Furthermore, the distances of the part of the bone and the water are shown the result modified in the same way as section 6.1.2.

Figure 14 shows the distances from the metal stem surface at z' =0 obtained from Fig.13 to the echo positions of outside and inside of the bone on the basis of the metal stem surface. The experimental results indicate the marks ● and ○. A solid line is the section form of the bone measured with the vernier calipers. From this figure, the thickness inside the bone is able to measure with fairly accuracy.

6.2.2 Bone inserted with a circular metal stem

Figure 15 shows the measurement result by the circular scanning method which is done section 5.3.2. In this case, the specimen is rotated at α=0°, 30°, 60°,...., 270°. The marks ●, ○ and ■ show the distances from the normal probe to the outside of the bone, the inside of the bone and the metal stem surface. Furthermore, the distances of the part of the bone and the water are the result modified in the same way as section 6.1.2.

Figure 16 shows the distances from the metal stem surface at z' =0 obtained from Fig.15 to the echo position of the outside and the inside of the bone on the basis of the metal stem surface. The experimental results indicate the marks ● and ○. A solid line is the section form of the bone measured with the vernier calipers. From this figure, the thicknesses of the bone and the distance from inside of the bone to the metal stem are able to measure with fairly accuracy.

7. CONCLUSIONS

The thicknesses of bone and bone marrow inside the femur inserted a square and a circular metal stems is measured using ultrasonic pulse echo method by immersion testing. Then, the linear and circular scanning methods are used to this measurement. On the other hand, the thickness inside the femur is measured with a vernier calipers. Both results are compared and the following conclusions are obtained.

(1) The thicknesses of bone and bone marrow inside the bone inserted with the metal stem by using ultrasonic technique agree fairly well with those of the vernier calipers. The present method is fairly practical.

(2) In the case of using the linear scanning method, if the measured point is the place near the center of the metal stem, the thickness inside the bone inserted with the square metal stem is able to measure. Also, if the measured point is in the position within the width of the metal stem, the distance between the metal stem and the inside of the bone is able to measure similarly. On the other hand, in the case of bone inserted with the circular metal stem, the thickness inside the bone is able to measure the only place near the center of the metal stem.

(3) In the case of using the circular scanning method, if the transducer face of the normal probe is parallel to the plane of metal stem, the thickness inside the bone inserted with the square metal stem is able to measure. On the other hand, if the sound wave from the normal probe is emitted at the center of the metal stem, the thicknesses of the bone and bone marrow is able to measure in all positions inside the bone.

Finally, the authors are deeply indebted to Professor Toshiaki Hara of Niigata University, to Professor Takashi Koizumi and Professor Toshikazu Shibuya of Tokyo Institute of Technology, for many valuable suggestions on this work.

REFERENCES

(1) Smith, H. W., De Smut, A. A. and Levine, A., Measurement of Cortical Thickness in a Human Cadaver Femur (Conventional Roentgenography versus Computed Tomography), Clin. Orthop. Rel. Res., No.169 (1982), p.269.
(2) Meema, H. E., CORTICAL BONE AND OSTEOPOROSIS AS A MEASUREMENT OF AGING, Am. J. Roentgenol, Vol.89, No.6 (1963), p.1287.
(3) Singh, S., Ultrasonic non-destructive measurements of cortical bone thickness in human cadaver femur, Ultrasonics, Vol.27, No.2 (1989), p.107.

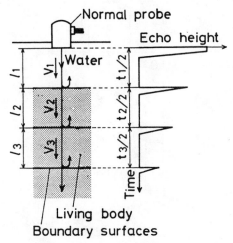

Fig.1 Principle of ultrasonic pulse echo method

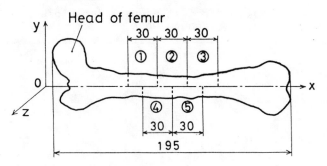

Fig.2 Cutting position and number of femur

Table 1 Wave velocity through bone (Specimen 1)

No.	Thickness of bone chip (mm)	Wave velocity (m/s)
①	2.20	2860
②	2.50	3000
③	2.30	2720
④	2.18	2775
⑤	2.00	2580

Table 2 Wave velocity through bone (Specimen 2)

No.	Thickness of bone chip (mm)	Wave velocity (m/s)
①	1.88	2680
②	2.22	2810
③	1.53	2820
④	1.27	2520
⑤	2.70	2990

151

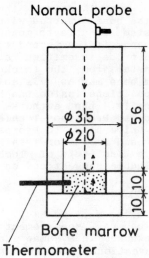

Fig.3 Measurement device of the wave velocity through bone marrow

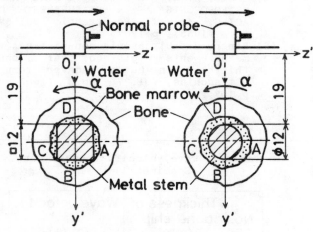

(a) Square stem   (b) Circular stem
Fig.4 Ultrasonic measurement by linear and circular scanning testings

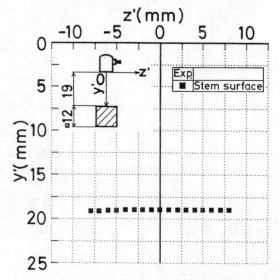

Fig.5 Echo points from a square metal stem (Linear scan)

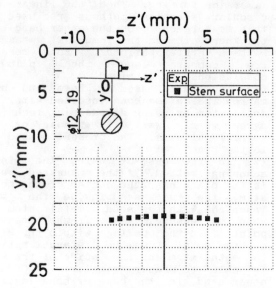

Fig.6 Echo points from a circular metal stem (Linear scan)

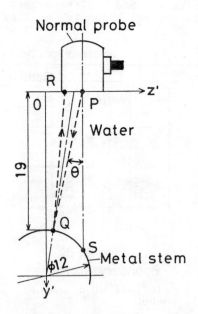

Fig.7 Shortest propagation process of sound wave

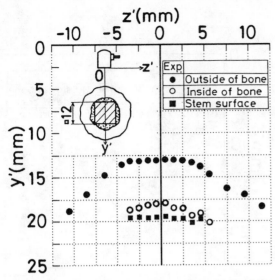

Fig.8 Echo points from the bone with
a square metal stem at C side
(Linear scan)

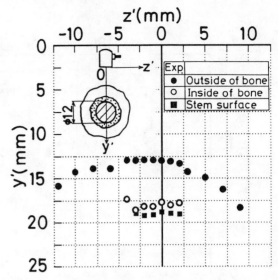

Fig.11 Echo points from the bone with
a circular metal stem at C side
(Linear scan)

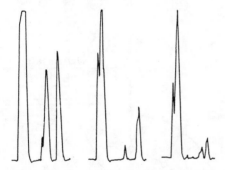

(a) z′=0   (b) z′=3   (c) z′=5

Fig.9 Echo wave forms of the bone with
a square metal stem at C side

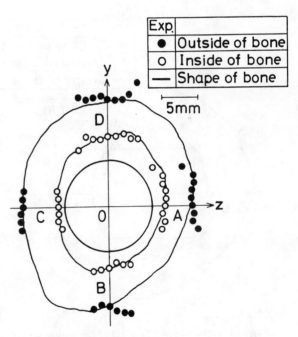

Fig.12 Cross section of the bone with a
circular metal stem (Linear scan)

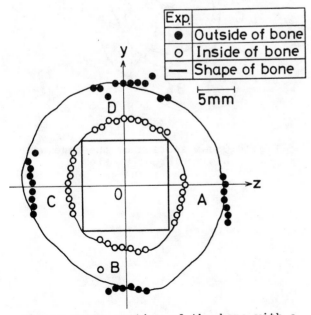

Fig.10 Cross section of the bone with a
square metal stem (Linear scan)

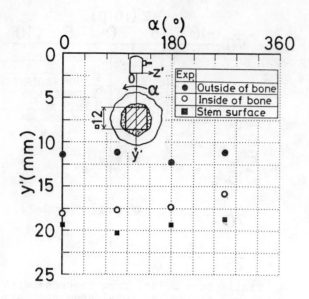

Fig.13 Echo points from the bone with a square metal stem (Circular scan)

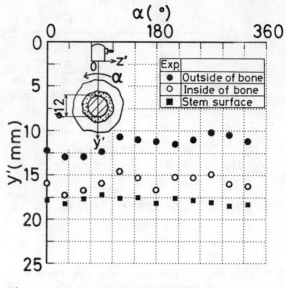

Fig.15 Echo points from the bone with a circular metal stem (Circular scan)

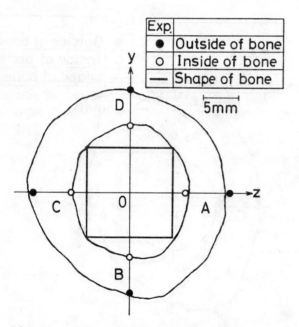

Fig.14 Cross section of the bone with a square metal stem (Circular scan)

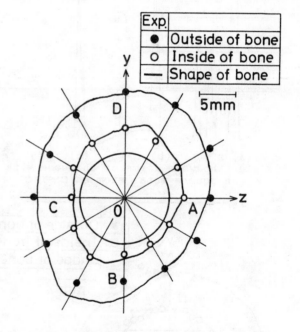

Fig.16 Cross section of the bone with a circular metal stem (Circular scan)

PREDICTION OF MOLAR ERUPTIVE FORCES CAUSED BY THE BITE PLATE FACE BOW

by

W. P. Hnat, S. Braun, and B. E. Johnson

INTRODUCTION

A test apparatus was constructed to simulate the force system present during application of the bite plate face bow. The bite plate face bow, sometimes called the Cervera face bow, is similar in design to the conventional cervical face bow, with the addition of a metal plate to the inner portion of the face bow as shown in Fig. 1. The plate presses against the maxillary incisors and prevents the patient from fully closing, thus acting as a bite plate.

This face bow has been reported to be "useful in the intrusion of maxillary and mandibular incisors for the correction of deep overbites while moving the teeth distally". [1,2] The intrusive forces on the maxillary incisors and the vertical eruptive forces on the first molars caused by the attachment of a bite plate face bow were studied using the test apparatus to simulate the actual force system. Molar vertical force comparisons are also made to the conventional cervical face bow.

W. P. Hnat is Assistant Professor, Mechanical Engineering Department, S. Braun is Associate Professor and B. E. Johnson is Associate Professor, Orthodontics Department, University of Louisville, Louisville, Kentucky, USA.

MATERIALS AND METHODS

The bite plate face bow is shown in position on a typical patient in Fig. 2. The dimensions shown are considered typical for the purposes of this analysis.

Impingement of the mandibular incisors on the underside of the inner bow plate is not predictable, since it is a function of whether the patient actually brings the mandibular incisors into contact with the plate, to what degree he or she occludes, and the length of time in contact with the plate. An analysis range of 0, 0.98, 1.96, and 4.9 N of total mandibular incisor impingement is thus considered to account for this variability. Overjet is also highly variable, and is assumed at 4 mm for this study.

The maxillary molar vertical components of the force system induced by a conventional cervical face bow are calculated using static equilibrium analysis. The equilibrium force equation based on the free body diagram of Fig. 3 is given by

$$F_2 = T \sin [180 - (\gamma + \theta)] , \qquad (1)$$

where F_2 is the molar eruptive force, T is the neck strap tension, γ is the angle between the neck strap and the outer bow following neck strap engagement, and θ the relative bow angle (i.e., the angle between the inner bow and the outer bow).

Force system analysis was performed with cervical neck strap tensions of 1.96 N and 3.92 N, and with relative bow angles of +30 degrees to -5 degrees, following engagement of the neck strap. A positive angle indicates the outer bow is above the inner bow, while a negative angle indicates that the outer bow is below the inner bow. When the maxillary and/or mandibular incisors impinge upon the bite plate, an additional unknown force is added to the face bow, and the number of indeterminants involved in the equilibrium equations exceeds the number of independent variables. To resolve the molar eruptive force, F_2, a test apparatus was constructed to simulate the force system present during the application of the face bow and allow measurement of the mandibular and maxillary incisor forces. The neck strap force and the mandibular and maxillary incisor forces were measured using high resolution strain gage based force transducers (Entran model ELH-TC400). Figures 4 and 5 are photographs of the test apparatus and associated instrumentation. The spatial dimensions were the same as described earlier and shown in Fig. 2.

The molar eruptive force, with no mandibular incisor force, is now calculated from the static force equilibrium equation based on the free body diagram of Fig. 6:

$$F_2 = T \sin [180 - (\gamma + \theta)] + F_3 , \qquad (2)$$

where F_3 is the maxillary incisor force.

The molar eruptive force with an applied mandibular incisor force is calculated from the static force equilibrium equation based on the free body diagram of Fig. 7:

$$F_2 = T \sin [180 - (\gamma + \theta)] + F_3 - F_4 , \qquad (3)$$

where F_4 is the mandibular incisor force.

For comparison purposes, the molar eruptive forces were calculated using eq (1) for a standard cervical face bow for neck strap tensions of 1.96 N and 3.92 N, and for relative bow angles of +30 degrees to -5 degrees, in 5 degree increments. The calculated molar eruptive force is plotted as a function of the relative bow angle in Fig. 8.

The molar eruptive forces of the bite plate face bow, absent lower incisor impingement, were calculated using eq (2) and experimental force measurements of the maxillary incisor intrusive forces. The results are shown graphically in Fig.9 for neck strap tensions of 1.96 N and 3.92 N.

Total molar eruptive forces, based on direct measurement of the mandibular and maxillary incisor impingement forces, are shown in Fig. 10 for various relative bow angles.

Because mandibular incisor impingement is highly variable and unpredictable, molar eruptive forces were calculated using the measured maxillary incisor intrusive forces for applied mandibular total incisor intrusive forces of 4.9, 1.96, 1.47 and 0.98 N. Neck strap tensions of 1.96 N and 3.92 N and relative bow angles between +25 degrees and -5 degrees were evaluated.

Total maxillary incisor intrusive forces, obtained by direct force measurement for various relative bow angles, are shown in Fig. 11.

Finally, Figs. 12 and 13 compare molar eruptive forces generated by the standard cervical face bow and the bite plate face bow.

DISCUSSION

For the conventional cervical face bow with 3.92 N neck strap tension, each molar is subjected to a maximal eruptive force of 1.63 N when the outer bow is at 30 degrees. This eruptive force diminishes almost linearly to 0.58 N when the inner bow angle is at -5 degrees. If the neck strap tension is reduced to 1.96 N, the molar eruptive force is reduced proportionally to 0.81 N at 30 degrees, and 0.29 N at -5 degrees (reference Fig. 8).

In the case of the bite plate face bow, the molar eruptive force without mandibular incisor impingement is markedly increased throughout the range of relative bow angles. At a 30 degree relative bow angle and 3.92 N neck strap tension, the molar eruptive force is 8.17 N; a 500% increase over the molar eruptive force induced by a conventional cervical face bow. This increased molar eruptive force occurs throughout the range of relative bow angles to a minimum increase of 192%, corresponding to 1.1 N at -5 degrees.

When the neck strap tension is reduced to 1.96 N, the molar eruptive force is 4.37 N at 30 degrees, and 0.46 N at -5 degrees. Comparing the molar eruptive forces to the conventional cervical face bow at 1.96 N of neck strap tension, the values are 537% above the cervical face bow at 30 degrees and 158% at -5 degrees (reference Fig.11).

Inspection of the molar eruptive force equations for the conventional cervical face bow, $F_2 = T \sin [180^\circ - (\gamma + \theta)]$, and the bite plate face bow, $F_2 = T \sin [180 - (\gamma + \theta)] + F_3$, reveals that the molar eruptive force is increased by the value F_3; the maxillary incisor intrusive force. The magnitude of F_3 was found to be significant and accounts for the large increases in the molar extrusive forces.

The molar eruptive forces do not change significantly when the patient occludes on the bite plate, irrespective of the magnitude of the occluding force or the relative bow angle. The molar eruptive forces remain highly extrusive. This is because the "$T \sin [180 - (\gamma + \theta)] + F_3$" term in the equilibrium equation exceeds F_4, the total mandibular incisor impingement force, for values up to 4.9 N (reference Fig. 11).

At a neck strap tension of 3.92 N, the total maxillary incisor intrusion without lower incisor impingement was found to be 13.1 N at 30 degrees and 1.2 N at -5 degrees. When the neck strap tension is at 1.96 N, these values are 7.37 N and 0.38 N, respectively.

If the patient occludes on the inner bow plate, the maxillary incisor intrusive force does not change significantly at the upper range of relative bow angles. At -5 degrees the total maxillary incisor intrusive forces are within the range of 1.7 N to 2.96 N, depending on the magnitude of lower incisor impingement.

CONCLUSIONS

The force system present during the application of the bite plate face bow was adequately simulated using the test apparatus. The apparatus allowed measurement of the mandibular and maxillary incisor forces under varying neck strap tensions and under controlled laboratory conditions. It is apparent that the choice of neck strap tension and relative bow angle are critical to the magnitude of the force system affecting the molars and maxillary incisors. The molar eruptive forces of the bite plate face bow can be exceedingly high, and may border on the non-physiologic at all relative bow angles above zero. It is important to recognize that there are no counter-balancing molar occlusal forces since the inner bow plate acts as a bite plate. It is therefore likely that overbite correction would occur primarily by maxillary molar eruption. If the neck strap tension is at 1.96 N, and the outer bow is adjusted below zero degrees, the molar eruptive force is less than 0.81 N. This may be more acceptable with regard to patient comfort and will likely result in a more physiological eruptive response, recognizing the absence of counter-balancing molar occlusion. During the period of time when the patient occludes on the bite plate, the molar eruptive forces are not materially affected.

The total intrusive force that is imparted to the maxillary incisors at 3.92 N of neck strap tension is considered non-physiologic[3], ranging from 13.1 N at 30 degrees to 1.2 N at -5 degrees. It is probable these intrusive forces would not be shared equally by the four incisors, as it is unlikely all of these teeth will be in equal simultaneous contact with the plate. When the strap tension is adjusted to 1.96 N, the maxillary incisor intrusive forces decrease to 7.37 N at 30 degrees, and to 0.29 N at -5 degrees. While the lower range of values may be more acceptable physiologically, the lack of continuous and constant maxillary incisor intrusive forces would likely make this an ineffective manner of obtaining true intrusion in the correction of deep overbites.

When the neck strap tension is either 1.96 N or 3.92 N, the data reveals that the maxillary incisor intrusive forces remain relatively high, and are not affected in any significant way by the magnitude of lower incisor impingement. The total maxillary incisor intrusive force is above those commonly accepted values as physiologic.[4]

BIBLIOGRAPHY

1. Cervera, A.J., Anclaji Extraoral "SC:", Sociedad Espanolas Ortodoncia Actas 13: 43-49,1967.

2. Sauer, G., Kuftinic, M., "Cervera Headgear," Journal of Clinical Orthodontics, 13: 351-356, 1981.

3. Dellinger, E.L., "A Histologic and Cephalometric Investigation of Premolar Intrusion in the Macaca Speciosa Monkey," Am. J. Orthod.1967; 53: 325-355.

4. Burstone, C.J., "Deep Overbite Correction By Intrusion," Am. J. Orthod. 1977; 72: 1-22.

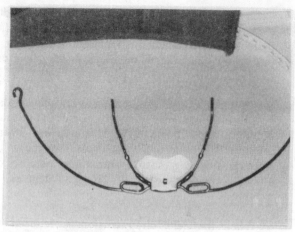

Fig. 1. Bite plate face bow.

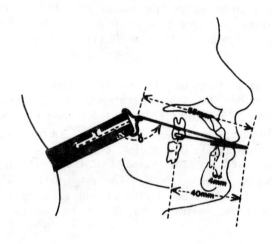

Fig. 2. Bite plate face bow in position.

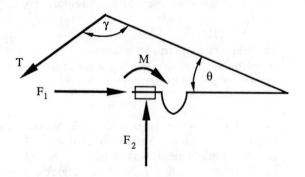

Fig. 3. Free body diagram of a conventional cervical face bow.

Fig. 4. Experimental test apparatus.

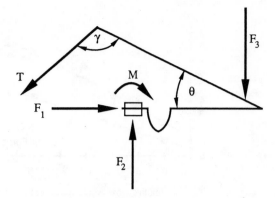

Fig. 6. Free body diagram of bite plate face bow without mandibular incisor impingement force.

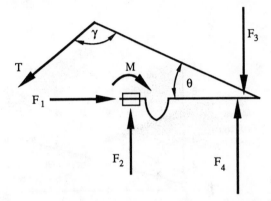

Fig. 7. Free body diagram of bite plate bow with mandibular incisor impingement force.

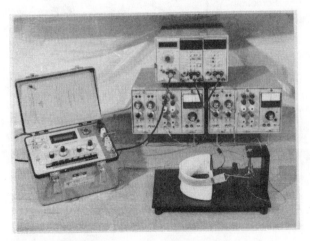

Fig. 5. Test apparatus and associated instrumentation.

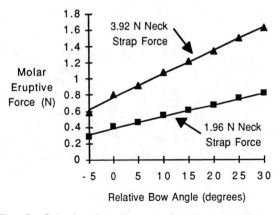

Fig. 8. Calculated molar eruptive force for the standard cervical face bow.

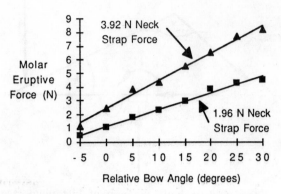

Fig. 9. Molar eruptive force for the bite plate face bow without the mandibular incisor impingement force.

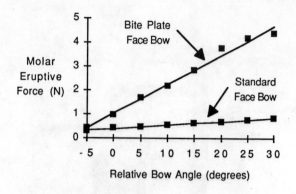

Fig. 12. Comparison of the molar eruptive force between the standard cervical face bow and the bite plate face bow for a neck strap tension of 1.96 N.

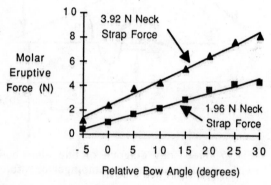

Fig. 10. Molar eruptive force for the bite plate face bow with the mandibular incisor impingement force.

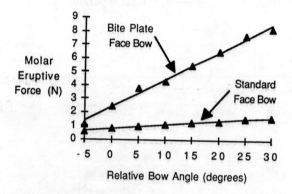

Fig. 13. Comparison of the molar eruptive force between the standard cervical face bow and the bite plate face bow for a neck strap tension of 3.92 N.

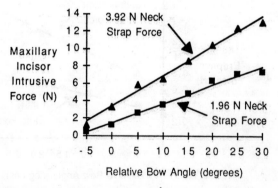

Fig. 11. Total maxillary incisor intrusive force following neck strap engagement.

HARMONIC ENERGY AS A MEASURE OF GAIT SYMMETRY

by
D.G.Berghaus and T.O.Woods
Georgia Institute Of Technology
Atlanta, Georgia 30332

Gait improvement is a fundamental objective when fitting artificial limbs or when rehabilitating hemiplegic patients. Good gait performance is important to a person's basic mobility and to his/her basic ability to compete or to share in the normal activities of life.

Experimental study of gait includes the use of foot force measurements, knee angle and stride length changes with time and optical studies of the walking individual (1). Each of the general methods is best used in a special laboratory.

Foot force measurements are made two different ways, both using force transducer plates. One type of transducer is able to measure the vertical as well as the horizontal (fore-aft and transverse) forces exerted by the foot on transducer plates which placed in walkways. The second type measures the distribution of forces in the vertical direction using an array of miniature transducers beneath the foot. These devices give good dynamic measurements for a single step, but require fairly precise placement of the foot to the transducer.

Knee angle measurements are made using goniometers. These devices are often potentiometric and readily permit temporal measurements. As previously noted, their deficiencies include their reduction of the knee to approximation as a simple hinge and the general lack of a reference angle. They also require running cables which can hamper natural gait. Stride length changes, in time, are also studied using walkways consisting of special mats which are fitted with electrical conducting surfaces. These surfaces can note the location of the feet of a walking individual, who is not encumbered by wires. There are no problems of an uncertain reference.

Optical methods for studying gait include video-computer systems and marker systems. Video computers can observe the motion of several points on the body. Using digitization methods, the motions of these points can be analyzed to determine velocity and acceleration as well as changes in angles on the body. It is possible, using more than one camera, to obtain a three dimensional view of the individual. Marker systems are more selective in being able to study certain points on the body which are marked for illumination and observation by photodetectors. These methods require special optical facilities, equipment and expertise, particularly with the computer-video interrelation.

The above are all effective methods for studying the many variables which are a part of gait for all people and they have contributed to the identification and understanding of their importance. They all require the use of a gait laboratory. No quantitative measure of gait symmetry has been developed from these methods.

This paper will describe a gait analysis procedure which is relatively easy to use and which can provide a quantified measure of gait quality. The method uses an accelerometer to observe motion of the torso and it studies the symmetry of gait. A gait performance index is obtained from the energy content of the harmonic response.

Gait Symmetry and Accelerometers

The use of an accelerometer to measure triaxial acceleration of the torso was reported by Gage(2), who also transformed the data into the frequency domain. He recognized the symmetry exhibited in the comparatively high response of the even harmonics, though there was no attempt to produce a "symmetry index".

The accelerometer approach to the study of gait has been used by Smidt, and his co-workers(3 - 5). They have also studied ratios of the harmonic responses to compare gait of different individuals, though they have not published any effort to deal with gait symmetry. Their work required the use of a dedicated facility with instrumentation, computer and walkway.

Small inexpensive desk-top computers and the availability of very small instrumentation and data storage packages make possible simplified procedures for gait analysis. The use of a digital oscilloscope and a personal computer have made harmonic gait analysis possible outside the laboratory(6). Small instrumentation and data storage modules have made the accelerometer significantly less intrusive for analysis of gait, as seen in the work of Sabelman and his co-workers(7). These advances provide for less restricted motion for the individual because connections to instrumentation pose constraints on motion and limit the path length to a few steps.

Stride Energy as a Measure of Symmetry

A measure of stride symmetry can be obtained by studying the energy associated with the various frequencies obtained in the harmonic response. The harmonic response is obtained from a discrete Fourier transform of the accelerometer signal(6). The energy is directly related to the work expended by the individual to support his/her motion.

For a mass moving with velocity, v, the kinetic energy at a given instant, i, may be given:

$$E_i = 1/2 \; m \; (v_i)^2 \; . \qquad\qquad 1$$

The average energy over a given time interval may be stated:

$$E_a = \frac{\sum_T [\; \frac{1}{2} m(v_i)^2 \, \Delta t_i\;]}{\sum_T \Delta t_i} \qquad\qquad 2$$

Which may be rewritten:

$$E_a = [\frac{1}{2} \; m \int_o^T v^2(t)\,dt\,]/T \qquad\qquad 3$$

For a single cycle of sinusoidal motion with $v(t) = K \sin \omega t$ and period $T = 2\pi/\omega$:

$$E_a = \frac{\frac{1}{2} m \int_o^{2\pi/\omega} K^2 \sin^2 \omega t \; dt}{2\pi/\omega} = \frac{1}{4} mK^2 \qquad\qquad 4$$

or the average energy during the cycle is proportional to the square of the amplitude of the velocity. The energy may be computed from the acceleration data using $v = \int a \; dt = \int C \sin (\omega t) \; dt = - (C/\omega) \cos (\omega t)$ where C is the amplitude of the acceleration signal for the given harmonic. Thus:

$$E_a = \frac{1}{4} \; m \; (\frac{C}{\omega})^2 \qquad\qquad 5$$

Noting that symmetric gait occurs with high response from even harmonics and low response from odd harmonics, an energy ratio may be employed which compares the even to the odd harmonics:

$$R_E = \frac{\sum E_{a_i} \quad i = 4,6}{\sum E_{ai} \quad i = 3,5,7} \qquad\qquad 6$$

162

Symmetry is seen in the several harmonics immediately following the second. The second harmonic is ordinarily very strong and its presence in R_E would overwhelm the smaller but most important contributions of higher harmonics. The first harmonic is also strong and is not especially valuable with respect to symmetry. It defines the "window" for the transformation. Finally, high harmonics beyond the seventh have a small energy content and may be omitted(8).

Experiments and Results

Data were taken from three individuals with different gait-associated variables. The procedure was described previously for the experiment and for the discrete Fourier transformation(6). Data were obtained in the fore-aft direction, parallel to the path of motion.

The individuals included two women and one man. One of the subjects (A) had calcium deposits in the heel. Another subject (B) had a diagnosed muscular deficiency in one leg. One of the subjects (C) had no diagnosed deficiencies.

The harmonic responses are given in Figure 1. Two separate data samples were taken for each subject and are shown as two plots. The results are normalized to the harmonic with the highest magnitude response, which is the second harmonic in every case. (Harmonic response results consist only of the even and odd values. They are connected only for convenience.) The energy ratios are also given. The energy ratios appear to give a reasonable index of the gait symmetry as seen in the harmonic responses.

Acknowledgement

This work was partially supported by the Veterans Administration Medical Center in Atlanta, GA.

References

1.   Hutton, W.C., "Gait Analysis: Measurements", Concise Encyclopedia of Biological and Biomedical Measurements, P.A. Payne, Editor-in-Chief, Pergamon Press, Manchester, UK, 1991, pp. 177-180

2.   Gage, H., "Accelerographic Analysis of Human Gait", American Society of Mechanical Engineers, Washington, D.C. Paper No. 64-WA/HUF 8, 137, 1964

3.   Smidt, G.L., Arora, J.S., and Johnston, R.C., "Accelerographic Analysis of Several Types of Walking", American Journal of Physical Medicine, v. 50, 1971, pp. 285-300

4.   Smidt, G.L., Deusinger, R.H., Arora, J., and Albright, J.P., "An Automated Accelerometry System for Gait Analysis", Journal of Biomechanics, v.10, 1977, pp. 367-375

5.   Robinson, J.L., Smidt, G.L., and Arora, J.S., "Accelerographic, Temporal and Distance Factors in Below-Knee Amputees", Physical Therapy, v. 57, n. 8, 1977, pp. 898-904

6.   Farris, D.A., Urquizo,G.C., Kilpatrick, D.L., Woods, T.O., and Berghaus, D.G., "A Simplified Accelerometer System for Analysis of Human Gait", Proceedings, 1990 Spring Meeting, Society for Experimental Mechanics, Albuquerque, NM, 1990, pp. 54-58

7.   Sabelman, E.F., Winograd, C.H., and Hoy, M.G., 1991, "Acceleromatic Body Motion in the Fall-Prone Elderly: a Pilot Study""A Rehabilitation R & D Progress Reports, 1989, pp. 353-354

8.   Winter, D.A., Sidwall, H.G., and Hobson, D.A., "Measurement and Reduction of Noise in Kinematics of Locomotion", Journal of Biomechanics, v. 7, 1974, pp. 157-159

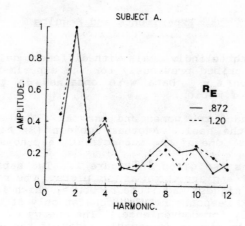

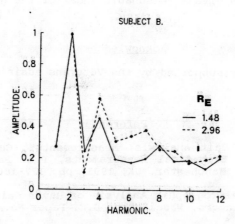

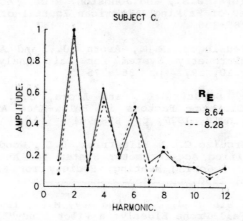

Figure 1: Harmonic response and energy ratio for three subjects, with two gait samples for each. Response amplitudes for first 12 harmonics are given. R_E uses harmonics from 3 to 7 (Eq. 6).

GRIP PRESSURE DISTRIBUTION UNDER STATIC AND DYNAMIC LOADING

R. Gurram
Ph.D. Student

G.J. Gouw
Assistant Professor

S. Rakheja
Associate Professor

CONCAVE Research Centre
Department of Mechanical Engineering
Concordia University
1455 de Maisonneuve West
Montréal, Québec, Canada H3G 1M8

ABSTRACT

Distribution of static and dynamic forces at a hand-handle interface is investigated using a grid of pressure sensors mounted on the handle. The pressure distribution is acquired for different values of static and dynamic grip forces in the range of 25-150 N. The dynamic measurements were conducted at various discrete frequencies in the 20 - 1000 Hz range with peak acceleration levels of 0.5 g, 1.0 g, 2.0 g and 3.0 g. The grip pressure distribution (GPD) under static loads revealed concentration of high pressures near the tips of index and middle fingers, and base of thumb. This concentration of high pressures, shifted towards middle of fingers under dynamic loads, irrespective of the grip force, excitation frequency and acceleration levels. The local pressure peaks are related to impairment of blood flow to finger tips and the possible causation of vibration white finger.

INTRODUCTION

High levels of vibrations transmitted to operators of hand-held power tools and off-road vehicles have been related to various occupational health disorders, operator discomfort and poor productivity. Several research investigations have established that prolonged exposure to such vibrations can cause *Vibration White Finger* (VWF) disease associated with impaired blood flow among the hand-tool operators and severe spinal and stomach disorders among the vehicle drivers [1,2,3]. The transmitted vibration levels, invariably measured using accelerometers, have been assessed in an attempt to identify the mechanisms related to VWF or spinal disorders. The transmitted hand-arm vibrations are measured either at the handle or at the operator's wrist [4,5], while the driver vibrations are acquired at the driver-seat interface using the three-axes seat accelerometer [6]. Although a measure of overall transmitted vibrations can be attained, such acceleration measurements do not provide distribution of dynamic forces at the human-machine interface.

The distribution of forces at the human-machine interface under static and dynamic loading can provide a considerable insight into transmission of localized forces and stresses experienced by the operators. In case of hand-held power tools, the grip pressure distribution (GPD) under dynamic conditions can thus be used to investigate hand injury and fatigue mechanisms, and to carry out design and ergonomic evaluations of handle grips [7]. The pressure distribution at the driver-seat interface can provide objective data to study the spine loads, and to design effective seat cushions and back-rests with load distributing capabilities. The measurement of pressure distribution at the human-machine interface, however, is highly complex due to associated curved surfaces and flexibility of the interface. In this paper two different types of flexible pressure sensors are investigated to acquire the pressure distribution at a hand-handle interface under static and dynamic conditions. The grip pressure distribution (GPD) measured at the hand-handle interface is analyzed to illustrate the influence of grip force and handle vibration characteristics on the occurrence of high localized dynamic pressures at the operator's hand.

INTERFACE PRESSURE SENSORS

Measurement of pressure distribution at a human-machine interface requires a comprehensive grid of thin and flexible sensors, such that the visco-elastic properties of the interface remain unaltered during static and dynamic measurements. In the recent past, a number of interface pressure measuring systems have been developed. Sensors such as rubber butterfly valves, manometers, sprung flat boards, strain gages, silicon diaphragms, foil capacitors have been used in conjunction with multi channel data acquisition systems to acquire distribution of static pressure at the human-seat interface [8,9]. All these sensors have severe limitations in view of the flexibility of the interface. These sensors either are applicable to hard surfaces or alter the elastic properties of human-machine interface. The pressure distribution at hand-tool interface has been acquired using a pressure resistive paint [10], conductive thioplastic sensors [11], and force sensing resistors [7] to achieve an accurate measurement of static grip forces. The flexible and thin resistive and capacitive sensors, which offer the potentials to acquire static as well as dynamic pressures, are investigated to acquire the GPD.

Piché *et al* [12] used force sensing resistors to study the static pressures at a human-seat interface. The basic sensing element comprises of ultra thin and flexible force sensing resistor and a film of foil conductors. The force sensing resistor consists of a polymer sheet with a layer of flexible sensing film. The foil conductor film is a mylar sheet with pattern of open ended conductors. The infinite resistance of open ended conductors is shunted by placing the force sensing resistor against the foil film. The resistance due to the force sensing resistor changes with changes in the applied load, the shunt resistance of the assembly is thus related to the force applied to the surface. The sensing assembly, comprising of two polymer sheets, is 0.25 mm thick and 9.75 mm diameter.

A pressure sensing grid was fabricated where each sensor is supplied with a 0.24 mA constant current at 1.5 V. A conditioning circuit is integrated and the sensors are calibrated to determine the resistance-force relationship, precision and repeatability, using a pneumatic actuator. The static calibration curve, shown in Figure 1, exhibits nonlinear characteristics with large hysteresis. Although the sensors showed good repeatability over a short period, the repeatability and dynamic range deteriorated quite rapidly due to oxidation of the foil conductors. These sensors were thus considered infeasible for the present study.

Alternatively, a pressure measurement system comprising of flexible variable capacitance sensors, conditioning circuit and data-acquisition software, referred to as *EMED System*, was employed to acquire the GPD. The sensors are calibrated and the calibration curve of each sensor is stored in the software. During measurements the software records the instantaneous pressures sensed by each sensor and its coordinates. The data acquisition and EMED system enable both static and dynamic measurements with a maximum speed of 150,000 samples/s.

The sensors are designed for a maximum pressure of 400 kPa and the calibration curve is approximated by a third order polynomial. The pressures in excesses of 250 kPa, however, yield poor resolution, since the calibration curve levels off beyond 250 kPa, as shown in Figure 1. A grid of 20 sensors is installed on the handle and calibration of each sensor is stored in the EMED software for later analysis of the measured data.

MEASUREMENT OF GPD

A 38 mm diameter, I - shaped handle was instrumented with a matrix of 20 flexible variable capacitance pressure sensors to measure the GPD under varied conditions of loading. The instrumented handle was mounted on an electro-dynamic vibration exciter such that either harmonic or stochastic vibration may be generated along its longitudinal axis. Strain gages were applied to measure the total grip force exerted by the subjects. The total grip force measured by the strain gages was displayed to the subject through a digital voltmeter to enable the subject to maintain nearly constant grip force. Figure 2 illustrates the schematic of the measurement system.

Two subjects were used to acquire the GPD under static and dynamic loading conditions. Each subject was advised to maintain an identical posture during all the experiments and to grip the handle with their dominant right hand while keeping the forearm horizontal with an elbow angle of 90 degrees. The subjects were advised to maintain constant total grip force by monitoring the strain gage signal displayed on the digital volt meter. The gripping hand of each subject was positioned on the handle in a specific manner to attain pre-determined sensor pattern, as shown in Figure 2.

The static and dynamic GPD was acquired for grip forces of 25 N, 50 N, 100 N and 150 N. The dynamic GPD measurements were performed under harmonic excitations of constant peak accelerations of 0.5 g, 1.0 g, 2.0 g and 3.0 g at discrete frequencies of 20 Hz, 50 Hz, 100 Hz, 200 Hz, 500 Hz and 1000 Hz. The static GPD measurements at 50 N grip force was performed five times and the data were examined for repeatability. Similarly, the repeatability of dynamic GPD was examined by measuring GPD for 50 N grip force and 2.0 g peak acceleration at 100 Hz. The experiments showed good repeatability.

RESULTS AND DISCUSSION

The measured data were averaged and analyzed for different static and dynamic test conditions to highlight the influence of magnitude of grip force, and characteristics of handle vibration on local concentration of pressures at the hand-handle interface. The measurements performed on the selected subjects revealed a high degree of consistency in terms of locations of peak pressures. The detailed results are, therefore, discussed in terms data obtained from a single subject.

Figure 3 presents the GPD measured under 50 N static and dynamic (2.0 g peak acceleration at 20 Hz) grip forces as a function of longitudinal and lateral coordinates of the hand. The sensor location on the hand is described in terms of its coordinates with reference to the approximate mid-point of the base of the hand. The location of sensors is described as distal and proximal along the longitudinal axis, and as lateral and medial along the lateral axis. The figure reveals high concentration of pressure at the index finger tip (sensor # 20) under static loads. The pressure at the base of the thumb (sensors # 4,5,10) and tip of the middle finger (sensor # 19) are also observed to be high. While the magnitude of peak pressure under static loads varies significantly with the level of grip force, the peak pressure occurs at the tip of index finger (sensor # 20), independent of the grip force. Under dynamic loads, the GPD data reveals concentration of high pressures on the lateral section of the hand, while the medial section is exposed to considerably lower levels of local pressure. A comparison of the GPD data reveals that the pressure peaks at the tips of index and middle fingers under static load (sensors # 20, 19) tend to shift towards the middle of fingers under application of dynamic grip force (sensors # 10,14,15). The magnitude of pressure peak at the index finger tip, measured under static load decreases considerably under the dynamic load, while the magnitude of the local pressure at its middle increases.

Figure 4 illustrates the GPD acquired for a static and dynamic grip force of 100 N. The dynamic measurements are performed for 1.0 g peak acceleration at 100 Hz. A comparison of the static and dynamic GPD data demonstrates the trend presented in Figure 3 for 2.0 g peak acceleration at 20 Hz. Various studies have established that the tips of index, and middle fingers are the first parts of the hand affected by the VWF disease [13,14]. Occurrence of excessive pressure at middle of these fingers can greatly reduce the blood supply to their tips. This factor, together with several other factors, such as prolonged exposure to vibration, may be related to the causation of VWF among hand-held power tool operators.

CONCLUSIONS

GPD at the hand-handle interface was measured under static and dynamic loading to study the influence of magnitude of grip force, and vibration characteristics on the local pressures at the interface. The FSR sensors were found to be inadequate due to their high hysteresis and poor repeatability. Variable capacitance pressure sensors were used to obtain GPD at various loading conditions. The dynamic tests were performed for 25 N, 50 N, 100 N and 150 N grip forces at 0.5 g, 1.0 g , 2.0 g and 3.0 g peak acceleration levels in the frequency range 20-1000 Hz. The results of the study revealed high concentration of pressure at the tips of index and middle fingers, and base of the thumb under static grip forces. These pressure peaks tend to shift towards middle of the fingers under application of dynamic loads, irrespective of grip force, vibration frequency and acceleration level. The magnitude of local pressure peaks, however, is strongly related to the grip force and acceleration level. High concentration of pressure at middle of the fingers can cause reduced blood flow to thier tips. This impairment of blood flow may contribute to causation of vibration white finger upon prolonged exposure.

REFERENCES

1. WASSERMAN, D.E. 1987, *Human Aspects of Occupational Vibration*, (Elsevier Science Pub.). 7-34.
2. BRAMMER, A.J. 1982, Relations between vibration exposure and the development of the vibration syndrome, In Brammer and Taylor eds., *Vibration Effects on the Hand and Arm in Industry*, (John Wiley & Sons, NewYork), 283-290.
3. GRUBER, G.J. 1976, Relationship between whole-body vibration and morbidity patterns among interstate truck drivers, *NIOSH Publication No.77-167*.
4. WASSERMAN, D.E., *et al* 1982, Vibration white finger disease in U.S. workers using pneumatic chipping and grinding hand-tools - Vol II - Engineering testing, *NIOSH Publication No. 82-101*.
5. PYKKÖ, I., *et al* 1976, Transmission of vibration in the hand-arm system with special reference to changes in compression force and acceleration, *Scandinavian Journal of Work, Environment & Health*, 2, 87-95.
6. Rasmussen, G. 1982, Human body vibration exposure and its measurements, *Brueil and Kjaer Technical Review No. 1*.
7. FELLOWS, G.L. and FREIVALDS, A., 1991, Ergonomics evaluation of a foam rubber grip for tool handles, *Applied Ergonomics,* 225-230.
8. LINDEN, O., *et al* 1965, Pressure distribution on the surface of the human body: I. Evaluation in lying and sitting positions using a bed of springs and nails, *Arch. of Phys. Med. & Rehab.*, 378-385.
9. HOLLEY, L.K., *et al* 1979, A new pressure measuring system for cushions and beds with a review of the literature, *Paraplegia*, 17, 461-474.
10. ABRAMS, C.F. 1971, Modeling the vibrational characteristics of the human hand by driving point mechanical impedance method, *North Carolina State University*, Raleigh, Ph.D Thesis (unpublished), 28-29.
11. KRAUSE, P., ORBAN, A., PANZKE, K.J. and POPOV, K. 1979, Critical assessment of common methods to determine vibrational stress of hand-arm system, *International Symposium Man under Vibration Suffering and Protection,* Udine (Italy), 261-274.
12. Piché , A., RAKHEJA, S., GOUW, G.J. and SANKAR, T.S. 1988, Development of an elastic human-seat interface pressure sensing system, *ICAART 88,* Montreal, 118-119.
13. BRUBAKER, R.L., MACKENZIE, C.J.G. and BATES, D.V. 1983, Vibration white finger disease among tree fellers in British Columbia, *J. of Occupational Medicine*, 25, 403-408.
14. HELLSTRØM, B. and ANDERSON, K.A. 1972, Vibration injuries in Norwegian forest workers, *British Journal of Industrial Medicine*, 29, 255-263.

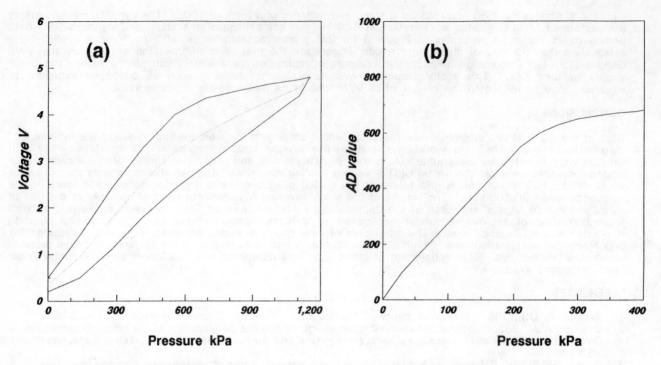

Figure 1: Calibration curves of the pressure sensors: (a) Force sensing resistors; (b) Variable capacitance sensor.

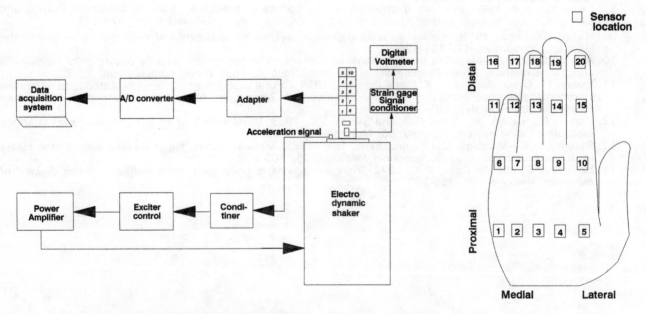

Figure 2: Schematic of the pressure sensing system and location of pressure sensors.

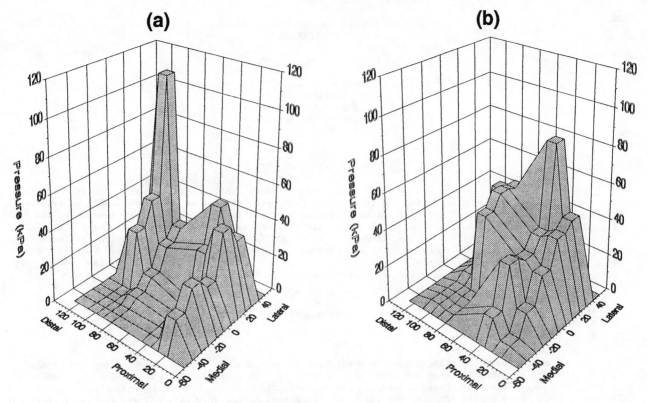

Figure 3: Static and dynamic grip pressure distribution under a 50 N grip force:
(a) Static; (b) 2.0 g peak acceleration at 20 Hz.

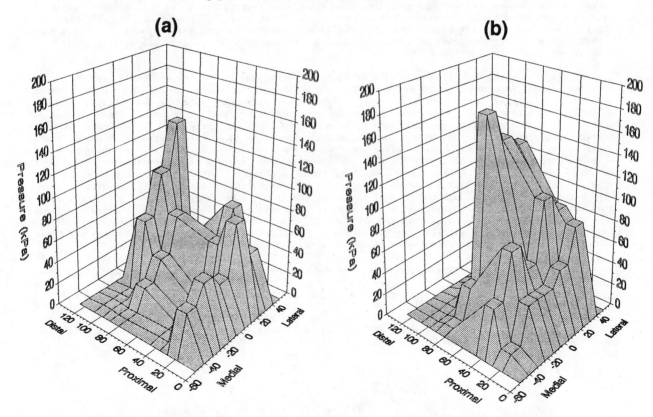

Figure 4: Static and dynamic grip pressure distribution under a 100 N grip force:
(a) Static; (b) 1.0 g peak acceleration at 100 Hz.

THE EFFECTS OF PHYSICAL AGING ON
COMPOSITE CREEP

by

J. L. Sullivan, E. J. Blais and D. Houston
Research Staff
Ford Motor Company
Dearborn, Mich. 48121

ABSTRACT

The creep behavior of a series of fiber reinforced plastics (FRP) and corresponding resins have been studied, with emphasis on elucidating the role of physical aging effects on FRP viscoelastic behavior. Thermosetting and thermoplastic composites were studied representing semi-crystalline, amorphous, and highly filled amorphous polymer matrix FRPs. It is found that physical aging effects are operative for all FRPs, including the semi-crystalline systems. Time-aging time and time-temperature superposition are found to be valid procedures for short term creep behavior; they cannot be applied to long term creep behavior. However, long term creep can be satisfactorily predicted from momentary creep using an effective time theory. Evidence of a universal, temperature shift factor temperature dependence is presented.

INTRODUCTION

The viscoelastic behavior of fiber reinforced plastics is dependent on stress, temperature, and physical aging. Although the importance of the first two factors has been appreciated in the composites community for a long time, the effects of physical aging on FRP viscoelastic behavior has not been elucidated until just recently [1-3]. As a matter of fact, the influence of physical aging on glassy polymer viscoelasticity has long been appreciated [4,5]; thermoplastic [4,5], thermosetting [6], and semicrystalline [7,8] polymer glasses have all been studied. The influence of physical aging effects on FRP viscoelastic behavior is similar to that of neat polymer glasses, i.e. upon aging at a temperature below the polymer's glass transition temperature (T_g), momentary creep curves (time under load much less than the aging time) shift to longer times. This was first shown for a unidirectional fiber vinyl ester resin system [1]. Since then, another study has been conducted on a high temperature thermoplastic composite (polyarylsulphone) where physical aging effects were found [9].

Physical aging is a manifestation of a slow evolution of a polymer to thermodynamic equilibrium. After a quench to below T_g, polymer glasses are generally not at thermodynamic equilibrium. This is manifested by time dependent changes in the extensive state variables such as volume, enthalpy and entropy, as well as the mechanical properties of the polymer. Such time dependence for the specific volume [10] and the viscoelastic functions [4,5] for polymers quenched below T_g is well documented. In fact, there is a strong correlation between changes in specific volume and the viscoelastic functions [4,5]. This correlation suggests at least a qualitative explanation of physical aging in terms of the time dependent free volume, the non-occupied volume component of the specific volume. When a polymer is quenched to a temperature below its glass transition temperature (T_g), there is a significant loss (about 3 orders of magnitude) in polymer chain and polymer segment mobility. System free volume strongly influences chain segment mobility which in turn affects the free volume through the rate of change of the free volume. This circle of influences describes an asymptotic approach to equilibrium, a very slow process which never equilibrates in a practical time frame for temperatures less than about T_g - 15° C. This slow evolution toward thermodynamic equilibrium has been termed by Struik as physical aging [5]. Above T_g, physical aging is not operative since a polymer reaches thermodynamic equilibrium almost instantly after a change in temperature.

There is little work in the literature devoted to the influence of physical aging on composite viscoelasticity. This paper extends what has been done before [1,2]. More specifically, the influence of physical aging on FRP viscoelasticity is discussed for a number of composite systems, including thermosets (structural and highly filled), an amorphous thermoplastic composite, and semicrystalline thermoplastic composites. In addition, the suitability of time-aging time and time-temperature superposition is discussed. Finally, it is shown that physical aging effects can be accounted for and long term creep can be predicted from short term creep using the Effective Time theory. A more in depth discussion of this material can be found in reference 3.

The constitutive equation for the time dependent strain of a linear viscoelastic material is

$$\epsilon_{ij}(t) = \int_o^t S_{ijkl}(t-s) \ \frac{d}{ds}\sigma_{kl}(s) \ ds \tag{1}$$

where ϵ_{ij}, σ_{kl}, and S_{ijkl} are the strain, stress, and compliance tensors, respectively, t and s are current and past times, respectively. For an isotropic material, there are only three compliance components needed for strain predictions; they are written in contracted notation: $S_{11}(t)$, $S_{66}(t)$, and $S_{12}(t)$. Only two of these are independent. For a transversely isotropic material, six independent material functions [11,13] could theoretically need to be determined; they are: $S_{11}(t)$, $S_{22}(t)$, $S_{66}(t)$, $S_{23}(t)$, $S_{12}(t)$, and $S_{21}(t)$. However, in practice there are only five to be determined since it has been shown experimentally [2,11,12] that $S_{12}(t)$ and $S_{21}(t)$ are the same. To avoid confusion with composite compliances, we henceforth denote $S_{11}(t)$ and $S_{66}(t)$ for isotropic materials as D(t) and J(t), respectively. Also, we adopt the usual composite material coordinate notation, i.e. 1-2 plane corresponds to the plane of the sheet from which samples are cut. For unidirectional FRPs, the fibers are assumed oriented in the 1-direction.

For polymer glasses [5] and the resin dominated compliances for an FRP [1-2], it has been shown experimentally that the momentary creep compliance at an arbitrary temperature, pre-age, and time can be related to the corresponding momentary compliance at a reference temperature (T_r) and age (t_{ar}) as follows:

$$M(t,T,t_a) = B(T) \ M(t/a,T_r,t_{ar}) \tag{2}$$

where $M(t,T,t_a)$ is a generic representation for any compliance component, B(T) is the ratio of the temperature dependence of the compliance at T and T_r. This ratio is found to have essentially no dependence on aging [5]. The momentary creep compliance is a response at constant age. Of course, since the glass starts aging the instant it is quenched below its T_g, a test of finite duration cannot be conducted at constant age. But it can be conducted at essentially constant age by assuring the test duration is no greater than about one tenth the preage (time elapsed between quenching and loading the sample). In eq. (3), "a" is the time scale shift factor, which is a function of both the temperature and age of the sample. When compared on log-log scales, momentary viscoelastic curves acquired at different temperatures and aging times are offset from one another by vertical and horizontal shift factors, namely B(T) and a, respectively. The generic compliance component, eq. (2), can be written more fundamentally in terms of its retardation spectrum, $\mathcal{L}(\tau)$, i.e.

$$M(t,T,t_a) = M_g + \int_{-\infty}^{\infty} \mathcal{L}(\tau) \ (1-e^{-t/\tau}) \ dln\tau \tag{3}$$

where M_g is the limiting glassy compliance at very short times and τ is a retardation time.

Writing the shift factor $a(t_a,T)$ as the product of aging and temperature shift functions [2] and taking the logarithm, we have,

$$\log a(T,t_a) = \log[\gamma t_a^{\mu}] + \log \overline{a_T} \tag{4}$$

where the first term is the aging contribution and the constants γ and μ are functions of T. The latter is often referred to as the aging shift rate. $\bar{a}_T$ is the temperature shift factor which is a function of both T and t_a for a glass; its above T_g counterpart, a_T, is a function of T only, because there is no aging at those temperatures.

Long term creep is fundamentally different than short term (momentary) creep. For long term creep, the test duration is not constrained to be less than $t_a/10$ and hence, significant aging occurs while the system is responding to load. Because long term creep is not a response due solely to an applied load, it can vary significantly with the pre-age, t_a. Hence, long term creep is not a fundamental material response. Nevertheless, long term creep behavior of polymer glasses and glassy matrix composites can be predicted from momentary creep behavior. For this purpose, the "effective time" theory has been derived and used with some success [5]. From the theory, the long term creep compliance $\overline{M}$ can be related to the corresponding momentary creep compliance M in the following manner:

$$\overline{M}(t,T,t_a) = M(\lambda,T,t_a) \tag{5}$$

where λ is the effective time. For systems where the aging shift rate, μ, is less than one [5] (true for most polymers), the effective time is

$$\lambda = t_a \frac{[(1 + t/t_a)^\alpha - 1]}{\alpha} \qquad (6)$$

EXPERIMENTAL

A summary of the resins used in this study and their designations appears in Table I; all the corresponding composites are glass fiber reinforced. Tests were conducted on neat resins (isotropic) and composites with three different types of fiber patterns, i.e. unidirectional fiber (UF), random chop fiber (SMC), and continuous strand mat (CSM). The CSM composites (PC, PP, and PBT) had a grain direction as indicated by the manufacturers; all creep samples were cut ninety degrees to that direction. Pertinent temperatures for the materials used in this study are also given in the table. The T_g values appearing in the table were determined from the peak of the log E" (loss modulus) vs temperature curve obtained using a Polymer Laboratories DMTA; the heating rate and frequency were 1° C/min and 1 hertz, respectively.

Details concerning sample dimensions, test machines, and temperature control can be found elsewhere [2]. Samples were loaded employing wedge action grips mated to wedge shaped end tabs on the specimens. End tabs were bonded to the samples with epoxy cement; to bond tabs to the Azdel samples (polypropylene), they were first plasma treated in an air atmosphere for 3 minutes. Strain measurements were made using strain gages; details concerning gage application and excitation have been discussed before [2].

For the unidirectional composites, samples of three different fiber orientations were used: transverse, longitudinal, and off-axis tensile specimens. For our off-axis specimens, the fiber angle was forty five degrees and hence only two strain gages (axial and transverse) were needed to determine $S_{66}(t)$. End effect corrections were small (less than 0.3%) and hence were not applied to off-axis strain data. $S_{44}(t)$ was calculated from $S_{23}(t)$ and $S_{33}(t)$ (plane of isotropic symmetry) both determined from strain data acquired from gages mounted to the sides of the transverse specimen. The determination of "through the thickness" compliance components for uni-directional materials is comparatively easy. For CSM materials on the other hand, the side surface is actually a plane of orthotropic symmetry and hence three compliance components need to be measured. However, due to thinness only two can be practically measured on typical plaque materials using side mounted gages i.e. $S_{23}(t)$, and $S_{33}(t)$. Some kind of off-axis test would have to be devised to determine $S_{44}(t)$; perhaps a forty degree off-axis compression specimen made from a laminate of CSM lamina could be used.

In this study, both short term (momentary) and long term creep tests were conducted. A schematic of the aging time / test sequence is shown in Figure 1. Remember, for short term creep, the condition $t \leq t_a/10$ defines the maximum test duration, whereas for long term creep, no restriction is placed on the test length. Before starting an aging sequence, a sample (unloaded) was placed in the creep oven of the test machine and the temperature was raised to the rejuvenation temperature T_{rej} (greater than $T_g + 20°$ C) for 2 hours. After that, the temperature was dropped to the test temperature and an aging time (t_a)/creep test sequence was commenced. Prior to running another aging sequence, specimen rejuvenation was affected by heating it in the test chamber for two hours at T_{rej}. The applied stress for each creep test was nominally 8 MPa. Maximum unrecovered strain between tests in an aging sequence was about $130\mu\epsilon$ for an applied strain of about $1500\mu\epsilon$. Of course, rejuvenation eliminates unrecovered strain. For a more complete discussion of these experiments, see reference 3.

RESULTS

In the following sections, results for creep tests on the materials studied are reported.

Recovery: Because total recovery following a creep test takes a very long time to complete, recovery strains associated with that test can in principle manifest themselves in a subsequent test. This is depicted in Fig. 1. However, in our case, recovery effects were not significant. Because our momentary aging times were typically 1, 2, 4, 8, 22, 70 hours, this resulted in test recovery times of at least nine times the test time. Hence, by the time the next test in an aging sequence comes up, the rate of recovery from the previous test is so low that corrections to the creep data were deemed unnecessary. We estimate that their omission results in a maximum error of about 2%. Incidentally, rejuvenation erases the effects due to load of all previous tests on the samples.

Physical Aging: In a previous study [1-2], it was shown that physical aging effects are operative in the compliance functions for the NV-UF system and its corresponding resin. Physical aging is also operative in all of the other systems reported on herein. Examples of this are shown in Figs. 2-6. All the data sets show the expected trend with aging time, i.e. both the compliance and its log rate of change decrease with increasing aging time. This is true for both the thermosetting and the thermoplastic composites. Note that even the SMC, which is 50% by weight calcium carbonate, shows aging effects.

Creep results for FRPs with the semi-crystalline polymer matrices (PP and PBT) are shown in Fig. 6. Note in the figure that for both materials physical aging effects are apparent at the lower temperature but not at the higher temperature. Since the elevated temperature (120° C) is much higher than the T_g of either polymer, the absence of physical aging effects at that temperature is as expected. In the case of the polypropylene composite, note in the figure that physical aging is evident at 30° C, which is still considerably higher than its T_g (see Table I). Supposedly, physical aging effects should not be operative above the glass transition temperature. An explanation of this has been given by Struik [11]. He argues that physical aging persist to temperatures well above a semi-crystalline polymer's nominal T_g because such materials demonstrate an "extended glass transition." It is felt that this is a consequence of lower segment mobility of amorphous chains near crystal surfaces, resulting in a distribution of T_g's.

For temperatures lower than T_g-30° C, test results for BPA-UF show that $S_{11}(t)$ has very little time dependence and is at best a weak function of temperature and aging time (data not shown). This is as expected for a fiber dominated compliance and consistent with previous results for the NV system [2]. For the same temperature range, the compliances $S_{12}(t)$ and $S_{21}(t)$ are found to be somewhat more strongly dependent on temperature and perhaps physical aging. Unfortunately, the data tended to be noisy and somewhat variable and hence are not shown. Due to these shortcomings, we are unable to conclusively show that $S_{12}(t)$ is equal to $S_{21}(t)$. However, at a given temperature, the time dependence of both functions appears to be about the same, suggesting that both functions are the same.

The compliance, $S_{44}(t)$, was calculated from data acquired on specimens with strain gages mounted to the sides. An example set of results is shown in Fig. 2. We find that these type of creep data are very reliable as is attested to by the excellent agreement observed between $S_{22}(t)$ data acquired from side mounted and face mounted strain gages.

<u>Time-Aging Time Superposition:</u>   For the amorphous polymer matrix composites, time-aging time superposition was applied to the isothermal momentary creep data to form momentary master curves [1-3]. An inspection of Figs. 2-5 reveals that good superposition is obtained. As reported before [2], horizontal shifts are found to be much larger than the vertical shifts; the latter are nearly zero and appear to be slightly positive (for shifting longer aging time curve to a shorter time curve). This is consistent with aging shift data on neat polymers [4,5] and recent results for a thermoplastic composite [9]. That the vertical shifts are small shows that the assumption of B(T) in eq. (3) being a function of T alone is an excellent approximation. Aging shift rate results determined from the horizontal shifts are similar to what has been reported before [1,2] and are discussed in more detail elsewhere [3]. But briefly, for the FRPs studied herein, μ varies between 0.7 to 0.9. Note that good superposition seen in Figs. 2-5 demonstrates that all retardation times for relaxation processes within the experimental time frame have the same aging dependence.

<u>Momentary Master Curves:</u>   The momentary master curves (MMC) for various compliance components of the BPA system are shown in Fig. 7. All curves were obtained from time temperature superposition using momentary creep data and as seen in the figures excellent superposition is obtained. To facilitate comparison of compliance components, the same reference curve has been drawn next to each compliance component. There are some interesting features to note in the figure. First, the shapes of D(t), J(t), and $S_{22}(t)$ are essentially identical to the reference curve. We point out that this equality of shape shows that all three compliances can be related to the same underlying retardation spectrum. Also note in Fig. 7 that $S_{66}(t)$ increases more rapidly than the reference curve. Further, $S_{44}(t)$ changes at about the same rate as the reference curve.

Horizontal shift factor data for these systems is shown in Fig. 8. Note that the data for all of our systems fall on the same curve when plotted on a reduced temperature scale, i.e. relative to a reduced temperature T_{red} which is defined here to be T_g-30°. The reference age (t_{ar}) is 70 hr. The superposition of all temperature shift factor data indicates that a common $\bar{a}_T$ vs temperature behavior exists for our systems, which includes neat bis-phenol A and Novolac vinyl ester resins, their composites, and polycarbonate composite. From a molecular point of view, this is not totally surprising since all of these materials have in part the bis-phenol A structure in the polymer network structure. However, the temperature dependence of $\bar{a}_T$ shown in Fig. 8 may be even more universal than just for BPA type resin systems. Also included in Fig. 8 are sub-T_g temperature shift factor data for a polyarylsulphone composite [9]; they also show the same temperature behavior. Molecularly this polymer is not as flexible as the BPA and NV based systems. Incidentally, for the superposition vertical shifts were also used, but they are discussed elsewhere [3].

No attempt has been made to compare BPA-CSM creep data with the BPA reference response, since the in-plane creep behavior of this system is expected to be much different than that of the unidirectional and neat resin systems. In fact, as seen in Fig. 7, the fiber constraint on the creep of the BPA-CSM system is sufficiently effective that the rubbery plateau is reached. For uni-directional systems, this constraint is much less restrictive of system compliance as is indicated by the near identical shapes of FRP transverse compliance and resin compliance curves.

For linear viscoelastic predictions of a composite at any arbitrary temperature, time, age, and loading (or deformation) condition, it is necessary to know B(T), M(t/a,T_r,t_{ar}), μ, and a(t_a,T). For the BPA-UF system discussed herein, the data in Figs. 7 and 8 together with B(T) and μ results [3] are sufficient to make such predictions. Stress relaxation is predicted by inversion of the compliance tensor $S_{ijkl}(t)$. On the other hand, for the CSM composite, not enough information has been obtained to make such general viscoelastic predictions. "Through the thickness" creep behavior for the CSM system also needs to be measured, which unfortunately is not easy to do as for uni-directional composites because of the combination of the orthotropy of the "through the thickness" plane and the thinness of the typical laminate.

There is one point that we want to make here. An important advantage of time temperature superposition over time aging time superposition is that the former yields momentary master curves with a broader time domain. This is so because relative to a longer aging time momentary creep tests no new information on the retardation spectrum, $\mathcal{L}(\tau)$, and hence relaxation processes are obtained from a shorter aging time test. Experimental support for this is shown in Fig. 2. Note that the 70 hr test data totally spans the domain of the function (momentary master curve). On the other hand, tests done at the longest aging time of aging sequences conducted at different temperatures extends information on the retardation spectrum.

Long Term Creep: Long term creep results for $S_{66}(t)$ and $S_{22}(t)$ of the BPA-UF system are given in Fig. 9. After an inspection of the experimental data in the figure, it is seen that the curves cannot be superposed, thus showing that time temperature superposition for long term creep data is not valid. Also note in the figure that the momentary master curves depart sharply from the long term counterpart. The reason for this is that during long term creep aging is retarding the creep process.

Overall the agreement between experimental and theoretical long term creep values is good; the maximum error is about 12%, which is about twice that reported before for the NV-UF system. The effective time theory curves were obtained from eqs. (2), (5), and (6) and momentary master curves given in Fig. 7.

CONCLUSIONS

An extensive study of the creep behavior of a variety of composite systems, including thermosetting and thermoplastic composites, has been conducted. The influence of physical aging on FRP viscoelastic behavior has been elucidated. The following conclusions have been reached:

• All composites (FRPs) and their resins demonstrate physical aging, including semi-crystalline polymer composites and a highly filled thermoset (SMC). The semi-crystalline FRPs continue to demonstrate physical aging effects in creep for temperatures somewhat above T_g but at elevated temperatures they creep relatively little.

• Time-aging time superposition works well, even for an SMC.

• Time-temperature superposition is successfully applied to momentary creep data but is not valid for long term creep.

• For both of our resins and composites, a common temperature shift factor vs temperature behavior is observed. Because this same temperature dependence is also observed for a structurally different FRP (polyarylsulphone based), this behavior could be more universally applicable.

• The similarity of the creep behaviors of resin and corresponding transverse tensile compliance suggest that they can be related to the same underlying retardation spectrum.

• Long term creep predictions based on the effective time theory are in good agreement with experiment.

REFERENCES

1.   Sullivan, J. L., Physical Aging and Creep of a Uni-Directional Fiber/Thermosetting Resin Composite, VI International Congress on Experimental Mechanics meeting, Portland, Oregon, June 6-10, 1988.
2.   Sullivan, J. L., Creep and Physical Aging of Composites, Compos. Sci. and Technol., 39, 207-232(1990).
3.   Sullivan, J., L., Blais, E. J. and D. Houston, Physical Aging in The Creep Behavior of Thermosetting and Thermoplastic Composites, submitted for publication in Composite Sci. and Technol.
4.   Struik, L. C. E., ' Physical Aging in Plastics and Other Glassy Materials', Polym. Eng. Sci. 17, 165-173(1977).
5.   Struik, L. C. E., 'Physical Aging in Amorphous Polymers and Other Materials,' Elsevier, 1978.
6.   Janas, V. F. and McCullough, R. L., " The Effects of Physical Aging on the Viscoelastic Behavior of a Thermoset Polyester," Comp. Sci. and Technol., 30, 99-118(1987).
7.   Ogale, A. A. and McCullough, R. L., 'Physical Aging of Polyether Ether Ketone', Comp. Sci. Technol. 30, 137-148(1987).
8.   Struik, L. C. E., The Mechanical Behavior and Physical Aging of Semi-crystalline polymers: 1, Polymer, 28, 1521-1533(1987).
9.   Hastie, R. L. and Morris, D. H., "The Effect of Physical Aging on the Creep Response of a Thermoplastic Composite, Masters Thesis, Department of Engineering Science and Mechanics, Virginia Polytechnic Institute and State University, (1991).
10.   Kovacs, A. J., 'La Contraction Isotherme Du Volume Des Polymeres Amorphes', J. Poly. Sci. 30, 131-147(1958).
11.   Halpin, J. C. and Pagano, N. J., "Observations on Linear Anisotropic Viscoelasticity", J. Comp. Materials, 2(1), 68-80(1968).

12. Morris, D. H., Brinson, H. F. and Yeow, Y. T., "The Viscoelastic Behavior of the Principal Compliance Matrix of a Unidirectional Graphite/Epoxy Composite, Polymer Composites, 1, 32-36(1980).
13. Rogers, T. G. and Pipkin, A. C., " Asymmetric Relaxation and Compliance Matrices in Linear Viscoelasticity", ZAMP, 14, 334-343(1963).

TABLE I

Glass Transition[a], Rejuvenation[b], and Melting Temperatures
of the Composites Studied Herein

Resin Type/Source	Designation	T_g (°C)	T_r (°C)	T_m (°C)
Thermosets				
Novolac vinyl ester (Dow Derakane 470-36)	NV	153	170	NA
Bis-Phenol A vinyl ester (Dow Derakane 411-C-50)	BPA	112	160	NA
Polyester Composite[b] (Rockwell RI-9466)	SMC	100 40	130	NA
Polycarbonate (Azloy)	PC	145	150	NA
Thermoplastics				
Polypropylene (GE Azdel)	PP	-2	130	138[d] 170[e]
Polybutylene Terephthalate (GE Azmet)	PBT	53	150	235

[a] T_g estimates obtained from peak of log E" vs T curve at ν=1 hz with a heating rate of 1° C/min.
[b] Two hours at temperature.
[c] Two component system.
[d] Syndiotactic
[e] Isotactic

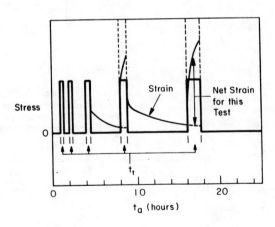

Fig. 1: A depiction of the load history for a set of momentary creep tests; the corresponding strain response, including recovery, is also depicted.

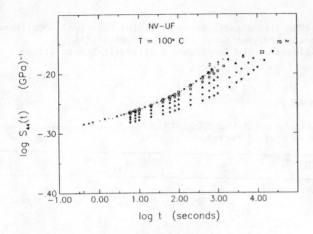

Fig. 2: Through the thickness, momentary shear creep curves for the NV-UF FRP; aging times in hours given in the figure; (•) denotes the momentary master curve at t_{ar} – 2 hr, (x) denotes the t_a = 70 hr creep data of the momentary master curve.

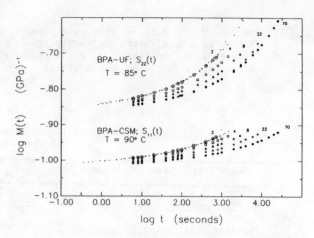

Fig. 3: Momentary creep behavior of two different BPA systems; (•) denotes the momentary master curve at t_{ar} – 2 hr; aging time in hours given in the figure.

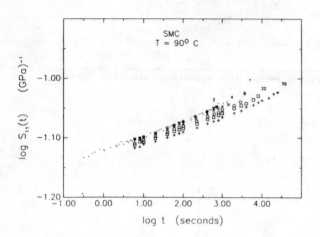

Fig. 4: Momentary creep behavior of the SMC at the aging times indicated; (•) denotes the momentary master curve at reference age (t_{ar}) of 2 hr.

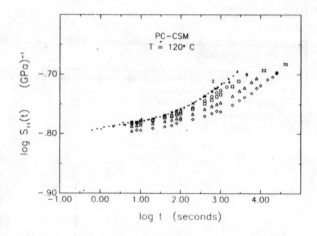

Fig. 5: Momentary creep behavior of the poly-carbonate FRP at the aging times indicated; (•) denotes the corresponding momentary master curve at reference age of 2 hr.

176

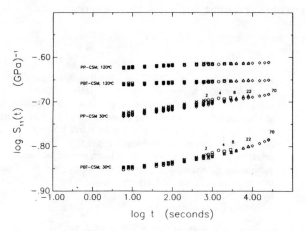

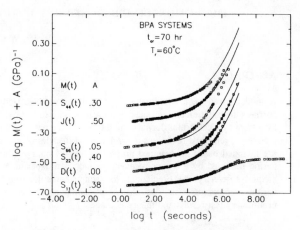

Fig. 6: Momentary creep behavior of two semi-crystalline thermoplastic composites at the aging times indicated.

Fig. 7: Momentary master curves obtained from time temperature superposition for various compliance components of the bis-phenol A resin system and composite.

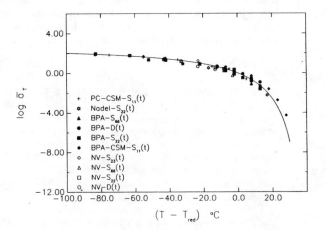

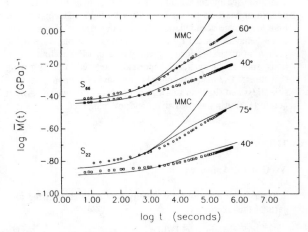

Fig. 8: The temperature shift factor vs departure from the reduced temperature, T_{red} (T_g-30°C).

Fig. 9: Experimental (○ & □) and theoretical (---) long term creep results for the shear and transverse creep compliance of the BPA-UF system; temperatures given in the figure, t_a=1 hr; μ=0.75.

PREDICTION OF CREEP STRAINS DURING CYCLICAL COMPRESSION OF COMPOSITES

E.G. Wolff, W.C. Hansen and K. Shenoy

ABSTRACT

A model based on a combination of non-linear viscoelasticity, stiffness degradation and physical aging was developed to predict long term cyclical strains during combined stress/temperature and recovery cycling. Predictions to over several decades of cycles are included based on assumed properties for a 4 hour loading period followed by a 1-hour recovery period. An experimental method to verify the predictions for compressive loading at various temperatures is described. A comparison between preliminary test results and theory is made.

INTRODUCTION

Many models of the creep behavior of polymer matrix composites assume viscoelastic behavior.[1-3] However, as Struik[4] has pointed out, the multiple integral theory for non-linear viscoelastic behavior alone will be insufficient because this theory assumes the material properties are invariant with time. Gates[5] includes viscoplastic behavior but it is difficult to separate mechanisms contributing to material property changes, such as matrix microcracking and physical aging.

The proposed model combines the mathematical formulation of non-linear viscoelastic theory with a stiffness reduction model (due to damage accumulation) and the description of changes in creep behavior caused by physical aging. The objective is the prediction of strains during stress and/or thermal cycling conditions, such as the cyclical compression expected in aircraft wing structures. The model is applied to the case of a 4 hour compressive stress and simultaneous high temperature followed by a short period (1 h) at no applied stress and low temperature.

THEORY

A) General Approach

Schapery's[11] equations are initially applied to each of the four parts of the creep curve:

a) initial strain = $g_o D(0) \sigma$ (1)

b) creep strain = $g_1 g_2 \sigma \Delta D(\psi)$ (2)

c) unloading strain increment =
$g_o D(0) \sigma + (g_1 - 1) \sigma g_2 \Delta D(\psi_1)$ (3)

d) recovery strain = $g_2 \sigma \left[\Delta D(\psi_1 + t - t_1) - \Delta D(t - t_1) \right]$ (4)

where $\psi = t/a_{\sigma,T}$ and $\Delta D(t)$, the creep compliance, can be a function suitable to the measured creep strain. Since the time in parts c) and d) is defined as $t > t_1$, we see that the recovery strain is in effect (g_2) times the continuation of the (linear) creep strain ($a_\sigma = 1$) past t_1 minus the same curve starting at t_1, but applied at the end of the nonlinear creep region. This assumes in effect that recovery process is independent of the non-linear parameters g_1 and $a_{\sigma,T}$. If for the time being, we do not make this assumption, then the recovery strain can be readily modeled by the following relation, starting after the unloading strain increment (c) has been applied.

$$e_r = g_1 g_2 \sigma \left[\Delta D(\psi) - \Delta D(\psi - t_1) \right] \quad (5)$$

Equation 1 can be written in terms of time dependent in-plane laminate stiffness A(t), in turn derivable from selected creep data on other arbitrary layups.[3] This approach will allow prediction of cyclical strain for arbitrary layups of a given material.

B) Damage Accumulation

Damage accumulation, such as matrix microcracking, fiber/matrix debonding, etc., causes a time/stress/temperature dependent reduction in stiffness. We have chosen a generalized formulation of Yang[6] to model this effect. Their data corroborate a power law decrease in E as N increases, with the functions f_1 and f_2 being linear relations with stress. Thus;

$$E(N) = E(0) (f_1) N^{f2} \quad (6)$$

where $-1 < f_2(\sigma) < 0$. For example, if $f_2(\sigma)$ is -0.1, there is 40% retention of initial stiffness E(0) after N = 10,000 cycles if $f_1(\sigma)$ is unity. Greater degradation requires a more negative value of $f_2(\sigma)$. If we keep this expression in terms of cycles, there will be no nonlinear effect, for the degradation is the same at the beginning and at the end of each cycle. Since degradation is assumed to occur during and not between cycles, eq. (6) is used with time and not cycles as the independent variable and the constant $f_2(\sigma)$ is adjusted accordingly.

The difference between the initial elastic load and the unloading strain in the same cycle according to Schapery (eq. (1) and (3)) is $(g_1 - 1) g_2 \Delta D(\psi) \sigma$. Thus there will be a net shrinkage of roughly $(g_1 - 1)/g_1$ times the magnitude of the positive creep strain through that cycle. The creep strain should be proportional to the change in loading/unloading strains since damage development affects both.

C) Physical Aging

The polymeric matrix will be used in the glassy state and as such is not in thermodynamic equilibrium. The resultant physical aging takes the form of volume shrinkage and decreasing

(E.G. Wolff is Associate Professor of Mechanical Engineering and W.C. Hansen and K. Shenoy are Graduate Research Assistants at Oregon State University, Corvallis OR 97331)

molecular mobility. Thus creep (due to applied load) strains will decrease during each cycle. Past work on thermosetting polymers[7-10] suggests that D(t) decreases as the aging time t_a increases. The aging related horizontal shift factor $a(t_a)$ increases as the free volume decreases. The effect of deformation on damage is complex, but generally opposite to that of t_a as the free volume is increased. Temperature tends to play a lesser role, for while the driving force T_g-T is reduced, the rate of aging increases. The shift factor $a(t_a)$ decreases slightly (de-aging) as the temperature increases but it needs a vertical as well as a horizontal shift to be modelled accurately. Sullivan[10] suggests that the total horizontal shift factor may be found from

$$\log a = \log \left\{ (1 - \mu)\, t_a^\mu \right\} + \log a_{o,t} \qquad (7)$$

Here the aging shift factor

$$\mu = d \log a(t_a)/d \log t_a \qquad (8)$$

increases slightly with temperature, from values around 0.5 at room temperature to about unity at T_g. Since damage accumulation at high temperatures reduces the effect of t_a slightly, our model must show a lesser effect of aging (lower μ) than one would expect from long term room temperature storage alone. If we assume a power relation in eq. (2), or $D(t) = C\, \psi^n$ combined with eqs. (7) and (8), we see that as t_a increases, a increases and the compliance D(t) decreases. There seems to be a negligible dependence of C on t_a.

D) Combined Effects

The second cycle (N = 2) must consider that recovery from the first cycle is incomplete. Combining this consideration with eqs. (1)-(4) shows that the strain at any time will be a combination of all prior creep and elastic strains, evaluated for times since their first appearance. Thus:

$$e(t) = \sum_{N=1}^{N} \left\{ g_o\, \sigma \left[f_1(\sigma)\, Q^{f2(\sigma)}\, E(0) \right]^{-1} + g_1\, g_2\, C\left[(t - Q)/a \right]^n \right.$$
$$\left. - g_o\, \sigma \left[f_1(\sigma)\, P^{f2(\sigma)}\, E_o \right]^{-1} - g_1\, g_2\, C\left[(t - P)/a_r \right]^n \right\}$$

Equation (9) gives predictions of strain at any time for an arbitrary number of creep/recovery cycles. The first two terms are evaluated for $t > N\tau$, the second two for $t > \psi$. The various terms and their assumed values for a parametric study are given as follows.

Q	= $N(\tau + \tau_o)$	g_o	= 1.0
P	= $N(\tau + \tau_o)$ - 1	g_1	= 1.4
a	= eq. (7)	g_2	= 0.9
$a_{\sigma,T}$	= eq. (7) = 0.3	μ	= eq. (8) = 0.7
C	= 5.5×10^{-6}	n	= 0.3
τ	= time of applied stress/temperature in each cycle = 4 h		
τ_o	= recovery time in each cycle = 1 h		
$f_1(\sigma)$	= eq. (6) = 1.0		
$f_2(\sigma)$	= eq. (6) = - 0.001		
E(0)	= 13.1 GPa (1.9×10^6 psi)		
σ	= applied stress level = 92.9 MPa (13473 psi)		

Figure 1 is plotted for selected cycles using the input parameters above.

EXPERIMENTAL VERIFICATION

The test specimens were 0.254 m × 0.0254 m 16-layer IM7/5260 graphite/bismaleimide tabbed tensile specimens in accordance with ASTM D3039. Unidirectionally reinforced samples were 0.254 m × 0.0127 m with 8 layers. In order to apply constant and cyclic compressive loads with either constant and cyclic temperatures, a special test fixture had to be developed. Requirements for this fixture included the need to test many samples simultaneously. The loading had to be constant over the length of the sample (no stress gradients), and the fixture had to be strong enough to prevent sample buckling. At the same time a minimal thermal mass was needed to facilitate concurrent heating/cooling with load application/removal.

The resulting fixture consists of two steel strips, 0.635 m × 0.078 m × 0.00635 m thick which are separated at each end and in the middle by three rectangular steel blocks which have a thickness just greater than the total thickness of the specimen and the tabs. These rectangular blocks are held in place by two 0.0158 m bolts which pass through the top steel strip, through the rectangular blocks and through the bottom steel strip. In the gap between the top and bottom strips, provided by the rectangular blocks, one specimen is placed against each end block. Parallel rows of small bolts on each side of the specimens are fastened between the top and bottom strip to prevent buckling along the length of each specimen. Two steel plates the thickness of the tabbed specimens act as sliders, and are placed in the gap between the center rectangular block and the other end of the specimen. These slider plates are wider than the steel strips and have two holes on each exposed end. Shims are used to fill the remaining gap between the top and bottom steel strips and the central untabbed section of the specimen. To minimize friction, sliding surfaces are covered with an adhesive Teflon tape. To apply the load, fixtures are placed end to end and the forward slider of the trailing fixture is attached by four steel strips to the rear slider of the leading fixture. This creates a chain where the specimens are in between links, so that when the chain is placed in tension, the specimens are loaded in compression.

To apply the load, the chain of fixtures is placed in a U-shaped foil lined wood channel. One end of the chain is fixed by a block, while the other is attached to a lever arm. The type of lever used depends on the type of load desired. For a constant load configuration, a 10:1 "L"- shaped lever arm is used. This extends the long arm of the lever back over the chain of fixtures. A steel pin welded into the long arm at the end allows for dead weight loads to be applied. For a cyclic loads configuration, an open "L" shaped lever arm is used. In this configuration, the lever arm extends ahead of the chain. To apply the load, timer controlled air cylinders, fixed to the wood channel, push up against the lever pulling the chain tight.

Figure 2 shows the top view of the specimen holder with the top piece removed. Figure 3 shows the side view. Figure 4 illustrates the chain and the applied load direction while Figs. 5 and 6 show the lever arm with a) constant load and b) air cylinder for applied loads.

PRELIMINARY RESULTS

Figure 6 shows creep and recovery curves for the first few cycles for three samples with a unidirectional layup loaded in the transverse (90°) direction to 92.9 MPa (13473 psi) at room temperature. The two lower curves are for samples in the same central fixture in a series of six fixtures subjected to the same cyclical load. The sample showing the higher strain was in an adjacent fixture. It is not known if the latter strain was due to sample or load variation in a different fixture. The first creep curves were fitted to a power law whose constants were used for Fig. 1 predictions. Good agreement continues with the 33rd cycle, where measured microstrains were also in the 7524-7581 range while recovery strains in the following hour dropped from about 492 to 436 μe.

DISCUSSION

The assumption that recovery is equally dependent on the non-linearizing parameters as the creep curve is based on the observation that the matrix or composite structure starts the recovery process from the same stress level that was responsible for the preceding (nonlinear) creep. Alternatively, one may consider that if creep is nonlinear, i.e., stress dependent, the recovery from this state will be equally stress dependent.

Modeling of the cyclical creep strains requires the summation of four processes during each cycle: an initial elastic loading, a creep strain, an elastic unloading strain and a recovery strain. Since the creep period is longer than the recovery time, there is a cumulative positive creep as the number of cycles increase. However, damage occurring during the creep stage means that the unloading step produces a greater (negative) strain than the initial load strain. This appears to be on the same order of magnitude as the creep strain during each cycle. The creep strain is further reduced by physical aging. The net result, substantiated by test data, is that the total strains may change very little on cycling, depending on the relative magnitudes of the various effects.

CONCLUSIONS

A model based on non-linear viscoelastic behavior, damage development and physical aging was used to predict long term creep and recovery strains of a graphite reinforced bismaleimide during intermittent compressive loading. It was found that long term changes in each of these effects are of the same order of magnitude. An experimental approach for verification of the model and initial model parameter inputs was developed. Continuing tests at high temperatures and various fiber layups will permit further tuning of the model to the experimental data.

ACKNOWLEDGMENTS

The authors wish to thank the Boeing Aircraft Company for sponsorship of this work. The Boeing monitor for this program was Mr. Ramesh Khanna who defined and helped guide the program and provided many helpful comments. The authors also wish to thank Professor Tim Kennedy for helpful discussions. Other OSU students who contributed to the project include Matt Norris, Xuimei Geng, and Robin Tenkate.

REFERENCES

1. Lou, Y.C. and Schapery, R.A., "Viscoelastic Characterization of a Nonlinear Fiber-Reinforced Plastic," *J. Comp. Mat. 5*, 208-234, 1971.

2. Tuttle, M.E. and Brinson, H.F., "Prediction of the Long-Term Creep Compliance of General Composite Laminates," *Exptl. Mech.*, 89-102, 1986.

3. Wolff, E.G. and Crane, S.T., "Prediction of the Micro-yield Strength of Polymer Matrix Composites," *J. Comp. Tech. & Res. 10*, 165-172, 1988.

4. Struik, L.C.E., "Physical Aging: Influence of the Deformation Behavior of Amorphous Polymers," Chapter 11 in *Failure of Plastics*, Ed. W. Brostow and R.D. Corneliussen, Hanser Publishers, New York, 1986.

5. Gates, T.S. "Effects of Elevated Temperature on the Viscoplastic Modeling of Graphite/Polymeric Composites," NASA-TM-104160, October 1991.

6. Yang, J.N., Jones, D.L., Yang, S.H., and Meskini, A., "A Stiffness Degradation Model for Graphite/Epoxy Laminates," *J. Comp. Mat. 24*, 753-769, 1990.

7. Bauwens, J.-C., "Physical Aging: Relation between Free Volume and Plastic Deformation," Chapter 12 in *Failure of Plastics*, Ed. W. Brostow and R.D. Corneliussen, Hanser Publishers, New York, 1986.

8. Vleeshouwers, S., Jamieson, A.M., and Simha, R., "Effect of Physical Aging on Tensile Stress Relaxation and Tensile Creep of Cured EPON 828/Epoxy Adhesives in the Linear Viscoelastic Region," *Polymer Science and Engineering 29*, May 1989.

9. Janas, V.F. and McCullough, R.L., "The Effects of Physical Aging on the Viscoelastic Behavior of a Thermoset Polyester," *Comp. Sci. and Tech. 30*, 99-118 1987.

10. Sullivan, J.L., "Creep and Aging of Composites," *Comp. Sci. and Tech. 39*, 207-232 1990.

Figure 2. Horizontal cross section of the fixture assembly

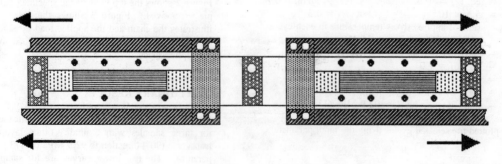

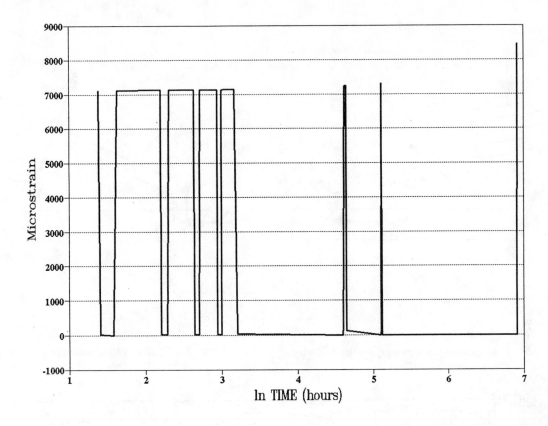

Figure 1. Selected cyclical strain predictions for 4 hour loading at 92.9 MPa, 1 hour recovery of a 90° IM7/5262 composite at room temperature

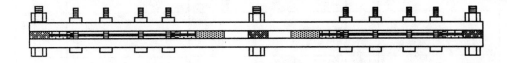

Figure 3. Side view of the fixture assembly

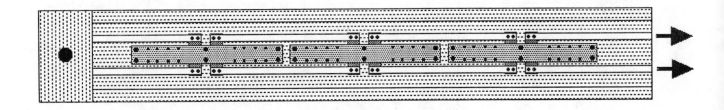

Figure 4. Fixture assembly under load showing direction of applied loading

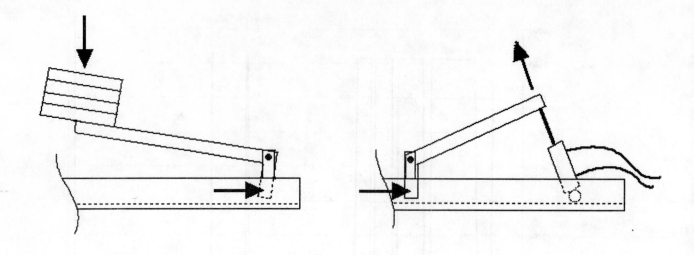

Figure 5. Constant loading configuration showing dead weights and lever arm

Figure 6. Cyclical loading configuration showing air cylinder supply, direction of loading, and lever arm

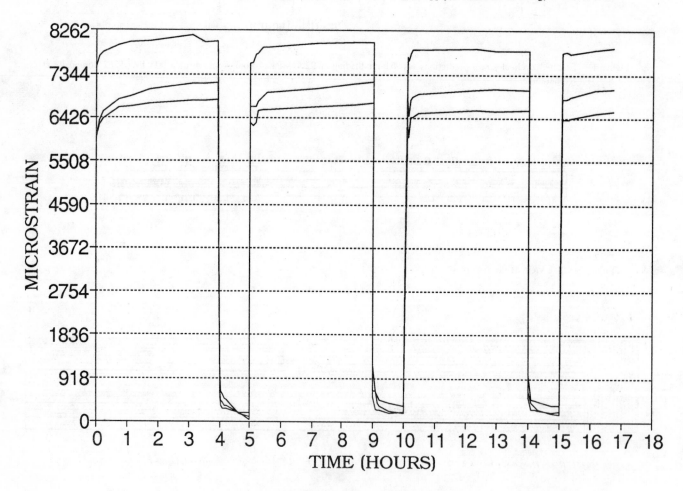

Figure 7. Long term creep and recovery data for a 90° sample loaded at 92.9 MPa at room temperature

The Effect of Physical Aging on the Creep Response of an Off-Axis Thermoplastic Composite

by R.L. Hastie Jr.[1] and D.H. Morris[2]

ABSTRACT

The effect of physical aging on the linear viscoelastic creep response of a Radel X/IM7 thermoplastic composite was studied. Momentary tensile creep tests were conducted at increasing aging times following a rapid quench from above the glass transition temperature (T_g) to a sub-T_g aging temperature. The resulting short-term creep compliance curves were shifted to form a momentary master compliance curve. The double-logarithmic aging shift rate μ and its dependence on sub-T_g aging temperature were determined. The aging characterization process was conducted on unidirectional specimens with 0, 90, and 45 degree fiber direction orientations. The results were used to determine the complete principal compliance matrix of the composite material with the effect of physical aging included. Theoretical predictions for long-term creep compliance were made using an effective time theory and compared to long-term experimental data for each of the specimen orientations used to characterize the composite. Finally, experimental results of a 30 degree fiber angle orientation specimen were compared to a theoretical prediction obtained by transforming the principal compliance matrix to the 30 degree orientation.

INTRODUCTION

Composite materials are proposed for use in advanced aerospace structures like the next generation high speed transport aircraft where the operating environment will be near 370°F (188°C) with a service life in excess of 60,000 hours at temperature. The time dependent or viscoelastic properties of the composite must be fully characterized in order to predict the long-term behavior of the structure. In this paper the experimental procedures used to characterize the effect of thermoreversible physical aging on the linear viscoelastic creep response of a composite in its glassy state are presented. Also included, are the characterization results used to develop a model to predict the long term creep response of unidirectional off-axis composites as the material experiences simultaneous physical aging and creep deformation associated with an applied load.

The term aging is used to describe the process that changes the properties of a material with time. Aging processes are generally grouped into either a physical aging or chemical aging category. Physical aging processes are characterized by the thermoreversibility of the change in the material properties. A polymer, quenched from the rubbery state above the glass transition temperature, T_g, to some lower temperature, does not achieve thermodynamic equilibrium[1]. This is due to the rapid increase in viscosity as T_g is approached from above. As the viscosity increases,

the motion of polymer chains are impaired and the polymer is unable to reach the equilibrium degree of packing before solidification. A characteristic of a polymer, in the quenched state, is that an excess of trapped free volume exists in the structure. As a result, the polymer exhibits volume relaxation with time as the structure tends toward the equilibrium state. Struik[2] refers to this slow gradual approach to volume equilibrium as physical aging. During the physical aging process, many of the physical and mechanical properties of the material change[3]. These changes include an increase in density, tensile yield stress, and elastic modulus. Also, a decrease occurs in impact strength, fracture energy, ultimate elongation, and creep rate. Sullivan[4] recently reported that viscoelastic creep properties of polymer-based thermoset composite materials are also significantly affected by physical aging. This study concentrates specifically on investigating how the creep response of a thermoplastic composite material is affected by physical aging.

PHYSICAL AGING MODELING

A procedure developed by Struik [2] was used to model the short and long term creep response of the composite material. Fundamental to Struik's model was the observation that momentary creep compliance curves exhibit a universal shape when plotted on double-logarithmic scales in the temperature range associated with physical aging. Momentary creep tests are essentially a "snapshot" of the compliance properties taken at a constant aging time. Struik found the shape of the momentary creep compliance curve could be described by the equation:

$$D(t) = D_0 \, e^{(t/t_0)^m} \qquad (1)$$

where D_0 represents the compliance immediately after stress application, t_0 is variable proportional to the mechanical relaxation time, and m is a material constant.

A master momentary compliance curve can be formed by shifting several momentary creep compliance curves as shown in figure 1. The individual compliance curves in figure 1 were obtained at different aging times (t_e) during a sequence of creep tests conducted at a constant temperature and stress level. The effect of aging time or temperature on short-term momentary creep compliance curves is seen as a horizontal shift of the curve on the log-time scale. The amount of horizontal shift, $-\log a$, required to shift each aging test to the referenced creep curve is also shown on figure 1. The last aging time in the test sequence was chosen as the referenced creep curve in figure 1 and is referred to as $t_{e,ref}$. The aging shift rate, μ, is determined by calculating the slope of a plot of $-\log a$ vs. $\log t_e$, shown inserted in the upper left corner of figure 1.

1 Associate Professor, Dept. of Engr. Mechanics USAFA, Colorado Springs, CO 80840

2 Professor, Dept. of Engr. Science and Mechanics VA Tech, Blacksburg, VA 24061

The time-temperature superposition procedure was applied to shift momentary creep compliance curves, obtained at different temperatures with a constant aging time and applied stress level, to form TTSP master momentary creep compliance curves that cover an extended time period. The effect of the constant physical aging of the material during long-term tests is accounted for by modifying the TTSP master momentary compliance curve using an effective time theory.

The effective time theory was developed to account for the effect of aging during long-term creep compliance tests. Although time-temperature superposition works well for momentary creep compliance curves at a constant aging state, it overestimates the creep response during long-term tests. Thus, it is necessary to use the effective time theory to account for the gradual stiffening of the material during physical aging.

Fundamental to the development of the effective time is the observation that the shift rate μ remains constant for very long periods of time. Struik [2] suggests that the shift rate, determined from short-term tests, should be close to unity (e.g., $0.7 < \mu < 1.0$) in order to obtain reliable long-term predictions. The analytical form of the effective time, λ, as derived by Struik [2] is given as:

$$\lambda = t_e \ln\left[1 + \frac{t}{t_e}\right] \qquad for \quad \mu = 1$$

(2)

$$\lambda = \frac{t_e}{\alpha}\left[\left(1 + \frac{t}{t_e}\right)^{\alpha} - 1\right] \qquad for \quad \mu < 1$$

where

$$0 < \alpha = 1 - \mu < 1$$

The two variables that influence the effective time and therefore the long-term compliance predictions are the aging rate μ, determined from short-term tests, and the aging time t_e, at the start of the long-term test. The long-term compliance predictions, associated with the real time axis, are made by substituting the effective time, computed using equation 2, into:

$$\overline{D}(t) = D_0\, e^{(\lambda/t_0)^m}.$$

(3)

In addition to the dependence on effective time, the long-term compliance prediction also depends on how well the variables D_0, t_0, and m define the momentary master compliance curve at t_e. Therefore, obtaining a correct representation of the momentary creep response of the material using TTSP is essential for accurate long-term predictions.

COMPOSITE RELATIONSHIPS

Fiber reinforced composites are considered to be orthotropic and require nine independent material variables [5] for a full three dimensional characterization in the elastic range. Typically, composites are used in the form of thin sheets with the loading applied in-plane. Under these conditions a two dimensional state of plane stress exists which requires only four independent material variables for analysis. The four material properties associated with creep testing are defined in terms of the compliance matrix in the material principal directions. The elastic constitutive equations relating stress, strain, and compliance for the two dimensional orthotropic unidirectional laminate (figure 2) are:

$$\begin{Bmatrix} \varepsilon_1 \\ \varepsilon_2 \\ \gamma_{12} \end{Bmatrix} = \begin{bmatrix} S_{11} & S_{12} & 0 \\ S_{21} & S_{22} & 0 \\ 0 & 0 & S_{66} \end{bmatrix} \begin{Bmatrix} \sigma_1 \\ \sigma_2 \\ \tau_{12} \end{Bmatrix}$$

(4)

This matrix equation, written in condensed notation, is given by:

$$\{\varepsilon\}_{12} = [S]_{12}\{\sigma\}_{12}$$

(5)

where

$\{\varepsilon\}_{12}$ = in-plane local strains

$[S]_{12}$ = principal compliance matrix

$\{\sigma\}_{12}$ = in-plane local stresses.

Determination of the principal compliance terms requires testing of unidirectional laminates at different angle orientations between the local material axis and the global load axis as shown in figure 2.

The four principal compliance terms S_{11}, S_{12}, S_{22}, and S_{66} were determined from the results of creep tests conducted at known aging times. The compliance was calculated by dividing the known stress level applied to the specimen by the measured strain response. The strain response was determined using foil resistance strain gages mounted on the specimens. Other methods of strain measurement such as extensometers, Moire interferometry, and laser-interferometry are possible, but were not used in this study.

A specific orientation of the unidirectional fibers, with respect to the global axis, was required in order to determine each principal compliance term. The S_{11} compliance term was obtained using a specimen with the fibers aligned along the global X axis. This orientation is referred to as a 0 degree specimen. S_{11} was calculated by substituting the axial strain measured in the specimen into the equation:

$$S_{11} = \frac{\sigma_1}{\varepsilon_1}.$$

(6)

The S_{22} compliance term was determined using a specimen with the fibers oriented perpendicular to the global X axis. This orientation is referred to as a 90 degree specimen. S_{22} was calculated by substituting the axial strain along the load axis into the equation:

$$S_{22} = \frac{\sigma_2}{\varepsilon_2}.$$

(7)

The S_{12} compliance term was obtained by using the measured strain in the transverse direction from the 0 degree specimen test. S_{12} was calculated using the equation:

$$S_{12} = \frac{\sigma_1}{\varepsilon_2}.$$

(8)

The compliance tensor was assumed symmetric such that $S_{12} = S_{21}$. This assumption has been confirmed by other investigators [4][6] for similar two dimensional orthotropic materials under in-plane loading. The symmetric assumption was not verified in this study due to the difficulty of accurately measuring the transverse strain in a 90 degree specimen. The small loads applied to the 90 degree specimen produced very small transverse strains in the 0 degree direction. Thus, it was impractical to accurately determine S_{21}.

The shear compliance term, S_{66}, is not as easily determined as the other compliance terms. Several test methods have been proposed to determine S_{66}. Possible methods include the rail-shear test, picture-frame test, and off-axis tensile specimen test. Among these, the off-axis tensile specimen test has gained wide acceptance. The 10 degree off-axis test, proposed by Chamis and Sinclair[7], has been used by several investigators [8][9] to characterize the shear compliance term. A disadvantage of this test is the requirement for a specimen gage-length to gage-width ratio of at least 14. The relatively long and narrow specimen is required to minimize the effect of the end constraint produced by the specimen grips. Unfortunately, the required length for 0.5 inch (1.27 cm) wide specimens, used in this study, was too long to fit in the available thermal chamber. The test configuration selected for shear characterization utilized a 45 degree off-axis specimen. Pindera and Herakovich[10] proposed this configuration to minimize the effect of end constraints. They found that, for even highly anisotropic composites, the effect of end constraints becomes negligible for off-axis angles greater than 45 degrees. The shear compliance, S_{66}, is determined by measuring the shear strain in the 45 degree specimen during uniaxial tension loading. The shear strain in the principal material axis, γ_{12}, is determined using the strain readings from a three strain gage rosette. The orientation of the strain gage rosette on the 45 degree specimen is shown in figure 3. The angle β, is defined as the angle between the X, global load axis, and a line parallel to the gage orientation. The shear compliance was calculated from the 45 degree specimen strain gage data using the following equation:

$$S_{66} = \frac{2(-\varepsilon_{g1} + 2\varepsilon_{g2} - \varepsilon_{g3})}{\sigma_x} \qquad (9)$$

The transformations between the local (1-2) axis and the global (X-Y) axis [5] can be used to determine the global system constitutive relationships. The relationships written in condensed notation are:

$$\{\varepsilon\}_{xy} = [\overline{S}]_{12}\{\sigma\}_{xy} \qquad (10)$$

where $[\overline{S}]_{12}$ is referred to as the transformed or rotated compliance matrix. It represents the material compliance in the global coordinate directions. The compliance in the direction of load application is computed using:

$$S_{xx} = \overline{S}_{11} = S_{11}\cos^4\theta + (2S_{12} + S_{66})\sin^2\theta\cos^2\theta + S_{22}\sin^4\theta. \qquad (11)$$

The load direction compliance is obtained from the experimental data by dividing the stress level applied in the x direction by the corresponding strain measured in the load direction.

EXPERIMENTAL

TESTING EQUIPMENT

Creep testing utilized a lever arm tester with a 20:1 load ratio and a 8000 lb (35.6 N) maximum load capacity. Friction type grips were used to apply load to the specimen. The frictional force was increased by inserting a fine steel mesh between the specimen and the grip face. Additionally, possible slippage of the specimen in the grips was eliminated by placing a 1/8 inch (0.3175 cm) steel pin through the grips and specimen. The grips were attached to the creep frame using 3/8 inch (0.9525 cm) steel pins in a conventional pin-thru-the-grip arrangement.

Mounted on the creep test frame was an oven used to provide the temperature environment for the tests. The temperature distribution in the oven was checked prior to creep testing. The temperature was measured at 3 locations equally spaced along an 8 inch (20.32 cm) length located in line with the load path using iron-constantan (ANSI symbol "J") thermocouples. Initial measurements, at oven temperatures up to 450°F (232°C), indicated ≈ 9°F (5°C) maximum temperature variation, from the top to bottom of the 8 inch (20.32 cm) test length. The temperature variation was improved by installing a simple aluminum air duct in the bottom of the oven. This air duct directed the heated air to the front of the oven and improved the mixing of the air within the oven. A repeated heating test revealed that the temperature variation had decreased to less than 4°F (2°C), over the 8 inch (20.32 cm) length. It is important to note that the temperature variation along the 1/2 inch (1.27 cm) length of the specimen where the strain gages were mounted was negligible.

SPECIMEN PREPARATION

The Radel X/IM7 composite material used in this study was received in 11 inch (28 cm) by 11 inch (28 cm) unidirectional panels with a 12 ply thickness. The material was consolidated using a 50 ton (445 KN) hot press. A grey scale imaging program was used to estimate the composite fiber volume fraction at 0.65. Upon receipt, the panels were C-scanned to locate any irregularities in the material. Panel regions with suspected irregularities were avoided during the fabrication of specimens. A 0 degree reference axis was produced on the panel by pealing off a thin strip of material along an edge parallel to the fibers. A water-cooled diamond wheel abrasive saw was used to cut the panels into 8 inch (20.32 cm) long by 1/2 inch (1.27 cm) wide specimens at 0, 90, and 45 degree angles from the reference fiber direction.

Since the same specimens would be used to characterize physical aging at various temperatures, a means of rejuvenating the specimen, i.e., erasing the previous physical aging history, was required. Booij and Palmen[11] recommended raising the material to a temperature of T_g + 18°F (10°C) to eliminate the effects of the previous thermal history. They stated that the volume equilibrium state is reached in a few seconds at this temperature. Other investigators have used rejuvenating temperatures ranging from T_g + 12.6°F (7°C) [12] to T_g + 72°F (40°C) [4]. The T_g of the Radel X/IM7 composite was determined to be 424°F (217.8°C) by Differential Scanning Calorimetry (DSC) at a 18°F (10°C) per minute heating rate. A temperature of 437°F (225°C) was chosen as a rejuvenating temperature for the Radel X/IM7 material. Preliminary tests verified the material was rejuvenated by holding at this temperature for 15 minutes as described by Hastie and Morris [13]

The Radel X/IM7 material was also subjected to a Thermal Gravimetric Analyzer (TGA) test in air at a heating rate of 18°F (10°C) per minute up to 1472°F (800°C) to determine if the material would degrade at the maximum testing temperature. The material experienced insignificant weight loss up to a temperature of 788°F (420°C) and lost only 5% of its original weight at a temperature of 1043°F (563°C). These temperatures were well beyond the 437°F (225°C) maximum temperature used during rejuvenation of the specimens.

Booij and Palmen [11] reported that the quench rate used to cool a specimen from above T_g to the aging temperature influences the linear viscoelastic properties of the resulting glassy material for a very long time. In order to compare viscoelastic properties at temperatures below T_g, it is essential to know the thermal history of the specimen as it passed through T_g during cooling. The method used to quench specimens from above T_g to the aging temperature varies between investigators. Booij and Palmen quenched their samples using liquid nitrogen. Kong [14] quenched his graphite/epoxy laminate specimens in an ice-water bath. A procedure used by Sullivan [4] utilized high pressure air to quench the specimen and was adopted for use in this study. This method provided the only practical means to quench the material when strain gages and wires are attached to the specimen.

The quench rate obtained using the high pressure air injection was determined using a specimen instrumented with an embedded J type thermocouple. The instrumented specimen, mounted in the test oven, was initially stabilized at the rejuvenating temperature. The specimen temperature was also monitored as a function of time during the air quench using a strip recorder. The specimen temperature vs. time data for five different quench cycles was plotted and fit using a linear regression routine. The air quench cooled the specimen at a rate of 9.5°F/sec (5.3°C/sec).

Another concern resulting from the quenching procedure was the formation of microcracks in the matrix material. This concern was investigated by polishing the edge of a 90 degree specimen and photoreplicating it before and after all heat treatments of the specimen. After the strain gage curing procedure a few small cracks were found in matrix-rich regions of the specimen. The maximum length of the cracks was about 4 times the fiber diameter of 0.197 mil (5 microns). The microcracks usually connected two fibers through the matrix-rich region. Subsequent repeated quenches and creep tests of the specimen revealed no further increase in crack formation or noticeable growth in the initially formed cracks. Quenching of laminates formed with various ply angle orientations will likely increase the formation of microcracks due to the high thermal expansion mismatch between plies.

Creep strain measurement was accomplished using resistance foil strain gages. The strain gages used were from the WK gage series made by Micro-Measurements. The normal operating temperature range of the WK gages is between -452° to 550°F (-269° to 290°C). WK-06-125TM-350 general purpose 2-element 90 degree tee rosette gages were used on the 0 and 90 degree specimens. WK-06-125RA-350 general purpose 3-element 45 degree rectangular rosette gages were used on the 45 degree specimens. Actual mounting of the strain gages on the specimens was done following the procedures recommended by Micro-Measurements [15] using M-bond 610 high temperature adhesive. The M-bond 610 was cured at 347°F (175°C) for 2 hours with the oven heated and cooled at 9°F (5°C) per minute. After curing, the specimens were subjected to a post cure cycle of 12 hours at 212°F (100°C) followed by 8 hours at 437°F (225°C). The specimens were then placed inside a desiccator until they were actually wired and used in the aging tests. Monitoring the weight of a sample specimen during this storage period revealed no significant increase or decrease in weight. Desiccant material was

also placed inside the oven to minimize any moisture absorption during the testing period.

During testing, both an active and a thermal compensating "dummy" specimen were placed in the oven. Strain gages were placed on both sides of each specimen. The active and dummy specimens were of the same fiber orientation and experienced the same thermal history. The four gages, two each from the active and dummy specimens, were wired in a full bridge Wheatstone circuit [16]. Specific placement of the active and dummy gages in the circuit allowed electronic cancelation of bending and thermal effects. Thus, the output signal is entirely due to the applied tension load.

AGING CREEP TEST PROCEDURES

Both short-term and long-term creep tests were conducted during this study. The results of the short-term (momentary) creep tests were used to characterize the aging rate of the material. The results of the long-term creep tests were used to verify the physical aging models. The procedures used to conduct both test types were identical, except for the duration of the test.

The testing sequence was started by heating the specimens to the rejuvenation temperature of 437°F (225°C) and holding for a minimum of 15 minutes. Next, the specimen was air quenched to the aging test temperature. Finally, a sequence of short-term tests were conducted at aging times, t_e, of 1, 3, 9, 27, and 81 hours after the quench. The duration t_i of the load application was varied so that a ratio of test time to aging time, t_i/t_e, of 0.1 was obtained throughout the aging experiments. The particular aging times selected allowed sufficient recovery time between tests and provided a manageable testing schedule. The actual creep strain for each creep test is obtained by subtracting the recovery strain from the previous test. This procedure is applicable since the specimen remained in the linear viscoelastic range where Boltzmann's superposition principle [2] is valid. An illustration of the sequence of creep and recovery tests and the strain response obtained during the sequence of creep tests is shown in figure 4.

RESULTS AND DISCUSSION

The four principal compliance terms S_{11}, S_{12}, S_{22}, and S_{66} were determined using momentary tensile creep tests of 0, 90, and 45 degree specimens. Before aging tests were conducted, each specimen was checked to insure that the test was conducted in the linear viscoelastic range and that effect of sequencing creep tests was insignificant.

90 DEGREE CHARACTERIZATION TESTS

The effect of physical aging on the transverse direction compliance, S_{22}, was determined using a sequence of short-term momentary creep tests conducted at five temperature levels on 90 degree specimens. The applied stress level on the 90 degree specimens was 400 psi (2.76 MPa). A representative compliance response from the 383°F (195°C) test is shown in figure 5. The symbols in this figure depict the actual test data with the solid line representing the numerical fit of Struik's equation (eqn. 1) to the data. An average m value of 0.4167 was used in the fitting program. This value was calculated by averaging the individual m values from the 338°F, 365°F, and 195°F

(170°C, 185°C and 195°C) aging sequences. The m values obtained from fitting individual creep curves varyed considerably from a low of 0.2921 to a high of 0.4894.

The momentary creep compliance curves were shifted to form master momentary compliance curves. The master curve data for the five test temperatures, referenced to the 81 hour aging time, is shown in figure 6. The shifting process used both a horizontal shift $-\log a$ and a small vertical shift $\log B$ for each creep compliance curve. The aging shift rate, μ, was determined for each aging test temperature using a linear regression routine. A plot of the aging data, $-\log a$ versus $\log t_e$, and the calculated aging shift rate, slope of the curve, are shown in figure 7.

TTSP master momentary compliance curves were formed by shifting momentary compliance curves, obtained at various temperatures with the same aging time, using the time-temperature superposition principle. The 90 degree long-term test was started at an aging time of 9 hours with the temperature at 338°F (170°C). Several data reduction techniques were examined for obtaining the TTSP master momentary compliance curve at this reference state.

The first method numerically fit the test data from various temperatures at an aging time of 9 hours to Struik's equation (eqn. 1) using the average m value of 0.4167. The resulting transverse direction master momentary compliance curve, referenced to 338°F (170°C) and t_e = 9 hours, is shown in figure 8. The second method utilized a graphical shifting procedure to determine the shift factors required to form the master curve. The resulting curve, again referenced to 338°F (170°C) and t_e = 9 hours, is shown in figure 9. An examination of the shift factor summaries, given in figures 8 and 9, shows that first and second methods give essentially the same shift factors. The final shift method utilized the graphical procedure to obtain the master curve referenced to 338°F (170°C) at an aging time of 81 hours instead of 9 hours. The resulting curve, referenced to 338°F (170°C) and t_e = 81 hours, is shown in figure 10. The aging shift rate, μ, at a temperature of 338°F (170°C), was 0.77. Using this aging rate the shift factor required to shift the t_e = 81 hours curve to t_e = 9 hours was determined. An additional small vertical shift was also included during shifting procedure. The resulting TTSP master momentary curves from the three shifting methods are shown in figure 11. The curves show essentially the same shape with a small variation between 10^4 to 10^6 seconds.

45 DEGREE CHARACTERIZATION TESTS

The 45 degree specimens were used to determine the shear direction compliance, S_{66}. The applied stress level σ_x of 800 psi (5.52 MPa) was found to produce a normal stress component σ_2 of 400 psi (2.76 MPa) in the matrix material. This was the same matrix normal stress used during the testing of the 90 degree specimens. An illustration of the load and material stress directions is shown in figure 2. The effect of physical aging on the shear direction compliance, S_{66}, was determined at three temperature levels. The upper two temperature levels, 399°F and 392°F (204°C and 200°C), that were used with the 90 degree specimen orientation, were not tested. The individual m values from the three aging sequences were averaged

resulting in an average m value of 0.4564. This value was used in the computer fitting program. The m values from the individual creep curves varied from a low of 0.3518 to a high of 0.5082.

TTSP master momentary compliance curves were formed using the same methods used for the 90 degree specimens. The resulting shear direction TTSP master momentary compliance curve, referenced to 338°F (170°C) and t_e = 9 hours, is shown in figure 12. Note that fitted curve is extrapolated beyond the test data at times greater than $10^{4.5}$ seconds. The average m value curve is shown with the curves obtained using the graphical methods in figure 13. Initially, the three curves are nearly identical. However, as the time increases beyond $10^{4.5}$ seconds, the curves start to separate. This time was observed to correspond to the end of the shifted compliance data shown in figure 12. The separation of the curves beyond $10^{4.5}$ seconds results from the extrapolation of the curves beyond the test data. Obtaining a better compliance representation beyond $10^{4.5}$ seconds would require testing at higher temperatures. Unfortunately, nonlinear effects, aging to equilibrium, and possible specimen rupture may occur as the test temperature approaches T_g.

0 DEGREE CHARACTERIZATION TESTS

The 0 degree specimen orientation was used to determine the fiber direction compliance, S_{11}, and the fiber/transverse coupling compliance, S_{12}. The 0 degree orientation is dominated by the properties of the elastic graphite fiber. Previous testing of graphite fiber composites [17] [18] [19] revealed little time-dependent behavior in the 0 degree fiber orientation. Results of creep tests conducted at 338°F (170°C) with an applied stress of 5000 psi (34.5 MPa) are shown in figures 14 and 15. As expected, neither S_{11} or S_{12} showed appreciable time-dependent behavior. Similar tests conducted at 399.2°F (204°C) yielded similar results. Thus, both S_{11} and S_{12} were considered temperature and aging independent.

LONG-TERM PREDICTIONS

A comparison of the transverse direction, S_{22}, long-term compliance predictions with the observed test data is shown in figure 16. The long-term test was conducted at a temperature of 338°F (170°C) with a starting age time of 9 hours. The test data is depicted with asterisk symbols, while the predictions obtained using each of the TTSP master momentary compliance curves from figure 11, along with the effective time theory, are shown as various line types. All of the long-term predictions with aging show the same shape as the test data. The predictions consistently under-predicted the compliance test data. The same under-prediction trend was noticed in long-term compliance data presented by Sullivan [4]. The cause of the under-prediction is believed to be related to drift of the strain gage voltages during long-term tests. The effect of strain gage drift was effectively canceled out during short-term tests by the subtraction of the recovery voltages from the previous test as described by Hastie and Morris [13]. The accumulation of the drift of the strain gage voltages could be responsible for the increased strain readings during long-term tests.

The sensitivity of the long-term compliance predictions to the short-term data fitting procedure is apparent in figure 16. The variation of the long-term predictions from the experimental data range from 7.3% for the m_{avg} = 0.41671 curve to 3.5% for the TTSP curve which was obtained at an aging time of 81 hours and shifted to the referenced aging time of 9 hours. The closeness of the predictions makes it difficult to determine if one data reduction technique is more reliable than another.

Also included in figure 16 is the compliance prediction calculated using the real time instead of effective time for the TTSP = 9 hr. data reduction technique. The prediction without aging effects included over-predicts the compliance data by 50% at 10^6 seconds. The corresponding prediction with aging effects under-predicts the compliance data by 5.7%. Clearly, the effect of physical aging must be included in order to use short-term momentary compliance data to predict the long-term compliance response.

Long-term shear direction compliance tests, S_{66}, were conducted at a temperature of 338°F (170°C) at starting age times of 9 and 3 hours are shown in figures 17 and 18. Noted on both figures is the region where the predictions were made using the extrapolation of the characterization data. The sensitivity of the long-term prediction to the short-term fitting procedure becomes more apparent in the extrapolated region. The best fit to the test data was the prediction obtained by graphically shifting the TTSP data to the aging time of the test. The predictions from this method were only 6.3% and 7.3% from the test data at starting age times of 9 and 3 hours respectively.

The effect of physical aging on the long-term compliance prediction becomes evident at smaller starting aging times. The compliance prediction without aging for the 9 hour starting age time, shown in figure 17, is 65% from the actual test data at the end of the test. The prediction without aging for a test at a 3 hour starting age time, shown in figure 18, is greater than 165% from the actual test data at the time corresponding to the end of the 9 hour aging time test. As the aging time before the start of the creep test was increased, the apparent effect of physical aging was shifted to longer test times. Significant variation between "with aging" and "without aging" predictions starts at about $10^{3.5}$ and 10^4 seconds respectively for 3 and 9 hours aging start times. Clearly, the aging time at the start of the creep test and the test duration determine if physical aging significantly changes the creep response of the material during the test.

The load direction compliance, referred to as S_{xx}, was determined using equation 11 and the four principal compliance terms S_{11}, S_{12}, S_{22}, and S_{66}. The TTSP momentary compliance curves used in the computations were determined using the graphical procedure at an aging time of 9 hours and referenced to a temperature of 338°F (170°C). Aging shift rate, μ, values of 0.77 and 0.93 were substituted, respectively for the S_{22} and S_{66} principal compliance directions, into equation 2 during the calculation of the effective time for long-term predictions. The test data and predictions for the load direction long-term compliance at a temperature of 338°F (170°C) and a starting age time of 9 hours is shown in figure 19. Predictions are shown for fiber angles of 29.5, 30 and 30.5 degrees to demonstrate the sensitivity of the compliance predictions to the possible misalignment of the fiber orientation during specimen fabrication or the misalignment of the strain gage. The 29.5 degree prediction matches the initial compliance value the best, but under-predicts the compliance at 10^6 seconds by 9.1%. This under-prediction of the compliance was also seen in the S_{22} and S_{66} long-term pre-

dictions. The compliance prediction obtained without physical aging effects over-predicted the test compliance value at 10^6 seconds by 137%.

Predictions of the load direction compliance, S_{xx}, for fiber orientation angles ranging from 0 to 90 degrees at a temperature of 338°F (170°C) and an aging start time of 9 hours are shown in figure 20. The 90, 45, 30 and 0 degree fiber angle long-term load direction compliance test data is also shown in figure 20 with asterisk symbols. The gradual stiffening of the material from physical aging is apparent in both the predictions and the test data. The predictions and test data compare quite well considering the possible sources of experimental error and specimen to specimen material property variations. Ideally, multiple specimens of each fiber orientation would be tested so a statistical distribution of the compliance response could be determined.

The shape of the compliance curve beyond the end of the test data at 10^6 seconds can be estimated by determining the double-logarithmic slope of the long-term creep curves. The shape of the double-logarithmic slope primarily depends on the aging shift rate μ. A μ value of 0.85 yields a nearly constant double-logarithmic slope value producing a straight line on the double-logarithmic plot of compliance versus time. Values of μ greater than 0.85 produce a slope that slightly decreases with time. When the value of μ is less than 0.85 the slope slightly increases with time. The proximity of the μ values for both the S_{22} and S_{66} compliance directions to 0.85 explains the nearly straight line prediction of the compliance at longer test times.

SUMMARY AND CONCLUSIONS

The creep response of Radel X/IM7 composite material has been found to be significantly affected by physical aging in the temperature range between 338°F (170°C) and 399.2°F (204°C). The effect of physical aging was determined on each term of the principal compliance matrix. The resin dominated transverse direction compliance, S_{22}, and shear direction compliance, S_{66}, were found to be time and aging dependent. The fiber direction compliance, S_{11}, and the fiber/transverse coupling compliance, S_{12}, were found to be virtually independent of time and aging effects.

The Time-Temperature Superposition Principle was successfully used to determine TTSP master momentary compliance curves at a specific referenced aging time. Long-term predictions using the TTSP master momentary compliance curves, without including effective time theory to account for the physical aging process, significantly overestimated the compliance response.

Momentary compliance data and the effective time theory were used to accurately predict long-term S_{22} and S_{66} compliance responses of the 90 and 45 degree specimens. Additionally, the four principal compliance terms were substituted into a laminate transformation equation to predict the load direction compliance for a 30 degree specimen. The long-term load direction compliance prediction matched the test data within normal error ranges associated with slight misalignments in the fiber orientation or strain gage direction.

References

1 Kovacs, A.J., La contraction isotherme du volume des polymeres amorphes, *Journal of Polymer Science*, Vol. 30, 1958, pp.131-147.

2 Struik, L.C.E., *Physical Aging in Amorphous Polymers and Other Materials*, Elsevier North-Holland Inc., New York, N.Y., 1978.

3 Tant, M.R. and G.L. Wilkes, "An overview of the Non-equilibrium Behavior of Polymer Glasses," *Polymer Engineering and Science*, Vol. 21, No. 14, Mid-October, 1981, pp. 874-895.

4 Sullivan, J.L., "Creep and Physical Aging of Composites," *Composite Science and Technology*, Vol. 39, 1990, pp. 207-232.

5 Jones, R.M., *Mechanics of Composite Materials*, McGraw-Hill, New York, NY, 1975.

6 Morris, D.H., H.F. Brinson, and Y.T. Yeow, "The Viscoelastic Behavior of the Principal Compliance Matrix of a Unidirectional Graphite/Epoxy Composite," *Polymer Composites*, Vol. 1, No. 1, Sept. 1980, pp. 32-36.

7 Chamis. C.C. and J.H. Sinclair, "Ten-deg Off-axis Test for Shear Properties in Fiber Composites," *Experimental Mechanics*, Vol. 17, No. 9, Sept., 1977, pp. 339-346.

8 Gramoll, K.C., D.A. Dillard, and H.F. Brinson, "Thermoviscoelastic Characterization and Predictions of Kevlar/Epoxy Composite Laminates," Virginia Polytechnic Institute and State University, VPI-E-88-12, Blacksburg, VA, May 1988.

9 Tuttle, M.E. and H.F. Brinson, "Accelerated Viscoelastic Characterization of T300/5208 Graphite/Epoxy Laminates," Virginia Polytechnic Institute and State University, VPI-E-84-9, Blacksburg, VA, March 1984.

10 Pindera, M.J. and C.T. Herakovich, "Shear Characterization of Unidirectional Composites with the Off-Axis Tension Test," *Experimental Mechanics*, Vol. 26, No. 1, March 1986, pp. 103-112.

11 Booij, H.C. and J.H.M. Palmen, "Viscoelasticity of ABS Samples Differing in Thermal History," *Polymer Engineering and Science*, Vol. 18, No. 10, Mid-August, 1978, pp. 781-787.

12 Vleeshouwers, S., A.M. Jamieson, and R. Simha, "Effect of Physical Aging on Tensile Stress Relaxation and Tensile Creep of Cured EPON 828/Epoxy Adhesives in the Linear Viscoelastic Region," *Polymer Engineering and Science*, Vol. 29, No. 10, May 1989, pp. 662-670.

13 Hastie, R.L. and D.H. Morris, "The Effect of Physical Aging on the Creep Response of a Thermoplastic Composite," CCMS-91-17, Virginia Tech Center for Composite Materials and Structures, Virginia Polytechnic Institute and State University, Blacksburg VA, July 1991.

14 Kong, E.S.W., "Sub-T_g annealing studies of advanced epoxy-matrix graphite-fiber-reinforced composites," *Journal of Applied Physics*, Vol. 52, No. 10, October 1981, pp. 5921-5925.

15 MM Bulletin B-130-12, "Strain Gage Installations with M-Bond 43-B, 600, and 619 Adhesive Systems," Micro-Measurements Division, Measurements Group, Inc., P.O. Box 27777, Raleigh, NC, 27611.

16 Dally, J.W. and W.F. Riley, *Experimental Stress Analysis*, 2nd Edition, McGraw-Hill, New York, NY, 1978.

17 Griffith, W.I., D.H. Morris, and H.F. Brinson, "The Accelerated Characterization of Viscoelastic Composite Materials," Virginia Polytechnic Institute and State University, VPI-E-80-15, Blacksburg, VA, April 1980.

18 Osiroff, R., "Damorheology Creep-Fatigue Interaction in Composite Materials," Ph.D Dissertation, Materials Engineering and Science Program, VPI & SU, Blacksburg, VA, June 1990.

19 Yeow, Y.T., D.H. Morris, and H.F. Brinson, "Time-Temperature Behavior of a Unidirectional Graphite/Epoxy Composite," *Composite Materials: Testing and Design (Fifth Conference)*, ASTM STP 674, S.W. Tsai, Ed., American Society for Testing and Materials, 1979, pp. 263-281.

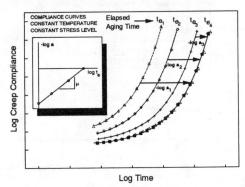

Figure 1 Illustration of Aging Shift Rate Determination by Shifting Momentary Creep Compliance Curves.

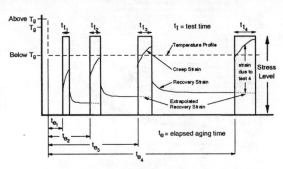

Figure 4 Illustration of the Sequence of Creep and Recovery Tests for Determining Aging Effects [4].

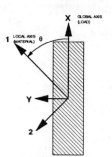

Figure 2 Coordinate Systems Used to Define Material Properties.

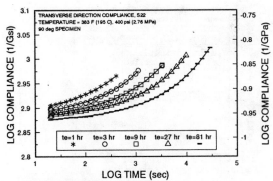

Figure 5 Transverse Direction Compliance for a Constant Temperature of 383 F (195 C) at Various Aging Times.

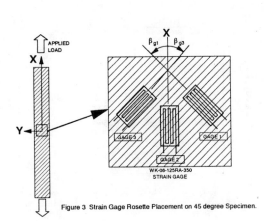

Figure 3 Strain Gage Rosette Placement on 45 degree Specimen.

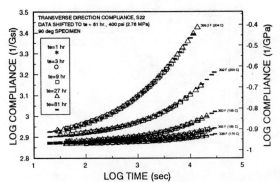

Figure 6 Transverse Direction Master Momentary Compliance Curves at Various Temperatures Shifted to the 81 hour Aging Time.

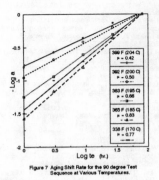

Figure 7 Aging Shift Rate for the 90 degree Test
Sequence at Various Temperatures.

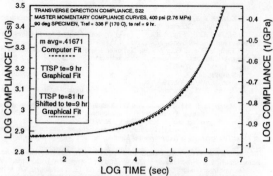

Figure 11 Comparison of Transverse Direction TTSP Master Momentary
Compliance Curves Referenced to T=338F (170C), te=9 hours.

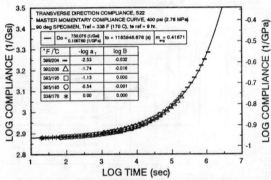

Figure 8 Transverse Direction TTSP Master Momentary Compliance Curve
Computer Fit with m avg = 0.4167 and Referenced to T=338F (170C), te=9 hours.

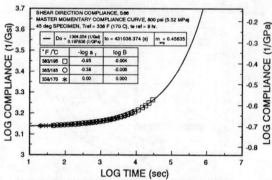

Figure 12 Shear Direction TTSP Master Momentary Compliance Curve
Computer Fit with m avg = 0.4564 and Referenced to T=338F (170C), te=9 hours.

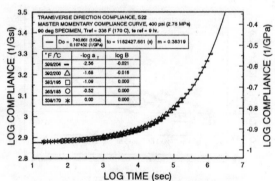

Figure 9 Transverse Direction TTSP Master Momentary Compliance Curve
Graphically Fit and Referenced to T=338F (170C), te=9 hours.

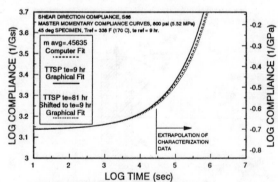

Figure 13 Comparison of Shear Direction TTSP Master Momentary
Compliance Curves Referenced to T=338F (170C), te=9 hours.

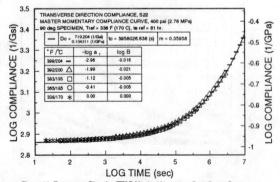

Figure 10 Transverse Direction TTSP Master Momentary Compliance Curve
Graphically Fit and Referenced to T=338F (170C), te=81 hours.

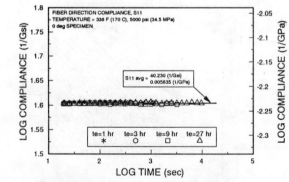

Figure 14 Fiber Direction Compliance for a Constant Temperature
of 338 F (170 C) at Various Aging Times.

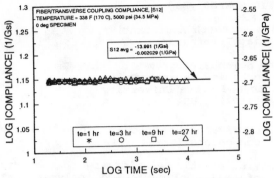

Figure 15 Fiber/Transverse Coupling Compliance for a Constant Temperature of 338 F (170 C) at Various Aging Times.

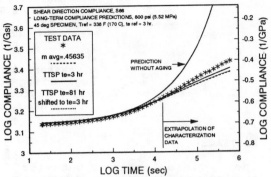

Figure 18 Shear Direction Long-Term Compliance Predictions and Test Data at 338 F (170 C) and te = 3 hours.

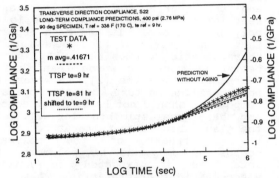

Figure 16 Transverse Direction Long-Term Compliance Predictions and Test Data at 338 F (170 C) and te = 9 hours.

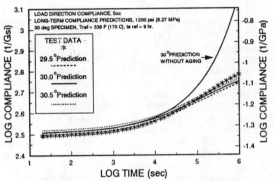

Figure 19 Load Direction Long-Term Compliance Predictions for the 30 degree Specimen at 338 F (170 C) and te = 9 hours.

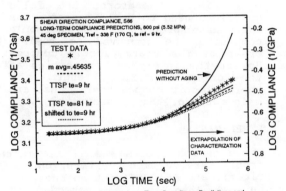

Figure 17 Shear Direction Long-Term Compliance Predictions and Test Data at 338 F (170 C) and te = 9 hours.

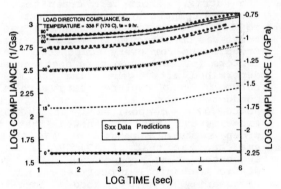

Figure 20 Load Direction Long-Term Compliance Predictions and Test Data at 338 F (170 C) and te = 9 hours.

THE INTERPHASE EFFECT ON THE TIME DEPENDENT PROPERTIES OF J2 THERMOPLASTIC COMPOSITES

*Yeou Shin Chang, Graduate Research Assistant
D. A. Dillard, Associate Professor

*Materials Engineering Science Program
Engineering Science and Mechanics Department
Virginia Polytechnic Institute and State University
Blacksburg, VA 24061-0219 USA

ABSTRACT

The viscoelastic behavior of thermoplastic composites (AU4/J2, AS4/J2, and AS4CGP/J2) was investigated. The interphases of the composites were created by employing the same fibers having different surface treatment (AS4) and epoxy sizing (AS4CGP). The ratios of the interfacial shear strength (ISS) for the AS4/J2:AU4/J2 and AS4CGP/J2:AU4/J2 were 1.22 and 1.24, respectively. The magnitude of the transverse (σ^f_{22}) and shear (τ^f) strengths of the composites were all in the order: AS4/J2> AS4CGP/J2> AU4/J2. This suggested that the transverse tensile and shear strengths of the AS4/J2 and AS4CGP/J2 composites were improved by altering the interphase properties. The transverse and shear moduli of the composites were insensitive to the ISS. The dynamic mechanical analysis results showed that the T_g of the composites was greater than the T_g of the matrix. Short term creep tests at elevated temperatures, ranging from 109°C to 160°C, were conducted and a master curve was constructed from the short term creep tests for every composite. Shift factors for each composite specimen were determined after generating the master curve. Creep rupture tests were also conducted for AU4/J2, AS4/J2, and AS4CGP/J2 composites at 120°C; experimental results showed that the creep rupture strength of AS4/J2 was smaller than that of AS4CGP/J2. This suggested that composites with good static mechanical properties might not necessarily have good long-term mechanical performance. SEM photomicrographs showed that the matrix maintained adhesion to the fibers in AS4/J2 and AS4CGP/J2 composites; whereas clean fiber surfaces were observed in AU4/J2 composites.

INTRODUCTION

The use of polymeric composites in the aerospace and automobile industries has increased. Traditionally, thermosetting polymers have been used as matrices for the polymeric composites. However, the brittle character of thermosetting polymers results in a low damage tolerance, which is often unacceptable in aerospace applications [1]. Therefore, thermoplastic polymers which have high T_g and fracture toughness properties are candidate matrices for structural components [1-2].

Viscoelastic behavior is a characteristic of all polymers and polymer matrix composites. It is generally believed that carbon fibers do not creep substantially under a long term loading; and the source for the viscoelastic behavior of polymeric composites is the polymer matrices. It has been reported that the viscoelastic behavior of thermoplastic composites will be no better or possibly worse than that of thermoset composites [2]. However, the non-crosslink nature of thermoplastic composites should not be of major concern for the viscoelastic behavior well below the glass transition temperature. Since the interphase of the polymeric composites is made of polymers, the interphase is expected to have a viscoelastic characteristic. Also, the interfacial adhesion between the fiber and thermoplastic polymer is found to be poor [3]. Therefore, the following questions need to be addressed. Can the interphase properties of thermoplastic composites be improved to resist the creep of the thermoplastic composites? How do the interphase properties affect the creep rupture strength of the thermoplastic composites? These are the main goals of the present study.

EXPERIMENTAL

Three carbon fibers - AU4, AS4 (with a proprietary surface treatment on the AU4 fiber), and AS4CGP (with an epoxy sizing on the AS4 fiber) - embedded in J2 polymer were used for this study. The J2 polymer is an amorphous polyamide copolymer produced and courteously supplied by the DuPont Corporation. Thus the properties of the interphase in each composite were expected to be different because of the final finishing on each fiber system. The consolidation procedures of making J2 composite panels were described in detail in Ref [5]. The quality of composite panels was examined by using the ultrasonic C-scan technique. Composite panels with poor quality were re-consolidated. Good quality composite panels were obtained after the second consolidation process. Specimens were cut in accordance with the requirements of the ASTM D3039 and D3518 standards. The specimens were annealed at 175°C for

48 hours and cooled to room temperature at a rate of 0.1°C/min. The annealed specimens were then stored in a desiccator prior to conducting mechanical tests. For the purpose of comparison, unannealed $[90°]_{12}$ specimens were also used for the creep tests.

The mesoindentation technique [4] was used to determine the interfacial shear strength of the composites. The ASTM D3039 and D3518 standards were followed to characterized the transverse tensile and shear properties of the composites. The tensile strengths of composite laminates ($[\pm45/90_2]_s$) were also determined, which were served as a reference for the creep rupture tests of the laminates. Static mechanical tests were performed by using a close loop hydraulic testing machine (MTS 445). Strain gages (CEA-06-250UN-350 from Measurement Group) bonded with M-Bond 610 were used to monitor the axial strains of the composite $[90]_{12}$ specimens. Strain gages (CEA-06-125UT-350 from Measurement Group) were used to determine the shear strains of the $[\pm45]_{2s}$ specimens. Creep rupture tests were conducted in lever arm machines equipped with temperature controlled ovens. The temperature of the creep rupture tests was controlled at 120°C. A scanning electron microscope was employed to examine the fracture surfaces of the failed $[90]_{12}$ and $[\pm45/90_2]_s$ specimens.

The dynamic mechanical analysis (DMA) technique was used to characterize E', E", tan(δ) and T_g of the composites. The DMA is capable of programming the creep/recovery tests at elevated temperatures. Thus, the DMA was also used to conduct short term creep tests at elevated temperatures, ranging from 109°C to 160°C, for $[90]_{12}$ and $[\pm45]_{2s}$ specimens.

RESULTS AND DISCUSSION

Mechanical Properties of J2 Composites

Table 1. contains the mechanical properties and ISS data for the three composites. Each entry in this table is an average of either four or five data points, as indicated by the parentheses. Typical stress-strain curves of the transverse tensile and shear tests for each composite system are shown in Figures 1 and 2.

The ISS of both AS4/J2 and AS4CGP/J2 composites is about 22% greater than that of the AU4/J2 composite. The surface treatment of the AS4 and AS4CGP fibers increases the fiber surface polarity and results in improved adhesion for J2 polymer to the AS4 and AS4CGP fibers [6]. Consequently, it is expected that the σ^f_{22} and τ^f of the AS4/J2 and AS4CGP/J2 composites should be greater than those

of the AU4/J2 composites. However, the E_{22} and G_{12} of the composites do not seem to be sensitive to the ISS. The authors have observed that the broken fibers randomly distributed in both inside and outside of the AU4/J2 composite specimens. These broken fibers result in increasing the values of E_{22} and G_{12} for the AU4/J2 composites [7]. The failure strengths of the AS4/J2 and AS4CGP/J2 laminates ($[\pm45/90_2]_s$) are nearly equal. These results imply that ISS has little influence on the strengths of these laminated composites (not lamina). However, the strengths of these two types of laminates are greater than that of the AU4/J2 laminates.

It has been shown that the intermingling of the epoxy sizing ($T_g = -10°C$) between the AS4CGP fibers after exposure to 295°C for 30 min [5]. This suggests that the epoxy sizing may form a thin layer around the fiber before applying consolidation pressure to make composite panels. On the other hand, because of the absence of a curing agent, the epoxy sizing will not fully cure and may mix with the J2 polymer at consolidation temperatures (295°C). This is supported by the fact that Thomason and Morsink [8] have shown the diffusion of epoxy sizing in the matrix. Thus, either one of these possible factors will yield the AS4CGP/J2 composites with a compliant interphase. As a result, σ^f_{22} and τ^f of the AS4/J2 composites are slightly larger than those of the AS4CGP/J2 composites. The compliant interphase effect may also explain why the E_{22} and G_{12} of the AS4/J2 composites are slightly larger than those of the AS4CGP/J2 composites.

Figure 3(a-c) shows the photographs of failed specimens. It is clear that fiber breakage is a dominant failure mode in the AS4/J2 and AS4CGP/J2 composites; whereas fiber slippage is a predominant failure mode in the AU4/J2 composites. SEM photomicrographs show clean fibers on the fracture surface of the AU4/J2 composites, as shown in Figures 4(a). On the other hand, Figure 4(b-c) show that the matrix remains on the fracture surfaces of the AS4/J2 and AS4CGP/J2 composites. These facts further reinforce the idea that the AS4/J2 and AS4CGP/J2 have better interfacial adhesion than AU4/J2. A careful comparison of Figure 4(b-c) shows that the matrix of the AS4/J2 composites was predominantly torn apart suggesting a brittle failure mode. However, hackles are dominant in the AS4CGP/J2 composites indicating a ductile failure mode. The

difference of the failure mode suggests a compliant interphase in the AS4CGP/J2 composites.

Dynamic Mechanical Properties of J2 Composites

The T_gs of the composites are shown in Table 2. The T_gs of the composites are ~20°C higher than that of the J2 polymer [9]. The increase of the T_g has been attributed to the interaction of the fiber and matrix restricts the mobility of polymer molecules and results in raising T_g [10,11]. The T_gs for each type of composite laminates do not differ significantly, as shown in Table 2. Ko et al. [12] have also shown that there is little difference in the T_g of the AU4 and AS4 fiber in EPON-828/mPDA. The present results are consistent with Ko's observations. Therefore, the fiber treatments do not have a significant effect on the T_g of the J2 composites.

Figures 5(a-b) show the traces of the log(E') and tan(δ) vs. temperature for $[\pm 45]_{2s}$ and $[90]_{12}$ specimens, respectively. It should be noted that the results in Figure 5(b) were obtained at 3.2 Hz because the tan(δ) (at 1 Hz) does not form a peak and tends to reach infinity at the T_gs. The authors have observed a "bump" (not a sharp peak) at about 275°C for $[\pm 45]_{2s}$ specimens. Thomason [13] has concluded that the bump was an artefact and was formed due to a complex combination of the instrument parameters and sample properties. Thus, the authors do not show the data for temperatures that are beyond 200°C in Figure 5(a). Figures 5(a) and (b) show only a small difference in the E' of the composites in the glassy state, suggesting a minor influence of the interphase. This also confirms a small difference in the E_{22} and G_{12} of the $[\pm 45]_{2s}$ and $[90]_{12}$ specimens. However, the difference of the E' becomes distinguishable in the glass transition and rubbery regions. The E' of the AS4CGP/J2 composites is the lowest perhaps because of the existence of the compliant interphase. The highest value for the E' in the AU4/J2 composites may be due to the broken fiber effect, as mentioned in the previous section.

The heights of the tan(δ) vs. temperature at T_g for $[\pm 45]_{2s}$ and $[90]_{12}$ specimens are also listed in Table 2. Since loss factor (tan(δ)) is the ratio of loss modulus (E") to storage modulus (E'), a smaller E' results in a higher tan(δ) value. For most advanced polymeric composites at a temperature below T_g, a storage modulus (E') was approximately equal to the corresponding Young's modulus, e.g., E_{22} of $[90]_{12}$ specimens. Figure 5 has shown that the trends of the E' for the $[90]_{12}$ and $[\pm 45]_{2s}$ specimens are consistent with the trends of the E_{22} and G_{12}. Thus the trends for the height of the tan(δ) peaks for the $[90]_{12}$ and $[\pm 45]_{2s}$ specimens are in a reversed order to those of the E_{22} and G_{12} of the composites. The present observations are consistent with the published results [12].

Creep and Creep Rupture of J2 Composites

Short term creep and recovery tests have been conducted at low stress levels. The stress levels, according to the DMA results, are all in the range between 10 and 20 MPa. Referring to Figure 5, the E' of the J2 composites are around 6.3 GPa from 80°C to 160°C. The temperature range of the creep/recovery tests is between 109°C and 160°C. Thus, it is believed that the creep/recovery tests were performed in the linear viscoelastic range.

A typical plot for creep compliance curves at elevated temperatures of AS4/J2 $[90]_{12}$ specimen is shown in Figure 6. Based on the time-temperature superposition principle (TTSP) [14], a master curve can be formed by shifting creep compliance curves horizontally to match a selected creep compliance curve (a reference curve.) The scheme to shift the creep compliance curve has been described in detail in Ref. [14]. A shift factor (log(a_T)) at each curve (or at each temperature) is obtained by counting the amount of each curve shifted along the log(time) axis. The reference temperature for all master curves is 109°C. The master curves of the annealed and unannealed composite $[90]_{12}$ specimens are shown in Figure 7. As expected, the annealed specimens become stiffer and thus the corresponding master curves shift to the right, when compared to the unannealed specimens. Figure 7 also shows that the AU4/J2 composites are stiffer than the AS4/J2 and AS4CGP/J2 composites, which is in good agreement with the E_{22}. To reach the same compliance level at elevated temperatures, the annealed specimens require more time, ~1.2 decades, than the unannealed specimens do for AU4/J2, AS4/J2, and AS4CGP/J2 composites. The same amount of time difference is within our expectation because the composites used for the DMA creep tests are $[90]_{12}$ laminates which are matrix dominated. Figure 8 is the master curves of the annealed $[\pm 45]_{2s}$ specimens, which shows a similar trend to that of Figure 7.

The Arrhenius type equation is commonly used to describe the log(a_T)-1/T below the T_g, as shown below

$$\log(a_T) = \frac{-H_a}{2.303R} \left(\frac{1}{T} - \frac{1}{T_0} \right) \qquad (1)$$

where H_a is the activation energy, T_0 is the reference temperature. The Arrhenius type equation is applicable below the T_g.

The activation energy can be obtained from the slope of the $\log(a_T)$ vs. $1/T$ plot. Typical Arrhenius plots for the tested composites are shown in Figure 9. It is apparent that the data falls onto two straight lines which are intersecting at approximately 145°C. The change of the slope can be confirmed by referring to Figures 5. Figures 5 shows that $\tan(\delta)$ starts to increase and $\log(E')$ starts to drop at approximately 145°C, which is the onset temperature of the glass transition region. Thus the change of the slope suggests a change of relaxation mechanism of molecular motion; i.e., from the glassy state to the glass transition region. At the glassy state, the relaxation is due to the motions of side-group [14]. However, at the glass transition region, the relaxation is mainly from the main-chain motions [14]. The main-chain motions require more energy than the side-group motions do. As a result, the activation energy at the glass transition region is higher than that at the glassy state, as indicated in Figure 9. It is noticed that the difference in the activation energy of the $[90]_{12}$ and $[\pm45]_{2s}$ is minor. Figure 9 shows that the slopes of the three sets of data for the $[90]_{12}$ specimens are very close to each other. This suggests the interphase have little influence on the activation energy. Similarly, one can see that the slopes of the three sets of data for the $[\pm45]_{2s}$ specimens are also nearly equal. This insensitivity of the ISS to activation energy has been also reported by Kimoto [15].

Figure 10 shows the creep rupture results for the AU4/J2, AS4/J2, and AS4CGP/J2 laminates ($[\pm45/90_2]_s$). The data are within the experimental scatter and show a distinguishable trend for each composite system. As shown in Figure 10, these lines are almost parallel to each other. This suggests that the degradation rate of the creep rupture strength for the J2 composite laminates is approximately the same. This also implies that the ISS does not affect the degradation rate of the creep rupture strength of the J2 composite laminates although the ISS does affect the static mechanical properties of the J2 composites. However, the final finishing of the fiber surface does play an important role in defining the long-term mechanical performance. As shown in Figure 10, the creep rupture strength of the AS4CGP/J2 composites is higher than that of the AS4/J2 composites. We have also shown that the static mechanical properties of the AS4/J2 composites are greater than those of the AS4CGP/J2 composites. This inconsistency is because of different interphase properties in the AS4/J2 and AS4CGP/J2 composites. The compliant interphase of the AS4CGP/J2 composites tends to blunt and/or arrest the cracks resulting in a

longer time to develop the cracks. It also implies that for a fixed life-time, it requires more energy to develop the cracks for the compliant interphase. Thus, the AS4CGP/J2 laminates last longer than the AS4/J2 laminates at the same stress level.

SEM photomicrographs of the fracture surfaces for specimens that failed with a long creep rupture life are shown in Figure 11. For AU4/J2 composites, the neat surface of the cleaved matrix suggests that the AU4 fibers were pulled out without causing debris or plastic deformation on the matrix. This phenomenon also confirms our previous observations about the poor interfacial adhesion between the AU4 fiber and J2 matrix. On the other hand, Figure 11 shows a much more pronounced plastic deformation of the J2 matrix in the AS4CGP/J2 composites than in the AS4/J2 composites. As a result, the creep rupture strength of the AS4/J2 composites is higher than that of the AS4CGP/J2 composites.

CONCLUSIONS

The following conclusions can be made based on the present observations: The transverse tensile and shear strengths of the J2 composites increase as the ISS of the J2 composites increases. The transverse tensile and shear moduli of the J2 composites are insensitive to the interphase properties. The dynamic mechanical properties of the J2 composites are similar at temperatures below the onset temperature of the transition region; however, they become distinguishable when the temperature is above the onset temperature of the transition region. For J2 composites, the interphase properties have little effect on the creep response. However, the creep rupture strengths of the J2 composites are affected by the properties of the interphase region.

ACKNOWLEDGEMENTS

The authors are grateful to Virginia Institute for Material Systems for financial support. We also appreciate the help of E. I. DuPont de Nemours and Co. for manufacturing and supplying the prepregs. Thanks are also due to Mr. Danny Reed for his help in preparing specimens for this study.

REFERENCES

1. Leach, D. C., "Continuous Fiber Reinforced Thermoplastic Matrix Composites," in Advanced Composites, Ed. by Patridge, I. K., Elsevier Applied Science, 1989.

2. National Materials Advisory Board, "The Place for Thermoplastics in Structural Components", National Research Council, USA, 1987.

3. Bascom, W. D., Yon, K. J., Jensen, R. M., Cordner, L., "The Adhesion of Carbon Fibers to Thermoset and Thermoplastic Polymers," Journal of Adhesion, Vol. 34, 1991, pp. 79-98.

4. Lesko, J.J., Carman, G. P., Dillard, D. A., and Reifsnider, K. L., "Indentation Testing of Composite Materials as a Tool for Measuring Interfacial Quality," submitted for publication ASTM STP, March, 1991.

5. Chang, Y. S., Lesko, J. J., Reifsnider, K. L., and Dillard, D. A., "The Effect of the Interphase/Interface Region on Creep and Creep Rupture of Thermoplastic Composites", presented at ASTM Symposium "High Temperature and Environmental Effect of Polymeric Composites", at San Diego, October 15-16, 1991.

6. Chang, Y. S., Commercon, P., Wightman, J. P., and Dillard, D. A., to be submitted to Journal of Adhesion, 1992.

7. Chang, Y. S., Ph.D. Dissertation, "The Effect of the Interphase/Interface Region on Creep and Creep Rupture of Thermoplastic Composites", Virginia Polytechnic Institute & State University, May, 1992.

8. Thomason, J. L. and Morsink, J. B. W., "Investigation of the Interphase in Glass-Fiber-Reinforced Epoxy Composites", in Interfaces in Polymer, Ceramic, and Metal Matrix Composites, Ed. by Ishida, H., Elsevier Science Publishing Co., 1988, pp. 503-512.

9. Krueger, W. H., Khan, S., Croman, R. B., and Chang, I. K., "High Performance J-2 Thermoplastic Matrix Composite Reinforced with Kevlar Aramid Fiber," in Proc. 33rd SAMPE Symposium, Anaheim, 7-10, March 1988, pp. 181-193.

10. Shalaby, S. W., "Thermoplastic Polymers", in Thermal Characterization of Polymeric Materials, Ed. by Turi, E. A., Academic Press, London, 1981.

11. Kodama, M., Karino, I., and Kuramoto, K., "Polar-Polar Interaction and Boundary Phase Structure Between Reinforcement and Matrix in a Polymer Composite", Polymer-Plastics Technology and Engineering, Vol.27, no. 1, pp. 127-153, 1988.

12. Ko, Y. S., Forsman, W. C., and Dziemianowicz, T. S., "Carbon Fiber-Reinforced Composites:Effect of Fiber Surface on Polymer Properties", Polymer Engineering Science, V. 22(13), 1982, pp. 805-814.

13. Thomason, J. L., "Investigation of Composite Interphase Using Dynamic Mechanical Analysis: Artifacts and Reality", Polymer Composites, Vol. 11, no. 2, pp. 105-113, 1990.

14. Aklonis, John J. and MacKnight, William J., Chapter 3, in Introduction to Polymer Viscoelasticity, Second Edition, John Wiley, New York, 1983.

15. Kimoto, M., "Flexural Properties and Dynamic Mechanical Properties of Glass Fiber-Epoxy Composites", Journal of Materials Science, Vol. 25, pp.3327-3332, 1990.

Table 1 Mechanical properties of J2 composites

	AU4/J2	AS4/J2	AS4CGP/J2
σ^f_{22} (MPa)	34.19±3.39 (5),[57.4%]	54.18±1.71 (4),[55.7%]	42.72±2.16 (5),[52.5%]
E_{22} (GPa)	8.95±0.22	8.47±0.35	8.34±0.26
τ^f (MPa)	94.83±3.50 (5)	159.87±2.79 (4)	153.46±5.12 (4)
G_{12} (GPa)	5.16±0.37	4.94±0.27	4.74±0.30
**σ^f_x (MPa)	196/182	316/303	316/309
***ISS (MPa)	69.6 [54%]	~84.8 [54.7%]	~86.2 [53.7%]

* Numbers in the round and square parentheses denote the number of tested specimens and fiber volume fraction, respectively.
** Tensile Strength for $[\pm45/90_2]_s$ laminates.
*** Measured by meso-indentation tests.

Table 2 T_g (°C) and Height of the tan(δ) Peak

T_g/Height	AU4/J2	AS4/J2	AS4CGP/J2
$[\pm45°]_{2s}$*	181°C/0.55	181°C/0.60	179°C/0.71
$[90°]_{12}$**	181°C/0.71	178°C/0.95	178°C/1.06

* : measured at 1 Hz; **: measured at 3.2 Hz.

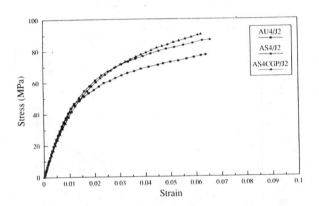

Figure 1. Typical stress-strain curves for J2 composite lamina [90]$_{12}$.

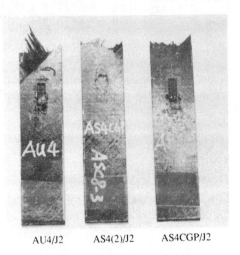

AU4/J2   AS4(2)/J2   AS4CGP/J2

Figure 2. Typical stress-strain curves for J2 composite laminates [±45]$_{2s}$.

Figure 3. Failed quasi-static tension specimens for J2 composite laminates [±45/90$_2$]$_s$.

(a)

(b)

(c)

Figure 4. SEM photomicrographs for the fractured (a) AU4/J2, (b) AS4/J2, and (c) AS4CGP/J2 composite lamina [90]$_{12}$.

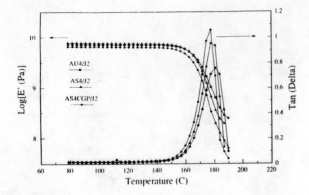

Fig 5(a). DMA results for J2 composite lamina [90]₁₂ at 3 Hz.

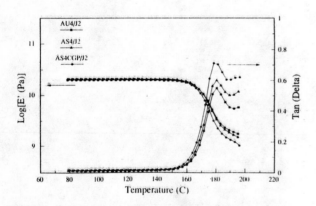

Fig 5(b). DMA results for J2 composite laminates [±45]₂ₛ at 1 Hz.

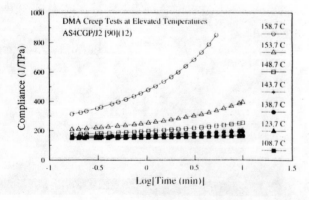

Figure 6. Typical creep compliance curves at elevated temperatures ranging from 109°C to 160°C for AS4CGP/J2 composite lamina [90]₁₂.

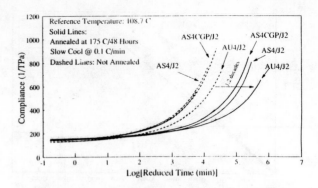

Figure 7. Master curves for annealed (solid line) and unannealed (dashed line) J2 composite lamina [90]₁₂, reference temperature: 109°C.

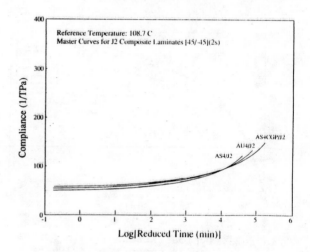

Figure 8. Master curves for annealed J2 composite laminates [±45]₂ₛ, reference temperature: 109°C.

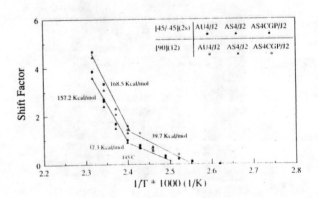

Figure 9. Arrhenius plots for both [90]₁₂ and [±45]₂ₛ laminates.

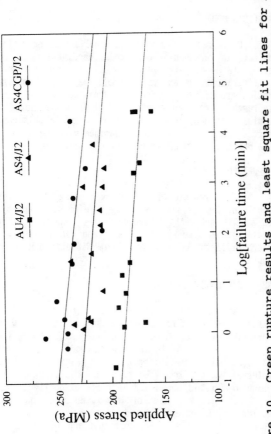

Figure 10. Creep rupture results and least square fit lines for AU4/J2, AS4/J2, and AS4CGP/J2 laminates [±45/90₂]ₛ at 120°C.

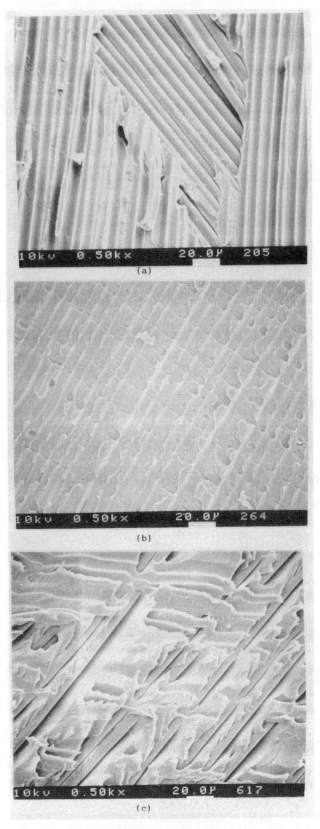

Figure 11. SEM photomicrographs for the fractured specimens with long creep rupture life; (a) AU4/J2, (b) AS4/J2, and (c) AS4CGP/J2.

ANALYSIS OF THE STRESS DISTRIBUTION AROUND FLAWS AND THE INTERACTION EFFECTS
BETWEEN FATIGUE CRACKS BY F.E.M

S.H. Song and J.B. Kim

ABSTRACT

Stress distribution around defects and stress interaction effects between defects existing on the surface of rectangular beam under bending was studied. In addition, effects of stress distribution on the interaction between fatigue cracks emanating from these defects was examined. F.E.M. was used to analyzed these effects with varing the size of defects and the interval between defects and these results were compared with the test results.

INTRODUCTION

The effect of defects and inclusions on the behavior of fatigue crack depends on the hardness of base material. However, if fatigue cracks initiate from these defects and inclusions then local areas including these become stress concentrator[1], and accordingly it is expected that the fatigue strength is affected by size and configuration of defects and inclusions. As it needs lots of time and effort to produce specimen controlling the size and configuration of defects and inclusions metallurgically , so the characteristic of micro defects is studied using artificial defects instead of natural defects.

Size and configuration of defects and inclusions in material is various and the interval between them is near and far[2]. Specially, if the interval between them is near then there are singular stress field by stress interaction and fatigue cracks incorporate rapidly. Accordingly, the analysis of stress distribution between defects is required to estimate the interaction effect between defects and cracks. However, as there are few exact solutions for stress distribution of defects and cracks,stress concentration diagram for the two dimensional configuration by Peterson [4] based on the results by Newber[3] is used. It is pointed out that there are lots of errors using these results to three dimensional problems. Lots of results for the stress distribution of 3-dimensional problem are reported to minimize the error and approximate the real problems.

These results can be classified into experimental method and analytical method, and problems are as follows . Measurement of stress at the surface of material is possible, but it is impossible at the inner part of material by experimental method[1], and configurations of defect and inclusion are spherical, semi-spherical,or semi-ellipsoid in analytical method[5]. The result of stress distribution for the cylindrical defect is reported by only H.Noguchi[6], despite of use of cylindrical configuration in experiment.

Considering problems mentioned above, stress distribution for the cylindrical defect is analyzed by F.E.M. and stress interaction effect between defects is examined in this study. In addition, historical effects of stress distribution on the crack emanating from defects are examined by rotary bending fatigue test for the artifical micro defects.

ANALYSIS MODEL

Fig.2 represents analysis model including surface defects in rectangular beam under bending stress. As size of defect is very small compared to total configuration of analysis model, magnified configuration around micro defect is shown at Fig.3. Fig.3 represents the configuration of twin micro holes as radius r is 300μm and depth h is same. In this case, stress interaction effect is examined with variation of the depth h and the interval between micro holes s.

EXPERIMENTAL MODEL

Fig.4 represents the rotary bending fatigue test specimen. The specimen was polished with sand papers up to #1,500 and with chrome oxide of 3μm and 0.05μm grain size. After that the specimen was drilled with micro drill of 300μum and 500μm diameter and 300μm depth.

RESULTS AND CONSIDERATIONS

Fig.5 represents σ_y/σ_0 (σ_y : y components of stress , σ_0 : nominal stress) around micro holes with variation of interval e(=s/r) between micro holes from 4 to 1(4→2→1). As total analysis model is symmetric at B',so only a guarter part is represented. If the interval varies from 4 to 1, stress distribution area which σ_y/σ_0 is above 1.8 increase gradually between B-B'. But the variation of σ_y/σ_0 does not appear at ouside of B-B' except limited area. Accordingly, the interaction effects of σ_y component appears at limited area around B-B', and there are no interaction effects at the other side of this area.

Fig.6 represents the interaction effects of σ_y/σ_0 between B-C for the case that h/r equals 2 and e equals 2. In this case, a solid line represents the stress distribution line formed by twin micro holes as the interal between them is near, and dashed lines represent the independent stress distribution line formed by each micro holes. In addition, deviant crease lines represent the area that stress affect each other.

S.H. Song is Professor of Mechanical Engineering and J.B. Kim a former Graduate Student(now in Korea Electrotechnology Research Institute) in Korea University of Korea,Seoul,Korea

For the case that h/r equals 2 and e equals 2, the interaction of σ_y/σ_o appears at $1.2 \leq x/r \leq 2.8$.

Fig.7 represents the σ_y/σ_o interation effects between unequal radius micro holes as the radius ratio is 1 versus 2. In this case, interaction effect of σ_y/σ_o appears at $1 \leq x/r \leq 2.8$. Comparing results of Fig.6 with Fig.7, the interaction area of σ_y/σ_o for the case of Fig.7 is larger than the case of Fig.6. In addition the interaction effect of σ_y/σ_o for the larger hole side is larger than the smaller one at Fig.7.

Fig.8 represents interaction effect factors γ which represents the degree of interaction effect of σ_y/σ_o between adjacent micro holes. In this case γ represents the ratio of stress concentration factor between two micro holes and a independent miro hole. For the case that γ equals one, there are no interaction effects at B. As h/r increases, the interval which affects the stress interaction increases, as shown in Fig.8. For the case that h/r equals one, γ for the case of unequal holes is smaller than for the case of twin holes. However, if h/r is larger than two, γ for the case of unequal holes is larger than for the case of twin holes except for the interval e(=s/r) ≤ 0.25. From the results, the range which there is no σ_y interaction effect is as follows ; (i) if h/r = 1 then e(=s/r) ≥ 1, (ii) if h/r=2 then e≥ 2 between twin micro holes, e≥ 3 between unequal holes.

Experimental results for the effects of stress on the behavior for fatigue cracks are as follows. Fig.9(a) represents the behavior of fatigue crack propagation for a hole as diameter of micro hole equals 300μm, Fig.9(b) is that of twin micro holes as d equals 300μm, and Fig.9(C) is that of unequal micro holes as d equals 300μm and 500μm. Crack length at N = 3 x 10^4 cycles is as follows for each cases : (a) 56 μm, (b) 59μm, and (c) 150μm.

Quantive results for stress effects on the initial fatigue crack is shown in Fig.10. Fig.10 represents the relation between numbers of stress and crack length. As crack length is almost same with 300μm for the case (a) and (b) until N = 2.3 x 10^4 cycles, independence of stress is maintained. However, if x/r is larger than 1.2 then crack length emanating from twin micro holes is larger than that from a single hole. The result is expected that stress interaction affects the behavior of fatigue crack between twin micro holes. Compaing results between Fig.8 and Fig.10 both results are same as the independance of σ_y is maintained at $1 \leq x/r < 1.2$ and the behaior of fatigue crack is affected by stress interaction at $x/r \geq 1.2$.

CONCLUSIONS

1. Stress interaction effects between twin miro holes is smaller than that of unequal micro holes.
2. For the case of unequal micro holes, stress inter-action effect of small hole side is larger than that of large side.

REFERENCES

[1] Brooksank, D. and K.W.Andrews, "Stress Fields around Inclusions and their Relation to Mechanical properties", Journal Iron & Steel Inst., pp.246-255, 1972.

[2] Trantina, G.G. and M. Barishpolsky, "Elastic - Plastic Analysis of Small Defect-Void and Inclusion", Engng. Fracture Mech., Vol.20, No.1, pp.1-10, 1984.
[3] Weuber, H., Theory of Notch Stresses, Springer, Berlin, 1957.
[4] Peterson, R.E., Stress Concentration Design Factors, John-Wiley & Sons, 1962.
[5] Fujita T., Tsuchida E.,Nakahara I., "Stress Concentration due to a Hemi-Prolate Spheroidal Pit at a Free Surface of a Semi-Infinite Body under All-around Tension", Bulletin of the JSME, Vol.23, No.181. pp.1048-1054, 1980.
[6] Noguchi, H., Nishitani, H., and Toto, H., "Semi-Infinite Body with a Drill-Hole Shaped Pit under Tension", Trans. J.S.M.E. (in Japanese), Vol.54, No.501,pp.977-982., 1985.

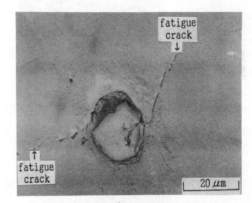

σ=1.176GPa N=1.9X10^4
(inclusion size = 20μm)

Fig.1 Crack propagation from a inclusion

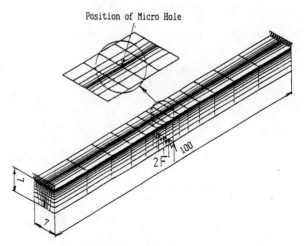

Position of Micro Hole

Fig.2 Configuration of analysis specimen

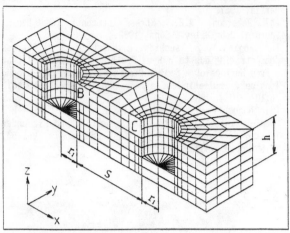

Fig.3 Configuration of twin micro holes ($r_1 = 25\mu$m)

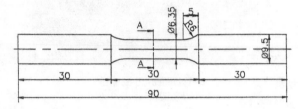

(a) Outline of fatigue test specimen (unit:mm)

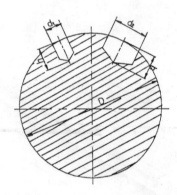

(b) Section of A—A of specimen

Fig.4 Fatigue test specimen

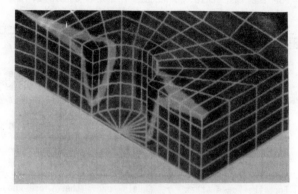

(a) e=4

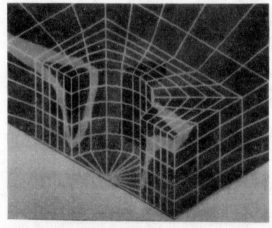

(b) e=2

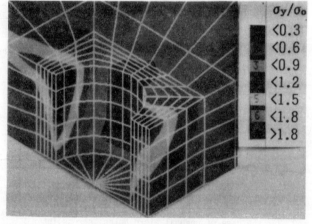

(c) e=1

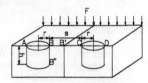

Fig.5 Distribution of σ_y/σ_o around micro holes with
variation of the interval e (e = s/r, h/r = 2)

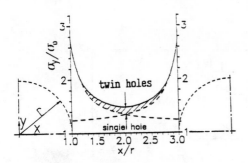

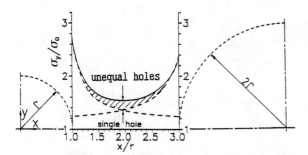

Fig.6 Comparison of σ_y/σ_0 between twin micro holes (B-C) and single micro hole (h/r=2, e=s/r=2)

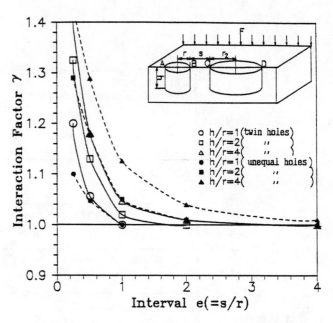

Fig.8 Comparison of effects of micro holes spacing e on stress concentration factor for twin and unequal micro holes (twin micro holes : r_2=r, unequal radius micro holes = r_2 = 2r)

Fig.7 Comparison of σ_y/σ_0 between unequal micro holes (B-C) and single micro hole (h/r=2, e= s/r=2)

(a) single hole(d=300μm)   (b)twin holes(d=300μm)   (c)unequal holes(d_1=300μm,d_2=500μm)
    (c=56μm)   (s=300μm,c=59μm)   (s=300μm,c=150μm)
★ c:crack length from B

Fig.9 Behavior of fatique crack propagation (N x 3 x 10⁴ cycles, σ=294MPA)

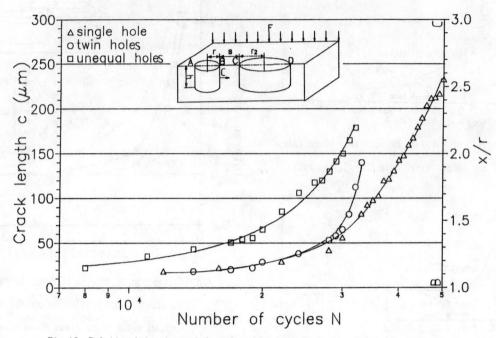

Fig.10 Relation between crack length and number of stress cycles (d = 300 μm, d$_2$

= 500 μm, s = 300 μm, c:crack length from B)

Application of the Strain Gage - Hole Drilling Method to Aircraft Transparencies

Thomas J. Whitney and Gregory J. Stenger[1]

INTRODUCTION

Crazing of the outer acrylic ply of laminated aircraft transparency systems results in a significant number of canopy or windshield changeouts annually. To understand the mechanisms of craze and thereby increase transparency durability, current efforts are focusing on relating laboratory craze data to field data from removed canopies. A number of factors are seen to contribute to craze, including exposure to chemicals, temperature, and stress in the material. As a first attempt at correlating these factors, the laminated F-16 canopy (Figure 1) has been targeted as the transparency system on which to concentrate the study.

A better understanding of crazing in the acrylic layer requires knowledge of the principal stresses in the transparency, be they of mechanical or residual origin (current craze initiation criteria are based on maximum principal stress). Measurement techniques for stresses should be non-destructive in nature in order to preserve optical integrity. Recent work [1], however, has shown the technology associated with scattered light photoelasticity and surface wave acoustics, to be insufficiently developed for use on the acrylic layers of laminated transparencies. The hole-drilling method was therefore selected as an "interim" method for measuring stress.

Although highly successful in applications in metals, the strain gage-hole drilling technique has not been used regularly in thermoplastics. Available literature does not consider optimum drilling methods or calibration techniques for thermoplastics. The purpose of this paper is to discuss recent work which validated the use of the strain gage-hole drilling method on acrylic laminated transparency material; designed a device to apply the procedure; successfully measured installation and service related stresses in F-16 transparencies.

VALIDATION OF METHOD

Using the hole-drilling method in this application required preliminary studies to resolve two issues. The first involved finding a means to drill the hole in a stress free manner. The second concerned accurately relating measured strains to residual stress in the laminated acrylic material.

Figure 2 presents results of a preliminary study to determine the optimum means of introducing the hole into acrylic in a stress free manner. The methods which were tested corresponded to those suggested by ASTM E837-85 and other references. A precision jig borer provided accurate speed and feed control for introducing holes into samples of "pre-shrunk" (annealed) cast acrylic under zero load. Measurements Group, Inc., type TEA-06-062RK-120 rosettes proved most convenient for these tests. A P3500 Strain Indicator and SB10 Switch and Balance Unit (also from Measurements Group, Inc.) displayed the relieved strain.

Reverse cone carbide cutters and end mills are frequently used in hole drilling of metals. They proved ineffective in the acrylic. The use of lubricants with the carbide cutter resulted in a decrease in residual strain, but not to a sufficient degree to warrant its use. High speed (100,000 RPM) drilling using the carbide cutter (another method widely employed in metals), conducted in unloaded preshrunk acrylic, resulted in enormous residual strains. The high speed most likely generated enough heat to degrade the polymer, resulting in high drill-induced stress. As the figure demonstrates, ordinary high speed steel twist drills (in a "sharp" condition) produced the lowest "machining induced" strains.

Figure 3 displays a portion of the results of additional jig borer tests and demonstrates the desirable feature of automatically controlled feed and speed. The jig borer on which tests were conducted drilled automatically at various rates and at 0.001"/rev. or 0.003"/rev. feed rate. Drill retraction occurred automatically at the same rate as penetration, or manually at much faster rates. Since feed rate was directly proportional to speed on the jig borer, the effects of speed and feed were indistinguishable. However, for the drill speeds being considered, the pressure of the tool on the acrylic, and hence the feed rate, most likely influences drill induced strain to a greater degree. The desire to reduce both drill pressure and drill time led to the compromise selection of 1200 RPM and 0.001"/rev. as the optimal feed and speed for drilling. Based on these tests, rapid drill retraction was also required.

[1] Associate Research Engineer and Research Engineer, respectively, Aerospace Mechanics Division, University of Dayton Research Institute, Dayton, Ohio 45469-0110.

The technique for reducing measured strains to stresses followed the calibration procedure recommended by ASTM E837-89. Annealed cast acrylic samples were loaded in a small tension fixture equipped with load cell instrumentation and drilled using the jig borer [2]. The results of calibration tests yielded a set a calibration constants for use in the data reduction equations. Because a twist drill introduces the hole, the conical shaped hole bottom prohibited incremental drilling. The constants are therefore valid for through holes. The fact that a soft interlayer separates the acrylic and polycarbonate plies of a laminated transparency suggests that relieved strains in the acrylic should not be constrained by the remaining polycarbonate. Through-hole constants should therefore be applicable to relieved strains from the canopy.

A complication arises in the calibration process because acrylic is a viscoelastic material. Each step in the procedure (loading, drilling, unloading) induces a new constant stress or strain state, which is accompanied by creep or stress relaxation, respectively. Since measured strains must be related back to a stress, a reference point is required. This reference was chosen to be the "relaxed" state, defined as the state at which creep or stress relaxation rates had decreased to some acceptable level (generally 1-2 $\mu\epsilon$/min). The resulting calibration constants related "relaxed" strain values (the strain achieved after allowing the material to creep after drilling) to a "relaxed" stress (the stress remaining after the specimen relaxed during centering of the drill). This process is depicted in Figure 4.

A series of hole drilling tests conducted after calibration, verified that the "relaxed" strain state could be correlated to residual stress originally in the material. The calibration fixture provided a means for inducing known principal stress levels in a variety of samples and load configurations. These included uniaxial tension and compression, uniaxial tension in transversely curved surfaces, biaxial stress in a curved surface (through pressurizing a tube), and uniaxial tension in laminated acrylic/silicone/ polycarbonate (including samples taken directly from an F-16 canopy). The results of these tests, summarized in Figures 5 and 6, indicate that the "relaxed" state indeed correlates to stress in the material and in a manner well within the acceptable error bounds. The results of tests on laminated samples also indicate that drilling through the acrylic layer into the silicone is correctly assumed to be a through hole. The soft inner layer essentially decouples the acrylic and polycarbonate plies and allows the acrylic to "freely" deform.

HOLE DRILLING DEVICE

Because the hole drilling method relies on accurate measurement of stress gradients in a small area, the means of introducing the hole must adhere to several critical requirements. These include the following:

· *Accuracy of aligning the hole in the center of the rosette*. ASTM E837-89 states that holes must be drilled to within ± 0.015 d (in which d is the diameter of the hole) of true center of the rosette gage circle to ensure accurate results. A 1/16" diameter hole must be drilled to within ± 0.001" to avoid significant error.

· *Accuracy in aligning the hole normal to the surface*. Little work in the literature addresses the issue of the accuracy in stress measurement for holes not drilled perpendicular to the surface. Non-perpendicular drilling creates holes that become "off-center" with depth, and results in elliptical holes. While no work could be found which addresses this issue, an error of 0.5° from perpendicular for a 0.0625" diameter drill creates a hole with a major axis of 0.062502". This is within uncertainty for the drill itself and represents acceptable error. The system requirement for perpendicularity was therefore chosen to be $\pm 0.5°$. Angles greater than this may result in rapidly increasing error.

· *Drilling stress free*. Stresses produced in the material by introduction of the hole will induce error in strain readings, since the rosette responds to strain relieved from all sources of stress. As suggested by the preliminary tests, automatically fed twist drilling induces the least amount of strain.

The above system requirements led to the design and fabrication of the device pictured in Figure 7. The unit consists of a base, alignment and drilling components, a control unit, and an external drill motor. The components were built with three design drivers in mind: portability, X-Y and θ adjustability, and the ability to automatically drill and retract.

The base of the unit is essentially an optical translation stage with a 2 inch diameter hole through the center. A split linear bearing serves as an aligning journal for the device. Vacuum cups at the bottom of the base's swivel feet allow quick and convenient attachment. The vacuum is sufficient to firmly attach the unit, oriented 90° to the upright position, to the side of an F-16 canopy. Figure 8 shows the alignment module, which consists of a 40x microscope for centering (to within 0.0006 in.) and a 0.5mW HeNe laser for aligning normal to the surface (to within 0.2°). Complete adjustment of the unit to center the journal over the rosette target and align the device normal to the drilled surface is an iterative process, since centering forces the alignment away from perpendicular, and vice-versa. Two or three iterations usually suffice. Figure 9 displays the drilling component inserted into the alignment bearing. The component consists of a steel sleeve around a handpiece from a flexible shaft electric drill. The cylinder and damper serve to power the drill feed and control the drill feed rate (1.2 ipm), respectively.

Hole drilling tests on instrumented samples loaded to known stress levels provided a means for verifying that the device would introduce holes in a stress free manner. Holes drilled at various uniaxial stress levels gave an indication of the machining induced stress. Figure 10 displays the results of these tests, based on the stress measured compared to the known stress. A large discrepancy between measured stress and the actual stress would indicate high drilling induced stress. The error band of less than 50 psi indicates the device performed within the required limits and specifications.

FULL SCALE TESTING

Hole drilling tests conducted on the 20 full scale F-16 canopies listed in Table 1 provided principal stress levels due to residual manufacturing stress, stress induced by deflecting the parts to install them in the aircraft, and stress due to cockpit pressurizing. The latter two tests were conducted by installing the canopies in a full scale F-16 cockpit fixture and pressurizing to 6 psig. The manufacturing residual stresses were measured as the canopy sat on a T-shaped support frame, essentially in a "free" undeformed state. The canopies tested represented a cross-section of bases, ages and states of craze damage.

The device performed well in measurements in all areas of the canopy, including those along the edge (using extension plates), and those in which the device was mounted 90° to the vertical (Figure 11). Measurements taken after drilling showed the hole misalignment to average 0.00104 inches, with 47 of the 60 holes misaligned less than 0.0006 inches (the resolution of the micrometer).

The residual stress results showed no discernable trends with canopy service location or age. However, results did show a possible stress relieving mechanism of craze, as maximum principal stresses appear compressive far away from craze, tensile near crazing, and tensile (of lower magnitude) in crazed regions (Figure 12). Installation and pressure stresses were determined by mounting 1 Sierracin and 1 Texstar canopy in a table-top fixture shown in Figure 11, and measuring strains using both regular rosettes and hole drilling. Figure 13 shows installation, pressure, and residual stresses from the Texstar canopy superimposed. "Sectioned" data is obtained by adding regular rosette readings for pressure and installation to residual stress data obtained by the sectioning method. "Drilled" data was obtained by installing, pressurizing, and drilling the canopy. The hole drilling data obtained from this procedure is therefore due to all three sources of stress. The results indicate relatively low stress levels induced by these mechanical loads, in comparison to uniaxial chemical craze thresholds which are generally in the 6.90 to 8.30 MPa range. The results also show drilled data to be slightly lower than "sectioned" data, since hole drilling responds to actual *stress* in the material, which may have relaxed, while regular rosettes respond to *strain*, which does not change if stresses relax.

CONCLUSIONS

· The strain gage hole drilling method is a viable means of measuring surface stress in acrylic materials and, in particular, outer transparency plies.

· A device for implementing the method in aircraft transparencies has been designed and fabricated. The device induces less than $15\mu\epsilon$ on the strain readings during the hole-drilling procedure. The result is an accuracy of $\pm10\%$ in stress measurement for this device. The device would also be capable of drilling holes in many other surfaces or components containing multiple curvature.

· Measurements made in selected full scale canopies showed stress levels induced by residual manufacturing stresses, installation, and cockpit pressurizing to be relatively low compared to laboratory craze thresholds.

ACKNOWLEDGEMENTS

The authors would like to acknowledge funding for this work from the U.S. Air Force Flight Dynamics Laboratory under contract F33615-84-C-3404, Russell E. Urzi, monitor. James Higgins contributed design concepts and fabricated the hole drilling device. John Murphy contributed suggestions for the optics and alignment system. Zhili Feng and Dr. Chon Tsai of the Welding Engineering Department of The Ohio State University conducted the high speed hole drilling tests on acrylic.

REFERENCES

1. Raju, B., Nondestructive Measurement of Residual Stresses in Aircraft Transparencies, WRDC-TR-89-3099, Wright-Patterson AFB, Ohio, 1989.

2. Whitney, T.J., and Stenger, G.S., "Measurement of Residual Stresses in Laminated Aircraft Transparencies by the Strain Gage - Hole Drilling Method", University of Dayton Research Institute Technical Report UDR-TR-90-106, November, 1990.

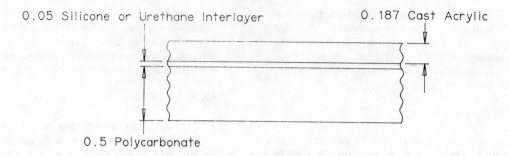

0.05 Silicone or Urethane Interlayer · · · · · · · · · · · · · · 0.187 Cast Acrylic

0.5 Polycarbonate

Fig. 1: Acrylic/Polycarbonate F-16 Cross-Section

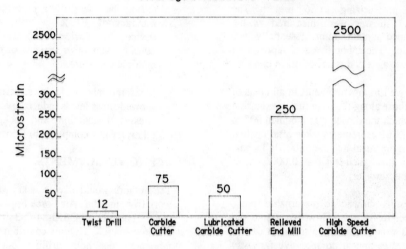

Fig. 2: Optimal Machining Methods for Acrylic

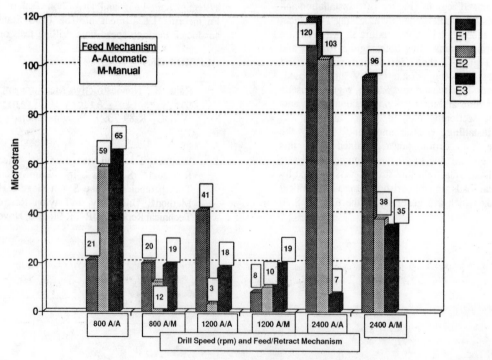

Fig. 3: Optimal Drilling Parameters

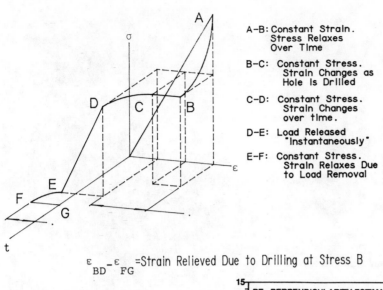

A-B: Constant Strain.
Stress Relaxes
Over Time

B-C: Constant Stress.
Strain Changes as
Hole Is Drilled

C-D: Constant Stress.
Strain Changes
over time.

D-E: Load Released
"Instantaneously"

E-F: Constant Stress.
Strain Relaxes Due
to Load Removal

Fig. 4: **Typical σ-ε-t Curve for Hole-Drilling Calibration in Viscoelastic Material**

$\epsilon_{BD} - \epsilon_{FG}$ = Strain Relieved Due to Drilling at Stress B

Fig. 5: Uniaxial Verification of Acrylic Hole-Drilling Constants

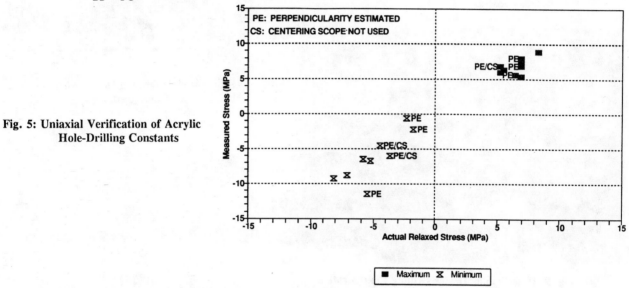

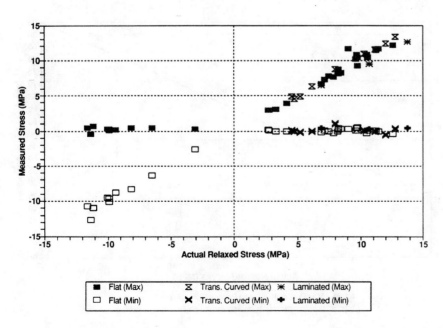

Fig. 6: Biaxial Verification of Acrylic Hole-Drilling Constants

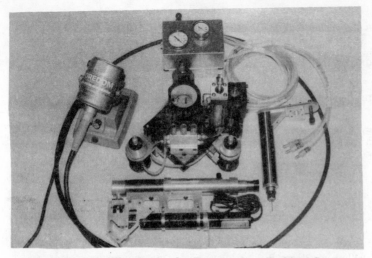

Fig. 7: Hole Drilling Device for Transparency Residual Stress Measurement

Fig. 8: Hole Drilling Device Alignment Configuration

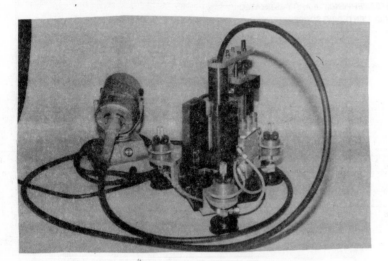

Fig. 9: Hole Drilling Device Drilling Configuration

Fig. 10:Uniaxial Verification of Hole-Drilling Device Performance

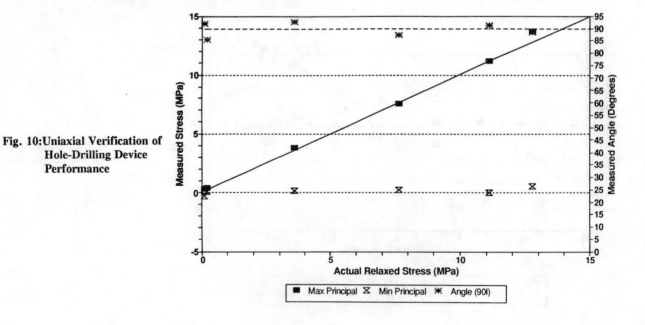

Fig. 11: Stress Measurement on an Installed F-16 Transparency

Fig. 12: Summary of Residual Stresses in 20 In-serviced Canopies

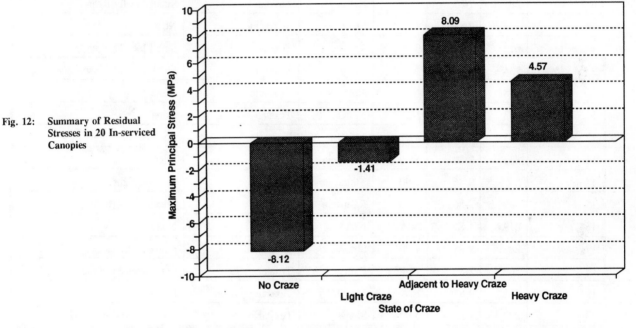

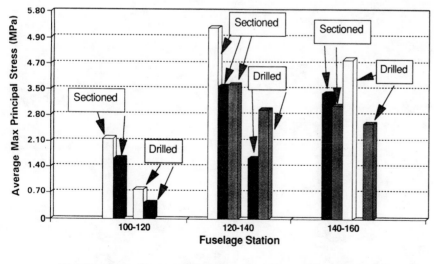

Fig. 13: Superimposed Stresses from a New Sierracin Canopy

Table 1: Full Scale Test Specimen Profile

SPECIMEN #	S/N	DOM	DOR	BASE	MANUFACTURER	CRAZE STATE
1	473	1-86	N/A	Shaw	Sierracin	None
2*	184	10-87	3-90	MacDill	Sierracin	None
3	373	10-85	4-90	Kunsan	Texstar	Small locally dense
4*	218	10-85	N/A	N/A	Texstar	Small locally dense
5	1476	9-87	2-89	Luke	Texstar	Small locally dense
6	289	7-85	4-89	Nellis	Texstar	Small locally light
7*	138	7-87	11-89	MacDill	Sierracin	None
8	612	5-86	3-90	Ramstein	Texstar	Small locally light
9	734	2-84	1-90	Kelly	Sierracin	Small locally dense; others light
10	1483	12-87	N/A	Nellis	Sierracin	None
11	133	4-84	N/A	Nellis	Texstar	None
12	1358	10-87	4-90	MacDill	Sierracin	Locally very light
13	835	9-86	5-90	Ramstein	Texstar	Locally dense
14	869	9-86	1-90	Tinker	Texstar	General light
15	499	2-86	12-89	Ramstein	Sierracin	Locally very light
16*	019	1-85	N/A	N/A	Sierracin	None
17	283	9-85	4-90	Shaw	Texstar	Locally dense
18	504	2-86	12-89	Ramstein	Texstar	Light deep local craze
19*	401	9-87	N/A	MacDill	Texstar	Locally light
20	279	7-85	3-90	Shaw	Texstar	Locally light, deep craze

*F-16C forward canopies

STRESS DISTRIBUTION IN A CONTINUOUSLY CAST INTERMETALLIC STRIP

G. Roy[1], Z. Wronski, M. Sahoo, and D. Kiff

ABSTRACT

Results of a study on the determination of the residual stress state in a nickel aluminide intermetallic strip by the hole drilling method (HDM) are presented. Special correlation functions that relate the relaxed surface strain and the original stresses before drilling were developed. It is shown that the HDM may be used to determine residual stresses in anisotropic materials such as intermetallic strips.

The results indicate that a complex stress field develops through the thickness and across the width of the strip. However, a suitable thermo-mechanical treatment may be applied to redistribute the stresses before aluminide strips can be used to make engineering components.

INTRODUCTION

Continuous-casting of metals and alloys at speeds 0.25 to 2 m/s is becoming an emerging technology to produce metal strips directly from molten metal. In the strip-casting process the liquid metal is delivered from tundish to the surface of a rotating cooling wheel[1,2]. Depending on the particular configuration of the tundish-wheel tandem, two casting processes can be identified, 1) planar casting, i.e. a meniscus is formed between the tandem orifice and the surface of the rotating wheel, and 2) melt overflow casting, i.e. the melt is poured over the wheel surface. In either case, the liquid is spread uniformly over the cooled surface and solidifies as a strip of uniform thickness. The processes are presented schematically in Figs.1a-b.

Although the thickness of the strip is uniform, high thermal gradients develop in the strip during the rapid heat transfer to the cooling wheel. Such thermal gradients are usually necessary to form strips with a fine-grained microstructure, which leads to an increase in the tensile strength, which in turn is beneficial for engineering applications[3]. However, the high thermal gradients generate residual stresses. The existence of such stresses and their distribution is of primary interest where the application of the strips is considered. Tensile residual stresses are detrimental to the fracture toughness of ordered intermetallics, in particular nickel aluminides. Moreover, a high stress concentration could generate preferred corrosion in intermetallic strips. Therefore, it is necessary to determine the stress state and develop an appropriate heat treatment that eliminates or redistributes the stresses.

Three nickel aluminides of the Ni_3Al family are now commercially available, IC-50, IC-218, and IC-221, of which only the IC-50 was subjected to extensive testing. The compositions and properties of these alloys have been reviewed recently by Sikka[4].

The alloys are candidate materials for high temperature applications, such as turbines, aircraft fasteners, and permanent mould materials, because of their increasing yield strengths with increasing temperature. Furthermore, tubes made of nickel Aluminides can be used in oil, gas, and other fields of petrochemical industry because of their excellent oxidation resistance at high temperatures (1100°C).

This paper presents the results of a study on the determination of the residual stress state in a strip-cast nickel aluminide IC-50. The study forms part of research and development on strip casting at CANMET/MTL[5].

MATERIALS AND METHODS

Materials

The strip was produced at Allegheny Ludlum by melting the alloy in a 1350-kg coreless induction furnace and single-roll casting it (Fig.1a) to a width of 310 mm, and a thickness of 1 mm [6], Fig.2. A cut of the strip was supplied to CANMET/MTL by Oak Ridge National Laboratory (ORNL).

---

[1] Drs. George Roy, Zbigniew Wronski, and Mahi Sahoo are Research Scientists, and Dave Kiff is a Technologist at Metals Technology Laboratories of CANMET, Department of Energy, Mines and Resources, 568 Booth Street, Ottawa, Ontario, K1A 0G1, Canada.

The chemical composition of the strip is 86.3% Ni, 11.9% Al, 1.05% Zr, and 0.016% B.

The strip is dull on the bottom side which comes in contact with the wheel and shiny on the top side which has no contact with the wheel, Fig.2.

Two specimens of dimensions, length 295 mm and width 145 mm were cut from the strip. One specimen was cut from one side of the strip, including its edges, and the second one was cut without the edges, denoted SP1 and SP2, respectively, Fig.3,

The second specimen, SP2, was subjected to a thermo-mechanical treatment. The treatment involved cold-rolling in multi-passes that resulted in the reduction (by 39%) of its thickness from 1.00 mm to 0.61 mm. The specimen was then heated to and maintained at the temperature of 1025°C in a furnace filled with argon for one hour.

Methods

The specimens were subjected to residual stress-, and microstructure measurements.

1)   Residual stress measurements

Residual stresses were determined by the hole drilling method[4]. The method consists of machining a blind hole in incremental steps in a specimen, Fig.4, and measuring the resulting change of strain in the vicinity of the hole, Fig.5. Measurements of strain in three different directions G_1, G_2, and G_3 of a rosette provide the necessary data from which principal components of the original residual stress state σ_p and σ_q (normal to the hole surface) at the hole location can be calculated, Fig.5.

Four locations were selected for hole drilling in SP1, 6, 61, 122, and 90 mm from the edge, denoted P1, P2, P3, and P4, respectively, and one location in SP2, 43 mm from the edge, denoted P5, Fig.3.

The hole drilling was performed in eight increments of 0.13 mm, to the total depth of 1.00 mm (through-holes) at each location of SP1 and four increments at the location of SP2.

To interpret the strains, a relaxation matrix, referred to as R-matrix, was developed to relate the measured surface strains and the principal stresses at depths h_i, $\sigma_p(h_i)$, $\sigma_q(h_i)$, i=1,2,...,N, where N indicates the number of subsurface layers identified during the incremental hole drilling. The method of strain interpretation by R-matrices is called the Relaxation Matrix Method and is abbreviated RMM[7].

$$
\begin{bmatrix} \varepsilon^1 \\ \varepsilon^2 \\ \cdot \\ \cdot \\ \varepsilon^i \\ \cdot \\ \cdot \\ \varepsilon^N \end{bmatrix} =
\begin{pmatrix}
R^{11} & 0 & . & . & . & 0 & . & 0 \\
R^{21} & R^{22} & 0 & . & . & 0 & . & 0 \\
. & . & . & . & . & . & . & . \\
. & . & . & . & . & . & . & . \\
R^{i1} & R^{i2} & . & . & R^{ii} & 0 & . & 0 \\
. & . & . & . & . & . & . & . \\
. & . & . & . & . & . & . & . \\
R^{N1} & R^{N2} & . & . & R^{Ni} & . & . & R^{NN}
\end{pmatrix}
\begin{bmatrix} \sigma^1 \\ \sigma^2 \\ \cdot \\ \cdot \\ \sigma^i \\ \cdot \\ \cdot \\ \sigma^N \end{bmatrix}
\tag{1a}
$$

where

$$
\varepsilon^i = \begin{bmatrix} \varepsilon_b^i \\ \varepsilon_s^i \end{bmatrix}, \ R^{ij} = \begin{pmatrix} R_{11}^{ij} & 0 \\ 0 & R_{22}^{ij} \end{pmatrix}, \ and \ \sigma^i = \begin{bmatrix} \sigma_b^i \\ \sigma_s^i \end{bmatrix}
\tag{1b}
$$

214

ε_b^i and ε_s^i are the biaxial and shear components of surface strain (h=O) around a hole of depth h_i; σ_b^i and σ_s^i are biaxial and shear components of the traction components $\sigma_p(h_i)$ and $\sigma_q(h_i)$; R_{kk}^{ij}, k=1,2, are called relaxation R-functions, and are elements of the relaxation submatrices R^{ij}; $R_{kk}^{ij}=0$ for j>i. The R-matrix is used to relate the relaxed surface strains to the stresses at the respective depths.

Represent the R-functions as

$$R_{11}^{ij}=\frac{1+\nu}{E}\frac{2E}{1+\nu}A^i(h_j) , \quad and \ R_{22}^{ij}=\frac{1}{E}2EB^i(h_j) \tag{1c}$$

However, in this case the constants $A^i(h_j)$ and $B^i(h_j)$ depend on the depths h_j.

Denote

$$A^{ij}=\frac{2E}{1+\nu}A^i(h_j) , \quad and \ B^{ij}=2EB^i(h_j) \tag{1d}$$

Then

$$R_{11}^{ij}=\frac{1+\nu}{E}A^{ij} , \quad and \ R_{22}^{ij}=\frac{1}{E}B^{ij} \tag{2}$$

$A^i(h_j)$ and $B^i(h_j)$ are called partial relaxation constants and were determined numerically by the finite element method.

2)   Microstructure characterization

The grain sizes, shapes, and their orientation at the top and bottom surfaces and along the cross section were determined by optical metallography. Killing's reagent was used to etch the surfaces and the cross section to identify the microstructural details.

RESULTS

1)   Residual stresses in specimen SP1

The results from residual stress analysis indicate that a complex stress field develops through the thickness and across the width of the strip. Close to the centreline, the stress ranges from 200 MPa on the bottom side to -200 MPa on the top side, varying from 50 MPa at depths 0.3 and 0.8 mm to -50 MPa in the middle (0.4 and 0.7 mm), Fig.6-P3. Closer to the edge, location P2, the stress is equal approximately 250 MPa below both surfaces and -250 MPa close to the top surface, and constant at 50 MPa in the middle, Fig.6-P2. The stress at location P4 (halfway between P3 and P2) increases from 0 MPA at the top surface to -500 MPa and decreases to 0 MPa at high gradients below the surface, Fig.6-P4. At the edge of the original strip, the stress varies with high positive and negative gradients, ranging from -700 MPA to 600 MPA, Fig.6-P1.

The stress state in the thermo-mechanically treated strip, SP2, is presented in Fig.7. The absolute magnitudes of the principal components are less than 75 MPA.

2)   Microstructure

Three distinct layers, each one of different degree of morphological inhomogeneity, were identified in the etched cross-section of the specimen SP1. The bulk layer can be described as having columnar-dendritic microstructure, Fig.8, whereas the top and bottom layers are equiaxial-dendritic, Fig.9. The top layer was thicker than the bottom one.

The cooling rate was determined from the dendrite arm spacing observed during the microstructural examination of the specimen SP1 at the magnification of 500X. The rate, dT/dt, was calculated from the power law

$$d=R(\frac{dT}{dt})^{-n} \tag{3}$$

where d is the spacing between the secondary arms of dendrites, and R=60 and n=41 are theoretically predicted parameters for solidified alloys[8]. For the experimentally determined spacing d=1-2 µm, the rate varied from 2.0×10^4 at the top and bottom surfaces to 4.0×10^3 Ks^{-1} in the middle of the specimen.

The dendritic structure of SP2 was changed after cold-rolling and annealing, the arms were shorter and randomly distributed. Thus, the material is homogeneous.

DISCUSSION

1) The origin of stresses

Usually the residual stresses result from different cooling rates at various depths below the surface. However, the cooling rate determined in this experiment did not vary substantially with depth. Therefore, another mechanism contributed to the generation of the stresses. To identify other sources of the stresses, the microstructure of the intermetallic strip was studied in details.

Inhomogeneity in the microstructure was observed, and this was to be expected, because of the non-equilibrium thermodynamic conditions during strip casting. In this case the equiaxial and columnar dendrites formed differently during solidification from the liquid state. Thus, interfacial strains of different magnitudes developed in the layers, i.e. different strain gradients developed across the thickness of the strip. Partial relaxation of this strain gradient was measured by the strain gauges during the hole drilling procedure.

The proof that the inhomogeneity is the major factor in the stress generation in the intermetallic strip is evident from stress measurements in the thermo-mechanically treated specimen, SP2. The stress level and its gradients decreased substantially, Fig.7, because its microstructure (after the heat-treatment) is homogeneous, Fig.10.

CONCLUSION

Results of a study on the determination of the residual stress state in a nickel aluminide intermetallic strip are presented.

Special correlation functions that relate the relaxed surface strain and the original stresses before drilling were developed.

It is shown that the hole drilling method may be used to determine residual stresses in anisotropic materials such as intermetallic strips. The results indicate that a complex stress field develops through the thickness and across the width of the strip.

The results indicate that a suitable thermo-mechanical treatment may be applied to redistribute the stresses before aluminide strips can be used. Such materials that have residual stresses reduced to acceptable levels are required for engineering applications in the petrochemical industry.

ACKNOWLEDGEMENT

The authors wish to thank Dr. V.K. Sikka, ORNL, Oak Ridge, Tennessee, for supplying the IC-50 strip, and Mr. B. Durocher for optical-microscopy analyses.

REFERENCES

1.   Carbonara, R.S., "Technology Development of the Thin Strip Metal Casting - Feasibility Study", U.S. Department of Energy, Report DOE(CE)12446, 1984.

2.   Sahoo, M., Morin, G., Cousineau, D., "Casting of Steel Strip Using a Single Roll Caster", Mtl Report 88-40(TR), 1988.

3.   Collins, L. E., Wronski, Z. S., "Rapidly Solidified Metals", MTL Report 86-54(OP-J), 1986.

4.   Sikka, W.K., "Nickel Aluminides - New Advanced Alloys", Material and Manufacturing Processes, Vol.4, No.1, pp.1-24, 1989.

5.   Sahoo, M., Lui, A., Morin, G., Sikka, V.K., "Mechanical Properties and Erosion Behaviour of Nickel Alumunides", Canadian Metallurgical Quarterly, Vol.30, No.1, pp.55-69, 1991.

6.   U.S. Department of Energy Newsletter, "Materials and Components in Fossil energy applications", pp.7-9, June 1, 1991.

7.   Roy, G., "Residual Stress Determination by the Hole Drilling Method: Theory and Applications", MTL Report 90-43(OP,J), submitted for publication to Experimental Mechanics.

8.   Brower, W.E, Stracham, R., and Flamings, M.C., "Effect of Cooling Rate on Structure of Ferrous Alloys", AFS Cast Metals Research Journal, Vol.6, p.176, 1970.

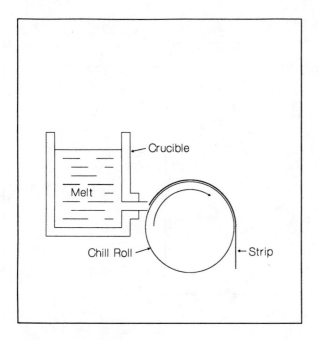

Fig.1a Schematic representation of continuous casting by the melt drag process.

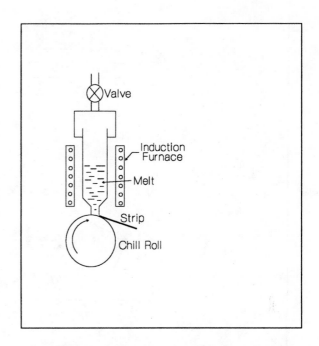

Fig.1b Schematic representation of continuous casting by the melt spinning process.

Top   Bottom

Fig.2 Top and bottom views of the strip; shiny and dull surfaces, respectively.

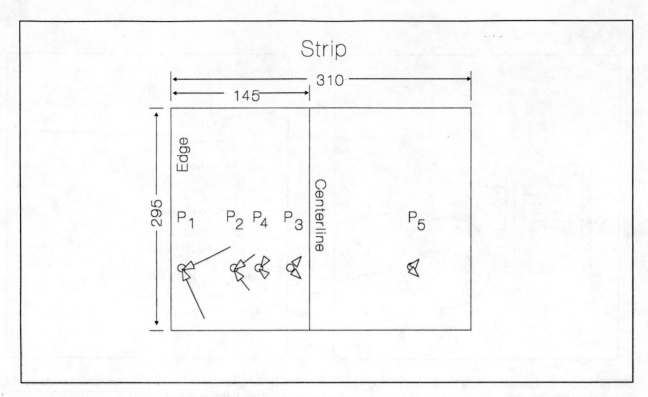

Fig.3 Geometry of specimens, locations of holes, and the orientation of principal stress components with respect to the edges of the strip.

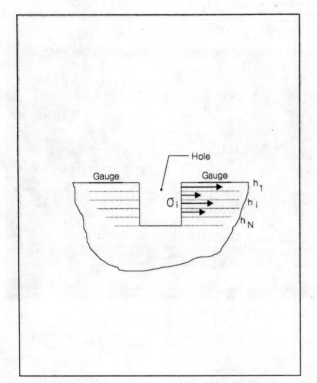

Fig.4 Schematic representation of hole drilling and the variation of the principal stresses below the surface, averaged at depths h_i

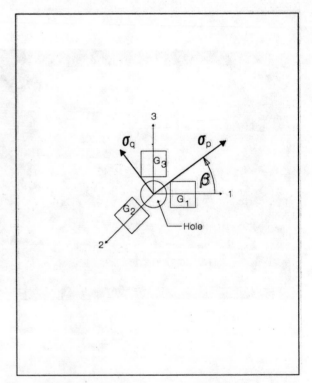

Fig.5 Strain gauge layout and the orientation angle ß of the maximum principal stress component σ^p with respect to the gauge G^1 of the strain gauge rosette.

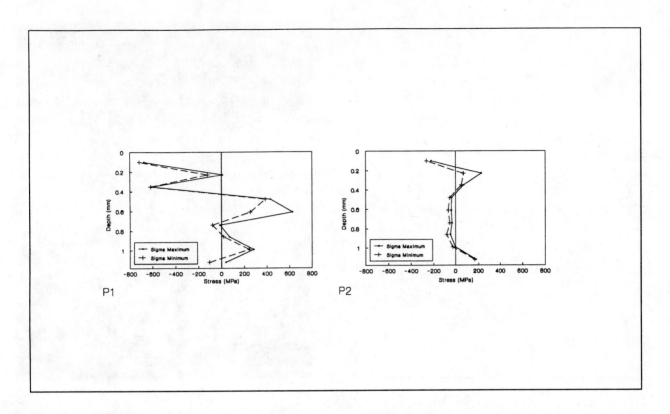

Fig.6a Variations of residual stresses through the thickness of the strip at the selected locations P1 and P2

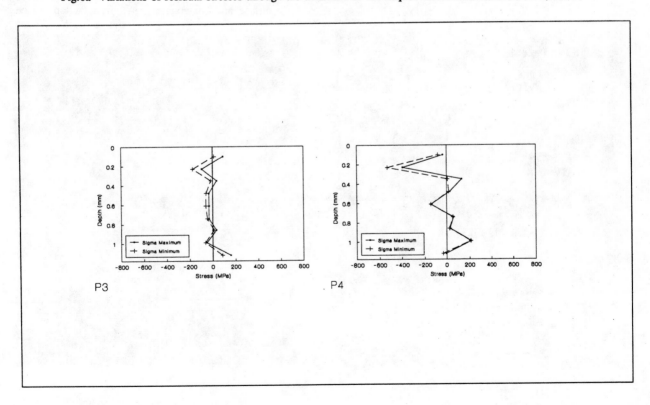

Fig.6b Variations of residual stresses through the thickness of the strip at the selected locations P3 and P4

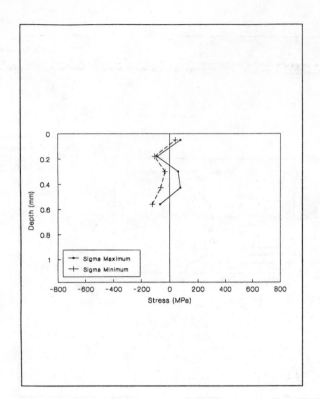

Fig.7　Variations of residual stresses through the thickness of the stress relived strip at the selected location P5

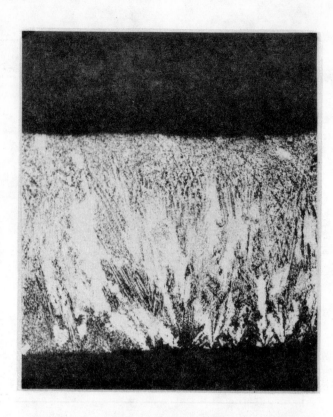

Fig.8　The microstructure of the cross-section of the strip. Distinct columnar dendritic growth from the bottom surface, and fine-grained growth from the top surface.

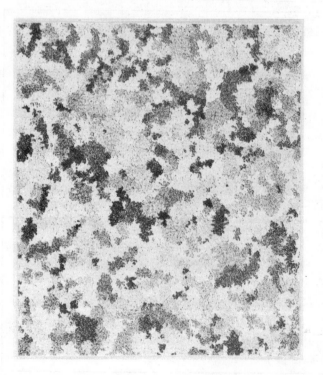

Fig.9　The top view of the equiaxial-dendritic microstructure of the fine-grained growth from the top surface

Fig.10 The microstructure of cold-rolled and annealed strip.

220

AN EXPERIMENTAL STUDY OF RESIDUAL STRESSES
IN MECHANICAL COMPONENTS

Khalid Khan, John Albers, David Atteridge,
Lemmy Meekisho, and Daniel Danks

ABSTRACT

Residual stresses in mechanical components are known to cause problems in a variety of ways. The task of characterizing these residual stresses in irregularly shaped parts has been approached from different angles. This investigation used the "blind-hole drilling" and the "Barkhausen noise" techniques to investigate residual stresses caused by a part's thermal history.

Results from the blind-hole drilling technique were quite consistent and showed a moderate level of residual stresses in tested components. This technique was independently "calibrated" against an etching technique of residual stress analysis on a specimen of known residual stress levels and gave comparable results which enhanced the authors' confidence in the blind-hole drilling technique.

The magnetic technique of Barkhausen noise analysis for residual stress measurement was also used to characterize some of the parts. This technique is based upon the well-known phenomenon of "Barkhausen noise" which is observed in ferromagnetic materials subjected to a time-varying magnetic field.

There was no correlation between the residual stress values obtained by the two techniques. This discrepancy should be taken into account when using the non-destructive techniques of residual stress analysis.

INTRODUCTION

Residual stresses in mechanical components have been known for a long time to cause problems such as cracking and premature failure during the service life of such components. The task of characterizing these residual stresses is not an easy one since the techniques used for such characterization are riddled with their own problems of application and interpretation. It is obvious that industrial users of these techniques want to have results available in a fast and timely manner if they can ever hope to incorporate these results into their manufacturing and quality control operations. These demands from the industrial user open up the field for makers of "special" equipment and "black boxes" which, according to the manufacturers' claims, can be used by technicians after minimal training and give not only the sign and magnitude but also the directions of residual stresses in a component. The industrial user is naturally attracted to such techniques since these are, at least superficially, easy to use and interpret. Some of the manufacturers of these black boxes also promise total automation, computer control, multichannel capabilities, and incorporation of all of this data into manufacturing and quality control functions of a company. One other attractive feature of these black box techniques is that they are, in general, completely non-destructive. Since these are all extremely attractive features of a technique or piece of equipment, industrial users often opt for such black boxes in favor of the tried and true but "old fashioned" techniques of residual stress analysis using strain gauges, sectioning, or boring.

In the present study, residual stress analysis was performed on a number of parts by the standard ASTM "blind-hole drilling" technique. Results from this investigation were compared with those obtained from the magnetic technique of Barkhausen noise analysis on the same parts. These parts were made of a proprietary iron-based alloy and had gone through different heat treatments involving water quenching, synthetic oil quenching, or slow cooling.

Khalid Khan is Associate Professor of Mechanical Engineering and John Albers is a former graduate student at the University of Portland, Portland, OR 97203-5798.

David Atteridge and Lemmy Meekisho are Associate Professor and Assistant Professor, respectively, at the Oregon Graduate Institute of Science and Technology, Beaverton, OR 97006-1999.

Daniel Danks is a tribologist with ESCO Corporation, Portland, OR 97210.

The blind-hole drilling technique involves the use of a special rosette strain gauge with three grids and a target area. This rosette is bonded to the part at the point of interest using standard cleaning and bonding procedures for strain gauges. Using a special jig, a hole is drilled at the target area in increments of 0.12 or 0.25 mm to a maximum depth of 1.5 or 3.0 mm depending upon the size of the rosette. Residual stresses in the component are released due to this hole drilling operation and can be easily computed by measuring the released strains in the three grids using a standard strain indicator (Ref. 1).

The magnetic technique depends upon the magnetoelastic phenomenon of Barkhausen noise in ferromagnetic materials. The movement of magnetic domain walls in such materials can be monitored by using a coil of conducting wire near the surface of the material. As the domain walls move, they induce an electrical pulse into the coil which can be monitored using standard equipment for measuring small electrical signals. These pulses come out of the material as bursts called "Barkhausen noise" after their discoverer Professor Barkhausen who observed this phenomenon in 1919. The Barkhausen noise has a spectrum ranging from magnetizing frequency to 250 kHz in most materials and is dampened by the material as a function of distance travelled inside the material. Measurement depths for practical applications vary between 0.01 and 1.5 mm. The Barkhausen noise signal is affected by two properties of the material, namely, the presence and amount of elastic stresses in the material and its metallurgical microstructure. It is also affected to some extent by the surface condition of the part (Ref. 2).

EXPERIMENTAL PROCEDURE

The testing procedure for evaluation of residual stresses in the parts under investigation was the standard ASTM blind-hole drilling technique. In this study, however, the "Air Abrasive Hole Drilling Technique" developed by Beany (Ref. 3) had to be used instead of the standard drill since the parts were made of abrasion resistant alloys of very high hardness (50-55 on the Rockwell C scale). A special jig was designed and built to handle these heavy parts and keep them level for the hole drilling operation (Fig. 1). Use of this jig in conjunction with accurate measuring tools allowed alignment of the part's surface to within ± 0.56° from the normal to the surface. A coating (Micro-Measurements PC-1 Adhesive) was used on the surface of these parts to facilitate the bonding of strain gauges. This coating was applied after the surface was prepared for standard strain gauge bonding. Rosette strain gauges (Micro-Measurements TEA-06-062RK-120) were then bonded to the surface using M-Bond 200 adhesive and standard procedures. The part was then installed in the jig assembly and the air abrasive drilling unit mounted onto the jig. By adjusting the knob shoe assembly and the jam nuts on the jig assembly, the part could be levelled properly. Lead wires were attached after this stage of leveling was complete. Strains were then recorded using a standard strain indicator after each increment of drilling. These strain values were converted to stresses using the standard conversion equations (Ref. 1).

The magnetic technique was applied in the field by the industrial sponsors of this project. Values of these readings are given in Table 1, along with residual stress values obtained by the hole-drilling method.

DISCUSSION

As can be seen from Table 1, values of residual stresses obtained by the blind-hole drilling method and the magnetic technique do not show much correspondence to each other. Since the hole-drilling method is a standardized technique and was also "calibrated" in the present study against a chemical etching technique, the level of confidence for this technique is quite high as far as the authors are concerned. If nothing else, this study has shown a need to be cautious when one is using techniques like Barkhausen noise analysis which, according to the trade literature, can give "everything one needs to know about the stress pattern in a part". Since the non-destructive techniques are quite sensitive to variables other than just stresses in the part, one should be very careful in applying these techniques without having a clear understanding of the variables involved. Some controlled experiments to calibrate such techniques before they are applied would be very useful in determining their limitations.

CONCLUSIONS

1. Residual stresses in mechanical components were successfully categorized using the standard ASTM Blind-Hole Drilling Technique. These stresses were of moderate magnitudes as compared to the yield strength of the parts under investigation.
2. There was no correlation between the residual stress values obtained by the blind-hole drilling method and the magnetic Barkhausen noise analysis technique. This

discrepancy should be taken into account when using the non-destructive techniques of residual stress analysis.

ACKNOWLEDGMENT

This research was supported by ESCO Corporation, Portland, OR.

REFERENCES

1. "Standard Test Method for Determining Residual Stresses by the Hole-Drilling Strain-Gage Method", ASTM Designation E 837-85, American Society for Testing and Materials, Philadelphia, PA.
2. "Nondestructive Inspection and Quality Control", Metals Handbook, Vol. 17, 9th Ed., ASM International, Metals Park, OH.
3. E.M. Beany, "Accurate Measurement of Residual Stresses on any Steel Using the Center Hole Method", Strain, July 1976, pp. 99-106.

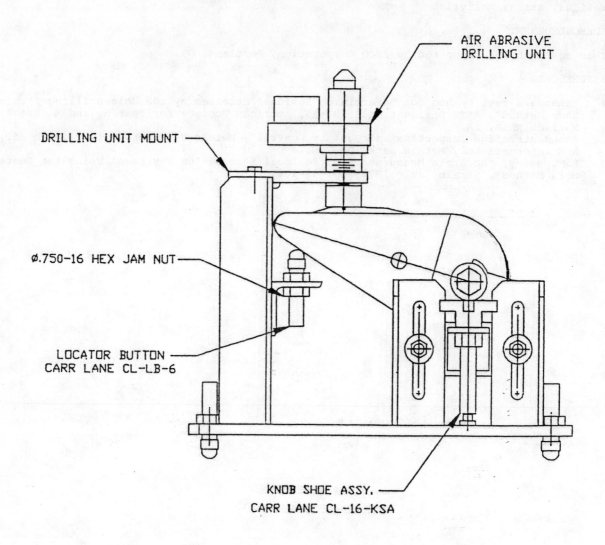

FIG. 1: Special jig for leveling of heavy parts for the hole-drilling operation.

Table 1: Residual Stress Levels and Barkhausen Noise Values (B.N.#) on Typical Parts

WATER QUENCHED # 1

POSITION	σ_1 (MPa)	σ_2 (MPa)	$\sigma_1 - \sigma_2$ (MPa)	B.N.#
1	-364.3	-393.7	29.4	Off-scale
2	-374.7	-437.7	63.0	160
3	-446.6	-496.3	49.7	145
4	-429.4	-510.5	81.1	176
5	-154.1	-287.2	133.1	Off-scale
6	-451.8	-597.1	145.3	165
7	-376.6	-412.2	35.6	Off-scale
8	-470.7	-481.8	11.1	179
9	-497.6	-545.7	48.1	170
10	-290.9	-485.3	194.4	Off-scale
12	-410.8	-585.0	174.2	165
13	-240.5	-493.4	252.9	n/a
14	-445.0	-597.5	152.5	n/a
15	-494.6	-577.2	82.6	n/a

WATER QUENCHED # 2

POSITION	σ_1 (MPa)	σ_2 (MPa)	$\sigma_1 - \sigma_2$ (MPa)	B.N.#
3	-100.5	-200.2	99.7	197
5	-212.3	-303.4	91.1	192
8	-138.6	-214.9	76.3	178
13	-185.5	-236.3	50.8	Off-scale
14	- 98.8	-350.7	251.9	n/a

RAPID AIR COOLED

POSITION	σ_1 (MPa)	σ_2 (MPa)	$\sigma_1 - \sigma_2$ (MPa)	B.N.#
3	-449.0	-464.2	15.2	Off-scale
5	-374.7	-390.1	15.4	Off-scale
8	-385.2	-466.0	80.8	Off-scale
13	-304.0	-351.1	47.1	n/a
14	-356.6	-365.1	8.5	n/a

SYNTHETIC QUENCH

POSITION	σ_1 (MPa)	σ_2 (MPa)	$\sigma_1 - \sigma_2$ (MPa)	B.N.#
3	- 70.4	-155.6	85.2	188
5	-105.2	-221.9	116.7	147
8	-137.9	-200.4	62.5	193
13	+ 4.0	-118.3	122.3	n/a
14	-189.5	-430.1	240.6	n/a

A STUDY OF RESIDUAL STRESS GRADIENT IN CERAMICS REINFORCED ALUMINIUM MATRIX COMPOSITES

J.Lu[1], B.Miège[2], P.Barbarin[2], J.F. Flavenot[1], J.Masounave[3]

ABSTRACT

This paper shows a study on the measurement of residual stress on the MMC components by the incremental hole drilling method and the X-ray diffraction method. The modified hole drilling method and the X-ray diffraction method are used for measuring the residual stress gradient in depth.

INTRODUCTION

Advanced composites show considerable promise for weight and volume critical applications , for example, aircraft and space vehicles. Aluminium alloys reinforced with ceramics (whiskers, particulates, and fibers) are new, potentially useful, structural materials with high strength and high modulus.

When a metal matrix composite (MMC) is cooled down to room temperature from the fabrication or annealing temperature, residual stresses can be induced in the composite due to the mismatch of the thermal expansion coefficients between the metal matrix and reinforcement. The magnitude of the residual stress has a very important effect on the yield stress and fatigue strength of the metal matrix composite.

Many techniques are available for residual stress measurement on mechanical parts. X-ray diffraction, bending deflection and hole drilling are three techniques which are commonly used [1]–[3]. In this study, the x-ray diffraction method and the hole drilling method are used and compared. In this paper, the residual stresses induced by mechanical origins will be analysed because very few research focus this problem today [4]-[6]. The major part of published research is about the residual stress due to thermal origins[7]-[8].

METHODS OF MEASUREMENT OF RESIDUAL STRESS
X-ray stress measurements

(a) General principle

When using atomic planes as strain gauges, it is possible to achieve non destructive X-ray stress measurements in crystalline materials.

The strain $\varepsilon_{\phi,\psi}$ in the ϕ,ψ direction (fig.1) is given by the general relation:

$$\varepsilon_{\phi,\psi} = \frac{1+\nu}{E} \{[\cos^2\phi\,(\sigma_{11}-\sigma_{33})+\sin^2\phi\,(\sigma_{22}-\sigma_{33}) + \sin2\phi\;\sigma_{12}]\sin^2\psi$$
$$+ [\cos\phi\,\sigma_{13}+\sin\phi\,\sigma_{23}]\sin2\psi\} + \frac{1}{E}[\sigma_{33}-\nu\,(\sigma_{11}+\sigma_{22})] \tag{1}$$

where E and ν are the bulk mechanical constants of the material.

Using X-ray elastic constants values S_1 and $1/2.S_2$ corresponding to the (hkl) set of atomic planes chosen for the measurement in the material, $\varepsilon_{\phi,\psi}$ can be written as follows:

$$\varepsilon_{\phi,\psi} = \frac{d_{\phi,\psi}-d_0}{d_0}$$

where $d\phi,\psi$ is the atomic interplanar spacing of the (hkl) set of planes in the ϕ,ψ direction and d_0 is the atomic interplanar spacing of the same set of planes for an unstressed specimen.

---

1 Research engineer and section head, respectively, Fatigue and fracture section, Centre Technique des Industries Mécaniques, 52 Avenue Félix-Louat, 60300 SENLIS, FRANCE

2 Research engineer and technician, respectively, Physical Analysis Section, CETIM, SENLIS

3 Professor, Ecole de technologie supérieur, Université du Québec, Canada

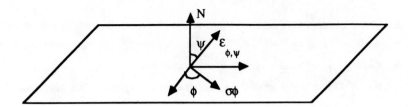

Fig.1

The last expression in equation 1 corresponds to the normal strain ε_N which can be written :

$$\varepsilon_N = \frac{d_N - d_0}{d_0}$$

where d_N is the spacing of (hkl) atomic planes which are parallel to the specimen surface.
Equation 1 can then be written :

$$\varepsilon_{\phi,\psi} = \frac{d_{\phi,\psi} - d_N}{d_0}$$

and as the unknown spacing d_0 can be replaced in the denominator by d_N with negligible error then:

$$\varepsilon_{\phi,\psi} - \varepsilon_N = \frac{d_{\phi,\psi} - d_N}{d_N} = \frac{1}{2} S_2 [A \sin^2\psi + B \sin 2\psi] \qquad (2)$$

where $\quad A = \cos^2\phi \, (\sigma_{11} - \sigma_{33}) + \sin^2\phi \, (\sigma_{11} - \sigma_{33}) + \sin 2\phi \, \sigma_{12}$

and $\quad B = \cos\phi \, \sigma_{13} + \sin\phi \, \sigma_{23}$

Differentiating the Bragg law $2d\sin\theta = \lambda$, equation 2 can then be written:

$$2\theta_{\phi,\psi} = 2\theta_N - 2 \, tg\theta_N \, \frac{1}{2} S_2 [A\sin^2\psi + B\sin 2\psi] \quad (3)$$

(b) Biaxial state

In a biaxial state, σ_{i3} expressions are equal to zero ($\sigma_{13} = \sigma_{23} = \sigma_{33} = 0$) and equation 3 can be written:

$$2\theta_{\phi,\psi} = 2\theta_N + K \, A \sin^2\psi$$

$$\text{where} \quad K = -2tg\theta_N \frac{1}{2} S_2$$

$$\text{then} \quad 2\theta_{\phi,\psi} = 2\theta_N + K \, [\cos^2\phi \, \sigma_{11} + \sin^2\phi \, \sigma_{22} + \sin 2\phi\sigma_{12}] \sin^2\psi \qquad (4)$$

From measurements carried out in 3 suitable ϕ directions (i.e. $\phi = 0°, 45°, 90°$), we can obtain by multiple linear regression the values σ_{11}, σ_{22} and σ_{12} of the biaxial stress tensor.

The measurement in only one ϕ direction gives a linear plot of $2\theta_{\phi,\psi}$ vs.$\sin^2\psi$:

$$2\theta_{\phi,\psi} = 2\theta_N + K \, \sigma_\phi \sin^2\psi \quad (5)$$

which slope is proportional to the stress σ_ϕ in the ϕ direction.

(c) Triaxial state

In this case σ_{i3} expressions are not equal to zero and equation 3 can be written:

$$2\theta_{\phi,\psi} = 2\theta_N + K\{[\cos^2\phi \, (\sigma_{11} - \sigma_{33}) + \sin^2\phi \, (\sigma_{22} - \sigma_{33}) + \sin 2\phi \, \sigma_{12}] \sin^2\psi$$
$$+ [\cos\phi \, \sigma_{13} + \sin\phi \, \sigma_{23}] \sin 2\psi\} \qquad (6)$$

Taking account of the fact that X-ray penetration depth is very weak in the irradiated specimen volume ($\leq 10\mu m$) we can consider that $\sigma_{33}=0$. Choosing suitable ϕ directions (i.e. $\phi = 0°, 45°, 90°$) with positive and negative ψ exposures, we can obtain by multiple linear regression the components $\sigma_{11}, \sigma_{22}, \sigma_{12}, \sigma_{13}, \sigma_{23}$, of the triaxial stress tensor.

The presence of shear stress σ_{13} and σ_{23} involves a misorientation of the stress tensor with respect to the main axis of the specimen.

For the measurement in only one ϕ direction with positive and negative ψ exposures, the plot of $2\theta_{\phi,\psi}.vs.\sin^2\psi$ gives an ellipse:

$$2\theta_{\phi,\psi} = 2\theta_N + K\,[\sigma_\phi \sin^2\psi + (\cos\phi\,\sigma_{13} + \sin\phi\,\sigma_{23})\sin2\psi] \qquad (7)$$

which main axis slope is proportional to σ_ϕ and which split is proportional to $(\cos\phi\sigma_{13} + \sin\phi\sigma_{23})$.

This non linear variation of $2\theta_{\phi,\psi}$ vs.$\sin^2\psi$ due to the presence of shear stress σ_{13} and σ_{23}, is generally observed in two phase materials after some hard mechanical treatment such as turning, milling, grinding [9]. In each phase these shear stresses have been found equal in intensity and opposite in sign [10] and the mean value is supposed to be equal to zero at the limit between each constituent.

For example, experiments have been carried out by [11] on carbon steels under the same conditions of severe grinding. Increasing the carbon content produces an increase of shear stress σ_{13} in the αFe phase as a result of an increase of the second phase Fe_3C.

(d) Experimental procedure

Experiments have been carried out on aluminium alloys reinforced with SiC particulates or whiskers, Al_2O_3, Al_2O_3-SiO_2 which volume fraction ranges from 15% to 40%. X-ray measurements were made using the portable equipment designed and built in CETIM. A position sensitive detector collects either X-ray chromium Kα photons diffracted by the (222) set of aluminium atomic planes for measurements in the matrix, or X-ray manganese Kα photons diffracted by the (208) set of silicon carbide atomic planes for measurements in the particulates. In both cases the stress measurement is obtained from the strain present at a depth of about 10 μm.

For all the measurements, the focal spot size was 2mm in diameter and we proceeded to 7ψ exposures in each ϕ direction.

These measurements were carried out in either 3ϕ directions (ϕ=0°, 45°, 90°) for the biaxial state or 6ϕ directions (ϕ=0°, 45°, 90°, 180°, 225°, 270°) in the triaxial state when necessary and in each case the whole stress tensor was obained by multiple linear regression using X-ray elastic constants reported in table 1.

Material	Set of atomic planes	$\frac{1}{2}S_2$ (MPa^{-1})	S_1 (MPa^{-1})
Al	(222)	17.9 10^{-6}	- 4.65 10^{-6}
SiCp	(208)	6.63 10^{-6}	- 1.82 10^{-6}

Table 1 X-ray elastic constants used for the stress calculation.

Hole drilling measurement

(a) Principle of the hole drilling method

The hole-drilling method involves monitoring the change in strains when a hole is drilled into a residually stressed component. Measurement is made by means of a special three-element strain gauge rosette. These strain measurements can then be related to the original residual stress in the analysed sample at the hole location .

To obtain the gradient of the residual stress with depth , the hole is drilled by steps . For each hole, the depth "z", and the surface strains ε_i (z) are measured. Once the hole drilling is complete, the residual principal stresses, σ_1(z) and σ_2(z) can be calculated from equations involving measured values of ε_i(z) and the calculated correlation coefficients. G.S.Schajer has carried out ([12]) an extensive review of the mathematical formulation for the stress calculation procedure. The integral method can be considered as the most "fundamental" of the four methods. CETIM uses this method for different kinds of materials and components [3]. The theoretical approach can be summarized as follows :

For determining the principal residual stresses (σ_{1hi} and σ_{2hi}, with $\sigma_{1hi} > \sigma_{2hi}$) and their directions with respect to any reference axis for each depth "hi", three independent strain measurements must be made . The equation for the radial strain corresponding to the principal residual stresses is :

$$\varepsilon_{in}(\theta_i) = A_{in}(\sigma_{1hi} + \sigma_{2hi}) + B_{in}(\sigma_{1hi} - \sigma_{2hi})\cos 2\theta_i \qquad (8)$$

The coefficients A_{in} and B_{in} depend on the following: the hole diameter, the position of the strain gauges, the position of the layer i, the depth of the hole, the elastic constants of the material. θ_i is the angle between the first strain gauge and the maximum principal residual stress. CETIM has developed a special finite element software (CATROR) for calculating A_{in} and B_{in}. Details of this are given in Ref.[3]. In the case of Al-SiC composite billets without extrusion, we consider that the composite is an isotropic material. In the case of whiskers reinforced extruded material, if the Young's modulus is not the same in the longitudinal direction and in the transversal direction. The calculation of an equivalent strain in each strain gauge direction is necessary.

MATERIALS

The first part of the composite materials investigated were aluminum alloys 2124 and 6061 reinforced with silicon carbide whiskers or particulates in volume fraction ranging from 15% to 40%. These materials are made by ACMC (Advanced Composite Materials Corporation, Greer, SC, USA) and were manufactured by powder metallurgy according to a classical process [13]. The heat treatment used is T6. The second part of the composites material investigated were aluminium alloy 5083 reinforced with short fibers Al_2O_3-SiO_2 and particulates Al_2O_3. These materials are made by IGM (Institut de Génie de Matériaux, Montreal) and were manufactured by squeeze casting[6].

Some of the different composites samples are shot-peened with the following peening conditions (table 2).

Shot	Shot diameter	Almen intensity (A)
Glass	300 μm	0.15 - 0.2 mm

Table 2 Shot-peening condition used

One example shows the results obtained on a laser-shocked test sample. In this case, laser-generated shock waves are used to harden and induce compressive stresses within the materials so as to improve their mechanical properties[14]-[15]. Laser-generated shock mainly results from a mechnical phenomenon based on a shock wave created by the explosion of a laser-irradiated matter. When a material is exposed to a laser beam with a sufficiently high fluence, a fine layer can evaporate thus forming a plasma. The pressure of the plasma, which may be very high (up to several ten of GPa) is transmitted to the matter due to a shock wave during sereral ns. After the shock wave has appeared at the surface, it propagates through the bulk material. Due to the high pressure, plastic flow occurs and the compressive residual stress can be generated.

RESULTS

X-ray method measurement

The residual stresses were measured before and after the shot-peening. The samples without the shot-penning are turned. Table 3 shows the residual stresses obtained on the matrix.

	Vf $_{(SiCp)}$	σ_{11}	σ_{22}	σ_{12}	σ_{13}	σ_{23}
turned	0	22 ± 5	44 ± 6	19 ± 7	- 2 ± 1	- 6 ± 2
	15 % SiCp	1 ± 6	8 ± 6	23 ± 6	- 3 ± 1	- 25 ± 2
	40 % SiCp	- 24 ± 9	- 41	25 ± 8	5 ± 2	30 ± 2
Shot peened	0	- 113 ± 8	- 119 ± 8	- 3 ± 9	0	0
	15 % SiCp	- 112 ± 9	- 111 ± 9	2 ± 8	0	0
	40 % SiCp	- 60 ± 13	- 65 ± 13	- 1 ± 12	0	0

Table 3 Residual stresses obtained in the turned samples

σ_{11} and σ_{22} respectively correspond to the axial and tranverse stress measured on the specimen which shapes are in all cases cylindrical. The error range corresponds to the statistical error which characterizes the reproducibility of the measurement for a confidence level of 99.7% (3σ).

The tensile residual stresses were observed for the case as turned. The stress level decreases and even became compressive when the volume fraction (Vf) of reinforcement increases. In the case of shot-peened samples, the residual stresses are in compression, but the level of the compressive residual stresses decreases when Vf increases. In fact, except for the yield stress, the effectiveness of shot peening also depends on hardness increase. For the same shot-peening intensity, the residual stresses and prestressed layer may be decreased for a higher Vf. So the shot-peening intensity must increase to increase the compressive residual stress.

As reported in Table 3, as turned reinforced billets show a systematical triaxial state with an average stress level which is quite low. Shot peening introduces compressive biaxial stress which level seems to depend on the particulates content.

We plotted fig.2, $2\theta_{\phi,\psi}$ vs.$\sin^2\psi$ for the mterial 2124+40% SiCp as turned and after shot peening.

The ψ splitting due to the presence of shear stress σ_{23} disappears with shot peening process. Figure 4 shows the effect of Vf on the shear stresses. When the Vf of the second phase (SiCp) increases, the residual shear stress increases. These results confirm the previous results obtained on steel.

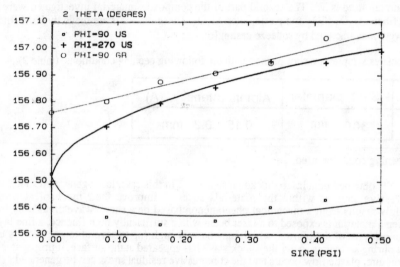

Fig.2 $2\theta_{\phi,\psi}$ vs.$\sin^2\psi$ before (MA) and after (SP) shot peening on the sample of 2124+40%

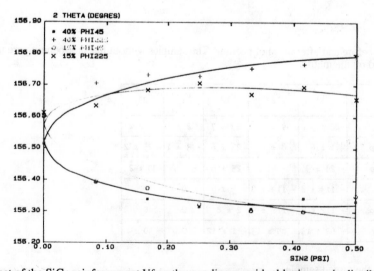

Fig.3 Effect of the SiCp reinforcement Vf on the non-linear residual lattice strain distribution vs.$\sin^2\psi$.

Table 4 shows measurements carried out in both Al and SiCp (40%) phases. In spite of the high statistical error observed in SiC measurements, we can notice that in the as turned state the stress level is quite low in both phases and shear stress seem to be opposite. Shot peening seems to be more efficient in SiC particulates than in the Al matrix.

	σ_{11}	σ_{22}	σ_{12}	σ_{23}	σ_{13}
As turned	- 6 ± 64	46 ± 58	33 ± 65	14 ± 14	- 10 ± 15
Shot peened	- 103 ± 56	- 127 ± 80	30 ± 55		

Table 4 X-ray measurements in matrix(2124) and in reinforcement (SiCp)

Hole drilling method measurement

Figure 4 and figure 5 show the results measured by the hole drilling method on the billet as received reinforced by 15% SiCp with two different matrix (2124 and 6061). It can be seen that in both cases , the level of residual stresses is very low and quasi isotropic (between -35 MPa and 25 MPa). The results of the X-ray diffraction method (table 4) confirm this observation. In this case, the nature of the matrix has no effect on the level and sign of residual stresses.

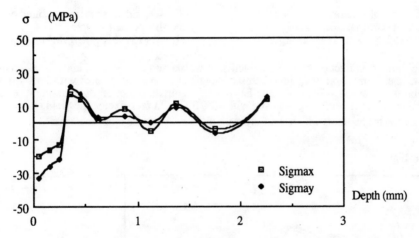

Figure 4 Residual stresses obtained by the hole drilling method on the as turned billet of 2124 matrix + 15% SiCp (±11 MPa).

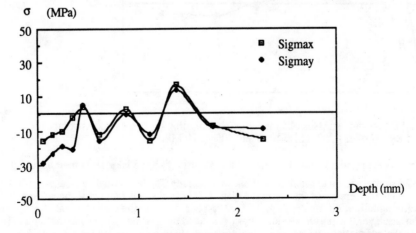

Figure 5 Residual stresses obtained by the hole drilling method on the as turned billet of 6061 matrix + 15% SiCp (±11 MPa).

Fig.6 and Fig.6[x] show the results measured by the hole drilling method on the shot peened billet reinforced by 15 % SiC$_p$ with two different matrix (2124 and 6061). The condition of shot peening is indicated in Table 2. In the both cases, the residual stresses are compressive and isotropic. But the level of the maximum residual stresses in the case of 2124 (fig.6) is more important than in the case of 6061 (fig.6[x]) matrix. In fact, the yield stress of the 6061 matrix composite is smaller than the 2124 matrix composite ([5] and [16]). The comparaison of results of the X-ray diffraction method are shown in table 5. It can be seen that the values obtained by the two methods of measurement are very close.

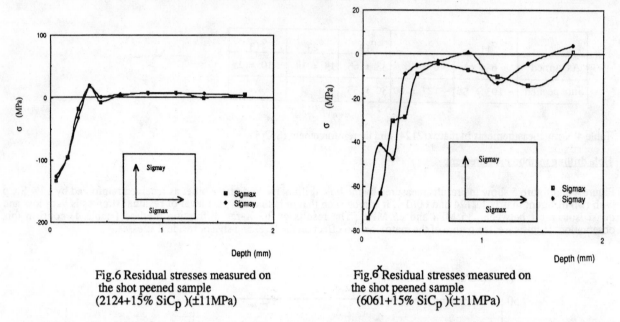

Fig.6 Residual stresses measured on
the shot peened sample
(2124+15% SiC$_p$)(±11MPa)

Fig.6[x] Residual stresses measured on
the shot peened sample
(6061+15% SiC$_p$)(±11MPa)

The following example shows the effect of the volume fraction of whisker on the extruded and blasted composite with a 2124 matrix. Figure 7 shows the comparison of residual stresses obtained on the composites with 25% SiCw and 40% SiCw reinforcement. It can be seen that the volume fraction has not an important effect on the maximum residual stress but the prestressed layer is smaller in the case of the composite with 40% SiC$_w$. In fact, except the yield stress, the effectiveness of shot peening depends also on the hardness which is different for different Vf of the reinforcements.

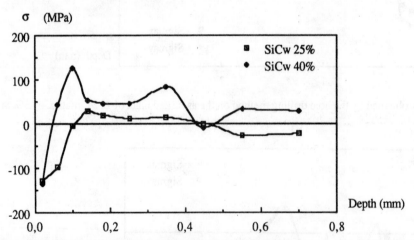

Figure 7 Comparison of the residual stresses obtained after shot peening on two extruded composites: 2124 reinforced with two volume fractions of SiC whisker (25% (±18MPa) and 40% (±20 MPa)).

Figure 8 and figure 9 shows the residual stress obtained in a composite 5083+35% Al$_2$O$_3$ manufactured by squeeze casting.

Tensile residual stresses are observed on the sample without shot peening.Those residual stresses are of thermal origins. These stresses are not only due to the difference of the thermal expansion coefficients between the matrix and the reinforcement but also due to the temperature gradient during cooling. After shot-peening, compressive residual stresses are observed on the surface and at the subsurface layer, the tensile residual stress generated by thermal origins are measured. This means that shot peening can only modify the surface residual stresses. Measurements are also carried out by X-ray diffraction technique. In the case of an as casted sample, it was impossible to measure the residual stresses due to the large grain size of the matrix and the texture. In the case of a shot peened sample, it was only possible to measure the residual stresses in the first 100μm of the hardened layer. The comparison between the residual stresses measured by the hole drilling method and the X-ray diffraction method are shown in figure 10. We can see that the results are very close. It can be noted that the X-ray technique measure the stresses on the matrix and the hole drilling technique measures the global residual stresses in the composite. In fact, in the case of the shot peening, the residual stresses occur in the matrix only during its plastification.

Figure 11 shows the comparison of the residual stresses obtained by X-ray and hole drilling method on a squeeze casted 5083 reinforced by Al_2O_3-SiO_2 short fibers. A quite good agreement between the results was observed.

Figure 12 shows the comparison of the residual stresses obtained in a shot peened sample and a laser shock treated sample. The results show that the laser shock treatment can induce more important residual stresses and for a higher depth. Another advantage of the laser shock treatment is the small roughness obtained after the treatment. This is very important for the fatigue behaviour of the MMC. In fact the MMC are very sensitive to the small defects like the modification of the roughness.

CONCLUSION

This study shows that the hole drilling method and the X-ray diffraction method are two suitable methods to evalute the residual stresses in ceramics reinforced aluminium matrix composite. The former measures the mean stress in composite, the latter can separate the residual stresses in the matrix and in the reinforcement. The X-ray method can measure the triaxial residual stresses but it is not applicable in the large grain size composites. Then both techniques must be used complementarily. In this study, the residual stresses induced by the manufacturing process (finishing and surface treatment) were analysed. The results obtained by the two methods are very similar in considering the scatter of those two methods, the stress gradient in the samples. Shot peening can generate compressive residual stresses but the laser shock treatment can induce higher residual stresses. In the future, the residual stresses generated by shot peening with different peening conditions (beads nature (glass, ceramic, steel), Almen intensity) will be systematically analysed. Other mechanical surface treatments will also be developed for metal matrix composite because the residual stresses can be easily modified in this way and it is quite difficult to induce favorable residual stresses by a heat treatment due to the multiphase state of MMC.

REFERENCES

1. Noyan , I.C., Cohen , J.B., "Residual stress measurement by diffraction and interpretation", Springer-Verlag, 1987

2. Flavenot , J.F. , Niku-Lari , A., "La mesure des contraintes residuelles", Mémoire Technique, No.31, CETIM, 1977

3. Lu , J., Niku-Lari , A. , Flavenot , J.F. , "Mesure de la distribution des contraintes residuelles en profondeur par la méthode du trou incrémentale", Mémoire et Etudes Scientifiques, Revue de la Métallurgie, Feb.1985, pp 69-81

4 Tohriyama, S., Kumano, M., Hisamatsu, S., "Influence of peening on fatigue life of SiC reinforced aluminium", Proceedings of the fourth international conference on shot peening, Tokyo, Japan, 1990, pp307-316

5. Lu ,J., Flavenot ,J.F., THERY ,S., "Study on the effect of the finishing treatment on the residual stress gradient in SiC reinforced aluminium metal matrix composite", Journal of composite technology and research, ASTM, Vol. 12, N.4, 1990, pp232-238

6. Masounave ,J., Lu, J., Arker, P., FLAVENOT, J.F., "Contraintes résiduelles de grenaillage dans les composites Al-SiO$_2$-Al$_2$O$_3$ et Al-Al$_2$O$_3$", Le recueil de conférence des journées nationales sur LES CONTRAINTES RESIDUELLES ET NOUVELLES TECHNOLOGIES, CETIM, SENLIS, FRANCE, Sept.1990, pp 289-297

7. Taya, M., Arsenault, R.J., "Metal matrix composites, Thermomechanical Behavior", Pergamon Press, 1989

8. Taya, M., Lulay, K.E., Lloyd, D.J., "Strengthening of a particulate metal matrix composite by quenching", Acta metall.mater. Vol.39, No.1. pp 73-87, 1991

9. Torbaty , S., Maisan , A., Lebrun, J.L., Maeder, G.,"Evolution of residual stress during turning and cylindrical grinding of a carbon steel, Annals of CIRP, Vol 31, pp 441-445, 1987

10. Hauk, V., Stuitje, P., " Zur Auswertung von gitter dehnungsmessungen en Zweithosen- werkstoffen", Coloque Franco-Allemand Freiburg 1983.

11. Castex, L., "Etude par diffraction X d'aciers au voisinage de la limite d'endurance et à différents stades de la fatigue", Thèse Université de Bordeaux 1, N.946, Dec 1987

12. Schajar, G.S. , "Measurement of non-uniform residual stress using the hole drilling method", Journal of Engineering Materials and Technology, Vol.110, October 1988, pp 338-349

13. Rack , H. J. , Niskanen , P. W. , Light metal age, Feb.1984

14. Fournier, J., Ph.D Thesis, Ecole Polytechnique, Paris, FRANCE, June 1989

15. Forget, P., Strudel, J.L., Jeandin, M., Lu, J., Castex, L., "Laser shock surface treatment of Ni-based superalloys", Materials and manufacturing processes, Vol.5, N.4, pp501-528, 1990

16. Barbaux, J., Hebert , J.P., Abiven ,H.,"Les composites à matrice métallique décollent :quelles technologies pour quelles applications ", Mémoire et Etudes scientifiques, Revue de Métallurgie July 1988, pp405-414.

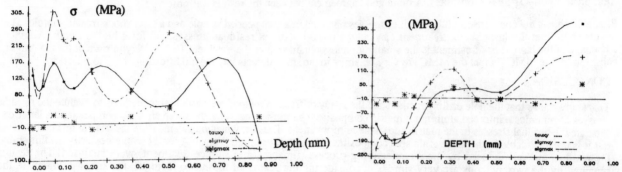

Figure 8 Residual stress obtained in a composite 5083+35% Al$_2$O$_3$ manufactured by squeeze casting (As casted sample)

Figure 9 Residual stress obtained in a composite 5083+35% Al$_2$O$_3$ manufactured by squeeze casting (Shot peened sample)

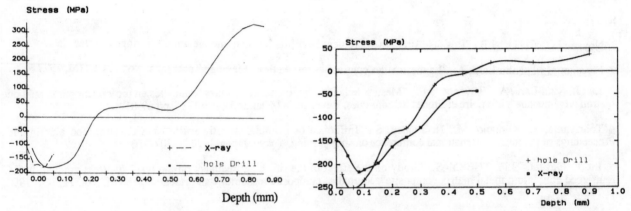

Figure 10 Comparison of two techniques (X-ray diffraction and hole drilling method), residual stress obtained in a composite 5083+35% Al$_2$O$_3$ manufactured by squeeze casting (Shot peened sample)

Figure 11 Comparison of two techniques (X-ray diffraction and hole drilling method), residual stress obtained in a composite 5083+10% Al$_2$O$_3$-SiO$_2$ manufactured by squeeze casting (Shot peened sample)

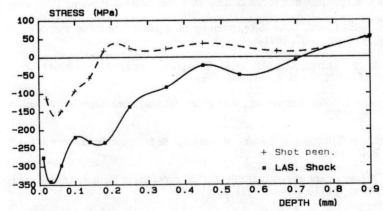

Figure 12 Comparison of residual stresses induced by shot peening and laser shock treatments on a 2124 + 40SiCw composite

THREE-DIMENSIONAL NONDESTRUCTIVE ISODYNE STRESS ANALYSIS
IN FRACTURE MECHANICS

Jerzy T. Pindera

ABSTRACT

Modern fracture mechanics requires more reliable and accurate data on the actual three-dimensional stress states in regions of cracks and notches than those which have been accepted in classical solutions and procedures. Paper presents experimental evidence that the newly developed isodyne stress analysis supplies reliable data on the actual three-dimensional stress states in plates with notches and cracks. Those data can be cross-checked by means of the new strain-gradient measurement procedures which are based on the strain-gradient light bending. Characteristic variations, of some major stress components along choses cross-sections are given for two typical specimens: ASTM Bend Specimen SE(B), and ASTM Compact Specimen C(T). To allow a critical assessment of the applied experimental procedures the basic theories of analytical and optical isodynes, and of strain-gradient analysis, are outlined. It is concluded that the capacities of both presented experimental methods satisfy the present requirements regarding the reliability of determination of actual static stress fields which exist when the crack propagation velocity is negligible with respect to sound velocity. The novel set of data on the actual stresses in the crack region presented in this paper indicates that a need exists to further develop theoretical bases of various analytical and experimental methods of stress analysis.

INTRODUCTION

Rapidly increasing requirements regarding the damage resistance of structures and the related damage tolerance studies result in more demanding requirements regarding the reliability of theoretical foundations of analytical, numerical, and experimental procedures of fracture mechanics. The knowledge of the actual, three-dimensional by definition, stress/strain fields is an inherent component of all fracture theories and hypotheses, regardless of whether they are formulated in terms of functions of stress or energy. Consequently, more attention is given recently to the reliability of the developed mathematical models and of the resulting analytical solutions for the stress/strain states in regions of cracks and notches.

It is already documented that the analytical, two-dimensional singular solutions of linear fracture mechanics yield only approximate information on the actual state of stresses in plates in regions of cracks, including the regions ahead of the crack tip. This pertains to plane stress solutions and plane strain solutions as well. Similar problems exist regarding the stress states in notches in plates. In both cases the actual stress states are strongly three-dimensional, that is the in-plane stresses vary with the distance from the plate faces, and there exist thickness stress components which are significant. This fact is known in advanced engineering for over 60 years [1]. The recently obtained comprehensive experimental evidence agrees with the results obtained by Thum et al, [2].

Such pronounced, but limited in space, three-dimensional stresses in plates are commonly denoted as "local effect". The analytical treatment of such stress states is complicated [3], the numerical treatment is promising but still expensive, and the theoretical basis of freezing techniques of transmission photoelasticity is still not reliably established regarding requirements of the linear elasticity. The surface measurement procedures (strain gages, moiré interferometry, speckle interferometry, etc.) supply valuable data on surface strains or stresses, only; such data are insufficient to infer the internal stress states. There is a need for an empirical method of three-dimensional stress analysis to be used for supplying reliable data on the actual stresses in crack problems and for testing analytical and numerical procedures. It was shown recently that the new nondestructive methods of isodyne stress analysis and strain-gradient light bending methods allow a satisfactory determination of three-dimensional stresses in local effects, [4] and [5].

Experimental data presented in this paper were obtained by means of the isodyne stress analysis and strain-gradient analysis. Theories of both nondestructive methods of three-dimensional stress analysis and of pertinent laboratory procedures are given in pertinent references, [6], [7]. The data on the distributions and values of stresses presented in this paper and in referred papers do not necessarily agree with some published data obtained either analytically, or by using methods of transmission photoelasticity or of caustics; such qualitative and quantitative differences or contradictions can be caused only by the differences in the theory of development of the mathematical models of a stress state or in the theory of the experimental procedures. Consequently, to allow a rational assessment of the reliability and accuracy of the isodynes and strain-gradient methods it is necessary to compare the basic

---

Jerzy T. Pindera is Professor Emeritus in the Civil Engineering Department, Solid Mechanics Division, Faculty of Engineering, University of Waterloo, Waterloo, Ontario, Canada N2L 3G1.

features of their underlying theories with the theoretical bases of other procedures. This will allow a better understanding of the causes of differences or contradictions between the results of various analytical or experimental evaluations of the stress fields when using different procedures.

PATTERNS OF APPLIED RESEARCH METHODOLOGY

The presented methods of nondestructive three-dimensional methods of stress analysis were developed, and the presented experimental results were obtained, within the framework of physical methodology presented in [8] and illustrated by examples in [9]. The experimental issues related to the local effects in plates are discussed in [10],and the influence of accepted methodology of analytical and experimental research is discussed in [11]. Two examples directly pertinent to the subject of this paper are presented in Figures 1 and 2.

Figure 1 presents two incompatible models of stress states in plates: the mathematical model of stress states in regions of notches and cracks, based on the notion of a generalized plane stress state, which is still often used in analytical and experimental research; and the experimental evidence of a strongly three-dimensional stress state in the region of a notch [2]. According to this evidence, all components of stress state in a plate vary with the distance from plate surface. A plane stress state exists only at the surface of the plate. Research presented in this paper was designed in accordance with this fact.

Figure 2 presents two incompatible sets of models of interaction between radiation and matter, the assumed phenomenological models, and the simplified physical models. Both sets of models are used concurrently in research, including the choice of foundations of theories of experimental methods and of evaluation procedures. In the reported research the physical models have been accepted as components of theoretical bases of the developed methods and procedures.

OUTLINE OF ISODYNE STRESS ANALYSIS

Theory of isodyne stress analysis consists of the theory of analytical isodynes and the theory and techniques of optical isodynes. Plane isodynes characterize plane stress fields; differential isodynes characterize three-dimensional stress fields in plates, when all stress components depend on the thickness coordinate.

Development

Theories and techniques of analytical and optical isodynes and the related procedures of isodyne stress analysis have been developed by Pindera with his co-workers during the last two decades. Detailed presentation of features and properties of plane and differential isodynes is given in [6]. Basic information on the relevant theories of observation, modeling, and measurement are given in [8,11,12,13,14,15]; components of the pertinent transfer functions are discussed in [16]. Design of isodyne recorder is presented in [17]. Reference [18] formulates requirements which follow from the actual viscoelastic responses of polymeric materials. Patterns of the actual light scattering are discussed in [19].

Plane Elastic Analytical Isodynes - an Outline

Two-dimensional (plane) stress state in a hypothetical, infinitesimally thin plate is considered. Material of plate is described by Hooke's body and complies with the notion of a material continuum. Plate is loaded by boundary tractions. Plate is co-planed with a (x,y)-plane. Using the notion of Airy Stress Function, Φ, we introduce the notion of an isodyne surface spanned over the plate. The isodyne surface is related to the first derivatives of the stress function, and to the direction of integration, or differentiation [20,6]:

$$\int \sigma_{yy}(x,y)dx = \int \frac{\partial^2}{\partial x^2} \Phi(x,y)dx = \Phi(x,y)dx = \Phi(x,y) + f_x(y) = p_y(x,y), \text{ etc.}, \tag{1}$$

where $\Phi(x,y)$ denotes the first derivative of Φ in x-direction, $f_x(y)$ is an integration function, and x is the characteristic direction.

Functions $p_y(x,y)$, which represent elevations of the x-isodyne surface over the (x,y)-plane called the characteristic plane, can be presented in a normalized form,

$$p_y(x,y) = S_s p_y^n(x,y) = S_s m_{sx}(s,y), \text{ etc.} \tag{2}$$

where S_s is a material coefficient, and $p_y^n = m_{sx}$ is a nondimensional parameter which is called order of the isodyne.

The functions

$$m_{sx} = m_{sx}(x,y) = \text{const} \tag{3}$$

are called plane analytical isodynes, and represent constant elevation lines on the isodyne surface. Projection of isodynes on the characteristic surface gives isodyne field, Fig. 3. Isodynes represent geometric loci of points at which the total force intensities along the characteristic direction, $p_y(x,y)$, are constant.

The cross-sections through the isodyne surface in the characteristic direction give normal isodyne functions,

$$m_{sxx} = m_{sxx}(x,y_i) = p_y^n(x,y_i) = S_s^{-1} p_y(x,y_i), \tag{4}$$

and the cross-sections in direction normal to characteristic direction give shear isodyne functions,

$$m_{sxy} = m_{sxy}(x_i,y) = t_y^n(x_i,y) \tag{5}$$

The slopes of isodyne functions, that is the slopes of the isodyne surface in corresponding directions, are proportional to the normal and shear stress components,

$$\sigma_{yy}(x,y) = -\frac{\partial}{\partial x} \Phi_x(x,y) = \frac{\partial}{\partial x} p_y(x,y) = S_s \frac{\partial}{\partial x} m_{sxx}(x,y) \tag{6}$$

$$\sigma_{yx} = \frac{\partial}{\partial y} \Phi_x(x,y) = \frac{\partial}{\partial y} t_y(x,y) = S_s \frac{\partial}{\partial y} m_{sxy}(x,y) \tag{7}$$

Thus two surfaces of plane analytical isodynes supply data on σ_{xx}, σ_{yy}, σ_{xy} and $\sigma_{yx} = \sigma_{xy}$.

Differential Elastic Analytical Isodynes

As discussed above, stress states in real plates of finite thickness is noticeably three-dimensional in regions of notches, cracks, contact loads, and other local effects. For such stress state one more family of characteristic lines of stress fields in plates is defined, and is called differential analytical isodynes. In the simplest case, when the characteristic plane is coplanar with the middle plane of the plate, the differential analytical isodynes are described by:

$$\Delta p_{y,z}(x,y,o) = p_y - p_z = \int (\sigma_1 - \sigma_3)dx = const., \tag{8}$$

and, for an arbitrary distance z_i,

$$\Delta p_{y,z}(x,y,z=z_i) = p_y - p_z = \int (\sigma_{yy} - \sigma_{zz})dx = S_s m_{sxx}^d(x,y,z=z_i) = const. \tag{9}$$

Plane and Differential Optical Isodynes

Surfaces and fields of analytical isodynes, plane and differential, can be determined experimentally, by using a particular scattered light technique. It must be noted that the light intensity fringes which are obtained by using techniques of the scattered light photoelasticity do not represent analytical isodynes. Lines of constant light intensity of a scattered light represent analytical isodynes only when the system of specific conditions is satisfactorily approximated [6,16,19]. The basic conditions are:

1. The basic features of the stress-induced birefringence are satisfactorily described by the simplified relations of photoelasticity which are derived on basic of the phenomenological model of photoelastic effect presented by Ramachandran and Ramasehan in [13].
2. The actual scattering of light is close to predictions of the mathematical model of scattering developed by Rayleigh [6,19,21], Figure 4.
3. The information collecting primary light beam is polarized either circularly or linearly with the vibration direction inclined by 45° to the middle plane of plate.
4. The recorded scattered light intensities satisfy the following restrictions at each scattering point:
   a - observation angles are very close to 90°.
   b - azimuthal angles are close to 0°, or 90°, or 45°.
5. The image plane of the recorded intensity distribution of the scattered light is parallel to the characteristic plane (object plane).
6. The optical paths of all rays of the three information-carrying light sheets are equal.

As it is presented in Figure 4 the scattering direction of the observed scattered light is usually given by two parameters which are related to the direction of the electric vector E, and to the direction of the light propagation $\bar{s}$, namely: the azimuthal angle Φ and the observation angle Θ. As it is shown in Figure 4 the direction of polarization of the scattered light vary with the varying observation and azimuthal angles, and the light is scattered in all directions, including the direction of the primary light beams.

When the above presented conditions are satisfied, then the suitable measurement instrument produces fields of intensity distributions of the scattered light, which have a common feature: the geometric loci of points of equal light intensity represent isodynes within the characteristic plane; those lines are called optical isodynes. It was shown that the optical isodynes have the same properties as the analytical isodynes [6,20].

The specified conditions are satisfied by the measurement system called the isodyne recorder. The details on the theory of measurement are given in [17]. Information on the isodyne field in a selected characteristic plane is collected by a very narrow, monochromatic, linearly polarized laser beam which propagates in the characteristic direction and is scanned within the characteristic plane. The angle between the vibration plane of the light entering plate and the plate middle plane is 45°. The collected fields of the scattered light intensities are given by lines of constant light intensities which are optical isodynes. In the case of a primary light beam, of intensity I_o, which propagates in the x-characteristic direction and is scanned in the (x,y,z_i)-characteristic plane of a plate, the lines of constant light intensity $I_x(x,y,\theta=90^{\circ}, \Phi_i)$ are given by:

$$\text{For } \Phi_i = 0^{\circ}: \quad I_x/I_o = I_x^n = \sin^2\pi m_{sx} = \sin^2\frac{\phi_{sx}}{2} = \text{const.} \tag{10}$$

$$\text{For } \Phi_i = 90^{\circ}: \quad I_x/I_o = I_x^n = \cos^2 m_s = \cos^2\frac{\phi_{sx}}{2} = \text{const.} \tag{11}$$

$$\text{For } \Phi_i = 45^{\circ}: \quad I_x/I_o = I_x^n = \text{const.} \tag{12}$$

Both parameters, the normalized linear relative retardation along the characteristic direction $m_{sx} = R_x/\lambda$, and the corresponding relative angular retardation (phase angle) ϕ_{sx}, are functions of the secondary principal stresses acting in the (y,z)-plane, σ_1^x and σ_3^x. The expressions (10) and (11) describe fields of complementary differential optical isodynes, and the expression (12) describes the reference beams whose intensities are constant when the thickness stresses are negligible. The following expressions describe the basic physical event, when the conditions presented earlier are satisfied,

$$m_{sx} = \frac{1}{2\pi}\phi_{sx} = S_s^{-1}\int (\sigma_1^x - \sigma_3^x) \, dx \cong S_s^{-1}\int (\sigma_{yy} - \sigma_{zz}) \, dx = \text{const.} \tag{13}$$

Two techniques of recording isodyne fields have been developed to date: the amplitude modulation technique, and the spatial frequency modulation technique [22], Figure 5, top and bottom, respectively.

The isodyne technique may be easily combined with transmission photoelasticity technique in regions when the thickness stress component is negligible. Reference [16] presents an example of such a stress analysis of a disk loaded diametrically.

EFFICACY OF ISODYNE STRESS ANALYSIS IN FRACTURE MECHANICS

Bibliography on analytical and experimental research in fracture mechanics is very extensive. A comprehensive review of contemporary research in fracture mechanics is presented by Kobayashi [23], thus it is not necessary to discuss this issue here.

Two examples presented below should allow to assess the efficacy of the isodyne stress analysis in determination of the actual stress states in the standardized specimens used in fracture mechanics. The presented examples pertain to the mode I crack in a plate loaded by a tensile stress normal to the crack plane. For such a case the classical solutions of the linear fracture mechanics, which are based on the notion of a generalized plane states (generalized plane stress state, or a generalized plane strain state) yield the following expressions for the stress components at the crack tip, in the plane of the crack, $(x,y=0,z)$:

$$\sigma_{xx}=\left(\frac{a}{2r}\right)^{1/2}\sigma; \quad \sigma_{yy}=\left(\frac{a}{2r}\right)^{1/2}\sigma; \quad \sigma_{xy}=\left(\frac{a}{2r}\right)^{1/2}\sigma; \tag{14a,b,c,}$$

$$\sigma_{zz} = 0 \text{ - plane stress state;} \quad \sigma_{zz} = \nu(\sigma_{xx} + \sigma_{yy}) \text{ -plane strain state;} \tag{14d,e}$$

where a is the semi-crack length and r denotes the distance from the crack tip.

Defining the stress intensity factor for mode I as [23]:

$$K_I = \sigma\sqrt{\pi a} \tag{15}$$

one can present the stresses in the crack plane as:

$$\sigma_{xx} = (2\pi r)^{-1/2} K_I; \quad \sigma_{yy} = (2\pi r)^{1/2} K_I; \quad \sigma_{xy} = 0 \tag{16a,b,c}$$

These expressions predict a monotomic decrease of values of the normal stress components, in the plane of the crack, with the increasing distance r from the crack tip. Question is what is the qualitative and quantitative correlation between the predicted and the actual, three-dimensional, stress components.

It must be noted that "the plane stress equations exhibit an inconsistency between the stress singularities and the compatibility of strain", as shown by Bui [24].

Isodyne specimens, which reproduce major features of stress states in selected ASTM fracture mechanics specimen, were tested in the constant deformation mode to eliminate the influence of the optical creep [6,18].

Stresses in Bend Specimen

Presented results pertain to the specimen described in the ASTM Testing Standards E399-83. Complete set of the results will be reported elsewhere [25]. The loading conditions deviate from those given in the ASTM Testing Standard E399-83; the central force acting in the crack plane is replaced by two forces which produce pure bending conditions in the crack region.

Normal Stresses in the Crack Plane

Both normal stress component acting along the crack plane close to the surface of the specimen, between the crack tip and outer boundary of specimen, are presented in Figures 6 and 7. Figure 6 presents the normal stresses acting in direction of the crack σ_{yy}. Stresses are equal to zero at the crack tip, reach the maximal value of the distance of about 3 mm from the crack tip, decrease to zero at the distance of about 19 millimetres from the crack tip, change the sign, and again decrease to zero at the outer specimen boundary. It may be noted that the normal stresses acting in the crack direction must be equal to zero at the crack tip, because the zero value of the crack tip curvature is physically inadmissible.

The variation of the second normal stress component with the distance from the crack tip is presented in Figure 7. The maximal value of this stress, which acts normally to the crack plane, occurs at the crack tip; with the increasing distance from the crack tip this stress decreases rapidly to zero, and changes its sign.

Comparing Figures 6 and 7 one notes that the normal stress component acting in direction of the crack is much smaller than the second normal stress components, with the exception of a small region when σ_{xx} approaches zero. Thus the relations (14) or (16) are not directly applicable in this case. It is shown elsewhere [26] that the value of the stress component normal to the crack plane is about 30% higher in the middle plane of a specimen than in the surfaces.

Normal Stresses Along the Crack Tip

As shown in Figure 1 and in [24] plane stress states at the crack tip are not admissible. A typical variation of the normal stress component acting along the crack tip with the distance from the specimen middle plane is shown in Figure 8. This stress component, called thickness stress, reaches maximal value in the middle plane of the specimen, and decreases monotomically to the zero value in the surface of specimen. Summarizing, both in-plane normal stress components, σ_{xx} and σ_{yy} are much larger in the middle plane of the specimen than in surfaces, and the thickness stress may reach 10-15% of the maximal surface stress. Thus, the value of the equivalent stress at the crack tip in the middle plane of a specimen, calculated according to Mises-Huber-Hencky hypothesis, may be 30-40% higher than the value which follow from a plane stress state solution.

One more interesting conclusion can be drawn from Figures 8. The actual value of the thickness stress, which is assumed equal to zero in the plane stress state solutions, equation (14d), is much smaller than that which is predicted by the plane strain state model, equation (14e).

Stresses in Compact Specimen

The isodyne compact specimen was designed to reproduce major features of the stress state in the ASME Compact Specimen C(T), which is described in the ASTM Testing Standard E399-83. The loading conditions simulate closely the loading conditions prescribed in the testing standards, with respect to stresses in the crack region. Examples of evaluated results are presented in Figures 9 and 10.

Normal Stress Components in Plane of Crack

Detailed data on the three-dimensional stress distribution in Compact Specimen are presented elsewhere [27]. Only one particular relationship is discussed here, namely the distribution and values of the normal stress component σ_{xx} which acts normally to the plane of the crack, ((y,z)-plane), in planes very close to surfaces of the specimen, $\bar{z} = 0.99$. The variation of this stress component with the distance from the crack tip is presented in Figure 9. Qualitatively, the distribution of this stress component is the same as the distribution of the corresponding stress component in the Bend Specimen, Figure 7. Quantitative differences are caused by different equilibrium conditions in the plane of the crack and by other evident factors.

It may be noted that the stresses presented in Figures 15 and 12 act in planes very close to free specimen surfaces and parallel to them, and therefore are components of plane stress states. Evidently, with increasing distance from the specimen surface the values of those stresses increase, and the location of the zero values of those stresses also depends on the thickness coordinate as shown in [2].

Stress Intensity Function

In the plane of crack stresses depend only on the distance r from the crack tip according to the linear fracture mechanics relations (14), (15) and (16). Thus the function

$$K_I = (2\pi r)^{1/2} \sigma_{xx}(r),$$ (17)

where K_I is a constant parameters, should be constant in the crack region.

It may be noted that the relation (17) is often taken as a theoretical foundation of various experimental procedures. Thus it is of a significant interest to test the reliability of that solution.

In paper [26] the function (17) was called the stress intensity function and was determined experimentally, using the isodyne stress analysis, for two bend specimens having cracks of different depths. It was shown that these functions are not constant, and also are not monotonic. The stress intensity function for the compact specimen, derived from Figure 9, is given in Figure 10. Because the maximal value of the actual stress at the crack tip is finite, the function K_I approaches zero with the decreasing distance from the crack tip. This function reaches maximum at the distance very close to the crack tip and again decreased to zero when the normal stress component σ_{xx} decreases to zero at a finite distance from the crack tip. Thus, with one only exception, this function assumes the same values for two different distances from the crack tip. The conclusions regarding the reliability of various experimental procedures which are based on the notion of a constant value of the stress intensity factor are evident.

STRAIN-GRADIENT STRESS ANALYSIS

Theoretically, the paths of any energy flow through inhomogeneous bodies must be curved [14]. It was reported independently in 1949 and 1955 that this light-path bending, depicted schematically in Figure 2, limits the resolution of the photoelastic systems. This effect modifies the fields of isochromatics in regions of high stress gradient, and - when accompanied by optical anisotropy - may result in noticeable separation of the conjugated light beams, Figure 11. This separation may be quite large - separations of 4 mm, produced along an optical path 200 mm long, were observed.

This strain-gradient effect is of a particular significance to the isodyne strain analysis. It requires that the material for isodyne specimens be carefully tested; on the other hand this effect is a source of complementary valuable data on the actual three-dimensional stress/strain field, as it is shown in [7]. When this natural occurrence is neglected, then the theoretical bases of some experimental methods may become questionable, as shown in [5]. A review of applications of the strain-gradient bending procedures is given in [28]. The example presented below illustrates the usefulness of this method in fracture mechanics.

The theory of the strain-gradient light bending is based on two models: (a) the model of energy flow through the inhomogeneous bodies which relates the rotation of the wavefronts to the gradients of velocity [14] (b) the phenomenological RR-model which relates linearly the components of the index tensor to the components of the stress or strain tensors [13]. It may be noted that the very drastic simplifications of the RR-model yield the known elementary relations of photoelasticity [6]. In practical applications a third model is needed, namely a satisfactorily reliable model of strain-gradient distribution across the thickness of the plate, which would allow convenient mathematical operations. Details of the theory and techniques of the strain-gradient stress analysis are given in pertinent bibliography [5,6,7,28].

TESTING THEORY OF TRANSMISSION CAUSTICS AND SOME FEATURES OF ANALYTICAL SOLUTIONS IN FRACTURE MECHANICS

The example presented below was taken from [5]. It provides an experimental evidence that it is inadmissible to neglect, or overlook, the actual patterns of light propagation in the theory of caustics in fracture mechanics; also presents an example of an experimental testing some features of the analytical solutions, in this case the testing the order of singularity in the singular solutions of linear fracture mechanics.

The specimen used to collect information on the actual patterns of light paths bending in the region of a crack tip is shown in Figure 12. Specimen was loaded in constant deformation mode. Information was collected along the plane of crack, using light beams polarized linearly in directions of principal stresses. The wavelength of light was 488 mm.

Typical characteristic results age presented in Figure 12. They present angles of rotation of wave fronts of light emerging from the specimen, α_1, in function of the distance from the crack tips. Four curves given in Figure 12 describe the influence of the orientation of the linearly polarized light, and the influence of the immersion fluid.

The presented results show that the birefringence in Plexiglas is not negligible and should be considered when the accurate measurements are made. They also show that the effect of the rotation of the plate surfaces at the crack tip contributes not more than about 60% to the total caustic effect.

Analysis of such results presented in [5] shows that in a certain region ahead of crack tip the singular solutions of linear fracture mechanics represent satisfactorily some features of the actual stress state, with respect to the stress gradients.

SUMMARY

Presented results document that the stress state ahead of crack in a plate is strongly three-dimensional. They present data on the actual stresses in regions of cracks, which may be used to test pertinent analytical solutions and experimental procedures of stress analysis in fracture mechanics. Presented evidence accentuates importance of a proper development of theoretical bases for the experimental and testing procedures.

ACKNOWLEDGEMENT

This research is supported by the Natural Sciences and Engineering Research Council of Canada under Grant No. A-2939.

REFERENCES

1. Thum, A., Peterson, C., and Svenson, O., "Verformung, Spannung and Kerbwirkung (Deformation, Stress and Notch Influence)", VDI-Verlag, Düsseldorf (1960).

2. Pindera, J.T. and Liu, Xianlong, "On the Actual Three-Dimensional Stresses in Notches and Cracks". Composite Engineering. In print (1991).

3. Ladevèze, Pierre (Ed), Local Effects in Analysis of Structures. Elsevier, New York (1985).

4. Pindera, J.T., "Local Effects and Defect Criticality in Homogeneous and Laminated Structures", Transactions of the ASME, Journal of Pressure Vessel Technology, 111, 136-150 (1989).

5. Pindera, J.T., Hecker, F.W., and Wen, Baicheng, "Testing Theoretical Bases of Caustic Methods in Fracture Mechanics". Theoretical and Applied Fracture Mechanics, 15, pp. 11-33 (1991).

6. Pindera, J.T. and Pindera, M.-J., "Isodyne Stress Analysis", Kluwer Academic Publishers, Dordrecht, The Netherlands (1989).

7. Pindera, J.T. and Hecker, F.W., "Basic Theory and Experimental Techniques of the Strain-Gradient Method. EXPERIMENTAL MECHANICS, 27 (3) 314-327 (1987).

8. Pindera, J.T., "Foundations of Experimental Mechanics: Principles of Modeling, Observation and Experimentation", in: J.T. Pindera (Ed.), "New Physical Trends in Experimental Mechanics", Springer-Verlag, 199-327 (1981).

9. Pindera, J.T. and Pindera, M.-J., "On the Methodologies of Stress Analysis of Composite Structures. Part 1: State of the Art - Phenomenological and Physical Methodologies", Theoretical and Applied Fracture Mechanics, 6(3), 139-151 (1986). Part 2: New Experimental Approaches", Theoretical and Applied Fracture Mechanics, 6(3) 153-170 (1986).

10. Pindera, J.T., "Local Effects in Plates - Theoretical and Practical Consequences", Theoretical and Applied Fracture Mechanics, 10, 1-18 (1988).

11. Pindera, J.T., "Advanced Experimental Mechanics in Modern Engineering Science and Technology", Transactions of the CSME, 11(3), 125-138 (1987).

12. Doeblin, E.O., Measurement Systems: Application and Design. McGraw-Hill Book Co., New York (1983).

13. Ramachandran, G.N. and Ramaseshan, S., "Crystal Optics", in: Flügge, S. (Ed.) Encyclopaedia of Physics, 25(1), 1-217, Springer Verlag, Berlin (1961).

14. Born, M. and Wolf, E., Principles of Optics, Pergamon Press, Oxford (1961).

15. Kac, M., "Some Mathematical Models in Science", Science, 166, 469-474 (1969).

16. Pindera, J.T. and Straka, P., "Response of the Integrated Polariscope", Journal of Strain Analysis, 8(1), 65-76 (1973).

17. Pindera, J.T., "Apparatus for Determination of Elastic Isodynes and of General State of Birefringence Whole-Field-Wise Using the Device for Birefringence Measurements in the Scanning Mode (Isodyne Polariscope)". United States Patent, No. 4,703,918, (Nov. 3, 1987).

18. Pindera, J.T. and Straka, P., "On Physical Measures of Rheological Responses of Some Materials in Wide Ranges of Temperature and Spectral Frequence", Rheologica Acta, 13(3), 338-351 (1974).

19. Krishnamurthy, A.R. and Pindera, J.T., "Study of Basic Patterns of Light Scattering in Aqueous Solution of Milling Yellow", EXPERIMENTAL MECHANICS, 22(1), 1-7 (1982).

20. Pindera, J.T., "Analytical Foundations of the Isodyne Photoelasticity". Mechanics Research Communications, 9(6) 391-397 (1981).

21. Kerker, M., "The Scattering of Light". Academic Press, New York (1969).

22. Pindera, M.-J., Pindera, J.T. and Ji, X., "Three-Dimensional Effects in Beams. Isodyne Assessment of a Solution". EXPERIMENTAL MECHANICS, 29, 23-31, (1989).

23. Kobayashi, A.S. [Ed.], Handbook on Experimental Mechanics, Prentice-Hall, Inc., Englewood Cliffs, New Jersey, (1987).

24. Bui, H.D., Theorie lineaire de la rupture. Revue Francoise de Mécanique. (3) 3-1 (1983).

25. Pindera, J.T., Zhang, Y-P, Unpublished Report (1991).

26. Pindera, J.T. and Krasnowski, B.R., "Determination of Stress Intensity Factors in Thin and Thick Plates using Isodyne Photoelasticity". In: L.A. Simpson [Ed.], Fracture Problems and Solutions in the Energy Industry, Pergamon Press, Oxford and New York, 147-156 (1982).

27. Pindera, J.T. and Wen, B., "Isodyne Evaluation of Three-Dimensional Stresses in Standard Compact Specimen". In: Proceedings of 1991 SEM Spring Conference on Experimental Mechanics The Society for Experimental Mechanics, Inc., 895-902 (1991).

28. Hecker, F.W., Pindera, J.T., Wen, B., "Actual Light Deflections in Regions of Crack Tips and Their Influence on Measurements in Photomechanics". In: Fu-Pen Chiang [Ed.], Speckle Techniques, Birefringence Methods and Applications to Solid Mechanics, Proceedings Volume 1554A, The Society of Photo-Optical Instrumentation Engineers, Washington, U.S.A. (1991).

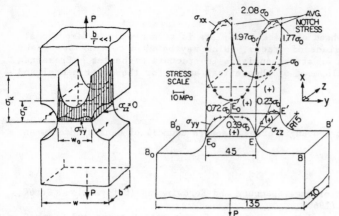

Fig. 1. Two incompatible models of stress state in regions of notches and cracks in plates and flat bars.
a - a generalized plane stress state model.
b - typical example of an actual stress state.

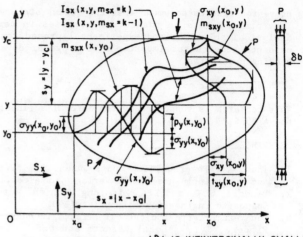

PLANE ELASTIC ANALYTICAL ISODYNES
PLANE ELASTIC OPTICAL ISODYNES
FIELD OF x – ISODYNES: $I_{sx} = I_{sx}(x, y, m_{sx})$

$(\delta b$ IS INFINITESIMALLY SMALL$)$

m_{sx}: PARAMETER OF x – ISODYNES IN (x,y) – PLANE
S_x: x – CHARACTERISTIC DIRECTION IN (x,y) – PLANE
s_x: x – CHARACTERISTIC SECTION
CONDITIONS FOR EXISTENCE:
 – ANALYTICAL ISODYNES: HOOKE'S BODY
 – OPTICAL ISODYNES: RAMACHANDRAN–RAMASESHAN BODY
   RAYLEIGH SCATTERING

Fig.3. Concept of plane analytical isodynes.

INTERACTION BETWEN RADIATION AND MATTER: SOME FEATURES OF COMMON PHYSICAL AND MATHEMATICAL MODELS OF ENERGY PROPAGATION THROUGH VARIOUS BODIES.

COMMON SPECULATIVE-HYPOTHETICAL MODELS:

ELEMENTARY PHYSICAL-THEORETICAL MODELS:

HOMOGENEOUS ISOTROPIC BODIES

INHOMOGENEOUS ISOTROPIC BODIES

INHOMOGENEOUS ANISOTROPIC BODIES

TWO HOMOGENEOUS ISOTROPIC BODIES IN CONTACT

BIREFRINGENT BODIES

SCATTERING BODIES

$\bar{\nu} = const$
$v = v(n)$
$\bar{s}$

$\bar{\nu} = const$
$v = v(n) = v(\lambda)$
$\bar{s}$

$\rho = \infty$
$\bar{\nu} = const$
$v = v(n)$
$\bar{s}$

$\bar{\rho}$ $\bar{\nu} \neq const$
$v = v(n) = v(\lambda)$
$\frac{1}{\bar{\rho}}\bar{\nu} = \frac{1}{n}(grad\, n - \frac{dn}{ds}\bar{s})$

$\rho = \infty$
$\bar{\nu} = const$
$v = v(n)$
$\bar{s}$

POLARIZED LINEARLY
$\bar{s}_1$
$\bar{s}_2$

TOTAL REFLECTION
$v_2 > v_1$

v_1
$v_2 > v_1$
EVANESCENT WAVE

$\frac{S(\lambda_1)}{S(\lambda_2)} = \frac{\lambda_1}{\lambda_2}$
where C = const

$\frac{1}{\lambda}dR = dm\frac{C}{\lambda}(\sigma_1-\sigma_2)db$
$= \frac{1}{S}(\sigma_1-\sigma_2)db$

$\frac{S(\lambda_1)}{S(\lambda_2)} = \frac{\lambda_1}{\lambda_2}\frac{C(\lambda_2)}{C(\lambda_1)}$
where C = C(λ)

PLANE OF SCATTERING
$\bar{s}$
SCATTERED LIGHT SHEET, LINEARLY POLARIZED IN PLANE

SIMPLEST CASE: RAYLEIGH MODEL
$\bar{s}$
SCATTERED LIGHT, LINEARLY POLARIZED DEPENDING ON ANGLE OF SCATTERING

Fig.2. Two sets of incompatible models of interaction between radiation and matter.
Left: typical simplified phenomenological models used in transmission photoelasticity, caustics, etc.
Right: physical models used in modern technology.

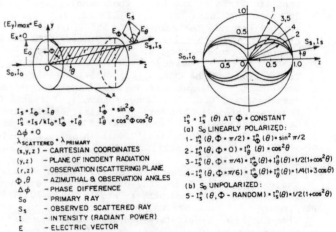

$I_s = I_\phi + I_\theta$
$I_s^n = I_s/kI_o = I_\phi^n + I_\theta^n$
$\Delta\phi = 0$
$\lambda_{SCATTERED} = \lambda_{PRIMARY}$

$I_\phi^n = \sin^2\phi$
$I_\theta^n = \cos^2\phi\cos^2\theta$

(x,y,z) – CARTESIAN COORDINATES
(y,z) – PLANE OF INCIDENT RADIATION
(r,z) – OBSERVATION (SCATTERING) PLANE
ϕ,θ – AZIMUTHAL & OBSERVATION ANGLES
$\Delta\phi$ – PHASE DIFFERENCE
S_o – PRIMARY RAY
S_s – OBSERVED SCATTERED RAY
I – INTENSITY (RADIANT POWER)
E – ELECTRIC VECTOR

$I_s^n = I_s^n(\theta)$ AT $\phi = $ CONSTANT
(a) S_o LINEARLY POLARIZED:
1 - $I_s^n(\theta, \phi = \pi/2) = I_\phi^n(\theta) = \sin^2\pi/2$
2 - $I_s^n(\theta, \phi = 0) = I_\theta^n(\theta) = \cos^2\theta$
3 - $I_s^n(\theta, \phi = \pi/4) = I_\phi^n(\theta) + I_\theta^n(\theta) = 1/2(1+\cos^2\theta)$
4 - $I_s^n(\theta, \phi = \pi/6) = I_\phi^n(\theta) + I_\theta^n(\theta) = 1/4(1+3\cos^2\theta)$

(b) S_o UNPOLARIZED:
5 - $I_s^n(\theta, \phi - RANDOM) = I_s^n(\theta) = 1/2(1+\cos^2\theta)$

Fig.4. Basic features of Rayleigh's mathematical model of scattering. Light is scattered in all directions.

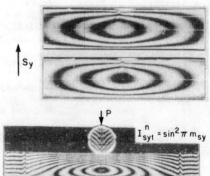

$I_{sy1}^n = \sin^2\pi\, m_{sy}$

Fig. 5. Beam under 3 point bending. y-optical isodynes. Top: amplitude modulation. Bottom: spatial frequency modulation.

242

$$\sigma_{yy}^n = (\sigma_0)^{-1} \sigma_{yy}^d = \sigma_{yy}^n \quad (x=0, \bar{y}, \bar{z}=0.87)$$

$$\sigma_0 = b^{-1} S_\sigma (\lambda, t); \quad \bar{y} = \frac{y}{h-a}; \quad \bar{z} = 2\frac{z}{b}; \quad \lambda = 632.8\,nm$$

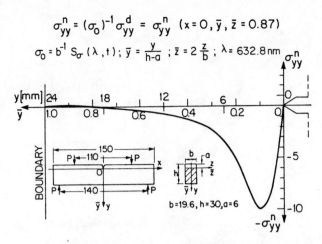

Fig.6. Isodyne bend specimen. Normal stresses at the surface in the plane of the crack and coplanar with it. Variation with the distance from the crack tip.

$$\sigma_{xx}^n = (\sigma_0)^{-1} \sigma_{xx}^d = \sigma_{xx}^d \quad (x=0, \bar{y}, \bar{z}=0.87)$$

$$\sigma_0 = b^{-1} S_\sigma (\lambda, t); \quad \bar{y} = \frac{y}{h-a}; \quad \bar{z} = 2\frac{z}{b}; \quad \lambda = 632.8\,nm$$

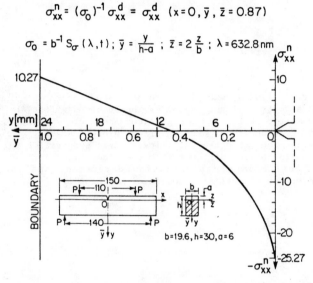

Fig.7. Isodyne bend specimen. Normal stresses at the surface in the plane of the crack and normal to it. Variation with the distance from the crack tip.

$$\sigma_{zz}^n = (\sigma_0)^{-1} \sigma_{zz}^d = \sigma_{zz}^n (x=0, y=0, \bar{z})$$

$$\sigma_0 = b^{-1} S_\sigma (\lambda, t); \quad \bar{z} = 2\frac{z}{b}; \quad \lambda = 632.8\,nm$$

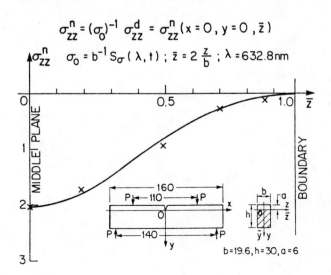

$$\sigma_{xx}^n = (\sigma_{xx}^d)^n = \sigma_{xx}^n \quad (x=0, y, \bar{z}=0.99)$$

$$= \frac{1}{\sigma_0} \sigma_{xx}^d \quad (x=0, y, \bar{z}=0.99)$$

$$= b \frac{\partial m_{syy}}{\partial y} \quad (x=0, y, \bar{z}=0.99)$$

Normalizing Factor
$$\sigma_0 = \frac{1}{b} S_\sigma (\lambda, t_0)$$

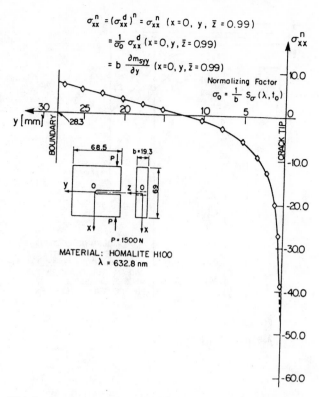

MATERIAL: HOMALITE H100
$\lambda = 632.8\,nm$

Fig.9. Isodyne compact specimen. Normal stresses at the surface in the plane of the crack and normal to it. Variation with the distance from the crack tip.

$$K_I^n = (2\pi r)^{1/2} \sigma_{xx}^n (y) = K_I^n (r)$$

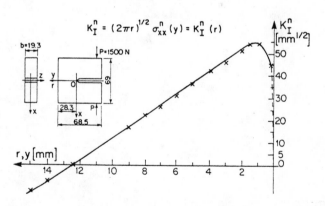

Fig.10. Isodyne compact specimen. Stress intensity function at the surface. Variation with the distance from the crack tip. This function is not unique and depends on the distance from the surface of the specimen.

Fig.8 (Left). Isodyne bend specimen. Normal thickness stresses at the crack tip. Variation with the thickness coordinate (with the distance from the middle plane of the specimen).

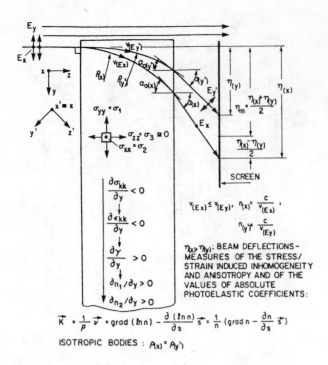

Fig.11. Influence of gradients of inhomogeneity and anisotropy caused by strain gradients on rotation and separation of wavefronts of a radiant power: strain-gradient light bending, the basis for the strain-gradien stress analysis.

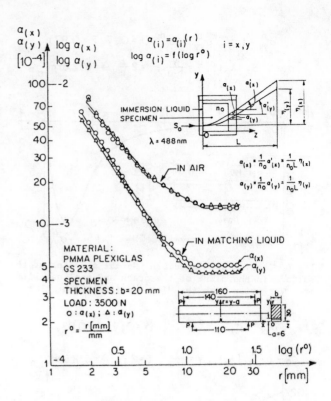

Fig.12. Typical example of rotation and separation of wavefronts of light caused by the combined effect of geometric refraction and gradient-index effect, and by the gradient-index bending effect alone. Angular deflections from the rectilinear light propagation in function of the distance from the crack tip. For two orientations of polarization direction, and two immersion fluids: air, and index-matching liquids.

The Method for Measuring the Mode I Stress Intensity Factor K_I Using the Chain Strain-Gage Consisting of 5 Measuring Grids

S. Kurosaki and S. Fukuda

ABSTRACT

This paper describes about the method to determine the opening-mode stress intensity factor K_I with using super small sized strain gage consisting of 5 measuring grids. In this paper, the two methods to determine K_I are proposed. One of them is the method to use only first term in the series of the strain, another one is the method to use first and second terms.

INTRODUCTION

It is important for Engineering to determine stress intensity factor by using strain gages experimentally. Some of paper are reported, which use strain gages for determining stress intensity factor.[1][2]

The stress singular region for the crack tip is small for comparing to the crack length. So the strain for the vicinity of the crack tip must be measured, if we determine the stress intensity factor with accuracy.

S.Kurosaki is associate professor of Mechanical Engineering, Tokyo National College of Technology, 1220-2 Kunugida machi Hatiouji-shi Tokyo, 193 Japan

S.Fukuda is professor of Tokyo Metropolitan Institute of Technology 6-6 Asahigaoka Hino-shi, 191 Japan

Recently super small sized strain gages consisting of 5 measuring grids(fig.1) are developed by the company which makes strain gages (KYOWA ELECTRIC Co. in Japan). This study is proposed to the two methods how to determine Mode I stress intensity factor K_I with use this super small sized strain gages, and the experiments for the tensile tests are carried out with two kinds of plate specimens to examine about the accuracy. (Center Cracked Plate Tension Specimens (CCT) and Single Edge Cracked Plate Tension Specimens(SECT)).

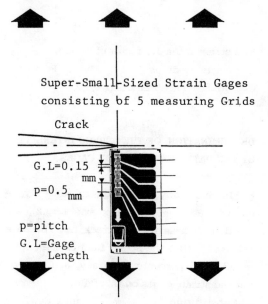

Fig1 Stress Intensity Factors Measurement by the Super-Small-Sized Strain Gages

STRAIN COMPONENTS OF CRACK TIP

The stress components of the crack tip are expressed in series form of the distance "r" from the crack tip, when the coordinate of crack tip is shown as fig 2. The first term of stress components for the crack tip are expressed as[3][4]

$$
\left.
\begin{aligned}
\sigma_x &= \frac{K_I}{\sqrt{2\pi r}} \cdot \cos\frac{\theta}{2}\{1 - \sin\frac{\theta}{2}\sin\frac{3\theta}{2}\} \\[2mm]
\sigma_y &= \frac{K_I}{\sqrt{2\pi r}} \cdot \cos\frac{\theta}{2}\{1 + \sin\frac{\theta}{2}\sin\frac{3\theta}{2}\} \\[2mm]
\tau_{xy} &= \frac{K_I}{\sqrt{2\pi r}} \cdot \cos\frac{\theta}{2}\{\ \sin\frac{\theta}{2}\cos\frac{3\theta}{2}\}
\end{aligned}
\right\}
$$

$$\cdots\cdots\cdots (1)$$

Consider a state of plane stress, the strain components are obtained by using the stress-strain relations. In this study, the strain components ε_y of the crack tip is treated. So the strain components ε_y is expressed as

$$E\varepsilon_y = C_K r^{-1/2} + C_0 + C_1 r^{1/2} + C_2 r^{2/2} + \cdots \quad (2)$$

where

$$C_K = \frac{K_I}{\sqrt{2\pi}} \cdot \cos\frac{\theta}{2}[(1-\nu)+(1+\nu)\sin\frac{\theta}{2}\cdot\sin\frac{3\theta}{2}]$$

$$(3)$$

K_I : stress intensity factor of mode I,
E : elastic modulus, ν : Poisson ratio,
C_i : unknown coefficients (i=0,1,2,$\cdots$)

DETERMINATION OF THE STRESS INTENSITY FACTOR BY THE DATA OF THE STRAIN GAGES

In this study, The angle to put a strain-gage on is $\theta = \pi/2$ for x axis (Fig.2), and the position is close for the crack tip. Because It is reported[2] that the strain field of the angle $\theta = \pi/2$ is 5 percents accuracy, and it is easy to put the strain-gages on this field.

Substituting $\theta = \pi/2$ into Eq.(3), strain component ε_y is obtained as

$$\varepsilon_y = \frac{(3-\nu)K_I}{4E\sqrt{\pi r}} + C_0 + C_1 r^{1/2} + C_2 r^{2/2} + \cdots$$

$$(4)$$

where the only first term Eq.(4) is represented in detail.

The two methods are proposed in this study, one of them is the method to use the first term only ("one point gage method"), and another one is the method to use first and second term in the series of the Eq.(4). ("the 5 point gages method")

CASE 1 : THE ONE POINT GAGE METHOD

This method treats the only one data for the close strain gage from crack tip. The analytical equation of this method is the first term of Eq.(4). Thus

$$K_I = \frac{4E\sqrt{\pi}}{3-\nu} \cdot \varepsilon_y \cdot \sqrt{r} \quad (5)$$

CASE 2 : THE FIVE POINT GAGES METHOD

This method treats strain data of 5 gages consisting 5 measuring grids. The first and second term of Eq.(5) are expressed as

$$\frac{4E\sqrt{\pi}}{3-\nu} \cdot \varepsilon_y \cdot \sqrt{r} = K_I + C_0'\sqrt{r} \quad (6)$$

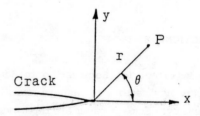

Fig **2** Coordinate of crack tip

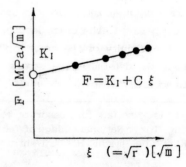

Fig **3** Extrapolation of K_I

By representing $\sqrt{r} = \xi$, $C_o' = C$ and the left part of Eq.(6)= F, the Eq.(6) becomes a linear equation for ξ. Thus

$$F = K_I + C \xi \qquad (7)$$

The equation (7) expresses a linear equation for ξ with inclination C and the cross point (K_I) at the F axis(Fig 3). In this experiment, strain gages consisting of 5 measuring grids are put on the angle $\theta = \pi/2$ and close to the crack tip. The strain ε_y of five gages are measured. The F value eq.(7) are calculated using the strain data of five gages. and The stress intensity factors are determined by the extrapolation method for the F value.

EXPERIMENTAL VERIFICATION

The test specimens in this study are two types, One is the center cracked plate tension specimens (Fig4), another is single edge cracked plate tension specimen (Fig5). The thickness of plate is 3.2mm. The material of this specimens is mild steel. The elastic modulus is 200MPa and Poisson ratio is 0.33.

The notch of the test specimen are cut by the electrical wire arc cutting machine. The wire of the machine is 0.2 mm diameter. The length of notch are 20, 30 and 50mm. The name of test specimen are called CCT or SECT before the crack length. Tensile test are carried out by the tensile testing machine with the capacity 100KN. Tensile test are carried out by using pin assembly gripping test specimen(fig 6), not to be affected by plate bending. The figure 7 show the experimental setup.

The RESULTS OF EXPERIMENTS

Load – strain relation near the crack tip

As the example, The load-strain relation of SECT50 is shown fig 8. Figure 8 is a straight line with every line as the elastic field. The strain of the gage near by the crack tip is maximum.

F Value – ξ ($\sqrt{r}$) relation

The figure 9 show the relation of F- ξ for the

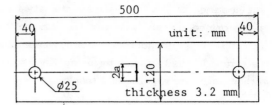

Fig 4 Center Cracked Plate Tension Specimen (CCT)

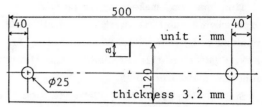

Fig 5 Single Edge Cracked Plate Tension Specimen (SECT)

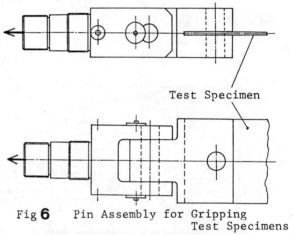

Test Specimen

Fig 6   Pin Assembly for Gripping Test Specimens

Fig 7 Experimental setup

test specimen CCT50. The stress intensity factor is determined by the method of the extrapolation with this F-ξ relation . This study determines the stress intensity factor by using least square method with the experimental result.

Comparison between experimental and theoretical value

This section makes a comparison between experimental and theoretical values which is published by The STRESS INTENSITY FACTOR HANDBOOK[5]. In this HANDBOOK, the theoretical function are expressed as

(1)Single Edge Cracked Plate Tension Specimen(SECT)

$$K_I = \sigma \sqrt{\pi a} \cdot U(\alpha) \qquad (8)$$
$$\alpha = a/W,$$
$$U(\alpha) = 1.12 - 0.231\alpha + 10.55\alpha^2$$
$$\qquad - 21.72\alpha^3 + 30.39\alpha^4$$

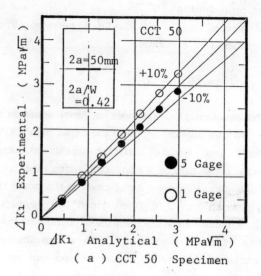

(a) CCT 50 Specimen

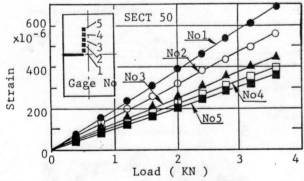

Fig 8 Load - Strain of SECT50

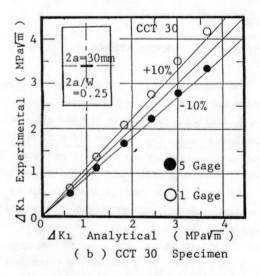

(b) CCT 30 Specimen

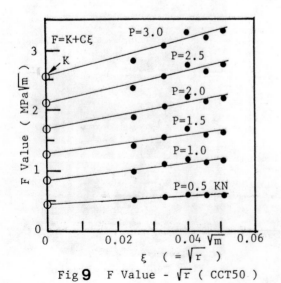

Fig 9 F Value - $\sqrt{r}$ (CCT50)

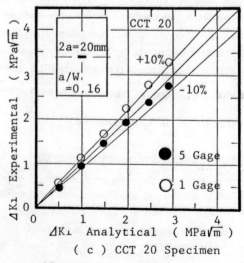

(c) CCT 20 Specimen

Fig 10 Accuracy of CCT Specimen

(2) Center Cracked Plate Tension Specimens (CCT)

$$K_I = \sigma \sqrt{\pi a} \cdot U(\alpha) \qquad (9)$$

$$\alpha = 2a / W,$$

$$U(\alpha) = (1 - 0.025\,\alpha^2 + 0.06\,\alpha^4)$$
$$* \sqrt{\sec(\alpha\,\pi/2)}$$

The comparative figure between experimental and theoretical value are shown fig 10 and 11. The stress intensity factor K is expressed as $\triangle$ K, because the K value of pre load is basis. The width of stress intensity factor $\triangle$ K is expressed as

$$\triangle K = K_{(load)} - K_{(preload)} \qquad (10)$$

where $K_{(load)}$ is K value with each load and $K_{(preload)}$ is K value when the test specimens is worked by the preload.

The error line of $\pm$ 10 percents is presented in the fig 10 and 11, and the experimental and theoretical value of stress intensity factor for test specimens of crack length 50, 20 mm are presented table 1-4.

The error of K value determined by 5 points gages method are within $\pm$ 10 % in comparison

Table 1 Experimental and analytical $\triangle$K value (SECT50)

Load	Experimental(MPa$\sqrt{m}$)		Analytical
KN	1 Gage	5Gages	(MPa$\sqrt{m}$)
0.4	0.92	0.94	0.94
0.8	1.97	1.92	1.88
1.2	3.04	2.95	2.82
1.6	3.94	3.79	3.76
2.0	4.99	4.83	4.70
2.4	5.91	5.66	5.64
2.8	6.83	6.44	6.58
3.2	7.75	7.37	7.51

Table 2 Experimental and Analytical $\triangle$K value (CCT50)

Load	Experimental(MPa$\sqrt{m}$)		Analytical
KN	1 Gage	5Gages	(MPa$\sqrt{m}$)
0.5	0.49	0.45	0.42
1.0	0.98	0.86	0.85
1.5	1.41	1.28	1.27
2.0	1.89	1.68	1.69
2.5	2.35	2.07	2.11
3.0	2.82	2.46	2.54
3.5	3.27	2.86	2.96

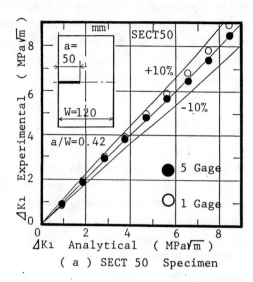

(a) SECT 50 Specimen

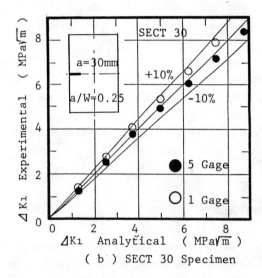

(b) SECT 30 Specimen

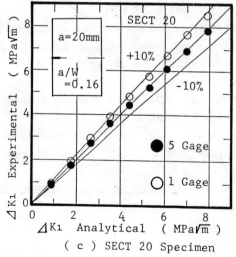

(c) SECT 20 Specimen

Fig**11**Accuracy of SECT Specimen

with theoretical value.   It is evident in this figure 10 and 11 that the accuracy of the 5 point gages method are better than one point gage method. The error of K value determined the one point gage method are within   ± 20 %.

SUMMARY

This report propose two methods to determine the stress intensity factor with using super small sized strain gages consisting 5 measuring grids.

The experiments are carried out to examine the accuracy of the stress intensity factor to be determined with these methods by using the two type of test specimen SECT and CCT, and the experimental value are compare with theoretical value. The results as follow

(1)

The stress intensity factors, which are determined with 5 points gages method, are within ± 10% errors compare with theoretical value.

(2)

The experimental value to be determined with one point gage method are within   ± 20% error.

REFERENCES

1. J.W.Dally and R.J.Sanford, " Strain-gage methods for measuring the opening-mode stress intensity factor, K_I", Experimental Mechanics , vol27,No4, pp381-388, 1987

2. J.R.Berger and J.W.Dally,"An overdeterministic approach for measuring K_I using strain gages", Experimental Mechanics ,vol28, No 2, pp142-145, 1988

3.H.Okamura "The linear fracture mechanics",(in japanese), baifuukan, pp20-23, 1976,

4. J.W.Dally and Riley, "Experimental stress analysis(Third Edition)", Mcgraw-Hill, pp104-107, 1991

5. Y.MURAKAMI edit; "STRESS INTENSITY FACTOR HANDBOOK", Pergamon Press, 1987

Table 3 Experimental and Analytical ΔK value   (SECT20)

Load	Experimental(MPa√ m)		Analytical
KN	1 Gage	5Gages	(MPa√ m)
1.0	0.97	0.94	0.88
2.0	1.98	1.82	1.75
3.0	2.94	2.75	2.63
4.0	3.89	3.57	3.50
5.0	4.82	4.40	4.38
6.0	5.73	5.21	5.26
7.0	6.65	6.05	6.13
8.0	7.57	6.92	7.01

Table 4 Experimental and Analytical ΔK value   (CCT20)

Load	Experimental(MPa√ m)		Analytical
KN	1 Gage	5Gages	(MPa√ m)
1.0	0.55	0.47	0.49
2.0	1.16	0.96	0.97
3.0	1.71	1.48	1.46
4.0	2.24	1.93	1.94
5.0	2.78	2.38	2.43
6.0	3.27	2.76	2.91

DETERMINATION OF STRESS INTENSITY FACTORS USING INTERFERENCE AND POLARIZATION BASED OPTICAL FIBER SENSORS

Arun Shukla*, Raman Singh* and Nadarajah Narendran**

* Dynamic Photomechanics Laboratory, Dept of Mechanical Engineering,
University of Rhode Island, Kingston, RI 02881.
** Mechanical Technology Inc.,
968 Albany Shaker Road, Lantham, N.Y. 12110.

ABSTRACT

Various interference and polarization based fiber-optics sensors have been used to determine the opening mode stress intensity factors in single edge notched specimens. The sensors are either attached or embedded in the fracture specimens and their performance is evaluated on the basis of sensitivity, ease of use, linearity, accuracy and freedom from environmental noise.

1. INTRODUCTION

An experimental investigation has been conducted to study the performance and applicability of fiber-optic (FO) sensors in fracture mechanics studies. In recent years both attached and embedded FO sensors have been used for damage detection studies[1,2,3,4,5] and for stress intensity factor measurements[6,7]. This study attempts to evaluate the applicability of various FO sensors such as the Mach-Zehnder, Michelson and Fabry-Perot interferometric sensors and the polarimetric sensor to fracture mechanics problems, with respect to the ease of use, sensitivity, durability, relative cost, etc.

2. DESCRIPTION OF THE SENSORS USED

This section presents the operating principles and the experimental setups for the various sensors used in our study.

2.1 Mach-Zehnder Interferometric Sensor

Figure 1 shows the experimental setup. The beam from a He-Ne laser is split into two beams. One of these is coupled into the reference fiber and the other into the sensing fiber. The sensing beam passes through the interaction region and is then recombined with the reference beam to produce an interference pattern, as shown in Figure 1. A strain applied to the sensing fiber causes a relative phase shift between the two light beams resulting in a corresponding movement of the fringe pattern. The fringes are detected by a photo-diode (EG&G 575-23). Data storage and analysis was done using a Lecroy data acquisition system. The relation between the axial strain, ε_x, acting on the fiber and the number of fringes passing past a given point is given by Eqn(1)[8].

$$\varepsilon_x = DN \tag{1}$$

where,

$$D = \left(\frac{\lambda}{nL}\right)\left[\frac{1}{1-c}\right] \tag{2}$$

and,

$$c = \left(\frac{n^2}{2}\right)\left[(1-\nu)p_{12} - \nu p_{11}\right] \tag{3}$$

λ is the vacuum wavelength of the optical beam; L and n are the gage length and the refractive index, respectively, of the optical fiber; p_{11} and p_{12} are the strain-optic coefficients; and ν is the Poisson's ratio of the fiber core. The above statement has been experimentally verified for attached fibers[8,9]. Recently, Sirkis and Haslach[10] have derived a more general phase-strain relationship for embedded interferometric optical fiber sensors. In our studies the fiber-optic sensors were embedded in plexiglass, which has a much lower stiffness than the glass fiber. Therefore, the phase-strain relationship given by Butter and Hocker[8] will give the same results as that by Sirkis and Haslach[10], as shown by Mathews and Sirkis[11].

2.2 Michelson Interferometric Sensor

The experimental setup for this sensor remains the same as for the Mach-Zehnder interferometer except that instead of recombining the two beams at the end they are both reflected back through the fibers by dipping the two fiber ends in mercury. These two returned light beams recombine at the beam splitter and result in an interferometric pattern similar to the one for the Mach-Zehnder interferometer. The output from this sensor can be analyzed in a similar manner as described for the Mach-Zehnder interferometer, except that in this case the effective gage length of the fiber-optic sensor is optically doubled due to the fact that the sensing beam travels over the sensing area twice. The Michelson interferometric sensor has been used effectively for measuring strains[12].

2.3 Fabry-Perot Interferometric Sensor

The experimental setup for the Fabry-Perot sensor is shown in Figure 2. The actual sensor is shown in Figure 3. It has a low finesse Fabry-Perot cavity which is formed by inserting two fibers with partially mirrored ends into a hollow-core fiber. Two separate reflections take place, as shown in Figure 3. These two light beams interfere to give an interference pattern. A change in the "air-gap", due to applied strain, causes the interference pattern to change and fringes are registered on the photodiode. This type of sensor is termed as an extrinsic Fabry-Perot interferometer and has been shown to be an effective strain sensor[4,5]. The relation between the number of fringes produced due to an axial strain, ε_x, can be expressed as,

$$N = \frac{\phi}{2\pi} = \frac{2L}{\lambda} \varepsilon_x \tag{4}$$

where 2L is the net optical gage length for the sensor and λ is the wavelength of light. The effective gage length for this sensor is twice the physical gage length, L, because the relative path between the two interfering beams difference is twice the "air-gap". Eqn.(4) has been experimentally verified[4,5]. Intrinsic Fabry-Perot interferometric sensors have also been developed and used effectively for strain sensing[1,2]. This sensor is based on the same operating principle as the above, but is constructed by splicing together fiber partially mirrored at the ends. The phase-strain relationship for the Intrinsic Fabry-Perot is slightly different from Eqn.(4) and has also been experimentally verified[1,2].

2.4 Polarimetric Sensor

The setup for this sensor is shown in Figure 4. Circularly polarized light is launched into a polarization maintaining fiber, is passed through the interaction region and is finally observed through another quarter-wave plate and analyzer combination. An axial strain applied to the fiber changes the beat length of the optical fiber which introduces a phase retardation between the two orthogonal modes propagating through the fiber[13]. This results in intensity modulation at the photodiode and fringes, similar to the ones observed for interferometric sensors, are recorded.
The number of fringes observed can be related to the strain using empirically determined phase-strain sensitivity.

3.0 EXPERIMENTAL PROCEDURE

The sensors were first calibrated to determine their phase-strain sensitivities and then used for the measurement of stress intensity factor, K_I, in fracture specimens.

3.1 Calibration

The attached sensors were calibrated using a cantilever beam setup, shown in Figure 5. The fiber-optic sensor was attached on one side and a strain gage was bonded on the other. The beam was displaced at its free end and the number of fringes moving across a given point was recorded along with the corresponding strain. This data was used to determine the phase-strain sensitivity for the sensor. Table 1 lists the phase-strain sensitivities for the different sensors used. The Michelson sensor has about twice the sensitivity than the Mach-Zehnder sensor. This is due to optical doubling of the fiber gage length, in

252

the Michelson sensor. The phase-strain sensitivity of the extrinsic Fabry-Perot was found to be different by 25% from the theoretical value. This could be due to an error in the measurement of the gage length, or, the presence of stress concentrations due to the steps at the ends of the hollow-core fiber (see Figure 3).

The polarimetric sensor was calibrated by attaching the fiber to a tension specimen and recording the number of fringes and corresponding strain with increasing axial load. Very long gage lengths had to be used because of the low sensitivity of this sensor. As can be seen from the phase strain sensitivity, listed in Table 1, this sensor is about a hundred times less sensitive than the interferometric sensors. Such a sensitivity was found to be too low for this sensor to be used in fracture studies for the measurement of K_I.

The embedded interferometric sensors were calibrated using a plexiglass beam having a transversely embedded sensor and subjected to tension. Again the fringe count versus strain data was used to get the phase-strain sensitivities, which are listed in Table 1.

3.2 Fracture Studies

A single edge notched (SEN) specimen machined out of 7075-T6 aluminum, shown in Figure 6, was used for K_I measurement using attached sensors. A crack was saw cut in the specimen and the sensor was bonded near the crack tip, as shown in Figure 6. The position and orientation of the sensor was selected to minimize three-dimensional effects[14] and to place it within the singularity dominated zone[15]. The specimen was loaded monotonically and the corresponding movement of fringes recorded along with the applied load. The fringe count data was converted to strain values which were used to determine the stress intensity factor using linear elastic fracture mechanics (LEFM)[15]. Figure 7 shows the comparison of experimentally determined K_I, using a Fabry-Perot sensor, with theoretical handbook values[16].

For the embedded sensor experiments a plexiglass SEN specimen was used. The sensors were transversely embedded straight through the plate thickness, near the crack tip, as shown in Figure 8. Again, the location of the sensor was selected so as to minimize three-dimensional effects[14]. The fringe count data was used to determine K_I, using LEFM[7,16]. Figure 9 shows the comparison of experimentally determined K_I, using an embedded Mach-Zehnder sensor, with theoretical handbook values[16]. Table 1 lists the deviation of the experimental values of K_I, from the theoretical values.

4. DISCUSSION

This section discusses the applicability and the performance of the different sensors used for the measurement of opening mode stress intensity factor, K_I.

The Mach-Zehnder and Michelson sensors are the cheapest and easiest to construct and use in a laboratory environment. However, they are not as useful in field applications. The setup is more elaborate as it requires the use of two separate fibers. Moreover the entire fiber is sensitive to environmental effects such as temperature, strain, vibration, etc. This requires either a close coupling of the reference and sensing fibers, or a controlled environment.

The Fabry-Perot sensor is not as easy to construct. However, its unique construction has a number of advantages. Only one fiber is required which simplifies the setup. Both the reference and sensing beams propagate through the same fiber which results in freedom from environmental effects. Also, the gage length can be controlled more accurately during sensor fabrication, as compared to the other two sensors. However, the presence of a thin hollow-core fiber makes the sensor relatively fragile, especially under bending and direct pressure, and makes surface attachment difficult. A possible alternative to this could be to use the Intrinsic Fabry-Perot sensor[1,2].

The polarimetric sensor requires only one fiber and is simple to construct. However, its low sensitivity does not allow it to be used for K_I measurements, using conventional fringe counting methods. However, using fractional fringe measurements one might be able to use this sensor also. This is currently being incorporated into our study.

When the Mach-Zehnder and Michelson sensors are used as transversely embedded sensors we observe greater deviations of the experimental data from the theoretical values, as shown in Table 1. These deviations are suspected to be mainly gage-length dependent errors. One possible reason for this is the shrinkage of the filler material (EnviroTex). After curing, the surfaces at the ends of the filler material maynot be perfectly flat and measurement of gage length becomes difficult.

Moreover, the effective gage length of the sensor would depend on the load transfer length of the embedded fiber. This load transfer length is currently being investigated so that effective gage length may be determined more accurately.

5. ACKNOWLEDGEMENT

The support of the National Science Foundation under Grant No. MSS-9101514 is gratefully acknowledged.

6. REFERENCES

1. Lee C.E., Taylor H.F., Markus A.M., and Udd E. "Optical-fiber Fabry-Perot embedded sensor". Opt. Lett., 14, 1225-1227, 1989.
2. Valis T., Hodd D. and Measures R. "Composite material embedded fiber-optic Fabry-Perot strain rosette". SPIE Vol. 1370, 154-161, 1990.
3. Udd E. "Embedded fiber optic sensors in large structures". Proc. OE/Fibers 1991, Boston, 1991.
4. Murphy K.A., Gunther M.F., Vengsarkar A.M. and Claus R.O. "Fabry-Perot fiber optic sensors in full-scale fatigue testing on an F-15 aircraft". Proc. OE/Fibers 1991, Boston, 1991.
5. Murphy K.A., Gunther M.F., Vengsarkar A.M. and Claus R.O. "Quadrature phase shifted, extrinsic Fabry-Perot optical fiber sensors". Opt. Lett., 16, 273-275, 1991.
6. Narendran N., Shukla A. and Letcher S. "Application of fiber-optic sensor to a fracture mechanics problem". Engineering Fracture Mechanics, 38, 491-498, 1991.
7 Narendran N., Shukla A. and Letcher S. "Determination of Fracture Parameters Using Embedded Fiber Optic Sensors". Expt. Mech., 31, 360-365, 1991.
8. Butter C.D. and Hocker G.B. " Fiber optics strain gauge". Appl. Opt. 17, 2867-2869, 1978.
9. Sirkis J.S. and Taylor C.E. "Interferometric-fiber-optic strain sensor". Expt. Mech. 28, 170-176, 1988.
10. Sirkis J.S. and Haslach H.W. Jr. "Complete phase-strain model for structurally embedded interferometric optical fiber sensors". J. of Intell. Materials Systems and Structures, 2(1), 3-24, 1991.
11. Mathews C.T. and Sirkis J.S. "Experimental verification of phase-strain models for structurally embedded optical fiber sensors". Proc. of the 1991 SEM Spring Conf., Milwaukee, 471-478, 1991.
12. Valis T., Tapanes E., Liu K. and Measures R. "Passive-Quadrature Demodulated Localized Michelson Fiber-Optic Strain Sensor Embedded in Composite Materials". Jour. Lightwave Tech., 9, no. 4, 535-544, 1991.
13. De Paula R.P., Flax L., Cole J.H. and Bucaro J.A. "Single-mode fiber ultrasonic sensor". IEEE J. Quantum Elect., QE-18, 680-683, 1982.
14. Rosakis A.J. and Ravi-Chandar K. "On crack tip stress state: An experimental evaluation of three-dimensional effects". Cal. Inst. Tech. Rep., SM 84-2, March 1984.
15. Dally J.W. and Sanford RJ. "Strain gage methods for measuring the opening mode stress intensity factor". Proc. of the 1985 SEM Spring Conf., Las Vegas, 851 - 860, 1985.
16. Broek D., Elementary Engineering Fracture Mechanics, (Martinus Nijhoff Publishers, 4th ed., 1986).

TABLE 1. Strain Sensitivities and Experimental Error for the Sensors used.

Sensor	Configuration	Strain sensitivity* (μmm/mm / fringe / mm)	Deviation of expt. K_I values from theory
Mach-Zehnder	Attached	610	6%
Michelson	"	315	3%
Fabry-Perot	"	403	5%
Polarimetric	"	107000	---
Mach-Zehnder	Embedded	630	11%
Michelson	"	310	17%

* This is the strain sensed corresponding to one fringe movement per mm of gage length.

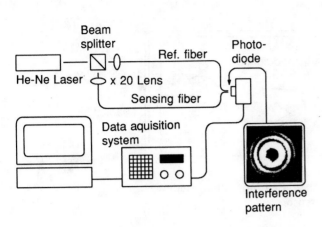

Fig. 1 Experimental setup for the Mach-Zehnder interferometric sensor.

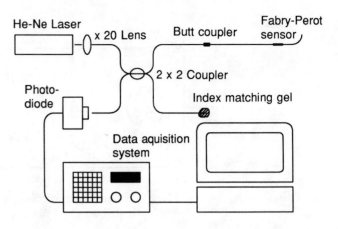

Fig. 2 Experimental setup for the Fabry-Perot interferometric sensor.

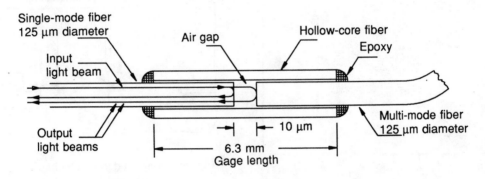

Fig. 3 The extrinsic Fabry-Perot sensor.

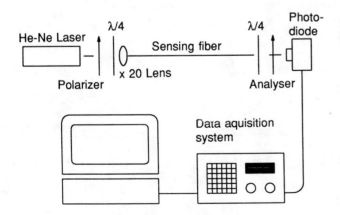

Fig. 4 Experimental setup for the polarimetric sensor.

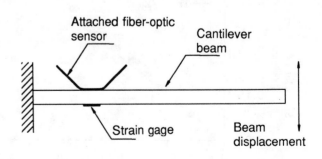

Fig. 5 Cantilever beam setup used to calibrate attached fiber-optic sensors.

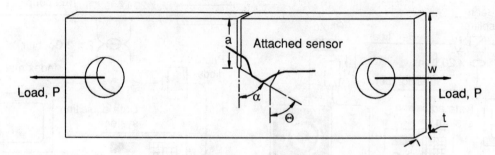

Fig. 6   Single edge notched specimen used for fracture studies
using attached fiber-optic sensors.

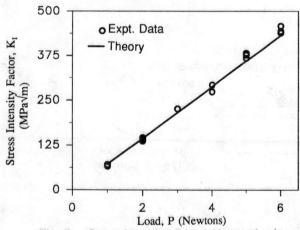

Fig. 7   Stress intensity factor measured using
an attached Fabry-Perot sensor.

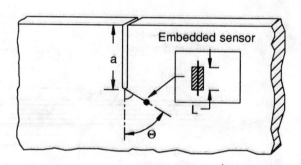

Fig. 8   Single edge notched specimen showing a
transversely embedded fiber-optic sensor.

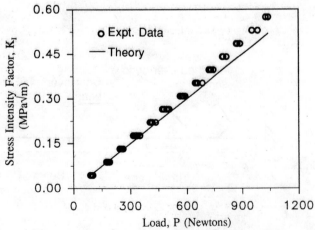

Fig. 9   Stress intensity factor measured using an
embedded Mach-Zehnder sensor.

MEASUREMENT OF THREE-DIMENSIONAL CRACK TIP DEFORMATIONS
BY DIGITAL IMAGE PROCESSING

Luo, P.F., Chao, Y.J., Sutton, M.A.
Department of Mechanical Engineering
University of South Carolina
Columbia, South Carolina 29205

ABSTRACT

A stereo imaging system was used to study the three-dimensional (3D) crack tip deformation in compact tension specimens made of AL 6061-T6 and 304L stainless steel. Both the in-plane and out-of-plane displacements were measured simultaneously. For AL 6061-T6, the plastic zone is very small even at the onset of crack growth. A K_I field was detected for the AL specimen, but no HRR field was found. For 304L, a K_I field was observed at lower loadings and an apparent HRR field was obtained at larger loadings. The two-dimensional J integral calculated using the experimentally determined in-plane displacements is path independent for each material. The J integral values for the aluminum specimen are close to the results obtained from both Merkle-Corten's formula and the EPRI report, but are 30% to 50% lower than the results obtained from the EPRI report for the stainless steel specimen. The contours of out-of-plane surface displacements are also presented in this paper.

INTRODUCTION

The J integral and HRR field[1, 2, 3] have been widely used as the theoretical bases for elastic-plastic fracture mechanics. In this paper, the stereo imaging system[4], of which the schematic drawing is shown in Figure 1, was used to measure the three-dimensional crack tip deformation and, thereby, study the J integral and crack tip singularity in both elastic-perfectly plastic and strain hardening materials.

SPECIMEN GEOMETRIES AND MATERIAL PROPERTIES

A uniaxial stress-strain tension test was performed for AL 6061-T6 and 304L SS. Figs. 2 (a) and (b) show the results obtained from the two materials. A Ramberg-Osgood relation was used to fit the stress-strain curves. The material properties obtained from the tests are shown in Table 1, which indicates that the AL 6061-T6 is close to the elastic-perfectly plastic material and the 304L SS is a strain hardening material.

Figure 3 shows CT specimens made of AL 6061-T6 with a/w=0.62 and 304L SS with a/w=0.34. A chevron notch was machined in the notch tip. A fatigue precrack was produced by cyclically loading the notched specimens with a sinusoidal waveform using standard ASTM procedures[5, 6]. A random pattern was produced on the surface using black and white spray paint.

PINHOLE CAMERA MODEL

A typical camera consists of a lens and a plane on which the image is formed. As illustrated in Figure 1, the camera can be modeled as a "pin-hole" camera with the image plane in front of the lens center, C. The stereo imaging system shown in Figure 1, based on a pinhole camera model, uses two images of the object obtained from two cameras to determine the global positions (X,Y,Z) for the interested points on a specific object region. See reference 4 for details.

EXPERIMENTAL PROCEDURE

The experimental setup of the stereo imaging system used in this work is shown in Figure 4 with $\theta \approx 22°$ and 26° for AL 6061-T6 and 304L tests, respectively. The digital cameras used in this experiment are the Videk Megaplus camera, developed by Kodak. The resolution of a Videk camera is 1280 by 1024. The camera system uses an IBM/AT computer for the acquisition and storage of images. Approximate in-plane magnification factors were 40 pixels/mm of object distance. After the two cameras were calibrated, an approximate error of 2 μm for each displacement component was obtained from a translation experiment.

Both specimens were loaded using displacement-control with a servo hydraulic MTS machine. For AL 6061-T6, when the loading reached 6995 N, crack growth occurred. For 304L SS, when the loading reached 20,470 N, substantial crack blunting occurred without crack growth. The images around the crack tip were taken at several loading stages and stored for later analysis. Detailed analysis of the data continues at this time. During the entire experiment, the load and load-point displacement were recorded with a 222.5 KN capacity load cell and a clip gage extensometer. Figure 5 shows the measured load vs. load-point displacement curve for the aluminum specimen.

Prior to loading of the specimens, two images of the specimen were obtained. For an AL 6061-T6 specimen, the global positions (X,Y,Z) for a 51 $\times$ 61 rectangular array of points on an approximately 12 mm $\times$ 14 mm object regions were determined. A plane was fitted to these 3111 global positions using a least-square procedure. The mean value of the perpendicular distance from (X,Y,Z) to the plane is ≈ 1 μm with a standard deviation of 0.80 μm. For 304L specimen, a similar result was also obtained. This indicates that the stereo vision system successfully constructs the undeformed surface of the CT specimen. The fitted plane was used as the *reference surface* for the determination of displacements and strains. *All displacement and strain components reported in this work are determined in a surface coordinate system, (x,y,z), which is located in the reference surface and has the origin at the estimated crack tip location* (see Figure 3). The z-axis is aligned with the outward normal to the fitted plane. Both the x and y axes are on the fitted plane, with the y-axis being perpendicular to the crack line at each loading and the x-axis is perpendicular to the y-z plane.

By subtracting the initial global positions from the final global positions for points on the reference plane and using a coordinate transformation, the (u,v,w) surface displacement fields were obtained, where (u,v,w) are displacement components in the (x,y,z) directions. A smoothing technique[7] was then used to smooth the displacement components individually and compute the total strains ϵ_{xx}, ϵ_{yy}, and ϵ_{xy}. After smoothing, 3-D rigid body rotations of the specimen surface were estimated by trial and error and removed from the displacement data. It is noted that, since symmetry is expected to be present in all components, this fact was used to determine when the rigid body rotation had been reasonably estimated. In addition, the in-plane displacements of the crack tip were estimated using displacements of points directly ahead of the crack tip and extrapolating back to the crack tip. It is assumed that the out-of-plane motion of points far from the crack tip can be used to estimate the rigid body out-of-plane motion. In the data analysis, the in-plane displacements of the crack tip were subtracted from the (u,v) displacement data, and out-of-plane displacement of a point located approximately 320 pixels directly above the crack tip was subtracted from the w-displacement data.

RESULTS

For the 304L SS specimen at a loading of 11,300 N, Figure 6 presents the contour plot for the smoothed w displacement field, and Figs. 7 (a), (b), and (c) present the contour plots for the smoothed ϵ_{xx}, ϵ_{yy}, and ϵ_{xy} strain fields, respectively. For Al 6061-T6 specimen at a loading of 6,995 N, Figure 8 portrays the contour plot for the smoothed w displacement field. The crack tip is located at (0,0) in each figure. Furthermore, Figures 9 and 10 show log ϵ_{yy}-log r plots for various radial lines for 304L specimens at the applied loads 11,300 N and 20,470 N, respectively. Figure 11 shows log ϵ_{yy}-log r plots for various radial lines for AL 6061-T6 specimen at the applied loads 6,995 N. In Figs. 9 to 11, r is the radial distance from the crack tip. Also, shown in Figures 12 through 14 are the two-dimensional J integral values plotted against distance measured from the crack tip to the path of the line integral.

DISCUSSION OF RESULTS

The out-of-plane displacement data, presented in Figs. 6 and 8, indicate that the largest deformation is located at 1 to 2 mm ahead of the crack tip. The results are similar to the results obtained by Chiang[8], but are different from the results obtained by Rosakis[9]. 3D finite element work is needed to verify the results. Figs. 9 and 10 indicate that for 304L SS, a K_I field is observed at the smaller loading and an apparent HRR field is detected at the larger loading. Fig. 11 indicates that for AL 6061-T6, a K_I field is still observed even when the crack started growing. Figs. 12 to 14 present a comparison of experimental J integral values to the results obtained using both the Merkle-Corten formula[10] and the EPRI report[11]. The J integral computed by the EPRI procedure is based on the plane stress case. It is noted that the experimental J integral values are also computed based on the plane stress assumption. The experimental in-plane displacement field was first smoothed to obtain the strain field. Using deformation theory, the strains were separated into elastic strain and plastic strain and the stresses were obtained. Then, the J integral was computed along several rectangular paths around the crack tip. Both materials show reasonable path independence. For AL 6061-T6, the J integral values are close to the results obtained from both Merkle-Corten's formula and EPRI report. For 304L SS the J integral values are close to the results obtained from EPRI report for the smaller loading but are 30% to 50% lower than the results from the EPRI report for the larger loading.

CONCLUSIONS

The in-plane and out-of-plane displacement fields in both 6061-T6 aluminum CT specimen and 304L stainless steel CT specimen have been obtained using stereo vision. The three displacement components are smoothed individually and the in-plane total strain field is obtained. Using the deformation theory of plasticity and plane stress assumption, the J integral values were computed and compared to the results obtained by Merkle-Corten's formula and EPRI report.

Initial results indicate that the J integral is reasonably path independent for both materials and the values are close to the analytical and numerical results, except for 304L at larger loadings. Much work remains before the complete analysis of the experimental data is finished.

ACKNOWLEDGEMENT

The authors wish to thank the National Science Foundation for the support of the project through grants MSM-9003973, ENGR-PYI-8451017, and engineering equipment grant MSM-8805569.

REFERENCES

1. Rice, J.R., "A Path Independent Integral and The Approximate Analysis of Strain Concentration by Notches and Cracks," **Journal of Applied Mechanics,** pp. 379-386, (1968)

2. Hutchison, J.W., "Plastic stress and strain fields at a crack tip," **Journal of the mechanics and Physics of Solids,** 16, pp. 13-31 (1968).

3. Rice, J.R. and Rosengren, G.F., "Plane Strain Deformation Near a Crack Tip in a Power Law Hardening Material," **Journal of the Mechanics and Physics of Solids,** 16, pp. 1-13 (1968)

4. Luo, P.F, Chao, Y.J, Sutton, M.A., and Peters, W.H., "Accurate Measurement of Three-dimensional Displacements In Deformable Bodies Using Computer Vision," In review with Experimental Mechanics.

5. ASTM standard E813-81, Annual Book of ASTM Standards, Vol. 03.01 (1981).

6. ASTM standard E399-83, Annual Book of ASTM Standards, Vol 03.01 (1983).

7. Sutton, M.A., Turner, J.L., Bruck, H.A., and Chae, T., "Full Field Representation of Discretely Sampled Surface Deformation for Displacement and Strain Analysis," **Experimental Mechanics,** Vol. 31, No.2, pp. 168-177 (1991).

8. Chiang, F.P. and Hareesh, T.V., "Three-dimensional Crack Tip Deformation: an Experimental Study and Comparison to HRR Field," **International Journal of Fracture,** 36, pp. 243-257 (1988).

9. Zehnder, A.T. and Rosakis, A.J., "Three Dimensional Effects Near a Crack Tip in a Ductile Three Point Bend Specimen, Part II: An Experimental Investigation Using Interferometry and Caustics," SM Report 88-7, California Institute of Technology, March 1988.

10. Merkle, J.G. and Corten, H.T., "A J Integral Analysis for the Compact Specimen, Considering Axial Force as well as Bending Effects," **ASME Journal of Pressure Vessel Technology,** Vol. 96, pp. 286-292 (1974).

11. Kumar, V., German, H.D, and Shih, C.F., "An Engineering Approach for Elastic-Plastic Analysis," EPRI NP-1931, Project 1287-1, Topical Report, July 1981.

	Material Properties	
	AL 6061-T6	304L SS
Yield stress	233 Mpa	341 Mpa
Elastic modulus	69 Gpa	127 Gpa
Strain hardening exponent	22.12	8.44
Strain hardening coefficient	1.12	1.95
Poisson's ratio	0.3	0.3

Table 1: Material Properties

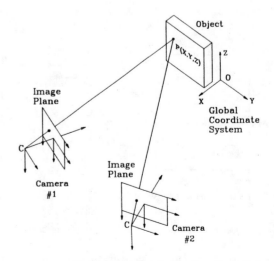

Figure 1: Schematic of Stereo Imaging Setup

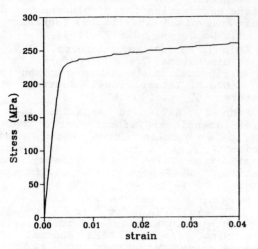

Figure 2 (a): Stress–Strain Curve for AL 6061–T6

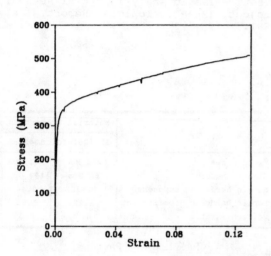

Figure 2 (b): Stress–strain curve for 304L SS

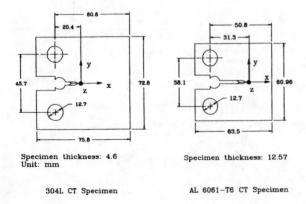

Specimen thickness: 4.6
Unit: mm

304L CT Specimen

Specimen thickness: 12.57

AL 6061–T6 CT Specimen

Figure 3: Specimen Configuration and Dimension

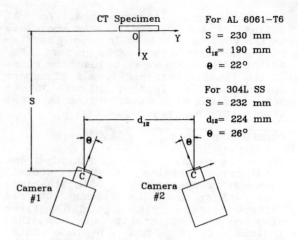

For AL 6061–T6
S = 230 mm
d_{12}= 190 mm
θ = 22°

For 304L SS
S = 232 mm
d_{12}= 224 mm
θ = 26°

Figure 4: Top View of Experimental Setup

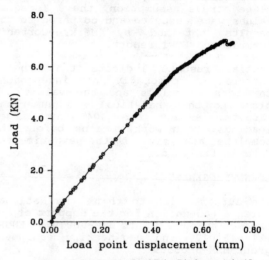

Figure 5: Load versus Load-Point Displacement in AL
6061-T6 CT Specimen

w–displacement field (mm)

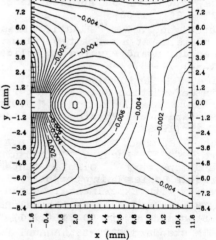

Figure 6: Out-Of-Plane Displacement Contour Plot, 304L
CT Specimen with 11,300 N Applied Load

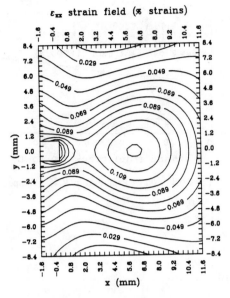

Figure 7 (a): ϵ_{xx} Contour Plot, 304L CT Specimen with 11,300 N Applied Load

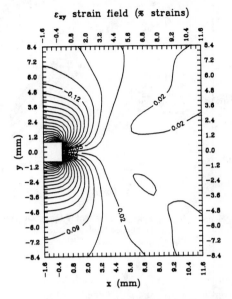

Figure 7 (c): ϵ_{xy} Contour Plot, 304L CT Specimen with 11,300 N Applied Load

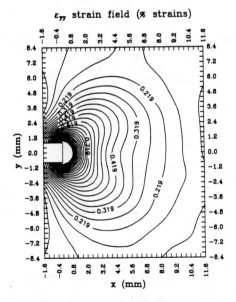

Figure 7 (b): ϵ_{yy} Contour Plot, 304L CT Specimen with 11,300 N Applied Load

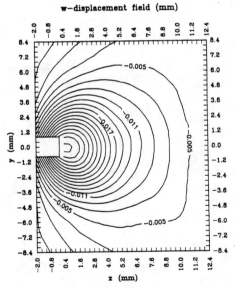

Figure 8: Out-Of-Plane Displacement Contour Plot, AL 6061-T6 CT Specimen with 6,995 N Applied Load

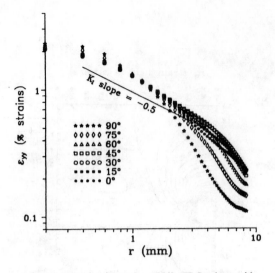

Figure 9: log-log Plots of ϵ_{yy}, 304L CT Specimen with 11,300 N Applied Load

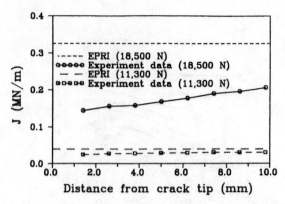

Figure 12: Distribution of J integral in 304L CT Specimen

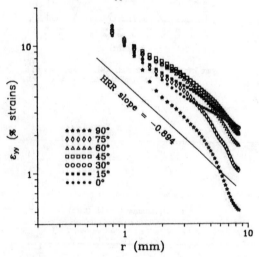

Figure 10: log-log Plots of ϵ_{yy}, 304L CT Specimen with 20,470 N Applied Load

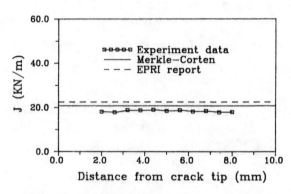

Figure 13: Distribution of J integral in AL 6061-T6 CT Specimen with Applied Load 6,657 N

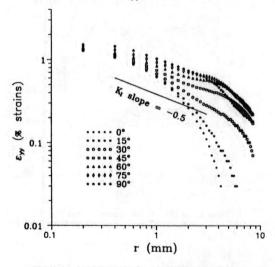

Figure 11: log-log Plots of ϵ_{yy}, AL 6061-T6 CT Specimen with 6,995 N Applied Load

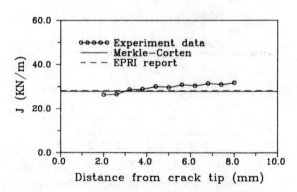

Figure 14: Distribution of J integral in AL 6061-T6 CT Specimen with Applied Load 6,995 N

STRESS INTENSITY FACTORS FOR AN ARBITRARY INNER EDGE CRACK OF PRESSURIZED ANNULUS

HIROHARU FUKUSUMI
Kumano Technical College
Kumano, Mie 519-43, JAPAN

EICHI MATSUMOTO, HIROSHI FUJIWARA AND ATSUSHI SAITO
Kinki University
Higashi-osaka, Osaka 577, Japan

ABSTRACT

The stress intensity factors of the pressurized annulus with an inner crack is investigated by a reflected photoelasticity. A suitable material for this experimental work is selected. Several kind of annulus models are prepared. The loading frame is made from steel holder with the reflector of thin stainless steel plate. The pressure load is applied through rubber tube connected to the compressor. The collected pictures are analyzed using a image data processing analyzer. The effect of crack depth and oblique angle to the stress intensity factor of the cracked annulus is fully summarized and compared each other.

INTRODUCTION

Annulus and cylinder subjected to the internal pressure load are frequently used to many structural components. If these components happen to have some structural defects like cracks, it is essential to ascertain the structural soundness of them. For a safety point of view of the structures, inner edge cracks would play an important role because these defects are not easy to find in advance nondestructively. There would be many problems of the annulus and cylindrical vessels with cracks which are subjected to internal pressure load whether the cracks are situated on the outer or inner surfaces.

In rather early time, A.S. Kobayashi had reviewed usefulness of applicability of photoelastic experimental methods to fracture problems of annulus[1],[2]. S. Takahashi and others gave many useful results for thick-walled vessels which had the longitudinal and radial outer surface cracks[3]. Recently, D. Chen and others solved the problems for an internal semi-elliptical surface crack of the cylindrical pressure vessels[4]. The stress of a disc with an elliptical hole subjected to the internal and external pressure loads was analyzed experimentally by the authors using the reflective photoelasticity[5]. In the case of a very thin elliptical hole, the similarity relation between the stress concentration factor and the stress intensity factor was affirmed in this paper.

In this work, the annulus with an oblique edge crack on the inner surface which is subjected to the internal pressure load will be analyzed by photoelasticity. The loading apparatus and the reflective photoelastic setup reported already in Ref. 5 are effectively used. The models with an inner edge crack are machined using the thin diamond disc saw. The isochromatic fringe pattern is observed at several steps of internal pressure load. The digital image data processing analyzer is fully utilized for getting the digital data from fringes. Collected data are used for analysis of stress intensity factors.

MODELS OF ANNULUS

Photoelastic model plates were molded and formed pouring the mixture of araldite CY 230, hardener HY 956 and thiokol LP-3. It is soft epoxy resin plate suitable for this experimental work. The annulus and beam for calibration was machined from the same plate. The configuration of annulus and crack are shown in Fig. 1. The outer diameter of the model is fixed to d_o=100mm. The inner diameter is selected to =60, 70, 80 and 90mm and the crack angle is changed to 0°,10°,20°,30° and 40°, respectively. The crack depth is changed from a=1mm to 8mm depending to the model configuration which is denoted definitely in Fig. 1. It was very difficult to make an inner edge crack of the annulus, the model was divided into two pieces by cutting through the diameter. Next, the crack is milled carefully in the form of defined configuration as shown in Fig. 1 using the thin diamond disc saw. After making the crack, the two pieces were set in position around dummy cores to form the exact annulus shape and adhered again to form the concentric annulus model with an edge crack[6].

EXPERIMENTAL APPARATUS AND METHOD

The reflective polariscope setup for this experimental work is shown in Fig. 2. Monochromic light emitted from the light source R is refracted its light path 90 degree by the half mirror G. The light goes through the loaded model T and reflected by the reflected plate M. Polished stainless steel thin plate of 0.5mm thick gave good reflected image. The reflected isochromatic image comes back the light path through the half mirror G and reaches on the film D in the end. The compressor C for pressure source and the pressure gauge P are also shown in the same figure. The square model holder case shown in Fig. 3 is made from a thick steel plate which has the dimension of 12mm thick and 220mm wide. At the center of the plate, a circular groove of 160mm in diameter and 6.5mm deep was cut out. In the deep end of the hole, the reflector plate is inserted.

A holding annulus made by urethane foam with the outer diameter of 158mm and the inner diameter of 101mm was set in the hole, which helped to hold the annulus model in the right position without any wrong constraint. A very thin gum tube was inserted in the center hole of the annulus model. This would give the internal pressure load on the internal surface of the annulus. A glass plate covers the photoelastic model case from the front outside and held firmly at four points as shown in Fig. 3. Thin cylindrical silicon gum packing and aluminum plate are put on the glass plate and held at four points.

Good holding state of the model is assured inserting a thin paper among the model and the glass plate. At the same time, the model appearance is checked not to be seen any isochromatic fringe from unfavorable constraint. The pressure load is applied carefully step-wise to 400 kPa and the variation of fringe pattern is observed. Selecting several good loading conditions for a model, isochromatic fringe is photographed.

STRESS INTENSITY FACTORS

An example of the isochromatic patterns is shown of a model with an oblique crack in Fig. 4. The isochromatic pattern for the every cases is stored in the image data processing system. A binary image is obtained after excluding some noisy data on the gray scale image and using a threshold of brightness. After the thinning process, the thinning image of the original pattern is obtained. A coordinate is affixed on the tip of the crack as shown in Fig. 5. The data (r_i, θ_i) are collected at several points on the thinning image of isochromatic fringe[6]. About 20 or more points were selected for analysis of this problems. The following equation has already proposed for the stress intensity factors K_I, K_{II} and a far field stress σ_{α} [6].

$$f(K_I, K_{II}, \sigma_{\alpha}) = \frac{1}{2\pi r} \left\{ (K_I \sin\theta + 2K_{II} \cos\theta)^2 + (K_I \sin\theta)^2 \right\}$$

$$+ \frac{2\sigma_{\alpha}}{\sqrt{2\pi r}} \sin\left(\frac{\theta}{2}\right) \left\{ K_I \sin\theta (1 + 2\cos\theta) \right. \tag{1}$$

$$\left. + K_{II}(1 + \cos\theta + 2\cos^2\theta) \right\} + \sigma_{\alpha}^2 - \left(\frac{n f_\alpha}{t}\right)^2 = 0$$

where n denotes a fringe number of the isochromatic pattern, t is the thickness of the model plate and fa is the material fringe value. For a large number of data set taken on the isochromatic fringes, some errors inevitable to the fitting process will be minimized by the least square method. For the initial estimates of K_I, K_{II} and σ_{α},

$$f_i(K_I + \Delta K_I, K_{II} + \Delta K_{II}, \sigma_{\alpha} + \Delta \sigma_{\alpha}) \neq 0$$

$$(i = 1, 2, 3, \cdots, m) \tag{2}$$

include errors and could not be fully satisfied. To correct these estimates, a series of iterative equations are derived from the Tailor series expansion of f_i.

$$f_i(K_I, K_{II}, \sigma_{\alpha}) + \Delta K_I \frac{\partial f_i}{\partial K_I} + \Delta K_{II} \frac{\partial f_i}{\partial K_{II}} + \Delta \sigma_{\alpha} \frac{\partial f_i}{\partial \sigma_{\alpha}} = v_i \tag{3}$$

The iterative condition of this equation gives an over-determined set of equations in terms of each corrections $\Delta K_I, \Delta K_{II}$ and $\Delta \sigma_{\alpha}$.

$$[g][\Delta \bar{K}i] = [f] \tag{4}$$

where

$$[g] = - \begin{bmatrix} \dfrac{\partial f_1}{\partial K_I} & \dfrac{\partial f_1}{\partial K_{II}} & \dfrac{\partial f_1}{\partial \sigma_{ox}} \\ \dfrac{\partial f_2}{\partial K_I} & \dfrac{\partial f_2}{\partial K_{II}} & \dfrac{\partial f_2}{\partial \sigma_{ox}} \\ \vdots & \vdots & \vdots \\ \vdots & \vdots & \vdots \\ \dfrac{\partial f_m}{\partial K_I} & \dfrac{\partial f_m}{\partial K_{II}} & \dfrac{\partial f_m}{\partial \sigma_{ox}} \end{bmatrix} , \quad [\Delta K_i] = \begin{bmatrix} \Delta K_I \\ \Delta K_{II} \\ \Delta \sigma_{ox} \end{bmatrix} , \quad [f] = \begin{bmatrix} f_1 \\ f_2 \\ \vdots \\ f_m \end{bmatrix} \quad (5)$$

The transpose of matrix [g] is multiplied from the left of this equation and the minimization of eq.(4) by the least square method is accomplished. In the final form, the matrix [ΔKi] is solved

$$[\Delta K_i] = [c]^{-1}[g]^T[f] \tag{6}$$

where $[g]^T$ means the transpose of matrix [g] and the matrix $[d]=[g]^T[g]$. The initial estimates Ki's will be improved to use the solutions of the eq.(6). After several iterations, a better fit of function f will be determined for the selected set of data. The validity of the solution could be confirmed to calculate the reconstructed isochromatic pattern using eq.(1).

RESULTS AND DISCUSSION

The results are summarized using a non-dimensional form of stress intensity factors

$$F_i = \frac{Ki}{p\sqrt{\pi\, d_0/2}} \quad (i=I,II) \tag{7}$$

where p is the internal pressure load applied and d_0 is the outer diameter of the model. Fig. 6 gives the variation of the stress intensity factor F_I to the crack depth for ϕ =0˚. The inner radius of the models are taken as a parameter. Figs. 7 and 8 show the variation of the stress intensity factors F_I and F_{II} for ϕ =10˚ to the crack depth. Similarly, the variation of F_I and F_{II} for ϕ = 20˚ is shown in Figs. 9 and 10. The similar results for ϕ = 30° and ϕ = 40° are summarized from Fig. 12 to Fig. 14. The value of the stress intensity factor F_I is higher in the thinner annulus and changes abruptly according to the crack depth. When the configuration of the annulus becomes thicker, the smaller F_I is attained and the variation to the crack depth turns gradual. For a small inclined crack of ϕ =10˚, the value of F_I decreases but F_{II} appears gradually. For a large inclined crack of ϕ =40˚, F_I decreases for some amount and the variation to crack depth becomes very moderate. On the contrary, the value of F_{II} becomes larger.

REFERENCES

1) A.S. Kobayashi(ed.): Experimental Technique in Fracture Mechanics, 1, Iowa State Univ. Press and SESA,p.19(1973)
2) A.S. Kobayashi(ed.): Experimental Technique in Fracture Mechanics, 2, Iowa State Univ. Press and SESA,p. 3(1975)
3) S. Takahashi, A. Shimamoto, F. Nogata and T. Ezumi: Photoelastic Determination of Stress Intensity Factors for Outer Surface Cracks of Internally Pressurized Thick-walled Vessels,Proc. Japan Soc. Photoelasticity,(in Japanese)3,1,(1981)p.24
4) D. Chen, H. Nishitani and K. Mori: Stress Intensity Factors for An Internal Semi-Elliptical Surface Crack in Cylindrical Pressure Vessels, Trans. JSME(Series A),(in Japanese) 35, 515(1989) p.1537
5) H. Fukusumi, H. Fujiwara and A. Saito: Stress Analysis of Disc with Elliptical Hole Subjected to Internal and External Pressure, Proc. Japan Soc. Photoelasticity, (in Japanese) 10,1,(1990)p.25
6) E. Matsumoto, H. Fujiwara, A. Saito and Y. Hirai: Stress Intensity Factor of Transient Thermal Stress of Annulus Cooled from Inner Surface, Asian-Pacific Congress of Strength Evaluation-91,(1991)P.990
7) R.J. Sanford and J.M. Dally: A General Method for Determining Mixed-mode Stress Intensity Factors from Isochromatic Fringe Patterns, Engineering Fracture Mechanics, 11(1979)p.621

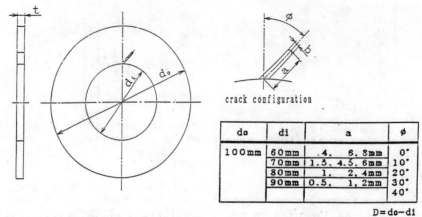

crack configuration

do	di	a	∅
100mm	60mm	.4. 6.8mm	0°
	70mm	1.5. 4.5. 6mm	10°
	80mm	1. 2.4mm	20°
	90mm	0.5. 1.2mm	30°
			40°

$D = do - di$

Fig. 1 Configuration of model and crack

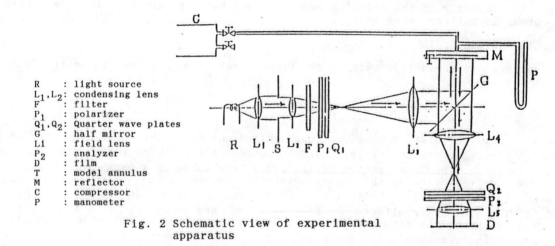

R   : light source
L_1, L_2: condensing lens
F   : filter
P_1 : polarizer
Q_1, Q_2: Quarter wave plates
G   : half mirror
L1   : field lens
P_2 : analyzer
D   : film
T   : model annulus
M   : reflector
C   : compressor
P   : manometer

Fig. 2 Schematic view of experimental
apparatus

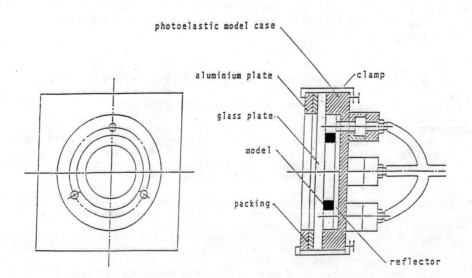

photoelastic model case

aluminium plate   clamp

glass plate

model

packing

reflector

Fig. 3 Holding setup of model and loading
frame for internal pressure load

Fig. 4 Isochromatic fringe for oblique
internal crack

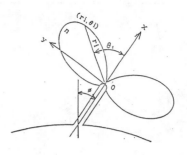

Fig. 5 Coordinates at the tip of crack

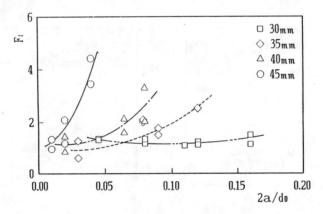

Fig. 6 Stress intensity factor F_I for
crack depth and $\phi = 0°$

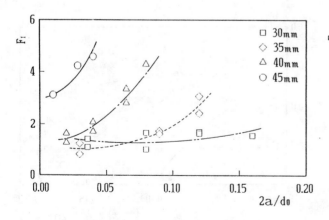

Fig. 7 Stress intensity factor F_I for
crack depth and $\phi = 10°$

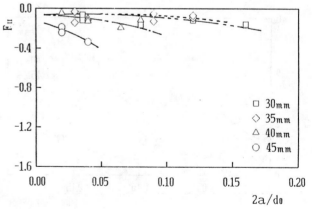

Fig. 8 Stress intensity factor F_{II} for
crack depth and $\phi = 10°$

267

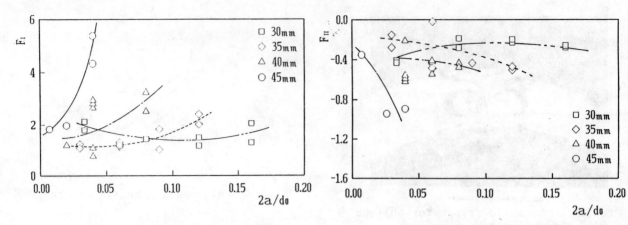

Fig. 9 Stress intensity factor F_I for crack depth and $\phi=20°$

Fig. 10 Stress intensity factor F_{II} for crack depth and $\phi=20°$

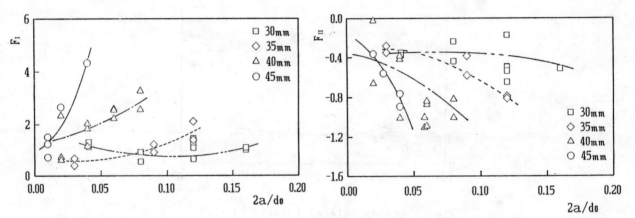

Fig. 11 Stress intensity factor F_I for crack depth and $\phi=30°$

Fig. 12 Stress intensity factor F_{II} for crack depth and $\phi=30°$

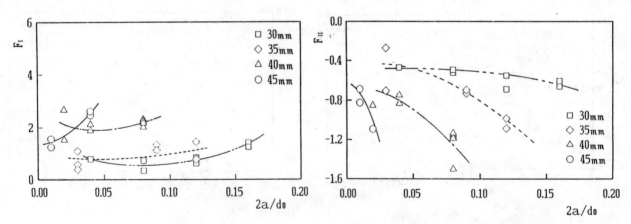

Fig. 13 Stress intensity factor F_I for crack depth and $\phi=40°$

Fig. 14 Stress intensity factor F_{II} for crack depth and $\phi=40°$

A New 1000 Tons Machine for Testing of
Tubular Products and Threaded Connections in Oilfield

Sergio Curioni   Alessandro Freddi   Antonio Podrini

ABSTRACT

A new testing facility to evaluate performances of oilfield tubular products and threaded connections has been designed and built, according to stringent test specifications which must prevent the in-service failures. Failures of steel tubular products are in fact currently costing the oil and gas industry more than one-half billion dollars annually, and are expected to worsen due to the harder environment (the wells are drilled deeper and tubulars and connections are subjected to higher state of stress). To perform full-scale fracture testing and/or to assess the stuctural integrity of tubulars and connections, a testing machine for combined loads was developed for single or simultaneous application of axial load (tensile load up to 10 MN, compressive load up to 5 MN), internally applied pressure (1000 bar) and bending moment (up to 100 $kN \cdot m$ i.e. 10 $ton \cdot m$), in several enviroments and temperatures.

INTRODUCTION

Failures of tubular joints are currently costing the oil industry many millions of dollars annually. Greater interest has been aroused in testing of tubular joints in order to prevent in-service failures. Severe environmental conditions and deeper drilled wells need an improve of well component performance, particularly the threaded connections, that must assure the structural integrity. This result can be obtained by a better design and pre-service verification of existing design. Manufacturers and oil company are also involved in design new connection solution that need to be tested with a qualification program. Subsea pipelines are subjected to many different loading conditions, ranging from tension and bending to high internal or external pressure. It is recommended to simulate this complex loadings, using a proper test apparatus. Due to large moments of inertia and loading regimes of the tubulars, pipe connectors design remains one of the most difficult of structural problems. According to API code RP 37, which recommends specific proof testing to simulate the testing conditions (internal pressure, external pressure, tensile loading, compressive loading, bending, temperature, make-up torque and any combination thereof) a servohydraulic machine for full-scale static testing of pipe connectors under combined axial, bending and internal pressure loadings, has been designed, built and tested. The aim of the machine is to investigate the feasibility and the structural reliability of a variety of pipe joining methods. The mechanical pipe connectors are composed of two separate half-joints which are factory welded at the ends of the pipe sections to be linked. The joint is completed by lowering the upper part of the tube and the mechanical system must assure a stable connection between the two pipes. There are different joints designed to guarantee also a gall-free make-up and break-out with leaktight performance.

S.Curioni, Professor in Nuclear Reactor,**A. Freddi**, Professor in Experimental Mechanics, Dip. DIEM - Facolta' di Ingegneria - Universita' di Bologna, Via Risorgimento, 2 - BOLOGNA, **A. Podrini**, Senior Researcher, C.S.M., Via di Castel Romano, 100 - ROMA- ITALY

SPECIMENS

Different types of loads are applied to the specimen : - tension (max. value 10 MN) - compression (max value 5 MN) - bending moment (max 100 $kN \cdot m$) - internal pressure (1000 bar)

Specimen length depends on pipe diameter D, wall thickness t and connector dimension. It is necessary to leave, before and after pipe connection, a length:

$$L = D + 6(D \cdot t)^{1/2} \qquad or \qquad L = 3 \cdot D$$

where the diameter D is variable from 60 mm to 244 mm (2"3/8−9"5/8) and wall thickness from 4.8 mm to 15.9 mm. The tubular specimens are prepared by threading each end in two sub-connectors which have pressure inlets and outlets and must be assembled to end caps with clevis pins, fig. 1 . Different sub-connectors, with ACME threads, have been built in order to assure the testing of the scheduled tubulars sizes. Threads allow rotation for alignement of pressure holes and pins during the test. An apparatus for a quick screwing of the end caps has been built. The specimen with the end caps is simply lowered, fig. 2 and connected to the clevis by two pins (260 mm diameter), pushed and pulled by two small hydraulic cylinders. Typical specimen handling time is reduced to 15 minutes. Also the replacing of different specimen sizes is greatly simplified and performed at low cost.

DESCRIPTION OF TESTING MACHINE

The consideration of cost and production time has played an important role in design decision process: a preliminary evaluation of the cost and of the necessary time has been done comparing several conceptual designs and technical solutions [1], [2]. The use of standard or stock sizes for all components has been choosen as first principle of cost reduction. A special effort has been done to select parts that are readily available, as hydraulic cylinders, bearings, fasteners etc. and to avoid the use of special components that would have increased costs and delivery time. This choice has permitted a total expended time for designing, production and preliminary tests of less than one year. Another constraint was the limitation of the room where the machine must be located. Several solutions was available with different number of cylinders and overall dimensions: the solution with only one cylinder of 10 MN capacity has been rejected for reasons of cost, delivery time of the cylinder and overall lenght of the machine. Solutions of only two cilinders of 5 MN capacity has been rejected for cost and delivery time. Only four cylinders of 2.5 MN capacity, readily available, have permitted a dramatic abate of the cost and a parallel reduction of the overall dimensions of the frame. Fig.3 and fig. 4 show general scheme of test facilities and machine. It has been designed with a movable cross head (with a maximum stroke of 300 mm), pushed and pulled by four cylinders having an external diameter of 376 mm , a length of 465 mm with a maximum pressure of 320 bar. The disadvantage of this choice is represented by the difficulty of mantaining the resultant of the four cylinder loads on the specimen axis. In order to overcome this handicap, two sturdy columns (250 mm diameter) support the movable cross head. The slide guides on the head are located at a proper distance to reduce at acceptable level the friction forces due to the cross head weight and to the jamming because of misalignment. The cylinders are connected to movable cross head by four special devices to absorb misalignment, fig.5. The cross head, made of steel plates (60 mm of thickness) and welded tubes, applies an axial load of 10 MN and a bending load of 100 $kN \cdot m$. At the head is fastened a clevis pin grip to connect the specimen, so to reduce to a minimum the horizontal misalignment and to apply at the specimen a pure bending (fig.6). Bending moment to the specimen is applied by two hydraulic cylinders placed in lower part of the structure, whose position on the slide guide fits the different specimen sizes. To prevent critical collapse of the pipe when compression load is applied, the specimen is supported by a movable framework put between the two pipe ends. The specimen is also supported by a structure to avoid pipe buckling when a compressive load is applied. Instrumented strain-gauges bars are utilized as load control unit calibration (one quarter and full range load machine capacity). A differential pressure transducer (pressures on the two chamber of actuator pistons are compared) as load read-out system is used; output is proportional to the force applied to the specimen.

LOAD TRAIN ALIGNMENT AND VERIFICATION

Under axial testing conditions the apparatus must have a good load train alignment. A accurately machined and strain gaged bar has been used to verify it. Clevis pin grips allow enough rotation to keep pipe centered and to minimize bending strain also at low loads.

Testing machine has been verified utilizing an elastic calibration device. Calibration bar has been placed between machine grips so that its center line coincides with the center line of the heads of the testing machine. To assure a stable zero the elastic device has been loaded from zero to maximum machine range several times. Follow-the-load method has been utilized : the load on the elastic calibration device is followed until the load reaches a nominal graduation on the load-readout scale of the machine. Load on the elastic calibration device is recorded. A suitable load test load increment has been used (.2 MN). Load has been applied slowly and smoothly during all verification measurements. A differential pressure transducer that measures and compares the pressure on each side of the actuator piston has been used for force readout. Differential transducer takes into account also internal actuator friction forces and, in order to calculate the load applied to the specimen, friction factors in hydraulic actuator must be evaluated . Friction is present in a servohydraulic actuator due to the internal fluid seals and actuator bearing. In high force testing is used only differential transducer and an electrical output proportional to the force is obtained. In lower force ranges a load cell that measures the force directly applied to the pipe has been utilized. In fig. 7 and 9 the relationships between calibration bar and machine display values in tension and compression load are shown. Fig. 8 and 10 show errors in machine display during tension and compression loading rate; error percentage is decreasing in higher force values.

TEST PROCEDURE

Repeated make-up and break-out tests are performed to verify the threaded connections. To carry out these tests the laboratory is equipped with a data acquisition system in order to evaluate connection response to different load combination. The specimen is loaded under specific load condition (tension, compression, internal pressure, bending and their combination) and several loads increment are applied before reaching maximum force. Connection answers to single load and to loads combination is obtained. Fig. 11 shows test procedure for internal gas pressure under tension and bending load. Strain gages are applied to control pipe bending and a monitoring bubble detection system is used; experiment is recorded on video tape. Loading forces are applied and released sequentially several times.

Loads combination are reported in fig. 12 as a function of material grade and pipe dimensions.

In fig. 13 one cycle load (49 min) is shown. Tension, bending and pressure, with different loading rate, are recorded as a function of time.

REFERENCES

[1] Makelt, H., (1961), "Die mechanischen Pressen", Munchen, Hanser

[2] Oehler, A., (1962), "Die hydraulischen Pressen", Munchen, Hanser

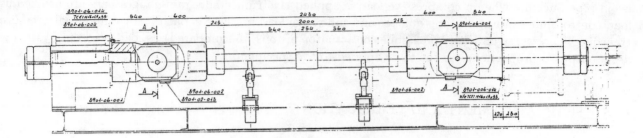

Fig. 1 - Tubular specimen

Fig. 2 - Specimen with end caps

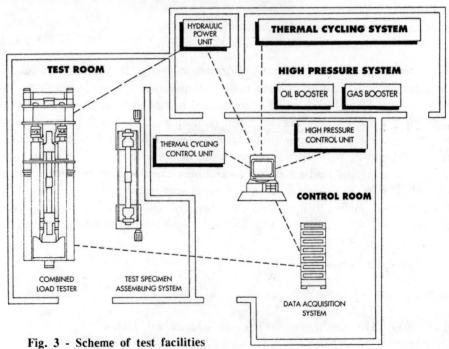

Fig. 3 - Scheme of test facilities

Fig. 4 - Test machine

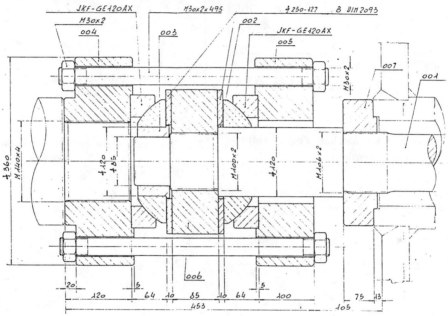

Fig. 5 - Device to absorb misalignment

Fig. 6 - Clevis pin grip

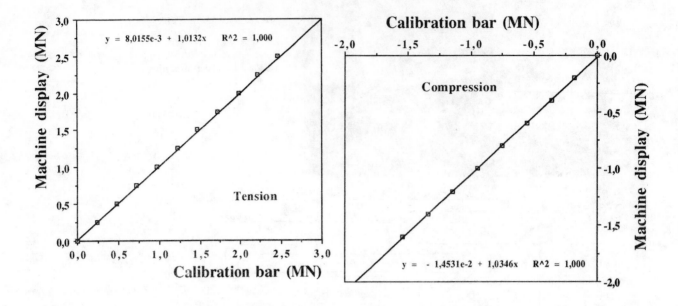

Fig. 7 - Calibration bar and machine display values (tension)

Fig. 9 - Calibration bar and machine display values (compression)

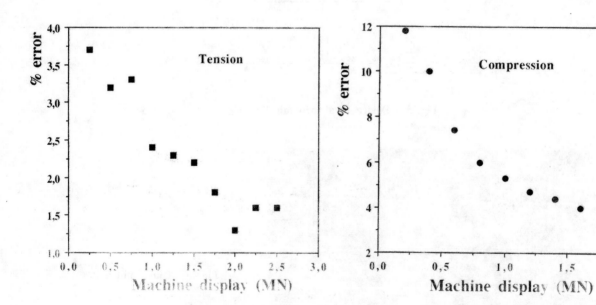

Fig. 8 - Machine display error (tension)

Fig. 10 - Machine display error (compression)

**DETAILED TEST PROCEDURE FOR INTERNAL GAS PRESSURE
UNDER TENSION AND BENDING**

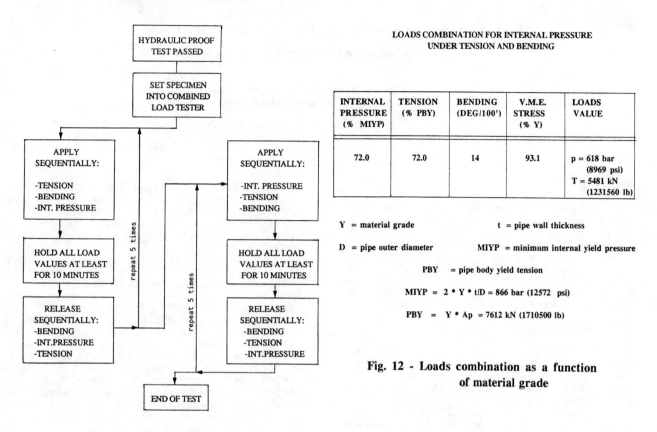

**LOADS COMBINATION FOR INTERNAL PRESSURE
UNDER TENSION AND BENDING**

INTERNAL PRESSURE (% MIYP)	TENSION (% PBY)	BENDING (DEG/100')	V.M.E. STRESS (% Y)	LOADS VALUE
72.0	72.0	14	93.1	p = 618 bar (8969 psi) T = 5481 kN (1231560 lb)

Y = material grade   t = pipe wall thickness

D = pipe outer diameter   MIYP = minimum internal yield pressure

PBY = pipe body yield tension

MIYP = 2 * Y * t/D = 866 bar (12572 psi)

PBY = Y * Ap = 7612 kN (1710500 lb)

**Fig. 12 - Loads combination as a function
of material grade**

Fig. 11 - Test procedure

LOADING DIAGRAMS FOR TENSION + BENDING + INT. GAS PRESSURE

TENSION LOAD = 3197 kN   BENDING = 980 μm/m   PRESSURE = 618 bar

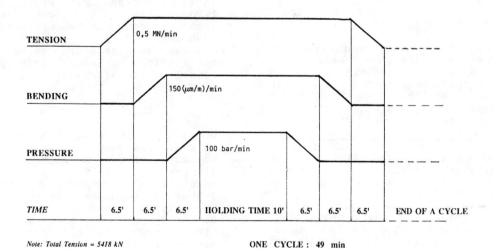

Note: Total Tension = 5418 kN   ONE CYCLE : 49 min

Fig. 13 - Cycle load

275

SIMPLE METHOD FOR MEASURING AXIAL TENSION OF BOLT

BY MEANS OF ULTRASONIC WAVES

Yoshihisa MINAKUCHI, Makoto FUKUI,
Tomiya IINO and Izumi SATO

ABSTRACT

A simple method for measuring the axial tension of bolt by using ultrasonic waves has been presented. The axial tension of bolt is obtained from the change rate of round trip propagation time of sound wave through the bolt. The experimental results are graphically presented and the utility of the proposed ultrasonic method is also discussed.

1. INTRODUCTION

The jointed parts in machines and apparatus are mainly assembled by a bolt connection. Accordingly, there is the fear that the loosen and the damage of bolt cause an important accident. In order to secure the reliability of the bolted joints, it is important to safely design bolted joints so that the bolt axial tension is precisely grasped.

Up to now the many measuring method is proposed to know the bolt axial tension. For example, there is the strain gauge method that utilizes the elongation of an axial part of bolt, the torque wrench method[1], the magnetic method that utilizes the change of magnetic characteristic by the stress acting on the bolt head[2], the eddy current method [3] and the ultrasonic wave method [4]~[8]. Especially, the method for measuring the bolt axial tension by the ultrasonic wave is measured by the change rate of round trip propagation time through the bolt under no loading and loading. In this ultrasonic wave method, the change rate

---

Y. Minakuchi is Associate Professor in the Faculty of Engineering, Yamanashi University, 4-3-11, Takeda, Kofu-shi, Yamanashi Pref. 400, Japan.
M. Fukui is a Graduate Student in the Faculty of Engineering, Osaka University, 2-1, Yamada-oka, Suita, Osaka 565, Japan.
T. Iino is Assistant in the Faculty of Engineering, Yamanashi University.
I. Sato is an Engineer, Tokimec Inc., 1-13-19, Yako, Tsurumi-ku, Yokohama 230, Japan.

of round trip propagation time from the head of bolt to the bottom of it is measured by using a counter. The measurement of the bolt axial tension is hardly found without using the counter[9].

The paper presents the method that the bolt axial tension is easily measured without using the counter. The round trip propagation time of ultrasonic wave through the bolt is transformed to the voltage by using B scope function equipped in the ultrasonic device. In the case where the material, the length and the axial diameter of the bolt differ, the relation between the bolt axial tension and the change rate of round trip propagation time through the bolt is checked. The utility of this measuring method is also investigated.

2. MEASURING METHOD

2.1 Principle of measurement

In order to know the bolt axial tension of length L_t as shown in Fig.1, the ultrasonic wave is propagated toward an axis from the normal probe which is attached to the bolt head. The change rate of round trip propagation time through the bolt under no loading and loading needs to be measured in this experiment.

In the case where the bolt is under no loading, the round trip propagation time T of the ultrasonic wave is given as follows:

$$T = \frac{2L_t}{c} \qquad (1)$$

where c is the wave velocity. When the bolt is fastened, the axial part occurs the axial stress and happens the elastic elongation. At this time, the wave velocity c' through the bolt barely decreases together with the increase of the axial stress σ and the propagation time through the bolt increases. In other words, the relation between the wave velocity through the bolt under loading and the axial stress is linearly given as follows:

$$c' = c(1 - \alpha \sigma) \qquad (2)$$

where α is the constant decided by the material. On the other hand, the length of bolt L_t' under loading is given as follows:

$$L_t' = L_t(1 + \frac{\sigma}{E}) \qquad (3)$$

where E is Young's modulus of the bolt.

When the elongation of the bolt under loading is ΔL_t and the change volume of the wave velocity is Δc, the round trip propagation time T of the supersonic wave under loading is given by the following equation.

$$T' = \frac{2L_t'}{c'} = \frac{2(L_t + \Delta L_t)}{c + \Delta c} \qquad (4)$$

As ΔL_t and Δc are sufficiently small, $\Delta T/T$ is given as follows:

$$\frac{\Delta T}{T} = \frac{\Delta L_t}{L_t} - \frac{\Delta c}{c} \qquad (5)$$

where $\Delta T(=T'-T)$ is the difference of the round trip propagation times under no loading and loading.

Both the change rate of elongation $\Delta L_t/L_t$ and the change rate of the wave velocity $\Delta c/c$ are proportional to the axial stress σ[5]. Accordingly, the $\Delta T/T$ of Eq.(5) is given as follows:

$$\frac{\Delta T}{T} = k\sigma \qquad (6)$$

where k is the proportional constant. σ is the value divided the axial tension by the cross-sectional area of the bolt. If k is the known value, the axial stress σ is obtained by measuring the value of $\Delta T/T$.

2.2 B scope function

Figure 2 shows the echo positions obtained from the bottom of the bolt which appear under no loading and loading on a CRT display of the ultrasonic device . These indicate a solid line and a dotted line. The B scope function equipped with the ultrasonic device is used in this experiment. The detail of it is explained below on the basis of Fig.2.

After gate starting point A and gate end B are determined in the detected range including two echoes, the threshold value of the echoes within gate is decided with a dot-dash-line. If this setting is done, the times from the point B to the points C and C' at the threshold value can be measured. In other words, the times in BC and BC' correspond to the voltage V_1 and V_2, respectively. This is B scope function. Accordingly, the change volume of round trip propagation time of the ultrasonic wave through the bolt is obtained by measuring the voltage difference ΔV (=$V_1 - V_2$).

3. EXPERIMENTAL METHOD

3.1 Round trip propagation time and voltage calibration

In order to check the relation between the round trip propagation time through the bolt and the voltage obtained by B scope function, an experiment is done by using the block specimens of different lengths (material: SS41, wave velocity:5960m/s) of h_1=45.077 mm and h_2=40.048mm.

First of all, a normal probe is attached on the block specimen of length h_1, and the ultrasonic wave is propagated. After the voltage V_n in BC detected by the bottom echo of the block specimen is electrically adjusted to become zero by using the B scope function, the voltage V_n in BC is measured by using the block specimen of length h_2. Also, the round trip propagation time T of the ultrasonic wave through each block specimen is calculated by divided the length with the wave velocity. Furthermore, as the voltage obtained by using B scope function is small, the value amplified with the voltage amplifier is adopted.

3.2 Measurement of the change rate of bolt axial tension and round trip propagation time

In order to check the relation between the bolt axial tension and the change rate of round trip propagation time $\Delta T/T$ through the bolt, an experiment is done by using the various bolt specimens with different material, length and axial diameter as shown in Fig.3. Furthermore, the head and the bottom of the bolt is processed in a plane with a lathe so that the normal probe is easy to be attached and the bottom echo is finely obtained.

Figure 4 shows the schematic diagram of a measurement device attached the bolt as shown in Fig.3 and the block diagram of a measurement system. The bolt axial tension is produced the tension by using the compressive device. The magnitude of the load is detected by a load cell. Also, the ultrasonic wave is propagated from the normal probe attached to the bolt head. After the voltage detected under no loading is electrically adjusted to become zero by using the B scope function, the voltage ΔV is measured under loading. The value of ΔV is equal to the voltage difference which occurs in the bolt under loading no loading. If the axial tension occurs in the bolt, the change rate of round trip propagation time $\Delta T/T$ is obtained by using the value of ΔV. Furthermore, the elastic elongation of the bolt under loading is measured by using the electric micrometer which is established to the head and the bottom of the bolt.

4. EXPERIMENTAL RESULTS AND CONSIDERATIONS

4.1 Relation between round trip propagation time and voltage difference.

Table 1 shows the relation between the round trip propagation time T_n and the voltage difference ΔV_n obtained on each block specimen by the experiment of section 3.1. In the case where the difference of the block length is $h_1 - h_2 = 5.029$mm, the change volume of round trip propagation time is $\Delta T_n = 1.688 \times 10^{-6}$ (s) and $\Delta V_n = 1.191$(V). Accordingly, if the axial tension occurs to the bolt, the change rate of the round trip propagation time $\Delta T/T$ is obtained in the following manner.

The change volume of round trip propagation time ΔT through the bolt is given by the following equation.

$$\Delta T = \frac{2\Delta L_t}{c} = \frac{2(h_1 - h_2)}{V_n} \times \frac{\Delta V}{c} \quad (7)$$

As seen from Eqs.(1) and (7), $\Delta T/T$ is sufficient to consider the only change volume of round trip propagation time where the bolt axial stress occurs in the part of the fastening length L_f. Accordingly, $\Delta T/T$ is given by the following equation.

$$\frac{\Delta T}{T} = \frac{h_1 - h_2}{V_n} \times \frac{\Delta V}{L_t}$$

$$= \frac{5.029\,(\text{mm})}{1.191\,(\text{V})} \times \frac{\Delta V}{L_f} \quad (8)$$

4.2 Effect of material

Figure 5 shows the relation between the bolt axial between and the change rate of round trip propagation time $\Delta T/T$. In this case, the axial diameter(ϕ20mm) and the length($L_t = 150$mm) are same, and the only bolt material differ. Here, the value of $\Delta T/T$ is obtained from Eq.(8). The horizontal axis is is the axial tension of the bolt. The vertical axis is the value that divided the change volume of round trip propagation time ΔT with the fastening length L_f of the bolt under no loading. $\Delta T/T$ is increasing like a straight line when the axial tension of the bolt is increasing. This trend is different by the material.

Figure 6 shows the relation between the axial stress and $\Delta T/T$ which correspond to Fig.5. Fig.6 shows a similar tendency as Fig.5. $\Delta T/T$ is different by the material in the case where the axial diameter and the length are the same bolt. Accordingly, in order to know the bolt axial tension, the proportional constant k in Eq.(6) must be previously requested.

4.3 Effect of length

Figure 7 shows the relation between the axial tension and the change rate of round trip propagation time $\Delta T/T$. In this case, the material (BsBD2) and axial diameter (ϕ20mm) are same, and the only length of bolt differs. From the figure, $\Delta T/T$ hardly changes by the length L_t of the bolt. This is reason why the change

volume of round trip propagation time divided by that of inside the fastening length L_f under no loading. Therefore, the value turns into none dimension. The actual change volume of round trip propagation time becomes large as the axial part of the bolt becomes long.

Figure 8 shows the relation between the axial stress and the $\Delta T/T$ which correspond to Fig.7. Fig.8 shows a similar tendency as Fig.7. From Fig.8, even if the length L_t of the bolt changes, $\Delta T/T$ is almost the same value. The influence of the length of a screw mountain part on the axial stress is hardly appeared.

4.4 Effect of axial diameter

Figure 9 shows the relation between the axial tension and the change rate of round trip propagation time $\Delta T/T$. In this case, the material (SS41) and length (110mm) are same and the only axial diameter differs. From this figure, $\Delta T/T$ becomes large as the axial diameter becomes small for the axial tension. If the same axial tension acts on the bolt, $\Delta T/T$ is to proportion to the axial stress occurred in the bolt as seen from Eq.(6).

Figure 10 shows the relation between the axial stress and the T/T correspond to Fig.9. If the axial diameter changes, $\Delta T/T$ is almost the same value.

5. CONCLUSIONS

This paper has been proposed the method that the bolt axial tension is easily measured by using the B scope function equipped with an ultrasonic device. In the case that the material, the axial diameter and the length of the bolt differ, the relation between the bolt axial tension and the change rate of round trip propagation time through the bolt are investigated, and the following conclusions are obtained.
(1) A simple method for measuring the axial tension of bolt by means of ultrasonic waves can be presented without using a counter.
(2) The proposed ultrasonic method is fairly practical.
(3) The relation between the bolt axial tension and the change rate of round trip propagation time is almost line.
(4) When the material of the bolt becomes soft, the change rate of round trip propagation time becomes large for the axial tension.
(5) Even if the fastening length of bolt changes, the difference in the change rate of round trip propagation time does not occur for the axial tension.
(6) When the diameter of bolt becomes large, the change rate of round trip propagation time becomes large for the axial tension.

Finally, the authors are deeply indebted to Professor Takashi Koizumi and Professor Toshikazu Shibuya of Tokyo

Institute of Technology, for many valuable suggestions on this work. We also wish to thank Mr. T. Nonaka, who was a student of Yamanashi University, for his help in carrying out the experiment.

REFERENCES

(1) Haruyama, S., Trans. Jpn. Soc. Mech. Eng., Ser.C, (in Japanese), Vol.53, No.495 (1987), p.2373.
(2) Mori. T., et al., Trans. Jpn. Soc. Mech. Eng., Ser. A, (in Japanese), Vol.47, No.413 (1980), p.102.
(3) Shimizu, S., et al., J. JSPE., (in Japanese), Vol.54, No.7 (1988), p.1357.
(4) Hughes, D. S. and Kelly, J. L., Physical Review, Vol.92, No.5 (1953), p.1145.
(5) Takahashi, S., et al., J. Materials Science, Vol.13 (1978), p.843.
(6) Yamamoto, E. and Motegi, R., J. Jpn. Soc. Mech. Eng., (in Japanese), Vol.82, No.731 (1979), p.1116.
(7) Sakai, T., et al., Trans. Jpn. Soc. Mech. Eng., (in Japanese), Vol.43, No.366 (1977), p.723.
(8) Makino, T., et al., J. JSPE., (in Japanese), Vol.43, No.2(1977), p.223.
(9) Suda, M., et al., J. Jpn. Soc. Mech. Eng., Ser A, (in Japanese), Vol.57, No.537 (1991), p.1240.

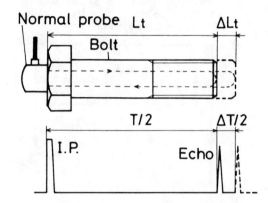

Fig.1 Propagation of ultrasonic wave and change of propagation time in a bolt

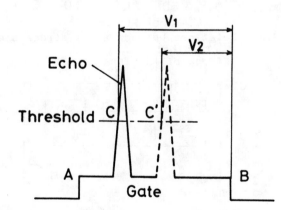

Fig.2 Measurement of propagation time by using B scope function

Table 1 Relations between propagation time and voltage in two specimens

	Material	h(mm)	T／2(sec)	V_h(V)
No.1	SS41	45.077	7.563×10^{-6}	0.000
No.2	SS41	40.048	6.719×10^{-6}	1.191

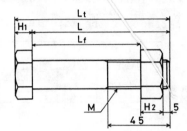

Material	M	H_1 (mm)	H_2 (mm)	L (mm)	L_f (mm)	C (m/s)	E (GPa)
SS41	M12	8	10	110	95	5960	206
	M16	10	13	110	92		
	M20	13	16	150	129		
	M20	13	16	110	89		
BsBD2	M20	13	16	150	129	4340	110
	M20	13	16	110	89		
	M20	13	16	70	49		
A5056DB	M20	13	16	150	129	6520	70

Fig.3 Shape and dimension of bolts

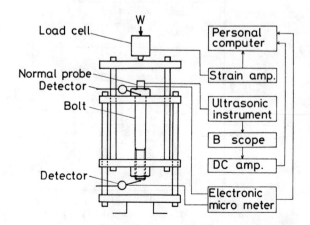

Fig.4 Schematic Diagram of experimental apparatus

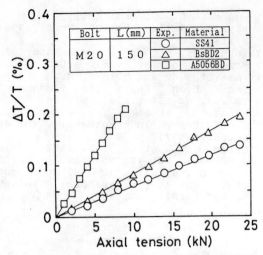

Fig.5 Relations between axial tension and
△T/T in bolts
(Effect of the material)

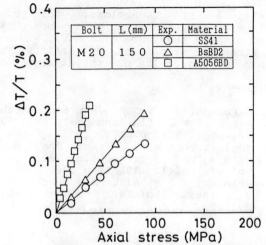

Fig.6 Relations between axial stress and
△T/T in bolts
(Effect of the material)

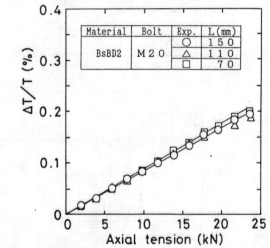

Fig.7 Relations between axial tension and
△T/T in bolts
(Effect of the length)

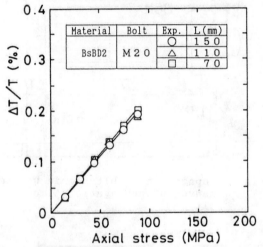

Fig.8 Relations between axial stress and
△T/T in bolts
(Effect of the length)

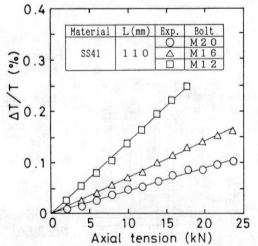

Fig.9 Relations between axial tension and
△T/T in bolts
(Effect of the axial diameter)

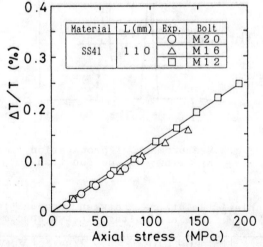

Fig.10 Relations between axial stress and
△T/T in bolts
(Effect of the axial diameter)

AN INSTRUMENTED FASTENER FOR SHEAR FORCE MEASUREMENTS
IN JOINTS

James Wayne Sawyer
NASA Langley Research Center
Hampton, VA 23665
and
Timothy M. Rothgeb
Lockheed Engineering and Sciences Company
Hampton, VA 23665

ABSTRACT

A preliminary investigation has been conducted on instrumented fasteners for use as sensors to measure the shear loads transmitted by individual fasteners installed in double splice joints. Calibration and load verification test were conducted for instrumented fasteners installed at three fastener torque levels. Results from calibration tests show that the shear strains obtained from the instrumented fasteners vary linearly with the applied load and that the instrumented fasteners can be effectively used to measure shear loads transmitted by individual fasteners installed in double splice joints. Tests were also conducted with three instrumented fasteners installed in a typical double splice joint. The test results showed that the load distribution between individual fasteners is dependent on the location of the fastener in the joint and the fastener torque level. The fastener located near the end of the joint with the single plate carried more load than the fasteners located near the end of the joint with the two plates. Installing the fasteners with a torque greater than finger tight results in a significant amount of the load being carried by friction between the faying surfaces of the plates even if the faying surfaces are polished and lubricated. Increasing the fastener torque increases the load being carried by friction between the faying surfaces of the joint. Increasing the fastener torque also results in a more uniform distribution of the loads between the individual fasteners for joints in aluminum plates with two fasteners, but did not have a significant effect for joints in steel plates with three fasteners.

INTRODUCTION

The development of new refractory composite materials that can be used for structural applications at temperatures between 1400 and 2500 K has resulted in many exciting possibilities for the structural design of advanced aircraft and space transportation systems. However, the application of these materials to high temperature aircraft structures is dependent on the availability of reliable joints that meet the strength and life cycle requirements of the vehicle.

Joint design techniques presently used were largely developed for metallic materials and modified or extended for use with conventional low-temperature composite materials. These design techniques were developed over a long period of time using a combination of analysis techniques and empirical data and are based on a large data base (ref. 1). However, most structural failures still occur at joints, and joints remain one of the structural designer's major concerns. The successful use of current joint design techniques is, in part, due to the forgiving nature of ductile metallic materials which have the capability to withstand relatively high strains before experiencing failure. The relatively high strain capability of ductile metallic materials allows local yielding of the material which reduces the stress concentrations due to uneven distribution of loads between fasteners in a joint. This local yielding of the material around highly loaded fasteners minimizes the requirement to know the individual loads carried by each fastener.

Advanced high temperature refractory composite materials generally have low strain-to-failure properties. Thus, the development of joint design techniques for these materials is dependent on a good understanding of how loads are distributed in the joint. For joints requiring multiple fasteners or multiple rows of fasteners, determining how the loads are distributed in the joint is difficult. Present techniques for measuring the load distribution in joints consists of measuring the surface strain and displacement of the fasteners and the surrounding areas. These measurements are useful but expensive to obtain for large areas and may not provide some of the most needed data especially for regions inside the joints. Analytical techniques have been developed that can be used to predict the performance of structural joints (ref. 1). However, experimental data are needed to verify the various analytical techniques especially for advanced high temperature refractory composite materials.

The present paper describes a preliminary investigation toward the development and application of an instrumented fastener as a sensor to measure the shear loads transmitted by individual fasteners installed in a double splice joint. The results presented were obtained using metal fasteners and joints to aid in the development and verification of the concept, but the resulting instrumented fasteners can also be used for the investigation of joints in advanced refractory composite materials. Results from calibration and load verification tests on joints with one and two instrumented fasteners, respectively, are presented and discussed for fasteners installed at three torque levels. Similar tests were also conducted with three instrumented fasteners installed in a typical double splice joint in which results from the calibration tests were used to determine fastener shear loads. Results from these tests are presented and discussed.

SENSOR DESCRIPTION

The shear force sensor consists of a steel fastener instrumented with strain gages installed on flat surfaces machined on the fastener as shown in figure 1. The location and length of the machined flat surfaces are indicated on the sketch in figure 1 and were selected based on the fastener being used in a double splice joint with 0.64-cm-thick plates. A groove 0.25 cm wide and 0.030 cm deep is machined around the fastener at the center of the machined flat surfaces. The purpose of the groove is discussed in the next section. Two 0.14-cm-long strain gages are installed in the center of each of the machined flat surfaces with the gage axes oriented at 90° to each other and at 45° to the axis of the fastener to measure shear strain. The gage leads are routed through small holes drilled in the fastener parallel with the axis of the fastener. The gage leads were potted in the holes to minimize the possibility of damage to the leads. For the present investigation, the fasteners were machined from 17-4 PH stainless steel heat treated to H-900 and had a nominal diameter of 0.953 cm. For measurements in a joint application, the actual fasteners to be used in the joint could be instrumented in the same fashion and used to make the measurements without affecting the joint load distribution.

PRINCIPLE OF OPERATION

A fastener installed in a double splice joint will experience a transverse shear load that varies along the length of the fastener as shown in the sketches presented in figure 2. If the loads are transmitted uniformly, then the transverse shear loads in the fastener are given by the shear diagram A. If the loads are concentrated in the center of the plates, the transverse shear loads in the fastener are given by the shear diagram B. In a real joint with fastener flexure and irregular bearing surfaces, the loads in the plates can be arbitrarily distributed, or concentrated at one point, which will result in transverse shear loads in the fastener that can vary at any location in the shaded regions shown in shear diagrams C and D. However, at the faying surfaces of the plates, which correspond to points 1 and 2 on shear diagram C, the transverse shear load will always be a maximum value. Placing the strain gages on the fastener in the plane of the faying surfaces will result in measurement of strains due to the maximum transverse shear load carried by the fastener. Since the strain gages have finite width, they will extend outside of the plane of the faying surfaces which could result in inaccurate measurements of the transverse shear strain for certain distributions of loads in the plates. This inaccuracy can be eliminated by cutting shallow grooves around the fastener that are slightly wider than the strain gages as shown in figure 1. The shear diagram for fasteners with grooves centered on the faying surface planes is shown by diagram D in figure 2. The grooves ensure that the transverse shear in the fastener will be constant at a maximum value over the width of the strain gages and thus will not be affected by the shear distribution through the thickness of the plates.

APPARATUS AND TEST PROCEDURE

Test Apparatus

Calibration, verification, and joint tests were conducted by applying a tensile load to the plates using a hydraulic actuated universal test machine. Pinned joints were used at each end of the test specimens to minimize the effects of alignment errors. The load was applied at a constant displacement rate of 0.13 cm/min. Tests were conducted with the fasteners tightened finger tight (approximately 0.5 N-m of torque) and with each instrumented fastener torqued to 5.6 and 11.3 N-m. Each of the strain gages were connected in a single active arm bridge using a 3-leadwire hookup system. Strain gage data and the applied load were recorded during each test using a computer controlled data acquisition system.

Calibration Tests

Each fastener was calibrated independently with a single fastener installed in the double splice joint fixture shown in figure 3. The fixture was fabricated using 17-4 PH stainless steel heat treated to H-900. Brass washers were used as shims to center the strain gages in the planes of the faying surfaces of the joint. The steel plates were fabricated by match drilling the holes in the plates with a clearance between the fastener and holes not greater than 0.005 cm. The fastener was rotated so that the strain gages and machined flat surfaces were parallel to the direction of the force applied to the fastener by the center plate. The faying surfaces of the calibration fixture were polished to a surface roughness of approximately 0.05 µm and lubricated with boron nitride powder to minimize friction between the surfaces. Calibration curves which indicate applied load as a function of measured shear strain were obtained for each fastener up to a maximum load of 4,500 N. In subsequent tests, the slope of the calibration curve for the appropriate fastener and torque load was multiplied by the measured fastener shear strain to obtain the measured shear load in the fastener.

Verification Tests

Tests were conducted to verify the use of the instrumented fasteners to measure the shear force transmitted by fasteners in an actual joint. The test fixture used for the verification tests is shown in figure 4. The fixture consists of a double splice joint in aluminum plates instrumented with strain gages and with two instrumented fasteners installed as shown in the figure. The faying surfaces of the joint were polished to a surface roughness of approximately 0.05 µm and lubricated with boron nitride powder to minimize friction during the load tests. The aluminum plates were fabricated by match drilling the holes in the plates with a clearance between the fasteners and the holes not greater than 0.013 cm. The strain gages were installed on the aluminum plates as shown so that the force carried by each fastener could be calculated from the strain measurements and the known properties of the aluminum plates. Verification tests were conducted for a maximum applied load of 6,800 N.

Joint Tests

The instrumented fasteners were used to measure the shear loads transmitted by individual fasteners in a typical double splice joint in steel plates. The joint contained three fasteners installed in two rows as shown in figure 5. The fasteners were spaced 2.86 cm apart across the width of the specimen and the rows were spaced 2.86 cm apart. The plates were 0.64 cm thick and were made of 17-4 PH stainless steel heat treated to H-900. The plates were ground flat and the faying surfaces were polished to a surface roughness of approximately 0.05 µm and lubricated with boron nitride powder. The fastener holes in the plates were match drilled and reamed to provide a maximum clearance between the fasteners and the holes of 0.005 cm. Joint tests were conducted for a maximum applied load of 11,000 N.

RESULTS AND DISCUSSION

Calibration Tests

Three fasteners were fabricated and calibrated for use in this investigation. Comparison of the shear strains at the two locations for the calibration tests showed up to 220 micro cm/cm strain difference at a maximum applied load of 4,500 N. Initial attempts at calibration of the fasteners at the higher torque levels resulted in poor repeatability and nonlinear load versus shear strain response. Also, torquing the fastener resulted in a residual shear strain in the fastener that was not removed when the applied torque was removed. This residual shear strain due to torquing the fastener was removed by the application of a slight negative torque to the fastener. Removal of the residual shear strain from the fastener was determined by observing the output from the strain gages and resulted in considerable improvement in the repeatability of the calibration data and a linear load versus shear strain response from the fasteners. This procedure for removing the residual shear strain in the fastener was followed for all the calibration, verification, and joint tests.

Typical calibration curves for one of the fasteners tightened finger tight and torqued to 5.6 and 11.3 N-m are shown in figure 6 where the applied load is shown as a function of the average shear strain at the two strain gage locations. The measured calibration data are given by the symbols and a linear least squares fit to the linear portion of data are given by the solid curves. A linear least squares fit to the data gives a slope of 11.67 N/micro cm/cm strain for the fastener installed finger tight and 11.05 and 11.24 N/micro cm/cm strain for the fastener torqued to 5.6 and 11.3 N-m, respectively. For the fasteners torqued to 5.6 and 11.3 N-m, there is a region at low applied load where changes in applied load produce very little change in measured strain. This lack of fastener response at low applied loads is due to friction between the faying surfaces in the calibration fixture which results in the load being transmitted primarily by friction between the faying surfaces of the plates and not by the fastener. For values of applied load above 400 N for the fastener torqued to 5.6 N-m and for values of applied load above 900 N for the fastener torqued to 11.3 N-m, the friction forces between the faying surfaces are constant and a linear least squares fit is a reasonable approximation to the applied load-strain relationship.

Slopes obtained from a linear least squares fit to repeated calibration curves are given in Table I for the three fasteners installed finger tight and those torqued to 5.6 and 11.3 N-m. The results in Table I show that repeated calibrations result in slopes that are within approximately $\pm$ 5 percent for the finger tight fasteners and within ± 8 percent for the torqued fasteners. Thus, some loss in repeatability of the calibration data is experienced when using the sensors in the torqued condition as compared with the finger tight condition. This loss of repeatability is probably associated with friction in the calibration fixture and the difficulty of obtaining consistent preloads on the fastener by using the fastener torque as a reference. Comparison of the calibration results for fastener number 1 at the three torque levels shows that the calibration constants are not highly dependant on the fastener torque level. This insensitivity of the calibration constants to the torque level suggests that it may be possible with better controlled calibration tests to obtain a calibration constant that is independent of the fastener torque level.

Verification Tests

Tests were conducted to verify that the instrumented fasteners could be used to measure the shear force transmitted by individual fasteners in an actual joint. The verification test setup shown in figure 4 allows two independent methods for verifying that the instrumented fasteners are giving correct values provided there is no friction in the joint. First the sum of the shear forces measured by the instrumented fasteners must be equal to the applied load. Second, the fastener loads calculated from the specimen strain gage measurements and the known properties of the aluminum plates must be equal to the shear force measured by the instrumented fasteners. If significant friction is present in the joint, as will be the case with the fasteners torqued to 5.6 and 11.3 N-m, the fastener loads calculated from the specimen strain gage measurements will include the fastener load and the load transmitted due to friction between the faying surfaces.

Typical results from the verification tests are given in figure 7 for the fasteners installed finger tight and in figures 8 and 9 for the fasteners torqued to 5.6 and 11.3 N-m, respectively. Measured loads are shown as a function of applied load. The individual fastener loads given by the instrumented fasteners (dashed lines) and calculated from the strain gages (solid lines) on the aluminum plates are indicated. The applied load (dotted line) is shown for comparison with the sum of the loads given by the instrumented fasteners (dashed line) and calculated from the strain gages (solid line). The individual fastener loads obtained from the strain gages on the aluminum plates were calculated as follows. For fastener number 1 (see figure 5), the fastener load is calculated from the strain gage data obtained from the two outside plates and the known properties and dimensions of the plates. For fastener number 2, the fastener load is calculated from the strain gage data obtained from the center plate and the known properties and dimensions of the plate.

Fastener Verification--Test results for the fasteners installed finger tight (see fig. 7) show good agreement between the shear forces measured by the individual instrumented fasteners and the shear forces calculated from the strain gages on the aluminum plates. Both the specimen strain gage data and the instrumented fastener data indicate that fastener number 1 carries more load than fastener number 2. The data from the instrumented fasteners show that fastener number 2 carries approximately 25 percent of the load as compared with 75 percent for fastener number 1. Theoretical results calculated for each fastener using a strength of materials approach are also shown on figure 7 at an applied load of 5,000 N. The points were calculated assuming that the strains between the two fasteners are equal in all three plates. The calculated points are in reasonably good agreement with the measured results and thus verify the measured results. There is also good agreement between the applied load and the sum of the shear loads obtained from the instrumented fasteners. The good agreement of the data verifies that the instrumented fasteners are valid instruments for measuring the shear forces transmitted by fasteners in a double splice joint.

Effects of Friction--Test results for the fasteners torqued to 5.6 and 11.3 N-m (see figs. 8 and 9) shows that torquing the fasteners introduces significant friction into the joint even with the faying surfaces polished and lubricated. The difference between the fastener loads calculated from the specimen strain gages and the instrumented fasteners highlights the differences. For low values of applied loads, friction in the joint accounts for a significant part of the joint load. For high values of applied load, the friction force between the faying surfaces become less dominant and fastener loads increase approximately linearly with the applied load. For an applied load of 6,000 N, approximately 18 percent of the joint load is carried by friction for the fasteners torqued to 5.6 N-m compared to 26 percent of the joint load for the fasteners torqued to 11.3 N-m. This increase in friction load with fastener torque level was expected.

The sum of the measured loads given by the strain gages are in good agreement with the applied load shown by the dotted line in figures 8 and 9. As was found for the finger tight fasteners, fastener number 1 carries more load than fastener number 2. However, for the joint with the fasteners torqued to 5.6 and 11.3 N-m, there is better sharing of the loads between fasteners 1 and 2 than was obtained for the finger tight joint. For the finger tight joint, fastener number 1 carried 3 times as much load as fastener number 2, whereas for the fasteners torqued to 5.6 and 11.3 N-m, fastener number 1 carried 2.5 and 2.0 times as much load, respectively as fastener number 2.

Joint Tests

Finger-Tight Fasteners--Test results obtained from the double splice joint with three fasteners installed finger tight are shown in figure 10. The measured shear load transmitted by each fastener and the sum of the fastener shear loads are shown as a function of the load applied to the joint. Fastener number 1 which is the single fastener, carries approximately 47 percent of the applied joint load. Fasteners 2 and 3 carry approximately 25 and 28 percent of the load, respectively. Theoretical results calculated for each fastener using a strength of materials approach and assuming that the strains between the fasteners are equal in the three plates are also shown on figure 10 at an applied load of 9,000 N. The theoretical fastener loads show that fastener number 1 carries 67 percent of the load and fasteners 2 and 3 each carry 16.5 percent of the load. The measured results show more sharing of the load between fasteners than given by the analysis. The sum of the measured shear loads transmitted by each of the fasteners is in good agreement (measured values are 5 percent higher than the applied load at 9,000 N applied load) with the applied joint load. This good agreement between the applied load and the sum of the measured shear loads indicates that the test technique is valid.

Torqued Fasteners--Test results obtained from the double splice joint with the fasteners torqued to 5.6 and 11.3 N-m, are shown in figures 11 and 12, respectively. The measured shear load transmitted by each fastener and the sum of the fastener shear loads are shown as a function of the load applied to the joint. For low values of applied load, most of the applied joint load is transmitted by friction between the faying surfaces of the plates and, as a result, the fasteners transmit very little load. As the applied load is increased, the fasteners start carrying a larger percentage of the applied load and the load transmitted by friction in the joint remains approximately constant.

For the fasteners torqued to 5.6 N-m (see figure 11) and an applied load of 9,000 N, approximately 87 percent of the applied joint load is transmitted by the fasteners. Increasing the fastener torque to 11.3 N-m (see figure 12) with an applied load of 9,000 N results in the fasteners transmitting approximately 83 percent of the applied load. Thus, as was noted for the aluminum joint with two fasteners, increasing the fastener torque level increases the load transmitted by friction in the joint. For the joint with the fasteners torqued to 5.6 and 11.3 N-m, fastener number 1 carries the largest load with fasteners 2 and 3 approximately equally sharing the remaining load. For both fastener torque levels, fastener number 3 carries approximately 3 percent more load than fastener number 2. This unequal sharing of the load may be due to a slight asymmetry in the joint configuration. Comparing the measured fastener loads for the fasteners installed finger tight (see figure 9) and torqued to 5.6 and 11.3 N-m (see figures 11 and 12) shows that for the three-fastener joint with the steel plates, increasing the torque level does not significantly change the distribution of loads between the various fasteners. This insensitivity of the load distribution between the fasteners to the fastener torque level is in contrast to the results shown for the two fastener joint with aluminum plates which showed a more uniform distribution of loads between the fasteners as the fastener torque was increased.

CONCLUDING REMARKS

A preliminary investigation has been conducted on instrumented fasteners for use as sensors to measure the shear loads transmitted by individual fasteners installed in double splice joints. Tests have been conducted for fasteners installed finger tight and installed at 5.6 and 11.3 N-m of torque. Results from calibration tests show that the shear strains obtained from the instrumented fasteners vary linearly with the applied load and that the instrumented fasteners can be used effectively to measure shear loads transmitted by individual fasteners in a double splice joint. The test results also show that for the fasteners installed with a torque greater than finger tight, care must be taken to ensure that there is no residual torsion in the fasteners when conducting calibration tests and making measurements in a joint.

Tests were also conducted with two instrumented fasteners installed in a double splice joint in aluminum plates and with three instrumented fasteners installed in a double splice joint in steel plates. The test results show that the load carried by the individual fasteners in a multiple fastener joint vary considerably depending on the location in the joint and the torque level of the fasteners. The fastener located near the end of the joint for the single plate carries more load than the fasteners located near the end of the joint for the two plates. Installing the fastener with a torque greater than finger tight results in a significant amount of the joint load being carried by friction between the faying surfaces of the plates in the joint even if the faying surfaces are polished and lubricated. Increasing the fastener torque increases the load carried by friction between the faying surfaces of the joint. Increasing the fastener torque also results in a more uniform distribution of the loads between the individual fasteners for joints in aluminum plates with two fasteners but does not have a significant effect for joints in steel plates with three fasteners.

Instrumented fasteners developed in this investigation can be used by researchers to develop a better understanding of how loads are distributed between fasteners in multifastener joints. For structural joints in advanced refractory composite materials that have relatively low strain-to-failure properties, understanding how the loads are distributed in joints will aid in the development of design criteria that are required for the structural application of these materials.

REFERENCES

1. Poon, C.: Literature Review on the Design of Mechanically Fastened Composite Joints. Published in Behavior and Analysis of Mechanically Fastened Joints in Composite Structures, AGARD-CP-427, April 1987.

TABLE I-CALIBRATION DATA FOR INSTRUMENTED FASTENERS.

FASTENER NUMBER	SLOPE OF CALIBRATION CURVE, N/MICRO cm/cm STRAIN				
	CALIBRATION TEST NUMBER			AVERAGE	PERCENT VARIATION
	1	2	3		
FASTENERS FINGER TIGHT					
1	12.38	11.67	11.35	11.80	-3.8, +5.0
2	12.76	11.92	11.67	12.11	-3.7, +5.3
3	12.26	12.29	11.72	12.08	-.2.9, +1.8
FASTENERS TORQUED TO 5.6 N-m					
1	11.05	11.05	11.19	11.10	-0.5, +0.8
2	9.95	10.43	10.64	10.34	-3.7, +2.9
3	10.18	10.73	9.54	10.14	-5.9, +5.8
FASTENERS TORQUED TO 11.3 N-m					
1	11.35	11.24	10.94	11.17	-2.1, +1.6
2	11.32	12.40	11.14	11.62	-4.1, +6.7
3	9.61	10.41	11.14	10.41	-7.6, +7.0

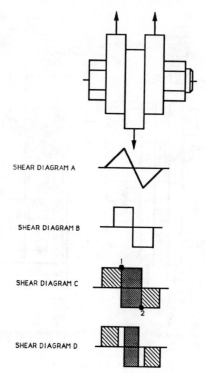

SHEAR DIAGRAM A

SHEAR DIAGRAM B

SHEAR DIAGRAM C

SHEAR DIAGRAM D

Figure 2.-Transverse shear load for instrumented fastener.

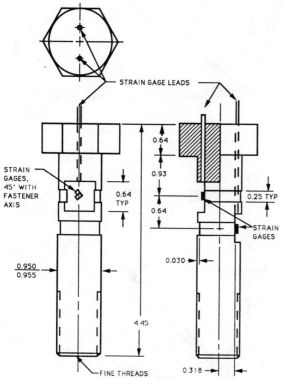

Figure 1.-Detailed description of instrumented fastener. Dimensions are given in centimeters.

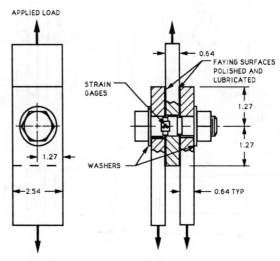

Figure 3.-Detailed description of double splice joint calibration fixture. Dimensions are given in centimeters.

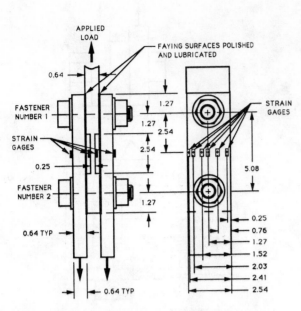

Figure 4.-Detailed Description of test fixture used for verification of instrumented fasteners. Dimensions are given in centimeters.

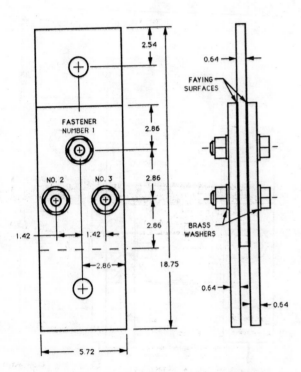

Figure 5.-Detailed description of double splice joint in steel plates. Dimensions are given in centimeters.

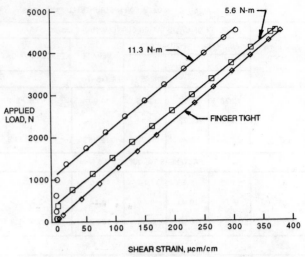

Figure 6.-Typical load calibration curves for instrumented fastener.

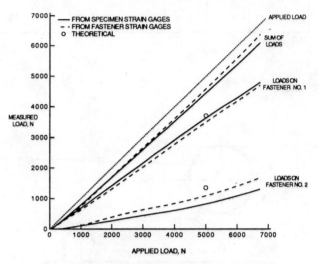

Figure 7.-Typical results from verification tests with fasteners installed finger tight.

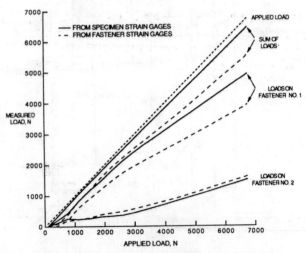

Figure 8.-Typical results from verification tests with fasteners installed with a torque of 5.6 N-m.

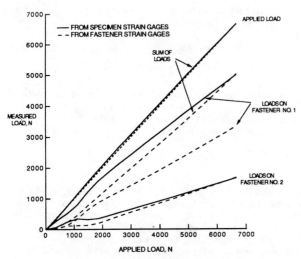

Figure 9.-Typical results from verification tests with fasteners installed with a torque of 11.3 N-m.

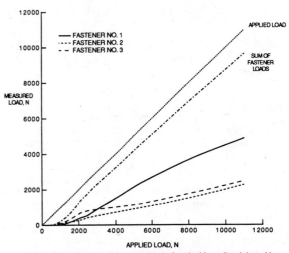

Figure 11.- Measured fastener loads for double splice joint with fasteners installed with a torque of 5.6 N-m.

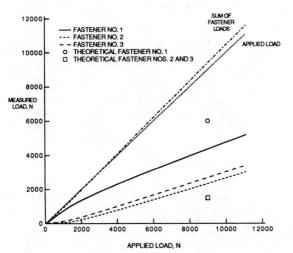

Figure 10.- Measured fastener loads for double splice joint with fasteners installed finger tight.

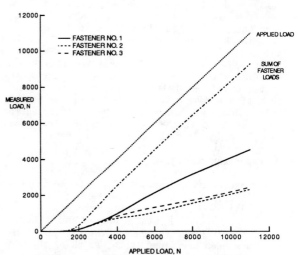

Figure 12.- Measured fastener loads for double splice joint with fasteners installed with a torque of 11.3 N-m.

On the Contact Stress in a Bolted Joint with a Tap Bolt

By Toshiyuki SAWA, Hiroyuki KUMANO and Tsuneshi MOROHOSHI

Abstract

The contact stress of a bolted joint, in which a hollow cylinder (clamped part) was fastened to a body (hollow cylinder) with a tap bolt, was measured by using sensitive pins and sensitive films and ultrasonic waves. The contact stress distribution was analyzed as a contact problem by an axisymmetrical theory of elasticity. The experimental results were compared with the analytical results. The characteristics of each method to measure the contact stress were discussed.

1. Introduction

The fastening with bolts has been usually used in the mechanical industry and in many other kinds of industries. Nowadays high strength bolts have come to be used in the architecture engineering, and a more strict design of bolted joints is demanded. Bolted joints such as cylinder heads, connecting rods and flange connections are subjected to repeated loads, therefore they are likely to be the source of rupture accidents and leakage accidents. From these viewpoints it is very important to examine the contact stress distribution and the load factor (the ratio of an increment of axial bolt force to an external load) in cylinder heads and flange connections of high pressure vessels fastened by bolts. The contact stress distribution at the interface of bolted joints has been investigated experimentally by Gould[1], Bradley[2] and Ito[3] and theoretically the analyses on a finite plate having a hole[4]-[6] and on a finite hollow cylinder[7][8] have been carried out by axisymmetrical theory of elasticity. However, these analyses dealt the case where a nut and bolt was used and clamped parts were symmetric. In addition, they regarded clamped parts as one body. The contact stress distribution in the case where a tap bolt is used has yet been sufficiently elucidated.

In this paper, the contact stress distribution of a bolted joint in an initial clamping state, in which a hollow cylinder (clamped part) is fastened to a cylindrical body with a tap bolt, is measured by using sensitive pins and sensitive films. In addition, the contact stress distribution of the joint is measured with the sensitive pins when an external load is applied to the joint. The contact stress distribution of the bolted joint included a metallic gasket is also measured by using ultrasonic waves and sensitive films. The load factor of the bolted joint is measured with strain gauges glued to the shank of bolt. Moreover, the contact stress distribution of a bolted joint with a tap bolt and the load factor are analyzed as a three-body contact problem by an axisymmetrical theory of elasticity. Numerical calculations are done and the experimental results are compared with the analytical results.

2. Experimental Method

2.1 Measurement of contact stress by means of sensitive pins

Figure 1(a) shows a bolted joint with a tap bolt. A hollow cylinder is fastened to a body by a tap bolt with an initial clamping force F_f. When an external load is applied to the joint, an increment of axial bolt force F_t is produced and a force F_c is eliminated from the contact surface as shown in Fig.1(b). In order to measure the contact stress distribution, sensitive pins shown in Fig.2 are used. Two strain gauges are glued to the shank of the pins. The strain gauges were previously calibrated. Figure 3 shows the experimental apparatus in which the clamped part is fastened with a tap bolt of M12 and an external load can be applied to this bolted joint. In the apparatus, the clamped part 6 is fastened to the body 7 with the tap bolt 1. After adjusting the position of the load application by the retaining ring 5, the frame 4 is attached. Since the inner face of the hollow cylinder 2 has internal threads, experiments can be carried out for various clamped parts by changing the frame. By three brims of the pedestal 3 the load is applied to the body 7 and the hollow cylinder 2. Putting a load cell on the frame 3 and applying a load to the apparatus by a material testing machine, the load is measured by the load cell. When a load is applied, an axial bolt force is measured by strain gauges attached to the shank of the bolt. Figure 4 shows the positions of five sensitive pins plugging into the body in which holes were drilled. Clamped parts are hollow cylinder and their inner diameter is 13 mm. The parts are prepared in three kinds of the dimensions for the outer diameter and the height, that is 52x26, 52x52 and 105x26 mm, respectively. In order to apply a load the outer circumference of the parts has external threads of M52x1.5 or M105x2. In order to improve the surface roughness, after finishing the surfaces of the body and the clamped parts by a surface grinder, the interfaces are finished by lapping. The flatness is obtained to about 6 μm for the body and 5 μm for the clamped parts. The surface roughness is about 0.6 μm R_{max}. After removing oil from the surfaces with acetone, experiments were carried out. Figure 5 shows the dimensions of tap bolt used in the experiments. The length L is varied as 48, 74, 58.5, 94.5, 89 and 115 mm in order to examine the effects of fastening positions on the contact stress distribution. Figure 6 shows the fastening positions of thread. The contact stress distribution is measured in three kinds of

T. SAWA is Associate Professor of Yamanashi university (4-3-11 Takeda, Kofu, Yamanashi, 400 Japan.)
H. KUMANO is Associate Prof. of Tokyo metropolitan institute of technology.
T.MOROHOSHI is an engineer of ASK Technica Co.,Ltd.(Japan)

fastening positions, that is, the upper, the middle and the lower.

2.2 Measurement of contact stress by means of ultrasonic waves

The contact stress distribution of a bolted joint with a metallic gasket was measured by using the ultrasonic waves based on the study by Ito[3]. Figure 7 shows an experimental setup. An ultrasonic transducer is set at the end surface of the body. The contact stress is measured at the distance r of 11.5, 13.5, 15.5, 17.5 and 20.0 mm. Figure 8 shows the dimensions of specimens. The clamped parts(hollow cylinders) were manufactured from steel for structural use (S45C, JIS) and the body from mild steel (SS41, JIS). The gaskets were manufactured from mild steel (SS41) and aluminum (A5056,JIS). The surface roughness R_{max} is 1.3 μm for the body, 1.1 μm for mild steel gasket and 0.6 μm for aluminum gasket. A relationship between a load and a reflected sonic pressure was previously calibrated.

2.3 Measurement of contact stress by means of sensitive films

The contact stresses are measured by using sensitive film (Fuji Film Co. Ltd., Prescale) in the cases of Figs.3 and 7.

2.4 Measurement of the load factor

When an external load W is applied to a bolted joint, an increment of axial bolt force F_t is produced as shown in Fig.1(b). The ratio F_t to W is named as the load factor. The value of the load factor is measured in the cases of Figs.3 and 7.

3. Theoretical Analysis

3.1 The contact stress

Figure 9 is a model for analysis. A clamped part is replaced with finite hollow cylinder [I] and its inner diameter and height are designated as $2a_1$ and $2h_1$, respectively. It is assumed that a compressive stress $P_0\{P_0=F_r/\pi(c^2-a_1^2)\}$ due to an initial clamping force F_r acts at the bearing surface ($a_1<r<c$). A gasket and a body are replaced with the finite hollow cylinders [II] and [III]. The inner diameter, the outer diameter and the height of hollow cylinders [II] and [III] are designated as $2a_1$, $2b_1$, $2h_1$, $2a_2$, $2b_2$ and $2h_3$, respectively. A shear stress $P_1\{P_1=F_r/2\pi a_2(h_3'-h_3'')\}$ due to the thread acts uniformly at the inner circumference of hollow cylinder [III] ($r=a_2, h_3<z<h_3'$). Expanding the stress at the bearing surface and the shear stress at the thread into a series of Bessel functions $C_0(\gamma_s r)$ and Fourier series, respectively, the boundary conditions are expressed by Eq.(1), where the shear stresses produced at the contact surfaces are neglected.

on the hollow cylinder [I](clamped part)

$r=a_1, b_1: \sigma_r=\tau_{rz}=0$

$z=h_1: \sigma_z=e_0+\sum_{s=1}^{\infty} e_s C_0(\gamma_s r), \tau_{rz}=0$

$z=-h_1: \tau_{rz}=0$

on the hollow cylinder [III](body)

$r=a_2: \sigma_r=0$

$\tau_{rz}=\dfrac{(h_3'-h_3'')}{2h_3}P_1$

$+\sum_{n=1}^{\infty}\{G_n\cos(n\pi/(h_3)z)+M_n\sin(n\pi/(h_3)z)\}$

$r=b_2: \sigma_r=\tau_{rz}=0$

$z=-h_3: \sigma_r=\tau_{rz}=0$

$z=h_3: \tau_{rz}=0$

on the hollow cylinder [II](gasket)

$r=a_1, b_1: \sigma_r=\tau_{rz}=0$

$z=\pm h_2: \tau_{rz}=0$

at the contact surface between [I] and [II]

$\left(\dfrac{\partial w}{\partial r}\right)_{z=-h_1}=\left(\dfrac{\partial w}{\partial r}\right)_{z=h_2}$

$(\sigma_z)_{z=-h_1}=(\sigma_z)_{z=h_2}$

at the contact surface between [II] and [III]

$\left(\dfrac{\partial w}{\partial r}\right)_{z=-h_2}=\left(\dfrac{\partial w}{\partial r}\right)_{z=h_3}$

$(\sigma_z)_{z=-h_2}=(\sigma_z)_{z=h_3}$

$\cdots\cdots(1)$

where

$e_0=-(c^2-a_1^2)P_0/(b_1^2-a_1^2)$

$e_s=\dfrac{-2P_0cC_1(\gamma_s c)}{\gamma_s\{b_1^2C_0^2(\gamma_s b_1)-a_1^2C_0^2(\gamma_s a_1)\}}$

$G_n=-P_1/(n\pi)\{\sin(n\pi h_3'/h_3)-\sin(n\pi h_3''/h_3)\}$

$M_n=P_1/(n\pi)\{\cos(n\pi h_3'/h_3)-\cos(n\pi h_3''/h_3)\}$ $n, s=1, 2, 3, \cdots\cdots\cdots$

In order to analyze each finite hollow cylinder [I], [II] and [III] under the boundary conditions (1), Michelle's stress functions are used.

3.2 The load factor

The load factor (the ratio of F_t to W) is obtained from the following equation, where K_t is the spring constant for a bolt, K_{cg} is the compressive spring constant for a clamped part and K_{pg} the tensile spring constant for the clamped part with a gasket.

$$\Phi_g=\frac{F_t}{W}=\frac{K_t}{K_t+K_{cg}}\left(\frac{K_{cg}}{K_{pg}}\right) \dots\dots\dots\dots\dots\dots\dots\dots\dots\dots\dots\dots\dots\dots(2)$$

The value of K_{cg} is obtained from the equation $K_{cg}=(F_r+F_t)/(\varepsilon_1+\varepsilon_2)$ using the mean displacement at the bearing surface ε_1 and ε_2 the displacement at the middle point in the fastening position ε_2 shown in Fig.10(a). The value K_{pg} is obtained from the equation $K_{pg}=W/(\varepsilon_1'+\varepsilon_2')$ using the mean displacement at the bearing surface ε_1' and the displacement ε_2' at the middle point of fastening position shown in Fig.10(b). The value K_b is obtained by the equation $K_b=(F_f+F_t)/(\varepsilon_b+\varepsilon_b')$ using the displacements shown in Fig.10(c). The analyses are carried out in the same way mentioned in Sec. 3.1.

4. Comparisons between experimental and analytical results

4.1 The contact stress distribution
Numerical calculations were done using the dimensions of the specimens used in the experiments. Figure 11 shows the comparisons among the measured values obtained by sensitive films and sensitive pins and the analytical results concerning the contact stress in the case of Fig.3. From the results, it is seen that the contact stress obtained by sensitive film tends to be uniform. The measured results obtained by sensitive pins are fairly consistent with the analytical results. However, it is difficult to measure the contact stress at many points by sensitive pins because the stiffness will be decreased. In the case of Fig.11 (c), it is noticed that a separation causes near the outer circumference of the contact surface. Figure 12 shows changes of the contact stress when loads are applied to bolted joints. In Fig.12 (a) and (b), the contact surface is completely in contact in the initial clamping, therefore the contact stress decreases linearly with the load application. When a separation is caused at a part of the contact surface the contact stress decreases along a curved line. In the case of Fig.12(c), a separation is caused at a part of the contact surface in the initial clamping.
Figure 13 shows the comparisons among the measured results obtained by ultrasonic waves and sensitive films and the analytical results. It is seen that the measured results are in fairly good agreement with the analytical ones. In addition, it is seen that the measured results obtained by sensitive film tend to be uniform in the case where mild steel gasket is used, because the sensitive films have the stiffness. However, they are consistent with the analytical results in the case where aluminum gasket is used.

4.2 The load factor
Figure 14 shows the comparisons of the load factor. Figure 14 (a) is the case where no gasket is used. Figure 14 (b) is the case where gasket is used. The value F_t slightly increases linearly with an application of load and after a separation of the contact surface is caused, F_t increases in a curve. Then, when the interface is completely separated, it becomes a straight line having a slope of 45 degrees. Namely, at this moment the load W is equivalent to the increment of the axial bolt force F_t. The load factor is defined by the incline of the initial line and this value is nearly constant and independent of an initial clamping force. The numerical values are expressed by the dotted lines. In the case of Fig.14(a), the value of the load factor obtained by the experiment is 0.0125 and the analytical result of the load factor is 0.0127. They show in fairly good agreement. In the case where a gasket is used, the experimental results are consistent with the analytical results. Table 1 shows the effects of the dimensions and the fastening positions and the stiffness ratio on the values of the load factor.

5. Conclusions

This paper dealt with the contact stress and the load factor in a bolted joint, in which a clamped part (hollow cylinder) is fastened to a cylindrical body with a tap bolt. The following results were obtained.
(1) The contact stress in initial clamping was measured by sensitive pins, ultrasonic waves and sensitive films. In addition, the contact stress was measured by sensitive pins when a load is applied to a bolted joint.
(2) When a load is applied to a bolted joint, the load factor was measured with strain gauges glued to the shank of tap bolt.
(3) The contact stress and the load factor were analyzed as a three-body contact problem using axisymmetrical theory of elasticity. It was shown that the experimental results of the contact stress were consistent with the analytical results.
(4) From the experimental results, it was seen that the contact stress obtained by sensitive films tends to be uniform because of the stiffness of the sensitive films.

References

(1) Gould, H. H. et al., Trans. ASME, Ser B, **94**-3(1972), 864.
(2) Bradly, T. L. et al., Trans. ASME, Ser E, **38**-2(1971), 452.
(3) Ito, M. et al., Trans. ASME, Ser D, **101**-4(1979), 330.
(4) Mitsunaga, K., Jour. Trans. Japan Soc. Mech. Engs., (in Japanese), **31**-23(1965), 1750.
(5) Fernlund, I., Konstruktion, **22**-6(1970), 218.
(7) Motosh, N., Trans. ASME, Ser B, **97**-1(1975), 157.
(8) Shibahara M. and Oda, J., Jour. JSME. (in Japanese), **72**-611(1969), 9.
(9) Sawa, T. et al., Bull. of JSME, **27**-228(1984), 1085.

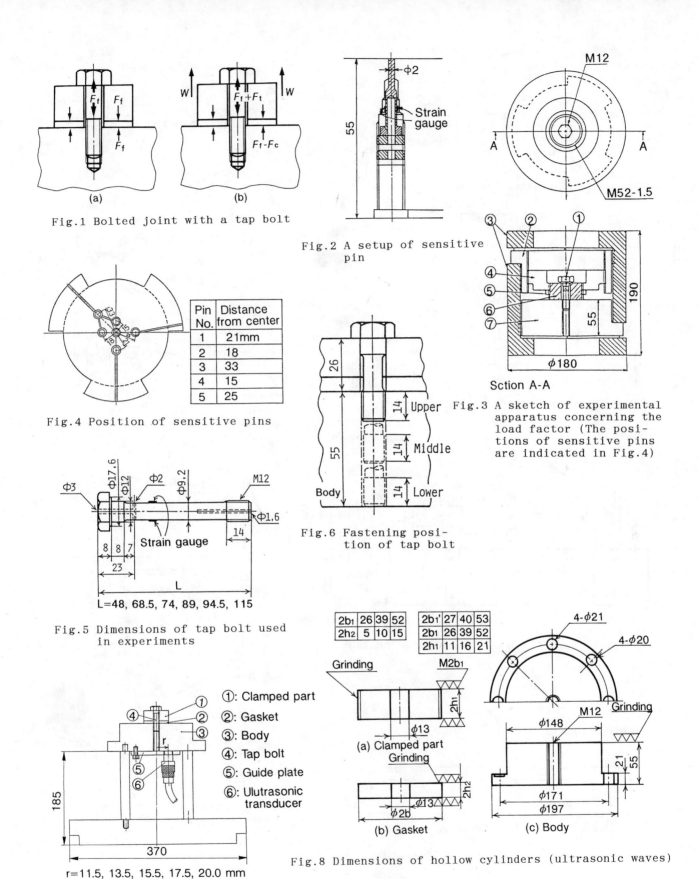

Fig.1 Bolted joint with a tap bolt

Fig.2 A setup of sensitive pin

Fig.4 Position of sensitive pins

Pin No.	Distance from center
1	21mm
2	18
3	33
4	15
5	25

Sction A-A

Fig.3 A sketch of experimental apparatus concerning the load factor (The positions of sensitive pins are indicated in Fig.4)

Fig.6 Fastening position of tap bolt

Fig.5 Dimensions of tap bolt used in experiments

L=48, 68.5, 74, 89, 94.5, 115

①: Clamped part
②: Gasket
③: Body
④: Tap bolt
⑤: Guide plate
⑥: Ulutrasonic transducer

r=11.5, 13.5, 15.5, 17.5, 20.0 mm

Fig.7 Sketch of experimental apparatus by means of ultrasonic waves

2b₁	26	39	52
2h₂	5	10	15

2b₁'	27	40	53
2b₁	26	39	52
2h₁	11	16	21

(a) Clamped part

(b) Gasket

(c) Body

Fig.8 Dimensions of hollow cylinders (ultrasonic waves)

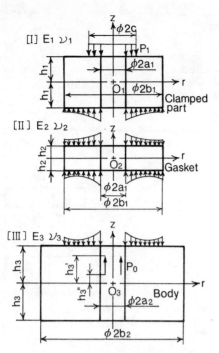

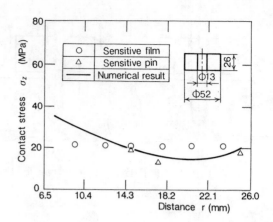

(a) $a_1=6.5$, $b_1=26$, $h_1=13$ mm

Fig.9 Model for analysis

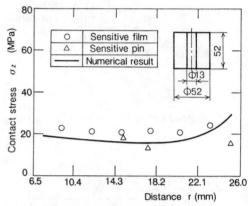

(b) $a_1=6.5$, $b_1=26$, $h_1=26$ mm

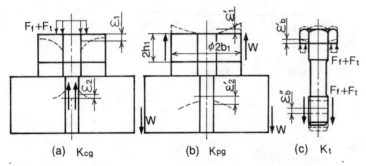

Fig.10 Definition of each spring constant

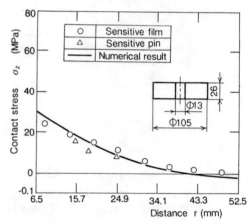

(c) $a_1=6.5$, $b_1=52.5$, $h_1=13$ mm

Fig.11 Comparisons between experimental
and analytical results
(in the case of the lower fastenig)

Table 1 Effects of some factors on the
load factor

No.	1	2	3	4	5	6	7
a_1				6.5			
b_1	13.0			19.5	26.0		
h_1	8.0						13.0
h_2	5.0						0.0
E_1/E_2	3	3	1	3	3	3	—
F,P,B	L	U	L	L	L	U	U
$\bar{\Phi}_g$ Exp	0.10	0.16	0.07	0.05	0.03	0.05	0.01
$\bar{\Phi}_g$ Num	0.120	0.185	0.081	0.056	0.036	0.052	0.013

F.P.B; Fastening position of bolt thread
U; Upper   L; Lower

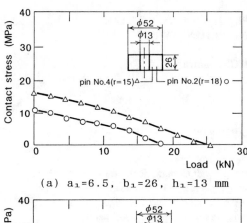

(a) $a_1=6.5$, $b_1=26$, $h_1=13$ mm

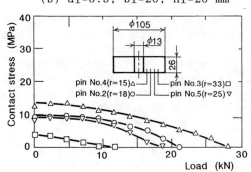

(b) $a_1=6.5$, $b_1=26$, $h_1=26$ mm

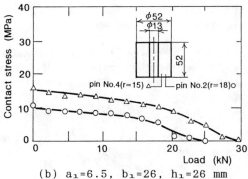

(c) $a_1=6.5$, $b_1=52.5$, $h_1=13$ mm

Fig.12 Changes in contact stress when load is applied (Initial clamping force is 29.4 kN and the fastening position is the lower)

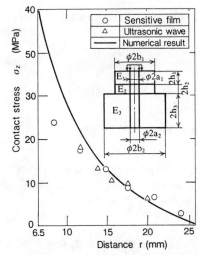

(a) the case where gasket is mild steel

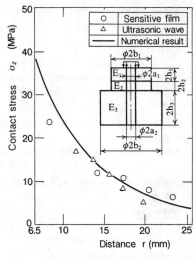

(b) the case where gasket is aluminum

Fig.13 Comparisons between experimental and numerical results concerning contact stress(case of $2a_1=13$, $2b_1=52$, $2a_2=12$, $2b_2=148$, $2h_1=16$, $2h_2=10$, $2h_3=55$, $F_f=20$kN and the lower fastening)

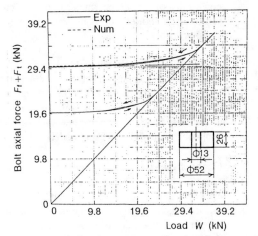

(a) the upper fastening

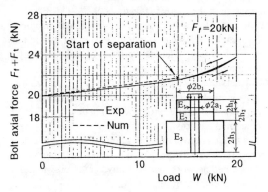

(b) the lower fastening ($2a_1=13$, $2b_1=52$, $2a_2=12$, $2b_2=148$, $2h_1=16$, $2h_2=10$, $2h_3=55$ mm)

Fig.14 Comparisons concerning the load factor

PARAMETER OPTIMIZATION OF VISCOPLASTIC CONSTITUTIVE EQUATION USING HIERARCHICAL NEURAL NETWORK

S. Yoshimura, H. Hishida and G. Yagawa

ABSTRACT

This paper describes a new method for optimizing multiple parameters of a viscoplastic constitutive equation using the hierarchical neural network.

At first, various behaviors of material under cyclic loading or creep conditions are obtained numerically for many combinations of the parameters of an inelastic constitutive equation. Each piecewise relation between the material behaviors and these parameters is called here "learning pattern". Next, the hierarchical neural network is trained using the learning patterns obtained, so that using the trained neural network, one can estimate the parameters optimized for real material behaviors measured in experiments.

To demonstrate the performance of the present method, it is applied to the parameter optimization of the Chaboche's viscoplastic model under uniaxial loading and stationary temperature conditions. Experimental data referred are cyclic hysteresis curves of about 60 cycles and a stress relaxation curve. The results clearly show that the present method is a powerful tool for the parameter optimization of a practical viscoplastic model, referring various material behaviors simultaneously.

INTRODUCTION

In various industrial fields, structural materials are often used under severe operating conditions such as cyclic loading, high temperature, high pressure and high irradiation. For the reliable evaluation of deformation behaviors of these materials, thermo-inelastic analyses are inevitable [1,2]. Various theoretical models to describe a wide range of viscoplastic behaviors of metallic materials have been proposed and studied by many researchers [3-15]. The viscoplastic constitutive equations derived from these theories involve many parameters, which greatly influence behaviors of the constitutive equations. Therefore, these parameters are requested to determine appropriately referring real behaviors of materials, i.e. cyclic loading tests, stress relaxation tests, and so on. Every constitutive equation has its own method for parameter determination, i.e. algebraic methods, least-square methods, and so on. However, these methods are not so good at optimizing the parameters referring various material behaviors simultaneously. This situation makes it difficult to fairly compare different inelastic constitutive equations.

Recently, the hierarchical neural networks have attracted notice because of the following features [16-22].

(1) One can automatically construct a nonlinear mapping from multiple input data to multiple output data in the network through a learning process of some or many learning patterns.

(2) The network has a feature of so-called "generalization", i.e. a kind of interpolation, that the trained neural network estimates appropriate output data even for unlearned patterns.

(3) The trained network operates quickly in an application process. The CPU power required for the operation of the trained network may be equivalent to only that of a personal computer.

The present paper describes a new method for optimizing multiple parameters of a viscoplastic constitutive equation using the hierarchical neural network.

At first, various behaviors of material under cyclic loading or creep conditions are obtained numerically for many combinations of the parameters of a constitutive equation . Each piecewise relation between the material behaviors and these parameters is called here "learning pattern". Next, the hierarchical neural network is trained using the learning patterns obtained, so that using the trained neural network, one can estimate parameters optimized for real material behaviors measured in experiments.

To demonstrate the performance of the present method, it is applied to the parameter optimization of the Chaboche's viscoplastic model under uniaxial loading and stationary temperature conditions. Experimental data referred are cyclic hysteresis curves of about 60 cycles and a stress relaxation curve. The results clearly show that the present method is a powerful tool for the parameter optimization of a practical viscoplastic model, referring various material behaviors simultaneously.

DEFINITION OF PROBLEM

To simplify the explanation of the present method without any loss of generality, we consider the Chaboche's viscoplastic theory in uniaxial loading and stationary temperature conditions. It should be noted here that the present method is applicable to any viscoplastic models.

Chaboche's Viscoplastic Theory [1, 9, 12]

The Chaboche's viscoplastic model is capable of describing cyclic hardening and softening behaviors with the yielding surface. Its formulation under uniaxial loading and stationary temperature conditions is given as follows :

S. Yoshimura is Associate Professor, H. Hishida a graduate student and G. Yagawa Professor in the Department of Nuclear Engineering, University of Tokyo, 7-3-1 Hongo, Bunkyo-ku, Tokyo 113, Japan.

$$F(\sigma, Y, R) = |\sigma - Y| - R \qquad (1a)$$

$$\varepsilon^P = \Lambda(\sigma - Y) / |\sigma - Y| \qquad (1b)$$

$$\Lambda = \begin{cases} (F/K)^n & , F > 0 \\ 0 & , F \leq 0 \end{cases} \qquad (1c)$$

$$Y = H\varepsilon^P - DY|\varepsilon^P| \qquad (1d)$$

$$R = (h - dR)|\varepsilon^P| \qquad (1e)$$

where state variables σ, ε^P, Y and R are the uniaxial stress, the uniaxial inelastic strain, the uniaxial back stress and the isotropic hardening variable, respectively. The initial value of R is taken to be k. Equation (1a) is the yield function, equations (1b) and (1c) the flow law, equation (1d) the cyclic hardening behavior of material, and equation (1e) the cyclic softening behavior, respectively.

Equation (1) involves seven parameters, i.e. K, n, H, D, h, d and k, which are determined so that equation (1) approximates well real viscoplastic behaviors of material. It should be noted here that all the parameters are assumed to be temperature-independent although they aren't in a general case.

Reference Material Behaviors

In the present study, the following four kinds of material behaviors are referred to optimize the seven parameters of the Chaboche's viscoplastic model :

(1) Tensile behavior
(2) Cyclic hysteresis behavior
(3) Cyclic strain hardening behavior
(4) Stress relaxation behavior

These data are obtained from a cyclic loading test and the subsequent strain-holding test under uniaxial loading and stationary temperature conditions as shown in figure 1. Temperature is set to be 200 ℃. In the cyclic test, strain range

and strain rate are fixed to be 0.4 % and 2.0×10^{-4} sec^{-1}, respectively, while strain is maintained at 0.2% in the strain-holding test. The number of cycles is above 60, and the hold time is over one hour. These conditions are chosen to achieve saturation of strain hardening and stress relaxation behaviors. These tests are performed on three specimens made of Type 316L stainless steel.

In conventional curve fitting approaches, the parameters of viscoplastic models are determined through the curve fitting process of the above behaviors one by one. These approaches are not good at optimizing all the parameters so that the viscoplastic model can approximate all the material behaviors well.

PARAMETER OPTIMIZATION USING NEURAL NETWORK

Network Architecture

Figure 2 shows a processing unit of the neural network which has multipe input and one output data. The relation between the input and the output data is formulated as follows [16, 17]:

$$O_j = f(U_j) = 1 / \{1 + \exp(-2U_j / U_o)\} \qquad (2)$$

$$U_j = \sum_{i=1}^{l} W_{ji} \cdot I_i - \theta_j \qquad (3)$$

where O_j is the output of the j-th unit, U_j the weighted input to the j-th unit, f the activation function, i.e. the sigmoid function here, U_o the temperature constant, W_{ji} the connection weight between the i-th and the j-th units, I_i the input from the i-th unit, θ_j the bais of the j-th unit, and l the number of input data.

The hierarchical neural network consists of multiple layers, each of which posesses a number of processing units. The basic idea of training the network is as follows. At first the following error E is defined :

$$E = E_p = 1/(2n) \sum_{k=1}^{n} (T_{pk} - O_{pk})^2 \qquad (4)$$

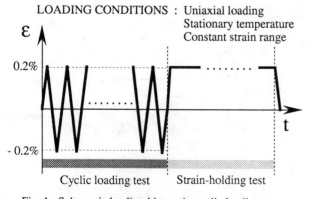

Fig. 1 : Schematic loading history in cyclic loading test and subsequent strain-holding test

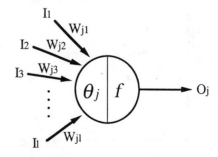

Fig. 2 : Single processing unit of neural network

where E p is the error for the p-th learning pattern, Tpk the teaching data corresponding to the k-th unit for the p-th learning pattern, Opk the output from the k-th unit for the p-th learning pattern, and n the number of learning patterns. In the training process, the connection weights Wji and the bais values θ j are modified iteratively based on the steepest gradient method to minimize the above error. Through the training, the network attains the ability of outputting the similar data to the teaching data. This training algorithm is called the back propagation [16, 17].

It is theoretically proven that the hierarchical neural network can approximate any kinds of continuous mappings [18]. However, the method has some limitation in reality because the number of available units is limited from a computational viewpoint.

Training Procedure

The basic principle of the present method is as follows. We utilize the simulation program of the Chaboche's viscoplastic model, i.e. equation (1), which can calculate material behaviors for a given parameter set of (K, n, H, D, h, d and k). By changing the combination of the seven parameters, we calculate the four kinds of material behaviors described previously. Figure 3(a) and 3(b) show the schematic view of cyclic hysteresis curve and that of stress relaxation curve, respectively. The obtained relationship between the parameter set and the calculated material behaviors are called the "learning pattern". We train the neural network to learn a number of learning patterns. After the error of equation (4) becomes sufficiently small, it is expected that the trained network approximates well the continuous relationship between the parameter set and the material behaviors. In the training process, the parameter set is given to the network as teaching data, while the material behaviors are given to it as input values as shown in figure 4. Here each material behavior is discretized into piecewise stress values as shown in figure 3. If real material behaviors such as cyclic hysteresis curve and stress relaxation curve are given to the trained network as input data, the network outputs the corresponding parameter set.

The input data employed here are as follows :
(1) Stress values at every strain interval of 0.01% from the yielding point on the tensile curve (8 values).
(2) Stress values at every strain interval of 0.02% from the minimum hysteresis tip to the maximum hysteresis tip on the 60-th cyclic curve (21 values).
(3) Maximum stress values at the hysteresis tip of the 1st, 2nd, 3rd, 6-th, 10-th, 20-th, 30-th and 60-th cycles on the cyclic strain hardening curve (7 values). It should be noted that the value of the 60-th cycle is already taken into account in (2).
(4) Stress values at 0, 1, 2, 3, 4, 5, 10, 20, 30 and 60 seconds in the stress relaxation curve (10 values).

The original values of the input data are sometimes not so sensitive to the variation of parameters to be optimized. This situation may result in less accuracy of parameter optimization. To improve accuracy of the method, the original values of the input data are modified so as to be more sensitive to the variation of the parameters. All the input data are taken to be the deviation of the original values from those corresponding to the parameter set of (K = 1.00 x 10^2, n = 3.5, H = 1.50 x 10^5, D = 1.50 x 10^3, h' = 1.20 x 10^2, d = 3.5, k = 8.00 x 10, which is taken from the the center point of the training ranges of parameters. The values of the input data are transformed into the range from - 0.5 to + 0.5 in the present study.

Table 1 shows the training range and the number of sampling points of the seven parameters. These ranges are roughly

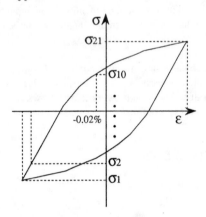

Fig. 3(a) : Schematic view of cyclic hysteresis curve

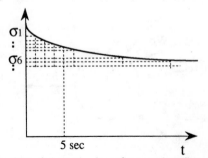

Fig. 3(b) : Schematic view of stress relaxation curve

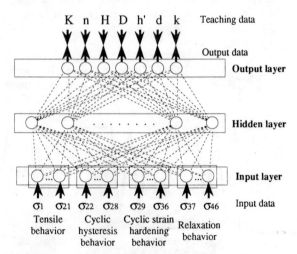

Fig. 4 : Architecture of the neural network used and the input / output data for parameter optimization

determined based on a conventional curve fitting method. In the table, h' is defined to be (h/d - k) for the purpose of convenience of training. Each training range is set to include possible parameter values.

Sampling points are usually chosen inside the training ranges at the regular interval. If sampling points are not chosen properly, the neural network would not learn well throughout the training ranges. The more sampling points are chosen, the more accurate results can be obtained, while the longer training time is required. In the present study, seven sampling points are chosen in each training range. The number of all the combinations of the seven parameters with seven sampling points becomes $7^7 = 823,544$. This is too many to prepare learning patterns and to train the network. To shorten these processes, 98 combinations are carefully selected considering the close relations between some parameters, that is, K and n are related to the flow law, H and D are related to the kinematic hardening behavior, and d and h are related to the isotropic hardening.

In general, it would take much calculation time for the preparation of the learning patters for all the combinations of the seven parameters. However, one can reduce significantly the effort on the preparation process because of the feature of generalization of the neural network.

RESULTS AND DISCUSSIONS

Table 2 summarizes the examined four cases, in which different material behaviors are referred to optimize the seven parameters of the Chaboche's viscoplastic model. For example, case 1 refers only the cyclic hysteresis behavior,

while case 4 does four kinds of material behaviors. Table 3 tabulates the parameter sets corresponding to cases 1 - 4 obtained with the present method. Table 4 also summarizes the configuration of the network used and the training conditions.

Figure 5(a) shows the comparison of experimental and estimated curves of cyclic hysteresis behaviors in case 1, while figure 5(b) does that of case 4. It is clearly shown from the figures that case 1 and case 4 give almost similar estimation curves as for cyclic hysteresis curve. Case 4 may be slightly less accurate than case 1 as for the cyclic hysteresis curve. Figures 6, 7 and 8 show the similar comparison of tensile curves, that of cyclic strain hardening curves, and that of stress relaxation curves, respectively. It can be seen from the comparison of figures 6, 7 and 8 that case 4 gives much better estimation for these three behaviors than case 1. The similar observation can be drawn from the comparison among cases 1 to 4. These results of case 4 are obtained due to the simultaneous reference of four kinds of material behaviors.

CONCLUDING REMARKS

The present study proposes the new parameter optimization technique of inelastic constitutive equations, refering various material behaviors simultaneously. This method is successfully applied to optimize the seven parameters of the Chaboche's viscoplastic model referring four kinds of material behaviors. It is expected that this method will become a powerful tool for fair comparison among different inelastic constitutive equations.

ACKNOWLEDGMENT

This work was financially supported by the Japan Atomic Power Company.

Table 1 : Parameter ranges and sampling numbers for network training

Parameter	K	n	H	D
Range	$0.5 \sim 1.5$ $\times 10^2$	$1.0 \sim 6.0$	$0.5 \sim 2.5$ $\times 10^5$	$0.5 \sim 2.5$ $\times 10^3$
Samples	7	7	7	7
Parameter	h' (= h/d-k)	d	k	
Range	$0.7 \sim 1.7$ $\times 10^2$	$1.0 \sim 6.0$	$0.4 \sim 1.2$ $\times 10^2$	
Samples	7	7	7	

Table 2 : Material behaviors referred for parameter optimization

Behavior / Case	Tensile	Cyclic hysteresis	Cyclic strain hardening	Stress Relaxation
1	-	◯	-	-
2	-	◯	◯	-
3	◯	◯	◯	-
4	◯	◯	◯	◯

Table 3 : Optimized parameter sets

Parameter / Case	K ($\times 10^2$)	n	H ($\times 10^5$)	D ($\times 10^3$)	h' (h/d-k) ($\times 10^2$)	d	k ($\times 10^2$)
1	1.18	4.61	1.18	1.27	2.60	1.97	1.03
2	1.13	4.63	1.35	1.34	0.94	1.67	1.08
3	0.94	4.18	1.51	1.72	1.52	1.29	1.20
4	1.02	3.76	1.34	1.39	1.85	1.38	1.22

Table 4 : Conditions of network training

Case	No. of learning patterns	No. of Units				No. of learning iterations
		Input layer	Hidden layer	Output layer	Total	
1	98	21	60	7	88	4,800
2	98	28	60	7	95	6,200
3	98	36	60	7	103	8,300
4	98	46	60	7	107	12,000

Note 1 : The same sigmoid function was employed in all cases.
Note 2 : Criterion for network training was : the error < 0.1%.

REFERENCES

1. Chiu, S. S., Eftis, J. and Lones, D. L. "Prediction of fatigue life with and without hold times using the Chaboche viscoplastic constitutive theory". Trans. ASME, J. Engng. Mater. and Tech., 112, 188, 1990.

2. Hishida, H., Diegele, E., Schinke, B. and Yagawa, G. "Parameter evaluation of Chaboche's viscoplastic constitutive equations to predict thermal fatigue of SS 316L SPH for fusion reactor first wall design". Nucl. Engng and Des., To be Submitted.

3. Perzyna, P., The constitutive equations for rate sensitive plastic materials". Q. All. Math., 20, 321, 1963.

4. Phillips, A. and Wu, H. C. "A theory of viscoplasticity". Int. J. Solids and Struc., 9, 15, 1973.

5. Bodner, S. R. and Partom, Y. "Constitutive equations for elastic-viscoplastic strain hardening materials". Trans. ASME, J. Appl. Mech., 42, 385, 1975.

6. Valanis, K. C. "On the foundations of the Endochronic theory of viscoplasticity". Arch. of Mech., 27, 857, 1975.

7. Robinson, D. N. "A unified creep-plasticity model for structural metals at high temperatures". ORN - TM- 5969, 1978.

8. Liu, M. C. and Krempl, E. "A uniaxial viscoplastic model based on total strain and overstress". J. Mech. Phys. Solids, 27, 377, 1979.

9. Chaboche, J. L. and Rousselier, G. "On the plastic and viscoplastic equations". Trans. ASME, J. Press. Vess. Tech., 105, 153, 1983.

10. Watanabe, O. and Atluri, S. N. "Internal time, general internal variable, and multi-yield-surface-theories of plasticity and creep". Int. J. Plasticity, 2, 37, 1986.

11. Yoshimura, S., Chen, K. L. and Atluri, S. N. "A study of two alternate tangent modulus formulations and attendant implicit algorithms for creep as well as high-strain-rate plasticity". Int. J. Plasticity, 3, 391, 1987.

12. Chaboche, J. L. "Constitutive equations for cyclic plasticity and cyclic viscoplasticity". Int. J. Plasticity, 5, 247, 1989.

13. Inoue, T. and Imatani, S. "A unified inelastic constitutive equation in terms of anisotropic yield function". Trans. 10th Int. Conf. Struc. Mech. in Reactor Tech., Anaheim, USA, L, 1, 1989.

14. Ohno, N. "Recent topics in constitutive modeling of cyclic plasticity and viscoplasticity, Appl. Mech. Rev., 43, 283, 1990.

15. Asada, Y., Okamoto, Y. and Hashimoto, T. "Creep-fatigue evaluation based on the overstress". Trans. ASME, J. Press. Vess. Tech., 113, 187, 1991.

16. Rumelhart, D. E., McClelland, J. L. and the PDP Research Group "Parallel distributed processing : Explorations in the microstructure of cognition". MIT Press, Cambridge, MA, 1986.

17. Rumelhart, D. E., Hinton, G. E. and Williams, R. J. "Learning representations by back propagation errors". Nature, 323, 533, 1986.

18. Funabashi, K. "On the approximate realization of continuous mappings by neural networks". Neural Networks, 2, 183, 1989.

19. Mochozuki, Y., Yagawa, G. and Yoshimura, S. "Inverse analysis by means of the combination of multilayered neural network and computational mechanics : Study on learning and estimating processes and its application to defect identification, Trans. JSME, 57A, 1922, 1991 (in Japanese).

20. Hajela, P. and Berke, L. "Neurobiological computational models in structural analysis and design". Comp. & Struc., 41, 657, 1991.

21. Wu, X., Ghaboussi, J. and Garrett, J. H. "Use of neural networks in detection of structural damage". Comp. & Struc., 42, 649, 1992.

22. Yoshimura, S., Yagawa, G., Toyonaga, K., Ohishi, T. and Mochizuki, Y. "Structure identification by means of the combination of neural network and computational mechanics : its application to one-dimensional beam, Trans. JSME, 58C, 1992, To be Published (in Japanese).

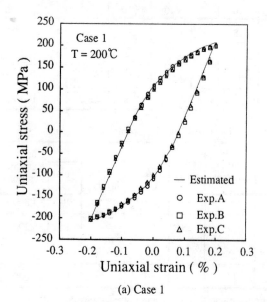

(a) Case 1

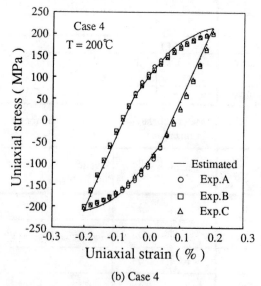

(b) Case 4

Fig. 5 : Comparison between experimental and estimated cyclic hysteresis behaviors

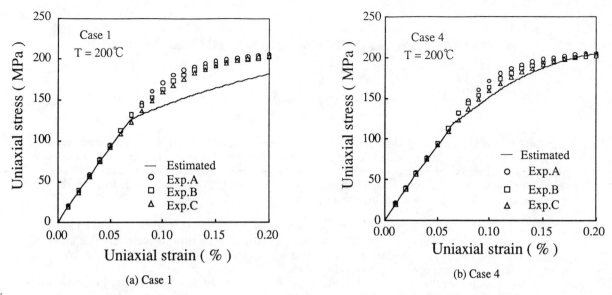

(a) Case 1

(b) Case 4

Fig. 6 : Comparison between experimental and estimated tensile behaviors

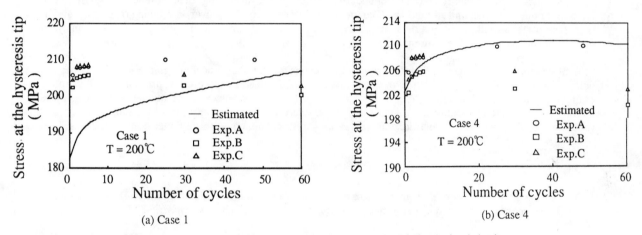

(a) Case 1

(b) Case 4

Fig. 7 : Comparison between experimental and estimated strain hardening behaviors

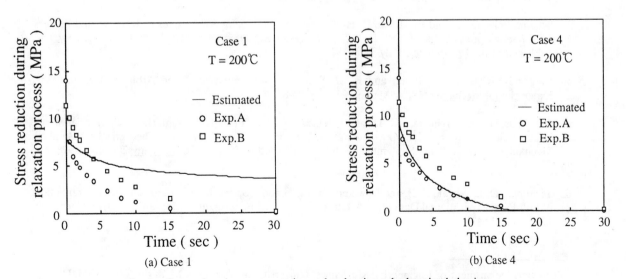

(a) Case 1

(b) Case 4

Fig. 8 : Comparison between experimental and estimated relaxation behaviors

HYBRID EXPERIMENTAL, THEORETICAL AND NUMERICAL ANALYSES

by

R. E. Rowlands[*]

Experimental techniques can be used to solve problems which are intractable theoretically or numerically, identify important unpredicted features, and guide theoretical or numerical analyses. However, they necessitate an existing physical component or model. Theoretical and/or numerical solutions are convenient for parametric studies and for conducting conceptual designs or analyses, but mathematical, computational or fiscal aspects can hamper their application to practical engineering problems.

Experience indicates that one can enhance reliability, reduce the amount of measured data needed and expedite a solution by hybriding experimental techniques with theoretical and numerical ingredients. For instance, combining theoretical and numerical features with experimental information permits one to do the following: (i) determine the individual stresses photoelastically at boundary and non-boundary locations without isoclinic information and in the presence of unreliable boundary data; (ii) enhance the quality of boundary thermoelastic data, smooth noisy measured thermoelastic stress information and determine the individual stresses thermoelastically at boundary and non-boundary locations notwithstanding the presence of questionable measured boundary data; and (iii) differentiate measured information. Moreover, combining theoretical and/or numerical methods with measured data can often enable a region of interest of a component to be analyzed without having to analyze the entire component.

Several synergistic advantages of hybriding a variety of experimental, theoretical and numerical techniques are detailed in Refs. 1 through 39. Results of those studies form the basis of the present presentation. Illustrative examples include fluid mechanics, moire, photoelasticity, holography, speckle, thermoelastic stress analysis, interferometry, finite elements, least squares, splines, fracture mechanics, composite, concrete, cellulosic and rubber materials, and involve inelastic, nonlinear, anisotropic, dynamic and three-dimensional responses.

REFERENCES

1. Rowlands, R. E., Liber, T., Daniel, I. M., and Rose, P. G., "Higher-Order Numerical Differentiation of Experimental Information," Experimental Mechanics, 13(3), March 1973, pp. 105-112.

2. Rowlands, R. E., Liber, T., Daniel, I. M., and Rose, P. G., "Holographic Stress Analysis of Composite Plates," presented at the 13th International Congress of Theoretical and Applied Mechanics, Moscow, USSR, August 1973 and published in AIAA Journal, 12(7), July 1974, pp. 903-908.

3. Sciammarella, C. A., and Rowlands, R. E., "Numerical and Analog Techniques to Retrieve and Process Information," presented at the 5th Int'l. Conference on Experimental Stress Analysis, Udine, Italy, and published in the Proceedings, Italy, May 1974.

4. Rowlands, R. E., J. A. Jensen and K. D. Winters, "Differentiation Along Arbitrary Orientations," Experimental Mechanics, 18(3), March 1978, pp. 81-86.

5. Rowlands, R. E., Winters, K. D., and Jensen, J. A., "Full-Field Numerical Differentiation of Photomechanical Information," presented at the 14th International Congress of Theoretical and Applied Mechanics, Delft, Holland, September 1976 and published in Jour. of Strain Analysis, 13(3), 1978, pp. 177-183.

6. Segalman, D. J., Woyak, D. B. and Rowlands, R. E., "Smooth Spline-Like Finite-Element Differentiation of Full-Field Experimental Data Over Arbitrary Geometry," Experimental Mechanics, (19)12, December 1979, pp. 429-437.

---

[*]Professor, Department of Engineering Mechanics, University of Wisconsin, Madison, WI 53706, USA

7. Rowlands, R. E., "Composite Strength Theories and their Experimental Correlation," Handbook on Composites, Vol. 3, ed. by A. Kelly and Y. Rabotnov, North-Holland, 1985, pp. 71-125.

8. AbdelMohsen, Hamdi M., and Rowlands, R. E., "Hybrid Analytical-Numerical Processing of Photomechanical Data," presented at the Society of Engineering Science Meeting, VPI, October 1984.

9. Rowlands, R. E., "Optical and Hybrid Methods of Stress Analysis," Proc. 10th U.S. National Congress of Applied Mechanics, Austin, TX, June 1986, pp. 227-232.

10. Feng, Z. and Rowlands, R. E., "Continuous Full-Field Representation and Differentiation of Two- and Three-dimensional Experimental Vector Data using Finite-Element Concepts," Computers and Structures, 26(6), 1987, pp. 979-990.

11. Rowlands, R. E., "Hybrid Photomechanics and Applications to Composites," presented at the 1986 SEM Fall Conference on Experimental Mechanics, Keystone, CO, November 1986.

12. Abu Gharbieh, N. I., "Numerical-Experimental Investigation of Singularity at a Crack in Nonlinear Elasticity," Ph.D. thesis, Mechanics Dept., University of Wisconsin, 1987.

13. Fuchs, E. A., Huang, Y. M., Yu, J. C., Feng, Z., and Rowlands, R. E., "Thermal Analysis using a Hybrid Experimental-Numerical Technique," presented at the Int'l. Conf. on Thermal Infrared Sensing for Diagnostics and Control, Orlando, FL, April 1988 and published in the Proceedings, pp. 172-179.

14. Huang, Y. M., Hamdi AbdelMohsen, M. H., Lohr, D., Feng, Z., Rowlands, R. E., and Stanley, P., "Determination of Individual Stress Components from SPATE Isopachics Only," Proc. VI Int'l. Cong. Exper. Mech., Portland, OR, June 1988, pp. 578-584.

15. Rule, W. K., and Rowlands, R. E., "A Simple Orthotropic Elasticity-based Constitutive Model for Reinforced Concrete," Experimental Mechanics, 20(4), Dec. 1989, pp. 448-454.

16. AbdelMohsen, H. H., Huang, Y. M., and Rowlands, R. E., "Hybrid Elastostatic and Thermostatic Analysis from Measured Data," Experimental Mechanics, 20(4), Dec.1989, pp. 474-480.

17. AbdelMohsen, H. H., and Rowlands, R. E., "Hybrid Stress Analysis of Flexed Isotropic and Composite Plates," accepted for publication in Computers and Structures.

18. Lee, C. A., Richard, T. G., and Rowlands, R. E., "Exact Interpretation of Moiré Fringe Patterns in Digital Images," Experimental Mechanics, 28(4), Dec. 1988, pp. 409-417.

19. Huang, Y. M., AbdelMohsen, H. and Rowlands, R. E., "Determination of Individual Stresses Thermoelastically," Experimental Mechanics, 30(1), March 1990, pp. 88-94.

20. Rowlands, R. E., Feng, Z., and Dudderar, T. D., "Quantitative Fluid Flow Analysis by Laser Speckle Velocimetry and Numerical Processing," Proc. ICALEO '89, Orlando, FL, Oct. 1989, pp. 74-81.

21. Huang, Y. M., Rowlands, R. E., and Lesniak, J. R., "Simultaneous Stress Separation, Smoothing of Measured Thermoelastic Information, and Enhanced Boundary Data," Experimental Mechanics 30(4), December 1990, pp. 398-403.

22. Feng, Z., and Rowlands, R. E., "Smoothing Finite-Element and Experimental Hybrid Technique for Stress Analyzing Composites," accepted for publication in Computers and Structures.

23. Huang, Y. M. and Rowlands, R. E., "Quantitative Stress Analysis Based on the Measured Trace of the Stress Tensor," Journal of Strain Analysis for Engineering Design, 26(1), 1991, pp. 58-63.

24. Kou, S., Feng, Z. and Rowlands, R. E., "An Effective Numerical Technique for Processing Measured Electric and Magnetic Fields," submitted for publication.

25. Feng, Z., Rowlands, R. E. and Sanford, R. J., "Stress Intensity Determination by an Experimental-Numerical Hybrid Technique," Jour. Strain Analysis, 26(4), 1991, pp. 243-252.

26. Feng, Z., Sanford, R. J. and Rowlands, R. E., "Determining Stress Intensity Factors from Smoothing Finite-Element Representation of Photomechanical Data," accepted for publication in Jour. Engineering Fracture Mechanics.

27. Lin, S. T., Suhling, J. C., Johnson, M. W. and Rowlands, R. E., "A Combined Analytical-Experimental-Numerical Analysis of the Burst Test for Paperboard Strength," presented at the Symposium on Mechanics of Wood and Paper, ASME Winter Annual Meeting, Texas, November, 1990, and published in AMD 112, pp. 71-84.

28. Huang, Y. M. and Rowlands, R. E., "Determining the Three Individual Stresses at Interior Locations from only Measured Boundary Thermoelastic Data," to be submitted for publication.

29. Huang, Y. M., Lin, G. H., Suhling, J. G. and Rowlands, R. E., "Determination of the Three Individual Stresses from Only Measured Isochromatic Fringe Data," Experimental Mechanics, 31(4), Dec. 1991, pp. 310-319.

30. Rowlands, R. E., "Determining Enhanced Edge Data and Individual Stresses from Measured Thermoelastic Information," Proceedings SEM Conference on Experimental Mechanics, Milwaukee, WI 1991, pp. 248-251.

31. Feng, Z., Zhang, D., Rowlands, R. E. and Sandor, B. I., "Thermoelastic Determination of the Individual Stresses in Loaded Composites," accepted for publication in Experimental Mechanics.

32. Rule, W. K. and Rowlands, R. E., "Predicting Behavior of Cyclically Loaded RC Structures," ASCE Jour. of Engineering Mechanics, 118(2), Feb. 1992, pp. 603-616.

33. Goetsch, D. P. and Rowlands, R. E., "Doppler-Interferometric (VPI) Stress Analysis of Flexed Isotropic and Composite Plates," Proceedings SEM meeting, Milwaukee, 1991, pp. 427-431.

34. Hyzer, J. B., Shih, J. and Rowlands, R. E., "Interferometric Moiré Analysis of Wood and Paper Structures," presented at the SPIE 2nd Int'l. Conference on Photomechanics and Speckle Metrology, and to appear in the Proceedings, San Diego, June 1991.

35. Saliklis, E., Klungness, J. H. and Rowlands, R. E., "Dynamic Water-Release of Filaments Pertaining to Contaminant Removal," published in Recycled Paper: From Fiber to Finished Product, TAPPI Press, November 1990.

36. Bazant, Z. P., He, S., Plesha, M. E. and Rowlands, R. E., "Rate and Size Effects in Concrete Failure: Implications for Dams," Int'l Conf. on Dam Fracture, Boulder, CO, September, 1991.

37. He, S., Plesha, M. E., Rowlands, R. E. and Bazant, Z. P., "Fracture Energy Tests of Dam Concrete with Rate and Size Effects," submitted for publication.

38. Feng, Z., Sanford, J. R. and Rowlands, R. E., "Stress Intensity Determination by Hybrid Moiré-Numerical Techniques," Proc. SEM Spring Conf. on Exper. Mechanics, Milwaukee, June 1991, pp. 370-377.

39. Rauch, B. J. and Rowlands, R. E., chapter entitled: "Thermoelastic Stress Analysis," to appear in the Handbook on Experimental Mechanics, 2nd edition, ed. by A. S. Koboyashi, 1992.

Three Dimensional Stress Distributions Surrounding an Elasto - Plastic Interface Crack Using a Combined Moire - Finite Element Approach

J.S. Epstein, W.R. Lloyd, W.G. Reuter[1] and E. Zywicz[2]

ABSTRACT

The three dimensional stress field surrounding an elasto plastic interface crack was investigated using a semi hybrid approach involving moire interferometry and the finite element method (FEM). Due to the extremely complex nature of the problem investigated, the approach taken was to utilize the superior post processing capability of the FEM to investigate the three dimensional crack tip stress fields using the experimental input as calibration. The experimental input data consisted of the material properties, bulk loading parameters such as load and load line displacement and the X, Y and Z displacement fields local to the bimaterial crack tip. The FEM output parameters consisted of the CTOD and the asymptotic stress fields through the specimen thickness and the J integral as function of bulk loading.

INTRODUCTION

The majority of in service flaws arise at sites of discontinuities in material properties. Typical of these sites are weldments. The process controlling the propagation of a flaw in weldment is extraordinarily complex, not only must one consider the issue of heterogeneous material properties and non linear material behavior, other issues arise such as residual stresses, large grain deformation or single crystal plasticity effects in the heat affected zone and finally geometry effects constraining plastic flow. In order to clearly separate out these complex effects, research has taken place on the issue of the mismatch in material properties across a mathematically sharp interface containing a crack. Material nonlinearity takes place in the form of plasticity emanating from the crack tip region. The problem of a sharp crack at a bimaterial interface with subsequent yielding has been the focus of intense research.[1,2,3,4] Computational studies indicate that a separable stress field does not necessarily exit local to the crack tip within realistic physical size scales which has significance on the applicability of HRR[5] like crack tip parameters such as J. However, the size of the asymptotic field appears to scale with the J parameter and the mixity parameter[2] M_p or phase angle[6] ζ_0 defined respectively as:

$$M_P = \frac{2}{\pi} \tan^{-1} \left| \lim_{r \to 0} \frac{\sigma_{\theta\theta}(r,\theta=0)}{\sigma_{r\theta}(r,\theta=0)} \right| \tag{1}$$

$$\xi_0 = \angle K + \varepsilon \ln \left(\frac{K\overline{K}}{\sigma_{ys}\pi\cosh^2(\pi\varepsilon)} \right) \tag{2}$$

1.   Fracture Behavior Section, The Idaho National Engineering Laboratory, Idaho Falls, ID, USA 83415-2218

2.   Univ. of California, Lawrence Livermore National Laboratory, Livermore, CA, USA 94550

This purpose of this note is two fold. First, we wish to report on the outline of the hybrid approach that has been developed from our joint investigation, significantly, the levels of calibration between the experiment and FEM. The approach while not fully hybrid, ie, using the measured displacement fields as direct input to a computational mesh[7,8,9,10] is, we postulate, very powerful and efficient. Our semi hybrid scheme utilizes the best capabilities of both methods, the experiment to calibrate the FEM and the FEM to extract post processing phenomena such as 3-D stress fields and crack tip parameters. The second purpose of this note is to explain briefly our initial results on the physics of an interface crack undergoing elasto plastic deformation and particularly the initial structure of the asymptotic fields that govern crack tip initiation.

This note will take the following outline, first we will discuss the material geometry and stress strain response. We will then describe the experimental procedure, the bulk response parameters such as load and load line deflection, the near tip measurements utilizing moire interferometry for the X and Y fields and a microtopography system for the out of plane deformations. We will then describe the levels of calibration between the experiment and FEM starting with the bulk loading parameters, then to driving the FEM with the moire measured CTOD and finally the detailed comparison between the moire X and Y displacement fields as well as the microtopography out of plane deformations. Finally we will describe the power that the FEM brings to the experimentalist by showing briefly the FEM 3-D the stress state and CTOD as well as the J integral as a function of load. The level of detail that the FEM provides in these 3-D post processing parameters are well beyond current experimental capability.

MATERIAL SYSTEM AND GEOMETRY

The material system chosen for this study is that of commercially pure titanium (CP Ti) diffusion bonded to 6Al-4V titanium (6Al-4V Ti). The stress strain response for the two systems is shown in figure 1. The specific material parameters for the two systems in found in Table 1.

TABLE 1

Material	E (GPa)	Poisson's Ratio	ε_0 (%)	σ_0 (Mpa)	α	n
CP Ti	112.3	0.24	0.33	366	0.60	11.0
6Al-4V Ti	115.1	0.28	0.72	886	0.349	31.8

where:

$$-\sigma/\sigma_0 = \sigma/E + \alpha(\sigma/\sigma_0)^n \qquad (3)$$

and the subscript 0, denotes the yield state.

The advantage of this system is the close elastic moduli and coefficients of thermal expansion to minimize residual bonding stresses. Thus the only parameter varied is the yield stress. The CP Ti yields while the 6Al-4V remaining essentially elastic. The J_{IC} of the 6Al-4V and CP Ti are 62.7 and 110.0 kJ/m^2 respectively. The bonding process begins with 50 mm diameter blanks that are 50 mm long and machined to produce parallel faces. The blanks are polished with a 1 micron diamond paste, etched and then inserted into 178 kN capacity hot press. They are then diffusion bonded at 870C at a nominal pressure of 3.44 MPa for 1 hour and cooled to room temperature by shutting off the furnace. The diffusion bonding process essentially produces a mathematically sharp interface. Figure 2 shows a micrograph of the bond line region using a Krolls etch. Figure 2 shows the large grained CP Ti and the long alpha structure of the 6Al-4V inter dispersed with the darker beta phases.

The material geometry and loading setup is shown in figure 3. The load and load line displacement were measured as well as the moire interferometry[11] X and Y displacement fields using 600 l/mm crossed gratings with multiplication of 2, or 0.8 microns per fringe order. Typical X and Y displacement fields are shown in figure 4. Of interest in figure 4 is the plastic zone extending into the CP material while the 6Al-4V shows a very small zone.

The parameter ε for the material combination is 7.2 x10^{-3} and the phase angle ζ_0 is relatively small at 1^0.

SEMI HYBRID APPROACH

The FEM utilized a finite deformation formulation based upon the Green-Naghdi stress rate and a rate independent elastic plastic power law hardening formulation. Both 2-D and 3-D full elasto plastic calculations were performed past limit load (P_0) of the bend bar (2.2 kN). A full 3-D calculation involved approximately 20 hours of Cray YMP time.

There are three levels of calibration between the experiment and FEM. The first level involves the accurate input of the material stress strain curves. This aspect is critical as material response local to the crack tip involves large strains. The material properties were fit well using equation (3). The next level of interaction involved driving the FEM with the experimental load and comparing to the bulk load line displacement. This comparison is shown in figure 5. It should be noted that the bulk deformation of the 4 point bend specimen at the contacting roller is asymmetric hence statically indeterminate. The static indeterminacy was bypassed by including in the FEM the upper roller that contacts the loading plate above the two loading pins. Finer levels of comparison take place. First the FEM is driven by the CTOD as measured from the moire Y field in a manner similar to Yu[12]. After driving the FEM with the moire CTOD, a detailed comparison between the X and Y moire fields and the FEM takes place. A major consideration of this process is that of locating the zero fringe in the moire pattern. For this experiment the coordinate system is taken at the crack tip. Normally one can assume planes of symmetry to discern zero fringe orders. However due to the inherent asymmetric deformation what appears to be a zero order fringe is not the case. For instance, Fig. 4a shows the Y displacement field and one would normally take the neutral axis and zero fringe at the inflection point on the pattern where the fringes become least dense and change direction. For this experiment the asymmetric deformation results in the zero fringe to be on the 6Al-4V side. A procedure was developed where the FEM produces Y or X field contours of the same apparent frequency as those of the moire pattern. The zero fringe from the FEM moire pattern is located and spatially superimposed upon the actual moire pattern. The experimental moire fringe that corresponds to this superposition is the zero fringe. Normally, one does not have concern on a difference in zero fringe location as this tends to be a rigid body displacement. However, as a large deformation formulation was employed, rigid body rotations can affect the stress tensor thus influencing the calibration and hence accuracy of the FEM results. Figures 6a and b detail the comparison at net section plasticity. In general the agreement is good with some offset that is unavoidable due to the large deformations and loss of fringe continuity in the crack tip caustic region of the CP Ti. Figure 7 details the unloaded out of plane field as produced by a microtopography system. Again the agreement is good indicating the FEM is accurately modelling the full three dimensional displacement field.

RESULTS

The power of the semi hybrid approach becomes evident with the post processing of the stress fields by the FEM. Figure 8 details the mesh response where the applied load P to limit load P_0 is 1.2. The plastic zone contours are also found in Fig. 8. Because the FEM is 3-D we are to produce plastics zone sizes as a function of thickness. Figure 9 details the CTOD as a function of thickness as well as the difference in CTOD curves between 2-D and 3-D computations. Figures 10a-c details the hoop stress first as function of thickness, then in comparison with the HRR field solutions and finally as a function of load. While some self similarity is evident for the hoop stress it does not necessarily agree, even deep within the plastic zone with the HRR field. Finally Fig.'s 11 and 12 details the normalized CTOD response as a function of load ratio and J as function of normalized distance from the crack tip. It is seen in Fig. 11 that the normalized CTOD is not a constant ratio of 0.5 (plane strain) as would be expected for an HRR dominant field. The hoop stress results, Fig. 9, indicate that because we have a rigid half space bonded to a yielding half space, the crack tip fields reach very high hydrostatic stress and that the interfacial normal tractions are 25% greater that the HRR values. Self similar stress field behavior appears asymptotically close, however, it does not compare with the HRR trend. Finally the stress fields are mixed mode due to the greatly different yield ratios for the bonded materials.

CONCLUSION

We have presented a hybrid stress analysis frame work that combines the best capabilities of both the FEM and experiment. The experiment has been used as strictly a tool for in depth calibration of the FEM. The FEM has been used to understand the physics of the phenomena: the three dimensional stress state as well dominance of the crack tip stress fields. The FEM has proved superior in its ability to process the stress state directly with non linear material behavior - an operation that is not readily amenable to the experimentalist using only displacement data. We have shown on a preliminary basis that the asymptotic fields local to a yielding interface crack are not necessarily HRR in character; however, some degree of self similarity is evident. Our future work will concentrate on more detailed comparisons of the displacement fields. The asymptotic fields nominally lie within 5% of the plastic zone. For the geometry studied, at full ligament plasticity, the outer portion of the asymptotic zone is thus roughly 250 microns. Moire interferometry can resolve spatial detail well within such a zone. However, the crack tip caustic effect due to plasticity causes a loss of fringe continuity hindering accurate analysis. We are now testing geometries that are 50 mm in height and 25 mm in depth. The 50 mm height will permit large plastic zones such that the inner 5% region will be at least 1250 microns which should be adequate even with the plastic caustic effect.

ACKNOWLEDGEMENTS

The experimental of this research was funded by the U.S. Dept. of Energy, Office of Basic Energy Sciences, Div. of Engineering and Geosciences under contract DE-AC07-76ID01570. The computational portion of this research was performed under contract No. W-7405-ENG-48 to Lawrence Livermore National Laboratory.

BIBLIOGRAPHY

1. Shih, C.F., Asaro, R.J., and O'Dowd, N.P., "Elastic - Plastic Analysis of Cracks on Bimaterial Interfaces: Part III - Large Scale Yielding", J. App. Mech., Vol. 58, pp. 450-463, June 1991.

2. Shih, C.F., and Asaro, R.J., "Elastic Plastic Analysis of Cracks on Bimaterials Interfaces: Part II - Structure of Small Scale Yielding Fields", J. App. Mech., Vol. 56, pp. 763-779, 1989.

3. Stout, M.G., O'Dowd, N.P., and Shih, C.F., "Interfacial Fracture Toughness of Alumina - Niobium Systems", Exp. in Micromechanics of Failure Resistant Materials, ASME AMD Vol. 130, ASME Press, N.Y., N.Y., pp. 9-16, Dec. 1991.

4. Varias, A.G., O'Dowd, N.P., McHugh, P.E., and Shih, C.F., "Computational Modelling of Interfacial Failure", J. Mech. Phys. Solids, Dec. 1991.

5. Hutchinson, J.W., "Singular Behavior at the End of a Tensile Crack in a Hardening Material", J. Mech. Phys. Solids, Vol. 16, pp. 13-31, 1968.

6. Zywicz, E., and Parks, D.M., "Elastic Yield Zone Around and Interfacial Crack Tip", J. App.. Mech., Vol. 56, pp. 577-584, 1989.

7. Diez, E., Engelstad, M., Eiland, R., Genge, G., Chambless, D., Swinson, W., and Turner, J., "Hybrid Structural Analysis", Report AFWAL-TR-86-2117, Final Report, 1986.

8. Laermann, K.-H., "A Hybrid Method to Analyze the Stress State in Piece Wise Homogeneous Two Dimensional Objects", Proc. Second Int. Conf. on Photomechanics and Speckle Metrology, San Diego, CA SPIE Vol. 1554A, Society for Photo optical Instrumentation Engineers, pp. 143-150, June 1991.

9. Tsai, M.Y. and Morton, J., "New Developments in Localized Hybrid Method of Stress Analysis", Exp. Mech., Vol. 31, No. 4, pp. 298-305, Dec. 1991.

10. Feng, Z., Sanford, R.J., and Rowlands, R.E., "Stress Intensity Determination by Hybrid Moire Numerical Techniques", Proc. 1991 SEM Spring Mtg., Milwaukee, Soc. Exp. Mech., pp. 370-377, 1991.

11. Post, D., "Moire Interferometry", Ch. 7, Handbook on Experimental Mechanics, A. Kobayashi ed., McGraw Hill Pub., 1987.

12. Yu, C.-T. and Kobayashi, A.S., Fracture Process Zone in Ceramics and Ceramic Composites", Proc. Int. Conf. on mech. Beh. of Matl., Kobe, Japan, Vol. 3, M. Jono and T. Inoue, ed.'s, pp. 423-428, Pergammon Press, 1991.

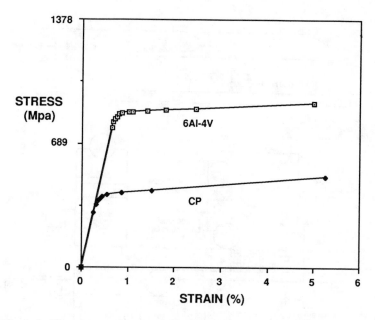

Figure 1. The stress strain response for the commercially pure and 6Al-4V titaniums

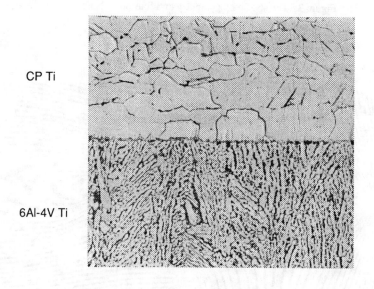

Figure 2. A 375X micrograph of the diffusion bond region.

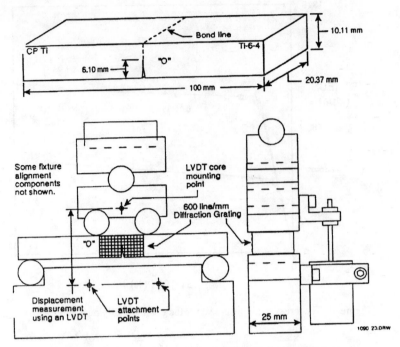

Figure 3. The specimen geometry and four point bend fixture.

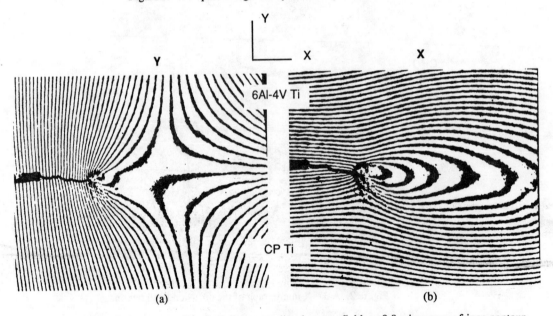

Figures 4a and b. The Y and X moire interferometry dispalcement fields at 0.8 microns per fringe contour.

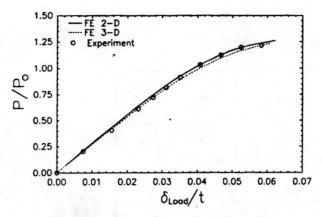

Figure 5. The load line calibration of the FEM.

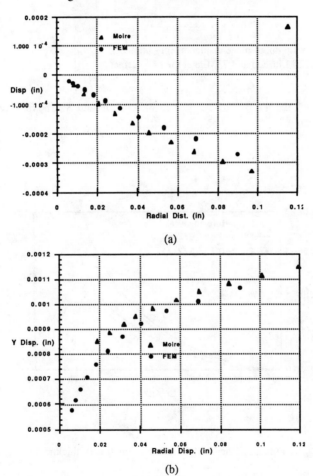

(a)

(b)

Figures 6a and b. The calibration of the FEM from the moire dispalcement fields at 4.73 MPa.

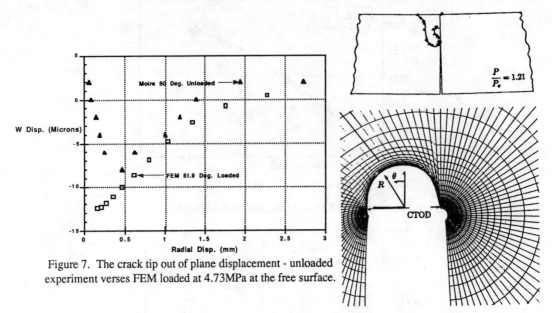

Figure 7. The crack tip out of plane displacement - unloaded experiment verses FEM loaded at 4.73MPa at the free surface.

Figure 8. The FEM mesh and plastic zone.

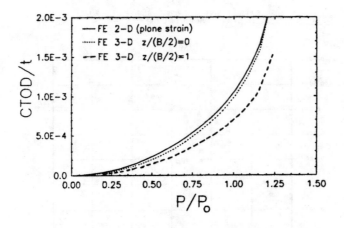

Figure 9. The FEM CTOD as a function of thickness.

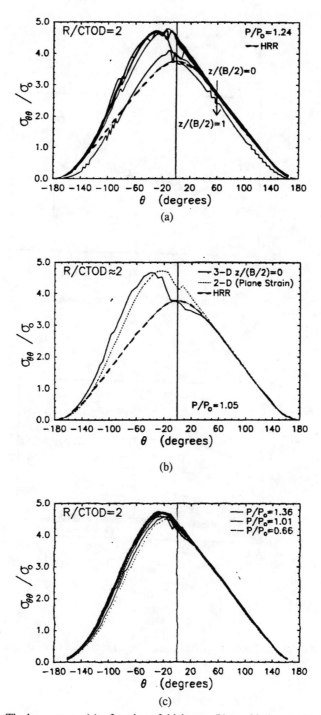

Figures 10a,b and c. The hoop stress (a) a function of thickness, (b) at mid plane and (c) as a function of load.

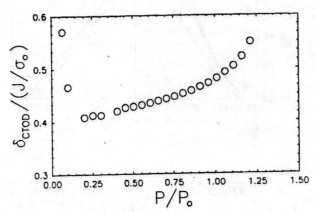

Figure 11. The normalized CTOD as a function of limit load.

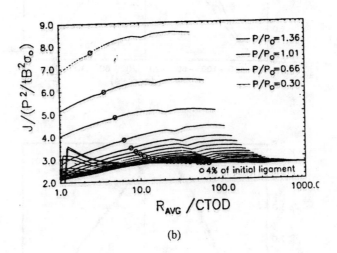

(b)

Figure 12. The normalized J integral as a function of crack tip distance.

HYBRID METHOD FOR RECONSTRUCTION OF BOUNDARY CONTOUR AND VALUE IN PHOTOELASTIC IMAGE DATA

Yoshika SUZUKI, Shizuo MAWATARI and Masahisa TAKASHI

Abstract

It is important to find specimen boundary contour and to determine values on it, if we perform accurate stress analysis on a deformed body by optical method such as photoelasyicity. Reconstruction of boundary contour with plane curves using disperse points extracted from image data is however difficult, because no suitable method has been developed for plane curve fitting. The author proposes a new plane-spline approximation method in which boundary is separated in several branches. An algebraic plane curve is applied to the set of measured data which corresponds to each branch. The method is successful in reconstruction of specimen boundary from photoelastic image data involving noise.

I. INTRODUCTION

When performing computer-aided stress analysis of photoelastic image data, several difficulties in the extraction of specimen boundary contour and of brightness distribution near boundary are often experienced since there exist many sorts of unavoidable noise due to fluctuation of source light intensity, inaccuracy in the optical equipment and its misalignment. It is, however, essential and important to determine the boundary contour of specimen and the image data on and near the boundary to improve and facilitate solving boundary value problems under a deformed state of elastic body. Accordingly, it will be expected to develop an efficient reconstruction method for specimen contour and boundary values which can preserve the original natures of experimental data.

In the current techniques of plane curve fitting with the spline function smoothing method, coordinates x_i and y_i at each measured point $(x_i \ y_i)$ are treated separately as single variables of x and y respectively in spite of importance of the treatment with a point in plane as an ordered pair of coordinates. Therefore, they are not always successful because of difficulties in selection of parameters, extraneous inflection and etc. It could, then, be pointed out that few examples of the approximation of plane curve are found up to date.

In this paper, the authors establish a new plane-spline function method for plane curve approximation which will be able to avoid difficulties mentioned above. An algebraic plane curve is applied to the sets of measured point which correspond to respective local ramification considering that the boundary divided into ramifications could be reconstructed by linkage of several simple arcs of a part of quadratic curve. A method for determination of functional value of the contour curve for boundary reconstructed is also proposed.

II. THE CURRENT TECHNIQUES OF PLANE CURVE FITTING

In the current techniques of plane curve fitting with the spline function method, a continuous plane curve C is expressed by a set of points ;

$$C = \{x(s), y(s) : a \leq s \leq \beta\} \tag{1}$$

Then two continuous function:

$$s \rightarrow x(s), \quad s \rightarrow y(s), \quad s \in [\alpha, \beta] \tag{2}$$

are respectively approximated using different single variable spline functions. In this type of current method, we can point out two disadvantages as follows,

(1) Extraneous Inflection

Although the approximated curve with a continuous function of eq.(2) can go through just on the given data point, unexpected extraneous inflection often occurs between node points.

(2) Selection of Parameters

Two different ways for selection of the parameter s of eq.(2) are considered.
1) to select the parameter s as one of x-y orthogonal coordinates, namely $x(s) = s$ or $y(s) = s$.
2) to take parameter s in term of arc-length of continuous plane curve C

The former is, however, possibly sensitive to noise involved in data. Although the latter is seemingly good at theoretical handling, it is usually impossible to know the arc-length of objective curve only with experimental data involving unavoidable noise. Therefore, it would not be easy to use the latter method for ordinary numerical analysis of curve fitting. There have been proposed various means to solve these difficulties[1, 2], it should be emphasized that the essential of the problem remains unsolved.

III. NEW METHOD FOR PLANE CURVE APPROXIMATION

The authors propose a new method for the approximation of a plane curve, which can efficiently draw specimen boundary contour using several points of data depicted from an image obtained through a CCD camera eliminating difficulties mentioned above. The basic concepts are summarized as follows;

Yoshika SUZUKI is a ph.D student in Department of Mechanical Engineering, Sizuo MAWATARI is Associate Professor of Industry and System Engineering and Masahisa TAKASHI is professor of Mechanical Engineering, Aoyama Gakuin University, 6-16-1, Chitosedai, Setagaya-ku, Tokyo, Japan

(1) Assume that an objective plane curve, e.g. a pattern of specimen boundary contour in photoelastic image data, is an ordinary curve, namely a group of plane curves which consist of several simple arcs crossing each other at finite numbers of point and that the sum-set of the curves is connected. Also measured data is considered as the actual values of the curve group which often involve noise. An approximated curve F of an arbitrary simple arc C is reconstructed with the following procedures by use of a corresponding set Q of discrete point data measured on boundary to C.

(2) The simple arc C is defined inside a plane rectangle region $I_x \times I_y \subset R^2$. In the parametric representation of C with arc-length s;

$$s \to C(s) \qquad s \in [0, L] \qquad (3)$$

C is assumed in C^2 class, and a Frenet frame $C(s)\xi_1\xi_2$ is designated at each point of C^2 class. Then, C is divided into n- branches, $(1 \leq n < \infty)$ $C_1, C_2, \cdots, C_n$;

$$s \to C_k(s) \qquad s \in [\alpha_k, \alpha_{k+1}] \qquad (4)$$
$$(k = 1, 2, \cdots, n; \alpha_1 = 0, \alpha_{n+1} = L)$$

(3) Denoting a mth-order$(m \geq 1)$ polynomial of variables x and y as $f_k(x, y)$ $(k = 1, 2, ..., n)$, a part of an algebraic plane curve determined by equation $f_k(x, y) = 0$ is represented as follows,

$$s \to F_k(s) \qquad s \in [\beta_k, \beta_{k+1}] \qquad (5)$$
$$(k = 1, 2, ... n; \beta_1 = 0)$$

Sum set F of $F_k(s)$;

$$F = F_1 \cup F_2 \cup \cdots \cup F_n$$
$$s \to F(s) \qquad s \in [\beta_k, \beta_{k+1}] \qquad (6)$$

corresponds to a simple arc in C^p class.

(4) A set of measured data Q is decomposed by the following procedure. Here, Q_k denotes the measured data at C_k (k = 1, 2, ..., n) and

$$Q = Q_1 \cup Q_2 \cup \cdots \cup Q_n.$$

Also it often involves noise in Q_k and the degree of noise distribution varies from a branch to the other. Except for the case of n = 1, it is assumed that C(s) at the end point s = 0 or L and the values of partial differentiate $D_xC(s)$ and $D_yC(s)$ are known.

(5) In order to obtain a well approximated curve F which satisfies the conditions mentioned above, we consider an optimization problem of;

$$\sum_{k=1}^{n} \sum_{Q_k} \{f_k(x,y)\}^2 + \int_F \{\sigma(F;s)\}^2 \to \min \qquad (7)$$

where $\sigma(F;s)$ is the curvature at point F(s) of approximated curve F. When we adopt an equation $f(x,y) = 0$ for determination of the function F, we have

$$\sigma(F;s) = -\frac{f_{xx}f_y^2 - 2f_{xy}f_xf_y + f_{yy}f_x^2}{\sqrt{(f_x^2 + f_y^2)^3}} \qquad (8)$$

where f_x, f_{xx} and etc. denote the first and second partial derivative of the function $f(x,y)$.

This type of treatment of the optimization problem aims twofold conditions, such as high fidelity to data obtained and smoothest connection of ramifications, simultaneously. It would be pointed out that the development could be compared with the extension of the current smoothing method with a single variable spline function and Whittaker spline[1] to the plane curve fitting problems.

(6) When we can find the optimal solution of eq.(7), the approximated functions f and y utilized for drawing of the plane curve will be explicitly determined solving the following differential equations with equation $f(x,y) = 0$ and the theorem of implicit function.

1. In the neighborhood of a point (x,y) where $f_y(x,y) \neq 0$
$$y = \phi(x) \qquad (9)$$
$$D_x \phi(x) = -\frac{f_x(x,y)}{f_y(x,y)} \qquad (10)$$

2. In the neighborhood of a point (x,y) where $f_x(x,y) \neq 0$
$$x = \psi(x) \qquad (11)$$
$$D_y \psi(x) = -\frac{f_y(x,y)}{f_x(x,y)} \qquad (12)$$

To draw automatically the plane curve mentioned above on a graphic screen of computer, we have to solve new problems such as, how to select a suitable algebraic plane curve in the clause (3), how to solve the optimization problems in the clause (5) and how to reduce the effect of unavoidable noise in reconstruction of a plane curve in the clause (6). We will discuss the three items in the subsequent sections 4. to 6.

IV SELECTION OF ALGEBRAIC CURVE

A simple arc C involved in an ordinary curve which explains the boundary contour of specimen can be often considered as a plane curve. It would be reasonably assumed that each branch C_k is approximated in sufficient accuracy with a low degree algebraic curve

Let us consider that there are several branches and that an approximated curve F can be reconstructed with various types of algebraic curve $f_k(x,y) = 0$. If f_k is in m-th degree, the approximated curve F could be only in C^{m-1} order. The lowest order of the algebraic curve applicable and suitable to our purpose seems $m = 2$. Thus, we adopt the following quadratic form as;

$$f_k(x,y) = a_k x^2 + 2h_k xy + b_k y^2 + 2c_k x + 2d_k y + e_k \qquad (13)$$

hen we have,

$$\left.\begin{array}{lll} f_{kx} = 2(a_k x + h_k y + c_k), & f_{ky} = 2(h_k x + b_k y + d_k) \\ f_{kxx} = 2a_k, & f_{kxy} = 2h_k, & f_{kyy} = 2b_k \end{array}\right\} \qquad (14)$$

where f_{ki} and f_{kij} denote the first and second derivatives of f_k in regard to i and j, respectively. The procedure for a plane curve approximation is briefly summarized as follows;

(1) As well known in the theory of conic section, if we explain the curve as,

$$f_k(x,y) = 0$$

and put

$$\Delta_k = a_k b_k e_k + 2 c_k d_k h_k - a_k d_k^2 - b_k c_k^2 - e_k h_k^2 \quad (15)$$

the condition $\Delta_k = 0$ is equivalent to the fact that eq.(15) shows linearity.

(2) Denoting the numerator in eq.(8) as Λ_k,

$$\Lambda_k = -8\Delta_k \quad (16)$$

(3) The curve of second order having the least absolute curvature is a linear line. The optimizing problem in eq.(7) is rewritten as,

$$\sum_{k=1}^{n} \left[\sum_{Q_k} \left\{ f_k(x,y) \right\}^2 + \Lambda_k^2 \right] \to \min, \quad (k=1,2,\ldots,n) \quad (17)$$

where,

$$f_{kx}^2 + f_{ky}^2 \neq 0. \quad (18)$$

(4) Referring to eqs.(8) and (16), curvature at each point on the plane curve F_k, under consideration holds its sign constant in the range designated. A point on F in eq.(6) at which the sign switches to opposite means a node between adjacent branches.

(5) If the coefficients in eq.(13) could be determined, the theory of conic section gives a shape of approximated plane curve.

Consequently, the proposed method for approximation of algebraic plane curve in this paper belongs to a parametric type in stead a non-parametric types of the current methods.

V. SOLUTION FOR OPTIMIZATION PROBLEM

Setting an initial point (x_k, y_k) of F_k, namely a node in F, and developing eq.(13) at the point by Taylor expansion with due regard to the sign of c_k and d_k we have,

$$\left. \begin{array}{l} f_k(x,y) = a_k(x-x_k)^2 + 2h_k(x-x_k)(y-y_k) \\ \qquad + b_k(y-y_k)^2 + 2c_k(x-x_k) + 2d_k(y-y_k) \end{array} \right\} \quad (19)$$

Then, let us solve the optimization problem mentioned above by the following procedure.

(1) Select several initial nodes (x_k, y_k), $(k = 1, 2, \ldots, n)$ of F.

(2) When F is in C^1 class at a point (x_{k+1}, y_{k+1}), from the relations,

$$\left. \begin{array}{l} f_{kx} = 2\left\{ a_k(x-x_k) + h_k(y-y_k) + c_k \right\} \\ f_{ky} = 2\left\{ h_k(x-x_k) + b_k(y-y_k) + d_k \right\} \end{array} \right\} \quad (20)$$

we obtain sequential equations as,

$$\left. \begin{array}{l} c_{k+1} = a_k(x_{k+1}-x_k) + h_k(y_{k+1}-y_k) + c_k \\ d_{k+1} = h_k(x_{k+1}-x_k) + b_k(y_{k+1}-y_k) + d_k \end{array} \right\} \quad (21)$$

then,

$$\left. \begin{array}{l} c_{k+1} = \sum_{j=1}^{k} \left\{ a_j(x_{j+1}-x_j) + h_j(y_{j+1}-y_j) \right\} + c_1 \\ d_{k+1} = \sum_{j=1}^{k} \left\{ h_j(x_{j+1}-x_j) + b_j(y_{j+1}-y_j) \right\} + d_1 \end{array} \right\} \quad (22)$$

where, c_1 and d_1 are given standing upon the assumption of (4) in the III section.

(3) Since,

$$\Lambda_K = 2 c_k d_k h_k - a_k d_k^2 - b_k c_k^2 \quad (23)$$

when a plane curve is represented by eq.(19), eq.(17) can be solved with the ordinary optimal algorithm.

(4) At a region of $Q_k = \varnothing$ F_k could be determined if vertices (x_k, y_k), and (x_{k+1}, y_{k+1}) as well as tangential at them are given. In necessity of extrapolation of algebraic curve, the procedure mentioned is adopted here.
However, several problems still remain unsolved in this procedure as follows;

(①1) The optimization of eq.(17) with eq.(23) turns out a higher order nonlinear optimization problem. Thus, it is not convenient since we have to adopt an iterating method in order to generate a point of convergence.

(②2) The relation $f_k(x,y) = 0$ for eq.(19) multiplied by any real number in both sides holds true. It seems too complicated in an optimization problem of solving eq.(17) to find an effective rule of the finish for calculation.

The following discussions and means, therefore, will be necessary for accurate solution of the optimization problem eq.(17).

V-1. Analysis of Error in Construction of a Plane curve

The major conditions for eq.(19) in our higher order nonlinear optimization problem are explained as follows,
1. c_k and d_k are determined with eq.(21).
2. a_k, h_k and b_k are determined with the least square method using observed data (x_1, y_1), (x_2, y_2), ... , (x_m, y_m).
In this situation, the relative error induced in each component of coefficient matrix is estimated as follows;

(i) in the case of a_k

$$\frac{(x+\varepsilon-x_k)^2 - (x-x_k)^2}{(x-x_k)^2} = \frac{\varepsilon}{(x-x_k)} \left\{ 2 + \frac{\varepsilon}{(x-x_k)} \right\}$$

(ii) in the case of h_k

$$\frac{(x+\varepsilon_1-x_k)(y+\varepsilon_2-y_k)-(x-x_k)(y-y_k)}{(x-x_k)(y-y_k)}$$

$$=\frac{\varepsilon_1}{(x-x_k)}+\frac{\varepsilon_2}{(y-y_k)}+\frac{\varepsilon_1}{(x-x_k)}\cdot\frac{\varepsilon_2}{(y-y_k)}$$

(iii) in the case of b_k

$$\frac{(y+\varepsilon-y_k)^2-(y-y_k)^2}{(y-y_k)^2}=\frac{\varepsilon}{(y-y_k)}\left\{2+\frac{\varepsilon}{(y-y_k)}\right\}$$

(iv) in the case of c_k and d_k

$$\frac{\left\{c_k(x+\varepsilon_1-x_k)+d_k(y+\varepsilon_2-y_k)\right\}-\left\{c_k(x-x_k)+d_k(y-y_k)\right\}}{c_k(x-x_k)+d_k(y-y_k)}$$

$$\leq\frac{(|c_k|+|d_k|)\cdot\max(|\varepsilon_1|,|\varepsilon_2|)}{|c_k(x-x_k)+d_k(y-y_k)|}=\begin{cases}\dfrac{\varepsilon_1}{x-x_k}, & \text{if } d_k=0\\[2mm]\dfrac{\varepsilon_2}{y-y_k}, & \text{if } c_k=0\end{cases}$$

Standing upon the discussions on errors mentioned above, we can emphasize that,

(1) the relative errors in the coefficients a_k h_k and b_k are as large as twice of those of the independent variables x and y.

(2) if $c_k\neq0$ and $d_k\neq0$, the relative error of the first order, $c_k(x-x_k)+d_k(y-y_k)$, seems so unstable that the error increases easily in the case that the absolute value of the term becomes relatively small. On the other hand, if $c_k=0$ or $d_k=0$, the error becomes stable and the degree is estimated as large as those of the variables.

It would be, therefore, recommended to shift the center of plane curve $f_k(x,y)=0$ to make artificially the value of c_k and d_k to be zero. But there exist the following difficulties such as, 1) the center does not always exist in all kinds of plane curve, and 2) since the location (x_0,y_0) of the center is a function of unknown coefficients a_k, h_k and b_k even if it exists, it is not easy to determine the location.

However, as mentioned previously in (iv) in this section, it is not necessary for both c_k and d_k to hold zero simultaneously. If either c_k or d_k could be zero, we can develop the following discussions.

V-2. Piecewise Coordinate System

Let us adopt a piecewise coordinate system (x_k,y_k)–X,Y on each branch C_k of a part of the object plane curve. Regarding a local plane curve $f_k(x,y)$ on a branch,

$$f_k(x,y)=a_k(x-x_k)^2+2h_k(x-x_k)(y-y_k)+b_k(y-y_k)^2$$
$$+2c_k(x-x_k)+2d_k(y-y_k)=0 \quad (k=1,2,\cdots,\ell)$$
$$(24)$$

the following three conditions are considered.

[Cond. 1]: c_k and d_k are known.

[Cond. 2]: $f_k(x_{k+1},y_{k+1})=0$ $\qquad(25)$

Under the condition, the initial point (x_k,y_k) of a branch C_k involved in the curve C is considered to be on an origin. Also, all of x-axes and all of y-axes are parallel, respectively.

The direction of the tangent line of C_k at (x_k,y_k) is known from the Cond. 1. Then we have the third condition as,

[Cond. 3]: Hereafter, C_k is explained on <u>a piecewise coordinate system</u> designated with the tangential and normal directions and with the origin at (x_k,y_k).

Eq.(24) is also explained on a piecewise coordinate (x_k,y_k)-X,Y as,

$$\tilde{f}_k(X,Y)=a_k'X^2+2h_k'XY+b_k'Y^2+2c_k'X+2d_k'Y=0 \quad(26)$$
$$(k=1,2,\cdots\ell)$$

The fact that c_k or d_k in eq.(26) becomes zero is shown as follows.

Now, let us assume $\partial f_k/\partial x$ at (x_k,y_k). In the case of $\partial f_k/\partial y$, we convert x-axes to y-axes. Then, y is explained explicitly as a function of x in the vicinity of the point (x_k,y_k). If C_k is expressed in a form of $y=\phi_k(x)$, we have the following equation according to Cond.1;

$$\phi_k'(x_k)=-\frac{c_k}{d_k}$$

Then, we obtain the angle α_k of a local coordinate to the global coordinate;

$$\tan\alpha_k=-\frac{c_k}{d_k}\qquad\left(|\alpha_k|<\frac{\pi}{2}\right)$$

Thus, the expression of eq.(24) on a piecewise coordinate system (x_k,y_k)-X,Y is easily derived. Using the well known coordinate transformation formulae,

$$\begin{pmatrix}X\\Y\end{pmatrix}=\begin{pmatrix}\cos\alpha_k & \sin\alpha_k\\-\sin\alpha_k & \cos\alpha_k\end{pmatrix}\begin{pmatrix}x-x_k\\y-y_k\end{pmatrix}$$
$$\begin{pmatrix}x-x_k\\y-y_k\end{pmatrix}=\begin{pmatrix}\cos\alpha_k & -\sin\alpha\\\sin\alpha_k & \cos\alpha_k\end{pmatrix}\begin{pmatrix}X\\Y\end{pmatrix}$$
$$(27)$$

we have the following relation substituting eq.(27) to eq.(24);

$$a_k(X\cos\alpha_k-Y\sin\alpha_k)^2$$
$$+2h_k(X\cos\alpha_k-Y\sin\alpha_k)(X\sin\alpha_k+Y\cos\alpha_k)$$
$$+b_k(X\sin\alpha_k+Y\cos\alpha_k)^2$$
$$+2c_k(X\cos\alpha_k-Y\sin\alpha_k)+2d_k(X\sin\alpha_k+Y\cos\alpha_k)$$
$$=a_k'X^2+2h_k'XY+b'Y^2+2c_k'X+2d'Y$$

where,

$$a_k'=a_k\cos^2\alpha_k+h_k\sin2\alpha_k+b_k\sin^2\alpha_k$$
$$2h_k'=2(b_k-a_k)\sin2\alpha_k+2h_k\cos2\alpha_k$$
$$b_k'=a_k\sin^2\alpha_k-h_k\sin2\alpha_k+b_k\cos^2\alpha_k$$
$$c_k'=c_k\cos\alpha_k+d_k\sin\alpha_k=0$$
$$d_k'=-c_k\sin\alpha_k+d_k\cos\alpha_k\ [=0,\ \because\text{eq.(26)}]$$
$$(28)$$

Then, we can conclude that either of c_k or d_k in eq.(26) becomes zero, where;

$$a_k'+b_k'=a_k+b_k$$
$$a_k'-b_k'=(a_k-b_k)\cos2\alpha_k+2h_k\sin2\alpha_k$$

$$\begin{pmatrix} a_k - b_k \\ 2h_k \end{pmatrix} = \begin{pmatrix} \cos 2\alpha_k & -\sin 2\alpha_k \\ \sin 2\alpha_k & \cos 2\alpha_k \end{pmatrix} \begin{pmatrix} a'_k - b'_k \\ 2h'_k \end{pmatrix}$$

From the discussion, we obtain the following transformation formula.for coefficients as,

$$a_k = \frac{1}{2}\{(a'_k + b'_k) + (a'_k - b'_k)\cos 2\alpha_k - 2h_k \sin 2\alpha_k\}$$

$$b_k = \frac{1}{2}\{(a'_k + b'_k) - (a'_k - b'_k)\cos 2\alpha_k + 2h_k \sin 2\alpha_k\} \quad (29)$$

$$h_k = \frac{1}{2}\{(a'_k - b'_k)\sin 2\alpha_k + 2h'_k \cos 2\alpha_k\}$$

V-3 Piecewise Optimization

To solve the problems ($\mathbb{P}$1) and ($\mathbb{P}$2) of optimization mentioned in the precious section, we transform eq.(17) as follows;

(1)Let us determine several nodes $(x_k, y_k)(k=1, 2, ..., n)$ in F as an branch C_k to be an approximated curve of F_k. which is a part of a proper quadratic curve or linear line. In our case of photoelastic data, it is easy to select several nodes on depicted configuration of image.

(2)On each branch C_k, an approximated curve F_k on a piecewise coordinate is derived by the following procedure,

1)Now we consider a problem in which the nonlinear term Λ_k^2 in eq.(17) is neglect ed. We, at first, determine each coefficients a'_k, h'_k, and b'_k in eq(26) by use of the ordinary linear least square method. Here,it is assumed that the [Cond.1] in the previous section is still holding. The curve obtained is in C^1 class on nodes.

2)On the other hand, an arbitrary linear line in a branch C_k:

$$g(x, y) = (y_{k+1} - y_k)(x - x_k) - (x_{k+1} - x_k)(y - y_k)$$

is determined on the original coordinate system using the linear least square method.

3) Comparing the errors in the second order norm both of a quadratic curve and a linear line against the set Q_k of measured data, F_k is determined by selection either of them as the error could be smaller than the other.

(3) The algorithm in 1) is briefly summarized as follows,

[Step1] The angle α_k is determined by the criteria,

(a)when $|c_k| \le (2 + \sqrt{3})|d_k|$,

$\tan \alpha_k = -c_k/d_k$, $\quad (|\alpha_k| \ge \pi/2)$

here, from eq.(28) we have,

$c'_k = 0$ and $d'_k = d_k/\cos \alpha_k$

(b)when $|c_k| > (2 + \sqrt{3})|d_k|$

$\tan \alpha_k = d_k/c_k$, $\quad (|\alpha_k| < \pi/2)$

$d'_k = 0$ and $c'_k = c_k/\cos \alpha_k$

[Step 2] Using eq.(27), a point $(x_i - x_k, y_i - y_k)$ is transformed to (X_i, Y_i) where (i = 1, 2, ..., m).

[Step 3] An optimization problem is solved as,

$$\sum_{i=1}^{m}\{\tilde{f}(a', h', b', X_i, Y_i)\}^2 \rightarrow \min \quad (30)$$

where

$$\tilde{f}(a', h', b', X_i, Y_i) = a'X^2 + 2h'XY + b'Y^2 + 2c'X + 2d'Y$$

[Step4] Finally, we calculate the coefficients a_k, h_k, b_k with eq.(29).

In the case that $(|\alpha_k| \ge \pi/2)$, X-axis and Y-axis on a piecewise coordinate are corresponded to the tangential and the normal at the initial point (x_k, y_k) taking the relation $\tan \alpha_k = -c_k/d_k$ into account. In the case of $5\pi/12 < |\alpha_k| \le \pi/2$, X-axis and Y-axis are changed to avoid the extraordinary increase of slope. On this coordinate system, it will be pointed out that either of c_k or d_k in eq.(30) becomes zero, thus, the error could be fairly reduced.

(4)The approximation method mentioned above is not always coincidence strictly with eq.(17). But it would be sufficient for our purpose.If it exhibit a little error, it is important to find the solution easily by linear least square method. Even if some error could arise in the results with the algorithm proposed, the effectiveness of the method in which a complicated non-linear optimization problem has been resulted in the linear least square calculation will be more than its defects.

V-4. Fitting of Plane Curves and Noise Reduction

It is important to take the effect of noise into account, when fitting plane curves reconstructed to a specimen boundary in photoelastic image from experiment. Since the coefficients of a plane curve are determined with the least square method, the degree of error can be studied by its variance.

The object function in eq.(30) for the least square approximation is rewritten as follows,

$$S(a', h', b') = \sum_{i=1}^{m} \frac{\{\tilde{f}(a', h', b'; X_i, Y_i)\}^2}{\sigma_i^2}$$

where $\tilde{f}(a', h', b'; X_i, Y_i)$ is the value of function obtained at a point (X_i, Y_i), and σi is the variance. The variance of error is considered as a measure of reliability for the results. Thus, we can explain the value of weight on each data point (x_i, y_i) adjusting the value of σ_i.

VI AUTOMATIC DRAWING OF A PLANE CURVE

All of the coefficients included in eq.(19) have, thus, been determined by the manner mentioned in the previous section. Utilizing the coefficients obtained, the differential equation, either eq.(10) or (12), has to be solved for the automatic drawing of a plane curve of eq.(6) with a computer. Taking f_{kx} and f_{ky} in eq.(20) into account, we can rewrite eqs.(10) and (12) as follows;

$$D_x\phi(x) = -\frac{f_{kx}}{f_{ky}} \tag{31}$$

$$D_y\phi(y) = -\frac{f_{ky}}{f_{kx}} \tag{32}$$

Then, eq.(31) or (32) is numerically solved from the initial point (x_1, y_1) with the Euler method, namely an itterative calculation with a step size $\Delta x, \Delta y$ (where $\Delta x = \Delta y$) of small positive value selected appropriately as follows.

1. if $|f_{kx}| \leq |f_{ky}|$

$$\left.\begin{array}{l} x_{j+1} = x_j \pm \Delta x \\ y_{j+1} = y_j + D_x\phi(x_j) \cdot \Delta x \end{array}\right\}$$

2. if $|f_{kx}| > |f_{ky}|$

$$\left.\begin{array}{l} y_{j+1} = y_j \pm \Delta y \\ x_{j+1} = x_j + D_y\phi(y_j) \cdot \Delta y \end{array}\right\}$$

Either of the double signs will be selected taking increase or decrease of x, y neighborhood of the point at which the above conditions are applicable.

VII APPLICATIONS TO SEVERAL TYPES OF DATA

VII-1. Test Data Made From Known Plane Curves

In order to verify adequacy and effectiveness, the curve drawing method was applied to a known plane curve, for example,

$$f(x,y) = x^4 - 2a^2x^2 - 2b^2y^2 + y^4.$$

Fig.2 shows a typical example of the results. It should be emphasized that the new method proposed here is so successful in automatic drawing of any type of complicated plane curves, although most of ordinary graphic tools on computer at present time can not draw such a type of plane curve automatically.

As shown in the previous sections we adopted the combination of locally connected algebraic curve of second order for reconstruction of specimen boundary. It will be the right way to show how the method can reconstruct a plane curve using a small number of point data made from a known curve, for example,

$$f(x,y) = 10x^2 + 12xy + 8y^2 + 2x + 4y + 1 = 0$$

in several cases with or without given noise of scattering. The conditions adopted in calculation are as follows,
* Number of branch of the curve C: 8 ($C_1, ..., C_8$)
* Four virtual data points on or near each branch Ck
* More than 1% error on several arbitrary data point.
The results obtained are shown in Fig.3 and Table 1. In the both cases without and with scattering noise, the curves are smoothly reconstructed. Thus, the method is expected applicable to reconstruction of specimen boundary contours in a photoelastic image data.

VII-2. Designed Data of Notch

Fig.4(a) shows another example of the results for notched specimen designed on a computer. The whole contour curve include both straight lines and complicated curves. The method proposed is successful and shows high fidelity to the original contour even if branches are of different order. Fig.4(b) is the case with scattering noise generated using random number on data points except nodes. A good result was also obtained as shown. Thus, we can say that most types of specimen boundary could be reconstructed successfully with the method proposed if several nodes and branches in addition to other data points even with scattering noise.

VII-3. Photoelastic Image Data

A typical example of photoelastic image of a concentric circular ring under diametral compression is shown in Fig.6. The authors are here interested in how to reconstruct the deformed boundary of specimen under loading with a function which can be utilized for designation of boundary conditions on it, and how to draw it automatically.

Fig.6 shows an example image of extracted boundary from the image in Fig.5 using a simple and ordinary edge detection processing. It is easily seen that there exist many vacant portions and scattering noise. Also, the configuration of depicted points is so irregular that selection of nodes for branch C_k becomes difficult.

Fig.7 shows the result obtained by application of the method proposed to Fig.6. In spite of considerable scattering noise and irregularities, fairly good reconstruction of the boundary is attained except near the initial point. As mentioned in previous section, the most important feature of the method is, moreover, in the fact that the approximated function of plane curve corresponding to each branch have been preserved. Thus, the method will be useful for reconstruction of deformed specimen boundary in photoelastic image and will be easily utilized to develop a computer-aided system for photoelastic analysis.

VIII CONCLUDING REMARKS

In the current state of the arts, it is usually pointed out that the difficulties in selection of parameter and extraneous inflection are fatal to a plane curve fitting problem in the framework with spline function. The method developed proposed here does not suffer from such difficulties.

It should be emphasized that the method introduces a new plane-spline function of parametric type standing upon the basic concept of spline. Then, the method could be considered as a hybrid one of mathematical representation of a plane curve and image processing for experimental data involving noise.

Application of the method to several test data of plane curve and experimental data proved its usefulness. The method can successfully reconstruct the shape of specimen boundary with a plane-spline function from an image data involving unavoidable noise. Since the geometric configuration of deformed specimen can be preserved and drawn continuously, it is expected for us to facilitate automatic designation of boundary conditions, also to develop an hybrid computer-aided system for photoelastic stress analysis.

ACKNOWLEDGEMENT

The authors appreciate the financial supports of the Center for Science and Engineering Research Institute of Aoyama Gakuin University, and of the Grant-in-Aid for Scientific Research, The Ministry of Education, Science and Culture.

REFERENCES

[1] Carl de Boor, <u>A Practical Guide to Splines</u>, Springer Verlag, 1978

[2] R. H. Bartels, et al., <u>An Introduction to Splines for Use in Computer Graphics and Geometric</u> Modeling, Morgan Kaufmann Publishers Inc., 1978

[3] R. L. Eubank, <u>Spline Smoothing and Nonparametric Regression</u>, Marcel Dekker Inc., 1988

[4] M. Mori, <u>Numerical Computation Programming</u>, (In Japanese. The title translated by author.), <u>The Iwanami Computer Science Series</u>, Iwanami, Tokyo, 1990

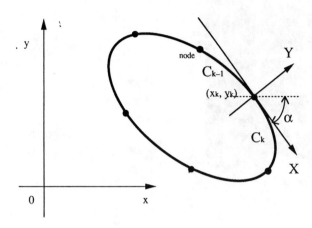

Fig.1 Piecewise Coordinate System

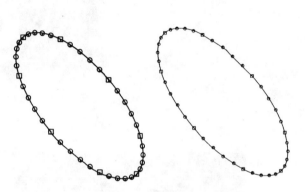

(a) Noiseless Data (b) Noise in 4 among 5 points in Each Branch

Fig.3 A Quadratic Curve
$$f(x,y) = 10x^2 + 12xy + 8y^2 + 2x + 4y + 1$$
Drawn by the Method.

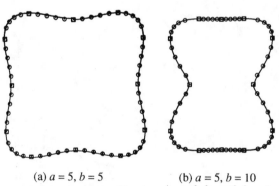

(a) $a = 5, b = 5$ (b) $a = 5, b = 10$

Fig.2 A Plane Curve $f(x,y) = x^4 - 2a^2x^2 - 2b^2y^2 + y^4$ by the Method

Table 1 Relative Error of Coefficients.

	Coefficients	a	h	b
	Given Value	10	6	8
Non-noise	Calculated	10.000003	6.000027	8.000026
	Relative Error	0.0003%	0.0005%	0.0003%
Noise on 1 point	Calculated	9.992876	5.991768	7.990514
	Relative Error	0.0712%	0.1372%	0.1186%
Noise on 2 points	Calculated	9.975258	5.970846	7.965685
	Relative Error	0.2474%	0.4859%	0.4289%

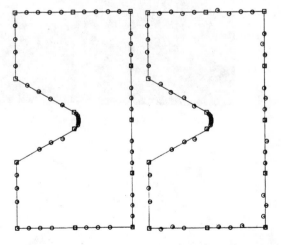

(a) Noiseless Data (b) Ramdom Noise Data

Fig.4 Result for a Designed Data of Notch Specimen

321

Fig.5 Photoelastic Image Data.

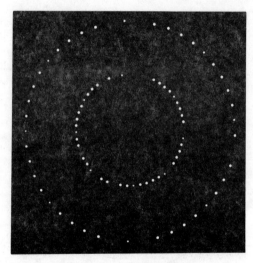

Fig.6 Extracted Boundary

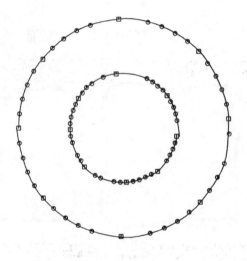

Fig.7 Reconstructed Boundary

PHOTO-VISCOELASTO PLASTIC STRESS ANALYSIS OF PUNCH INDENTATION

Shigeru TADANO and Hiromasa ISHIKAWA

ABSTRACT

The elasto-plastic analysis of punch indentation was carried out by the photo-viscoelasto plastic method with cellulose acetate. A cellulose acetate plate of 80mm width and 30mm height was examined in plane strain state during indentation with a rigid circular punch. The distribution of stress or strain and the development of plastic zone in the plate were obtained taking the rate effect into account.

INTRODUCTION

The fringe order gives important information on the nonlinear mechanical properties of a transparent polymer. It is possible that the values of stress and/or strain of a model material under elasto-plastic deformation can be estimated by use of its optical properties. Many researchers, therefore, have investigated the photoplastic method. The authors have previously reported that cellulose acetate was one of the most effective model materials for photoplasticity for the following reasons [1]. (1) Cellulose acetate is optically more sensitive than celluloid. (2) Cellulose acetate does not show either the necking or luder's bands at the yield point that appears in polycarbonate. (3) The stress-strain relation of cellulose acetate shows a behavior similar to a perfectly elastoplastic material. Namely, the perfectly plastic behavior of cellulose acetate is helpful only when the prototype is also perfectly plastic and not when strain hardening is involved. (4) Though the mechanical and optical behavior of cellulose acetate depends essentially on viscosity, the stress-strain-optic laws of the material can be uniquely represented in their nondimensional forms in terms of yield stress, yield fringe order and yield strain, and do not depend on strain rate and temperature. (5) The yield stress and the yield fringe order are linearly related both to temperature and to the logarithm of strain rate, while the value of the strain rate can be determined from the fringe order as well as the fringe order rate. Therefore, a new method of photoplastic stress analysis considering the rate effect has been proposed by authors. Using this method, the distribution of strain rate and that of stress or strain in the photo-viscoelasto plastic model of cellulose acetate can be obtained easily by the fringe order measured at constant intervals during loading. This method has also been applied to the stress analysis of a finite plate with a circular hole under uniaxial tension[2,3].

In this paper, the elasto-plastic analysis of punch indentation was carried out by the photo-viscoelasto plastic method with cellulose acetate. As is typical in the elasto-plastic contact problem, the considerable researches have been attempted by many numerical methods [4-7]. In order to confirm that both sliding wear and the initiation of contact fatigue cracks are attributed to plastic deformation, the stress distribution and the deformation pattern in the vicinity of contact surface under the repeated rolling or sliding contact were analysed by the finite element methods [6,7]. However, there is a few effective experimental method for this problem. Therefore, a cellulose acetate plate of 80mm width and 30mm height was examined in plane strain state during indentation with a rigid circular punch. The distribution of stress or strain and the development of plastic zone in the plate were obtained taking the rate effect into account.

A METHOD OF PHOTO-VISCOELASTO PLASTIC STRESS ANALYSIS CONSIDERING RATE EFFECT

The stress-strain relation of cellulose acetate shows a behavior similar to an elastic perfectly plastic material[1]. The yield point of this material was defined as the commencement

---

Shigeru Tadano is associate professor and Hiromasa Ishikawa is professor of Mechanical Engineering II in Hokkaido University, Kita-13, Nishi-8, Kita-ku, Sapporo, 060 JAPAN.

of the plastic flow. The uniaxial yield stress σ_Y (MPa) and the yield fringe order N_Y of cellulose acetate are represented by the rate of principal strain difference $\Delta\dot{\varepsilon}$ (1/hr) and room temperature T(°C), as eqs (1) and (2), respectively.

$$\sigma_Y = 5.70 \log \Delta\dot{\varepsilon} - 0.57\,T + 49.6 \quad \text{(MPa)} \tag{1}$$

$$N_Y = 0.48 \log \Delta\dot{\varepsilon} - 0.08\,T + 8.62 \tag{2}$$

By eliminating $\log \Delta\dot{\varepsilon}$ from eqs (1) and (2), the relationship between the yield stress and the yield fringe order can be expressed as,

$$\sigma_Y = 11.88\,N_Y + 0.38\,T - 52.76 \quad \text{(MPa)} \tag{3}$$

The stress-strain relation can be uniquely represented by the following nondimensional formulation in terms of yield stress, yield fringe order and yield strain.

$$\frac{\Delta\varepsilon}{\varepsilon_Y} = 0.55\left(\frac{\Delta\sigma}{\sigma_Y}\right) + 0.45\left|\frac{\Delta\sigma}{\sigma_Y}\right|^{20} \tag{4}$$

where $\Delta\sigma$ and $\Delta\varepsilon$ are the principal stress difference and the principal strain difference, respectively. The yield strain ε_Y is the values of $\Delta\varepsilon$ at the yield point, and is nearly equal to 5.7%, which does not depend on either strain rate or temperature.

Similarly, the stress-fringe order relation can be represented by eq (5).

$$\frac{N}{N_Y} = 0.82\left(\left|\frac{\Delta\sigma}{\sigma_Y}\right|\right) + 0.18\left(\frac{\Delta\sigma}{\sigma_Y}\right)^{20} \tag{5}$$

By eliminating $(\Delta\sigma/\sigma_Y)^{20}$ from eqs (4) and (5), the stress-strain-optic laws of cellulose acetate are obtained,

$$\frac{N}{N_Y} = 0.40\left(\frac{\Delta\varepsilon}{\varepsilon_Y}\right) + 0.60\left(\frac{\Delta\sigma}{\sigma_Y}\right) \tag{6}$$

The fringe order-strain relation is represented by eqs (7) and (8).

$0 < (\Delta\varepsilon/\varepsilon_Y) \leq 1$:

$$\frac{\Delta\varepsilon}{\varepsilon_Y} = 0.25\left(\frac{N}{N_Y}\right) + 0.75\left(\frac{N}{N_Y}\right)^{2.1} \tag{7}$$

$(\Delta\varepsilon/\varepsilon_Y) \geq 1$:

$$\frac{\Delta\varepsilon}{\varepsilon_Y} = 2.36\left(\frac{N}{N_Y}\right) - 1.36 \tag{8}$$

The rate of the principal strain difference $\Delta\dot{\varepsilon}$ is expressed by the fringe order N and the fringe order rate $\dot{N}$ (fringe order/hr) as follows,

$$\log \Delta\dot{\varepsilon} = \frac{\log \dot{N} + (a_2 T + a_3)\,N^2 - b_2}{b_1 - a_1 N^2} \tag{9}$$

where, $a_1 = -1.65 \times 10^{-3}$, $a_2 = 2.97 \times 10^{-4}$, $a_3 = 4.95 \times 10^{-3}$, $b_1 = 1.01$ and $b_2 = 2.24$.

Since $\dot{N}$ becomes a constant value in the plastic region as shown in ref. [1], $\Delta\dot{\varepsilon}$ beyond the yield point can be determined by the value of $\dot{N}$ only. Therefore, by eliminating $\Delta\dot{\varepsilon}$ from eq (2) and an equation given by substitution of $N=N_Y$ into eq (9), the relation between N_Y and $\dot{N}$ was represented approximately by eq (10).

$$N_Y = 0.48 \log \dot{N} - 0.08\,T + 7.79 \tag{10}$$

By using these relations (1)~(10) described above, the photoplastic stress analysis with consideration of the rate effect in the model of cellulose acetate can be performed by the following procedure. Square network must be marked on a a surface of the model specimen to trace the fringe order produced during loading. First, the fringe order at several nodal points of the networks in the model must be measured carefully at every constant intervals during loading. Therefore, the fringe order and fringe order rate at all points can be obtained. Second, the yield fringe order at this fringe order rate is calculated from eq (10). If the fringe order measured is less than the N_Y obtained from calculation, then the current stress state is below the yield point. On the other hand, if the fringe order measured is larger than N_Y, the current stress state is in the plastic flow region. From this judgment, the elastic-plastic boundary in the model can be determined easily. Third, the values of $\Delta\dot{\varepsilon}$ at any points before the yield point, are obtained from eq (9) by substitution of N and $\dot{N}$ measured. Since $\dot{N}$ becomes a constant value in the plastic region, $\Delta\dot{\varepsilon}$ at any points in plastic region are obtained from the same eq (9) with $N=N_Y$. Finally, the values of $\Delta\sigma$ and the values of $\Delta\varepsilon$ in the plastic region can be determined from eqs (6) and (8), while those in the elastic and transition region can be obtained from eqs (6) and (7), where the value of N_Y in eqs (6), (7) and (8) is obtained already from eq (10). The value of σ_Y can be calculated easily by substitution of this value of N_Y into eq (3), or by substitution of the value of $\Delta\varepsilon$ into eq (1).

EXPERIMENTAL PROCEDURE FOR PUNCH INDENTATION

The elasto-plastic analysis of punch indentation was carried out by the photo-viscoelasto plastic method with cellulose acetate as described above. As is typical in the elasto-plastic contact problem, the considerable researches have been attempted by many numerical methods[4-7]. In order to confirm that both sliding wear and the initiation of contact fatigue cracks are attributed to plastic deformation, stress distribution and the deformation pattern in the vicinity of contact surface under the repeated rolling or sliding contact were analysed by the finite element method [6,7]. However, there is a few effective experimental methods for these problems.

Indentation experiments were performed on the model specimen of 80mm width, 30mm height and 4mm thickness, as shown in Fig.1. On a surface of the model specimen, square networks of 2x2mm at the whole region and 1x1mm at the central region of 40x20mm were marked carefully by a height gauge. Figure 2 shows the experimental apparatus for punch indentation. Specimen was sandwiched between two hard glass plates with 10mm thickness to restrict the deformation in the direction of thickness of the plate. Therefore, under indentation loading by a rigid circular punch, the specimen deforms nearly in plane strain state. Three steel circular punches with D=20, 30 and 40mm diameter and 4mm thickness were used to examine the effect of punch diameter on the stress distribution in a model and the contact width. Silicon grease as lubricant was applied to the cleaned contact surface of punch. The model specimen is fixed only in the direction of compression at the lower surface, and free in the biaxial direction at the other surfaces. Isochromatic patterns that appeared in the model during indentation were recorded photographically. Photographs were taken at 1 minutes intervals during indentation at the speed of 1 mm/min. Since the mechanical and optical properties of cellulose acetate are greatly influenced by temperature, all of the tests were carried out at a constant temperature of 20°C.

RESULT AND DISCUSSION

Figure 3 shows the distributions of the principal strain difference $\Delta\varepsilon$ along the depth from the center of the contact surface. These strain values were obtained taking the effect of the strain rate into account. Points within the plastic zone are represented by the closed circles in each figure. It is clear from these figures that the strain distribution during indentation depends on a punch diameter. In every case, the peak of the strain distribution occurs in the subsurface in early stage of indentation, and moves toward deeper region with increase of load. This tendency is emphasized at larger diameter of a punch. Though the indentation loads are the same, the maximum strain shows a higher value in indentation of a punch with smaller diameter.

Figure 4 shows the distribution of principal stress difference $\Delta\sigma$ along the depth from the center of contact surface during indentation with various punch diameters. Points within the plastic zone are also represented by the closed circles in each figure. The development of a plastic region during indentation can be observed clearly in Fig.4. The plastic region develops gradually from the contact surface to deeper area with increasing of loads, and its development at the same loads does not depend on punch diameter.

Figure 5 shows the stress distribution of $\Delta\sigma$ at the same punch of D=40mm diameter with increase of indentation loads. In comparison with these figures, the development of the stress during indentation can be observed clearly. The maximum stress occurred in the subsurface of the center of contact area in early stage of indentation, and then spread toward inner region. In following stages, they separated into the both edges and below the punch contact area. The value of the maximum stress at P=1.1kN was almost the same at P=2.0kN.

Figure 6 shows the stress distribution of $\Delta\sigma$ under the same indentation loads of P=1.4KN at punches of three different diameters. From this figure, the stress distribution below 20MPa was confirmed to be observed in the same region, regardless of punch diameter. Otherwise, the higher stress region beyond 30MPa spread in wider area from the contact surface with decrease of diameter. In addition, the contact width at the same indention loads did not depend on the punch diameter. In Figs.5 and 6, the region of zero stress or tensile stress fields were distributed in the vicinity of the upper free surface. The tensile stress region spread with increase of indentation load.

CONCLUSIONS

From this investigation, the following results were confirmed:

(1) The maximum values of the difference of the principal stress or of the difference of the principal strain occurred in the subsurface of the center of the punch contact area in early stage of indentation. In the following stages, they appeared in the both edges and below the punch contact area.

(2) Under the same load, the distribution of the lower stress level and the width of punch contact did not depend on the diameter of punch.

(3) The plastic zone started from the subsurface of the punch contact area, and spread gradually insider.

ACKNOWLEDMENT

This research has been supported by Grants in Aid for the Scientific Research from the Japanese Ministry of Education, Science and Culture (Grant No.02555020).

REFERENCES

1. Ishikawa, H. and Tadano, S., "Mechanical and Optical Characterization of Cellulose Acetate", Experimental Mechanics, 28, 221-225(1988).

2. Ishikawa, H. and Tadano, S., "Photoplastic Stress Analysis Considering Rate Effect", Experimental Mechanics, 29, 49-53(1989).

3. Tadano, S. and Ishikawa, H., "Photo-Viscoelastic Plastic Stress Analysis on Cellulose Acetate," Proc. VI Int.Cong. on Exp. Mech., 1, 907-912(1988).

4. Lee, C.H., Masaki, S. and Kobayashi, S., "Analysis of Ball Indentation", Int. J. mech. Sci, 14, 417-426(1972).

5. Akyuz, F.A. and Merwin, J.E., "Solution of Nonlinear Problems of Elastoplasticity by Finite Element Method", AIAA Journal, 6, 1825-1831(1968).

6. Merwin, J.E., and Johnson, K.L., "An Analysis of Plastic Deformation in Rolling Contact", Proceeding of Institution of Mechanical Engineers, 177(25), 678-685(1963).

7. Ishikawa, H., Ishii, H. and Uchida, T., "An analysis of Deformation of Steel Coated with Ceramics in Rolling-Sliding Contact", Trans. ASME, J. of Tribology, 113, 349-354(1991).

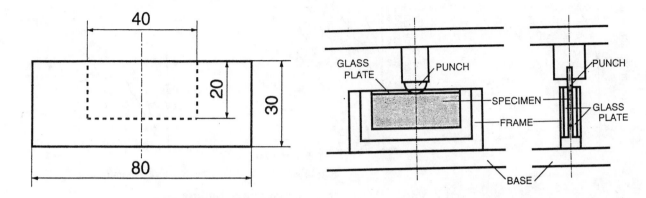

Fig.1 - The model specimen

Fig.2 - Experimental apparatus for punch indentation

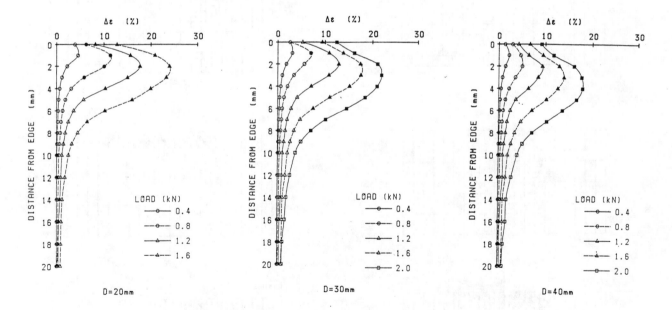

Fig.3 - Variations of the principal strain difference $\Delta\varepsilon$ with depth from the center of contact surface

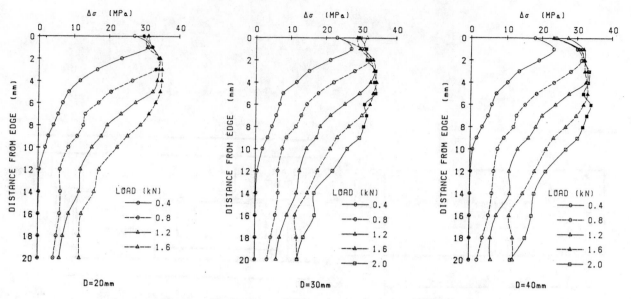

Fig.4 - Variations of the principal stress difference Δσ
with depth from the center of contact surface

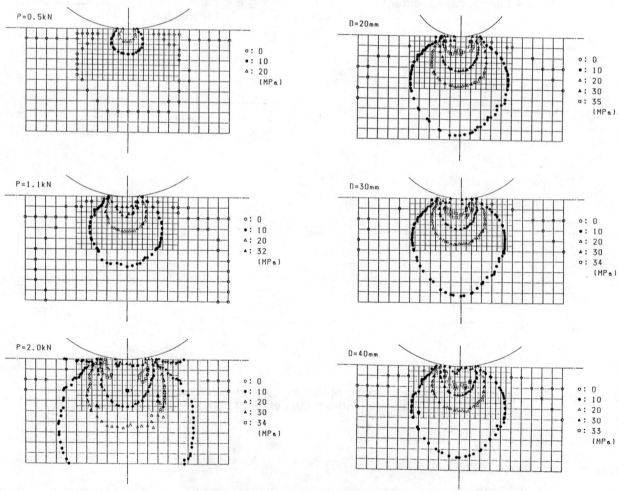

Fig.5 - Stress distribution under indentation
loads at the same punch diameter
(D=40mm)

Fig.6 - Stress distribution at various punch
diameters under the same indentation
load

DYNAMIC MATERIAL PROPERTIES OF BIREFRINGENT POLYMERS

S.S. Marlor
Civil Engineering Department
Michigan Technological University
1400 Townsend Dr.
Houghton, MI 49931

I. Miskioglu
Mechanical Engineering-Engineering Mechanics Dept.
Michigan Technological University
1400 Townsend Dr.
Houghton, MI 49931

J.B. Ligon
Mechanical Engineering-Engineering Mechanics Dept.
Michigan Technological University
1400 Townsend Dr.
Houghton, MI 49931

Abstract

The significant material properties in modelling stress wave propagation by photoelasticity are evaluated based on the elastic wave speeds in the photoelastic material using a Cranz Schardin Camera and digital image analyzer.

Introduction

Birefringent materials that exhibit sufficient sensitivity to loading for stress wave propagation studies are typically polymers. Since the effect of loading rate on the material properties is more pronounced in these materials [1], accurate measurement of model properties is essential in a dynamic photoelasticity study. The material properties that are needed in the study of elastic waves by photoelasticity are Young's Modulus, E, Poisson's ratio, ν, mass density, ρ, and the photoelastic material fringe value, f_σ. From the elastic wave propagation theory the speed of propagation in one and two dimensional models are related to the Young's Modulus, Poisson's ratio and the mass density of the material. Hence a careful measurement of the wave speeds in both a bar and a plate model using the birefringent material, together with the mass density, would yield these properties. The dynamic material fringe value of the birefringent material can be approximated using the creep test method proposed in [2]. An alternative method is presented in [3], where strain gages and a photodiode were employed to perform the measurement of the material properties of the photoelastic material.

In the current study, the wave speeds were extracted from dynamic photoelastic fringe patterns with the help of a digital image analyzer. These data were then used to determine E and ν. The creep method was used to determine dynamic f_σ.

<u>Experimental Method</u>

From elastic stress wave propagation theory, the speed of propagation in a one-dimensional model, C_B, is related to the density and Young's Modulus of the material [4]:

$$C_B = \sqrt{\frac{E}{\rho}} \tag{1}$$

The speed of propagation of the primary wave in a two-dimensional plate, C_L, is related to the mass density, Young's Modulus and to Poisson's ratio [4]:

$$C_L = \sqrt{\frac{E}{\rho(1 - \nu^2)}} \tag{2}$$

Thus, by careful determination of the wave speeds in a one dimensional and a two dimensional model, the necessary material properties can be determined.

In the past, accurate determination of the two wave speeds from photoelastic fringe patterns have been difficult since the difference between the two wave speeds is small and the location of the exact wave front is hard to establish. With a digital image analysis system, the wavefront from a typical dynamic photoelastic fringe pattern can be located accurately. If the wave front is defined as the point where the fringe order approaches zero ahead of an elastic wave, this point can be precisely determined from a light intensity scan on the photographic negative of the fringe pattern. The light intensity scans were performed on the negatives of the light field isochromatic fringe patterns as recorded by a high-speed 9 frame Cranz-Schardin camera. Fig. 1 shows a typical light intensity scan on a negative after it was smoothed by a spline fitting routine. The wavefront identified in Fig. 1 was established at the point where the light intensity from the first half fringe order dropped down to the background level.

In determining the wave front location, it was found that the optimum magnification level was obtained when 100-150 linear millimeters of the model were displayed along the x-axis of the display monitor. Hence a spatial resolution of 0.2mm/pixel was achieved, and, thus, the wave front could be located within that degree of accuracy. Any higher order magnification of the image introduced unacceptable noise in the light intensity scan and smaller magnification levels decreased the spatial resolution.

In order to determine the time interval between photographs from the high-speed camera, a lite mike together with a storage oscilloscope were used to sense and record the sparks from the Cranz-Schardin camera. A typical oscilloscope trace is shown in

Fig. 2 where each peak corresponds to the rise time during which a fringe pattern was recorded on the photographic negative. Again, the image analyzer was used to locate the peaks from the lite mike trace as displayed on the oscilloscope. Accurate determination of the time of each photograph was required in order to determine the wave speeds. The digitized oscilloscope traces were sharpened by using a gradient filter which improved the accuracy in the determination of the time each photograph was recorded and consequently the elapsed time between two consecutive photographs. The results of sharpening is shown in Fig. 3. It should be noted that since the exact starting time of the dynamic event cannot be recorded, the times obtained from the oscilloscope trace are relative.

After the relative times of the 9 frames from the Cranz Schardin camera were determined, the position of the wave front was measured with respect to a convenient origin on the negatives. The data obtained from the one dimensional and the two dimensional models are shown in Fig. 4. The wave speeds were determined from the slope of the best fit lines through the data which were in turn used to determine the dynamic value of Young's Modulus and Poisson's ratio using Eqs. 1 and 2.

In addition to these two material properties, a third property that is necessary for a dynamic photoelastic analysis is the dynamic material fringe value, f_σ. In methods based on work by A. B. J. Clark, [2] a creep test was performed on a beam in four point bending. The material fringe value could then be determined at various times by [5]:

$$f_\sigma = \frac{y}{N}\left(\frac{Mh}{I}\right) \tag{3}$$

where $\frac{y}{N}$ is the slope of the y location versus fringe order, h is the material thickness, M is the constant moment in the section and I is the moment of inertia for the cross-section of the beam.

If the value of f_σ is plotted versus the log of the time after the application of the load, the result is linear. This linear relationship can be extrapolated back to time in the dynamic region (time = 10 μsec). Clark noted that, in the dynamic region, there is approximately a 10% increase in f_σ over the "straight line" value for CR-39 (Homalite 911).

The material fringe value, f_σ, is also dependent on the wavelength of the polariscope light source. In order to avoid errors due to the mismatch of the light sources from a static polariscope and the spark camera, the calibration was performed using the spark camera.

To determine the dynamic value of f_σ, the beam shown in Fig. 5 was loaded and each frame of the spark camera was covered except one. The camera was then fired at the required time for the creep test which resulted in just one frame per time value. The isochromatic fringe patterns were digitized and sharpened using the gradient filter, and the location of each fringe with respect to the top of the beam was determined using the image analyzer. Fig. 6 shows the sharpened photoelastic fringes of the calibration beam. The data collected was then used to compute the slope $\frac{y}{N}$ in Eq.3 and to compute the average f_σ for the beam for each discrete time.

From this analysis, a plot of f_σ versus log of time was made (Fig. 7) and a dynamic value of f_σ computed for the model material. Since the value of f_σ changes with time, the polymer used in this study was calibrated in this manner at the approximate time of usage.

Results

The model material used in this study was Homalite-100. The longitudinal and the bar wave speeds were obtained from the slopes of the lines in Fig. 4 as 2220 m/sec for the plate and 2110 m/sec for the bar. The mass density of the polymer was measured by weighing a sample of known dimensions and determined to be 1200 kg/m^3. It was assumed that the density does not significantly change during the stress wave propagation.

The dynamic modulus of elasticity was determined using Eq. 1:

$$E = C_B^2\rho = 2110^2 \times 1200 = 5.34 \; GPa \tag{4}$$

and Poisson's ratio was determined from the two wave speeds using Eqs 1 and 2:

$$\nu = \sqrt{1 - \frac{C_B^2}{C_L^2}} = \sqrt{1 - \frac{2110^2}{2220^2}} = 0.311 \tag{5}$$

The calibration beam was made from the same sheet of Homalite that was used for the one and two dimensional models. The results of the creep test are shown in Fig. 7. The value of f_σ in the dynamic region was determined to be 24.68 kN/m/fringe. All of the dynamic material properties for Homalite 100 that were measured in this study are summarized in Table 1. These values compare favorably with the reference values given in Ref. [5, 6].

Conclusions

Use of the digital image analysis system greatly enhanced the capabilities of the dynamic photoelastic method. The precise location of the wave front as well as fringe centers were established for the desired frames in the analysis. These determinations are difficult to accomplish and highly susceptible to human error without the means of image analysis.

The accurate determination of the wave front and of the time interval between successive pictures resulted in a calculation of dynamic material properties with a high degree of confidence.

References

1. Arenz, R.J. and U. Soltesz, "Time-dependent Optical Characterization in the Photoviscoelastic Study of Stress-Wave Propagation, Experimental Mechanics, Vol.21, 227-233, 1981.

2. Clark, A.B.J., "Static and Dynamic Calibration of a Photoelastic Model Material, CR-39,"Proceedings SESA, Vol. 14, No.1, 195-204, 1956.

3. Dally, J.W., " An Introduction to Dynamic Photoelasticity," Experimental Mechanics, Vol. 20, No. 12, pp. 409-416, 1980

4. Achenbach, J.D., Wave Propagation in Elastic Solids, North-Holland Pub. Co., Amsterdam, 1973.

5. Dally, J.W. and W.F. Riley, Experimental Stress Analysis, McGraw-Hill Book Co., New York, 1978.

6. Toivonen, Paul, "Stress Wave Interaction with Simulated Multiple Rectangular Mine Openings," Master's Thesis, Michigan Technological University, 1983.

Table 1: Dynamic Material Properties of Homalite 100

Dynamic Property	Measured Value
Bar Wave Speed	2110 m/sec
Plate Wave Speed	2220 m/sec
Rayleigh Wave Speed	1090 m/sec
Dynamic Material Fringe Value	24.68 kN/m/fringe
Dynamic Modulus of Elasticity	5.34 GPa
Dynamic Poisson's Ratio	0.311
Density	1200 kg/m^3

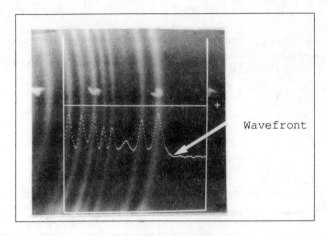

Figure 1. Image Showing the Location of the Wavefront and the Fringe Locations.

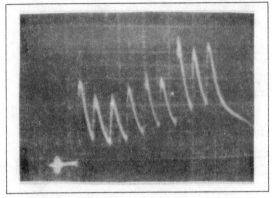

Figure 2. Oscilloscope Trace Showing Spark Occurances.

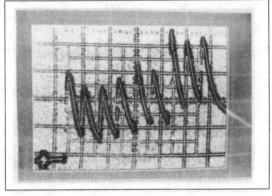

Figure 3. Oscilloscope Trace After Fringe Sharpening.

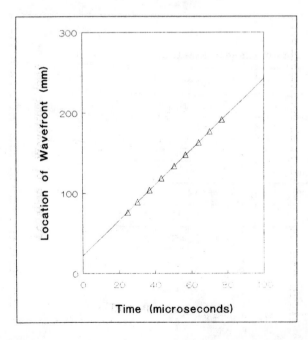

Figure 4a. Wavefront Velocity Data for the Primary Wave

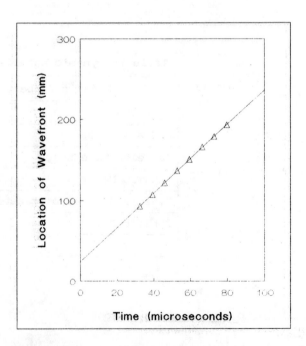

Figure 4b. Wavefront Velocity Data for the One-Dimensional Wave.

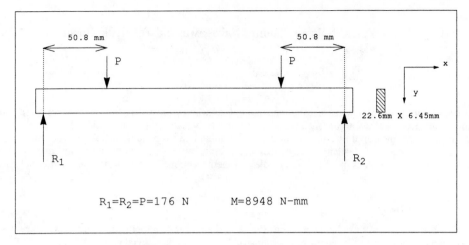

Figure 5. Beam Used in the Creep Calibration

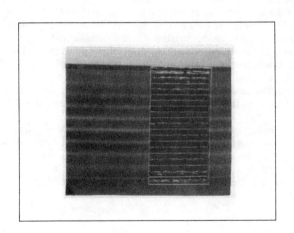

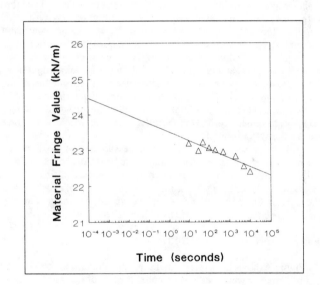

Figure 6. Beam Calibration used in the
Determination of Dynamic f_σ.

Figure 7. Material Fringe Value Creep Test.

PHOTOELASTIC MEASUREMENT OF THERMAL STRESS IN BUTT ADHESIVE JOINTS

Yuichi Nakano, Fumito Nakagawa and Toshiyuki Sawa

ABSTRACT

This paper dealt with the thermal stress distributions in a butt adhesive joint where two finite strips were bonded by an adhesive having rigid fillers and circular holes, and was maintained in certain steady-state temperature field. The thermal stress in an epoxide plate modeled as the adhesive was measured by a photoelastic experiment and also the thermal stress distribution in the joint was analyzed using the two-dimensional theory of elasticity. The experimental results were similar to the numerical ones obtained from the thermal stress analysis. The effects of the sizes of a filler and a hole and their locations in an adhesive on the thermal stress distribution were clarified numerically.

INTRODUCTION

Adhesive joints are increasingly used in many industries with the recent development of structural adhesives themselves and the substantial improvement in the strength of adhesive by adding rubbery, aluminum, metal particles and so on as fillers[1],[2]. Particularly in the manufactures of vehicles, aerospace and electric devices, adhesively joining method becomes one of the key technologies in place of other conventional joining methods such as bolted, riveted and welded joints. In adhesive joints, however, thickness of an adhesive bond is extremely thin and the material properties of adherends and an adhesive bond are generally quite different each other. Thus a fracture initiates mostly at the interface between the adherend and the adhesive in adhesive joints subjected to external loads. Up to now, many investigations have been done concerning the strength of adhesive joints under various loading conditions such as tensile, bending, torsional, alternative and impact loads. On the other hand, thermal properties of an adhesive bond such as a coefficient of thermal expansion and thermal conductivity are also quite different generally from those of adherend material. Therefore, internal stress will remain in an adhesive bond during its cure and cooling processes and thermal stress due to temperature difference will be generated easily in the joint, and in a severe case, the adhesive joint might be ruptured or damaged by the thermal stress as well as by mechanical loadings. In most adhesive, small hole defects are contained in joining process, particularly in case of mixing type adhesive for example epoxide resin with hardening one, and small particles are added to improve its static and dynamic strength as mentioned above. A few studies on the strength of adhesive joints subjected to some loading condition considering effects of such fillers and hole defects in an adhesive have been carried out recently. However, studies on thermal strength of the adhesive joints which have fillers and hole defects in an adhesive are quite few.

This study deals with a photoelastic measurement of the thermal stress in butt adhesive joints which have fillers and hole defects and are maintained in a steady-state temperature field. An epoxide resin plate containing circular fillers and holes in it was modeled and used as an adhesive bond in the experiments and photoelastic fringe pattern in the plate was observed. Then the thermal stress in plane stress state was analyzed using the two-dimensional theory of elasticity and compared with the photoelastic experimental results. Moreover, the effects of a coefficient of thermal expansion, thickness of an adhesive and sizes and locations of a hole and a filler on the thermal stress distribution were clarified by numerical calculation.

EXPERIMENTAL PROCEDURE

Figure 1 shows the experimental setup and dimensions of a butt adhesive joint used in the photoelastic measurement. Three holes of 5 mm diameter were made on an epoxide plate of the width of 80 mm, the height of 20 mm and the thickness of 6 mm by water jet machining in order to reduce the residual stress generated in machining. Then, in the case of the joint which has two holes and a filler in an adhesive as shown in Figure 1, a pin of 5 mm diameter and the length of 6 mm was inserted into a center hole of the plate (x=0,y=0) and adhesively bonded as a filler. The epoxide plate having two holes and a filler was joined with two adherend plates which have a hole of 8 mm diameter to insert a rod type heater (100V, 300W). The adherends and the filler were made of steel for structural use (S45C, JIS) and its Young's modulus of 206 GPa was about 60 times as large as that of the epoxide plate of 3.3 GPa so that the adherends and the filler were considered to be relatively rigid. A coefficient of thermal expansion ß, thermal conductivity K and Poisson's ratio ν of the epoxide plate were 67x10⁻⁶/K, 0.28 kcal/mhK and 0.38 from the measurements, respectively. After bonding and curing, the joint was maintained at room temperature and the internal stress generated during manufacturing process of the joint was confirmed to be negligibly small from an observation of an isochromatic line on the epoxide plate. In the photoelastic measurement, both the adherends were heated by the heaters inserted into each adherend and side surfaces of the joint were surrounded with air of room temperature 25°C (298 K). The temperature distribution in the adherend plate was measured by thermocouples mounted on it and when the joint was in the steady-state temperature, photoelastic fringe pattern on the epoxide plate produced by the thermal stress was observed.

THERMAL STRESS ANALYSIS

Figure 2 shows an analytical model of a butt adhesive joint where two similar adherends are joined by an adhesive having circular

Y. Nakano is an Associate Professor in the Department of Mechanical Engineering, Shonan Institute of Technology, 1-1-25 Tsujido Nishi-kaigan, Fujisawa, Kanagawa 251,Japan, F. Nakagawa is an Associate Professor of Tokyo Metropolitan College of Aeronautical Engineering, Tokyo, Japan and T. Sawa is an Associate Professor of Yamanashi University, Kofu, Japan.

holes and rigid fillers in it and both the adherends are kept at a certain constant temperature T_I and side surfaces of the joint are surrounded with air of another constant temperature T_O and a heat transfer coefficient between the side surfaces of the joint and air is denoted as α. An adhesive layer is replaced with a finite thin strip of which the height and the width are denoted as $2h$ and $2l$, and a_f and a_h denote the radii of a filler and a hole, respectively. Young's modulus, Poisson's ratio, a coefficient of thermal expansion and a thermal conductivity of the adhesive are denoted as E, ν, β and K, respectively. In the analyses, following assumptions, i.e., (1) these material properties are constant and are independent of temperature change, (2) there is no temperature changes in the z-direction in order to conduct as the two-dimensional problem and (3) the adherends and fillers are rigid, are made.

Temperature distribution

In the thermal stress analysis, first, the temperature distribution in an adhesive joint is calculated. In the case of the steady-state, the basic equation of heat transfer is expressed as Eq.(1), where the temperature distribution is denoted by $T(x,y)$.

$$\nabla^2 T(x,y) = 0 \tag{1}$$

Thermal boundary conditions in the joint considered in this study are written as Eq.(2) from the relationships that the temperature is constant T_I at the interface between the adherend and an adhesive and heat flux is constant at side surfaces of the adhesive.

$$T(x,y) = T_I \;\cdots\; (y = \pm h), \qquad -K\frac{\partial T(x,y)}{\partial x} = \pm \alpha\{T(x,y) - T_O\} \;\cdots\; (x = \pm l) \tag{2}$$

Temperature distribution in the adhesive is solved by a variable separation method and expressed as follows;

$$T(x,y) = \sum_{s=1} \frac{A_s}{\cosh(\lambda_s h)} \cosh(\lambda_s y)\cos(\lambda_s x) + \sum_{s=1} \frac{B_s}{\cosh(\alpha_s l)} \cosh(\alpha_s x)\cos(\alpha_s y) \tag{3}$$

where, $\alpha_s = \dfrac{2s-1}{2h}\pi$, $\lambda_s = \dfrac{2s-1}{2l}\pi$ $(s = 1,2,3,\cdots)$

A_s and B_s $(s=1,2,3,\cdots)$ in Eq.(3) are unknown coefficients and are determined by confirming Eq.(2).

Thermal stress

Thermoelastic potential $\Omega(x,y)$ is adopted to analyze the thermal stress in this study which is expressed as Eq.(4) using the temperature distribution $T(x,y)$ and the thermal stresses (σ_{xo}, σ_{yo}, τ_{xyo}) and the displacements (u_{xo}, v_{yo}) are obtained from $\Omega(x,y)$ [3].

$$\nabla^2 \Omega(x,y) = T(x,y) \tag{4}$$

Using Eqs.(3) and (4), the thermoelastic potential $\Omega(x,y)$ of the adhesive is written as Eq.(5).

$$\Omega(x,y) = \sum_{s=1} \frac{A_s y}{2\lambda_s \cosh(\lambda_s h)} \sinh(\lambda_s y)\cos(\lambda_s x) + \sum_{s=1} \frac{B_s x}{2\alpha_s \cosh(\alpha_s l)} \sinh(\alpha_s x)\cos(\alpha_s y) \tag{5}$$

However, in practice, these solutions can not be satisfied with the boundary conditions of the joint concerning the stresses and the displacements, which are expressed as Eq.6(a) at the interface between the adherend and the adhesive and at the side surfaces of the adhesive and as Eq.6(b) at the peripheries of a hole and a filler when the joint is not subjected to any external load.

$$\sigma_x = \tau_{xy} = 0 \cdots (x = \pm l),\quad u_x = \frac{\partial v_y}{\partial x} = 0 \cdots (y = \pm h) \quad \text{(a)} \qquad u_r = v_\theta = 0 \cdots (r = a_f),\; \sigma_r = \tau_{r\theta} = 0 \cdots (r = a_h) \quad \text{(b)} \tag{6}$$

where, u_x, v_y, u_r and v_θ denote the displacements in the x-, y-, r- and θ-direction, respectively and σ_r and $\tau_{r\theta}$ the stresses at the periphery of a hole.

In the present analysis, a solution which satisfies the above boundary conditions Eq.(6), is obtained by an alternating method of the following steps.

Step 1 : In order to satisfy the boundary conditions Eq.6(a), the thermal stress distributions and the displacements in the adhesive which has no filler and hole, is analyzed using Airy's stress function χ in rectangular coordinate [4] under the conditions of eliminating the stresses σ_{xo} and τ_{xyo} and the displacement u_{xo} and $\partial v_{yo}/\partial x$ which have been obtained from the thermoelastic potential $\Omega(x,y)$, as shown in Figure 3 (a). Then the displacements u_r and v_θ at each filler periphery and the stresses σ_r and $\tau_{r\theta}$ at each hole periphery are obtained from this solution.

Step 2 : In order to satisfy the boundary conditions Eq.6(b), first, an infinite plate which has a circular hole is solved using Airy's stress function φ_h in polar coordinate, which is expressed as Eq.(7) [3],[4], under the conditions of eliminating the stresses σ_r and $\tau_{r\theta}$ at the hole periphery obtained in Step 1, as shown in Figure 3 (b).

$$\varphi_h = B_0 \log r + A_1 r \log r \cos(\theta) + B_1 r\theta \sin(\theta) + \sum_{n=2} \{A_n r^{-n} + B_n r^{-n+2}\}\cos(n\theta) \tag{7}$$

where, B_0, A_n, B_n $(n=1,2,3,\cdots)$ are unknown coefficients and are determined from the coefficients in Fourier series of the stresses σ_r and $\tau_{r\theta}$ at the hole periphery. Next, similarly, an infinite plate which has a rigid filler is solved using Airy's stress function φ_f in polar coordinate, which is expressed as same as Eq.(7) under the conditions of eliminating the displacements u_r and v_θ at the periphery of a filler obtained in Step 1, as shown in Figure 3 (c). The stresses σ_x and τ_{xy} and the displacements u_x and $\partial v_y/\partial x$ are generated again by the two Airy's stress functions φ_h and φ_f at the boundaries of the adhesive (x=±l, y=±h) and they should be eliminated again in the same manner as described in Step 1. In the case where an adhesive contains two or more fillers and holes, the displacements u_r and v_θ of each filler and the stresses σ_r and $\tau_{r\theta}$ of each hole are eliminated in the same manner mentioned above and the stresses σ_x and τ_{xy} and the displacements u_x and $\partial v_y/\partial x$ at the boundaries of the adhesive are added in sequence. These two steps are repeated until the boundary conditions Eq.(6) are satisfied sufficiently and finally the thermal stresses and the displacements in the adhesive can be obtained.

RESULTS

Experimental results and Comparison with numerical results

Figure 4 shows examples of photoelastic experiments. In (a), isochromatic lines were observed on an epoxide plate modeled as an adhesive which contained a filler at the center (x=0) and two holes at x=±20 mm from the center of it and as a special case, (b) shows the case where the plate contained three fillers at the positions of x=-20, 0 and 20 mm and (c) shows the case where the plate contained two holes at the positions of x=±15 mm. The temperature of the adherends was 75°C (=348 k) and that of air surrounding the side surfaces of the joint was 25°C (=298 K).

Figure 5 shows numerical result of the principal stress difference in an epoxide plate, which coincide with the isochromatic line in principle, were calculated by the analytical method in the case where an adhesive contained a filler and two holes corresponding to Figure 4(a), using the above measured temperature conditions of the plate. It is seen that the thermal stress concentrates at the peripheries in the thickness direction ($\theta=\pm90°$) of the filler and the hole and in the width direction ($\theta=0°$, $180°$) of the hole and from the comparison of Figures 4(a) and 5, some slight distortions are seen on the isochromatic lines, but generally, the experimental result is similar to the numerical one.

Numerical results

In order to estimate the strength of a butt adhesive joint due to the thermal stress and an initiating point of fracture in the joint which has circular holes and rigid fillers in the adhesive, the maximum principal stresses at the interface between an adherend and an adhesive and at the peripheries of a filler and a hole are examined numerically. In the numerical calculations, a filler radius and a hole one are the same ($a_f = a_h = a$) and the following two types of adhesive are examined, i.e., type (1) : a hole is located at the center (x=0, y=0) and two fillers are at the positions x=±0.5ℓ, y=0 and type (2) : a filler is located at the center (x=0, y=0) and two holes are at the positions x=±0.5ℓ, y=0, symmetrically. In both cases, a temperature of the adherends is 100°C(373 K) and that of air surrounding the side surfaces of the joint is 0°C (273 K) with a coefficient of heat transfer of 10 W/m^{2}K. The number of terms N of the series in the analysis is taken as 80 and the number of alternating steps as 6. The difference of the thermal stresses of 5-th and 6-th alternations are within 3 % in the following calculations so that a satisfactory degree of convergence is expected.

Figure 6 shows the effects of the ratio a/h of a filler or a hole radius to the half thickness of the adhesive on the maximum principal stress distributions (a) at the interface between the adherends and an adhesive, (b) at the periphery of a filler and (c) at the periphery of a hole in the case of type (1), i.e., a hole is located at the center of the adhesive and two fillers are at the positions of x=±0.5ℓ, y=0. In the figures, the maximum thermal principal stresses are normalized as σ_1 /(E$\beta\Delta$T), where ΔT denotes the temperature difference between the adherends and the air. Moreover, the normalized maximum thermal stress distributions at a half interface of adhesion are shown in (a) and also those at half peripheries of the filler and the hole are shown in (b) and (c), because of symmetry of the stress distribution. From (a), these are seen that the thermal stress is tensile near the end of the interface and is singular at the end of it, the tensile thermal stress is generated around the interface where the filler is contained beneath, and it becomes large with an increase of the ratio a / h. On the other hand the compressive stress is generated around the center of the interface where the hole is contained beneath and it also becomes large with an increase of the ratio a / h. From (b), at the filler periphery, the normalized maximum tensile stress occurs around positions in the thickness direction of the adhesive ($\theta=\pm90°$) and the maximum value of it increases from 0.81 to 1.00 with an increase of the ratio a / h from 0.1 to 0.3, on the contrary, from (c), the normalized maximum tensile stress occurs around positions in the width direction of the adhesive ($\theta=0°$, $180°$) at the hole periphery and the maximum value of it decreases from 1.02 to 0.79 with an increase of the ratio a / h.

Figure 7 shows the effect of the filler position in the adhesive on the normalized maximum principal stress at the peripheries of the hole and the filler in type (1). The abscissa x_a /ℓ in the figure denotes the normalized distance from the center of the adhesive to the filler. The maximum value of the principal tensile stress at the hole periphery, which occurred at the positions θ of 0°and 180°and shown by a solid line in the figure, is 1.26 when x_a /ℓ is small, i.e., the two fillers are located close to the hole, and decreases with an increase of x_a /ℓ, and the normalized maximum principal stress is not affected by the filler and is kept constant 0.80 when x_a /ℓ is larger than 0.25. At the filler periphery, the maximum value of the principal tensile stress, which occurred around the positions θ of ±90° and shown by a dotted line in the figure, is about 1.00 in the range of x_a /ℓ from 0.07 to 0.7 and then increases steeply with an increase of x_a /ℓ, i.e., the filler is located close to the side surface of the adhesive.

Figure 8 shows the effect of the hole position in the adhesive on the normalized maximum principal stress at the peripheries of the hole and the filler in type (2). In this case, the maximum value of the principal tensile stress at the filler periphery, located at the center of the adhesive and shown by dotted line in the figure, varies only between 0.97 and 1.10 in all range of the hole position x_a /ℓ. At the hole periphery, the maximum value of the principal tensile stress, shown by a solid line, is 1.18 when the ratio x_a /ℓ is small and then decreases gradually to 0.81. However, similarly to the filler periphery in the type (1), the maximum value of the principal tensile stress at the hole periphery increases steeply when the hole is located close to the side surface of the adhesive.

Figure 9 shows the effect of the diameters of a filler and a hole on the maximum normalized principal stress at the peripheries of the filler and the hole in type (1). The maximum value of the principal tensile stress at the periphery of the filler which is located at x=±0.5ℓ and shown by dotted line in the figure increases with an increase of the ratio a /ℓ, on the other hand, that at the periphery of the hole which is located at the center of the adhesive and shown by solid line, decreases with an increase of the ratio a /ℓ.

From these results, it is not easy to decide an initiating point of fracture in the joint due to the thermal stress by comparing the maximum values of the thermal principal stresses at the peripheries of the filler and the hole with that at the interface between the adherend and an adhesive, because the thermal stress becomes singular at the end of the interface as shown in Figure 6 (a), however, the maximum value of the thermal principal stress at the filler or the hole periphery seems to have a large effect on the joint fracture, in particular, when the filler or the hole is located close to the side surface of the adhesive.

CONCLUSIONS

This study dealt with the thermal stress distributions in butt adhesive joints where two rigid plates were bonded by an adhesive having rigid fillers and circular holes. The thermal stress distribution in an epoxide plate modeled as an adhesive, was measured using photoelastic experiment when a butt adhesive joint was in the steady-state temperature field. Moreover, the thermal stress distribution was analyzed using the two-dimensional theory of elasticity and the effects of the sizes and the locations of a filler and a hole on the thermal stress distribution were clarified numerically. The results obtained in this study are as follows;
1 Isochromatic lines on an epoxide resin plate modeled as an adhesive having fillers and holes, were measured by photoelastic

experiment and the experimental result was similar to the principal stress difference in the plate obtained from the thermal stress analysis.

2 The thermal stress concentrated at the peripheries of the filler and the hole in the thickness and in the width directions of the adhesive.

3 The thermal stress distribution in a butt adhesive joint in the steady-state temperature field where an adhesive contained rigid fillers and circular holes, was analyzed using the two-dimensional theory of elasticity.

4 Tensile stress was generated near the interface between an adherend and an adhesive and around the interface where the filler was contained beneath, while compressive stress was around the interface where the hole was contained beneath in an adhesive when the adherend was kept at higher temperature and the side surfaces of the joint was surrounded by air of lower temperature.

5 The thermal principal stress was tensile and singular at the end of the interface, while those at the peripheries of the filler and the hole increased when the filler or the hole was located near the side surfaces of the adhesive.

REFERENCES

1. Sohn.J.E., "Improved matrix-filler adhesion". J. Adhesion, 19 (1985) 15-27.

2. Jakusik,R., Jamarani,F. and Kinloch.A.J.,"The fracture behavior of a rubber-modified epoxy under impact fatigue". J. Adhesion, 32 (1990) 245-254.

3. Timoshenko.S.P. and Goodier, J.N.,"Theory of elasticity". McGraw-Hill, New York 1970.

4. Temma,K., Sawa,T., Uchida,H. and Nakano,Y.,"A two-dimensional stress analysis of butt adhesive joints having a circular hole defect in the adhesive subjected to external bending moments", J. Adhesion, 33 (1991) 133-147.

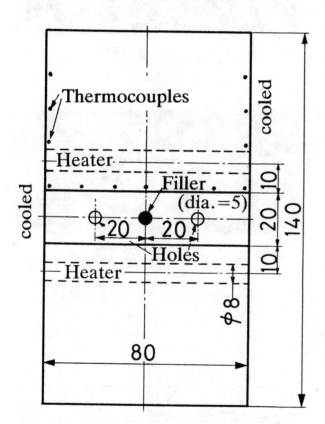

Fig. 1 Experimental setup and dimensions of a joint in the photoelastic measurement

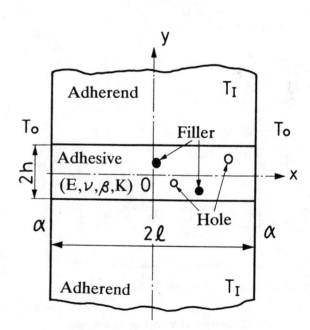

Fig. 2 Model for analysis of butt adhesive joint having rigid fillers and circular holes in an adhesive

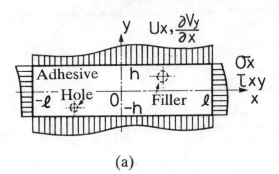

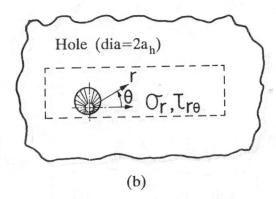

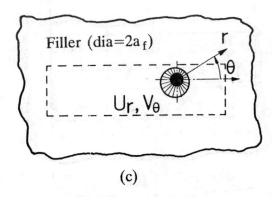

Fig. 3 Analytical model of an adhesive

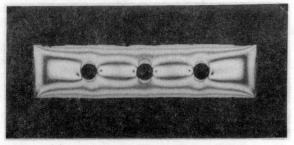

(a) in case of a filler and two holes
(filler position x=0 mm, y=0 mm
hole positions x=±20 mm, y=0 mm)

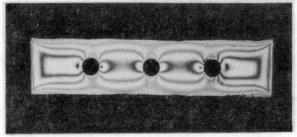

(b) in case of three fillers
(filler positions x=-20, 0, 20 mm, y=0 mm)

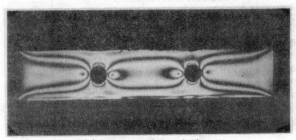

(c) in case of two holes
(hole positions x=±15 mm, y=0 mm)

Fig. 4 Photoelastic measurements
(T_I = 75°C (= 348 K), T_O = 25°C (= 298 K))

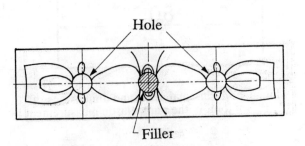

Fig. 5 Numerically calculated fringe pattern
in case of a filler and two holes
(filler position x=0 mm, y=0 mm
hole positions x=±20 mm, y=0 mm)

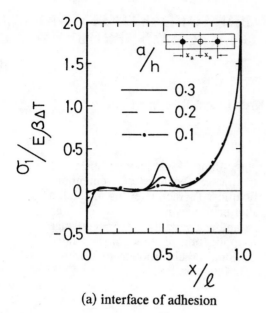

(a) interface of adhesion

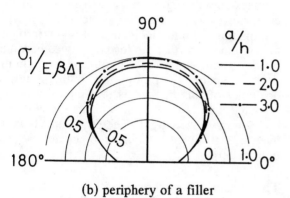

(b) periphery of a filler

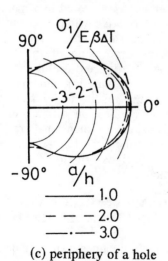

(c) periphery of a hole

Fig. 6 Principal thermal stress distribution in case of type (1)

hole position x=0, y=0 : filler positions x=±0.5l, y=0
(h / l = 0.1, E = 3.3 GPa, ν = 0.36, β = 0.67x10^{-6}/K,
T_I = 100°C (= 373 K), T_O = 0°C (= 273 K))

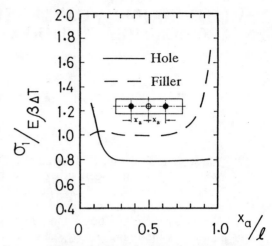

Fig. 7 Effect of filler position on the maximum thermal principal stresses at peripheries of filler and hole in type (1)

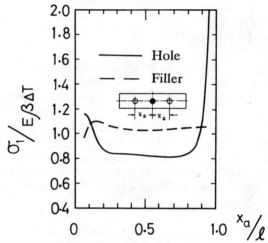

Fig. 8 Effect of hole position on the maximum thermal principal stresses at peripheries of filler and hole in type (2)

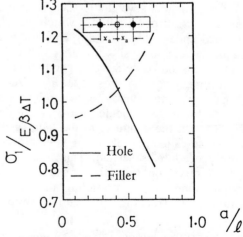

Fig. 9 Effect of diameters of hole and filler on the maximum thermal principal stresses at peripheries of filler and hole in type (1)

COMPUTER-AIDED SCATTERED LIGHT PHOTOELASTICITY AND ITS APPLICATION TO THREE-DIMENSIONAL CRACK PROBLEM

Akihiro KATOH, Jian RAO, Masahisa TAKASHI, and Takeshi KUNIO

ABSTRACT

The scattered light method,the classical techniques in three-dimensional photoelastic stress analysis, have not been utilized so often in practical cases because of tremendous elaboration for data analysis and of experimental difficulties. To facilitate this method, a compact set of polarized light source of thin and parallel band was made up using a high intensity Argon laser beam and a few cylindrical lenses, and analyzed the integrated fringe pattern as the digital image data. In this paper, as an application of the computer-aided stress analysis, the authors try to analyze three-dimensional crack problem of CT type specimen with the improved devices of the Scattered Light Photoelasticity.

I. INTRODUCTION

As well known, ordinary photoelastic method is useful and effective for the analysis of (average) plane stress of a plate, the thickness of which is very small compared with the other dimension. But, in case that the thickness is not so thin, the stress analyzed by this method only gives the average value over the thickness, so that the stress analysis must be performed three-dimensionally for obtaining more accurate stress value of such a problem.

Two techniques, stress freezing method and scattered light method, have been so far proposed as the photoelastic method available to the three-dimensional stress analysis. However, they have some merits and demerits in their own ways. In the former method, several slice cut mechanically from a stress frozen model, which has been performed under a high freezing temperature, are needed for the analysis. In other words, this method is a kind of destructive photoelastic one. Furthermore, since the stress state is frozen at a high freezing temperature, i.e. in a rubbery state, it is that for a low modules and Poisson's ratio being 0.5. On the contrary, in the latter method, since the so-called optical slicing is employed, no slicing procedure is needed. This indicates that nondestructive photoelastic stress analysis is possible under a direct loading to the model without the freezing procedure involving troublesome slicing of the frozen model. In this case, however, the immersion method is needed for making straight incidence of light into the loaded model, so that the loading device becomes rather complicated because it must be set up in the limited space of immersion bath. Another difficulty of this method is that intensity of the scattered light is very weak compared with that of incident polarized light. Therefore, much more intense light source is requisite to get the scattered light pattern.

This paper is concerned with computer-aided scattered light photoelasticity. Since the principal stress difference is scattered light photelasticity is given as a derivative value of fringe order, the computer-aided treatment of the data including digital image processing of the fringe pattern seems to be effective and useful not only to avoid bothersome data handling but also to improve accuracy of the results to be analyzed. In this paper, as an application of the computer-aided stress analysis, three-dimensional crack problem of CT-type specimen is demonstraited, with the improved devices of the scattered light photoelasticity.

II. FUNDAMENTAL EQUATION OF SCATTERED LIGHT METHOD

When polarized light passes in a model, which is in three-dimensional stress states, the fringe order N at any point of the scattered isochromatic fringe

Akihiro KATOH is a graduate student in Department of Mechanical Engineering, Masahisa TAKASHI is a professor of Mechanical engineering, Aoyama Gakuin University, 6-16-1, Chitosedai, Setagaya-ku, Tokyo,Japan, RAO Jian is a ph.D student in Department of Mechanical Engineering, Takeshi KUNIO is a professor of Mechanical Engineering, Kanto-Gakuin University, 4834, Mutsuura-chou, Kanazawa-ku,Yokohama,Japan

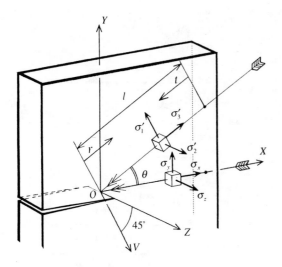

Fig. 1 Scattered Light Photoelastic Effect

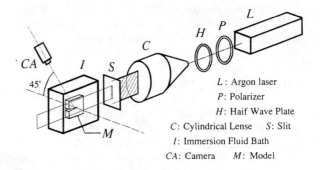

L : Argon laser
P : Polarizer
H : Haif Wave Plate
C : Cylindrical Lense S : Slit
I : Immersion Fluid Bath
CA : Camera M : Model

Fig. 2 Optical System

pattern is given by equation (1) on the assumption the secondary principal stress direction dose not rotate along the incident light path.

$$N = \alpha \int_0^t (\sigma_1' - \sigma_2') dt \tag{1}$$

where σ_1' and σ_2' are secondary principal stress with respect to the incident direction, t, of the polarized light, and α is the photoelastic stress sensitivity of the model material. In equation (1), the lower and upper limit values of the integral give the incident points to the model and an arbitrary points on the light path in the model, respectively. By differentiating equation (1) with respect to t, the fundamental equation is derived as follow;

$$\frac{dN}{dt} = \alpha (\sigma_1' - \sigma_2') \tag{2}$$

Now, let transform the equation (2) into a form appropriate to analysis of CT-type specimen. The three dimensional coordinates are taken as shown in Fig.1, the origin of which is on the crack front and in the middle plain(x,y-plain). For the sake of simplicity of explanation, assume that the incident light is in the middle plain and makes σ_r with x-axis. And, using the polarcoordinates(r,θ,z) instead of (x,y,z), equation (2) is transformed as;

$$\frac{dN}{dr} = -\alpha (\sigma_\theta - \sigma_z) \tag{3}$$

because σ_r provides no photoelastic effect and $\sigma_{rz}=\sigma_{zr}=0$ in the middle plain.

As a special case, if $\theta=0$, i.e. r-axis coincide with x-axis, then equation (3) can be represented by the following equation;

$$\frac{dN}{dr} = -\alpha (\sigma_y - \sigma_z) \tag{3'}$$

As for the light incidence in other planes parallel to the middle plain of the specimen, equation (3) and (3') are given in somewhat complicated forms involving other stress components.

III. EXPERIMRNTAL METHOD AND APPARATUS

Experimental optical system used in this study is shown in Fig.2. High power light of argon laser (higher than 1600mW) with a single wave length of 514.5 nm was used. The light of laser itself has a character of polarization. But, for the purpose of making it more strict polarized light, Kramtom type polariscope is used, through which the light turns into a complete linearly polarized light. Also, a half wave length plate is usual for make a rotation of the above polarized light by any angle.

On the other hand, for clear observation of a whole scattered fringe pattern, a layer of incident polarized light is made by means of a cylindrical lense together with a slit having 0.8 mm in width.

Even in the ordinary photoelastic experiment, the so called immersion method is sometimes adopted for taking a pretty photoelastic fringe pattern. This method is always needed in the scattered light photoelasticity, because individual polarized light beam constructing a light layer must pass straightly through a model without showing any refraction at its curved surface boundary. Moreover, adjustment of the index of refraction of immersion liquid must be made precisely. In this experiment, mixture of 1-1-2-2 tetrabromoethane (Nd=1.634) and silicone oil(Nd=1.440) is used. The mixing ratio is determined accurately so that the refractive index of the immersion liquid may have the same value of a figures as that of the model, using the precision refract meter.

Since the scattered fringe pattern is observed at the angle of 45 degree with model surface, the fringe picture is generally disturbed between the upper and lower parts. The reform of this distortion is made, taking a picture by means of an optical bent module camera. And, positioning of the scattered fringes in such picture is performed, taking the reform procedure into consideration. On the other hand, at the crowded part of fringes like crack tip, the fringe position is decided directly from the digital image data obtained by CCD camera.

IV. MODEL SPECIMEN FOR SCATTERED PHOTOELASTICITY

In addition to the requested characteristics to the model material for ordinary photoelastic experiment, desirable characteristics as the materials used in scattered light photoelasticity are listed up as follows;

(1) less absorptiveness of light intensity along the light path in the material,
(2) no luminous site in the material, and
(3) higher scattering coefficient.

In the present experiment, epoxy resin, which is composed of Araldite B and hardening agent HT 901, is used. The hardening and curing procedures are described in the following.

First, Araldite B is conditioned about at 120 °C for more than 5 hours, then HT 901 is mixed with the Araldite in the weight ratio of 100:32 and this mixture is stirred at 130 °C for 30 minutes, when it is in considerably lower viscous state. Next, the above mixture is filtered through a fine sieve to remove impurities. Then, after vacuum degassing at 130 °C, it is poured into a mold and cured in a furnace. Control of the curing temperature after the molding is conducted carefully lest any initial stress and mottle should be produced.

The specimen employed is similar to the Compact Tension type of ASTM standard as shown in Fig.3, and a crack is introduced as a sharp notch (ρ=0.4mm) by a fine cutter under water cooling. Also, stress induced by working is relieved with annealing treatment. On the other hand, the surface of the specimen is polished so well thus

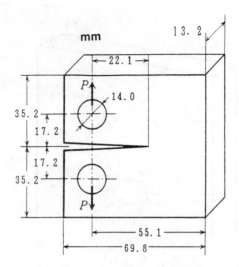

Fig. 3 Compact Tension Specimen

loss of incident light due to refraction and reflection at the boundary may be reduced.

The present experiment can be conducted without use of the stress freezing method. However, from the reason of complicated arrangement of loading device set up within a limited space of a immersion bath as mentioned before, the freezing method easy to handle was employed. To obtain the exact stress distribution at crack tip, introduction of a sharp crack to the specimen is needed. But, for fear lest the crack should develop into the fracture during stress freezing process owing to a load enough to make a clear scattered fringe pattern, a sharp notch was used instead of a crack.

V. IMAGE OPERATION OF SCATTERED LIGHT FRINGE

A typical photograph of scattered light fringe pattern is shown in Fig.4. If this pattern is given numerically as digital image data, the correct position of each fringe can be extracted from the data. In the present image processing, the whole fringe pattern was taken as digital image data of 512x480 pixel having 256 ranks of brightness with CCD camera and computer. The image data of an ordinary photoelastic fringe pattern generally show a smooth brightness distribution, while those of the scattered light fringe are not always so smooth because of various noise involved. Furthermore, the brightness is in low contrast. therefore, in order to extracting correctly the positions having the extreme value of brightness, it is essential to perform the noise reduction and other procedures against image data.

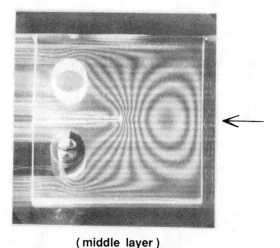

(middle layer)
← : incident direction

Fig. 4　Scattered Light Fringe Pattern

The type of noise are mainly classified into;
   (1) noise due to electric vibration of hard ware (camera and computer etc.),
   (2) noises due to impurities and very small voids in the specimen, and
   (3) noise of the scattered light itself.

To make reduction of noise (1), superposition of several image data at the same position is effective. As for noise (2), soft ware filter is available. But, in case of noise (3), it seems generally difficult to distinguish between brightness of scattered light and noise, so smoothing by the basic spline technique was used. A typical example of such a smoothing curve is shown in Fig.5, together with the original brightness distribution of the image data.

Since the extreme of each amplitude in fringe brightness distribution corresponds to the dark line or bright line of a scattered fringe pattern, fringe order at the position of the extreme is assigned to N or N+0.5, where N=integer.

A series of procedure; acquisition of image data, smoothing of brightness distribution, positing of the brightness extreme and assignment of fringe order, are all performed on computer soft program.

VI. STRESS INTENSITY FACTOR OF CT-TYPE SPECIMEN

When a polarized light layer passes through in the middle plain of the specimen with an incident

angle of θ, the scattered light fringe order N at r can be expressed from equation (3) as;

$$\frac{dN}{dr} = -\alpha \cdot F(r, \theta)$$
(4)

For a specimen having an ideal crack like CT-type specimen, equation (4) can be given in the following form;

$$\frac{dN}{dr} = -\alpha \cdot \frac{K_1}{\sqrt{2\pi r}} \cdot \cos^3\frac{\theta}{2} + F_1(r, \theta)$$
(5)

according to the theory of linear fracture mechanics. In the above equation, K_1 is stress intensity factor, $F_1(r,\theta)$ is nonsingular term, which becomes negligible small near the crack tip in comparison with the first term of the right side of the equation. Thus, in the vicinity of crack tip, the following relation holds.

$$\frac{dN}{dr} = -\alpha \cdot \frac{K_1}{\sqrt{2\pi r}} \cdot \cos^3\frac{\theta}{2}$$
(6)

or

$$\frac{dN}{dr} = -\alpha \cdot \frac{K_1}{\sqrt{2\pi r}}$$
(6')

for light incident along x-direction(θ=0)

From equations (6) or (6'), dN/dr is found inversely proportional to the square root of r near the crack tip. This indicates that plot of N against $\sqrt{r}$ gives a straight line, the slope of which is proportional to K_1 value, in the vicinity of crack tip.

$$\frac{dN}{d\sqrt{r}} = -\alpha \cdot K_1 \cdot \sqrt{\frac{2}{\pi}}$$
(7)

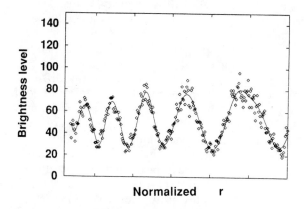

Fig. 5　Brightness Distribution

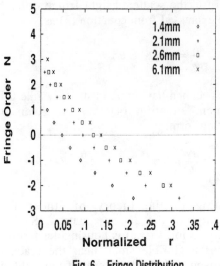

Fig. 6 Fringe Distribution

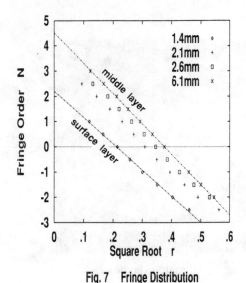

Fig. 7 Fringe Distribution

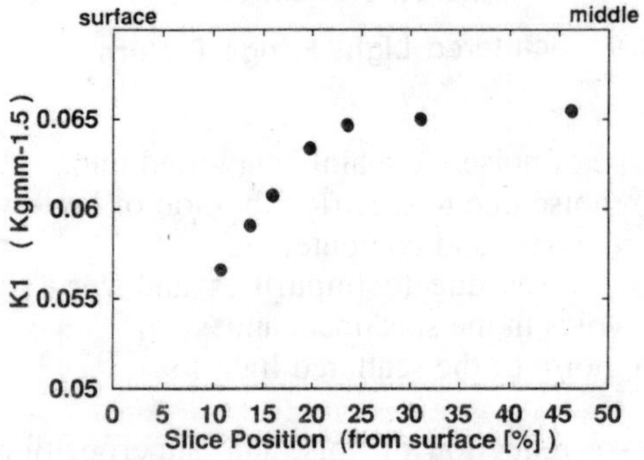

Fig.6 shows fringe order N against the normalize r, say r/l, where l is the ligament width l, with an angle of θ=0 in a few light layer incidence (z=constant) parallel to the middle plain (z=0), while in Fig.7 the relationship between N and the square root of r/l, which was derived from Fig.6, is given as additional data.

As seen from this figure, the curves of fringe order against normalized value of $\sqrt{r}$ are almost linear near the notch tip, so that the K_1 value for z=0 (in the middle plain) and its equivalent values for z=constant (in the plains parallel to the middle plain) were determined from the slopes at r=0 of the extrapolated curves. The experimental results in this ways are given in Fig.8.

VII. EXPERIMNTAL RESULTS AND DISCUSSIONS

The experimental values given in Fig.8 may not all the values of valid stress intensity factor, because the value for the middle plain involves the stress component of z-direction and the other values does shear stress components. This means that for determination of more exact stress intensity factor, supplementary light incidence from different direction may be required. This is possible to do in the scattered light method because of it being a nondestructive method. In this case, however, attention should be paid to the rotation of polarized light along its path. In fact, fringe pattern for a plain except the middle one grows a little faint because of the rotation mentioned above. It is noteworthy, nevertheless, that the equivalent K_1 values vary along crack front as seen in Fig.8

Fig. 8 Stress Intensity Factor

VIII. CONCLUDING REMARKS

In this paper, possibility of three-dimensional photoelastic analysis for crack problem by use of computer-aided scattered light method without any slicing of a stress frozen model was shown, taking CT-type specimen having a finite width, which is widely used for the fracture mechanics as an example. As results, it turned out that computer aided technique including digital image processing is available and very effective to treatment of scattered light fringe pattern containing various noise.

ACKNOWLEDGEMENT
The authors appreciate the financial support of the center for Science and Engineering Research Institute of Aoyama Gakuin University.

REFERENCES
[1] Paipeties,S.A. and Holister,G.S., Photoelasticity in Engineering Practics, Elsevier Applited Science Publishers, (1985)
[2] Nishida,M. and Kawata,K., Photoelasticity, Proceeding of the International Symposium on Photoelasticity, (1986),p.251-258

DIGITAL FRINGE MULTIPLICATION
OF PHOTOELASTIC IMAGES – A NEW APPROACH

* T. Y. Chen

ABSTRACT

A simple and new approach for digital fringe multiplication of photoelastic images is described and demonstrated. By using image-division technique and the power relations of cosine function, the fringes can be multiplied to 16 times or more. The use of a PC-based image-processing system eliminates the photographic process and optical equipment of the conventional methods of fringe multiplication.

INTRODUCTION

In normal photoelastic analysis, light- and dark-field isochromatic fringe patterns are obtained which allow the determination of half- and whole-order fringes. However, in certain applications the ordinary isochromatic fringe pattern may be inadequate to allow an accurate evaluation of the stress. Thus a procedure to increase the number of fringes is required. Currently several methods can be used to accomplish this objective. Methods of compensation [1] can be applied to evaluate the fractional fringe orders except that they are tedious and time-consuming. And, the superimposition of two negatives (light- and dark-field) using photographic techniques increases the number of fringes by twice [2,3]. In doing so, good darkroom techniques are required to produce good results. A better way to multiply the fringes can be done by inserting a partial mirror into the field of a lens polariscope on both sides of the model [4,5]. However a considerable loss of light intensity of the multiplied fringe pattern is accompanied with this method. In recent years, applications of digital techniques for data acquisition and data analysis of photoelastic fringe patterns have made photoelastic method more efficient. A digital method of photoelastic fringe multiplication was reported [6]. The concept used is similar to the photographic technique, and is done by substracting the pixel intensities of the dark-field image from the light-field image. The fringes can be increased by a factor of 4. In this paper another approach based on image-division (or normalization) technique is applied for fringe multiplication. With a carefully calibrated image-processing system, the normalized image data can be used for fringe multiplication directly. By using the power relations of cosine function, the fringe multiplication can be increased to many times.

THEORETICAL BACKGROUND

In photoelastic analysis, the circular polariscope as shown in Figure 1 is used to obtain the isochromatic field. The intensity of a light-field isochromatic fringe pattern is given by:

$$I = I_m \cos^2(\Delta/2) \qquad (1)$$

where I is the intensity of the light emerging from the analyzer, I_m is the maximum intensity of light emerging from the analyzer, Δ (= $2N\pi$) is the relative retardation, and N is the fringe order. Let I_1 and I_2 be the light-field intensities of the unloaded and loaded photoelastic model, respectively. Then dividing I_2 by I_1 gives the

---

* T. Y. Chen is Associate Professor of Mechanical Engineering, National Cheng Kung University, Tainan, Taiwan, R. O. C.

resultant intensity,

$$I_r = I_2 / I_1 = \cos^2(\Delta/2) \qquad (2)$$

Thus the relative retardation can be computed from the following relationship.

$$\Delta = 2 \cos^{-1}(I_2/I_1)^{1/2} \qquad (3)$$

For this equation to be used without ambiguity, the maximum fringe order in the field of interest must not exceed 1/2. For the purpose of fringe multiplication, the resultant intensity, I_r, in equation (2) can be directly substituted into a power relation of cosine function, such as

$$\begin{aligned} I_p = \cos^2\Delta &= 4 \cos^4(\Delta/2) - 4 \cos^2(\Delta/2) + 1 \\ &= 4 I_r^4 - 4 I_r^2 + 1 \qquad (4) \end{aligned}$$

In equation (4), the extinction of the intensity, I_p, occurs when $\Delta=(2n+1)\pi/2$ for $n = 0, 1, 2, ...$ Thus the order of the fringe observed on this image is $N = (2n+1)/4$, i.e.; the fringe order is 1/4, 3/4, etc. Therefore the number of fringes in the computed image is increased twice. Besides using equation (4), other power relations of cosine function can also be used for fringe multiplication with various time.

SYSTEM CONFIGURATION

The system, as shown in Figure 1, consists of a standard diffused-light polariscope for producing isochromatic fringe patterns, a CCD camera, a DT-2851 frame grabber with two frame buffers, a PC/AT 386 computer with 2 Mbytes of RAM, and other peripheral devices. Each frame buffer has 256K bytes memory which is organized as 512 X 512 pixels with 256 gray levels. The fringe pattern is presented to the CCD camera directly and is digitized at a rate of 30 frames per second.

CALIBRATION

CCD camera accumulates signals generated by light falling on it between one readout cycle and the next. Then the signals are amplified to produce usable electronic signals for later conversion of digital values. However this process may not be linear. Besides that, dark current generated by thermal excitation may limits the readout in low-light areas. Hence a careful calibration of the system is needed to obtain an accurate result. The image-processing system is calibrated by using a standard density-step tablet. Firstly the tablet is put into the polariscope and digitized. Then the digitized density values are fitted by a polynomial regression. And, a set of data is generated from the polynomial to form a new look-up-table for later acquisition of image data. Figure 2 shows the grey-level responses of the image-processing system and the calibrated results. Apparently this calibration procedure is very effective. However the response at the low-light region is bad and should be avoid in the data acquisition process.

EXPERIMENTAL TESTS AND RESULTS

The photoelastic model (made of PSM-1 material) used is a circular disk of diameter 50mm subjected to a concentrated diametral load. The load was increased until having two fringes on the model in the light-field setting. Figure 3 shows the images of the unloaded model, the loaded model and the fringe pattern after multiplication. It is noted that because the intensity value obtained from equation (2) did not fall into the interval (0,1) exactly, an adjustment of the image data was made before using equation (4) for fringe multiplication. Further use of equation (4) repeatedly, the fringe multiplication can be increased by a factor of 4 as shown in Figure 4, and even to a factor of 16 as shown in Figure 5. Theoretically the fringes can be multiplied to a higher time. However a computer simulation of this approach reveals that it is limited by the system resolution and quantization errors.

CONCLUSIONS

A simple and new approach for digital fringe multiplication of photoelastic image is described and demonstrated. Results have shown that the fringe multiplication can be increased up to 16 times. With a PC-based image-processing system, the time-consuming photographic process and the requirement of additional equipment for fringe multiplication are eliminated. The linearity of the system has been studied and calibrated using a standard density tablet and the polynomial regression method. This effort makes the following image-division operation more accurate. Although This approach is somewhere comparable with the method described in Ref. 6, it is a new and more effective approach.

ACKNOWLEDGMENTS

The author is thankful to the National Science Council of the Republic of China for supporting this research under grant NSC81-0422-E006-01. This project is directed by Dr. Hong-Sen Yan and Dr. Rong-Shean Lee.

REFERENCES

1. Dally, J.W. and Riley, W.F., Experimental Stress Analysis, Mcgraw-Hill Book Co., 1978.

2. Post, D.,"Isochromatic Fringe Sharpening and Fringe Multiplicationin Photoelasticity," Proc. SESA, XII (2), 143-157, 1955.

3. Talukder, N.K.D. and Ghosh, P.,"On Fringe Multiplication by Superimposition of Negatives," Experimental Mechanics, 15(6), 237-239, 1975.

4. Dally, J.W. and Ahimaz, F.J.,"Photographic Method to Sharpen and Double Isochromatic Fringes," Experimental Mechanics, 2(6), 170-175, 1962.

5. Bynum, D.J.,"On the Accuracy of Fringe Multiplication with Mirrored Birefringent Coatings," Experimental Mechanics, 6(7), 381-382, 1966.

6. Toh, S.L., Tang, S.H. and Hovanesian, J.D.,"Computerized Photoelastic Fringe Multiplication," Experimental Techniques, 14(4), 21-23, 1990.

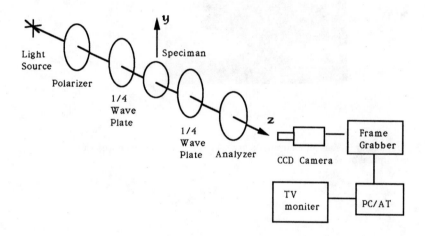

Figure 1 Schematic of experimental setup

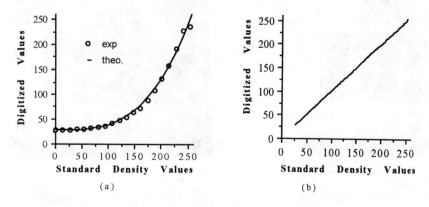

Figure 2 Grey-level response of the image system . (a) original , (b) calibrated .

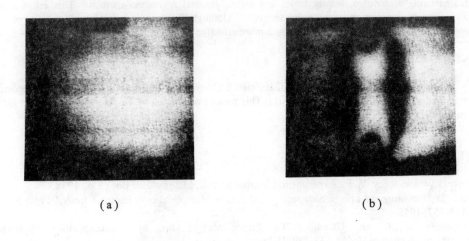

(c)

Figure 3   Light-field images of a circular disk. (a) unloaded, (b) loaded, (c) after multiplied by 2.

Figure 4   Light-field image of a circular disk after multiplied by 4.

Figure 5   Light-field image of a circular disk after multiplied by 16.

A PHOTOELASTIC STUDY ON THE
FATIGUE LIMIT OF SPHEROIDAL GRAPHITE IRON

Hideto SUZUKI*   and   Tsuneo NAGAI**

* Professor, Department of System Engrg., Faculty of Engrg.,
Ibaraki University,
1-12-4, Nakanarusawa, Hitachi, Ibaraki, 〒316 JAPAN
** Professor emeritus, Ibaraki University

ABSTRACT

It has been found by micro fractography using SEM that a fatigue crack initiates at micro porosity and it propagates through voids formed by separating spheroidal graphite,SG from the matrix microstructure in the high-strength Spheroidal Graphite Iron,SGI. Then, the singular stress field around crack-tip under interacting by crack and voids was experimentally analyzed by photoelastic method. Based on the present analysis, it could be interpreted that SG at crack tip variously effected fatigue crack propagation,FCP.

INTRODUCTION

Recently, Spheroidal Graphite Iron,SGI has been notified as a new structural material with high strength and toughness, because of the advance of processing technique such as Austempered Ductile Iron, ADI and also new utilizations like the cask for abandoned used atomic fuel[1~5]. However, the fatigue reliability of SGI has not been made clear yet and the design concept against SGI fatigue in machines and structures has not been competent. In order to estimate and improve fatigue reliability of SGI, it has become important to study the behavior of crack initiation and propagation under the lower stress near the fatigue limit. Especially, it should be attended to that the high-strength SGI is ruptured under over 10

cyclic loading[6]. In the domain of long fatigue life, the rate of fatigue crack propagation, FCP is extremely lower and then microstructural factors such as spheroidal graphite can affect FCP.

Furthermore, by comparing the microstructre of SGI with that of general carbon steels, it was found that the microstructure of SGI could be recognized as the compound of SG and the micro-structure of carbon steels. Then, the effects of SG on the fatigue behavior should be made clear in order to guarantee the fatigue reliability of SGI[7]. However, the rolls of SG on the fatigue behaviors of the high-strength SGI have not been sufficiently studied by experimental mechanics.

On the other hand, by photoelastic experiment, the stress concentration, α around circular particle and void like SG, and also stress intensity factor, SIF of crack have been analyzed[8]. Thus, based on photoelastic study, it may be possible to make clear effects of interacting by SG and fatigue crack on the singular stress field around crack-tip and then fatigue crack propagation, FCP.

In the present paper, the effects of SG on FCP was studied in order to guarantee the fatigue reliability of high-strength SGI through two approaches based on experimental mechanics which were micro fractography using SEM and photoelastic method.

FRACTOGRAPHY OF SPHEROIDAL GRAPHITE IRON

First of all, in this section, a typical example of the fatigue process in spheroidal graphite iron, SGI was demonstrated by fractography as shown in Fig.1~4. This high-strength(UTS of 900MPa) SGI with full pearlite matrix fractured in fatigue after long life of 10 cyclic loading. A macro fracture surface of SGI in Fig.1 shows Fish Eye pattern.

This part was enlarged in Fig.2 and 3. The casting defect of micro porosity appeared at the center of Fish Eye pattern, that is the first stage of fatigue fracture. In addition, many SG particles could be observed around the porosity. Furthermore, it should be noticed that SG was separated from pearlite matrix microstructure and then a void was formed as shown in Fig.4.

From the above observation, it could be understood that the fatigue crack initiated at the micro porosity and then FCP passed through the void capsulating SG. in high-strength SGI as illustrated in Fig.5. The reason why the fatigue crack can initiate at the casting defect of micro porosity is the higher notch-sensitivity of harder matrix microstructure in high-strength SGI. However, the rolls of SG on FCP have been wrapped in mystery. As expressed simply, " SG is stopper or accelerator for FCP ? " Thus, the effects of SG on FCP should be made clear to guarantee the fatigue reliability of SGI.

Based on the above fracture analysis, in the following section, the effects of SG on the local stress condition around the fatigue crack tip were examined by photoelastic method using the plates with a crack and holes simulated to voids capsulating SG.

Fig. 1. Macroscopic fractography.

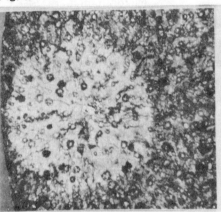

Fig. 2. Fish Eye pattern.

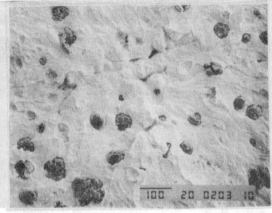

Fig. 3. Porosity on center of Fish Eye.

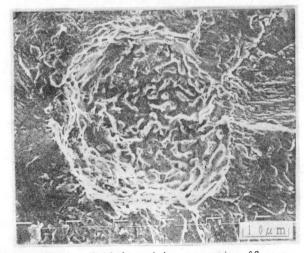

Fig. 4. Void formed by separating SG.

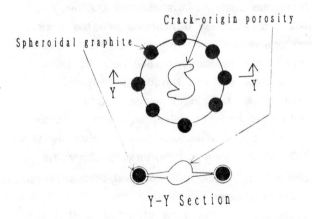

Fig. 5. The effect of porosity and SG on micro mechanism of fatigue crack.

PHOTOELASTIC EXAMINATION FOR EFFECTS OF SPHEROIDAL GRAPHITE ON FCP

In order to discuss the effects of SG on FCP, the interaction of voids and crack on the local stress condition around crack tip and holes, and Stress Intensity Factor SIF were examined by photoelastic experiments.

Local Stress Condition around Crack Tip and Holes

(1) Single Hole and Crack:

The specification of tested model plates of Epoxy resin for photoelastic experiment was shown in Fig.6. The positions of holes were tabulated in Tab.1. Two types of model plates were prepared to be varied in the horizontal distance or the vertical distance of a hole from the crack tip.

Enlarged isochromatic pattern around the crack tip in TPH-1 of the horizontal type was shown in Fig.7. As the hole closes to the crack tip, the remarkable interaction between the stress concentration by hole and the stress singurality by crack is displayed in the horizontal type of model plates. Thus,

it could be understood from photoelastic experiment that the local stress at the edge of SG would be increased when the fatigue crack approached to SG as simulated in TPH. While, the other isochromatics in TPV-7 of the vertical type displayed the rotation of local stress around crack tip which was controlled with the vertical distance of hole as shown in Fig.8.

From the above facts, it might be suggested that FCP was accelerated by the void capsulating SG. Also, a micro crack can be initiated at the edge of void ahead of main fatigue crack by the high local stress. Then, the main fatigue crack joints easily with this micro crack and rushes into the void. While, FPC can be curved by the rotation of local stress if the position of SG is vertically disoriented for FCP as simulated in TPV type of plate. Therefore, the micro behaviors of FCP of SGI could be understood as illustrated in Fig.9.

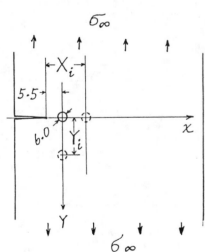

Fig. 6. Test piece with single hole for photoelastic study.

Fig. 7. Enlarged isochromatics on TPH-1

Fig. 8. Enlarged isochromatics on TPV-7

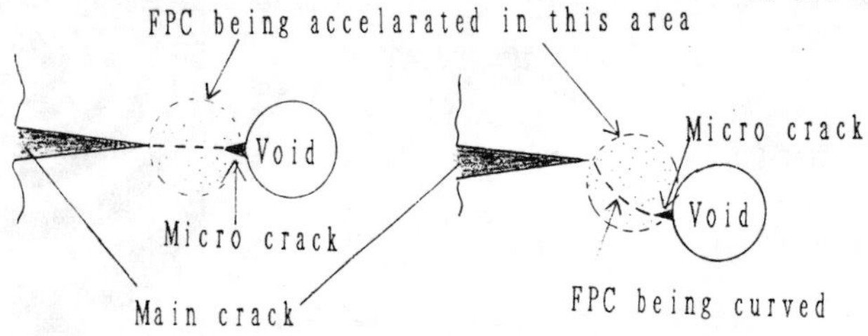

Fig. 9. Illustration of the effect of void formed by separating SG on FPC.

TPH-No.	-1	-2	-3	-4	-5	
$X_i/3$	1.8	2.2	2.8	4.8	5.8	

TPV-No.	-6	-7	-8	-9	-10	-11
$Y_i/3$	0.64	1.1	1.6	2.5	4.2	4.6

Tab. 1. The position of hole

(2) Plural Holes and Crack:

The specifications of plural holes in tested model plates were shown in Fig. 10 for double holes in T. P. 3~6 and also Fig. 11 for triple holes in T. P. 7~11 respectively. As compared with each other, enlarged isochromatic patterns at crack tips interacted by single hole, double and triple holes were shown in Figs. 12, 13 respectively. Furthermore, Figs. 14, 15 indicated isoclinic and principal stress lines in the same manner as isochromatic patterns. These figures displayed the remarkable interaction on the local stress by holes and a crack.

Therefore, the stress concentration factor, α at the edge of hole in each model plates determined with the photoelastic fringe was indicated in Figs. 16~18. It could be understood from Fig. 16 that the local stress at the edge of hole in the side of crack would be increased considerably as a crack had approached to the holes within the dimension of hole radius. Also, Fig. 17 shows that the local stress at the edge of hole could be increased by a crack and other two holes. Thus, in the case of three holes the stress concentration at the hole close to the crack was remarkably higher than that at two other holes. On the hand, the crack is ineffective on increasing the local stress at the edge of hole in the opposite side to crack as shown in Figs. 16 and 18.

While, the isochromatics on plural-holes plate displayed the rotation of local stress around crack tip and hole as shown in Figs. 12, 13, which was observed in just same manner on one-hole plate of the vertical type. Also, this fact might suggest that FCP would be curved and the fatigue crack rushed into the void as illustrated in Fig. 9.

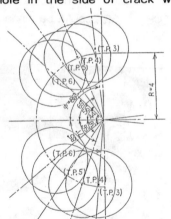

Fig. 10. Test piece with two holes for photoelastic study.

Fig. 12. Isochromatics on T. P. 6.

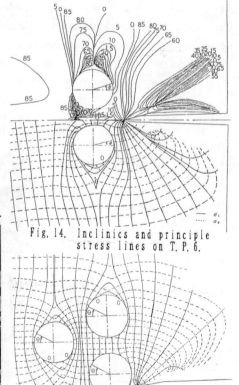

Fig. 14. Inclinics and principle stress lines on T. P. 6.

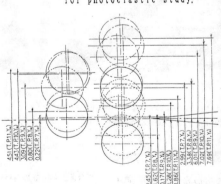

Fig. 11. Test piece with three holes for photoelastic study.

Fig. 13. Isochromatics on T. P. 10.

Fig. 15. Principle stress lines on T. P. 6.

EDM SURFACE EFFECTS ON THE FATIGUE STRENGTH OF A 15 Vol% SiCp/Al METAL MATRIX COMPOSITE MATERIAL

M. Ramulu and G. Paul
Department of Mechanical Engineering
University of Washington, FU-10
Seattle, WA 98195 USA

ABSTRACT

The effects of Electric Discharge Machining (EDM) on the mechanical properties of 15 vol% SiCp/A356 aluminum are studied. Preliminary investigation includes EDM machined surface and subsurface characterization, assessment of the depth of the EDM affected zone, fatigue testing, and fractographic analysis. Fatigue tests show reduction in the fatigue strength of the coarse machined material in comparison to the finely polished material, and microhardness tests show changes in subsurface hardness due to EDM sparking.

INTRODUCTION

Metal matrix composites (MMCs) are gaining increasing attention for applications which demand properties not easily obtainable by traditional homogeneous materials. However, the reinforcing components in MMCs often make them difficult or uneconomical to machine by traditional methods. Consequently, non-traditional machining processes such as Electric Discharge Machining (EDM) have become candidates for processing of MMCs.

Recent studies have demonstrated the machinability of SiC reinforced aluminum metal matrix composites by EDM process [1]. However, Jeelani and Collins [2] noted that EDM machining, like traditional machining, leaves surface defects that cause slight reduction in fatigue life of an Inconel 718 alloy. Therefore, the optimization of EDM for production use in composite materials necessitates the study of its effect on surface integrity.

Other studies have accumulated base data on the fatigue properties of a variety of reinforced aluminum composite materials, establishing in general that reinforced aluminum exhibits superior fatigue strength to that of the un-reinforced aluminum matrix [3-9]. These studies characterized the fatigue behavior of the MMCs under conditions where surface defects have been carefully minimized. Little is known about the fatigue strength of MMCs with imperfect surface integrity brought about by effects of material processing, specifically thermal damage induced by EDM sparking.

An experimental investigation is underway to study the effect of EDM surface effects on the fatigue behavior of 15 vol% SiCp/A356 Al. This material has an excellent strength-to-weight ratio and good fatigue strength. Preliminary data on the effect of coarse (fast cutting) EDM sparking versus fine polishing on the surface integrity of the material has been obtained, and the study of similar effects of fine (slow cutting) EDM sparking is currently being conducted. Surface integrity was assessed by measuring surface roughness, depth of surface effect on the microstructure, and effect on fatigue properties. The purpose of this paper is to report our ongoing research results on the surface integrity of SiCp/Al metal matrix material.

EXPERIMENTAL SETUP AND PROCEDURE

MATERIAL
The base material was 15 vol% SiCp/A356-T6 metal matrix composite provided by Alcan International in the form of extruded rods 9.5 mm (3/8 in.) in diameter. Microstructure of the as-received material is shown in Figure 1, and the particulate size ranges from 3 to 12 μm.

SPECIMEN PREPARATION
Cylindrical axial fatigue test specimens of 15 vol% SiCp/A356 Al were machined from the rods of the base material. The design of the specimens conforms approximately to the recommendations outlined in ASTM Standard E466-82 [10]. The specimen test sections were turned to a diameter of 5.4 mm (0.21 in.) using a carbide tool (grade C6) with a 1/4 in. nose radius, zero rake angle, and 7 degree clearance angle. Figure 2 shows the fabricated specimen EDM geometry and its configuration. Three sets of specimens were fabricated for evaluating the effects of surface roughness on the mechanical properties. The first series of as-machined test specimens were polished with 400 grit SiC sandpaper, followed by 600 grit and by crocus cloth. The other two sets of specimens were uniformly surface sparked in their test sections by EDM using a specially designed and fabricated concave semi-cylindrical shaped copper electrode. The EDM used was a servo-controlled ram type Hansvedt model SE-380. EDM machining conditions were either coarse (maximum current of 6 amperes) or fine (maximum current of 1 ampere). Average material removal rates were obtained by dividing the reduction in specimen mass by total machining time.

EXPERIMENTAL PROCEDURE
The surface finish of each specimen after polishing or sparking was quantified by measuring roughness average (Ra). Roughness was measured using a Taylor-Hobson Surtronic 3 surface profilometer with a traverse length of 7.5 mm and cut-off length of 0.8 mm. Stress-strain tests were conducted on some representative specimens to establish yield and tensile strengths. Remaining specimens in all three sets were subject to constant amplitude zero-to-maximum (R=0) axial loading at 5 Hz by an MTS servo-hydraulic machine in air at room temperature.

Vickers hardness testing was used to measure the microhardness of the polished material and the EDM sparked material to assess the depth of the heat affected subsurface zone. The fracture surfaces of representative sample specimens from all sets were examined by SEM to investigate crack origins and fracture mechanisms.

RESULTS AND DISCUSSION

Figure 3 shows a typical monotonic stress-strain curve up to ultimate tensile strength for the material. The ultimate tensile strength of the material was determined to be 237 MPa, and the 0.2% offset yield stress was found to be 183 MPa. This data clearly shows the enhancement in properties over the base A356 material [11]. Vickers microhardness measurements were also made on the polished material and yielded an average hardness of 69 HV.

Figure 4 shows the fatigue lives of polished and EDM coarse machined specimens. Fatigue tests were stopped beyond 1 million cycles if no fracture occurred. Clearly the fatigue strength of the coarse EDM sparked material is significantly less than that of the polished material. At high cycles ($N_f > 10,000$) the fatigue strength is reduced by 15 to 20% for the same life. The maximum stress shows a clear power relationship with the number of cycles to failure for both data sets, as shown by the linear scatter of the data points on log-log scaling. Additional testing is in progress to confirm this data and to study the fatigue behavior of the material under EDM fine machined conditions.

Figure 5 shows a portion of the fatigue fracture surface of a coarse EDM sparked specimen. Multiple radial lines indicate multiple crack origins. Observation of specimens in all fatigue test series indicated that the crack initiation life was much greater than the propagation life; specimens typically failed with little or no warning.

Figure 6 shows a low magnification view of the surface of a specimen machined by EDM under coarse conditions. Significant thermal damage due to melting and solidification is evident, and surface examination at higher magnification revealed pullout of particulates in the recast layer. The EDM recast layer penetrates approximately 50 μm into the material. Table 1 gives average surface roughness data for the polished specimens, EDM coarse machined specimens, and EDM fine machined specimens, along with the average mass removal rates for fine and coarse sparking. The data shows that the EDM fine machined surface and the EDM coarse machined surface are about 17 and 70 times rougher, respectively, than the polished surface. This increase in roughness may be the cause of the decrease in fatigue life in the EDM sparked specimens.

CONCLUSIONS

Experimental investigation on the effect of surface roughness generated by an EDM machining process on the mechanical properties of 15 vol% SiCp/A356 aluminum metal matrix composite material was carried out. Based on the preliminary results the following conclusions were made:

1. Yield and ultimate strength of 15% Vol. SiCp/Al were found to be 183 and 237 MPa respectively.

2. Coarse EDM produced a rougher surface than polishing, which in turn contributed to the decrease in the fatigue strength of the material by 15 to 20% for the same life at high cycles (N_f>10,000).

3. The direct physical effects of EDM machining included high surface roughness and disruption of the microstructure in the form of recasting of the matrix aluminum and pullout of the silicon carbide particulates which promoted the initiation of surface cracks and eventual failure.

REFERENCES

1. Ramulu, M. and Taya, M., "EDM Machinability of SiCw / Al Composites," Journal of Materials Science, v. 24 (1989) pp. 1103-1108.

2. Jeelani, S. and Collins, M. R., "Effect of Electric Discharge Machining on the Fatigue Life of Inconel 718," International Journal of Fatigue, v. 10, n. 2 (1988) pp. 121-125.

3. Bonnen, J. J., Allison, J. E., and Jones, J. W., "Fatigue Behavior of a 2xxx Series Aluminum Alloy Reinforced with 15 Vol Pct SiCp," Metallurgical Transactions A, v. 22A (May, 1991) pp. 1007-1019.

4. Lee, E. E., "Fatigue Behavior of Silicon Carbide Whisker / Aluminum Composite," Naval Air Development Center (Warminster, PA) Report no. NADC-89037-60, 1988.

5. Masuda, C., Tanaka, Y., Yamamoto, M., and Fukazawa, M., "Effect of Volume Fraction on Fatigue Strength of SiC Whisker or SiC Particle Reinforced Aluminum Composites," Nihon Fukugo Zairyo Gakhaishi (Journal of the Japan Society for Composite Materials), v. 17, n. 2 (1991) pp. 66-73.

6. Srivatsan, T. S., Auradkar, R., Lavernia, E. J., and Prakash, Amit, "High Strain Cyclic Fatigue and Fracture Behavior of a SiC Reinforced Cast Aluminum Alloy Composite," Materials Transactions, JIM, v. 32, n. 5 (1991) pp. 473-479.

7. Tsangarakis, N., Andrews, B. O., and Cavallaro, C., "Mechanical Properties of Some Silicon Carbide Reinforced Aluminum Composites," Journal of Composite Materials, v. 21 (May 1987) pp. 481-492.

8. Hasson, D. F., Crowe, C. R., Ahearn, J. S., and Cooke, D. C., "Fatigue and Corrosion Fatigue of Discontinuous SiC/Al Metal Matrix Composites," <u>Failure Mechanisms in High Performance Materials</u>, Proceedings of the 39th Meeting of the Mechanical Failures Prevention Group, National Bureau of Standards, James G. Early, et. al eds., Cambridge University Press, New York, 1985, pp. 147-156.

9. Karayaka, M. and Huseyin, S. , "Thermomechanical Fatigue of Particulate-Reinforced Aluminum 2xxx-T4," <u>Metallurgical Transactions A</u>, v. 22A (March, 1991) pp. 697-707.

10. ASTM E466-82: "Standard Practice for Conducting Constant Amplitude Axial Fatigue Tests of Metallic Materials", 1982/1991.

11. Metals Handbook, Vol. 2, 10th Ed., ASM International, 1990, pp. 164-167.

Table 1. Surface finishes of 15 vol% SiCp/A356 Al fatigue specimens

Surface Process	Average Mass Removal Rate (mg/s)	Average Ra (μm)
Fine polish	---	0.24
EDM fine	0.0445	3.96
EDM coarse	0.411	16.8

Figure 1. Microstructure of 15 vol% SiCp/A356 Al (1000x)

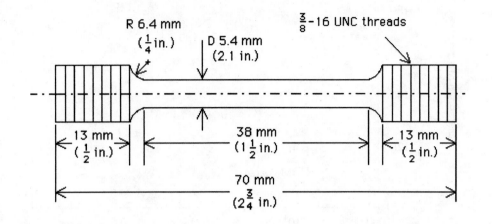

Figure 2. Test specimen configuration

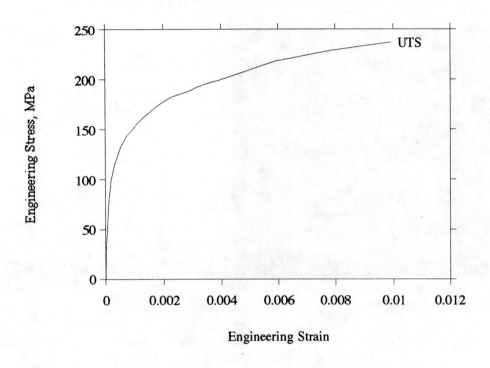

Figure 3. Stress-strain diagram for 15 vol% SiCp/A356 Al

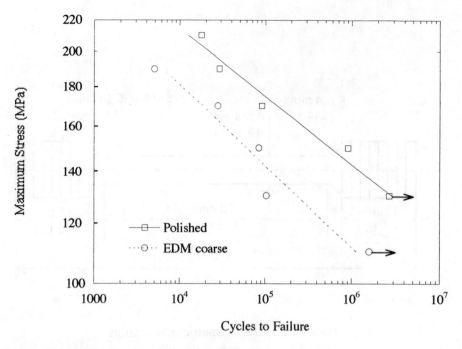

Figure 4. S-N curves for polished and EDM coarse specimens

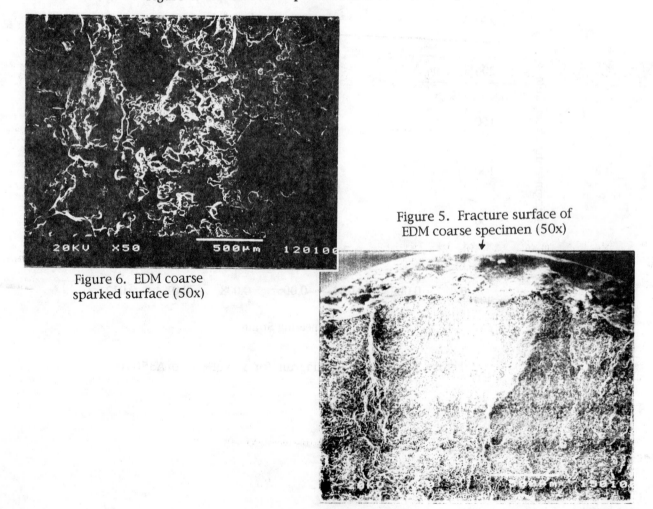

Figure 6. EDM coarse
sparked surface (50x)

Figure 5. Fracture surface of
EDM coarse specimen (50x)

Resistance Curves for Monolithic and Phase Blended γ-TiAl Alloys

Mahyar S. Dadkhah

Rockwell International Science Center
1049 Camino Dos Rios
Thousand Oaks, CA 91360

I. Abstract

The phase blending technique was used to reveal the potential to increase fracture toughness and ductility of γ-TiAl. Moiré interferometry was used to measure resistance curves for monolithic and phase blended γ-TiAl alloys. This whole-field measurement technique was used to record both vertical and horizontal displacements associated with crack growth and to evaluate the crack opening displacement (COD) for compact tension specimens. The result showed that, although fracture toughness of phase blended sheet was noticeably improved, ductility was low. The low ductility is consistent with that of other as-HIP'ed Ti aluminides. Thus, while phase blending increases toughness and further refinement of processing parameters may lead to additional improvements, the as-HIP'ed ductility needs to be improved before the full effects of phase blending can be realized. Increase in toughness in the composite is due to formation of crack face bridging, crack path deviation, blunting and multiple cracking.

II. Introduction

Phase blending has been proposed as a method of improving the ductility of Ti aluminides [1]. Phase blending involves incorporating a ductile phase into the matrix of a brittle material to serve as a crack arrestor or restrict crack propagation by forming ductile ligaments to bridge the crack front [2]. Tractions produced by the bridges reduce crack tip stress intensities. Ductile phase reinforced composites often experience large-scale bridging effects [3], especially for short cracks or in components with small dimensions. The overall load displacement characteristic $P(\delta)$ of a reinforced component is governed by traction law $p(u)$ for the ductile phase, as well as the effective crack tip fracture resistance of the composite, Γ_t and the elastic modulus E' [4]. In addition, important secondary toughening mechanisms have been demonstrated, which arise from crack particle interaction processes [4]. These mechanisms include crack trapping and renucleation leading to increases in Γ_t and crack branching and deflection. The toughening contributions from these mechanisms may be significant and depend on the combined properties of the ductile phase, interface reaction layer and matrix. Numerous studies of the fracture behavior of brittle matrices containing ductile particles show that, if bonded to the matrix, the inclusions toughen the matrix, the toughening increases with volume fraction and inclusion size, and the toughening derives from a bridging zone of unbroken ductile material behind the crack tip. Difficulty in applying phase blending has resulted from excessive interdiffusion of components during consolidation and mechanical working. Typically the high temperatures used to HIP, roll, and extrude γ-TiAl result in a variable composition within the mixture, while deformation produces a nonuniform distribution of the ductile phase. These factors limit the effects of phase blending. The availability of ductile γ-TiAl in thin sections would greatly increase the number of potential applications for this material and, as a result, the use of γ-TiAl powder.

A collaborative research and development effort at Rockwell International Science Center (RISC) and Nuclear Metals, Inc.

(NMI) has been carried out to determine if powder metallurgy techniques can be used to fabricate "phase blended" sheet. PREP™ powders exhibit good uniformity and may be capable of producing a sound composite product with good fracture toughness characteristics. A low temperature (1800°F) high pressure (45 ksi) HIP cycle was selected for consolidation. The microstructures and properties of monolithic Rockwell 1.3 γ-TiAl having a composition of Ti-48Al-2.5Nb-0.3Ta were compared to HIP sheet of Rockwell 1.3 alloy phase blended with Ti-30Nb.

III. Experimental

Tensile Testing

Machining was performed at MET-CUT Research Associates in Cincinnati, Ohio. Flat tensile specimens, having a nominal gauge section of 2 mm x 9.4 mm x 25.4 mm long, were tested at room temperature. Tensile test pieces were machined using low stress grinding techniques. Two tensile specimens were tested for each material. Tests were conducted at room temperature on a 20 kip closed loop servo-hydraulic test machine per ASTM E8. Strain control was set so that a strain rate of 0.005 / sec was maintained through 0.2% yield and the head rate was 1.27 mm/min. after that. Extensometers were used on all specimens.

Crack Growth Experiments (Resistance Curves and Fracture Toughness)

Cracks were grown stably under measured loading conditions in compact tension fracture mechanics specimens of dimension 30 x 32 x 2 mm. A loading fixture that could attach to the stage of an optical microscope was used, to allow in situ observation of the crack tip and wake zones. An improved four-beam moiré interferometry system was used to measure two orthogonal in-plane displacement fields simultaneously [5]. This technique involves replicating a diffraction grid to the surface of the compact tension specimen before growing the crack, and then, during loading to extend the crack, illuminating the surface with an Argon-ion laser (wavelength 514 nm). In this set up, part of the incident beam impinged directly onto the specimen surface, while the other part, after reflection from three plane mirrors, was incident in a symmetrical direction to produce a virtual reference grating. The combination of this reference grating and the diffraction grating bonded to the specimen produced the moiré pattern, which was recorded photographically. The moiré pattern consists of a set of fringes, which represent contours of constant displacement in the x_1 and x_2 directions, the increment between adjacent fringes being equal to the period of the reference grating (0.417 μm). In the present experiments, this technique allowed strain resolution of 10^{-3} over gauge lengths as small as 40 μm. The testing environment for toughness testing was ambient laboratory air at room temperature. Digitized recordings of the moiré patterns were converted to strains automatically [6]. The evaluation of the J-Integral is essentially a numerical integration along a loop encompassing the crack where the three strain components must be evaluated at identical points along the chosen path [6].

J-Integral requires the strain components, the stress components and the strain energy density. The three stress components are calculated using J_2-deformation theory of plasticity for multi-axial states with a power hardening stress-strain relation. Stress intensity factors were evaluated using $k=(JxE)^{0.5}$. Fracture toughness values were obtained by marking the maximum in K_R vs crack extension curves.

IV. Results

Micrographs of the as-HIP'ed microstructures are shown in Figure 1a-b. The monolithic Rockwell 1.3 microstructure transformed into equiaxed γ grains. The surface appearance of phase blended microstructure consisted of spherical γ-TiAl powder encompassed by a nearly continuous array of binary Ti-30Nb alloy as shown in Fig. 1b. The γ powder is made up of γ grains (20 μm diameter) with a featureless matrix. A 10 μm reaction zone exists between the two alloys. Monolithic Rockwell 1.3 and phase blended sheets had densities of 3.76 and 3.97 g/cc, respectively.

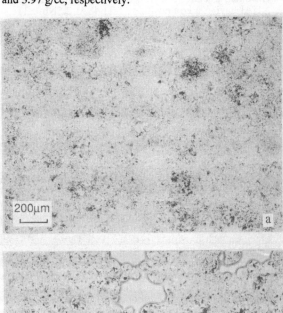

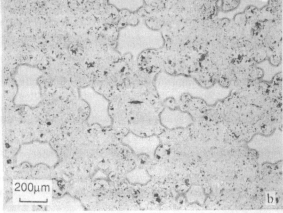

Fig.1 Micrographs of the as-HIP'ed microstructures for a) Monolithic and b) Phase Blended Alloys.

The uniaxial stress-strain relations for monolithic and phase blended alloys with the two coefficients for the power hardening relations are shown in Figure 2. Room temperature elongations were below 1% for both the monolithic and phase blended sheet. All fracture surfaces showed occasional flat cleavage facets and ductile tearing. There was no evidence of intergranular fracture. Although the phase blended fracture surface was more rough, grain boundary facets and prior powder boundary facets were not observed.

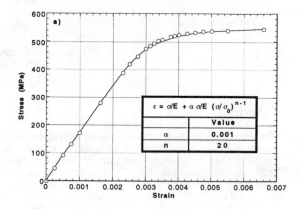

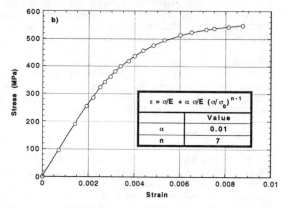

Fig.2 The uniaxial stress-strain relations for a) monolithic and b) phase blended alloys.

A typical moiré fringe pattern and its processed image are shown in Figure 3. An example of x_2 displacement field for stable crack growth in the compact specimen is shown in Figure 4. Crack opening profiles for monolithic and composite γ-TiAl alloys, measured by moiré interferometry, are shown in Figure 5. Comparison of crack opening profiles show that in the composite material the crack is bridged. In this case bridging is supplied by ductile ligaments that remain connected to both fracture surfaces behind the crack front. The bridging tractions acting on the fracture surfaces of cracks could be determined from measurements of such crack opening profiles [7].

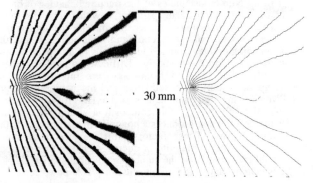

Fig. 3 A typical moiré fringe pattern and its processed image.

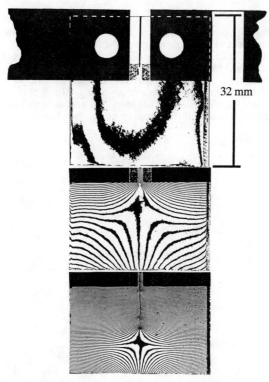

Fig. 4 An example of x_2 displacement field for stable crack growth in the compact specimen.

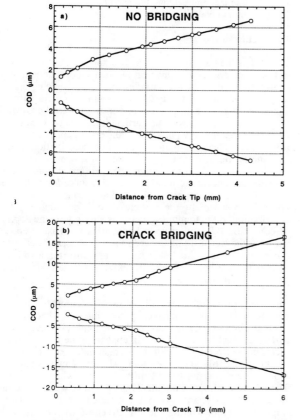

Fig. 5 COD profiles for a) monolithic and b) composite γ-TiAl alloys, measured by moiré interferometry.

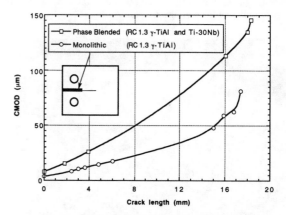

Fig. 6 Crack mouth opening displacement (CMOD) vs crack length.

K_R-Δa resistance curves are shown in Figure 7. For the monolithic alloy crack extension has practically no effect on the toughness, when the crack is fully grown out of semi-chevron zone. The average toughness for monolithic alloy is ≈11 MPa√m. In contrast, some resistance curve behavior is observed for the phase blended composite. K_R increases from an apparent initiation value of ≈ 15 MPa√m to ≈19 MPa√a at $\Delta a \geq 10$ mm. The toughness for phase blended alloy is ≈19 MPa√m, which is a significant improvement in toughness of γ-TiAl alloys.

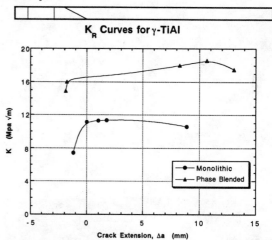

Fig. 7 K_R-Δa curves for Monolithic and Phase blended alloys.

Figures 8a-8c show micrographs taken along the crack path in the compact tension specimen. Ductile ligaments along the fracture surface remain intact as shown in Figs. 8a-c. These ligaments simply pull out when the bridging zone is saturated. With reference to work of Ashby [8], by allowing for the constraint of the surrounding matrix, the average flow stress of the ductile particles increases significantly. The crack growth sequence in phase blended alloy is: crack grows in γ phase toward the reaction zone, crack blunts when it grows into ductile zone, crack renucleates behind the ductile ligament, (at this point crack is bridged), and series of microcracks develop parallel to the second crack and grow toward Ti-30Nb phase (Fig. 8b). Blunting and microcrack development allow the particles to stretch out as the crack faces separate, forming bridging ligaments that hinder the crack advance (Fig. 8c). Due to these ligaments, the value of K_{Ic} will increase as the crack length increases up to the point at which the Ti-30Nb particle pulls out through the reaction zone.

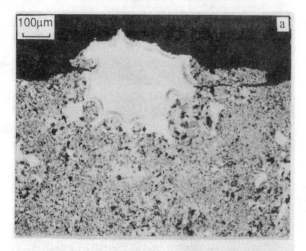

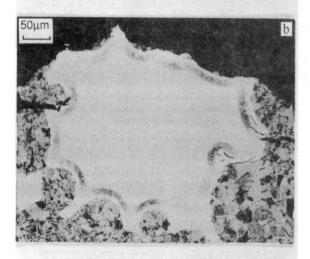

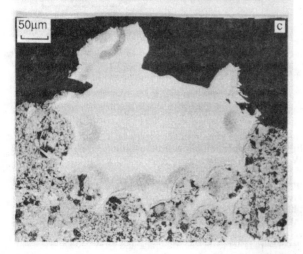

Fig. 8   Micrographs of phase blended alloy taken along the crack path.

Fracture toughness could increase with mechanisms such as; increases in surface roughness, formation of fracture surface steps at particle-matrix interfaces (crack trapping), decohesion of particles and changes in crack shape at the particles. Figure 9 shows typical crack deflection and branching in phase blended alloy. Additional study using ultra high sensitive moiré interferometry is needed [9] to reveal contribution of different toughening mechanism in the phase blended alloys.

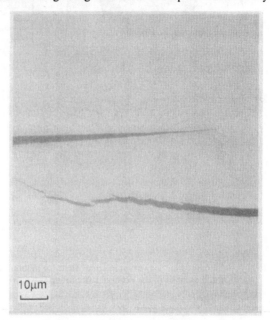

Fig. 9   Typical crack deflection and branching in phase blended alloy.

V. Discussion

Bridging is the most puissant way of improving the toughness of brittle materials. The physical mechanism of toughening is straightforward: if ductile particles span the advancing crack, they must stretch as the crack opens until they fracture or decohere: the work-of-stretching contributes to the overall toughness of the solid. If the particle is so weakly bonded to the matrix that it easily pulls free as the crack approaches, then it is not stretched and there is almost no contribution to the toughness. But if it is strongly bonded, it is constrained; and then its force-displacement curve is very different from that of the unconstrained material as measured in an ordinary tensile test. This is an important difference because the energy absorbed in stretching the particle, crucial in calculating the contribution to the toughness, depends strongly on the degree of constraint. Reaction zone boundaries in phase blended sheet are the weakest link between the two phases. Therefore, optimization of the HIP cycle for minimization of interdiffusion between the Rockwell 1.3 and Ti-30Nb powders is crucial.

The sheet ductility's were all below 1% demonstrating the need for subsequent mechanical processing as has been found in other studies on compaction of Ti aluminide powders. Thus as-HIP'ed ductility of the matrix appears to be a controlling factor in the overall behavior of this material. The yield stress of the phase blended sheet was slightly lower than the monolithic sheet, but the ductility was somewhat improved. The nearly continuous ductile Ti-30Nb phase would account for this. The toughness of phase blended sheet was greatly improved demonstrating the effectiveness of the Ti-30Nb phase. The quantitative contribution of different mechanisms of fracture toughness enhancement is being investigated.

VI. Conclusions

The major conclusions of this study are as follows:

A) It has been demonstrated that PREP powders of Rockwell 1.3 alloys and a ductile binary Ti-30Nb alloy can be physically blended and compacted into thin sections using hot-isostatic-pressing.

B) Compared to monolithic Rockwell 1.3 sheet, the phase blended sheet showed a slight increase in ductility and a noticeable increase in fracture toughness. Techniques to assure homogeneous distribution of the ductile phase and improve the as-HIP'ed ductility must be developed to realize the full potential of this material.

C) Increase in toughness in the phase blended composite is due to formation of crack face bridging, crack path deviation, blunting and multiple cracking.

These results are promising and provide useful guidance to alloy development efforts and additional fundamental studies of ductile phase toughening. Methods to assure homogeneous distribution of the ductile phase and improve the as-HIP'ed ductility must be developed to recognize the full potential of the phase blended composite material.

VII. Acknowledgments

The powder for this program was supplied by North American Aircraft, Rockwell International Corporation, Los Angeles, California. The HIP cycles and containers were supplied by Industrial Materials Technology, Inc., North Andover, Massachusetts. Specimens were made by the Nuclear Metals, Inc., Concord, Massachusetts. I am grateful to Dr. Mark A. Ohls for supplying alloys and helpful discussions.

VIII. References

1. M.A. Ohls, W.T. Nachtrab and P.R. Roberts, "Processing and Properties of Gamma Titanium Aluminide Sheet Produced from PREP Powder" to be published

2. C.K. Elliott, G.R. Odette, G.E. Lucas and J.W. Sheckard, " Toughening Mechanisms in Intermetallic γTiaAl Alloys Containing Ductile Phases" MRS Proc. 120, p. 95 (1988).

3. F. Zok and C. Hom, "Large Scale Bridging in Brittle Matrix Composites" ,Acta Metall. Mater.

4. G.R. Odette, H.E. Deve, C.K. Elliott, A. Harigowa and G.E. lucas, "The Influence of the Reaction Layer Structure and Properties on Ductile Phase Toughening in Titanium Aluminide-Niobium Composites" in Interfaces in Ceramic Metal Composites, R.J. Arsenault, R.Y. Lin, G.P. Martins and S.G. Fishman (eds), TMS-AIME, Warrendale, PA, 443 (1990)

5. Dadkhah, M.S., Wang, F.X. and Kobayashi, A.S., "Simultaneous On-Line Measurement of Orthogonal Displacement Fields by Moire Interferometry," Experimental Techniques 12 (1988) 28-30.

6. Dadkhah, M.S., Kobayashi, A.S. Wang, F.X. and Graesser, D.L., "J-integral Measurements Using Moire Interferometry," Proc.. of the VI Int'l Congress on Experimental Mechanics (1988) 227-234.

7. B.N. Cox and C.S. Lo, "Load Ratio, Notch, and Scale Effects for Bridged Cracks in Fiberous Composites" Acta Metall. Mater. Vol. 40, No. 1, pp. 69-80, 1992

8. M.F. Ashby, F.J. Blunt and M. Bannister, "Flow Characteristics of Highly Constrained Metals Wires" Acta Metall. 37, 1847 (1989).

9. B. Han, "Ultra-high Sensitivity Moiré Interferometry," Second International Conference on Photomechanics and Speckle Metrology, SPIE Proceedings, Vol. 1554 A-B, July 1991.

TESTING AND MODELING OF CREEP
IN TITANIUM-BASED METAL MATRIX COMPOSITES

M.R. Eggleston
Material Research Center
GE Corporate Research and Development
Schenectady, NY 12301

ABSTRACT

The creep deformation of continuous fiber, titanium-based metal matrix composites was studied in the transverse orientation. The model composite material was SCS-6 silicon carbide fibers in a matrix of commercially pure titanium with a fiber volume fraction of 28%. Tests were performed at 427°C (800°F) in an air environment. The creep of the transverse composites was generally faster than that of the monolithic matrix material. Replicas of the specimen surface were made at multiple times during selected creep tests, to study the development of surface cracking. A comparison of the test results with simple model predictions provided insight into the behavior of the weakly bonded fiber/matrix interface.

INTRODUCTION

Silicon carbide reinforced titanium metal matrix composites are being considered as candidates for advanced aerospace applications. A primary goal of most composite applications is to replace existing monolithic metals with materials that possess higher temperature capabilities. This requires composites with higher tensile strengths, more creep resistance, and matrices with greater oxidation resistance. Of these many material design considerations, composite creep seems to have received the least amount of attention. While creep resistance in the longitudinal fiber direction is a strong function of the fiber strength, transverse behavior is not as easily characterized. The matrix creep resistance is obviously important, but the roles of the fiber, the fiber-matrix interface, and the residual stresses in the composite are complex and vary between different composite systems.

A significant number of studies have been performed for whisker or short fiber composites. Kelly and Tyson [1] found that short tungsten fibers significantly improved the creep resistance of silver. Nieh and colleagues [2,3] performed tests on SiC reinforced aluminum alloys and determined that SiC whisker provided more creep resistance than a particulate form. Lilholt and Taya [4,5] also studied the beneficial effects of SiC whiskers in Aluminum 2124 and 6061 at 300°C.

Although continuous fiber composites have been studied, only a limited number of researchers examined the creep in the transverse orientation. Shimmin and Toth [6] found that the SiC coated boron fiber failed by filament splitting when embedded in Ti-6Al-4V matrix. A graphite and 6061-T6 aluminum system was tested by Min and Crossman [7]; they found the transverse creep affected by the geometry of the fiber distribution, debonding between the fiber and matrix, and splitting of the fiber. Only the primary creep region appeared to be affected by residual stresses in the composite. In this system, significant creep occurred at stress levels far below those that would cause creep in the unreinforced aluminum. Lucas and McNelly [8] found that in a boron-aluminum system, separation of the fiber-matrix interface occurred at elevated temperatures (300°C). This separation led to an increased creep rate. Gambone and colleagues [9] performed a large series of tests on SCS-6/Ti-24Al-11Nb composites in both the longitudinal and transverse directions from 650°C to 870°C. Their transverse creep data possessed a steady-state creep region for the majority of the creep life.

In this paper, a study will be made of the transverse creep behavior of titanium-based composites with SCS-6 continuous, unidirectional fiber reinforcements. Commercially-pure titanium will be used as the matrix, to separate this study from any complicated microstructural effects that might occur during composite processing. The fiber volume fraction for the composites is 28%. Constant load creep tests will be performed at 427°C (800°F) in an air environment.

As noted by previous researchers [9-13], the strength of the interface between the SCS-6 fiber and titanium matrix is very weak. During fabrication, a number of brittle compounds, including titanium carbides and silicides, are formed near the fiber's carbon coating [14,15]. While the debonding of this interface is known to affect tensile properties [11,13], the role it plays in creep deformation is unknown and will be studied.

Analytical prediction of steady-state creep deformation will be compared to measured test results to provide insight into the role of the interface during composite creep. Finally, a series of interrupted creep tests will be performed to examine the evolution of damage during creep, and to suggest some areas for further study.

TESTING

There are a number of titanium-based matrices currently being used with the SCS-6 fiber for composite systems. While many of these alloys provide significant strength and oxidation resistance advantages over unalloyed titanium, there is also a need to carefully control the microstructure, in order to assure consistent properties. For the simplicity of material fabrication, and to assure more uniform material during the test program, composites were made with a matrix of commercially pure titanium and Ti-6Al-4V; only the results from the CP Ti/SiC work will presented in this paper.

The material used in this study was consolidated from single fiber layer tapes. These monotapes were created with a rf-plasma spray system using carbon-coated SiC fiber (SCS-6) purchased from Textron, Inc. The composites were consolidated at 900°C using four layers of fibers (Figure 1). Specimens were EDM machined from plates, and then five mils was ground from the machined surface to remove any material that may have been degraded. The specimen geometry is provided in Figure 2. Only results from specimens with transversely oriented fibers are presented in this paper.

All composite creep tests were performed in an ATS Series 2410 creep testing machine. For this portion of the work, all tests were performed in air. The specimen was heated to 427°C during the tests. A cage extensometer was attached to the specimen at the points shown on Figure 2. A finite element calculation was performed to estimate the creep in the gage section of the specimen from the displacements measured by the extensometer. Comparison with monolithic creep tests has validated this analysis. All the tests were constant load creep tests. Since the strain to failure for the transverse composite specimens is small (approximately 6%) and they did not neck, the true stress on the specimen during the entire test is approximately constant.

CONTINUOUS TEST RESULTS

Creep tests were performed at 69, 83, and 103 MPa (10, 12, and 15 ksi). Figure 3 and Figure 4 provide typical test results from composite creep tests. The creep failure strain is approximately 6 percent; this is very close to the failure strain during monotonic tensile tests. The majority of the creep life is spent in near steady-state creep. For the 103 MPa test, the specimen spent 80 percent of life around a creep rate value of 0.05%/hour. The test at 83 MPa exhibited a larger primary creep region, and over half of the creep life was spent close to a creep rate value of 0.02%/hour. The composite tests performed to date have shown that the variability in this steady-state rate between tests is no more that 30% (see Figure 15). Additional tests have shown that at the lower stress levels, the primary creep region is a larger portion of the test. In each test, the tertiary stage is small, and lasts 5 to 20 hours.

Additional insight can be gained by comparing the composite creep behavior to that of the titanium matrix. Typical creep behavior of the matrix is shown in Figure 5. This test was performed at 103 MPa and 427°C in an argon environment. Although this test was stopped after 300 hours and 7 percent strain, the typical strain to failure in this material is over 20 percent; failure is caused by necking of the specimen. The creep rate in these tests gradually increases during the deformation and seldom exhibits a steady-state regime. A series of tests has shown the variability in the minimum creep rate to be less than 20%.

The behavior of the titanium matrix significantly differs from that of the composite in Figure 3. While the titanium creep rate gradually increases, the composite possesses a large near steady-state creep region. The minimum creep rate of the titanium occurs at the beginning of life and is approximately 0.01%/hour. For the composite, the minimum creep rate is the near steady-state value of 0.05%/hour. These rates differ by a factor of five. If the comparison is made at the composite mid-life strain (taken as 3%), the difference in rates is a factor two. In either case, the composite exhibits a significantly greater creep rate than the titanium matrix. In addition, while the matrix exhibits a gradual increase in creep rate with life (continuing on until failure), the composite has a dramatic increase in the creep rate shortly before failure.

A SEM micrograph of the failed composite specimen of Figure 4 in shown in Figure 6. The surface is made up of troughs, where the transverse fibers used to sit, and ligaments of matrix that failed in a ductile fashion. Note that the opposing failure surface contains the fibers, which have remained in place. All the creep specimens exhibited this type of failure, where the plane of failure was along a plane of transverse fibers.

Figure 7 is a replica that was made of the composite surface after failure. After the creep test is completed, the gage section of the surface is covered with cracks or tears. The figure shows that these cracks lie colinear on the specimen surface at regular intervals. This interval corresponds to the spacing between fibers, with the cracks occurring in regions above the outer layer of fibers. These cracks exist not only at the failure surface, but for some distance away; Figure 7 was made 10 mm away from the failure surface. The existence of these cracks at the fracture surface is illustrated in Figure 8. Although the cracks do exist on this surface, they do not grow to a major portion of the cross-sectional thickness. While the matrix is initially very ductile at these high temperatures, the surface of the specimen is embrittled by the absorption of oxygen. In titanium alloys, this embrittled region is referred to as alpha-case. The cleavage in the surface layer is clearly shown on Figure 8. Note that the region adjacent to the cleavage contains a very ductile failure, similar to the failure on the internal matrix ligaments. This type of cleavage can be found at numerous locations on this and other transverse creep specimens.

SPECIMEN REPLICATION

A creep test was performed to measure the growth of these cracks. A specimen was loaded to 86 MPa (12.5 ksi) at 427°C. The test was interrupted at regular intervals by unloading and then cooling the specimen to room temperature. Replicas were made of the specimen surface without removal from the grips. During each test, the replication process was repeated a number of times. The data from this test are presented in Figure 9; the open circles represent the points during the test when the specimen was examined. After over 500 hours, the specimen was removed prior to failure with less that 4 percent creep strain.

The initial examination of this specimen, after 44 hours, revealed no surface cracking. Another replica was then made after 106 hours (Figure 10). This replica exhibited a significant amount of cracking throughout the gage section. While the cracks did not cover the entire surface, small regions of cracks were distributed evenly along the gage. By locating one of the biggest cracks, which was 0.82 mm in length, and referencing that location on the 44 hour replica, the beginning of this crack at 44 hours was identified (0.17 mm long). This was true for many, though not all, of the cracks at 106 hours. The next replica, at 145 hours, showed a significantly increased number of cracks. From this point, until the final replication after 500 hours (Figure 11), the number of surface cracks did not increase. Instead, the cracks

opened up in certain regions of the specimen as the creep process continued. The "tongue" of replica material representing each crack became longer as the crack depth increased.

Therefore, it was observed that cracks form along the entire gage section of the specimen very early in the test. The creep deformation process causes these cracks to increase slightly in length, and substantially in depth. As the test progresses, certain regions along the gage experience more rapid crack growth than others. It is unclear whether one of these rapid crack growth regions eventually becomes the point of failure. Although the surface cracks appear to play some role in the fracture process, these tests are not sufficient to quantitatively evaluate their effect on creep life and strain to failure. A series of tests in an argon environment are currently being performed. It is expected that the surface cracking will be significantly decreased without the oxygen exposure at elevated temperatures. These tests should also help to quantitatively evaluate the effect of the surface embrittlement on creep performance.

INTERRUPTED CREEP TESTS

Perhaps more interesting than the replicas themselves was the effect that the interrupted tests had on the creep of the composite. A comparison can be made by examining two creep tests performed at 103 MPa (Figure 3 and Figure 12). In the first case, a continuous test was performed, while the second test involved unloading and cooling the composite in order to obtain a replica. As the comparison indicates, the two tests had very similar creep rate behavior prior to replication. After the replica was made on the second test, the creep rate upon reloading was an order of magnitude lower than before.

Two tests were performed on a transverse specimen to better understand this behavior. Both specimens were tested at 103 MPa and 427°C. After the first specimen (Figure 13) had crept for 28 hours and 1.4 percent creep, it had reached a near steady-state creep rate of 0.04%/hour. It was then unloaded. After over 16 hours at temperature, it was loaded again. The creep rate then returned to approximately the same level as before. After the second specimen (Figure 14) had crept for 37 hours and 0.9 percent creep, it had reached a near steady-state creep rate of 0.02%/hour. It was then unloaded and also cooled to room temperature. It was then reheated and, after 16 hours at temperature, reloaded. The specimen now returned to a creep rate of less than 0.005%/hour, over four times lower than the rate before unloading and cooling. This observation is consistent with those made during the replication tests.

While the mechanisms for this creep rate change cannot be verified at this time, a number of observations can be made. First, a similar set of experiments conducted on monolithic cp titanium did not show a change in creep rate after unloading and/or cooling. The interactions between the fiber and matrix are therefore the most probable cause of the composite's behavior. Examination of the specimens after testing indicates that the fiber and matrix have debonded. Comparisons with simple models imply that this debonding occurs very early in the creep deformation. When the specimen is unloaded in the middle of the test, the interface is allowed to close and experiences a near-zero stress state. When cooled to room temperature, however, large compressive residual stresses are created at this interface. It is possible that these compressive forces "rebond" the matrix to the fiber, thus yielding a composite with improved creep resistance. Future tests are planned to investigate how much cooling is necessary to improve the creep resistance, whether the rate of cooling and heating has an effect, and whether a simple heating and loading in the elastic region can provide the same type of benefits.

COMPARISON WITH MODEL

As previously noted, a number of researchers have measured and modeled the effect of the weak interface of the titanium/SCS-6 system on the transverse tensile behavior of the composite. Comparison of these new creep results with some model predictions should provide insight into the role of the interface in creep deformation. While a number of researchers have attempted to account for weak composite interface within analytical models [8,16,17], we will use a finite element method similar to the earlier work of Crossman, Karlak and Barnett [18] and, more recently, Nimmer and colleagues [11]. In this approach, the fiber is modeled as a linear elastic material, while the matrix is described by an elastic-plastic constitutive relationship that is rate-independent, along with a time-dependent creep deformation. For this study, the dependence of strain rate on the applied stress will approximated by the power creep relation

$$\dot{\epsilon}_{crp} = 3.5E{-}10 \ \sigma^{3.50}. \qquad [1]$$

The finite element analysis was performed with the interface between the fiber and matrix taken to be either (1) a perfect bond, or (2) a sliding frictional interface with no strength in the normal direction. Experience with this model has shown that the steady-state results are relatively independent of the friction coefficient chosen. ABAQUS was used to implement this micromechanical model.

Figure 15 compares the creep rates predicted for these two model assumption. Also shown is the power creep relation for the pure matrix. Notice that the slope of the creep rate versus stress line is the same for the matrix and either of the composite models. This is consistent with observations of transverse creep modeling first noted by Crossman, Karlak and Barnett [18]. Also shown on the figure are letters that represent creep tests performed on the actual composite. Note that for the interrupted creep tests, the roman letter represents the creep rate prior to unloading/cooling, while the italic letter represents the creep rate attained when the test was ended (the smallest value during the entire test).

The continuous creep tests above 70 MPa, and the initial portions of the interrupted creep tests, all lie very close to the model predictions with a weak fiber/matrix interface. The two points from the later portions of the interrupted tests lie closer to the perfectly bonded model predictions. In addition, the continuous creep test performed at 69 MPa also lies closer to the perfectly bonded curve.

An additional set of analyses was performed to examine the effect of variable fiber/matrix bond strength on the composite. The sliding friction interface was modified, so that it contained a certain normal strength. The interface would not debond unless the normal force exceeded a certain level. Figure 16 provides the steady-state creep rate results for an applied stress of 86 MPa. Once there is enough normal load to debond the fiber from the matrix at one point, the rest of the interface also quickly debonds. Therefore, there is a bimodal result: If the interface strength is sufficient to prevent any debonding, the composite remains intact and the resulting creep rate is lower than for the pure matrix, and is independent of the actual assumed interface strength. If the interface strength is insufficient, the interface debonds and the composite creeps at a more rapid rate, that is once again independent of interface strength.

In examining Figure 15 again, one could postulate that test **C** at 69 MPa had insufficient load to debond the fiber, while test **B** at 86 MPa had enough. This hypothesis also might describe the uninterrupted tests, but it does not explain the decreased creep rate during the interrupted tests. The finite element model, in its present form, does not predict this change in creep rate from unload/cooling of the composite.

CONCLUSIONS

Creep tests were performed on Ti/SiC composites in the transverse orientation. These tests were performed at 427°C in an air environment. The specimen failure surfaces showed that the fiber and matrix debonded, and the continuous matrix ligaments failed in a ductile fashion. Surface cracks or tears developed during the test along the gage section. The cracks initiated very early in the creep test. The effect of these cracks on the overall fracture of the composite is unclear.

The comparison of the measured steady-state creep behavior with that predicted by a finite element model, showed that assumptions of a weakly bonded interface provided good predictions of composite creep deformation. The analyses also implied that if the applied creep stress is low enough, the fiber and matrix do not debond, and the rate of creep deformation is significantly decreased.

Additional work is needed to understand the role of limited thermal cycles on the creep deformation of the composite. The data presented in this paper suggest that a small number of thermal cycles might improve the creep resistance of the composite. This behavior is not consistent with prediction made with the finite element model

ACKNOWLEDGEMENTS

The author would like to thank Mr. Scott Weaver and Mr. William Catlin for their assistance in performing the creep tests. The review and criticism of this manuscript by my advisor at Rensselaer Polytechnic Institute, Prof. Erhard Krempl, and my colleague at GE, Dr. A.M. Ritter, are very much appreciated.

REFERENCES

1. A. Kelly and W.R. Tyson, "Tensile Properties of Fiber Reinforced Metals - II. Creep of Silver-Tungsten," *J. Mech. Phys. Solids*, **14**, 1966, pp. 177-186.

2. T.G. Nieh, "Creep Rupture of a Silicon Carbide Reinforced Aluminum Composite," *Met. Trans.*, **15A**, 1984, pp. 139-146.

3. K. Xia, T.G. Nieh, J. Wadsworth and T.G. Langdon, "The Creep Properties of Aluminum Composites Reinforced with SiC," *Fundamental Relationships Between Microstructures and Mechanical Properties of Metal Matrix Composites*, P.K. Liaw and M.N. Gungor, Eds., TMS, 1990, pp. 543-556.

4. H. Lilholt and M. Taya, "Creep Behavior of the Metal Matrix Composite Al 2124 with SiC Fibers," *6th International and 2nd European Conference on Composite Materials*, Elsevier, 1987, pp. 2234-2244.

5. T. Morimoto, T. Yamaoka, H. Lilholt and M. Taya, "Second Stage Creep of SiC Whisker/6061 Aluminum Composite at 573K," *J. Appl. Mech.*, **110**, 1988, pp. 70-76.

6. K.D. Shimmin and I.J. Toth, "Fatigue and Creep Behavior of Aluminum and Titanium Matrix Composites," *Fracture Modes in Composites*, I. Toth, Ed., TMS, 1972, pp.357-393.

7. B.K. Min and F.W. Crossman, "Analysis of Creep for Metal Matrix Composites," *J. Comp. Mat.*, **16**, 1982, pp. 188-203.

8. G.F. Lucas and T.R. McNelley, "A Comparison Between Creep of Laminated Aluminum and the Transverse Creep Behavior of a Unidirectional Boron-Aluminum Composite," *Met. Trans.*, **7A**, 1976, pp.1317-1324

9. M.L. Gambone, "Fatigue and Fracture of Titanium Aluminides," *WRDC-TR-89-4145*, 1989.

10. R.R. Kieschke and T.W. Clyne, "Control Over Interfacial Bond Strength in Ti/SiC," *Fundamental Relationships Between Microstructures and Mechanical Properties of Metal Matrix Composites*, P.K. Liaw and M.N. Gungor, Eds., TMS, 1990, pp. 325-340.

11. P. Wright, R. Nimmer, G. Smith, M. Sensmeier and M. Brun, "The Influence of the Interface on Mechanical Behavior of Ti-6Al-4V/SCS-6 Composites," *Interfaces in Metal-Ceramics Composites*, R.Y. Lin, et al., Eds., TMS, 1989, pp. 389-409.

12. Y. LePetitcorps, R. Pailler and R. Naslain, "The Fibre/Matrix Interfacial Shear Strength in Titanium Alloy Matrix Composites Reinforced by SiC or Boron CVD Filaments," *Comp. Sci. Tech.*, **35**, 1989, pp. 207-214.

13. W.S. Johnson, S.J. Lubowinski and A.L. Highsmith, "Mechanical Characterization of Unnotched SCS-6/Ti-15-3 Metal Matrix Composites at Room Temperature," *Thermal and Mechanical Behavior of Metal Matrix and Ceramic Matrix Composites*, ASTM STP 1080, J.M. Kennedy, et al., Eds., 1990, pp. 193-218.

14. C.G. Rhodes and R.A. Spurling, "Fiber-Matrix Reaction Zone Growth Kinetics in SiC-Reinforced Ti-6Al-4V as Studied by Transmission Electron Microscopy," *Recent Advances in Composites in the United States and Japan*, ASTM STP 864, J.R. Vinson and M. Taya, Eds., ASTM, 1985, pp. 585-599.

15. E.L. Hall, A.M. Ritter and N. Lewis, "Microstructural Studies of Reaction Zones and Fiber Coatings in Ti-1421/SiC Composites," *GE Corporate Research and Development Report 90CRD173*, September, 1990.

16. C.A. Bigelow, W.S. Johnson and R.A. Naik, "A Comparison of Various Micromechanics Models for Metal Matrix Composites," *Mechanics of Composite Materials and Structures*, J.N. Reddy and J.L. Teply, Eds., ASME, 1989, pp. 21-31.

17. S. Goto and M. McLean, "Modeling Interface Effects During Creep of Metal Matrix Composites," *Scripta Met.*, **23**, 1989, pp.2703-2078.

18. F.W. Crossman, R.F. Karlak and D.M. Barnett, "Creep of B/Al Composites as Influenced by Residual Stresses, Bond Strength, and Fiber Packing Geometry," *Failure Modes in Composites II*, J.N. Fleck and R.L. Mehan, Eds., TMS, 1974, pp. 8-21.

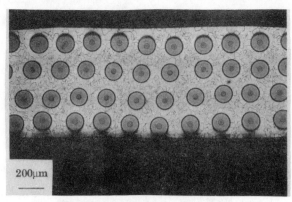

Figure 1: Metal Matrix Composite

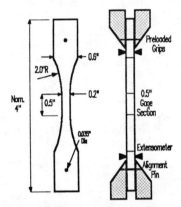

Figure 2: MMC Creep Specimen Geometry

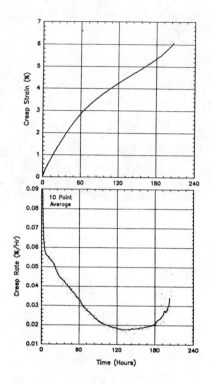

Figure 4: Continuous MMC Creep Test
at 83MPa, 427°C in Air

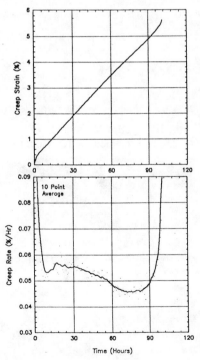

Figure 3: Continuous MMC Creep Test
at 103MPa, 427°C in Air

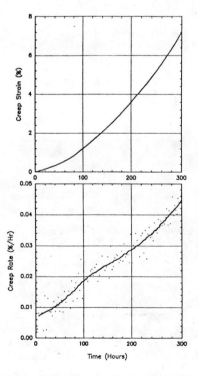

Figure 5: Continuous Matrix Creep Test
at 103 MPa and 427°C in Argon

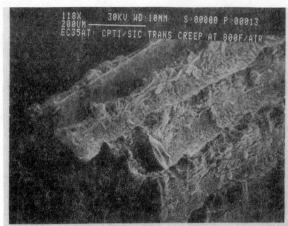

Figure 6: SEM Micrograph of
MMC Creep Failure Surface

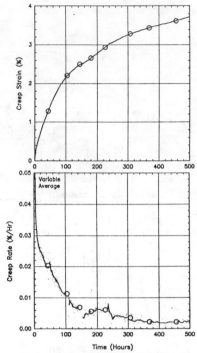

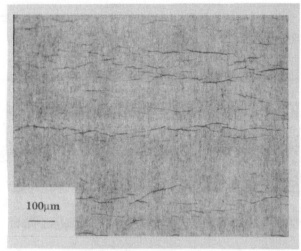

Figure 7: Replica Micrograph of
MMC Creep Specimen Surface

Figure 9: Replica MMC Creep Test
at 86 MPa and 427°C in Air

Figure 10: Replica Micrograph of
MMC Creep Specimen At 106 Hours

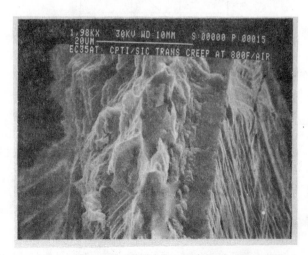

Figure 8: SEM Micrograph of
MMC Creep Failure Surface (Close-Up)

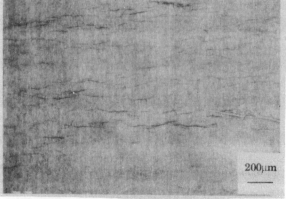

Figure 11: Replica Micrograph of
MMC Creep Specimen at 525 Hours

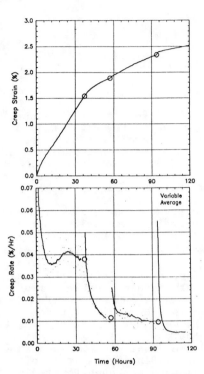

Figure 12: Replica MMC Creep Test
at 103 MPa and 427°C in Air

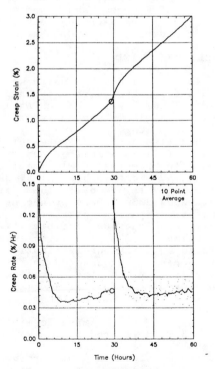

Figure 13: Interrupted MMC Creep Test
at 103 MPa and 427°C in Air
(Unloaded Only)

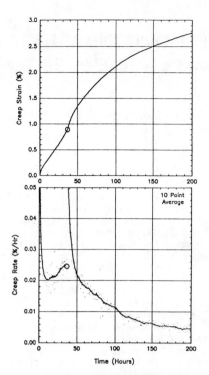

Figure 14: Interrupted MMC Creep Test
at 103 MPa and 427°C in Air
(Unloaded and Cooled)

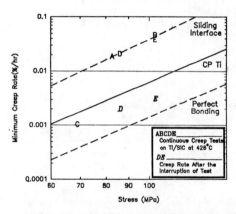

Figure 15: ABAQUS Model Predictions and
Measured MMC Minimum Creep Rates

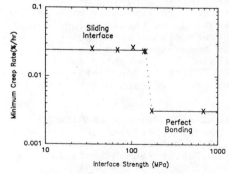

Figure 16: ABAQUS Model Predictions
for Varying Interface Strength

THE THERMOVISCOPLASTIC RESPONSE OF SiC/Ti MMC's AT ELEVATED TEMPERATURES

J.R. Rogacki and M.E. Tuttle

ABSTRACT

The thermoviscoplastic response of fiberless Ti-15-3 and fibered Ti-15-3/SCS$_6$ laminates were investigated under constant load (creep), constant strain rate, and cyclic constant strain rate conditions at temperatures ranging from 482 to 649°C. Material parameters for three unified constitutive models (Bodner Partom, Miller, and Walker models) were determined for Ti-15-3 from the experimental data. Each of the models was then incorporated into a classic rule of mixtures formulation for a unidirectional laminate, compared to experimental results, and evaluated for ease of use and predictive accuracy.

INTRODUCTION

In recent years, metal matrix composites (MMCs) have been widely investigated for use in satisfying structural requirements in high temperature, high performance aerospace applications. Titanium alloys reinforced with silicon carbide fibers are currently under consideration for use on the National Aerospace Plane. Although the thermoviscoplastic behavior of titanium and other metals has been modeled by a number of researchers, the presence of stiff, brittle fibers complicates modeling the elevated temperature behavior of MMCs.

Three thermoviscoplastic constitutive models--the Bodner-Partom, Miller, and Walker models--were selected for this study. The goal was to develop a combined experimental-analytic methodology for predicting the thermoviscoplastic behavior of unidirectional MMC laminates at elevated temperatures. Since the experimental parameters associated with each of these models can be derived from roughly the same database, by generating an appropriate database for Ti-15-3, the predictive power of each of the models

J.R. Rogacki (SEM Member) is Materials Division Chief, Department of Engineering Mechanics, USAF Academy, CO 80840. M.E. Tuttle (SEM Member) is Associate Professor of Mechanical Engineering, Mechanical Engineering Department, University of Washington, Seattle, WA 98195.

could be assessed for the "neat" (fiberless) material. Each model would then integrated into an appropriate form for a unidirectional laminate using a "rule of mixtures" approach.

This study was initiated via a grant from the NASA Langley Research Center (LARC). The project was completed in three phases: **Phase 1** consisted of extensive testing using neat Ti-15-3 specimens at the University of Washington (UW) and LARC. During this first phase an extensive database for the thermoviscoplastic response of Ti-15-3 at elevated temperatures was established, and parameters for the three thermoviscoplastic constitutive models were determined. During **Phase 2**, the thermoviscoplastic behavior of unidirectional SCS$_6$/Ti-15-3 MMC's was measured. Finally, a "rule of mixtures" formulation was used to predict the thermoviscoplastic behavior of unidirectional SCS$_6$/Ti-15-3 MMC's during **Phase 3**. This entailed combining the results of Phases 1 and 2 and comparing the predictions with the measurements obtained during the MMC tests.

MATERIALS USED

The specific MMC studied was manufactured by Textron Specialty Materials of Lowell, MA, using a Timet Ti-15-3 matrix reinforced with continuous SCS$_6$ fibers made by Textron. The neat laminates consisted of thirteen layers of Ti-15-3 foil joined by hot isostatic pressing (HIP). The fibered laminates, eight layers thick, had alternating layers of Ti-15-3 foil and continuous SCS$_6$ fibers joined by hot isostatic pressing. Micrographs revealed the volume fraction of fibers (V_f) to be approximately 29%. The fibers were treated as being purely elastic over the strain ranges encountered in this analysis, and thus the viscoplastic behavior of the MMC was assumed to be solely attributable to the matrix material.

In order to optimize formability, Ti-15-3 is delivered in its metastable beta state. Metastable β-Ti alloys decompose into an α+β mixture upon aging, wherein the α phase has a hexagonal close packed crystalline structure and the β is body centered cubic. Hence, after forming is completed, the alloy is strengthened by causing it to a undergo a phase transformation to its stable α+β form. This aging process is generally accomplished at temperatures 85-195°C below the β transus (760 ± 8.33°C) for varying lengths of time, depending on the aging temperature. For this study, all specimen material was received in the annealed (beta) condition and subsequently aged at 649°C for one hour prior to testing.

General Description of Models Used

The three models employed in this study are alike in that they are all "unified" models. Unified models do not separate inelastic strain into plastic and creep components as so-called "uncoupled" models do. The unified constitutive models of inelastic behavior are based upon a number of internal state variables (ISV's), including such quantities as applied stress, Young's modulus, inelastic strain, thermal strain, etc. Three ISV's of special interest here are inelastic strain, back stress, and drag stress.

Inelastic strain (ϵ_i), as used in this work, is the total strain minus elastic and thermal strain. It includes both plastic and creep strains.

Back stress (B) is the parameter used to account for strain hardening. During inelastic deformation, dislocations pile up on slip planes at barriers in the crystal. The pile ups produce a back stress which opposes the applied stress on the slip plane. When the slip direction is reversed, dislocations that previously piled up aid in dislocation movement. This ISV relates to kinematic hardening or the "Bauschinger effect" whereby the tensile plastic deformation of a metal increases the tensile yield strength and decreases the compressive yield strength, or vice-versa. Back stress has also been referred to as "rest" or "equilibrium" stress in the literature.

Drag stress (D) corresponds to the average dislocation density which produces isotropic hardening. This ISV accounts for cyclic hardening or softening of the material. The effect of drag stress is similar to isotropic hardening in time-independent classical plasticity. Physical mechanisms and microstructural features contributing to drag stress might include grain boundaries, subgrains, dislocation tangles, solute atoms, and precipitate particles.

Bodner Partom Model

The Bodner-Partom theory, more fully described in Refs 6-8, 14, and 23, is a microphenomonologically based constitutive theory for characterizing inelastic behavior. It assumes that the total deformation rate is separable into elastic and inelastic components which are functions of two ISV's: inelastic strain ϵ_I, and drag stress, D. Strain hardening is related to plastic work. The Bodner-Partom model assumes isotropy and isothermal conditions. The theory is independent of a yield criterion and loading or unloading conditions. Although later modifications to the theory included back stress as an ISV, the presently used form, chosen for its simplicity and ease of use, has no back stress parameter, so the theory cannot account for the Bauschinger effect. The Bodner-Partom model is considered especially useful for metals at elevated temperatures where the back stress saturates to a constant value. It is relatively simple to construct, well verified, and requires a minimum of experimentation.

The Bodner Partom theory requires two types of tests:
  - constant strain rate tensile tests at various strain rates and temperatures, and
  - creep tests at several stress levels and temperatures.

The data analysis procedure described in Refs 1, 4-8, 14, 15, 18, and 23 was used to obtain the Bodner Partom parameters for Ti-15-3.

Miller Model

Like the Bodner Partom model, Miller's constitutive model is strongly related to underlying microscopic physical mechanisms. Miller's theory consists of a hyperbolic sine strain-rate equation, which generates all of the inelastic strain, plus work hardening/recovery equations for the two history variables. It contains all three ISV's: inelastic strain, back stress, and drag stress. Details concerning Miller's theory can be found in Refs 16 and 17.

This model was developed for and has produced accurate results for strongly workhardening materials, such as stainless steels. Miller's model has a demonstrated ability to simulate annealing; the effects of warm working; cyclic hardenening, softening, and the Bauschinger effect; and various transient phenomena. It does not contain an explicit yield stress.

Miller's theory requires three types of tests:
- fully reversed cyclic stress-strain tests over various strain rates, strain extremes, and temperatures;
- creep tests at several stress levels and temperatures; and
- constant strain rate tests at several strain rates and temperatures

The data analysis procedure described in Refs 5, 14, 16, and 17 was used to obtain the Miller paramenters for Ti-15-3.

Walker Model

Walker's constitutive theory (Ref 26) is based upon a nonlinear modification to a three-parameter solid (spring and Voigt element in series). It all contains three ISV's: back stress, drag stress, and inelastic strain. The growth law for the back stress contains both dynamic and static recovery terms, although the static recovery term is assumed insignificant compared to the dynamic recovery term at "high" strain rates, and the back stress becomes independent of strain rate. Only dynamic recovery terms are included in the growth law for the drag stress. Creep, relaxation and strain rate effects are modeled by a power law for the inelastic strain rate, and all of the material constants in the theory are functions of temperature and must be determined experimentally for each temperature of interest.

Walker's theory requires three types of tests:
- fully reversed cyclic stress-strain tests over various strain rates and temperatures;
- creep tests at several stress levels and temperatures;
- stress relaxation tests starting from different points on steady state hysteresis loops.

The data analysis procedure described in Refs 18 and 26 was used to determine the Walker parameters for Ti-15-3.

EXPERIMENTAL PROCEDURES AND EQUIPMENT

Test Matrix

Tables 1 & 2 contain details of the creep, constant strain rate, and cyclic constant strain rate tests completed in this program. The purpose of these tests was to build a data base for Ti-15-3, determine the experimental parameters required for the three constitutive models, and to verify and evaluate each of the models for use in a rule of mixtures formulation for unidirectional laminates. The following abbreviations are used in the tables:

SSC - Single Step Creep
MSC - Multistep Creep
CSR - Constant Strain Rate
CCSR - Cyclic Constant Strain Rate

Test Procedures and Equipment

Testing for this program was accomplished at the University of Washington and at NASA Langley Research Center. Some additional follow-up work took place at the United States Air Force Academy.

Creep tests were accomplished at UW using a SATEC Model G creep rupture tester. The tester features a power positioning resistance furnace, automatic load leveling, and a choice of 6:1 or 30:1 lever arm ratio. Three type K Chromel-Alumel thermocouples monitored temperature in the gage length (center two inches) of each specimen. The temperature data was recorded on a Fluke model 2200B Datalogger. Displacements were measured by a SATEC Model 200 extensometer in conjunction with an ATS Linearly Varying Displacement Transducer (LVDT). The LVDT was used to measure displacements and hence strains over a 5.08 cm (2.0 in) gage length. The LVDT had a linear displacement range of 0.050 inches. The input voltage (6.5V) for the LVDT was supplied by a Fluke 3330B Programmable constant voltage calibrator. Displacement data was recorded on an IBM PC/AT using an IBM PC Data Acquisition and Control Adaptor.

Two types of creep tests were accomplished: single step creep (SSC) and multi-step creep (MSC). During the creep tests, constant tensile loads were applied to each specimen using the lever arm creep frame. The resulting axial strain was recorded as a function of time. SSC tests on neat specimens were conducted at three temperatures--482, 566, and 649°C (900, 1050, and 1200°F)--and five stresses--34.5, 69, 103.4, 138, and 172.4 MPa (5, 10, 15, 20 and 25 ksi). The MSC tests were designed to represent a "complex" load history. Two creep tests were accomplished using fibered specimens.

CSR and CCSR tests were accomplished at LARC using two MTS Model 810 Servo-hydraulic Material System Testers with Instron hydraulically activated grips. One tester featured an induction furnace which used two infrared pyrometers for temperature control, while the other had a quartz lamp heating system equipped with thermocouples for temperature control. Displacements were measured by quartz-rod extensometers having a 1 inch gage length and a +/-0.15 inch linear range. Data was recorded with Nicolet XF-44 Data Storage systems backed by an X-Y analog plotter.

In the CSR tests, a variable tensile load was applied such that a constant strain rate was induced in the specimen. The CSR tests were accomplished at five strain rates (1×10^{-4}, 5×10^{-4}, 1×10^{-3}, 5×10^{-3}, and 1×10^{-2}/sec) and three temperatures--482, 566, and 649°C (900, 1050, and 1200°F)--for a total of 15 tests. These 15 tests were done on Neat (fiberless) specimens.

CSR tests were also completed on four fibered specimens. The neat CSR specimens were strained to approximately 6%, while the fibered specimens were strained to approximately .67%

Fully-reversed strain-controlled loading was required for the CCSR tests. In these tests, a variable tensile load was applied such that a constant strain rate was induced in the specimen. At a predetermined strain limit (normally 0.9 or 1.0% strain), the load was reversed. In most cases, the specimens were tested for a minimum of 20 cycles, or until the hysteresis loop stabilized. Five strain rates were used for the CCSR tests--1×10^{-4}, 5×10^{-4}, 1×10^{-3}, 5×10^{-3}, and 1×10^{-2}/sec--and three temperatures--482, 566, and 649°C (900, 1050, and 1200°F)--for a total of 15 tests. These 15 tests were done on neat specimens.

Three of the CCSR tests (tests L22, 23, and 24) were specifically modified to accomodate the Walker model. After the material response was stabilized during the CCSR tests, the strain was stopped at a predetermined value and stress relaxation behavior was measured. After a period of time the cycling was reinitiated until the response was again stabilized, and then the strain was stopped at a different value. This process was continued until relaxation was measured at a total of five different strain values.

Three other CCSR tests were altered to accomodate the Miller model (tests L25, 26, and 27). In these tests, the strain limits were increased in five increments from ±.2 to ±1.2%. The specimens were cycled approximately 30 to 40 times within each of the limits before proceeding to the next.

EXPERIMENTAL RESULTS

Neat Specimens

Sample creep test results for neat specimens are depicted in Figures 1 and 2. Figure 1 shows the creep response of Ti-15-3 at 566°C and five different stress levels. Figure 2 shows the creep response of Ti-15-3 at 138MPa and three different temperatures.

Sample CSR results for neat specimens are shown in Figures 3 and 4. During the constant strain rate tests, stress was controlled so as to produce a predetermined strain rate. In Figure 3

the CSR response of Ti-15-3 at 649°C and five different strain rates is shown. Figure 4 shows the CSR response at .0001/s and three different temperatures.

The predictive accuracy of the Bodner Partom model for Ti-15-3 is demonstrated in Figure 5, which shows the B.P. model prediction vs experimental results at 566°C and .0001 m/m/sec. In this study, the B.P. model was used only to model creep and CSR behavior, while the Walker and Miller theories were used to model CCSR response.

Sample CCSR results for a neat specimen are shown in Figure 6. During the CCSR tests, stress was controlled so as to produce a predetermined strain rate until a limiting strain was reached (usually +/- .01) at which time the loading was reversed. In Figure 6 the CCSR response of Ti-15-3 at 649°C and .0001/s is shown. Note the upper/lower yield point phenomenon experienced on the first cycle. Figure 7 shows the predictive accuracy of the Miller model for Ti-15-3 at 482°C and .001 m/m/sec, and Figure 8 shows Walker model predictions vs experimental results at 566°C and .01 m/m/sec.

It should be emphasized that the CCSR tests were difficult to accomplish. Many of the tests had to be repeated; one was attempted five times before usable results could be attained. Additionally, data was contaminated by electronic noise. Although the source of the noise has not been clearly established, it most likely can be linked to the induction furnace used in many of the tests. Where possible the data obtained during these tests was smoothed using a commercially available software package called VuPoint (Ref 25). The quartz lamp heating system provided a much "quieter" elctronic environment in which to record the CCSR data. This data never required smoothing.

Laminted Specimen Results

Two creep tests were completed using laminated specimens. The results of the first, shown in Figure 9 are for a 0° laminate at 566°C and 262 MPa. The creep predictions of the Bodner Partom and Walker models are shown on the same figure. The Miller model blew up computationally at this stress level, although it didn't have such problems at lower stress levels. Figure 10 shows the creep response of a 90° laminate at 566°C and 48.3 MPa, along with the response predicted by the three constitutive models. Note that all three models substantially underpredict the deformation. The suspected, but as yet unverified, reason is a weak fiber-matrix interface.

Four constant strain rate tests were completed using laminated specimens. The results of test L33, shown in Figure 11 are for a 0° laminate at 649°C and a strain rate of .0001 m/m/sec. Response predicted by the three constitutive models are also shown in the figure. Figure 12 shows the experimental and predicted CSR results of a 90° laminate at 566°C and .0001 m/m/sec. It is readily apparent that all three models significantly overpredicted the stresses. Once again, the suspected cause is a weak fiber-matrix interface. Although Ti-15-3 exhibited an upper-lower yield point phenomenon in a majority of the neat tests, this characteristic was observed in only the 649°C 90° laminate CSR test.

Overall Assessment of Models

Ease of Use

All three models required extensive testing and considerable curve fitting. Several parameters for each of the three models were temperature dependent, so tests over a range of temperatures is required in each case. Also, Ti-15-3 exhibits an upper-lower yield point phenomenon and strain softening. These characteristics greatly complicated the analysis for all three models. Although each of the three models required a certain amount of "curve fitting", parameters for the Walker model seemed easiest to obtain for Ti-15-3.

The Bodner Partom model was easiest to use for two reasons. First, the procedure to determine the parameters is more clearly described in the literature than for the other two models. Second, the version of the Bodner Partom model used did not require elevated temperature CCSR testing, which is a great benefit. On the other hand, the version of the Bodner Partom model used was not designed to model CCSR response.

Predictive Accuracy

As shown in Figure 11, all three constitutive models predicted the 0° laminate CSR response within about 10 percent, with the Miller model being the most accurate. The Bodner Partom model agreed most closely with experimental results in predicting 0° laminate creep response, shown in Figure 9, followed by the Walker model. Both overpredicted the inelastic deformation. The Miller model blew up computationally at 262 MPa, and so was unusable in this case. The predictive accuracy of the three models for the 90° creep and CSR tests is still an open question because of the unexpected weakness of the specimens in the transverse direction.

Conclusions

Each of the three constitutive theories, combined with a classic rule of mixtures, produced accurate results for a 0° laminate at 649°C under constant strain rate conditions. The Bodner Partom and Walker models produced good results for a 0° laminate at 566°C under constant load (creep) conditions. All three of the models underestimated the creep strain response and overestimated the constant strain rate stress response for the 90° specimens.

The suspected reason for this is a low strength fiber-matrix interface.

REFERENCES

1. Allen, D.H. & Beek, J.M., "On the Use of Internal State Variables in Thermoviscoplastic Constitutive Equations," Mechanics and Materials Center, Texas A&M University, College Station, TX, #MM NAG3-491-84-12, May 1984.
2. Ankem, S., & Seagle, S.R., "Heat Treatment of Beta Titanium Alloys," in Beta Titanium Alloys in the 1980's, Edited by R.R. Boyer & H.W. Rosenberg, AIME 1983, pp.107-128.
3. Bania, P.J., Lenning, G.A., & Hall, J.A., "Development and Properties of Ti-15V-3Cr-3Sn-3Al (Ti-15-3)," in Beta Titanium Alloys in the 1980's, Edited by R.R. Boyer & H.W. Rosenberg, AIME 1983, pp.209-230.
4. Beaman, Rebecca L., "The Determination of the Bodner Material Coefficients for IN 718 and Their Effects on Cyclic Loading," M.S. Thesis, AFIT, WPAFB, OH, AFIT/GAE/AA/84M-1, March 1984.
5. Beek, J.M., Allen, D.H., & Milly, T.M., "A Qualitative Comparison of Current Models For Nonlinear Rate-Dependent Materials Behaviour of Crystalline Solids," Mechanics and Materials Center, Texas A&M University, College Station, TX, #MM 4246T-83-14, Nov 1983.
6. Bodner, S.R., and Partom, Y., "Constitutive Equations for Elastic-Viscoplastic Strain-Hardening Materials," JRNL APPL MECH, Vol 42, pp. 385-389 (1975).
7. Bodner, S.R., Partom, I., and Partom, Y., "Uniaxial Cyclic Loading of Elastic-Viscoplastic Materials," JRNL APPL MECH, Vol 46, pp. 805-810 (1979).
8. Bodner, S.R., "Representation of Time Dependent Mechanical Behavior of Rene 95 by Constitutive Equations," Tech Report AFML-TR-79-4116, Aug 1979.
9. Boyer, Rodney R., "Titanium and Titanium Alloys," ASM METALS HANDBOOK, 1988, pp. 458-475.
10. "Continuous Silicon Carbide Metal Matrix Composites," Product Information Brochure, Textron Specialty Materials, Textron, Inc., Lowell, MA.
11. Duerig, T.W. & Williams, J.C., "Overview: Microstructure and Properties of Beta Titanium Alloys," in Beta Titanium Alloys in the 1980's, Edited by R.R. Boyer & H.W. Rosenberg, AIME 1983, pp.20-68.
12. Hall, J.A., "Primary Processing of Beta and Near Beta Titanium Alloys," in Beta Titanium Alloys in the 1980's, Edited by R.R. Boyer & H.W. Rosenberg, AIME 1983, pp.129-144.

13. Hicks, A.G., & Rosenberg, H.W., "Ti-15-3 Foil Properties and Applications," in Beta Titanium Alloys in the 1980's, Edited by R.R. Boyer & H.W. Rosenberg, AIME 1983, pp.231-238.

14. Imbrie, P.K., Haisler, W.E., & Allen, D.H., "Evaluation of the Numerical Stability of Material Parameter Variations for Several Unified Constitutive Models," Aerospace Engineering Department, Texas A&M University, College Station, TX, #MM 4998-85-6, May 1985.

15. Merzer, A., & Bodner, S.R., "Analytical Formulation of a Rate and Temperature Dependent Stree-Strain Relation," ASME JRNL ENG MATLS AND TECH, Vol 101, July 1979, pp. 254-257.

16. Miller, A., "An Inelastic Constitutive Model for Monotonic, Cyclic, and Creep Deformation: Part I - Equations Development and Analytical Procedures," ASME JRNL ENG MATLS AND TECH, April 1976, pp. 97-105.

17. Miller, A., "An Inelastic Constitutive Model for Monotonic, Cyclic, and Creep Deformation: Part II - Application to Type 304 Stainless Steel," ASME JRNL ENG MATLS AND TECH, April 1976, pp. 106-113.

18. Milly, T.M., & Allen, D.H., "A Comparative Study of Nonlinear Rate-Dependent Mechanical Constitutive Theories for Crystalline Solids at Elevated Temperatures," M.S. Thesis, #VPI-E-82-5, VPI, Blacksburg, VA, March 1982.

19. Rogacki, J. and Tuttle, M., "Experimental Measurement of the Viscoplastic Behavior of SiC/Ti Metal Matrix Composites at Elevated Temperatures," Presented at the 1989 SEM Fall Conference, Nov 6-8, Kansas City, MO.

20. Rogacki, J. and Tuttle, M., "Thermoviscoplastic Behavior of SCS_6/Ti Metal Matrix Composites," Presented at the 1990 SEM Spring Conference, June 6-8, Albequerque, NM.

21. Rosenberg, H.W., "Ti-15-3 Property Data," in Beta Titanium Alloys in the 1980's, Edited by R.R. Boyer & H.W. Rosenberg, AIME 1983, pp.409-432.

22. Rosenberg, H.W., "Ti-15-3: A New Cold-Formable Sheet Titanium Alloy," JRNL OF METALS, Vol 35, No. 11, pp 30-34 (1986).

23. Stouffer, D.C., & Bodner, S.R., "A Relationship Between Theory and Experiment For a State Variable Constitutive Equation," Tech Report #AFWAL-TR-80-4194, January 1981.

24. Tuttle, M. and Rogacki, J., "Thermoviscoplastic Response of Ti-15-3 Under Various Loading Conditions," NASA CR 187621, NASA Langley Research Center, Hampton, VA, Oct 1991

25. "Vu-Point II," Maxell Laboratories, Inc., WS-Cubed Division, La Jolla, CA, 1991.

26. Walker, K.P., "Research and Development Program for Nonlinear Structural Modeling With Advanced Time-Temperature Dependent Constitutive Relationships," NASA Tech Report #CR-165533, NASA Lewis Research Center, Cleveland, OH, 1981.

TABLE 1   TESTS CONDUCTED AT U.W.

Test #	Type	Nominal Stress(MPa)	Test Temp°C
U1	NEAT/SSC	34.5	482
U2	NEAT/SSC	34.5	482
U4	NEAT/SSC	34.5	566
U5	NEAT/SSC	34.5	649
U6	NEAT/SSC	34.5	649
U7	NEAT/SSC	69	482
U8	NEAT/SSC	69	482
U9	NEAT/SSC	69	566
U10	NEAT/SSC	69	566
U11	NEAT/SSC	69	649
U12	NEAT/SSC	69	649
U13	NEAT/SSC	103.4	482
U14	NEAT/SSC	103.4	482
U15	NEAT/SSC	103.4	538
U16	NEAT/SSC	103.4	566
U17	NEAT/SSC	103.4	649
U18	NEAT/SSC	103.4	649
U19	NEAT/SSC	138	482
U20	NEAT/SSC	138	482
U21	NEAT/SSC	138	566
U22	NEAT/SSC	138	566
U23	NEAT/SSC	138	649
U24	NEAT/SSC	138	649
U26	NEAT/SSC	172.4	482
U27	NEAT/SSC	172.4	566
U28	NEAT/SSC	172.4	566
U29	NEAT/SSC	172.4	649
U30	NEAT/SSC	172.4	649
U31	NEAT/MSC	48.3/96.6	482
U32	NEAT/MSC	48.3/96.6	482
U33	NEAT/MSC	48.3/96.6	566
U34	NEAT/MSC	48.3/96.6	566
U35	NEAT/MSC	48.3/96.6	649
U36	NEAT/MSC	48.3/96.6	649
U38	0°/MSC	Various	566
U41	90°/MSC	48.3/96.6	566

TABLE 2   TESTS CONDUCTED AT LARC

TEST #	TYPE	STRAIN RATE(1/s)	TEMP °C
L1	NEAT/CSR	1X10-4	482
L2	NEAT/CSR	1X10-4	566
L3	NEAT/CSR	1X10-4	649
L4	NEAT/CSR	5X10-4	482
L5	NEAT/CSR	5X10-4	566
L6	NEAT/CSR	5X10-4	649
L7	NEAT/CSR	1X10-3	482
L8	NEAT/CSR	1X10-3	566
L9	NEAT/CSR	1X10-3	649
L10	NEAT/CSR	5X10-3	482
L11	NEAT/CSR	5X10-3	566
L12	NEAT/CSR	5X10-3	649
L13	NEAT/CSR	1X10-2	482
L14	NEAT/CSR	1X10-2	566
L15	NEAT/CSR	1X10-2	649
L16	NEAT/CCSR	1X10-4	482
L17	NEAT/CCSR	1X10-4	566
L18	NEAT/CCSR	1X10-4	649
L19	NEAT/CCSR	5X10-4	482
L20	NEAT/CCSR	5X10-4	566
L21	NEAT/CCSR	5X10-4	649
L22	NEAT/CCSR	1X10-3	482
L23	NEAT/CCSR	1X10-3	566
L24	NEAT/CCSR	1X10-3	649
L25	NEAT/CCSR	5X10-3	482
L26	NEAT/CCSR	5X10-3	566
L27	NEAT/CCSR	5X10-3	649
L28	NEAT/CCSR	1X10-2	482
L29	NEAT/CCSR	1X10-2	566
L30	NEAT/CCSR	1X10-2	649
L33	0°/CCSR	1X10-4	649
L34	90°/CCSR	1X10-4	482
L35	90°/CCSR	1X10-4	566
L36	90°/CCSR	1X10-4	649

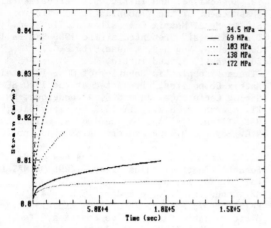

Figure 1   Ti-15-3 Creep Strains
Measured at 566°C

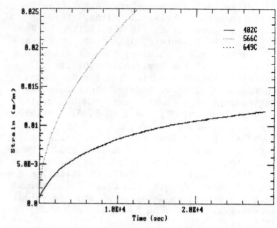

Figure 2   Ti-15-3 Creep Strains
Measured at 138 MPa

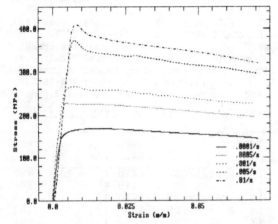

Figure 3   Ti-15-3 Constant Strain Rate
Response at 649°C

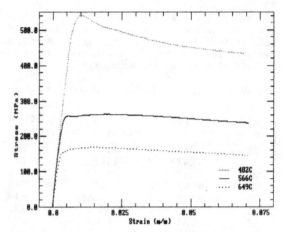

Figure 4   Ti-15-3 Constant Strain Rate
Response at .0001 m/m/sec

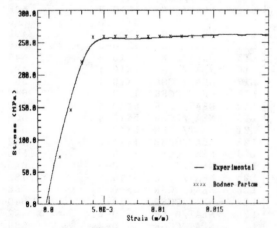

Figure 5   Bodner Partom model
prediction vs experimental results for
Ti-15-3, CSR test at 566°C, .0001
m/m/sec.

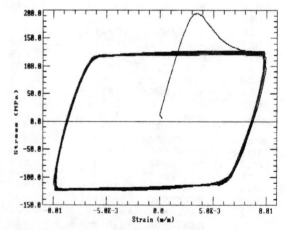

Figure 6   Ti-15-3 Cyclic Constant
Strain Rate Response at 649°C, .0001
m/m/sec

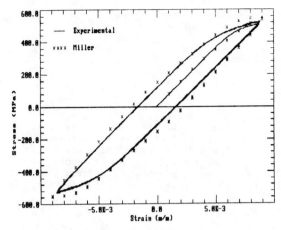

Figure 7   Miller model prediction vs
experimental results for Ti-15-3, CCSR
test at 482°C, .001 m/m/sec.

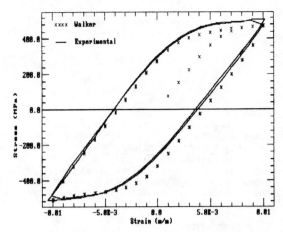

Figure 8   Walker model prediction vs
experimental results for Ti-15-3, CCSR
test at 566°C, .01 m/m/sec.

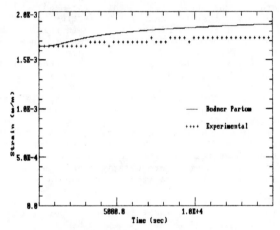

Figure 9   Experimental creep results
and predicted response of a .29 V_f 0°
laminate at 566°C and 262 MPa

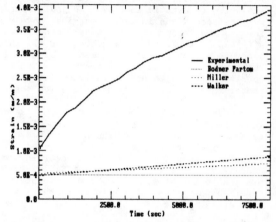

Figure 10   Predicted creep response of
a .29 V_f 90° laminate at 566°C and 48.3
MPa

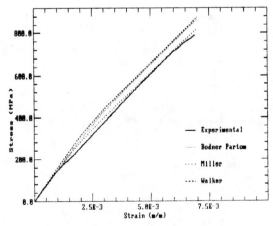

Figure 11   Experimental results and
predicted response of a .29 V_f 0°
laminate at 649°C and a strain rate of
.0001 m/m/sec.

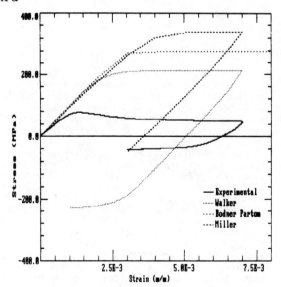

Figure 12   Experimental and Predicted
CSR results of a .29 V_f 90° laminate
tested at 566°C and a strain rate of
.0001 m/m/sec.

NUMERICAL AND EXPERIMENTAL INVESTIGATION INTO THE FATIGUE BEHAVIOUR OF PLAIN CONCRETE.

D.A. Hordijk and H.W. Reinhardt

ABSTRACT

Fatigue of concrete received considerable attention in the last fifteen years. The investigations, however, were mainly phenomenological and therefore, the knowledge about the cause and mechanism of concrete fatigue is still limited. This paper reports about a research project in which fatigue of concrete is studied by applying nonlinear fracture mechanics. With a description of the crack cyclic behaviour of concrete crack growth could be studied numerically. Qualitatively promising results were found. Also a number of fatigue experiments are described in which the development of deformations with the number of cycles is followed as accurately as possible. For that purpose, a data-acquisition system was specially designed.

1. INTRODUCTION

In the last fifteen years, the fatigue behaviour of concrete has received considerable attention from investigators in the field of concrete structures. There are several reasons for the interest in this loading type for concrete. Firstly, the use of new types of structures, like offshore platforms, that are subjected to dynamic loadings. Secondly, the use of higher strength concrete and lightweight concrete, as well as reductions in safety margins, have resulted in more slender structures in which the dead load forms a smaller part of the total load. Thirdly, it is recognized that the material properties may be affected by repeated loading. Despite all this, the importance of fatigue of the concrete in reinforced concrete structures is sometimes doubted, mainly because no clear concrete fatigue failures are known from the literature. However, in a study by CEB General Task Group "Fatigue of Concrete Structures" [1], it was concluded that although no fatigue collapses of concrete structures were found, fatigue was a contributory factor in the progressive deterioration observed in most of the cases studied.

Codes for concrete structures comprise more and more design rules for concrete fatigue calculations. These rules are based on the Palmgren-Miner hypothesis [2,3] in which the supposition is that damage accumulates linearly with the number of cycles applied at a particular stress level. The material input in the analyses are the so-called S-N curves. From these curves the number of cycles until failure for each relative stress level can be obtained. In the past concrete fatigue research activities have mainly been addressed to the determination of S-N curves. Although these investigations were very valuable from a pratical point of view, they did not explain the cause and mechanism of concrete fatigue behaviour. In order to gain more insight in the mechanism, it is necessary to study the fatigue phenomenon on a theoretical basis.

Fatigue investigations for steel structures deal with crack growth. Cracks initiate at points of stress concentrations which may be due to flaws present in the material or may be caused by discontinuities in the geometry of the structure. After the crack is initiated, its propagation is studied with the aid of fracture mechanics. In the research project that is described in this paper, a similar local approach is also applied to fatigue of concrete. Here only some principal results will be presented. For more detailed information the reader is referred to [4]

2 CONCRETE FATIGUE BEHAVIOUR

For a comprehensive review of the fatigue behaviour of concrete, the reader is referred to [5] and [6]. Here, some main findings for concrete fatigue behaviour will be presented, with emphasis being placed on the observed tendencies rather than on quantitative descriptions. Like in the case of static loading, a distinction can be made between the different loading types, as there are compression, tension, bending and bond between concrete and steel. It appeared, however, that qualitatively more or less the same results were found for these different loading types.

The main characteristic of fatigue behaviour of concrete, but also of other materials, is that the number of load cycles, N, that can be performed before failure occurs, increases for a decreasing upper load level. When the relative upper load (or stress) level is plotted against the logarithm of the number of cycles to failure, then a linear relation will be found (see Fig. 1a). These types of curves are known as Wöhler curves or S-N curves. If the deformations are recorded during a fatigue test on concrete and plotted against the number of cycles performed, then a curve will generally be obtained that is known as a cyclic creep curve (Fig. 1b). This curve is characterized by three specific parts. In the secondary branch the increase of deformation per cycle is constant. Just before failure occurs, the deformations increase rapidly. A similar relation, but than turned upside down, is found for the development of the secant modulus of elasticity in a compression test [8] (see Fig. 1c). Finally, it can be mentioned that there is a strong relation between the increase of strain per cycle in the secondary branch of the cyclic creep curve and the number of cycles to failure. This indicates that there may be a fatigue failure criterion for concrete that is based on ultimate strain or deformation.

D.A. Hordijk is Senior Research Engineer in the Department of Structural Engineering of TNO Building and Construction Research, Lange Kleiweg 5, NL-2288 GH Rijswijk, The Netherlands. H.W. Reinhardt is Professor for Engineering Materials at Stuttgart University and Managing Director of Otto-Graf Institute, Pfaffenwaldring 4, D-7000 Stuttgart 80, Germany.

3 APPROACH FOR THE CONCRETE FATIGUE STUDY

3.1 General

In this investigation an attempt is made to explain concrete fatigue behaviour based on crack growth due to cyclic loading. For this local approach the knowledge of fracture mechanics for concrete is applied. Concrete is a heterogeneous material for which is has been demonstrated that conventional fracture mechanics approaches can not be applied for normal-sized structures. In 1976, Hillerborg and coworkers [9] proposed the fictitious crack model in which it is assumed that there exists a fictitious crack (also called "softening zone") ahead of a visible crack (see Fig. 2). In the fictitious crack stresses can still be transferred, depending on the crack opening. With this model it became possible to analyse the behaviour of different types of concrete structures properly. A very important material property of concrete is now the relation between stress and crack opening in the softening zone. This relation can be determined in deformation-controlled uniaxial tensile tests (Fig. 3). For these tests it is known that fracture occurs very locally. Therefore crack openings can directly be obtained from the measured stress-deformation relation. By now, the stress-crack opening relation for concrete is reasonably well known [4].

If in a deformation-controlled uniaxial tensile test a load cycle is performed in the descending branch, then a result as sketched in Fig. 3 is found. The fact that after such a load cycle the maximum attainable stress is lower than the stress at the start of the load cycle, is the basic material behaviour for the concrete fatigue approach in this study. If the solid line in Fig. 2 represents the stress distribution after n loading cylces (n≥0) then by the observed post-peak cyclic tensile behaviour it is known that the stresses in the softening zone will be lower after the next loading cycle. Since the external maximum load will be the same, a stress redistribution has to take place which causes the length of the softening zone to increase.

3.2 Numerical investigation

In order to study crack growth numerically with the above presented approach it is necessary to describe the complete post-peak tensile behaviour of concrete and to implement it in a numerical programme. Based on a great number of experiments such a complete constitutive model "continuous-function model" for the tensile behaviour of concrete was proposed [4]. The structure that was chosen for the investigation of crack growth is a notched four-point bending specimen, while a multi-layer model was applied for the analyses. With these analyses it was intended to investigate to what extent results from cyclic loading correspond with results that are usually found in fatigue experiments.

3.3 Experimental investigation

In the past, the increase of deformations with the number of cycles, as measured in tensile fatigue tests, was mostly assumed to be the result of increased strains. By now it is known that in a static tensile test fracture occurs locally. In this research project the intention was to investigate to what extent fracture in tensile fatigue tests also occurs locally and to investigate whether the descending branch in a static test is the failure envelope in a fatigue test. Therefore a number of fatigue experiments were performed in which deformations were measured very accurately. With these tests it was furthermore intended to study the development of the shape of the loops with the number of cycles. Some details about the applied measuring technique will be given in the next Section.

4 EXPERIMENTS

A limited number of tensile-tensile and tensile-compressive fatigue tests were performed. For these tests as well as for the accompanying deformation-controlled uniaxial tensile tests a very stiff testing rig was applied (Fig. 4). Initially, it was intended to use unnotched specimens. However, due to the fact that fracture mostly occurred near a glue platen, this proved to be impossible. Nevertheless, two experiments on unnotched specimens, one loaded statically and one loaded dynamically, were successful. For the rest of the experiments, notched specimens were applied. The middle cross-sectional area of the specimens was 50*50 mm², while the length was 150 mm. A normalweight concrete with a 8 mm maximum aggregate size and a cube compressive strength equal to 47 MPa, was applied. For the deformation measurements eight LVDTs (Linear Variable Differential Transducers) were applied with a base of 35 mm and 110 mm respectively. Four 50 kN load cells placed under the lower loading platen were used for the load measurement. For more information about the testing rig and the procedure for deformation-controlled uniaxial tensile tests, the reader is referred to [4].

The test ran load-controlled with cycles between an upper and lower load level that could be chosen freely. For measuring the deformations at different loading points in a loop, it is necessary to have a measuring system which is able to measure very accurately. This is understandable if it is realized that for a measuring length of 35 mm, the deformations of the unloading and reloading curves in a loop differ less than 1 μm. On the other hand, the measuring system must be very fast. In order to get some idea about the shape of a loop, the number of measuring points in such a loop must not be too small. It is very hard to meet these two requirements at the same time: a measuring system that is accurate as well as fast. A new data-acquisition equipment was specially built for these experiments.

In the data-acquisition system a fast A/D-converter was chosen for the analog-digital conversion. The resolution and accuracy that could be attained with that converter was not enough. Therefore, for each measurement, eight samples were averaged. The frequency of the fatigue loading was 6 Hz. This means that every second, 6 loops are performed (see Fig. 5a). The principle of the data-acquisition system is such that the first half of each second is used to sample and the second half of the second is used to process the data. In the three loops that are recorded, 75 measuring points are available. For each measuring point, the deformation of eight LVDTs and the load in the four load cells are recorded. Consequently, 900 (=75*12) measurements are taken in 0.5 seconds (sampling frequency: 14400 Hz). As an example, an experimental result is shown in Fig. 5b. So far, the procedure for measurements at regular intervals is described.

The most interesting part of the experiment is certainly the last part. In that part, the deformations increase strongly. Since it was intended to compare deformations at the envelope curve in a static test and at failure in a fatigue test, it was necessary to record data near failure. For that reason a buffer is used, in which the data of the last 20 seconds are stored. This buffer is updated in each second half of a second in which data processing takes place and therefore contains 20 times the data of three loops. As soon as the test is stopped, the data in the buffer can be read and stored in a data-file. In order to detect the ending of the experiment, the recorded load at the upper load level is checked. After failure of the specimen, the upper load level will no longer be reached. When this had occurred a preset number of times, the test and measurements were stopped.

As far as the above described measurements are concerned, the following remarks can be made. It is not claimed that the data-acquisition system is able to measure reproducible deformations of less than 0.1 μm. It was only intended to improve the measurements in such a way that the unloading and reloading curves in a loop do not cross each other. It is realized that some hysteresis may be present in the measurements. Nevertheless, the development of loops can very well be studied. Furthermore, a difference in temperature between day and night, as well as a difference in temperature due to an open door, may influence these measurements significantly. Therefore, an environmental chamber was built around the specimen, in which the temperature could be kept more or less constant during the experiment.

5 NUMERICAL ANALYSES

By applying a multi-layer model (for details see [4]) and the constitutive relation for the crack cyclic behaviour it was possible to study the behaviour of a notched four-point bending specimen. For a continuous increasing deformation a load-deflection curve with a maximum of 1403.6 N was found (Fig. 6). Then the analysis was repeated until a load level equal to 94% of the maximum load was reached, whereafter the structure was unloaded until a zero load level. Because a softening zone exists at the upper load level, it could be expected that crack growth occurs with cyclic loading (see also Fig. 2). That indeed was observed when more loading cycles were performed. Besides the growth of the length of the softening zone (crack) with the number of cycles, a change in shape and position of the loops could be observed. After 146 cycles were performed, the maximum load level could no longer be reached and the descending branch, as found in the static analysis, was then followed. As could be expected, the descending branch acted as a failure criterion. Whether the development with the cycle ratio of parameters like deflection and secant stiffness shows a curve as usually found in experiments (Fig. 1) could not be said in advance. Therefore it is very promising that such curves were indeed found in the analysis (see Figs. 7a, 7b and 7c). Furthermore, a number of analyses with different upper and lower load levels were performed. The results of these analyses plotted in S-N diagrams showed qualitatively good similarity with experimental results [4]. Although the proposed model could so far only be applied for low cycle high amplitude fatigue, the obtained preliminary results are very promising.

6 EXPERIMENTAL RESULTS

With the uniaxial tensile fatigue tests it was mainly intended to compare deformations in a static test with those in a fatigue test and to get an answer to the question of whether the descending branch in a static test is also the failure envelope in a fatigue test. Initially, it was intended to use unnotched specimens. The reason for that was that the process of localization in a fatigue test was also to be investigated. Notches in the specimens cause such a local increase in stress that one may not draw conclusions on the phenomenon of localization when notched specimens are used. Tests on unnotched specimens, however, are very difficult to perform. In most of the experiments, fracture occurred near a glue platen. Nevertheless, one fatigue experiment and one static experiment were successful. Furthermore, a number of fatigue experiments were performed on notched specimens. The applied upper and lower stress levels and the number of cycles to failure, can be obtained from Table 1. Additionally, four specimens were loaded under a continuous increasing deformation (denoted as static tests). The results of these tests were used as reference for the fatigue tests.

In the experiment on the unnotched specimen, fracture fortunately occurred within the base of the 35 mm LVDTs. In Fig 8a, the stress-deformation relation for a number of loops is plotted, while deformation is the average of the four 35 mm LVDTs. In the same figure the stress-deformation relation for the static test on the unnotched specimen is plotted. As can be seen, the deformation at the upper stress level for the last loop that was recorded more or less coincided with the descending branch of the static test. However, two remarks need to be made. First of all, it is not known whether the last recorded loop is also the last loop that was performed. There is a possibility that three more loops were performed. Since the increase in deformation is the greatest in the last loops, this may have a significant effect on the measured deformation at failure. In actual fact the real value for the deformation at failure is equal to or larger than the last one recorded. The second remark concerns the result of the static test. Here, only the result of one experiment is shown. It should be borne in mind, however, that due to scatter, the position of the descending branch may vary [4].

Table 1. Upper and lower stress levels in the fatigue tests and number of cycles to failure.

experiment	notched/unnotched	upper stress (MPa)	lower stress (MPa)	number of cycles
1	unnotched	2.51	-2.75	12812
2	notched	3.18	-5.30	86
3	notched	3.00	0.67	13026
4	notched	3.00	0.05	1951
5	notched	2.75	-5.20	2378
6	notched	2.69	-5.14	10784
7	notched	2.50	-4.82	50720

In order to quantify the damage that occurred outside the final fracture zone, the deformations obtained with the 35 mm LVDTs were subtracted from the deformations obtained with the 110 mm LVDTs. This results in a deformation pertaining to a measuring length of 75 mm (two parts of 37.5 mm each), which does not encompass the final fracture zone. It appeared that the shape of the stress-deformation curve of a loop varied only a little in the beginning of the test, while it remained more or less the same during the subsequent cycles to failure. The shape of the last cycles is shown in Fig. 8b. The irreversible deformation is about 1 μm, which is equal to about 13 $\mu strain$. This result shows that also in a tensile fatigue test, fracture mainly occurs in a small zone. This can also be seen when the deformations at the upper stress level in a cycle are plotted versus the cycle ratio n/N (see Fig. 9a). The result of the experiment on the unnotched specimen has also been used to calculate the development of the secant stiffness and the energy within a cycle respectively, with the cycle ratio. In Fig. 9b and 9c, it can be seen that the obtained relations show good similarity with those found in the fatigue analyses.

In order to show the relation between deformations in a fatigue experiment and in a static test, results are plotted in one diagram (see Fig. 10). In the upper part of Fig. 10, the average σ-δ relation for the static experiments is plotted, while in the lower part of the same figure, the cyclic creep curve for fatigue test 7 is plotted in such a way that the axes for the deformation correspond. Characteristic points in the cyclic creep curve denoted as B, C and D are projected in the σ-δ diagram. Similarly, the points B, C and D for all the fatigue experiments are plotted in Fig. 11. No distinct relation can be obtained from the results. Except for the result of the unnotched specimen, the deformation for the upper stress level at failure in the fatigue experiments is larger than the deformation at the descending branch in the static experiments, even if the scatter in the static experiments is taken into account. So far, possible explanations for this observed result deal with the influence of the notches and distributed cracking due to compressive loading in the lower parts of the loops (see also [4]). Although the authors believe that a failure criterion based on ultimate deformations exists, further research along the presented lines is necessary to prove it.

7 CONCLUDING REMARKS

From the analyses and experiments the following main conclusions can be drawn:
- The local approach to fatigue of plain concrete showed very promising results and offers good prospects for further research in this direction.
- The specially developed data-acquisition system is suitable for studying the tensile fatigue behaviour more thoroughly.
- Tensile fatigue failure is a local phenomenon like tensile failure in a static experiment.
- As regards a failure criterion based on deformations more research is required before conclusions can be drawn.

REFERENCES

1. CEB Fatigue of concrete structures; State of the art report. CEB Bulletin No. 188, 1988.
2. Palmgren, A., Die Lebensdauer von Kugellagern. Zeitschrift Verein Deutscher Ingenieur, 68(14), 1924, pp. 339-341.
3. Miner, M.A., Cumulative damage in fatigue. J. of Applied Mechanics, Trans. ASME, 12(1), 1945, pp. A159-A164.
4. Hordijk, D.A., Local approach to fatigue of concrete. Doctoral Thesis, Delft University of Technology, Delft, 1991, 210 pp.
5. RILEM committee 36-RDL, Long term random dynamic loading of concrete structures. RILEM Materials and Structures, 17(97), pp. 1-28.
6. Cornelissen, H.A.W., State of the art report on fatigue of plain concrete. Stevin report 5-86-3, Delft University of Technology, 62 pp. and Chapter 3 "Fatigue performance of concrete", CEB Bulletin No. 188.
7. Cornelissen, H.A.W., Fatigue failure of concrete in tension. Heron 29(4), 1984, 68 pp.
8. Holmen, J.O., Fatigue of concrete by constant and variable amplitude loading. Doctoral Thesis, NTH Trondheim, 1979, 218 pp.
9. Hillerborg, A., Modeer, M. and Petersson, P.E., Analysis of crack formation and crack growth in concrete by means of fracture mechanics and finite elements. Cement and Concrete Res., 6, 1976, pp. 773-782.

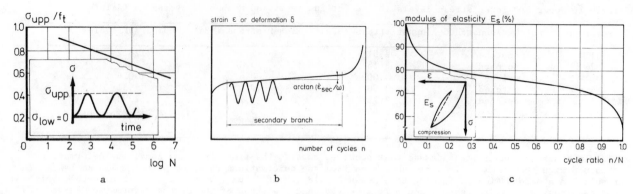

Fig. 1 Concrete fatigue results; S-N curve (a), cyclic creep curve (b) and development of the secant modulus of elasticity with n/N (c).

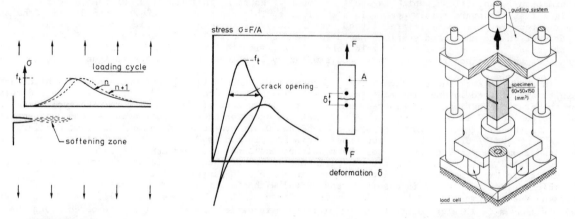

Fig. 2. Stress distribution according to the "fictitious crack model" [9].

Fig. 3 Concrete tensile behaviour.

Fig. 4 Schematic representation of the applied testing rig.

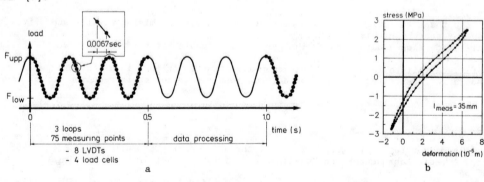

Fig. 5 Principle of the data-acquisition for the fatigue tests (a) and an example of an experimental result (b).

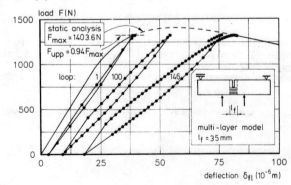

Fig. 6 Load-deflection relations obtained with the numerical analyses.

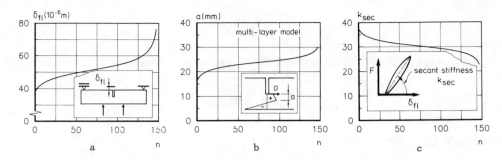

Fig. 7 The variation of the deflection (a), length of the softening zone (b) and secant stiffness (c) with the number of cycles as found in the fatigue analysis.

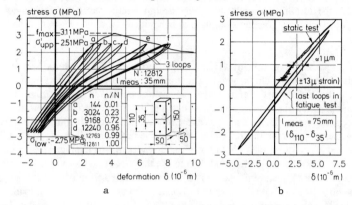

Fig. 8 Stress-deformation relation from a static and a fatigue tensile experiment on an unnotched specimen.

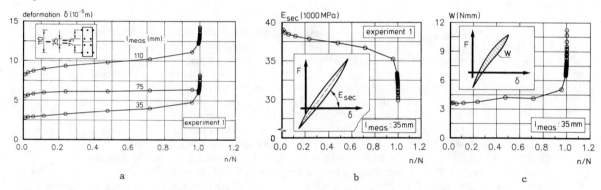

Fig. 9 Deformations at the upper stress level (a), secant stiffness (b) and energy within a cycle (c) versus cycle ratio.

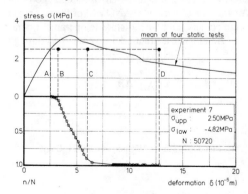

Fig. 10 Average stress-deformation relation of the static tests and the cycle ratio versus deformation of fatigue test 7.

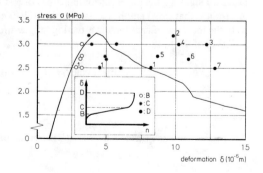

Fig. 11 Characteristic points in the cyclic creep curves of fatigue tests compared with the average σ-δ relation of the static tests.

FATIGUE TESTING OF A TOUGHENED FIBER-REINFORCED COMPOSITE SYSTEM

A.N. Baumgarten

EXTENDED ABSTRACT

Although it is well established that aircraft structures constructed of carbon fiber reinforced plastic (CFRP) materials have significantly improved fatigue performance compared to those made of commonly used metals [1], it is still necessary to establish the durability of important CFRP design details, particularly when constructed using a new fiber-resin system, in order to establish predictable structural behavior.

Two experimental fatigue test programs involving a toughened resin CFRP material were undertaken in support of a new commercial airplane development program. These tests constitute a small part of a much larger test program, an example of which has been previously described [2], whose objective is to demonstrate structural integrity for purposes of certification. An open hole (i.e. notch) detail, evaluated in the first experimental program, may be considered variously as a material screening device and as a severe representation of a manufacturing flaw or in-service damage. In the second experimental program, mechanically fastened specimens representing joints subject to significant load transfer were evaluated . The objective of both test programs was to first characterize fatigue behavior in terms of S-N curves for constant amplitude cyclic loading and then to use the S-N curves as a tool for predicting fatigue life under block spectrum loading. Block spectrum loading is a highly simplified form of variable amplitude loading which is characteristic of the operating loads environment of a commercial air transport. Test loading significantly exceeded realistic operating load levels in order to satisfy test objectives. Specimens were fabricated using a unidirectional tape form of Toray T800/3900-2, a toughened composite material system [3].

In the first test program, a $(+45/90/-45/0/+45/-45)_s$ laminate was tested with rectangular dimensions 38 mm (1.5 inch) wide, 305 mm (12 inch) long, and 2.3 mm (.09 inch) thick, and with a centered 6.35 mm (.25 inch) open hole. This stacking sequence was chosen because it represents a practical laminate in that its strength is fiber-dominated, but an extreme laminate in that the large percentage of off-axis plies can be expected to be associated with lateral (matrix and delamination) damage propagation under cyclic load with a consequence of reduced strength. Specimens were supported against buckling. All testing was conducted under a regime of constant amplitude cyclic load to evaluate the effects of stress amplitude, stress ratio, waveform, temperature, and moisture on fatigue life. Parameter values are shown in Table 1. Stress amplitude was defined as the percentage of the open hole static compression strength under respective hygrothermal conditions. Relative dwell was defined as the ratio of time at maximum load to the time at minimum load for the trapezoidal waveform used in testing. The test matrix, comprising sixteen unique combinations, was structured as a statistically designed experiment [4] of the form 2^{k-p}, where k is the number of independent variables and p is the fractional reduction. The base "2" signifies that each variable can have only two values within the framework of the test matrix, a "high" value and a "low" value, chosen (on the basis of prior experience) to maximize the potential for consistent specimen behavior in terms of damage growth mode and failure mode for significantly different combinations of test variables. An analysis of variance (ANOVA) of the test results determined that stress amplitude, stress ratio, relative dwell, moisture content, and the moisture-temperature interaction were the most significant factors affecting fatigue life, in that order. An empirical life model was obtained through ANOVA of the form

$$y \text{ (life, cycles)} = Mean + Coeff_A*A + Coeff_B*B... + Coeff_{AB}*AB...$$

A.N. Baumgarten is an engineer at the Boeing Commercial Airplane Group , P.O. Box 3707, Seattle, Washington, 98124, USA.

where terms A, B... are identified as test parameter main effects (Table 1) and terms AB... represent two-way interactions. Four additional constant amplitude tests were run to validate the model (using all terms) under conditions differing from those of the designed experiment, Table 2. The empirical life model was then used as a basis for predicting the life of the open hole specimen under simple spectrum loading comprising a sequence of constant amplitude loading blocks. The objective of these tests was to evaluate the applicability of the linear damage accumulation hypothesis (Miner's Rule). Cycles-to-failure (N) were predicted for each loading block defined by stress amplitude, stress ratio, waveform, temperature, and moisture. Test conditions are identified in Table 3 (where multiple entries in single cell indicate the conditions of various loading blocks). A damage ratio (n/N) was calculated for each loading block, where n represents the number of applied test cycles. Failure was predicted when $\Sigma(n/N)=1$. Test-prediction correlation is shown in Figure 1.

In the second ongoing test program, single lap shear T800/3900-2 specimens were tested under sinusoidal constant amplitude loading and room temperature, ambient environmental conditions. Specimens were constructed of 16 ply $(45/0/-45/90)_{2s}$ plates (with a width-to-fastener diameter ratio of 5) fastened together with one 6.35 mm (.25 inch) diameter titanium protruding head fastener or 20 ply $(45/90/-45/0/45/-45/90/45/-45/0)_{2s}$ plates with fastened together with two such protruding head fasteners (one per row). Fasteners were "fully" torqued to approximately 11.3 Nm (100 lb in.). Specimens were supported against buckling. In Figure 2, constant amplitude test results illustrate similar performance between T800/3900-2 and previously tested CFRP tape (IM6/3501-6) and fabric (AS4/3501-6, T300/5208) specimens. The T800/3900-2 specimens assembled with one fastener failed either in laminate bearing (that is, hole elongation) or by failure of the fastener at the first thread engaged by collar. The 20 ply T800/3900-2 two-fastener specimens failed similarly in the fastener, but at a lower life than the 16 ply one-fastener specimens for the same laminate bearing stress. This is explained by the higher fastener load for thicker laminate specimen. Based on the data in Figure 2, the fastener stress in the 20 ply specimen is approximately 15% higher than in the 16 ply specimen. An S-N curve for a comparable two-bolt aluminum joint specimen is included to illustrate the significant improvement in "typical" fatigue life of CFRP relative to aluminum. Note that the slopes of the S-N curves are nearly the same although the damage modes are different.

Finally, four block spectrum tests were run on previously identified two-fastener T800/3900-2 specimens to evaluate the applicability of the linear damage accumulation hypothesis (Miner's Rule) to CFRP joint fatigue life prediction under spectrum loading. Loading comprised a sequence of constant amplitude loading blocks, identified in Table 4 (where multiple entries in single cell indicate the conditions of various loading blocks), under room temperature ambient environmental conditions. Specimen life was predicted two ways. First, the damage ratio calculation (n/N) for each loading block was determined based on the S-N curve in Figure 2 with the bearing stresses increased by a "stress correction" factor of 1.15 to account for observed lower failure life of the two-fastener specimen relative to the S-N curve. Failure was predicted when $\Sigma(n/N)=1$. A second separate failure prediction was made based on a bolt bending analysis coupled with the use of an appropriate S-N curve for a titanium bolt. The bolt was idealized as a beam fully fixed at one end and fixed only against rotation at the other end. Test-prediction correlations are shown in Figure 3.

SIGNIFICANT RESULTS

1. A statistically designed experiment is an effective means for modeling fatigue life, including hygrothermal effects, for CFRP test specimen displaying a consistent mode of damage propagation and failure.
2. Bolted joint fatigue performance for a toughened composite system is similar to that of materials with which we have prior experience.
3. Fastener failure is a common CFRP joint failure mode.
4. Once a failure mode has been identified, CFRP fatigue life (for open hole specimens and bolted joint specimens) under simple block spectrum loading (and, perhaps, more complex spectrum loading) may be predicted with sufficient engineering accuracy using the linear damage accumulation hypothesis (Miner's Rule).

REFERENCES

1) Rouchon, J.,"Certification of Large Airplane Composite Structures, Recent Progress and New Trends in Compliance Philosophy," 17th ICAS Congress, Stockholm 1990.

2) McCarty, J.E., Johnson, R.W., and Wilson, D.R., "737 Graphite-Epoxy Horizontal Stabilizer Certification, A Collection of Technical Papers," Part 1: Structures and Materials, AIAA No. 82-0745, AIAA/ASME/ASCE/AHS 23rd Structures, Structural Dynamics and Materials Conference, New Orleans, May 1982.

3) Odagiri, N., Muraki, T., Pobukuro, K., "Toughness Improved High Performance TORAYCA Prepreg T800H/3900 Series," 33rd International SAMPE Symposium, March 7-10, 1988.

4) Montgomery, D.C., Design and Analysis of Experiments, John Wiley & Sons, 1984.

ACKNOWLEDGMENTS

The author wishes to acknowledge Boeing Company employees D.M. Hoyt and D. Dupertuis for technical support, G.B.Doty and D.P.Mooney for their review of the manuscript, and D.R. Ostgaard as the source of the S-N curve used in the fastener analysis.

Table 1: Open Hole Designed Experiment Test Parameters

Parameter	Low Value	High Value
Stress Amplitude (A) (% of ultimate)	60	72.5
Stress Ratio (B)	-1	10
Relative Dwell (C)	50	1/50
Temperature $^{\circ}$C ($^{\circ}$F) (D)	-59 (-75)	49 (120)
Moisture (%) (E)	0	1.25

Table 2: Constant Amplitude Verification Test Conditions for Open Hole Specimen

Parameter	Specimen No. 16	Specimen No.18	Specimen No. 64	Specimen No. 51
Stress Amplitude (% of ultimate)	70	72.5	60	68
Stress Ratio (R)	-1	-1	-1	10
Relative Dwell	1	1	1/50	50/1
Temperature ($^{\circ}$C)	21	71	49	71
Moisture (%)	1.25	1.25	0	0

Table 3: Block Spectrum Testing Used to Evaluate Miner's Rule for Open Hole Specimens

Parameter	Specimen No. 58	Specimen No.60	Specimen No. 61	Specimen No. 88
Stress Amplitude (% of ultimate)	70,60,60,65,70,70	50,65,60,70	50,65,60,60,70	57,65,62,60,70
Stress Ratio (R)	10,-1,-1,-1,10	-1,10,-1,10	-1,10,-1,-1,10	-1,10,-1,-1,10
Relative Dwell	1	1	1	1
Temperature ($^{\circ}$C)	21,21,54,54,21,21	38,71,21,54	49,49,21,-54,54	54,49,-54,21,54
Moisture (%)	0	0	0	1.25
Applied Test Block Cycles	20000,50000, 30000,125000, 20000,3900	100000,100000, 30000,25500	100000,100000, 50000,120000, 10200	195000,250000, 150000,130000, 108000

Table 4: Block Spectrum Testing Used to Evaluate Miner's Rule for Bolted Joint Specimens[1]

Parameter	Specimen No. DH57	Specimen No.DH58	Specimen No. DH63	Specimen No. DH64
Normalized Block Bearing Stress	.35,.50	.35,.20,.40,.25,.45 ,.35	.25,.35,.20,.45	.25,.3,.45,.22,.37,. 3
Stress Ratio (R)	-1	-1	-1	-1,-1,-.8,-1,-.8,-1
Applied Test Block Cycles	200000, 29300	100000,275000 70000,100000, 63780,35370	100000,100000, 350000,16200	100000,150000, 75000,250000, 150000,89466

1   Room temperature, ambient environmental conditions.

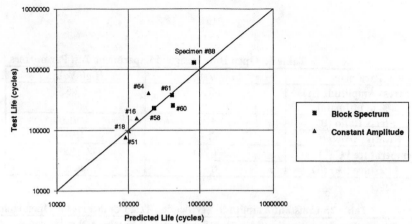

Figure 1: Prediction-Test Correlation for T800/3900-2 (+45/90/-45/0/+45/-45)ₛ Laminate with 6.35 mm Open Hole

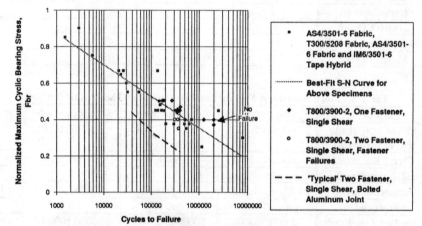

Figure 2: CFRP and "Typical" Aluminum Bolted Joint S-N Curves: Fully Reversed Loading (R=-1), Protruding Head Fasteners, and Room Temperature, Ambient Environmental Conditions

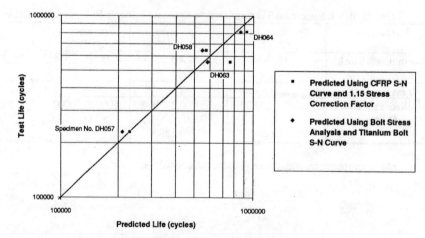

Figure 3: Prediction-Test Correlation for CFRP Bolted Joint Specimens with Protruding Head Fasteners Under Block Spectrum Loading and Room Temperature, Ambient Environmental Conditions

CONSTITUTIVE RELATIONS FOR FLEXURAL FATIGUE BEHAVIOR OF FIBER REINFORCED CONCRETE

V.Ramakrishnan, Bjorn J. Lokvik and Henning Selstad

SYNOPSIS
This paper presents the results of an analytical investigation to compare and determine flexural fatigue strength of plain and fiber reinforced concrete (FRC) subjected to flexural loading. Four different types of fibers were used: straight steel, corrugated steel, hooked end steel, and polypropylene fibers. These fiber mixes were investigated in two different quantities (0.5% and 1.0% by volume). The same basic mixture proportions had been used for the concrete. About 300 beams subjected to flexural fatigue with third point loading at a frequency of 20 load cycles per second in a range of one to four million cycles were investigated. For a better accuracy in generating the S-N curves, statistical and probabilistic concepts are introduced to predict the fatigue life expectancy of the concrete beams. Fiber reinforced concrete reaches an endurance limit at about two million cycles.

INTRODUCTION
The use of fiber reinforced concrete has passed from experimental small-scale applications to routine factory and field applications involving the placement of many hundreds of thousands of cubic yards annually throughout the world[1to10]. FRC has been successfully used for many applications, for instance in the construction industry, as highway and airport runway overlays, nuclear reactor shielding, pile caps, tunnel wall linings and refractory materials, and in the building industry as pipes, flat and corrugated sheets, roof, floor and decorative panels [1 to 12].

The addition of fibers in the concrete matrix has many important effects. Most notable among the improved mechanical characteristics of fiber reinforced concrete (FRC) are its superior fracture resistance and resistance to impact and impulsive or dynamic loads [7,10]. Secondly they impart additional strength under all modes of loading which include tensile, shear, and flexural loads. The degree of improvement of the mechanical characteristics of FRC are influenced by the specimen size, loading configuration, size and type of fibers.

However a better understanding of using these improvements in design and specifications for different fiber composites and for different applications is clearly needed. With rationally acceptable procedures for specifying the performance characteristics, FRC may be utilized to its fullest potential.

OBJECTIVES
The primary objectives of this study were:
1. to collect and combine experimental data from plain and fiber reinforced fatigue tests, subjected to nonreversed flexural fatigue loading, and
2. to conduct a statistical and probabilistic analysis to develop constitutive models for the prediction of the flexural fatigue life, and to determine prediction intervals describing fatigue life expectancy as an aid to calculate design fatigue life.

THE FATIGUE TESTING PROGRAM
Four types of fiber reinforcement were analyzed: straight steel, corrugated, hooked end, and polypropylene fibers. The fiber mixtures were tested for two different quantities (0.5 and 1.0% by volume), using the same basic mixture proportion for all concretes. The specimens used for the flexural fatigue tests were concrete beams measuring 150 X 150 X 525 mm, subjected to third point loading. Data from 300 test specimens were collected and investigated.

Dr.V. Ramakrishnan is Professor of Civil Engineering,and Bjorn J. Lokvik and Henning Selstad are former Graduate students, South Dakota School of Mines and Technology, Rapid City, South Dakota, U.S.A

For each type of fiber mixture and fiber volume 36 fatigue test results were collected. For each series six beam specimens were subjected to static flexural test according to ASTM C1018 (third point loading). The average of these results was taken as the static modulus-of-rupture of that particular concrete. For flexural fatigue test, non-reversed third point loading at a frequency of 20 cycles per second (20 Hz) was used.

The procedure adopted for all the fatigue tests was as follows: The lower load limit was set at 10% of the average maximum load (f_r) obtained from the static flexural test. For the first beam in each mix series the upper (f_{max}) load was set at 90% of average maximum flexural load (f_r) for the set. If the beam failed before completing 2 million cycles, the upper limit (f_{max}) was reduced for the next specimen. If the beam survived, another beam was tested at the same upper load as a replicate. Three specimens were tested at each maximum load (stress) level [6].

The data analyzed in this investigation were collected from five different M.S. theses [1,2,3,4,5]. The same mixture proportions and fiber types had been used in all these investigations.

FLEXURAL FATIGUE

In recent years, considerable interest has developed in the flexural fatigue strength of concrete members. The widespread adoption of ultimate strength design, and use of higher strength materials require that structural concrete members perform satisfactorily under high stress levels subjected to a large number of load cycles. In many structural applications (like pavements, bridge deck overlays, crane beams, and offshore structures) the flexural fatigue and endurance limit are important design parameters.

To be able to come up with an economical design for these structures that are designed on the basis of fatigue load cycles, the relation between load and fatigue strength must be established. It must be emphasized that there are two different ways of defining and measuring endurance limit for fiber reinforced concrete:

1. Endurance Limit expressed as a percentage of the Modulus of Rupture of Plain Concrete:
The endurance limit is defined as the maximum fatigue flexural stress at which the beam could withstand two million cycles of non-reversed fatigue loading, expressed as a percentage of the modulus of rupture of plain concrete [6].

2. Endurance Limit expressed as a percentage of its modulus of Rupture:
Endurance limit of concrete can be defined as the fatigue stress at which the beam could withstand two million cycles of non-reversed fatigue loading, expressed as percentage of its modulus of rupture.

AVAILABLE MODELS

Even after several decades of experimental research, and the preparation of comprehensive reviews of current knowledge there is not much guidance available to the designer. In an effort to help the designer, Butler et al.[9] conducted tests on 50 beams 220 X 200 X 1500mm reinforced with 1.2, 2.3, and 3.3% volume of steel fibers. The steel fibers used in their investigation were Melt-Extract stainless steel fibers (25X0.5mm). Some supplementary testing of concretes containing hook ended (40X0.4mm) and indented fibers (50X0.5mm) was also done. The test specimens were loaded with a triangular wave form varying between a minimum stress level (S_{min}) of 10 percent of S_{max} to a selected maximum stress level S_{max}, at frequencies ranging from 4Hz to 20Hz.

Butler et al.[9] argued that the fatigue strength is dependent on the stress rate, and the ultimate strength is obtained by testing at the stressing rate appropriate to the fatigue test.

Since the fatigue strength of fiber reinforced concrete is highly dependent on the fiber type and the fiber volume, Ramakrishnan, et al.[10] conducted a comparative evaluation of fatigue properties of four different fiber types (hooked end steel, straight steel, corrugated steel, and polypropylene) in two different quantities (0.5 and 1.0% by volume) using the same basic mixture proportions for all concretes. Third point loading was used in the flexural and fatigue strength tests. The test beams had a span of 450mm and were subjected to non-reversed fluctuating load at a frequency of 20 Hz.

On the basis of their investigation, Ramakrishnan developed two figures (fig.1 and 2) for the prediction of the fatigue life of a test specimen. In the figures, the stress is obtained by taking the stress level fmax/fr obtained from the graph times the modulus of rupture of the concrete.

Fiber types in fig.1 and fig.2 :
    Type A: 50 mm long hooked end fibers
    Type B: Low carbon straight steel fibers
    Type C: 50 mm long corrugated steel fibers
    Type D: Collated 19 mm long polypropylene fibers

FLEXURAL STRENGTH AFTER FATIGUE

Later investigations by Ramakrishnan et al.[10] have shown that there seems to be an increase in flexural strength for both plain and fiber reinforced concretes after they were tested for fatigue. This observed increase of post first crack flexural strength for the runouts seems to be higher than the strength gain due to the aging of the test specimens.

The increase in flexural strength seems to depend on the flexural fatigue stress (f_{fmax}) to which the specimens were subjected to during the fatigue test. With lower f_{max} values the increase in flexural strength is higher.

The effects of stress rate may also be a factor of this increased post fatigue strength. In a rapid stress rate test, cracks are forced to develop along shortest possible path lengths in a very short time, generally through stronger matrix zones, resulting in higher material strength. It is also known that most fiber reinforced concretes are linearly elastic up to about 80% of the matrix tensile strength, and that the microcracking process starts beyond this point. This leads to the conclusion that beam specimens subjected to rapid cyclic flexural stress below this level are not likely to have decreased first crack flexural strength.

ENDURANCE LIMIT

In the published papers there are some differences in the definitions attached to the term endurance limit. Most interpret it as the maximum flexural fatigue stress at which the beam can withstand two million cycles of nonreversed load. According to ACI 215R [11], plain concrete is not believed to exhibit a fatigue endurance limit. Contrary to this view, recent extensive research [1 to 6] has shown that both plain and FRC have definite endurance limits when subjected to flexural fatigue loading. Beams which have survived two million cycles, never failed even when they were tested upto 23 millions under the same load [12]. The beams that survived 23 million cycles had higher static flexural strength than their corresponding beams which were not subjected to fatigue loading [12]. Therefore, the maximum flexural fatigue stress at which a beam survives two million cycles can be considered as the endurance limit.

For FRC, endurance limit is influenced by several factors like fiber aspect ratio, fiber bonding, and fiber spacing. Endurance limit can be investigated only by studies involving cycles in excess of two million cycles. So far, no equations or other constitutive relations than the graphs produced by Butler, and Ramakrishnan are available for the designer to predict the fatigue strength and the endurance limit for fiber reinforced concrete.

DEVELOPMENT OF THEORY

INTRODUCTION

Most studies on the fatigue of concrete have so far been directed to interrelate the applied fatigue stress and fatigue life of concrete. The results of fatigue tests usually show considerable scatter even in a given stress level under very carefully controlled testing environment. It is therefore desirable to apply probabilistic or expected value procedures to insure adequate resistance of concrete structures. Several mathematical models have been used for statistical description of the fatigue life. The 1963 edition of American Society for Testing and Materials (ASTM) guide for fatigue testing and statistical analysis of fatigue data suggested that the fatigue life is normally distributed. However it is misleading to assume that this is true for all fatigue life models.

It has been shown that a simple relationship between applied-fatigue stress and the fatigue life is difficult to obtain. Fatigue is a progressive fracture of a material. This may account for a closer correlation between the fatigue strength and the tensile strength than between the fatigue strength and other mechanical properties.

PREDICTION OF AVERAGE FATIGUE LIFE

Even when identical parts are subjected to the same fluctuating stress, they generally fail at different cycles due to non-homogenity in material properties i.e. variation in the aggregate, and type and volume of fibers. To predict the average life of a part, a number of test specimens are tested at various stress levels until failure. Since the best estimate of a sample is generally the average value, the average life is commonly used to describe the fatigue characteristics of the specimens.

The fatigue results can either be plotted on log-normal or log-log paper with the stress on the ordinate and corresponding lives on the abscissa. A line representing the average life is fitted through the test points. For this investigation the two most common models tried for the best fit are given below:

1. The logarithmic equation:
   $y = a + b*ln(x)$
   (log-normal plot)

2. The power equation:
   $y = ax^b$; $a > 0$
   (log-log plot)

The selection of the model to predict the fatigue life is based on the correlation coefficient. The assumption of normality of the data must also be checked. This is done by producing a normal probability plot of the residuals and checking whether the points have formed approximately a straight line. For all data analyzed the power equation gave the best fit for the test data. Both equations are transformed to linear form by taking logarithm of both sides. Since the life is expressed in logarithm, the underlying stress distribution reduces to a normal distribution. All tools and principles applicable to normal distribution would then apply here.

THE FATIGUE LIFE MODEL

Most of the fatigue experimental studies have been carried out in the high-cycle region, in the range of 10^3 to 10^7 cycles. The models adopted to describe the fatigue life have usually been modelled by a straight line Log function. Investigations by Su et al.[13] have shown that the S-N fatigue curve can not be fitted by a straight line as assumed earlier. They suggested that the test data should be expressed by a curve which has a steeper slope in the "low-cycle" region, and a less steeper slope in the "high-cycle" region. This separation of low and high cycle regions can be avoided by fitting the model by a power equation:

$$Y = ax^b \qquad\qquad\qquad ...(1)$$

The power equation is linearized and transformed by taking logarithms of both sides which yields the equation:

$$\ln(Y) = \ln(a) + b*\ln(X) \qquad \ldots(2)$$

This relationship between cycles to failure versus stress is commonly used for metals, and in the application of fracture mechanics to model the fatigue crack propagation. The proposed expression to determine the fatigue life of fiber reinforced concrete is:

$$S = f_{fmax}/f_r' = C_0(N)^{C_1} \qquad \ldots(3)$$

in which C_0 and C_1 are coefficients, f_{fmax}/f'_r is the fatigue stress ratio. The proposed expression is valid only in the range of 10^3 to $2*10^6$, which is the type of loading that may be expected in concrete pavements and bridge decks.

FATIGUE TEST RESULTS

The flexural fatigue strength had increased substantially with the addition of fibers to the unreinforced concrete. In this investigation the fatigue strengths shown in fig.3 and fig.4 are given as a percentage of their own modulus of rupture. Expressed in terms of stresses, the fatigue strength increased with an increase in volume of fibers for all types of fibers tested except for the polypropylene fiber which had the least increase in fatigue strength as shown in fig.5 and fig.6. For the polypropylene fibers the quantity of fibers upto one volume percent did not have any specific effect on the static ultimate strength. All fiber reinforced beams in this investigation had better fatigue performance when compared to plain concrete beams.

LIMITATIONS

Although there is no current standard for flexural fatigue performance, testing similar to that employed for the conventional concrete has been conducted using the reversing and nonreversing loads, with applied loads normally corresponding to 10 to 90 percent of the static flexural strength. The short beam specimens as analyzed in this investigation requires small deflection movements, and have been successfully tested at 20 cycles per second (20 Hz), since adequate testing equipment have been available. Large beam specimens, however, with large deflections needed to produce the required stress level, are tested at reduced rates of 1 to 3 (Hz), to minimize inertia effects.

Due to the large number of load cycles required per specimen, fatigue testing is a time consuming experiment. Each specimen requires up to 55 hours if the specimen is tested all the way to 4 million cycles at 20 Hz. This limits the number of specimens to be tested. The reduced number of available fatigue data will make it more difficult to apply the available statistical methods. This will also reduce the accuracy of the results.

THE FATIGUE S-N CURVE

One of the goals of this investigation was to improve the accuracy of the S-N curve. As discussed by Su the S-N curve can not represent the fatigue data with adequate accuracy in a semi-logarithmic scale from 100 to 2 million cycles. It was found that the number of cycles to failure was too high in the mid fatigue stress region. This problem can simply be solved by using a log-log scale. The correlation coefficient of the regression line was greatly improved and the data points were scattered on both sides of the estimated regression line.

CONCLUSIONS

1. The ultimate flexural strength (modulus of rupture) of concrete is highly dependent upon the fiber volume and fiber type.
2. The average flexural strength is significantly dependent upon the amount and type of fiber reinforcement. Increased volume of fibers increases the average flexural strength of concrete.

3.   The fatigue strength is highly dependent upon the bond strength of the fiber reinforcement. Higher bond strength of fiber reinforcement increases the fatigue strength of the concrete, as shown by the beams reinforced with the hooked end steel fibers.
4.   The fatigue strength is highly dependent upon the distribution of the fibers in the concrete beam, particularly in the tension zone.
5.   The polypropylene fibers,do not appear to increase the flexural strength of concrete. However the fatigue BEHAVIOR has been enhanced by adding polypropylene fibers.
6.   The fiber reinforced concrete reaches an endurance limit around two million cycles. Specimen withstanding two million cycles will probably never fail due to the increase in flexural strength caused by the fatigue loading.
7.   Since the fatigue-test data of plain and fiber reinforced concrete show considerable scatter and are random in nature, it is desirable to use probabilistic concepts to ensure adequate fatigue resistance of concrete structures.

REFERENCES

[1]   Dhakshinamurthy, D.,"Properties and Behavior of Steel Fiber Reinforced Concrete," Thesis submitted to South Dakota School of Mines and Technology, 1988.
[2]   Hossali, G., "Properties of Steel Fiber Reinforced concrete and Effects of Fiber Volume," Thesis submitted to South Dakota School of Mines and Technology, 1988.
[3]   Nasser,   H., "Fiber Reinforced Concretes-an Experimental   Investigation," Thesis submitted to South Dakota School of Mines and Technology, 1988.
[4]   Wang, Z., "Steel Fiber Reinforced Concrete," Thesis submitted to South Dakota School of Mines and Technology, 1988.
[5]   Venkatasamy, V., "Fatigue properties and performance characteristics of Hooked end steel and polypropylene fiber reinforced concrete," Thesis submitted to South Dakota School of Mines and Technology, 1988.
[6]   Selstad, Henning., "Constitutive Relations for Flexural Fatigue Behavior of Fiber Reinforced Concrete," M. S. Thesis, South Dakota School of Mines and Technology, 1990.
[7]   Vondran, G.L., Nagabhushanam, M., and Ramakrishnan, V., "Fatigue strength of polypropylene fiber reinforced concretes," Elsevier Applied Science, Crown House, Linton road, Barking, Essex UK. 1989, pp. 533-543.
[8]   Aas-Jacobsen K., "Fatigue of concrete beams and columns," Bulletin No 70-1, NTH Institute of Betongkonstruksjoner, Trondheim September 1970, 148pp.
[9]   Butler,J.E.,"The Performance of Concrete containing high proportions of steel fibers with particular reference to Rapid Flexural and Fatigue Loadings,",Fiber Reinforced Cements and Concretes: Recent developments, Edited by R.N Swamy, and B. Barr, Elsevier Science publishers LTD. 1989, pp. 544-552.
[10] Ramakrishnan V., Wu Y.G. and Hossali G., "Flexural fatigue strength, endurance limit and impact strength of fiber reinforced concretes," Transportation Research Board, Washington,D.C. 1989.
[11] ACI Committee 215, "Considerations for Design of Concrete Structures subjected to Fatigue Loading," Report American Concrete Institute, Detroit, USA, ACI 215R-74, Revised 1986.
[12] Punit.C.Prakash., "Performance characteristics of hooked end steel fiber reinforced concerete pavement." Thesis submitted to South Dakota School of Mines and Technology, 1989.
[13] Su,Eric., and Hsu.T.C.Thomas., "Biaxial compression fatigue of concrete," University of Huston, Department of Civil Engineering, Research report UHCE-86-17.

ACKNOWLEDGEMENTS

The research work of the authors has been supported by a grant from the US National Science Foundation, grant no. MSM-8652082.   The support of NSF is gratefully acknowledged.   The authors also express their gratitude to Ms.Thenmozhi, graduate student for the help in preparing this paper.

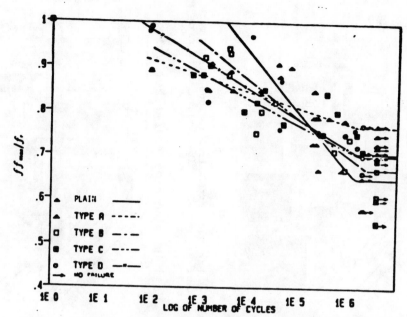

Fig. 1   Ratio of fatigue stress to flexural stress versus Log N for 0.5% fiber beams [12].

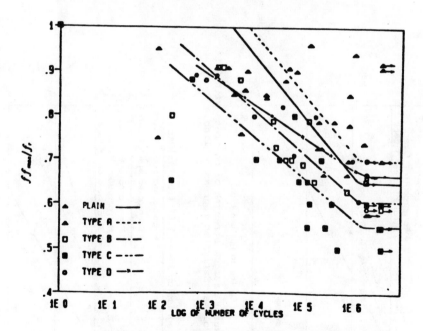

Fig. 2   Ratio of fatigue stress to flexural stress versus Log N for 1.0% fiber beams [12]

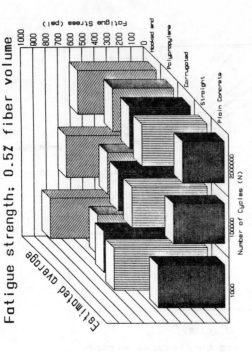

Fatigue strength; 0.5% fiber volume

Fig. 5 Bar chart of flexural fatigue stress of concrete with 0.5% fiber volume; Est. regr. eq.

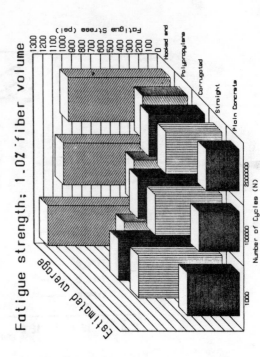

Fatigue strength; 1.0% fiber volume

Fig. 6 Bar chart of flexural fatigue stress of concrete with 1.0% fiber volume; Est. regr. eq.

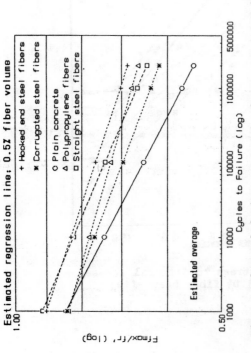

Estimated regression line; 0.5% fiber volume

+ Hooked end steel fibers
* Corrugated steel fibers
○ Plain concrete
△ Polypropylene fibers
□ Straight steel fibers

Estimated average

Fig. 3 Flexural fatigue strength of concrete with 0.5% fiber volume; Estimated regression line.

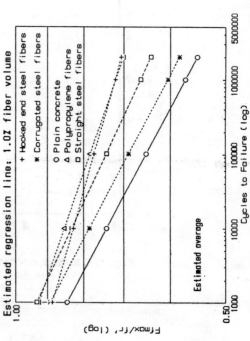

Estimated regression line; 1.0% fiber volume

+ Hooked end steel fibers
* Corrugated steel fibers
○ Plain concrete
△ Polypropylene fibers
□ Straight steel fibers

Estimated average

Fig. 4. Flexural fatigue strength of concrete with 1.0% fiber volume; Estimated regression line.

FATIGUE AND FRACTURE OF PLAIN AND REINFORCED CONCRETE BEAMS: ON THE SUITABILITY OF FRACTURE MECHANICS

S. E. Swartz

ABSTRACT

Recent work dealing with fatigue testing and analysis of plain concrete includes approaches which may be categorized as statistical (empirical-probabilistic), damage mechanics and fracture mechanics. These are: Wöhler or S-N curves; damage functions; non-linear and linear fracture mechanics--fictitious crack model, Paris' law, fracture toughness and size effect law. In the past, difficulties in implementing linear elastic fracture mechanics (LEFM) concepts to the problems of crack growth and fracture in plain concrete subjected to statically-applied tractions have precluded their use in describing fatigue behavior. In the work presented here, it is postulated that these problems with using LEFM are near resolution through an understanding of the influence of the process zone and reasonable ways to model this - eg. via the Size Effect Law or Effective Crack Model to obtain valid fracture toughness data. This then leads the way to use of fracture mechanics to model the fatigue behavior of plain concrete beams. The possibility that this approach may be applied to reinforced concrete beams is demonstrated with experimental data obtained from fatigue-loaded model beams reinforced in such a way that debonding, yielding or rupture of the reinforcement is prevented. The primary cause of fatigue failure is then due to propagation of one or more macro-cracks through the matrix which completely penetrates the beam even though crack width is controlled by the reinforcement.

INTRODUCTION

Fatigue of plain and reinforced concrete members subjected to essentially uniaxial stress states has been studied for many years [1,2]. The process of fatigue, which is due to progressive and irreversible deterioration, may lead to excessive deformations, excessive crack widths, debonding of reinforcement, and rupture of reinforcement and/or matrix leading to structural collapse.

Fatigue-life estimates for concrete have traditionally been based on test data expressed in form of Wöhler, or S-N, curves in which each curve represents the locus of points of average values of life N obtained at different maximum stress levels S. Different curves are obtained for different stress ranges, types of load cycle/frequency, etc. A recent study in which the frequency of occurrence, or data dispersion, in terms of stress level, has been presented by Oh [3].

The determination of confidence limits in terms of stress level is based on a Weibull probability density function $f_N(n)$ and the related cumulative distribution function which is

$$F_N(n) = 1 - \exp\left[-\left(\frac{n}{u}\right)^\alpha\right], \; n \geq 0 \tag{1}$$

By plotting $\ln \ln 1/(1 - F_n)$ versus $\ln n$, the constants α and u (the characteristic extreme value) may be obtained provided the plotted data fall on a straight line. The term α is the shape parameter and is related to the variance or standard deviation a. When $\alpha \to \infty$, a $\to$ 0.

The variation of α with stress level, f_r^{max}/f_r' (max stress in cycle/static strength) as given by Oh [3] for three stress ranges is shown in Fig 1. This indicates that the dispersion of data <u>increases</u> with <u>increasing</u> fatigue life and therefore $F_N(n)$ itself is a function of stress ratio f_r^{max}/f_r'.

Another approach is to use the method of damage mechanics which is directed to obtaining damage indices to describe the reduced function of the structural component in terms of load cycles. Typically, the damage function is of the form

$$\Psi = \Psi_{ref}(1 - D) \tag{2}$$

where Ψ is the current stiffness parameter, Ψ_{ref} is the original (considered to be undamaged) reference state and D is a damage parameter. As noted by Alliche and François [4], this approach to describing damage--as opposed to considering stresses--yields less scatter and therefore strain- -or equivalently deflection--may be better correlated with damage.

S. E. Swartz is Professor of Civil Engineering, Kansas State University, Manhattan, KS 66506-2905.

The damage concept may be utilized with fracture mechanics methods to model the damage process directly. Apparently Gylltoft [5] was the first to use a fracture mechanics model in this way to study low-cycle fatigue behavior of a concrete beam. More recently, this approach has been used by Hordijk [6] and Hordijk and Reinhardt [7] by modeling uniaxial, cyclic damage obtained from tests on concrete and then implementing this in a finite element program (DIANA) applied to a beam in four-point bending. The obtained results appear to be quite realistic.

FRACTURE MECHANICS METHODS

The explicit use of fracture mechanics concepts to evaluate concrete fatigue data will be described in this section. An approach commonly used for metals relates crack growth with number of cycles according to the so-called Paris' Law [8,9]:

$$da/dN = C(\Delta K)^m \tag{3}$$

where C, m are experimental constants and K is the stress intensity factor. In the logarithmic form

$$\log(da/DN) = \log C + m \log(\Delta K) \tag{4}$$

and the resulting data should plot as a straight line. The difficulties implementing this approach are: measurement of crack length a; calculation of $K = K(P, a, geometry)$; calculation of da/dN and ΔK. Inherent to this are the questions of the influence of process zone size and use of LEFM.

Compliance Calibration

Using a compliance-calibration technique, Baluch, et al. [10] used cracked specimens with crack length measurement based on surface observations. Their results are presented in Fig. 2a for three different stress ratios R. The fitted straight lines all have about the same slope. Similar work by Perdikaris and Calomino [11] is shown in Fig. 2b. However, a and k were based on notched beam compliance calibration and LEFM.

Size Effect Law

Work by Bazant and Xu [12], which exploited the principle of the size effect law, resulted in a modified-or generalized, size-adjusted Paris' law:

$$\frac{\Delta a}{\Delta N} = C\left(\frac{\Delta K_I}{K_{IC}}\right)^m \tag{5}$$

where K_{IC} is a size-dependent fracture toughness given by

$$K_{IC} = K_{If}\left(\frac{\beta}{1 + \beta}\right)^{\frac{1}{2}} \tag{6}$$

In this K_{If} is the fracture toughness of an infinitely-large beam and the brittleness number $\beta = d/d_o$ where d is the beam depth and d_o is an empirical constant which is considered to be the transition size between LEFM and strength behavior. Results are plotted in Fig. 3a for a value of $d_o = 2.86$ in. (72.6 mm) which was obtained from static tests. In this it is seen that a size effect still is present. They postulate that d_o may vary according to the ratio $\Delta K_I/K_{If}$. In their tests this was 0.8 (and the minimum load was zero). By arbitrarily adopting a value of $d_o = 28.6$ in. (726 mm), or ten times the value for static loading, improved results are shown in Fig. 3b in which it is seen that the size effect virtually disappears. Thus, they conclude that the size of the fracture process zone is greatly enlarged by load cycling.

Effective Crack Length

The problem of the process zone has plagued researchers trying to apply LEFM to concrete and other materials. For beams in bending subjected to quasi-static loads, results from using a dye technique to reveal the crack fronts are presented in Fig. 4 [13,14]. The development of the process zone is conceptualized, based on this evidence, in Fig. 5. In this it is seen that once the zone forms, it propagates with an approximately constant shape until the crack front approaches the compressed boundary. This occurs at about 60-70% of the depth of the beam. Tests on different beam sizes have shown this zone to be essentially size-independent for beam depths greater than 8 in. (203 mm) for a maximum aggregate size of 0.75 in. (19 mm) [13].

This observation has led to the concept of the effective crack length, a_e, proposed by Jenq and Shah (J/S)[15], Karihaloo and Nallathambi (K/N)[16] and Go, Refai, Swartz (G/R/S)[14]. The idea basically is to determine an effective crack length which approximates the process zone effect, and is thus longer than an open crack or a notch. Using this length, LEFM formulas are utilized to find K_{IC}. As shown in Fig. 6, this approach yields values which are approximately constant with respect to crack length provided a_e/w is less than about 0.7 (for the beams shown here).

This approach was applied to beams fatigue tested in three point bending (TPB) using two sizes and two mix designs [17]. The crack lengths were determined using compliance calibration [17,18]. The fatigue loading was done using CMOD strain control and was stopped at $N = 1 \times 10^6$ cycles. A typical group of data plots is shown in Fig. 7. The objective was to grow true fatigue cracks of different lengths but with about the same elapsed time ($1 \times 10^6/4$ Hz = .25 $\times 10^6$s). After cracking, the beams were loaded to failure and P-CMOD plotted. In each case a companion beam was cracked such that the slope of the ascending P-CMOD curve matched that of the fatigued beam. Then this was also loaded to failure. In both cases, K_{IC} was computed using P_{max} and LEFM with the crack length corresponding to the slope of the ascending curve.

The results of these tests are presented in Table 1. Based on the compliance-calibration method of crack measurement, K_{IC} (fatigue)/K_{IC} (static) = 0.90, CV = 6%. Corresponding results were obtained from the Jenq/Shah method [15]. These results are contradictory to those presented by Perdikaris and Calomino [19].

The effective crack approach also is evidently contradicted by the results presented by Bazant and Xu [12] since if the size of the process zone is associated with the load ratio used in the fatigue test, then the effective crack length a_e should be substantially different for the statically-loaded beams as compared to the fatigue-loaded beams. Yet a review of the J/S results in Table 1 indicate this is not the case.

REINFORCED CONCRETE BEAMS

The term "reinforced concrete" (R/C) implies here the use of conventional rebars or prestressed, steel cable or bars. Previous work done on R/C beams subjected to long term (high N) fatigue loadings is described in reference 1. In general, fatigue failures in such members are due to reinforcement debonding or rupture. For post-tensioned, prestressed beams fatigue failure may occur at the anchorages. It is mentioned that in a properly designed unbonded, prestressed concrete beam for which precompression is such that the section will remain uncracked during its service load cycle, the consequences of fatigue have not been a major factor in design. However, a conceivable failure mechanism could occur by a fatigue crack starting initially in a tensile region and extending through the compression zone.

Two small beam models were tested by Swartz and Noory [20] with the geometry and reinforcing shown in Fig. 8. The reinforcement consisted of smooth bars anchored at the beam ends to steel plates. Cracks were monitored using a photoelastic coating bonded to the beam surface at midspan as shown. This was Photoelastic PS-2A which had a thickness of 3mm, a k factor of 0.13 and f = 750 μm/m/fringe. Prior to starting fatigue testing the beam was loaded to its computed service level and cracks were induced in the central portion. Following this the beam was loaded in fatigue at 4 Hz with $P_{max} = 3.56$ kN, $P_{min} = 2.67$ kN (R = 0.75). The crack growth versus load cycles is shown in Table 2. These data were obtained from the photoelastic coating photographs, one of which is shown in Fig. 9. The failed beam is shown in Fig. 10. It may be seen that the primary mode of failure was by penetration of a flexural crack completely through the compressed region after which the load was carried solely by the reinforcement. This induced a yield mechanism in the steel bars. The fatigue lives for the two beams were 4.83×10^6 cycles and 17.68×10^6 cycles.

This model study revealed that (1) it is possible for flexural cracks to propagate through the concrete matrix due to fatigue in a mode which is not normally considered in design and (2) serviceability requirements in terms of crack widths need to be considered with respect to fatigue loads.

CONCLUSIONS

From the work presented here the following conclusions may be drawn:

1. Recent advances in the understanding of the static cracking behavior of concrete subjected to mode 1 deformation behavior, eg. the Size Effect Law [12] and Effective Crack Model [14,15,16], have shown promise of more realistic modeling of fracture behavior in fatigue with fracture mechanics.

2. Nevertheless, problems remain in understanding the influence of the fatigue mechanism on crack formation, coalescence and bridging, ie. the process zone effect. The size-effect law evidently predicts a large increase in the process zone due to fatigue [12] whereas the effective crack model [15] does not. Clearly, more detailed experimental evidence of the actual crack growth process - especially due to repeated, low-level loads - is needed.

3. When these problems are resolved, it appears that the Paris' Law, in some modified form, may reasonably model crack growth versus load cycles for plain concrete.

4. Future work on testing plain concrete in bending to determine fatigue damage behavior and life should incorporate the concepts presented here.

5. Extension of this work to reinforced concrete should be done with particular emphasis on very lightly reinforced beams, over-reinforced beams and post-tensioned (unbonded) beams.

ACKNOWLEDGEMENTS

The work of the author and his colleagues reported here has been supported over the years by a number of grants from the National Science Foundation : ENG78-07829, CEE-8305120, MSM-8317136, INT-8812995 and MSM-8919449. This support is gratefully acknowledged.

REFERENCES

1. Shah, S.P., ed., Fatigue of Concrete Structures, ACI SP-75, American Concrete Inst., Detroit, 1982.

2. ACI Committee 215, "Consideration for Design of Concrete Structures Subjected to Fatigue Loading", ACI Journal, Vol. 71, No. 3, Mar. 1974, pp. 97-121.

3. Oh, Byung Hwan, "Fatigue-Life Distributions of Concrete for Various Stress Levels", ACI Materials Journal, Vol. 88, No. 2, Mar.-Apr. 1991, pp. 122-128.

4. Alliche, A. and François, D., "Fatigue Damage of Concrete", Fracture of Concrete and Rock, eds. S.P. Shah and S.E. Swartz, Springer-Verlag, New York, 1989, pp. 88-95.

5. Gylltoft, K., "Fracture Mechanics Models for Fatigue in Concrete Structures", PhD Thesis, Lulea University of Technology, 1983.

6. Hordijk, D.A., "Local Approach to Fatigue of Concrete", PhD Thesis, Delft University of Technology, 1991.

7. Hordijk, D.A. and Reinhardt, H.W., "Growth of Discrete Cracks in Concrete Under Fatigue Loading", Toughening Mechanisms in Quasi-Brittle Materials, ed. S.P. Shah, Kluwer Academic Publisher, Dordrecht, 1991, pp. 541-554.

8. Paris, P.C., "The Growth of Fatigue Cracks Due to Variations in Load", PhD Thesis, Lehigh University, 1962.

9. Paris, P.C. and Erdogan, F., "A Critical Analysis of Crack Propagation Laws", Transactions of ASME, Journal of Basic Engineering, V. 85, 1963, pp. 528-534.

10. Baluch, M.A., Qureshy, A.B. and Azad, A.K., "Fatigue Crack Propagation in Plain Concrete", Fracture of Concrete and Rock, eds., S.P. Shah and S.E. Swartz, Springer-Verlag, New York, 1989, pp. 80-87.

11. Perdikaris, P.C. and Calomino, A.M., "Kinetics of Crack Growth in Plain Concrete", Fracture of Concrete and Rock, eds. S.P. Shah and S.E. Swartz, Springer-Verlag, New York, 1989, pp. 64-69.

12. Bazant, Z.P. and Xu, K., "Size Effect in Fatigue Fracture of Concrete", ACI Materials Journal, Vol. 88, No. 4, July-August 1991, pp. 390-399.

13. Refai, T.M.E. and Swartz, S.E., "Fracture Behavior of Concrete Beams in Three-Point Bending Considering the Influence of Size Effects", Report 190, Engineering Experiment Station, Kansas State University, Manhattan, July 1987.

14. Swartz, S.E. and Refai, T.M.E., "Cracked Surface Revealed by Dye and Its Utility in Determining Fracture Parameters", Fracture Toughness and Fracture Energy-Test Methods for Concrete and Rock, eds. H. Mihashi, H. Takahashi and F.H. Wittmann, A.A. Balkema, Rotterdam, 1989, pp. 509-520.

15. Jenq, Y.S. and Shah, S.P., "Two-Parameter Fracture Model for Concrete", Journal of Engineering Mechanics, ASCE, Vol. 111, No. 10, Oct. 1985, pp. 1227-1241.

16. Karihaloo, B.L. and Nallathambi, P., "Notched Beam Test: Mode I Fracture Toughness", Ch. 1 of Fracture Mechanics Test Methods for Concrete, eds. S.P. Shah and A. Carpinteri, Chapman and Hall, London, 1991, pp. 22-30.

17. Swartz, Stuart E., Huang, Chen-Ming James and Hu, Kuo-Kuang, "Crack Growth and Fracture in Plain Concrete--Static Versus Fatigue Loading", ACI SP-75, ed. S.P. Shah, American Concrete Institute, Detroit, pp. 47-69.

18. Swartz, Stuart E., Hu, Kuo-Kuang and Jones, Gary L., "Compliance Monitoring of Crack Growth in Concrete", Journal of Engineering Mechanics Division, ASCE, Vol. 104, No. EM4, Aug. 1978, pp. 789-800.

19. Perdikaris, Philip C., Calomino, Anthony M., and Chudnovsky, Alexander, "Effect of Fatigue on Fracture Toughness of Concrete", Journal of Engineering Mechanics, Vol. 112, No. 8, Aug. 1986, pp. 776-790.

20. Swartz, S.E., and Noory, A.K., "Photoelastic Coatings to Monitor Crack Growth in Concrete", Experimental Techniques, Vol. 5, No. 3, Sept. 1981, pp. 2-3.

Table 1. Stress intensity factors at unstable crack growth-fatigue and static precracking

W^1 mm	Load² Type	f'_c MPa	P_m kN	$\frac{a_e^3}{W}$	K^s_{Ic} kN-m$^{-3/2}$	$\frac{a^4}{W}$	K_{Ic} kN-m$^{-3/2}$	$\frac{F}{S}$
102	F3	48.9	4.54	.352	1192	.195	769	.84
102	S3	48.9	4.94	.297	1116	.245	916	
102	F3	54.2	1.92	.525	740	.510	727	.93
102	S3	54.2	2.02	.527	780	.520	782	
102	F3	51.7	2.06	.605	1117	.612	1102	.86
102	S3	51.7	2.31	.605	1252	.618	1276	
203	F3	22.5	12.37	.072	595	.160	842	.83
203	S3	23.4	13.71	.065	642	.180	1016	
203	F3	24.8	5.70	.350	631	.490	880	
203	S3	24.8	5.83	.350	646	.515	972	.91
203	F3	26.0	4.91	.380	590	.580	1032	
203	F3	52.7	11.35	.230	902	.374	1263	.95
203	S3	52.7	10.24	.290	963	.438	1329	
203	F3	53.1	3.90	.590	857	.740	1670	
203	S3	53.1	4.05	.760	1710	.742	1752	.95
203	F3	53.2	1.07	.770	1110	.830	779	

[1] For W = 102 mm, B = 76 mm, S = 381 mm. For W = 203 mm, B = 102 mm, S = 610 mm.

[2] F = fatigue precracking, S = static precracking, 3 = TPB.

[3] Method of Jenq and Shah [15]

[4] Compliance Calibration [18]

Table 2. Crack size versus number of cycles.

$N \times 10^3$	$\dfrac{\text{Crack Depth}}{\text{Beam Depth}}$	% Change in Crack Width
0	0.232	--
25	0.344	5
850	0.376	11
1174	0.400	74
4300	0.600	137

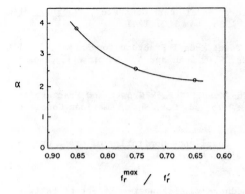

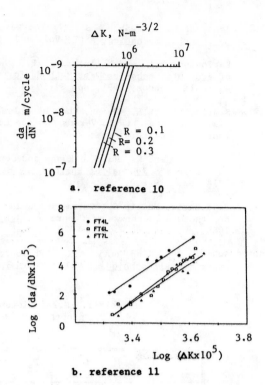

a. reference 10

b. reference 11

Fig. 1. Variation of shape parameter according to the applied fatigue stress levels [3].

Fig. 2. Crack growth da/dN versus Δ [10,11]

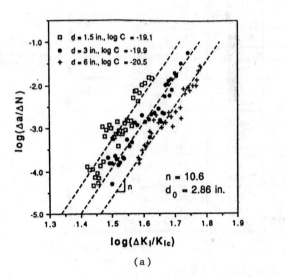

(a)

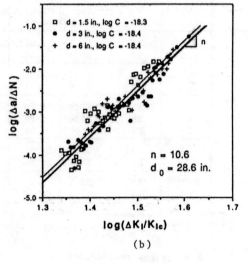

(b)

Fig. 3. Crack growth, three beam sizes, after Ref. 12
(a) d_o from monotonic tests, (b) d_o ten times larger.

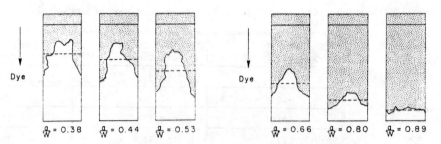

Fig. 4. Cracked surfaces, beams tested by Refai [13]
W = 8 in. (203 mm), B = 3 in. (76 mm).

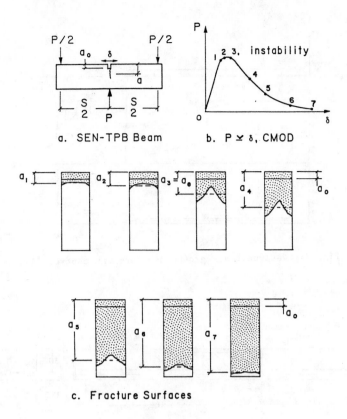

a. SEN-TPB Beam

b. $P \simeq \delta$, CMOD

c. Fracture Surfaces

Fig. 5. Crack growth from a notched beam.

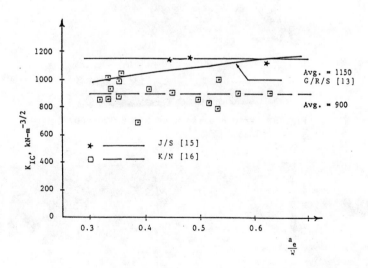

Fig. 6. K_{IC}, series B beams, W = 203 mm [14].

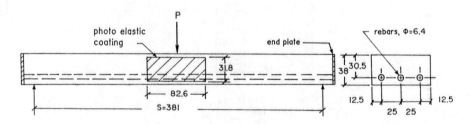

Fig. 7. Fatigue crack growth-displacement control [17].

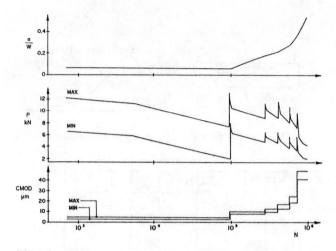

Fig. 8. Model beam with end-anchored reinforcement (after ref. 20).

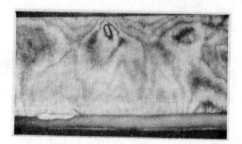

Fig. 9. Fringe pattern at N = 4,300,000

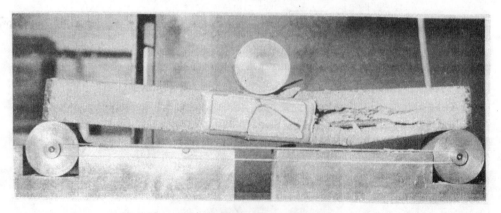

Fig. 10. Fatigue failure of reinforced concrete beam.

HIGH SPEED POSITIONING AND ANALYSIS OF AN NC TURRET PUNCHING PRESS BY EXPERIMENTAL TRANSFER FUNCTIONS

Yoshitaka MORIMOTO[*1], Takeshi YASUI[*2] and Masashi TYUJYOU[*3]

ABSTRACT

The dynamic characteristics of an NC Turret Punching Press has been evaluated by decomposition of the positioning system into two units :one is control system, the other is mechanical one, by using the transfer function between the input command and the resultant carriage motion measured directly. It includes not only control system but also mechanical one.

Next, a new control method for the carriage motion has been developed by using the experimental transfer function. This method is based on the idea that an input-output relation between a control command and the resultant carriage motion can be described in a linearized form constructed by the transfer function measured at a representative position of a carriage. The control input which realizes a carriage motion to move with the desired trajectory and the rapid motion has been easily calculated by our method. The experimental results showed considerable surpression of the over shoot and the vibratory motion.

1.INTRODUCTION

Numerical controled machines which play an important part for automation and high productivity have been improving in functions along with computer advances. Because of the high speed positioning and the high productivity, the NC Turret Punching Press is a representative NC machine from the point of the motion speed and reaches the speed of over 1 m/s of carriage motion. This demand for the high speed positioning will be required more and more. But the higher carriage motion increases in speed, the more it increaes in the over shoot and in the vibratory motion. In order to solve these problem, increasing the structual rigidity and selecting the powerfull motor cause a vicios circle. Thus research on the analysis and control[1][2] has been conducted. But one of the most important issues in controling NC machines has been how to describe and design the system with sufficient accuracy for use in control. In our previous study[3][4], we propose the method to control a flexible robot arm by using an experimrntal modal analysis technique. In this study, we propose a method based on our previous study by which the carriage moves with the enough accurate trajectory and without the over shoot and the vibratory motion also by using a experimental transfer function calculated from the input command and the resultant carriage motion. The main issues in this paper are :(1)analysys of motion by decomposing NC system into the control system and the mechanical system,(2)how to measure the transfer function for use in control,(3)control method to supress the overshoot and the vibratory motion by our proposed method.

2.ANALYSIS OF DYNAMIC CHARACTERISTICS

An AC servo motor and a ball-screw driving mechanisim are equiped for the motion control of a carriage in an NC Turret Punching Press. The digital feedback system is applied to the position control system with an AC servo motor. Thus, it is needed to make clear whether the cause of the overshoot and the vibratory motion in the case of positioning is in the control system or in the mechanical system.

Measuring the transfer function between the input command and the carriage motion, it is the most common method to evaluate the dynamic characteristics for control system and/or mechanical system. As shown in Fig.1, a position signal at the end of the servo motor is only fed back to the NC system and the mechanical system including the carriage after the servo motor is left out of control system in a conventional machine. We should note that the needed control output for us is not the signal of the rotatory position angle but the one of carriage motion. Further, two units of dynamic characteristics are defined:(1) the dynamic characteristics between the input and the output of a motor axis,(2) the one between a timing pulley and the carriage motion. These are used for the evaluation of the total dynamic characteristics of a carriage positioning so that the cause of the over shoot and the vibratory motion is specified clearly.

2.1 EVALUATION OF DYNAMIC CHARACTERISTICS

In this study, we describe the dynamic characteristics by using a transfer function between the input and the motion at a representitive point on a carriage. The experimental transfer function between the input and the motion at a representitive point on a carriage is described as Eq.(1).

$$H(j\omega) = O(j\omega) \, / \, I(j\omega) \qquad (1)$$

where $H(j\omega)$ is a frequency transfer function. $I(j\omega)$ is the input (frequency domain input). $O(j\omega)$ is a carriage motion (frequency domain output).

*1 Yoshitaka MORIMOTO is an engineer of the Industrial Research Institute of Ishikawa Pref. Department of Mechanics and Electronics. Ro-1 Tomizu-machi KANAZAWA 920-02, JAPAN, Phone +81 762-67-8082, Fax. +81 762-67-8090
*2 Takeshi YASUI is Professor of Department of Mechanical System Engineering, Fucalty of Engineering, Kanazawa University
*3 Masashi TYUJYOU is a graduate student of Department of Mechanical System Engineering, Fucalty of Engineering, Kanazawa University

In the conventional NC system, because the input in the time domain is not known, the input $I(j\omega)$ in Eq.(1) can not calculate. We need special technique to get the information about it. The NC system equipes a check board for monitoring velocity command, torque and position during motion. By using this borad, the input $i(t)$ can be derived as Eq.(2).

$$i(t) = Vcmd / Pg + \int_0^t Venc \, dt \qquad (2)$$

where Vcmd is the velocity command. Pg is the position gain. Venc is the velocity from the pulse-corder of the motor .

2.2 DECOMPOSITION METHOD OF CONTROL SYSTEM AND MECHANICHAL SYSTEM

We suppose the model shown in Fig.2 for decomposing the total dynamic characteristics into the control system and the mechanical system. Where point 1 is the input point of desired target value. Point 2 is the only point connecting an element "a" (motor axis) to an element "b" (timing pulley of carriage). Point 3 is a representitive point of a carriage. According to the method of sructual modification using frequency response functions [6], outputs of three points are derived from following equations using transfer functions G^a_{12}, G^a_{22}, G^b_{22}, G^b_{23}.

$$X^a_2 = VG^a_{12} + FG^a_{22} \qquad (3)$$

$$X^b_2 = - FG^b_{22} \qquad (4)$$

$$X^b_3 = - FG^b_{23} \qquad (5)$$

Where X^a_2, X^b_2 and X^b_3 are the outputs of an each point of elements in frequency domain. In Eq.(3), the desired target value V can be derived from Eq.(2). The motor torque can be also measured by using the check borad. Suppose that this torque approaches zero after positioning, this can be Fouurier Transformed as T (frequency domain). G^b_{22} and G^b_{23} can be derived directory from Eq.(4) and Eq.(5). However G^a_{12} and G^a_{22} can not be derived from Eq.(3). We prepared another condition. In the case that the motor is not connected to the ball-screw of a carriage, the output at the point 2 of element "a" is described using Eq.(6).

$$X^a_{2n} = V_n G^a_{12} + F_n G^a_{22} \qquad (6)$$

Where n denotes the unconnected condition.

We can calculate G^a_{12} and G^a_{22} easily. Because NC system including a servo motor is as one assembly unit for a designer, we define its system as the control system. The other part which is driving mechanism of a carriage is defined as the mechanical system. Hence the motion trajectory of an each term calculated from Eq.(3), Eq.(4) and Eq.(5) indicates the effect of positioning by inverse Fourier transform of X_i as described Eq.(7).

$$x_i(t) = \int_0^t \{F^{-1}[X_i(j\omega)]\} dt \qquad (7)$$

Where i denotes point as shown in Fig.2. Where F^{-1} denotes the inverse Fourier transform of [].

2.3 EXPERIMENT

The NC Turret Punching Press used has two axes, each driven by AC digital servo motors, the maximum speed of 1.08m/s. The experiments were carried out by using Y axis motion (another X axis was fixed) of this carriage (weight:800kgf) in such a way that we gave the conventional input command whose acceleration and deceleration pattern is linear and whose maximun speed of 280 mm/s had 0.17 s duration time. The velocity input measured by the check board and the velocity output measured by a laser position system were Fourier transformed to get a transfer function at one position by a personal computer as shown in Fig.3. Because the coherence function calculated by using data measured five times showed the good results from DC to 23 Hz(except around 12-13Hz), this measurement has enoutgh accurate to evaluate the dynamic characteristics and to decompose the sytem which includes the control system and the mechanichal one.

The results of each trajectory computed by using Eq.(3)-(5) were shown from Fig.4. The first peak of 12Hz (G^a_{12}) was the resonant frequency of the feed back system according to the vibratory motion which appears at the unconnected condition. Though there were some peeks, these did not affect the positioning which was required the least positioning resolution of 50 μm. Figure 5 shows the posiotoning processes of a desired target value, calculated and measured trajectry of terms. This figure shows that the over shoot is caused by the control system and the vibratory motion is generated by a carriage due to the motor torque.

3.CONTROL OF CARRIAGE MOTION USING INVERSE DYNAMICS

3.1 Control method

The motion control of a carriage can be described as the inverse problem of prediciton of motion Eq.(7). In this case, the transfer function and a desired output are known and the input is unknown. Hence we use Eq.(1) and get a input i(t) immediately by using the experimental transfer function and a desired output as Eq.(8).

$$i(t) = \int_0^t \{ \ F^{-1}[O(j\omega)/H(j\omega)] \ \}dt \qquad (8)$$

Because we can only teach the final position of a carriage to the conventional NC system, the positioning of a carriage depends on the CPU of the control part which calculates its own control input. We took a special technique to control the carriage motion, that was DNC(Direct Numerical Control) with the RS232c interface connecting between a host CPU and the control part to realize our control method as shown in Fig.6. The calculated input is directly fed to the digital servo amplifier of the control part. Because the calculated data is transmitted at the speed of 9600 bps (0.004 sec./datum and 1000 data continueously), we have to execute the calculation to syncronize with the transmission speed of an experimental system.

3.2 DYNAMIC CHARACTERISTICS USED WITH CONTROL

The transfer function between a personal computer and carriage motion would be different from the one measured in the conventional NC system. Thus we have to measure the transfer function once again as same as the method mentioned above. Though the experiment was carried out, in this case the input was the calculated one by a personal computer. The least resolution of this NC system is 1 μm. When the desired position output is designed with a linear accelation and deceleration, the specter to contain over the 1 μm is in a range from DC to 12Hz. Thus we have to measure the transfer function acuurately within the frequency range.

4. EXPERIMENT

4.1 MEASUREMENT OF TRANSFER FUNCTION AND CALCULATION OF INPUT COMMAND

The experiments of measuring the transfer function were carried out by using Y axis motion (another X axis was fixed) of this carriage as same as chapter 2. The velocity input whose acceleration and deceleration pattern were linear and whose maximun speed was 140 mm/s and whose duration time was 0.17 s. The measured transfer function was calculated by a personal computer as shown in Fig.7.

4.2 CONTROL EXPERIMENT

The control experiments was carried out by a designed output whose motion was linear acceleration and deceleration and maximum speed of 85 mm/s and duration of 0.17 s. Figure 8 shows the comparison of the measured position of the carriage driven by (a) our control results, and by (b) conventional input only. This figure shows that considerable vibration has been generated by our method. This results shows that the more improvment of our control method is required.

5. REPETITIVE COMPENSATION OF TRANSFER FUNCTION

5.1 COMPENSATION METHOD OF TRANSFER FUNCTION

The control results showed the vibratory motion. Thus the cause of the vibratory motion can be considered that the computed input does not have enough exiting force to calculate the accurate transfer function. Next the compensation of transfer function was carried out the following way as shown in Fig.9.

Suppose that the input has not enough exiting force at a representitive frequency, the measured output contains the error which is larger or smaller than the original transfer function as described Eq.(9).

$$H_{1l} > H_r > H_{1h} \qquad (9)$$

Where H_{1l} is smaller, H_{1h} is larger than the original H_r of a transfer function.

Then we compute the transfer function H_2 from Eq.(1) by using the input obtained I_1 and the output O_1. Because this transfer function contains the dynamic characteristics of vibratory motion, the computed input should be compensated and changed the value as Eq.10.

$$I_{2l} > I_r > I_{2h} \qquad (10)$$

Where I_{2l} denotes the second computed input which is lager than the original input I_r.

Each input compensates the transfer function H_l or H_h by increasing or decreasing the exiting force. Thus we repeat this operation untill the over shoot and the vibratory motion approach to the given tolerance.

5.2 COMPENSATION OF TRANSFER FUNCTION AND CONTROL RESULTS

The compensation of a transfer function was carried out according to the method described above. Figure 10 shows the compensation result of the transfer function . The specter changed at certain frequency range in which the vibratory motion occured. The control result by using the transfer function compensated four times is shown in Fig.11. Because the fourth results shows the considerable surpresion of the over shoot and the vibratory motion, the transfer function was measured accurately enough to use in control.

Next we changed the desired output a new output of 25mm movement with 240 mm/s. Figure 12 shows the comparison of motion by (a) the first positioning, by (b) the second positioning used our repetitive compensation method and by (c) the conventional positioning. The second positioning by our repetitive compensation method has reached at the desired position with 0.22 s compared with 0.53 s of the conventional positioning.

6.CONCLUSION

(1) A transfer function was used to describe the dynamic charasteristics of a NC turret punching press. Based on the composition method of transfer functios, the dymamic characteristics has been decomposed into the mechanical system and the control one.

(2) Based on the results obtained (1), it was revealed that the motion of a carriage consists of the over shoot due to the control system and the vibratory motion due to the mechanical system.

(3) DNC was applied to control the carriage motion of an NC Turret Punching Press.

(4) A new control method to compensate a transfer function has been developed. Experimental results showed that this method was effective and had wide applicability.

(5) Because the experiments have been limited to the case of one axis motion, further study including the case of multiaxial control is required to verify the practical value of the proposed method.

ACKNOWLEDGMENT

The authors would like to express their siscere gratitude to Mr. H.Yamahachi, T.Nakayabu and Y.Ichimaru for their kind support during this study. KOMATSU Ltd., who offered the use of the NC turret punching press during experiments, is also greatfully acknowledged.

REFERENCES

1. Young, K. D., "Controller Design for a Manipulators Using Theory of Variable Structure Systems",IEEE Trans. SMC, 8-2, 101-109, 1978

2. Yeung, K. S. and Chen, Y. P., "A New Controller Design for a Manipulatores Using Theory of Variable Structure Systems", IEEE Trans. AC, 33-2, 200-206,1988

3. Morimoto, Y., Inamura, T. and Mizoguchi, K., "Dynamic Control of a Flexible Robot Arm by Using Experimental Modal Analysis", Proc. of the ASME Winter Annual Meeting, Modeling and Control of Robotic Manipulators and Manufacturing Processes, DSC-6, 337-343,1987

4. Morimoto, Y., Inamura, T. and Makita, R., "Analysis and Control of a Flexible Robot Arm by Using Experimental Modal Analysis", JSME Inter National Trans. SIII,Vol.33, 634-640, 1990

5. Hara, S., Omata,T. and Nakano,M., "Synthesis of Repetitive Control Systems and Its Application" Proc.24th CDC, pp.1384-1392(1985) 6. S.Hara, Y.Yamamoto, T.Omata and M.Nakano "Repetitive Control System: A New Type Servo System for Periodic Exogenous Signsls", IEEE Trans. Automatic Contrpl, AC-33-7, 659-668, 1988

6. Crowley, J., Klosterman, A., Rocklin, G. and Vold, H., "Direct Structural Modification Using Frequenncy Response Functions", International Modal Analysis Conference Proceedings, February, 1984

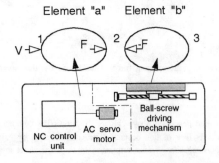

Fig.1　Schematic diagram of an NC turret punching press

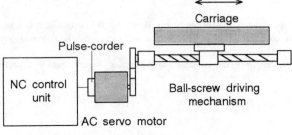

Fig.2 Decomposition of an NC positioning system

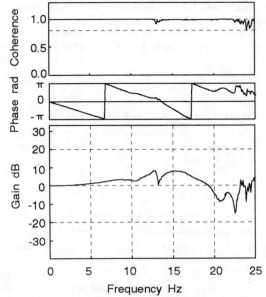

Fig.3　Example of measured transfer function and its coherence

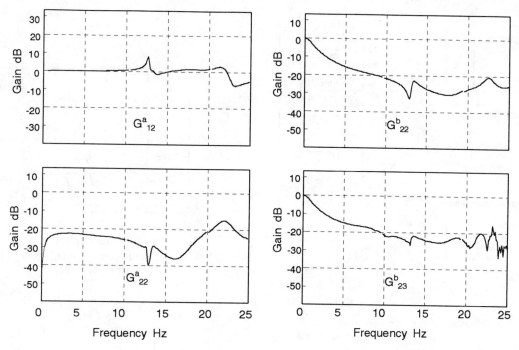

Fig.4   Calculated transfer functions of decomposed elements

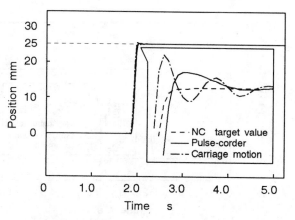

Fig.5   Calculated motion at representative points

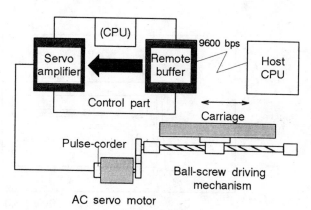

Fig.6   Schematic diagram of a DNC system

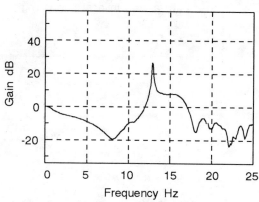

Fig.7   Measured transfer function of a DNC positioning system

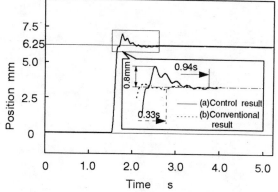

Fig.8   Comparison of motion driven by (a)our proposed method and by (b) a conventional input

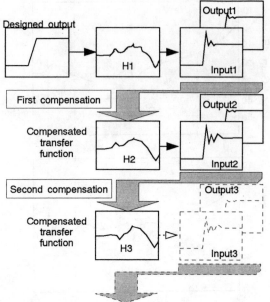

Fig.9　Method for compensating transfer function by repetitive measurement

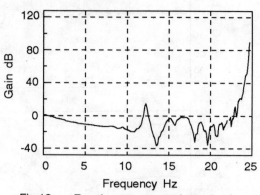

Fig.10　Fourth compensated result of a transfer function

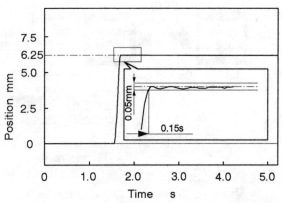

Fig.11　Control result by four times' repetitive compensation of transfer function

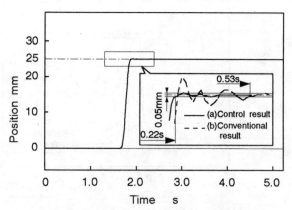

Fig.12　Comparison of motion driven by (a) the proposed method and by (b) a conventional positioning

Transmission Error for a Stepping Motor-Timing Belt Drive System

Hyunsoo Kim : Associate Professor, Department of Mechanical Engineering,
Sungkyunkwan University, Chonchon-dong 300, Suwon, 440-746, Korea
Hyuk   Wee : Hyundai Motor Company, Ulsan, Korea

ABSTRACT

Transmission error for a stepping motor drive timing belt system was investigated experimentally and analytically. From FFT analysis of the experimental results, it was found that the transmission error consists of three periodic errors: (1) error by the stepping motor per one resolution angle(θ_m), (2) error by the pulley eccentricity per one revolution(θ_e) and (3) error by the meshing interference between the belt and the pulley teeth per one pitch revolution(θ_p). In order to investigate the effects of some design parameters on the transmission error, the dynamic model of the stepping motor drive timing belt system was derived by using Bondgraph. According to the simulation results, as the belt total tension increased, θ_m and θ_e decreased due to the nonlinearity of the belt. In addition, the numerical and experimental results showed that θ_m and θ_e of the loaded case were larger than those of the unloaded case. The theoretical results were in good accordance with the experimental results.

1. INTRODUCTION

One of the outstanding features of timing belt drives is their ability to position shafts accurately. Because of this characteristic, timing belt drives are used in machines requiring precise linear and angular positioning or synchronous motion such as office automation or factory automation machines. However, in spite of the high transmission accuracy, the transmission error becomes a problem in printing machines, copying machines, faximilies and high quality machine tools which require high transmission accuracy and positioning.

The transmission error of timing belt drives is defined by lead or lag of the revolution angle of the driven shaft to the revolution angle of the driving shaft. The transmission error causes the overstriking of lines, smearing of characters in copying and printing machines and also causes vertical lines to be printed in a zigzag pattern in dot matrix printers. Although such a machine with high precision is equipped with backlashless timing belt, an improvement in transmission error characteristics are desired.

As for the transmission error characteristics, only a few studies have been reported by Kagotani and Koyama[1-6]. They found that the transmission error is generated by the elastic deformation of the belt and the polygonal action of the pulley under an initial tension and by the meshing interference between the belt and pulley teeth. Their works have been performed based on the assumption of perfect alignment of the machine components and constant driving torque as an input energy source. However, a perfect alignment can hardly be obtained due to many reasons such as pulley eccentricity, production errors and so on. Also, as can be seen in stepping motor drives which are widely used in the precision machines, the motor torque varies periodically during the operation.

In this paper, the transmission error characteristics of a stepping motor drive timing belt system were investigated analytically and experimentally considering the torque variation of the stepping motor and the pulley eccentricity.

2. EXPERIMENT

Since there are few works on the transmission error characteristics for the stepping motor torque variation and the pulley eccentricity, preliminary experiments were performed to investigate the trends of the transmission error.

2.1 Experimental apparatus

Figure 1 shows the experimental apparatus for a stepping motor drive timing belt system. Stepping motor(1) drives the driver pulley (3) and the power is transmitted to the driven pulley via timing belt(5). The torque transmitted to the driven side is balanced with the torque load which is applied by a torque disk(7) with dead weight(18). The torque disk converts a given weight to a torque. A variety of torque loads can be obtained by adding and subtracting dead weight. The torque disk and the driven pulley are mounted on a transverse sliding plate which is bolted to linear bearings(16). The initial belt tension is supplied by a lead screw(9) through a cantilever(8). Various tension can be applied by adjusting the lead screw.

The stepping motor has a resolution of 1.8 degree and is controlled by a computer through a drive circuit(13). The stepping motor output torque is measured by a torque transducer(2). The timing belt total tension is measured by a tension transducer which consists of the cantilever and strain gauges(10).

The transmission error is measured by encoders(4) which are connected to the driver and the driven shafts. The number of output pulses of each encoder is 2000 PPR, which can be augmented by 5 times through a post processing program. The pulse signals from the encoders are processed continuously through signal converting citcuits(14) and stored in the RAM of a computer. A pulse generator(15) is used in order to measure the real time of each pulse. The transmission error is obtained by post processing the pulses of the driver and driven sides.

Timing belt, 32XL037, with 9.5 mm wide and 160 teeth and pulley, 18XL037 with 5.08 mm pitch and 18 teeth were used for the experimental study. In the study, the experimental apparatus were assembled with almost zero misalignment and only the pulley eccentricity was allowed to investigate its effects on the transmission error. The experiments were performed at transmission ratio 1:1 and motor speed 36 rpm for various tensions $T_1 + T_2 = 100N$, $200N$, $300N$, $400N$.

2.2 Preliminary experimental results

Figure 2(a) shows the transmission error of the stepping motor drive timing belt system without torque load with $T_1 + T_2 = 100N$. As shown in Fig. 2(a), the transmission error consists of many frequency components. In order to analyze the frequency components, Fourier transformation of the experimental data in Fig. 2(a) was performed and the results were plotted in the frequency domain in Fig. 2(b). It is seen in Fig. 2(b) that the transmission error consists of three dominant frequencies: $f = 0.6$ Hz, $f = 10.8$ Hz, $f = 120$ Hz. $f = 0.6$ Hz corresponds to the frequency of the pulley revolution at 36 rpm and $f = 10.8$ Hz is about 18 times of the pulley revolution frequency, where 18 is the number of the pulley teeth. $f = 120$ Hz corresponds to the cycle of the stepping motor resolution angle, 1.8 degree, in other words, 200 times per one revolution of pulley.

Figure 3 shows the tension fluctuation of the timing belt at zero torque load with $T_1 + T_2 = 300N$. As shown in Fig. 3, the belt tension changed with the period $T = 1.6667$ sec, which is the period of the pulley revolution. This tension variation was induced by the pulley eccentricity. Close investigation of the experimental curve shows that the tension fluctuates 18 times in one revolution of the pulley, which corresponds to the number of the pulley teeth. This tension fluctuation results from the meshing inteference between the pulley and the belt teeth per one pitch revolution. Above tension fluctuation causes the deformation of the belt and results in the transmission error.

From the experimental results in Fig. 2 and Fig. 3, it is found that the transmission error of the stepping motor drive timeing belt system consists of three components: (1) error by the stepping motor per one pitch revolution angle(θ_m), (2) error by the pulley eccentricity per one revolution(θ_e) and (3) error by the meshing interference between the pulley and belt teeth per one pitch revolution(θ_p). The error by the meshing interference, θ_p was studied in detail by Kagotani at al[2,3]. They found that magnitude of θ_p was less than 200 μ radian and the effect of θ_p on the performance of the system was negligible. Therefore, in this paper, the effects of θ_m and θ_e on the transmission error were investigated.

3. BONDGRAPH MODEL

3.1 Transmission error by stepping motor

The stepping motor has a torque fluctuation per one revolution angle[7], which results in the tension variation. In this paper, neglecting the electrical characteristics inside the motor, only the output torque of the stepping motor was considered. The output torque T(t) of the stepping motor can be represented as

$$T(t) = T_m + T_a\sin(\omega_R t) \qquad (1)$$

where T_m is an average output torque, T_a is an amplitude of torque variation, ω_R is a motor speed.

Figure 4 shows a bondgraph model of timing belt drive system with stepping motor. As shown in Fig. 4, an effort source T(t) is used as an input which is indicated by dotted line(1). In order to investigate the effect of the stepping motor on the transmission error, let us assume that there is no pulley eccentricity. Then the inlet and the outlet where the belt enters and goes out of the pulley can be modelled as TF(transformer) with a coefficient n. The coefficient n is a driver pulley radius. At TF, the rotational motion of the belt is changed into a linear motion and vice versa. Since there is no eccentricity in the pulleys, MTF(modulated transformer) at the driven pulley becomes just a TF with a coefficient $R_1 = R_2 = n$.

Enen if the timing belt drive used in this study has a fixed tensioning system, the cantilever of the tension transducer can be considerd to be a linear spring as it should be. Thus, the driven pulley on the sliding plate was modelled at 1-juction with an equivalent mass, M and a transducer spring of constant Kn.

Now, let's consider a nonlinear characteristic of the belt. Since the belt tension between the driver and the driven pulley is carried by two components: (1) belt teeth made of rubber and (2) load carrying cord made of wire or glassfiber, we can not say that the relation between the tension and the belt deformation is linear. Assuming that the relationship is a 3rd order polynomial as follows,

$$T = C_1X^3 + C_2X^2 + C_3X + C_4 \qquad (2)$$

where T is a tension, X is a belt deformation, $C_1 \sim C_4$ are coeffients which can be determined from simple tensile experiment. Nonlinear belt is modelled as a nonlinear spring element C in the bondgraph in Fig. 4.

It can be seen in Fig. 4 that the bondgraph model has 6 state variables as: driver pulley angular momentum h_R, tight side belt deformation X_t, slack side belt deformation X_s, driven pulley angular momentum h_N, driven side linear momentum P, driven side spring displacement X_N. In Fig. 4, J_R and J_N are inertias of the pulleys, b_t and b_s are damping coefficients of the belt, b_R and b_N are damping coefficients of the bearings.

From the bondgraph in Fig. 4, the following state space equations are derived.

$$\dot{h}_R = T(t) - b_R\frac{h_R}{J_R} - n\left[b_t\left(n\frac{h_R}{J_R} - \frac{h_N}{J_N} - \frac{P}{M} \right)\right.$$

$$\left. - b_s\left(-n\frac{h_R}{J_R} + n\frac{h_N}{J_N} - \frac{P}{M} \right) + T_t - T_s \right] \qquad (3)$$

$$\dot{X}_t = n\frac{h_R}{J_R} - R_1\frac{h_N}{J_N} - \frac{P}{M} \qquad (4)$$

$$\dot{X}_s = - n\frac{h_R}{J_R} + R_2\frac{h_N}{J_N} - \frac{P}{M} \qquad (5)$$

418

$$\dot{h}_N = -b_R \frac{h_R}{J_R} - T_L + R_1 \left[b_t \left(n \frac{h_R}{J_R} - R_1 \frac{h_N}{J_N} - \frac{P}{M} \right) \right.$$

$$\left. + T_t \right] - R_2 \left[b_s \left(-n \frac{h_R}{J_R} + R_2 \frac{h_N}{J_N} - \frac{P}{M} \right) - T_s \right] \quad (6)$$

$$\dot{P} = \left[b_t \left(n \frac{h_R}{J_R} - R_1 \frac{h_N}{J_N} - \frac{P}{M} \right) + b_s \left(- n \frac{h_R}{J_R} \right. \right.$$

$$\left. \left. + R_2 \frac{h_N}{J_N} - \frac{P}{M} \right) + T_t + T_s \right] - b_1 \frac{P}{M} - K_N X_N \quad (7)$$

$$\dot{X}_N = \frac{P}{M} \quad (8)$$

where T_t is a tight side tension, T_s is a slack side tension and T_L is a load torque. Solving the above equations numerically gives the angular momentum of the driver and driven pulley, i.e. angular velocities of the pulleys. The transmission error can be obtained from a difference between the angular displacements of the pulleys which can be calculated by integrating the angular velocities over time.

3.2 Transmission error by pulley eccentricity

Fig. 5 shows a pulley which has an eccentric center. In Fig. 5, pulley radius R can be represented as

$$R = r + \varepsilon \cos\theta \quad (9)$$

where r is a pulley radius from a true center C, ε is an amount of the eccentricity and θ is an angular position.

A bondgraph model of the timing belt system with eccentric pulley is basically same with the model in Fig. 4 except the input energy source. In order to examine the effect of pulley eccentricity, the stepping motor was considered as an input flow source, $\omega(t)$. The capacitance K_c was introduced between the flow source and the driver pulley to avoid numerical difficulties[8]. The flow source and the capacitance are indicated by dottd line(2) in Fig. 4. Considering the eccentrcity only in the driven pulley, MTF was used for the pulley radius instead of TF. The radii of the inlet and outlet positions of the driven pulley are

$$\left. \begin{array}{l} R_1 = r + \varepsilon \cos(\theta_N + \phi) \\ R_2 = r + \varepsilon \cos(\theta_N + \phi + \pi) \end{array} \right\} \quad (10)$$

where θ_N ia an angular position of the driven pulley and ϕ is an initial phase angle.

The state space equations for the transmission error due to the pulley eccentricity can be represented with the same equations of the previous case in section 3.1 except the equation(3) and a new state variable θ_c which was introduced to describe the driver shaft angular displacement. The equation(3) is replaced by the following equations with the speed input $\omega(t)$.

$$\dot{\theta}_c = \omega(t) - \frac{h_R}{J_R} \quad (11)$$

$$\dot{h}_R = \theta_c K_c - b_R \frac{h_R}{J_R} - n \left[b_t \left(n \frac{h_R}{J_R} - R_1 \frac{h_N}{J_N} - \frac{P}{M} \right) \right.$$

$$\left. - b_s \left(-n \frac{h_R}{J_R} + R_2 \frac{h_N}{J_N} - \frac{P}{M} \right) + T_t - T_s \right] \quad (12)$$

4. RESULTS AND DISCUSSION

4.1 Transmission error by stepping motor

Figure 6 shows the numerical results for the transmission error due to the stepping motor. In numerical analysis, torque load $T_L = 0.52$ N-m was used as an input for various belt tensions. The numerical simulations were performed for the nonlinear and linear belt model. As for the the the nonlinear belt coefficients in equation(3), $C_1 = 8.8561$, $C_2 = 7.7009$, $C_3 = 33.241?$ $C_4 = 0$ were used from simple experiments for the tension-deformaton relationship while $C_1 = C_2 = C_4 = 0$, $C_3 = 200$ were used for the linear model. The coefficient of linear model was determined based on the assumption that the tension-deformation relationship is linear in the experimental range. The steady state response were plotted in Fig. 6. As shown in Fig. 6, for the nonlinear belt model, the amplitude of θ_m decreased as the belt tension increased while the amplitude and the mean of θ_m remained constant for the linear model with the increased tension.

Figure 7(a) shows the experimental results for the transmission error at $T_1 + T_2 = 300$N with no torque load. The wave in Fig. 7(a) is a zoom of the experimental results in steady state. Referring to Fig. 7, it can be seen that the transmission error fluctuates with the period of $T = 0.00833$ sec, which is the frequency of stepping motor resolution angle. However, the experimental results in Fig. 7 consists of three components: the error due to the stepping motor θ_m, the error due to the pulley eccenticity θ_e and the error due to the meshing interference θ_p. Thus, in order to separate the effect of θ_m from the experimental results, FFT analysis was performed. Figure 7(b) shows the results of FFT analysis in the frequency domain. The peak at $f = 120$ Hz in Fig. 7(b) is caused by the stepping motor. The transmission error due to the stepping motor can be obtained by eliminating the frequency components below and above $f = 120$ Hz of the original wave in Fig. 7(a). Taking the cut-off frequencies as $f = 106$ Hz and 134 Hz, the transmission error wave is created by inverse Fourier transformation of the remaining frequency components, which is plotted in Fig. 7(c).

Figure 8 shows the comparison of the experimental and the numerical results of θ_m for various tensions. The amplitudes of θ_m obtained from an average of the five FFT analysis for the experiments were compared with the numerical results for the nonlinear and the linear belt models. As shown in Fig. 8, the amplitude of the experimental transmission error decreased for the unloaded and loaded case as the belt tension increased. Comparing the transmission error for the unloaded and the loaded case, θ_m for the loaded case were lager than those of the unloaded. The numerical results of the nonlinear model also showed the same trend with the experiment and agreed well with the experimental results. For the linear model, the amplitude of θ_m remained constant with the increased tension. Referring to Fig. 8, it is found that the nonlinear belt model describes the experimental trends better than the linear model.

The reason why the transmission error θ_m decreased with the increased tension can be explained as follows: As the tension increases, the tight side and the slack side tension increase. The tension difference between the tight side and the slack side causes the belt deformation and the amount of deformation at higher tension is smaller than that of lower tension because of the nonlinear characteristic. Since the transmission error depends on the difference in the angular displacement between the pulleys which is directly related with the belt deformation, the transmission error decreases as the tension increases. Thus higher tension is required for smaller transmission error. However, exccesive belt tension results in the reduction in the belt life and causes the exccesive load on the driving parts such as bearings, which has detrimental effects on the performance of the high precision machines.

4.2 Transmission error by pulley eccentricity

Figure 9 shows the numerical results for the transmission error θ_e due to the pulley eccentricity. In simulations, the eccentricity $\varepsilon = 0.08$ mm was used with the torque load $T_L = 0.52$ N-m for various belt tensions. The amount of eccentricity was determined from the experiment. The numerical analysis was carried out for the nonlinear belt model. The steady state response for a step input $\omega(t) = 36$ rpm were plotted in Fig. 9. As shown in Fig. 9, the amplitude and the mean of θ_e decreased as the belt tension increased.

Figure 10(a) shows the transmission error in the frequency domain. The peak at f = 0.6 Hz in Fig. 10(a) is induced by the pulley eccentricity. Taking the cut-off frequencies as f = 0.4 Hz and 0.6 Hz, the modified transmission error wave due to the pulley eccentricity is created in Fig. 10(b) by the inverse Fourier transformation of the remaining frequency components.

Figure 11 shows the comparison of the experimental and the numerical results of θ_e for various tensions. As shown in Fig. 11, the amplitude of the experimental transmission error θ_e decreased for the unloaded and the loaded case as the belt tension increased. Comparing the transmission error for the unloaded and loaded case, θ_e for the loaded case were larger than those of the unloaded. The numerical results of the nonlinear model also showed the same trend with the experiment and agreed well with the experimental results.

It can be seen in Fig. 8 and Fig. 11 that the transmission error θ_m and θ_e decrease as the belt tension increases. Therefore high belt tension is required for the improvement of the transmission error.

4.3 Tension fluctuation

Fig. 12 shows the experimental and the theoretical belt tension for $T_1 + T_2 = 300$N without torque load. The experimental curve shows a fluctuation due to the stepping motor, the pulley eccentricity and the meshing interference of the pulley and the belt. Referring to Fig. 12, the effect of the stepping motor can not be observed in the experimental curve because its magnitude of the tension fluctuation is small respectively compared

to those of the remainings. The theoretical curve was obtained from the superposition of the simulation results for the stepping motor and the pulley eccentricity. Since the effect of the meshing interference was not included in the theoretical results, the tension fluctuation due to the meshing interference was not observed in the experimental curve. As shown in Fig. 12, the theoretical curve follows the experimental results and predicts the tension fluctuation closely except the effect of the meshing interference.

4.4 Comparison of θ_m, θ_e, θ_p

Fig. 13 shows the comparison of the transmission error due to the stepping motor θ_m, the pulley eccentricity θ_e and the meshing interference θ_p at $T_1 + T_2 = 300$N for the unloaded and loaded cases. The amplitude of each error from the FFT analysis was compared in Fig. 13. As swown in the figure, the relative magnitude of θ_p is small enough to be neglected compared to those of θ_m, and θ_e. Thus, in order to reduce the overall magnitude of the transmission error, θ_m and θ_e should be reduced. Since θ_m is related with the electrical characteristics of the stepping motor, the the reduction of θ_m by the improvement of the mechanical part has a limitation. The reduction of θ_e can be achieved by minimizing the eccentricity or increasing the belt tension. If the production error is innevitable, the last choice is to increase the belt tension. However, exccesive belt tension results in the reduction in the belt life and causes wear of the precision parts. Therefore a compromise should be made for the best performance of the machine, which is a matter of common but an integral part in design work.

5. CONCLUSIONS

From the experimental and the theoretical analysis for the transmission error characteristics of the stepping motor drive timing belt system, the following results have been obtained.

(1) The transmission error consists of: ① error due to the stepping motor per one resolution angle(θ_m), ② error due to the pulley eccentricity per one revolution(θ_e) and ③ error due to the meshing interference between the pulley and the belt teeth per one pitch revolution(θ_p).

(2) As the belt initial tension increases, θ_m, θ_e decrease because of the nonlinear characteristic of the belt.

(3) θ_m, θ_e increase as the applied torque load increases.

(4) The theoretical results based on the bondgraph model are in good accordance with the experimental results.

REFERENCES

[1] Kagotani, M., Aida, T., Koyama, T., 1982, "A Study on Transmission Characteristics of Toothed Belt Drives, 1st report, Effect of Initial Tension on Tight side and Slack side Tensions," Bulletin of the JSME, Vol. 25, pp. 459~466.

[2] Kagotani, M., Aida, T., Koyama, T., 1983, "A Study on Transmission Characteristics of Toothed Belt Drives, 2nd report, Transmission Error under a State of Applied Initial Tension, Theoretical Analysis," Bulletin of the JSME,

Vol. 26, pp. 132～139.

[3] Kagotani, M., Aida, T., Koyama, T., 1983, "A Study on Transmission Characteristics of Toothed Belt Drives, 3rd report, Transmission Error under a State of Applied Initial Tension, Experimental Results, " Bulletin of the JSME, Vol. 26, pp. 1238～1244.

[4] Kagotani, M., Aida, T., Koyama, T., 1984, "A Study on Transmission Characteristics of Toothed Belt Drives, 4th report, Transmission Error at Normal and Reverse Revolution under a State of Initial Tension," Bulletin of the JSME, Vol. 27, pp. 2553～2559.

[5] Kagotani, M., Aida, T., Koyama, T., 1984, "Load Distribution on Toothed Belt Drives under a State of Initial Tension," Bulletin of JSME, Vol. 27, pp. 1780～1787.

[6] Kagotani, M., Aida, T., Koyama, T., 1986, "A Study on Transmission Characteristics of Toothed Belt Drives, 5th report, Relative Shifting between Belt and Pulley in Normal and Reverse Revolutions under a State of Initial Tension," Bulletin of JSME, Vol. 29, pp. 609～616.

[7] Kuo, B., 1974, "Step Motors", West Publishing.

[8] Rosenberg, R. C., Karnopp, D. C., 1983, "Introduction to Physical System Dynamics", McGraw-Hill.

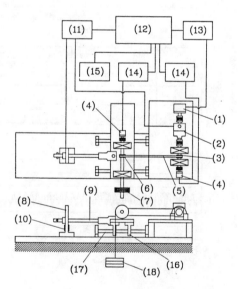

Fig. 1   Experimental apparatus for stepping motor drive timing belt system

(1) Stepping motor
(2) Torque Sensor
(3) Driver pulley
(4) Encoder
(5) Timing belt
(6) Driven pulley
(7) Torque disk
(8) Tension transducer
(9) Lead screw
(10) Strain gauge
(11) Amplifier, A/D Converter
(12) Computer
(13) Drive circuit
(14) Signal converting circuit
(15) Pulse generator
(16) Linear bearing
(17) Linear bearing rail
(18) Dead weight

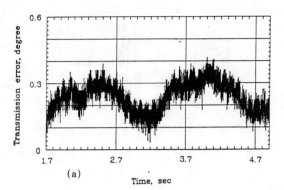

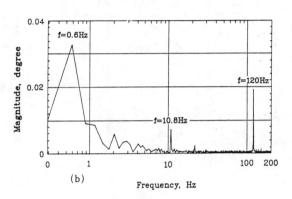

Fig. 2(a) Transmission error for $T_1 + T_2 = 100N$, $T_L = 0$
     (b) Transmission error in frequency domain

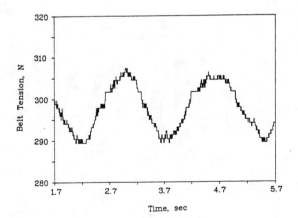

Fig. 3   Tension fluctuation for $T_1 + T_2 = 300N$, $T_L = 0$

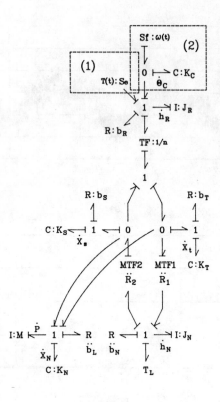

Fig. 4   Bondgraph model for a stepping motor
          drive timing belt system

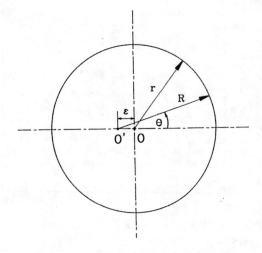

Fig. 5   Eccentric pulley

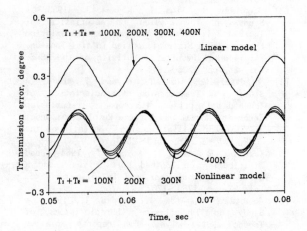

Fig. 6   Numerical results of θ_m for linear and
          nonlinear belt model

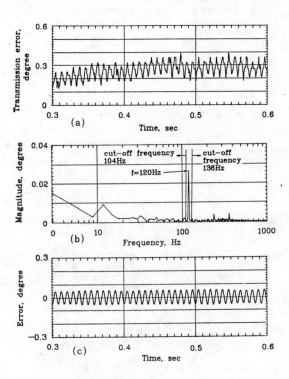

Fig. 7(a) Experimental results of transmission error
           for $T_1 + T_2 = 100N$, $T_L = 0$
     7(b) Transmission error in frequency domain
     7(c) Modified transmission error for θ_m

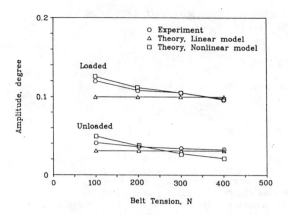

Fig. 8   Comparison of experimental and numerical
results for θ_m

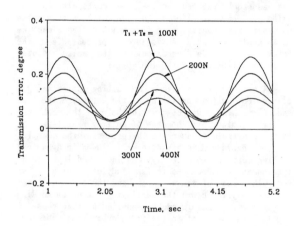

Fig.9   Numerical results of θ_e for various
tensions

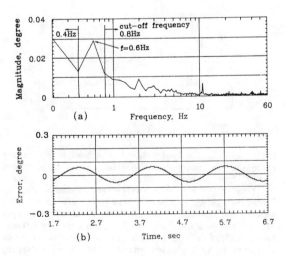

Fig. 10(a) Transmission error in frequency domain
(b) Modified transmission error for θe

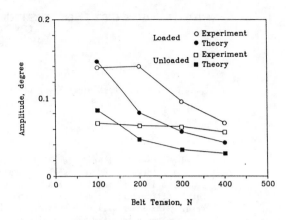

Fig. 11   Comparison of experimental and numerical
results for θ_e

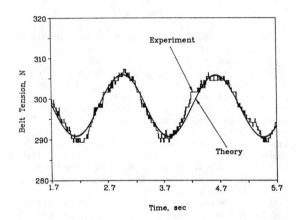

Fig. 12   Comparison of experimental and numerical
results for belt tension

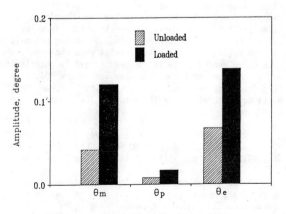

Fig. 13   Comparison of experimental results for
θ_m, θ_e, θ_p

EFFECT OF CUTTING SYSTEM'S DYNAMICAL CHARACTERISTICS ON CUTTING NOISE

ZHANG Jian   YI Chuijie   YE X. B.   C. H. KU

Institute of Mechanical Eng., Xi'an Jiaotong University, 710049 Xi'an, P. R. China

ABSTRACT

Based on Power Input Analysis (PIA) of copuled structures, effect of dynamical characteristics of a large cylindrical shell's turning system on cutting noise is studied in this paper. Noise radiated from each main radiator in the system and its contribution to the total cutting noise is determined, too. Results show that the cutting noise generated in turning the inner wall of a cylindrical shell is mainly determined by the sound radiation from the workpiece. And the dynamical characteristics of the tool-holder and the cutting tool system has much effect on the total cutting noise, although the effect of noise radiated from them is negligible.

INTRODUCTION

Cutting noise generated in the process of turning the inner wall of a large cylindrical shell is much high, even more than 115 dB(A) when machining a drying-cylinder in a paper-making machinery factory, which is much harmful for operators health and production environment. Unfortunately, study on cutting noise may be the most poor part in the field of noise analysis and control. The general characteristics of cutting noise [1] has shown that the noise is mainly determined by the noise radiated from the workpiece (a cylindrical shell here) and the tool-holder (a beam-like structure) if the both have higher modal densities. The other noise components, such as the increment of machine tool noise in cutting process, has negligible effect on totatl cutting noise. Because a cutting process is a feedback one and the main excitation on the cutting system is the dynamical cutting force, the dynamical characteristics of the system must have a heavy influnce on the cutting force, and hence on the vibration of and noise from the main radiators in the system.

As cutting noise is changing with cutting position, it is difficult for triditional analysis theory or experimental methods to be applied directly to the study. Based on Power Input Analysis (PIA) of Coupled structures [2], effect of dynamic characteristics of a large cylindrical shell's turning system on cutting noise is studied mainly in the paper. Results show that the cutting noise generated in the process is mainly contributed by the sound radiated from the work-piece under cutting, and the dynamical characteristics of the tool-parts has much effect on the noise as the dynamical cutting force dependend on it.

POWER INPUT ANALYSIS (PIA)
IN THE STUDY OF CUTTING NOISE GENERATED
IN TURNING THE INNER WALL OF A LARGE CYLINDRICAL SHELL

It has been shown in [1] that machine tool noise in cutting process is nearly the same as that in idle operation. This noise component is negligible in deal with the cutting noise from machining a large cylindrical sheel, which is generally 10 dB higher than machine tool noise. Therefore, it is acceptable that in the process of turning the inner wall of the sheel, noise from

the headstock, the bed and the other parts else of the lathe will have no effects on the total cutting noise so that the radiation efficiencies of those machine parts could be considered as zero in process, ie., the total cutting noise depends only on the noise radiated from the workpiece and the tool parts.

A cutting process makes a cutting system being a closed-loop system consisting of the workpiece, the tool and the machine. Direct coupling between the workpiece and the tool occurs, because of cutting operation. As there is dynamic feedback in the process, the coupling can be considered to having been included in dynamical cutting forces, so the system in closed-loop can be treated as an opened one in the study of cutting noise and vibration of the workpiece and the tool subsystem respectively. Therefore, the cutting system corresponding to the turning process can be modelled as that shown in Fig. 1, where the first to the fifth subsystems represent

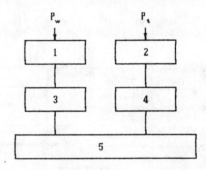

Fig.1 PIA model (I)

the workpiece, the tool-holder, the headstock (include spindle), the tool-post and the bed of the lathe respectively. Power items P_w and P_t are power input to subsystem 1 and 2 respectively, which are caused by cutting forces in the process, and P_w and P_t are correlative because the cutting force actting simultaneously upon both of the workpiece and the tool. The coupling between subsystems in cutting process can be considered to be conservative in the study because the coupling damping between them is much small in general. Based on Power Input Analysis of coupled systems developed in ref. [2], time averaged vibration energy of subsystems in Fig.1

can be represented as in the following

$$E_1=(P_w/\omega)/(\eta_{1t}-\eta_{31}\eta_{13}/\eta_{3t}) \quad (1a)$$

$$E_2=(P_t/\omega)/(\eta_{2t}-\eta_{42}\eta_{24}/\eta_{4t}) \quad (1b)$$

$$E_3=(\eta_{13}/\eta_{3t})E_1 \quad (1c)$$

$$E_4=(\eta_{24}/\eta_{4t})E_2 \quad (1d)$$

$$E_5\approx 0 \quad (1e)$$

where

$$\eta_{1t}=\eta_1+\eta_{13}$$

$$\eta_{2t}=\eta_2+\eta_{24}$$

$$\eta_{3t}=\eta_3+\eta_{31}+\eta_{35}$$

$$\eta_{4t}=\eta_4+\eta_{42}+\eta_{45}$$

$$\eta_{5t}=\eta_5+\eta_{53}+\eta_{54}$$

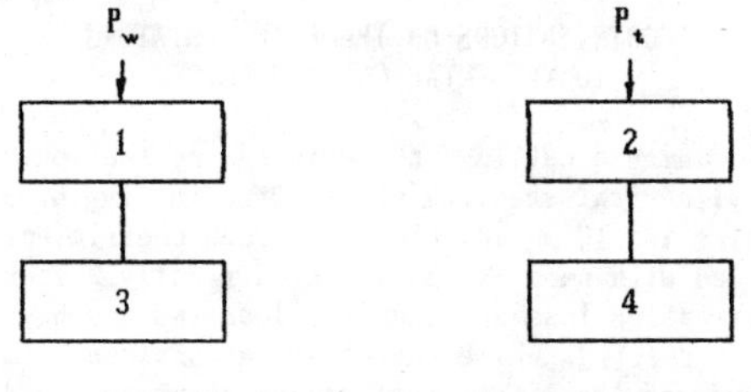

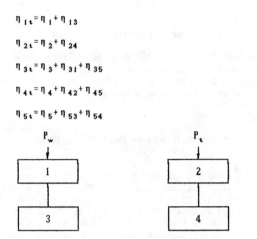

a) subsystem for the work   b) subsystem for the tool

Fig.2 PIA model (II)

and η_i is the internal loss factor of the ith subsystem, η_{ij} is the coupling loss factor between the ith and the jth. The equations show that the vibration energy of the bed is negligible compared with the other subsystems else so that the model in Fig.1 can be simplified to two blocked systems, as shown in Fig.2. It is much convenient to evaluate the cutting noise and to determine the contribution of each sub-system to total cutting noise if the fact that the only radiators in cutting system are the workpiece (a cylindrical shell) and the tool-holder (a beam) has been noticed. The sound power from the workpiece and the tool-holder can be determined respectively from

$$W_1=(\rho_o c\sigma_1 S_1/M_1)(P_w/\omega)/(\eta_{1t}-\eta_{13}\eta_{31}/\eta_{3t}) \quad (2a)$$

$$W_2=(\rho_o c\sigma_2 S_2/M_2)(P_t/\omega)/(\eta_{2t}-\eta_{42}\eta_{24}/\eta_{4t}) \quad (2b)$$

where σ_1, σ_2 are sound radiation efficiencies of the respected structures, S_1 and S_2 are the surface areas, M_1 and M_2 are the masses of the workpiece and the tool-holder, ρ_o and c are density of medium and velocity of sound in the medium, respectively. Modal averaged sound radiation efficiency of a cylindrical shell (the workpiece) is approximately equal to unity in the range of frequency above its critical frequency, and in the band of frequency below the critical it is [3]

(1) when $f_R/f_c<0.52$ and $1<\upsilon_o<f_c/f_R$

$$\sigma=\frac{\left(\frac{h}{Ra^2}\right)^{1/2}\ln\left[\frac{1+(f_o/f_c)^{1/2}}{1-(f_o/f_c)^{1/2}}\right]+\frac{2[f_o/f_c)]^{1/2}}{1-(f_o/f_c)}}{\pi[12(1-\mu^2)(\upsilon_o^2-1)]^{1/4}[1-(f_o/f_c)]^{1/2}} \quad (3a)$$

(2) else

$$\sigma=\left[\frac{\upsilon_o^{3/2}(f_R/f_c)}{2B(U-1/U)}\right]\{1-\upsilon_o[1-\upsilon_o^2(f_R/f_c)^2]^{1/2}\}\times$$

$$\times\left[\frac{1}{(1/U-\upsilon_o)^{1/2}}-\frac{1}{(U-\upsilon_o)^{1/2}}\right][12(1-\mu^2)]^{1/2} \quad (3b)$$

where (f_oU) and (f_o/U) are equal to the upper and the lower frequency of a band; f_o is the center frequency of the band and υ_o is the dimensionless one respectively; $\upsilon_o=f_o/f_R$, f_R is the ring frequency of the shell; μ is Poisson's ratio; U is a bandwidth factor and U=1.122 for one third octave band and U=1.414 for an octave one; B is a factor related to modal density and $B=(h/2a)n(f_o)$, $n(f_o)$ is the modal densisty of the shell and [3]

$$n_1(f_o)=\begin{cases}\frac{10Ra}{hc_L}\upsilon_o^{1/2} & \upsilon_o<0.48\\ \frac{14.4Ra}{hc_L}\upsilon_o & 0.48<\upsilon_o<0.83\\ \frac{4Ra}{hc_L}\left[2+\frac{0.596}{U-1/U}U\cos\left(\frac{1.745}{U^2\upsilon_o^2}\right)-\frac{1}{U}\cos\left(\frac{1.745U^2}{\upsilon_o^2}\right)\right] & \upsilon_o>0.83\end{cases} \quad (4)$$

Sound radiation efficiency of the tool-holder can be evaluated from [4]

$$\sigma=\begin{cases}17.5(\pi R_b^2)\Theta(f/c)^3(1-f_c/f)^{-1/2} & f_c<f\leqslant\chi f_c\\ 11.0(\pi R_b^2)\Theta^{-2}(1-f_c/f)^{-1/2} & f>\chi f_c\end{cases} \quad (5)$$

$$\chi=0.5+[0.25+(298/f_c\Theta)]^{1/2}$$

where Θ is the perimeter of cross section of the tool-holder (a beam-like structure) and R_b is the equavalent radius of the holder. The modal density, which is usful for coupling loss factors evaluation besides presentation of energy store ability, of a rectangular beam can be obtained from [5]:

$$n_b(f)=L_b(\rho'/D)^{1/4}(2\pi f)^{-1/2} \quad (6)$$

where $D=EI_b$ is the bending stiffness, I_b is the second moment of the cross section, L_b is the length of the beam and ρ' is the mass per unit length.

It can be proved that power input to either the workpiece or the tool-holder can be represented as:

$$P_{ay} = P_{ayy} + P_{azy} \tag{7a}$$

$$P_{az} = P_{ayz} + P_{azz} \tag{7b}$$

where:

$$P_{ayy} = 2\pi \int_{o}^{+\infty} \mathrm{Re}[H_{ayy}(f)]G_{fy}(f)df$$
$$+ 2\pi \int_{o}^{+\infty} \mathrm{Re}[H_{ayz}(f)]G_{fyz}(f)df$$

$$P_{azy} = 2\pi \int_{o}^{+\infty} \mathrm{Re}[H_{azy}(f)]G_{fy}(f)df$$
$$+ 2\pi \int_{o}^{+\infty} \mathrm{Re}[H_{azz}(f)]G_{fyz}(f)df$$

$$P_{ayz} = 2\pi \int_{o}^{+\infty} \mathrm{Re}[H_{ayz}(f)]G_{fz}(f)df$$
$$+ 2\pi \int_{o}^{+\infty} \mathrm{Re}[H_{ayy}(f)]G_{fzy}(f)df$$

$$P_{azz} = 2\pi \int_{o}^{+\infty} \mathrm{Re}[H_{azz}(f)]G_{fz}(f)df$$
$$+ 2\pi \int_{o}^{+\infty} \mathrm{Re}[H_{azy}(f)]G_{fzy}(f)df$$

here alphabet "a" represents the structure under analysis, while a=w and a=t denote the parameters are corresponded to the workpiece and the tool respectively, H_{ayy} and H_{azz} are direct effective admittances of structure "a" in Y and Z directions at cutting point respectively, both H_{azy} and H_{ayz} are cross effective admittances between Y and Z directions of the structure "a", P_{ay} and P_{az} represent power input to structure "a" by cutting forces in Y and Z directions, P_{ayy} and P_{azy} are those in Y and Z directions caused by cutting forces in Y-direction, and P_{ayz} and P_{azz} are that caused by cutting force in Z-direction, G_{fy}, G_{fz}, G_{fyz} and G_{fzy} are single side auto-spectral or cross-spectral densities of the cutting force in or between Y and Z-directions respectively.

It can be found from Eq.7 that the measurement of power input needs to know each effective admittance (or impedance) and the cutting forces. But in the practical cutting process, the cross-impedance between the workpiece and the tool at cutting point can be neglected compared with the other ones else if the subsystems are weakly coupled, and because the cross-impedances meet reciprocity rule, it needs to measure only six of direct and cross impedance before determining the input power.

Principle for the dynamic cutting force evaluation, which is dependent on the characteristics of cutting force meter, is mentioned in ref.[2]. Main parts of cutting force are that in Y and Z directions, whose effect on cutting noise and vibration of cutting system is much important. Effect of cutting force in X-direction on those can be neglected because

(1) It is much less than that in Y or Z directions.

(2) It is a logitudinal excitation for the workpiece so that it can not cause much vibration and noise from the workpiece.

(3) Moment caused by it on the tool-holder is also much small if the suspending length of the tool ($\triangle a$ in Fig.3) is designed to be small enough.

Cutting force meter used in cylindrical shell's cutting process is shown in Fig.3, which is located on

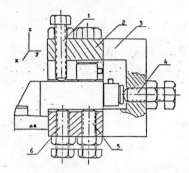

Fig.3 Cutting force meter used in the study

the beam-like tool-holder. With the different suspending length of the holder, dynamical characteristics of the meter is different, too. Therefore, transfer functions of the meter must be measured again if the suspending length is changed.

CONTRIBUTIONS OF THE MAIN RADIATORS TO THE TOTAL CUTTING NOISE

To analyze cutting noise in tuning the inner wall of a cylindrical sheel, which is 700mm in length, 300 mm in radius and 10 mm in thickness, some coefficients PIA concerned with need to be measured firstly. Techniqes for evaluating loss and coupling loss factors have been given in ref.[2], while the other factors can be measured by use of the instrument set-up shown in Fig.4. The

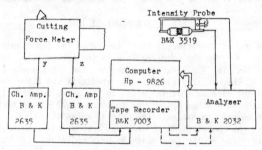

Fig.4 Test set-up

tool used in the test is 45° throw-away insert one, with a rectangular beam-like tool-holder, on which the tool is put, of 40×40 mm in cross section and a maximum suspending length of 390 mm.

Results from PIA analysis and experiments with sound intensity measure-ments are shown in Fig.5, where Lww and Lwt represent sound power levels radiated from the workpiece and the tool-holder in the cutting process respectively, Ww and Wt are the corresponded sound power, Lwm is the total cutting noise power levels obtained from PIA method. L is the suspending length of the tool-holder and L=350 mm in the test, the distance from cutting point to the clamped end of the workpiece is about 150mm, the workpiece turns in 40 rpm with a feed rate of 0.056mmpr and a cutting depth of 1.2mm. It can be found from the figures that the cutting noise radiated from the workpiece is much higher than that from the tool system because the radiation resistance of the latter is much less than the former. Furthermore, because

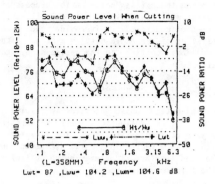

Fig.5 Contribution of the workpiece and the
tool-holder to total cutting noise

of the much higher modal density of the shell, high vibration level can reach with no difficulty in much wide frequency range so that the total cutting noise is determined mainly by that from the workpiece while the radiation of the other structures else in the system can be neglected. But the dynamic characteristic of every structure in the system do affect the cutting force, and then has influnce on the total noise.

EFFECT OF CUTTING SYSTEM DYNAMICAL CHARACTERISTICS ON LARGE CYLINDRICAL SHELL'S CUTTING NOISE

As mentioned above, the cylindrical shell's cutting noise is mainly determined by the noise radiated from the workpiece (the shell) which is under excitation of dynamical cutting force in the cutting process. So the noise must be concerned with mechanical impedance and sound radiation efficiency of the workpiece, as well as the value of dynamical cutting force. Because of the closed-loop characteristics of a cutting process, the quantity and the spectral structures of the force depend not only upon the dynamical characteristics of the workpiece, but also on that of the tool parts and that of the machine used. So the effect of dynamical characteristcs of the tool parts, espatially the tool-holder and the tool-post, can not be neglected, although the contribution of the noise radiated from them to the total is much less.

Theoretically, effects of dynamical characteristics of both the workpiece and the tool parts could be studied by application of cutting noise analysis theory mentioned in ref.[2]. But, because the cutting technological system is much complicated and the measurement or the evaluation of all statical and dynamical parameters of the cutting process is difficult, pure theoretical analysis can reach only the determinate level but can not reach the quatitative level. And for a cutting process, workpiece under cutting is generally inchangible. Therefore in the following, the effect of cutting system dynamical characteristics on cutting noise is studied experimentally, and only by changing the suspending length of the tool-holder to obtain different dynamical characteristics of the tool parts, and hence the whole cutting system. The experimental procedures are as follows

(1) Measure the transfer functions of the cutting force meter and admittance (response) fuctions of the tool parts and the workpiece respectively, at different suspending length of the tool-holder.

(2) For different suspending length of the tool-holder, evaluate or measure the loss factors and coupling loss factors used for the determination of the distribution of noise and vibration energy in the system.

(3) For different suspending length of the tool-holder, evaluate the dynamical cutting force in concerning directions and the space averaged cutting noise intensity, as well as the sound power.

In the study, three kinds of suspending length of the tool-holder are selected, which are 100mm, 200mm and 350mm respectively. The effect is mainly studied by PIA and on-line measurement. Direct driving mobilities in decibel of the tool parts in Y and Z directions at different suspending length are shown in Fig.6, which reveals that the shorter the suspending length, the higher the anti-vibration ability of the tool parts in the whole analysis frequency range, because the stiffness of the tool-holder is increasing with the decrease of its suspending length. It can also be seen from the figure that the spectra of driving point mobilities are different in different suspending condition.

Cylindrical shell's cutting noise power in different suspending length is shown in Fig.7, where Lwc is that obtained by PIA and Lw is that by on-line intensity measurement, subscripts of "1", "2" and "3" represent that the tool-holder is suspended with a suspending length 100mm, 200 mm or 350 mm respectively. It can be seen from the figure that with the suspending length of the tool-holder decreasing, spectra of cutting noise are changing correspondingly and the total cutting noise is decreasing. The decrease of the total noise is nonlinear with the increase of tool parts impedance.

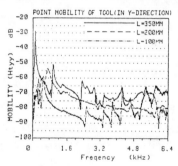

a) in Y-direction

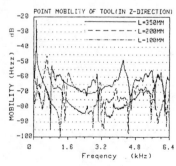

b) in Z-direction

Fig.6 Direct driving point mobilities of the tool-
holder at different suspending length

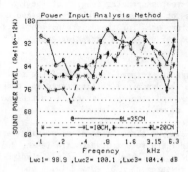

a) PIA analysis

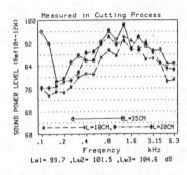

b) in-situ measurement

Fig.7 Total sound power level of cutting noise at different suspending length of the tool-holder

It can be deduced that both of the dynamical cutting force and the cutting noise in the process of turning the inner wall of a large cylindricall shell will be decreased or controled by improving the dynamical characteristics of the whole cutting system, either by adding additional damping to the system or by increase its stiffness.

CONCLUSIONS

1. The total cutting noise generated in turning the inner wall of a cylindrical shelllike workpiece is mainly determined by that from the workpiece under cutting. The effect of noise radiated from the tool-holder and another structure in the cutting system on the total one are much small.

2. Although the effect of noise radiated from the tool-holder can be negnected, the characteristics of the holder and the tool system do affect the dynamical cutting forces and the power input to the system by them, so as to influence the noise radiated from the workpiece, as well as the total cutting noise.

REFERENCES

[1] ZHANG J., Ye X. B and Ku C. H., "Effect of Cutting System Dynamic Characteristics on Cutting Noise". Proc. of the 5th Int. Manufacturing Conf. (IMCC'91), Apr. 1991, China, pp.C37-C42

[2] ZHANG J., "Energy Analysis and Experimental Study of Cutting Noise". Ph.D Thesis of Xi'an Jiaotong Univ. Jan., 1989

[3] Szechenyi E., J. Sound & Vib., (1971)19(1), pp.65-81

[4] Richards E.J. et. al, J. Sound & Vib., (1970)65(3), pp.419-451

[5] Lyon R.H., "Statistical Energy Analysis of Dynamical Systems: Theory and Applications". MIT, 1975.

ON THE MECHANICAL IMPACT STRENGTH OF PMMA

I.Maekawa, A.Shoda and H.Shibata

ABSTRACT

Charpy test is a popular method to evaluate the impact strength of materials. However, the Charpy test is inconvenient to use directly for machine design because it is expressed by energy unit. In addition to this, Charpy test is performed under its own low impact velocity. Therefore, a Charpy value is available only for the velocity tested, if it depends on the impact velocity. In this study, a new experimental method is used to evaluate the impact strength of materials. By this method,impact tensile and bending strengths of PMMA specimen are evaluated over the impact velocity of 0-70m/s. These strengths are denoted as Im,t or Im,b and expressed by stress unit. Although Im,t value and Im,b showed scattering,it is increased with increase of strain rate,and Im,t value is higher than Im,b value. At 77K,Im,t value increased with loading rate,but Im,b did not increased clearly. Density of parabola pattern observed on the fracture surface in the case of impact bending is higher than that of impact tension.

INTRODUCTION

In order to evaluate the impact strength of materials, Charpy value is used popularly. However, Charpy value is expressed in terms of energy unit. Therefore, it is inconvenient to use directly for machine design. Although instrumented Charpy test[1] is improved one to investigate the time history of the relation between the impact force and the deformation for a specimen, the impact velocity of Charpy test is low, that is, it is usually at most 3-5 m/s. Therefore, Charpy value is not available for more higher impact velocity, if the impact strength depend on the loading velocity. Then, it is desirable to express the impact strength of materials in terms of stress unit instead of energy unit concisely by using a new type testing machine over wide range of loading velocity.

Thus, the purpose of this paper is to show the practical availability of new testing method by using PMMA specimens, because this material is convenient to investigate the dynamic properties.

EXPERIMENTAL

According to our previous studies, impact strengths of steel and PMMA showed size dependence. Those behavior were called the mechanical size effect [2],[3]. That is, a stress pulse is formed by the superposition of many reflected stress waves in a specimen with a finite length and influences on the strength of a specimen. Those stress waves propagate with a high velocity in a specimen. Then the measurement for such a complicated stress state is not easy.

By the way, PMMA is convenient to investigate the effect of stress waves which plays important role on the dynamic behavior of a specimen, because wave velocity in it is low compared with structural steel.Therefore,so the complexity of dynamic stress state which is produced by the superposition of waves can be reduced. In addition to this,it is apparently brittle material. Then, the fracture behavior may be discussed based on the elastic consideration. Thus, PMMA specimens were used in this study.

The dimensions of tensile and bending specimens are shown in Figs.1(a) and (b), respectively. The thickness of both ends of each tensile specimen was increased by additive daubing with a plastic resin to reinforce the strength around the pin holes. Bending specimens were standard Charpy type one.

Impact experiments were carried out by using a setup shown in Figs.2(a) and (b). In this figure, high pressure nitrogen gas was supplied into an accumulator from a gas bomb,and a flyer was accelerated when ABS plate set in the accumulator was broken out. The thickness of a plate was 2mm and a couple of groove was engraved on the one side. The diameter and the length of the steel flyer were 10mm and 100mm, respectively. The velocity of a flyer as controlled by selecting an appropriate ABS plate with a suitable depth of groove.

I.Maekawa is Professor of Mechatronics and Precision Engineering,H.Shibata is research associate and A.Shoda is Graduate student,Tohoku University,Aramaki,Aoba-Ku,Sendai, Japan

In the case of impact tension, a flyer shoots the tip of tension lever as shown in Fig.2 (a) and give an impact tension to a specimen. Both ends of specimen were pinned to the bed and to the tension lever, respectively.

In the case of impact bending experiment, a flyer shoots the impact rod and gives an impact bending to a specimen which was supported by two supporters as shown in Fig.2 (b).

Impact velocity was measured by using two sets of photo cell. Each specimen was immersed in liquid nitrogen in a small vessel in the case of low temperature experiments.

Impact behavior of a specimen was measured by using a strain gage pasted at the center of each specimen as shown in Figs.2(a) and (b). The typical examples of strain history are shown in Figs.3(a) and (b). In each figure, little change of gradient can be observed at point f on the strain diagram. It was considered that this point correspond to the fracture strength of each specimen. Then, fracture strength Im was evaluated for this strain by multiplying elastic constant. And the relation between Im and impact velocity V is shown in Figs.4(a) and (b). But, these results seem to be somewhat strange and difficult to understand.

In order to get correct result, it was considered that it needs a correction for the plastic behavior probably included in the fracture behavior. Therefore, constitutive relations were obtained as shown in Fig.5(b) by using one more strain gage pasted at point B beside of point A as shown in Fig.5(a). That is, in the plastic range, fracture stress was estimated by using this relation for the fracture strain measured at point A.

A falling weight type apparatus was also used for low impact velocity. That is, a steel weight of 3.5Kgr was naturally dropped to a flange connected to the lower end of a tensile specimen or to the impact rod put on the middle point of a bending specimen with the lift of 400mm in order to give an impact force for each specimen. The impact velocity was 2.8m/s. Beside of these impact experiments, static experiments were also carried out by using a servohydraulic testing machine. The loading rate was 2 X 10-3 m/min.

DISCUSSION

Experimental results are shown in Figs.6(a) and (b). In these figures, fracture strength of a specimen are expressed in terms of stress unit instead of energy unit, and it is denoted by the mechanical impact strength Im in order to emphasize that it is available for machine design directly. Furthermore, appropriate suffix is added to show the loading condition, for example, Im,t or Im,b was used for impact tension or impact bending.

In Figs.6, impact tensile strength Im,t and impact bending strength Im,b are shown against strain rate, and Im values are increased with increase of impact velocity in all cases, although some scatterings of data are seen. And it can also be seen that Im,t value is higher than Im,b.

The similar results were obtained for impact tension and impact bending at 77K. It can also be seen that Im,t value at 77K is about four times higher than Im,t value at 293K. On the other hand, Im,b value at 77K is about twice higher than Im,b at 293K.

It is well known that yielding strength is increased with increase of loading rate for metals[4]. The results obtained above are also the similar to them, although many more studies will be necessary to make clear the mechanism of such a dynamic properties of material in future.

The experimental results of impact bending are shown in Figs.4(b) and 6(b). In these figures, Im,b are expressed by nominal stress. That is, impact bending fracture strengths shown on those ordinate are the stress divided value by the stress concentration factor, α=2.3[5], of the notch introduced in bending specimen. In general, bending strength of ductile materials is higher than tensile strength. But, above results obtained in this study is contrary to those well known results. This reason may due to the brittleness of PMMA. That is, the stress concentration effect may be more effective to cause the fracture for this material.

Strictly speaking, stress waves produced by an impact force are so complicated that the analysis is not easy in general. However, these macroscopic studies on dynamic stress analysis will also be necessary to explain the difference between the impact tensile strength and bending strength in addition to the studies on the microscopic considerations on materials. Although the detailed discussions are remained in future, the results obtained above will provide new data for those discussions.

On the fracture surface, characteristic patterns were observed as shown in Figs.7(a) (d). On a static bending fracture surface,many dimples were observed as shown in Figs.7(a) or (b) for tension and bending. And parabola patterns were observed on impact fracture surface as shown in Fig.7(c) or (d). More many parabolas were observed in the case of impact bending compared with the case of impact tension.

A parabola pattern is produced by an interference between the stress wave produced by an applied force and spreading of cracks initiated at the front of the stress wave. Then, the density of parabola on a fracture surface is proportional to the number of crack initiated at week points in a specimen.

According to our previous investigation, the density of parabola was increased with increase of strength in the case of impact tension[6]. But, the density on a bending fracture surface was rather higher than that of tensile fracture surface. Then, it is considered that the density of parabola produced on a impact fracture surface is also depend on the loading condition. It may be increased under a complicated stress state such as in the case of bending, although the strength is lower than tensile strength.

CONCLUSION

Impact strength of PMMA was evaluated over the impact velocity 0 80 m/s by using a new method developed by authors. The results are denoted by mechanical impact strengths, $I_{m,t}$ and $I_{m,b}$ for impact tension and impact bending, respectively, and expressed in terms of stress unit. According to these results, difference between impact tensile strength and impact bending strength were shown clearly. And these new results will be more useful machine design compared with Charpy value.

(1) Impact tensile strength $I_{m,t}$ was increased slightly with increase of loading rate at 293K.
(2) Impact bending strength $I_{m,b}$ was increased only little with increase of loading rate at 293K.
(3) Impact bending strength $I_{m,b}$ was evaluated by taking into account the stress concentration effect at the notch root of a specimen. It was rather lower than impact tensile strength $I_{m,t}$ over the loading rate tested.
(4) $I_{m,t}$ value at 77K increased about four times of $I_{m,t}$ at 293K. However, $I_{m,b}$ at 77K increased about twice of $I_{m,b}$ at 293K.
(5) More high density of parabola pattern was observed on the impact bending fracture surface compared with the case of impact tensile fracture.

REFERENCES

[1]Instrumented Impact Testing,ASTM STP 563(1974),pp.214.
[2]I.Maekawa et al.;Impact Stress in a Finite Rod, Int.J.JSME, Vol31, No.3 (1988),554-559.
[3]I.Maekawa;On the Mechanical Size Effect of Impact Strength,Proc.Oji Int.Seminar on Dynamic Fracture, (1989),275-286.
[4]M.F.Kanninen et al.;Behavior of Materials under Dynamic Load,Ed., by U.S.Lindholm(1967),96.
[5]STRESS CONCENTRATION DESIGN FACTORS, R.E.Peterson,JohnWiley & Sons Inc., (1965),pp.155.
[6]I.Maekawa and K.Katagiri; Proc. Int. Semi.on Impact Fract.of Polymers Mater.Sci. and Test.Tech. (1991)p1.

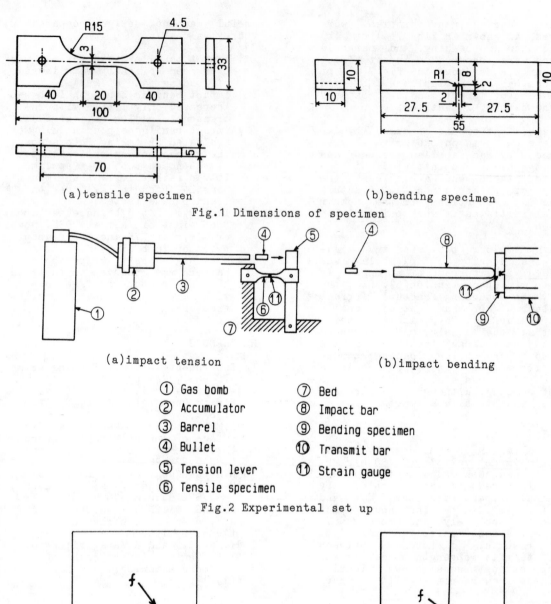

(a)tensile specimen   (b)bending specimen

Fig.1 Dimensions of specimen

(a)impact tension   (b)impact bending

① Gas bomb   ⑦ Bed
② Accumulator   ⑧ Impact bar
③ Barrel   ⑨ Bending specimen
④ Bullet   ⑩ Transmit bar
⑤ Tension lever   ⑪ Strain gauge
⑥ Tensile specimen

Fig.2 Experimental set up

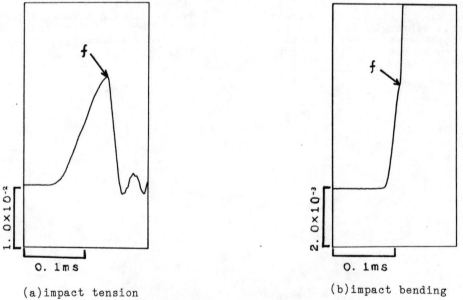

(a)impact tension   (b)impact bending

Fig.3 Typical examples of strian history

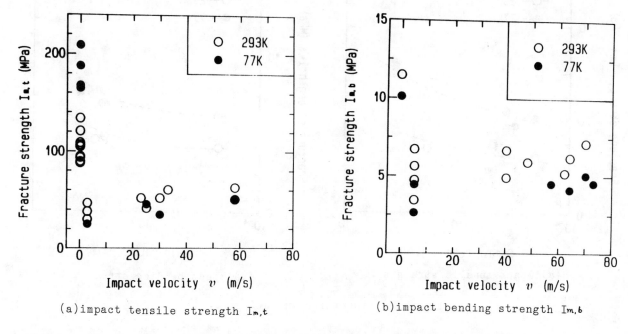

(a)impact tensile strength $I_{m,t}$

(b)impact bending strength $I_{m,b}$

Fig.4 Experimental results(I_m vs. V)

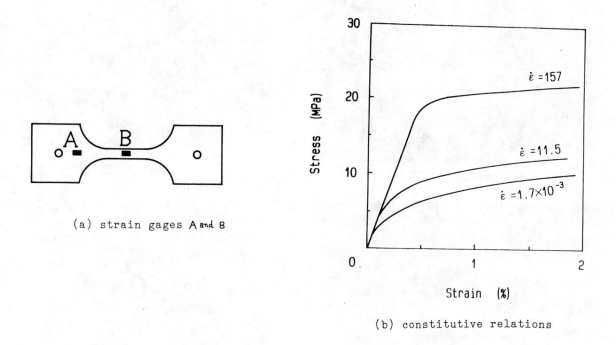

(a) strain gages A and B

(b) constitutive relations

Fig.5 Measurement of constitutive relation

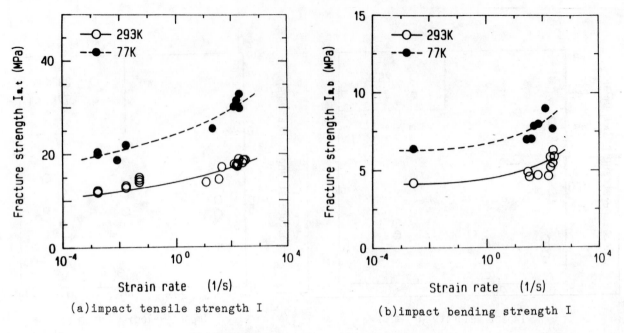

(a)impact tensile strength I

(b)impact bending strength I

Fig.6 Experimental results(I   vs.   )

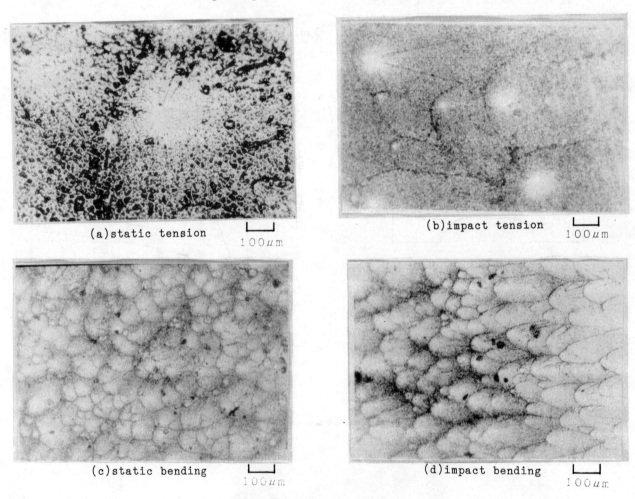

(a)static tension   100μm

(b)impact tension   100μm

(c)static bending   100μm

(d)impact bending   100μm

Fig.7 Fracture surfaces

INVESTIGATION OF THE LOW TEMPERATURE INDUCED STRAIN IN MICROELECTRONIC PACKAGES

Pei-Haw Tsao and Arkady S. Voloshin

Department of Mechanical Engineering and Mechanics

Lehigh University

Bethlehem, Pa 18015

Abstract

Due to the wide applications of microelectronic packages, proper assessment of the reliability of the packages became very important. The mismatch in the coefficient of thermal expansion of the materials used in the packages leads to the mechanical strains which may lead to thee package failure under the thermal load. Low temperature induced thermal load may be applied during thermal cycling in reliability studies or during service life of the package. An experimental method of the Digital Image Analysis Enhanced Moiré Interferometry (DIAEMI) was used to investigate those strains. This technique monitors the actual surface displacements and can operate on small and complex geometries. The specimens investigated here were prepared from the microelectronic packages manufactured by Cypress Semiconductor. They were subjected to a temperature change from 20^0C to -50^0C and the thermal strain was monitored at selected locations. The results obtained from the analysis of moiré patterns show that the significant mechanical strains are induced because of thermal loading. It was also found that the change in material properties of the constituents of the package significantly influence the strain level in the chip.

1. Introduction

The materials used in the contemporary microelectronic packages are usually chosen according to their electrical and chemical properties. This leads to the significant mismatch in the coefficients of thermal expansion of the materials used which induces the severe mechanical strains on the chip when it is subject to various temperatures during testing and service. Several approaches, such as an analytical modeling [1], numerical analysis [2] and piezo-resistance measurements [3], were utilized to assess the strain induced in the packages under thermal load. Due to the complexity of the package geometry, the lack of the exact knowledge of temperature dependent properties of each constituent material and the boundary conditions, those techniques [1,2] are not quite successful. Use of the piezo-resistive elements relies on a correct temperature dependent calibration which is difficult to obtain [3,4].

Thus, this paper introduce an experimental approach capable of *in-situ* measurements of the thermally induced strain in the variety of microelectronic packages. The technique of the digital image analysis enhanced moiré interferometry (DIAEMI) was used to evaluate the low temperature induced strains.

1.1 Fractional Fringe Moiré Interferometry

Moiré interferometry [5] is a high resolution, full-field displacement measurement technique. Due to its high accuracy, moiré interferometry is suitable for direct strain determination. Moiré interferometry is based on the interference of the two high frequency gratings – one attached to the specimen surface (specimen grating), the other, known as the virtual grating, is created by the interference of the two coherent rays, A and B, at a given angle β (Figure 1). The specimen grating with the frequency of *1200 lines/mm* is produced from a photographic mold by a replication technique [5]. This grating is attached to the specimen surface and deforms with the specimen as loading is applied. In front of the specimen surface, the virtual grating is produced. The frequency f of this grating is given by

$$f = (2/\lambda)\sin\beta \qquad (1)$$

where λ is the wavelength of the light used. The specimen grating interacts with the virtual grating to form a moiré pattern. To utilize the first order diffraction, the frequency of the virtual grating is set to be twice of the frequency of the specimen grating. The virtual grating frequency f is equal to *2400 lines/mm*, which corresponds to a sensitivity of *0.417μm* per fringe order.

The obtained moiré pattern characterizes the in-plane displacements at every point on the specimen surface. Quantitatively, the displacement is related to the fringe value by the following expression

$$U = N_x/f \qquad (2)$$

where U is component of displacement in the x direction and N_x is the fringe value when lines of the virtual gratings are perpendicular to the x direction. If crossed grating are used, the other component can be monitored simultaneously.

By using the digital image analyzer and fractional fringe analysis technique [6], the displacements can be computed not only at full fringe locations (dark bands in the moiré pattern), but at every locations throughout the pattern. This is accomplished by using a basic optical law [7] that relates light intensities in a moiré field to corresponding displacements as follows

$$U(x) = U_0 + (1/2\pi f)\cos^{-1}[(I(x) - I_0)/I_1] \qquad (3)$$

where U_0 is the displacement at the starting point and x is

zero at that point. $I(x)$ is the light intensity at the point under consideration, I_1 is the intensity amplitude of the first harmonic term in the optical law for the field and I_0 is the average background intensity. Equation (3) can be applied over any half fringe. The value of I_1, I_0 are determined by the image analyzer for each half fringe separately. Since the digital image analyzer has a light intensity resolution of 256 grey levels, one can hope for effective fringe multiplication of 512, however in practice multiplication of 10 to 50 are more reliable.

2. Experimental Approach

2.1 Specimen and Experimental Setup

Two types of the packages were analyzed here. They had identical geometry. The only difference between the packages was in the material properties of one of the constituents. Those packages will be identified as type A and type B specimens. The samples were prepared from the microelectronic packages by slicing the package along the longitudinal plane in order to expose the chip and the leadframe. Crossed gratings with a frequency of *1200 lines/mm* in both horizontal and vertical directions were replicated on the specimen surfaces. Figure 2 displays a schematic view of the experimental equipment when the specimen is illuminated from all four directions in order to evaluate both components of the displacement vector. Light from an Helium-Neon laser (Spectra Physics model 127-25 mW) is decollimated through a convex lens, purged of off-axis reflections by a spatial filter and then collimated to a large beam diameter (100 mm) by means of a parabolic mirror. The resulting expanded beam is then projected onto the specimen at the angle β. The second beam, required to

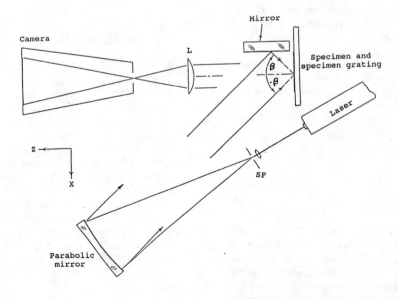

Figure 1   Schematic of the moiré interferometry setup.

436

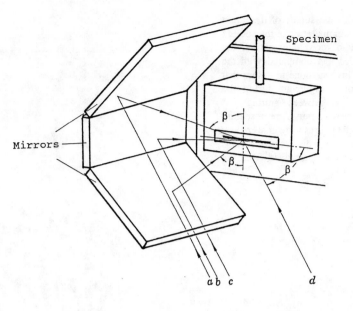

Specimen

Mirrors

β

β

β

a b c   d

Coherent light

Figure 2   Optical arrangement for *U* and *V* measurements.   Beams a & b produce *V*-field while c & d produce *U*-field.

create the virtual grating, is generated by reflection of the part of the expanded beam by a plane mirror to the specimen at an angle -β.   To be able to monitor both vertical and horizontal displacement components, two identical arrangements were used.   Optical separation of the two field becomes necessary for this case.   The interference pattern emerging from the specimen is acquired by a CCD video camera which is connected to a PC-based digital image processor [4].

2.2 Experimental Procedure

The specimen was placed at a room temperature in a cooling chamber (Figure 3) which allows for an uniform cooling of the package.   This was confirmed by temperature measurements at several locations on the chip.   Liquid nitrogen was used as a cooling agent because of its availability and easy of handling.   The cooling process reduced the specimen's temperature from 20^{0}C to -50^{0}C.   Then, the specimen's temperature was raised to room temperature.   In order to secure a virtual grating frequency of *2400 lines/mm*, the apparatus and specimen were adjusted for proper optical alignment and orientation.   The optical axis and the focus of the viewing camera was adjusted to get a proper view on the screen.   Actually, some deviations from ideal setting exist in practice.   This resulted in an initial pattern of relatively few fringes (null or zero field).   In such a case, the effect of the initial field had been subtracted from the final displacement field to obtain the net load induced displacements.

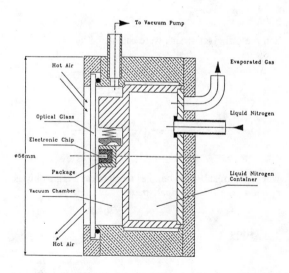

Figure 3   Cooling chamber

After the null field for each displacement component had been recorded, the specimen was cooled to -50^{0}C, while fringe patterns for both displacement components were continuously recorded. After this the supply of the liquid nitrogen was stopped. When the temperature of the cooling chamber and specimen raised to room temperature, the resulting null field was recorded and compared with the initially recorded null field. This was done to assure that the system had kept the proper alignment during the operation and that the bonding between grating and specimen did not fail. Several frames representing deformation field at selected temperatures were analyzed by the image processing software. The displacement maps were produced and the strains were determined from the strain-displacement relations as follows

$$\varepsilon_x = \frac{\partial U}{\partial x}$$

$$\varepsilon_y = \frac{\partial V}{\partial y} \qquad (4)$$

$$\gamma_{xy} = \frac{\partial U}{\partial y} + \frac{\partial V}{\partial x}$$

These equations provide total strain components. To get the net mechanical strains, the free expansion strain $(\alpha \cdot \Delta T)$ for each material in the package has to be subtracted from the total strain. Thus:

$$\varepsilon_{x,m} = \varepsilon_x - \alpha \bullet \Delta T$$

$$\varepsilon_{y,m} = \varepsilon_y - \alpha \bullet \Delta T \qquad (5)$$

and the principal strains were calculated by

$$\varepsilon_1 = \frac{\varepsilon_{x,m} + \varepsilon_{y,m}}{2} + \sqrt{(\frac{\varepsilon_{x,m} - \varepsilon_{y,m}}{2})^2 + (\frac{\gamma_{xy}}{2})^2}$$

$$\varepsilon_2 = \frac{\varepsilon_{x,m} + \varepsilon_{y,m}}{2} - \sqrt{(\frac{\varepsilon_{x,m} - \varepsilon_{y,m}}{2})^2 + (\frac{\gamma_{xy}}{2})^2} \qquad (6)$$

where the m subscript denotes mechanical strains only and ε_1 and ε_2 are the principal strains.

3. Results

The typical fringe patterns of a specimens at -50^0C and 20^0C were shown in Figure 4. Because of symmetry, only right half of the pattern was shown. The null field patterns (at 20^0C) shown in Figure 4a and 4c has several fringes for both U and V directions. These must be taken into consideration when processing the final fringe pattern for the displacement at -50^0C as shown in Figure 4b and Figure 4d. Each fringe (dark line) is a line of constant displacement (i.e. all points along that line have undergone the same amount of displacement in the direction considered). To assign fringe values, a reference point of

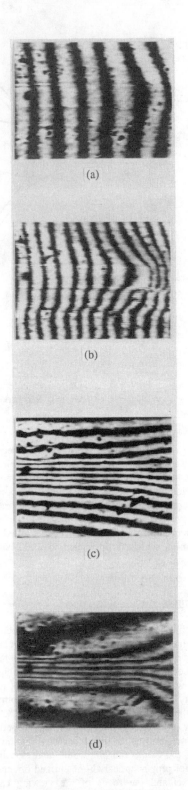

(a)

(b)

(c)

(d)

Figure 4 Typical fringe patterns in a coated chip specimen.
(a) U-fringe pattern at 20^0C (null field).
(b) U-fringe pattern at -50^0C.
(c) V-fringe pattern at 20^0C (null field).
(d) V-fringe pattern at -50^0C.

438

zero displacement must be known. In our case the package was not constrained at any point and was free to expand in all directions. Therefore, any arbitrary point may be considered as a reference point and the displacements may be defined relative to it. For analysis of strains, the reference point displacement is immaterial, since only relative displacements are needed for the strain computations (equation 4) and not the absolute values.

Numerical values for displacements in the chip for both A and B type packages were determined by DIAEMI procedure and then smoothed by a least square fitting. Figure 5 shows the displacements along both directions in the chip area at -50^0C, the principal strains are calculated along a chip cross section by equation (6) (Figure 6). There is clear evidence that the mechanical strains which are due to mismatch in the coefficients of thermal expansions of the chip, leadframe, and encapsulant are on the order of thousands microstrains. This implies that the there are severe strain concentrations in a package under thermal loads.

Comparison of the two different specimens, type A and type B, (Figure 6) reflects the effect of the material modification on the strain levels. It is obvious that the thermally induced strains in the type A package are lower than those in the type B package. This shows that the type A material is preferable considering the strain induced on the chip. Normal strains were also calculated at several locations throughout the chip at various temperatures. The obtained results are shown in Figure 7. These results provide an important information for package design.

4. Conclusions

Variety of analytical and numerical assessments of package deformations under thermal loads are not completely successful because of the complexity of the package geometry and the boundary conditions. Also the small magnitude of the deformations due to the loading conditions in microelectronic packages make detection very difficult for many experimental displacement measuring techniques. The presented work shows that digital image analysis enhanced moiré interferometry can be used successfully to investigate the strain distributions in the microelectronic packages due to the temperature change.

Full displacement fields in the chips in microelectronic devices subject to uniform cooling were measured by DIAEMI technique. The strains were computed from this field data and analyzed. The effect of the material modification of the strain on the chip surface was quantitatively evaluated. The obtained experimental data may provide an important reference for package design.

5. Acknowledgement

Partial support for this work from the SRC under contract No. SRC 91-MP-071 is gratefully acknowledged. One of the authors (A. Voloshin) appreciate the input of Dr. Lazar Trachtenberg from Drexel University during productive discussions and his help with data processing.

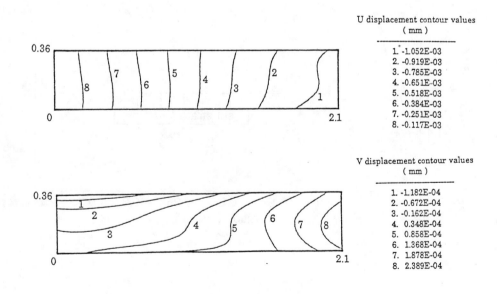

Figure 5   U and V displacement pattern in the right half of the type A package.

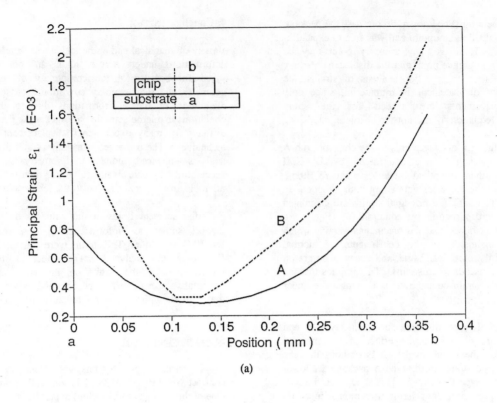

(a)

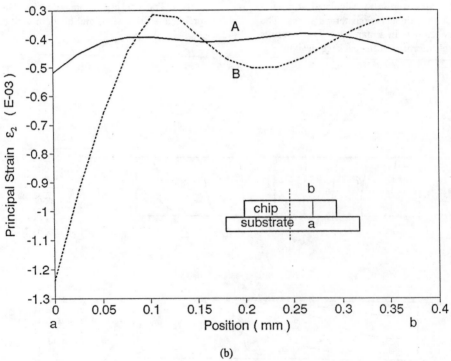

(b)

Figure 6 Principal strain distribution along an a-b section (due to temperature change from 20^0C to -50^0C).

(a) ε_1

(b) ε_2

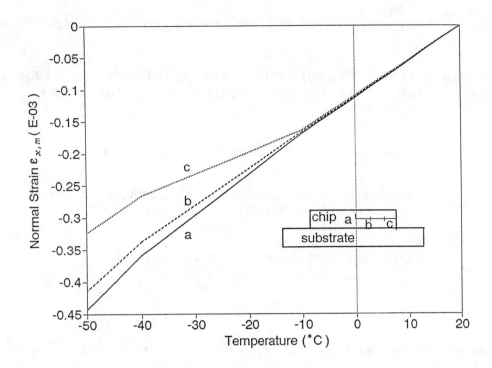

Figure 7   Normal strains at the several locations (due to cooling from 20^0C to -50^0C).

6. References

[1]   Barrie S. H. Royce, " Differential Thermal Expansion in Microelectronic System ", IEEE Transactions on Components Hybrid and Manufacturing Technology, vol.11, no.4, pp.454-463, Dec. 1988.

[2]   S. Groothius, W. Schroen and M. Mortuza, "Computer Aided Stress Modelling for Optimizing Plastic Package Reliability", Proceedings of 23rd Annual Reliability Physics, 1985.

[3]   B. Natarajan and B. Bhattacharyya, "Die Surface Stresses in a Molded Plastic Package", Proceedings of 36th Electronic Components Conference, pp.74, 1986.

[4]   A. F. Bastawros and A. S. Voloshin, "In Situ Calibration of Stress Chip ", IEEE Transactions on Components Hybrid and Manufacturing Technology, vol.13, no.4, pp.888-892, Dec. 1990.

[5]   D. Post and W. A. Baracat, "High-Sensitivity Moiré Interferometry - a Simplified Approach", Experimental Mechanics, vol.21, pp.100-104, 1981.

[6]   A. S. Voloshin, C. P. Burger, R. E. Rowland and T. S. Richard, "Fractional Moiré Strain Analysis using Digital Imaging Technique", Experimental Mechanics, vol.26, no.3, pp.254-258, March 1986.

[7]   C. A. Sciammarella, " Basic Optical Law in the Interpretation of Moiré Pattern Applied to the Analysis of Strain-Part I ", Experimental Mechanical, vol.5, no.5, pp.154-160, May 1965.

THERMAL DEFORMATION ANALYSIS FOR INTERCONNECTIONS IN ELECTRONIC PACKAGING BY MICROSCOPIC MOIRE INTERFEROMETRY

Bongtae Han*, C. K. Lim**, Yifan Guo** and Daniel Post*

*Engineering Science and Mechanics Department
Virginia Polytechnic Institute & State University
Blacksburg, VA 24061

**Technology Laboratory, IBM Corporation
Endicott, NY 13760

Abstract

Microscopic moire interferometry is used to conduct a thermal deformation analysis of interconnections in second level electronic packaging. A significant bending deformation was documented at the corner pin brazed to the multi-layer ceramic module. Enhanced sensitivity and high spatial resolution provided by the method makes it ideally suited for the study of deformations of electronic components.

Introduction

Thermal strains are the major cause of fatigue failures of interconnections of electronic assemblies, or packages. As the components and structures involved in high-end electronic packaging are made smaller, the thermal gradients increase and the strain concentrations become more serious. Numerical analyses by the finite element method, FEM, have been used extensively to estimate stresses and strains in packaging structures.[1,2] However, numerical methods are subject to limitations for analysis of anisotropic materials and multi-body problems. The models and results usually require verification by other means. Accordingly, advanced experimental techniques are in high demand to correlate numerical methods, and thus to provide accurate solutions for deformation studies of electronic packaging.

For the analysis of small components and structural elements involved in electronic packages, the relative displacements within the small field can be very small even when the strains are large. Accordingly, very high sensitivity is needed to map the displacement fields. Recently, a whole-field in-plane displacement measurement method—*microscopic moire interferometry*—was developed for micromechanics studies.[3,4] The method increases the sensitivity of moire interferometry by an order of magnitude and it utilizes an optical microscope to achieve high spatial resolution. The sensitivity and spatial resolution provided by the method makes it ideally suited for the deformation study of electronic packages.

The component investigated here was a 28mm multi-layer ceramic (MLC) module connected to a glass/epoxy circuit board. The dimensions are shown in Fig. 1. The MLC module has a thickness of 2.3mm and a stand-off of 1.7mm from the board. The module and board are connected by Kovar pins. One end of the pin is brazed to the module; the other end is inserted into a plated-through hole in the board and then wave-soldered to form the connection as illustrated in the insert in Fig. 1. The overall deformation of the assembly subjected to thermal loading was documented by conventional moire interferometry and can be found in Ref 5. It revealed that the module and board were significantly bent as a result of the thermal expansion mismatch between the module and board. Note that the pins were sufficiently strong and stiff to produce high forces between the module and board. It is important that each pin and brazed joint be capable of withstanding the applied bending moment. Accordingly, a detailed experimental analysis of the pin was needed to optimize the design. In this work, microscopic moire interferometry was used to investigate thermal deformations of the pin. In-plane U and V displacement fields of the corner pin, induced by a temperature change of 80°C, were documented. The deflection and the bending strains were determined from the displacement fields.

Microscopic Moire Interferometry

Microscopic moire interferometry was developed for two goals: high spatial resolution and enhanced sensitivity of displacement measurements. The desired spatial resolution was achieved by employing an optical microscope as an imaging system. Two techniques were utilized to enhance the sensitivity. They are the *immersion interferometer*[3] and the *optical/digital fringe multiplication* (O/DFM) method.[4]

The immersion interferometer and the complete optical and mechanical arrangement is illustrated in Fig. 2 and described in Ref. 3. The two channels for U and V fields are illustrated in the insert in Fig. 2. The basic sensitivity provided by the interferometer was 4.8 fringes/μm displacement (a contour interval of 208nm displacement per fringe order), which exceeds the previously conceived theoretical limit.[6] This was accomplished by creating a virtual reference grating inside a refractive medium. Thus, the wavelength of light was reduced by a factor equal to the index of refraction, and this reduction enabled the formation of a virtual reference grating of 4800 lines/mm. The configuration of the interferometer made it inherently stable and relatively insensitive to environmental disturbances. This allowed a robust scheme to shift the fringes for fringe multiplication.

The O/DFM method consists of optical fringe shifting and a digital process to sharpen and combine the shifted fringes. With the configuration shown in Fig. 2, the moire fringes were shifted by translating the interferometer relative to the specimen grating by a fraction of its pitch, g.[4] This was done by controlling a piezo-electric actuator to which the interferometer was attached. A series of β shifted moire patterns was obtained by sequential shifts of the immersion interferometer by a constant increment, g/β, where β is the fringe multiplication factor; in terms of phase, each pattern was shifted by an increment of $2\pi/\beta$ relative to its neighbors. Shifting and grabbing the series of β patterns was accomplished within a fraction of second. Then, the series of shifted patterns was sharpened and combined into a single contour map. The result is a map with β times as many fringe contours as the original moire pattern. The resultant pattern then represents in-plane specimen displacements U and V by

$$U = \frac{N^*_x}{\beta f} \qquad\qquad V = \frac{N^*_y}{\beta f} \qquad\qquad (1)$$

where N^* is the fringe order in the final pattern and f is the frequency of the virtual reference grating (4800 lines/mm in this case). Equation 1 defines the measurement sensitivity of the method, i.e., the number of fringes per unit displacement, as $N^*_x/U = \beta f$. Clearly, the sensitivity is increased by the factor β, compared to that of the basic moire pattern.

Experiment and Results

A special implementation of moire interferometry[7] was used for the steady-state thermal deformation analysis. A uniform cross-line diffraction grating was produced on the specimen at an elevated temperature of 102°C. The grating deformed as the specimen cooled to room temperature and the deformation was recorded at room temperature by microscopic moire interferometry.

The U and V displacement fields are depicted in Fig. 3 for the portion of the corner pin outlined by the dashed box. They represent the total deformations which include a free thermal contraction caused by the temperature change and a stress-induced deformation caused by the bending moment. The temperature change was $\Delta T = 80°C$. The fringe multiplication factor was $\beta = 4$ and the contour interval was 52nm per fringe contour.

The deflections (x displacements) relative to the ceramic module were determined from the U displacement pattern (Fig. 3) and they are plotted in Fig. 4. It shows a substantial bending of the pin shank relative to the pin head. The relative y displacements across the end of the shank were also determined from the corresponding V displacement pattern and they are plotted in Fig. 5. It shows a nearly uniform slope at the junction of the head and shank, caused by bending of the pin.

In order to examine the bending strains, the carrier fringe technique[8] was used to transform the V field in Fig. 3 to that illustrated in Fig. 6. The carrier fringes cancelled the free thermal contraction part of the pattern to reveal the remaining stress-induced part depicted in Fig. 6. Here, $\beta = 6$ and the contour interval is 35nm. The pattern in the shank region is typical of bending.

The experimental procedure utilized observation of the central pin to establish the correct carrier pattern. The shank of the central pin was free of stress; its strain was caused by thermal contraction alone. The interferometer was adjusted to produce a null field (a field devoid of fringes) in this region, and thus cancel the strain of free thermal contraction. This adjustment was retained for observation of the corner pin. In addition, carrier fringes of rotation were introduced to cancel the rigid by rotation. This procedure revealed the stress-induced fringes of Fig. 6.

The ε_y strain across AA' was determined from Fig. 6 and its distribution is shown in Fig. 7. The maximum tensile and compressive strains occurred at each end, where they were 0.28% and -0.21%, respectively. The strains caused by an 80°C temperature change are large. The results will be used to evaluate the geometric design and the material selection, as well as to evaluate the companion FEM analysis. The influence of cutting away half of the assembly in order to expose the cross-section for the experiment will be considered in the assessment.

Conclusions

Microscopic moire interferometry was employed successfully to investigate thermal deformations of interconnections in second level electronic packaging. A significant bending deformation was documented at the corner pin. With the enhanced sensitivity and high spatial resolution provided by the method, it is ideally suited for the analysis of deformations occurring in electronic packages.

Acknowledgements

Sponsorship by IBM Corp. (Grant No. Z909162) and the National Science Foundation (Grant No. MSS-8913942) is greatly appreciated and graciously acknowledged.

References

1. J. H. Kelly, C. K. Lim and W. T. Chen, "Optimization of Interconnections between Packaging Levels", *IBM Journal of Research and Development*, vol. 28, no. 6, Nov. 1984.

2. L. S. Goldman, "Mechanical Optimization of Brazed Pins", *International Society for Hybrid Micromechanics Conference*, Chicago, IL, 1981.

3. B. Han and D. Post, "Moire Interferometry with Increased Sensitivity," *Proc. 1991 Spring Conference of Society for Experimental Mechanics*, Milwaukee, Wisconsin, 1991; also B. Han and D. Post, "Immersion Interferometer for Microscopic Moire Interferometry," *Experimental Mechanics* (to be published).

4. B. Han, "Ultra-high Sensitivity Moire Interferometry," *SPIE Proceedings No. 1554, The 2nd International Conference on Photomechanics and Speckle Metrology*, San Diego, California, July 22, 1991; also B. Han, "Higher Sensitivity Moire Interferometry for Micromechanics Studies," *Optical Engineering* (to be published).

5. Y. Guo and C. G. Woychik, "Thermal Strain Measurements of Solder Joints in Second Level Interconnections using Moire Interferometry," *ASME Journal of Electronic Packaging*, (will be published in March 1992).

6. E. M. Weissman and D. Post, "Moire Interferometry near the Theoretical Limit," *Applied Optics*, vol. 21, no. 9, May 1982.

7. D. Post and J. D. Wood, "Determination of Thermal Strain by Moire Interferometry," *Experimental Mechanics*, vol. 29, no. 3, pp. 318-322, Sept. 1989.

8. Y. Guo, D. Post and R. Czarnek, "The Magic of Carrier Patterns," *Experimental Mechanics*, vol. 29, no. 2, pp. 169-173, June 1989.

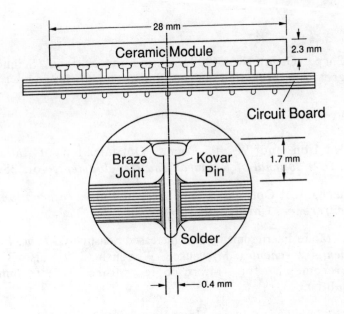

Fig. 1 Schematic illustration of the cross section of the specimen.

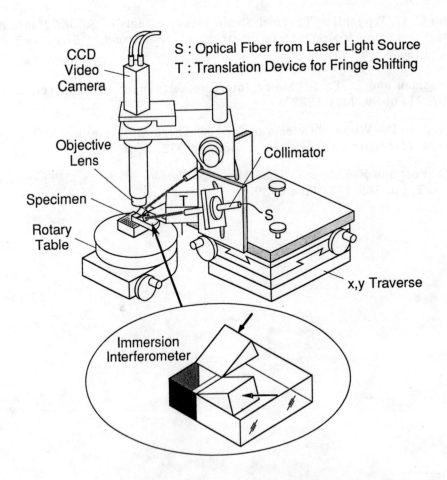

Fig. 2 Optical and mechanical assembly of the microscopic moire interferometry apparatus.

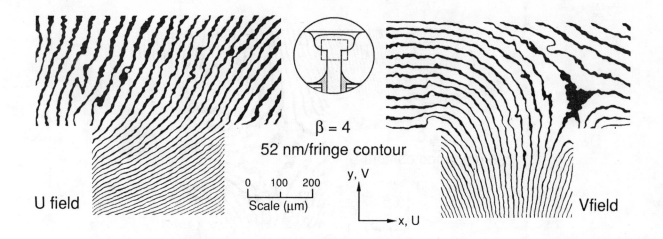

U field

β = 4

52 nm/fringe contour

0   100   200
Scale (μm)

y, V

x, U

V field

Fig. 3 U and V field depicting total displacements for ΔT = 80°C.

y (μm)

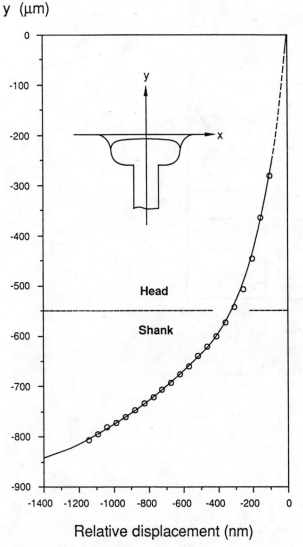

Head

Shank

Relative displacement (nm)

Fig. 4 Deflection along y, relative to the module.

V displacement (nm)

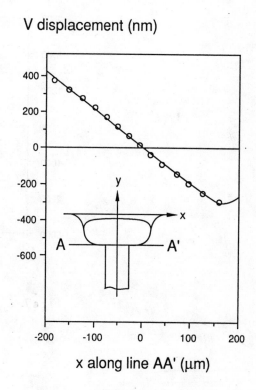

x along line AA' (μm)

Fig. 5 Vertical displacements along line AA'.

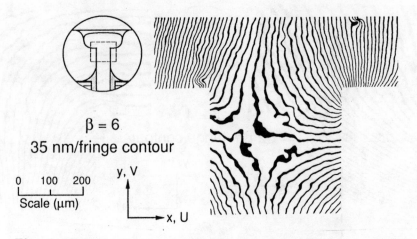

β = 6

35 nm/fringe contour

0   100   200
Scale (µm)

y, V
x, U

Fig. 6 V field with carrier fringes of extension and rotation.

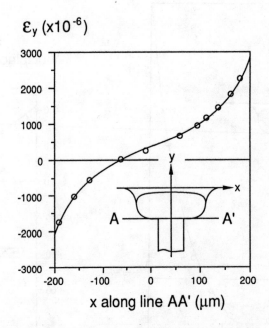

ε_y (x10^{-6})

x along line AA' (µm)

Fig. 7 ε_y distribution along line AA'.

Moire Study of Effect of Near Plate Edges on
Residual Strain Created by Coldworking
Fastener Holes

Gary Cloud, P.E.
Michigan State University, East Lansing, MI 48823

Rajab Sulaimana
Sargent and Lundy Corp., Chicago, IL

Abstract

The effects of near plate edges upon the residual strains near coldworked holes were measured. A moire technique which incorporated grating photography, optical Fourier processing and computer data reduction was employed. Coldworking a hole or a row of holes introduces undesirable tensile strain in the plate edge. Order of coldworking is important, and the strains fields are often adversely affected when a row is treated.

INTRODUCTION

Studies of fatigue crack initiation and growth indicate that introducing residual strains (and so residual stresses) by drawing an oversized mandrel through a mechanical fastener hole in a machine assembly markedly improves the fatigue life of the structure. This procedure is particularly useful in the aerospace industry because one of the major problems common to aircraft is that of structural fatigue beginning at joints.

Structures in which flaw-induced fracture may be responsible for failure are common. In a turbine, for instance, bolt holes in high speed rotating parts, such as the engine fan and compressor disks, act as stress raisers. The local stresses and strains around the hole are higher than the nominal values in the bulk of the material. Flaws, which are always induced by the hole generation process, form a focus in a high-stress region for the beginning of crack growth and eventual failure.

Most engineering structures are primarily load-transmitting devices in which ductility allows yielding in small regions of stress concentration under static or cyclically changing stresses. Stress concentrations are blunted by plastic flow so that crack initiation and failure of the machine part are prevented. This design approach, however, is relatively uneconomical, especially when weight considerations are critical.

The process of drawing an oversized mandrel through the fastener hole is considered to be one of the most economical and effective approaches to fatigue life improvement. The essential principle is the same for the various types of fatigue improvement fastener systems. That is, the material around the fastener hole is coldworked and the material adjacent to the hole is left in a state of residual compression.

In order to utilize prestressing effectively, one must understand the ways in which the residual strain fields are affected by having the fatigue-rated fasteners installed near the edge of a plate. Also, it is important to learn how the strains are redistributed when a row of holes is placed near an edge and then coldworked, as is the usual practice in aircraft manufacture. The placement of holes and the order of coldworking would seem to be important factors in the development of an advantageous strain/stress environment, particularly if stress corrosion might be a factor.

OBJECTIVE AND SCOPE

This paper reports the results of some experiments to investigate the effects on the residual strain field of a plate edge near a single cold-expanded hole and near a row of treated holes. It is part of a larger study which also examined the effects of compressive in-plane loads as well as the effects on the residual strain field of the sequence of coldworking the holes in an array.

The coldworking technique studied in this research is the seamless sleeve method marketed by J.O. King, Inc., 711 Trabert Avenue, N.W., Atlanta, Georgia, 30318. The findings should be relevant to other coldworking systems, including the Boeing split-sleeve technique, but no work has been performed to validate such an extrapolation.

Figure 1 shows a schematic of the seamless-sleeve coldworking process. A pilot hole is first drilled and then reamed to size. A mandrel and sleeve are then inserted into the hole from the head side. With the help of a puller nose piece, the mandrel is installed into a puller and the mandrel is pulled through the sleeve and hole.

This study deals only with surface residual strains. The implications in terms of residual stress are not addressed here, although some qualitative inferences can be drawn without involving plasticity calculations.

METHODS OF MEASUREMENT

The measurement of strain in the vicinity of coldworked holes is complicated by several factors including the following: (1) The strains range from about −10% to about +5%; (2) There is considerable out-of-plane displacement; (3) The strained surface is often rippled in the regions of large deformation; (4) Strain gradients near the hole are large; (5) The area of primary interest is close to a boundary; (6) The sleeve protrudes from one side and the sleeve head covers part of the other side; (7) Experiments take place in several nonreversible, nonrepeatable stages, and data are to be recorded at each stage; (8) Whole-field maps of two principal strain components are needed.

These conditions dictate that a noncontacting optical method be used. A moire

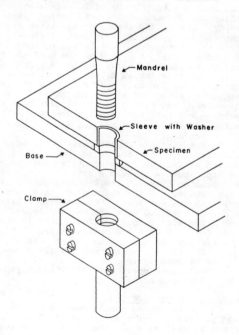

Figure 1.
Schematic of coldworking using mandrel and sleeve with attached anvil washer.

method which creates grating records at each specimen stage for subsequent optical processing and data reduction was developed. It provides permanent grating photographs, and the sensitivity may be chosen to some extent during optical processing after the experiment is completed.

The developed technique has been adequately described in other publications [1-3], so only a summary is needed here. Gratings of 1000 lines per in. (39.4 lines per mm) were printed onto the specimens using photoresist. The specimen grating was photographed using high-resolution techniques for the original state, the as-coldworked state, and each subsequent loaded state. These photographic replicas were superimposed with one or more submaster gratings in on optical Fourier processing system [4,5] in order to form separate baseline (original state) and at-load (other states) moire fringe patterns. Fringe multiplication and pitch mismatch of appropriate sign and magnitude were introduced at this stage in order to improve interpolation and increase precision. The fringe orders and their positions along chosen axes were obtained from the photographs in digital form. Displacement and strain distributions were generated and plotted using a mainframe computer.

It is important to realize that the technique is a differential one in that a set of baseline (or any other state) data and at-load data are required by the data reduction routine. False strains which would be caused by magnification errors and such are thereby removed. This approach also automatically attends to the apparent strain induced by pitch mismatch, so there is no need to determine the mismatch accurately. The only requirement is that the photographic system is not changed during any one experiment. Proper scaling and elimination of distortion errors are established by the use of abundant fiducial markings on the specimen. The locations of these marks are input as the fringe patterns are digitized, and scaling is handled by the data reduction scheme.

Figure 2 is a moire fringe pattern which is typical of those obtained with the technique described above.

MATERIALS AND SPECIMEN PREPARATION

Two groups of specimens were used in this phase of the investigation. All the specemins were cut from a single plate of 7075-T6 aluminum (Aluminum Company of America) having 1/4 in. (6.35 mm) thickness. Specimens of the first group contained only one hole at three different distances from the plate edge. The remaining specimen carried a 4-hole array. A sketch of the multi-hole edge effect specimen is shown in Fig. 3. Hole diameters were held constant at 0.261 in. (6.63mm).; radial interference for each specimen was maintained by proper selection of sleeve thickness and mandrel diameter. The machining of the near edge was held uniform and care was taken to keep machining stresses negligible. Mandrel drawing rate was set to 0.5 cm/min.

The variable of interest is the edge distance/hole diameter ratio (e/d). In conventional design of fatigue improvement fastener systems, e/d is kept above a threshold ratio of 2.0. Values of e/d greater than 2.0 are known to give fatigue improvement, but the reasons for this value being critical are not known. The effect on life of using e/d less than 2.0 have not been explored.

The single-hole specimens used in this study were designed with e/d ratios of 1/8, 2.0, and 2.25. The e/d for the multi-hole pattern was set at 1.8.

The radial interference, which controls the degree of coldworking, was 0.0089 in. (8.9 mils) for the single-hole specimens and 0.006 in (6 mils) for the multi-hole array.

RESULTS AND DISCUSSION

The following strain components were evaluated and plotted for each specimen: (1) normal strain along several axes parallel to the long specimen edge and between the hole and the edge - this component is called the "hoop strain"; (2) normal strain along the transverse axis from hole center to specimen edge - this component is called "radial strain". Typical plots and summary results for the several different cases are presented below.

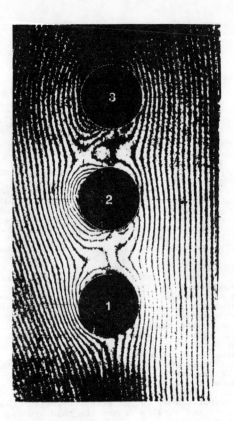

Figure 2.
Typical moire fringe pattern from edge effect investigation.

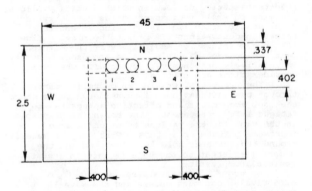

Hole Separation
= 1.75 D

D = Hole Diameter

Figure 3.
Dimensions and fiducial marks of typical in-plane edge-effect specimens. Dimensions inches.

Additional results and more thorough discussion can be found in the related reports [6-9].

Hoop Strain Distributions

Figure 4 displays a typical hoop strain plot for various axes between hole and edge for a single coldworked hole at e/d = 1.8. This graph is representative of those that are produced by the computerized data reduction scheme. A significant feature of this plot and the others from the series is that the hoop strain becomes very small midway between the hole and the plate edge, but it increases again as the edge is approached. The implication is that significant tensile strain is created at the plate edge, which could result in serious problems in a stress-corrosion environment.

Figure 5 is a summary of the peak hoop strains created between hole and edge for all three of the single-hole specimens. Peak residual hoop strain was plotted as a function of distance from the fastener hole edge for e/d=1.8, 2.0, and 2.25. The specimen with e/d=1.8 had the highest strain at the free edge, approximately 0.5%. The remaining specimens had lower residual strains at about 0.25%.

Figure 6 is a summary of the residual hoop strain distribution along the plate edge for the specimen with a row of holes. The order of coldworking was 1, 2, 4, then 3. Observe first that the plate edge strain varies by a factor of two within the span of the 4 holes. Also significant is the fact that the strain near hole no. 3, the last one coldworked, is the minimum for the entire set. This minimum is almost equal in magnitude to that of the single fastener hole in a semi-infinite plate, as is shown on the same graph. This plot also shows that the maximum strain magnitude along the plate edge increases by a factor of almost 2 in comparison with the single hole result. The hoop edge strain increases in magnitude and extent when only one fastener hole of a row is coldworked in comparison with the strain produced when there is only one coldworked hole in a semi-infinite plate.

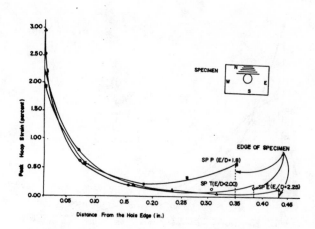

Figure 5.
Peak residual hoop strain along radial line from hole boundary to plate edge for single holes having 8.9 mils radial interference and various e/d.

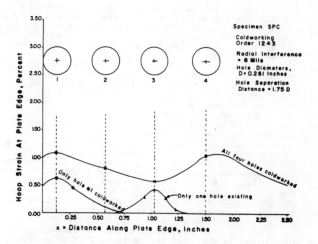

Figure 6.
Residual hoop strain along specimen edge for a single hole, for a row with only one hole coldworked, and for a row with all holes coldworked. Radial interference is 6 mils and e/d=1.8.

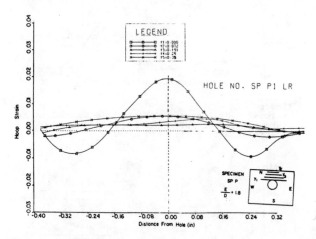

Figure 4.
Residual hoop strain distributions along several axes near a plate edge at different radial distances for 8.9 mils radial interference and e/d=1.8.

Radial Compressive Strain

Figure 7 summarizes the effect of edge distance on the residual radial strain for the single-hole specimens. In general, these results are in accord with the expectation that the radial strain at the fastener hole boundary increases with increasing edge-to-hole distance for a given level of radial interference during coldworking. Plastic expansion of a hole in an infinite plate would represent a limiting state. The shape of the curve for e/d=1.8 is peculiar, but its value at the hole edge is consistent with expectations. The shapes of the curves for distances from the hole exceeding 0.2 in. are not entirely consistent with one another.

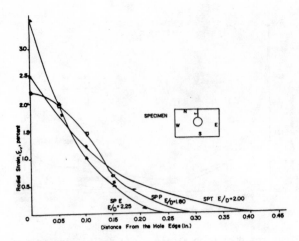

Figure 7.
Residual radial strain from hole boundary to plate edge for single holes having 8.9 mils radial interference and various e/d ratios.

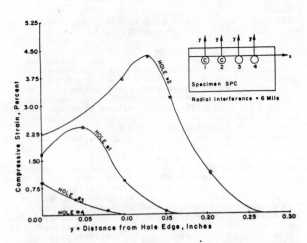

Figure 9.
Residual radial strain between hole boundaries and plate edge after only two holes are coldworked. Radial interference is 6 mils and e/d=1.8.

Figures 8 through 11 are the radial strain results for the 4-hole in-line array. Fig. 8 compares the radial strain between hole no. 1 and the plate edge after only that hole is coldworked and after all the holes are coldworked. Three serious modifications of the residual strain are apparent. First, the strain at the hole edge is reduced from 2.5% to 1.6% by coldworking the adjacent holes. Second, the area of compressive radial strain is reduced from .25 in. to .15 in. Finally, the peak radial strain is shifted away from the hole boundary. Clearly, the plastic expansion of a hole adversely affects the strain distribution and magnitudes around adjacent holes.

The plots of Figures 9 - 11 show radial strain between each hole and the plate edge as the holes are coldworked in order 1, 2, 4, and 3. The effects of coldworking adjacent holes and of order of coldworking are very striking. For example, look at the modifications of strain near hole 2 as hole 4 is expanded, then observe the effect on radial strain near hole 4 of coldworking hole 3. None of these radial strain fields are similar to those obtained for a single hole near a plate edge. Especially noteworthy is the relative inefficacy of coldworking

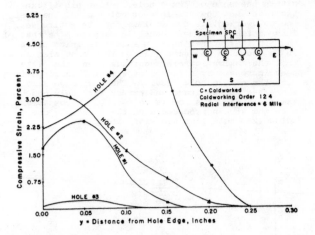

Figure 10.
Residual radial strain between hole boundaries and plate edge after coldworking 3 holes. Radial interference is 6 mils and e/d=1.8.

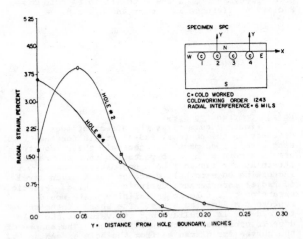

Figure 8.
Residual radial strain near one hole in a row after only one is coldworked and after all are coldworked. Radial interference is 6 mils and e/d=1.8.

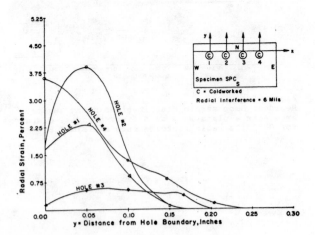

Figure 11.
Residual radial strain between hole boundaries and plate edge after coldworking all holes. Radial interference is 6 mils and e/d=1.8.

452

hole 3 after the ones on either side of it are coldworked. The final radial strain at the boundary of hole 3 is nearly zero. Recall that the minimum hoop strain was also found near hole 3. One should not assume that expanding all holes in a row has created helpful stress environments near all the holes.

Finally, it was observed that, during coldworking of a row of holes, the individual holes underwent a sort of "rigid body motion" which was larger than the actual deformation imposed by the mandrel. This behavior was more pronounced in the specimens with smaller e/d.

CONCLUSIONS

Methodology

The moire method developed for strain analysis problems of this type has been very successful. With this technique, the measurement of small and large elastic and plastic strains occurring in several stages over an extended field can be accomplished.

Optical spatial filtering proved to be indispensible in separating the u-field and v-field isothetics while improving visibility of fringes obtained with grating records which were recorded photographically.

The fringe analysis system minimized data reduction problems. The microprocessor-controlled digitizer was instrumental in obtaining reliable displacement field data. This was an extremely important factor since the data must be differentiated to find the strains. Additionally, mismatch techniques were introduced in the fringe formation process to improve the accuracy of the measured displacement gradients in the x and y directions.

Residual Strain

The effects of near plate edges on the strain fields created by coldworking a single hole and a row of holes carry serious implications for the designer. The findings can be summarized as follows:

1. The coldworking of a single fastener hole or a row of holes near an edge of a plate creates an undesirable tensile strain environment in the plate edge.

2. The residual strain fields depend on the e/d ratio for a given level of cold expansion.

3. The order of coldworking the holes in a row has an important effect on the residual strain field.

4. The tensile strain along a plate edge adjacent to a row of coldworked holes will vary by a factor of 2.

5. The minimum tensile strain in a plate edge adjacent to a coldworked row will exceed that produced by having a single hole near the edge.

6. For a single fastener hole near a plate edge, residual hoop strain attains a high value at the hole boundary and diminishes to a minimum at approximately 0.168 in from the hole. This strain then increases as the plate edge is approached.

7. The residual radial strains near some holes in a row are adversely affected by coldworking the others in the row. The maximum strain is shifted away from the hole edge, the strain at the *hole boundary is diminished, and the area of compressive strain is reduced.

8. When coldworking a row of holes, the resultant radial strain near some of the holes will be near zero after all are treated.

9. The strain distributions near a row will vary wildly as successive holes are coldworked.

10. The holes in a row actually move as adjacent holes are expanded.

ACKNOWLEDGEMENT

This research was supported by the Air Force Materials Laboratory, Wright-Patterson Air Force Base, Ohio under contract number F33615-78-C-5123. Project Engineer was Dr. Robert C. Donath.

REFERENCES

1. Cloud, G.L., "Measurement of Strain Fields near Coldworked Holes," Exp. Mech., vol. 20, no. 1, pp 9-16 (Jan 1980).
2. Cloud, G., "Residual Surface Strain Distribution Near Holes Coldworked to Various Degrees," AFML-TR-78-153, Air Force Materials Laboratory, Wright-Patterson AFB, Ohio, Nov. 1978.
3. Cloud, G. "Measurement of Elasto-plastic Strain Fields using High-resolution Moire Photography, Coherent Optical Processing, and Digital Data Reduction," Proc. 8th Congress of International Measurement Confederation, Moscow, USSR, May 1979.
4. Cloud G., "Simple Optical Processing of Moire Grating Photographs," Exp. Mech., vol. 20, no. 8, pp 265-272 (Aug 1980).
5. Chiang, F., "Techniques of Optical Spatial Filtering Applied to the Processing of Moire-Fringe Patterns," Exp. Mech., Vol. 9, pp 523-526 (Nov. 1969).
6. Cloud, G. and R. Sulaimana, "An Experimental Study of Large Compressive Loads Upon Residual Strain Fields and the Interaction Between Surface Strain Fields Created by Coldworking Fastener Holes," Tech. Report. AFWAL-TR-80-4206, 219pp, WPAFB, OH (Feb 1981).
7. Cloud, G. and M. Tipton, "An Experimental Study of the Interaction of Strain Fields Between Coldworked Fastener Holes," Tech. Report AFWAL-TR-80-4205, 123pp, WPAFB, OH (Mar 1981).
8. Sulaimana, R., "An Experimental Study of Large Compressive Loads Upon Residual Strain Fields and the Interaction Between Surface Strain Fields Created by Coldworking Fastener Holes," Ph.D. Dissertation, Michigan State University, E. Lansing, MI, 1980.
9. Tipton, M., "An Experimental Study of the Interaction of Strain Fields Between Coldworked Fastener Holes," M.S. Thesis, Michigan State University, E. Lansing, MI, 1980.

A MODIFIED MOIRE INTERFEROMETRY SYSTEM FOR REAL-TIME THERMAL STRAIN MEASUREMENTS

Y. Guo, H. C. Choi and W. R. LaFontaine

Technology Laboratory, IBM Corporation, Endicott, NY 13760

ABSTRACT

A moire interferometry system for real-time thermal strain measurements is introduced. The system provides very stable fringe patterns when thermal loadings are applied to specimens, and it is relatively insensitive to vibrations from the testing environment. Sub-micron sensitivity measurements can be conducted off optical tables. Real-time fringe patterns can be recorded continuously with a video camera, and a small power laser can be used as the light source. Thermal strains and deformations developed under high temperatures, especially time and temperature dependent deformations, can be determined.

INTRODUCTION

Thermal strains have great importance in characterizing mechanical and electrical performance of materials and structures used under elevated temperatures. In micromechanical studies, high sensitivity measurements are also needed in order to investigate thermal effects on a small and localized area. Recently, moire interferometry has been successfully used in determining thermal strains with a high sensitivity, and many methods have been developed to apply thermal loadings in complementing moire systems for high sensitivity thermal strain measurements [1-5]. In a real-time thermal strain measurement using moire interferometry, the major difficulty is the thermal instabilities of fringe patterns caused by the thermal loading and vibrations from the testing environment.

Moire interferometry is a high sensitivity optical technique [6]. Measurements using moire interferometry are usually conducted in optical laboratories with all optical elements, specimens and loading devices attached to an optical table in order to minimize vibrations and to obtain stable fringe patterns. In the cases where thermal strains are measured, a heating device has to be used together with the optical system to create thermal deformations. The thermal current caused by the heat convection and the vibrations induced by the testing environment cause unstable fringe patterns, which makes real-time observations and recordings difficult. In Reference [7], a vibration insensitive moire interferometer was introduced. By using a high frequency real reference grating, the sensitivity of the system to vibrations was greatly reduced. Actually, this system also improved fringe stability under thermal loadings.

In this paper, a modified system, specifically designed for conducting thermal strain and time/temperature dependent measurements, is introduced. This new system has excellent thermal stabilities and is also relatively insensitive to vibrations. It records stable and high contrast real-time fringe patterns at elevated temperatures. The technique provides a practical way to determine thermal strains with a high displacement sensitivity. In an experimental evaluation, the new system was used to investigate thermal deformations in an electronic package, and the information obtained from the experiment was very valuable in the analysis of failure mechanisms and reliability of micro electronic packaging.

MOIRE INTERFEROMETRY SYSTEM USING A REAL REFERENCE GRATING

The principle of moire interferometry is shown in Fig. 1. Two coherent beams diffracted by the specimen grating form a interference pattern – a fringe pattern – which can be recorded by a camera focused on the specimen surface. The principle can also be explained by using an approach from the geometric moire concept. The two-beam interference (B1 and B2) produces a virtual reference grating which interacts with the specimen grating to form a fringe pattern. The fringe pattern, similar in the geometric moire, is a contour map of in-plane displacement of the specimen. When a wavelength is chosen, the displacement sensitivity of a moire interferometry system is a function of the frequency of the reference grating which, in order, is determined by the intersection angle (2α) between the two incident beams (B1 and B2). The relation can expressed as

$$f_r = 2 \sin\alpha / \lambda$$

where f_r is the frequency of the reference grating, α is half of the intersection angle and λ is the wavelength. A large angle α will result in a high frequency virtual grating and a high displacement sensitivity for the measurement.

In the vibration insensitive system introduced in Reference [7], a real diffraction grating is employed. The purpose is to reduce the system's sensitivity to vibrations which could cause low contrast or no contrast in fringe patterns. In the system shown in Fig. 2, two coherent beams illuminate the real reference grating with a small intersection angle $\Delta\alpha$. The displacement sensitivity is low in front of the real grating according to the previous analysis. However, after the real grating, the 0th diffraction order from the beam B1 and the 1st diffraction order from B2 are used. These two beams (0th and 1st order) form a large intersection angle before they reach to the specimen grating, and the high sensitivity for measurements is recovered in front of the specimen. They carry the displacement information and are recorded as I1 and I2 by the camera after they are diffracted from the specimen grating. In a real system, the real reference grating is attached to the specimen in such a way that they move together by rigid body motions but do not constrain each other from deformations. The relative rigid body motions in the system exist only between the real grating and the incident beams, and the sensitivity there is low so that certain degree motions, such as a vibration, can be tolerated. Using this system, measurements can be conducted off the optical tables and very stable fringe patterns can be achieved.

In the design of the system (Fig. 2), one of the incident beam is striking the reference grating from an angle α, and the other one has a small angular deviation $\Delta\alpha$ from the direction of the incidence. When a HeNe laser is used (wavelength 633 nm), the frequency of the specimen grating (f_s) is 1200 lines/mm and the frequency of reference grating (f_r) is 2300 lines/mm, the angle α should be 49.4 degree and the angle $\Delta\alpha$ should be 5.2 degree. The modified system for thermal strain measurements has a similar design.

MODIFIED SYSTEM FOR THERMAL STRAIN MEASUREMENTS

The modification of the system for thermal strain measurements can also be introduced using Fig. 2. An ultra low expansion glass (ULE) is used to replace a regular glass substrate to carry the real reference grating, so that the frequency of the reference grating is maintained as a constant when a thermal loading is applied. In experiments, the real reference grating is also used as the window for the heating chamber, and it is attached to the specimen grating with a very small clearance t (less than 1 mm). The virtual reference grating (2400 lines/mm) is formed inside the heating chamber with an elevated temperature. Using a very small t (Fig. 2), the two rays from the incident beams B1 and B2, which create the interference pattern at a point P of the specimen, are very close to each other in their optical paths. In comparison, a regular moire system has to use two incident beams (B1 and B2' in Fig. 2) with a large intersection angle. To create the interference pattern at point P, the two rays have a much greater separation between their optical paths. Therefore, their phase difference could easily be disturbed and is very unstable if a thermal current or a temperature gradient is introduced in their optical paths. The unstable phase difference can cause a drifting, dancing and low contrast fringe pattern, which makes real-time observation and recording difficult.

By attaching a real grating to the specimen, the two rays (B1 and B2) almost follow the same optical path to create the fringe pattern. The thermal effects on their phase difference are greatly eliminated and that is why this system is insensitive to the thermal current and temperature gradient. In addition, the system is relatively insensitive to vibrations from the testing environment as discussed before. Since the real reference grating is attached to the specimen grating, they move together in harmony when disturbances such as vibrations are introduced by the environment. The elimination of relative motions between the two gratings provides mechanical stability to ensure high contrast fringes patterns.

A system using the principle demonstrated in Fig. 2 was built to perform real-time thermal measurements in a field condition (Fig. 3). A high frequency transparent grating was replicated on a ULE glass substrate using a thin layer of clear epoxy. It had a frequency of 2274 line/mm. A collimated beam was formed by a parabolic mirror and directed to the interferometer which consists of a full mirror and a partial mirror. A small intersection angle ($\Delta\alpha$) of the two incidence beams was used to illuminate the reference grating, such that the two beams almost follow the same optical path when they reach the specimen grating. The effect of temperature gradients on their phase difference was minimized. The whole setup was built on a 24 x 36 in.(0.6 x 0.9 meter) bread board and the experiments were conducted on a counter top with a forced air oven to apply thermal loadings. The system provided very stable fringe patterns on the TV screen when the thermal loadings were applied. Real-time fringe patterns were monitored and recorded for analyzing the time/temperature dependent deformations.

In the system shown in Fig. 2, when the incident beams pass through the reference diffraction grating, the 0th diffraction order of beam B1 and the 1st diffraction orders of beam B2 are used to create the fringe pattern. The diffraction efficiency in the 0th and 1st diffraction order is usually different for a diffraction grating. The intensity ratio of 0th and 1st order is also a function of the polarization direction of the incident beams relative to the direction of the grating lines. In the design, the reflection/transmission ratio of the partial mirror was chosen to compensate the efficiency ratio of the 0th and 1st order diffraction from the ULE grating. The objective is to equalize the intensities of the two information beams (I1 and I2) such that the highest fringe contrast can be achieved. A half-wave plate can also be used to change the polarization direction of the incident beams relative to the direction of the reference grating to optimize the intensity ratio of the two information beams.

EXPERIMENTAL EVALUATION

In electronic packaging, surface mount technology using solder interconnections is very popular and important. The reliability issue related to the thermal strains in the solder is a much discussed and greatly interested topic [8, 9, 10]. Because of the small dimensions of the solder interconnections, conventional experimental techniques for measurements of strain distributions cannot be readily applied. In addition, high strain concentrations usually exist in solder interconnections, and the solder itself usually responds non-linearly to applied forces and temperatures, so that the need for direct experimental measurements becomes especially important. The experimental data is also in great demand for verifying and guiding numerical and mathematical models in analyses.

Figure 4 shows an electronic package using solder ball interconnections to connect a multi layer ceramic (MLC) module and a printed circuit board (PCB). The components used in the package have different coefficients of thermal expansion (CTE). The CTE mismatch between the MLC and the PCB induces the mechanical strains to the solder interconnections whenever temperature changes occur. The magnitudes of thermal strains in solder determine the thermal fatigue life and the reliability of the interconnections.

The specimen shown in Fig. 4 is a strip cut from the MLC to PCB package. The interconnections are 35 mil. (890 μm) diameter solder balls. A specimen grating of 1200 lines/mm was replicated on the cross-section at room temperature. The process of producing a specimen grating can be found in Reference [1] and [5]. The specimen was mounted on a rotary stage such that its in-plane rotation could be adjusted. A heating chamber was used to apply the thermal loading by circulating hot air from a forced air oven. A ULE grating of 2274 lines/mm was mounted on the thermal chamber and attached to the specimen mount. A thermal couple was also attached on the specimen to monitor the temperature. In the experiment, the temperature was slowly increased from the room temperature (22 °C) to 92 °C in 35 minutes corresponding to a heating rate of 2 °C/minute. The fringe patters were monitored by a video system and recorded by taking pictures from the TV screen using a Polaroid camera.

Fig. 5 shows the fringe patterns taken at the temperature of 40, 60, and 80 °C. The fringe patterns are U fields corresponding to the x-direction displacements of the specimen. The two solder balls in the pictures are located at the far left side of the package which is shown by the dashed line box in Fig. 4. The relative displacements in x-direction between the ceramic module and the printed circuit board are obtained from the fringe order across the solder ball. Since the rigid body rotation is canceled by adjusting the carrier fringes of rotation, the average shear strain in the solder ball can be calculated using the relative displacement divided by the height of the solder ball. Figure 6 shows the displacements and strains as a function of the temperature. The data is taken from the center line of the left most solder ball as shown in Fig. 5. The deformations respond non-linearly to the temperature changes, and strain concentrations were developed at the corners of the solder balls. The information obtained from this experiment can be used to analyze the thermal strains and mechanical properties of the package. The strain concentrations are usually responsible for the initiations of fatigue cracks in the solder interfaces. The thermal fatigue life and the reliability of the interconnections are closely related to the strain levels in the solder.

CONCLUSIONS

A new system has been developed to measure time/temperature dependent properties of materials and structures. By attaching a real reference grating to the specimen, the system's sensitivity to temperature gradients and vibrations is greatly reduced. The fringe patterns are very stable under thermal loadings. The thermal stability of the system enhanced the capability of real-time thermal strain measurements. The new system can be used off the optical table to conduct experiments in a field environment.

The system introduced has all the adjustability of the regular moire interferometry system. The null-field is easily aligned and carrier fringes of extension and rotation are easily introduced. The system also has a simple structure and high light efficiency. The technique is practical for investigating thermal strains in materials and structures, such as electronic packages, with real-time observation.

ACKNOWLEDGMENTS

The research work presented in this paper was accomplished with help from J. Woods, S. Merrilll and D. Strope. The technical discussions on electronic packaging conducted with Dr. C. Lim and Dr. W. Chen are also greatly appreciated.

REFERENCES

[1]   D. Post and J. Wood, "Determination of Thermal Strains by Moire Interferometry," Experimental Mechanics, Volume 29, No. 3, September, 1989.

[2]   B. Kang, F. X. Wang and Q. K. Liu, "High Temperature Moire Interferometry for Use to 550 °C," Proceedings of the 1990 SEM Fall Conference on Hologram Interferometry and Speckle Metrology, Baltimore, Nov. 1990.

[3]   A. F. Bastawros, and A. S. Voloshin, "Thermal Strain Measurements in Electronic Packages Through Fractional Fringe Moire Interferometry," Journal of Electronic Packaging, Vol. 112, pp. 303, December 1990.

[4]   R. Czarnek, J. Lee and S. Y. Lin "Testing of Composite Materials at Elevated Temperatures Using Moire Interferometry," Proceedings of the International Conference on Composite Materials (ICCM/8), Paper number 36-O, Honolulu, Hawaii, July 1991.

[5]   Y. Guo and C. Woychik, "Thermal Strain Measurements of Solder Joints in Second Level Interconnections Using Moire Interferometry," to be published in ASME Journal of Electronic Packaging, March, 1992.

[6]   D. Post, "Moire Interferometry", Chap. 7, Handbook of Experimental Mechanics, A. S. Kobayashi, Editor, Prentice–Hall, Englewood Cliffs, NJ, 1987.

[7]   Y. Guo, "Developments in Moire Interferometry: Carrier Pattern Technique and Vibration Insensitive Interferometers", Ph.D Dissertation in Virginia Polytechnic Institute and State University, Feb. 1989.

[8]   P. M. Hall, "Force, Moment and Displacement during Thermal Chamber Cycle of Leadless Ceramic Chip Carrier Soldered to Printed Circuit Board." IEEE CHMT–7, No.4, Dec. 1984.

[9]   J. R. Wilcox, R. Subrahmanyan and Che–Yu Li, "Thermal Stress Cycles and Inelastic Deformation in Solder Joints," Proceeding of 2nd ASM International Electronic Materials and Processing Congress, Philadelphia, PA, April 1989.

[10]   W. Chen and C. Nelson, "Thermal Stress in Bonded Joints," IBM Journal of Research and Development 23, No. 2, pp. 179–180, 1979.

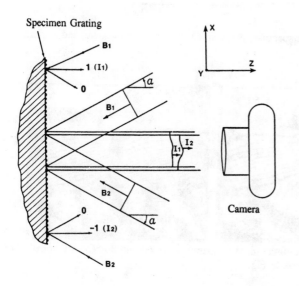

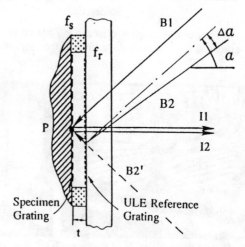

Fig. 2. A moire interferometry system using a real reference grating attached to the specimen. The two incident beams (B1 and B2) follow almost the same optical path if the gap t between the two gratings is very small.

Fig. 1. Diagram of a regular moire interferometry system

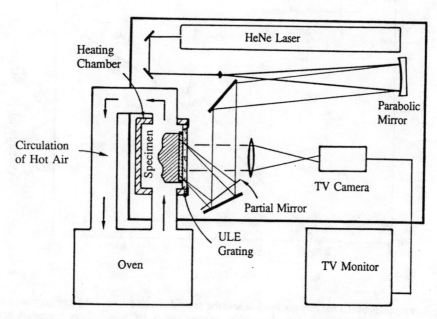

Fig. 3. The optical system and the setup for thermal strain measurements. A real reference grating formed on a ULE glass was attached on the specimen and used as the window of the heating chamber. The specimen is heated by circulating hot air from an oven.

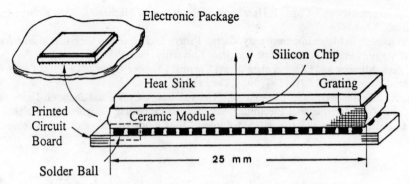

Fig. 4. An electronic package with solder ball interconnections. The specimen is a strip cut off from the package, and a specimen grating is replicated on the surface of the cross section.

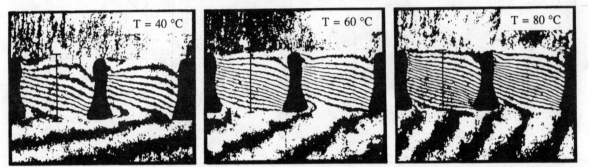

Fig. 5 U field fringe patterns of the thermal deformations in the x–direction at temperature 40, 60 and 80 °C. The location of the two solder balls in the package is shown by the dashed box in Fig. 4.

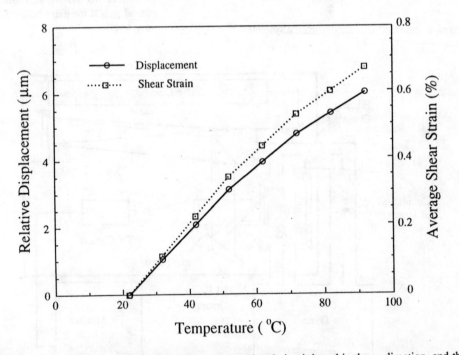

Fig. 6. Relative displacements between the ceramic module and the printed circuit board in the x–direction, and the average shear strain in a solder ball as a function of temperature. The heating rate is 2°C/min.. Shear strains are obtained by using the relative displacements divided by the height of the solder ball. The displacement and strain data are taken from the center line of the left most solder ball as shown in Fig. 4.

CONSIDERATIONS IN EVALUATING BRIDGE CONDITIONS: LESSONS LEARNED FROM NONDESTRUCTIVE AND DESTRUCTIVE TESTING OF A THREE SPAN REINFORCED CONCRETE BRIDGE

by R. Miller[1], A. Aktan[2] and B. Shahrooz[1]

ABSTRACT

A series of nondestructive tests were performed on a three span, skewed, reinforced concrete bridge to determine the extent of damage on the bridge. Nondestructive truck load testing and modal testing revealed damage to the shoulder areas of the bridge, even though this damage was hidden by an asphalt layer over the deck.

After the nondestructive testing, the bridge was loaded to failure. The failure load was about 700,000 pounds, which is equivalent to 22 trucks, far more than could ever fit onto the bridge. This showed that slab bridges have far more capacity than is predicted by usual methods of analysis and rating, even when damaged.

The final failure was in shear in a large circular arc around the loading points. The crack followed the rebar cutoff points near the support line. Although the shoulder rebar was exposed, it did not pull out. Later pull out tests confirmed that there was enough bond to yield the bar even though it was partially exposed. It is also interesting to note that at failure, the shear stress along the failure line was very low. Finally, analysis showed that the load carrying mechanism of the bridge changed, indicating that service load tests may not be accurate predictors of ultimate load behavior.

INTRODUCTION

It is often difficult to evaluate the effect of damage on structural performance. Damage in existing structures is often hidden. Even when damage is visible or when hidden damage is detected, it is often difficult to determine when damage is critical or only cosmetic. Of the major engineering codes, only the AASHTO specifications[1] have any method of evaluating the effect of damage on a structure. However, the AASHTO method is extremely simplified. There is also no accepted method of accounting for damage in finite element analysis.

In order to fully understand the effect of damage on structural performance, it is necessary to carefully evaluate the damage in a structure and then test the structure. This paper describes a series of nondestructive and destructive tests performed on a reinforced concrete bridge. These tests confirmed the usefulness of nondestructive test methods for evaluating damage in existing structures. The final destructive tests offered insight into the actual behavior and capacity of an existing structure.

---

[1] Assistant Professor of Civil and Environmental Engineering, M/L 71, The University of Cincinnati, Cincinnati, Ohio 44221-0071

[2] Professor of Civil and Environmental Engineering and Director of the Cincinnati Infrastructure Institute, M/L 71, University of Cincinnati, Cincinnati, Ohio 45221-0071

DESCRIPTION OF THE BRIDGE

Figure 1 shows the test bridge, which was a 38 year old, three span, skewed concrete slab bridge having span lengths of 9.75 m (32') for each end span and 12.2 m (40') in the midspan. The bridge was 11 m (36') wide and had one lane and a shoulder in each direction. The abutments and piers were skewed at 30° to the traffic lanes. The bridge slab was 450 mm thick (17.75") and was reinforced with #9 bars. Core tests indicated that the concrete had obtained an average strength of 54 MPa (7800 psi). The reinforcing bar was tested and found to be Grade 40 with a yield strength of 330 MPa (48000 psi).

Originally, the surface of the bridge was covered with asphalt, so the actual concrete surface was not visible. When the asphalt layer was removed, it was found that the driving lane concrete was sound but shoulder areas has severe deterioration down to the level of the rebar (about 65mm or 2.5"). There was also severe deterioration on the sides of the bridge. The bottom of the bridge, however, was still in good shape with some minor cracking and spalling. Figures 2 and 3 illustrate some of the damage.

PRELIMINARY CONSIDERATIONS

The goal of this research was to determine the ultimate load capacity of slab bridge. An additional goal was to verify the usefulness of nondestructive testing techniques for damage detection in bridges. Before any work was done, careful analysis of the bridge determined the best position for load placement. It was decided that one of the end spans would be loaded since it would probably have the lowest collapse load due to the boundary conditions (one end continuous and the other pinned). It was easier to load and instrument this span since it was not over water. The decision was also made to load only one lane so that possible twist and out of plane motion could be studied.

TRUCK LOAD TESTING

Three gravel loaded dump trucks, each weighing 690 kN (32000 pounds) were used to load the bridge. Six different loading combinations were used (Figure 4), all in the span which was to be destructively tested. LVDTs (Linear Variable Displacement Transducers) were placed under the bridge to measure deflections.

Figure 5 shows the deflection along the midspan of the span (line D in Figure 8). The dashed line in Figure 5 is the deflection predicted by a linear finite element program (SAP 90). Note that the bridge is more flexible in the damaged shoulder region. Deflections in the shoulder area, parallel to the traffic lanes (line 3 in Figure 8) are shown in Figure 6. Note that the graph again shows the damaged shoulder areas are more flexible. At the time the truck load tests were conducted, the asphalt layer was still on the bridge, so the damaged shoulders were not visible. This indicates that truck load testing can be used to detect hidden damage.

The linear finite element model was modified in an attempt to account for the damage. This was done by making the shoulder elements 65 mm (2.5") thinner to simulate the loss of concrete from the top surface. The result is a very good match between measured values of deflection and predicted values of deflection. The linear finite element model worked in this case because: 1) The truck loads did not exceed the maximum load which had ever been applied to this bridge. As a result there was no new cracking. 2) The stress levels induced by the truck load test were low, so linear analysis is a sufficient approximation.

MODAL TESTING

In addition to truck load testing, modal tests were performed on the bridge. Modal testing consists of placing accelerometers on the bridge deck at known points and then striking the bridge with an instrumented hammer. The accelerometers record the bridge vibrations under the known impact load. Complete data about bridge vibration is obtained by striking the bridge deck with the hammer at various places (usually a grid is used). The accelerations recorded can be processed to produce various mode shapes of the bridge. From the modal information, it is also possible to calculate a flexibility matrix for the bridge. Complete information about modal testing can be found in literature.[2]

Using the flexibility matrix obtained from the modal test, it was possible to predict the bridge deflection behavior. Figure 6 shows a sample comparison of the deflections predicted by modal testing and the deflections predicted by a linear finite element model. The figure shows a cut perpendicular to the direction of traffic (line I in Figure 8) with a load placed at point I3 (see Figure 8). Again, the shoulder damage is seen by the additional flexibility in this area.

DESTRUCTIVE TESTING

The destructive load was applied to the bridge using four Sheffer 1560 kN (350 kip) capacity hydraulic actuators (total capacity of 6225 kN or 1400 kips). The actuators were set in concrete blocks sized to simulate the foot print of the tires of a tandem axle. Rock anchors consisting of 178 mm (7") diameter prestressing cables grouted 13.7m (45') into a rock layer below the bridge were attached to the actuators using button head connectors (Figure 7). The actuators were controlled using a two channel digital controller (each channel controlled two cylinders in a "master/slave" relationship). Using a personal computer equipped with special software, it was possible to monitor the load vs. bridge deflection at one point in real time.

Figure 8 shows the positions where deflections were measured. Two types of deflection instruments were used: wire potentiometers with a 255 mm (10") range were used in the loaded span and LVDTs with a 50 mm (2") range were used in the other spans. In addition to the deflection instruments, LVDTs were used to measure pier cap and abutment rotations. Strain gages were used to measure rebar strain at 13 places. Concrete strains were measured at 16 places (top and bottom of slab at eight separate places) over a 153 mm (6") gage length using LVDTs. In all, over 150 instruments were used.

The instruments were read using two data acquisition systems. Periodically during the test, data was downloaded to a spreadsheet and checked to assure that the data system and instruments were operating properly.

Load was applied in 70 kN (16 kip) increments and data was collected at the end of each increment. It took three days to complete the total test. The bridge was unloaded at the end of each day.

ANALYSIS OF BRIDGE RESPONSE

The bridge responded in a linear fashion up to a load of about 710 kN (160 kips). At a load of 995 kN (224 kips) there was an abrupt change in the rotational stiffness in the center of the south abutment (point A6 in Figure 8). Figure 9 shows this response. At 1280 kN (288 kips), a change in the rotational response of the pier cap occurred at point G8. The west end of the slab (points A8 to A10, Figure 8) begins to lift off the south abutment at 1700 kN (384 kips). When the load reached 2275 kN (512 kips), the deflection instruments along the "9" line (Figure 8) begin to stiffen as shown in Figure 10. Cracks begin to form on the bottom of the slab, perpendicular to the skew, at this same load. Final failure occurred at 3120 kN (700 kips). The lines of failure are shown in Figure 11.

After careful examination of the bridge response, the authors have formed a hypothesis about the bridge behavior. Finite element analysis indicated that a skewed bridge carries load parallel to the skew (Figure 12). However, at the early stages of the test, the bridge carried the load parallel to the traffic lanes. This may be the result of some degree of fixity in the abutment. At 995 kN (224 kips), the abutment suddenly loses the fixity, indicating that this fixity may have been cause by some type of a frictional effect. Once the rotational stiffness changes at the abutment, the bridge begins to carry the load parallel to the skew. Note, however, that the change happens gradually. The stiffening in the instruments along the "9" line is probably an unloading (remember that the load shown in Figure 10 is the load applied by the cylinders, not the local load). The unloading in this area probably occurs because this area is no longer along the primary load path.

The formation of cracks perpendicular to the skew serves to strengthen the hypothesis. These cracks appear to be flexural cracks and their direction (perpendicular to the skew) would indicate that the direction of primary bending is parallel to the skew.

Note that this change in the load carrying path during the test has important consequences since the change occurs between the service load and the ultimate load. The bridge had different behavior and boundary conditions at service load levels than it does at ultimate load levels. Therefore, models based on service behavior may not correctly predict ultimate behavior and models based on ultimate behavior may not correctly predict service load responses.

The final failure was in flexural shear. This was not expected since analysis had indicated that shear should not be a problem. This final failure does not appear to be related to the mechanisms previously discussed and is believed to be caused by exceeding the shear capacity of the weakened and deteriorated shoulder region. Once the shear capacity of the shoulder region was exceeded, the crack propagated as shown in Figure 11, following the ends of cutoff bars at the top of the slab.

It must be again noted that analysis indicated the bridge had sufficient shear capacity to hold the failure load and the failure is thought to have occurred because of lower shear capacity in the deteriorated shoulder region. The shear strength of the shoulder region cannot be determined because no method exists for determining the capacities of deteriorated concrete. However, the shear stress along the failure plane has been estimated to be $0.95(f'_c)^{0.5}$, about half of the usual value of $2(f'_c)^{0.5}$. More work is needed in this area.

It is interesting to note that top bars in the deteriorated shoulder section did not pull out, even though they exposed. After the conclusion of the destructive test, one of the exposed rebars on the damaged shoulders was subjected to a pull out test. This test was performed away from the loaded span so the failure damage would not affect the test. The bar was 3.6m (12') long and only about 1/2 the perimeter of the bar was embedded in the concrete. In spite of the fact that the entire top of the bar was exposed, the bar did not pull out and it was possible to yield the bar. Unfortunately, time did not permit further testing, but another project testing the pullout strength of bars in deteriorated concrete is underway.

BRIDGE RATING

The bridge was rated using the 1983 AASHTO Manual for Maintenance and Inspection of Bridges (with 1989 revisions)[3] and the 1989 Guide Specifications for Strength Evaluation of Existing Steel and Concrete Bridges[1]. For a bridge built in 1954, both specifications recommend using f'_c = 3000 psi or 21 MPa for the concrete. The steel is assumed to have a yield strength of f_y = 33000 psi or 230 MPa. The critical rating using these properties are given in Table 1. The bridge was rated again using the actual measured properties (Table 1). The results show that the bridge would be rated as deficient if the assumed properties are used but adequate using the measured properties.

The 1989 Guide Specifications[1] also allow for rating the bridge using finite element analysis. Such a rating was performed and is shown in Table 1. Use of a finite element analysis greatly increased the rating. However, it is important to note that rating does not give a clear picture of the actual bridge capacity. The rating is the ratio of the supply (capacity) to the demand (load). Using the actual capacity measured from the destructive load test, the rating would have been about 20. This is an order of magnitude above the highest critical rating in Table 1. It should also be noted that AASHTO rating method would have rated the bridge as deficient (using the recommended material properties), yet the bridge held a far greater load than could ever be placed on it. The final failure load was equivalent to 22 eighteen wheel truck, but it would have been impossible to fit any more nine such trucks on the bridge even if the shoulder areas were used.

Table 1 - Bridge Rating

| | Critical Rating Factor | |
	Assumed Material Properties	Actual Material Properties
1983 AASHTO Maintenance Specifications[3]	0.99	1.76
1989 AASHTO Guide Specifications[1]	0.80	1.64
Finite Element Analysis	1.53	2.90

Note: The Critical Rating Factor was for the moment over the south pier line in all cases.

CONCLUSIONS:

1) Bridge testing can provide a large amount of information about bridge condition and performance. Nondestructive tests, such as truck load tests and modal tests, can detect hidden damage and the information from such tests can often be used in modeling the damage in an analysis.

2) Service load testing can be used to determine structural performance under normal loading conditions, but the results cannot always be extrapolated to ultimate load conditions. Changes in the structure which occur during loading (especially in structural stiffness or boundary conditions) may invalidate the extrapolation.

3) Slab bridges are not being used to their full capacity. The damaged bridge in this test still held the equivalent of 22 eighteen wheel trucks, a greater load than could ever be realistically imposed on this bridge. Yet, this bridge was rated as deficient and scheduled for demolition. There is an obvious need for a better method of analysis for slab bridges.

4) There is also a need for better method of judging the properties of deteriorated concrete. The final shear failure of the bridge was probably caused by exceeding the shear capacity of the deteriorated shoulders. However, this failure could not be predicted since no information is available on shear strength of deteriorated concrete.

ACKNOWLEDGEMENTS

The authors gratefully acknowledge the support of the Ohio Department of Transportation and the Federal Highway Administration (Contract #14482 (O)) and the National Science Foundation (Grant #MSM-9002820, Dr. Ken Chong, Program Director). They also wish to thank Mr. W. Edwards, Engineer of Research and Development; Mr. V. Dalal, Research and Development Bureau; Mr. D. Hanhilammi, Engineer of Bridges; Mr. R. Eltzroth, District 8 Bridge Engineer; and Mr. W. Fair, District 8 Chief of Operations; all of the Ohio Department of Transportation. This project was done in association with the firm of Wiss, Janney, Elstner Associaties, Northbrook, Illinois. Some of the instrumentation used in this project, the installation of that instrumentation and one of the data acquisition systems was provided by WJE under and NSF contract. The authors thank WJE for their cooperation.

REFERENCES

1. Guide Specification for Strength Evaluation of Existing Steel and Concrete Highway Bridges, American Association of State Highway and Transportation Officials, Washington, D. C., 1989.

2. Raghavendrachar, M. and Aktan, A. E., "Flexibility by Multi-Reference Impact Testing for Bridge Diagnostics," Journal of the Structural Division, ASCE, August, 1992

3. Manual for Maintenance and Inspection of Bridges, American Association of State Highway and Transportation Officials, Washington, D. C., 1983, revisions 1989.

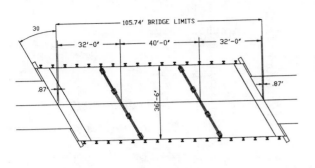

Figure 1: Test Bridge

Figure 2: Damaged Shoulders with Exposed Rebar

Figure 3 Damaged Sides

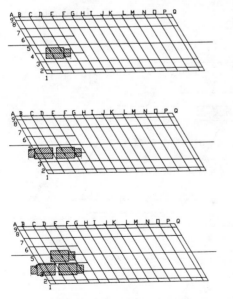

Figure 4: Truck Load Test Positions (Load Cases 1 - 3, top to bottom, left; Load Cases 4 - 6, top to bottom, right)

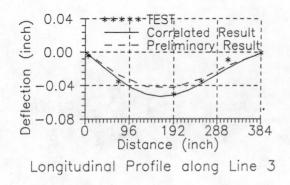

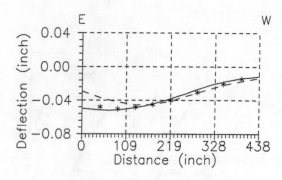

Longitudinal Profile along Line 3

Transverse Profile along Line D

Figure 5: Comparison of Truck Load Test Results with Analytical Models

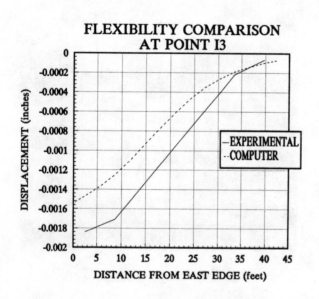

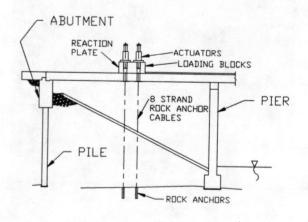

Figure 6: Comparison of Modal Test Results with Analytical Model

Figure 7: Loading System

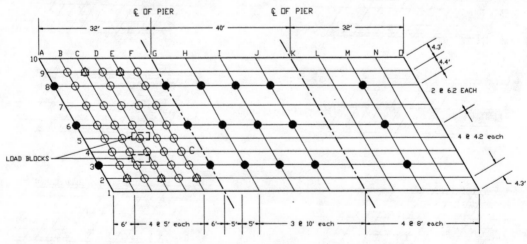

○ Vertical Wire Pot (qty. 38)
● Vertical DCDT Instrument location (qty. 18)
△ Horizontal DCDT Instrument Location (qty. 6)

Figure 8: Deflection Instrumentation Grid

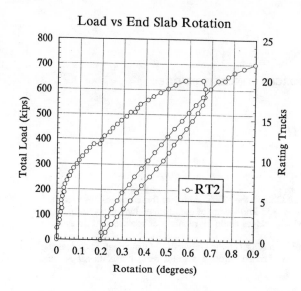

Load vs End Slab Rotation

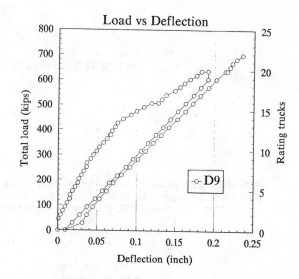

Load vs Deflection

Figure 9: Load vs. Rotation at Point A6

Figure 10: Load vs. Deflection at Point D9

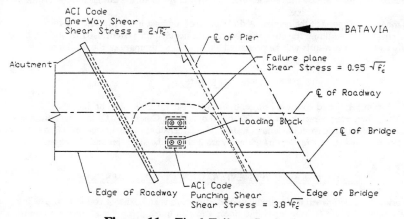

Figure 11: Final Failure Surface

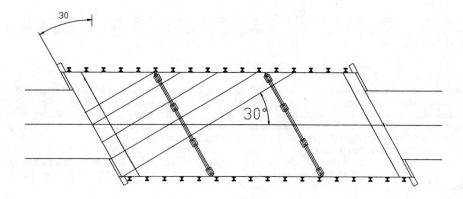

Figure 12: Load Carrying Mechanism for a Skew Bridge

DESTRUCTIVE TESTING OF A REINFORCED CONCRETE BRIDGE

F. Dirk Heidbrink

INTRODUCTION

A large number of reinforced concrete bridges were built in the state of Ohio in the 1950's. Many of these bridges have reached their design life and are badly deteriorated. It has become desirable to gain knowledge of the ultimate load capacity in order to determine which bridges need to be immediately replaced and which bridges could be repaired or replacement delayed.

A test program was initiated with the Ohio Department of Transportation (ODOT), the University of Cincinnati (UC) and the firm of Wiss, Janney, Elstner Associates, Inc. (WJE). The project was funded through a grant from the National Science Foundation.

The test program included choosing a suitable bridge to be tested, performing a computer structural analysis of the bridge and performing non-destructive tests and a destructive load test on the bridge to failure. At the conclusion of the test, the values obtained from the load test were input into the computer analysis to more accurately estimate the ultimate capacity of the bridge. The data will be archived for future use by universities and the private sector in the design of new bridges.

This paper describes the testing aspects of the bridge. A description of the load test frame and the instrumentation installed on the bridge will be discussed. In addition, the computer-based data acquisition system used to acquire the data will also be discussed. A brief discussion of the results will be presented along with a summary of the findings.

TEST SPECIMEN

The test structure is a 3-span reinforced concrete bridge, built in the early 1950's. The bridge, shown in Fig. 1, is located on Route 222 in Clermont County, approximately 48 Km (30 miles) outside of Cincinnati, Ohio. The abutments and piers of the bridge are skewed at a 30 degree angle from the lane of traffic. The dimensions of the bridge are 9.8 m (32 ft) at the end spans, 12.2 m (40 ft) in the center span and 11.1 m (36.5 ft) wide. Figure 2 shows the site plan and elevation.

COMPUTER ANALYSIS AND BRIDGE CONDITION SURVEY

An inspection of the bridge was performed to document as-built dimensions and existing conditions. The information obtained along with drawings supplied by ODOT were input into linear and non-linear computer analysis programs. The results from the computer study were used to locate instrumentation for the load test. It was decided that the first span of the bridge would be loaded since it has both a free-end (simple) support and a continuous support condition.

After the bridge was closed to traffic, an asphalt overlay was removed from the bridge deck. During this process, spalled and deteriorated concrete was also removed. The concrete was found to be deteriorated below the level of top reinforcing steel over a large area of the bridge deck.

LOAD TEST FRAME

The application of load was placed in the center of the south end-span in the northbound lane. Load was applied to the bridge through the use of rock anchor cables. A total of 4 eight-strand anchors were grouted into core holes drilled 13.7 m (45 ft) into bed-rock, and extended through core holes drilled in the bridge deck. Two concrete blocks were cast integrally into the concrete deck with the use of dowel bars. The block dimensions were chosen to simulate the footprint of a typical tandem-wheel trailer. Two holes were cast through the height of each concrete block over the holes cored through the concrete bridge deck. As shown in Fig. 3, a 305 mm (12-in) stroke 20,600 KPa (3,000 psi) servo controlled hydraulic actuator was placed over each rock anchor, on top of the concrete block. Each of the four actuators had a capacity of 1500 KN (340,000 lbs). This permitted loading the bridge with up to 6200 KN (1.4 million lbs). A computer-controlled servo system was used to control the application of load to the bridge.

F. Dirk Heidbrink is a Senior Engineer with Wiss, Janney, Elstner Associates, Inc., Northbrook, Illinois 60062

INSTRUMENTATION

A variety of instruments were required to adequately monitor the behavior of the bridge during the load test. Vertical displacements of the bridge were monitored using wire potentiometers and Linear Variable Differential Transformers (LVDT's). The wire pots were located at points of large deflections, each pot having a stroke of 254 mm (10 in). The LVDT's were used at supports and non-loaded spans where displacements would be less than their allowable stroke of 51 mm (2 in). The locations of the 56 vertical displacements are shown in Fig. 4.

LVDT's were also used to monitor column rotations and strains in the concrete bridge deck. Column rotations were monitored by mounting two LVDT's horizontally a known distance apart, as shown in Fig. 5. Strain in the concrete deck was monitored by measuring the displacement of an LVDT over a 254 mm (10-in) gage length (Fig. 6). LVDT's were mounted directly over each other on the top and bottom of the bridge deck in both the longitudinal and transverse directions.

Strain in the reinforcing steel was monitored by installing strain gages directly on exposed bars. A pachometer was used to locate the embedded steel. Concrete was chipped away until a sufficient amount was removed to apply the gages. On each bar, two strain gages were installed opposite each other and wired together to subtract out bending effects.

Load was monitored at each load point by installing a load cell in-line with the hydraulic actuators. Each load cell had a capacity of 1300 KN (300,000 lbs).

The lead wires from the instruments were brought to a central location inside a trailer. The wires were terminated on panel boards. The UC data acquisition system was capable of acquiring data on up to 64 channels of data. As shown in Fig. 7, the data system consisted of an OPTIM Megadac which was controlled by a PC computer. The remaining 81 channels of data were monitored by the system provided by WJE. The data system included a Hewlett-Packard (HP)3497A data acquisition unit interfaced to a portable PC computer (Fig. 8). The HP3497A has an internal 5-1/2 digit voltmeter capable of resolving voltages to the nearest microvolt. Software was designed by WJE to acquire data through manual keypress. Voltage readings were saved to hard disk with a date/time stamp after completion of each scan.

Commercial spreadsheet software was utilized in reducing the data from the two systems. After importing the scans for each load stage into the spreadsheet, formulas were written to reduce the data to engineering units. Plots of each instrument were readily obtained through the use of the spreadsheet software. A printer was used to make hard-copy plots in the field for use in determining the bridge behavior during testing.

DESTRUCTIVE TEST

A series of low load tests were performed on the bridge prior to the destructive test. The first tests were conducted to verify the output of the instrumentation and the performance of the loading system. Once the system was checked out and operating properly, additional load tests were conducted to check for gage drift and possible local yielding.

The destructive test was designed to be performed as a series of tests, each increasing in load until failure occurred. Between tests, the load was removed from the bridge to check for yielding of any members and to observe for consistencies or abnormalities between the different test series. A plot of a typical vertical displacement instrument is shown in Fig. 9.

The tests were performed over a period of three days. On the final day, the bridge was loaded to 780 KN (176,000 lbs) per actuator, or 3100 KN (704,000 lbs) of total load on the bridge. After obtaining readings on the instruments, a sudden and unexpected failure in the bridge occurred. The bridge failed in the region near the first interior column of the loaded span. As shown in Fig. 10, the failure mode was a shear failure in the bridge deck. The failure occurred earlier and at a lower load level than expected. Spalling of the concrete on the top reinforcing steel occurred from years of damage from freeze-thaw cycling and corrosion of the reinforcing steel. Since insufficient concrete covered the reinforcing steel, the bars near the surface of the bridge deck did not behave as would normally be expected.

For a bridge with sufficient concrete cover over the top reinforcing steel, the expected behavior of the bridge during loading would be increasing load with increasing deflection downward. At some point, the load would drop off while downward deflection would continue. The failure would be gradual and the bridge would creak and groan as various structural members failed and other members carried the load.

DISCUSSION

Although the failure load was lower than expected, the value was much higher than could be physically applied to the bridge. The 3100 KN (704,000 lbs) applied to fail the bridge is equivalent to approximately 18 fully loaded trucks. Since only one truck would fit on the span at a time, it would be virtually impossible to place that many trucks on the bridge and cause a failure.

The failure mode is a more interesting finding from this load test. The sudden shear failure was unexpected and was not taken into account in the computer analyses. In order to prevent this type of failure, periodic maintenance and renovation of the bridge deck under extreme conditions must be performed.

Currently, the data from the load test are being analyzed and archived. It is hoped that the data will be useful in the future in the design and analysis of bridges.

ACKNOWLEDGEMENTS

The author wishes to acknowledge the support of the National Science Foundation and the contribution of Mr. Vic Dalal and the staff at the Ohio Department of Transportation who provided the bridge and many hours of their time during the conduct of the load test. The author also wishes to thank Drs. Aktan, Miller and Shahrooz and the graduate students at the University of Cincinnati for their tireless support in conducting the load test.

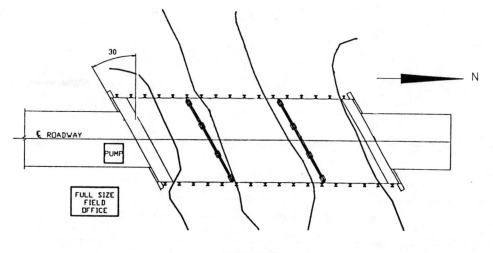

SITE PLAN

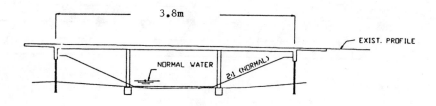

SITE ELEVATION

Fig. 2 - Site plan and elevation

Figure 3 - Loading system

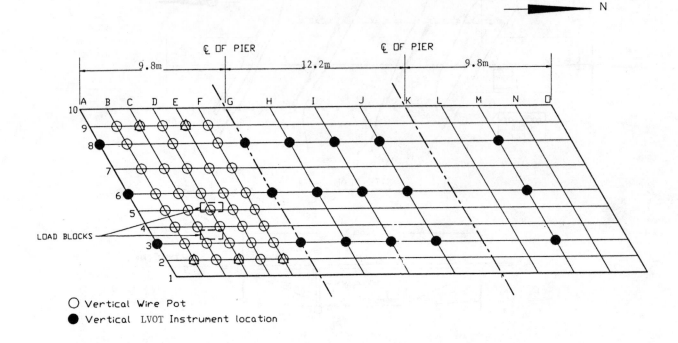

Fig. 4 - Location of vertical displacement instrumentation

Fig. 5 - Column rotation instruments

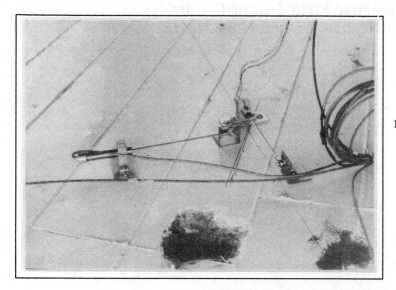

Fig. 6 - Measurement of concrete
strains on underside of
bridge deck

Fig. 7 - UC data acquisition system

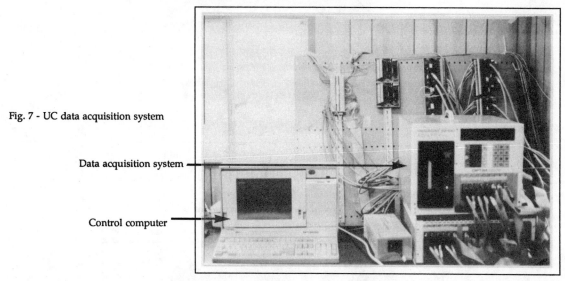

Data acquisition system

Control computer

Fig. 8 - WJE acquisition system

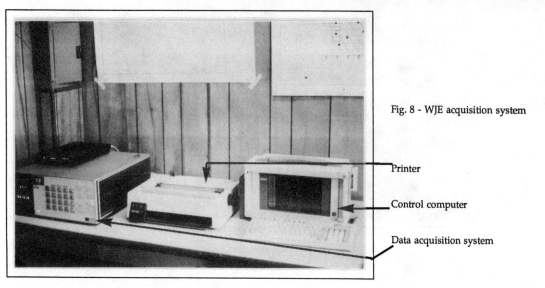

Printer

Control computer

Data acquisition system

Destructive Field Test of R/C Bridge
Vertical Deflection Gage No. D5

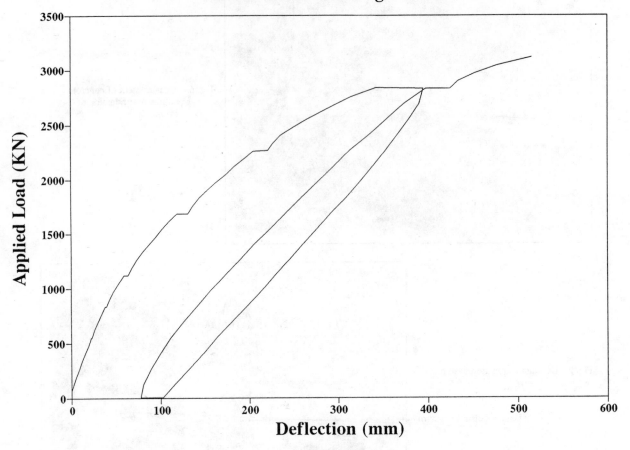

Fig. 9 - Typical vertical displacement plot

Location of failure

Fig. 10 - Failure mode

INVESTIGATION OF REBAR CORROSION IN
A REINFORCED CONCRETE SUBWAY TUNNEL

Ashok M. Kakade, Harvey Haynes, P.E., and Kerri M. Howell, P.E.[1]

ABSTRACT

The paper presents findings of an investigation of corrosion damage in a box type reinforced concrete subway tunnel in Oakland, California. The tunnel is situated about 9.8 m (30 ft) below ground level and passes under an estuary which carries seawater to an artificial lake. The tunnel is used for local commuter trains which are powered by a high voltage third rail system.

The tunnel walls exhibited spalling from rebar corrosion in certain locations. Hence, an investigation was conducted to identify the cause of rebar corrosion and determine if the exterior face of the tunnel in contact with soil was also delaminated from rebar corrosion.

The investigation consisted of sounding tests to identify delaminations on the interior surfaces, and impact-echo tests to determine the wall thickness and identify delaminations on the exterior wall surfaces. Cores were drilled at potential delamination locations identified by impact-echo tests. Half-cell potential tests were conducted to determine degree of variation in potential, as an indication of corrosion activity. Stray current tests were performed to determine the effects of the system operating voltage on rebar potentials. Soil borings were taken adjacent to the tunnel to obtain soil samples for chloride analysis. Concrete cores from the walls were tested for compressive strength and chloride contents.

The findings showed that the rebars were corroding for a combination of reasons. The running rails, which act as the return path for the operating current, appeared to be not sufficiently insulated. This allows some current to flow along the reinforcement. High chloride contents on both the interior and exterior face of the wall and low cover to rebars were another contributing factors to the corrosion of the reinforcement on the interior of the tunnel.

INTRODUCTION

The subway tunnel was located about 9.8 m (30 ft) below ground level and 6.6 m (20 ft) below ground water level. Part of the tunnel passed under an estuary, which provides seawater to a man made lake. Figure 1 shows a cross-sectional view of the tunnel. The tunnel was a dual-box type reinforced concrete structure; the west side tunnel was referred to as tunnel A1 and the east side as tunnel A2. The structure was constructed around 1970 to carry local commuter trains. The trains operate on a third rail direct

[1]Ashok M. Kakade is Senior Engineer and Harvey Haynes is President of Haynes & Associates. Kerri Howell is Manager, Engineering Services, with V & A Associates.

current system.

The tunnel showed significant corrosion of reinforcement by delaminating the concrete cover to the reinforcing steel in numerous areas. The tunnel had a design wall thickness of 61 cm (24 in) and two mats of reinforcing steel: one mat near the interior and the other near the exterior of the wall. Only the interior mat of reinforcing was visible regarding corrosion activity. The owner was concerned whether the exterior reinforcing mat was corroding, which may impair the strength of the tunnel wall.

This paper presents the findings of a limited investigation to determine if the exterior reinforcing steel was corroding and to determine if stray currents or chloride ions were the cause of the existing corrosion.

FIELD INVESTIGATIONS

The field investigations were conducted in two phases. Phase I consisted of a delamination survey of the interior surfaces of tunnels A1 and A2 to determine the extent and distribution of corrosion activity. This survey used a sounding technique of hitting the walls with either a hammer or a steel rod.

A non-destructive test, using the impact-echo method, was also conducted to identify potential delaminations on the exterior wall surface in a 19.7m (60 ft) long section of tunnel A1 and two 9.8m (30 ft) long sections of tunnel A2. The impact-echo test is a sonic test and typically involves hitting one side of the wall with a small instrumented impactor or hammer and recording the reflected wave energy with a receiver. The reflected frequency data were processed using Fourier transform operations to identify delamination areas. These areas were potential sites for drilling cores in the walls.

Phase II consisted of obtaining cores from the walls of tunnel A1 and tunnel A2 to determine the condition of the exterior reinforcing steel and whether delaminations existed on the exterior of the walls. The coring procedure required injecting polyurethane resin into three 15mm (0.6 in) diameter holes surrounding the core location. The polyurethane was required in order to create a waterproof plug behind the core locations as the cores were removed below the watertable and to fill any gaps from delaminations.

The coring operation consisted of drilling a six-inch diameter core, to the exterior steel, and then a two-inch diameter core through the remainder of the wall thickness. The concrete cores were tested for compressive strength and analyzed for chloride content. The chloride analysis was performed in accordance with the test method described in American Society for Testing and Materials (ASTM) C 1152-90. The cores taken through the wall were at a 19.7m (60 ft) section in tunnel A1, and a 8.8m (30 ft) section in tunnel A2.

Corrosion tests were conducted at the 19.7m (60 ft) section in tunnel A1. The tests included electrical continuity of the reinforcing steel, half cell potential tests, and stray current tests. Soil samples were obtained from borings located adjacent to the external walls of tunnels A1 and tunnel A2. The soil samples were then tested for resistivity and analyzed for pH, chlorides and sulphate contents.

RESULTS & DISCUSSION

Delamination Survey

Delaminated areas were found on the interior surfaces of the walls, roof, floor slab and rail support pads. In some locations the delaminations coincided with leaks occurring at cracks or construction joints. However, delaminations had also occurred where there was no evidence of leaking water. Figure 2 shows a typical portion of wall having delaminations and corroded reinforcement. The rail support pads showed extensive delaminations, as seen in Figure 3.

The data obtained during impact-echo tests was used to select coring locations at areas which showed probable delamination cracks in the walls. In actuality, the cores did not show any delaminations, so the usefulness of the impact-echo data was questionable.

Tests on Cores

Wall Thickness
Two cores obtained from tunnel A1, and one core from tunnel A2, measured 60.2, 61.0, 62.2 cm (23.7, 24.0, and 24.5 inches) as opposed to 53.6, 69.1, 62.5 cm (21.1, 27.2, and 24.6 inches) estimated by impact-echo test. The impact-echo results overestimated the wall thickness by a range of 0.25 to 8.1 cm (0.1 to 3.2 inches).

The design thickness of the walls was 61cm (24 inches). Hence, the as-built thickness of the wall, in the regions tested, had a tolerance variation of minus 0.8 cm (0.3 inches) and plus 1.3 cm (0.5 inches) as compared to the design dimensions.

Compressive Strength
The compressive strengths of the three cores obtained from the 19.7 m (60 ft) section of the wall in tunnel A1 were 36.3, 41.2, 45.0 MPa (5,260, 5,970, 6,530 psi); the average was 40.8 MPa (5,920 psi) with a coefficient of variation of 11 percent. The compressive strength of the core from the 9.8 m (30 ft) section of wall in tunnel A2 was 54.1 MPa (7,840 psi).

Corrosion and Cover
The exterior reinforcement in the wall was examined for corrosion after the coring operations. The exterior reinforcement did not show corrosion.

Concrete cover to the exterior reinforcement was an average of 114 mm (4-1/2 inches) of concrete. On the interior face, the average cover was 32 mm (1-1/4)inches and the steel showed signs of corrosion. At certain other locations on the interior face, where delamination had occurred, the concrete cover was measured at 19 mm (3/4 inches).

Waterproof Coating
The exterior surface of the cores was examined for evidence of waterproof coating upon removal of the core. A bituminous coating was found on only one core in tunnel A2. The cores from tunnel A1 did not show evidence that a coating had been applied.

<u>Chloride Content</u>
The chloride content of the cores are shown in Figure 4. The chloride concentration for cores from tunnel A1 was higher than tunnel A2. In tunnel A1, the chloride concentration was 2.67 kg/m^3 (4.5 lb/cy) of concrete at 25 mm (1 inch) from the exterior face of the wall. The chloride level decreased to an average 0.45 kg/m^3 (0.75 lb/cy) in the middle two-thirds of the wall thickness and again increased to 2.55 kg/m^3 (4.3 lb/cy) at 25 mm (1 inch) from the interior surface. In tunnel A2, the chloride levels at 13 mm (1/2 inch) from the exterior face, in the middle two-thirds, and 25 mm (1 inch) from the interior face were 1.92, 0.08, 0.77 kg/m^3 (3.24, 0.13, and 1.3 lb/cy), respectively.

From the distribution pattern of chloride ions in the wall, it was apparent that water containing chlorides entered the concrete at the exterior face and evaporated on the interior face, leaving behind chloride salts. Over the years the chlorides accumulated at the interior face. The absence of a bituminous coating on the exterior surface in tunnel A1 allowed for passage of more water and thereby more chlorides to enter the concrete. The lower chloride level in tunnel A2 was probable due to a bituminous coating on the exterior surface, due to higher quality concrete, or both. The concrete in tunnel A2 likely had lower permeability characteristics than that of the concrete of tunnel A1, as evidenced by the higher compressive strength.

The chloride contents near the faces of the concrete walls were sufficiently high to contribute to corrosion activity of the steel. The National Association of Corrosion Engineers suggest a chloride content of 0.59 kg/m^3 (1.0 lb/cy) of concrete as the threshold level for corrosion initiation.

Oxygen is a critical element in the corrosion process. On the interior wall of the tunnel, the low concrete cover to the steel allowed for sufficient oxygen to be available, in the presence of the chlorides and moisture in the concrete, to drive an active corrosion cell. On the exterior wall of the tunnel, the availability of oxygen was limited; hence, corrosion was not found on the exterior reinforcing steel mat.

Corrosion Tests

<u>Electrical Continuity</u>
Electrical continuity tests showed that the interior and exterior reinforcement in the concrete wall was electrically continuous. Because no reinforcing steel was exposed on the floor of the tunnel, no measurements were made to determine continuity between the floor and wall.

<u>Soil Tests</u>
The soil resistivity was low, which meant it represented a "very corrosive environment". Chemical analyses showed that the soil was slightly alkaline with a pH value of 8.4. The sulphate content was found to be low and not harmful to concrete. The chloride content averaged 1810 ppm, with a maximum value of 3,600 ppm. (The sea water has a chloride content that can vary from 4,000 to 20,000) Hence, the water in contact with the tunnel could be defined as brackish.

<u>Half Cell Potential Tests</u>
The half cell potential test is a non-destructive test to determine the degree of corrosion inside reinforced concrete. The test was used to calculate differences in potentials at

various locations. Corrosion activity is the result of variations in potential values of metals contained in a single electrolyte or environment. The test results showed that the highest potential values were on the floor slab, but the highest differences in potentials were occurring in an area near the bottom of the wall. The lower part of the walls was the location that showed rebar corrosion.

<u>Stray Current Tests</u>

Stray current tests consisted of measuring the electrical potentials of reinforcement over a 24 hr period, which included both train maintenance and train operation time. The tests showed that the potential between the front and the back reinforcing steel mats varied by an average 0.20 millivolt. An experiment was conducted to estimate the current flowing through a 3.9 m (12 ft) span of reinforcement. The average current was estimated at 0.45 amperes.

The system was designed for current to return to the station via the return rails, that is the train track. Where track isolation is not entirely effective, current can discharge into or be picked-up by the track from reinforcing steel in the concrete. Corrosion occurs at locations were current leaves the reinforcing steel. The presence of delaminations in the rail support pads indicates that stray currents flow from the reinforcing steel to the track. Results from the delaminations survey show much distress in the rail support pads, especially at the track fasteners.

Stray current is believed to be a relatively minor contributor to the corrosion activity found at the tunnel walls. Reinforcement corrosion at these locations were likely due to the presence of a high chloride content in the concrete and availability of oxygen and moisture to drive the corrosion cell. The lack of sufficient concrete cover to the reinforcing steel has permitted to corrosion to occur sooner than if the cover were thicker. Although the exterior reinforcing steel had an environment with a high chloride and moisture content, the lack of oxygen prevented the reinforcement from corroding.

RECOMMENDATIONS

Further investigations are recommended to determine the extent of existing damage to the structure. Electrical tests should be conducted in the rail support pads, at track fastener locations, to investigate further the stray current corrosion problem.

Corrosion in the floor slab needs to be investigated further to determine if the high potential values, from the half cell potential tests, actually indicate significant on-going corrosion. After the investigative work is accomplished, a suitable cathodic protection system should be designed for the tunnel to assure an extended life for the structure.

CONCLUSIONS

The investigation findings showed that the reinforcement on the interior face was corroding and the major causes of corrosion were high chloride content in concrete, low concrete cover, and availability of oxygen and moisture. The exterior reinforcement did not show corrosion, even though the chloride content was high; however, oxygen availability was low.

The results of the stray current tests indicated that a small current was flowing along the reinforcing steel in the walls; this stray current was a minor contributor to the corrosion activity in the walls.

It was likely that stray currents were the cause of rebar corrosion in the rail support pads. The extent of rebar corrosion next to the track fasteners was significant, which indicated ineffective insulators.

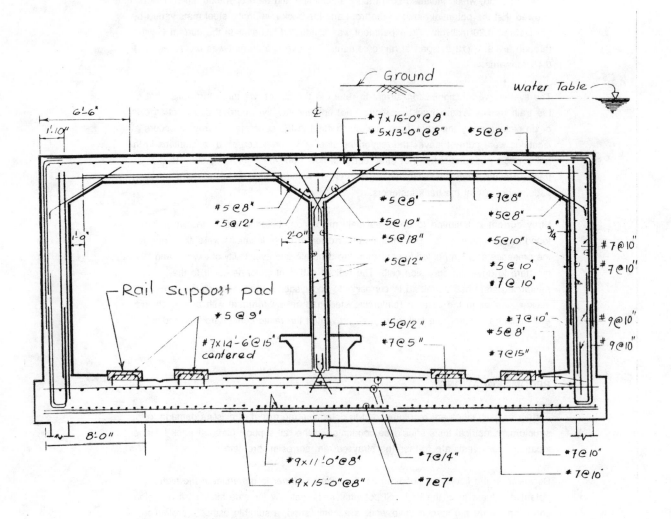

Figure 1. Cross sectional details of the tunnel.

Figure 2. Delaminated concrete cover removed from corroded reinforcing steel in wall of tunnel A1.

Figure 3. Delaminated area at the rail support pad.

Tunnel A1, Location: 961+57-2

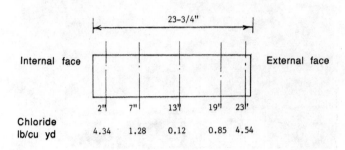

Internal face   External face

	2"	7"	13"	19"	23"
Chloride lb/cu yd	4.34	1.28	0.12	0.85	4.54

Tunnel A2, Location: 962+05-4

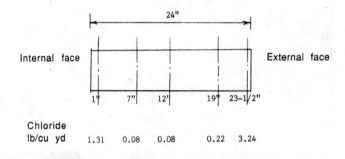

Internal face   External face

	1"	7"	12"	19"	23-1/2"
Chloride lb/cu yd	1.31	0.08	0.08	0.22	3.24

Figure 4. Chloride analyses results.

INFLUENCE OF COMPACTOR FOOTPRINTS ON PAVEMENT PERFORMANCE

Jeff Budiman[1], Johan Wibowo[2]

ABSTRACT

The subgrade soil was mixed in the laboratory and compacted using compactors of three different footprint types. The study was conducted through triaxial tests and pavement section model tests under dynamic loading. The results show significant variation in the response; samples compacted by the compactor with pyramid frustum protrusion base showed the highest lateral stiffness followed by samples compacted with cylindrical protrusion and finally those compacted with the smooth footprint. However, samples compacted with the flat/smooth-base showed the stiffest response in the vertical direction. In the pavement section model tests, the results show that although the subgrade of the models were of the same density, the monitored displacements of elements within each pavement system were significantly influenced by the type of footprint used during compaction.

INTRODUCTION

The performance of a flexible pavement is influenced by many factors such as the type of asphalt, asphalt content, type of aggregate, gradation, density, type of subgrade, method of compaction, temperature, climate, magnitude and frequency of loads, and other variables. The complex interaction of all these factors yields a composite behavior for a particular pavement structure that can become evident in the form of distress (or perhaps failure) such as cracking, rutting, potholes and so forth.

When the wheel load is transmitted to the pavement, it causes the in situ stresses within the pavement system to change. Figure 1 illustrates the major principal stress within the pavement system under a wheel load, it shows that the magnitude and the orientation of the major principal stress varies from element to element within the system. The direction of the major principal stress directly under the contact area is primarily vertical and gradually rotates to other directions as the stresses are distributed away from the loaded area. As the traffic continues to flow, the pavement system will be subjected to repeated loads of various rates and intensities, which in turn cause the in situ principal stress magnitudes and directions to change constantly, similar to the stress field shown in Figure 1. If the subgrade soils were isotropic, the rotating principal stress field would have no influence on the material response. Unfortunately, real soils are anisotropic.

Research findings [2, 4, 5, 8, 9] indicate that soils have the weakest constitutive response in the direction perpendicular to the past major principal stress direction. As seen in Figure 1, the vertical deflection of the pavement is not only controlled by the stiffness of the material in the vertical direction, but is also significantly affected by the stiffness moduli of the material in other directions, including the stiffness in the lateral/horizontal direction which possesses the lowest value. Therefore, if the lateral stiffness modulus of the material can be increased during construction, the vertical deflection will be significantly reduced.

During construction, the subgrade soil is compacted using various types of compacting equipment depending on the type of soil. The selection of a compactor is primarily based on the effectiveness of the energy transferred to a given volume of soil to achieve a certain density, while the lateral stiffness modulus of the compacted material has not been considered as a design criterion. Since a smooth wheel roller compacts the soil by a kneading mechanism while the sheepsfoot roller type by a combination of shearing and kneading mechanisms, the soil fabrics thus produced are also different, which directly affect their stiffness moduli. In this investigation, three different types of compactor footprint were used to study their influence on the stress-strain behavior of compacted soil. The three types of compactor footprints were flat (smooth), cylindrical protrusion base, and pyramid frustum protrusion base.

---

[1]Assistant Professor of Civil Engineering, Illinois Institute of Technology, Chicago, Illinois, USA

[2]Graduate Student, University of Colorado, Boulder Colorado, USA. Formerly Research Assistant, Illinois Institute of Technology, Chicago Illinois.

TEST MATERIAL

A mixture of 65% Ottawa sand No. 30, 5% silica silt, and 30% Kaolin clay represented the subgrade material. The soil had a Liquid Limit of 25%, a Plastic Limit of 19% and a Plasticity Index of 6%. This soil was classified as A-2-4 according to the AASHTO classification system and rated as excellent to good for subgrade. A compaction test was performed according to AASHTO Standard T-99 (ASTM D-1557) to determine the variation of the dry density with respect to water content. The value of optimum moisture content (OMC) was 9.75% with the maximum dry density 2.03 g/cm^3. The specimens were compacted to 95% relative compaction, the dry density of the soil was 1.93 g/cm^3 and the moisture content was 11.5%.

SPECIMEN PREPARATION

The soil mixture was compacted in a large, stiff walled mold in layers using the static undercompaction technique [3] to achieve dry density of 1.93 g/cm^3. After each layer was compacted, the surface was scratched/roughened to ensure continuity with the following layer. The compaction load was applied to the specimen through a rigid metal plate in a universal loading machine. Three different metal bases were used, each represented a type of footprint of the compactor, namely: the flat smooth base, the sheepsfoot type with cylindrical protrusion, and the tampingfoot type with the pyramid frustum protrusion as shown in Figures 3, 4 and 5. The cylindrical protrusion was 12.7 mm in diameter and 25.4 mm high. The spacing of the protrusions was 3.5 times the diameter and was arranged in a triangular pattern. The pyramid frustum protrusion had the same height and volume as the cylindrical ones. The position of the projection on each layer was unchanged during compaction, i.e. the location of each protrusion on the footprint of each succeeding layer was exactly above the previous one.

For the triaxial tests, in order to simulate the rotation of the principal stress direction relative to the material principal axes of elements within the subgrade, three specimens were prepared from each block sample, each specimen was cut and trimmed in a different orientation relative to the direction of compaction load, i.e., vertical, inclined (45°), and horizontal as shown in Figure 3. By this trimming method, a relative rotation of the principal stress direction with respect to the material's plane of anisotropy (resulting from the maximum past pressure due to compaction) could be achieved. These three specimens represented the three elements at different coordinates in the pavement system where the major principal stress rotates from the vertical, inclined and to the horizontal directions. The triaxial specimen was 71 mm (2.8 in.) in diameter and 152 mm (6 in.) in height. After trimming the specimen to the required size and orientation, the specimen was carefully placed in the triaxial cell following the standard procedures. The outer cell was then mounted to the base and the chamber was filled with water for testing.

TRIAXIAL TEST RESULTS AND DISCUSSION.

The loading machine used in this experiment was the Material Testing System (MTS) Closed-Loop Servo Hydraulic System Model 810. It has the capability to deliver dynamic loads of various rates and shapes to the specimen. The initial seating load was chosen to be 34 kPa (5 psi) to simulate the overburden pressure. The water content of the specimen was inadequate to permit full saturation of the pores, and thus there was no porewater pressure buildup during loading; therefore, the experiment was conducted under drained conditions. The confining pressure of 172 kPa (25 psi) was applied to the cell, the maximum deviator stress was 275 kPa (40 psi), and the cyclic haversine load was applied to the specimen. The 275 kPa deviator stress represented average wheel pressure within the subgrade soil. The effects of confining pressure and rate of loading in the cyclic triaxial tests have been studied by many investigators and in literature, e. g.: [1, 6, 7]. The number of recorded deformations during the test was selected according to the following intervals; every cycle for the first 50 cycles, every tenth cycle between 51-150 cycles, and every 50th cycle between 151-10,000 cycles. The response included the maximum and minimum stress-strain relationships for a particular cycle of loading, meanwhile detailed data on every cycle was stored in an output file. The test was stopped after 10,000 cycles where the strains were relatively constant under the given load.

The triaxial tests results are shown in Figures 4,5 and 6. Figure 4 shows the response of samples compacted with the smooth flat base compactor. For the vertical specimen ($\Psi=0°$, specimen trimmed with longitudinal axis in vertical direction), the total strain after 10,000 load cycles is about 0.56%, with a large percentage of the strain accumulated in the first few load cycles and very little thereafter. The maximum strain is defined here at maximum load while the minimum strain is at the end of unloading, the curves show very little increase in strain after the first few cycles. For the specimen with $\Psi=45°$, the response is similar to that observed in the vertical specimen, however, the magnitude of the strain is higher. For the same stress level and number of load application, e.g. first cycle, the maximum strain in the vertical sample is 0.46% while in the inclined sample the strain is 0.96% or more than two magnitudes of the strain in the vertical sample, and the permanent strain at the end of the test is also significantly higher in the inclined sample. The response of the horizontal sample (Ψ=90°) under the same loading conditions shows a significant decrease in the stiffness modulus; here, the strain at the end of the test is 2.56% or 460% higher than that of vertical sample for the same loadings. In addition, the total strain increases rather gradually compared to the other two tests mentioned earlier.

The results of the tests for specimens compacted with the cylindrical protrusion compactor base are shown in Figures 5. The figure shows that the trends of the soil responses are similar to those observed in the sample compacted with the flat smooth base, i.e., the largest total strain occurs in the horizontal sample followed by the inclined sample and vertical sample. Furthermore, a significant percentage of the total strain is accumulated during the earlier load cycles. However, the magnitude of the total strains for the horizontal and inclined samples are lower than the corresponding strains for specimens compacted with the flat base for the same loading condition. On the contrary, the total strains in the vertical samples are higher than the corresponding strains for samples compacted with the flat base.

The response of specimens compacted with the pyramid frustum base compactor are shown in Figure 6. In general, the accumulation of the strain is similar to the previous cases, i.e., the strains for the horizontal samples are always the largest compared to those of inclined and vertical samples, where the vertical samples produced the smallest strains. After ten thousand cycles of loading, the vertical sample produced about 1.05% strain, while the horizontal sample has a strain of 1.65%, or about 57% more strain than the vertical sample, and the inclined sample produced 1.45% strain, or about 38% more than the strain in vertical sample. Again, the stiffness modulus of the vertical sample is higher than the other two samples. The difference in response is also shown in Figure 7, where the total strain of all samples are superimposed. It is shown that significant variation in strain occurred in the samples compacted with the flat base compactor, as indicated by the steeper slope of the line drawn through the three points of the total strain. The slope the curve for the samples compacted with pyramid protrusion base is the flattest among the three, showing less variation in the stiffness moduli of the material. An isotropic material would yield a flat horizonal line.

These results show that regardless of the type of footprint used, the specimens become anisotropic due to compaction, and thus they possess different characteristics in different directions with respect to the orientation of the compaction load (maximum pressure). In general, they are stiffer in the direction of maximum past pressure and softer/weaker in the direction perpendicular to the maximum past pressure. However, the effects of the footprints on the constitutive response are also clearly depicted. For the three vertical samples, the sample compacted with a flat base produced the lowest strain compared to those compacted with bases with cylinder or pyramid protrusions. However, for horizontal samples, the sample of flat base produced the largest strain. The strain from the three inclined samples show the same tendency as for the horizontal samples, but to a lesser degree. The results show that samples compacted with a protruded base compactor result in lesser variation in the stiffness of the samples in various directions. This observation also indicates that the lateral stiffness is significantly increased and thus the degree of anisotropy is reduced. The protrusion of pyramid frustum type is more effective than of cylinder type in increasing the horizontal stiffness of the soil. This shows the significant effect of the protrusion shape. It is believed that the effectiveness of the pyramid protrusion in compacting the soil is that when the soil is being compressed, the inclined walls of the pyramid also caused the soil to be displaced and thus compacted laterally as the protrusion penetrates into soil. At this stage, the lateral pressure in the soil generated by the inclined wall of the protrusion is higher than the lateral pressure generated within the soil when compacted with flat base compactor, or even with the cylinder type protrusion base.

MODEL TEST RESULTS AND DISCUSSION

In order to observe the influence of the types of compactor footprints on the deformation of soil within the subgrade layer, three model tests were performed in the laboratory. These models represented roadway cross section. Since the wheel load is symmetrical about the center of each lane, only one half of the section was necessary for modeling. Three models were compacted with compactors having three different types of footprint similar to those used for preparing triaxial specimens. The models were constructed in a plexiglas box, the 1 in. plexiglas wall was reinforced with steel C-channels from the outside to provide rigid boundaries for plane strain conditions. The transparent walls allowed direct observation to the subgrade. The subgrade layer of 10.16 x 50.8 x 30.48 cm was compacted in twelve layers using the undercompaction method similar to that used in preparing the triaxial samples. For the asphalt layer of the model, ready cold mixed asphalt was used and compacted to the

485

density of 2 ton/m^3. Thin teflon sheets were placed between the walls and the soil to eliminate friction at the interface. The deformation within the subgrade was observed by monitoring the displacements of twelve slender steel rods of 2.5 mm. in diameter which were penetrated into the subgrade model. Holes were drilled on one side of the wall to allow the penetration of these monitoring rods, the rods were inserted in the subgrade at specified coordinates. In addition, deformation within the subgrade was also observed through the movement oh pinheads which were implanted in the subgrade. To implant these pins, the wall opposite to the side where the steel rods were penetrated was temporarily removed, and 88 monitoring pins were inserted into the subgrade in a grid formation through the teflon sheet leaving only the pinheads exposed. During loading, the horizontal and vertical displacements of the rods that were implanted in the subgrade were monitored by utilizing Linear Voltage Displacement Transformers (LVDTs) and recorded periodically. Photographs were also taken periodically to trace the movement of the pinheads that were inserted into the subgrade. The magnitude and direction of displacement of each pinhead could then be measured from reference coordinates of the grids on the photographs using an x-y digitizer.

The same MTS Machine Model 810 used previously for dynamic triaxial tests was also utilized in this experiment. The dynamic loads of passing vehicles were assumed as haversine loads. A square plate of 10.16 x 10.16 cm was mounted to the base of the loading ram, in turn the dynamic contact pressure of 448 kPa (65 psi.) was transferred to the center of the model through this plate.

The results of the three model tests were plotted as shown in Figure 8. It was observed that the deformations of five rods that were located relatively far away from the loaded area were too small to be analyzed. The analysis was then focused on the results of the remaining seven rods, i.e. Rods No. 1, 2, 3, 5, 6, 7, and 9. For Rod No. 1, which was located at the top of subgrade and below the center of the loaded area, it was observed that for the model compacted with the flat base footprint, a vertical displacement of 4 mm occurred after 500 load cycles; while for models compacted with cylinder or pyramid frustum footprints, the same magnitude of displacement for Rod No. 1 was reached after only 25 load cycles. These observations show that the model compacted with the flat base compactor is stiffer in the vertical direction than the models compacted with cylinder or pyramid frustum compactor. After 10,000 load cycles, it was also observed that on Rods No. 2 and 6, the horizontal displacements were larger in the model compacted with the flat base compactor than in the models compacted with the cylinder or pyramid frustum compactors. To the contrary, the largest vertical displacement for these two rods occurred in the model compacted with the pyramid frustum compactor, followed by the displacement in the model compacted with the cylinder and flat base compactors respectively. Rods No. 3 and 4 moved away from the loaded area and upward, however, the magnitude was minuscule. Rods No. 5 and 9 on the model compacted with the flat base compactor deformed the least compared to the models compacted with cylinder or pyramid frustum base compactors. This shows that the model compacted with the flat base compactor is stiffer in the vertical direction than the other two models.

The results of these model tests were consistent with the results of the dynamic triaxial tests. It is obvious that the subgrade layer is anisotropic and the degree of that anisotropy can be reduced by using a compactor with a protrusion base. These model tests will provide very valuable data for future verification of the mathematical material constitutive models and numerical analyses.

CONCLUSIONS

During construction, the subgrade layer of pavement becomes anisotropic due to the loading by compaction equipment. The compacted soil is stiffer in vertical direction than in horizontal direction. The type of compactor footprint used in the compaction process also significantly influences the load-deformation behavior of the soil. This is illustrated by the fact that all specimens in this study were compacted to the same dry density, however they possessed different characteristics. This study also shows the importance of recognizing the material anisotropy, since using the stiffness modulus in the vertical direction alone as a design criteria may result in a faulty prediction of the service life of the pavement. It should be noted here that the laboratory specimens were compacted using static compaction and did not simulate the conditions of field compaction, primarily to control the density and uniformity of the specimens. The results above suggest that the combination of flat and pyramid footprints would result in higher stiffness moduli of the material. Further investigation on specimens compacted with rollers having different types and sizes of footprint should reveal other critical information regarding the improvements resulting in higher stiffness moduli of the subgrade material in highway construction.

ACKNOWLEDGEMENTS

The financial support for this research provided by Engineering Foundation under Grant No. RI-A-89-2 is greatly appreciated.

REFERENCES

[1] Brown, S.F. and Hyde, A.F.L. "The Significance of Cyclic Confining Stress in Repeated Load Triaxial Testing of Granular Materials," Transportation Research Record 537, TRB, National Research Council, Washington D.C., 1975.

[2] Budiman, J.S., Sture, S., Ko. H-Y. "Constitutive behavior of stress induced anisotropic cohesive soil" to be published, ASCE, Geotechnical Engineering Journal, September 1992.

[3] Ladd, R.S. "Preparing Test Specimen Using Undercompaction," ASTM, Geotechnical Testing Journal, Vol. 1, pp. 16-23, 1978.

[4] Lambe, T.W. "The Engineering Behavior of Compacted Soil," Journal SMFE, ASCE, vol 84, Proc. Paper 1655, 1958.

[5] Oda, M. "Anisotropic Strength of Cohesionless Sands," J. Geotechnical Div. ASCE, Vol. 107, GT9, pp 1219-1231, 1981.

[6] Pumphrey Jr, N.D. and Lentz, R.W. "Deformation Analysis of Florida Highway Subgrade Sand Subjected to Repeated Load Triaxial Tests. Transportation Research Record 1089, TRB, National Research Council, Washington D.C., 1986.

[7] Saada, A.S. and Ou, C.D.,"Strain-Stress Relations and Failure of Anisotropic Clays," Journal SMF Division, ASCE Vol. 99, No. SM12, 1973.

[8] Seed, H.B. and Chan, C.K. "Effect of Duration of Stress Application on Soil Deformation Under Repeated Loading," Proc. Fifth International Conference on Soil Mechanics and Foundation Engineering, Paris, 1961.

[9] Sture, S., Budiman, J.S., Ontuna, A.K., and Ko, H-Y. "Directional Shear Cell Experiments On a Dry Cohesionless Soil," ASTM, Geotechnical Testing Journal, Vol.10, No.2, 1987.

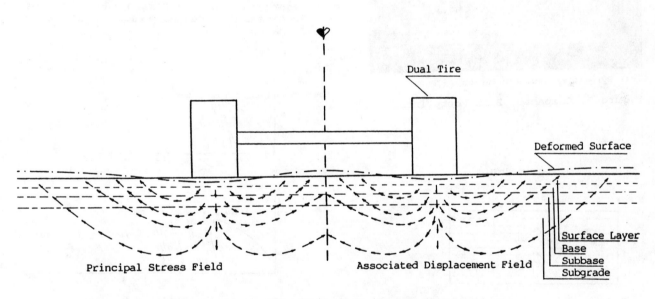

Figure 1. Approximate In Situ Principal Stress Field and the Associated Displacement Field

(a). Flat Base

(b). Cylindrical Protrusion

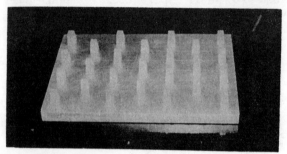

(c). Pyramid Frustum Protrusion

Figure 2. Compactor Base Footprints

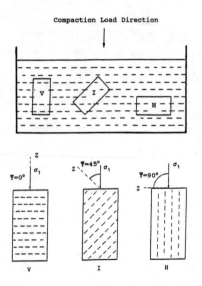

Figure 3. Triaxial Specimens

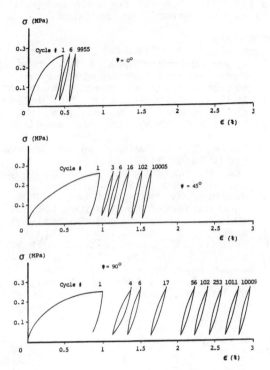

Figure 4. Stress-Strain Response of Specimens Compacted with Flat Base Compactor

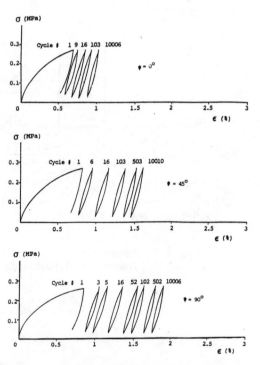

Figure 5. Stress-Strain Response of Specimens Compacted with Cylindrical Protrusion Base Compactor

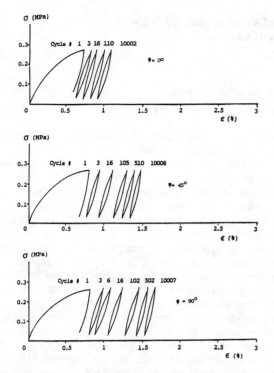

Figure 6. Stress-Strain Response of Specimens Compacted with Pyramid Frustum Protrusion Base Compactor

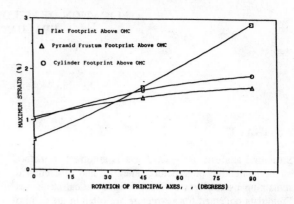

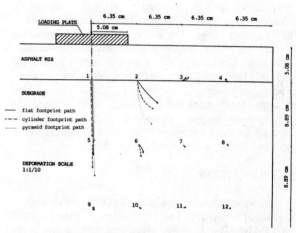

Figure 7. Strain after 10,000 Load Cycles

Figure 8. Displacement of Rods within Pavement Models after 10,000 Load Cycles

489

APPLICATION OF FIELD DATA TO FATIGUE PERFORMANCE
EVALUATION OF STRUCTURES

Jamshid Mohammadi[1] and Ramakrishna Polepeddi[2]

ABSTRACT

Structural analysis using field data is an effective method in the evaluation of structural integrity and prediction of remaining useful lives of many fatigue-critical structures. Field data collected for a structure are often in the form of internal strain (or stress) distribution at fatigue-critical structural components and/or in the form of parameters describing the dynamic behavior of the structure. Often information on a structure's different acceleration components is obtained to describe the dynamic behavior of the system. Depending on the type of data collected for a structural system, a specific analysis scheme needs to be developed consistent with the type of structure and the available field data for fatigue damage evaluation purposes. This paper presents an overview of different types of field data commonly collected for various structures and the corresponding fatigue analyses methods that are suitable to be used for these structures. The structures discussed are bridges, aircraft and railroad freight cars.

INTRODUCTION

Many structural systems experience fatigue damage as a result of the dynamic load environment they are subjected to. Bridges, for example, experience damage due to the internal stress fluctuation which happens as a result of vehicles passing over them. Aircraft are subjected to internal stress variation as a result of change in the cabin pressure or their different maneuvers (mainly in military applications). A railroad freight car develops fatigue damage due to its many different modes of vibration which occur as a result of the track irregularities. Marine structures are also develop fatigue damage due to their special dynamic load environment. For example, off-shore platforms are affected by periodic forces and pressures from wind, waves and currents that promote fatigue damage.

It is now recognized that an effective procedure for tracking the structural integrity of these and other fatigue-critical systems is only through a program of field observation and data collection. The availability of many modern data acquisition systems now permits the utilization of a cost-effective automated field observation program for most fatigue critical structures without an interruption in their routine service activities.

The method of analysis for fatigue damage evaluation, to a great extent, depends on the type of structure, the type of filed data and the type of information available on the fatigue damage characteristics of the structure's individual critical components. To optimize the efficiency of the field observation effort, it is important to consider the type of fatigue analysis scheme most suitable for the structure in the initial design of the data acquisition process. Due to the random nature of the load intensity and frequency, special attention should be paid on the estimation of the duration of the data acquisition period so that a reasonable representation of all load ranges, including those with rare occurrences but with greater damage-producing potentials, can be made. The type of fatigue damage model selected for the structure should also consider the availability of damage tolerance data on the typical structural components. This would determine whether to select a damage initiation analysis or a crack propagation scheme for the structure. The selection of one method over the other may require the adoption of a different strategy for collecting field data.

DESCRIPTION OF FIELD DATA AND FATIGUE ANALYSIS METHODS

Three different fatigue critical structures and their specific types of field data are discussed in this paper. For each type of structure, the fatigue analysis scheme suitable for the collected data is described and discussed. Furthermore, the period of the data acquisition process that needs to be considered to capture a nearly complete load spectrum is described for each application. The structures discussed are:

1. Highway and railway bridges.
2. Airframe structures.
3. Railroad freight cars.

Highway and Railway Bridges

Damage in bridge structures is in the form of fatigue of steel girders and crack in reinforced concrete beams and slabs.

Fatigue in steel girders has been investigated much in detail. appropriate formulations representing fatigue failure and behavior of almost all typical structural steel details has been established (see for example Ref. 1). The main cause of fatigue damage in steel components is stress fluctuation in structural members due to the passage of heavy vehicles and their dynamic action on the bridge.

---

1   Associate Professor, Civil Engineering Department, Illinois Institute of Technology, Chicago, Illinois

2   Graduate Student, Civil Engineering Department, Illinois Institute of Technology, Chicago, Illinois

The stress variation in a steel girder as a result of passage of a heavy truck often contains a peaks preceded and followed by a series of secondary peaks. The stress range experienced by structural members is often low (about 3-5 ksi, Ref. 2). However, upon repeated application of such loads, the bridge structural components suffer damage in the form of fatigue. When stress ranges from all types of trucks are compiled, the stress distribution shows a random pattern that can be described with a probability distribution diagram.

Damage in reinforced concrete is mainly in the form of cracks. Initial cracks may develop due to creep and shrinkage. Cracks will grow to critical sizes upon repeated application of load (Ref. 3). Large size cracks (cracks with large width) will further promote deterioration of concrete elements by allowing moisture and harmful chemicals reach the rebars.

Field data in the form of internal strains are often collected by states departments of transportation at fatigue-critical components (e.g., at the cover plate locations in steel girders) for highway bridges. Such data are then converted to and presented in the form of live load stress ranges and their corresponding frequencies of occurrence. The process of stress range data computation generally follows a cycle counting method called "rainflow." The technique is explained by ASTM standards (Ref. 4) and can easily be programmed for on-site implementation. Figure 1 shows a sample of stress range data collected over a two-day period at a W-section with welded cover plates (Ref. 5) using the rainflow method. As seen in Fig. 1, only a small percentage of the stress range data appears in values above 3 ksi.

Truck loads data are also collected for many bridges using weigh-in-motion systems. In this case, the data is arranged in the form of load distribution by truck type (in terms of the number of axles). An example of such data is presented in Fig. 2 for a bridge near Danville, Illinois (Ref. 6). The data in Fig. 2 represents the load distribution of 5-axle trucks only.

Both types of data (i.e., the direct stress data and truck load data) are useful in fatigue reliability analysis of bridge structures. The type of analysis currently being used for bridges is a crack initiation approach utilizing the S-N data known for many typical structural details recommended in design codes. References 1 and 2 describe the probabilistic methods that are used for fatigue reliability analyses. A similar approach can also be used for railroad bridges. However, suitable S-N data for railroad bridges should be used in the analysis. Such S-N relations for many bridges with riveted joints and cover plates and special details may not readily be available especially for many older railroad bridges.

The duration of field strain data collection for highway bridges is often limited to a few days. For most bridges this period is adequate to obtain a complete history of various stress ranges experienced by a bridge (except maybe for the very high stress levels generated by heavy trucks which are allowed to pass the bridge by special permits from the states departments of transportation). Compared with highway bridges, railroad bridges are expected to experience a much more uniformly distributed load. Thus a shorter period of data collection is perhaps adequate.

The method of fatigue analysis comprises of:

1. Development of theoretical stress-range distribution models obtained from the field data. The use of Beta probability density functions has been suggested in Refs. 1 and 6.

2. Use of the Palmgren-Miner damage rule for fatigue damage analysis along with an appropriate S-N relationship for the critical structural details

3. Use of a probability function (e.g., Weibull) to describe the reliability of a critical component in terms of a desired fatigue life. A complete description of this method can be found in Ref. 1.

Alternatively, the stress data (such as that in Fig. 1) can directly be used to determine the fatigue life expended and the remaining life of the structural component. In such a case, the number of stress frequencies in a specific range is used in the S-N diagram to determine how much fatigue life has been expended for that stress range and for the period the data was collected. Fatigue life expended for all ranges are then added. The result represents the damage accumulated over the period the data was collected considering all possible stress ranges experienced by the bridge. This information can then be used to estimate the fatigue life expended since the bridge started its service life.

Airframe Structures

Aircraft data consists mainly of:

1. Strain data at fatigue critical locations of the wings and fuselage.

2. The cabin pressure.

3. The normal and lateral accelerations.

4. Other flight dynamics characteristics.

The duration for the strain data acquisition activity could range between 200-1000 of accumulated flight hours. Aircraft with more severe flight activities and with different flight missions require more hours of data. For these aircraft the longer duration of data acquisition is needed to capture the statistics associated with rare high strain levels. Aircraft load factor (normal acceleration) and strain data are often compressed and described in the form of "exceedance" statistics. Exceedance data describe the number of times a parameter (e.g., strain) exceeds a predetermined threshold level in a typical 1000 hours of flight. Generally, exceedances that are below the endurance limits are not counted. The exceedance statistics are then used in fatigue analysis of critical components for which strain data has been compiled.

Both crack initiation and crack propagation methods have been used for the analysis of fatigue-critical components of airframe structures. The crack propagation technique is especially useful when fatigue analysis of special structural details around holes or around crack arresters is desired. The crack propagation analysis utilizes the following crack-growth relation (Ref. 7).

$$da/dN = A(\Delta K)^m \qquad (1)$$

in which a=crack size, N=number of stress cycles, ΔK=stress intensity factor and A and m are constants. The stress-intensity factor can be expressed in terms of the stress range S and crack length through the following equation.

$$\Delta K = Y(a,X)S\sqrt{(\pi a)} \qquad (2)$$

in which Y defines the geometry of the detail and is a function of the crack size and a series of crack parameters X. For a constant Y (say y), Eqs. 1 and 2 can be solved for the crack size a.

$$a = [NA(1-m/2)(y\sqrt{\pi})^m S^m]^\alpha \qquad (3)$$

in which $\alpha = 2/(2-m)$. Knowing the probability density function of S, the probability that the crack size is less than a critical level (say a_C), i.e., $P(a < a_C)$, can be obtained. In a more general case, where Y is a function of the crack size, a numerical integration and analysis method will be required to solve Eqs. 1 and 2 simultaneously for the calculation of the crack size for a given number of stress cycles.

The extent of damage occurred to a structural components (damage in terms of crack growth or damage accumulated using the crack initiation method) is used in computing the expended fatigue life of an aircraft.

Railroad Freight Car

Structural components of a freight car are subjected to stress fluctuation resulting from various motions of the car body moving along a track with irregularities. Track irregularities follow a random pattern and cause random stresses in the structural components of the car.

Two types of field data are collected to investigate the effect of track irregularities on structural components of a freight car. These include:

1. Acceleration data for different components of a car traveling along a given route.

2. Data of loads generated on certain bearing elements and support systems of the car during a typical ride (Ref. 8).

The acceleration data is often preferred because of the lesser cost involved in the needed data acquisition system. Acceleration data are filtered and presented in the form of power spectral density (PSD) functions. Figure 3 shows a typical PSD (Ref. 8) obtained from acceleration time-history data.

The data should be collected during a ride along a several hundred-mile track so that a wide spectrum of nearly all frequencies can be made and a complete picture of all potential track irregularity modes can be captured. The fatigue analysis of the freight car can effectively be conducted using the acceleration PSD data. For this purpose the PSD data is used as an input to a comprehensive structural dynamic analysis of the car to obtain the stress variation results at the critical components of the car. Specifically, PSD's of critical stresses can be used to determine the statistics of stress peaks in the form of probability density function, $f_s(s,t)$, of the peak stresses (t=time). If M is a random variable describing the number of cycles of the stress S=s in unit time, the following approximation can be made (Ref. 9).

$$mf_s(s,t|m)f_M(m)dm \approx E[M(t)]f_s(s,t) \qquad (4)$$

in which $f_M(m)$ is the probability density function of M and $f_s(s,t|m)$ is the conditional probability density function of S given a specific number of stress cycles such as M=m. Assuming a stationary process for S and using the Palmgren-Miner damage rule, it can be shown that the damage E(d) is:

$$E(d) = E(M) \int_0^\infty [f_s(s)/N(s)]ds \qquad (5)$$

in which E(M) is the number of cycles of stress S=s in unit time and N(s) describes the number of cycles of stress S=s to failure (note that this number of stress cycles can be obtained if the S-N relation for the structural component is available). If f_e is the expected equivalent frequency (i.e., the mean number of cycles/second), the damage for one cycle of stress will be $E(d)/f_e$ and for n cycles $E(D) = nE(d)/f_e$. Since failure occurs when damage approaches unity, equating E(D) with unity results in the following relation for the average life of the structural component.

$$\bar{n} = f_e/\{E(M) \int_0^\infty [f_s(s)/N(s)]ds\} \qquad (6)$$

in which N(s) denotes the S-N relation describing the fatigue behavior of the component. This equation can now be used in the fatigue reliability analysis of the component (Ref. 8).

In cases where the field data collected consist only of the load statistics at the bearing and support elements, the fatigue life evaluation analysis constitutes the following procedure:

1. Static analysis of the car components using the load data as input to find the stresses at the critical locations.

2. Development of theoretical probability density functions for stress ranges.

3. Crack-initiation analysis of the critical details to determine their fatigue reliability for a given service life.

This procedure was used in Ref. 8 to determine the fatigue reliability of several details for 2,000,000 cycles of fatigue life. The results indicated that for a welded connection in the supporting bolsters of a freight box-type car, the probability of failure was 2.0×10^{-4} for a detail with welded cover plate and 7.0×10^{-4} for a detail with butt welds. The corresponding average fatigue lives $\bar{n} = 3.618 \times 10^9$ and 1.080×10^9 for these details, respectively.

SUMMARY AND CONCLUSIONS

This paper presents an overview of the application of field data to the fatigue reliability analysis of structures.

Specifically, three different types of structures (bridges, aircraft and railroad freight cars) are described. The type of field data currently collected for each group of structures and the method of fatigue analysis suitable for each type of data are described. For each type of data and the corresponding structures group, the duration of data acquisition period needed to obtain a complete spectrum of internal stresses in the critical components and all potential variations in the system's dynamic load parameters is described. The importance of the method of fatigue analysis (i.e., crack initiation versus crack propagation) in the design of a data acquisition system for a structure is also explained and discussed.

REFERENCES

1.   Ang, A. H.-S., and Munse, W. H., "Practical Reliability Basis for Structural Fatigue," ASCE National Structural Engineering Convention, Preprint 2494, April, 1975.

2.   Moses, F. Schilling, C. G., and Raju, K. S., "Fatigue Evaluation Procedures for Steel Bridges, NCHRP 299, Transportation Research Board, Washington, DC, Nov., 1987.

3.   Mohammadi, J. and Yazbeck, G., J., "Strategies for Bridge Inspection Using Probabilistic Models," Proc., ICOSSAR, 89, International Association for Structural Safety and Reliability, IASSAR, Columbia University, New York, 1989.

4.   American Standard for Testing of Materials, Annual Book of ASTM Standards, Section 3, Volume 03.01, Test Methods and Analytical Procedures, "Standard Practices for Cycle Counting in Fatigue Analysis," E1049, 1991.

5.   Mohammadi, J., Guralnick, S.A. and Polepeddi, R., "Effect of Increased Truck Load Upon Illinois Highway Bridges," FHWA Report FHWA/IL/RC/013, 1991.

6.   Mohammadi, J. and Shah, N., "Statistical Analysis of Truck Overloads," Journal of Transportation Engineering, American Society of Civil Engineers, New York, Vol. 118, November, 1992.

7.   Barsom, J. M., and Rolfe, S. T., Fracture & Fatigue Control in Structures, Applications of Fracture Mechanics, Second Edition, Prentice-Hall, Inc., Englewood Cliffs, N. J., 1987.

8.   Mohammadi, J., Garg, V. K., and Subei, N., "Data-Based Evaluation of Fatigue Reliability of Railroad cars," ASME Paper #84-WA/DE-11, 1984.

9.   Lin, Y. K., Probabilistic Theory of Structural Dynamics, R. E. Kreiger Publishing Company, Hunting, N. Y., 1976.

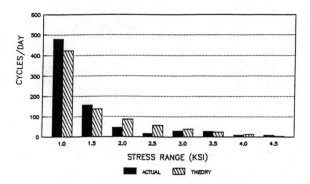

Fig. 1 Sample of Bridge Stress Data (Ref. 6)

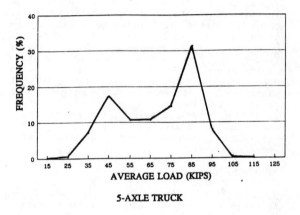

Fig. 2 Sample of Truck Load Data (Ref. 7)

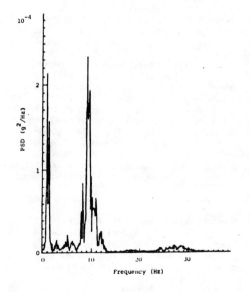

Fig. 3 Carbody Lateral Acceleration Data (Ref. 8)

PHOTOELASTIC STRESS ANALYSIS OF ORTHOTROPIC MATERIALS
BY USING AN ISOTROPIC PLATE

T. Hayashi and Y. Morimoto

ABSTRACT

Based on the two dimensional theory of elasticity for the orthotropic plate, the relations between two stress fields produced in two different orthotropic plates are considered and the conditions to realize the similar stress fields in different orthotropic plates are studied. On the basis of the similarity law, a convenient photoelastic method to analyze stress fields in an orthotropic plate using an isotropic plate is presented. Three examples are treated. One is the stress concentration problem around a circular hole in a strip with edges parallel to the symmetric axis of elasticity. In the second example, the edges of the strip are assumed to be inclined by angle 30° to the symmetric axis. Third example is a semi-infinite plate with a hole. The experimental results are compared with theoretical ones.

INTRODUCTION

Orthotropic materials, such as fiber reinforced composites, have been increasingly favored for high performance structures because of their high strength-to-weight ratio. They have a set of orthogonal elastic axis of symmetry and the behavior of the materials under applied forces differs from isotropoic body. The stress fields in these orthotropic plates were studied theoretically by several authors[1,2] by the use of the two dimensional stress functions.

As to the experimental approach to the problem, photoelastic investigations were performed developing a transparent filament-resin composite[3] as a photoelastic material, or employing birefringent coatings[4,5] bonded to an orthotropic plate, and general methods[4,6] of photoelastic analysis for the plane stress fields of the aeolotropic plate were developed. Stress fields in various orthotropic plates under the same boundary conditions differ to each other depending on their elastic moduli.

T. Hayashi is Emeritus Professor of Osaka University.(Private Address: Tsunoe, 3-23-22, Takatsuki, Osaka, 569, Japan.)
Y. Morimoto is Associate Professor, Department of Mechanical Engineering, Faculty of Engineering Science, Osaka University, Machikaneyama, 1-1, Toyonaka, Osaka, 560, Japan.

And so, it is desired in the experimental research of these plates to make the elastic properties of the model coincide with the actual material as well as possible. For this purpose, a method of equivalent stress field[7] was proposed previously by one of the authors. In the present paper, this method is applied to photoelastic study to analyze the stress fields in any orthotropic plate by using an isotropic plate.

TWO DIMENSIONA, STRESS FUNCTION FOR AN ORTHOTROPIC PLATE

A set of orthogonal axes x and y is taken along elastically symmetric axes of an orthotropic plate as shown in Fig. 1. Then, the stress-strain relations of the plate are expressed by the following equations.

$$\left. \begin{array}{ll} \varepsilon_x = \dfrac{1}{E_x}\sigma_x - \dfrac{\nu_y}{E_y}\sigma_y \ , & \varepsilon_y = \dfrac{1}{E_y}\sigma_y - \dfrac{\nu_x}{E_x}\sigma_x \\[3mm] \gamma_{xy} = \dfrac{\tau_{xy}}{G_{xy}} \ , & \dfrac{\nu_x}{E_x} = \dfrac{\nu_y}{E_y} \end{array} \right\}$$

$$\cdots\cdots\cdots\cdots (1)$$

where E_x, E_y : Modulus of elasticity in the x, y directions respectively.

G_{xy} : Modulus of rigidity.

ν_x, ν_y : Poisson's ratio in the x, y directions respectively.

Regardless of the sorts of materials, we obtain the compatibility equation and the equations of equilibrium as follows.

$$\frac{\partial^2 \varepsilon_x}{\partial y^2} + \frac{\partial^2 \varepsilon_y}{\partial x^2} = \frac{\partial^2 \gamma_{xy}}{\partial x \partial y} \qquad \cdots\cdots\cdots\cdots (2)$$

$$\frac{\partial \sigma_x}{\partial x} + \frac{\partial \tau_{xy}}{\partial y} = 0 \ , \qquad \frac{\partial \sigma_y}{\partial y} + \frac{\partial \tau_{xy}}{\partial x} = 0$$

$$\cdots\cdots\cdots\cdots (3)$$

from which the stress components are expressed by using a stress function F as follows.

$$\sigma_x = \frac{\partial^2 F}{\partial y^2} \ , \quad \sigma_y = \frac{\partial^2 F}{\partial x^2} \ , \quad \tau_{xy} = -\frac{\partial^2 F}{\partial x \partial y}$$

$$\cdots\cdots\cdots\cdots (4)$$

From equations (1),(2) and (4), governing equation of the stress function F is obtained in the following form with elastic moduli in its coefficients:

$$\frac{E_x}{E_y}\frac{\partial^4 F}{\partial x^4}+\left(\frac{E_x}{G_{xy}}-2\nu_x\right)\frac{\partial^4 F}{\partial x^2 \partial y^2}+\frac{\partial^4 F}{\partial y^4}=0$$

$$\cdots\cdots\cdots\cdots(5)$$

As the solution of this biharmonic equation, stress function of an orthotropic plate is given in the following form,

$$F(x,y)=\mathrm{Real}[f(x+i\ p\ y)+g(x+i\ q\ y)]$$

$$\cdots\cdots\cdots\cdots(6)$$

where p and q are orthotropic constants related to the elastic moduli by the following relations.

$$\left.\begin{array}{l}p^2\ q^2=(E_x/E_y)\ ,\\p^2+q^2=(E_x/G_{xy})\ -2\nu_x\end{array}\right\}\ \cdots\cdots(7)$$

SIMILARITY LAW OF STRESS FIELDS IN DIFFERENT ORTHOTROPIC PLATES

Suppose that there are two orthotropic plates, plate I and plate II, whose orthotropic constants have the following relations

$$(p_1/p_2)=(q_1/q_2)=k\qquad\cdots\cdots\cdots\cdots(8)$$

Suffix of each character means that the character belongs to the corresponding plate. From the relation (8) described above, following relations are obtained.

$$(E_x/E_y)_1=p_1^2\ q_1^2=k^4\ p_2^2\ q_2^2=k^4(E_x/E_y)_2$$

$$\cdots\cdots\cdots\cdots(9)$$

Namely, the ratio of the elastic modulus $(E_x/E_y)_1$ of the plate I is k^4 times larger than the ratio of the elastic modulus $(E_x/E_y)_2$ of the plate II.

Instead of the physical plane (x_1,y_1) of the plate I, consider now a mathematical plane (ξ,η) defined by the following relations.

$$\xi=x_1\ ,\quad \eta=k\ y_1\qquad\cdots\cdots\cdots(10)$$

Then, from equation (8), stress function $F_1(x_1,y_1)$ of the plate I is expressed on the mathematical plane (ξ,η) in the following form.

$$F_1(x_1,y_1)$$
$$=\mathrm{Real}[f_1(x_1+i\ p_1\ y_1)+g_1(x_1+i\ q_1\ y_1)]$$
$$=\mathrm{Real}[f_1(\xi+i\ p_2\ \eta)+g_1(\xi+i\ q_2\ \eta)]$$

$$\cdots\cdots\cdots\cdots(11)$$

This is the same form as stress function $F_2(x_2,y_2)$ of the plate II on its physical plane. Accordingly, if the plate II is submitted to the same boundary conditions as the plate I has on the mathematical plane (ξ,η), then both of the stress functions become the same one.

$$F_1(\xi,\eta)=F_2(x_2,y_2)=F\qquad\cdots\cdots\cdots(12)$$

This fact shows that an experimental stress analysis of an orthotropic plate can be performed by using another plate with different elastic constants. The space variables on each plane have following relations

$$x_2=\xi=x_1,\qquad y_2=\eta=k\ y_1\ \cdots\cdots\cdots\cdots(13)$$

From eq. (13), relations between second derivatives of the stress function F on each plane become as follows:

$$\left.\begin{array}{l}\sigma_{x2}=\dfrac{\partial^2 F}{\partial y_2^2}=\dfrac{\partial^2 F}{\partial \eta^2}=\dfrac{1}{k^2}\ \dfrac{\partial^2 F}{\partial y_1^2}=\dfrac{1}{k^2}\sigma_{x1}\\[2mm]\sigma_{y2}=\dfrac{\partial^2 F}{\partial x_2^2}=\dfrac{\partial^2 F}{\partial \xi^2}=\dfrac{\partial^2 F}{\partial x_1^2}=\sigma_{y1}\\[2mm]\tau_{xy2}=-\dfrac{\partial^2 F}{\partial x_2 \partial y_2}=-\dfrac{\partial^2 F}{\partial \xi \partial \eta}=-\dfrac{1}{k}\ \dfrac{\partial^2 F}{\partial x_1 \partial y_1}\\[2mm]\qquad\quad=\dfrac{1}{k}\tau_{xy1}\end{array}\right\}$$

$$\cdots\cdots\cdots\cdots(14)$$

Assume that the shape and the boundary stresses of the plate I are given with a parameter s as follows.

contour line of the boundary:

$$x_1=\mathrm{a}(s),\quad y_1=\mathrm{b}(s)\qquad\cdots\cdots\cdots\cdots(15)$$

boundary stresses:

$$\sigma_{x1}=\mathrm{X}(s),\sigma_{y1}=\mathrm{Y}(s),\tau_{xy1}=\mathrm{S}(s)\ \cdots\cdots(16)$$

Then, to obtain the same stress function on the plate II, boundary conditions on the plate become as follows.

contour line of the boundary:

$$x_2=\mathrm{a}(s),\quad y_2=k\ \mathrm{b}(s)\qquad\cdots\cdots\cdots\cdots(17)$$

boundary stresses:

$$\sigma_{x2}=\mathrm{X}(s)/k^2,\sigma_{y2}=\mathrm{Y}(s),\tau_{xy2}=\mathrm{S}(s)/k$$

$$\cdots\cdots\cdots\cdots(18)$$

Instead of the boundary conditions (16), normal and tangential stresses, $\sigma_1(s)$ and $\tau_1(s)$, are given usually along the boundary on the plate I.

$$\sigma_1(s)=\mathrm{N}(s),\quad \tau_1(s)=\mathrm{T}(s)\ \cdots\cdots\cdots(19)$$

Then, after some calculation, the boundary conditions (18) become as follows.

$$\left.\begin{array}{l}\sigma_2(s)=\dfrac{\mathrm{N}(s)}{k^2\cos^2\theta+\sin^2\theta}\\[3mm]\tau_2(s)=\dfrac{\mathrm{T}(s)}{k}+\dfrac{\mathrm{N}(s)\ (k^2-1)\sin\theta\cos\theta}{k\ (k^2\cos^2\theta+\sin^2\theta)}\end{array}\right\}$$

$$\cdots\cdots\cdots\cdots(20)$$

where θ is the angle between the x_1 axis and the normal to the boundary line on the plate I as shown in Fig. 1. Under the boundary conditions (15) and (19) on the plate I, and (17) and (20) on the plate II, each stress component at the corresponding point has a simple relation as shown in eqs. (14).

EXPERIMENTAL PROCEDURE

In the present experiment, a transparent isotropic material is used as photoelastic specimens to study the stress fields in an orthotropic plate, whose elastic moduli are assumed as follows.

$$E_x/E_y = K^4 \qquad \cdots\cdots\cdots (21)$$

In the isotropic plate, elastic moduli are independent on directions, and so

$$E_x/E_y = 1 \qquad \cdots\cdots\cdots (22)$$

Then, from eq. (9), expansion factor k becomes equal to K.

$$k = K \qquad \cdots\cdots\cdots (23)$$

In the present work, the value of k is taken to be 1.5, and so the experimental results correspond to the stress field in an orthotropic plate with modulus ratio $(E_x/E_y) = 1.5^4 \fallingdotseq 5$.

First example is a stress concentration problem around a circular hole in a strip under tension as shown in Fig. 2. Lateral edges of the strip are assumed to be parallel to the elastically symmetric axis, x, of the plate. To satisfy the condition (17), we design a photoelastic specimen as shown in Fig. 3. A rectangle $A_1 B_1 C_1 D_1$ with a circular hole shows the given figure of the orthotropic plate. The figure is expanded in the y direction by 1.5 times, and we obtain a rectangle $A_2 B_2 C_2 D_2$ with a elliptic hole, whose major axis is vertical to the lateral edges of the strip. Isotropic photoelastic material is machined after the shape of this figure. By using the specimen, photoelastic fringe pattern in this case is obtained as shown in Fig. 4.

Second example is also a stress concentration problem around a circular hole in a strip. Lateral edges of the strip, however, are assumed to be inclined to the symmetric axis of elasticity by angle 30^0 as shown in Fig. 5. The process to obtain the shape of the specimen is shown in Fig. 6. A rectangle AB_1CD_1 with a circular hole is the figure of the orthotropic plate, which is expanded in the y direction by 1.5 times, and a rhombic strip AB_2CD_2 with an elliptic hole is obtained. In this case, the major axis of the elliptic hole is oblique to the lateral edges of the strip. Thus the shape of the photoelstic specimen is obtained. Tensile force is applied normal to the terminal edge AB_1 or CD_1 on the orthotropic plate and the edge is oblique to the elastic axis of symmetry as shown in Fig. 5. In this case, it should be noted that the force applied at the corresponding point on the specimen has both normal and tangential components as shown in the boundary conditions (20). After some calculations, the line of resultant force applied at the terminal edge of the specimen is proved to be parallel to the lateral edge of the specimen. Photoelastic pattern obtained in this case is shown in Fig. 7.

Third example is shown in Fig. 8. Semi-infinite plate with a circular hole is submitted to a concentrated force applied normally to the straight edge of the plate, and the edge is assumed to be inclined by angle 30^0 to the elastically symmetric axis, y, of the plate. The process to obtain the shape of the specimen is shown in Fig. 9. Rectangle $A_1 B_1 C_1 D_1$ with a circular hole is the given shape of the orthotropic plate. Rohnbic $A_2 B_2 C_2 D_2$ with an elliptic hole in the figure is the shape of the specimen. In the experiment, a concentrated force is applied obliquely to the straight edge $C_2 D_2$ of the specimen and the angle α between the line of the resultant force and the straight edge is given from eqs. (20) as follows.

$$\left. \begin{array}{l} \tan\alpha = \dfrac{k}{(k^2-1)\sin\theta\cos\theta} \\[2mm] \theta = 30^0, \quad k = 1.5 \end{array} \right\} \qquad \cdots\cdots (24)$$

To apply a oblique force to the specimen, a wedge shape loading device is employed. Photoelastic pattern obtained in this case is shown in fig. 10.

EXPERIMENTAL RESULTS

From the photoelastic fringe patterns shown in Figs. 4, 7, and 10, stress components at any point in each specimen are obtained by the usual photoelastic method for isotropic material. Corresponding point on the orthotropic plate can be found easily from the relations (13) for space variables on both plates, and the stress components on each orthotropic plate are obtained from the stress values measured on the specimen by using the conversion formulae (14).

Along a free edge of a plate, only one principal stress is the periphery stress σ_θ. In such a uniaxial stress state, the conversion formulae (14) become simple for the periphery stress as shown below.

$$\sigma_{\theta 1} = \frac{k^2}{k^2\cos^2\theta + \sin^2\theta}\, \sigma_{\theta 2} \qquad \cdots\cdots\cdots (25)$$

Where θ is the angle between the x axis and the normal to the free edge on the orthotropic plate. By using the relation, stress distribution around a circular hole in an orthotropic plate is obtained. Figure 11 shows the stress distribution around a hole for the first example. Periphery stress σ_θ is normalized by the tensile stress σ_0 at the position far from the circular hole. Solid line is the stress distribution around a hole in a strip obtained in the present experiment. Dotted line is the theoretically calculated stress distribution around a circular hole in a infinite plate. In this example, line of the applied force coincides with the elastic axis of symmetry, and so, stress distribution is symmetric with respect to the x axis. Stress concentration factor in this case is larger than that of the isotropic plate. (But if the tensile force is parallel to the y axis, stress concentration factor becomes smaller.)

Figure 12 shows the stress distribution for the second example. In this case, elastic axis of symmetry does not coincide with the geometric axis of symmetry nor the line of the applied force. Solid line is the stress distribution around a circular hole obtained in the present experiment. Dotted line is the theoretically calculated stress distribution around the circular hole in an infinite plate. From the experimental method mentioned above, it is clear that with increase of the ratio (E_x/E_y) of an orthotropic plate, expansion factor k becomes larger and the elliptic hole in the specimen becomes slender, and maximum stress in the specimen occurs near the end of the major axis of the ellipse. This point corresponds to the crossing point of the y axis to the periphery of the circular hole on the orthotropic plate. And so, with increase of the ratio (E_x/E_y) of the plate, position of maximum stress moves along the periphery of the circular hole toward the y axis. In the present experiment, maximum stress concentration is observed at a point on the periphery removed about 15⁰ from the neck section of the specimen. Theoretical result for a circular hole in an infinite plate shows that the maximum stress occurs at a point on the periphery removed about 13⁰ from the section vertical to the force line. Agreement between the experimental and theoretical results obtained for first and second examples is good enough.

Figure 13 shows stress distribution for third example. In this case, there is no theoretical work available for comparison to the experimental result, and absolute value of stresses around the circular hole is presented. In this case, a concentrated force is applied along the geometric axis of symmetry, but the elastically symmetric axis of the orthotropic plate is oblique to these axes by angle 30⁰, and complicated stress distribution appears around a circular hole. Maximum stress occurs at the periphery of the hole near the y axis of the plate.

SUMMARY

Based on the similarity law of stress fields, photoelastic stress analysis are performed for an orthotropoic plate. In the present experiment, isotropic material is used as the specimen and so we have no need to prepare any special photoelastic material nor special method for analysis. Present method is very simple and yet adaptable for the orthotropic plate with any value of the modulus ratio (E_x/E_y). Present experiments have made clear some special features of the orthotropic plate under loading. If the force is applied along a elastic axis of symmetry with larger elastic modulus, the orthotropic material shows larger stress concentration than the isotropic one. Even if the loading axis coincides with geometric axis of symmetry, complicated stress distributions are obtained when the elastic axis of symmetry intersects these axes obliquely, and in these cases, the maximum stress point around a hole moves toward the y axis, one of the elastically symmetric axes with smaller elastic modulus. But attention should be paid to the following matter.

As shown in eq. (5), there are two factors which affect the behavior of the orthotropic plate. One is the first coefficient (E_x/E_y) and the other is the second coefficient $[(E_x/G_{xy})-2\nu_x]$. In the present study, only the first coefficient is considered. To take account of the second coefficient, we must perform the experiment by using several kinds of orthotropic plates as mentioned in the previous work.[7] But to know the behavior of an orthotropic plate under the given boundary conditions, first factor is most important and the effect of the second term on the stress distribution in the plate is rather small compared with the first term, and so, present method is useful especially to clarify the distinguishing feature of the stress field in the orthotropic plate.

ACKNOWLEDGMENTS

The experiments described here was supported by Mr. M.Inoue and Mr M.Nishiyama. The author would like to express their hearty thanks to them especially for their skilful work to prepare the specimen and to perform the experiments.

REFERENCES

1. Ikeda, K. "On the Plane Stresses in Orthogonal Anisotropic Plates having a Circular or Elliptic Hole". Jour. of Science and Culture Association Japan, 2, 3,(1947),22- in Japanese
2. Hayashi, T. "On the Tension in an Orthogonally Aeolotropic Strip with a Circular Hole". Bulletin of JSME, 3, 10(1960), 265-270.
3. Hayashi, Tu. "Photoelastic Method of Experimentation for orthotropic materials ". Japanese Jour. Appl.Phys. 31, 10(1961), 808-811 in Japanese
4. Hayashi, T. "Some Problems on the Photoelastic Experiment by a Birefringent Coating Method". Bulletin of JSME,8, 31(1965), 337-343.
5. Dally, J. W. and Alfirevich, I. "Application of Birefringent Coatings to Glass-fiber-reinforced Plastics". Experimental Mechanics, March 1969, 97-102.
6. Sampson, R. C. "A Stress-Optic Law for Photoelastic Analysis of Orthotropic Composites". Experimental Mechanics. may 1970, 210-215.
7. Hayashi, T. "Some Experimental Studies on Plane Stresses by Use of the Equivalent Orthotropic Plate". Bulletin of JSME, 4, 15(1961), 431-437.

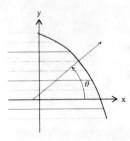

Fig. 1 : Co-ordinate system

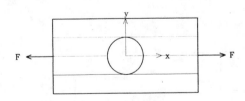

Fig. 2 : First example

497

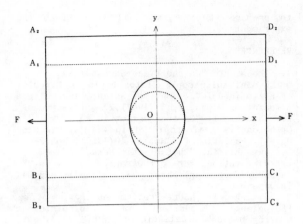

Fig. 3 : Specimen design process for the first case

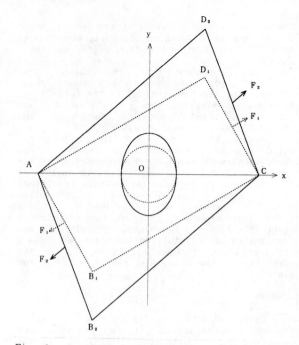

Fig. 6 : Specimen design Process for the second case

Fig .4 : Photoelastic pattern for the first case

Fig. 7 : Photoelastic pattern for the second case

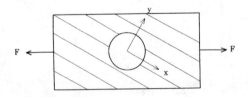

Fig. 5 : Second example

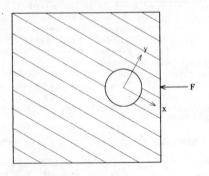

Fig. 8 : third example

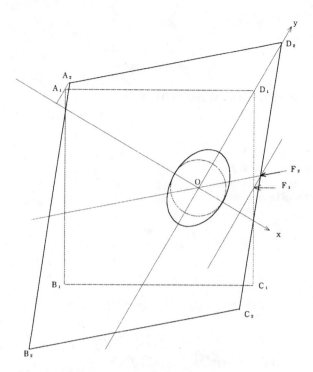

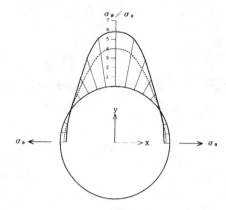

Fig. 11 : Stress distribution around a circular
hole for the first case

Fig. 9 : Specimen design process for the third
case

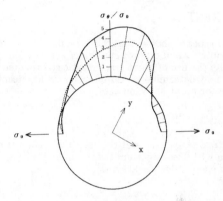

Fig. 12 : Stress distribution around a circular
hole for the second case

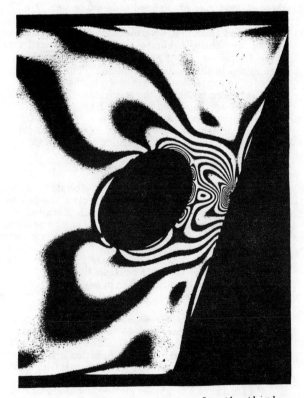

Fig. 10 : Photoelastic pattern for the third
case

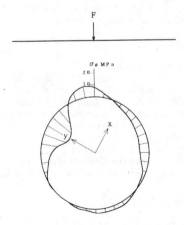

Fig. 13 : Stress distribution around a circular
hole for the third case

STRESS INTENSITY FACTORS FOR 45° V-NOTCHES

Freire, J.L.F. and Carvalho, E.A.
Mechanical Engineering Department
Catholic University of Rio de Janeiro

ABSTRACT

This paper shows that the singular stress fields for 45° V-notches and cracked specimens are very similar and suggests the use of blunt crack elastic stress equations to study and determine stress intensity and concentration factors for blunt 45° V-notches.

INTRODUCTION

Stress singularities at the vertex of reentrant corners in bars with free-edges under tension or bending depend on the eigen-value equation [1],

$$\lambda \sin 2\alpha = \pm \sin 2\lambda\alpha \qquad (1)$$

where the degree of singularity of the stress, $\lambda - 1$, is maximum when the angle α of the V-notch is zero. For this case, $\lambda = 1/2$ and the notch assumes a crack shape.

Mahinfalah and Zachary [2] applied photoelasticity to determine mode I and II stress intensity factors for 90° reentrant corners using the overdeterministic least squares technique in conjunction with the Newton-Raphson method as proposed by Sanford [3,4]. Mode I and II stress intensity factors were generically defined by:

$$K_{I,II} = \lim_{r \to 0} (2\pi)^{1/2}\, r^{1-\lambda_{I,II}} \sigma_{I,II} \qquad (2)$$

where $\sigma_{I,II}$ are nominal stress.

In the present paper the Mahifalah-Zachary approach was applied to show that the singular stress fields for 45° V-notches in finite bars under tension and bending are very similar to the crack-like stress fields. Based on this conclusion the paper shows that it is possible to determine the stress field for the region near the root of a blunt 45° V-notches by coupling the isochromatic photoelastic response to the Creager-Paris equations [5] and to the Sanford's overdeterministic approach [3,4].

SINGULAR V-NOTCHES

After William's [1], Mahinfalah and Zachary [2] developed stress equations for points in the neighborhood of the vertex of reentrant corners for mixed mode I and II such that

$$\sigma_r = K_I r^{\lambda^+ - 1} Q^+ [f_1(\theta)] - K_{II} r^{\lambda^- - 1} Q^- [f_2(\theta)]$$

$$\begin{aligned}
\sigma_\theta &= K_I r^{\lambda^+ - 1}(1 + \lambda^+) Q^+ [f_3(\theta)] - \\
&= K_{II} r^{\lambda^- - 1}(1 + \lambda^-) Q^- [f_4(\theta)]
\end{aligned} \qquad (3)$$

$$\tau_{r\theta} = K_I r^{\lambda^+ - 1} Q^+ [f_5(\theta)] + K_{II} r^{\lambda^- - 1} Q^- [f_6(\theta)]$$

where K_I and K_{II} are defined as in expression (2). The values of λ^+ and λ^- are solutions of the eigenvalue equations (1) and their first determination (smaller values of $\lambda \neq 0$) are shown in Figure 1. It can be noticed that $\lambda^- > 1$ when $\alpha > 103.5°$. For this case there are not singularities in the mode II stress field. The other terms presented in expression (3) are given in the Appendix.

The determination of the stress intensity factors K_I and K_{II} are accomplished by using the overdeterministic approach proposed by Sanford [2,3,4].

The present paper modified expressions (3) by adding to σ_r a polynomial expansion term such that

$$\sigma^* = \Sigma_{i=0}^m \Sigma_{j=0}^i C_{ij}\, x^{i-j} y^j \qquad (4)$$

to take into account the influence of the non-singular field in the isochromatic fringe distribution around the V-notch corner. Therefore, isochromatic data can ben collected far from the near field and still can be analysed to furnish reliable K_I, K_{II} information. In the present case, the authors preferred to use σ^* instead of using other non singular λ terms which are also roots of the eigenvalue function (1) as is usual in the case of cracks [2]. It should be notices that when $m = 0$, σ^* corresponds to the constant stress terms proposed by Irwin [6] for the crack problems.

As an application, stress intensity factors for mode I were determined for bars with 45° V-notches and varying a/w geometry, tested under tension and bending. Figure 2 shows the region used for data acquisition in a specimen with $a/w = 0.29$ under tension load (nominal fringe order at the gross section equal to 3).

Figure 3 shows computer plotted isochromatic fringe distributions for a crack-like and a 45°V-notched specimen with $a/w = 0.05$. It can be noticed that the fringe distributions are very similar showing that they are only slightly affected by the differences in their λ expoents. So, it can be concluded that 45° V-notches with singular stress distributions and cracks have very similar K_I values. Figures 4 and 5 prove this showing experimentally determined K_I values for 45° V-notches under tension and bending compared to K_I values for cracks determined for specimens with the same a/w ratios.

BLUNT V-NOTCHES

Creager and Paris [5] developed elastic stress field equations (5) presented below for blunt cracks (small ρ/a) in a form equivalent to the usual sharp crack tip stress fields. They showed that their difference was a simple function of the curvature radius at the crack tip. For these equations, the origin of the coordinate system (r, θ) is located $\rho/2$ away from the notch root (Figure 6).

$$\sigma_x = \frac{K_I}{(2\pi r)^{1/2}} cos\frac{\theta}{2}\left[1 - sin\frac{\theta}{2}sin\frac{3}{2}\theta\right] - \frac{K_I}{(2\pi r)^{1/2}}\frac{\rho}{2r}cos\frac{3}{2}\theta$$

$$\theta_y = \frac{K_I}{(2\pi r)^{1/2}} cos\frac{\theta}{2}\left[1 - sin\frac{\theta}{2}sin\frac{3}{2}\theta\right] - \frac{K_I}{(2\pi r)^{1/2}}\frac{\rho}{2r}cos\frac{3}{2}\theta$$

$$\tau_{xy} = \frac{K_I}{(2\pi r)^{1/2}} sin\frac{\theta}{2}cos\frac{\theta}{2}cos\frac{3}{2}\theta - \frac{K_I}{(2\pi r)^{1/2}}\frac{\rho}{2r}sin\frac{3}{2}\theta \quad (5)$$

Considering that $\lambda \simeq 1/2$ in mode I for V-notches with opening angle $0 < \alpha < 60°$, equations (5) can be used to determine the stress fields near the root of the blunt V-notches. In the present paper the equations of Paris-Creager were coupled to the overdeterministic method of Sanford [2] to determine K_I, K_{II} parameters in blunt 45° V-notches. In this case, data can be collected very close to the notch root once the effect of the non-singular stress concentration field is taken into consideration in the equations.

For data collected in the far field, a polynomial series term can be added to the Creager-Paris equations. In the present case only one term (constant σ_o) was used, once data was collected very close to the notch root as shown in Figure 6.

Figure 6 shows the locations of the data points and the regenerated isochromatic distributions for an application analysis using a Charpy V-notch specimen ($a/w = 0.2$, $\rho/a = 0.125$) subjected to tension load. The regenerated isochromatic fringes were computer plotted using the K_I and σ_o values determined from the overdeterminstic method.

The K_I determined value agreed very well (less than 1% difference) with the K_I value determined using Figure 4. In this case, the effective sharp crack length should be determined from the origin of the system of coordinates.

The value of the maximum stress ($\sigma_y = \sigma_{max}$) at the notch root ($\rho/2$, 0) can be determined using equations (5). In terms of isochomatic fringe response, this value was calculated to be $N_{max} = 8.6$ which is very close to the photoelastic direct observation ($N_{max} = 8.8$).

Using σ_{max} or N_{max} and a norminal stress or fringe order, the stress concentration factor for the Charpy V-notch can be calculated as $K_t = N_{max}/N_{nom}$. In the present case, the presence of bending in the net section was considered in the calculation of σ_{nom} as suggested by Noda and Nisitani [7] and then

$$N_{nom} = \frac{N_{gross}w}{w - a}\left(1 + \frac{3a}{w - a}\right) \quad (6)$$

The values of K_t determined in this analysis were 3.4 and 3.5, respectively for the overdeterministic approach and the photoelastic direct observation. Theoretical results from Noda and Nisitani [7] for $\alpha = 60°$ give $K_t = 3.7$. Recent results from Demelio et al. [8] approximated to the Charpy geometry and considering the N_{nom} calculated as in (6) give $K_t \simeq 3.6$.

Figure 7 gives the stress separation for the photoelastic analysis in locations very near to the notch root. This separation is possible if equations (5) are calculated independently for each point (r, θ) using ρ and the determined K_I value.

REFERENCES

[1] Williams, M.L., "Stress Singularities Resulting from various Boundary conditions in Angular Corners of Plates in Extension," J. Applied Mechanics, 526-528, December, 1952.

[2] Mahinfalah, M. and Zachary, L., "Photoelastic Determination of Stress Intensity Factors for Reentrant Coorners," Proceedings of the 1989 Conference on Experimental Mechanics, SEM, 147-153, 1989.

[3] Sanford, R. J., "Application of the Least Squares Method to the Photoelastic Analysis," Experimental Mechanics, 20 (6), 192-192, 1980.

[4] Sanford, R.J., "Determining Fracture Parameters with Full-Field Optical Methods," Experimental Mechanics, 29 (3), 241-247, 1989.

[5] Creager, M. and Paris, P.C., "Elastic Field Equations for Blunt Cracks with Reference to Stress Corrosion Cracking," International Journal of Fracture, Mechanics, v.3, 247-252, December, 1967.

[6] Irwin, G.R., Discussion of "The Dynamic Stress Distribution Surrounding a Running Crack" - A Photoelatic Analysis," by Wells, A.A. and Post, D., Proc. SESA, 16 (10), 92-96, 1958.

[7] Noda, N.A. and Nisitani, H., "Stress Concentration of a Strip with a Single Edge Notch," Engineering Fracture Mechanics, v. 28, n. 2, 233-238, 1987.

[8] Demelio, G., Papalettere, C. and Pastore, C., "Stress Concentration Factor for V-Notches," Proceedings of the 1989 Conference on Experimental Mechanics, SEM, 147-153, 1989.

APPENDIX

$$f_1(\theta) = [(3 - \lambda^+)cos(\lambda^+ - 1)\theta - (1 + \lambda^+)\beta_1 cos(\lambda^+ + 1)\theta]$$

$$f_2(\theta) = [(3 - \lambda^-)sin(\lambda^- - 1)\theta - (1 + \lambda^-)\beta_2 sin(\lambda^- + 1)\theta]$$

$$f_3(\theta) = [cos(\lambda^+ - 1)\theta + \beta_1 cos(\lambda^+ + 1)\theta]$$

$$f_4(\theta) = [sin(\lambda^- - 1)\theta + \beta_2 sin(\lambda^- + 1)\theta]$$

$$f_5(\theta) = [(\lambda^+ - 1)sin(\lambda^+ - 1)\theta + (\lambda^+ + 1)\beta_1 sin(\lambda^+ + 1)\theta]$$

$$f_6(\theta) = [(\lambda^- - 1)cos(\lambda^- - 1)\theta + (\lambda^- + 1)\beta_2 cos(\lambda^- + 1)\theta]$$

$$\beta_1 = -\frac{(\lambda - 1)sin(\lambda - 1)\alpha}{(\lambda + 1)sin(\lambda + 1)\alpha}$$

and

$$\beta_2 = -\frac{\sin(\lambda - 1)\alpha}{\sin(\lambda + 1)\alpha}$$

$$C_1 = Q_1 K_I$$

$$C_2 = -Q_2 K_{II}$$

where Q_1 and Q_2 are:

$$Q_1 = 1/(2\pi)^{1/2}(1 + \beta_1)(\lambda^+)(1 + \lambda^+)$$

$$Q_2 = 1/(2\pi)^{1/2}(\lambda^-)[\lambda^- - 1 + \beta_2(\lambda^- + 1)]$$

$$Q^+ = \lambda^+(Q_1)$$

$$Q^- = \lambda^-(Q_2)$$

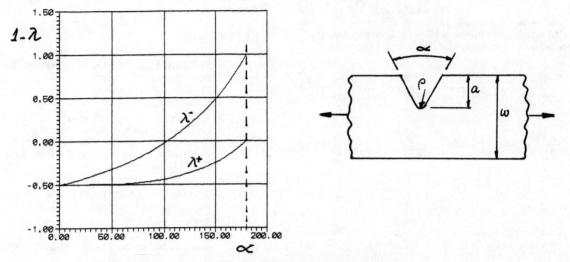

Figure 1 – Degree of singularity of reentrant V-notched specimens and nomenclature

Figure 2 – Isocromatic fringe distribution for a 45° V-notched specimen under tension load

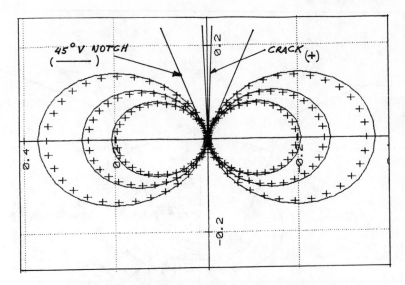

Figure 3 – Computer-plotted isochromatic fringe
distributions for a crack and for a 45°
V-notched specimen under tension
$a/w = 0.05$, near field

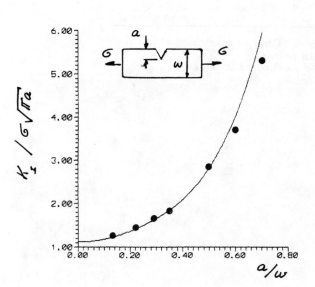

Figure 4 – Stress intensily factors for
45° V-notches under tension

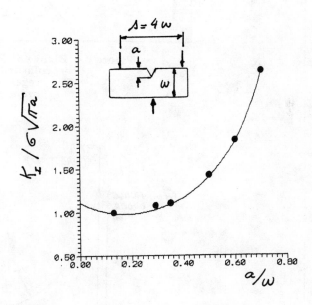

Figure 5 – Stress intensity factors for
45° V-notches under bending
 • V-notch
 — crack

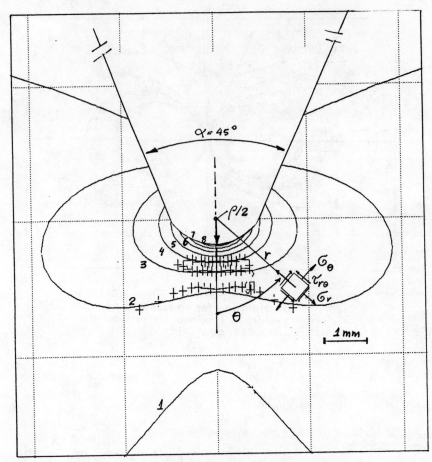

Figure 6 – Blunt 45° V-notch (Charpy specimen)
+ collected data points
— regenerated isochromatic fringe order

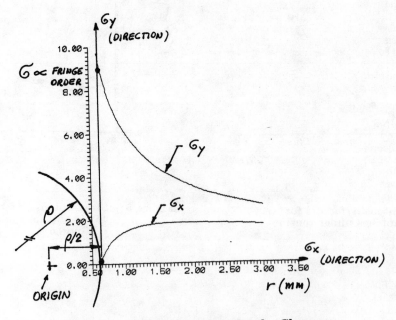

Figure 7 – Stress separation for the Charpy
V-notched specimen under tension

EVALUATION OF FULL FIELD AUTOMATED PHOTOELASTIC ANALYSIS BASED ON PHASE STEPPING

S.J.Haake*, Z.F.Wang* and E.A.Patterson†

ABSTRACT

A full field automated polariscope designed for photoelastic analysis and based on the method of phase-stepping is described. The system is evaluated through the analysis of five different photoelastic models using both the automated system and using manual analysis employing the Tardy Compensation method. Models were chosen to provide a range of different fringe patterns, orders and stress gradients and were (a) a disc in diametral compression, (b) a constrained beam subject to a point load, (c) a tensile plate with a central hole (d) a turbine blade and (e) a turbine disc slot.

The repeatability of the full field system was found to compare well with point by point systems. The worst isochromatic error was approximately 0.007 fringes and the corresponding isoclinic error was 0.75°. Results from the manual and automated methods showed good agreement. It is concluded that automated photoelastic analysis based on phase-stepping procedures offers a potentially accurate and reliable tool to stress analysts.

INTRODUCTION

A full-field automated polariscope for photoelastic analysis has been developed in the authors' laboratory and has been described in detail elsewhere [1]. Briefly, the system uses phase-stepping to determine both the fractional isochromatic fringes and isoclinic parameter at all points in the field of view independently of their neighbouring points. A wrapping algorithm is then employed to produce continuous isochromatic and isoclinic data, which can subsequently be used in stress separation procedures. The idea of using phase stepping in photoelasticity is a fairly recent innovation [2] and can be described as changing incrementally the absolute phase of the reference wave, by rotating the output elements of the polariscope, and measuring the local light intensity after each step.

A number of full field techniques have been developed. Voloshin and Redner [3] have developed half fringe photoelasticity and two laboratories in Japan [4,5], are working on the technique of phase stepping. It appears, however, that no detailed evaluation has been made of the accuracy and reliability of the results generated by the technique. The objective of the work described in this paper has been to provide such an evaluation. Five different models were selected for analysis using the automated system and manually using the Tardy compensation method: (a) a disc in diametral compression, (b) a constrained beam subject to a point load, (c) a tensile plate with a central hole, (d) a turbine blade, and (e) a turbine disc slot. These models provided a range of different fringe patterns, orders and stress gradients to test the performance of the system.

ANALYSIS USING THE AUTOMATED POLARISCOPE

The experimental configuration is shown in Figure 1. A monochromatic CCTV camera records images from the output of the polariscope which are then amplified and digitized and sent to a personal computer. The computer subsequently processes the digitized images. The computer also controls the optical element controller which rotates the analyser and output quarter wave plate to the desired positions using stepper motors. A TV monitor is used to aid the positioning of the photoelastic samples.

Five models were analysed using the full field automatic polariscope and a standard polariscope. The isochromatic fringe order was determined manually using the method of Tardy compensation [6]. These will be described in the following sections.

*S.J.Haake and Z.F.Wang are Research Associates in the Department of Mechanical and Process Engineering, University of Sheffield, Mappin Street, Sheffield, S1 3JD.
†E.A.Patterson is a lecturer in the Department of Mechanical and Process Engineering, University of Sheffield, Mappin Street, Sheffield, S1 3JD.

Disc in diametral compression

A 76 mm diameter, 4.65 mm thick disc of epoxy resin (mixed in the ratio 100 CT200:30 HT901 by weight) was loaded across its diameter with 17.8N and the stresses "locked in" using the method of stress freezing. The method of stress freezing was developed by Oppel [7] and has been described in many subsequent publications [6,8]. Figure 2 (a) contains a photograph of the disc using a circular polariscope and a white light source. Figure 2 (b) gives a comparison of the isochromatic values obtained using the Tardy compensation method and the automatic polariscope (Full Field method) for the diameter perpendicular to the line of load. It can be seen that the two techniques show good agreement and that they are both consistent with values expected from theory. Figures 3 (a) and (b) show the isochromatic and isoclinic patterns respectively as obtained by the automated polariscope. The continuous isochromatic pattern is shown on screen using eight colours from red to green with red indicating the larger value. As the photograph here is in black and white a scale has been provided. The graph to the right of the image shows the normalised value of the isochromatic parameter along the horizontal line on the full field image. Similarly, the graph to the right of the isoclinic image shows the isoclinic values along the vertical line.

Tensile plate with a central hole

Figure 4 (a) shows a photograph of a plate with a central hole obtained using a circular polariscope. The plate was 229 mm long between the loading points, 4.63 mm thick and 76 mm wide. The diameter of the hole was 15 mm and the plate had been loaded and stress frozen with an axial tensile load of 40.1 N. Figure 4 (b) shows the isochromatic fringe order along the centre line perpendicular to the direction of the load obtained using both Tardy compensation and the automatic polariscope. The shapes of the curves and the values obtained using the two methods agree well, although there is some disagreement very close to the hole.

Constrained beam with a point load

Figure 5 (a) contains a photograph of a 90 mm long 15 mm wide 6.5 mm thick constrained beam that had been stress frozen with a load of 19 N (the model geometry is identical to that seen in Figure 6.15 on page 193 of reference 6). Figure 5 (b) shows the isochromatic fringe order along the vertical section through the loading point obtained using Tardy compensation and the automatic polariscope. In general, the shape of the curves are very close. However, in the region of the loading where stress gradients are high the automatic polariscope gives low values of the isochromatic parameter.

Model of turbine slot and blade

Figures 6 (a) and (b) show the images of a turbine slot and blade obtained in a circular polariscope set for a dark field. The lines on the images indicate the lines that were analysed using a conventional polariscope and the automated polariscope. The models were supplied by Le Societe National d'étude et de Construction de Moteurs D'Aviation (SNECMA).

Figures 7 and 8 show the isochromatic parameter of the turbine blade and slot along the sections shown in Figure 6 using both the automatic and manual methods. It can be seen that, in general, there is good agreement between the results from the two techniques. Figure 9 and 10 show the isoclinic parameters for the same two models. The parameter shown is that defined as the isoclinic parameter by Frocht (reference 6, page 177) and varies between 0 and 90° and thus isoclinic values of 90° and 0° are in effect the same angle. In general there is good agreement between the automatic and manual methods. but the isoclinic parameter along line AB of the turbine blade (Figure 9 (a)) has been affected by noise.

DISCUSSION

An estimate of the accuracy is necessary when comparing results from two different techniques. Using manual analysis it is possible to determine isoclinic angles to an accuracy of about ±1° while retardations can be measured to within ±0.02 fringes [9]. A better estimate of the photoelastic parameters can be obtained by taking multiple readings. All results from the manual analysis represent an average of five readings. This can involve a considerable amount of time since each reading can take around 30 seconds.

The automatic analysis results represent only one reading, i.e. one set of images. These images take approximately 3 minutes to be obtained with perhaps another 5 minutes of subsequent processing time. In comparison to manual analysis, the automated polariscope results in full field images of 256 by 256 pixels. Repeated analysis of the same model was carried out to determine the repeatability of the automatic polariscope. It was found that for 20 randomly chosen points on a model, the worst isochromatic error was ±0.007 fringes while the worst isoclinic error was found to be ±0.75°. This compares favourably with the repeatability ascribed to point-by-point systems of around ±0.005 fringes and ±0.1° [10] or of about ±0.01 fringes [11].

Discrepancies between manual analysis and automatic analysis can be divided into systematic errors due to positioning and orientation and random errors due to noise. Systematic errors are caused by incorrect alignment of the model in either the automated or manual polariscopes. This would primarily effect the isoclinic parameter since it is orientation dependent. As far as possible no lines or marks were placed on the model as these tended to produce large amounts of interference in the automated polariscope images. Thus, positioning of the models and the determination of the sections to be analysed was carried out using geometrical features of the model. The selection of slightly different lines of analysis in the automatic polariscope in comparison to those used in the manual method could cause discrepancies between the two sets of data.

A further systematic error can be introduced in the calibration of the isochromatic parameter. The only input required by the operator of the automatic polariscope is the identification of a point of the fringe order. This fixes the isochromatic value at all points on the image. It is achieved by placing the cursor on a fringe and entering the appropriate fringe value. To minimise the error associated in identification it is necessary to use a well defined fringe in the centre of the screen. Repeated analysis of the same image using different points on a particular fringe for the calibration procedure showed a range of isochromatic values for any point on screen of ± 0.007 fringes. This systematic error is smaller than that associated with errors in measuring the isochromatic parameter using manual analysis [9].

The effects of noise can cause very noticeable jumps in the data produced by the automatic system. Noise in the image comes from a number of sources. Initially there is an element of noise in the model arising from bubbles formed in the curing of the epoxy resin and from surface scratches. The former can be minimised by appropriate selection of materials while the latter can be minimised by polishing the model surface prior to analysis.

A primary cause of noise is the camera used to obtain the photoelastic images. The choice of lens affects this since a wide angle lens transmits more light than a longer focal length lens. An unavoidable amount of noise occurs in the electronics of the camera. This may be alleviated by switching to a CCD (Charge Coupled Device) camera.

The amplifier and digitiser used to boost and prepare the image signal for processing introduces a large element of random noise. Unless an expensive digitiser containing noise filters is used, the only way to reduce the noise is to maintain the amplifier gain at a low level.

Noise affects the processing of the photoelastic images in two ways. The first affects the boundary routine causing it to fail in its determination of the background and the second causes errors in the "stacking" or "wrapping" of the fractional isochromatics and isoclinics to make up continuous maps. The boundary routine searches for areas of background where the light intensity is constant. Noise causes variations in the background and the routine therefore fails.

An improved digitiser and a CCD camera are to be evaluated to determine their effectiveness in reducing noise in the system. It is hoped that the use of these will greatly improve the processing of the isoclinic parameter.

Figure 9 (a) shows a good example of a "noise" type interference although it is not caused by any of the processes above. The six original images contain both the isochromatic and the isoclinic patterns superimposed on top of each other. A mathematical problem occurs where a half order isochromatic cuts an isoclinic. At this point the isoclinic becomes undefined (a feature of the mathematics of the analysis). To overcome this problem the isoclinic is extrapolated from its value on one side of the half fringe order to its value on the other side of the half fringe order. Inspection of Figure 7 (a) shows that much of the line of analysis lies along the half order isochromatic. Thus, at most of the points along this line the isoclinic parameter has been estimated and not calculated. This causes large discrepancies with results from manual analysis. The most suitable method of overcoming this problem is to replace the line of analysis with a neighbouring line near the original along which the isochromatic is not predominantly half a fringe order.

It was found during analysis that the automatic polariscope gives low values of the isochromatic parameter in regions of high stress gradient. Analysis of this discrepancy reveals that the automatic system fails to determine the isochromatic when the fringe density is greater than one fringe per ten pixels. It is possible to increase the number of pixels per fringe by moving the model closer to the camera or by using a longer focal length lens with extension tubes. In the latter case the image quality decreased because of the increase in length of lens required to gain a close image of the region of interest.

CONCLUSION

Five models were successfully analysed using the automated polariscope; a disc in compression, a constrained beam under a point load, a semi-infinite plate with a central hole and models of a turbine blade and slot. It was found that the isochromatic parameter found with the automated polariscope agreed closely with results found using the Tardy compensation method. Lower than expected values of the isochromatic parameter were found in regions of high stress gradient greater than about 10 pixels per fringe on screen. The isoclinic parameter was only evaluated in the slices from the model of a turbine; results from manual and automatic analysis agreed well except in one case. This was caused by interaction between the isochromatic and isoclinic patterns.

A full field analysis of a model took place in about 8 minutes, comprising about 3 minutes to collect the images and 5 minutes to process them. It was found that results from the system were repeatable to around ±0.007 fringes for the isochromatic parameter and about 0.75° for the isoclinic parameter. This compares well with results from point-by-point systems.

ACKNOWLEDGEMENTS

The authors would like to thank the Science and Engineering Research Council (SERC) for their generous help and assistance during this project and Le Societe National d'étude et de Construction de Moteurs D'Aviation (SNECMA) for supplying models for analysis.

REFERENCES

1. Patterson, E.A., Wang, Z.F., "Towards full-field automated photoelastic analysis of complex components," *Strain*, **27**(2): 49-56, (1991).

2. Hecker, F.W., Morche, B., "Computer-aided measurement of relative retardations in plane photoelasticity", in *Expt. Stress Anal.*, ed. H. Weirunga, Martinnus Nijhoff Publ., Dordrecht, pp. 532-542, (1986).

3. Voloshin, A.S. and Burger, C.P., "Half fringe photelasticity - a new approach to whole field stress analysis", *Expt. Mech.*, **23**, 304-314 (1983).

4. Kihara, J., "Automated whole-field measurement of photoelasticity using linearly polarised light", *Proc. 9th Int. Conf. Expt. Mech.*, **2**; 821-827, (1990).

5. Takashi, M., Mawatara, S., Toyoda, Y., Kunio, T., "A new computer aided system for photoelastic stress analysis with structure driven type image processing", in Applied Stress Analysis, eds. T.H.Hyde and E. Ollerton, Elsevier Applied Science, London, 516-525, (1990).

6. Frocht, M.M., "Photoelasticity", Volume 1, John Wiley and Sons, Inc., New York, (1941), fourth reprint (1954).

7. Oppel, G., "Polarisationoptische untersuchang rammerlicher spanmings und deliunggzustande", Forsch, Geb. Ingenieurw., 7, 240-248, (1936).

8. Dally, J.W. and Riley, W.F., "Experimental Stress Analysis". McGraw Hill, 3rd Edition, (1991), 639pp.

9. Allison, I.M. and Blakemore, R.H., "The analysis of photo elastic data for stress separations". Recent Advances in Stress Analysis, Royal Aeronautical Society, London, 4-7 to 4-12, (1968).

10. Fessler, H., Marston, R.E., Ollerton, E., "A micropolariscope for automatic stress analysis", *Journal of Strain Analysis*, **22**, 25-35 (1987).

11. Voloshin, A. S., Redner, A. S., "Automated Measurement of Birefringence: Development and Experimental Evaluation of the Techniques", *Expt. Mech.*, **29**, 252-257 (1989).

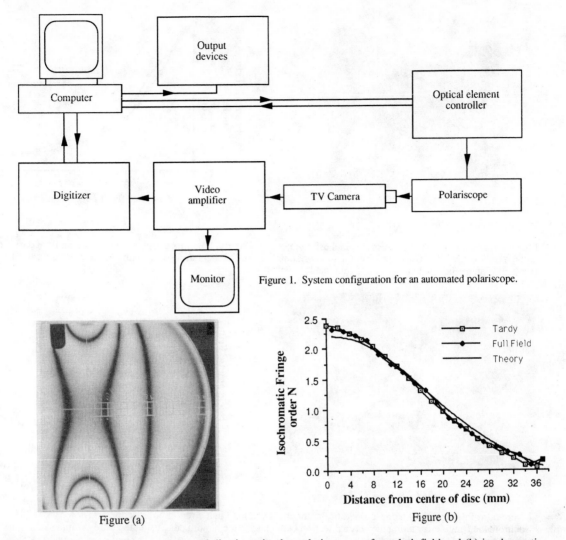

Figure 1. System configuration for an automated polariscope.

Figure (a)

Figure (b)

Figure 2 (a) Photograph of a frozen stressed disc in a circular polariscope set for a dark field and (b) isochromatic fringe order across the diameter normal to the line of load using the Tardy compensation method and the Full Field (automatic) method. Also shown is the theoretical curve as given by Frocht [6].

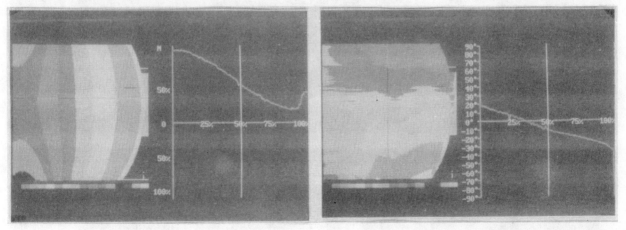

Figure (a) Isochromatic parameter. The graph to the right shows the normalized isochromatic parameter along the selected line seen in the full field image.

Figure (b) Isoclinic parameter. The graph to the right shows the normalized isoclinic parameter along the selected line seen in the full field image.

Figure 3. Photoelastic images of a stress frozen disc obtained using an automated polariscope.

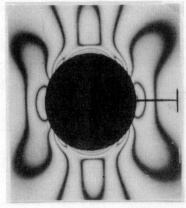

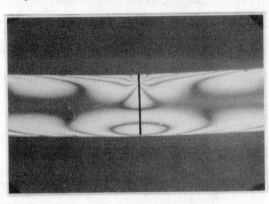

Figure (a)

Figure (b)

Figure 4. (a) Photograph of a stress frozen tensile plate with a central hole in a circular polariscope set for a dark field and (b) the isochromatic fringe order along the horizontal centre line beginning at the edge of the hole using the Tardy compensation method and the Full Field (automatic) method.

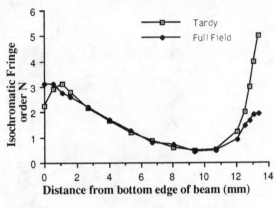

Figure (a)

Figure (b)

Figure 5 (a) Photograph of a constrained beam under a point load in a circular polariscope set for a dark field and (b) isochromatic fringe order along the vertical section beginning at the bottom edge using the Tardy compensation method and the Full Field (automatic) method.

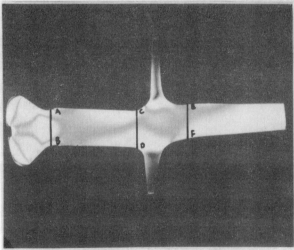

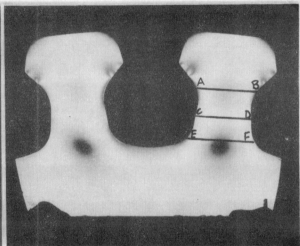

Figure (a) Turbine blade

Figure (b) Turbine slot

Figure 6 Photographs of (a) turbine blade and (b) turbine disc slot in a circular polariscope set for a dark field. The lines shown are the sections that were analysed (photographs courtesy of SNECMA).

510

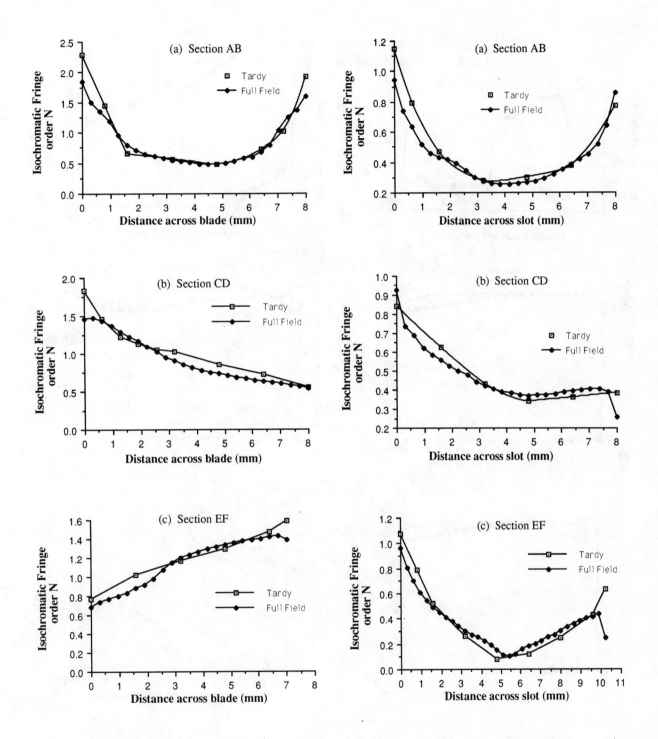

Figure 7. The isochromatic fringe order across the three sections of the turbine blade shown in Figure 6 (a) obtained using the Tardy compensation method and the Full Field (automatic) method.

Figure 8. The isochromatic fringe order across the three sections of the turbine slot shown in Figure 6 (b) obtained using the Tardy compensation method and the Full Field (automatic) method.

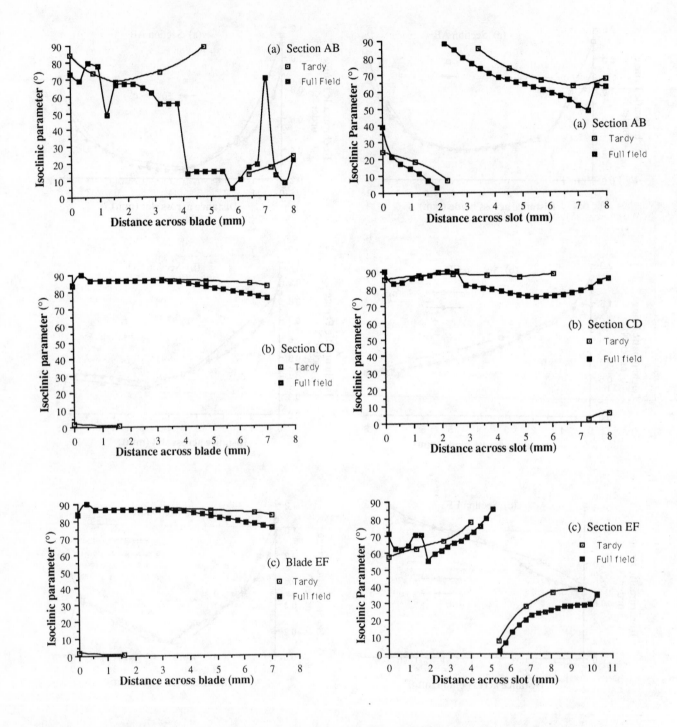

Figure 9. The isoclinic parameter across the three sections of the turbine blade shown in Figure 6 (a) obtained using manual analysis and the Full Field (automatic) method.

Figure 10. The isoclinic parameter across the three sections of the turbine slot shown in Figure 6 (a) obtained using manual analyis and the Full Field (automatic) method.

FUNCTIONAL APPROXIMATION METHOD FOR ANALYSIS OF COLLAPSED PHOTOELASTIC IMAGE DATA AROUND STRESS SINGULARITY

Makoto HARA, Yoshika SUZUKI, Shizuo MAWATARI and Masahisa TAKASHI

ABSTRACT

Although photoelastic experiment has a great advantage in visualization of two-dimensional stress state, several difficulties still exist in the accurate measurement of fringe distributions around a singular point such as a concentrated load or a crack tip, because of significant deformation there and insufficient resolving power of ordinary equipment. This paper is concerned with a proposal of the functional approximation method to overcome these types of difficulty. Collapsed data of photoelastic fringe pattern in the neighborhood of a singular point will be well reconstructed, using a general form of stress functions, unknown parameters of which are determined by a nonlinear optimizing approximation. And, as an typical example, the stress intensity factor determined as one of the unknown parameters are derived from application of this method to a cracked specimen, together with several disscusion.

I. INTRODUCTION

The last four decades, many investigations on photoelastic analysis of crack problem have been published. In 1950s, post[1] and Wells[2] et al published several papers on experimental analysis of stress intensity factor, using a photoelastic isochromatic fringe pattern around a crack. Irwin[3] proposed a method in which Westergaard's stress functions[4] involving two parameters(K_I,σ_{0x}) is employed for the purpose of taking the effects of nonsingular terms into consideration. Smith[5] and Dally[6], [7] et al extended Irwin's method and determined K_I value using multiple-parameters method. Recently, Sanford and Dally[8]~[11] have made a proposal for determining unknown parameters in Westergaard's stress functions which contains extra nonsingular terms expressed by power series. The aim of these methods is to remove restrictions on the analysis within a limited region of the vicinity of crack tip, thus to improve the accuracy of analysis successfully by introduction of additional nonsingular terms.

For development of the above studies into more general problems having another stress singularity, such as stress state near a concentrated load, the following two items to overcome will be pointed out.

Firstly, since almost all researches mentioned above are based on use of Westergaard's stress function, they are not always appropriate for application to other stress singularity problems than the crack problems as mentioned above.

Secondly, the data used in determination of unknown parameters for analysis are limited to the fringe values only on a isochromatic pattern, so that other data left unused, even though these data contains significant information for determining the unknown parameters.

The authors have already proposed a method for two dimensional photoelastic stress analysis, in which a structure driven type image processing is introduced. This method is an effective and useful to photoelastic analysis, because making it possible to provide a set of isochromatics and isoclinics separated each other through superimposing for kinds of image data obtained under a plane polariscope [12]~[15]. On the other hands, authors proposed a functional approximation method[16], in which Goursat's stress functions are used for compensation and reconstruction of condensed isochromatic fringe near a concentrated load like a diametrically compressed circular disk, and showed its usefulness.

In order to solve the first items mentioned above, Goursat's stress functions will be used in this paper for functional approximation instead of Westergaard's stress functions. This comes from the reason that Goursat's one has much more generality applicable to the singularity problems than Westergaard's stress functions. In other words, the former can be applied not only to a crack problem but also to general two-dimensional problems, while use of the latter is mainly limited to crack problem.

To overcome difficulty described in the second items, employment of the functional approximation method seems effective, because the whole data obtained from a fringe pattern, which contains the data not only near singular point but far points apart from singular point are available to the analysis. Also, in this method, the optimization of the difference between the observed distribution and calculated brightness distribution reconstructed Goursat's stress functions is easily performed. Because Goursat's stress functions have nonsingular terms expressed by power series for taking the effects of far field stress into account, thus unknown parameters in the stress functions can be determined with high accuracy like Sanford's method[11].

By means of the functional approximation method connected with nonlinear optimization technique, authors succeeded in determination of K_I value and other unknown parameters from the isochromatic fringe data far from a crack tip, which were extracted from clear reconstructed image data with high contract surrounding the area having stress singularity.

II. STRESS FUNCTIONS IN THE VICINITY OF CRACK

II-1 Principal Stress Difference Expression Using Goursat's Stress Functions

Since the isochromatic fringe order in photoelastic experiments is proportional to the principal stress difference, it is the first step for photoelastic stress analysis of a crack problem to express the stress difference in terms of stress functions. If Goursat's stress functions are employed as the stress functions for the present problem, they are given by the

Makoto HARA is Graduate Student ,Yoshika SUZUKI is Ph. D. Student in Department of Mechanical Engineering, Shizuo MAWATARI is Associate Professor ,and Masahisa Takashi is Professor in Science and Engineering, Aoyama Gakuin University, 6-16-1,Chitosedai, Setagaya-ku, Tokyo, Japan.

following equations in term of a complex variable, $z = x + iy$, the origin of which is at crack tip;

$$\phi(z) = \frac{1}{\sqrt{2\pi}}\sqrt{z}\left\{K_I + \sum_{n=1}^{\infty} a_n z^n\right\}$$

(1)

$$\psi'(z) = \frac{1}{\sqrt{2\pi}}\sqrt{z}\left\{K_I + \sum_{n=1}^{\infty} b_n z^n\right\}$$

(2)

taking the singularity due to crack into consideration, the first and second terms in the right side of the above equations give the singular and nonsingular ones, respectively, and n is a positive integer.

Derivation of eq.(1) and (2) with respect to z give the following equation;

$$\phi''(z) = \frac{K_I}{4\sqrt{2\pi}z^{\frac{3}{2}}} + \frac{1}{\sqrt{2\pi}}\sum_{n=1}^{\infty}\left(n^2 - \frac{1}{4}\right)a_n z^{n-\frac{3}{2}}$$

(3)

$$\psi''(z) = \frac{K_I}{\sqrt{2\pi}\sqrt{z}} + \frac{1}{\sqrt{2\pi}}\sum_{n=1}^{\infty}(n+\frac{1}{2})b_n z^{n-\frac{1}{2}}$$

(4)

From these equation, the principal stress difference at any point z is given as;

$$\sigma_1 - \sigma_2 = \left|\bar{z}\phi''(z) + \psi''(z)\right|$$

(5)

Although general relationship between coefficients a_n and b_n in the nonsingular term of stress functions are not evident, the following relation could be assumed for the purpose of reduction number of coefficients without loosing their generality

$$\left(n^2 - \frac{1}{4}\right)a_n = \left(n + \frac{1}{2}\right)b_n$$

(6)

where $a_n = a_{n1} + ib_{n2}$ and $b_n = b_{n1} + ib_{n2}$.

Using eqs.(3)~(6), the following function $G(r,\theta)$ representing principal stress difference $\sigma_1 - \sigma_2$ is derived in terms of polar coordinates,

$$G(r,\theta) = \sigma_1 - \sigma_2 = \left|\bar{z}\phi''(z) + \psi''(z)\right|$$

$$= \frac{1}{\sqrt{2\pi}}\left[\left\{\frac{K_I}{\sqrt{r}}\sin\frac{3}{2}\theta\sin\theta\right.\right.$$

$$\left. + 2\cos\theta\sum_{n=1}^{\infty}\left(n+\frac{1}{2}\right)\left\{b_{n1}\cos\left(n-\frac{3}{2}\right)\theta - b_{n2}\sin\left(n-\frac{1}{2}\right)\theta\right\}r^{n-\frac{1}{2}}\right\}^2$$

$$+\left\{\frac{K_I}{\sqrt{r}}\cos\frac{3}{2}\theta\sin\theta\right.$$

$$\left.\left. + 2\cos\theta\sum_{n=1}^{\infty}\left(n+\frac{1}{2}\right)\left\{b_{n2}\cos\left(n-\frac{3}{2}\right)\theta + b_{n1}\sin\left(n-\frac{1}{2}\right)\theta\right\}r^{n-\frac{1}{2}}\right\}^2\right]^{\frac{1}{2}}$$

(7)

Eq.(7) is applicable to the whole area in a specimen. If unknown parameters, K_I, b_{11}, b_{21}, , , b_{n1}, b_{12}, b_{22}, , , and b_{n2} in Eq.(7) are determined using clear and stable photoelastic image data of brightness distribution or fringe order values extracted from the whole field stress state can be

calculated by use of Goursat's stress functions. This is due to the facts that the singularity hardly exert influence upon the stress state dominated by nonsingular terms.

II-2 Functional Approximation Method

The following conditions are assumed concerning the brightness distribution of photoelastic image by reference to the photoelastic fringe pattern shown in Fig. 1,

(1) Within the domain near a crack tip (this is referred to as U_1 hereafter), accurate isochromatic image data for quantitative analysis can not extracted from the fringe pattern because of it being excessively crowded together.

(2) On outside domain of U_1 domain (this is referred to as U_2 hereafter), there are a lot of highly contrasted and sufficient data to analysis and no singular point exists.

According to the stress optics law in two dimensional photoelasticity, the well known relationship between isochromatic fringe order and principal stress difference holds as

$$N = \frac{cd}{\lambda}(\sigma_1 - \sigma_2)$$

(8)

where c is the photoelastic coefficient, d is the specimen thickness and λ is the wave length of polarized light.

Since the brightness F in the dark field photoelasticity is given by

$$F = A\sin 2N\pi + C$$

(9)

an approximated function of brightness distribution $F(r,\theta)$ at any point $c(r,\theta)$ on isochromatic fringe pattern can be expressed, by substituting eq.(8) into eq.(9), as follows;

$$F(r,\theta) = A\sin^2\left\{\frac{cd}{\lambda}G(r,\theta)\pi\right\} + C$$

(10)

Now, let $I(r_k,\theta_j)$ be noted as the brightness at a point $c(r_k, \theta_j)$ in the domain U_2 in Fig. 1. To determine unknown parameters involved in eq.(7), sum of second order residue between the eq.(10) and $I(r_k,\theta_j)$ have to minimized. This leads to an optimization problem, that is

$$\sum_{k=1}^{m}\sum_{j=1}^{n}\left[I(r_k,\theta_j) - F(r_k,\theta_j)\right]^2 \to min$$

(11)

where m and n are positive integer, or

$$\sum\left[I(r_k,\theta_j) - \left\{A\sin^2\left\{\frac{cd}{\lambda}G(r_k,\theta_j)\pi\right\} + C\right\}\right]^2$$

$$\to min$$

(12)

II-3 Procedure for Determining Unknown Parameters in an Approximated Brightness Distribution Function

Parameters A and C in eq.(10) can be easily determined from photoelastic image data; i.e. A is the difference of the maximum and minimum value of I_{kj}, and C is the minimum value of I_{kj}. Other parameters are determined by following procedure.

Eq. (12) is written in the following form;

$$\sum \left[\frac{I_{kj} - C}{A} - \sin^2 \left\{ \frac{cd}{\lambda} G(r_k, \theta_k) \pi \right\} \right]^2 \to \min \tag{13}$$

In a sense of optimization, eq. (13) would be equivalent to

$$\sum \left[\frac{1}{2} \left\{ 2 \left(\frac{I_{kj} - C}{A} - \frac{1}{2} \right) + \cos 2 \left\{ \frac{cd}{\lambda} G(r_j, \theta_j) \pi \right\} \right\} \right]^2 \to \min \tag{14}$$

Thus the most fitted solution are obtained by satisfying the following equation.

$$\frac{cd\pi}{\lambda} \sum \left[\frac{\lambda}{2cd\pi} \cos^{-1} \left\{ 2 \left(\frac{I_{kj} - C}{A} - \frac{1}{2} \right) \right\} + G(r_k, \theta_j) \right]^2 \to \min \tag{15}$$

Eq. (15) is in a linear form with respect to A and C, but it is given in a nonlinear one with respect to other parameters. In other words, the problem must be solved as a nonlinear optimization problem. Thus, for the purpose of determining the unknown parameters in Eq. (15) effectively and successfully, a well known program system of Statical Analysis with Least-Square fitting (SALS) on a super-computer (NEC SX-1EA) was employed. On using SALS, only thing that user should do is to make FORTRAN subroutine to which the model functions and the observed data are admitted[17]. In treating the nonlinear optimization problem by SALS, however, the difficulties sometimes arise that the solution obtained does not always converge to the intrinsic minimum value of model function. It is very important, therefore, to give initial value appropriate to the given problem so that unknown parameters may converge.

III. APPLICATION OF THE MODEL TO THEORETICAL DATA

III-1 Construction of Theoretical Isochromatic Image Data from Westergaard's Stress Functions

Before applying the method developed in the previous section to an actual experimental data, its availability together with accuracy of the results obtained was examined using isochromatic image data constructed by a theoretically analyzed problem. The theoretical isochromatic data used for this purpose is adjusted with the same format in a current image processor; i.e. brightness gradation of 256 and 480 ×512 pixels.

A model data was constructed, using the strict Westergaard's solution of two-dimensional cracked body subjected to a biaxial tension as illustrated in Fig. 2. Principal stress difference by Westergaard's solution is given for opening mode, i.e. mode I of an infinite plate with a crack follows,

$$\sigma_1 - \sigma_2 = 2\sqrt{2} y \, \text{Im} \left[Z_I'(z) \right] \tag{16}$$

Using bipolar coordinates as shown in Fig. 3, eq. (16) gives

$$\sigma_1 - \sigma_2 = 2\sqrt{2} \frac{\sigma a^2}{\sqrt{r_1} \left(\sqrt{r_2} \right)^3} \sin \theta_1 \sin 3 \left(\frac{\theta_1 + \theta_2}{2} \right) \tag{17}$$

Therefore, the theoretical isochromatic intensity, L is expressed as

$$L = A \sin^2 \left\{ \frac{cd}{\lambda} (\sigma_1 - \sigma_2) \pi \right\} + C \tag{18}$$

in which numerical values of A and C are taken as 255 and 0, respectively.

In practice, theoretical isochromatic brightness at each point in the whole field is constructed as image data by substituting eq. (17) into eq. (18). In this case, since one pixel of ideal image data corresponds to the area of 0.25×0.25 mm^2, crack length $2a$ of 60 mm comes to equal 240 pixels on display.

III-2 Results of Optimization for Theoretical Data

The followings are description of the results of practical nonlinear optimization using the theoretical image data prepared by the methods discussing in the previous section.

Fig. 4 shows two types of data which were obtained by different loading conditions (σ=0.196MPa, and 0.329MPa). Brightness distributions of these theoretical data alone a line having a coordinates parameter $\theta_1 = \pi/2$ are given in Fig.5(a) and (b). Several sets of data ranging from a fixed point, which is located at 60 mm distant from the crack tip, to another reference point on the $\theta_1 = \pi/2$ line were used for the analysis. The position of the above reference point was measured with a distance l from crack tip to boundary of two domains U_1 and U_2 mentioned before. This means that the longer l is selected, the larger the domain becomes, thus collapsed image data in domain U_1 come to increase.

On the other hand, the effect of optimum order n in eq. (7) on the stability of the obtained parameters was examined by changing n from 0 to 10. As a results, it turned out that each parameter shows unstable value for n greater than 5. Particularly, in the case of n=0, the principal stress difference is given by only the singular term, so that it is equivalent to the expression without nonsingular terms, which is used in an ordinary approximation for a crack problem.

Taking the above results into consideration, the approximation method proposed in this paper was examined for a infinite plate having a crack under various conditions; taking six integer from 0 to 5 as n and 6 steps of 1, 2, 3, 5, 10, and 20 mm as l. In Fig. 6 (a), (b) and (c), are shown three typical examples(l = 1, 5, and 10 mm, for n = 0, 3, 5) of the principal stress difference distribution determined in the optimization procedure, together with those calculated by theoretical analysis.

It is found from these figures that the proposed approximation method gives a satisfactory optimized results if appropriate number of order n is adopted, thus the principal stress difference distribution over the whole field of specimen can be reconstructed.

On the other hand, it is also recognized from these figures that for a large value of l that means employment of a wide domain as U_1, the principal stress difference distributions determined with the optimization become more unstable. This implies that its dependence on the data dominated by nonsingular stress field become much stronger than that on the data dominated by singular stress field.

However, it is concluded that even in the case of large value of l, the reconstruction of principal stress difference distribution around the crack tip is possible with the data dominated by the nonsingular stress field. It is a matter of course that employment of a smaller distance of l leads to more accurate optimization of parameters in eq. (7) on the whole area of specimen.

III-3 Results of the parameter K_I

Relative errors of the stress intensity factor which was determined as a parameter of the approximated stress function given as eq(7) against theoretically calculated value under two loading conditions are compared in Table 1. The white columns in the table give excellent results within 3 percent error, and the darker columns indicate ones having larger errors dependent on the employed combination of n and l.

On both loading conditions, for a smaller value of l against the crack length a, in other word, for employment of the experimental data holding the accuracy near the crack tip, the present method will provide the K_I with a small error irrespective of the order of n. On the other hand, in the case of $n=0$, i.e. use of an model approximated stress function constructed only with singular term will accompany the error which increase with l. However, if an approximate value of n is selected between 2 and 3, the K_I value could be evaluated accurately in a wide variation of l/a ranging from 1/10 to 1/3.

Fig. 7 shows a typical example of the brightness distributions reconstructed by taking $l=5$(mm) and $n=2$. The square points dotted in this figure indicates the brightness before the reconstruction of the principal stress difference expressed with Westergaard's strict solution involving nonsingular term, and the solid line gives the brightness distributions after the reconstruction. This figure shows an excellent reconstruction of brightness distribution of isochromatics. Thus, it turns out that the proposed method is useful for determination of isochromatic fringes not only around the crack tip but .also over the whole field of a specimen.

As described above, each parameters in eq(7) may vary in accordance with the variety of l and n. However, a rough estimation of appropriate parameters would be possible through several calculations of the relative error resulting from these factors.

Figs. 8 (a), (b) are shown pictures of the theoretical isochromatic fringe distribution (a) and the reconstructed one (b) performed by means of the optimization procedure to determine the principal stress difference expressed with Goursat's stress functions containing the effects of nonsingular term The circle domain which radius is 5 mm and corresponds to domain U_I in Fig. 8 (a) corresponds to Fig. 8 (b). In view of these pictures, it is found that the collapsed area in Fig. 8 (a) has been well reconstructed.

III-4 Discussion

Some studies have been published on experimental analysis of the crack problem using the stress functions including nonsingular term with power series[5], [8]~[11]. It can be said, however, that the functional approximation method presented in this paper has the characteristic advantages summarized as follows;

1) Isochromatic image data in the whole specimen except the area where the isochromatic fringes are extremely crowded are available for determining the unknown parameter of model approximated function.

2) The procedure of this system for determination of unknown parameters is carried out by comparing the equation of brightness distributions given by a model approximation function with the brightness distribution observed in photoelasticity. Therefore, the numerical differentiation of maximum shearing stress expressed by Westergaard's stress function is not needed.

3) The present system can widely use for analyzing any problem concerning the singularity, because it utilizes the Goursat's stress functions, instead of Westergaard's functions.

However, it is noteworthy that the model function contains nonlinear term, so there is no definite way to determine the initial conditions or order n of the model function. Therefore, before appropriating this method to the practical analysis, careful attentions must be paid as for selection of suitable initial conditions and order n so that the unknown parameters may converge.

IV. CONCLUSION

In this paper a method for determining the unknown parameters including the stress intensity factor K_I in the Goursat's stress functions by use of the nonlinear optimum method was proposed. And, validity of this method was verifyed by applying it to the theoretical isochromatic fringe data constructed by Westergaard's stress function. Thus, it turned out that the proposed method is very effective to analysis not only K_I value but also the distribution of the whole area in a cracked specimen with a high accuracy.

Acknowledgement

The authors appreciate the financial support of the Center for Science and Engineering Research. Institute of Aoyama Gakuin University.

Reference

[1] Post,D.,"Photoelastic Stress Analysis for An Edge Crack in Tensile Field", Proc. SESA 12(1954), 99-116.
[2] Wells, A. A, and Post, D., "The Dynamic Stress Distribution Surrounding A Running Crack - A Photoelastic Analysis", Proc. SESA, 16(1958), 69-92.
[3] Irwin, G. R., Discussion of paper: "The Dynamic Stress Distribution Surrounding A Running Crack - A Phototelastic Analysis", Proc. SESA, 16(1958), 93-6.
[4] Westergaard, H. M., "Bearing Pressure and Cracks", Jour. of appl. Meck., 6(1939), 49-53.
[5] Schroedl, M. A., McGowan, J. J. and Smith, C. W., "Determination of Stress Intensity Factors from Photoelastic Data with Applications to Surface-fraw Problems", ,Exp. Mech., 14(1974), 392-399.
[6] Etheridge, J. M. and Dally, J. W., "A Three-parameter method for Determining Stress Intensity Factors from isochromatic fringe patterns", Eng. Fract. Mech. 10(1978), 91-94.
[7] Etheridge, J. M., Dally, J. W.and Kobayashi, T., "A New Method of Determining the Stress Intensity Factors from Isochromatic Fringe Loops", Eng. Fract. Mech., 10(1978), 81-93
[8] Sanford, R. J., "Application of Least-Squares Method to Photoelastic Analysis", Exp. Mech., June(1980), 192-197.

[9] Sanford, R. j., "Determining Fracture Parameters with Full-field Optical Methods", Exp.Mech., **29**(1989), 241-247.

[10] Dally, J. W., "Agawal, R. K. and Sanford, R. J., "A Study of Hysteresis in The K_{ID}-a Relation", Exp. Mech., **30**(1990), 177-183.

[11] Sanford, R. J. and Kirk, M. T., "A Comparison of Boundary and Global Collocation Solutions for K$_I$ and CMOD Calibration Functions", Exp. Mech., **31**(1991), 52-59.

[12] Mawatari, S., et al, Trans. of JSME, **55**-511, A(1989), 598-607 (in Japanese).

[13] Mawatari,.S., et al,.Trans. of JSME, **55**-514, A(1989), 1423-1428 (in Japanese).

[14] Mawatari, S., et al ,Proc. 9th Int. Conf. on Exp. Mech, **5**(1990), 2069-2087.

[15] Takashi, M., et al, Appl. Stress Analysis, Elservier Appl. Science, London & New York(1990), 516-525.

[16] Suzuki, Y., et al, Trans. of JSME, **57**-538, A(1991), 171-177, (in Japanese).

[17] Nakamura, T., et al, "Program System SALS for Nonlinear Least-square Fitting in Experimental Science" in Recent Developments in Statical Inference and Data Analysis, Matukawa, K., editor, 221-225, (North Holland Publishing Co.,(1980).

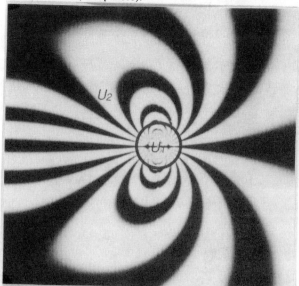

Fig.1 Domain division in vicinity of crack tip

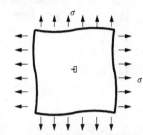

Fig.2 Theoretical model for Westergaard's solution

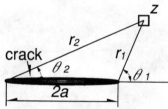

Fig. 3 Bipolar coordinates for expression of Westergaard's stress function

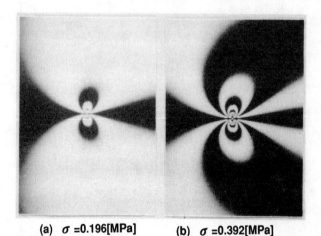

(a) σ =0.196[MPa]   (b) σ =0.392[MPa]

Fig. 4 Theoretical data

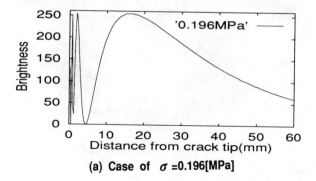

(a) Case of σ =0.196[MPa]

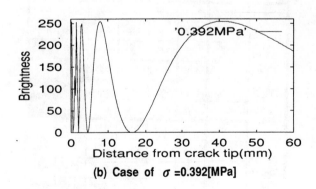

(b) Case of σ =0.392[MPa]

Fig. 5 Brightness distribution of isochromatic fringe along the line on $\theta_1 = \pi/2$

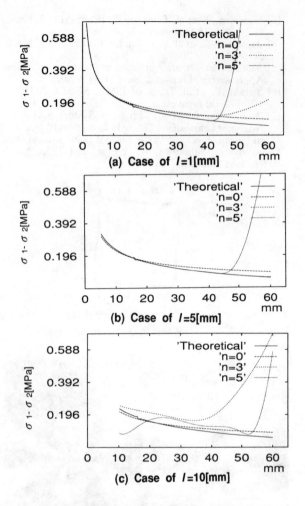

(a) Case of l =1[mm]

(b) Case of l =5[mm]

(c) Case of l =10[mm]

Fig. 6 Principal stress difference distribution
along the line on $\theta 1 = \pi/2$

Table 1 Relative error against theoretical K_l [%]

Stress	l/a	$n=0$	$n=1$	$n=2$	$n=3$	$n=4$	$n=5$
σ =0.196 (MPa)	1/30	1.24	1.57	1.21	2.05	0.50	3.04
	1/15	3.07	1.58	1.60	0.47	0.04	0.56
	1/10	3.05	1.68	1.43	0.73	0.67	7.37
	1/6	4.82	2.69	0.48	0.65	13.49	1.77
	1/3	9.43	5.27	2.44	13.50	63.52	388.77
	2/3	18.06	8.41	3.51	6.42	23.35	722.90
σ =0.392 (MPa)	1/30	1.07	1.57	0.81	0.57	0.17	0.29
	1/15	2.04	1.62	2.01	0.21	0.54	1.60
	1/10	2.94	1.71	0.02	0.51	0.10	4.11
	1/6	4.76	2.38	0.51	0.24	6.33	17.10
	1/3	9.31	4.33	0.01	1.57	16.41	48.52
	2/3	17.79	8.92	2.95	9.96	145.10	21.90

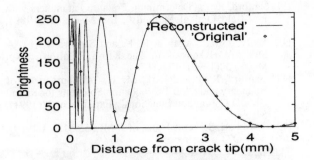

Fig. 7 Original and reconstructed data

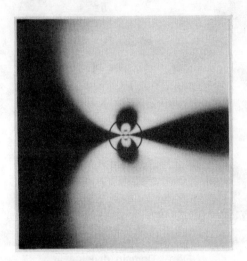

(a) Before reconstruction

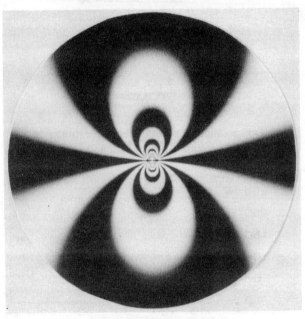

(b) After reconstruction

Fig. 8 Reconstructed isochromatic
fringe distribution

518

Development of Photoelastic ExperimentalMethod for the Measurement of
Stress Intensity Factor Around the Interface Crack of Bimaterial

Jae-Guk Sur, Jai-Sug Hawong, Sun-Ho CHoi

ABSTRACT

Photoelastic experimental model materials for bimaterial are manufactured by bonding method which is to bond two materias by adhesive and molding method which is to fabricate the bimaterial through the curing cycle after pouring the solution of polymer into molding box with another material. we characterize the properties of those specimens about the role of photoelastic experimental model material of bimaterial and develop the photoelastic experimental method for bimaterial.

It is better to utilize the molding method than the bonding method in manufacture of photoelastic experimental model material for bimaterial. Althrough experimental values obtained from photoelastic experiment for bimaterial fabricated by molding method were greater than values of computational analysis, the inclinations of experimental value are similor to the result of computational analysis.

Therefor we can know that the process of photoelastic experiment for bimaterial developed in this reseach is effective in the stress analysis of bimaterial with interfacical crack.

INTRODUCTION

It goes without saying that present and future advance in the engineering and the technology are dependent on the development of new and innovative materials. In the recent years, composite materials have been developed countlessly and used in engineering field such as

Jae-Guk Sur is graduate student in Ph.D. Course,
Jai-Sug Hawong is Professor, department of mechnical Engineering,
Sun-Ho Choi is Professor, Department of Machine design, Yeungnam University, Dae-dong, Gyungsan City, Gyung-buk, Korea, 713-749.

aircraft, automobiles and rocket. The bimaterials, a kind of composites, are made of dissimilar materials which are bonded to each other.

The bimaterials are diversely used each part of the structure in the engineering field. The particular important thing in the bimaterial is the strength of the interface between bimaterials. The manufacturing cavities which are developed during bonding or molding process and flaws resulting from the residual stresses in welded materials should be seriously taken into consideration for estimating the strength of the interface of bimaterial.

The plane problem of interface in the bimaterials has been theoretically studied. The stress field in the vicinity of interface crack tip of bimaterial was initially studied by Williams.[1] He definded stress singularity which is osicillated at the crack tip in the interface of bimaterial(1959). But he did not define the value of stress components in the vicinity of the crack tip in the interface of bimaterial. Stress components in the vicinity of the crack tip of bimaterial was given by England[2], Erdogan[3] and Rice and Sih[4] etc..

THE STRESS COMPONENTS IN THE VICCINITY OF THE INTERFACE CRACK TIP OF BIMATERIAL

We consider two homogeneus, isotropic elastic materials numbered 1 and 2 ,which occupy the upper $(y>0)$ and lower$(y<0)$ half-planes (Fig.1). The materials 1 and 2 are characterized by the physical properties G_1, v_1, and G_2, v_2. when $G(i=1,2)$ are the shear moduli and v $(i=1,2)$ are the Piosson's ratios. The two materials are bonded to each other along the X-axis except for a finite segment of length $2a$ forming an internal horizontal crack.

We suppose that the crack surfaces are not loaded and the bimaterial plate is loaded at infinity. Eq.(1) describe the stress state in the region near the crack tip for material 1 ($0° \leq \theta \leq 180°$)

$$\sigma_{1x} = \frac{K_1}{2\sqrt{2\pi r} \cdot \cosh \pi \beta} \left[\frac{1}{2} e^{-\beta(\pi-\theta)} \left[5\cos\left(\frac{\theta}{2} + \beta \log \frac{r}{2a}\right) + \cos\left(\frac{5\theta}{2} + \beta \log \frac{r}{2a}\right) + 4\beta \sin\theta \cos\left(\frac{3\theta}{2} + \beta \log \frac{r}{2a}\right) \right] - e^{\beta(\pi-\theta)} \cos\left(\frac{\theta}{2} - \beta \log \frac{r}{2a}\right) \right] - \frac{K_{11}}{2\sqrt{2\pi r} \cdot \cosh \pi \beta} \left[\frac{1}{2} e^{-\beta(\pi-\theta)} \left[5\sin\left(\frac{\theta}{2} + \beta \log \frac{r}{2a}\right) + \sin\left(\frac{5\theta}{2} + \beta \log \frac{r}{2a}\right) + 4\beta \sin\theta \sin\left(\frac{3\theta}{2} + \beta \log \frac{r}{2a}\right) \right] + e^{\beta(\pi-\theta)} \sin\left(\frac{\theta}{2} - \beta \log \frac{r}{2a}\right) \right] - \sigma_{ox}$$

$$\sigma_{1y} = \frac{K_1}{2\sqrt{2\pi r} \cdot \cosh \pi \beta} \left[\frac{1}{2} e^{-\beta(\pi-\theta)} \left[3\cos\left(\frac{\theta}{2} + \beta \log \frac{r}{2a}\right) - \cos\left(\frac{5\theta}{2} + \beta \log \frac{r}{2a}\right) - 4\beta \sin\theta \cos\left(\frac{3\theta}{2} + \beta \log \frac{r}{2a}\right) \right] + e^{\beta(\pi-\theta)} \cos\left(\frac{\theta}{2} - \beta \log \frac{r}{2a}\right) \right] - \frac{K_{11}}{2\sqrt{2\pi r} \cdot \cosh \pi \beta} \left[\frac{1}{2} e^{-\beta(\pi-\theta)} \left[3\sin\left(\frac{\theta}{2} + \beta \log \frac{r}{2a}\right) - \sin\left(\frac{5\theta}{2} + \beta \log \frac{r}{2a}\right) - 4\beta \sin\theta \sin\left(\frac{3\theta}{2} + \beta \log \frac{r}{2a}\right) \right] - e^{\beta(\pi-\theta)} \sin\left(\frac{\theta}{2} - \beta \log \frac{r}{2a}\right) \right]$$

$$\tau_{1xy} = \frac{K_1}{2\sqrt{2\pi r} \cdot \cosh \pi \beta} \left[\frac{1}{2} e^{-\beta(\pi-\theta)} \left[\cos\left(\frac{\theta}{2} + \beta \log \frac{r}{2a}\right) + \cos\left(\frac{5\theta}{2} + \beta \log \frac{r}{2a}\right) + 4\beta \sin\theta \sin\left(\frac{3\theta}{2} + \beta \log \frac{r}{2a}\right) \right] - e^{\beta(\pi-\theta)} \sin\left(\frac{\theta}{2} - \beta \log \frac{r}{2a}\right) \right] + \frac{K_{11}}{2\sqrt{2\pi r} \cdot \cosh \pi \beta} \left[\frac{1}{2} e^{-\beta(\pi-\theta)} \left[\cos\left(\frac{\theta}{2} + \beta \log \frac{r}{2a}\right) + \cos\left(\frac{5\theta}{2} + \beta \log \frac{r}{2a}\right) + 4\beta \sin\theta \cos\left(\frac{3\theta}{2} + \beta \log \frac{r}{2a}\right) \right] + e^{\beta(\pi-\theta)} \cos\left(\frac{\theta}{2} - \beta \log \frac{r}{2a}\right) \right] \quad \text{(1)}$$

In eq. (1), r and θ are the polor coordinates of the point considered from the tip of the crack and β is a bimaterial constant given by

$$\beta = \frac{1}{2a} \log \beta_o \quad \text{(2)}$$

where $\beta_o = \frac{G_1 + k_1 G_2}{G_2 + k_2 G_1}$

$$k_j = 3 - 4v_j \quad \text{for plane strain}$$

$$k_j = \frac{3 - v_j}{1 + v_j} \quad \text{for plane stress}$$

The stress intensity factors K_1 and K_{11} are independen of the coordinate r, θ and depend on the physical constants of two materials and loading conditions of the bimaterial plate.

Complex stress intensity factor for the interface crack of bimaterial was obtained by Sih and Rice[4] as following equation.

$$K_1 - iK_{11} = \frac{\sqrt{a}}{\cosh \pi \beta} (1-i2\beta)(2a)^i (\sigma - i\tau) \quad \text{(3)}$$

Sun and Jih[5] suggested the previous equation as eq.(4).

$$K_1 - iK_{11} = \frac{\sqrt{a}}{\cosh \pi \beta} (1-i2\beta)(\sigma - i\tau) \quad \text{(4)}$$

In this paper, the complex stress intensity factors are defined as following equation.

$$K_1 - iK_{11} = (1-i2\beta) \sqrt{a} (\sigma - i\tau) \quad \text{(5)}$$

We can know through the equation (2) that bimaterial constant β_o is between 1/3 and 3. Bimaterial constants 1/3 and 3 respectively correspond to $G_2/G_1=0$ and ∞ with $k_{1,2} = 3$(corresponding to the value of the Poisson's ratio $v = 0$)

It can be easily established from symmetry consideration that the stress σ_{2x}, σ_{2y}, τ_{2xy} in the material 2($-180° < \theta < 0°$) could be determined from the stress σ_{1x}, σ_{1y}, τ_{1xy} in material 1 by substituting the quantities β and θ for the values $-\beta$ and $-\theta$.

When materials 1 and 2 have the same physical properties, equation (1) is identical the stress compoments in the vicinity of the crack tip in an infinite plate of isotropic material.

BASIC THEORY OF PHOTOELASTIC EXPERIMENT

Equation (6) represents stress optic law in the plane stress

$$\frac{Nf}{t} = \sigma_1 - \sigma_2 = \sqrt{(\sigma_x - \sigma_y)^2 + 4\tau^2_{xy}} \quad \text{(6)}$$

where σ_1, σ_2: The principal stresses

    f: Stress fringe value

    t: The thickness of the specimen

    N: Fringe order

Putting equation (1) into equation (6),

equation (6) is expressed by terms K_1, K_{11} and σ_{ox}. Material constants(E_1, E_2, ν_1, ν_2, f and t) are measured by experiments.

To obtain three unknown parameters K_1, K_{11}, σ_{ox}, m numbers of polar coordinates(r, θ) and fringe orders(N) are put into equation (6) and an interative procedure based on the Newton Raphson method[6] will be applied to the equation (6). Equation (6) can be transformed into equation (7)

$$G_k(K_1, K_{11}, \sigma_{ox}) = (\sigma_x - \sigma_y)^2 + 4\tau^2_{xy} - (\frac{fN}{T})^2 \quad (7)$$

Applying Taylar's series to equation (7) and neglecting high order, the following equation is obtained.

$$(G_k)_{i+1} = (G_{ki}) + (\frac{\partial G_k}{\partial K_1})_i \Delta k_1 + (\frac{\partial G_k}{\partial K_{11}})_i \Delta k_{11}$$
$$+ (\frac{\partial G_k}{\partial \sigma_{ox}})_i \Delta \sigma_{ox} \quad (8)$$

Where i refer to the (i)th interation step and K_1, K_{11} and σ_{ox} are respectively stress intensity factor and singularity in the bimaterial with the crack along interface.

Since $(G_k)_{i+1} = 0$, eq (8) can be transformed into eq (9).

$$- (G_k)_i = (G_k)_i + (\frac{\partial G_k}{\partial k_1})_i \Delta K_1 + (\frac{\partial G_k}{\partial k_{11}})_i \Delta K_{11}$$
$$+ (\frac{\partial G_k}{\partial \sigma_{ox}})_i \Delta \sigma_{ox} \quad (9)$$

By matrix notation, Equation (9) becomes:

$$\begin{pmatrix} G_1 \\ G_2 \\ \cdot \\ G_m \end{pmatrix} = \begin{pmatrix} \frac{\partial G_1}{\partial K_1} & \frac{\partial G_1}{\partial K_{11}} & \frac{\partial G_1}{\partial \sigma_{ox}} \\ \frac{\partial G_2}{\partial K_1} & \frac{\partial G_2}{\partial K_{11}} & \frac{\partial G_2}{\partial \sigma_{ox}} \\ \cdot & \cdot & \cdot \\ \frac{\partial G_m}{\partial K_1} & \frac{\partial G_m}{\partial K_{11}} & \frac{\partial G_m}{\partial \sigma_{ox}} \end{pmatrix} \begin{pmatrix} \Delta K_1 \\ \Delta K_{11} \\ \Delta \sigma_{ox} \end{pmatrix} \quad (10)$$

The simple expression of equation (10):

$$[G] = [a][\Delta K] \quad (11)$$

The least-squares process is the same as following process

To multiply both sides of equation (11) by transpose of the coefficient matrix:

$$[a]^T \times [G] = [a]^T \times [a][\Delta K] \quad (12)$$
$$[d] = [c] \times [\Delta K] \quad (13)$$

where $[d] = [a]^T[G]$
$[c] = [a]^T[a]$

Finally, if matrix [c] has an inverse, the soultion of equation (11) is given by

$$[\Delta K] = [c]^{-1}[d] \quad (14)$$

$$K_1 = K_1 + \Delta K_1$$
$$K_{11} = K_{11} + \Delta K_{11} \quad (15)$$
$$\sigma_{ox} = \sigma_{ox} + \Delta \sigma_{ox}$$

where $[c]^{-1}$ is the inverse of [c]

About 20 points of coordinates and fringe orders were measured on the fringe patterns. And put them into equation (7)

Through equation (13), (14) and (15). We can obtain K_1, K_{11} and σ_{ox}.

EXPERIMENT

1. FABRICATION OF PHOTOELASTIC EXPERIMENTAL MODEL FOR THE BIMATERIAL

In this paper, specimens are made by bonding method and molding method. The bonding method is to bond two materials by adhesive, the molding method is to fabricate the bimaterial through the curing cycle after pouring the solution of polymer into molding box with another material.

In the bonding method, epoxy plate were respectively bonded to aluminum plate and brass plate by adhesive(Alteco-EE) and the crack was formed by using teflon molding method[7] between epoxy plate and aluminum plate or brass plate. After 24 hours on bonding, the epoxy plate of bimaterial plates were examined about residual stress at room temperature and we perform an experiment on the bonded bimaterial plate without residual stress.

In molding method, photoelastic bimaterial plate were fabricated by the molding method that glass mats were inserted the half side of epoxy solution during molding process and were molded through the same curning cycle as shown in Fig. 2. Glass surface mats have not directional properties. The internal crack was formed along the interface of specimen by mechanical cutter.

2. PHOTOELASTIC EXPERIMENT

Epoxy plate was respectively bonded with aluminum and brass by the bonding method and bimaterial plate for photoelastic experiment was fabricated. We performed photoelastic experiment on the bimaterial bonded with aluminum and epoxy or brass and epoxy. We did not obtain precise experimental stress intensity factors of the interface crack of the above bimaterial under tension by using photoelastic experiment because adhesive strength was not constant and too strong on the interface of bonded bimaterial plate. The configuration of the fringe pattern for each crack length of the bimaterials(aluminum and epoxy, brass and epoxy) is shown in Fig.3.

The specimen which glass surface mat reinforced epoxy plate and pure epoxy plate is fabricated by the molding method developed in this research is very good photoelastic experimental model material for bimaterial because adhesive state and adhesive strength between the material 1(epoxy) and material 2(glass fiber reinforced epoxy) are constant and strong on the interface of bimaterial plate. Plate which glass surface mat is inserted into the epoxy plate is called glass surface mat reinforced epoxy. We can fabricated many kinds of photoelastic experimental model material for bimaterials by changing number of glass surface mats. That is to say, we can change the physical constant of materia 2 with the change of V_r(glass surface mat volume/glass surface mat volume + epoxy volume). Therefore, we can measure experimental stress intensity factor with various step of E_2/E_1. Photoelastic experiment was reinforced with the ratio E_1/E_2 in high temperature to perform model experiment with the great ratio of E_1/E_2. That is, stress freezing method was used in this research. Stress freezing curing cycle is shown in the Fig.4. Strain gauge for high temperature was used to measure physical constants(E: Young's moduli, ν: Poisson's ratio) in high temperature(about 120℃)

EXPERIMENTAL RESULTS

Physical constants of epoxy and glass surface mat reinforced epoxy in high and room temperature is shown in table 1.

The isochromatic fringe patterns of epoxy of isotropic material with crack length (2a/w) under mode I load are shown in Fig.5. The isochromatic fringe patterns of bimatrial (material 1: epoxy ,material 2: glass surface mat reinforced epoxy) with crack length(2a/w) under mode I load are shown in Fig.6 and Fig.7.

Comparing isochromatic fringe patterns(Fig.5) of the pure epoxy with those(Fig.6 and Fig.7) of the bimaterials, we may know that r_{max} of isochromatic fringe of pure epoxy in the vicinity of the crack tip is directed to Y-axis as general fringe patterns of isotropic materials and that r_{max} of fringe pattern in the vicinity of the interface crack tip of bimaterial is very inclined from Y-axis to X-axis(or crack surface).

Isochromatic fringe patterns of pure epoxy

under mode II load are shown in Fig.8. In this case, the r_{max} of the fringe patterns in the vicinity of the crack tip are inclined to X-axis and the values of stress intensity factors are shown in table 2. Comparing isochromatic fringes of Fig.6 and Fig.7 obtained from bimaterials under mode I as external load with those of Fig.8 from pure epoxy under mixed mode, we can know that considerable shear stress acts in the vicinity of interface crack tip of bimaterial under mode I as external load . The value of K_1/K_o of bimatrial 1 in the table 1 is shown in Fig.9. When experimental values obtained from the photoelastic experiment process used in this research were compare with the result of B.E.M. in condition which $E_2/E_1=10$ and $\nu_1=\nu_2=0.3$ experimental values are greater than the result of B.E.M.. But although the physical properties in Fig.9 are different from thoses of model material of B.E.M., the inclinations of experimental values are vary similar to those of B.E.M. results. The values of K_{11}/K_o of bimaterial 1 in table 1 are presented in Fig.10. Comparing exeperimental values of bimaterial 1 with the results of B.E.M, it is known that the experimental values of bimaterial 1 are greater than the results of B.E.M..

CONCLUSION

In this paper, we may know that it is better to utilize the molding method than the bonding method when we fabricate phtoelastic experimental model material for bimaterials.

(1) It is known that the bimaterial which epoxy plate and glass surface mat reinforced epoxy are molded play a role as photoelastic experimental model material for bimaterial.

(2) It is assured that the bimaterials bonded by adhesive can not be used as photoelastic experimental model material for bimaterial. But the bimaterial bonded by adhesive can be used as photoelastic experiment model material both using high technology of bonding and considering bonding larger as matrial 3.

(3) Althrough experimental values obtained from phtoelastic experiment developed in this reseach as photoelastic experiment for bimaterials were greater than B.E.M. results , the inclinations of experimental values are similar to B.E.M. rsults. There was considerable problem in determination of location of the crack tip. If this problem is

solved, it is inferred that we can obtain the better results in the experiment.

REFERENCE

(1) M.L. Williams, "The Stress around a Fault or Crack in Dissimilar Media", Bull Seism. Soc. Am. 199-204 (1959)

(2) England, A. H., "A Crack between Dissimilar Media" J. Appl. Mech. 400-402 Vol.32 (1965)

(3) Erdogan, F., "Stress Distribution in Bonded Dissimilar Materials with Crack", J. Appl. Mech. 403-410 Vol.32

(4) Rice, J.R. and Sih, G.C., "Plane Problems of Crack in Dissimilar Media", J. Appl. Mech. 418-423 (1965)

(5) Sun, C.T. and Jih, C.J., "On Strain Energy Release Rates for Interface Cracks in Bimaterial Media", Eng. Fract. Mech. 13-19 Vol.28 (1987)

(6) Robert, J. Sanford, "Application of the Least-squares Method to Photoelastic Analysis", Exp. Mech. 192-197 (1980)

(7) S.B. Cho and R. Yuuki, "Boundary Element Analysis of Crack Problems in Dissimilar Materials Using Hetenyi's Solution", Proceedings of 2nd Conference of APCS, Seoul, Korea, 495-500 (1986)

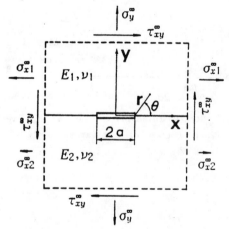

Fig.1   Infinite plate with a crack subjected to stress at infinity

Table.1 Properties of materials

Specmen	Room Temp.		High Temp.		Remark
	E_1(MPa)	ν_1	E_2(MPa)	ν_2	
Epoxy	2.279	0.4	8	0.3	
Glass mat reinfoced Epoxy	5.321	0.45	97	0.26	V_f=2.5%
Aluminum	71	0.33			

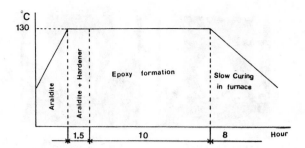

Fig.2   Epoxy curing cycle

(a) Epoxy + aluminum   (b) Epoxy + brass
2a/w=0.5, σ_o=2.92 MPa   2a/w=0.6, σ_o=4.62 MPa

Fig.3   Isochromatic fringe pattern for bonding bimaterial plate in mode I load

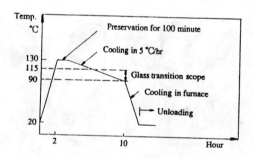

Fig.4   Stress freezing cycle

(a) 2a/w=0.3, σ_o=3.92 MPa (b)2a/w=0.4, σ_o=3.92 MPa
   K_1/K_o=1.045 K_1/K_o=1.140

Fig.5   Isochromatic fringe pattern for pure epoxy plate in mode I load

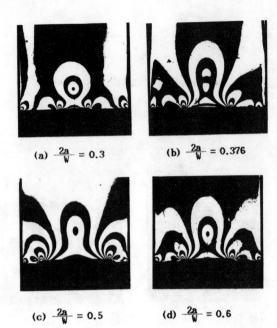

(a) $\dfrac{2a}{W} = 0.3$ (b) $\dfrac{2a}{W} = 0.376$

(c) $\dfrac{2a}{W} = 0.5$ (d) $\dfrac{2a}{W} = 0.6$

Fig.6   Isochromatic fringe pattern for molding bimaterial plate with V_f=2.5% in mode I load

(a) 2a/w=0.6, θ =30°   (b) 2a/w=0.4, θ =60°

K_1/K_o=0.978 K_{11}/K_o=0.475 K_1/K_o=0.33 K_{11}/K_o=0.507

Fig.8   Isochromatic fringe pattern for pure epoxy plate in mode II load

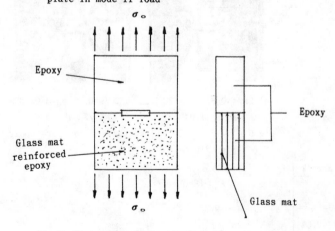

Fig.7   The shape of the specimen of molding bimaterial

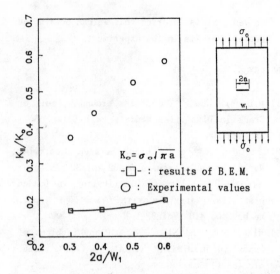

Fig.9   Stress intensity factors(K_1/K_o) versus 2a/w for molding bimaterial plate with V_f=2.5% in mode I load

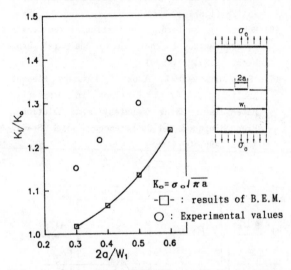

Fig..10   Stress intensity factors(K_{11}/K_o) versus 2a/w for molding bimaterial plate with V_f=2.5% in mode I load

EXPERIMENTAL INVESTIGATION OF HIGH PRESSURE
WATERJET PIERCING PROCESS

M. Ramulu and H. Yeh

Department of Mechanical Engineering, FU-10
University of Washington
Seattle, WA 98195 USA

ABSTRACT

Dynamic photoelastic technique was used to investigate the high pressure waterjet impacting and piercing process on a polycarbonate material. A high speed camera system was used to record the photoelastic fringe pattern associated with the jet-material interaction. Transient stresses associated with the jet penetration process were evaluated.

INTRODUCTION

Waterjet cutting is a well known technique used in industry for cutting paper, cloth, wood, plastics, and coal. Recently, with the improvement in waterjet nozzle design and high pressure supply systems, combined with numerical control technology, the high pressure waterjet has became a novel machining tool in cutting of hard-to-cut fiber-reinforced composites, in food processing, and in medicine and surgery.

Research on high pressure waterjet impact on solid surfaces can be traced back to the early 1960's. Brunton [1] applied the high-speed photography technique to record the impact on a solid by a small mass of liquid at ultra-high speed. Bowden & Brunton [2] further applied this method on the study of the solid deformation modes caused by the impact of a small mass of liquid at supersonic speeds as well as the behavior of the liquid. Daniel et. al. [3] in the mid-1970's focused on water jet impact fracture phenomena in brittle materials by varying such experimental parameters as nozzle geometry, specimen materials, and jet velocity. Their results showed that the fracture involved in waterjet impacting processes consists of almost immediate cratering formation and was enhanced by a shear wave, followed by quasi-state crater pressurization resulting in crack opening and extension. They also observed that there exists a threshold velocity for each material below which no fracture occurs. All of these studies have undoubtedly enhanced an understanding of jet impacting process, but very little is known about the jet penetration process. In order to optimize the use of the supplied energy, it is necessary to know the role played by the water and the stress associated with jet piercing. The purpose of this study is to use the two dimensional dynamic photoelasticity to visualize the stress field accompanied with high pressure waterjet piercing on a polycarbonate material.

EXPERIMENTAL SETUP AND PROCEDURES

In a series of experiments, a high pressure waterjet system was used in combination with a photoelastic setup. The apparatus consists of a Powerjet model 20-35 high pressure waterjet system capable of generating pressures up to 240 MPa at an exit water flow rate of 2.50 liters/min. was related through a pure waterjet nozzle (Figure 1) which has a 0.30 mm diameter jewel orifice assembly with an exit of diameter of 1.59 mm. The specimen to be impacted is an annealed sheet of polycarbonate of thickness 3.2 mm sandwiched between two sheets of polymethylmethacrylate (PMMA) and bonded by epoxy was held by a workpiece assembly. The high speed photoelastic photographic setup was configured to enable the capture of the rapidly changing stress fields accompanying the changes in the depth on the waterjet penetration into the polycarbonate. Detail of the whole setup including the camera system was described by Wong [4].

Dynamic photoelastic experiments were conducted for various supply pressures at a constant stand-off distance for a jet exposure time of 1 second. The photoelastic fringe patterns were recorded by a high speed camera system. From photographs, the variation of the depth of cut with time was evaluated.

RESULTS

Figure 1 and 2 shows the typical photoelastic record of the high pressure waterjet impacting and piercing process at a supplied pressure of 83 MPa and 69 MPa respectively. The high pressure waterjet upon impact immediately penetrated through the material and the depth of penetration is clearly a function of supply pressure.

The results of the jet penetration depth over time corresponding to different supply pressures are listed in Table 1. The depth of penetration in 65 millisecond of jet exposure versus supply pressure was plotted (shown in Figure 3) in order to determine the threshold pressure of the waterjet piercing process . The threshold pressure was determined to be about 54 MPa (7.8 ksi).

At a supply pressure of 83 MPa (12 ksi), the jet did not enlarge the crack and the cutting depth did not increase significantly after the initial penetration. These effects are more pronounced at the pressure of 69 MPa (10 ksi), at which the highly concentrated normal force only created a shallow hole at the onset of impact. After the initial impact the back flow of water reduced the strength of the oncoming jet stream, preventing any further growth of the hole. This is a physical illustration of the existence of a threshold pressure below which there is no effect of the pure waterjet on the material.

As was observed before [5], upon initial impact, the waterjet generated dilatational waves at high supplied pressures. These waves generated high stress field at the impact zone resulted in immediate jet penetration in the workpiece material as given in Table 1.

The results of the comparative study of the depth of penetration as a function of time under different pressures are shown in Figure 4. At the beginning stage of piercing, the depth of cut increases rapidly, as shown by the steep slope of the curve in the figure. The higher the supply pressure, the higher the rate of increase. As the continued jet produced a quasi-static pressurization of the initial craters, the cracks opened further and the craters enlarged. Here we observed a decrease in the penetration rate, as shown by the lower slope of the curves in the same figure. The bottom of the drilled hole became blunt at the end of the impact process, when the depth growth rate slowed down.

CONCLUSIONS

Based on the results of this investigation, the following conclusions can be made:

1. There exists a threshold pressure for the waterjet impingement process. Below this pressure the energy contained in the water jet is not strong enough to produce penetration.

2 When the impact hole reaches a certain depth, most of the energy is being used to widen the existing crack, as well as being absorbed by the back flow. To produce a deeper hole, a higher supply pressure is needed.

REFERENCES

1. Brunton, J. H., "The High Speed Photography of Liquid/Solid Impact", Proceedings of the Fifth International Congress on High Speed Photography, Paper N-3, Washington D. C., USA, Oct. 22nd, 1960.

2. Bowden, F. P., and Brunton, J. H., "The Deformation of Solids by Liquid Impact at Supersonic Speeds", Proceedings of the Royal Society of London, A 263, pp. 433-450, Oct. 1961.

3. Daniel, I. M., Rowlands, R. E., Labus, T. J., "Photoelastic Study of Water Jet Impact", Proceedings of the Second International Symposium on Jet Cutting Technology, Paper A1, Cambridge, England, Apr. 2nd-4th, 1974.

4. Wong, K.P., "Photoelastic Investigation of Abrasive Waterjet Machining", Master thesis, University of Washington, 1991

5. Ramulu, M., Yeh H. and Raju, S.P., "Photoelastic Investigation of Jet Piercing Process", Proceedings of the 6th American Water Jet Conference, pp.1-15, Houston, Texas, USA, Aug. 24-27,1991

TEST NUMBER	SUPPLY PRESSURE	DEPTH OF CUTTING	
		0.065 SECOND	0.865 SECOND
HWJ292-1	68.9 MPa (10 ksi)	0.6560 mm	0.6560 mm
HWJ292-2	68.9 MPa (10 ksi)	0.6364 mm	0.6364 mm
HWJ292-3	82.7MPa (12 ksi)	0.6000 mm	1.4718 mm
HWJ292-4	82.7MPa (12 ksi)	0.7009 mm	1.2150 mm
HWJ292-5	82.7MPa (12 ksi)	0.6825mm	1.1564 mm
HWJ292-6	110.2 MPa (16 ksi)	1.7172 mm	2.9293 mm
HWJ292-7	110.2 MPa (16 ksi)	1.7143 mm	3.8095 mm
HWJ292-8	110.2 MPa (16 ksi)	1.8269 mm	2.7885 mm
HWJ292-9	110.2 MPa (16 ksi)	2.2406 mm	3.4434 mm
HWJ292-10	165.4MPa (24 ksi)	2.3113 mm	3.8208 mm
HWJ292-11	165.4MPa (24 ksi)	2.2820 mm	4.4951 mm
HWJ292-12	165.4MPa (24 ksi)	2.0952 mm	4.6190 mm
HWJ292-13	165.4MPa (24 ksi)	1.9118 mm	4.5588 mm
HWJ292-14	192.9 MPa (28 ksi)	3.0000 mm	6.5000 mm

Table 1

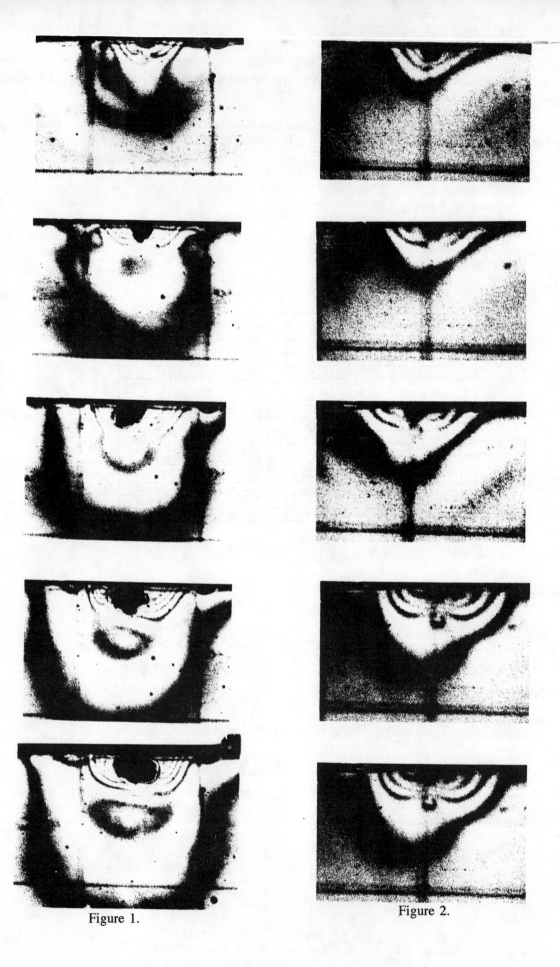

Figure 1.

Figure 2.

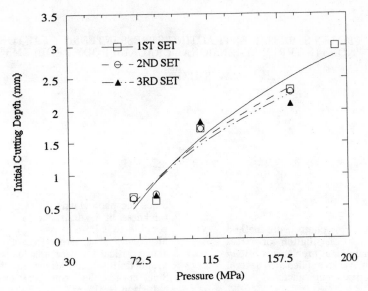

Figure 3.   Initial Cutting Depth vs. Pressure

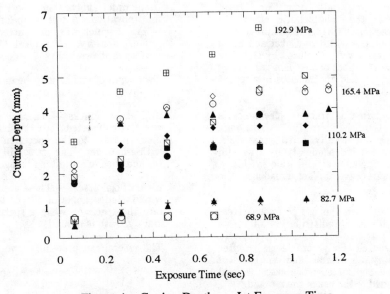

Figure 4.   Cutting Depth vs. Jet Exposure Time

"USE OF FROZEN STRESS IN EXTRACTING STRESS INTENSITY FACTOR DISTRIBUTIONS IN THREE DIMENSIONAL CRACKED BODY PROBLEMS"

C.W. SMITH[1]

ABSTRACT

The adaptation of the frozen stress photoelastic method to the determination of the distribution of stress intensity factors in three dimensional problems is briefly reviewed. The method is then applied to several engineering problems of practical significance.

INTRODUCTION

Although concepts leading to the theory of light can be dated to several hundred years B.C., the origins of photoelasticity appear to result from Sir David Brewster's discovery of the "photoelastic effect" or temporary double refraction in 1816. A comprehensive treatise of the subject was provided by Coker and Filon in 1931 [1] and frozen stress was introduced by Oppel in 1937.[2] Subsequently, a number of excellent texts have been written on the subject and are included in a recent survey of the field by Burger.[3]

The first attempt to formalize fracture mechanics is found in a paper by Griffith [4] in 1921. Although initially proposed only for ideally brittle materials, foundations were extended independently by Irwin [5] and Orowan [6] to include small scale yielding. Subsequent developments have further broadened the theory.[7]

The present paper deals with the use of frozen stress photoelasticity to estimate the distribution of stress intensity factors (SIF) around the border of cracks in three dimensional cracked body problems. After reviewing the necessary algorithms and methods of analysis for the mode I and mixed mode cases, several examples will be provided of the use of the method.

METHODS OF ANALYSIS

When a frozen stress experiment is conducted on a cracked body, thin slices are removed mutually orthogonal to the crack surface and the crack border for analysis in a polariscope for the local fringe pattern. One then needs an appropriate algorithm to accept the stress fringe data and estimate the value of the stress intensity factor for each slice. Such algorithms for loading modes I and I & II are presented in the Appendix.

---

[1]Alumni Professor
Department of Engineering Science and Mechanics
Virginia Polytechnic Institute and State University
Blacksburg, VA 24061

Since the photoelastic effect averages data through the thickness, it is desirable to cut the slices as thin as possible to minimize averaging along the flaw border. Moreover, since stress freezing material is quite soft above critical temperature, loads must be kept small to avoid finite deformations in the measurement zone. Since both of these considerations result in a significant reduction in the number of stress fringes available, it is necessary to modify standard polariscopes so as to optically increase the number of fringes occurring near the crack tip. This may be accomplished by the tandem application of the Tardy Method [8] for the fractional fringe order analysis and the Post Method [9] for fringe multiplication. A test setup for this procedure is shown in Fig. 1 which was constructed by Epstein [10] and is self explanatory. A typical Mode I multiplied fringe pattern is shown in Fig. 2.

Two types of cracks may be employed, depending upon the interests of the investigators:

a) Natural cracks — These cracks are surface cracks which are inserted into the body by holding a sharp blade normal to the specimen surface and striking it with a hammer. The crack will emanate from the blade tip and then arrest after propagating into the material.

b) Artificial cracks — These are really sharp vee notches with included angle of 30° or less which are machined into the specimen when a specific crack shape with no crack growth is desired.

The general test procedure involves the following steps:

i) Cut or cast test specimen
ii) Insert crack
iii) Heat to critical temperature
iv) Apply loads and extend the natural starter cracks
v) Cool slowly under reduced lead
vi) Remove thin slices mutually orthogonal to the crack surface and its border at intervals along the flaw border
vii) Analyze for stress fringe pattern
viii) Use fracture algorithm to estimate the stress intensity factor.

APPLICATION OF METHOD AND RESULTS

Example I — Crack Emanating from a Hole in a Plate Loaded Through a Rigid Pin in the Hole. The test geometry is shown in Fig. 3. The cracks were all natural cracks. Tests were conducted covering the following range of dimensionless ratios (See Fig. 3)

a/c:	1.08 to 2.08
a/T:	0.19 to 0.88
c/T:	0.34 to 1.68
2F/T:	0.50 and 1.00

The near tip fringe patterns obtained showed Mode I patterns (Fig. A·2·a) at H and Mixed Mode patterns (Fig. A·2·b) at S. Fig. 4 shows the extrapolation of the test data across a near tip non—linear zone to estimate K^* at H and S, respectively using the algorithms described in the Appendix. Since Mode II was absent at H, $K_H^* = K_{1H}$. SIF values for the pin loaded holes were from two to four times higher than for holes without pins loaded remotely.[11] Details of this study are found in Ref. [12]

Example II — Stress Intensity Factor Distribution Around a Surface Crack in a Model of a Nuclear Pressure Vessel Nozzle. A photograph of a test model constructed by glueing together four pieces (two domes and two semi—cylindrical sections each containing an integrally cast nozzle) is shown in Fig. 5. A natural starter crack was located at the re—entry nozzle corner in a vertical diametrical plane bisecting the nozzles on each nozzle. The loading was internal pressure. Cracks were grown above critical temperature to various depths in different models, and, after stress freezing under pressure, slices from around the crack border were analyzed photoelastically. Fringe loops indicated pure Mode I loading and $\bar{\sigma}$ was replaced by p in Eq. A·1. Prior finite element analyses had predicted contradictory SIF distributions along the crack front, some predicting a dish shaped SIF distribution, and others predicting an inverted dish shaped distribution. Results of this study are shown in Fig. 6. The results show that, for a very shallow crack, the SIF distribution is dominated by the reentrant corner boundary and is dish shaped. However, as the crack grows deeper, its shape changes as it comes under the influence of the outer boundary and the SIF distribution becomes an inverted dish. Moreover, crack shapes are not quarter—elliptic as assumed by analysts. Details of this study are found in Ref. [13].

Example III — SIF Distribution Around the Border of a Crack Emanating from the Tip of a Star Finger in a Rocket Motor Grain Geometry. The test geometry and slice locations for this problem are shown in Fig. 7. Data for the tests are presented in Table I. In determining the normalized SIF values, the remote stress $\bar{\sigma}$ in Eq. (A·1) is replaced by p/Φ where p is the internal pressure and

$$\Phi = \int_0^{\frac{\pi}{2}} [(\tfrac{a}{c})^2 \sin^2\phi + \cos^2\phi]^{1/2} d\phi \qquad (1)$$

Experimental results, shown in Fig. 9, suggest little variation of the SIF along the crack front, even for the shallow cracks. This study is continuing and progress to date is found in Ref. [14].

TABLE I

Test No.	a(mm)	a/c	a/T	Φ^1	p(KPa)^2
T0	3.6	.54	.28	1.23	26.9
T1	3.2	.52	.25	1.22	47.6
T2	4.1	.55	.32	1.24	47.6
T3	6.2	.46	.45	1.18	47.6
T4	6.6	.52	.52	1.22	42.1
T5	7.3	.43	.56	1.16	47.6
T6	8.4	.44	.66	1.17	47.6
T7	7.9	.45	.62	1.17	47.6

1. See figure 8 and Eq. (1).
2. Internal pressure.

SUMMARY

After briefly describing the use of the frozen stress method to determine SIF distributions in three dimensional cracked body problems, three examples of such application with results were given. It is clear from these (and other studies [15]) that real cracks are not always plane and usually do not exhibit straight crack fronts. For problems of this type the approach described here provides a useful way for determining what kind of geometry should be used in formulating such problems analytically.

ACKNOWLEDGEMENTS

The author wishes to acknowledge the contributions of a number of former students as noted in the references. He is also indebted to NASA Langley Research Center, Oak Ridge National Laboratory, Wright Patterson Flight Dynamics Lab, and the National Science Foundation for past support of parts of this work and the current support of Phillips Laboratory under contract No. FO—4611—88K—0025 and the advice of Dr. C.T. Liu.

REFERENCES

[1] Coker, E.G. and Filon, L.N.G. "Photoelasticity," Cambridge University Press, New York, (1931)

[2] Oppel, G. "Polarisationsoptische Untersuchung Raumliche, Spannungs and Dehnungszustande," Forsch. Geb. Ingenieurw, p. 240—248 (1936).

[3] Burger, Christiaan P. "Photoelasticity," Chapter 5 of Handbook on Experimental Mechanics, A.S. Kobayashi, Ed. (Society for Experimental Mechanics) Prentice—Hall Inc. Englewood Cliffs, NJ., p. 162—281 (1987).

[4] Griffith, A.A. "The Phenomena of Flow and Rupture in Solids," Phil. Trans. of Roy. Soc. London, V—A221, p. 163—198 (1921).

[5] Irwin, G.R. "Fracture Dynamics," Fracturing of Metals, Am. Soc. Metals, p. 147—166 (1948).

531

[6] Orowan, E. "Fracture and Strength of Solids," Progress in Physics VXII, p. 185 (1948).

[7] Anderson, T. L. Fracture Mechanics – Fundamentals and Applications, CRC Press, Boca Raton, Fla. (1991).

[8] Tardy, M. H. L., "Methode Pratique D'examen de Messure de la Birefringence des verres D'optique," Rev. Optics, V. 8 pp. 59–69, (1929).

[9] Post, D. "Isochromatic Fringe Sharpening and Fringe Multiplication in Photoelasticity," Prof. of Soc. for Expr Stress Anal. (now Society for Experimental Mechanics) VXII, pp. 143–156 (1955).

[10] Smith, C. W., Epstein, J. S. and Rezvani, M., "Measurement of Dominant Eigenvalues in Cracked Bodies," Structural Integrity, Theory and Experiment E. S. Folias, Ed., See also Int. J. of Fracture, V. 39, N.1, pp. 15–24 (1989).

[11] McGowan, J. J. and Smith, C. W., "Stress Intensity Factors for Deep Cracks Emanating from the Corner Formed by a Hole Intersecting a Plate Surface," Mechanics of Crack Growth, ASTM–STP 590 pp. 460–476 (1976).

[12] Smith, C. W., Jolles, M. and Peters, W. H. "Stress Intensities for Cracks Emanating from Pin–Loaded Holes," Flaw Growth and Fracture, ASTM–STP 631, pp. 190–201, (1977).

[13] Smith, C. W., Peters, W. H. and Jolles, M. I., "Stress Intensity Factors for Reactor Vessel Nozzle Cracks," J. of Pressure Vessel Technology, V. 100, pp. 141–149 May (1978).

[14] Smith, C. W., Wang, L. and Mouille, H., "Observations of Material and Geometric Effects on Crack Opening and Growth for Particulate Composites," Experiments in Micromechanics of Failure Resistant Materials, K. S. Kim, Ed., Applied Mechanics Division of ASME, Vol. 130, pp. 119–130 (1991).

[15] Smith, C. W., "Analytical and Experimental Studies of the Surface Flaw," J. of Expr. Mech., V–XLV, pp. 194–200, June (1988).

[16] See Ref. [3] Chapter 20, "Experimental Fracture Mechanics," pp. 891–956 (1987).

Appendix – Photoelastic Algorithms for SIF

The general cracked body geometry and notation used in the development of appropriate algorithms for converting stress fringe data into SIF values is shown in Fig. A–1 where the coordinate system tnz is a local one which slides along the crack front in the t direction. The form of the algorithms are developed elsewhere [16] and only the results are given below for the reader's convenience.

i) Mode I – (Fig. A–2–a) We compute a truncated form of τ_{max}^{nz} (Fig. A–1, $\bar{\tau} = 0$) along $\theta = \pi/2$ for a two parameter model. The result is:

$$\frac{K_{Ap}}{\bar{\sigma}(\pi a)^{1/2}} = \frac{K_I}{\bar{\sigma}(\pi a)^{1/2}} + \frac{B(8)^{1/2}}{\bar{\sigma}}\left[\frac{r}{a}\right]^{1/2} \quad (A-1)$$

where $K_{Ap} = \tau_{max}^{nz}(8\pi r)^{1/2}$ is defined as an "apparent" SIF.

$\bar{\sigma}$ = remote stress
a = crack depth
K_1 = Mode I SIF
B = Non–Singular stress parameter
r = Distance from crack plane along $\theta = \pi/2$

Equation A–1, when plotted as

$$\frac{K_{Ap}}{\bar{\sigma}(\pi a)^{1/2}} \text{ versus } \left[\frac{r}{a}\right]^{1/2} \quad (A-2)$$

yields a straight line which when extrapolated to the origin will yield $K_I/\bar{\sigma}(\pi a)^{1/2}$ the normalized SIF (See Fig. 4).

ii) Mixed Mode – (Fig. A–2–b) Here both $\bar{\sigma}$ and $\bar{\tau}$ (Fig. A–1) are present. Proceeding as before, but not specifying θ, $K_{Ap}^* = \tau_{max}^{nz}(8\pi r)^{1/2}$ as before, and plotting, $\frac{K_{Ap}^*}{\bar{\sigma}(\pi a)^{1/2}}$ vs $\left[\frac{r}{a}\right]^{1/2}$ as before, we obtain $K^*/\bar{\sigma}(\pi a)^{1/2}$ (See Fig. 4). Here

$$K_{Ap}^* = \left[\left\{\left[K_I\right]_{Ap}\sin\theta_m + 2\left[K_{II}\right]_{Ap}\cos\theta_m\right\}^2 + \left\{\left[K_{II}\right]_{Ap}\sin\theta_m\right\}^2\right]^{1/2} \text{ and}$$

$$K^* = \left[\left[K_I\sin\theta_m^0 + 2K_{II}\cos\theta_m^0\right]^2 + \left[K_{II}\sin\theta_m^0\right]^2\right]^{1/2} \quad (A-3)$$

where θ_m^0 is obtained from a plot of θ_m vs. r/a (Fig. A–3). Moreover, from a near tip geometric fringe condition,

$$\frac{K_{II}}{K_I} - \frac{4}{3}\left[\frac{K_{II}}{K_I}\right]\cot 2\theta_m^0 - \frac{1}{3} = 0 \quad (A-4)$$

Knowing θ_m^0, Eqs. (A–3) and (A–4) may be solved for K_I & K_{II} the Mode I and Mode II SIF values.

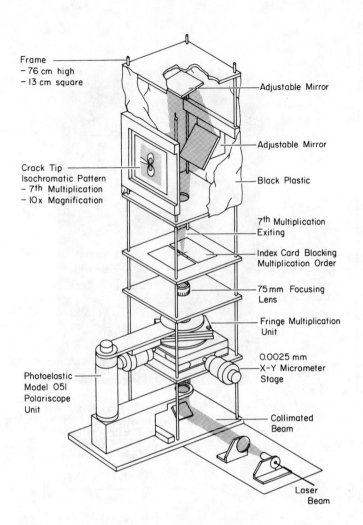

Frame
– 76 cm high
– 13 cm square

Adjustable Mirror

Adjustable Mirror

Black Plastic

Crack Tip
Isochromatic Pattern
– 7th Multiplication
– 10x Magnification

7th Multiplication
Exiting

Index Card Blocking
Multiplication Order

75 mm Focusing
Lens

Fringe Multiplication
Unit

0.0025 mm
X-Y Micrometer
Stage

Photoelastic
Model 051
Polariscope
Unit

Collimated
Beam

Laser
Beam

Fig. 1. Refined Polariscope [Ref. 10].

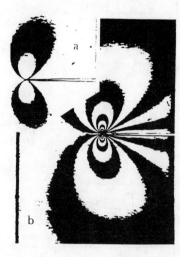

Fig. 2. Typical Mode I Stress Fringe Pattern
a) Unmultiplied **b)**Fifth Multiple.

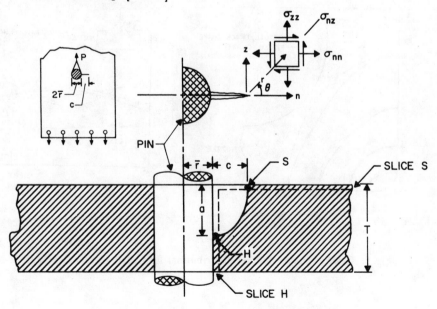

Fig. 3. Pin–Loaded Cracked Hole Geometry.

533

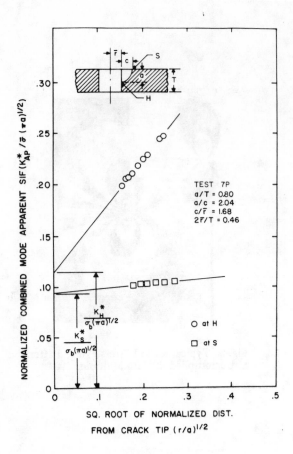

TEST 7P
$a/T = 0.80$
$a/c = 2.04$
$c/\bar{r} = 1.68$
$2\bar{r}/T = 0.46$

○ at H

□ at S

Fig. 4. Typical Data Sets for Estimating K* [Ref. 12].

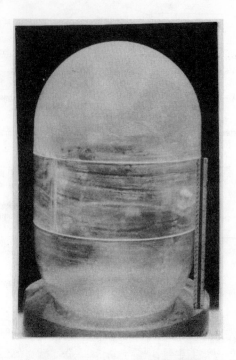

Fig. 5. Photo of Photoelastic Model of a Nuclear Pressure Vessel for Cracked Nozzle Analysis.

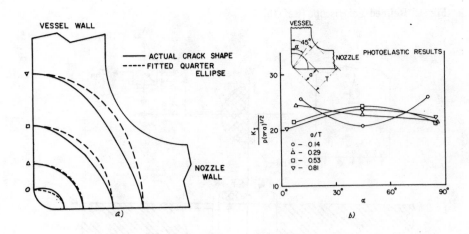

Fig. 6. Cracked shapes and SIF Distributions for Nozzle Corner Cracks [Ref. 13].

534

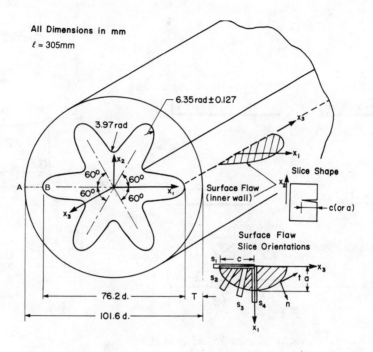

Fig. 7. Motor Grain Model Geometry and Slice Orientation.

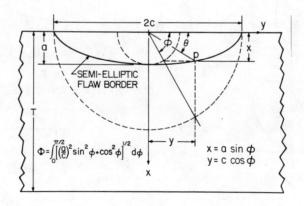

$$\Phi = \int_0^{\pi/2} \left[\left(\frac{a}{c}\right)^2 \sin^2\phi + \cos^2\phi \right]^{1/2} d\phi$$

$$x = a \sin\phi$$
$$y = c \cos\phi$$

Fig. 8. Semi—Elliptic Crack Notations.

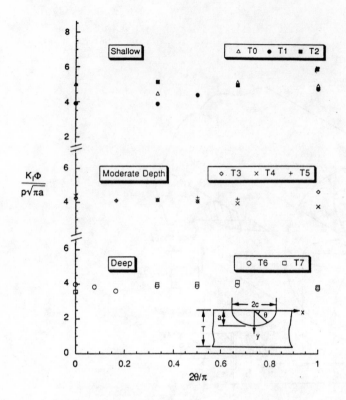

$$\frac{K_I \Phi}{p\sqrt{\pi a}}$$

Shallow △ T0 ● T1 ■ T2

Moderate Depth ◇ T3 × T4 + T5

Deep ○ T6 □ T7

$2\theta/\pi$

Fig. 9.   Normalized SIF Distributions Around Crack Borders in Motor Grain Models [Ref. 14].

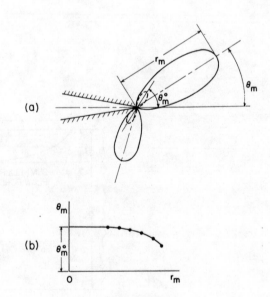

Fig. A–1.   General Cracked Body Geometry, Loading and Notation.

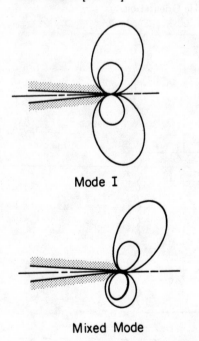

Mode I

Mixed Mode

Fig. A–2. Stress Fringe Signatures for a) Mode I and b) Mode Loading.

(a)

(b)

Fig. A–3. Determination of θ_m^0 from θ_m (Note that only forward leaning loops are used).

536

FOURTH DIMENSIONAL EFFECTS IN THE COLD EXPANSION OF LARGE HOLES IN THICK ALUMINIUM AIRCRAFT MATERIAL USING PHOTOSTRESS AND STRAIN GAUGES

E W O'BRIEN

MANAGER, EXPERIMENTAL STRESS ANALYSIS, BRITISH AEROSPACE AIRBUS LTD.
BRISTOL, U.K

ABSTRACT

Fatigue protection by the application of cold expansion by the 'split sleeve and mandrel' system to holes in aircraft components and other high performance structures has become common practice for sizes up to 15 mm diameter. Recent advances particularly in large aircraft mean that the process is now applied to holes up to twice that size. Theoretical analyses of the stress field surrounding cold expanded holes have been developed over many years, involving very complex close form solution estimates based on the resultant balance between bi-axial plastic and elastic deformation. Experimental stress analysis techniques reveal that the 2-D solutions of the past are inadequate to describe stress fields around the larger sizes of holes. In fact for a full description of the strain state of the expanded hole the *fourth dimension* of time must be considered. The effects of high strain rates discovered in the experiments is also examined with respect particularly to 7010 aluminium, which has sponsored a tool modification programme.

INTRODUCTION

The split sleeve system of cold expansion is ingeniously designed for single side application to components of high performance structures. Expansions to provide fatigue protection are typically of the order of 2–5% depending on the particular material involved. The enhancement is particularly effective as it is achieved for no additional weight. Two main assumptions are made in the theoretical analyses: (a) the material being expanded is infinitely thin, and (b) the expansion occurs instantaneously.

None of the theoretical solutions to describe the stress state around an expanded hole are exact, only very recent research workers hint at the necessity to consider third dimension effects to achieve better precision. The previous theoretical work although approximate was adequate to assure improved fatigue performance. However as the process is applied to more exotic materials, particularly the less ductile alloys, the existing explanations of the strain state have proved to be not rigorous enough.

This paper reports on experimental work done to detect more precisely the strain behaviour in material surrounding a 'split sleeve' cold expanded 25.4 mm dia hole in 25.4 mm thick forged 7000 series aluminium.

TECHNICAL CONSIDERATIONS

In order to improve on previous classical experimental work a review of the extent and limitations of those experiments is necessary. In the early days Nadái [1] conducted experiments by expanding copper tubes into the end plates of steam boilers to create leak proof joints. His technique was to use a roller bearing type tool which expanded as it rotated to generate the interference fit with the end plate. His accompanying analysis, however, was for an instantaneous expansion, which is more appropriate to the mandrel or split sleeve expansion.

More recent experimenters attempted to simulate the apparent phases of the mandrel expansion process. Schneider and Schwarmann [2] for example measured strains on one face only of a plate first with a modified mandrel that expanded the hole to its maximum diameter for the full depth of the plate. They then measured the strains on the same surface after the removal of the mandrel to record the final retained strains. The second measurements are clearly valid as data for generating theoretical formulations to describe the phenomenon. The results for maximum expansion, however, ignore the transient nature of the maximum expansion as it passes through the depth of the hole. This approach although clearly approximate is thought to be adequate for holes and plate up to 6.5 mm diameter and 6.5 mm thick. Many researchers like Cloud [3] for example have used moiré interferometry to determine the strain distribution on one face due to expansion, Link and Sandford [4] used the technique on both faces and noted that the strain distributions were not identical.

After a few years of applying existing 'small size' theories to large diameters and thicknesses combined with less ductile materials it became evident that more rigorous measurements and analysis were necessary.

EXPERIMENTAL TECHNIQUES

Initial trials of 3% applied expansion to 25.4 mm diameter holes in 25.4 mm 7010 light alloy plate were conducted using reflective photoelastic coatings. The strain patterns were recorded on high quality video for both faces of the plate being expanded, observation instantly revealed a double stress wave on the exit side which could not be explained by any of the known theories. It also became apparent that the range of strains being measured was extreme with the highest strains being well into the non-linear plastic region of the material. Subsequent investigations utilised arrays of 32 miniature strain gauges monitored at 200 Hz combined with photoelastic coatings off differing sensitivities to record both high and low strain effects.

The specimens were chosen to demonstrate a variety of parameters:

a) Real structure with representative reinforcings, flanges, ribs ··· etc. — see Fig. 1.

b) Quasi infinite sheet with two representative holes to assess interaction effects— see Fig. 2.

c) As above, but with holes near to a free edge to assess finite sheet size effects— see Fig. 3.

The specimens were mounted with two reflection polariscopes aimed at each face of the hole to be cold expanded. Each polariscope was aligned with a high quality Betacam video camera and recording system, which were equipped with linked in-frame time codes. The strain gauge arrays were linked into 32 conditioning amplifiers and a 200 Hz data acquisition and storage unit. The experimental procedure entailed a careful sequence of events in a period of only 15 seconds. The video and strain recording devices were started followed by the operation of the cold expansion gun, all before the limited computer storage facility filled up with the 100 000 data points generated.

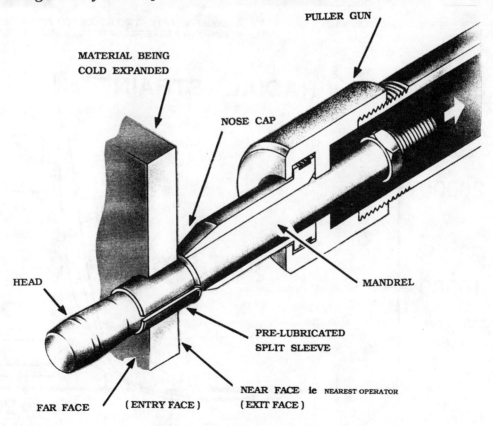

Details of the cold expansion process

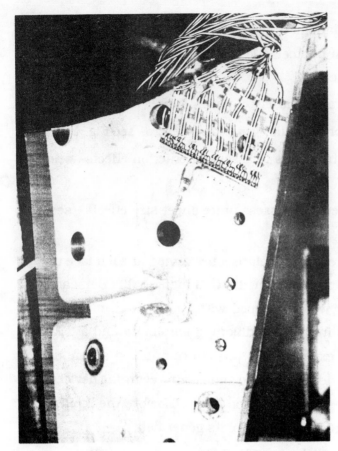

Fig. 1   REAL STRUCTURE SPECIMEN

Fig. 2   INFINITE PLATE - TWO HOLES FOR PROXIMITY EFFECTS
Fig. 3   FINITE PLATE - SIMILAR TO Fig. 2 BUT HOLES CLOSE TO EDGE

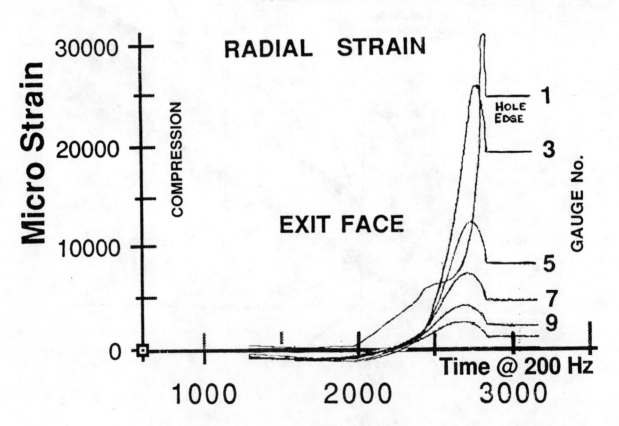

SUMMARY OF EXPERIMENTAL RESULTS

- The record of strains indicate clearly a significant difference in level and extent on the entry compared to the exit side.

- The material nearest the mandrel on the exit face is shown to be in a dead zone until the very end of the process.

- A double wave of photoelastic isochromatic stress fringes was observed on the exit face during the progress of the expansion process.

The strains on the entry face have a marked effect through the material and account for the first stress wave in the double stress wave phenomenon observed. The second stress wave was due to expansion effects near the exit face and in fact the peak strains on the exit side were also seen to have an effect on the entry face. This effect was observed in the strain gauge traces (Fig. 4) for the exit face in that the second radial gauge indicated much higher levels than the radial gauge nearest to the hole until very late in the mandrel pull through. The first gauge then overtook the second gauge in very dramatic style and proceeded to record the peak strain of the whole system.

The slope of the strain curves is the strain rate, it is clear from the slope of the first strain gauge data curve on the exit face that the strain rate is exceedingly high, therefore merits particular attention. Strain rate trials on the 7010 light alloy being used indicate that at the strain rates measured (between 0.4 sec^{-1} and 1.0 sec^{-1}) the strain to failure is reduced significantly compared to the standard rate values.

All the strain information on the surfaces can be explained by reference to the internal effects and their phasing during the expansion.

THEORETICAL CORRELATION

It is clear that none of the close form solutions generated to explain the cold expansion process in the past consider the fourth dimensional or time effects. It is certain that for the large sizes under consideration that the equations published are, at best, only true for one plane through the thickness of the plate and possibly only true at one time in the process.

To try and replicate the process and establish the stressstate as well as the strain state, finite element (FE) analyses were undertaken using the state of the art methods at the time. It was soon clear that both geometric and material non-linearity must be represented. Several innovations were introduced by the FE software houses in response to the particular problem. Full anisotropic material characteristics were required as well as complicated manipulation of slide lines to represent both the action of the mandrel and the split sleeve.

The most successful FE analysis of the cold expansion problem followed what is becoming known as an 'organic' technique whereby test results are used to guide the precise analysis steps. This method determined that it was necessary to analyse the pull through of the mandrel at five equal quasi-static steps through the thickness.

CONCLUSIONS

It may be surprising to find so much complication coming from an apparently simple hole in a plate. However, the fatigue benefits are so significant that full understanding must be achieved in order to permit an orderly approach to further research and development. One area of further work being undertaken which will allow more detailed comparisons with numerical techniques is to detect the boundary of the plastic zone through the thickness of the plate. After attempting many non-productive methods, electron back-scatter microscopy is starting to give encouraging results based on non-linearities caused by lattice distortion due to the presence of plasticity.

Cold expansion has been used in the past to yield fatigue protection almost as if there were no limitations caused by size or material. In this work a variety of experimental stress analysis techniques have been combined to identify limitations due to size and material that have not previously been considered.

Manufacturers of the split sleeve expansion system are in the process of modifying the equipment to make it more displacement controlled rather than exclusively force controlled as it is at the moment. This modification should overcome any problem specifically related to high strain rates in 7010 light alloy.

REFERENCES

[1] Nadái A., *Theory of the expanding of boiler and condensed tube joints through rolling*, Transactions of the ASME 1943.

[2] Schneider E. , Schwarmann L., *On improving the fatigue performance of a double-shear lap joint*, International Journal of Fatigue Vol. 5 1983.

[3] Cloud G., Sulaimana R., *Experimental study of large compressive loads upon residual strain fields created by cold working fastener holes*, AFP 2418 AFWAL 1980.

USE OF PHOTOSTRESS TO CHARACTERIZE THE
MECHANICAL BEHAVIOR OF WELDMENTS

S. C. Gambrell, Jr.
Professor of Engineering Mechanics
The University of Alabama
Tuscaloosa, Alabama 35487

ABSTRACT

Welded aluminum constitutes an important part of many space structures. Knowledge of the properties of weld material and of the material surround the weld is important for design and modeling of the structure containing the welded joints. Photoelastic coatings (Photostress) were used to determine stress-strain curves in uniaxial tension for the weld material and the material in the heat affected zones. Contraction ratios for the material were determined using a tangent modulus approximation and were used in calculations after the material reached its proportional limit. After converting the maximum shearing strain obtained from the Photoelastic coating to maximum normal strain, stress versus normal strain curves were plotted. Since photoelastic coatings provide a method to measure strain at a point rather than over a finite gage length, use of the coatings may improve the accuracy of the data over that normally obtained using strain gages applied to the specimen in the different zones.

NOMENCLATURE

γ_{max}	=	maximum in-plane shearing strain
N	=	fringe order
λ	=	wavelength of light
t_p	=	thickness of coating
K	=	calibration constant for coating
f	=	$\lambda / 2t_p K$
μ	=	Poissons ratio
α	=	contraction ratio
E	=	modulus of elasticity
E_t	=	tangent modulus
ϵ_1	=	maximum principal strain
ϵ_2	=	minimum principal strain

BACKGROUND

Photoelastic coatings are useful to view strains in a large field and to examine strain gradients in the field. Contrary to extensometers and strain gages which average strains along their length, photoelastic coatings provide measurements of strain over a gage length of essentially zero (at a point). When testing is done using specimens having welds between parent material, there are, in general, three primary zones in which strains may be significantly different. These zones are (a) the weld material, (b) the heat affected zone, and (c) the parent material. To date, most all strain measurement on welded specimens has been done using electromechanical extensometers or strain gages to measure strain in and across the various zones, thereby averaging across strain gradients and across zone boundaries. [1][2]

BASIC TECHNIQUE

In an effort to eliminate strain averaging, photoelastic coatings were used to characterize the mechanical behavior of weldments when tested in uniaxial tension. Data were taken at various points along the centerline of the specimen and were used to construct stress-strain curves. The basic strain-optic law states that

$$\gamma_{max} = \epsilon_1 - \epsilon_2 = \frac{N\lambda}{2t_p K} = Nf \qquad (1)$$

Since $\epsilon_2 = -\mu\epsilon_1$ for uniaxial tension, equation [1] may be written for the elastic range as

$$\epsilon_1 = \frac{Nf}{(1 + \mu)} \qquad (2)$$

For the inelastic range, Poisson's ratio must be replaced by the contraction ratio, α, which Chakrabarty [3] approximates as

$$\alpha = 0.5 - (0.5 - \mu)(\frac{E_t}{E}) \qquad (3)$$

Thus, equation (2) becomes

$$\epsilon_1 = \frac{Nf}{(1 + \alpha)} \qquad (4)$$

for the inelastic range. The contraction ratio may be calculated for each value of uniaxial stress using a tangent modulus curve constructed from an engineering stress-strain curve. Contraction ratios for the weld material and parent material were calculated. Since strains exceeding the 0.2 percent offset are seldom allowed in design, data collection was limited to maximum strains of from two to three percent where the engineering and true stress-strain curves are essentially the same.

Specimens tested were of the standard "dog bone" type (see Figures 3-7) having different dimensions and different thickness of weld material. Parent material on either side of the weld was aluminum, 2219-T87 plate or 2219-T352 forged, depending upon the specific application for which the test was made. Weld material was 2319 filler. Since relatively large strains were to be measured (2% to 3%), PS-1 plastic sheets 0.011 inches thick were used for strain measurement on all specimens that had the welds ground off flush with the parent material. PL-1 liquid plastic was poured 0.070 inches thick and contoured on the specimens that had the full weld left in place. Thus, specimens using contoured plastic were restricted to measurement of strains much less than that for flat sheets. PC-1 cement was used sucessfully, but it was found that PC-8 did a better job when strains exceeded 2 percent. Maximum shearing strains were measured using a digital recorder/printer equipped with a uniform field compensator. All plastic, cement, and Photostress equipment was obtained from Measurements Group, Inc., Raleigh, N.C. (4)

RESULTS

The contraction ratio data for 2219-T87 parent material and 2319 weld material were obtained from regular stress-strain curves for each material by obtaining the tangent modulus versus stress curve and then using equation (3). In order to associate the contraction ratio with inelastic stresses only, contraction ratio data were plotted as inelastic stress minus the proportional limit stress versus the contraction ratio. To test the theory previously described, maximum in-plane shearing strains obtained by Photostress were plotted against stress-strain curves obtained by use of universal testing machines for parent material (Figure 1) and weld material (Figure 2). Curves of stress versus maximum normal strain were plotted by obtaining the maximum normal strain from the maximum shearing strain by use of equation (4). It is clear from Figures 1 and 2 that use of Photostress to obtain data for plotting curves of stress versus maximum normal strain is sufficiently accurate to characterize the material's behavior.

For most of the welded test specimens, points for data collection were located each 0.25 or 0.50 inches along the centerline of the specimen (see Figures 3-7) beginning at the centerline of the weld. These locations provided for preparation of stress-strain curves at the weakest point (the weld centerline) and for other points in the heat affected zone of the specimen. The sample stress-strain curves included herein clearly demonstrate that different degrees of yielding did occur at all points in the welded joint and that material properties are significantly different as the points chosen approach the centerline of the weld. Figures 3 through 7 indicate results of several tests on different types of test specimens. Figure 3 shows the yielding characteristics on a point by point basis of as-welded and heat treated specimens up to a location of one inch from the centerline of the weld. Note the sub-

stantial effects of heat treatment on the weld material of the specimen. Other points in the as-welded specimens were similarly affected by heat treatment. Figure 4 shows similar information for specimens of the same material as for Figure 3 but which were thinner and had a smaller cross sectional area. One can note again the substantial effects of heat treatment on the weld material of the specimen. Also, by comparing Figure 3 with Figure 4, one can note the effects of specimen size on yield behavior. The specimen for Figure 3 had a weld thickness of 0.50 inches whereas the specimen for Figure 4 had a weld thickness of only 0.125 inches. Therefore, much less heat was required to weld the thinner specimen resulting in less yielding at a given stress level than for the thick specimen.

Figure 5 shows yielding characteristics of a welded joint having different parent material on each side of the weld. Forged aluminum (2219-T352) behaved quite differently from plate aluminum (2219-T37) and from weld material (2319 filler). The plate aluminum never yielded whereas the forge and weld material exhibited pronounced yielding.

Figures 6 and 7 indicate the yielding characteristics of 2219-T87 welded specimens which had full welds in place rather than having the welds ground off to a flat surface in the same plane as the parent material. The results of different heating on the thick side of the weld (Figure 6) are readily apparent when compared to the results for the thin side of the weld (Figure 7). Parent material (2219-T87) for the specimens of Figures 6 and 7 was 0.50 inches thick and the two weld/parent material interfaces were tapered through the thickness. Therefore, more heating of the material occurred on the side of the specimen having the thick part of the weld than it did on the side having the thin part. Thus, the material on the thick side yielded more at a given stress level than the material on the thin side.

CONCLUSION

Color photographs of fring patterns in the coatings clearly showed the strain gradients and the three zones previously mentioned. In comparison to use of strain gages, more technical expertise, calculations, and care are required to successfully use the photoelastic coating technique. However, strain averaging is eliminated and, up to a maximum strain of from two to three percent, photoelastic coatings provide a useful method to characterize material behavior on a point by point basis at closely spaced points in a weldment.

REFERENCES

(1) Burghard, H.G., Jr., and Norris, E.B., "Development of Welding Techniques and Filler Metals for High Strength Aluminum Alloys," Final Report, Projects 07-1603 and 07-1757, Southwest Research Institute, May 27, 1966.

(2) Verderaime, V., "Weld Stresses Beyond Elastic Limit," NASA Technical Paper 2935, G. C. Marshall Space Flight

Center, 1989.

(3) Chakrabarty, J., Theory of Plasticity, McGraw Hill Book Co., Inc., New York, 1987.

(4) "Operating Instructions and Technical Manual-Strain Measurement with the 030-Series Reflection Polariscope," Measurements Group, Inc., Raleigh, NC.

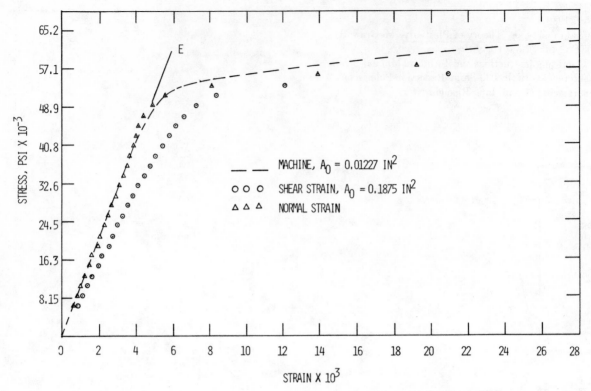

Figure 1.   Characteristics of 2219-T87 Parent Material

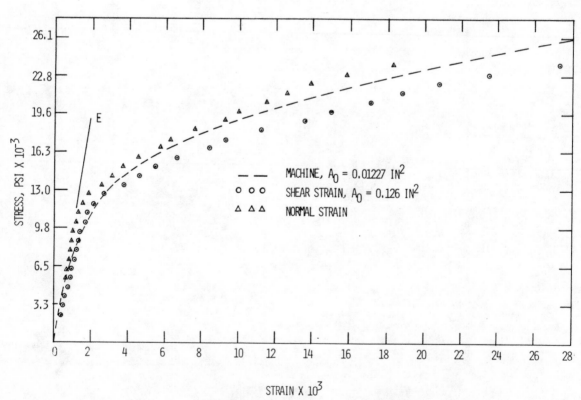

Figure 2.   Characteristics of 2319 Weld Material

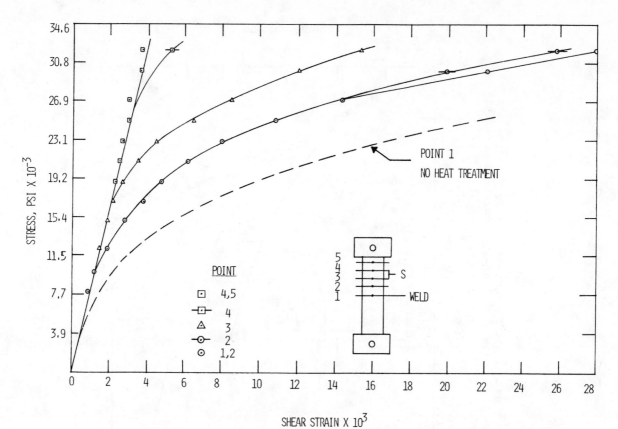

Figure 3. Plate-Weld-Plate, 2219-T87, Heat Treated
S = 0.25 in, A_0 = 0.65 in^2

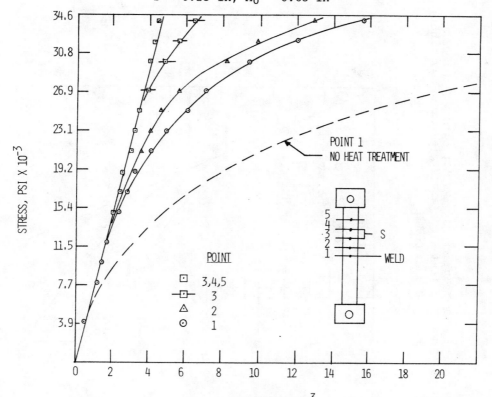

Figure 4. Plate-Weld-Plate, 2219-T87, Heat Treated
S = 0.25 in, A_0 = 0.1875 in^2

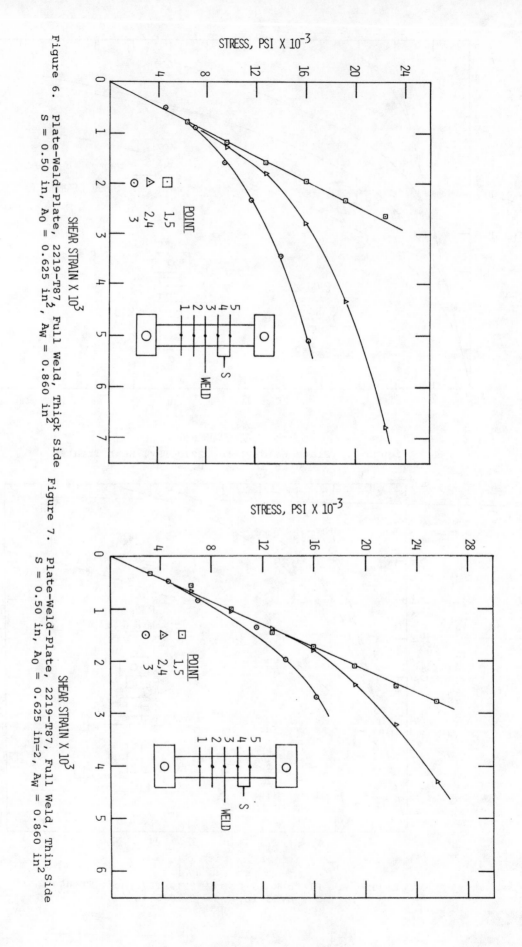

Figure 6. Plate-Weld-Plate, 2219-T87, Full Weld, Thick Side
S = 0.50 in, A_0 = 0.625 in², A_w = 0.860 in²

Figure 7. Plate-Weld-Plate, 2219-T87, Full Weld, Thin Side
S = 0.50 in, A_0 = 0.625 in=2, A_w = 0.860 in²

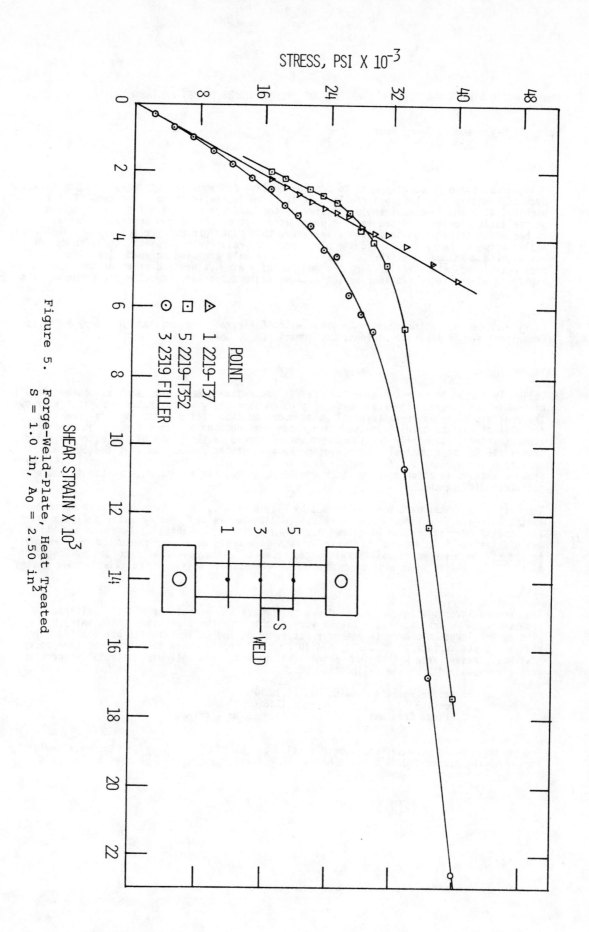

Figure 5. Forge-Weld-Plate, Heat Treated
S = 1.0 in, A_0 = 2.50 in^2

PHOTOELASTIC STRESS ANALYSIS OF A PATTERN OF OBLIQUE HOLES IN JET ENGINE HARDWARE

Larry J. Meyer and H. Jerry Macke

ABSTRACT

Oblique holes are frequently used to provide cooling passages in various jet engine parts, such as combustors or hollow airfoils. It is often desirable to have the axes of such holes machined at a small oblique angle relative to the hardware surface. The frozen-stress photoelastic studies reported in this paper were part of the design process on cooled combustors. In relation to previous analyses, this paper presents relatively small oblique angles between the hole axis and the plate surface, relatively large thickness to diameter ratios, and a staggered pattern of holes. Both tensile and bending loads were applied. The most notable effects revealed were the unexpectedly high values and rates of increase in the highly localized concentrations as the oblique angle decreases. Results are compared with those of previous investigators.

Larry J. Meyer is Photomechanics Engineer with GE Aircraft Engines, and H. Jerry Macke is Consultant for GE Aircraft Engines, Cincinnati, Ohio, USA.

INTRODUCTION

Obliquely formed holes are frequently used in jet engine components, such as cooled airfoils or combustion liners. The real physical problem is usually approximated experimentally by the analysis of holes or patterns of holes machined into flat plates. Several previous analyses of oblique holes in plates have shown that such holes can produce high stress concentrations, especially for the component of stress in the plane of the plate which is transverse to the normal plane containing the axes of the holes. Besides the obvious variation in results as a function of skew angle, results of the various investigators also show variations as a function of thickness to hole diameter ratio, hole patterns, and other geometric differences.

Theoretical analyses have been performed by Ellyin et al.,[1,2] containing fairly stringent limits on angle of obliquity and thickness to diameter ratio. Photoelastic analyses using the stress-freezing process have been performed by Leven[3,4], Daniel[5,6], McKenzie and White[7], and Ozaki et al.[8] At General Electric, strain gage tests have been conducted over a long period of time with very small strain gages, some of which have been recorded by Jongensen et al.[9,10,11] Ellyin[12] has also conducted tests with strain gages for relatively thin plates.

MODELS

The present investigation was carried out to compare concentrations of hole patterns in combustors. Two Araldite epoxy blanks were machined to the dimensions shown in Figure 1, with rather large thickness to diameter ratios (4.0) and oblique angles between the hole axis and plate surface of 20°, 30°, and 40°. A calibration bar, cast from the same epoxy mix, was stress-frozen with a four point bending load. The following material properties were then obtained from the calibration bar:

$$
\begin{aligned}
\text{Frozen Young's Modulus} &= 18.20 \text{ MPa} \\
\text{Density} &= 1.2315 \text{ g/cm}^3 \\
\text{Fringe Constant} &= 0.3466 \text{ N/mm - fringe}
\end{aligned}
$$

Photoelastic tests were set-up in both tension and bending, as shown in Figures 2 and 3. Photos of the stress-frozen tension model, in polarized light, can be seen in Figure 4.

PROCEDURE

The nominals used to calculate the stress concentrations were taken from each tested model. Three sections equally spaced across the beam width were taken above and below the angled holes as well as between each hole pattern. Five readings were taken at equally spaced distances through the beam thickness.

The resulting stresses from the sections above & below each hole pattern were averaged and used as the nominal for that hole pattern.

Determining the nominals for the bending model was slightly more complicated. Five readings through the thickness of each section, as defined above, were used to determine an equation for the bending stress in that section. The equations from each nominal section were used to determine an overall equation describing the bending stresses along the length of the beam. This overall equation was determined for the depth through the thickness for each slice. Analyzed nominal stresses were then calculated at the distance (along the beam length) for holes analyzed in each hole pattern.

Models were cut in sections so that, for each of the three sets of holes, a piece with a middle hole and a piece in the same row with a hole near an edge were obtained. Each piece, which contained a complete hole, was cut into 11 slices through the thickness. First analysis of these slices was done by passing the light beam parallel to the axes of the holes (using index matching fluid), to obtain the stresses around the holes for all slices. These stresses are the average through the slice thickness. It was noted that the highest values of stress occurred in the end slices at the acute corners. Hence, it was decided to obtain more accurate values at the acute corners themselves by extrapolation to the surface of the plate. The end slices were then immersed in fluid and analyzed as illustrated in Figure 5, where successive readings of fringe order and thickness were made along the axis of symmetry leading to the acute corner. In all cases, the calculated stress (actually principal stress difference), when plotted as in Figure 5, showed a rapid increase as the coordinate x, from the acute corner, approached zero. At x = 0, the extrapolated stress is used to define the stress concentration.

This kind of extrapolation was performed for both ends of the holes for the three angles α, for both tension and bending, and for both the middle holes in the pattern, and the holes near the edge of the plate. Fringe readings were made as close as 0.06 mm from the sharp edge and then extrapolated to x = 0. In all cases the curves rose more steeply than expected as they approached x = 0. Polariscope set-ups were made at 20x and 50x, making it possible to read fringe orders with thicknesses as small as 0.023 mm. Because of the small thickness and steepness of the curve, the extrapolated stress ratio values had sufficient scatter that it was difficult to separate the effects of tension, bending, and nearness to the edge of the plate; but all rose dramatically as x → 0. Hence all of the extrapolated stress concentrations have been combined in a single plot.

RESULTS

Figure 6 shows the stress concentrations as a function of the oblique angle α, for which all data have a distinct and consistent variation. In general, values at both ends of holes have been averaged, to reduce the number of overlapping points. An average curve has been drawn through the plotted points and the known value at $\alpha = 90°$. Stress concentrations (K_{tg}) are based on the gross cross sections.

Stress distributions through the plate thickness are shown in Figure 7 for the tension case. Here, the concentrations at the end of the hole are combined with the average stresses in the slices.

Figure 8 shows the distribution of the principal stresses in the surface slice for the tension case, along a line of symmetry proceeding away from the hole. These principal stresses were obtained by oblique incidence.

CONCLUSION

Figure 9 shows how the present maximum concentrations compare with those from other sources. It would appear that the large thickness to diameter ratio and the hole pattern have caused the concentrations to increase, especially at low values of the angle α, and also caused the peak concentrations to move to the surface of the plate.

Some comparisons were made with the strain-gage results of Jongensen [9, 10, 11] which were also at a fairly large T/d ratio. If we visualize the smallest available strain gage width to be placed on the curves of Figure 5 or Figure 7 adjacent to the acute corner, then because of the steep gradient, the recorded strain might be as low as 60% of the peak value. Thus it appears that Jongensen's points are as accurate as could be done with strain gages and also tend to confirm the magnitude of the present results (see Figure 9).

Other writers have observed that the peak stress does not occur at the extreme ends of the holes. We have previously noted that this condition is nearly always true, especially with holes drilled normal or nearly normal to the surface.[13] However, in this study, the peak always occurred at the surface of the plate.

In the study reported here all hole edges were sharp. However, in another study, the effect of rounding the edges of the holes was also studied. As noted by Daniel[6] and others[14], there is usually an increase in peak stress, together with a shifting of the peak away from the surface of the plate.

ACKNOWLEDGMENT

Contributions to the investigation were made by RP Zieger of the GE Aircraft Engine design organization; and the usual assistance was made by technicians in the GE Photoelastic Lab.

REFERENCES

1. Ellyin, F., Lind, A.M., and Sherbourne, A.N., "Elastic Stress Field in a Plate with a Skew Hole", Journal of the Engineering Mechanics Division, ASCE, Vol 92, Feb 1966, pp. 1-10.

2. Ellyin, F. and Sherbourne, A.N., "Effect of Skew Penetration on Stress Concentration", Journal of the Engineering Mechanics Division, ASCE, Vol 94, Dec 1968, pp. 1317-1336.

3. Leven, M.M., "Determination of Stresses Around an Oblique Hole ($\alpha=45°$) in a Flat Plate", Westinghouse Report 64-9D7-520-R1, 8/12/64.

4. Leven, M.M., "Photoelastic Determination of the Stresses at Oblique Openings in Plates and Shells", Welding Research Council Bulletin 153, 1970, pp. 52-59.

5. Daniel, I.M., "Photoelastic Analysis of Plates with Rows of Oblique Holes", IIT Research Institute Project No. D6025 for General Electric Company, March 1968.

6. Daniel, I.M., "Photoelastic Analysis of Stresses Around Oblique Holes", Experimental Mechanics, Vol 10, Nov 1970, pp. 467-473.

7. McKenzie, H.W. and White, D.J., "Stress Concentration Caused by an Oblique Round Hole in a Flat Plate Under Uniaxial Tension", Journal of Strain Analysis, Vol 3, April 1968. pp. 98-102.

8. Ozaki, T., Sugiura, M. and Wada, H., Photoelastic Analysis of Stresses Around an Oblique Circular Hole", Bulletin of the JSME, Vol 19, July 1976, pp. 719-722.

9. Jorgensen, A.W. and Laflen, J.H., "Experiments to Determine the Elastic Stress Concentration Factors of Various TF-39 DCIP Film Cooling Hole Geometries", GE Aircraft Engine Group Report TM 70-684, 6/26/70

10. Jorgensen, A.W. and Locke, E.H., "Experimental Determination of the Elastic Stress Concentration Factors of Various ATEGG HPT Blade Cooling Hole Geometries", GE Aircraft Engine Group Report TM72-603, 6/29/72.

11. Locke, E.H, & Jorgensen, A.W., "Experimental Determination of Theoretical Stress Concentration Factors Produced in a Flat Plat by Skew Holes of Circular and Elliptical Cross Sections", GE Aircraft Engine Group Report TM73-574, 8/7/73.

12. Ellyin, F. "Experimental Study of Oblique Circular Cylindrical Apertures in Plates", Experimental Mechanics, SESA, Vol 10, May 1970, pp. 195-202.

13. Macke, H.J., "Refinements in the Analysis of Photoelastic Stress Concentrations for Thick Members", GE Aircraft Engine Group Report TM84-299, 8/31/84.

14. Macke, H.J., "Effects of Chamfers and Rounded Edges on Stress Concentrations", GE Aircraft Engine Group Report TM80-393, 8/21/80.

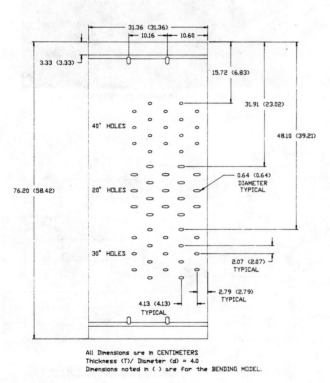

All Dimensions are in CENTIMETERS
Thickness (T)/ Diameter (d) = 4.0
Dimensions noted in ( ) are for the BENDING MODEL.

FIGURE 1 - DIMENSIONS OF PHOTOELASTIC MODELS

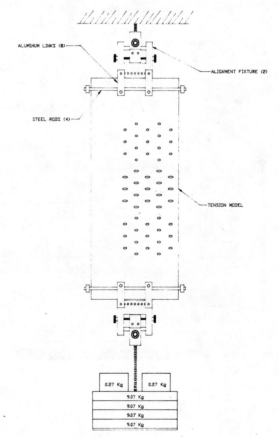

FIGURE 2 - TENSILE TEST SET-UP

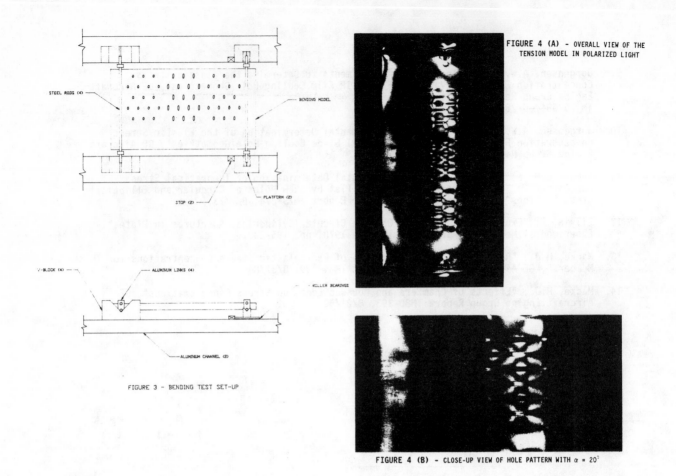

FIGURE 4 (A) - OVERALL VIEW OF THE
TENSION MODEL IN POLARIZED LIGHT

STEEL RODS (4)

BENDING MODEL

STOP (2)

PLATFORM (2)

V-BLOCK (4)

ALUMINUM LINKS (4)

ROLLER BEARINGS

ALUMINUM CHANNEL (2)

FIGURE 3 - BENDING TEST SET-UP

FIGURE 4 (B) - CLOSE-UP VIEW OF HOLE PATTERN WITH α = 20°

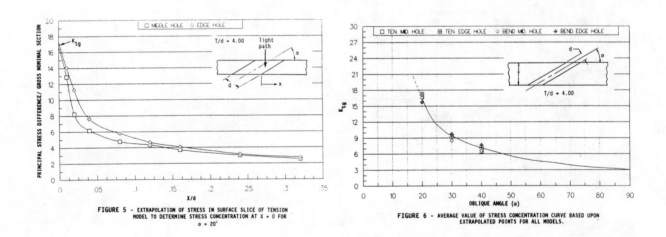

FIGURE 5 - EXTRAPOLATION OF STRESS IN SURFACE SLICE OF TENSION
MODEL TO DETERMINE STRESS CONCENTRATION AT X = 0 FOR
α = 20°

FIGURE 6 - AVERAGE VALUE OF STRESS CONCENTRATION CURVE BASED UPON
EXTRAPOLATED POINTS FOR ALL MODELS.

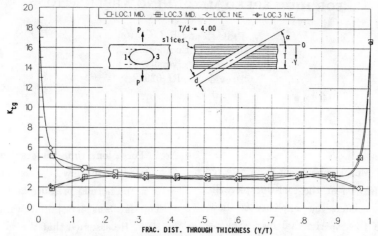

FIGURE 7 - STRESS CONCENTRATION THROUGH THE PLATE THICKNESS FOR TENSION MODEL WITH
α = 20°

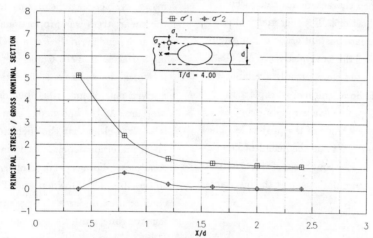

FIGURE 8 - STRESS DISTRIBUTION ALONG X - AXIS AWAY FROM HOLE FOR SURFACE SLICE IN
TENSION MODEL WITH α = 20°

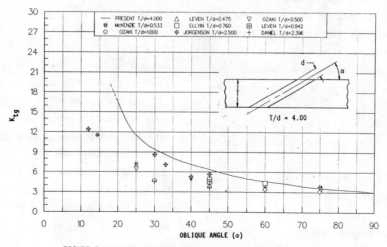

FIGURE 9 - STRESS CONCENTRATION CURVE FROM FIG. 6 AND DATA FROM OTHER SOURCES

PRESSURE-SHEAR PLATE IMPACT MEASUREMENT OF DYNAMIC FRICTION
FOR HIGH SPEED MACHINING APPLICATIONS

V. Prakash and R.J. Clifton
Division of Engineering
Brown University
Providence, RI–02912

ABSTRACT

A pressure-shear plate impact experiment is introduced to study time-resolved friction at the tool-workpiece interface. The configuration offers the simplicity of allowing the interpretation of the experimental results by using the framework of plane-wave analysis. Experiments are conducted which simulate the local conditions of pressure, slipping velocity and surface characteristics that occur in high speed machining applications. The tool material used for the present study is a wear-resistant grade of tungsten-carbide provided by GTE and the work-pieces are AISI4340 VAR steel (425° C temper) and commercially available Ti-6Al-4V. The conditions of slip at the tool-workpiece interface are varied by changing the surface roughness of each plate and by varying the skew angle of the projectile. The experimental results indicate that the coefficient of kinetic friction increases with the surface roughness of the tungsten-carbide tool-plate and with cumulative slip at the interface.

INTRODUCTION

Friction between the tool and the material being machined plays an important role in the mechanics of machining. Reduction of friction between the chip and the tool-rake reduces chip 'build-up' in front of the tool, thereby having a strong effect on chip formation. The stick-slip character of frictional response results in unsteadiness of the relative motion between the chip and the tool. The lack of steadiness in the motion tends to cause unwanted undulations in the surface of the finished material. Stick-slip behavior is also understood to have an effect on the morphology of the chips - an important consideration in the cost and convenience of recovering the removed material. Frictional heating affects the temperature at the tool and consequently the tool life. In view of the importance of friction in machining, and the sensitivity of critical mechanisms such as shear-band development and chip formation to the frictional response of the interface between the tool and the workpiece, there is need for an in-depth understanding of the frictional behavior at such an interface.

For a long time the science of surface friction was restricted to the law $\tau = \mu N$ where τ is the shear force, N is the normal pressure and μ the coefficient of friction. This law was first put forward by Leonardo da Vinci in 1508. He assumed that the value of μ was a constant and independent of the normal pressure. In 1699 the French physicist Amontons[1] formulated a friction law based on his experience in polishing optical lenses. He stated that the shear stress was proportional to the normal stress and was independent of the size and the combination of the mating surfaces. In 1778 Coulomb[2] proposed a frictional law in which the coefficient of friction was not a constant for a given pair of materials, but depended upon the applied pressure. As the knowledge of surface friction accumulated it became clear that the coefficient of friction for a pair of given materials depended on many factors e.g. the surface roughness, sliding speed, temperature, the environment and so on. In 1930, Bowden and Tabor[3], measured the real contact area under a sliding interface, accounting for surface roughness and the contact stresses analyzed by Hertz[4] (1882). They established the appearance of high temperature flashes at contact points and formulated their theory of welded junctions between rubbing surfaces. At the same time in the Soviet Union a molecular-mechanical theory was put forward. This theory was based on the dual nature of the friction force, which is comprised of the inter-molecular interaction force between the contacting surfaces and the mechanical resistance to sliding resulting from the ploughing action of the asperities. In 1939 Kragelsky[5] introduced the concept of the formation of a third phase between rubbing bodies. He showed that the frictional force between the mating bodies was controlled by this third phase and depended on the state of the surface, the pressure between the bodies, the contact time and the rate of the application of load. Bowden and Persson[6] (1961) studied surface friction at high sliding speeds (1/10 of the speed of sound or more) and showed that the coefficient of friction falls with increasing sliding speeds to values of 0.02-0.03 both at high and low normal pressure. More recently, a deeper understanding of friction laws has come from the work of Dieterich[7] (1978) and Rabinowicz[8,9](1958,1959), Johnson[10](1981) and Ruina[11](1980). Their work led to a general class of friction laws that involve the introduction of state variables. The frictional response modeled by these laws is similar to that resulting from the conventional friction law, but with the coefficient of friction μ depending on cumulative slip, slip rate, and time.

In the field of metal-cutting the response at the tool-workpiece interface continued to be treated as a problem of classical friction, i.e. the frictional response described by the Coulomb-Amontons relationship. Zorev[12] (1963) provided evidence that both sticking and sliding could occur at the interface and questioned the applicability of the Coulomb-Amontons relationship with a constant value for μ. Trent[13] (1963) published metallographic evidence that seizure is the common condition at the work-tool interface when machining iron and steel with cemented carbide tool materials. Rowe and Spick[14] (1967) published an analysis, not based on the concept of a coefficient of friction, but based on modeling the response of an interfacial layer between the tool and the work piece. However, much work since that time has continued to be expressed in terms of a coefficient of friction and the direction of research continues to be focused on the determination of the shear angle. Since it is widely understood that the practice of metal cutting is largely controlled by the tribology of the work-tool interface, experiments are required which simulate the local conditions of pressure, slipping velocity, surface characteristics, and temperature that occur in machining. These conditions need to be realized in a simple geometry for which the local tractions and the relative velocity at the interface are readily measured so that the mathematical models of the frictional behavior of the interface can be developed for use in computer simulation of machining.

THE PRESSURE-SHEAR FRICTION EXPERIMENT

An attractive geometry for studying friction between the machine stock and the machine tool is the pressure shear plate impact configuration as shown in Fig. 1. This configuration, which is a modification of configurations used for studying the shearing resistance of metals[15], polymers and lubricants at high strain rates[16], involves the impact of the flyer plate of the machine stock with a target plate having the material and surface characteristics of the machine tool. The pressure-shear plate impact occurs as a

moving projectile carrying a flyer impacts a stationary target. The impacting plates are flat and parallel, but inclined relative to the direction of approach. The projectile consists of a fiberglass tube with a aluminum cap (the piston) at the rear end. The piston holds a sealing O-ring and a plastic key which slides in a keyway in the barrel to prevent rotation of the projectile. A 63.5mm single stage gas gun, capable of launching projectiles at velocities up to 0.3 mm/μs using compressed nitrogen gas, is used to accelerate the flyer. The velocity of the projectile is measured, to an accuracy of 1% or better, by recording the times at which a series of voltage-biased thin wires are shorted out by contacting the flyer. The target is mounted in a chamber evacuated to a pressure of 50 μm Hg before the shot in order to minimize the air cushion between the flyer and the target. To ensure the generation of plane waves with wavefronts that are sufficiently parallel to the impact face, the two flat impacting faces are aligned to be parallel (within $2.0 \times 10^{-5} radians$), by means of an optical alignment technique due to Kumar and Clifton[17] in 1979. The actual tilt between the two plates at impact is measured by recording the times at which four isolated, voltage biased pins, that are flush with the surface of the target plate, are shorted to ground. The tilt obtained in the experiment is usually of the order of 0.3 milliradians or less. The first contact of a tilt pin with the flyer provides the triggering signal for the recording system.

Wave propagation in the specimen

Both the flyer and the target plates are unstressed initially. The target is at rest while the flyer is carried by a moving projectile at a known velocity V. Thus, the initial normal and the transverse particle velocities u_o and v_o of the flyer are

$$u_o = V \cos\theta, \quad v_o = V \sin\theta \qquad (1)$$

where θ is the skew angle. At impact, both normal and transverse components of velocity are imposed on the impact face of the target. Two stress waves propagate into the target as well as into the flyer plate: a longitudinal wave propagating at the elastic longitudinal wave speed c_1 and a transverse wave propagating at the elastic shear wave speed, c_2. The propagation of these waves is shown schematically in a t-X diagram (Fig. 2). Solid lines indicate the main normal wavefronts while the dashed lines indicate the shear wave fronts. The velocity and the skew angle of the projectile are controlled such that the flyer and target plates remain elastic throughout the experiment. Thus one dimensional elastic stress wave theory can be used in the interpretation of the experiments. The governing equations which hold along the characteristics are

$$\sigma \pm (\rho c_1)u = \text{constant}; \quad \text{along } \frac{dx}{dt} = \mp c_1 \quad (2)$$

$$\tau \pm (\rho c_2)v = \text{constant}; \quad \text{along } \frac{dx}{dt} = \pm c_2 \quad (3)$$

where σ, τ are the normal and shear stresses, u, v are the normal and the transverse components of the particle velocity, ρ is the mass density of the flyer and the target material. The quantities (ρc_1) and (ρc_2) are the longitudinal and the shear impedances, respectively. The constants in both equations are obtained from the initial and boundary conditions.

The components of the traction at the interface between the flyer and the target are

$$\tau = \frac{(\rho c_2)_t}{2} v_{fs}(t) \quad \text{(shear-stress)} \quad (4)$$

$$\sigma = \frac{(\rho c_1)_t}{2} u_{fs}(t) \quad \text{(normal-stress)} \quad (5)$$

where $v_{fs}(t)$ and $u_{fs}(t)$ are, respectively, the transverse and the normal components of the velocity of the free surface of the target plate, and the subscript t denotes the properties of the target.

From equations (2) and (3) the free surface velocities of the target under conditions of no-slip between the flyer-target interface are

$$u_{fs} = \frac{2(\rho c_1)_f}{[(\rho c_1)_t + (\rho c_1)_f]} V \cos\theta, \quad (6)$$

$$v_{fs} = \frac{2(\rho c_2)_f}{[(\rho c_2)_t + (\rho c_2)_f]} V \sin\theta. \quad (7)$$

where the subscript f denotes the properties of the flyer material. Based on the elementary definition of the friction between two dry contact surfaces under no-slip conditions, the coefficient of static friction, μ_s, satisfies

$$\mu_s \geq \frac{\tau}{\sigma}. \quad (8)$$

From equations (4) through (8), μ_s satisfies the inequality

$$\mu_s \geq \tan\theta \frac{(c_2)_t (c_2)_f}{(c_1)_t (c_1)_f} \frac{[(\rho c_1)_t + (\rho c_1)_f]}{[(\rho c_2)_t + (\rho c_2)_f]}. \quad (9)$$

From equation (9), a fully elastic impact, with no slip at the interface, provides a lower bound for the static coefficient of friction, μ_s. When the no-slip condition is violated, i.e. slipping occurs at the flyer-target interface, the measured free-surface velocity of the target plate can be used along with equations (4), (5) and (8) to obtain the coefficient of kinetic friction

$$\mu_k = \frac{\tau}{\sigma}. \quad (10)$$

Tool-Workpiece Materials and Specimen Preparation

The tool-material used for the present study is a wear-resistant grade of tungsten-carbide in a cobalt matrix, provided by GTE. The workpiece materials are AISI 4340 VAR steel (425° C temper) and commercially available Ti-6Al-4V alloy. The physical properties of these materials are given in Table 1. The Tungsten-Carbide plates were 40 mm in diameter and ≈ 3.4 mm in thickness. The workpiece materials were 50 mm in diameter and ≈ 4.5 mm in thickness. These dimensions provided a useful recording time of $\approx 2\mu s$ before unloading waves from the lateral boundaries reach the center of the plates. Both sides of the target and the flyer are ground flat using a surface grinder. Four copper pins, isolated electrically from the specimen, are placed in slots near the periphery of the impact face. These pins are used to determine the inclination between the faces at impact. Both the specimen and the flyer are lapped flat on both sides to within 1-2 Newton's rings over the diameter. Lapping is done on a Lapmaster machine using 14.5 μm aluminum oxide powder in mineral oil for 4340 steel and Ti-6Al-4V and 15μm boron-carbide for tungsten-carbide.

A DEKTAK surface analyzer was used to determine the surface roughness profiles of the lapped tool and the workpiece plates. These profiles were digitally filtered to remove high frequency noise. A statistical analysis was performed on the filtered data to obtain the RMS value of the surface roughness. Typical surface profiles measured on a tungsten-carbide plate and 4340 steel plate are shown in Fig. 3. The surface roughness for the tool and the workpiece is varied for each shot by polishing the specimen surfaces on Texmeth cloth using 3μm diamond paste. This procedure allows the surface roughness of the tungsten-carbide plate to be varied from 0.02 to 0.3 μm (RMS) without losing optical flatness. The corresponding ranges for the workpiece materials are 0.05 to 0.5 μm and 0.18 to 0.67 μm for 4340 steel and Ti-6Al-4V, respectively.

Interferometeric Technique

A laser interferometer technique is used to obtain the particle-velocity at a central point on the rear surface of the target plate. An Argon-ion laser with wavelength of 514.5 nm is used to provide a coherent monochromatic light source. Both the normal and transverse particle displacements are measured using a combined Normal displacement interferometer (NDI), introduced by Barker and Hollenbach[18], and Transverse displacement interferometer (TDI), introduced by Kim et al.[19]. The optical set up is shown in Fig. 4. The NDI monitors the normal displacement of the rear surface by combining a reference beam and a beam reflected from the target such that one peak-to-peak variation of the intensity of light corresponds to a displacement of $\lambda/2$. The operation of the transverse displacement interferometer is based on the phase difference between two N^{th} order beams diffracted from a grating deposited on the rear surface of the target. The transverse displacement at the rear surface of the target is given by $d = n\Delta$, where $\Delta = p/(2N)$ is the transverse displacement corresponding to one peak-to-peak variation in intensity, p is the line spacing of the grating and n is the number of fringes recorded. In the present experiments the first order diffracted beams from gratings having a frequency of 800-1200 lines/mm are used. To deposit the holographic gratings, one side of the target plate is polished to a mirror finish. After being cleaned, the surface is coated with a thin layer of Shipley Microposit Photo Resist S1400-17. The coated plate is then exposed to a virtual grating produced with an Argon-ion laser of wavelength 514.5 nm (green light). The grating is then processed in a solution consisting of one part of Shipley Microposit Developer 303A and eight parts of fresh water. The quality of the grating is checked by monitoring the diffracted beams from the grating surface. Since the Shipley photoresist is not very sensitive to normal lights, all exposure and developing procedures are carried out under room lights.

Data Recording and Processing

The interference signals from the NDI and the TDI are detected by the Monsanto MD-2 photodiodes having a risetime of 1.5 nsec. The ouput of the photodiodes is amplified by wide-band amplifiers and then recorded by LeCroy waveform digitizers having a sampling rate of 1.34 gigasamples/second (742 psec between points), with a bandwith of 250 MHz to 400 MHz. LeCroy's waveform CATALYST software, resident on an IBM AT compatible, remotely controls the operation of the digitizers and trnsfers the digitized data across an IEEE-488 bus into the hard disk of the computer. A digital data processing program is used to reduce the recorded experimental data. The program first analyzes the frequency spectrum and then filters the high frequency noise by the digital implementation of the Fast-Fourier Transform method. The filtered data is adjusted to account for variations in the amplitude of the fringes. After obtaining the normal and transverse displacement-time profiles, the velocity-time profiles are obtained by numerical differentiation (see Tong[20]).

EXPERIMENTAL RESULTS

A series of experiments are conducted using the pressure-shear friction experiment configuration. In all cases the tool material was tungsten carbide and the workpiece material was either 4340 steel or Ti-6Al-4V. The condition of slip at the interface was varied by either altering the surface roughness of the impacting plates or by varying the skew angle of the projectile. In all cases the velocity of impact was kept low enough to prevent yielding of either of the two plates. In order to ensure the validity of the plane wave analysis, measurements were restricted to the time interval (2 μs) before any unloading waves from the lateral boundaries reach the center of the plate.

A typical set of experimental velocity-time profiles for the impact of tungsten carbide and 4340 steel are shown in Fig. 5 to Fig. 7. In each case the chain line represents the predicted transverse velocity if no slipping occurs. The dashed line represents the predicted history of the transverse velocity if slipping occurs according to a Coulomb friction law with the value of the kinetic friction coefficient μ_k equal to the average value given in the figure. For Shot FRIC2 (Fig. 5) the surface roughness of the tungsten carbide plate is 0.023 μm. The skew angle is 26.6°. This angle assures a 2:1 ratio of the normal stress to the shear-stress at the flyer target interface. The transverse velocity jumps initially to the elastic prediction and shows sticking for less than 40μs followed by slipping. Once slipping begins there appears to be a tendency for the effective coefficient to increase. The slipping velocity at the interface is given, from (3) and (4), by

$$v_{slip} = V \sin\theta - \frac{(\rho c_2)_t + (\rho c_2)_f}{2(\rho c_2)_f} v_{fs}. \qquad (11)$$

For Shot FRIC2 (Fig. 5) the average slipping speed at the interface is 12.0 m/s. For Shot FRIC1 (Fig. 6) the

559

surface roughness of the tool plate is altered significantly to $0.28\mu m$ in comparison to the tool plate of Shot FRIC2 while maintaining the same skew angle of 26.6°. As anticipated the interface transmits a much larger shear stress and the transverse velocity is much closer to the elastic prediction of 44m/s. The sliding speed of the interface is reduced to 6.83 m/s. The oscillations present in the transverse velocity may be due to a weak interferometric signal during the latter part of the experimental record. In Shot FRIC5 (Fig. 7) the surface roughness of the tool-plate is kept the same as that of Shot FRIC1 but the skew angle is reduced to 22° from 26.6°. The transverse velocity profile comes very close to the elastic prediction initially and eventually reaches the elastic limit indicating that sticking occurs at the interface. The average slipping speed is reduced to 2.9 m/s. Thus by systematically changing the surafce roughness of the tool material and varying the skew angle of the projectile the slip condition at the interface changes from slipping to sticking.

Fig. 8 and Fig. 9 show transverse-velocity time profiles for the case of tungsten carbide/ Ti-6Al-4V interface. As before the chain line represents the elastic prediction based on the no-slip condition and the dashed line represents the predicted history of the transverse velocity if slip occurs according to the Coulomb friction law. The skew angle for both shots is 26.6° but the surface roughness of the tungsten carbide plate for Shot FRIC6 is 0.318 μm whereas for Shot FRIC7 is 0.042. As expected the interface corresponding to the smoother tool plate (Fig. 8) transmits a smaller shear stress and slides at a much higher average slip speed. The interface, in the case of Shot FRIC6, sticks initially and then starts to slip and then sticks again as the coefficient of kinetic friction increases with slip.

Table 2 and Table 3 summarize the experiments conducted for the present study. Higher sliding speeds and hence lower values for the coefficient of kinetic friction are obtained for the case of tungsten carbide against 4340 steel. Moreover, the slip character of the interface is determined not by the surface-roughness of the workpiece materials but by the surafce roughness of the harder tungsten carbide plate.

Fig. 10 shows a plot of the coefficient of kinetic friction as a function of the surface roughness of the tungten carbide plate for both the tungsten carbide/steel interface and tungsten carbide/Ti-6Al-4V interface. The solid symbols represent the μ_k values for Ti-6Al-4V and the open symbols represent the values for steel. The coefficient of ki-

netic friction for both interfaces increases with the surface roughness of the tungsten-carbide tool. Also, for a given surface roughness of the tungsten carbide plate the coefficient of kinetic friction is higher for Ti-6Al-4V than for 4340 steel. Also, for both machine stocks the coefficient of kinetic friction increases with cumulative slip as shown in Figs. 11 and 12 for Ti-6Al-4V and 4340 steel, respectively.

Once these limiting conditions for no-slip and for slip are established, flyer plates backed by a variable acoustic impedance plate will be used to impose a varying normal pressure at the flyer-target interface. By using a back-up plate in which the impedance decreases (say, linearly with distance through the thickness), the normal stress at the interface is lowered while the shear stress remains constant. This loading promotes the initiation of slipping under conditions in which no-slipping was encountered previously. By using a back-up plate in which the impedance increases with distance, the normal stress at the interface is increased and makes it possible to study the initiation of sticking under conditions in which slipping was encountered earlier. These stick-slip instabilities will be studied for both the tungsten carbide/4340 steel and the tungsten carbide/Ti-6Al-4V combinations.

ACKNOWLEDGEMENT This research was supported by the National Science Foundation's Program in Design and Manufacturing Systems. Partial support and the tungsten-carbide plates were provided by GTE.

REFERENCES

[1] Amontons, M. ' De Resistance Causee Dans les Machines'. Memoires de l' Academie Royale, 203-222, 1699.

[2] Coulomb, C.A. ' Theorie des Machines Simples'. Memoires de mathematique et de physique de l' Academie des sciences, t.10, 161-331, 1785.

[3] Bowden, F.P., Tabor, D. ' The Area of Contact between Stationary and Moving Surfaces'. Proc. Royal Society, Vol. 169, N938, 391-413, 1939.

[4] Hertz, H. 'Über die Berührung fester elastischer Körper'. J. reine und angewandte Mathematik, 91 156-171, 1882.

[5] Kragelsky I.V. 'Friction of Unlubricated Surfaces'. In All-Union conference on friction and wear of machines, Vol. 1 Acad. Science USSR, Moscow, 543-561, 1939.

[6] Bowden, F.P., Persson, P.A. ' Deformation, Heating and Melting of Solids at High-Speed Friction'. Proc. Royal

Soc., Series A, Vol. 260, N 1303, 433-458, 1961.

[7] Dieterich, J.H. ' Time-Dependent Friction and Mechanics of Stick-Slip'. Pure Applied Geophysics 116, 790-806, 1978.

[8] Rabinowicz, E. ' The Intrinsic Variables Affecting Stick-Slip Process'. Proc. Royal Soc. of London, 71, 668-675, 1958.

[9] Rabinowicz, E. ' A Study of Stick-Slip Process in Friction and Wear'. edited by Davies, 149-164, Elsevier, New York, 1959.

[10] Johnson, T. ' Time-Dependent friction of Granite – Implications for Precursory Slip on Faults'. J. of Geophysics, Res. 86, 6017-6028, 1981.

[11] Ruina, A. ' Frictional Laws and Instabilities– A Quasistatic Analysis of some Dry Frictional Behavior'. Ph.D. Thesis, Brown Univ., Providence RI., 1980.

[12] Zorev, N.N., International Research in Production Engineering, ASME, Pittsburg, PA., 1963.

[13] Trent, E.M., Journal of Iron and Steel Inst. London, Vol. 201, pp. 1011-, 1963.

[14] Rowe, G.W. and Spick, P.T., Journal of Engrg. Ind., pp. 530-, 1967.

[15] Clifton, R.J. and Klopp, R.W. ' Pressure–Shear Plate Impact Testing, Metals Handbook, Ninth edition(ASM International, Metals Park, OH–1985) Vol. 8, p230-, 1985.

[16] Ramesh, K.T. and Clifton, R.J.' A Pressure-Shear Plate Impact Experiment to Study the Rheology of Lubricants at High Pressures and Shearing Rates' Journal of Tribology, Vol. 109, pp. 215-, 1987.

[17] Kumar, P., Clifton, R.J. ' Optical Alignment of Impact Faces for Plate Impact Experiments'. J. of App. Phy., Vol. 48, 1366-1367,1979.

[18] Barker, L. and Hollenbach, R.E., Review of Scientific Instruments, Vol. 36, pp.1617-, 1965.

[19] Kim, K.S., Clifton, R.J., Kumar, P. ' A Combined Normal and Transverse Displacement Interferometer with an application to Impact of Y-cut Quartz'. J. of App. Phy., Vol. 48, 4132-4139, 1977.

[20] Tong, W. 'Pressure-Shear Impact Investigation of Strain-Rate History Effects in OFHC Copper', Ph.D. thesis, Brown University, 1991.

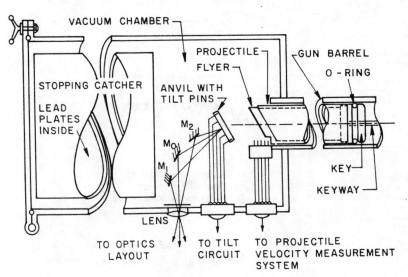

Fig. 1 Muzzle end of the gas gun used for the Pressure-Shear Friction Experiments.

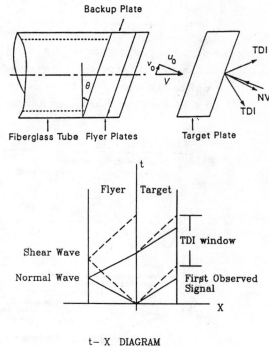

t– X DIAGRAM

Fig. 2 Schematic of the Pressure-Shear Friction experiment and the time-distance diagram.

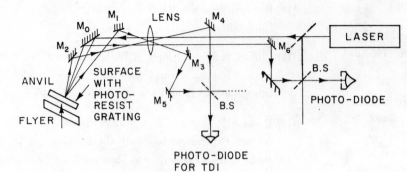

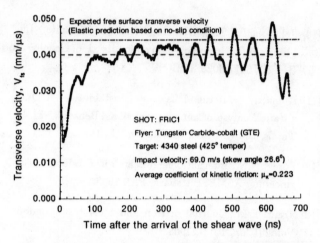

Fig. 4 Combined normal-displacement and transverse-displacement interferometer.

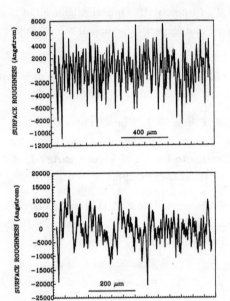

Fig. 6 Transverse-velocity versus time profile for tungsten-carbide against 4340 steel. (surface-roughness of tungsten- carbide plate is 0.28 μm).

Fig. 3 Surface-roughness profiles obtained using DEKTAK profilometer. The upper profile is for tungsten carbide (surface-roughness 0.217 μm) and the lower profile is for 4340 steel (surface-roughness 0.39 μm).

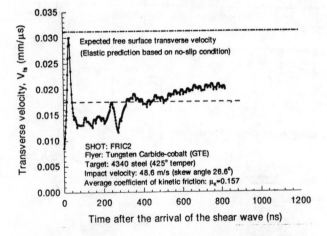

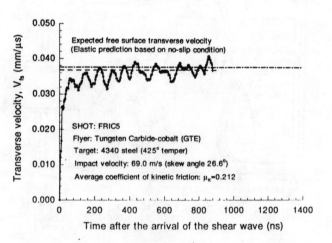

Fig. 7 Transverse-velocity versus time profile for tungsten-carbide against 4340 steel. (surface-roughness of tungsten carbide plate is 0.28 μm).

Fig. 5 Transverse-velocity versus time profile for tungsten-carbide against 4340 steel. (surface-roughness of tungsten- carbide plate is 0.023 μm).

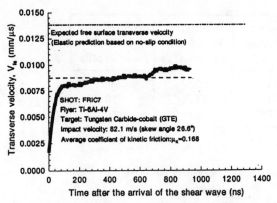

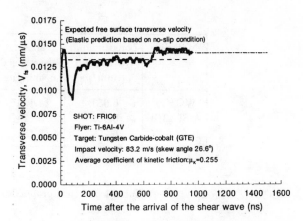

Fig. 8 Transverse-velocity versus time profile for tungsten-carbide against Ti-6Al-4V. (surface-roughness of tungsten carbide plate is 0.042 μm).

Fig. 9 Transverse-velocity versus time profile for tungsten-carbide against Ti-6Al-4V. (surface-roughness of tungsten-carbide plate is 0.318 μm).

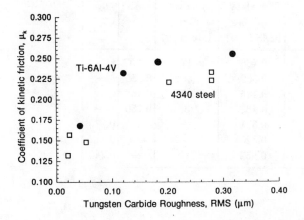

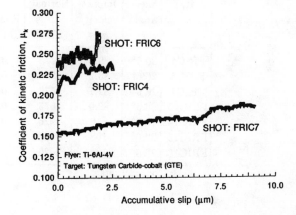

Fig. 10 Coefficient of kinetic friction as a function of the surface-roughness of the tungsten-carbide tool plate.

Fig. 11 Coefficient of kinetic friction as a function of cumulative slip (for tungsten-carbide/Ti-6Al-4V interface).

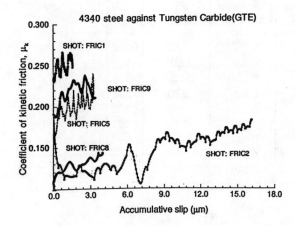

Fig. 12 Coefficient of kinetic friction as a function of cumulative slip (for tungsten-carbide/4340 steel interface).

Material	Longitudinal Wave-speed c_1 mm/μs	Transverse Wave-speed c_2 mm/μs	Acoustic Impedance GPa/mm/μs	Shear Impedance GPa/mm/μs	Proportional Limit in Shear k, MPa
WC/Co	6.650	4.125	97.12	60.23	2200
AISI 4340	5.983	3.124	45.47	23.74	750
Ti-6Al-4V	6.255	3.151	27.58	13.96	450

Table 1 Physical properties of the tool and the workpiece materials.

SHOT #	Skew Angle θ	Impact Velocity m/s	Normal Stress MPa	WC Roughness RMS (μm)	Ti-6Al-4V Roughness RMS (μm)	Average Slip Rate(m/s)	μ_k	μ_s $\geq$
FRIC4	26.6°	89.2	1715	0.121	0.466	6.17*	0.232	—
FRIC6	26.6°	83.2	1590	0.318	0.669	1.35*	0.255	—
FRIC7	26.6°	82.1	1576	0.042	0.185	12.93	0.168	—
FRIC10	26.6°	82.0	1575	0.210	0.485	1.38	0.250	—
FRIC14	18.0°	110	2226	0.310	0.521	—	—	0.170
FRIC15	22.0°	108	2150	0.263	0.525	—	—	0.212
FRIC16	25.0°	104	2020	0.291	0.552	—	—	0.245

$\star$ No slip initially.

Table 2 Summary of shots (Tungsten-carbide/Ti-6Al-4V).

SHOT #	Skew Angle θ	Impact Velocity m/s	Normal Stress MPa	WC Roughness RMS (μm)	4340 steel Roughness RMS (μm)	Average Slip Rate (m/s)	μ_k	μ_s $\geq$
FRIC1	26.6°	69.0	1910	0.280	0.510	6.83	0.223	—
FRIC2	26.6°	48.6	1340	0.023	0.067	12.0*	0.157	—
FRIC3	26.6°	62.1	1718	0.053	0.104	14.39	0.148	—
FRIC5	22.0°	70.5	2010	0.280	0.466	2.90	0.233	—
FRIC8	26.6°	73.9	2046	0.020	0.083	17.43	0.132	—
FRIC9	26.6°	86.1	2384	0.203	0.210	7.73	0.221	—
FRIC11	18.0°	109	3210	0.275	0.482	—	—	0.178
FRIC12	14.0°	114	3425	0.298	0.483	—	—	0.137
FRIC13	15.0°	108	3230	0.298	0.510	—	—	0.147

$\star$ No slip initially

Table 3 Summary of shots (Tungsten-carbide/4340 steel).

MEASUREMENTS OF THE FRONT SHAPES OF DYNAMICALLY PROPAGATING CRACKS IN PLATES

T.Nishioka, M.Nishi, T.Ishihara, T.Fujimoto and K.Sakakura

ABSTRACT

In the present study, the shapes of dynamically propagating crack-fronts in relatively thick DCB specimens of PMMA(polymethyl methacrylate) were taken by using a high-speed camera. The nature of mirror-like fracture surface in PMMA was utilized to visualize the instantaneous crack shapes in high-speed photographs. This feature was also used in the trigger system for the light source of the high-speed camera. Precise measurements of instantaneous crack-fronts appearing in the high-speed photographs were made by using an image processor. The crack-front angles to the free surfaces are investigated in connection with the singularity behavior at the corner points.

Key Words: Crack Propagation, Brittle Fracture, Curved Crack-Front, Dynamically Propagating Crack-Front, Crack-Front Angle, High-Speed Photograph, Three-Dimensional Dynamic Fracture Mechanics, Crack Arrest

INTRODUCTION

Recent experimental evidences reveal that the shape of a rapidly propagating crack-front in a plate is not necessarily straight-line. Postmortem investigations on ultrasonically induced "Wallner-line" patterns in brittle materials often indicate curved crack-fronts. This is more evident in relatively thick plates.

In most dynamic fracture experiments, the dynamic crack propagation lasts only about several hundred micro-second after the onset of the event. There were many theoretical and experimental difficulties in dynamic fracture mechanics, since the highly transient phenomena have to be treated. The two-dimensional dynamic fracture mechanics has greatly advanced in recect years, due to recent developments in the theory, simulation method and measurement technique for this field. However, contrary to the advaces in the two-dimensional dynamic fracture mechanics, few investigations on three-dimensional dynamic fracture mechanics have been made because of further difficulties.

Although the dynamic crack propagation and arrest problems in plates have been treated as two-dimensional plane problems, the curved crack-fronts in relatively thick plates may give rise to the necessity of three-dimensional dynamic fracture mechanics.

On the other hand, several researchers[1,2,3] pointed out that the stress singularity at the intersection between the straight crack-front and the free surface is weaker than the well known $r^{-0.5}$ singularity. The weaker singularity at the intersection theoretically means that the energy release rate for the straight crack decays as the free surface is approached. By energy arguments, Bazant and Estenssoro[4] proposed a hypothesis which the inclination of the crack-front to the free surface must be such that the singularity coincides with the internal $r^{-0.5}$ stress singularity.

Recently Takahashi[5] has measured the shapes of the crack-front marked on the fast fracture surfaces using the ultrasonic fractography technique. Suzuki and Yoshiyama[6] have measured instantaneous shapes of curved crack-front propagating in relatively thick PMMA plates, using a pulsed holographic microscopy technique. However, no continuous high-speed measurements of dynamically propagating curved crack-fronts have been made,so far, to the best of our knowledge. The curved crack-fronts suggest the necessity of the establishment of three-dimensional dynamic fracture mechanics.

T.Nishioka is Professor of simulation engineering; M.Nishi, T.Ishihara, T.Fujimoto are graduate students; and K.Sakakura is an engineer in Department of Ocean Mechanical Engineering, Kobe University of Mercantile Marine, Higashinada-ku, Kobe, 658, Japan.

In the present study, the shapes of dynamically propagating crack-fronts in relatively thick double-cantilever-beam (DCB) specimens of PMMA(polymethyl methacylate) are taken by using a high-speed camera. Precise measurements of the instantaneous crack-front shapes are made by using an image processor. The crack-front angles to the free surfaces are investigated in connection with the singularity behavior at the corner points.

EXPERIMENTAL METHOD

• Specimen

Figure 1 shows the typical geometry of the DCB specimen of the PMMA that was used in the present experiment. As shown in this figure, the thickness of each specimen is about 20mm, which is relatively thick comparing with the other dimensions. The refractive index of the PMMA is 1.49. Five specimens of similar type were tested as listed in Table 1. The radii of the initial notch roots were set as 0.45mm or 1.0mm in order to control the total amount of dynamic crack propagation.

The side-surface of the plate is coated with very thin layer of liquid paraffin, which has the similar refractive index of 1.48 with 1.49 of the PMMA, in order to make the side-surface clear and smooth. Since the refractive index of the PMMA is larger than 1.414, the PMMA has mirror-like fracture surfaces. This feature is utilized to visualize the instantaneous crack shapes in the high-speed photographs.

• High-speed photography

The experimental set-up for measurering the shape of dynamically propagating crack-fronts in the DCB specimens of the PMMA is shown in Fig.2. A displacement-controlled load was applied to the specimen through a wedge between the pins inserted in the pinholes(see Fig.1).

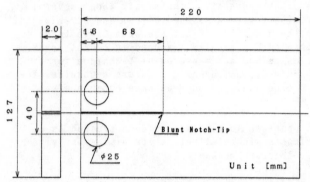

Fig.1: DCB specimen

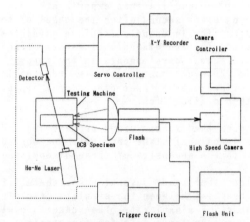

Fig.2: Experimental set-up

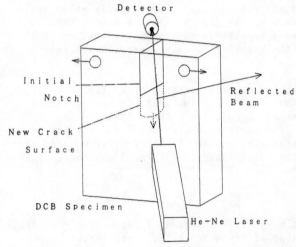

Fig.3: Trigger system

Table 1 Experimental conditions and results

SPECIMEN NO.	NOTCH-ROOT RADIUS (mm)	FRACTURE LOAD (kN)	INPUT ENERGY (Joule)
3D-1	0.45	1.31	3.9
3D-2	0.45	1.63	6.0
3D-3	0.45	1.42	4.7
3D-4	1.0	3.09	22.7
3D-5	1.0	2.40	13.6

The nature of the mirror-like fracture surface is also used in the the trigger system for the light source of the high-speed camera (Cordin 330A; muximum framing rate of two million frames per second). The trigger system is shown in Fig.3. In this system, the trigger laser beam transmits in front of the initial notch-tip and impinges to a photo-detector, then newly created mirror-like fracture surfaces intercept the trigger beam. This signal is sent to a Xenon flash unit of the high-speed camera system. The flash light impinges from a downward direction. Then this flash light is reflected by the dynamically propagating crack surface and reaches to the high-speed camera. In the present experiment, high-speed photographs were taken with the framing rate of about one hundred thousand to two hundred thousand frames per second.

• Image processing

The crack-front shapes recorded in the films of the high-speed camera are slightly distorted due to the non-uniform distribution of the refractive index in the plates. In order to evaluate the crack-front shapes precisely, a test pattern was used. The estimation procedure of the crack-front shape is schematically shown in Fig.4. The test pattern with 2 mm uniform meshes was placed between the two parts of the fractured specimen. The photographs of a test pattern were taken by the high-speed camera under the same optical conditions with each dynamic fracture experiment. Both types of the photographs were taken into an image processor by a CCD camera. The following steps were used in the image processor, for the evaluation of accurate crack-front shapes.
(1) First, the distance of crack propagation at the center of the plate was determined by mapping the crack-front position to the test pattern.
(2) Next, the measurement points in the thickness direction (P0~P10) were determined using the meshes of the test pattern.
(3) The positions of the crack-front along the lines P0~p10 were determined relatively to the position at the center (P5).

EXPERIMENTAL RESULTS

Figure 5 shows the high-speed photographs of dynamically propagating crack-front in the 3D-1 specimen. These photographs were rearranged in an image processor. The framing rate of the photographs was 150,333 frames/sec. Thus, the time intervals of the photographs were 6.65 μ sec. The numbers in the photographs indicate the crack-propagation time after the initiation of the brittle fracture.

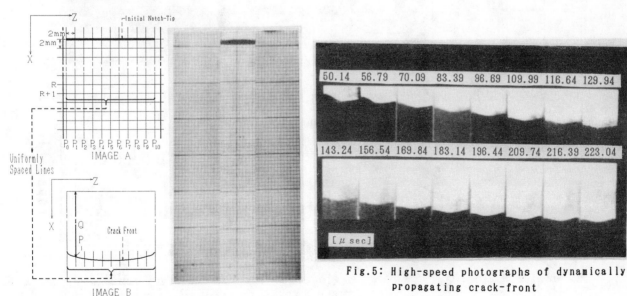

(a) Mapping of crack front
to test pattern

(b) Test Pattern

Fig.4: Estimation procedure of crack-front shape

Fig.5: High-speed photographs of dynamically propagating crack-front

Figure 6 illustrates the coordinate system employed in the DCB specimen and the plate surfaces appearing in the high-speed photograph. Since the plate surfaces of z=0 and z=h also appears near both left and right ends of each high-speed photograph in Fig.5, the shapes of the mirror image of the crack-front are also seen in the photograph. It is seen in Fig.5 that the crack-front at the center of the specimen goes in advance of those at the plate surfaces.

The time variation of the crack length at the center of the plate in the 3D-1 specimen is shown in Fig.7. The circles indicate the data points of the crack length. These data were least-squares fitted by a polynomial of the ninth order. Differentiating the polynomial for the a-t curve with respect to time t, the time variation of the crack velocity is obtained and depicted also in Fig.7. The maximum crack velocity observed in this specimen is about 186 m/sec. The crack propagated with the almost constant speed of 170 m/sec until 160 μ sec. The crack arrested at t=229.5 μ sec.

In order to find a correlation between the crack-frant shapes in the high-speed photographs and the actual one, the fracure surfaces were investigated. Figure 8 shows the photograph of the fracture surface of the 3D-1 specimen. The left and right crack-front angles to the free surfaces are indicated by α and β, respectively.

The crack-front angles appearing in the high-speed phtographs should be modified to obtain the correct angles, because of the distortion of the image in the high-speed photograph due to thenon-unforn distribution of refractive index in the specimen. This modification is done as follows:
(1) determine the magnification factors in the x and z directions, Mx and Mz, near the free surfaces of z=0 and z=h.
(2) evaluate the acual angle by using the following formula,
$$\alpha = \tan^{-1}(Mx/Mz \cdot \tan \alpha_{ph}) \qquad (1)$$

In this specimen, the crack-front angles marked on the fracture surface are α_f=101.8° and β_f=106.3°. The crack-front angles appearing in the high-speed photograph at the crack arrest (see Fig.5) were measured as α_{ph}=102.9° and β_{ph}=107.3°. Using Eq.(1), the actual angles were estimates as α=101.4° and β=105.2°, which are very close to α_f and β_f. The crack-front angles α_f and β_f in all specimens are summarized in Table 2.

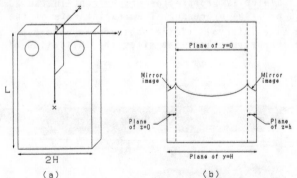

(a)　　　　　　　　(b)

Fig.6: Coordinate system in DCB specimen and planes appearing in high-speed photograph

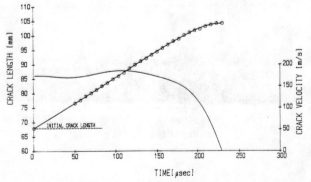

Fig.7: Crack propagation history

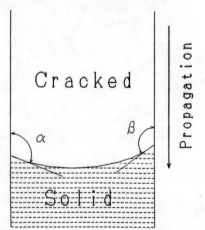

Fig.8: Arrested crack-front shape marked on fractured surface

Bazant and Estenssoro[4] have proposed a hypothesis that a crack advances maintaining the $r^{-0.5}$ singularity even at the corner point in order to produce non-zero energy release rate. They have also shown the crack-front angles with the corner singularity of $r^{-0.5}$, for various Poisson's ratios in quasi-static cases. The calculated crack-front angle in Ref.[4], for PMMA (ν =0.39) is 104.7°. This value is very close to the experimentally obtained average values of α_f =106.1° and β_f =104.1°.

Using the procedures described in the previous section, the positions of the crack-front were measured in the image processor. The time vatiations of the relative positions of the points P0~P10 (see Fig.4(a)) on the crack-front, with respect to the center point P5 are shown in Fig.9. In the early stage of dynamic crack propagation, the crack-front shape is greatly unsymmetrical since the initiation point of the brittle fracture locates around z=15 mm along the initial notch-tip. Contrary to the early stage, the relative positions of the left hand portion(P0~P4) at the arrest stage are slightly closer to the center position.

Table 2 Arrested crack-front angles

SPECIMEN NO.	(LEFT) α_f (DEGREE)	(RIGHT) β_f (DEGREE)
3D-1	101.8	106.3
3D-2	101.9	98.3
3D-3	98.3	97.5
3D-4	not arrested	not arrested
3D-5	104.3	114.1
AVERAGE	101.6	104.1

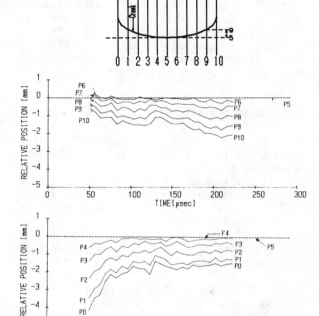

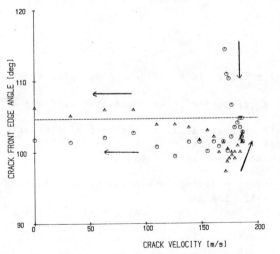

Fig.10: Variation of crack-front shape during dynamic crack propagation and arrest

Fig.9: Relative positions of crack-front with respect to the center position

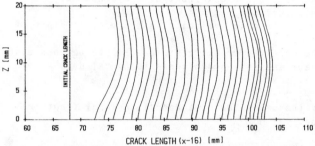

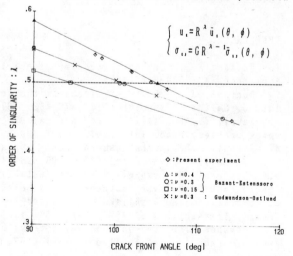

Fig.11: Variation of the crack-front angle with crack velocity

$$\begin{cases} u_i = R^{\lambda} \bar{u}_i (\theta, \phi) \\ \sigma_{ij} = G R^{\lambda-1} \bar{\sigma}_{ij} (\theta, \phi) \end{cases}$$

◇ : Present experiment

△ : ν =0.4
○ : ν =0.3   Bazant-Estenssoro
□ : ν =0.15
× : ν =0.3 : Gudmundson-Ostlund

Fig.12: Relations between the corner point singularity and crack-front angle

The variation of the crack-front shape during dynamic crack propagation and crack arrest is shown in Fig.10. In order to obtain accurate crack-front shapes, the crack-front positions at addtional points betweeen P0 and P2, and between P8 and P10 were measured and used in Fig.10. It is seen that the crack-front tends to become symmetrical after some amount of crack propagation.

The crack-front angles obtained in the present experiment were plotted against the crack velocities in Fig.11. The arrows in the figure indicate the order of the high-speed photograph. Except the data in the early stage of propagation, the crack-front angles slightly decrease for increasing crack velocity, as pointed out in Ref.[6].

The corner singularities for dynamically propagating crack-fronts in an elastic material with ν =0.3 have been evaluated based on the numerical results by Gudmundson and Ostlund[7]. Their quasi-static results for the order of singularity at the corner points with various angles are summarized in Fig.12, together with those of Bazant and Estenssoro[4] for different Poisson's ratios. As seen in the figure, the order of singularity for the Poisson's ratio of 0.3 varies linearly with the crack-front angle. The crack-front angles evaluated from the fracture surfaces at the crack-arrest in the PMMA(ν =0.39) are also plotted in Fig.12. It is seen that the singularities at the corner points of the arrested crack-fronts distribute between 0.45 and 0.55.

CONCLUDING REMARKS

Precise measurements of instantaneous crack-fronts appearing in the high-speed photographs were made by using an image processor. The following points were deduced from the present experimental results:
(1) In the present DCB specimen with 20 mm thickness, the crack-front at the center of the specimen goes in advance of those at the plate surfaces.
(2) The crack-front angle is not much influenced by the crack velocity in the present range of crack velocity
(3) The singularities at the corner points of the arrested crack-fronts distribute between 0.45 and 0.55. Therefore, the hypothesis of Bazant and Estenssoro seems to be valid in an average sense.

However, further studies are required to clarify the mechanism of three-dimensional fracture process, especially for dynamic crack propagation.

ACKNOWLEDGEMENTS: The present study was supported by the Grant-in-Aid for Scientific Research from the Minstry of Education, and in part by the Science and Technology Grant from the Toray Science Foundation.

REFERENCES

1. Folias, E.S. "On the three-dimensional theory of cracked plates" Trans. ASME, Journal of App. Mech. 42, 663-672, 1975.
2. Benthem, J.P. "State of stress at the vertex of a quarter-infinite crack in a half-space" Int. J. Solids & Structures 13, 479-492, 1977.
3. Kawai, T., Fujitani, Y. and Kumagai, K. "Analysis of singularity at the root of the surface crack problem, Proc. Int. Conf. Fract. Mech. and Tech., Hong Kong, Vol.II, 1157-1163, 1977.
4. Bazant, Z.P. and Estenssoro, L.E. "Surface singularity and crack propagation" Int. J. Solids and Structures 15, 405-426, 1979.
5. Takahashi, K. "Dynamic fracture instability in glassy polymens as studied by ultrasonic fractography", Polymer Engineering and Science 27, 25-32, 1987.
6. Suzuki, S. and Yoshiyama, I. "Pulsed holography for photographing fast propagating crack front", Transactions of JSME. Ser.A 56, 1107-1115, 1990.
7. Gudmundson, P. and Ostlund, S. "Stress singularity at the free surface of a dynamically growing crack", J. of Applied Mechanics 57, 112-116, 1990.

A BAR IMPACT TESTER FOR DYNAMIC FRACTURE TESTING OF CERAMICS AND CERAMIC COMPOSITES

L. R. Deobald and A. S. Kobayashi[*]

Abstract

A bar impact test was developed to study the dynamic fracture responses of precracked ceramic bars, Al_2O_3 and 15/29% volume SiC_W/Al_2O_3. Crack opening displacement was measured with a laser interferometric displacement gage and was used to determine the crack velocities and the dynamic stress intensity factor, K_I^{dyn}. The crack velocities and K_I^{dyn} increased with increasing impact velocities while the dynamic initiation fracture toughnesses, K_{Id}, did not vary consistently with increasing impact velocities.

1. Introduction

Available configurations of new ceramics and ceramic composites are often restricted to bar geometries of about 10 x 10 mm in cross section due to the historical precedence of using modulus of rupture (MOR) tests for determining the mechanical properties of early experimental materials. These MOR specimens are ideally suited for single-edge notched, three-point bend tests in determining fracture toughness despite the inherent experimental difficulties associated with the small dimensions. These specimens are also extremely sensitive to the interaction of reflected stress wave with the propagating crack tip as evidenced by the copious fluctuations in the dynamic stress intensity factor during the dynamic fracture process [1,2]. Moderate fluctuations in dynamic stress intensity factor in relatively large three-point bend specimens of 75 mm height x 10 mm thickness and 89 mm height x 9.5 mm thick were documented in [3] and [4], respectively, but not to the extent shown in [1,2]. Such superfluous reflected stress waves do not exist in the one-dimensional split Hopkinson tensile bar test of Duffy and his colleagues [5,6]. However, this clean test configuration uses explosives for loading which requires special training and laboratory facilities. Thus a need exists for a similar clean test which can be executed without the special facilities. The objective of this paper is to describe such a dynamic fracture test procedure involving a bar impact test.

2. Experimental Procedure

The bar impact experiment consists of a 50.8 mm long, rectangular bar specimen which is impacted on its end by a 25.4 mm long bar impactor of the same material. Ideally the reflected tension wave from the free end of the specimen bar interacts with the incoming compressive wave and generates a tensile stress pulse of 5.2 µs duration in the middle of the bar specimen with the transit of approximately 3/4 of the compressive pulse as shown by the Lagrangian diagram of Figure 1. In practice, the impact typically produces a stress wave of 1.6 µs rise time propagating in both the impactor and specimen. The superposition of the incoming ramping portion of the stress wave causes a tension pulse, which rises in about 0.8 µs and is sustained for another 3.6 µs, at the crack plane.

The schematic of the experimental apparatus is shown in Figure 2. The specimen and impactor bars are held by molded urethane holders which are mounted in two carriages. Both the specimen and the impactor carriage run on guide rails. An air gun propels the impactor carriage down the guide rails towards the stationary specimen carriage. The ceramic bars impact well before the collision of the urethane holders. The resultant compressive stress is proportional to the impact velocity which is determined by a laser velocity measurement system.

The specimen geometry is shown in Figure 3. The ceramic materials tested and the corresponding nominal mechanical properties are shown in Table 1. A sharp precrack with an approximate initial length of 3 mm was generated by the single-edge-precracked-beam (SEPB) method [7] from a shallow chevron notch. This sharp crack is transparent to the incoming compressive wave but reflects the tensile wave which initiates dynamic crack propagation. The crack opening displacement (COD) at the location X was measured using the laser interferometric displacement gage (LIDG) system [8]. LIDG targets were mounted at the precrack tip such that the reflective indentations, 0.4 mm apart, straddled the precrack as shown in Figure 3. Also a short strain gage of 1.6 mm gage length was mounted at the mid-length of the bar on the surface opposite to the precrack. This strain gage was used to determine the initial rise in the stress history and its relation to the LIDG signal. The measured impact velocity was used to determine the level of sustained tension stress after the initial stress rise had been measured.

3. Data Reduction Procedure

3.1 Theoretical Preliminaries

The dynamic initiation fracture toughness, K_{Id}, was determined by using the solution to a stress wave impinging on a stationary crack [10]. A non-dimensional parameter, Ψ, was derived by the simple inversion of the dynamic displacement equation as follows [11].

---

[*] L.R. Deobald is a Senior Specialist Engineer, The Boeing Company, Defense & Space Group, Seattle, WA 98124 USA, and A.S. Kobayashi is Boeing Pennell Professor in Structure Mechanics, Dept. of Mechanical Engineering, University of Washington, Seattle, WA 98195 USA.

$$\Psi = (4\hat{f})^{-1} \sqrt{\pi/2} = \frac{K_I^{dyn} \sqrt{a-X} \; f(V)}{E' \; COD} \qquad \text{where } \hat{f}(V) = \frac{\beta_1 (1-\beta_2^2)}{(1-v) \; D(V)} \tag{1}$$

$$D(V) = 4 \beta_1\beta_2 - (1+\beta_2^2)^2 \tag{2}$$

$$\beta_1^2 = 1 - V^2/C_1^2 \qquad\qquad \beta_2^2 = 1 - V^2/C_2^2 \tag{3}$$

where a is the crack length, X is the distance along the crack at which the COD is determined, COD is the crack opening displacement, K_I^{dyn} is the dynamic propagation stress intensity factor, $E' = \dfrac{E}{1-v^2}$, E is the modulus of elasticity and V, C_1 and C_2 are the crack velocity, dilatational and shear wave velocities, respectively.

For the near field asymptotic solution of a semi-infinite crack propagating at constant velocity in an infinite plate, $\hat{f} = 1$ and the theoretical value of Ψ becomes $\Psi_{theo.} = \sqrt{\pi/32}$. As will be shown later through dynamic finite element analysis, Ψ remains essentially constant during the short crack propagation time in this small specimen.

A second non-dimensional parameter, Ω, was also derived based on an empirical relationship between the energy consumed at the crack tip and the strain energy flux into the crack tip region. Details of this derivation can be found in [11].

$$\Omega = 4\sqrt{2/\pi} \; \hat{f} \; X\sqrt{\hat{k}/W} = \frac{X \; E' \; COD}{(a-X) \; W \; \sigma_0 \; f(V) \; g(V)} \tag{4}$$

where $\hat{k}$ is a proportionality constant

$$g(V) = \left(\frac{C_1 C_2^2 D(V)}{2(1+v) \; V^3\beta_1} \right)^{1/2} \tag{5}$$

3.2 Dynamic Finite Element Analysis

3.2.1 Impacted SEPB Specimen

A commercial finite element code, ABAQUS[1], was used to simulate the dynamic fracture of the impacted ceramic bar. The purpose of this study was to determine the calibration parameters, Ψ and Ω, for the specimen configuration considered. Although the impact phenomenon was not symmetric, the stress state and the stress wave propagation become completely symmetric after the stress wave has propagated about the length of the bar and thus only half of the bar was modeled. Stress wave propagation was simulated in the finite element model by ramping the initial static compressive stress at the impact end to zero over a 1.6 μs duration. This loading created a tension pulse which propagated towards the center of the bar. As shown in Figure 1, two tension pulses, which met at the crack plane at a post impact time of 8.6 μs, produced a sudden net tension stress. This tension pulse was modeled by the tension wave which reflected off of the rigid boundary along the crack plane as a tension wave in the one-half finite element model. This reflected tension wave in the finite element method (FEM) model represented the tension wave passing from the back half of the bar in a real test. The crack was then allowed to open at the time the crack plane was in tension as predicted by Figure 1. After a delay of about 0.6 μs, a constant crack velocity was then prescribed and the energy release rate, G_I, was calculated from the change in the total energy in the model as the crack propagated.

The FEM analysis was used to also justified the above use of the theoretical solution for a semi-infinite crack, which is either stationary or moving at a constant velocity and impacted by a one-dimensional wave, in an infinite domain despite the finite geometry of the specimen. This analysis consisted of prescribing the impulse of Figure 1 on the impacted end of a finite element model of the *whole* specimen bar, without a precrack, and computing the dynamic state of stress at the crack plane. Figure 4 shows the wave front of the reflected tensile pulse, σ_y, through the width of the specimen prior to impacting the crack surface. Also shown is the secondary stress, σ_x, which is perpendicular to the tensile pulse, at this instant. The negligible distribution of the secondary stress, σ_x, shows that the one-dimensional wave front is maintained at this instant. Figure 5 shows a comparison between the computed stress and that determined by the strain gage located on the specimen edge in front of the crack tip. The good agreement between the two stresses indicate that the thickness-wise strain, which is zero in the plane strain FEM analysis, is negligible and thus the plane strain assumption is valid in this data reduction procedure.

3.2.2 Determination of Ψ_C and Ω_C

The parameter, Ω, listed as Equation (4), was calculated in a series of dynamic finite element analyses for the W = 8.89 mm specimen. The crack velocities varied from 1201 to 2222 m/s. Two different initial crack lengths were included and different load levels were simulated. From this analysis, a constant $\Omega = 0.95$ was obtained as the calibration constant, Ω_C. This Ω will not model correctly the dynamic fracture phenomenon near crack initiation where the crack velocity jumps from zero to a high constant velocity used in the simulation. An additional finite element analysis of the specimen geometry with W=7.24 mm yielded a calibration constant of $\Omega_C=1.37$.

---

[1] Hibbit, Karlsson and Sorensen, Inc., Providence, RI 02906-4402 USA.

The parameter, Ψ, was calculated from the finite element analyses for four different crack velocities. The parameter Ψ remained constant before dropping off slightly as the cracks passed $\alpha = a/W = 0.85$. A constant value line was fit to the data yielding the calibration constant, $\Psi_C = 0.34$. This value compares well with the constant velocity crack solution in an infinite medium where $\Psi_{theo.} = \sqrt{\pi/32}$. A single finite element solution was used to determine Ψ_C for the FEM model with W=7.24 mm. The result for the 7.24 mm wide model was $\Psi_C = 0.35$ which is within 3% of Ψ_C for the 8.89 mm wide model. A speculation is made that the coarse FEM mesh causes the models to be overly stiff and the underestimated COD yielded a numerically determined Ψ_C which is slightly higher than the theoretical value, $\Psi_{theo.}$.

Although many finite element analyses were done to verify the data reduction procedure, only one analysis was required per specimen geometry. The resulting calibration constants, Ω_C and Ψ_C, are given in Table 2 for the two geometries used here.

The crack length history, a(t), using the experimental mid-plane stress, $\sigma(t)$, was computed by the crack opening displacement, COD(t). $K_I^{dyn}(t)$ computation required the use of a(t) and COD(t). These relations are shown in the following as functions of the two non-dimensional parameters which are referred to as calibration parameters Ω_C and Ψ_C.

$$a(t) = X \left(1 + \frac{E' \, COD(t)}{\Omega_C \, W \, \sigma(t) \, f(V) \, g(V)} \right) \tag{6}$$

$$K_I^{dyn}(t) = \Psi_C \frac{E' \, COD(t)}{f(V) \, \sqrt{a(t) - X}} \tag{7}$$

The crack length history, determined by Equation (5), is a function of two functions, f(V) and g(V). Hence, the crack length history, a(t), must be determined in an iterative fashion. An initial guess was made of the crack velocity, V, to calculate f(V) and g(V). a(t) was then calculated with Equation (6) and least squares fitted with a straight line. The slope (crack velocity) was used to determine new estimates of f(V) and g(V). The process was repeated until the crack velocity converged to the correct value, which is the measured crack velocity in this case. The final value of f(V) was used with a(t) in Equation (7) to calculate $K_I^{dyn}(t)$, explicitly.

4. Experimental Results

As mentioned previously, an accurate measurement of the impact velocity is important since it is used to calculate the stress level. Simple bar wave theory predicts a square stress pulse of magnitude $\sigma_y = EV_0/2C_b$ while the actual stress, as determined by dynamic finite element analysis, ramps up and oscillate around the stress level predicted by the bar wave theory as shown in Figure 5. A typical stress pulse, which is the first compressive pulse, measured with a single strain gage is also shown in Figure 6. The reasonable agreement between the computed and measured stress pulses, show that the specimen bar is in a uniaxial state of stress and that the stress wave dispersions at the edges are minimal. The reflected tension pulse was of the same shape except that the higher frequency oscillations diminished. The initial ramping at the beginning of the measured wave was combined with the maximum stress based on the measure impact velocity. This combined stress history is shown as a shaded area in Figure 6 and was used to calculate the experimental a(t).

A typical photomultiplier tube (PMT) output representing the COD variation with crack propagation in a specimen (15% vol. SiC_W/Al_2O_3) impacted at 8 m/s is shown in Figure 7. The crack began to run shortly after the arrival of the tension stress wave. This fringe history was combined with the other PMT output to obtain the COD history. The COD data was then curve fitted with a higher order polynomial which was used to analyze the data at the same time increments as the stress history.

4.1. Crack Histories

The procedure presented previously was used to obtain the crack length histories of the ceramic specimens impacted at velocities of approximately $V_0 = 5.8$, 8, and 10 m/s for each of the four materials. Figure 8 shows a typical crack length history for 15% vol. SiC_W/Al_2O_3 where the crack velocity, V, increased with increasing impact velocity, V_0. The crack velocity for hot pressed alumina and the two composite materials were similar but was 11-31% higher for the 99.5% dense alumina.

The initial crack lengths, a_0, for 10 of the 12 specimens were determined by observing the fracture surface with a binocular microscope. All materials exhibited a distinct fracture initiation site with the exception of the 99.5% dense alumina. For the last test of the 99.5% dense alumina, dye penetrant was baked onto the precrack area for a_0 determination prior to testing. The initial crack was generally curved along the crack front and thus the measured initial crack length was taken as the average distance of a_0 measured at the side surfaces and in the mid-plane.

4.2. K_I Determination

The dynamic stress intensity factor, K_I^{dyn}, variation for 15% volume SiC_W/Al_2O_3 bars impacted at three velocities each is shown in Figure 9. The fracture toughness increased with increasing impact velocities within each material group. The K_I^{dyn} data was plotted as a function of the non-dimensional crack length, $\alpha = a/W$. K_I^{dyn} increased rapidly to begin with, then increased more slowly as the crack approached the boundary. The increase in K_I^{dyn} as a function of time is even more pronounced. Figure 10 is a plot of K_I^{dyn} versus the average crack velocity, V, for all the materials in this study.

The dynamic initiation fracture toughness, K_{Id}, was calculated by the technique presented in Section 3. All results are summarized in Table 3. All specimens impacted at 10 m/s showed macroscopic crack branching. Also, the hot pressed alumina impacted at 8 m/s showed crack branching. The crack branching stress intensity factor, K_{Ib}, was determined by measuring the crack branch length, a_b, then choosing $K_{Ib} = K_I^{dyn}(\alpha = a_b/W)$ from the dynamic stress intensity factor curves e.g., Figure 10. The crack branching toughness [13], K_{Ib}, is also listed in Table 3. K_{Ib} was typically 2 to 2.5 times the magnitude of K_{Id} which is in accordance with previously reported results [12]. Surpassing K_{Ib} was a necessary, but not a sufficient condition for the crack to branch and is in agreement with some tests where K_I^{dyn} exceeded K_{Ib} without crack branching.

5. Discussions

Before proceeding to the analysis of experimental data, it was important to verify that the numerically determined calibration constants, Ω_c and Ψ_c would determine the correct crack length history, a(t) and K_I^{dyn} as determined by the finite element model. A verification, which used Ω_c and Ψ_c and the known stress history and COD from the FEM analysis to calculate a(t) and K_I^{dyn}, was thus conducted. In regard to K_I^{dyn}, the initial oscillation in Ψ did introduce a discrepancy of about 10% immediately after the crack began to propagate. However, K_I^{dyn} matched closely in the range of $0.5 < \alpha = a/W < 0.85$. The difference between $\Psi_{theo.} = \sqrt{\pi/32}$ and Ψ may be due to an overly stiff finite element mesh.

The crack velocities were nearly the same for the hot pressed alumina and the two composites. This indicates that the toughening mechanisms in the composite were ineffective under this severe dynamic fracture. The higher crack velocity in the lower density alumina was in accord with other published data[1,2].

Crack propagation initiated at the respective values of K_{Id} for each material and reached values of K_I^{dyn} as high as 4 times K_{Id}. K_I^{dyn} plot was terminated where crack branching occurred. A unique relationship between V and K_I^{dyn} was not apparent from the results of this experiment. Other researchers have reported similar results for ceramic materials [1,2]. The uniqueness of the K_I^{dyn} versus V curve continues to be a source of controversy and the results of this study did not resolve this question due to the insufficient resolution in determining the crack velocity.

A great advantage of this technique was that the crack was loaded by a relatively "clean" tension stress which happens to be uniform across the crack plane and loads the crack in mode I opening only. The duration of the experiment was less than the time for the primary release waves to return to the crack.

6. Conclusions

1) A new type of experiment was designed to study the dynamic fracture behavior of ceramic materials. The new test method provided several distinct advantages over current experimental methods.

   - A predictable, unidirectional stress pulse was suddenly applied at the crack plane.
   - A sharp precrack better estimate of K_{Id}.
   - Once set up, this experiment was relatively easy to perform and was comparable to the popular instrumented Charpy impact test.
   - The method gave consistent results for a(t) and K_I^{dyn}.

2) A new method of analysis was developed for converting the measured COD and stress to useful K_I^{dyn} data. The technique provided the following contributions:

   - Two non-dimensional invariant parameters, Ω and Ψ were derived. The constants defined as Ω_c and Ψ_c were used to analyze a number of experiments of similar materials at a variety of impact velocities.
   - Only one dynamic finite element analysis was needed per specimen geometry to analyze a series of tests. This makes dynamic fracture study more economical.

3) The toughening mechanisms for SiC_W/Al_2O_3 composites were ineffective when the material was subjected to severe dynamic fracture conditions.

7. Acknowledgement

This research was supported by the Office of Naval Research Contract No. 0004-87-K032. The authors express their sincere gratitude to Drs. Yapa Rajapakse and Steve Fishman for their patience and encouragement during the course of this investigation.

8. References

1. Yang, K.H., Kobayashi, A.S., Emery, A.F., "Dynamic Toughness of Ceramic Composites," Ceramic Engineering Science Proceedings 9(7-8) (1988) 795-802.

2. Takagi, Y. and Kobayashi, A.S., "Further Studies on Dynamic Fracture Response of Alumina and SiC_W/Al_2O_3 Composite," Proc. of Symp. on Elevated Temperature Crack Growth, eds. S,. Mall and T. Nicholas, ASME MD-Vol. 18 (1990) 145-148.

3. Kalthoff, J.F., Winkler, S. and Beinert, J., "The Influence of Dynamic Effects in Impact Testing, " International Journal of Fracture, Vol. 13, (1977) 528-531.

4. Mall, S., Kobayashi, A.S. and Urabe, Y., :Dynamic Photoelastic and Dynamic Finite Element Analyses of Dynamic Tear Test Specimens," Experimental Mechanics, Vo. 16, December 1978, 449-458.

5. Marchand, A., Duffy, J.F. Christman, T.A. and Suresh, S., " An Experimental Study of the the Dynamic Mechanical Properties of an Al-SiC_W Composite," Engineering Fracture Mechanics, Vol 30, No. 3,1988, 295-315.

6. Suresh, S, Nakamura, T., Yeshurun, Y., Yang, K.-H. and Duffy, J.F., "Tensile Fracture Toughness of Ceramics Materials: Effects of Dynamic Loadings and Elevated Temperature," Journal of American Ceramic Society, Vol 73, No. 8, 1990, 2457-2466.

7. Nose, T. and Fujii, T., "Evaluation of Fracture Toughness for Ceramic Materials by a Single-Edge-Precracked-Beam Method." J. of the Amer. Cer. Soc.. 71 (5) (1988) 328-333.

8. Sharpe, W.N., Jr., "A New Optical Technique for Rapid Determination of Creep and Fatigue Thresholds at High Temperatures," AFWAL TR 84-4028, Air Force Wright Aeronautical Laboratories, WPAFB, 1984.

9. Freund, L.B., "Crack Propagation in an Elastic Solid Subjected to General Loading-III. Stress Wave Loading," J. Mech. Ph6s. Solids, 21 (1973) 47-61.

10. Ravichandran, G. and Clifton, R.J., "Dyanmic Fracture Under Plane Wave Loading," Brown University Report No. AD-A178 594. U.S. Army Research Office, Report No. ARO 223067EG, December 1986.

11. Deobald, L. R., "Experimental/Numerical Characterization of the Dynamic Fracture Behavior of Ceramic Materials," a PhD thesis submitted to University of Washington, June 1991.

12. Ramulu, R. and Kobayashi, A.S., "Mechanics of Crack Curving and Branching," Int'l J. of Fracture, 27 (1985) 187-201.

Table 1. Mechanical properties

Materials	E (GPa)	ν	ρ (g/cc)	C_b (mm/μs)
Al_2O_3[1] 99.5%	372	.22	3.89	9.78
Al_2O_3[2] 99.9% —HP[3]	387	.22	3.97	9.87
15% v SiC_W/Al_2O_3[2] —HP	398	.23	3.85	10.17
29% v SiC_W/Al_2O_3[2] —HP	408	.23	3.73	10.46

C_b is the bar wave velocity

Table 2. Calibration constants, Ω_c and Ψ_c, calculated by FEM.

W (mm)	X (mm)	Ω_c	Ψ_c
8.89	2.5	0.95	0.34
7.24		1.37	0.35

Table 3. Summary of Experimental Results

Material	V_0 m/s	V m/s	V/C_2	K_{IC} MPa√m	K_{Id} MPa√m	K_{Ib} MPa√m
Al_2O_3	5.8	1975	0.32		5.3	–
	7.9	2317	0.37	3 - 4	5.9	–
	10.3	2605	0.42		5.2	12.4
Hot Pressed Al_2O_3	5.7	1546	0.24		5.9	–
	8.1	1830	0.29	4	6.8	14.9
	10.1	2465	0.39		5.8	13.6
15% vol. SiC_W/Al_2O_3	5.8	1457	0.22		9.0	–
	8.0	1872	0.29	6	6.5	–
	10.0	2210	0.34		6.7	14.2
29% vol. SiC_W/Al_2O_3	5.8	1536	0.23		6.5	–
	8.0	2383	0.36	7	5.7	–
	10.1	2383	0.36		9.8	14.2

[1] Coors Ceramic Company, 600 9th Street, Golden, CO 80401 USA.
[2] Advanced Composite Materials Corporation, 1525 S. Buncombe Road, Greer, SC 29651 USA.
[3] Hot pressed processing.

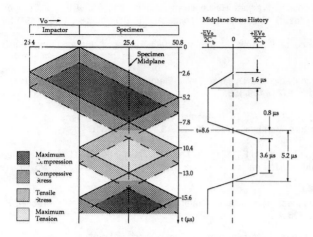

Figure 1 Lagrangian diagram for impact experiment, C_b = 9.8 mm/μs

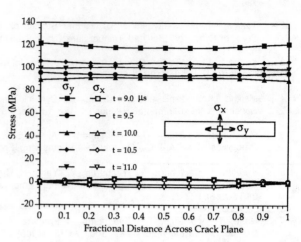

Figure 4 Computed stresses at the crack plane.

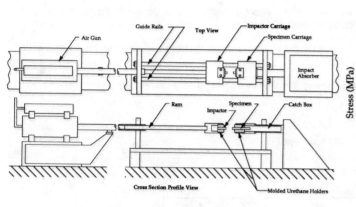

Figure 2 Impact apparatus and air gun.

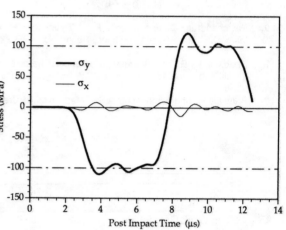

Figure 5 Computed stresses at strain gage location.

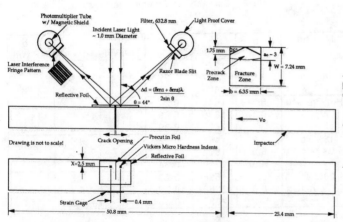

Figure 3 Specimen geometry and LIDG technique.

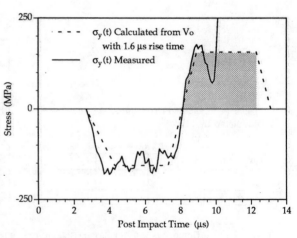

Figure 6 Typical measured stress and Ideal stress.

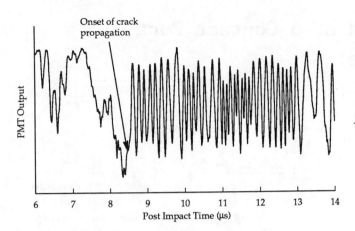

Figure 7 Typical PMT Signal representing LIDG fringe motion.

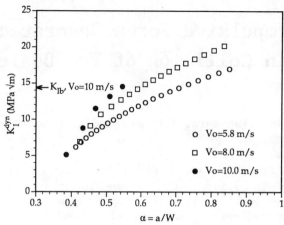

Figure 9 Dynamic stress intensity factor for 15% vol. SiC$_w$/Al$_2$O$_3$.

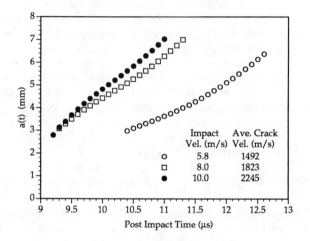

Figure 8 Typical crack length histories, 15% vol. SiC$_w$/Al$_2$O$_3$.

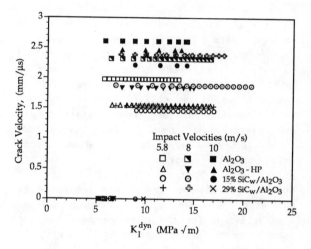

Figure 10 Influence of K$_I^{dyn}$ on the crack velocity for all materials.

Impulsive Force Generated at a Contact Part in Collision of Two Bodies

By S.Tanimura, Y.Chuman and K.Kaizu

ABSTRACT— A new method has been devised for measuring impulsive force generated at a contact part in collision. This new method, here called sensing block method, is based on a simple structure which is made of steel cylindrical block with a small cylindrical projection, the top of this projection serves as the contact plane in collision. The impulsive force generated at the contact part can be measured using small strain gages mounted on the side surface of the projection. Through the calibration tests, it was confirmed that the new method is more effective for direct measurement of impulsive force with relatively high sensitivity for both normal and oblique impacts. The obtained measurements are almost entirely free from disturbances caused by interference from the reflected waves. Using this method, impact experiments were performed using commercial pure aluminum bars of different lengths and spherical ends. The impact was generated by colliding these bars against a sensing block. Time variation for the force generated at the spherical end of the specimens collided with the sensing block, and the duration of the impact, were measured at various impact velocities. It was found that the volume of the deformed part at the contact end was proportional to the potential energy of the bars before impact and, the generated mean stress on the contact part was constant independent of the length of the specimen and the impact velocity.

Shinji Tanimura is Professor, Koichi Kaizu is Assistant Professor, Department of Mechanical Engineering, University of Osaka Prefecture, Sakai, Osaka 591, Japan and Yoshitaka Chuman is Associate Professor, Department of Mechanical Engineering, Osaka Prefectural College of Technology, Neyagawa, Osaka 572, Japan

INTRODUCTION

In recent years, research and development in high speed machining methods and fast transport services have made remarkable advances. Consequently, collision of machine parts or structures with each other and, collision of flying objects against a structure, has become a serious problem.

In designing machine parts or structures which should withstand an impact load, it is fundamentally important to know the dynamic deformation of the materials at its contact part and the impulsive force generated at that part. In a collision of machine parts or structures against each other, or in a collision of a flying object against a structure, the impact range is usually from a few meters per second to tens of meters per second; the damage number[1] D is $10^{-5} < D < 10^{-2}$. The impulsive force and the duration of impact depend on the shape, size and material properties of both bodies as well as the impact velocity. In addition, the contact surface area undergoing plastic deformation varies during collision. Even where the impact velocity is only a few meters per second, an inelastic deformation or a crash may sometimes occur at the contact part: Such an occurrence make conditions as the impact ends in elastic-plastic impact of bodies, very complicated.

In experiments where a one-dimensional or a tension-torsion combined load is applied impulsively to a specimen, conventional methods for measuring the stress or displacement produced at the impact end is often by means of strain gages mounted on an elastic cylindrical bar[2,3] or tube[4], or by means of a piezoelectric element[5], or by using diffraction gratings[6]. When plastic deformation or a crash occurs at a contact part and the contact surface area varies during the collision, the above stated conventional methods for measuring the impact force, are sometimes not very accurate because of disturbances caused by interference from the reflected waves[7].

TANIMURA et. al.[8-11] devised a measuring method for achieving an effect that is equivalent to the embedment of small strain gages in a solid body. Experimental results were obtained from aluminum bars with a variety of truncated cone-shaped ends which were collided against a devised sensing plate. In our previous sensing plate method, problems sometimes occurred in maintaining a close contact between the sensing plate and the sensing block during the repeated impacts. This problem created certain difficulties in resetting the sensing plate.

In the present paper, a new measuring method which has been devised for measurements of impulsive force generated at the contact part is presented. The basic principle involved in this new technique and the device set up are very simple. This apparatus can also be easily reconditioned following damage to the impact surface of the sensing block, which may result from large impulsive forces. From experimental deductions, it was confirmed that the new sensing block method is more effective for taking measurements of impulsive force than the sensing plate method proposed in our previous papers. The new measurements were almost entirely free from disturbances caused by interference with the reflected waves. Using this new method, impact experiments were performed using commercial pure aluminum bars of varying lengths and spherical ends, these bars were collided with an elastic wall.

Method of Measurement

Figure 1 shows the schematic diagram of a new apparatus for calibration testing. The devised sensing block was made of high carbon steel cylindrical block of 200 mm in diameter and 300 mm in height, with a small cylindrical projection of 15 mm in diameter and 20 mm in height on the surface of one side of the block. Small strain gages are mounted on the side surface of the small cylindrical projection for measuring impulsive force generated at the impact end, as shown in Fig.2. The characteristics of the sensing block can be calibrated by allowing stress pulses of known magnitude, propagate in an elastic input bar which is perpendicular to a small area of the impact surface of the sensing projection(see Fig.1) and, by recording the output pulses from the sensing block.

The calibration test of the sensing block was performed by means of the stress-bar technique. The input bar and striking bar were both made of a rod of SUS 304, 20 mm in diameter and 750 mm in length. As shown in Fig.1, the striking bar impacts axially against the input bar, which is perpendicular to the impact surface of the sensing projection of the block. An incident pulse produced by the impact of the striking bar is recorded by two strain gages mounted on the input bar in an axial direction at axisymmetric positions of 60 mm above the end which gets in contact with the sensing projection. At the same time, an output pulse generated in the projection of the sensing block is recorded by four strain gages which are located perpendicularly to the impact surface on the surface of the projection of the sensing block as shown in Fig.2.

Figure 3(a) shows an example of the oscillograms recorded simultaneously from both the input bar and the sensing block in the calibration test, using a digital memory scope. For the strain gages used in this test, for the input bar, had gage length of 2mm, resistance was 120Ω and gage factor was 2.16. While the strain gages used for the sensing block, had gage length of 0.5mm, resistance was 350Ω and the gage factor K was 2.06. The upper trace in the figure is the output pulse from the sensing block and the lower one is the input pulse from the stress bar.

As seen in Fig.3 (a), the upper trace from the sensing block, show smooth pulse apparently free from disturbances caused by the interference with reflected waves. However, the lower trace reveals the repeated propagation and reflection of stress waves in the bar. Both the incident and output pulses remained at almost constant levels after a rise time of approximately 30–40μs. For reference, an example of the incident and output pulses in the sensing plate method we had proposed earlier in our previous studies is shown in Fig.3 (b). Comparing Fig.3(a) with Fig.3(b), it was concluded that there is no evident significant differences between output pulses from the sensing block method and the sensing plate method. The sensitivity of the sensing block could therefore, be tested by comparing the constant output voltage from the sensing block, e_{po}, with that from the input bar, e_b.

Variations in the sensitivity of the sensing block with the impact position is given in Fig.4 (a) and (b). In this test, the striking position on the impact surface of the block was changed along the lines designated by L–R, U–D and so on, as shown in Fig.2. The end of the input bar which gets in contact with the impact surface was reduced to a circular plane of 3 mm in diameter by cutting off the edge. The vertical axis in Fig.4 is the ratio, e_p/e_{po}, which was defined as 1.0 at the center of the sensing projection and the abscissa is the moving distance from the center of the projection.

Figure 5, show the results of the calibration test on the sensitivity of the sensing block. The experimental points were obtained by impacting the input bar of 20 mm in diameter upon the center of the sensing projection with four-gage configuration. In this experiment, we used bars with six different ends which ranged from 3 mm to 15 mm in diameter. The contact ends in these bars were made by cutting them off perpendicular to the longitudinal axis. The results showed that the output voltage was nearly proportional to the applied load over a wide range except in the 12 mm and 15 mm end diameters. This relationship was also seemingly not affected by the size of the contact area of up to 9 mm in diameter. Therefore, it can be expected that when a body with a protruding end collides perpendicularly against an elastic wall, to produce an elastic-plastic deformation at the contact part, and when the contact area is varied during such a collision, the impulsive force generated at the contact part can be measured directly with high accuracy by means of the sensing block. For the sensing block used, therefore, impulsive force F(kN) generated at the contact part was calculated as follows:

$$F = 3.653e_{po} + 0.453 \qquad (1)$$

IMPACT OF ALUMINUM BAR

Using this proposed method , impact experiments were performed using commercial pure aluminum bars of 40 mm in diameter with different lengths and spherical ends as shown in Fig.6. The specimens used had varying radius of curvature of 10, 20, 40 mm and four different lengths of 200, 400, 800 and 1600 mm. These specimens were dropped on to the surface of the sensing projection from various heights.

Figure 7 shows the typical record of the generated force in the experiments of axial, perpendicular collision of aluminum specimen of 800 mm in length and 10mm in radius of curvature at a 2m/s impact velocity against the impact surface of the sensing block. Figure 8 shows the relation between the maximum force of the record ,Fmax, and potential energy of the specimen, E. It is seen from Fig.8, that the maximum force, Fmax, gradually increases proportionally to the square root of potential energy, $E^{1/2}$, for each radius of curvature, ρ, and that Fmax increases when ρ becomes larger. Figure 9 shows the relation between the volume of deformed part at the contact top end after impact ΔV and the potential energy,E,of the bar before impact. As

seen in Fig.9, the deformed volume,ΔV,is nearly proportional to the energy,E, independent of the radius of the curvature, ρ.

From the maximum force, Fmax, the mean stress on the contact part at the impact end was obtained by using $\sigma_1 = 4Fmax/\pi d_1'^2$, where d_1' is a diameter of deformed part at the impact end. Figure 10 shows the relation between the mean stress,σ_1, obtained and the potential energy,E. In Fig.10, it is shown that mean stress,σ_1,is constant independent of the radius of curvature of sphere ρ and of the impact velocity, Vo. Figure 11 shows the relation between T and, Tu which are the duration of deformation and unloading, respectively, as shown in Fig.7 and, the impact velocity Vo for the specimen length L=400 mm. From Fig.11, it can be observed within the range of experiment procedure used, that the duration of deformation,T, is not affected by the impact velocity but it is affected by the radius of curvature of the impact end. It was also found that the duration of unloading, Tu, was constant independent of the impact velocity and the radius of curvature .

CONCLUSION

A new method for measuring impulsive force generated at a contact part was devised by cementing small strain gages on the side surface of the small cylindrical projection on one side of the block. By this method, the impulsive forces generated at the impact end of a body in perpendicular impact against another body can be measured directly. The measurement procedure suggested is almost entirely free from disturbance caused by interference with reflected waves.

The principle involved in the measurement technique and the device used are very simple. This method is effective for taking measurements of the impulsive force generated at an impact end even when elastic or plastic deformations arise at the impact end as well as, when the contact area varies with time.

Some of experiments performed using this method, which involved collision of commercial pure aluminum bars of several lengths and spherical ends, with an elastic wall have shown that the maximum force generated gradually increased proportionally to the potential energy of the colliding bar before impact. The deformed volume at the contact part, was nearly proportional to the energy. The mean stress on the contact part was found to be constant independent of the impact velocity and the radius of curvature. The duration of deformation was apparently not affected by the impact velocity but it was however, affected by the curvature, while the unloading time was constant independent of the impact velocity and the curvature.

REFERENCES

1. Johnson,W., "Impact Strength of Materials", Edward Arnold(1972).

2. Kolsky, H. and Douch, L.S., "Experimental Studies in Plastic Wave Propagation", J.Mech. Phys.Solids, 10, 195-223(1962).

3. e.g., Tanimura, S. , Igaki, H. , Majima, H. and Tada, M., " A Combined Tension-Torsion Impact Testing Apparatus and an Experimental Study in Incremental Wave Propagation", Bul. JSME, 21, 1455-1461(1978).

4. Hayashi, T. and Tanimoto, N., "Behavior of Aluminum Simultaneously Subjected to Dynamic Combined Stress of Torsion and Tension", Proc. 19th Japan Cong. on Mat. Res., Soc. Mat.Sci., Japan, 53-56(1976).

5. Ripperger, E.A., "Dynamic Plastic Behavior of Aluminum,Copper and Iron", Behavior of Materials Under Dynamic Loading, ed, N.J.Huffington, Jr., ASME(1965).

6. Bertholf, L.D., Buxton,L.D., Thorne, B.J., Byers, r.k., Stevens, A.L.and Thompson, S.L., "Damage in Steel Plates from Hypervelocity Impact II, Numerical Results and Spall measurement", J.Appl. Phys., 46, 3776-3783(1975).

7. Lundberg, B. and Henchoz, A., "Analysis of Elastic Wave from Two-Point Strain Measurement, "EXPERIMENTAL MECHANICS", 17, 213-218(1977).

8. Tanimura, S. and Aiba, M., "A Trial to Detect the Generated Impulsive Force Directly with High Sensitivity", Trans. JSME(in Japanese), 49, 1565-1571(1983).

9. Tanimura, S. and Aiba, M., "On the Deformation and Impulsive Force at a Protrudent Impact End in Collision of an Aluminum Bar against a Wall", Trans.(in Japanese), 50, 2009-2016(1984).

10. Tanimura, S., "A New Method for Measuring Impulsive Force at Contact Parts", EXPERIMENTAL MECHANICS, 24, 271-276(1984).

11. Daimaruya, M., Naitoh, M., Kobayashi,H. and Tanimura, S., "A Sensing-Plate Method for Measuring Force and Duration of Impact in Elastic-plastic Impact of Bodies", EXPERIMENTAL MECHANICS, 268-273(1989).

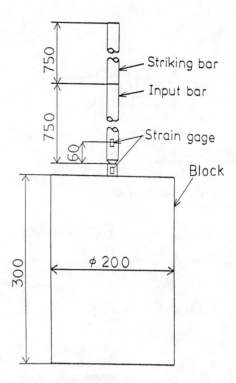

Fig.1 Schematic diagram of an apparatus for calibration testing

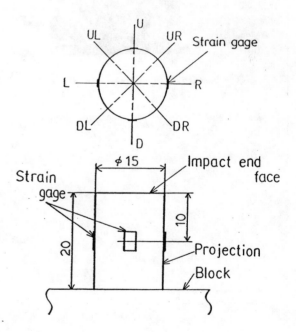

Fig.2 Detail of the projection of the sensing block

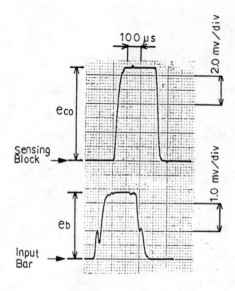

(a) Example from the sensing block

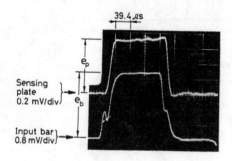

(b) Example from the sensing plate

Fig.3 Examples of the incident and output pulses

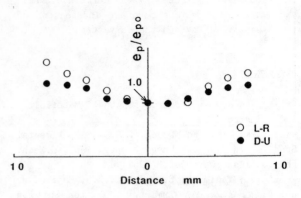

(a) Along L-R and U-D lines

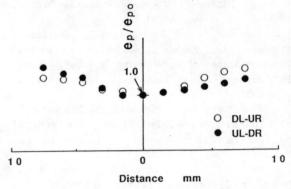

(b) Along DL-UR and UL-DR lines

Fig.4 Sensitivity of the sensing block

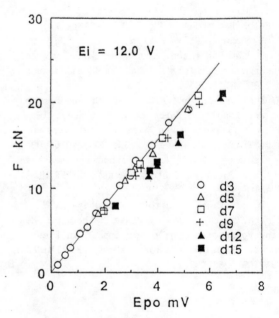

Fig.5 Applied load vs. output voltage e_{po} from the sensing block

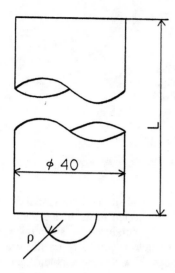

Fig.6 Configuration of the specimen

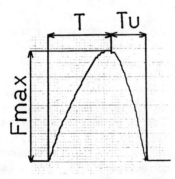

Fig.7 Typical record of the generated impulsive force

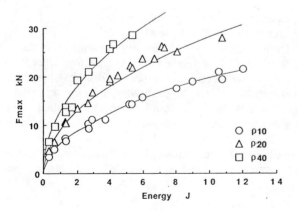

Fig.8 Maximum impulsive force Fmax vs. potential energy E

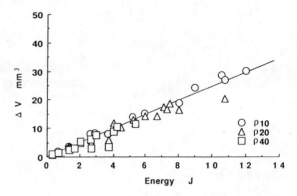

Fig.9 Volume of deformed part ΔV vs. potential energy E

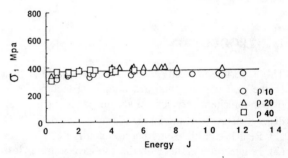

Fig.10 Mean stress σ_1 vs. potential energy E

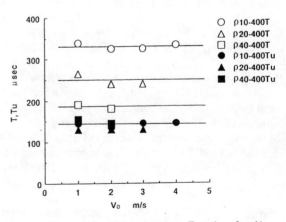

Fig.11 Duration of deformation T and unloading time Tu vs. impact velocity Vo

INFLUENCE OF PARTICLE SHAPE ON STRESS WAVE PROPAGATION IN GRANULAR MEDIA

Arun Shukla and Raman Singh

Dynamic Photomechanics Laboratory,
Department of Mechanical Engineering,
University of Rhode Island, Kingston, RI 02881.

ABSTRACT

An experimental study has been conducted to investigate the effect of particle shape and size on inter-granular load transfer, velocity and wavelength of a stress wave transmitted through granular media subjected to explosive loading. Dynamic photoelasticity was used to study stress wave propagation through granular media simulated by assemblies of elliptical particles in contact. The results indicate that the effect of the shape of the particle is primarily on the velocity of the transmitted stress wave pulse. The wavelength and the load transfer characteristics show no appreciable dependence on the particle shape.

1. INTRODUCTION

This experimental study attempts to investigate the influence of particle shape on the dynamic response of granular materials. In the past experimental and numerical techniques have been used to study the load-transfer, wave velocity and wave dispersion characteristics, for various loading parameters and stacking geometry, using granular media simulated by circular disks[1-6]. However, modelling a granular media using circular discs has the following limitations.
(1). Real life particles are not necessarily circular.
(2). In general a granular media can have more or less number of contacts per particle than those for circular discs.
(3). For non-circular particles the contact normals may or may not pass through the centers of the particles in contact.

In this study the granular media was modelled using elliptical particles of different shape and size. The ellipse was chosen for its simple yet more generalized shape than the circular disc. Moreover, now the circular disc can be treated as a special case of an ellipse with an aspect ratio of one.

2. EXPERIMENTAL PROCEDURE AND ANALYSIS

The experimental setup was comprised of various assemblies of Homalite-100 ellipses which were loaded by exploding a small amount (10-15 mg) of Lead Azide in a specially designed charge holder. Figure 1 shows one such single chain setup used for simulating one dimensional granular media. A Cranz-Schardin multiple spark-gap camera was used to capture 20 separate photoelastic images of the dynamic process, at predetermined timings. A typical sequence of 5 photographs for one of the single chain setups is shown in Figure 2. These images capture the wave propagation process at discrete time frames and can be used to provide data for determining contact loads, wavelength and velocity for the transmitted stress wave pulse. Dynamic photoelasticity was chosen as the experimental technique as it provides full field information and enables one to see the shape of the stress wave front, as it propagates down the granular assembly.

The elliptical particles were routed out of Homalite 100, a photoelastic material. The template used for routing was machined out of aluminum using a CNC milling machine. The routing was carefully monitored so as to avoid producing any heat related residual stresses in the material.

To separate the effect of particle shape and particle size the single chain experiments have been designed such that the number of contacts per unit length remain constant while the aspect ratio is being varied. That is, while varying the aspect ratio of the elliptical particles within a set of comparative experiments the axis length along the direction of wave propagation is kept constant and the other axis length is varied. See Figure 3 for a definition of the particle width and length and the particle aspect ratio.

The photoelastic images were enlarged using a Beseler enlarger and then data was collected with a Hicomscan digitizer linked to an IBM PC-AT. Contact load calculation at a particular contact and time is done by assuming a Hertz contact stress field and applying the multi-point, non-linear least square method suggested by Shukla and Nigam[2]. The plot of the wave propagation distance as a function of time is used to obtain the stress wave velocity. The average velocity was calculated using a linear least-square fit through the experimental data points. The wavelength λ of the stress wave pulse can be measured directly from the photographs of the wave propagation process as shown in Figure 2. It can also be calculated using the duration of contact at any given contact point and the average velocity of the stress wave.

3. RESULTS AND DISCUSSION

3.1 Effect of Particle Shape on Wave Velocity and Wavelength.

Four different single chain setups were used, with contacts at 25.4 mm intervals. For the four chains the width of the elliptical particles was increased from 12.7 mm to 38.1 mm while the length was kept constant at 25.4 mm. This allows us to have single chain granular assemblies with varying particle shapes but a constant contact interval. Figure 4 shows the plot of distance propagated by the wavefront as a function of time for the single chain of 12.5 x 25.4 mm ellipses. The average velocity obtained from the slope of this plot is also shown. Average wave velocities obtained from the four different single chain setups are listed in Table 1. As the particle width is decreased from 38.1 mm to 12.7 mm the wave velocity is seen to increase from 950 m/s to 1250 m/s. Table 1 also lists the wavelength, λ, of the transmitted stress wave pulse as it travels down the single chain assembly. The wavelength shows no appreciable change as the particle aspect ratio is changed. Earlier experiments done with circular discs[6] have shown that changing the length of the particles changes the velocity and the λ/D ratio, where D is the contact interval (i.e., the particle length). In this set of experiments the λ/D ratio remains constant, as expected, as the particle width rather than the particle length is changed.

Changing the width of the particle changes the radius of curvature at the contact point. This change of curvature at the contact can influence the contact stiffness. The radii of curvature, at the contact point and the theoretically expected half contact width, b, as given by the Hertz contact theory for a contact load of 1000 N, are listed in Table 1 for all the different single chain assemblies. As shown, the half contact width, b, increases with the radius of curvature at the contact point. These values of half contact width, b, were used for theoretically generating the fringe pattern using Hertz contact field equations. The fringe patterns obtained for different particles in contact are given in Figure 5. As the particle width is increased more fringes are observed. Since everything else, including the material properties and the applied contact load, is being held constant the appearance of more fringes most probably implies a decrease in the contact stiffness. Thus, as the radius of curvature at the contact point increases the contact stiffness decreases, which would imply a lower stress wave velocity at the contact. So, one of the factors explaining the variation of wave velocity with the particle width is the change in contact stiffness due to the change in the radii of curvature at contact.

Photographs obtained from the experiments also show how the stress wavefront tends to take the shape of the particle, as shown in Figure 6. Figure 7 shows the change in the aspect ratio (defined in Figure 6) of the wavefront fringe contour as the stress wave propagates down any given particle. Near the contact area the fringe contour aspect ratio is nearly unity for all the different particles. However, further down the particle the wavefront shape shows a greater dependency on the particle shape. Near the contact area circular fringes are expected as the Hertz contact stress field is valid. Away from the contact zone the free boundary effects start gaining prominence and the particle shape starts influencing the shape of the wavefront fringe contour. The Hertz contact stress field does not take care of free boundary effects, and is thus valid only near the contact zone. A comparison of Figures 5 and 6 shows the influence of particle shape on the wavefront shape, especially near the free boundary of the particle. Figure 8 shows the almost linear relationship between the wave velocity and the fringe contour shape. Wave propagation through a granular media occurs by contact mechanisms which result in load transfer from particle to particle. Within a particle, however, the wave propagation process is through a reflection mechanism. The stress wavefront observed is a resultant of the various reflection of the stress wave from the free boundaries of the granular particle. For a wider particle the time taken by the stress wave to reach the sides and reflect back would be more than for a narrower particle, leading to a broader wavefront and a lower wave velocity.

3.2 Load Transfer Characteristics

Data from different single chain assemblies was used to determine the normal contact loads, at different contact points. Figure 9 shows the typical normal contact load variation for a single chain assembly. The contact loads have been normalized with respect to the peak contact load occurring between particles 5 and 6. This normalization allows for easy comparison between different experiments[4]. The normalized contact loads for the 25.4 mm (1") diameter circular disc chain were available from earlier experiments done using circular discs[4].

Normalized contact load plots provide information about load attenuation as the stress wave travels from contact to contact. They also provide information about the duration of contact which can be used along with the wave velocity to give the wavelength of the transmitted stress wave pulse. No appreciable difference has been observed in the load attenuation plots for the various single chain setups and there is no obvious relationship between particle aspect ratio and load attenuation.

4. CONCLUSION

The results obtained from the experiments done show that
(1) Wave velocity shows a strong dependence on the particle shape. The velocity increases from 950 m/s to 1250 m/s as the particle width is decreased from 38.1 mm to 12.7 mm, the particle length being kept constant at 25.4 mm. This change in the stress wave velocity can be attributed to change in contact stiffness, due to changing radius of curvature at the contact, and to the influence of the particle shape on the reflection mechanism of wave propagation within a particle. The influence on the reflection mechanism is also seen in the form of the influence of particle shape on the wavefront shape. The wavefront tends to take the shape of the particle as the stress wave travels down through the chain.
(2) The wavelength of the stress wave pulse shows no appreciable change as the particle shape is changed, as long as the contact interval is kept constant.
(3) The load transfer characteristics do not seem to change with change in particle shape. There are no significant differences in the load attenuation curves for the different shaped particles considered here. However, data is still lacking in this aspect for a conclusive statement to be made.
Further experiments are currently being conducted to study the effect of particle length and of the shape of the loading pulse on the wave propagation phenomenon. This is necessary to reach a better understanding of the influence of both particle size and particle shape on wave velocity and wavelength, and to be able to distinguish between their effects. Experiments are also being conducted to study two-dimensional assemblies of elliptical particles. One such experimental photograph is shown in Figure 11.

REFERENCES

1. Rossmanith, H.P. and Shukla, A. "Photoelastic Investigation of Dynamic Load Transfer in Granular Media". Act. Mech. 42, 211-225, 1982.
2. Shukla, A. and Nigam, H. "A Numerical Analysis of Contact Stress Problem". J. Strain Analysis, 20(4), 241-245, 1985.
3. Shukla, A. and Rossmanith, H.P. "Dynamic Photoelastic Investigation of Wave Propagation and Energy Transfer Across Contacts". J. Strain Analysis, 21(4), 213-218, 1986.
4. Shukla, A. and Damania, C. "Experimental Investigation of Wave Velocity and Dynamic Contact Stress in An Assembly of Disks". J. Expt. Mech. 27(3), 1988.
5. Sadd, M.H., Shukla, A., and Mei, H. "Computational and Experimental Modeling of Wave Propagation in Granular Materials". Proc. 4th Int. Conf. on Computational Methods and Experimental measurements, Capri, Italy, 325-334, 1989.
6. Xu, Y. and Shukla, A. "Stress Wave Velocity in Granular Medium", Mechanics Research Communications, 17(6), 383-391, 1990.

ACKNOWLEDGEMENT

The authors would like to acknowledge the support of the U.S. Air Force Office of Scientific Research under grant number F49620-89-C-0091.

Table 1 Variation of various parameters with change in particle size.

Particle size	Average Wave Velocity	Wavelength	Radius of Curvature at the point of contact	Half Contact Width expected for a load of 1000 N	Average Fringe Aspect Ratio
25.4 x 12.7 mm	1250 m/s	101 mm	3.2 mm	0.358 mm	1.56
25.4 x 19.05 mm	1140 m/s	103 mm	7.1 mm	0.522 mm	1.27
25.4 mm dia.	1070 m/s	102 mm	12.7 mm	0.681 mm	1.05
25.4 x 38.1 mm	950 m/s	104 mm	28.6 mm	1.025 mm	0.64

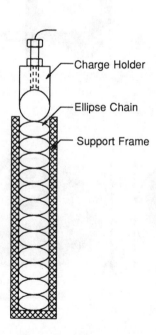

Fig. 1 Experimental setup for the single chain assembly.

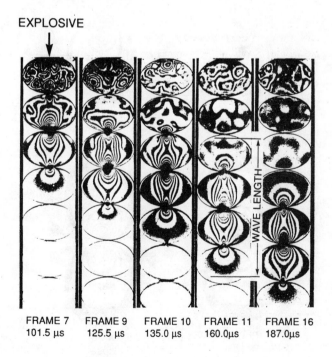

Fig. 2 Typical set of photoelastic fringe patterns obtained for a single chain setup.

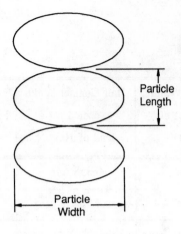

Particle Aspect Ratio = $\dfrac{\text{Particle Length}}{\text{Particle Width}}$

Fig. 3   Definition of the particle width, length and aspect ratio.

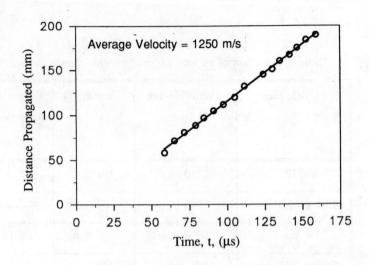

Fig. 4   Wavefront position as a function of time for the 25.4 x 12.7 mm particle assembly.

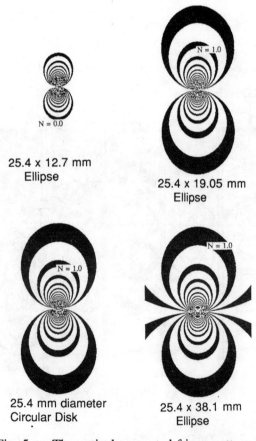

25.4 x 12.7 mm
Ellipse

N = 1.0

25.4 x 19.05 mm
Ellipse

N = 1.0

25.4 mm diameter
Circular Disk

N = 1.0

25.4 x 38.1 mm
Ellipse

N = 0.0

Fig. 5   Theoretical generated fringe patterns for different particles in contact.

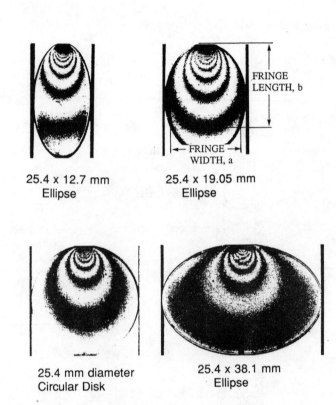

25.4 x 12.7 mm
Ellipse

FRINGE
LENGTH, b

FRINGE
WIDTH, a

25.4 x 19.05 mm
Ellipse

25.4 mm diameter
Circular Disk

25.4 x 38.1 mm
Ellipse

Fig. 6   Wavefront shapes observed for single chain assemblies of different particles.

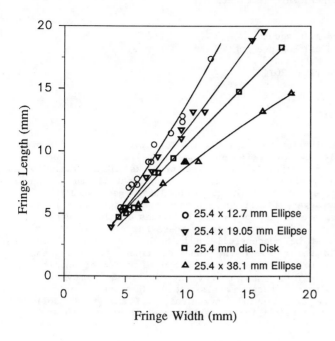

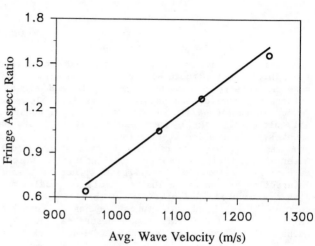

Fig. 7   Fringe contour length as a function of the contour width for different particles.

Fig. 8   Variation of the fringe contour aspect ratio with the wave velocity.

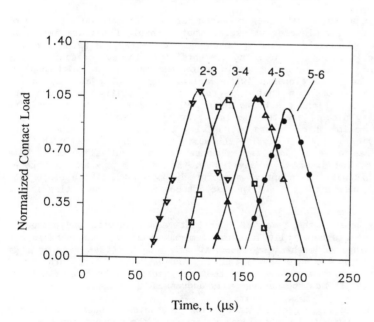

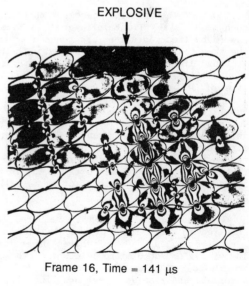

Frame 16, Time = 141 µs

Fig. 9   Normalized contact loads as a function of time for the 25.4 x 38.1 mm particle assembly.

Fig. 10   Typical photoelastic fringes for a two dimensional assembly of elliptical particles.

MECHANICS ISSUES IN INTELLIGENT STRUCTURES

J. S. Sirkis and A. Dasgupta
Department of Mechanical Engineering
University of Maryland
College Park, Maryland 20742

ABSTRACT

This paper describes many of the fundamental mechanics issues currently inhibiting the realization of the "intelligent structures" concept. We view what is commonly referred to as "intelligent structures" more as sensory and adaptive materials and structures that use distributed networks of structurally integrated actuator and sensor devices to achieve self-monitoring and self-adapting capabilities. (The reader is cautioned that their is not yet a consensus as to the form in which "intelligent structures" will ultimately take.) Each embedded micro-device has a very localized response on the microscale to an input stimulus, which combines with the localized response of the other micro-devices in the network to produce a metered response in the macroscale structure. All length-scales posses inherent geometric, material, and time dependent non-linearities which must be successfully addressed. The goal of the mechanics research in "intelligent structures" should be to model the inherent linear and nonlinear interaction mechanics so that accumulating modification to structural response can be predicted and then either accounted for, or actively changed in some way. This paper is not intended to be a review of current "intelligent structures" mechanics research, mainly because this field of endeavor is very immature. Instead, this paper describes some of the experimental, numerical, and analytical solid mechanics research we believe should be undertaken in order to realize reliable "intelligent structures."

1. INTRODUCTION

Adaptivity in structural materials requires that a load bearing structure includes devices which will in some way provide the ability to monitor itself and its environment, and provide musculature of one form or another for adaptive motor response [1]. The monitoring capability comes from sensors, the musculature is provided by actuators, and communication between the sensors and actuators is achieved via local processors. The materials which are most commonly suggested as actuator/sensor materials include shape memory alloys, piezoelectric materials, electrostrictive materials, magnetostrictive materials, thermally controllable materials, electrorheological fluids, and ferrofluids. Resistance strain gages and optical fiber sensors are the most commonly quoted devices devoted strictly to sensing functions.

One of the principal research thrusts in actuator materials research has been to develop actuators of such small size, i.e multilayer thin film or microdiameter whiskers, that mechanical failure mechanism caused by these actuators are reduced to the microscale. This approach brings the failure mechanics into the same regime as those associated with the indigenous reinforcing elements of laminated, braided, woven, stitched thick and thin composite materials. Such tailoring would allow the inclusions which provide adaptability to be treated as additional reinforcing elements (with variable reinforcing action, in the case of actuators). The advantage of this approach is that the geometric obtrusivity, and resulting stress concentrations, associated with large inclusions can be avoided. Microdevices are very promising but high authority actuation requirements may necessitate the use of a few strategically located larger wafer scale inclusions (approximately 250μm to 2mm thick) whose obtrusivity is significant. Actuator and sensor devices will represent a wide variety of active and passive thermomechanical inclusions in the host structural components. Each microdevice has a very localized response to an input stimulus. This response, combined with similar responses of the other micro-devices in the network produces a metered response in the macroscale structure. In this way, the adaptive structure behaves much like a biological system with the microdevices acting as cells, neurons, etc. and the macrostructural response acting as the motor system.

A fundamental approach is required to achieve the level of quantitative mechanistic understanding required to model these distributed networks of structurally integrated microactuators, microsensors and microelectronics. This involves understanding the mechanics issues at all length scales ranging from individual embedded microdevices and other microscale heterogeneities, all the way to the structural macro length scale. Mechanics phenomena at each length scale possess their respective inherent geometric, material, and time dependent non-linearities which must be successfully addressed.

This paper heuristically outlines the local-to-global interaction mechanics issues confronting "intelligent structures." The interaction issues between individual devices and the surrounding host are addressed in Sect. 2; the interactions of the device with neighboring microdevices and other heterogeneities in the host are addressed in Sect. 3. Homogenization issues to obtain macroscale "smoothened" partial differential equations are discussed in Sect. 4. The major issues are summarized in Sect. 5.

2. MICROSCALE INTERACTIONS BETWEEN INDIVIDUAL DEVICES AND THE HOST MATERIAL

The microscale interactions are of crucial importance in formulating the system-level transfer functions for two different reasons. First, they form the building blocks for the overall macroscale transfer function and hence the accuracy of the whole approach hinges on how accurately the microscale interaction phenomena are recognized and modeled. Second, the concentrations of stress/strain/temperature caused by the interactions may induce damage under static, cyclic, or shock loads in the device, host, or their interface. The damage may cause either a gradual, time-dependent drift/nonlinearity in the transfer function of the device, or in extreme cases, catastrophic failure of the device, electronics, interconnects, or the host. This drift needs to be understood and characterized for long-term reliability of the sensing and control functions. For the above reasons, addressing microscale interaction issues between structurally integrated passive and active inclusions is of prime importance.

From a mechanics perspective, microdevices can be treated as inclusions with a mismatch of constitutive properties between the host and the device. The constitutive properties which need to be addressed include not only hygro-thermo-mechanical behavior, but also magneto-electro-mechanical and opto-mechanical behavior in the case of many actuator and sensor materials. These misfitting inclusions (or heterogeneities) affect the system dynamical response in two different ways: 1) by generating internal stress fields which can be considered as perturbations to the strain energy distribution and/or as effective forcing functions, and 2) by altering the effective properties of the dynamical system. These perturbations may either be unintentional, a result of environmental "loads" such as hygro-thermo-mechanical fields and intrinsic nonlinearities of the constituent materials; or they may be intentional as in electro-mechanical, magneto-mechanical, etc. actuation loads. Quantifying the interaction phenomena, which is essential for robust control development, becomes more complicated when one considers all the nonlinearities listed below.

> 1. Nonlinearities in the microscale transfer functions as a result of nonlinearities such as viscoplasticity and hygro-thermo-mechanical behavior of host and inclusion materials.
>
> 2. Nonlinearities and time-dependent changes in the microscale transfer functions as a result of local damage in the host material (such as local crushing, composite fiber microbuckling, interlaminar shear failure) and due to interfacial debonding between host and inclusion.
>
> 3. Catastrophic failures induced by local stress fields in the form of brittle fracture of inclusions, failure of electronics and/or interconnects, loss of integrity of host, and excessive drift of transfer function beyond an acceptable limit.
>
> 4. Characterization of residual stresses induced during processing, and their influence on micromechanical interactions.

The damage-induced drift of the device transfer function is extremely important since it is inevitable during the service life of the system due to gradual accumulation of fatigue damage, and it has to be quantitatively compensated for, if reliable actuation, sensing, and control functions are to be maintained. The fatigue damage can occur either as interfacial debonding between the host and the device or as one or more fatigue mechanisms within the host material. Fig. 1 shows an example of just such a case where an interfacial microcrack has occurred between an optical fiber sensor and its graphite/epoxy host material that is subjected to high cycle fatigue.

The accumulation of damage can be thought of as changes in the effective residual mechanical properties of the host. Important damage modes are matrix microcracking and crushing due to wafer-scale and thin-film inclusions, localized delaminations, and microbuckling of embedded slender devices and of reinforcing fibers in adjacent layer of host composite.

The damage modes discussed above can ultimately lead to catastrophic failure due to loss of integrity of the embedded device and/or unacceptable drift of the microscale transfer function due to excessive local damage in the host. Figures 2a and 2b are provided as an example of the complexity of embedded active inclusions and of both microlevel damage and catastrophic failure. This figure shows micrographs of wafer scale piezoelectric actuators which have experienced in-service failures. Figure 2a provides a feel for the complexity of the system, and it shows a catastrophic failure. Figure 2b shows a microcrack in the vicinity of a catastrophic failure. The capabiltiy to predict catastrophic failure such as this is required in order to develop robust control algorithms and to develop design guidelines to increase structural life.

The residual stresses resulting from the adaptive material manufacturing processes or the thermo-mechanical load environment will obviously have a pronounced effect on all mechanical interactions. As an example, Fig.3 shows the residual vertical displacement field with moiré interferometry around a local processor embedded in a host epoxy system. This residual field resulted from the thermo-mechanical stress field generated by thermal dissipation of the processor. Including these types of residual stresses in mathematical and numerical models is straight forward. However, knowing the actual residual stress state local to the inclusion is another matter all-together. Methods to measure residual stresses on the microscale, such as microindentation techniques, will be required if modeling the effects of residual stresses on the local behavior are to be successful.

3. INTERACTIONS WITH NEIGHBORING MICROSTRUCTURAL HETEROGENEITIES

Quantitative identification of all the microscale interactions leads to a set of spatially discrete and localized transfer functions for each microscale device interacting in isolation with a host of much larger dimensions. At the next length scale, the task is one of modeling the interactions between neighboring microdevices (or distributions of microdevices) or between microdevices and geometric boundaries of finite-sized hosts. Finally, the discrete interaction must be "homogenized" to produce spatially continuous/distributed partial differential equations. In making the transition from the local to the global problem, the critical issues at the next length scale are load transfer mechanisms from the microscale to the structural macroscale and the role of the host composite micro-architecture (such as braided, stitched, or woven composites) on the propagation of interaction effects to macroscale. These features will affect not only the interactions between neighboring devices in nondilute dispersions of distributed device networks, but also the synthesis of the spatially discrete microscale interaction models into a homogenized distributed transfer function to facilitate macroscale modeling. Statistically smooth distributions of embedded devices are discussed in the this section and discontinuous clusters of embedded devices are discussed in Sect. 4. In the case of macroactuators, various researchers have proposed "active" finite element formulations (see for example, Refs. [2] or [3]) which can be effectively utilized to solve the problem.

The two most challenging interaction issues that have to be addressed are:

1. Interactions between neighboring inclusions in the case of distributed microactuators and sensor-networks.

2. Interactions with other neighboring microstructural heterogeneities such as finite geometry, free surfaces, interfaces, microarchitectural features of the composite host, etc.

The first issue determines how the local discrete microscale transfer function for isolated device inclusions undergoes modifications due to the influence of surrounding microdevice inclusions. When there are nondilute concentrations of distributed devices, the thermomechanical interactions between the perturbation fields of neighboring inclusions modifies the microscale transfer function obtained in Sect. 2. Such cases will be encountered for microactuators and sensor networks, as well as for multilayered thin-film devices.

The second issue is somewhat different since it addresses interactions with the inherent heterogeneities of the host microarchitecture and finite geometry effects. The inherently heterogeneous microstructure of composite hosts may create additional complications in the micromechanics analysis. The perturbation of the interaction field due to the presence of planar interfaces is just one example. In the case of anisotropic hosts, numerical or experimental methods methods are necessary. Similar techniques are also required if the microarchitecture of the composite host is of the same length scale as the microdevices being modeled. Such situations may arise in the case of microsensors and microactuators embedded in braided or woven composites where the characteristic length scale of the periodic weave reinforcement may be extremely large.

4. MACROSCALE HOMOGENIZED SYSTEM

The localized and discrete micro-scale interaction models identified in Sects. 2 and 3 need to be homogenized before they can be integrated into the system dynamical partial differential equations (PDEs). These PDEs are intended for used in the design of appropriated control strategies. Often, the density of microdevice distributions may be piecewise continuous in a structure, leading to further interaction and homogenization issues. The heterogeneities at this length scale not only include discontinuous clusters of microdevices, but also macrolevel interactions between the device and structural deformations, boundary conditions, geometry effects and external loads. Specific examples of special-purpose techniques applied to specific geometries can be found in the literature, but the generic underlying theory still needs to be developed. The ultimate goal professed in this section is to evolve stable and robust differential equations for the system by recognizing quantitatively all the nonlinear transfer functions and the inherent reliability risks due to damage accumulation. Such a differential description of the system is necessary for developing the necessary control algorithms [3,4].

The important issues at this length scale are:

1. Homogenization of nonlinear discrete interaction models into piecewise continuous "smoothened" PDEs for developing macroscale dynamical equations.

592

2.   Developing a novel framework to describe the structural dynamics
of systems with discontinuous discrete distributions or clusters of
embedded sensors and actuators.

3.   Determination of critical density of device for effective
control.

4.   Effects of distributed damage on the macroscale strength and
effective   behavior.

The critical density of embedded devices refers to the issue of estimating the number, type, and
location of sensors and actuators required to achieve the desired adaptability.

5.   SUMMARY

The research issues that have been presented in the preceding sections are by no means exhaustive,
nor are they unique to "intelligent structures." They do, however, serve to illustrate the roles that
experimental and theoretical solid mechanics can play in the development of the ever-expanding technology
field of "intelligent structures."   It is the authors' (arguable) opinion that the local-to-global
mechanistic approach to identifying, quantifying, and understanding the important interaction mechanisms
will provide the most rewards for the "intelligent structures" technology.   For this reason, the research
tasks have been divided into three major groups or thrust areas: microscale interactions, interactions
with other neighboring devices, and homogenization and system PDEs.   In all cases non-linear materials and
interactions have been emphasized, and the overall goal is to develop the mechanics-based PDEs which can
be used for robust system control.   These tasks, and there interrelation, are illustrated schematically in
Fig. 4.   This diagram constitutes an integrated analytical and experimental approach to the fundamental
science underlying the unsolved research issues crucial to the success of adaptive structures technologies
of the future.

6.   ACKNOWLEDGEMENTS

Many of the ideas presented in this paper evolved from discussions with our colleagues at the
University of Maryland and elsewhere.   We gratefully acknowledge their continual stimulating exchanges on
the subject of "intelligent structures."   We also would like to thank Mr. Leland Melvin of the NASA
Langley Research Center for running the fatigue tests that ultimately lead to Fig. 1, and Mr. Russ May and
Dr. Rick Claus and Electro-Optic research Center at Virginia-Tech. for providing the specimen used to
produce Fig.3.

7.   REFERENCES

1.   Rogers, C.A., "An Introduction to Intelligent Material Systems and Structures" in *Intelligent
Structures* Edited by Chong, K.P., Liu, S.C. and Li, J.C. in *Proceedings of the International Workshop on
Intelligent Structures*, pp. 3-41, 1990.

2.   Ha, S-K., Keilers, C. and Chang, F-K., "Analysis of Laminated Composites Containing Distributed
Piezoelectric Ceramics," *J. Intelligent Material Systems & Structures*, 2

3.   Hagood, N.W., Chung, W. von Flotow, A., "Modelling of Piezoelectric Actuator Dynamics for Active
Structural Control," *J. Intelligent Material Systems & Structures*, 1990.

4.   Hanagud, S., Savanur, S.G. and NageshBabu, G.L., "Control-structure Interaction in a Delaminated
Beam: An Experimental Investigation," *SEM Spring Conf.*(presented only), Milwaukee, 1991.

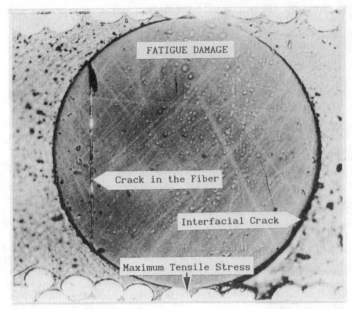

FATIGUE DAMAGE

Crack in the Fiber

Interfacial Crack

Maximum Tensile Stress

Figure 1.
Interfacial Microcrack Between an Optical-Fiber Sensor and its Graphite/Epoxy Host Due to High Cycle Tension-Tension Fatigue.

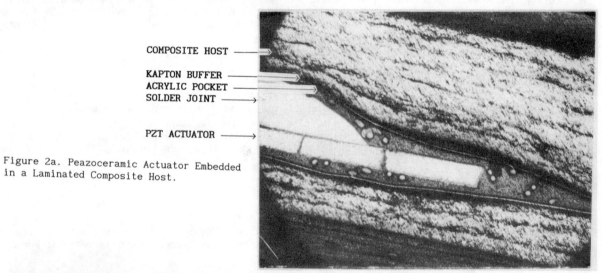

COMPOSITE HOST

KAPTON BUFFER
ACRYLIC POCKET
SOLDER JOINT

PZT ACTUATOR

Figure 2a. Peazoceramic Actuator Embedded in a Laminated Composite Host.

Figure 2b. Damage Mechanisms in the Peazoceramic Actuator.

MICROCRACK

PZT ACTUATOR

ACRYLIC POCKET

Figure 3. Residual Verticle Displacement Field Near an Embedded Local Processor.

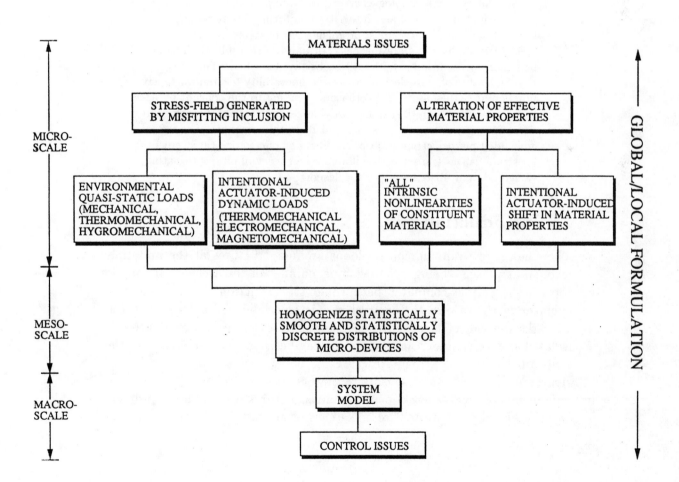

Figure 4. Schematic of Interrelated Local-to-Global Mechanics Issues in "Intelligent Structures."

Sensors for Intelligent Structures

Tomas Valis

FiberMetrics Corporation
4925 Dufferin Street, Downsview, Ontario
M3H 5T6 Canada

Abstract

Several sensing technologies are expected to play a key role in structures with shape-control and integrity-monitoring functions built into them. At present, the two most promising sensor types for structurally-embedded applications are piezoelectrics and optical fibers. The embeddment procedure for both will be briefly described. The most appealing feature of piezoelectric devices is their ability to simultaneously function as both sensors and actuators—leading to the concept of 'active composites.' Optical fibers provide sensing capability only, but do so in a geometrically-versatile and dielectric manner. The use of embedded piezoelectrics and optical fibers as one-to-one replacements for strain gauges is discussed, followed by a survey of path-integrating, -weighted, and -distributed sensor designs.

1 Introduction

The concept of wrapping control loops around structures at the materials level is, at present, being explored by a number of researchers. It has its roots in the 'ship-as-computer' backdrop of science fiction. In taking control engineering right down to the level of micromechanics and shape control, it marks the end of mechanical engineering research as a pure discipline, isolated from electronics and computer engineering. To some extent, the well-tested notion of 'strong structures' is being superseded by 'intelligent structures' with entangled sensors, actuators, and controllers.

Much of the early work in intelligent structures was of the 'top-down' variety, wherein one started from sketches of aircraft, spacecraft, etc., and inked in networks of sensors and actuators tied to local processors. The specific purpose and design of any particular sensor or actuator was subsumed in the overall conceptual framework. More recently, the user community (e.g., airframers) has begun to identify specific structural concerns that may be best met with the application of 'intelligent structures' technology. This 'bottom-up' approach has a more robust developmental quality to it.

To date, the design of sensors for intelligent structures is being pursued by a handful of academic and industrial groups. Traditional sensor design groups tend to ignore 'intelligent structures' for lack of a well defined market. Instead, most of the development is being carried out by structures and dynamics groups. Perhaps this is a reflection of the highly interdisciplinary nature of of the subject matter.

The sensing parameter most intimately related to structures is strain. From strain, one can directly infer the structures' response to applied loads, and, indirectly, structural damage (e.g., delamination). The three most prominent strain sensing technologies for intelligent structures are based on:

1. resistive foil,

2. piezoelectric materials,

3. optical fibers.

Semiconductor strain gauges are used for performing on-chip diagnosis in the integrated circuit industry, but their development has not been actively pursued in an intelligent structures context. Magnetostrictive devices have received attention as actuators, but not as sensors. Biological and molecular strain gauges are still in the basic research phase, but are expected to play a significant role in the future. This paper will focus on the three strain sensor technologies enumerated above. As a further restriction, the discussion will focus of those sensors that can be *embedded* in composite materials.

2 Resistive Foil Sensors

An embedded strain gauge technique for testing boron/epoxy composites was developed in the early 1970s by Daniel et al. at the Illinois Institute of Technology Research Institute[1]. Their method involved modifying commercially available resistive-foil strain rosettes so that they could be laminated between plies. They succeeded in measuring the laminate Modulus and Poisson's Ratio through the thickness of representative laminates. To date, their work represents the most extensive study of embedded strain gauges. Neither piezoelectric, nor optical fiber technology has advanced to the point of being able to make a number of strain tensor measurements through a laminate. Measurements Group Inc. published an Applications Note dealing with the practical aspects of embedding resistive foil strain gauges[2]. Surprisingly, little else has been published on the subject. This may be a reflection of limited interest in embedded strain sensors, or the impracticality of this method. Resistive foil gauges will likely play an important role in intelligent structures, if for no other reason than their ease of use.

A wide variety of resistive-foil gauges are available; although none of them have been developed specifically for intelligent structures. The decision *not* to use resistive foil gauges in an intelligent structures application is usually based on the need to meet a requirement that cannot readily be met using resistive foil technology. Some of the intrinsic limitations of resistive-foil gauges are:

- limited temperature range (-200 to +300 °C),

- electromagnetic interference susceptibility,

- Joule self-heating,

- conductive leads,

- galvanic potential relative to the host material,

- limited fatigue life ($10^4 - 10^6$ cycles),

- limited gauge length (3 - 100 mm).

A detailed investigation of the merits of resistive foil gauges for intelligent structures has yet to be performed. Once piezoelectric and optical fiber technology become further commercialized, a complete comparison can be made.

3 Piezoelectric Strain Sensors

Piezoelectric materials are widely used as acoustic radiation transducers. Their use as strain gauges has been limited by their capacitive nature (i.e., they are better as strain-rate sensors). Piezoelectric materials are commonly

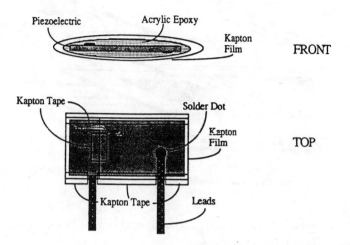

Figure 1: Insulation of piezoceramic components embedded within an electrically conductive composite (after [Hagood:89]).

available as either piezoceramics or piezopolymers. The ceramics are used as both sensors and actuators, the polymers are overwhelmingly used as sensors. Of the two, only piezoceramics have been successfully embedded in composites. The polymer materials cannot withstand most composite material processing temperatures.

Piezoceramic wafers have been embedded in glass/epoxy and graphite/epoxy. The piezoelectric element, and the leads must be insulated. The approach used by the MIT Space Engineering Research Center [3] was to encapsulate the piezoceramic wafer segment in acrylic epoxy sandwiched between Kapton sheets (see Fig. 1). Transformer-coil style insulated leads were used. The size of the piezoceramic sensor/actuator necessitated cutting out sections of the laminae, as illustrated in Fig. 2.

The difficulties of embedding piezoelectrics are akin to those associated with resistive foil gauges. The brittle nature of ceramics makes them more difficult to embed than resistive foil gauges. Sufficiently high temperature piezopolymers would likely be much easier to embed. Spatially weighted piezopolymers for modal and wave sensing have been developed[4]. Their application to embedded sensors would represent a further advantage.

The most useful attribute of piezoelectrics for intelligent structures is

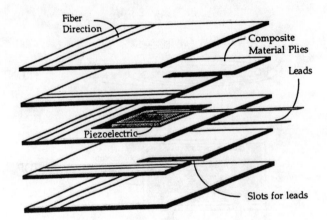

Figure 2: A piezoceramic sensor/actuator embedded inside a composite laminate (after [Hagood:89]).

their dual sensor/actuator capability. The sensors and actuators can either be collocated or noncollocated. The ultimate case of collocation is simultaneous sensing and actuation with a piezoelectric element. This approach has been pursued in both a passive[5] and active[6] forms.

Some anticipated future work on piezoelectrics as sensors/actuators are listed below:

- high-temperature embedable piezopolymers,

- fiber-form embedable piezoceramics,

- impedance-shunted piezo fiber composites,

- actively controlled piezo fiber composites

- embedded control and power switching electronics

If piezo fiber composites (i.e., matrix, reinforcing fiber, piezoelectric sensing/actuating fibers) become reality, they will represent 'active materials.'

4   Fiber-Optic Strain Sensors

It is unclear who, and exactly when, made the discovery that optical fibers are compatible with composite materials. As neither was designed for the other, this compatibility can only be viewed as a coincidence.

In the most elementary sense, optical-fiber/composite-material compatibility refers to the fact that ordinary optical fibers—designed for telecommunications—can be laid between laminae of a composite prior to material processing, survive the processing, and fail at loads comparable to those of the laminate. In a structural design sense, it means that the embedded fibers do not adversely affect the properties of the host composite. Taking advantage of this compatibility to do something useful is the subject of *composite-material embedded fiber-optic sensors*[1].

Embedded fiber-optic strain gauges for intelligent structures may span the gauge length range from 0.5 mm for acoustic radiation sensing to 5 m integrating gauges for civil engineering applications.

Some of the properties of optical fiber that make it compatible with composite materials are itemized below:

- Same shape as the reinforcing fibers: *geometric compatibility*.

- Comparable size to the reinforcing fibers[2]: *dimensional compatibility*.

- Thermally and chemically stable in the host composite: *environmental compatibility*.

In addition, composite embedded fiber-optic sensors share the following common attributes with fiber-optic sensors in general:

- electrically nonconductive

- electromagnetic interference (EMI) immune

- thermally nondissipative

- (almost) linearly elastic to failure

- high elastic-modulus (70 GPa)

- broad strain-response bandwidth (dc – 1 GHz)

- broad temperature operating-range (–200 to 1000 °C)

---

[1]Composite-material embedded optical fibers can also be used as information conduits à la fly-by-light.

[2]At present, optical fibers are one order of magnitude larger (i.e., 100 μm) in diameter, but they can be made smaller (i.e., 20 μm)—sacrificing only attenuation performance and ease of handling.

Sensor Type	Typical Gauge Lengths	Modulation
Bragg[7]	10 mm	Spectral
Intrinsic Fabry-Perot[8,9,10,11,12]	3–30 mm	Phase
Extrinsic Fabry-Perot[13]	5–10 mm	Phase
Polarimeter[14]	30 mm – 3 m	Phase
Modal Interferometer[15]	30 mm – 3 m	Phase

Table 1: The most prominent fiber-optic strain sensors under development. Commercial versions are available.

- high ultimate-strain (2-3%)

- high fatigue-life (expected)

- range of gauge-lengths possible (1 mm - 1 km)

At present, all of the above points are offset by a lack of experience, and the generally high costs involved.

A variety of fiber-optic strain sensors have been developed, each with its own niche. They are summarized in Table 1.

Distinct from the sensors are the various strain demodulation optoelectronic circuits. These tend to be much more complicated and expensive compared to the Wheatstone bridges or charge amplifiers that are used with resistive foil and piezoelectric sensors, respectively. It is the performance of the 'demodulation boxes' in *conjunction* with a particular sensor that allows one to evaluate the strain resolution and dynamic range.

The performance specifications of a commercial fiber-optic strain gauge system based on the intrinsic Fabry-Perot[12] are given in Tables 2 and 3. An illustration of the sensor is provided in Fig. 3. A block diagram of the entire system is given in Fig. 4.

An emerging technology in fiber-optic communications is dense wavelength division multiplexing (WDM) for local area networks and multiprocessor networks. Fiber-optic strain gauges can take advantage of this emerging technology to allow one to locate many gauges along a single fiber (see Fig. 5). This leads to so-called distributed sensing networks. An intermediate step between path-integrating sensors and distributed sensor networks is the use of spatially weighted fiber-optic sensors[16], similar in concept to the weighted piezopolymer sensors.

Sensor type: Intrinsic Fiber Fabry-Perot (FFP)

Gauge length: 5 - 20 mm   Cable length: 1 - 10 m
Gauge diameter: 125 µm   Cable diameter: 3 mm
Gauge material: fused silica glass   Cable type: Kevlar reinforced

Connector type: PM-FC single mode

Ultimate Strain: 2 000 µε   (Tension)
                  10 000 µε   (Compression)

Transverse strain sensitivity: ±1%   (surface adhered)
Thermal apparent strain: C.T.E. + 6 [µε/°C]

Table 2: Performance specifications of a commercial fiber-optic Fabry-Perot strain gauge.

Strain range: ±50 000 µε
Strain resolution: 10 µε
Strain rate: dc - 10^6 µε/s

Input: PM-FC single mode,
         5 - 20 mm FFP gauge lengths

Output: analog and 12 bit digital

Power: 110 VAC, 12 - 30 VDC

Table 3: Performance specifications of a commercial fiber-optic strain demodulation unit for use with Fabry-Perot strain gauges.

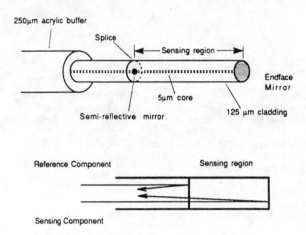

Figure 3: A detail of an intrinsic fiber-optic Fabry-Perot strain gauge.

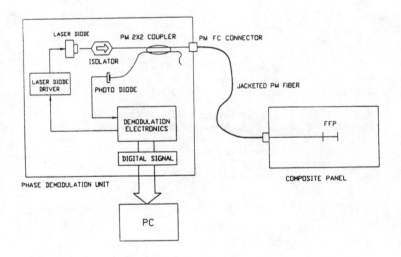

Figure 4: A block diagram of the intrinsic fiber-optic Fabry-Perot strain gauge system.

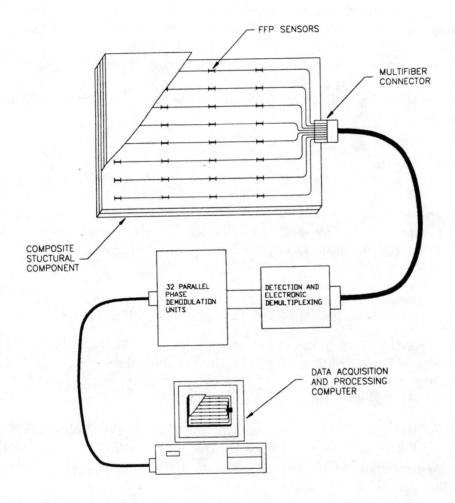

Figure 5: A wavelength division multiplexed network of fiber-optic strain gauges embedded in a composite laminate.

5 Conclusion

A variety of sensor technologies are emerging to meet the needs of intelligent structures. The most actively pursued ones are those based on resistive foil gauges, piezoelectric materials, and optical fibers. The primary advantage of resistive foil gauges are their ease of use, of piezoelectric materials are their dual sensor/actuator capabilities, of optical fibers are their capacity to form dense wavelength division multiplexed sensing networks. As each of these technologies becomes more refined, objective comparisons will be possible.

References

[1] Daniel, I.M., J.L. Mullineaux, F.J. Ahimaz, and T. Liber, 'The Embedded Strain Gauge Technique for Testing Boron/Epoxy Composites,' *Composite Materials: Testing and Design (Second Conference)*, ASTM STP 497, American Society for Testing and Materials, pp. 257–272, 1971.

[2] Measurements Group, Inc., 'Interlaminar Gaging of Composites,' Applications Note, Raleigh, North Carolina 27611, 1988.

[3] Hagood, N.W., E.F. Crawley, J. de Luis, and E.H. Anderson, 'Development of Integrated Components for Control of Intelligent Structures,' in Proc. *Intelligent Materials, Structures, and Mathematical Issues*,' C.A. Rogers, Ed., Blacksburg, VA, pp. 80–104, 1989.

[4] Collins, S.A., D.W. Miller, and A.H. von Flotow, 'Piezopolymer Spatial Filters for Active Structural Control,' in Proc. *Recent Advances in Active Control of Sound and Vibration*, Blacksburg, VA, April 15–17, pp. 219–234, 1991.

[5] Hagood, N.W., and A.H. von Flotow, 'Damping of Structural Vibrations with Piezoelectric Materials and Passive Electrical Networks,' *J. Sound & Vibration*, vol. 146, pp. 243–268, 1991.

[6] Hagood, N.W., and E.H. Anderson, 'Simultaneous Sensing and Actuation Using Piezoelectric Materials,' in Proc. *Conference on Active and Adaptive Optical Components*, SPIE vol. 1543, paper no. 1543-40, 1991.

[7] Morey, W.W., G. Meltz, and W.H. Glenn, 'Fiber optic Bragg grating sensors,' in Proc. *Fiber Optic & Laser Sensors VII*, SPIE vol. 1169, pp. 98–106, 1989.

[8] Lee, C.E., and H.F. Taylor, 'Interferometric optical fiber sensors using internal mirrors,' *Electron. Lett.*, vol. 24, pp. 193–194, 1988.

[9] Lee, C.E., W.N. Gibler, R.A. Atkins, and H.F. Taylor, 'In-Line Fiber Fabry-Perot Interferometer with High-Reflectance Internal Mirrors,' in Proc. *Fiber Optic & Laser Sensors IX*, pp. 396–399, 1991.

[10] Valis, T., D. Hogg, and R.M. Measures, 'Composite Material Embedded Fiber Optic Fabry-Perot Strain Rosette,' in Proc. *Fiber Optic Smart Structures & Skins III,*, SPIE vol. 1370, pp. 154–161, 1990.

[11] Valis, T., D. Hogg, and R. M. Measures, 'Fiber Optic Fabry-Perot strain Gauge,' *IEEE Photonics Technol. Lett.*, vol. 2, No.3, pp. 227–228, March 1990.

[12] Hogg, D., B. Mason, T. Valis, and R.M. Measures, 'Development of a Fiber Fabry-Perot (FFP) Strain Gauge System,' in Proc. *Fiber Optic Smart Structures & Skins IV*, SPIE vol. 1588, pp. 300–307, 1991.

[13] Murphy. K.A., M.F. Gunther, A.M. Vengsarkar, and R.O. Claus, 'Quadrature phase-shifted, extrinsic Fabry-Perot optical fiber sensors,' *Opt. Lett.*, vol. 16, no. 4, pp. 273–275, 1991.

[14] Varnham, M.P., A.J. Barlow, D.N. Payne, and K. Okamoto, 'Polarimetric strain gauges using high birefringence fibre', *Electron. Lett.*, vol. 19, no. 17, pp. 699–700, Aug. 1983.

[15] Blake, J.N., S.Y. Huang, B.Y. Kim, and H.J. Shaw, 'Strain Effects on Highly Elliptical Core Two-Mode Fibers,' *Opt. Lett.*, vol. 12, no. 9, pp. 732–734, 1987.

[16] Vengsarkar, A.M., K.A. Murphy, B.R. Fogg, W.V. Miller, J. Greene, and R.O. Claus, 'Two-Mode, Elliptical-Core, Weighted Fiber Optic Sensors for Vibration Analysis,' in Proc. *Smart Materials and Structures Workshop*, Blacksburg, VA, April 3-4, 1991.

SOME INTERESTING MECHANICS ISSUES FOR SMART MATERIAL SYSTEMS

Professor Craig A. Rogers, and C. Liang
Center for Intelligent Material Systems and Structures, Virginia Polytechnic Institute
and State University, Blacksburg, Virginia 24061-0261

ABSTRACT

Over the past decade, tremendous advancements have been made in the development of structural control paradigms and in the necessary supporting technologies. The fundamental paradigm that has driven these advancements is the desire to create "biologically inspired", controllable structures. In search of these structures with adaptive and lifelike features, modern-day alchemists have developed several approaches, based on natural systems, to incorporate adaptability into structures. This paper will describe four specific examples of adaptive behavior and the applications which might benefit from such lifelike functions.

INTRODUCTION

Man has always used nature as a source of inspiration for his engineering, both in design and process. The development of ideas within the area of intelligent material systems and structures is no exception. William Zuk (1970), in the book Kinetic Architecture, writes, "Life itself is motion, from the single cell to the most complex organism, man ... It is these attributes of motion, mobility, of change, of adaptation that place living things on a higher plateau of evolution than static forms. Indeed, survival of these living species depends on their kinetic abilities: to nourish themselves, to heal themselves, to reproduce themselves, to adapt to changing needs and environments ..." It is this concept of creating a higher form of material systems and structures by providing the "life" functions of sensing, actuation, control and intelligence to materials and structures which has inspired and motivated the initiation of this "new" field of endeavor.

In the search for biologically-inspired material systems and structures, researchers have become inspired by the science of biomimetics. However, as Vladimir Nabokov (1966) wrote so elegantly in Speak, Memory, organisms adept at mimicry often have aspects far removed from the sciences -- art, aesthetics and grace may be important as well.

"The mysteries of mimicry had a special attraction for me. Its phenomena showed an artistic perfection usually associated with man-wrought things ... When a certain moth resembles a certain wasp in shape and color, it also walks and moves its antennae in a waspish, unmothlike manner. When a butterfly has to look like a leaf, not only are all the details of a leaf beautifully rendered but markings mimicking grub-bored holes are generously thrown in. `Natural selection', in the Darwinian sense, could not explain the miraculous coincidence of imitation aspect and imitative behavior nor could one appeal to the theory of `the struggle for life' when a protective device was carried to a point of mimetic subtlety, exuberance and luxury far in excess of a predator's power of appreciation. I discovered in nature the nonutilitarian delights that I sought in art. Both were a form of magic, both were a game of intricate enchantment and deception."

However, in light of the "nonutilitarian delights" that nature has provided us, nature still seems to obey one law fairly consistently . . . natural systems seem to operate in a mode to reduce energy consumption while continuously performing adaptive functions. Recent advances in structural control with smart/intelligent material systems have followed this same mode of operation. It is my desire for smart materials to have the goal of: "replacing mass and energy with intelligence". By using this goal as the driving force behind new structural control concept development, we can begin looking at structural control in a more natural way. We can investigate the different methods by which nature creates adaptive functions and develop synthetic methods to mimic those of nature.

In general, the modes of adaptability in nature and in smart material systems can be classified as follows:

- Variations in material properties, i.e., stiffness;
- Changes in the stored strain energy of a system;
- Application of forces, moments and torques;
- Shifting of energy from one mode to another.

Each of these four classes of adaptability will be discussed in the following four sections by means of examples resulting from research undertaken in the last few years.

Example 1. Variations in Material Properties - Active Vibration Control

Shape memory alloys (SMAs) have several unique characteristics, including their Young's modulus-temperature relations, shape memory effects, and damping characteristics. The Young's modulus of the high-temperature austenite of SMAs is about three to four times as large as that of low-temperature martensite. Therefore, a spring made of SMA can change its spring constant by a factor of four. Since an SMA spring can vary its spring constant, provide recovery stress (shape memory effect), or be designed with a high damping capacity, it can be very useful in adaptive vibration control. It is expected that using SMA springs as control elements will have a significant impact on active/adaptive vibration control.

Shape memory alloy springs have been used as actuators in many applications, although their use in the vibration control area is very recent. Since shape memory alloys differ from conventional alloy materials in many ways, the traditional design approach for springs is not complelely suitable for designing SMA springs. Some design approaches based upon linear theory have been proposed for SMA springs (Liang and Rogers, 1991). A more accurate design method of SMA springs based on a new non-linear thermomechanical constitutive relation of SMA has also been presented (Liang and Rogers, 1991).

Shape memory alloys have been commercially available since the 1970s, although their applications have been very limited. Most applications of shape memory alloys are as force and displacement actuators. Rogers (1988) suggested that SMA fibers could be embedded into conventional composites such as graphite/epoxy to control the structural response including static deformation, vibration, buckling, and structural acoustic radiation/transmission. Nagaya et al. (1987) suggested that shape memory alloys could be used to control the critical speed of rotating shafts. A great deal of research and development related to SMAs is currently in progress; this section will address possible applications of SMA springs in vibration control.

Active vibration control can be realized by either tuning material properties or by applying controllable stimulus. Shape memory alloys have a tunable elastic modulus and recovery force. Since tuning the properties or recovery stress of SMA requires heating or cooling, SMA may not be suitable for high-frequency vibration control, but it may be used for low-frequency vibration control and quasi-static response control. The high damping capacity of the martensitic phase of shape memory alloys can be used in passive vibration control. The hysteric damping of pseudoelastic SMAs can be exploited in passive/adaptive vibration control. To demonstrate the possibility and feasibility of using SMA springs in vibration control, only one case shall be discussed, namely vibration control utilizing the variable stiffness of SMA springs.

The Young's modulus of shape memory alloys changes as a function of temperature. The modulus of high-temperature austenite is 3 to 4 times higher than that of low-temperature martensite; the shear modulus of SMA has the same relation. The spring constant of an SMA spring, as a linear function of its shear modulus, changes by three times over a small temperature range. The transition temperature range for the Young's modulus of SMA is about ten to thirty degrees. So far, most of the applications of SMAs as variable stiffness elements, such as shape memory alloy hybrid composites (Rogers, Liang and Jia, 1989), have utilized only the high-temperature modulus or the low-temperature modulus; it is difficult to achieve an intermediate Young's modulus by simply controlling the temperature. The reason is that the Young's modulus of

SMA is a function of its martensitic fraction which is affected by both the temperature and stress. In the following discussion of the applications of SMA springs as variable stiffness control elements, it is considered that an SMA spring has only two spring constants, K_SA (high-temperature austenitic spring constant) and K_SM (low-temperature martensitic spring constant).

Consider the natural frequencies of a simple structure, a cantilever beam with an SMA spring on one end of the beam, as shown in Figure 1. It is a simple problem and its solutions are given in virtually any vibration textbook. However, this problem is now different because the notion of elastic support having a variable stiffness has not previously been considered.

The governing equation for the system can be written as:

$$\frac{\partial^4 y}{\partial x^4} - k^4 y = 0$$

where k = ω2ρ/EI. Its boundary conditions are:

$$\begin{cases} y|_{x=0} = 0 \\ \frac{\partial y}{\partial x}|_{x=0} = 0 \end{cases}$$

and

$$\begin{cases} \frac{\partial^2 y}{\partial x^2}|_{x=L} = 0 \\ EI\frac{\partial^3 y}{\partial x^3}|_{x=L} = K_s y \end{cases}$$

where E is the Young's modulus of the beam, I is the moment of inertia of the cantilever beam, ρ is the density of the beam, and K_S is the spring constant. The natural frequency of the system can be solved from the following equation:

K(sin kL cosh kL - cos kL sinh kL) + $(k$L$)^3$(1 + cosh kL cos kL) = 0

where K = $K_S L^3$/EI is the ratio of the spring stiffness to the bending stiffness of the beam. The relative natural frequency, k_nL, can be solved from the equation above and the first five of them are listed in Table I.

When K is zero, the beam system is simply a cantilever beam. If K is infinite, the beam system is a clamped-simply supported system. The calculated k_n clearly indicates this point. Another point worth mentioning is that low-order natural frequencies are sensitive to a relatively small change of the stiffness of the support when K is small. The high-order natural frequencies, on the contrary, seem not to respond to the change of the stiffness of support as much when K is small. The above conclusion will be reversed at large K values. For example, when K increases from zero to 5, the first natural frequency increases by about 26% and the second natural frequency by only 1%, while higher-order natural frequency hardly changes. When K increases from 1000 to 10^{10}, there are not many changes for the first natural frequency, while changes are obvious for the fourth and fifth modes.

Example 2. Change in Stored Strain Energy - Adaptive Alternate Resonance Tuning

When adjacent sound-transmitting panels in a structure are tuned to resonate above and below a particular frequency such that they oscillate and radiate sound with equal source strength and opposite phase, incident sound is readily attenuated by the structure at and near the frequency to which the panels are tuned. This concept is known as alternate resonance tuning (ART). A simply-supported shape memory alloy (SMA) hybrid composite panel can be locally stiffened by selectively activating embedded SMA fibers to achieve ART adaptively, thereby enabling the panel to attenuate sound over several activation-dependent frequency ranges.

Bliss and Gottwald (1990) experimentally demonstrated the concept of alternate resonance tuning by arranging arrays of panels with adjacent panels tuned to resonate above and below a given operating frequency. Acoustic incidence at that frequency was observed to excite the panels to oscillate with nearly equal amplitude and opposite phase, thereby radiating sound with comparable source strength but opposite phase; causing high near-field acoustic interaction, and effectively reducing sound transmission to the far-field. In this work, ART was presented as a passive technique for reducing sound transmission through a panel-like structure when exposed to acoustic excitation at or near a particular frequency.

SMA hybrid composites are a class of materials which combine the strain recovery and stiffness transformation capabilities of SMA fibers with the structural characteristics of advanced composite materials to produce intelligent material systems with potential utility in numerous adaptive applications. Embedding SMA fibers in structures provides active material properties with transformation capability as well as capability to actively alter the state of stored strain energy. These characteristics can be utilized in a controlled fashion to manipulate the stiffness, stress and strain distribution throughout a structure, thereby altering its configuration and dynamic response. Intelligent material systems possess actuation along with sensing and control capabilities which can be utilized in many applications requiring adaptibility to changing external conditions (such as environment, load, or the desire to alter the scope, geometry or purpose of a structure) or internal conditions which may include damage to or failure of isolated portions

of the material or structure (Rogers, Liang and Jia, 1989).

The concept of embedding SMA fibers in composite materials was presented in 1988 (Rogers, 1988). Since then, several potential applications for these materials have been investigated (Rogers and Robertshaw, 1989), and extensive research has been conducted to characterize the recovery stress and strain recovery behavior of SMA fibers (Liang and Rogers, 1989), as well as the constitutive relations of SMA-reinforced laminates and their micromechanical behavior (Jia and Rogers, 1989).

The theory behind the concept of structural modification and control of SMA hybrid composites by general activation has already been developed and presented (Rogers, Liang and Barker, 1989) and (Rogers, Liang and Jia, 1989). General activation, which induces a spatially uniformly distributed transformation of material properties and recovery forces throughout SMA hybrid composites, was shown by Rogers, Fuller and Liang (1990) to alter the lower order modes of the structure (i.e., the third, fourth, fifth and sixth mode shapes) and to adaptively alter the transmission loss and directivity patterns of transmitted sound. The first and second modes were found to be generally difficult to modify with global activation, which provided the motivation to refine this concept.

The theory developed for globally activated SMA hybrid adaptive composite panels was expanded to consider localized activation by Anders and Rogers (1991). Analytical case studies for various arrangements of localized and global activation indicated that localized activation enhances adaptive structural acoustic control capability over certain frequency ranges. Localized activation also demonstrated the ability to slightly alter the first and second mode shapes; however, the geometric mode shapes were still not significantly modified.

An investigation of the utility and performance of adaptive ART by localized activation of SMA hybrid composites was initiated to address the issue of low frequency structural acoustic control. Selectively activating the SMA fibers embedded near the center of a panel induces localized stiffening and produces a "rigid" section interposed between two compliant sections. The stiffened section may be regarded as a pseudo-stiffener or support which couples the two adjacent "compliant" panel sections, i.e., the complete panel is adapted into sub-panel regions. This coupling influences the modal and structural acoustic behavior of the panel as a whole. The concept of adaptive ART using a single panel differs significantly from the passive control concept using an array of independently supported panels introduced by Bliss and Gottwald (1990), as dynamic and structural acoustic panel behavior can be actively tuned to exploit the advantages of ART over several frequency ranges by strategic placement of the activated SMA fiber region in order to adapt the panel configuration in response to changing input disturbances.

Previous investigations considering locally and globally activated panels showed no significant modification of the first and second mode shapes. Analysis of a unidirectional SMA hybrid fiberglass (NiTi/GFRP) panel with a narrow band of fibers considered activated at its center has demonstrated the ability to effectively modify the first two mode shapes, such that the two unactivated panel sections appear to assume their own separate modal identities, with a finite amount of coupling introduced in the activated region (see Figure 2).

Displacing the region of activation-induced stiffening from the center of the panel introduces a stiffness imbalance between the two unactivated sections, thereby tuning them to resonate at different frequencies. Moving the activated section about the central region of the panel changes the modal response of the entire panel and the stiffnesses of the unactivated panel sections, stiffening one section, making the other more compliant, and retuning the alternate resonance behavior. Sound transmission through SMA hybrid composite panels can be adaptively mimimized by strategically activating fibers to best attenuate incident sound over a range of frequencies by exploiting the concept of ART, thus enabling broad-band structural acoustic control capability, as shown in Figure 2.

Example 3: Application of Forces and Moments - Active Structural Acoustic Control

In many applications, the sound fields radiated by vibrating elastic structures is an important noise problem. Examples are machinery noise in factories, marine hull radiated noise and interior noise in aerospace applications. An understanding of the behavior of such systems, with a view to controlling them, involves the field of structural acoustics. Structural acoustics is the study of how elastic structures radiate or receive sound (Junger and Feit, 1986) and in its most fundamental form involves the simultaneous solution of the differential equations describing the structure and fluid media with appropriate coupling conditions between the two (a "fully coupled" analysis).

The usual methods of control of such radiated noise fields involve passive techniques such as added mass, damping, stiffness and system modification through re-design.
However, these techniques have proven unsatisfactory in many applications for a number of reasons. Passive techniques usually imply a significant mass increase and do not work well at low frequencies and, due to the "coupled" nature of the problem, it is difficult to predict their effect except in the simplest of applications. One approach that shows much potential to overcome these difficulties is active control. Active control has recently re-emerged as a very promising technique to reduce radiated sound fields (Williams, 1984). The main reason for this has been advances in high-speed data acquisition and processing enabling active control to be implemented in "real time". The

traditional active approach to the problem of reducing sound radiation from structures is to use a number of secondary acoustic control sources arranged around the structural noise source (see, for example, Hesseleman, 1978). This technique can be seen to have a number of disadvantages. From an implementation point of view, it is often impracticable to have secondary acoustic sources located away from the structure (as well as error microphones). More importantly, the use of acoustic control sources leads to a generation of additional unwanted noise, termed "control spillover". This situation is overcome by using additional strategically positioned acoustic sources. Thus, for example, a machine radiating noise requires a large number of active acoustic sources arranged around it to produce global (here global means throughout an extended volume or space) noise reduction (Hesseleman, 1978).

In terms of controlling sound radiation from structures using active or adaptive means applied directly to the structure while sensing some state or parameter of the structural acoustic system, very little previous work has been done. Knyasev and Tartakovskii (1967) demonstrated in a brief experiment that it was possible to reduce sound radiation from a panel using an active damping force. Vylayshev et al. (1986) analytically considered sound transmission through a one-dimensional plate and showed an increase in the plate transmission loss with one active control force applied to the plate. Fuller and Jones (1987) and Jones and Fuller (1988) showed both experimentally and analytically that sound transmission into a model elastic fuselage can be globally controlled with a small number of point force control inputs applied to the structure. This early work (Fuller and Jones, 1987; Jones and Fuller, 1988) provided the basis for further research; while the control inputs are applied to the structure, the error information is taken from the acoustic field and thus the controlled system includes the natural coupling between the structural response and the acoustic field. This approach has been shown, for low-frequency applications, to markedly reduce the dimensions of the controller.

Structural acoustics is directly concerned with the coupling between the motions of elastic structures and their radiating (or receiving) sound fields. The response of these systems must be solved simultaneously (or in a coupled sense) as in heavy fluids or highly reactive environments the back loading (radiation impedance) of the acoustic field affects the motion of the radiating structure (Junger and Feit, 1986). Obviously this natural "feed-back" loop has important implications on the design of active systems for such situations. This section will discuss some of the important characteristics of structural acoustic coupling and how they relate to the present problem. One important aspect of how structures radiate sound is known as radiation efficiency, σ, which is defined as the ratio of the acoustic power that a structure radiates to the power radiated by a piston of equivalent area vibrating with an amplitude equal to the time-spatial average of the structure. Obviously, the higher σ is, the more sound energy will be radiated for a given structural response. As an example, Figure 3 shows the radiation efficiency of various modes of vibration of a baffled circular clamped plate versus non-dimensional frequency $k_0a = 2\pi fa/c$, where f is frequency of excitation, a is plate radius, and c is the speed of sound (Hansen and Bies, 1976). For low frequencies, σ is seen to vary strongly with modal order, (m,n) where m and n are circumferential and radial mode numbers, respectively. The most efficient mode is the (0,1) or monopole-like mode. All modally responding structures exhibit behavior related to Figure 3. Thus, if a structure is vibrating in a number of modes of nearly equal amplitude, then only a few of these will radiate sound in the low-frequency region (which is our frequency region of interest). This implies that only one or two control inputs need be applied to the structure to reduce the radiated field as long as the error information is constructed from radiated acoustic variables.

Figure 4 shows results from an experiment in which sound transmitting through an elastic clamped circular panel located in a baffle is reduced by active point force inputs applied to the panel (Fuller et al., 1989). The error points are two microphones in the radiated acoustic field. In this experiment, the aluminum plate was 0.4572 m in diameter and 1.27 mm thick. The incident acoustic wave was planar at an angle of incidence of 45° and was at a single frequency of 112 Hz. Substantial reduction in radiated noise is observed in this off-resonance case where there are many panel modes present in the response. In contrast, Figure 5 shows the same situation except that the error information is taken from two accelerometers mounted on the panel (i.e., directly controlling panel vibration). The results show that, although panel vibration is attenuated by around 20 dB at the error points, the noise radiation increases.

Example 4: Moving Energy from One Mode to Another - Active Fatigue Control

Active damage control is a new technique evolving with the development of intelligent materials and structures. This technique, mimicking the self-repairing function of biological beings, can greatly increase the lifespan and reliability of the structures of the future. The first paper published in this area (Rogers, Liang and Li, 1991) described the active damage control mechanisms that can be applied in various scenarios.

The mechanism of active damage control is to redirect the energy flow in the structure, resulting in less high-energy concentration, or high-stress concentration in the structure. The energy flow direction can also be altered by inputing energy from outside. The total energy of the system may increase, but the energy that is deteriorating the structure can be decreased. This concept has been demonstrated in the

active fatigue control of adhesive bonding joints using piezoelectric actuators. The flexural energy that debonds the adhesive joints is associated with the stress and strain field that is perpendicular to the bonding layers. This energy is transferred into longitudinal energy by activating the PZT actuators mounted close to the joints to create a new stress-strain field that is parallel to the bonding layers.

To investigate active fatigue control, a simple experiment has been conducted. As shown in Figure 6, a composite beam was bonded on an aluminum bracket and subjected to a fatigue loading from a motor. Two PZT actuators were mounted on the roof of the beam. The actuators operated at the same frequency as the fatigue loading, but the induced stress from the actuators in the bonding area was out-of-phase with the fatigue loading. Through reducing the fatigue stress amplitude, the fatigue cycles of the bonding joint were increased significantly. The fatigue life of the bond without the active control was 52,000 cycles, while this number increased to more than 500,000 cycles when the actuators were activated. At the same time, the vibration amplitude of the beam was also greatly reduced.

The explanation for this type of damage control from a stress-strain point of view is very straightforward. However, it is more difficult to explain where the energy goes. In the above experiment, both the motor and the actuators input energy to the composite beam, but yet the energy associated with the vibration of the beam and the peeling of the bond decreases. Stress analysis indicates that although the stress amplitude in the vertical direction (with respect to the adhesive joint) decreases, the stress in the parallel direction increases. Thus, we may conclude that the flexural energy that tends to de-bond the adhesive joint has been transfered into longitudinal energy which governs the longitudinal vibration of the beam.

SUMMARY

"Whoever, in the pursuit of science, seeks after immediate practical utility, may generally rest assured that he will seek in vain."

Hermann von Helmholtz
Academic Discourse, 1862

ACKNOWLEDGMENTS

The author gratefully acknowledges the support for this work by the National Science Foundation Presidential Young Investigator Award Program, NSF Grant No. MSS-9157080, and Dr. Ken Chong, Program Manager.

REFERENCES

Anders, W. S. and Rogers, C. A., 1991. First Joint U.S./Japan Conference on Adaptive Structures (Maui, HI, 13-15 November, 1990), B. K. Wada, J. L. Fanson and K. Miura, Eds., Technomic Publishing Co., Inc., Lancaster, PA, pp. 285-303.

Bliss, D. B., and J. A. Gottwald, 1990. AIAA Journal of Aircraft; in press.

Fuller, C. R. and Jones, J. D., 1987. Journal of Sound and Vibration, 112, 389-395.

Fuller, C. R., Silcox, R. J., Metcalf, V. L. and Brown, D. E., 1989. Proceedings, American Control Conference, Pittsburgh, PA, 2079-2084.

Hansen, C. H. and Bies, D. A., 1976. Journal of the Acoustical Society of America, 60(3), 543-555.

Hesseleman, N., 1978. Applied Acoustics, 11, 27-34.

Jia, J., and C. A. Rogers, 1989. Failure Prevention and Reliability (Proceedings of the 8th Biennial Conference on Failure Prevention and Reliability, Montreal, Canada, 18-20 September).

Jones, J. D. and Fuller, C. R., 1988. Proceedings, 6th IMAC Conference, Orlando, FL, 315-321.

Junger, M. C. and Feit, D., 1986. Sound, Structures and their Interaction, MIT Press, Cambridge, MA.

Knyasev, A. S. and Tartakovskii, B. D., 1967. Soviet Physics-Acoustics, 13(1), 115-117.

Liang, C., and C. A. Rogers, 1989. Proceedings, Seventh International Conference on Composite Materials, Beijing, P.R. China, 1-4 August.

Liang, C. and Rogers, C. A., 1991. Proceedings, Conference on Recent Advances in Active Control of Sound and Vibration, Blacksburg, VA; Technomic Publishing Co., Inc., Lancaster, PA, pp. 177-198.

Nabokov, V. V., 1966. Speak, Memory, Putnam, NY.

Nagaya, K., Takeda, S., Tsukui, Y. and Knmaido, Y., 1987. Journal of Sound and Vibration, 113(2), 307-315.

Rogers, C. A., 1988. Proceedings, the American Society for Composites 3rd Technical Conference on Composite Materials, Technomic Publishing, Co., Lancaster, PA.

Rogers, C. A., Liang, C. and Li, S., 1991. Proceedings, AIAA/ASM/ASCE/AHS/ASC 32nd Structures, Structural Dynamics, and Materials Conference, AIAA, Inc., Washington, DC, Part II, pp. 1190-1203.

Rogers, C. A., Fuller, C. R. and Liang, C., 1990. Journal of Sound and Vibration, 136(6), 164-170.

Rogers, C. A., Liang, C. and Barker, D. K., 1989. Smart Materials, Structures and Mathematical Issues, (C. A. Rogers, Ed.), Technomic Publishing Co., Inc., Lancaster, PA, pp. 39-62.

Rogers, C. A., Liang, C. and Jia, J., 1989. Proceedings, 30th Structures, Structural Dynamics, and Materials Conference, Mobile, Al, 3-5 April 1989, AIAA Paper No. 89-1389, pp. 2011-2017.

Rogers, C. A., and Robertshaw, H. H., 1989. Engineering Science Preprints 25, Society of Engineering Sciences, Inc., ESP25.88027.

Vylayshev, A. I., Dubinin, A. J. and Tartakovskii, B. D., 1986. Soviet Physics-Acoustics, 32(2), 96-98.

Williams, J. E. Ffowcs, 1984. Proceedings of the Royal Society of London, A395, 63-88.

Zuk, W., 1970. Kinetic Architecture, Van Nostrand Reinhold, NY.

K	k_nL				
	n=1	n=2	n=3	n=4	n=5
0	1.88	4.69	7.85	11.00	14.14
0.1	1.89	4.70	7.86	11.00	14.14
0.5	1.95	4.70	7.86	11.00	14.14
1.0	2.01	4.70	7.86	11.00	14.14
5.0	2.37	4.74	7.87	11.00	14.14
20.0	2.97	4.90	7.90	11.01	14.14
50.0	3.40	5.20	7.96	11.03	14.16
100.0	3.64	5.62	8.04	11.07	14.17
1000.0	3.90	6.88	9.55	11.95	14.58
10^{10}	3.93	7.07	10.21	13.38	16.49

Table 1. The First Five Relative Natural Frequencies of the Beam System

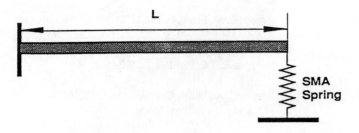

Figure 1. Cantilever beam with an SMA spring support at one end.

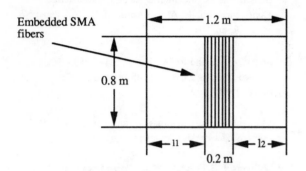

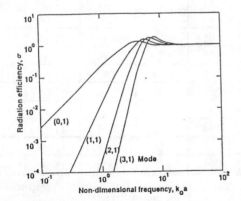

	Unactivated	$\frac{l_1}{l_2} = 1.0$	$\frac{l_1}{l_2} = 0.9$	$\frac{l_1}{l_2} = 0.8$	$\frac{l_1}{l_2} = 0.7$
mode 1					
frequency (TL)	27.7 Hz (9.3 dB)	57.3 Hz (17.8 dB)	56.2 Hz (21.2 dB)	53.6 Hz (18.5 dB)	50.8 Hz (16.3 dB)
mode 2					
frequency (TL)	52.6 Hz (26.8 dB)	64.3 Hz (9.2 dB)	65.9 Hz (10.7 dB)	69.6 Hz (12.6 dB)	75.0 Hz (14.0 dB)

Figure 2. Adaptive alternate resonance tuning: panel geometry (above) and mode shape and transmission loss response (below).

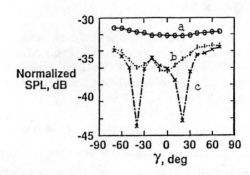

Figure 4. Radiation directivity, microphone error sensors: no control (a); one control (b); two controls (c).

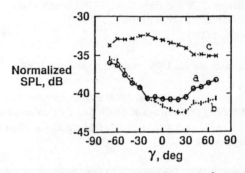

Figure 5. Radiation directivity, accelerometer error sensors: no control (a); one control (b); two controls (c).

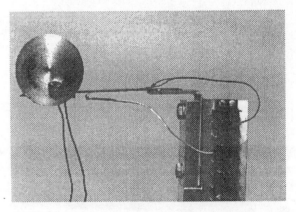

Figure 6. Active fatigue control of adhesive bonding joint using PZT actuators.

Figure 3. Modal radiation efficiency of clamped circular panel in a baffle.

CONTROL ISSUES FOR INTELLIGENT STRUCTURES

Harry H. Robertshaw and William R. Saunders

Center for Intelligent Material Systems and Structures, Virginia Polytechnic Institute
and State University, Blacksburg, Virginia 24060-0261

ABSTRACT

Opportunities in control of structures that are afforded by the introduction of intelligent material systems with large numbers of integral, inexpensive, sensors and actuators (with wide choices of local and global topologies) has created the need for and expectations of control strategies which can perform effectively and reliably over large ranges of temporal and spatial scales. Two applications are introduced along with a numerical example to illustrate the requirements for control approaches and to discuss the current state of technology. Examples from biology and the natural world are discussed to suggest methods to respond to the opportunities of intelligent material systems.

INTRODUCTION

The emerging field of intelligent material systems and structures has provided new opportunities for control technology and science. Much time has been spent in defining and attempting to find the extent of this area (see for example Ahmad et. al. 1990). We'll not add to this discussion here except to note that one way to "cut the diamond", to provide a structure, for this field is to propose categories of: actuators, sensors, and controls. Some have observed that uses of the terms "smart" (as in Smart Structures) and "intelligent" (as in Intelligent Materials) in a name for this field emphasizes the most developed of the three areas. This presentation will address this assumption from aspect of suitability of current approaches in the light of opportunities presented and expectations that have been raised.

The opportunities afforded to the control practitioner by the field of intelligent material systems and structures is the possibility of having very large numbers of sensors and actuators that can be interconnected by wide ranges of topologies for information and energy flow. The sensors and actuators, if connected properly, will be capable of global (over the entire structure) sensing and actuation as well as finely textured local sensing and actuation. In addition to the need to address wide structural spatial scales, wide scales of time responses will be expected to be controlled by or in intelligent structures. This expectation results, in part, from the extensive comparison that have been made of this field to that of biological systems which have been very successful in carrying out the control tasks that are needed for their goals. One of the important questions is: what are the goals and subgoals of biological and natural systems?

The classical approach to control system design is that the control engineer will choose the format and the details of the information and energy flow topologies. A general goal to be met by these choices is that the resulting system will follow reference variables (or concepts) as closely as possible despite the influence of disturbances, measurement noise, and system variations. In the case of feedback control systems this goal partially accomplished by 1)moving the system response sensitivities to predictable components 2) using the sensors and actuators and control laws to change the (effective) system dynamic and steady-state characteristics to those desired and 3) performing these tasks with minimum energy and constrained parameters and variables.

A powerful, and commonly-used approach to control system design is to add so-called (full) state feedback. The state feedback method requires the sensing (or on-line construction) of "N" linearly independent variables which are then used to control the system inputs, where "N" is the order of the mathematical model used to represent the uncontrolled system. The state feedback method guarantees the designer the ability to change the transient response to any desired one. However, this method of control will break down in the implementation when a large numbers of sensors and a large number of actuators are available for use because the state feedback method requires the association of all sensor outputs with each actuator input. Therefore, for a equal number of sensors and actuators, an N×N matrix multiply is required at each control instant. This could be an insurmountable computational burden since some intelligent material systems are anticipating at least hundreds, if not thousands, of sensors and actuators.

Additionally, the performance of the resulting controlled system will be significantly degraded if the mathematical model utilized for system design does not well-represent, for all time, the system being controlled. This performance degradation can be very sensitive to modelling errors for many applications. Intelligent structures will be expected to be able to maintain performance, as biological and other natural systems do, in the face of changing conditions both internal to and external to the structure. Current control approaches are not able to provide this performance.

Two examples of applications of intelligent structures will be outlined and the implications of their requirements for control strategies will be discussed. This will be followed by a quantitative example with a review of current control approaches. Finally, a discussion of advanced control functions will be presented with suggestions for further areas of development.

TWO APPLICATIONS

Critical issues for control of intelligent structures will vary, depending on the application physics. The role of control paradigms is expected to range in complexity from relatively simple strategies such as position control to advanced mimicry of biomechanical systems. Two qualitative applications of intelligent structural systems are discussed next. The first application focuses on the active control of turbulent boundary layer noise (TBLN). The second application is concerned with the development of a free-swimming, autonomous, underwater marine vehicle.

Active Turbulent Boundary Layer Noise Control

A variety of important hydroacoustical problems are related to turbulent flow over structural surfaces. Viscous fluid flow past a solid boundary produces a boundary layer adjacent to the surface. Turbulence in the boundary layer results with the development of a field of disordered vorticity. The turbulent motion in the boundary layer induces fluctuating wall pressures which may excite the adjacent structure, causing vibration and subsequent radiation from the boundary. The dominant TBLN phenomena which must be addressed by an active control strategy include flexural radiation of turbulence-induced

vibration, trailing edge sound radiation, direct radiation from turbulent boundary layer, and acoustic sensor self-noise (Blake, 1984).

Successful methods of TBLN control might be developed using an intelligent structural system approach. The relationship between the control paradigm, the material system component design and the performance of the smart system depends on a variety of parameters associated with the physical laws governing the TBLN phenomena. For example, the flexural radiation component is governed by spatial scales on the order of the structural dimensions. The corresponding time scales have relatively large bandwidths, particularly for the sampled-data controller implementations in intelligent structures. However, direct modification of the turbulent boundary layer formation would possibly require tracking of much smaller spatial and temporal scales, on the order of correlation lengths of convected eddies in the turbulent boundary layer. The variation in participating spatial and temporal scales imposes important design criteria on the intelligent control. The controller must be able to address changeable topologies of sensory transducers, depending on the performance criteria. This selectivity must realizable in the system network hardware and be compatible with a control hierarchy which is responsible for satisfying possibly concurrent control objectives. Finally, active TBLN control would be dominantly feedback-based in its approach strategies, e.g. minimization of trailing edge noise would be accomplished by direct feedback of the corresponding edge velocities. Integration of such diverse hydro-acoustic silencing techniques into a single material systems and hardware design will require control theory approaches which confront the present technology limits.

Swimming Marine Vehicles

Nature provides abundant inspiration for possible applications of intelligent structures. One of the more interesting ideas is the biomechanical locomotion of aquatic animals. It is intriguing to consider the development of an intelligent material system into an autonomous swimming vessel. Several methods of locomotion dominate the fish population (Lighthill, 1974). The undulatory wing motion of the rays, the carangiform motion of the fish body and the rigid, oscillatory beating of the lunate caudal fin of large, fast-swimming fishes are examples which a swimming vessel could mimic. Next, the flight of the Manta ray will be the basis for discussion of some control issues associated with the design of an intelligent swimming vessel.

Forward underwater flight for the Manta ray is very similar to the aerodynamic flight of birds. Both lift and thrust are generated by the flapping of strong pectoral fins. The ability to reproduce this type of motion depends on selection of the smart material system and the control methods which link the behavior of the swimming vehicle to appropriate performance indices. Combined flexibility and strength are required for the wing material. The characteristic flapping produces large curvature at various stages of the cycle and large pressure loadings during the downward thrust motion. The travelling-wave motion of the pectoral 'wings' demands large displacements along the span, sequential spatial events coordinated over some time scale, and significant force requirements at the junction of the body and wing structure. Actuator and sensor placement for a swimming ray vehicle needs to conform to these physical requirements. Observations of a swimming ray indicate that the control paradigm might be quasi open-loop. Phased firing of actuators could be largely anticipatory, based on recognition of an appropriate incoming signal to a local sensory area. A hierarchical control approach would unify the swimming function with other performance objectives such as navigation, buoyancy control, and soaring. The controller needs to be inherently adaptive and stable for this variety of tasks. The control tools which are currently available for problems of this nature are discussed next.

A REVIEW OF CURRENT APPROACHES

Current approaches to the design of control algorithms depend on the modelling approach utilized and the goals for the controlled system. For differential equation models (including transfer function models), the state feedback method is widely used with for both single-input and multiple-input applications. The use of integral performance indexes has become common to produce either state feedback designs, along with Kalman filters, or to produce some polynomial compensator feedback designs. This approach will yield good results (using a known, constant, linear system model and known descriptions of the measurement noise and the nature of the disturbances) in the face of reference inputs to be followed with both persistent and transient disturbances. These methods can also be utilized with the performance being described by a "model" or "desired" system description.

However, in all cases, the system performance is degraded when the system being controlled deviates from the mathematical description utilized in the design process. When the form of these deviations can be anticipated apriori methods of "robust system design" such as H_∞ analysis along with μ-synthesis can be utilized to strike a happy medium between performance and stability.

Adaptive methods due to Widrow (1985) and others have been used with excellent results for a class of applications directed at rejection of harmonic and narrow-band disturbances. However, these methods have not been extended to transient control or to large numbers of inputs; additionally, they are dependent on model fidelity as are the above-mentioned methods. Model-based adaptive methods such as self-tuning control and model-reference adaptive control (Astrom and Wittenmark, 1989) require an explicit on-line system identification in order to be effective. This is not computationally feasible for the large-scale systems mentioned above.

The use of artificial neural systems as control and identification algorithms is increasing (Simpson 1990 and e.g. Cui and Shin 1991, Narendra and Mukhopadhyay 1991) and offers promise for the intelligent structural system application. They have not, as yet, been applied to large numbers of sensors and actuators. Work on decentralized control (Gundes and Desoer 1990, Rudie and Wonham 1991) has progressed well and may be ready to offer some alternatives.

Work in hierarchical control (e.g. Zhong and Wonham 1990) and in knowledge-based, inductive-learning-based control (Silva and McFarlane 1989) has the most promise for application to intelligent structural systems; however, much development must be carried out. Some examples of biological control may be illustrative for the needs in control approaches.

ADVANCED CONTROL FUNCTIONS AND CLOSURE

Examples abound in living systems and natural systems of the abundance of "regulation" or control that occurs and is needed for performance of function. The control of many physiological variables such from blood carbon dioxide, to body temperature. to control of protein biosynthesis. Yates (1990) has concluded that modern control theory "...cannot be brought to bear on the richness of modern genetic control ...". We find that this is true also. For example, in the modelling of the human thermoregulatory process, classical ideas of sensors and actuators can be applied to reproduce the short-term, quantitative thermoregulatory response of humans. The classical idea of homeostasis is reproduced in these simulations; however, as Iberall (1972 and others) has observed temperature control in humans follows a limit-cycle-like oscillation of significant amplitude over large time scales as do most physiological variables. Hence, the term "homeokinetics" coined by Iberall. This suggests a collection of non-linear, limit-cycle oscillators in the body.

Iberall (in Yates 1990) has proposed the definition of "complex systems" that applies to both biological and natural systems and implies that the control function has been "concurrently designed" into each of the systems:

> To say that a complex system exists is to say that a set of macroscopic processes has stabilized in action space by cycling the materials and energies at hand through persistent patterns and forms. We call this process *homeokinetics* – a term that emphasizes the role of kinetic processes as dynamic regulators of the internal environment of the complex field system.

We suggest that a "complex-system approach" be taken to the design of the control function in intelligent structural systems.

REFERENCES

1. Astrom, K. J., and B. Wittenmark (1989), *Adaptive Control*, Addison-Wesley, 1989.

2. Ahmad, I, A. Crowson, C. A. Rogers, and M. Aizawa, Eds.(1990), 'U.S.-Japan Workshop on Intelligent Materials and Systems,' March 1990, Technomic Press, Lancaster, PA.

3. Blake, W.K. (1984) 'Aero-Hydro Acoustics for Ships, Vol I and II', DTNSRDC-84/010.

4. Cui, Xianzhong and Kang G. Shin (1991),'Intelligent Coordination of Multiple Systems with Neural Networks', Proceedings of ACC, 1991.

5. Gundes, A.N. and C.A. Deseor (1990), 'Algebraic Theory of Linear Feedback Systems with Full and Decentralized Compensators,' Springer-Verlag, 1990.

6. Iberall, A.S (1972), *Toward a General Science of Viable Systems*, McGraw-Hill, 1972.

7. Lighthill, J.(1979), 'Animal Flight', Proceedings of the Symposium on Swimming and Flying in Nature, Cal Tech, Pasadena, CA, 1974, pp. 423-492.

8. Narendra, Kumpati S. and Snehasis Mukhopadhyay (1991), 'Intelligent Control Using Neural Networks', Proceedings ACC, 1991 pp. 1069-1074.

9. Rudie, Karen, W. Murray Wonham (1991), 'Think Globally, Act Locally: Decentralized Supervisory Control', Proceedings ACC 1991 pp.898 -903.

10. de Silva, C.W. and A.G.J. MacFarlane (1989), *Knowledge-Based Control with Application to Robots*, Springer-Verlag, 1989

11. Simpson, P. K. (1990), *Artificial Neural Systems*, Pergammon Press, 1990.

12. Widrow, B, and S. D. Stearns (1985), *Adaptive Signal Processing*, Prentice-Hall, 1985.

13. Yates, F. Eugene, Ed.(1987) *Self-Organizing Systems: The Emergence of Order*, Plenum, 1987.

14. Zhong, Hao and W. Murray Wonham (1990), 'On the Consistency of Hierarchical Supervision in Discrete-Event Systems', IEEE Transactions on Automatic Control, Vol. 35, No. 10, October, 1990, pp.1125-1134.

FUNDING ISSUES IN INTELLIGENT STRUCTURES AT AFOSR

Walter F. Jones

Considerable effort within the Department of Defense research community has been recently focused on the development of intelligent materials and structures. These materials and structures have the ability to adapt to their environments through shape and/or material property modification. Applications of this technology include vibration and instability suppression, shape modification, and noise suppression. Actuators within aircraft wings can be used to apply bending and twisting moments which counter the aerodynamic forces on the wing. In-service health (damage) monitoring of aerospace structures is also an important application of this technology. The payoffs for space subsystems technology will include the ability to control the deployment and ultimate shape of large space structures. All of these applications are directly related to the design of future Air Force aircraft/spacecraft systems, and will provide tremendous improvements in several important areas, including aerodynamic shape control and stealth characteristics. The U.S. Army is also working to develop intelligent structures for use in its future helicopter fleet, as is the U.S. Navy research community for use in future submarines and aircraft.

Despite the resources that have been focused on intelligent structures technology development by the Air Force Office of Scientific Research and other Department of Defense funding agencies, it is clear that there are numerous key issues that must be settled before this technology reaches its full potential. For example, a fundamental understanding of the interactions between sensors, actuators, and the host materials must be developed using appropriate micromechanical modeling. An understanding of the possible detrimental effects on the host structure resulting from the embedding of inclusions (sensors and actuators) must also be developed. Inherent material and geometric nonlinearities must be studied in order to consider the effects of internal damage on the controllability of intelligent structures. Other issues will also require further study, and these issues must be clearly identified by the research and development community in order to justify the continued spending of funds on the development of intelligent structures technology.

In times of limited resources, members of the research community must work closely with the appropriate government agency program managers in order to define the technical issues that need further study and to relate these needs to senior management within the Department of Defense and other government funding agencies. Interaction with government laboratory researchers is also critical to ensure that the results obtained from university and industrial laboratory research teams can be transitioned to government research and development programs as soon as possible. Numerous opportunities exist for this interaction, including workshops sponsored by the Society for Experimental Mechanics and other professional societies. Government research agencies also frequently sponsor their own workshops to address the basic research issues associated with the development of a particular technology. Participation in these workshops is encouraged, and is an excellent way to learn of current and future government research and development programs and to influence the future direction of research efforts within the U.S. government.

Walter F. Jones manages the Mechanics of Materials program within the Directorate of Aerospace Sciences at the Air Force Office of Scientific Research, AFOSR/NA, Bolling Air Force Base, Washington, DC 20332-6448.

EFFECT OF MICROSTRUCTURES ON CHARACTERISTICS OF FATIGUE
CRACK GROWTH IN HYPO-EUTECTOID GRAPHITIC STEELS

N. Kawagoishi, H. Sueyoshi
Faculty of Engineering
Kagoshima University
Kagoshima 890, Japan

H. Nisitani
Faculty of Engineering
Kyushu University
Fukuoka 812, Japan

ABSTRACT

The influence of microstructural factors, i.e., the volume fraction of graphite, the size of graphite nodules and so on, on the crack growth was investigated in several hypo-eutectoid graphitic steels. the crack growth rate increases to some degree by the existence of the graphite nodules. This is mainly brought by the change of the crack propagation mechanism, namely graphite nodules cause voids and intergranular facets. Graphitic steels, however, has a sufficient resistance for crack growth as structural materials.

INTRODUCTION

It has been recognized that a graphitic steel containing graphite nodules in the matrix of steel has superior properties in machinability, workability, wear resistance and so on in comparison with plain carbon steels (1-7). Therefore, this steel is expected to be applied to many structural parts, for example as the material for slide bearing working under a high contact pressure. However, the influences of graphite nodules on mechanical properties especially the fatigue property which is highly sensitive to microstructures, are not fully clarified (8). In the present paper, rotating bending fatigue tests were carried out on specimens with a small blind hole of a ferritic single phase steel and several hypo-eutectoid graphitic steels which have different volume fractions, sizes and distributions of graphite nodules, in order to clarify the effect of graphite nodules on the crack growth. Furthermore, the fatigue crack growth resistance of hypo-eutectoid graphitic steels was evaluated in comparison with those of plain carbon steels and a spheroidal graphite cast iron. Recently, many works on the spheroidal graphite cast irons with superior strength and toughness have been conducted actively (9, 10). Although the present study is related to those works, the size and volume fraction of graphite nodules are fairly small and low in graphitic steels compared with the cast irons.

MATERIALS, SPECIMENS AND EXPERIMENTAL PROCEDURES

The materials used are forged round bars (about 14 mm in diameter) of four kinds of steels whose carbon content alone are different one another. The chemical compositions of the materials are shown in Table 1. The heat treatments for preparing the materials having various microstructures are shown in Table 2. Tables 3 and 4 show their microstructural factors and mechanical properties, respectively. Each material is described by a symbol noted in Tables 3 and 4 hereafter. Microstructural factors change widely as seen from Table 3. These graphitization treatments improve remarkably the wear resistance and the machinability (4,5). Little influence on the tensile strength σ_B due to these graphitization is recognized, though the ferrite grain size slightly affects to σ_B. Figure 1 shows microstructures for each steel. Although these photographs show the cross sections of the forged bars only, the anisotropy was scarcely observed. Figure 2 shows the shape and dimensions of specimen. Prior to fatigue testing, all the specimens machined were polished by buff and annealed in vacuum at 600°C for one hour. The measurement of crack length was made using plastic replicas under an optical microscope. The crack length was measured in the circumferential direction of specimen surface including the diameter of the small blind hole (0.3 mm). The fatigue tests were performed by using the Ono type rotating bending fatigue machine operated at a frequency of 50 Hz.

EXPERIMENTAL RESULTS AND DISCUSSION

S-N curve

S-N_f curves for all steels are shown in Fig.3. The number of cycles to failure N_f decreases with increasing the volume fraction of graphite nodules and the influence of other microstructural factors on the value of N_f is very small. These results suggest that the influence of graphite nodules on the fatigue life can be evaluated through the volume fraction of graphite nodules approximately. The reason why the fatigue life decreases by the existence of graphite nodules will be discussed in the following sections.

Influence of microstructural factors on the crack growth

Graphite nodules can become an initiation site of crack in plain specimens of all graphitic steels. On the other hand, in all of ferritic and graphitic steels, cracks initiate at early stage of stress repetition, and most of fatigue life is occupied by the growth of small crack from the crack initiation to the length 1-2 mm even in a plain specimen (11). Therefore, the influence of graphite nodules on the fatigue life can be evaluated by the one on the crack growth life, moreover it may be investigated using specimens with a small blind hole. The examples of crack growth curves are shown in Fig.4 as a function of cycle ratio N/N_f. The relation between ln l and N/N_f is almost independent of stress amplitude and can be approximated by a single straight line when the crack is small in each steel. Figure 5 shows the crack growth rates as a function of crack length. In the figure, the results obtained by using pre-cracked specimens under low stress levels are shown in addition to the ones under high stress levels. For every constant stress range, a straight line can be drawn approximately for the crack length smaller than about 3 mm. The slope of a straight line depends on the stress level, and they are about unity when the stress level is high and about 2 when the stress level is low, that is, $dl/dN \propto l$ at a high stress level and $dl/dN \propto l^2$ at a low stress level. Figure 6 shows the crack growth rates as a function of the stress intensity factor range ΔK ($= \frac{2}{\pi} \Delta \sigma \sqrt{\pi l/2}$). Under a low stress level, crack growth rates can be determined uniquely by ΔK. At a high stress level, however, the relation between dl/dN and ΔK depends on the stress level, namely ΔK is not a controlling parameter for crack growth in this range. The stress amplitude where the parameter ΔK is available is below about 60 per cent of the yield or 0.2 % proof stress. These results as mentioned above were similar in many steels not only the examples in Figs.4-6. Figure 7 shows the stress dependence of crack growth under high stress levels where ΔK is not applicable. The relation between the logarithm of the crack growth rate and that of the stress amplitude can be expressed approximately by a straight line in each material, namely $dl/dN \propto \sigma_a^n$. Although the slope of the line, n, is different to some degree in each steel, the results in Figs.5 and 7 mean that the crack growth rates are nearly proportional to $\sigma_a^7 l$ in all steels. Figure 8 shows the relation between the crack growth rate and $\sigma_a^7 l$. The crack growth rates are uniquely determined by $\sigma_a^7 l$ in all steels. Therefore, the evaluation of the influence of graphite nodules on the crack growth rate can be done through the change of constant C_1 in the following equation (12,13);

$$dl/dN = C_1 \sigma_a^n l \quad \text{(n=7 for all steels)} \tag{1}$$

Figure 9 shows the relation between C_1 and several microstructural factors. As seen from Figs.8 and 9, crack growth rates in graphitic steels are higher than those of the ferritic steel, furthermore, crack growth rates increase with increasing the volume fraction of graphite nodule and the correlations between C_1 and other microstructural factors are very small. From these results, the influence of graphite nodules on the number of cycles to failure as mentioned before can be understood.

Fractographic observation

Figure 10 shows the examples of crack observed on the specimen surface, and Fig.11 shows the magnified photographs of crack pass. Although cracks propagate zigzag in all steels, cracks in graphitic steels propagate threading through graphite nodules and intergranular cracks are also observed. These results observed at the specimen surface are also confirmed from examples of fractographs shown in Fig.12. Figure 12 shows the fracture surface of a ferritic steel and a graphitic steel 6C-C which has the least resistance to crack growth in graphitic steels. Although fatigue striations are observed in most of fracture surfaces of all steels, the surface of graphitic steel is rough, and voids and intergranular facets which are related to graphite nodules are partially observed in addition to striations. The static fracture mode increases with the increase in the volume fraction of graphite. These results suggest that the decrease in crack growth resistance due to the existence of graphite nodules is mainly brought by the change of the crack propagation mechanism.

Evaluation of fatigue crack growth resistance of graphitic steels

As mentioned above, crack growth rates increase by the existence of graphite nodules and, in all of a ferritic and graphitic steels, the crack growth rates are uniquely determined by the stress intensity factor range ΔK under low stress levels and by $\sigma_a^n l$ under high stress levels, respectively. Therefore, the resistance for fatigue crack growth of graphitic steels can be evaluated through the two parameters stated above. In this section, the crack growth resistance of graphitic steels is compared with several materials. Materials compared are annealed low and medium carbon steels and a spheroidal graphite cast iron FCD45 (mean ferrite grain size: 35 μm, mean graphite nodule size: 42 μm) (14). Figures 13 and 14 show the results under low and high stress levels, respectively. In Fig.14, the crack growth resistance is evaluated through the constant C_2 in the following equation (15,16);

$$dl/dN = C_2 (\sigma_a/\sigma_B)^n l \tag{2}$$

Equation (2) is derived from Eq.(1) by introducing σ_B in order to consider the material properties partially. As seen from Figs. 13 and 14, the resistance to crack growth in graphitic steels is not inferior to the ones in carbon steels and a spheroidal graphite cast iron, since the matrix of graphitic steels have a sufficient resistance to crack growth and the reduction of resistance due to the existence of graphite nodules is comparatively small.

CONCLUSIONS

Fatigue crack growth tests were carried out on a ferritic single phase steel and several hypo-eutectoid graphitic steels in order to investigate the influence of microstructural factors, i.e., the volume fraction, the size and the distribution of graphite nodules on the crack growth. Main results obtained are summarized as follows: (1) The crack growth rates are uniquely determined by the stress intensity factor range ΔK under low stress levels and $\sigma_a^n l$ under high stress levels, respectively. (2)

The crack growth resistance decreases by the existence of graphite nodules and the main microstructural factor controlling the resistance is the volume fraction of graphite. (3) Voids and intergranular facets increase with the increase in the volume fraction of graphite. This is main reason for the reduction of resistance due to the existence of graphite nodules. (4) Graphitic steels have a sufficient resistance to crack growth as structural materials.

REFERENCES

1. Bonte, F.R. and Fleishman, M., "Developments in Graphitic Steel for Tools and Dies," Metal Progress, 31, 409-410(1937).
2. Honma, M., Meguro, H., Minato, A. and Abe, Y., "On the Various Properties of Nodular Graphite Cast Steel," J. Japan Found. Soc., 31, 9-19(1959).
3. Ototani, T. and Masuko, Y., "Study on Nodular Graphite Steel Rolls," J. Iron and Steel Inst. Japan, 46, 669-677(1962).
4. Sueyoshi, H., Ohshige, T., Suenaga, T. and Tanaka, R., "Machinability of Hypo-Eutectoid Graphitic Steel," J. Japan Inst. Metals, 52, 1285-1292(1988).
5. Sueyoshi, H., Suenaga, K. and Tanaka, R., "Cold Forgeability and Machinability after Cold Forging of Hypo-Eutectoid Graphitic Steels," J. Japan Inst. Metals, 53, 206-211(1989).
6. Sueyoshi, H. Suenaga, K. and Tanaka, R., "Effect of Microstructural Factors on the Tensile Properties of Hypo-Eutectoid Grphitic Steels," Trans. Japan Inst. Metals, 26, 397-404(1985).
7. Sueyoshi, H., Suenaga, K. and Tanaka, R., "Ductile Fracture of Hypo-Eutectoid Graphitic Steels," J. Japan Inst. Metals, 51, 1139-1144(1987).
8. Sueyoshi, H., Suenaga, K. and Tanaka, R., " Effects of Microstructural Factors on Fatigue Limit of Hypo-Eutectoid Graphitic Steels," J. Japan Inst. Metals, 48, 965-971(1984).
9. Suzuki, H., Ueki, T. and Kobayashi, T., "Effects of Composite Microstructures on Threshold of Fatigue Crack Propagation, ΔK_{th} in Toughened Austempered Ductile Cast Iron," Trans. Japan Soc. Mech. Eng., 57, 1029-1034(1991).
10. Sugiyama, Y., Asami, K. and Kuroiwa, H., "Fatigue Crack Propagation Characteristics of Ductile Cast Iron Austempered from ($\alpha + \beta$) Phase Region," J. of the Soc. of Mater. Sci., 39, 65-71(1990).
11. Kawagoishi, N., Sueyoshi, H. and Nisitani, H., "Evaluation of Fatigue Crack Growth Resistance of Graphite Steels based on the Small-Crack Growth Law," Trans. Japan Soc. Mech. Eng., 55, 416-423 (1989).
12. Nisitani,H., "Unifying Treatment of Fatigue Crack Growth in Small, Large and Non-propagating Cracks," ASME AMD, 47, 151-166(1981).
13. Nisitani, H. and Kawagoishi, N., "Fatigue Crack Growth Laws in Small and Large Cracks and Their Physical Background," JSME Int. J. Ser. I, 35, 1-11(1992).
14. Nisitani, H. and Tanaka, S., "Initiation and Propagation of Fatigue Crack in Cast Irons (Rotating Bending Fatigue Tests of FC25 and FCD45)," Trans. Japan Soc. Mech. Eng., 51, 1442-1447(1985).
15. Hisitani, H. "Behavior of Small Cracks in Fatigue and Relating Phenomena, Current Research on Fatigue Cracks(eds. Tanaka, T., Jono, M. and Komai, K.),The Soc. of Mater. Sci., 1-22(1985).
16. Nisitani, H. and Goto, M. "A Small Crack Growth Law and Its Application to the Evaluation of Fatigue Life," The Behavior of Short Fatigue Cracks, EGF, Pub., 9, 461-478(1986).

Table 1 Chemical composition

(Mass %)

Steel	C	Si	Mn	Al	P	S	Cu	Ni	Cr	Mo
F	0.004	1.17	0.34	0.039	0.005	0.004	<0.01	2.01	0.01	0.01
2C	0.21	1.20	0.31	0.039	0.005	0.005	<0.01	2.05	0.01	0.01
4C	0.41	1.19	0.31	0.039	0.005	0.003	<0.01	2.02	0.01	0.01
6C	0.59	1.19	0.31	0.039	0.005	0.003	<0.01	2.04	0.01	0.01

Table 3 Microstructural factors

Steel	F	2C-A	2C-B	4C-A	4C-B	6C-A	6C-B	6C-C
$f (\times 10^{-2})$	–	0.726	0.726	1.41	1.41	2.02	2.02	2.02
$d_g (\mu m)$	–	22	24	4.8	4.4	7.4	4.9	21
$\lambda (mm)$	–	2	0.22	0.22	0.2	0.24	0.16	0.07
$d_f (\mu m)$	35	20	13	12	35	39	28	20

f: volume fraction of graphite
d_g: mean graphite nodule diameter
λ: mean ferrite path between graphite nodules
d_f: ferrite grain size

Table 2 Heat treatment

Steel	Graphite steel	Pre-treatment (0.5h)	Graphitization time at 680℃(h)
F	–	960℃ A.C.	—
2C	2C-A	960℃ A.C.	30
	2C-B	900℃ A.C.	7
4C	4C-A	850℃ A.C.	8
	4C-B	850℃ W.Q.	7
6C	6C-A	960℃ A.C.	18
	6C-B	830℃ A.C.	9
	6C-C	830℃ W.Q.	5

A.C.: Air cooled   W.Q.: Water quenched

Table 4 Mechanical properties

Steel	σ_{s1}(MPa)	σ_B(MPa)	σ_T(MPa)	ψ(%)
F	375	493	1691	88.5
2C-A	365	500	1173	78.8
2C-B	354	522	1156	69.6
4C-A	374	524	1051	63.8
4C-B	'293	487	952	63.6
6C-A	'298	482	697	39.0
6C-B	'299	492	886	56.9
6C-C	'298	508	933	57.2

'$\sigma_{0.2}$

σ_{s1}: yield stress, σ_B: tensile strength
σ_T: ultimate tensile strength,
ψ: reduction of area

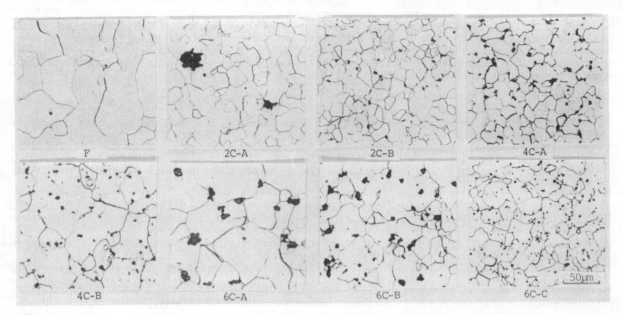

Fig. 1 Microstructures

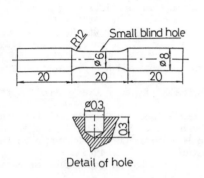

Fig.2 Shape and dimensions of specimen

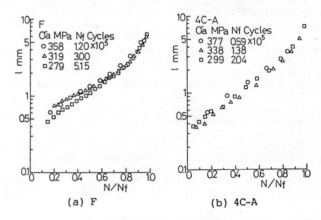

(a) F   (b) 4C-A

Fig.4 Crack growth curves

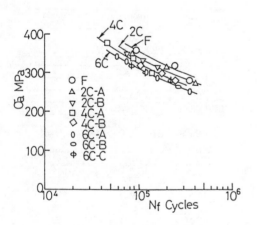

Fig.3 S - N_f curves

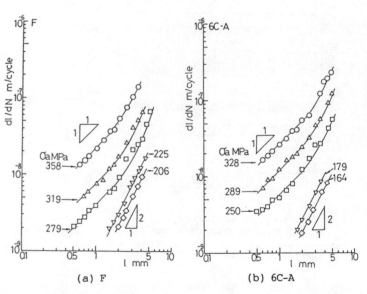

(a) F   (b) 6C-A

Fig.5 Relation between crack growth rate and crack length

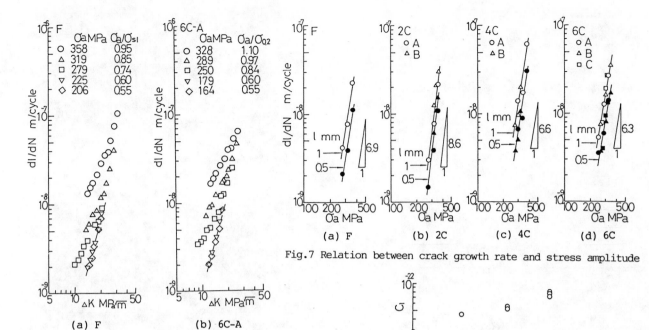

Fig.7 Relation between crack growth rate and stress amplitude

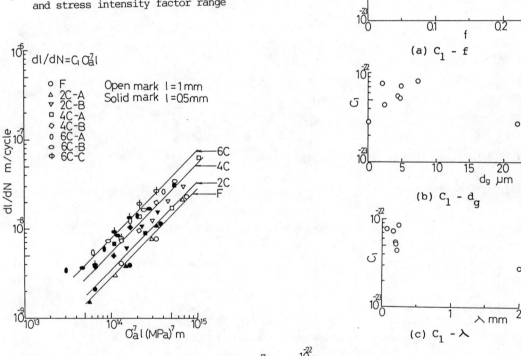

Fig.6 Relation between crack growth rate and stress intensity factor range

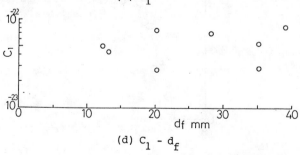

Fig.9 Relation between C_1 and microstructural factors
(The definition of notations is found in Table 3)

$dl/dN = C_1 \sigma_a^7 l$

Open mark $l = 1mm$
Solid mark $l = 0.5mm$

○ F
△ 2C-A
▽ 2C-B
□ 4C-A
◇ 4C-B
⬡ 6C-A
⬡ 6C-B
Φ 6C-C

Fig.8 Relation between crack growth rate and $\sigma_a^7 l$

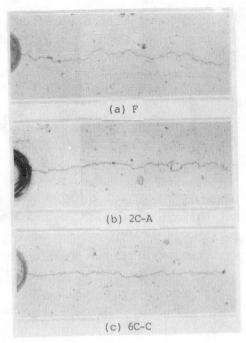

(a) F

(b) 2C-A

(c) 6C-C

Fig.10 Cracks observed on the specimen surface

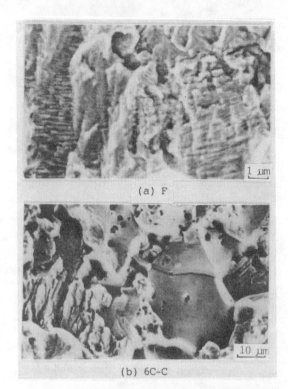

(a) F

(b) 6C-C

Fig. 12 Fractographs

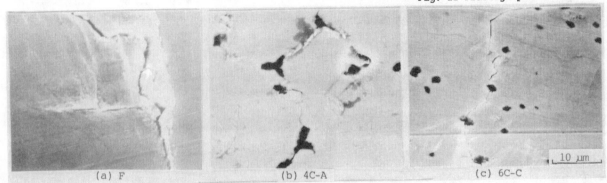

(a) F   (b) 4C-A   (c) 6C-C

Fig.11 Surface cracks magnified by SEM

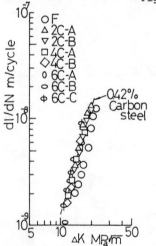

Fig.13 Relation between crack growth rate

and stress intensity factor

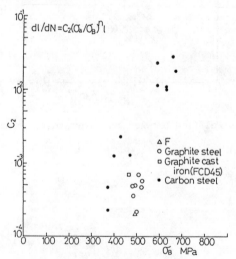

Fig.14 Relation between C_2 and σ_B

BEHAVIOR OF FATIGUE CRACKS FROM HOLE DEFECTS
IN THE SURFACE OF STEEL PLATES FOR PRESSURE VESSEL

S. H. Song and K. R. Lee

ABSTRACT

Two differnt hole defects are machined adjacently in steel plates for pressure vessel and it is investigated the behavior of fatigue cracks under constant bending fatigue stress and examined about transient fatigue crack growth rate following the single-overlaod.

According to the interaction effects of stress fields around the hole defects, the initiation and the growth of fatigue cracks between two hole defects were faster than that of outside. In addition, at an early stage, fatigue crack growth to the direction of the depth was faster than that of the surface. Right after the single-overload, the fatigue crack growth rate was reduced rapidly, it was showed that it was related to the behavior of crack opening and ΔCOD.

INTRODUCTION

The reduction of the number of fracture cycles or the fatigue limit is caused mainly by the existence of flaws. The influence of flaws on the behavior of fatigue crack growth depends on the geometry , size, direction and location of flaws[1, 2, 3, 4, 5]. Specially in case of more than two flaws, it varied in accordance with the spacing between the center of the two flaws. Murakami and Nemat-Nassaer [1] reported that the stress intensity factor calculated by body force method was increased rapidly in the range of $L \leq (2a_1 + a_2)/2$, where a_1, a_2 are small and large crack radius respectively and 2L is the spacing between the center of the two cracks. When the ratio of depth and radius of twin hole defects h/r is 2, and the spacing between the center of the two holes is 4r, stresses between two flaws interact to each other [2]. Saito[4] reported that the stress field was distributed to about 3r as the result of analyzing the problem with uniaxial tension, in case the flaw was presented as a pit on the surface of semi-infinite elastic body. In addition to this, in the case of the materials under rotary bending stress, the range of the interaction of a stress field is $L/r \leq 3$ by experiment when the radius of hole is r, the distance between the center of holes is 2L [5]. Similarly, many researches on the flaws that are distributed variously in the materials and the mutual interferences of cracks that are initiated and propagated between the flaws have been performed by analytical or experimental methods. However, a detailed investigation on the crack behavior is still important assignment in the case where the defects have interference of stress field, or have independent stress field, and it is needed to be investigated the variation of internal and surface crack.

On the other hand, the machine components or structural elements are subjeted to variable stresses according to environments and driving conditions, and the research on the fatigue crack behavior under the variable stresses is practically very important. There have been many researches on the influence of the variable stresses on the behavior of crack propagation. Ward-Close [6] explained that the phenomenon of crack retardation was occured when the 100% single overload was acted on the cracked titanium alloy, and investigated it as the crack closure mechanism's viewpoint. McMillan and Pelloux [7] investigated the influence of the overload on the crack propagation rate by measuring the spacing of the striation of Al alloy, and reported that the COD ratio of before and after overload have influenced on the crack growth behavior. Song [8] reported that the acceleration of the crack growth rate arose, in case the high-low step load acted on the hole-defected circular beam and it was related to the failure zone of around the fatigue crack tip. Kurihara [9] reported that the transitional phenomenon of the crack propagation rate under the high-low, low-high step loading can be explained by considering the change of the effective stress range ratio U after the change of load amplitude. But the above investigations are mostly related to the long crack and it is hardly able to find the influence of variable stresses on the short crack. All kinds of fatigue failures are started from the growth of a short crack. As the mechanism of a short crack growth differs from that of a long crack, a consideration on the influence of a step load on the short crack seems to be very important.

On the basis of the above researches, the followings have been investigated.
1. Studies and comparisons on crack behavior for the hole defects with the interaction of stress fields and without the interaction of stress field.
2. Investigation and comparison of surface and internal crack growth.
3. Crack growth behavior and variation of COD in case a single-overload acts on the short crack in the range of interaction of stress field.

SPECIMEN AND EXPERIMENTAL PROCEDURES

The materials used in this investigation are Cr-Mo steel plates for pressure vessel, and its chemical composition and mechanical properties are showed in Table 1 and Table 2. The fatigue test was examined under out of plane bending fatigue stress, Fig.1 (a) shows the specimen geometry and (b) indicates the shape of hole defects as well as the crack length. The hole defects are drilled, and are specified the diameter of a small hole as d_S, depth h_S, diameter of a large hole d_L, depth h_L and spacing between two hole edges S. When the interaction of stress fields exists, S/ds is set to 1 in order to investigate the crack growth behavior. It is compared and studied on the behavior of the cracks occured from the hole defects and the cracks occured to the outside from the hole defects which maintain the independence of stress fields. h_L/d_L is set to 1 , the aspect ratio of a small hole h_S/d_S is varied to 2, 4, 6, and 8 respctively in order to investigate the influence

Professor and Graduate Student, respectively, Department of Mechanical Engineering, Korea University, Seoul, Korea.

of the change of the hole defects on the crack behavior. Table 3 represents the specimens PB1, 2, 3 and 4 respctively.

The stress model which is performed in this study is specified in Fig. 2, where (a) R=-1, σ_{1max}=166.7MPa, (b) R=-0.5, $\sigma_{2max}=2\sigma_{1max}$=333.4MPa in case a single overload is acted on. In order to investigate the influence of the variable stresses at the range which has a short crack and occurs a stress concentration and an interaction of stress fields, a single overload is acted on the specimens when the crack occured between the flaws is about 0.2mm. And, in order to measure the COD according to the stress change , the microvickers indentation is treated along the cracks and the plastic replica method is used.

RESULTS AND DISCUSSION

1. Crack behavior occured from the two adjacent hole defects.

Relations for the number of stresses, N, and the crack length, a, for specimens PB1 and PB3 are indecated in Fig. 3 and Fig. 4, and that for the crack growth rate ,da/dN, and the crack length, a, are specified in Fig. 5 and Fig. 6. From the above figures, the initiation and propagation rate of crack a_2 and a_3 which occured in the section having an interaction of the stress field is much faster than that of crack a_1 and a_4, and the crack propagation rate which just before the two crack coalesces is similar to that leads to unstable fracture. This phenomenon can be explained in two ways. First, since the distance between the hole defects is 0.5 mm, a crack occured between them is regarded as a short crack [10]. The crack propagation rate of this short crack is faster than that of a long crack in the same ΔK because of the crack closure phenomenon and the plastic zone formulated in notch and crack tip [11]. Second, it is because of the interaction of the stress fields occured between both edges of the hole defects. The first phenomenon is understood by the behavior of cracks a_1 and a_4 in Fig. 5 and Fig. 6, and the crack propagation rate in an early stage of crack growth is found to be very high. While, a propagation rate of cracks a_2 and a_3 is faster than that of cracks a_1 and a_4, this implies that the interaction of the stress fields between the edge of hole defects has much influence on the initiation and growth of cracks, and this also explains the 2nd phenomenon and can be understood that a crack reacts sensitively on the stress fields from defects as well.

Fig. 7, 8 and Fig. 9, 10 shows the crack behaviors propagated to each direction for the specimens PB1, 2, 3 and 4. In Fig. 7 and Fig. 9, it can be understood that a fatigue life, N_f, increases in the order of PB4, 3, 2 and 1. This is because the stress concentration in a small hole becomes relatively high as h_S/d_S increases. In Fig. 9, the propagation of a crack at the same crack length also has a tendency of increase in an early stage of crack growth as h_S/d_S increases. But in Fig. 8 and 10, it is showed somewhat different tendency, this tendency is regarded that the crack growth behavior is influenced not only by the stress field but also by the metal structure when the crack length is short.

The crack behavior occured between holes is showed in Fig. 8 and 10, the propagation rate of a_2 is faster than that of a_3 in the initiation of crack and a_2 is longer in the crack position when it coalesces. This is because the stress concentration factor for a small hole

is higher than that of a large hole, and also because the larger the ratio of h_S/d_S is, the higher the stress concentration coefficient is [2]. And, just before a_2 and a_3 coalesce as in Fig. 10, the crack propagation rate has a very high value, this is because the stress intensity factor becomes very high when two cracks coalesce[1]. While, it is observed that da_1/dN increases steeply until a_1 is 0.23mm, then it dropped suddenly as in Fig. 9, this implies that the plastic zone occured at a small hole defect is about 0.23mm, and it is because the effective stress range U is increase up to the range occured the plastic zone [12].

Photo 1 represents the crack growth behavior of specimen PB3, crack a_2 represents the fastest initiation and propagations, and the position of crack coalescence of it is also much longer than a_3. But, a crack a_1 which occured from a small hole exceeds 0.5mm, a crack a_4 which occured from a large hole also increases same rate as a_1, this proves above results as well.

2. Behavior of surface and internal crack growth.

The behavior of surface and internal crack growth for specimens PB1, 2, 3, and 4 is specified in Fig. 11 and 12, it shows that the internal crack growth is faster than the surface crack growth in an early stage of crack growth, but surface crack growth is gradually faster than internal crack growth as crack propagates. The sepcimen PB1, 2, 3, and 4 are performed a temper color through heat treatment on the cross section after beach marking, and they are indicated in photo2, it shows the behavior of internal cracks as well as that of surface cracks. As before, a growth of internal crack is faster than that of surface crack in an early stage of crack growth, this is because the initial stress field occured around defect.

On the other hand, a change of surface crack and internal crack from a small hole defects which the aspect ratio of hole defects changes according to specimens as in Fig. 11. But, in the case of large hole defects which the aspect ratio of hole defects is constant, it is understood that the change of cracks is showed to be a curve as in Fig. 12. Thus, the relation of relative crack depth b/t and the crack aspect ratio b/t is indicated in semi-log graph as in Fig. 13 and 14. The slopes of these graphes are varied according to the shapes of small hole defects, but in case the of a large hole defect which the aspect ratio of defects is constant, since b_4/t and b_4/a_4 is in the narrow scattered band, this can be specified as a straight line, and it has the relation that $b_4/t = -A \times \ln(b_4/a_4)+B$. It is resulted out that A=0.277 and B=0.283 in this study.

3. Crack growth behavior in case acted on single-overload

A crack behavior is experimented when a single-overload acted upon the short crack occured between the edges of two holes. The influence of a single overload acted on the behavior of crack a_2 for a specimen PB1 is showed in Fig. 15. It occured a sudden decrease of crack propagation rate just after a single overload of $2\sigma_{1max}$ is acted on the specimen when a_2 is 0.173mm. When a crack a_2 is about 0.26mm, it is recovered to the original propagation rate. These mechanisms are based on concepts as follows: (1) residual stresses, where the higher strain generated by the overload results in the residual compressive stress field ahead of the crack on unloading[6]; (2) crack closure , where the residual stresses lead to enhanced

628

plasticity-induced closure in the wake of the advancing crack[13] ; (3) plastic blunting of the crack tip at the overload ; (4) crack deflection, and so on. Since the effects of residual stresses, phenomenon of crack closure and plastic blunting have to do with the change of COD, the change of COD is focused on this study.

Changing the stresses between A and B which just before the single overload is acted on, and between C and D right after the single overload is acted on [Fig.2(b)], it is observed the change of COD as in Fig.16 and Fig.17. Photo 3 is a microphotograph of replica which is made in experiment. A stress amplitude $\Delta \sigma$ and a effective stress range ratio U can be defined as follows,

$$\Delta \sigma = \sigma_{max} - \sigma_{min} \qquad (1)$$
$$U = (\sigma_{min} - \sigma_{op})/\Delta \sigma \qquad (2)$$

where, σ_{op} is a crack opening stress. Thus, da/dN and the effective stress intensity factor range ΔK_{eff} is specified as follows,

$$da/dN = C(\Delta K_{eff})^m = C(U \cdot \Delta K)^m \qquad (3)$$

That is, the larger the U, the faster the da/dN. In comparision with Fig.16 and 17, U before an overload is acted on is 0.5, but U after overloading is 0.15. Thus, from eq (3), it is understood that da/dN after overloading is much smaller than before, and the magnitude of ΔCOD, which is about 50% of that before an overload is acted on, can also be ascertained the decrease of da/dN [7].

CONCLUSIONS

It is studied on the case that a constant cyclic stress and a single overload acted on the steel plate for pressure vessel which is machined two hole flaws having different size and depth, and acquired the results as follows.

1. The growth behavior of initial crack occured at the edges of defects responds sensitively to the stress fields which is distributed around the hole defects, specially, in case there is an interaction of stress fields between the edges of holes, a crack growth rate is faster than that of no interaction case.

2. The growth behavior of surface crack and internal crack differs according to the aspect ratio of the flaws. A relative crack depth b/t and a crack aspect ratio b/a have the relation that b/t = -A× ln(b/a)+B. In this study, A=0.267 and B=0.283 is acquired in case of $d_L = h_L = 1.5mm$.

3. The influence of a single-overload on a short crack subjected to the stress concentration and the interaction of the stress fields is studied. The decrease of a crack propagation rate is observed after a single overload is acted on. This results from the decrease of effective stress range ratio and ΔCOD after the overloading.

REFERENCES

[1] Y.Murakami and S.Nemat-Nasser, "Interaction Dissimilar Semi-elliptical Surface Flaws under Tension and Bending", Engi., Frac., Mech., Vol.16, No3, pp 373-386, 1982.

[2] J.B.Kim, "A Study for the Stress Interaction between Surface Micro Defects and The Effects of Stress Field for Initiation and Propagation of Cracks Emanating from Surface Micro Defects", Korea University, Seoul, Korea, Dept. of Mech., Engi. 1992.

[3] H.Tada, P.C.Paris and G.R.Irwin, "The Stress Analysis of Cracks Handbook", pp 20.1-20.2, Del Research Corporation, Hellertown, Pennsylvania, 1973.

[4] K.Saito, I.Nakahara, "Uniaxial Tension of a Semi-Infinite Body with a Hemispherical pit", Trans. of the JSME, Vol.33, No.247, pp 343-350, 1967.

[5] S.H.Song and W.S.Oh, "Behavior of Initiation and Propagation of Fatigue Cracks around Microhole", Proc. of the First Conference on Mechanical Behavior, Seoul, korea, pp 251-258, 1987.

[6] C.M.Ward-Close and R.O.Ritchie, "On the Role of Crack Closure Mechanism in Influencing Fatigue Crack Growth Following Tensile Overloads in a Titanium Alloy : Near Threshold versus Higher ΔK Behavior", ASTM STP 982, pp 93-111, 1988.

[7] J.C.McMillan and R.M.Pelloux, Engineering Fracture Mechanics, 2, p81, 1970.

[8] S.H.Song and S.T.Won, "Behavior of Initiation and Propagation of Fatigue Crack under Periodic Overstressing(Ⅱ)", Trans. of the KSME, Vol.10, No.2, pp 188-197, 1986.

[9] M.Kurihara, A.Katoh and M.Kawahara, "Effects of Stress Ratio and Step Loading on Fatigue Crack Propagation Rate", Current Japanese Materials Research, Vol.1, pp 247-265, 1987.

[10] S.Suresh and R.O.Ritchie, "Propagation of Short Fatigue Cracks", International Metals Reviews, Vol.29, No.6, pp 445-475, 1984.

[11] S.J.Hudak, "Small Crack Behavior and the Prediction of Fatigue Life", Trans. of the ASME, Vol. 103, pp 26-35, 1981.

[12] K. Ogura, Y.Miyoshi and I.Nishikawa, "Fatigue Crack Growth and Closure of Small Cracks at the Notch Root", Current Japanese Material Research, Vol.1, pp 67-91, 1987.

[13] W.Elber, "Damage Tolerance in Air Craft Structures", ASTM STP 486, Philadelpia, pp 230-242, 1971.

Table 1 : Chemical Composition of the Testing Material.

Material	Composition(Wt%)							
	C	Si	Mn	P	Ni	Cr	Mo	Cu
SA 387	0.12	0.55	0.53	0.007	0.03	1.40	0.55	0.2

Table 2 : Mechanical Properties of the Testing Material.

Yield strength (MPa)	Ultimate strength (MPa)	Elongation (%)	Reduction of Area (%)	Elastic Modulus (Mpa)
281.26	480.20	24.39	60.53	156368.8

Table 3 : Types of the specimens

	h_L/d_L	d_S (mm)	h_S (mm)	h_S/d_S
PB1	1	0.5	1.0	2
PB2	1	0.5	2.0	4
PB3	1	0.5	3.0	6
PB4	1	0.5	4.0	8

(d_L = 1.5mm, h_L = 1.5mm)

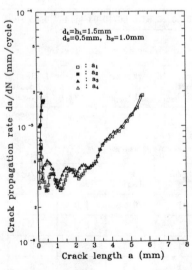

(detailed drawing of A)

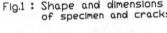

(near the holes at the cross section of B-B)

(b) Shape of cracks

Fig.1 : Shape and dimensions of specimen and cracks

(a) Geometry of specimen

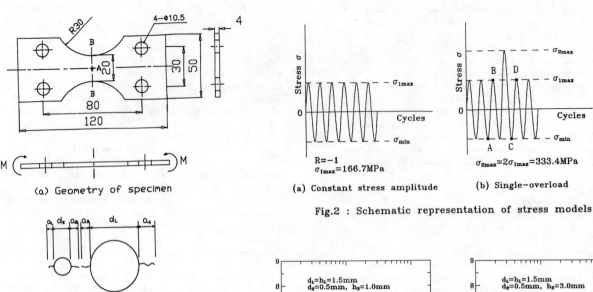

(a) Constant stress amplitude

$R=-1$
$\sigma_{1max}=166.7MPa$

(b) Single-overload

$\sigma_{2max}=2\sigma_{1max}=333.4MPa$

Fig.2 : Schematic representation of stress models

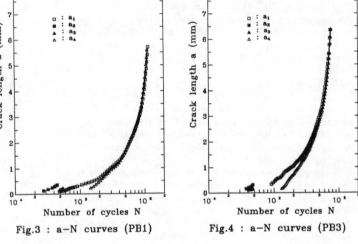

Fig.3 : a–N curves (PB1)

Fig.4 : a–N curves (PB3)

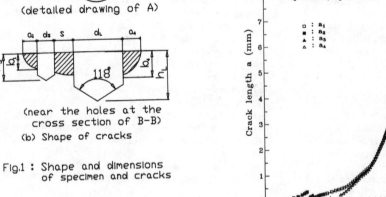

Fig.5 : da/dN–a curves (PB1)

Fig.6 : da/dN–a curves (PB3)

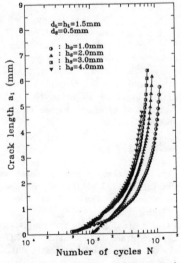

Fig.7 : a_1–N curves (PB1,2,3,4)

630

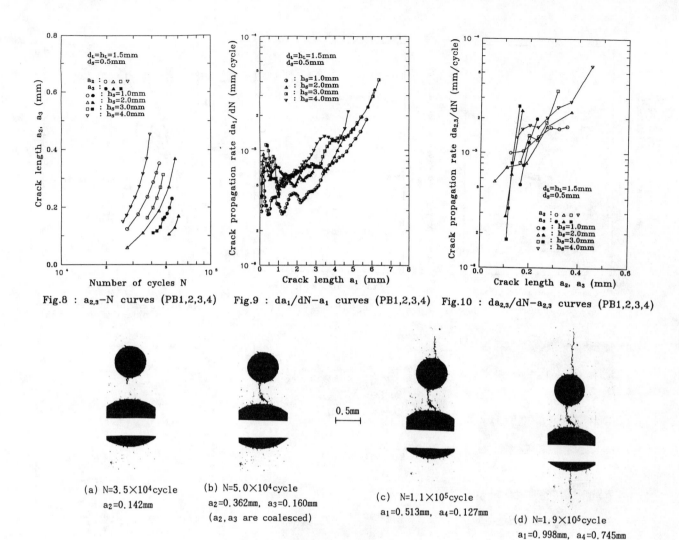

Fig.8 : $a_{2,3}$–N curves (PB1,2,3,4)　　Fig.9 : da_1/dN–a_1 curves (PB1,2,3,4)　　Fig.10 : $da_{2,3}/dN$–$a_{2,3}$ curves (PB1,2,3,4)

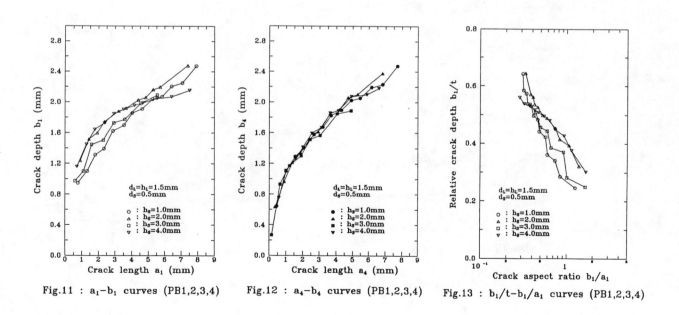

(a) $N=3.5×10^4$cycle
$a_2=0.142$mm

(b) $N=5.0×10^4$cycle
$a_2=0.362$mm, $a_3=0.160$mm
(a_2, a_3 are coalesced)

0.5mm

(c) $N=1.1×10^5$cycle
$a_1=0.513$mm, $a_4=0.127$mm

(d) $N=1.9×10^5$cycle
$a_1=0.998$mm, $a_4=0.745$mm

Photo 1 : Crack initiation and propagation (PB3 ; $d_L=h_L=1.5$mm, $d_S=0.5$mm, $h_S=3.0$mm)

Fig.11 : a_1–b_1 curves (PB1,2,3,4)　　Fig.12 : a_4–b_4 curves (PB1,2,3,4)　　Fig.13 : b_1/t–b_1/a_1 curves (PB1,2,3,4)

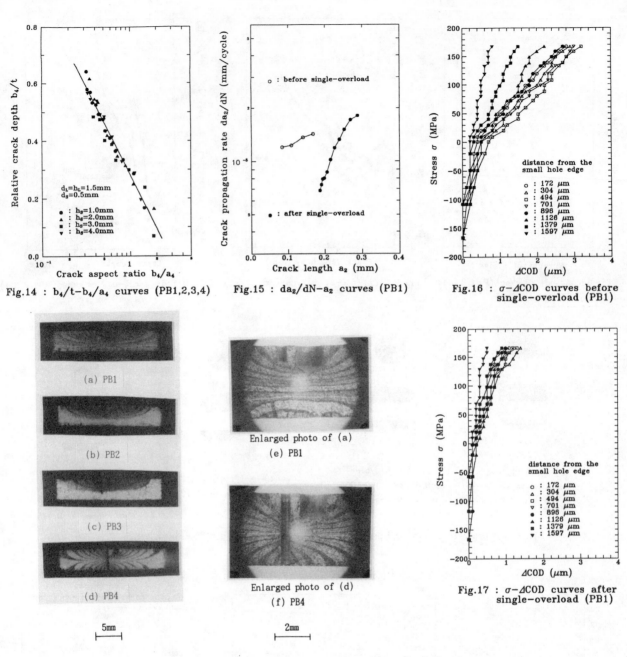

Fig.14 : $b_4/t-b_4/a_4$ curves (PB1,2,3,4)

Fig.15 : $da_2/dN-a_2$ curves (PB1)

Fig.16 : $\sigma-\Delta$COD curves before single-overload (PB1)

Fig.17 : $\sigma-\Delta$COD curves after single-overload (PB1)

(a) PB1

(b) PB2

(c) PB3

(d) PB4

Enlarged photo of (a)

(e) PB1

Enlarged photo of (d)

(f) PB4

5mm

2mm

Photo 2 : Shapes of surface and internal cracks

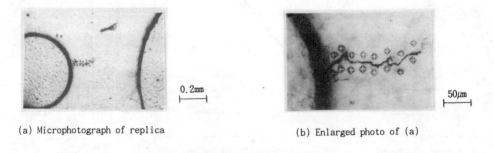

(a) Microphotograph of replica

0.2mm

(b) Enlarged photo of (a)

50μm

photo 3 : Microvickers indentation and cracked small hole (PB1)

632

UNIAXIAL RATCHETTING AND CREEP BEHAVIOR OF TYPE 304 STAINLESS STEEL AFTER CYCLIC LOADING

K. SASAKI and H. ISHIKAWA

Department Mechanical Engineering II
Hokkaido University
Sapporo, 060 Japan

ABSTRACT

A series of tests for creep and uniaxial ratchetting of type 304 stainless steel after cyclic preloading were carried out at room temperature. Namely, the specimens were subject to intermittent creep at several stress levels or subject to uniaxial ratchetting after stabilization of a stress-strain loop of cyclic tension-compression preloading with a constant strain amplitude under a constant stress rate. As a result, creep strain could be represented by the modified Bailey-Norton law with stress levels from the current center of the yield surface (back stress), which was determined by the constitutive model proposed. It was also appear that the model could be applicable to predict uniaxial ratchetting.

INTRODUCTION

Many parts of space crafts, airplanes, nuclear systems are subject to complex load histories combined cyclic plasticity, creep, and ratchetting. The constitutive model available for the design of these parts is required and many models have been proposed [1,2]. Chaboche [1] proposed a unified constitutive model, and verified its applicability from the experiment with type 304 stainless steel. However, there is few constitutive model to explain uniaxial ratchetting and creep after cyclic loading.

Experimental observation is very important to construct the unified constitutive model. Kujawski [3] conducted creep and stress relaxation tests at several stress levels during cyclic tension-compression loading. The following interesting observation was obtained that creep strain progresses outside of the hysteresis loop at the maximum or the minimum stress level of the loop, and inside of the hysteresis loop at the zero stress during unloading. These results suggest that the stress level at which creep strain does not progress should exist. Unfortunately, they did not pay their attentions to this stress level. On the other hand, Krempl [2] conducted combined tests of cyclic plasticity and uniaxial ratchetting, and he achieved to predict them with the model based on the concept of overstress.

The authors have proposed the constitutive model for cyclic plasticity in which the following assumptions were included[4]: (1) The plastic-deformation-induced anisotropy and the motion of the center of the yield surface are incorporated in the yield function. (2) The associated plastic flow is derived from the normality of the plastic strain increment to the yield surface. (3) The Ziegler type of kinematic hardening is used as the evolution equation of the center of the yield surface. (4) All the stress-strain curves in cyclic loading are represented by the modified Ramberg-Osgood law. These four assumptions have been confirmed to be adequate from the experiment of proportional and nonproportional loading, and the computer simulations.

In this paper, using type 304 stainless steel, the center of the yield surface (back stress) in cyclic plasticity was confirmed to play an important role to describe the creep behavior following cyclic preloading. Namely, after the specimen was subjected to cyclic tension-compression loading until the stress-strain loop was stable, intermittent creep tests were conducted at several stress levels. The subsequent creep curves were expressed by the effective stress which measured from the center of the yield surface prescribed by the proposed model. Moreover, using the proposed model, the simulations of uniaxial ratchetting after cyclic tension-compression loading were also performed.

EXPERIMENTAL APPARATUS

The specimens used in this work have the gauge length of 50mm, and the inner and the outer radii of 20mm and 23 mm, respectively. The specimens were made of type 304 stainless steel subjected to a solution heat treatment at 1070°C ; its chemical compositions were 0.05C, 0.38Si, 1.56Mn, 0.037P, 0.003S, 9.22Ni, 18.49Cr and Fe balance in weight percent. Young's modulus at room temperature was equal to E=198GPa, while shearing modulus G=73.5GPa.

The servo-controlled axial-torsional testing machine (Shimazu EHF-EB10), together with both the Shimazu 4825 controller and the computer (NEC PC-9801vm), was used for computerized testing and data acquisition accomplished by the program written in Machine Word. Strains were measured using two strain gauges applied on diametrically opposite side of the specimens. The axial force and torque were measured using load cells incorporated in the machine.

The stress controlled mode was used for creep and uniaxial ratchetting tests. The resulting stress-strain responses were recorded on a floppy-disk by the computer. A data point was recorded whenever stress changed by 5MPa for both the cyclic tension-compression and the uniaxial ratchetting tests, or whenever time changed by 0.5 seconds for creep tests.

EXPERIMENTAL PROCEDURE

Intermittent creep tests were performed at several stress levels, as shown schematically in Fig. 1, after stabilization of a stress-strain loop of cyclic tension-compression preloading with the constant strain amplitude of 1% under the constant stress rate of 10MPa/s. The values of the stress levels at a ~ k are also shown in Fig. 1. Creep tests were conducted at these stress levels during time interval 300 seconds.

Uniaxial ratchetting tests were performed as the following procedure: The specimens were subjected to cyclic tension-compression preloading with the strain amplitude of 1% under the stress rate of 10MPa/s until the hysteresis loops were stabilized. At the tensile maximum point of the stabilized loop, the stress σ_{max} was recorded, which was corresponded to the maximum ratchetting stress level. Unloading from σ_{max} to zero stress with the constant stress rate, 20 cycles between zero stress and ratchetting stress level were conducted with the constant stress rate. Three constant stress rates of 5, 10 and 20MPa/s during uniaxial ratchetting tests were chosen in order to examine the effect of the stress rate on the uniaxial ratchetting.

CONSTITUTIVE MODEL

A brief summary of the mathematical structure of the proposed model is reproduced from [4]. Combined the von Mises stress hardening form with the kinematic hardening, the following yield function (1) is chosen for cyclically stable material at temperature T,

$$f = \frac{1}{2} C_{ijkl} (\sigma_{ij} - \alpha_{ij}) (\sigma_{kl} - \alpha_{kl}) - \frac{1}{3} R^2 (\kappa, T) = 0 \tag{1}$$

where C_{ijkl} is plastic-deformation-induced-anisotropy coefficient tensor of 4th rank, σ_{ij} and α_{ij} are stress and the coordinate of the current center in the stress space, R is the flow stress and κ is the hardening or softening parameter. Associated to (1), the modified Lévy-Mises equations of cyclic plasticity are obtained from the normality of the plastic strain increment to the yield surface,

$$d\varepsilon_{ij}^p = \frac{3 d\bar{\varepsilon}^p}{2R} C_{ijkl} (\sigma_{kl} - \alpha_{kl}) \tag{2}$$

where $d\varepsilon_{ij}^p$ and $d\bar{\varepsilon}^p$ are the plastic strain increment and the equivalent plastic strain increment, respectively. Using Ziegler type of assumption as the evolution equation of the center of the yield surface, then the motion of the center is given by,

$$d\alpha_{ij} = \frac{3}{2R^2} \{ C_{klmn} (\sigma_{mn} - \alpha_{mn}) d\sigma_{kl} \} (\sigma_{ij} - \alpha_{ij}) - \left(\frac{dR}{dW^p} \right) (\sigma_{ij} - \alpha_{ij}) d\bar{\varepsilon}^p \tag{3}$$

where dW^p is the modified plastic work increment. The hardening or softening parameter κ is reasonably assumed to be a scalar proportional to the modified plastic work.

$$d\kappa = dW^p = Rd\bar{\varepsilon}^p = (\sigma_{ij} - \alpha_{ij}) d\varepsilon_{ij}^p \tag{4}$$

Let us assume that all the stress-strain curves in cyclic loading are represented well by the modified Ramberg-Osgood law which should be applied from the current center of the yield surface,

$$\varepsilon_t - e_t = \frac{\sigma_t - \alpha_t}{E}\left[1 + K\left\{\frac{\bar{\sigma}}{\sigma_{0(n)}}\right\}^{m_{(n)}}\right] \tag{5}$$

where σ_t, ε_t, α_t and e_t are the uniaxial stress, uniaxial strain, the center of the yield surface and the strain at the center, and $\bar{\sigma} = \sqrt{\frac{3}{2}\,C_{ijkl}(\sigma_{ij} - \alpha_{ij})(\sigma_{kl} - \alpha_{kl})}$ is the equivalent stress. $\sigma_{0(n)}$ and $m_{(n)}$ are the stress at the proof strain $\varepsilon_0 = 500\mu m/m$ and the exponent of hardening or softening after the (n-1)th inversion of loading, and they depend on the modified plastic work according to the following Eqs. (6, 7),

$$\sigma_{0(n)} = \sigma_{0(\infty)}\left[1 \stackrel{-}{_+} \alpha \exp\left\{-\frac{W^p_{(n-1)}}{W_0}\right\}\right], \qquad (n > 2) \tag{6}$$

$$m_{(n)} = m_{(\infty)}\left[1 \stackrel{-}{_+} \beta \exp\left\{-\frac{W^p_{(n-1)}}{W_1}\right\}\right], \qquad (n > 2) \tag{7}$$

where $\sigma_{0(\infty)}$, α, W_0, $m_{(\infty)}$, β and W_1 are material constants prescribed by the history of loading or effected by a strain path memory.

Let us assume that the flow stress R after (n-1)th inversion of loading can be prescribed by the Eq. (8) following Eq. (6),

$$R_{(n)} = R_{(\infty)}\left[1 \stackrel{-}{_+} \lambda \exp\left\{-\frac{W^p}{W_2}\right\}\right] \tag{8}$$

where W^p is the accumulated plastic work which is equal to $W^p = W^p_{(n-1)} + dW^p$ with the modified plastic work increment dW^p during loading in the current stage of deformation. $R_{(\infty)}$, λ and W_2 are constants prescribed by the history of loading or effected by a strain path memory.

CREEP DURING CYCLIC LOADING

The specimens were subjected to stress-controlled tension-compression loading with the strain amplitude of 1% under the stress rate of 10MPa/s until the hysteresis loops were stable. Creep periods were then introduced around the loops. Figure 2 shows the intermittent creep periods of 300 seconds duration during strain cycling between 1%. After stabilization of cyclic straining by 5th cycle, the creep periods start at point a. All consecutive creep-hold periods are designated by the alphabet letters ending at k. In spite of the same stress levels at a and j, b and i, d and g, and at e and f, creep in the nearly straight sections of the hysteresis loop is very small or nonexistence. At c and h, which are points of zero stress, the magnitude of strain decreases by a small but noticeable amount. Due to the conventional creep theory, the creep rate depends on stress and time. The results shown in Fig. 2, however, are at variance with these theories. The additional observation of the results in Fig. 2 shows that at maximum stress level of the cycle the greatest amount of creep is found which subsequently subsides and then increases in the opposite direction as the curvature of the stress-strain curve increases. Therefore, a point of zero creep must exist by continuity arguments. However, this point of zero creep cannot be well defined only from Fig. 2, as pointed out by [3].

Physical instinct suggests that the point zero creep should corresponds with the current center of the yield surface. Nevertheless, the point cannot be defined from an experiment because the back stress is an internal variable. It is reasonable that the origin of the stress space should move due to the plastic deformation as presented in many constitutive models for cyclic plasticity; namely, the center of the yield surface (kinematic back stresses) evolved during cyclic preloading. The authors have succeed in defining the evolution of back stress from the computer simulation based on the model shown in the previous section.

Figure 3 shows the simulated stress-strain curve of cyclic tension-compression preloading with the constant strain amplitude of 1% under the constant stress rate of 10MPa/s, using the proposed model. The movement of the center of the yield surface during cyclic preloading is traced by the dash-dot lines. The value of the kinematic back stress during compression in the stabilized stress-strain loop is 150MPa. The stress at the point b shown in Fig. 2 corresponds to this back stress.

The creep curves corresponded to Fig. 2 are shown in Fig. 4, where the absolute values of total strain measured from back stress are plotted during 300 seconds. The numerals in Fig. 4 represent the effective stress measured from the back stress. The solid lines and the marks ($\bigcirc$, $\triangle$, $\square$) show the creep along the tension side of the stress-strain loop, while the broken lines and the marks ($\bullet$, $\blacktriangle$, $\blacksquare$) along the compression side. In Fig. 4, the results of intermittent creep tests after the preloading with the strain amplitudes of 1, 1.5 and 2% are also shown by the marks $\bigcirc$, $\triangle$, $\square$ ($\bullet$, $\blacktriangle$, $\blacksquare$), respectively. Two creep curves under the same effective stress level have a good agreement. It is clear from Fig. 4 that intermittent creep does not depend on the strain amplitude of preloading. It is important to note that creep depends on stress and time if stress is measured from the back stress. Therefore, the evolution of back stress during cyclic preloading plays an important role to prescribe the following creep behavior.

From the experimental results of creep during cyclic loading, the following conventional creep law has been obtained,

$$\varepsilon^c = 1.90 \times 10^{-5} \, \sigma^{1.72} \, t^{0.0181} \tag{9}$$

where σ is the effective stress measured from the back stress, and t is time in second. Equation (9) is the modified Bailey-Norton law. Figure 5 shows the results calculated from Eq. (9). Comparing Fig. 5 with Fig. 4, it is clear that the experiments are represented well by Eq. (9).

UNIAXIAL RATCHETTING

Figure 6 shows, for example, the experimental result of the uniaxial ratchetting test under the constant stress rate of 10MPa/s after the hysteresis loop of the cyclic tension-compression loading was stable. It is noticeable that the inelastic strains (ratchetting strain) developed during uniaxial stress cycling. Figure 7 shows the relations between accumulate ratchetting strains and cycles during uniaxial ratchetting test under the three stress rates. The marks ($\bigcirc$, $\triangle$, $\square$) show the experimental results of the stress rates of 5, 10, 20MPa/s, respectively. Figure 7 indicates that the accumulated ratchetting strain strongly depends on the stress rate.

Figure 8 shows the computer simulation corresponding to Fig. 6 based on the proposed model. Comparing Fig. 6 with Fig. 8, experiments are predicted well by the model. The solid lines in Fig. 7 show the accumulated ratchetting strain predicted by the model. It is appear that the model can be applicable to uniaxial ratchetting, irrespective of the strain rate. Thus, the proposed model could be applied to uniaxial ratchetting under the arbitrary constant stress rate.

CONCLUSIONS

A series of tests for creep and uniaxial ratchetting of type 304 stainless steel after cyclic preloading were carried out. The verifications of the center of the yield surface (back stress) for explaining creep behavior after cyclic preloading, and of the applicability of the proposed model for the prediction of uniaxial ratchetting were made. As a result, intermittent creep strain after cyclic preloading could be represented well by the modified Bailey-Norton law with stress levels from the back stress determined by the proposed model. It was also appear that the model could be applicable to predict uniaxial ratchetting under arbitrary constant stress rate.

REFERENCES

[1] Chaboche, J.L., and Nouailhas, D., "A unified Constitutive Model for Cyclic Viscoplasticity and Its Applications to Various Stainless Steels", ASME Journal of Engineering Materials and Technology, Vol. 111, 1989, pp. 424-430.
[2] Krempl, E., and Ruggles, M.B., "The Interaction of Cyclic Hardening and Ratchetting for AISI Type 304 Stainless Steel at Room Temperature-II, Modelling with the Viscoplasticity Theory based on Overstress", Journal of Mechanics and Physics of Solids, Vol. 31, 1990, pp.587-597.
[3] Kujawski, D., Kallianpur, V., and Krempl, E., "An Experimental Study of Uniaxial Creep, Cyclic Creep and Relaxation of AISI Type 304 Stainless Steel at Room Temperature", Journal of the Mechanics and Phsics of Solids, Vol. 28, 1980, pp. 129-148.
[4] Ishikawa, H., and Sasaki, K., "Yield Surfaces of SUS304 Under Cyclic Loading", ASME Journal of Engineering Materials and Technology, Vol. 110, 1988, pp. 364-371.

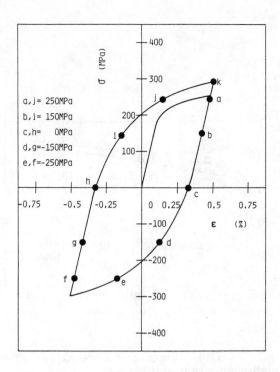

Fig. 1 Test procedure for intermittent creep

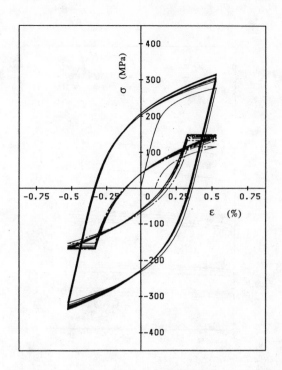

Fig. 3 Predicted stress-strain relation of cyclic tension-compression loading ($\Delta\varepsilon = 1\%$, $\dot{\sigma} = 10$MPa/s)

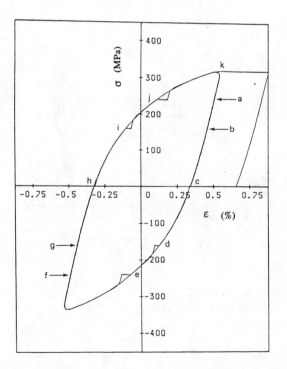

Fig. 2 Intermittent creep behavior during cyclic tension-compression loading ($\Delta\varepsilon = 1\%$, $\dot{\sigma} = 10$MPa/s)

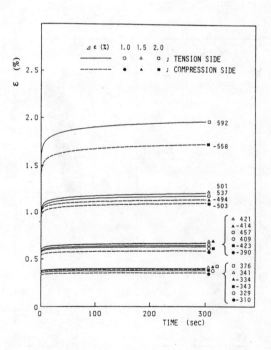

Fig. 4 Creep curves after cyclic tension-compression loading

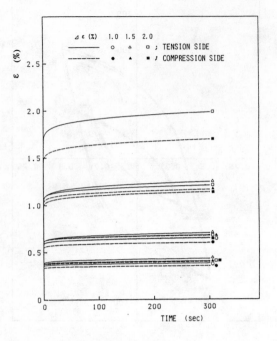

Fig. 5 Calculated creep curves

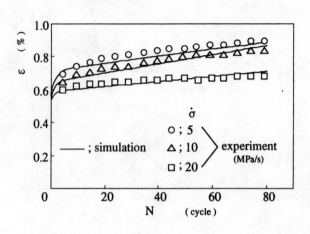

Fig. 7 The relation between uniaxial ratchetting strain and cycles

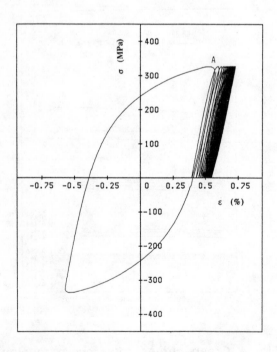

Fig 6 Stress-strain relation during uniaxial ratchetting test ($\dot{\sigma} = 10$MPa/s, experiment)

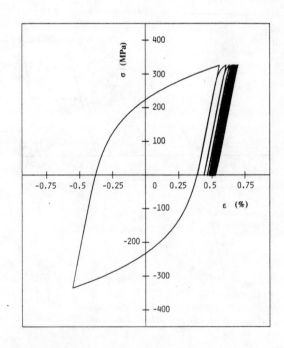

Fig. 8 Stress-strain relation during uniaxial ratchetting test ($\dot{\sigma} = 10$MPa/s, simulation)

INVESTIGATION OF CRACK CLOSURE
DURING THERMAL-MECHANICAL CYCLING

J. J. Pernot[1] and S. Mall[2]

ABSTRACT

A technique, incorporating the laser interferometric displacement gage, was developed to measure fatigue crack closure (or opening) during thermal-mechanical cycling.

INTRODUCTION

Fatigue crack closure has been an item of great interest during the past twenty years [1, 2]. Of particular concern is the effect crack closure has on component life prediction. For components of gas turbine engines, life prediction is more complex as a result of the thermal and mechanical loads that components experience. The objective of this investigation is to develop a technique for studying the effects of crack closure during thermal-mechanical cycling. In this study, crack opening displacements are measured during a thermal-mechanical fatigue (TMF) cycle using a laser interferometric displacement gage (IDG), in order to determine the crack closure load. Using this load, the corresponding effective values of stress intensity range, i.e. ΔK_{eff}, can be calculated.

BACKGROUND

Elber discovered that a crack under zero-to-tensile load fatigue was closed at zero load because of the plastic deformations in the wake of the propagating crack. A crack is only fully open for a portion of the loading cycle even if the cycle is entirely tensile [3, 4]. Studies [3-7] have shown that loads exerted on the specimen when the crack is closed do not contribute to crack propagation; therefore, an effective range of stress intensity, ΔK_{eff}, is used to correlate the crack growth rates instead of using the stress intensity range, ΔK. This effective value only considers the loads during the open portion of the loading cycle; therefore, ΔK_{eff} is defined as the difference between the maximum and opening stress intensities, K_{max} and K_{op}:

$$\Delta K_{eff} = K_{max} - K_{op} \tag{1}$$

The mechanisms most often attributed to crack closure during the tensile portion of a fatigue cycle include: 1) residual plasticity, 2) fracture surface asperities, and 3) surface corrosion [3, 8]. Plasticity induced closure involves the reverse slip in the plastic region around the tip of a propagating crack. This is most often used to describe the variation in load ratio, R, and the retardation associated with an overload. Surface roughness closure is significant when there is a mismatch of fracture surfaces. This type of closure can be significant only when the grain size of the material is large enough to develop a surface roughness comparable to the opening displacement [8]. The oxide-induced closure results from the oxide deposits on the exposed surfaces of the crack when a material is subjected to a corrosive environment. In addition to the three mechanisms described above, others which are also believed to contribute to the crack closure phenomenon are: 4) load-transition effects, 5) phase-transformations, and 6) grain boundaries [9].

Ever since the investigations of Elber [3, 4], studies of crack closure have been performed with various techniques, which include: 1) strain gages, 2) extensometers, 3) ultrasonic techniques, 4) photoelastic models, 5) DC electric potential, 6) Moires's grid with photomicrographs, 7) eddy current, 8) photographic techniques, and 9) interferometry. Extensive reviews of these techniques can be found in References 1 and 2. Majority of these techniques can be classified as either compliance measurements (bulk closure) or as direct observations of closure at the crack surfaces. Compliance

---

1. Material Directorate, Wright Laboratory, WL/MLLN, Wright-Patterson AFB, OH 45433
2. Department of Aeronautics and Astronautics, Air Force Institute of Technology, Wright-Patterson AFB, OH 45433

measurements, both mechanical and electrical, are used most often to measure closure, since these methods have been adopted from crack length measurement techniques; furthermore, the components used for these techniques are relatively inexpensive. A problem with all the compliance techniques is determining the point on the load vs. displacement traces where the crack opens. Moreover, experimenters cannot agree on the best position of strain gauges and extensometers, and the results are not consistent between different studies. Of the techniques involving compliance measurements, the most questionable one is the DC electric potential. An oxide layer can form on the crack surface and act as an insulator, or asperities can cause electrical bridging across the crack. In cases where thermal cycling is present along with mechanical fatigue, another complicating factor has to be considered. The electric potential across the crack is highly dependent on temperature. For the potential method to be successful, not only the oxide formation or bridging must be eliminated, but also, the potential dependence on temperature must be accounted for. The only published results of closure measurements during thermal-mechanical fatigue were obtained using an electric potential technique [10, 11]. Direct observations are the most reliable methods of determining the exact load at which the crack opens during the fatigue cycle; therefore, this type of technique was used in the current investigation to measure fatigue crack closure under thermal-mechanical cycling. The equipment developed in this study to directly measure displacements near the crack surface is described in the following section.

MATERIAL AND EXPERIMENTAL EQUIPMENT

The material used in this investigation is the nickel-base superalloy, Inconel 718, which has been studied and modeled under TMF conditions for the same temperature range previously [12]. The specimen geometry is a compact tension (C(T)) specimen with a nominal width of 40.0 mm and thickness of 2.54 mm. This thin geometry is used to maximize the heating and cooling rates without causing thermal gradients through the thickness. The specimen is polished to a 3 micron finish for making visual crack length measurements and crack displacement measurements with a laser interferometry system, described later.

The experimental equipment consists of components to control both the load and temperature on the specimen, as well as measuring the displacement between the crack surfaces. Before the displacement measuring technique is discussed, the load and temperature components are discussed briefly.

Mechanical loading is performed with a closed-loop MTS servohydraulic system. The temperature is maintained by both heating and cooling the specimen. The heating is accomplished by four quartz lamp heaters, two in front and two behind, and the cooling is accomplished using jets of compressed air. The advantage of using radiant heat lamps is that the specimen can be heated rapidly with very accurate temperature control across the surface of the specimen. The temperature is controlled with a Micricon microprocessor which powers the lamps and activates the compressed air cooling. The microprocessor uses four K-type thermocouple for feedback; one for each of the lamps. A fifth thermocouple is placed in the center of the other four thermocouples to monitor the temperature independently for the microprocessor. The load and temperature are monitored and controlled by a microcomputer. Further details of these systems are provided in references [13] and [14].

The system used to measure the crack opening displacement is a laser interferometric displacement gage, also referred to as an IDG. This method of measurement, pioneered by Sharpe [15, 16] and later modified [17], was employed in this study, which is shown schematically in Figure 1. Using a steering mirror, light from a five-milliwatt HeNe laser is directed toward two microhardness indents on the specimen, one above and one below the crack plane. The two indents cause two sets of fringe patterns to occur in space. The two linear array detectors monitor the fringes caused by the indents, and the movements of the indents can be tracked. This is shown in Figure 2. The translation (rigid body motion) of the indents can be accounted for by subtracting the two displacements, yielding the relative displacement. Details of this measurement system are provided in reference [17].

There are a few difficulties when using the IDG setup with radiant heating, since the signals used to measure displacement are altered with light sources such as those used to heat the specimen. In fact, early in the investigation, the fringe patterns were deteriorated completely by the light, and modifications to the setup were needed to ensure that the fringes could be detected without interference. The components required to reduce the light from interfering with the measurements are shielding plates, light filters, apertures, tubes, and seals. These components, which are shown in Figure 3, are described below.

The lamps that heat the back side of the specimen face directly toward the two detector arrays of the IDG system, which makes the use of the IDG under these conditions (lamp heating) very difficult. Two 76 mm x 140 mm light shields, constructed from 1.0 mm thick stainless steel, were used to shield a large portion of the light energy away from the detectors without disrupting the control of the temperature on the C(T) specimen. These plates are placed in front of the specimen, one just above the specimen and one just below the specimen.

The specimen is polished to a 3 micron finish to make high quality indents for the IDG system; therefore, the light reflecting from the two front lamps also is a concern. Since the front lamps heat at large angles to the left and right of the IDG system, the light from the heat lamps is not reflected directly into the detectors. However, light does enter into the array housings, and other techniques of eliminating excess light interference are employed.

Filters and slotted apertures attached to either end of a 102 mm aluminum tube shown in Figure 3, reduce the interference of the heat lamps. These filters are standard 25.4 mm (1.0 in) optics and the apertures were constructed from 25.4 mm aluminum disks. The slot widths used in this study were 3.18 mm and 1.59 mm. The filters allow for passage of the laser light; however, as the intensity of the lamp energy varies, the light can disrupt displacement measurements. Filters of two different bandwidths were tried, 10.0 nm and 1.0 nm, each centered on 632.8 nm, which is the wavelength of HeNe laser light. Each of the filters tends to reduce the intensity of the fringe pattern making it more difficult to detect the fringe patterns. Therefore, one has to make a compromise when selecting the amount of optical filtering necessary with the degradation of the system performance. Later in the investigation, the IDG system was upgraded by replacing the electronic components to increase the resolution of the system from approximately 100 angstroms to better than 50 angstroms, and one filter of each type was used (one at either end of the aluminum tube).

By using the two filters along with two slotted apertures, the light from the heaters was cut down tremendously. The only difficulty is the alignment of the fringes with the detectors. The slots in the apertures need to be lined up directly with the incoming path of the fringes; however, this allows for only the light traveling along that path to reach the array. Since there are no lamps in the path of the fringes, only reflected and refracted light from the heaters will travel up the tube through the apertures and filters and reach the detectors. The entire tube is black anodized (including the interior) to help reduce the light from entering the front slot and reflecting through the second slot. The front slot is 1.59 mm and the rear slot is 3.18 mm. Although two 1.59 mm slots are sufficient to pass the fringes through the tube, that configuration was nearly impossible to align.

Every effort was made to ensure light did not enter the box where the array detectors was housed. This arrays are housed in black anodized aluminum boxes with felt rear covers to make sure light from the rear does not effect them. Felt was used to allow heat to escape from the box while not allowing light to enter. A two-axis adjustable base is mounted on the front of the box, to which the aluminum tube is attached, and a rubber seal is placed between the steering mechanism and the box.

EXPERIMENTAL PROCEDURE

Before the displacement measurements can be made, a few preliminary steps must be taken. First, the specimen is thermal-mechanically cycled under constant K_{max} condition until a constant crack growth rate is established using the DC electric potential drop technique. (This type of test is selected to save time.) The crack growth rate data from the three in-phase TMF tests performed in this study (ΔK = 25, 30, and 40 MPa m$^{1/2}$) compared very well with those obtained by Nicholas et al. [12] for the same test conditions. Second, the specimen is removed and indents are placed on either side of the crack plane as shown in Figure 4. The dimensions of these indents are 40 × 40 microns, and are placed 50 microns above and below the crack plane. Typically these indents are placed 50 microns behind the crack front. Third, the specimen is placed back into the test rig and a thermal profile must be established on the specimen. This requires the positioning of the lamps, setting the control parameters, adjusting the air flow, and placement of the air jets, which is discussed in reference [13]. A typical thermal profile, as measured by the fifth thermocouple on the C(T) specimen, is shown in Figure 5. Fourth, the laser is aligned with the power to the lamps off. The lights in the room are turned off, and the laser beam is steered toward the indents until fringes appear on white paper cards placed in front of the detectors. Then the aluminum tubes are adjusted until the fringes are aligned with the detectors. Fifth, the power is restored to the lamps, and the light shields are moved into position. Then, the crack opening displacement measurements are made.

The crack opening displacement measurements are obtained in the following manner: A thermal-mechanical fatigue cycle is established on the specimen. It takes one or two cycles to check the phase angle. Then the crack length is measured using DC electric potential drop, and during the next two cycles, the differential fringe count is obtained from each array detector. During the first of these, the load and temperature are cycled. During the second, only the temperature is cycled; however, a minimum tensile load is maintained to preserve the alignment of the laser. The differential fringe count, m, is converted to relative displacement, δ, with the following expression [17]:

$$\delta = m\ \lambda\ /\ \sin(\theta) \qquad (2)$$

where λ is the laser wavelength, and θ is the enclosed angle between the incident and reflected laser beam. Following a procedure similar to that used by Pelloux and Marchand [10] in the measurement of closure during TMF using DC electric potential, the relative displacement of the indents during the thermal cycle are subtracted from the relative displacements during the TMF cycle. The thermal displacement (δ_{th}), when subtracted from the thermal-mechanical displacement (δ_{tmf}), yields the mechanical displacement (δ_m):

$$\delta_m = \delta_{tmf} - \delta_{th} \tag{3}$$

The mechanical displacement can be used for determining the crack opening load during the thermal-mechanical cycling, since the thermal displacements have been accounted for.

RESULTS AND DISCUSSION

Using Equation (2) the relative displacements of two microhardness indents, which are 101.2 microns apart and 0.86 mm behind the crack tip, are calculated for an in-phase TMF cycle between 427 and 649°C with $\Delta K = 25.0$ MPa m$^{1/2}$. These displacements are shown in Figure 6A. The thermal displacements for the very next cycle are shown in Figure 6B. Note that the total thermal displacement is approximately 1/25 of the total TMF displacement. The thermal displacement is verified with a simple linear thermal expansion calculation. Assuming that the crack surfaces do not separate, the total relative displacement of two points on Inconel 718 that are 101.2 microns apart at room temperature would equal to 0.381 microns when cycled between 427 and 649°C. From Figure 6B, the measured total thermal displacement is 0.385 microns. Using Equation (3), the data in Figure 6B is subtracted from those in Figure 6A to obtain the mechanical displacement data presented in Figure 6C. It is obvious that the data in Figure 6A and 6C are nearly identical, and when either are used to obtain the opening (or closure) loads, the results are nearly the same. This will not be necessary the case for thermal-mechanical cycles of various other phase angles. However, in this case, the peaks and valleys of both traces occur simultaneously, and subtracting them does not affect their shape substantially.

A plot showing load (P) versus mechanical displacement (δ_m) for the data described above is shown in Figure 7. The opening and closure load levels are calculated in the following manner: Linear fits to the upper and lower regions of the loading and unloading portions of the load-displacement trace are performed. The intersection of these lines is the point of crack opening for the loading portion of the trace, and closure for the unloading portion of the trace. Note that the opening load level is slightly greater than the closing level. $P_{op}/P_{max} = 0.38$ and $P_{cl}/P_{max} = 0.37$. All of the displacement data for the in-phase tests for ΔK values of 25, 30, and 40 MPa m$^{1/2}$, regardless of the location of the indents, show this behavior. This feature needs to be investigated further.

It is well understood [1] that the amount of closure measured with this technique is strongly dependent on the measurement location. The purpose of this study is not to identify the specific closure levels for each stress intensity level, but to validate the technique to measure closure. However, an indication of this dependence can be seen in Figure 8. Initial data indicate that the opening load level continues to drop as the crack propagates away from the indents, which is consistent with the findings of other isothermal results [1]. The normalized opening and closing levels do not stabilize to a constant value for the distances from the crack tip studied here; however, this is being investigated in order to obtain the values of ΔK_{eff} as defined in Equation (1).

SUMMARY

A technique for measuring fatigue crack opening (or closure) during thermal-mechanical cycling was developed. This technique incorporates the use of a laser interferometric displacement gage. Future investigations are being considered which include: additional optical filtering of the light, use of a higher power laser, other load-temperature phase angles, the calculation of ΔK_{eff} for the various phase angle tests, and the mechanism of closure.

ACKNOWLEDGEMENTS

The authors gratefully acknowledge the technical support of Mr. G. Hartman, University of Dayton Research Institute during the course of this study. The authors are also indebted to Air Force Office of Scientific Research, AFOSR/NA, Bolling AFB, D.C. for sponsoring this research.

REFERENCES

1. Allison, J. E., "Crack Closure Measurement During Fatigue Crack Growth", *Fracture Mechanics 18th Symposium*, STP 945, American Society for Testing and Materials, Philadelphia, 1988, pp. 913-933.

2. Banerjee, S., "A Review of Crack Closure", Air Force Wright Aeronautical Laboratories Report AFWAL-TR-84-4031, Wright-Patterson Air Force Base, OH, 1984.

3. Elber, W., "Fatigue Crack Closure Under Cyclic Tension", *Engineering Fracture Mechanics*, Vol 2, 1970, pp. 37-45.

4. Elber, W., "The Significance of Fatigue Crack Closure", *Damage Tolerance in Aircraft Structures*, STP 486, American Society for Testing and Materials, Philadelphia, 1971, pp.230-242.

5. Sehitoglu, H.,"Characterization of Crack Closure", *Fracture Mechanics*, STP 868, American Society for Testing and Materials, Philadelphia, 1985, pp. 361-380.

6. Sehitoglu, H., "Crack Opening and Closure in Fatigue", *Engineering Fracture Mechanics*, Vol 21, 1985, pp 329-339.

7. Schijve, J., "Fatigue Crack Closure: Observations and Technical Significance", *Mechanics of Fatigue Crack Closure*, STP 982, American Society for Testing and Materials, Philadelphia, 1988, pp. 5-34.

8. McEvily, A.J., "On Crack Closure in Fatigue Crack Growth", *Mechanics of Fatigue Crack Closure*, STP 982, American Society for Testing and Materials, Philadelphia, 1988, pp. 35-43.

9. Lindley, T.C. and Richards, C.E., "The Relevance of Crack Closure to Fatigue Crack Propagation", *Materials Science and Engineering*, Vol 14, 1974, 281-293.

10. Pelloux, R.M. and Marchand, N., *Thermal-Mechanical Fatigue Behavior of Nickel Base Superalloys*, NASA CR 175048, March 1986.

11. Marchand, N., Pelloux, R.M., and Ilschner, B., "Non-Isothermal Fatigue Crack Growth in Hastelloy-X", *Fatigue Fract. Engng Mater. Struct.*, Vol 10, 1987, pp 59-74.

12. Nicholas, T., Heil, M.L., and Haritos, G.K., "Predicting Crack Growth Under Thermo-Mechanical Cycling, *Int. J. Fract.*, Vol 41, 1989, pp 157-176.

13. Pernot, J.J. and Mall, S., "A Thermal-Mechanical Fatigue Crack-Growth Testing System", *Exp. Techniques*, Vol 13, 1989, pp 24-28.

14. Hartman, G.A., III, "A Thermal Control System for Thermal Cycling", *J.Test Eval*, Vol 13, 1987, pp 363-366.

15. Sharpe, W.N., Jr., "Interferometric Surface Strain Measurement", *International Journal of Nondestructive Testing*, Vol 3, 1971, pp 59-76.

16. Sharpe, W.N., Jr., "Benchmark Cyclic Plastic Notch Strain Measurements", *Journal of Engineering Materials and Technology*, 1983, pp. 235-240.

17. Hartman, G. and Nicholas, T., "An Enhanced Laser Interferometer for Precise Displacement Measurement", *Exp. Techniques*, 1987, pp 24-26.

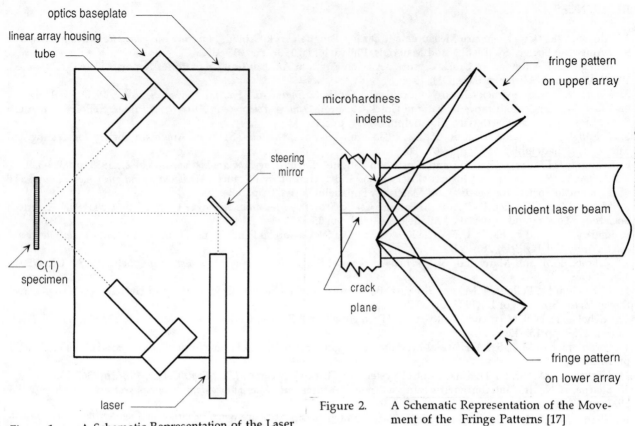

optics baseplate

linear array housing

tube

steering mirror

C(T) specimen

laser

Figure 1.   A Schematic Representation of the Laser Interferometric Displacement Gage [17]

microhardness indents

crack plane

fringe pattern on upper array

incident laser beam

fringe pattern on lower array

Figure 2.   A Schematic Representation of the Movement of the Fringe Patterns [17]

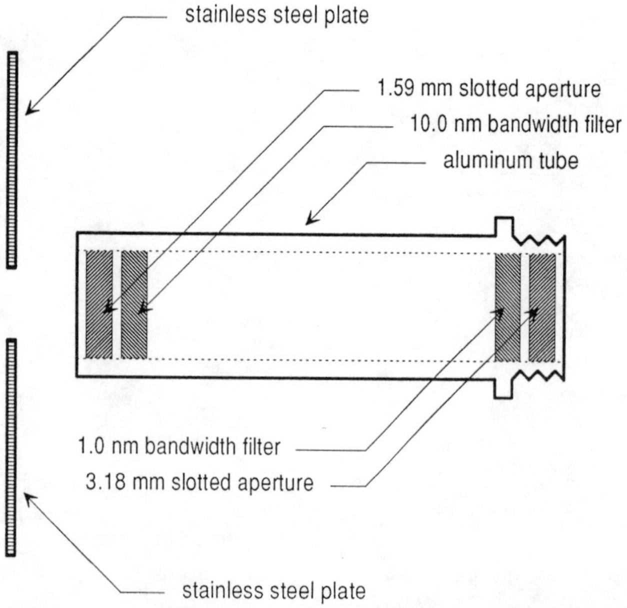

stainless steel plate

1.59 mm slotted aperture
10.0 nm bandwidth filter
aluminum tube

1.0 nm bandwidth filter
3.18 mm slotted aperture

stainless steel plate

Figure 3.   Arrangements of Components Required to Reduce the Light from Interfering with the IDG Measurements

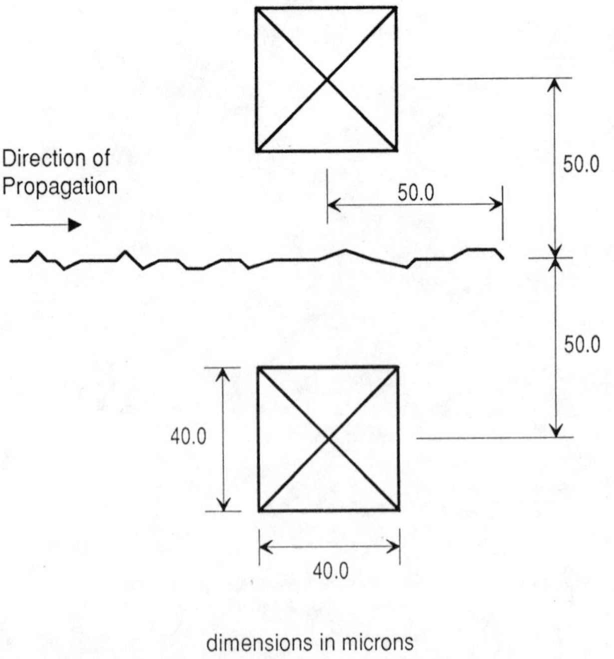

Direction of Propagation

50.0

50.0

50.0

40.0

40.0

dimensions in microns

Figure 4.   A Schematic Representation of Indents on Either Side of the Crack Plane

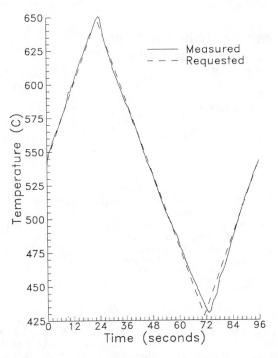

Figure 5. A Typical Thermal Profile on the C(T) Specimen

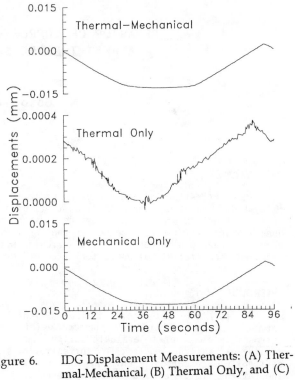

Figure 6. IDG Displacement Measurements: (A) Thermal-Mechanical, (B) Thermal Only, and (C) Mechanical Only

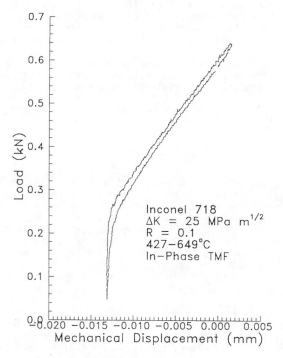

Figure 7. A Plot of Load (P) Versus Mechanical Displacement (δ_m)

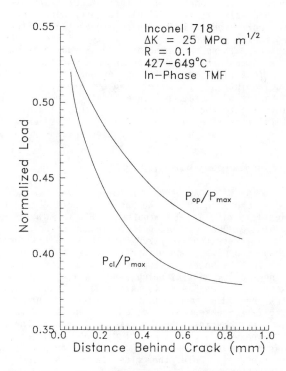

Figure 8. Normalized Opening and Closure Load Levels as a Function of Distance Behind the Crack Tip

BEHAVIOR OF CORROSION PIT AND FATIGUE CRACK OF
A HEAT-TREATED STEEL IN 3% NaCl SOLUTION

M. Goto and H. Nisitani

ABSTRACT

When estimating fatigue damage quantitatively, it is important to clarify its physical background. In this study, rotating bending fatigue tests of a heat-treated 0.45 % carbon steel were carried out in 3 % NaCl solution, in order to clarify the physical background of corrosion fatigue damage from successive observations of fatigue processes by the replication technique. By analyzing the experimental data, the generation and growth behavior of a corrosion pit, the initiation and propagation behavior of a fatigue crack and the statistical characteristics of corrosion fatigue behavior were investigated.

INTRODUCTION

It is important to clarify the physical background of fatigue damage when quantitatively assessing fatigue damage. Therefore, the crack initiation and propagation behavior in air have been studied extensively in order to evaluate fatigue damage. On the other hand, the investigation of physical background of fatigue damage in corrosive environment has not been made fully because of its experimental difficulty. In corrosive environment, a crack initiates even under the stresses sufficiently lower than the fatigue limit in air and it propagates until the fracture of specimen occurs. This means that an estimation of fatigue damage is crucial to the safe design of machines and structures operating in corrosive environments.

The analysis of fatigue behavior in a corrosive environment is difficult if compared to that in air, because electrochemical factors affect fatigue behavior, as well as metallurgical and mechanical factors. Accordingly, it is difficult to infer corrosion fatigue damage from "in-air" results. As typical phenomena in corrosion fatigue, there are the generation and growth of corrosion pits, the wedge action caused by corrosion products, the dissolution of the crack surface, and the interaction and coalescence of numerous cracks. These phenomena have been studied by many researchers [1-11], however, the physical background of the corrosion fatigue phenomena has not been discussed fully.

In this study, rotating bending fatigue tests of a heat-treated carbon steel were carried out in 3 % NaCl solution. The generation and growth behavior of a corrosion pit and the initiation and propagation behavior of a crack are investigated through the successive observations of plastic replicas. In order to investigate the statistical characteristics of corrosion fatigue behavior, the distributions of crack initiation life and crack length were also examined. A few studies have used the plastic replica technique for the investigation of corrosion fatigue problems [11-15].

EXPERIMENTAL PROCEDURES

The material used is a rolled round bar (about 18mm in diameter) of 0.45 % carbon steel. Specimens were machined from the bar after normalizing for 30 minutes at 845°C, quenching for 30 minutes at 845°C and tempering for 60 minutes at 600°C. The chemical composition (wt%) is 0.45C, 0.25Si, 0.79Mn, 0.01P, 0.01S, 0.09Cu, 0.03Ni, 0.18Cr, remainder Fe and the mechanical properties are 750 MPa yield stress, 833 MPa ultimate tensile strength, 1510 MPa true breaking stress, and 61.6 per cent reduction of area. The shape and dimensions of specimens are shown in Fig.1. Figures 1(a) and (b) show specimens for tests in air and in NaCl solution respectively, and these are called plain specimen in this study. In some specimens, a fine shallow partial notch (see Fig.1(c)) was machined in the middle of the specimen. The specimen having such a notch has a strength reduction factor close to 1 and can be regarded as a plain specimen. Before testing, the specimens were electropolished to remove about 20 μm from the surface layer in order to facilitate observations of changes in the surface state.

All tests were carried out under the constant stress amplitude using a rotating bending fatigue machine with a capacity of 100 Nm operating at 3600 rev/min. The environment for corrosion fatigue tests was a NaCl solution with a concentration of 3 % at room temperature (25±1°C). The solution was dripped continuously onto the midsurface of specimen during tests and was circulated between a test chamber and

M. Goto is Associate Professor in the Department of Mechanical Engineering, Oita University, Oita, 870-11 Japan. H. Nisitani is Professor in the Department of Mechanics and Strength of Solids, Kyushu University, Higashi-ku, Fukuoka, 812 Japan.

a large reservoir bottle at a rate of about 1000 cc/min. The solution was renewed for each test.

The observations of fatigue damage on the specimen surface and the measurements of corrosion pit size and crack length were made via plastic replicas using an optical microscope at a magnification of x400. The corrosion pit size, l_p, and crack length, l, signify the length along the circumferential direction of the specimen surface. The value of stress, σ_a, is the nominal stress amplitude at the minimum cross section and, when appropriate, neglects the existence of the shallow notch.

EXPERIMENTAL RESULTS AND DISCUSSION

Figure 2 shows the S-N curve for plain and notched specimens. The fatigue limits exist in air. However, the fatigue limits disappear in NaCl solution [11,15-17]. The fatigue life to failure, N_f, in NaCl solution is less than in air with an exception at high stresses near the lower yield point. The difference in N_f between NaCl solution and air tests increases with decreasing stress amplitude. The fatigue life of notched specimens is always smaller than that of plain specimens for both environments. The difference in N_f between a plain and notched specimen is small in the NaCl solution and the difference tends to be small with a decrease in stress amplitude. Note that at σ_a =300 MPa, although N_f for the notched specimen is nearly equal to N_f for the plain specimen, the initiation site, which led to the fracture, in the notched specimen was not within a notched zone.

In what follows, the crack initiation and propagation behavior in a corrosive environment are investigated from the results of plain and notched specimens. That is, notched specimens were used mainly for experiments in which the behavior of a major crack was examined, and plain specimens were used for the statistical investigation of the behavior of cracks. The statistical characteristics of the fatigue behavior is examined by applying the Weibull distribution to each set of data. The three-parameter Weibull distribution function F(x) is given by the following equation [18]:

$$F(x)=1 - \exp[-(\frac{x-\gamma}{\eta})^m] \qquad (1)$$

where the three constants m, η and γ are the shape parameter, scale parameter and location parameter, respectively. Determination of three Weibull parameters is made by the correlation factor method [19]. That is, the Weibull parameters are determined so that the correlation coefficient for the linear regression becomes the maximum value.

Generation and growth behavior of a corrosion pit

In this section, the behavior up to the initiation of a major crack in notched specimens are discussed, along with the result at σ_a =300 MPa amplitude for the plain specimen.

Figures 3(a) and (b) show the changes in surface state around a major crack in air and NaCl solution, respectively. The stress amplitude σ_a is 500 MPa. In air, a major crack in many specimens is initiated from a small surface defect, although a major crack in some specimens is initiated from a slip band [20]. The crack initiation time in air is about 20-30 % of the total fatigue life. On the other hand, in NaCl solution, the specimen surface is corroded as a whole in the very early stages of cycling. Then corrosion pits are generated within the heavily corroded region. After the generation of corrosion pits, a great many cracks are initiated from corrosion pits and those cracks propagate by interactions and coalescence of cracks.

Figures 4 and 5 show the change in surface states around the initiation site of a major crack at the stress amplitude of 400 and 300 MPa, respectively. Corrosion pits are generated at the extremely early stages of cycling, then they grow gradually with the progressive cycling. A crack is initiated from a corrosion pit after the growth of the pit. From Figs. 3, 4 and 5, the number of cycles over which the generation of a corrosion pit is first observed is hardly affected by the stress level i.e. the generation of a corrosion pit is usually observed after 5000 repetitions at each stress level. However, a corrosion pit initiated at σ_a =500 MPa seems to be rather different in its character from the one at σ_a =400 and 300 MPa. At σ_a =500 MPa, comparatively small corrosion pits are generated but with a high density. At σ_a =400 and 300 MPa, however a small number of corrosion pits, whose sizes are relatively large, are generated. On the other hand, in air, many slip bands are generated during the early stages of cycling of σ_a =500 MPa, while only a few slip bands are generated at σ_a =400 MPa and no slip bands are observed at σ_a = 300 MPa. These results suggest that the density of corrosion pits at σ_a =500 MPa nearly corresponds to that of slip bands in air and a corrosion pit is generated from a slip band at a stress above σ_a =500 MPa. For the generation of a corrosion pit at the stresses below 400 MPa, no close relation between a corrosion pit and a slip band is observed, and both the pit size and the number of pits after the same number of repetitions tend to become large with an increase in the stress level. It has been reported that a corrosion pit in an aluminium single crystal is generated from a slip band [21], and the generation of corrosion pit in SUS405, a ferritic stainless steel, is hardly affected by a slip band [22].

In order to examine the effect of stress on the generation of a corrosion pit, zero loading fatigue tests (σ_a =0 MPa) were performed and the change in surface states were examined. A corrosion pit is generated at an extremely early stage. Although a pit grows after its generation, the growth soon ceases. Following this, the different corrosion pits are generated close to the corrosion pits whose growth is stopped. However, the newly generated corrosion pit also soon stops growing.

The above results concerning the behavior of a corrosion pit can be summarized as follows : Although the generation of a corrosion pit does not necessarily need stress cycling, the repetition of relatively high stresses at which a slip band is generated in air contribute definitely to the generation of a corrosion pit, because a corrosion pit is generated from a slip band. As for the behavior of a corrosion pit at a low stress amplitude, no generation of a corrosion pit from a slip band is observed. On the other hand, the pit growth and crack initiation behavior are affected by stress cycling. The growth rate of a pit increases with an increase in stress level. However, all corrosion pits do not necessarily grow up to a sufficiently large pit from which a crack is initiated. This indicates that the electrochemical factors around a corrosion pit are also closely related to the growth of a corrosion pit.

Crack initiation from a corrosion pit

As for the initiation time of a crack from a corrosion pit, Figs. 3, 4 and 5 give some informations. They show that a crack at σ_a =500 MPa is initiated very soon after the generation of a pit, however, a crack at σ_a =300 and 400 MPa is initiated after a corrosion pit grew up to the certain size which produced a sufficiently large stress concentration for crack initiation.

The relation between the corrosion pit size and whether the pit has a crack or not was examined for each stress level in order to estimate the threshold size of a corrosion pit from which a crack is initiated. That is, both the sizes of small pits with a crack and large pits without a crack were measured from all the corrosion pits observed. Figure 6 illustrates the relation between the corrosion pit size, l_p, and stress. Here, the diameter of corrosion pit was defined as the corrosion pit size for convenience sake, whereas the depth of corrosion pit is seemed to play more important role in crack initiation rather than the diameter. It is found that the threshold size of a pit with a crack increases with a decrease in the stress level. The average threshold corrosion pit size is about 100 μm for σ_a =300 MPa, about 40 μm for σ_a =400 MPa and about 25 μm for σ_a =500 MPa.

Figure 7 shows the crack initiation life, N_i, in which the cracks are initiated from corrosion pits, plotted on the Weibull probability paper. Each full line is the distribution function analyzed by Eq.(1), and it is well fitted to the experimental results. Namely, the two-parameter Weibull distribution (γ=0) holds for σ_a =500 and 600 MPa. However, the distribution of N_i for σ_a =400 MPa can be expressed by a three-parameter Weibull distribution. On the other hand, the distribution of N_i in air can be expressed by a Weibull distribution of mixed type [23], where N_i in air is defined by the number of cycles when the crack length reaches 25 μm. The Weibull distribution of mixed type results from the physical background that the starting sites of the crack in air can be divided into two sites, small surface defect and slip band. In corrosive environment, however, the distinction of starting site of crack needs not because all the cracks are initiated from corrosion pits. Figure 8 shows the CV, coefficient of variance, versus σ_a and the m versus σ_a relations for the crack initiation life distribution.

Propagation behavior of a corrosion fatigue crack

Figure 9 shows the propagation curves of a major crack of the notched specimens in air and in NaCl solution. In the figure, the numbers of cycles for crack initiation from a corrosion pit are also shown by the ○mark. After the initiation of a crack, a crack continues to propagate below the fatigue limit in air, σ_w =380 MPa. The logarithm of crack length versus number of cycles, relation in air is approximated by a straight line or a slight concave curve, however, the corresponding relation in NaCl solution is approximated by a convex curve with the exception of the extremely high stress range. Thus, the ratio of propagation life for a comparatively long crack to the total fatigue life is larger in an NaCl solution than in air. The main reason for the decreasing growth rate of a comparatively long crack in NaCl solution is probably the wedge action caused by the corrosion products, as is proposed for other materials [4-8, 15].

Figure 10 shows the cross section of a crack just after it has initiated from a corrosion pit. It is found that the crack surface is dissolved by the corrosion action, even near the crack tip. Thus a major reason for the accelerating growth rate of a short crack as indicated in Fig.9, is corrosion dissolution. A crack may propagate by corrosion dissolution alone, while at the same time corrosion dissolution causes the decrease in crack closure level.

Figure 11 shows the N/N_f versus δ relation obtained from plain specimens, where the crack density δ is the mean value of the number of cracks in 1 mm² and without including a corrosion pit. The crack density for a high stress range increases with increasing N/N_f, however, δ for 400 MPa tends to saturate in the range N/N_f >0.4. It is found that the value of δ in NaCl solution is more than 10 times of that in air [20].

Figure 12 shows the crack length distribution plotted on the Weibull probability paper. The stress levels are 400 and 500 MPa for Figs. 12(a) and (b), respectively. The crack length distribution is expressed by the three-parameter with the exception of N/N_f =0.88 under 400 MPa. The distribution of crack length for the last stages of cycling can be expressed by the two-parameter Weibull distribution. Figure 13 shows the relation between the shape parameter of crack length distribution and the relative number of cycles. The value of m is nearly equal to unity. In air, m takes about unity for high stress level and it is smaller than unity for the stress near the fatigue limit [23].

CONCLUSIONS

In order to assist an understanding of the physical background of corrosion fatigue damage, rotating bending fatigue tests of a heat-treated 0.45 % carbon steel were carried out in 3 % NaCl solution.

Successive observations on the specimen surface were made by the plastic replica method. The main results obtained are summarized as follows:

(1) In a corrosive environment, many corrosion pits are generated at an extremely early stage of cycling. The number of corrosion pits increase with increasing stress amplitude. After the generation of a corrosion pit, the pit grows gradually with continued cycling. A crack is initiated from a pit when the pit has grown to a certain size and when a sufficient stress concentration is attained. The corrosion pit size at the time of crack initiation is controlled mainly by the stress amplitude, and it increases with a decrease in the stress amplitude.

(2) When the stress amplitude is relatively high, but in the range of stress for which slip bands are generated in air, a large number of corrosion pits whose sizes are comparatively small are generated. These corrosion pits seem to be generated from slip bands. When the stress amplitude is relatively low, a comparatively large size of corrosion pits (whose numbers are significantly decreased) are generated. No relation between the generation of a pit and slip bands is observed.

(3) The generation of a corrosion pit does not necessarily require the repetition of stress, because a corrosion pit is generated in the early stages of cycling even in the case of a zero load test. However, the growth rate of a corrosion pit is affected by the repetitions of stress. The growth rate of a pit increases with an increasing stress amplitude.

(4) The logarithm of crack length versus number of cycles in air is approximated by a straight line or a slight concave curve. However the corresponding relation in NaCl solution is approximated by a convex curve. Thus the ratio of the long crack propagation life to the total fatigue life in a corrosive solution is larger than that in air.

(5) The crack initiation life from a corrosion pit under the stresses above and below the fatigue limit in air are expressed by two- and three-parameter Weibull distribution, respectively. Its relative scatter increases with a decreasing stress level.

(6) The crack length distribution is expressed by the three-parameter Weibull distribution independent of both the stress level and number of cycles, with the exception of the case just before the fracture under a low stress level. Such a case, a two-parameter Weibull distribution nearly holds.

REFERENCES

1.   Uhlig, H.H., Editor, "The Corrosion Handbook". Wiley, New York, 1948.
2.   Komai, K., Minoshima, K., Kinoshita, S. and Kim, G., "Corrosion fatigue crack initiation of high-tensile strength steels in synthetic sea water". Trans. JSME **53**, 496. 2267-2273, 1987.
3.   Hattori, S. and Okada, T., "Corrosion fatigue crack initiation behavior of a structural steel in salt solution with various concentrations". Proc. of Fatigue-90. 1617-1622, 1990.
4.   Nordmark, G. E. and Fricke, W. G., "Fatigue crack arrest at low stress intensities in a corrosion environment". J. Testing Evaluation **6**, 301-303, 1978.
5.   Dorward, R. C., Hasse, K. R. and Helfrick, W. J., "Marine atmosphere stress corrosion tests on precracked specimens from high-strength aluminium alloys; effect of corrosion product wedging". J. Testing Evaluation **6**, 268-275, 1978.
6.   Endo, K., Komai, K. and Shikida, T., "Crack growth by stress-assisted dissolution and threshold characteristics in corrosion fatigue of a steel". ASTM STP **801**, 81-95, 1983.
7.   Kobayashi, H., Ishizaki, S. and Gao, H.B., "Near-threshold corrosion fatigue growth characteristics of high strength steel in seawater". Trans. JSME **52**, 1778-1785, 1986.
8.   Murakami, R. and Ferguson, W. G., "The effects of cathodic potential and calcareous deposits on corrosion fatigue crack growth rate in seawater for two offshore structural steels". Fatigue Engng Mater. Structures **9**, 477-488, 1987.
9.   Endo, K., Komai,K. and Matsuda,Y., "Mechanical effect of corrosion products on the corrosion fatigue crack growth of a steel". Trans. JSME **46**, 1337-1343, 1980.
10.   Kitagawa, H., Fujii, T. and Miyazawa, K., "Small randomly distributed cracks in corrosion fatigue". ASTM STP **642**, 98-114, 1978.
11.   Goto, M., Matsuda, Y., Nisitani, H. and Miyagawa, H., "Statistical property of fatigue behavior of a heat-treated 0.45% C steel in 3% NaCl solution". Trans JSME **57**, 2641-2646, 1991.
12.   Akid, R and Miller, K. J., "The initiation and growth of short fatigue cracks in an aqueous saline environment". Environment Assisted Fatigue (Edited by Scott, P. and Cottis, R.A.) EGF/ESIS Publication 7, MEP, 415-434, 1990.
13.   Akid, R. and Ghulam, M., "Corrosion fatigue crack growth modelling of a high strength steel under fully reversed torsional loading". paper read at the 3rd NACE Inter. Symposium on Life prediction of corrodible Structures, Cambridge, England, 1991.
14.   Tokaji, K., Ando, Z. and Mizutani, H., "On statistical property of fatigue crack length of high strength steel". J. Soc. Mater. Jpn **31**, 1204-1209, 1982.
15.   Noguchi, H., Nisitani, H. and Ogawa, T., "Corrosion fatigue process of annealed 0.50% carbon steel under rotating bending". Trans. JSME **55**, 386-391, 1989.
16.   Jaske, C. E., Payer, J. H. and Balint, V. S., "Corrosion Fatigue of Metals in Marine Environment". Springer/Battelle Press, Berlin, 1981.
17.   Ragab, A., Alawi, H. and Sorein, K., "Corrosion fatigue of steel in various aqueous environments". Fatigue Engng Mater. Structures **12**, 469-479, 1989.
18.   Weibull, W., "A statistical distribution function of wide applicability". J. Appl. Mech. **18**, 293-297, 1951.

19. Sakai, S. and Tanaka, T., "Estimation of three parameters of Weibull distribution in relation to parameter estimation of fatigue life distribution". J. Soc. Mater. Sci. Jpn. 29, 17-23, 1980.
20. Goto, M. and Nisitani, H., "Relation between scatter characteristics of fatigue life and crack initiation and small-crack growth behaviour of a heat-treated carbon steel". presented in Inter. Conf. on Short Fatigue Cracks, to be published.
21. Endo, K., Komai, K. and Nakamuro, N., "Estimation of corrosion fatigue strength by corrosion resistance and notch sensitivity of materials". Trans. JSME 35, 2154-2165, 1969.
22. Kimura, Y., Yagasaki, T. and Kunio, T., "On the generation process of corrosion fatigue crack in a ferritic stainless steel". Trans. JSME 50, 33-40, 1984.
23. Goto, M., "Statistical investigation of the behaviour of microcracks in carbon steels". Fatigue Engng Mater. Structures 14, 833-845, 1991.

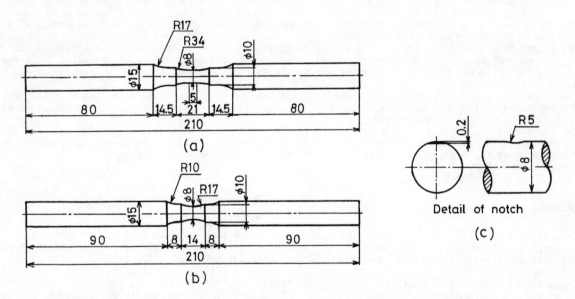

Fig. 1 : Dimensions (in mm) of (a)"in-air" specimen, (b) specimen tested in NaCl solution, and (c) the local shallow notch

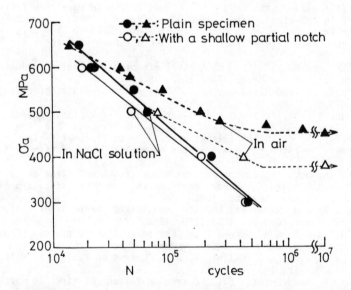

Fig. 2 : Fatigue endurance curves in air and in NaCl solution for plain and notched specimens

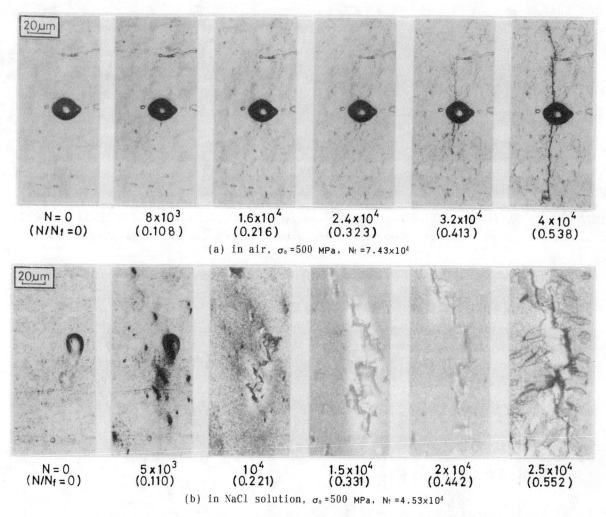

(a) in air, σ_a =500 MPa, N_f =7.43×10^4

(b) in NaCl solution, σ_a =500 MPa, N_f =4.53×10^4

Fig. 3 : Changes in surface states around a major crack of shallow notch

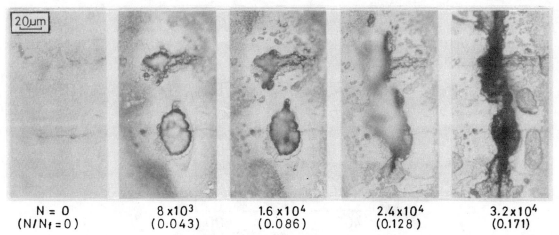

Fig. 4 : Changes in surface states around a major crack in NaCl solution
in a shallow notched specimen, σ_a =400 MPa, N_f =1.87×10^5

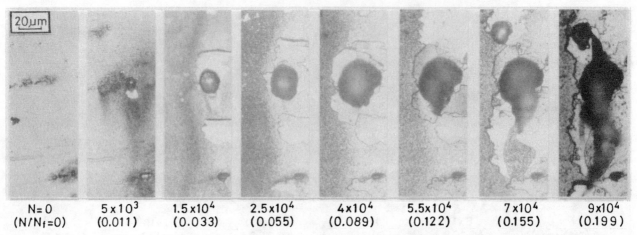

Fig. 5 : Changes in surface states around a major crack in NaCl solution in a plain specimen, σ_a =300 MPa, N_f =4.51×10⁵

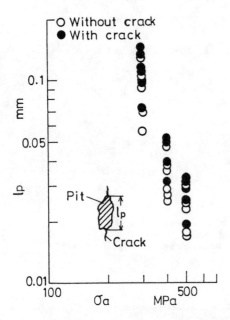

Fig.6 : Relation between pit size at the time of crack initiation and stress level

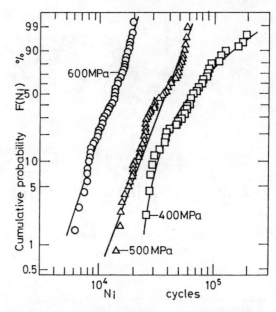

Fig. 7 : Crack initiation life distribution plotted on Weibull probability paper

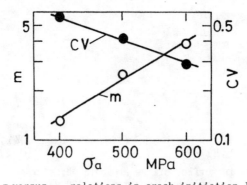

Fig. 8 : The cv, m versus σ_a relations in crack initiation life distribution

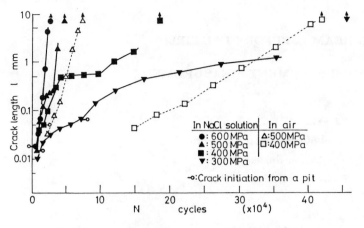

Fig. 9 : Propagation curves of major cracks

$\sigma_a = 400\,MPa$
50 μm

Fig. 10 : Cross section of a crack just after the crack initiation

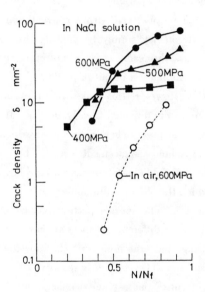

Fig. 11 : Relation between crack density and cycle ratio

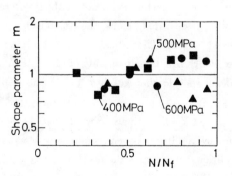

Fig. 13 : The m versus N/N_f relation in crack length distribution

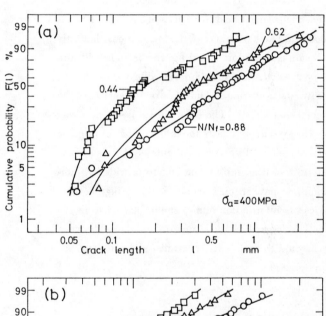

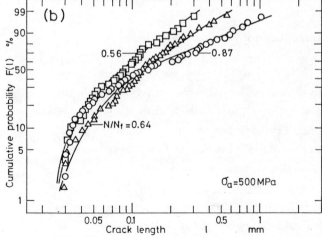

Fig. 12 : Crack length distribution plotted on Weibull probability paper; (a) 400 MPa, (b) 500 MPa

SHEAR BEAM ESPI FOR FULL-FIELD

IN-PLANE DISPLACEMENT MEASUREMENT

Jie Gu   Fang Chen

Department of Mechanical Engineering

Oakland University

Rochester, Michigan 48309

Abstract

A novel technique for the measurement of in-plane displacement field referred as Shear Beam ESPI is proposed. The key feature of the technique is that only one beam is needed in the set up, the beam is split into two parts and each of them is deviated by a shear device. The two parts overlap and interfere on the surface of the object being tested. The shear device is set in a way that the system eliminates the influence of out-of-plane displacement. A TVcamera-computer system is used to perform real time subtraction and to provide live full-field fringe pattern on a monitor. The fringe pattern carries the information of in-plane displacement in the direction along which the beams are deviated. Theory of the method as well as its experimental demonstrations are presented.

1. Introduction

In the past three decades, development of new methods of experimental mechanics seems to be in the area of optics. Optical methods enjoy the advantages of being extremely fast response, noncontacting, and generally full-field. The introduction of image processing system to optical method facilitates its progress a great deal. Electronic Speckle Pattern Interferometry (ESPI) has been widely used as a technique for displacement measurement and vibration analysis[1]. Most of such works have been done on conventional ESPI system with the viewing axis combined with a conjugate reference beam. This arrangement has a sensitivity vector parallel to the line of sight and is ideal for observing

displacement that are predominantly normal to the object surface. For the other problems, the displacement may be predominantly parallel to the surface. This type of problem can be observed with a conventional out-of-plane interferometry simply by viewing the object obliquely, so that the resulting fringe patterns are sensitive to the combination of out-of-plane and in-plane components[2]. However, this makes interpretation of the result much more difficult. Clearly, in these circumstances it would be preferable to use a system which can measure the in-plane displacement directly. Leendertz developed a whole field measurements with in-plane sensitivity in which the object is illuminated by two coherent wavefronts[3]. The speckle patterns generated by these wavefronts at different instances are correlated to produce a fringe patterns indicating the movement of the object surface. The method is sensitive to one resolved component of the in-plane displacement. Variations on this method have been successfully applied to the measurements of static displacement and strain[4][5]. However, since the pattern is formed by the interference of two widely separated beams, the coherent length of the source is crucial. The optical set up is also relatively complex, which results in instability of the system. The single beam speckle photography[6] enjoys the simplicity of its optical set up in recording a specklegram, but in order to get Young's fringes or whole field fringe pattern, one has to filter the specklegram in a second step. This additional step makes the real time processing impossible. Electronic Shearography is excellent in both simplicity and real time performance[7][8], but is mainly sensitive to the displacement derivative. A simple arrangement is introduced in this paper with the merit similar to that of Electronic Shearography, but sensitive only to the in-plane displacement.

2. Principle of the method

The object to be studied is illuminated by a coherent light source as shown in Fig.1. The object is imaged by a TVcamera-Computer system. A prism is placed between the light source and the object. The prism produce two wavefronts of equal amplitude, which are brought to illuminate the object symmetric to the horizontal axis. This is not obvious in Fig.1 because this figure is a vertical view from top down to the table. A side view is shown in Fig.2. The bending angle is

$$\alpha = (n_o - 1)\beta \qquad (1)$$

where n_o is the refractive index of the prism glass. In this arrangement, the interferometer is sensitive to vertical in-plane displacement. As the object is illuminated by a coherent light, the two wavefronts interfere with each other producing a random interference pattern referred as a speckle pattern. When the object is deformed, this speckle pattern is slightly modified. Subtraction of the two speckle patterns (deformed and undeformed) by the image processing system yields a fringe pattern depicting the in-plane displacement field of the deformed object.

In Fig.2, wave front due to w_1 and w_2 are

$$U_1 = aexp(j\varphi_1)$$
$$U_2 = aexp(j\varphi_2)$$

where φ_1 and φ_2 are random phase angles, a is the amplitude of the wavefront. For simplicity the magnification is assumed to be unity. Reaching the detector,

$$U = U_1 + U_2 = a[exp(j\varphi_1) + exp(j\varphi_2)]$$

The intensity received is

$$I = UU^* = 2a^2(1 + cos\varphi) \qquad (2)$$

Where $\varphi = \varphi_1 - \varphi_2$ represents a random phase angle. When the object is deformed, an optical path change occurs due to the surface displacement on the object. This optical path change produces a relative phase change δ

between the two wavefronts. Similar to eq.(2), the second exposure of light intensity is

$$I' = 2a^2[1 + cos(\varphi + \delta)] \qquad (3)$$

Performing a subtraction, the intensity shown on the monitor is

$$I_s = | I' - I| = 2a^2|cos(\varphi + \delta) - cos\varphi|$$
$$= 4a^2|sin(\varphi + \frac{\delta}{2})||sin\frac{\delta}{2}| \qquad (4)$$

The part $4a^2|sin(\varphi + \frac{\delta}{2})|$ is a random background[7]. Examining the second part, $|sin(\frac{\delta}{2})|$, it is obvious that the dark fringes occur when

$$\delta = 2n\pi \quad n = 0, 1, 2, ... \qquad (5)$$

δ is the relative phase change due to the surface displacement. Suppose that the illumination lights are plane wave fronts. The cases where there is only out-of-plane displacement, W, or horizontal in-plane displacement, U, are shown in Fig.3 and Fig.6. Where O is the original point of interest, and O' is the point position after the deformation. Fig.3 is a three dimensional view of the situation. To get a better picture of the situation, please look at Fig.4 and Fig.5 for the views along inverse x and y directions, respectively. Because the waves W_1 and W_2 are symmetric to each other with respect to x axis, $DO = CO$. So the path difference between the two exposures in Fig.3 is

$$\Delta = (A'O' - B'O') - (AO - BO)$$
$$= (A'O' - AO) - (B'O' - BO)$$
$$= DO - CO = 0 \qquad (6)$$

Similarly, from Fig.6, we have

$$\Delta = (A'O' - B'O') - (AO - BO)$$
$$= CO' - DO' = 0 \qquad (7)$$

There is no fringe at all in these conditions. In the case where only vertical component take place, see Fig.7, we have

$$\Delta = (A'O' - B'O') - (AO - BO)$$
$$= CO' + DO = 2vsin\alpha \qquad (8)$$

Where v is the vertical displacement. In a combination of all three dimensional displacements, one can think of the movement goes through three steps: step 1, step 2, and step 3, corresponding to Fig.3, Fig.6, and Fig.7. And because the displacement is so smaller that angle α is virtually not changed during the deformation. Finally, we obtained the governing equation to represent the optical phase change caused by the displacement:

$$\delta = \frac{2\pi}{\lambda}\Delta = \frac{4\pi}{\lambda}v\sin\alpha \qquad (9)$$

There is only one displacement component shown up in the equation as we expected. substitute eq. (9) into eq.(5), it turns out

$$v = \frac{n\lambda}{2\sin\alpha} \quad n = 0, 1, 2, \ldots\ldots \qquad (10)$$

Where n is the fringe order, λ is the wavelength of the light. By processing the fringe pattern image, we can derive the full field displacement distribution, which is not discussed in this paper.

The fringe sensitivity is given by

$$d = \frac{\lambda}{2\sin\alpha} \qquad (11)$$

Where d is the object displacement in the sensitive direction between adjacent fringes. α can be ranged from very small angle to nearly 90°, chosen according to the displacement range of the problem. The shear device suitable for different angle ranges are recommended as the following. For very small α, one may use a Wollaston prism coupled with a polarizer. For about $0.5^o < \alpha < 5^o$, Fresnel prism is pretty good. For example, take $\alpha = 1^o$, and $\lambda = 0.6328\mu m$, eq.(11) gives $d \simeq 20\mu m$. This is the typical displacement quantity measured in the conventional speckle photography. In the range of $\alpha > 1^o$, one can set up the system shown in Fig.8 using double mirrors as a shear device. Similar to Fig.1 and Fig.2, the double mirror do not block the view of the camera since it is off-axis. When $\alpha > 45^o$, there will be no obvious advantage for the technique suggested here than the conventional dual beam speckle interferometry because the two beams are widely separated.

The two illumination waves in Fig.1 and Fig.2 almost go through a common path. So the set up preserves most stability and reduces the coherent length requirement. α is adjustable by using different prism angles. The set up show in Fig.8 is a little bit more complex, it offers the advantage of adjustable angle on the spot but introduce some instability. Anyway, both schemes enjoy much more stability than the conventional dual beam speckle interferometry.

Ideally, the beam should be collimated in order for the fringe sensitivity to be constant across the object surface. But sometime it is convenient to approximate plane wavefront by diverging the beam over a large distance relative to the object dimension. To complete the in-plane study, it is necessary to rotate the illumination beam with the prism (or the object) through 90 degree about the viewing axis to make the system sensitive to horizontal in-plane displacement. If this technique is used along with the ordinary ESPI, one can determine 3-D displacement without much difficulty.

3. Experiment Result

As in Fig.1, the object is viewed along its surface normal with a TV camera. The camera is connected to a computer via a FG-100 image processing board. A computer program is designed to control the testing procedure. Real time subtraction mode is triggered immediately after an initial image is taken. Then the live fringe patterns are shown on the monitor if one changes the load exerted on the object. The first example chosen to demonstrate the method is a circular disk subject to rigid body in-plane rotation. Fig.9 shows its fringe patterns at three instants. The fringes are equal spaced vertical straight lines. This means the vertical displacement component is linear along the horizontal axis, which is consistent to the geometric theory of a rotated disk.

The second example is meant to verify that out-of plane displacement has no influence on the fringe formation in the fringe pattern. The fringe pattern of a thin edge clamped plate subjected to uniform presure in its surface normal direction is shown in Fig.10. The in-plane displacement in this case is negligible. Therefore there is no fringe in Fig.10, and hence confirms our conclusion that out-of-plane displacement is eliminated in this technique. Experimental also observation show that out-of-plane displacement and the in-plane displacement which is perpendicular to the direction the beams are deviated do not contribute to the fringe formation. However, they do cause decorrelation.

The technique permits full-field observation of surface displacement in structures. Fig.11 shows the fringe patterns of a cantilever beam with a concentrated force at the free end. They were taken from the live pattern at three instants.

To show the two dimensional nature of the full-field approach, the technique is applied to a disk under diametral load. Fig.12 shows the V and U isothetic patterns, respectively.

4. Comparison of the Shear Beam ESPI with the conventional ESPI and Single Beam Speckle Photography

Since they can all be used to depict in-plane displacement, it seems appropriate to compare them. All of the three methods enjoy the advantages of being full-field and noncontacting. However the Shear Beam ESPI offers several advantages over the other two. These can be summarized as follows :

1. It requires a very simple optical set up, thus eliminate the optical alignment problem.
2. The slow and cumbersome process of film registration and development is totally avoided.
3. It relaxes the vibration isolation requirement, thus, it is more suited for inspection in production environments.
4. The coherent length requirement is greatly reduced, thus relax the problem of maintaining laser running at single mode.
5. It provide a wider and more controllable range of sensitivity, thus extend the range of deformation to be measured.
6. Its real-time processing nature makes it possible to implement the technique for transient deformation measurement.
7. The fringe pattern quality is much higher because its stability and high contrast.

5. Conclusion

Theory and experiment show that the Shear Beam ESPI is unique in many aspects as a technique for in-plane displacement measurement. It combines the real-time capabilities, short exposure, high repetition. It is therefore be very attractive for fast and trouble free testing in research, and posses the potential of being developed into a fully automated practical tool for measurement in industry.

6. Reference

1. O. J. LOkberg, " ESPI the Holographic Tool for Vibration Analysis ? " J. Acoust. Soc. Am. vol. 75, no. 6, 1783-1791 (1984).
2. O. J. LOkberg, " Mapping of the in-plane vibration modes by Electronic Speckle Pattern Interferometry, " Opt. Eng. vol. 24, no. 2, 356-359 (1985).
3. J. A. leendertz, " Interferometric displacement measurement on scattering surface utilizing speckle effect, " J. Phys E3, 214-218 (1970).
4. Y. Y. Hung and J. D. Hovanesian, " Full-field Surface-strain and displacement analysis of three-dimensional object by speckle interferometry, " Exp. Mech. vol. 12, no. 10, 454-460 (1972).
5. Fermando Mendoza Santoyo, Michael C. Shellabear, and John R. Tyrer, " Whole field in-plane vibration analysis using pulsed-stepped ESPI, " Appl. Opt. vol. 30, no.7, 717-721 (1991).
6. R. P. Khetan, R. P. Chiang, " Strain analysis by one-beam laser speckle interferometry. 1: single aperture method, " Appl. Opt., vol. 15, no. 9, 2205-2215 (1976).
7. Y. Y. Hung, " Shearography: a new method for strain measurement and nondestructive testing, " Opt, Eng. vol. 21, no. 3, 391-395 (1982).
8. Y. Y. Hung, " Nondestructive Evaluation by Electronic shearography, " 16th Symposium on Nondestructive Evalution, San Antonio, Texas, April 21-23, (1987).

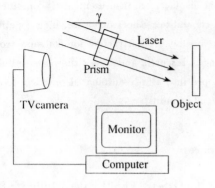

Fig. 1. The Shear Beam ESPI set up

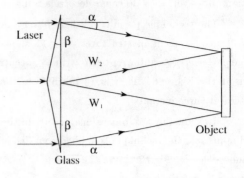

Fig. 2. A side view of the Shear Beam ESPI set up

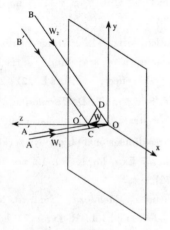

Fig. 3. The effect of out-of-plane displacement

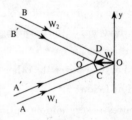

Fig. 4. The view along the inverse x direction of an out-of-plane displacement

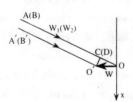

Fig. 5. The view along the inverse y direction of an out-of-plane displacement

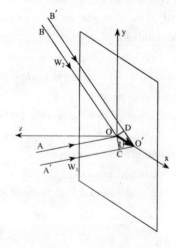

Fig. 6. The effect of horizontal displacemant

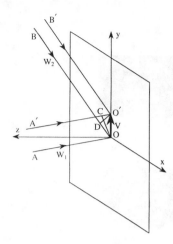

Fig. 7. The effect of vertical displacement

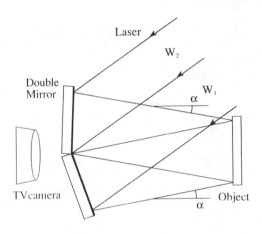

Fig. 8. Double mirror shear device

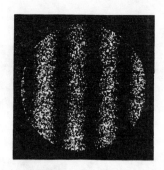

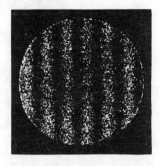

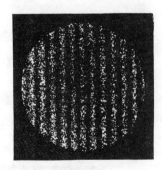

Fig. 9. Isothetics of a disk under rigid body
in-plane rotation for various rotation angles
(Vertical displacement field)

Fig. 10. The
pattern of an
edge clamped
plate subject to
normal pressure
(No fringe on it)

659

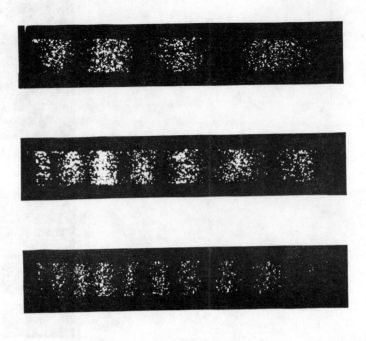

Fig. 11. Isothetics of the full-field
pattern of a cantilever for various loads

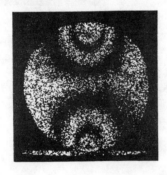 

Fig. 12. Isothetics of a disk under
diametral load (V field and U field)

BIAXIAL CREEP STRAIN MEASUREMENTS AT NOTCH ROOTS AT 250C

William N. Sharpe, Jr. and H. Zeng
Department of Mechanical Engineering
The Johns Hopkins University
Baltimore, MD 21218, USA

Abstract

This paper describes the first measurements of biaxial notch root creep strains using a laser-based interferometric technique which has a very short gage length. The technique, called the Interferometric Strain/Displacement Gage or ISDG, uses three tiny indentations placed in the specimen surface with a Vickers microhardness tester as reflective targets. When these indentations, which are only 150 μm (0.006 inch) apart are illuminated with a laser, interference patterns are formed. The motions of these fringe patterns are monitored with linear diode arrays and a microcomputer-controlled system to provide realtime strain measurement. The ISDG is simply an optical lever, so the stability of the measurement system is independent of the stability of the electronics. It is therefore useful for creep studies.

The principle of the ISDG and a description of the test setup and measurement system are given in the paper. Strains are recorded during loading and during creep tests lasting as long as 1000 hours. The results from tests at 250C on zirconium alloy pressure-tube material are then presented; biaxial creep strains are measured at the roots of notches with a 1 millimeter radius.

INTRODUCTION

The core of a Canada Deuterium Uranium (CANDU) reactor consists of hundreds of horizontal zirconium alloy pressure tubes which contain the fuel bundles and coolant. Small blunt flaws can form in the pressure tubes during operation due to fretting of the fuel bundle bearing pads and small trapped debris. These small flaws or notches are stress concentrations and must be assessed for the possibility of crack initiation from the flaw due to fatigue [1] and delayed hydride cracking [2].

A nonlinear finite element model is being developed to predict the elastoplastic and creep deformation at the roots of these stress concentrations. This will replace the current assessment procedure which is empirical and is considered to be very restrictive in determining pressure tube life. The validity of the new model can be determined by comparison of its predictions with experimental measurements of strain at the notch roots.

This paper describes the first measurements of notch root creep strains using a laser-based interferometric technique which has a very short gage length. The technique, called the Interferometric Strain/Displacement Gage or ISDG, uses three tiny indentations placed in the specimen surface with a Vickers microhardness tester as reflective targets. When these indentations which are only 150 μm (0.006 inch) apart are illuminated with a laser, interference patterns are formed. The motions of these fringe patterns are monitored with a microcomputer-controlled system to provide realtime strain measurement. The ISDG is simply an optical lever, so the stability of the measurement system is independent of the stability of the electronics.

The principle of the ISDG and a description of the test setup and measurement system are given in the next section. The results from tests at 250C on zirconium alloy pressure-tube material are then presented. These results include the biaxial strains as the notched specimen is loaded and then the creep strains from tests lasting as long as 1000 hours. These are the first results from an ongoing experimental program sponsored by Ontario Hydro Research of Canada.

THE CREEP STRAIN MEASUREMENT SYSTEM

The measurement system consists of a constant-force load frame and the laser-based ISDG for creep strain measurement. The ISDG is the novel feature of the current setup and it is described next.

Principles of the ISDG

The ISDG is very simple in concept, and the basics are very briefly described in this section. A more thorough explanation is available in [3].

Two tiny indentations are made in the surface of a specimen with a Vickers microhardness tester. When a coherent, monochromatic light source is incident upon them, the reflected light is diffracted because of the small size of the indentations. The two cones of light emanating from the indents intersect and form interference fringes in space. As the distance between the two indents changes because of loading of the specimen, the fringes move, and this motion is related to the relative displacement between the two indentations.

The optical principle is simply Young's Two-Slit Interference phenomenon from elementary optics except that it is in reflection instead of transmission through two slits or pinholes. Both diffraction and interference are involved to create the fringes. First, the impinging light is diffracted by the reflecting sides of the indentations. The wavelength of a He-Ne laser is 0.6328 μm , whereas a representative dimension of a reflecting side is about 15 μm ; this ratio of wavelength to 'slit width' of ~ 0.04 is small enough to cause appreciable spreading by diffraction. Second, these reflected rays of light interfere because they are coherent and have been shifted along the lines to the observation positions by an amount $d \sin\alpha$ where d is the distance between the indentations and α is the angle between the incident laser beam and the observation positions. One sees straight, parallel fringes at the observation positions because the angle α changes slightly as one moves to different positions on the screen.

The equation used with the ISDG is :

$$\epsilon = \frac{\Delta m_1 + \Delta m_2}{2\, d_o} \frac{\lambda}{sin\alpha_o}$$

where Δm_1 and Δm_2 are the fringe movements at two observation positions. The wavelength of light is λ and the spacing between the indentations is d_o. The angle α_o is the angle between the incident laser beam and a fixed measurement position and is approximately 42 degrees because of the shape of the Vickers diamond. So the 'calibration factor', $\lambda/sin\alpha_o$, is ~ 1 μm . A fringe shift of one, i.e. a fringe moving to occupy the position of a neighbor, corresponds to a relative displacement between two indentations of ~ 1 μm .

To measure biaxial strains, one simply places three indentations in an orthogonal pattern. It is then necessary to monitor four fringe motions, but the equation and procedures are the same as for a uniaxial measurement. The fringe pattern is checkered because of the overlapping of parallel fringes and this requires a larger aperture on the fringe sensing devices to get smooth signals. A more thorough description of a biaxial system is given in reference [4].

Larger displacements, say more than 5 or 10 μm , can be measured simply by recording the fringe motions versus load on an X-Y plotter, determining the loads at which maxima and minima occur, and plotting the load-displacement curve. The basic displacement resolution is therefore 0.5 μm which is too coarse for strain measurement. The microcomputer-controlled system which measures fractions of fringe motion is described in the next section.

The Creep Strain Measurement System

Figure 1 is a schematic of the ISDG as used for creep strain measurement (only two diode arrays are shown; the actual system has four). A 30 milliwatt He-Ne laser is used in this particular setup — the laser does not have to be that powerful; a 10 milliwatt one would be quite sufficient. For notch root measurements, the laser may be focussed with a lens onto the indents in the notch so that the reflections from the corners of the notch are reduced. The laser is mounted on a frame attached to the test machine and its beam is directed onto the specimen with an adjustable mirror. The fringe patterns shine directly onto linear diode arrays that are mounted on adjustable stages attached to the test machine.

The key to stability of the measurements is the mechanical stability among the laser, mirrors, specimen and diodes. The variation in intensity of the laser beam, the oxidation of the indentations (as long as they remain partially reflective), and the variation in intensity output of the diodes does not affect the measurement because the *position, not the amplitude* of the fringes is monitored.

Each linear diode array contains 512 individual photodiodes on 25 μm centers; each diode is 2.5 mm wide. The total length of the array is 12.8 mm and it is mounted in a standard 22-pin IC package. Each diode array is mounted on a small (5 cm by 11.4 cm) satellite circuit board containing the signal amplifying circuits; the assembly is mounted in a plastic mini-box attached to a translation stage. Each array requires a larger mother board containing the clock, trigger, and sampling circuitry. The mother boards for the diode arrays are mounted in the scanner controller along with the power supply and are connected to their satellite boards by six-foot long cables.

Each mother board has an adjustable internal clock and provides an output trigger signal for synchronization; however, it will also accept an external clock and trigger. The current setup uses an external variable frequency TTL function generator which produces the clock signal for the mother boards and for the A/D converters of the microcomputer. The fringe patterns are scanned continually, but are recorded only on demand of the microcomputer. The trigger output from the mother board for Channel 1 is connected to the microcomputer. When the controlling program determines that a strain measurement is to be made, it calls an A/D routine that initiates the data acquisition of 512 values from Channel 1 followed immediately by 512 values from each of the other three channels. The result is a record of intensity versus angle (diode location) for each of the four channels.

The fringe patterns are monitored on two oscilloscopes which use the trigger signal from the scanner controller for synchronization. Load from a load cell in the test frame and temperature from the temperature controller are also recorded and stored by the microcomputer. Data points are taken at a slow rate in creep tests, so they can be printed as the test progresses; this provides a permanent record and permits continual evaluation of the results.

The relative fringe shift, e.g. Δm_1, is computed by the strain measurement program as follows. The minimums of the central fringe and the two adjacent fringes are located and temporarily stored. The two spacings between the three fringe minimums are computed and averaged. The location of the central minimum is then compared with its previous location (for the previous strain computation) to determine the amount of fringe shift. This fringe shift is divided by the spacing to compute the relative fringe shift Δm . The location of the minimums is first found by locating the minimum intensity value in the neighborhood of the central fringe (i.e. near diode # 250). The resolution is increased by fitting a quadratic curve to the 20 values surrounding that point and then computing the minimum of the fitted curve. This procedure enables the minimum to be located to within 1/100th of the spacing between diodes and thereby increases the sensitivity proportionally.

The results of a 100 hour drift test at small load on a specimen show variations of less than ± 100 microstrain. The variations appear to originate from temperature variations in the laboratory. This amount of drift is acceptable in view of the large creep strains to be monitored.

The speed at which data is taken is not a serious concern in creep testing. The current system can record strain at the rate of one data point every 4 seconds. The data acquisition is slowed because of the printer. Also, in this initial version, the fringe intensities of both patterns are stored for later analysis if necessary. The ISDG has been extensively used for cyclic plasticity studies, and the data rate there is 10 points per second [3].

The ISDG is simply an optical strain measurement system with the indentations serving as the gage and the laser, diode arrays, and microcomputer serving as the signal conditioner. Its advantages are a very short gage length and excellent stability.

The Creep Loading System

The creep frame consists of a lever system constructed and mounted on a 20 kip electrohydraulic test frame; this was simply for convenience. The small specimen, which is approximately 8 cm long, is pin-mounted in grips attached to long pull-bars. It is desirable to monitor the very early stages of creep, so a continuous loading apparatus was constructed with the load applied by water flowing into a counterbalanced tank hanging on the end of the lever. The ISDG system measures on an incremental basis and if the increments of strain are too great it cannot follow the changing strain; this is another reason for smooth load application. The load cell in the test frame is monitored to see if there is any load change due to evaporation; only very small changes have been observed.

The specially constructed resistance furnace contains four 57 watt heaters; two mounted on each side of the cavity. The outer aluminum shell is insulated by fireboard panels that are 4 cm thick. Five openings are cut in the furnace — one for the incident laser beam and four for exiting fringe patterns. Fused quartz windows cover these openings. Temperature control is achieved through a commercial controller and a locally constructed power circuit. Temperature is maintained at 250C ± 1C.

TEST PROCEDURES AND RESULTS

Description of Specimens

The zirconium alloy tested has the following properties at 250C: an elastic modulus of 95 GPA, a proportional limit of 450 MPa, and a yield stress of 650 MPa.

Specimens were supplied by Ontario Hydro Research. Figure 2 is a sketch of the notched specimen shape; the smooth specimen had the same dimensions but no notch. The semicircular shape of the notch is chosen to approximate the stress concentrations observed in the pressure tubes and to allow for exit of the two fringe patterns. The gage area of the specimen was mechanically polished with a final 0.1 μm abrasive.

Oxidation of the specimens is of course a concern; if the indentations lose their reflectivity, the strain can no longer be measured. One approach is to provide an inert atmosphere in the furnace, and another is to apply a protective coating to the sample. The best coating was found to be vapor-deposited gold with the indentations applied either before or after the coating. Coatings of this type have lasted more than 1000 hours.

The polished circular notch acts as a mirror to reflect the incident laser beam into the diode arrays. The notch area must therefore be covered with a nonreflective coating except for the small region around the indentations. This was accomplished by applying a temporary mask approximately 0.5 mm wide across the width of the notch and then spraying the notch with a molybdenum disulfide lubricant. When the lubricant dried, it produced a diffuse gray coating that remained stable at 250C.

Smooth Specimen Results

A smooth specimen was tested at a creep stress of 520 MPa which is between the proportional limit and the yield stress of the material; only the uniaxial strain was measured in this early test. Figure 3 shows the stress and strain data from the initial portion of the smooth specimen test. The microcomputer program was set up to take data at the rate of 3 points per minute for 80 minutes, and the valve on the water loading tank was manually adjusted so that the creep stress would be reached in approximately 20 minutes. Note that an initial stress was applied to the specimen so that it would not move out of the laser beam as the linkages straightened out.

The stress data in Figure 3 shows that, after some initial adjustment of the valve, the stress increased linearly with time. However, the strain did not increase in a linear manner up to the proportional limit of 450 MPa as would be expected. This indicates that creep is occurring during the slow application of load to the specimen.

After the maximum stress was reached, considerable creep (over 2500 microstrain or 0.25 percent) occurred in the next 60 minutes. This demonstrates the importance of the ability to record strain continuously during loading.

Notched Specimen Results

Five tests in which biaxial strain was measured and two in which only the uniaxial strain was measured have been conducted to date. Two remote net stresses (load divided by the minimum cross-section area) of 350 MPa and 400 MPa have been applied.

The cumulative results of these seven loading tests are plotted in Figure 4. Bearing in mind the anisotropy of the material due to its processing and the inhomogeneity of the pipe sections from which samples were taken, the overall scatter among the specimens is acceptable. The axial strain is more reproducible from specimen to specimen than is the lateral, but the lateral consistently shows little plastic deformation as would be expected from the constraint at the notch. An elastoplastic finite element analysis of the specimen shows the lateral strain to be linear throughout the loading. It also shows the axial strain going plastic at approximately the same point as the measurements, but at the higher loads it shows a smaller total strain. This is because it does not account for the creep during loading.

Creep results for the seven tests are shown in Figure 5. The strain on the ordinate is the strain at the ends of the plots in Figure 4, and it is seen that it is difficult to achieve identical strains for supposedly identical loads. It would be possible to control the load application by monitoring the strains. Nevertheless, the creep rates at the two applied stresses are very consistent among the tests with rates of approximately 1.0 microstrain per hour at 350 MPa and 1.5 microstrain per hour at 400 MPa.

CLOSING COMMENTS

These are the first biaxial creep strain measurements over a short gage length using the laser-based ISDG. Crack opening displacements have been measured under creep conditions by the ISDG with equally good results [5]. It therefore appears that this is a technique that will be useful for the measurement of strains over short gage lengths for long periods of time.

There are some obvious improvements that could be made. A better oxidation-resistant coating can probably be found; the first version used did enable the tests to run for usefully long time periods. A controlled atmosphere furnace would extend the duration of the tests. A different creep frame with more precisely aligned loading rods and grips would improve the initial strain readings considerably.

Finally, as in any new and different experimental setup, replicate tests are needed to build confidence in the results. Also, creep tests at various stress levels must be conducted to complete the picture for this particular material and geometry.

ACKNOWLEDGMENTS

The authors acknowledge the support of Ontario Hydro Research and the guidance of Mr. Doug Scarth and Mr. Bill Lee. The assistance of Mr. R.L. Tregoning and Mr. C.H. Yang in the design and fabrication of the creep setup is greatly appreciated.

REFERENCES

1. D.A. Scarth, E. Nadeau, and R.G. Sauve. "Assessment of the Structural Integrity of CANDU Zr-Nb Pressure Tubes for the Fuel Channel Spacer Repositioning Operation". Proceedings of the 1990 ASME Pressure Vessels and Piping Conference, vol. 192, 1990, pp. 75-83.

2. B.A. Cheadle, C.E. Coleman, and J.F.R. Ambler. "Prevention of Delayed Hydride Cracking in Zirconium Alloys". Zirconium in the Nuclear Industry: Seventh International Symposium, ASTM STP 939, 1987, pp. 224-240.

3. W.N. Sharpe, Jr. "Applications of the interferometric strain/displacement gage." Optical Engineering, vol. 21, 1982, pp. 483-488.

4. W.N. Sharpe, Jr. and K.C. Wang. "Evaluation of a Modified Monotonic Neuber Relation." Journal of Engineering Materials and Technology. vol. 113, 1991, pp. 1-8.

5. W.N. Sharpe, Jr. and J.J. Shen. "A New Method for Determining Threshold Values of Creep Crack Growth." Failure Prevention and Reliability - 1983, ASME, 1983, pp. 53-58.

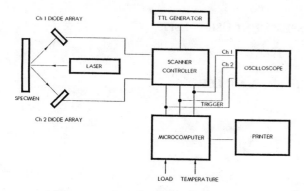

Figure 1. Schematic of the creep strain measurement system.

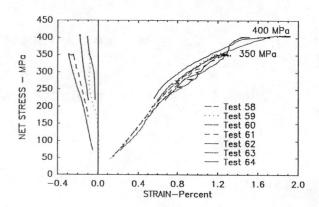

Figure 4. Cumulative axial and lateral notch-root strains at 250C during loading.

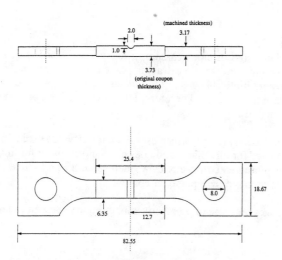

Figure 2. Dimensions of the notched test specimen.

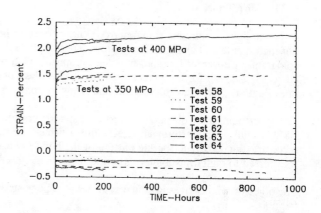

Figure 5. Cumulative axial and lateral notch-root strains at 250C during creep.

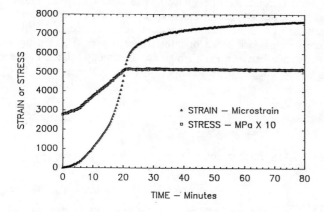

Figure 3. Stress and strain as load was applied to the smooth specimen at 250C.

BONE/IMPLANT STRAIN ASSESSMENT USING ESPI

B. CHITSAZ, D. WHEELER, G. MILLER

ABSTRACT

An electronic speckle pattern interferometry system was developed and tested on a cylindrical object and was adopted for use in the biomedical field. The displacement field on the surface of a cylinder subjected to in-plane bending as well as displacement gradients were plotted. A femur with and without a hip implant was examined and the change in the physiological strain was reported.

INTRODUCTION

Although holographic interferometry (HI) has proven to be a viable tool in biomechanics, it has many shortcomings (1). Through simple 2-D analysis HI can provide out-of-plane displacement, however, to extract in-plane displacement, multiple holograms at different locations must be examined which requires multiple changes in the optical setup (2). Additionally, HI requires a laser for image reconstruction and analysis of displacement fringes. Therefore, HI is a very tedious procedure to evaluate the surface displacement and strain in bone reconstructions.

HI's shortcomings are obviated by electronic speckle pattern interferometry (ESPI) which uses the latest in video technology. ESPI is a full-field interferometric technique which eliminates the need for film plates and does not require a laser for image reconstruction (3). The speckle pattern of the bone's image is captured electronically by a video camera in real-time and transferred to digital pixel information which is then stored and processed by a personal computer.

The objective of this investigation was to asses the bone strain changes seen due to prosthesis implantation in human cadaver femurs.

THEORY

ESPI is an established method for non-destructive and non-contact strain analysis. ESPI uses two expanded beams of laser light to illuminate the bone. The light reflected from the bone is perceived as light and dark speckles. These speckles move with respect to one another and their original position as the bone is deformed or displaced. The speckle patterns before and after deformation are captured by a video camera and stored through A/D conversion on an IBM PC in two separate data files. When the speckle images are electronically compared, the areas in which the speckles were displaced a distance equal to an even multiple of the wavelength of laser light are seen as dark bands or interference fringes. These fringes represent areas of constant displacement. Theoretically, the distance between each fringe (Δ) is directly related to the wavelength of laser light (λ) and inversely related to the illumination angle (Θ) as follows (3):

$$\Delta = \lambda / (2 \sin\Theta)$$

Displacement information can be numerically differentiated to yield surface strain.

B.Chitsaz is a Research Student in the Department of Engineering Mechanics, D. Wheeler is an Assistant Researcher and G. Miller is Faculty of Biomechanics in the University of Florida, Gainesville, Florida.

DISCUSSION

Studying the cylindrical object, one can appreciate ESPI better. From the displacement gradient plot (Figure 4b), the effects due to the fixed end of the cylindrical model show an offset value in the displacement gradient, which is non- existence in the theoretical model.

The cobalt-chromium cemented hip prosthesis stiffened the femur and, therefore, reduced the amount of deformation per unit load. This was reflected in a reduction in fringe frequency. Additionally, the fringes were evenly spaced proximal to the prosthesis tip. This would indicate a significant change in displacement gradient (strain) at the distal tip of the prosthesis. The sudden change in the slope as represented in Figure 7, reveals the location of tip of the implant. Our preliminary qualitative results prove ESPI is a promising method for detecting surface strain in bone. We are currently developing methods to quantify interference fringes to deduce surface strain. ESPI has many advantages over other currently used strain evaluation techniques in biomechanics. It is non-contact and provides a full-field map of the surface strain. Additionally, it eliminates the time-consuming process of developing optical film plates or tedious application of strain gauges.

PROCEDURE

An intact embalmed human femur was potted in a base fixture and securely mounted to the optical table as shown in Figure 1. The femur was pre-loaded in a manner to simulate physiological loading (4). The optical setup to capture the mediolateral and longitudinal displacements is shown in Figure 2. An image of the anterior femur was captured by the CCD video camera and stored in the PC. A small load was added to the preload and a second image was captured. The digitized speckle patterns of these two images were then electronically processed through digital subtraction and filtering to yield a reconstructed video image of the bone with a superimposed fringe pattern representing the amount of surface deformation occurring due to the application of the load increment. This process was repeated using the same femur and optical setup after implantation of an orthopaedic implant. For this particular presentation, a cobalt-chromium cemented hip prosthesis was implanted into the femur.

RESULTS

A cylindrical model simulating the femur and subjected to in-plane bending and axial load was examined (Figure 3). Figures 4a and 4b show the plots of lateral displacement versus position and displacement gradient for both experimental and theoretical case. Studying the displacement gradient plot (Figure 4b), one can see the differences between the experimental and theoretical cases more predominantly.

For the femur the same parameters as above were studied. The implantation of the cemented femoral hip prosthesis changed the surface displacement of the femur under applied load. A typical photograph of the fringe pattern produced under application of incremental load is shown in Figure 5a and the location of fringe center for the same photograph is shown in Figure 5b. These fringes represent lines of constant mediolateral displacement. Fringe order was determined with respect to the longitudinal axis of the bone, distal to proximal. The most distal fringe, adjacent to the base fixture, was considered the zero order fringe where no displacement occurred. The curves in Figure 6 display the change in the fringe order with respect to the longitudinal axis of the bone (displacement versus distance) which are similar to curves produced using HI previously by Wheeler (5). The displacement plot for the intact femur is overlaid by the plot of the same femur with a hip implant experiencing the same load increment. The change in fringe frequency can be detected by a gradient plot of displacement (Figure 7).

REFERENCES

(1) Manley, M.T., Ovryn, B. and Stern, L.S.: Evaluation of Double-Exposure Holographic Interferometry for Biomechanical Measurements In Vitro. J. Orthop. Res. 5(1):144-149, 1987.
(2) Vest, C.M.: Holographic Interferometry, John, Wiley & Sons. 70-77, 1979
(3) Wykes, C.: Use of Electronic Speckle Pattern Interferometry (ESPI) in the Measurement of Static and Dynamic Surface Displacements. Optical Eng. Vol. 21, No. 3, 400-406, 1982
(4) Rohlmann, A.; et al.: J. Biomech. 16(9):727-742. 1983.
(5) Wheeler, D.: The Use of Holographic Interferometry to Measure Surface Deformations of the Femur Due to a Cementless Prosthesis. Thesis, 1987.

ACKNOWLEDGEMENT

VA Rehabilitation Research and Development Service; Project #A100-4RA

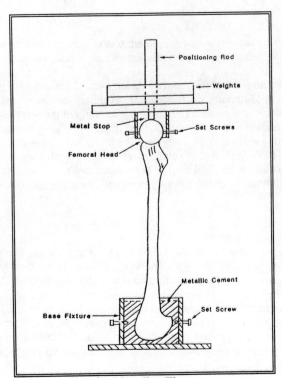

Figure 1: Sketch of Loading Fixture and femur

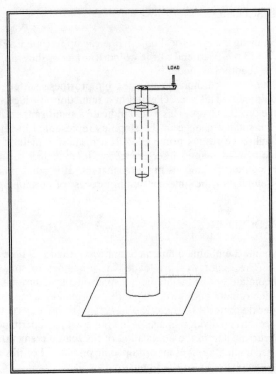

Figure 3: Cylindrical Model

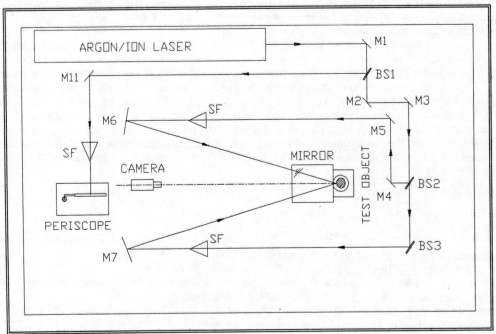

Figure 2: Optical Setup for Mediolateral and Anterior-Posterior displacement

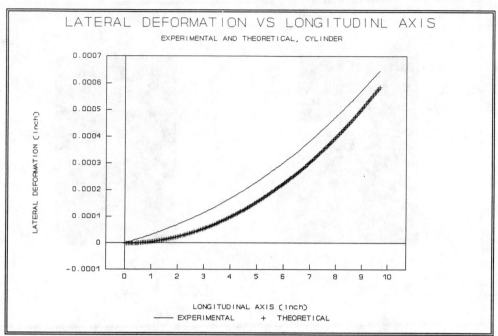

Figure 4a: Lateral Displacement plot

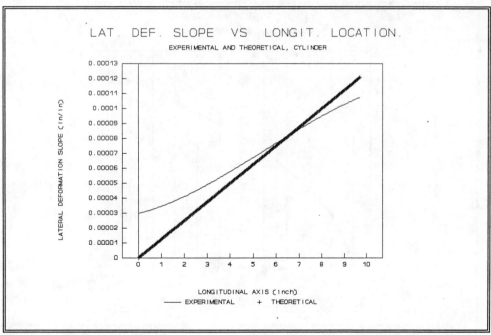

Figure 4b: Displacement Gradient plot

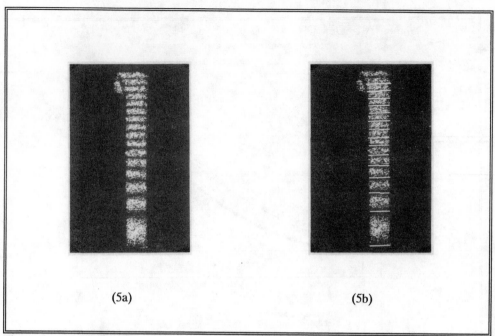

Figure 5a and 5b: Photographs of a typical fringe pattern and fringe centers.

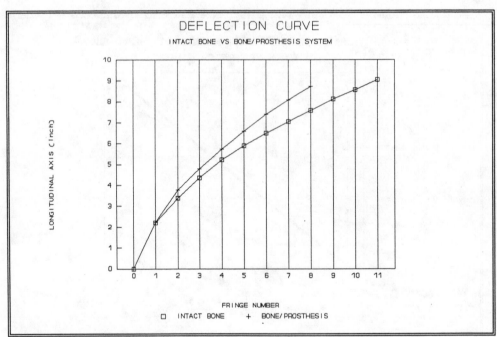

Figure 6: Plot of Fringe Order versus
Longitudinal Distance

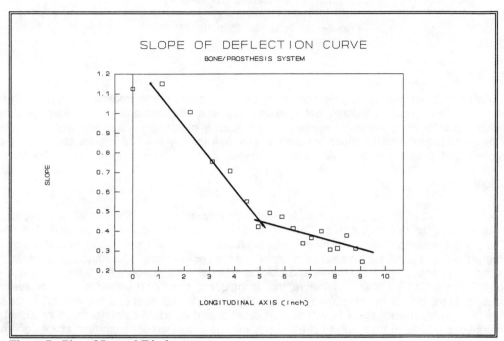

Figure 7: Plot of Lateral Displacement
Gradient for Bone/Prosthesis.

ELECTRONIC SHEAROGRAPHY FOR MEASUREMENT OF TIME-DEPENDENT DEFORMATION

Y.Y. Hung
Department of Mechanical Engineering
Oakland University
Rochester Hills, Michigan 48309

ABSTRACT

In the conventional shearography, a fringe pattern comparing two states of deformation in the object is formed from the two speckle images before and after deformation. This paper presents a novel technique allowing time-dependent deformation in an object to be studied by continuously digitizing the speckle images. Instead of generating fringe patterns, the deformation variation versus time for any point of interest can be studied by plotting the corresponding phase variation versus time after recording.

INTRODUCTION

Shearography[1] is an interferometric method for full-field measurement of derivatives of surface displacement. The technique requires the test object to be illuminated with laser light and imaged by an image-shearing camera. The camera equipped with a shearing device produces two laterally sheared images in image plane, and hence the technique is given the name shearography. In the conventional shearography, a fringe pattern is formed from the two speckle patterns before and after deformation and it depicts the difference between the two states of deformation in the object. Therefore, the technique is somewhat limited to the measurement of static deformation. In the case of double-pulsed shearography, the deformation at only two discrete times can be compared. In this paper, shearography is extended to allow time-dependent deformation in an object to be studied by continuously digitizing the intensity of the speckle images. Instead of generating fringe patterns, the phase variation versus time for any point of interest can be studied by plotting the corresponding pixel gray level versus time after recording.

DESCRIPTION OF THE TECHNIQUE

The technique employs a scheme of electronic shearography. Electronic shearography is a computerized process which eliminates photographic recording and wet processing. A typical set-up of electronic shearography is illustrated in Fig. 1. The object to be studied is illuminated with a point source of coherent light and it is imaged by an image-shearing video camera. The shearing device used here is different from that of the photographic version(1). It consists of a birefringent crystal which splits one object point into two in the image plane. Thus, a pair of laterally sheared images is produced on the image sensor of the camera. In other words, two neighboring points are brought to meet in the image plane. The key to the video recording in electronic shearography is the birefringent crystal serving as a shearing device. The shearing crystal brings two nonparallel beams scattered from two different points on the object surface to become colinear or nearly colinear. As a result, the spatial frequency of the speckle pattern is very low, and thus it is resolvable by video image sensors such as CCD.

In the study of a time-dependent deformation of a test object, the speckle patterns received by the image-shearing video camera are continuously digitized at a predetermined rate depending on the deformation rate via a frame grabber into a computer such as a PC, and stored in the memory of the computer. After recording, the displacement derivative versus time for any point of interest can be extracted by plotting the phase change of the speckle pattern at the point versus time from the computer memory. Fig. 2 shows a typical phase variation versus time plot obtained with the proposed technique. It is a plot of the fringe intensity variation of the point versus time as the object is being deformed. As expected, the intensity varies cyclically as the phase increases. The total phase change can be obtained by integrating the phase curve.

PRINCIPLES OF THE TECHNIQUE

While a detailed description of shearography can be found in reference (1), a physical explanation of the principles is given here. An image-shearing camera of shearography brings the rays scattered from one point on the object's surface to interfere with those scattered from a neighboring point. Since the object is illuminated by laser light (note that laser light is coherent, i.e., it has the ability to interfere), the rays from the two points interfere producing a random interference pattern (commonly known as speckle pattern). This speckle pattern modulates the object image and it may be represented by:

$$I_s = I_o (1 + \cos\phi) \qquad (1)$$

where I_s is the speckle image; I_o is the object image and ϕ is random phase.

When the object is deformed, a relative displacement between the two points occurs. This relative displacement induces a relative phase change which slightly modifies the interference speckle pattern. If the deformation is time-dependent, this speckle pattern will vary with time and it may be represented by:

$$I_s' = I_o \left\{ 1 + \cos\phi \left[\phi + \Delta(t) \right] \right\} \qquad (2)$$

where $\Delta(t)$ is the phase change induced by the time-dependent deformation, and it is a function of time. The intensity difference I_d between the deformed state and the undeformed state is therefore given by

$$I_d = I_o \left\{ \cos\left[\phi + \Delta(t) \right] - \cos\phi \right\} \qquad (3)$$

The square of the above intensity difference is used as the output I_{out} which can be shown to be

$$I_{out} = 2I_o^2 \cos^2\left[\phi + \frac{\Delta(t)}{2} \right] \cdot \cos^2\left[\frac{\Delta(t)}{2} \right] \qquad (4)$$

ϕ in the above equation has a random value and it is of high spatial frequency. The present image digitization hardware has a low resolution, typically 512x512 (or 1024x1024 for higher definition one) digitization points over the entire image. Therefore, a pixel in the digitized image generally has an area covering several speckles. Consequently, an averaged intensity over one pixel area should be considered. Assuming equal probability for the value of ϕ varying from 0 to 2π in a pixel area, the averaged pixel intensity is thus:

$$I_a = \frac{1}{2\pi} \int_0^{2\pi} I_{out} \, d\phi$$
$$= I_o^2 \cos^2\left[\frac{\Delta(t)}{2} \right] \qquad (5)$$

where I_a is the averaged pixel output intensity. In the measurement, the speckle images of the object undergoing deformation are continuously digitized at a rate depending on the deformation rate and they are stored in the computer memory. To study the deformation of a point as a function of time, I_a versus time for the corresponding pixel can be retrieved and thus the phase change $\Delta(t)$ at any particular time can be deduced. The total deformation at that time can be determined by integrating the phase change from the beginning to that particular time. It should be noted that although the postrecording data display is point by point, the recording is full-field. Normally, a full-field fringe pattern for a certain time represented by Eq.5 is first generated to visualize the deformation distribution and thus determine the critical points to be studied.

$\Delta(t)$ in Eq.5 is related to the derivatives of the surface displacement. If the shearing crystal is so oriented that the rays are deviated in a direction parallel to the x-axis, two points separated in the x-direction are brought to interfere. And if the magnitude of the shearing is small, $\Delta(t)$ depicts the derivatives of the displacements with respect to x as:

$$\Delta(t) = \frac{2\pi}{\lambda} \left(A\frac{\partial u}{\partial x} + B\frac{\partial v}{\partial x} + C\frac{\partial w}{\partial x} \right) \delta x \qquad (6)$$

Where δx is the amount of shearing, and A, B, C are the sensitivity factors given by:

$$A = \frac{x_s - x}{R_s} + \frac{x_o - x}{R_o}$$

$$B = \frac{y_s - y}{R_s} + \frac{y_o - y}{R_o}$$

$$C = \frac{z_s - z}{R_s} + \frac{z_o - z}{R_o} \qquad\qquad (7)$$

where (x_s, y_s, z_s) is the location of the illumination; (x_o, y_o, z_o) is the position of the camera, and $R_s^2 = x_s^2 + y_s^2 + z_s^2$, $R_o^2 = x_o^2 + y_o^2 + z_o^2$.

For a general case, three measurements with different sensitivity factors are needed for the three derivatives in Eq(6) to be separated. However, with the viewing and illuminating directions parallel to z-axis, the system is mainly sensitive to the derivatives of the z-displacement component only.

Should the shearing be in the y-direction, the displacement derivatives of the above equation becomes with respect to y.

EXPERIMENTAL DEMONSTRATION

To demonstrate the proposed technique, a pressure vessel is chosen to be the test object. The vessel has a leakage in the seal. Due to the leak, it deforms continuously when pressurized. With the setup of the Fig. 1, the time-dependent deformation of the vessel due to leakage is monitored. Since the vessel leaks slowly, the speckle images are digitized at a relatively slow rate of about one frame per second. Fig. 3 shows a full-field fringe pattern depicting primarily the derivative of the out-of-plane displacement of the pressure vessel. The fringe pattern reveals an internal crack and therfore, a point near the crack tip is a point of interest and its plot of the phase change versus time retrieved from the computer memory is shown in Fig. 2. High frequency noises are observed. These are likely electronic noises in the camera and the A/D frame grabber. Fortunately, the noises are of high frequency compared with the signal. Therefore, they can be easily removed my means of low-pass frequency filtering. Fig. 4 shows the result of the filtered signal. Clearly, the high fequency noises have been removed. Fig. 5 is a plot of the total phase change versus time obtained by the integration of the plot of Fig. 4.

CONCLUSION

This paper has added a time dimension to shearography which allows time dependent deformation to be studied. The highest deformation rate that can be studied depends on the speed of the digitization hardware. An alternative way is to continuously acquire the time-dependent speckle images on a magnetic tape by means of a video recorder. The speckle images are then digitized from the playback video images. Recording on a magnetic tape is inexpensive and it can store a large number of images. However, the signals are generally much noisier. It should be noted that shearography is a more practical method than holography, as it does not employ a reference beam and hence the requirement for environmental stability is greatly reduced.

ACKNOWLEDGMENT

This investigation is, in part, supported by the National Science Foundation (Grant No. MSS-9100627). The support of Dr. John Scalzi is greatly appreciated. The author is also grateful to Ms. Mary Sue Perria for her help in preparing this manucript.

REFERENCES

1. Y.Y. Hung "Shearography: a new optical method for strain measurement and nondestructive testing", Optical Engineering,Vol. 21, No.3, pp 391-395, May/June, (1982).

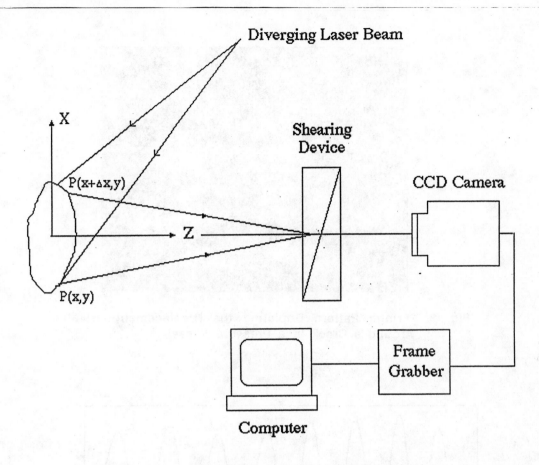

Fig. 1 **Schematic Diagram of Electronic Shearography**

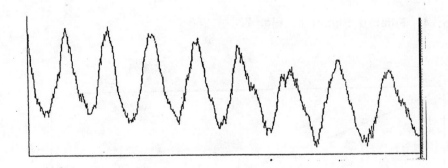

Fig. 2 **Phase Variation vs Time**
(Depicting the time-dependent deformation near the crack tip of a
leaking   pressure vessel)

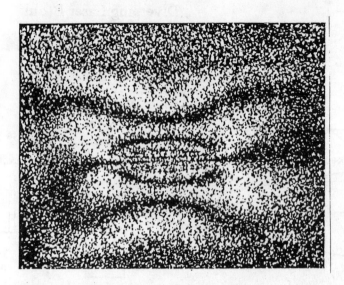

Fig. 3   Fringe Pattern Depicting the Displacement-derivative
Around a Crack in a Pressure Vessel

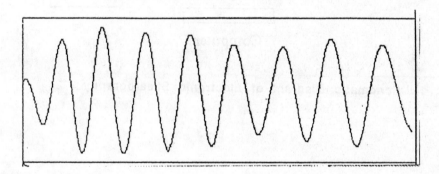

Fig. 4   Filtered Signal of Fig. 2.

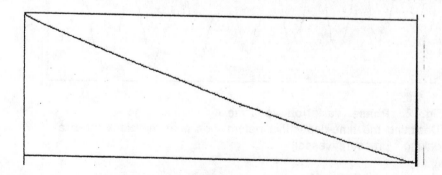

Fig. 5   Total Phase Change vs Time Obtained by Integrating the
Plot of Fig. 4

DETECTION OF IMPACT STRESS WAVES
BY PULSE LASER SHEAROGRAPHY

VPW Shim, SL Toh, HM Shang, CJ Tay and FS Chau

ABSTRACT

The propagation of an elastic disturbance (stress wave) generated by transverse point impact on a bar between clamped supports is observed using pulsed laser shearography - the double exposure of holographic film to a laser-illuminated object at different instants of its deformation. Sequential images are captured via a camera which has a thin, wedge-shaped prism placed in front of half its lens. The prism produces another image which is sheared in the direction of the wedge, with a net result that two images - sheared with respect to each other - are recorded by the camera. When the structure is deformed and a second exposure is superimposed on the first, a series of fringes is produced; these are visible when observed via high-pass optical Fourier filtering. The fringe pattern obtained represents loci of constant out-of-plane *displacement derivatives* with respect to the direction of image shear. These can be integrated to give the out-of-plane displacement. By adjusting the delay between the first and second laser pulses, the propagation of the out-of-plane displacement caused by bending can be investigated.

INTRODUCTION

Early experimental studies and measurement of stress wave transients relied extensively on the use of strain gauges [1-4]. Although effective in quantifying surface strains, strain gauges provide only localised information and not a full field description of the dynamic deformation which a structure experiences. However, the data is continuous timewise at the gauge locations. For fuller spatial information, more strain gauges must be employed. This engenders two disadvantages; strain gauging involves surface contact and this may affect the structure's response; secondly, the fast recording of a large number of channels of dynamic data entails high equipment cost. Optical methods of observing stress transients provide an alternative which is non-invasive since no contact is made, and also yields full field visual information. One such approach employs photoelasticity to study continuous and interconnected structures [5-7]. The main drawbacks of this approach are the requirement of model construction and the interpretation of photoelastic data. More recently, laser interferometry has begun to find application in the area of strain evaluation [8-9], as the wavelength of laser light is suitable for detecting small deformations. Much of such work pertains to quasi-static deformation. However, the advent of pulse lasers has facilitated the detection of dynamic deformation. This often assumes the form of pulsed-laser holography [10-13] whereby instantaneous out-of-plane displacement fields are captured. The main limitations of holography arise from its sensitivity to rigid body movement and the rapid increase in fringes with displacement, which makes the reading and determination of fringe orders difficult. An approach which is insensitive to rigid body motion and generally has sparser fringes is shearography [14-15], which measures displacement gradients rather than displacements.

SHEAROGRAPHY

Fig. 1 shows an object illuminated by a coherent light source. Its image is captured by a camera which has a glass wedge of small angle covering half the lens. Light reflected from a generic point $P(x,y)$ converges on two points in the image plane - P_1 and P_2 (for the ray passing through the glass wedge); i. e. the presence of the wedge results in the generation of a second image sheared in the direction of the wedge slope. The two images interfere with each other, producing a speckle pattern. If the structure is then deformed, a modified speckle pattern is generated. Superposition of these two patterns via double exposure yields a shearogram containing a fringe pattern which describes the displacement gradient of the surface in the direction of image shear. Fig. 2 shows two neighbouring points $P(x,y,z)$ and $P_1(x+\delta x, y, z)$ on the undeformed surface which displace to $P'(x+u, y+v, z+w)$ and $P'_1(x+\delta x+u+\delta u, y+v+\delta v, z+w+\delta w)$ respectively after deformation. The optical path length of the ray from the light source S to the camera O is altered from SPO to SP'O, giving a path length change of dl. Similarly, the change in path length for the neighbouring point P'_1 is δl_1. Hence, the relative path difference between the two points is $(\delta l_1 - \delta l)$. This corresponds to a relative phase change Δ of :

$$\Delta = \frac{2\pi}{\lambda}\left(A\frac{\partial u}{\partial x} + B\frac{\partial v}{\partial x} + C\frac{\partial w}{\partial x}\right)\delta x \qquad (1)$$

VPW Shim, SL Toh, HM Shang, CJ Tay and FS Chau are academic staff of the Department of Mechanical and Production Engineering, National University of Singapore, 10, Kent Ridge Crescent, Singapore 0511, Republic of Singapore.

where A, B and C are termed sensitivity factors [14] and are functions of the positions of the light source, the camera and the point P. λ is the wavelength of the laser light and δx is the shear in the x-direction caused by the glass wedge; this is related to the object distance D_o, the wedge refractive index μ and the wedge angle ϕ by :

$$\delta x = D_o(\mu-1)\phi \qquad (2)$$

If the optical arrangement is such that the light source and camera lie in the x-z plane, O is on the z-axis and the angle between the illumination and viewing directions is small, equation (1) is approximated by :

$$\Delta = \frac{2\pi}{\lambda}C\left(\frac{\partial w}{\partial x}\right)\delta x \qquad (3)$$

When a shearogram is viewed via high-pass optical Fourier filtering, the dark fringes observed correspond to areas where the phase difference Δ is equal to $(2n+1)\pi$, where n $(=0,\pm1,\pm2,\pm3,...)$ denotes the fringe order. By combining equations (1) and (3) and determining the respective fringe orders from the shearogram, the displacement gradient in the x-direction is given by :

$$\frac{\partial w}{\partial x} = \frac{\lambda}{2C\delta x}(2n+1) \qquad (4)$$

If the surface of the undeformed object is perpendicular to the optical axis of the camera, then $(\partial w/\partial x)$ is the slope of the deformed surface with respect to the x-axis. One significant advantage of shearography is that it detects *relative* displacements (displacement gradients) and is thus not affected by rigid body motion. Also, unlike holography which yields high fringe orders (and therefore a high fringe density) with large displacements, the fringes in shearography indicate slopes or displacement gradients and these may not be large even though the absolute displacements are. The displacements may be obtained by integrating the displacement gradients.

EXPERIMENTAL PROCEDURE

Figure 3 shows a schematic diagram of the experimental arrangement. A 25 mm wide, 3 mm thick, mild steel bar is supported by clamps at points about 1.5 m apart. The bar surface is painted white to increase reflectivity. A compound pendulum, in the form of a thin wooden strip pivoted at its upper end, is positioned to transversely strike the center of the bar after its release. The lower end of the pendulum is attached to a round-head screw which makes contact with the bar on impact. By adjusting the initial height of the free end of the pendulum, the speed and impulse of the impact can be varied. An infra-red beam emitter and photo-diode detector pair is placed in the trajectory of the pendulum. This emitter-detector pair is mounted on a micrometer to facilitate fine adjustment of its position with respect to the pendulum trajectory. Interruption of this infra-red beam by the pendulum prior to impact triggers the emission of the first laser pulse which illuminates the bar in its undeformed state. Although there is approximately an 800 μs delay after triggering before the first pulse is emitted, this first illumination occurs before impact. The laser used is a 3 joule, Q-switched pulse ruby laser (λ = 694 nm) which can operate in single or multiple pulse mode. Recording of the images of the bar is done by a large-format single lens reflex camera which uses 6 cm x 7 cm film. The glass wedge fitted over half its lens is aligned to shear the images in the direction of the length of the bar. Hence, the fringes in the shearograms represent slopes in the direction of the bar length.

The pendulum and steel bar form part of an electrical circuit which is closed when contact is made upon impact. By incorporating a digital storage oscilloscope into this circuit, the instant of impact is recorded. For the particular laser used, the choice of time interval between the first and second pulse affects the distribution of energy between the pulses. To ensure roughly equal illumination intensities, this interval is set at 400 μs. Hence, control of the duration between impact and the second exposure is achieved by adjusting the position of the infra-red sensor. Moving the sensor closer to the bar causes a later triggering of the first and second pulses; a shearogram thus obtained depicts a later stage of deformation after impact. By varying the position of the sensor, a series of shearograms showing the development and progression of deformation is obtained. The time at which emission of the second pulse occurs is also captured by the oscilloscope. Figure 4 shows the sequence of events recorded by the oscilloscope. The energy and impulse imparted to the bar at impact are determined separately by repeating the impacts and recording the rebound of the pendulum using another camera aimed at the pendulum and with its shutter kept open during this phase.

After each test, the doubly-exposed film is developed and viewed via an optical arrangement (Fig. 5) incorporating a light source, lenses and an opaque stop which serves as a Fourier filter. The resulting shearographic fringe pattern becomes visible at the output plane and this is photographed to provide hard-copy output for fringe interpretation and measurements.

RESULTS AND DISCUSSION

For the set of test results presented, the impact velocity was 0.822 ms^{-1}. The optical elements used produced a horizontal shear δx of 9.6 mm and the sensitivity factor C in equation (3) had a value of 2.18 which resulted in equation (4) assuming the form :

$$\frac{\partial w}{\partial x} = 1.658 \times 10^{-5}(2n+1) \qquad (5)$$

Figure 6(a-d) shows selected photographs taken from a series of shearograms depicting the propagation of out-of-plane deformation generated by impact of the pendulum on the rear of the steel bar. Since deformation is essentially symmetrical about the vertical through the impact point, the camera is positioned such that the impact point is near the left of its field of view. This facilitates the observation of stress wave propagation to points farther from the site of impact. Fig. 6(a-c) are close-ups of the region surrounding the point of impact, showing the nature and extent of deformation at 16 µs, 21 µs and 40 µs after impact respectively. Fig. 6(a) depicts a very early stage of deformation. The impact-generated transverse bending of the bar in this experiment is basically a one-dimensional phenomenon and hence should give rise to straight fringes running across the width of the bar. However, the effect of point contact between the pendulum and bar is clearly evident during this early phase. This initial two-dimensional response manifests itself via the closed loops and curved loci observed. The bright central fringe containing the vertical axis of symmetry denotes the location of impact and maximum displacement. Hence, the displacement gradient here is zero and corresponds to a fringe order of n = -0.5 in equation (4). By moving to the right, along the centreline of the bar, the first dark fringe encountered is of order n = -1 and substitution of this value into equation (5) yields a slope of -1.658x10^{-5}. This is consistent with the fact that the out-of-plane displacement decreases to the right of the impact point. The second dark fringe is of order n = -2 and denotes a steeper negative slope. The fringe order increases numerically to a maximum of n = -4 which corresponds to the fourth dark fringe in the form of a dark spot and defines the location of the steepest slope. This defines the point of inflexion as the fringe orders decrease numerically thereafter back to n = -0.5 (bright fringe) where the slope is zero again and corresponds to the undeflected portion of the bar at the stress wavefront.

Figure 6(b) shows a transition from the two-dimensional nature of the initial stages of deformation to the essentially one-dimensional expected behaviour. This shearogram taken at 21 µs after impact shows the curved and closed loop fringe loci exhibiting an evolution to straighter fringes traversing the bar width. The number of fringes and fringe orders increase in magnitude, indicating the steepening of displacement gradient as the out-of-plane deformation grows. Progression of the deformation wavefront is also evident from the expanded distance between the impact location and the position of the right fringe edge. Fig. 6(c) indicates that by 40 µs after impact, the out-of-plane bending is basically one-dimensional. There is now more than one point of inflexion to the right of the impact location, implying that out-of-plane deflection has both positive and negative values. This can be seen in Figs. 7 and 8 which show respectively the displacement gradient and out-of-plane displacement along an axis running through the centreline of the bar as functions of distance from the impact point at various times after impact. Figure 8 is obtained by integrating the displacement gradients in Fig. 7 and ascertaining an appropriate reference point where the displacement is zero (e.g. the wavefront) to facilitate the integration. Note in Fig. 6(c) that fringes further from the impact site are more spread out, since deformation near the wavefront comprises out-of-plane ripples of small amplitude but long wavelengths. Figure 6(d) shows a longer portion of the bar at 188 µs after impact and this fringe pattern is typical of an advanced stage of deformation. The corresponding displacement gradient and out-of-plane displacement are illustrated in Figs. 7 and 8; the latter shows that the displacement distribution has characteristics somewhat similar to that of a zero-order Bessel function of the first kind - a series of ripples of decaying amplitude. This correlates with numerical results and experiments in holography [10]. By noting the successive positions of the wavefront, the present results show that the flexural wave propagates at a speed of about 1980 ms^{-1}.

It can be seen that as deformation develops, some limitations can arise. Firstly, the wavefront moves out of the field of view of the camera, thereby making it difficult to locate a reference point of zero deflection to facilitate integration of $(\partial w / \partial x)$ to obtain the absolute deflection. If the deflected *shape* rather than the deflection itself is required, then the (impact) point could be used as the (zero deflection) reference point for integration. This will yield a deflection curve which is offset from the actual one by the displacement of the impact point. However, even if the actual deflection is necessary, a good estimate of the offset can be determined by examining the offset deflection curve at the region furthest from the impact point. Here, the amplitude of the deflection ripple has decayed to a small value (e.g. see Fig. 8), thereby providing a narrow band defined by the ripple peak and trough within which the zero deflection line must pass. A second possible limitation is that there can be a large change in deflection gradient over a short segment of the bar, thus causing a high fringe density which makes fringe resolution and interpretation difficult. One method of overcoming this is to change the glass wedge or the optical arrangement to reduce the shear δx in equation (2). Equation (4) shows that a reduction in δx would mean that a larger change in displacement gradient is required to produce a change of one fringe order. Another approach is to employ progressive double exposure - i.e. the first pulse is emitted when the bar is in a state of deformation already evaluated from a previous test. The shearogram thus obtained will depict the displacement gradient relative to the earlier deformed state and therefore exhibit a lower fringe density. The total displacement and displacement gradient can then be evaluated by summing the results of the two stages. Determination of the exact location of the flexural wavefront at later times after impact involves more approximation as the slope at the wavefront tends to reduce with time after impact. Consequently, the slope only becomes large enough to manifest itself as a dark fringe at some distance behind the actual wavefront. If the object of interest is the wavefront position, then this distance can be reduced by increasing the shear δx to make the change in fringe order more sensitive to slope changes.

Although these possible limitations exist which require additional effort to circumvent, pulsed shearography has some inherent advantages over its holographic counterpart which make its employment attractive. Shearographic fringes represent displacement gradient and therefore if the bar curvature ($\partial^2 w / \partial x^2$) were required to evaluate the instantaneous bending moment distribution to examine the current state of the flexural wave, only one numerical (or graphical) differentiation is necessary. With pulsed holography, the displacement from experimental data must be double-differentiated, thus error amplification occurs twice, since numerical differentiation is an error magnifying process. Conversely, integration is a smoothing process and therefore integration of shearographic data to obtain deflection reduces the effect of fluctuations in the original experimental data.

CLOSURE

An optical technique to obtain sequential, instantaneous full-field visual data on the propagation of impact-induced deformation in a beam has been described. Pulse laser shearography provides an interferometric means of analysing the development of out-of-plane displacement gradients in a dynamically loaded structure. The displacement gradients may be integrated to obtain the current deformed surface contour, or differentiated to evaluate curvature and the accompanying bending moment distribution. Although presently applied to investigating a one-dimensional dynamic phenomenon, it has potential in the study of dynamic two-dimensional surface deformation.

REFERENCES

1. Dohrenwend, C.O., Drucker D.C. and Moore, P. "Transverse impact transients". Proc. Society for Experimental Stress Analysis, 1, 1-10, 1944.
2. Hoppmann, W.H. II "Impulsive loads on beams". Proc. Society for Experimental Stress Analysis, 10, 157-164, 1952.
3. Goland M., Wickersham, P.D. and Dengler M.A. "Propagation of elastic impact in beams in bending". Journal of Applied Mechanics, Trans. ASME, 77, 1-7, March 1955.
4. Ripperger E.A. and Abramson, H.N. "A study of the propagation of flexural waves in elastic beams". Journal of Applied Mechanics, Trans. ASME, 24, 431-434, September 1957.
5. Schwieger H. "A simple calculation of the transverse impact on beams and its experimental verification". Experimental Mechanics, 378-384, November 1965.
6. Clark, J.A. and Durelli A.J. "Optical stress analysis of flexural waves in a bar". Journal of Applied Mechanics, Trans. ASME, 37, 431-434, June 1970.
7. Shukla A. and Damania C. "Experimental investigation of wave velocity and dynamic contact stresses in an assembly of disks". Experimental Mechanics, 268-281, September 1987.
8. Erf, R.K. "Holographic nondestructive testing". Academic Press, 1974.
9. Vest, C.M. "Holographic interferometry". John Wiley, 1979.
10. Aprahamian R., Evensen D.A., Mixon J.S. and Wright J.E. "Application of pulsed holographic interferometry to the measurement of propagating transverse waves in beams". Experimental Mechanics, 11, 309-314, July 1971.
11. Aprahamian R., Evensen D.A., Mixon J.S. and Jacoby, J.L. "Holographic study of propagating transverse waves in plates". Experimental Mechanics, 11, 357-362, August 1971.

12. Fallstrom, K.-E., Gustavsson H., Molin N.-E. and Wahlin, A. "Transient bending waves in plates studied by hologram interferometry". Experimental Mechanics, 29, 378-387, December 1989.

13. Fallstrom, K.-E., Lindgren, L.-E., Molin N.-E. and Wahlin, A. "Transient bending waves in anisotropic plates studied by hologram interferometry". Experimental Mechanics, 29, 409-413, December 1989.

14. Hung, Y.Y. and Durelli, A.J. "Simultaneous measurement of three displacement derivatives using a multiple image shearing interferometric camera". Journal of Strain Analysis, 14, 81-88, 1979.

15. Hung, Y.Y. "Shearography : A new optical method for strain measurement and nondestructive testing." Optical Engineering, 21, 391-395, June 1982.

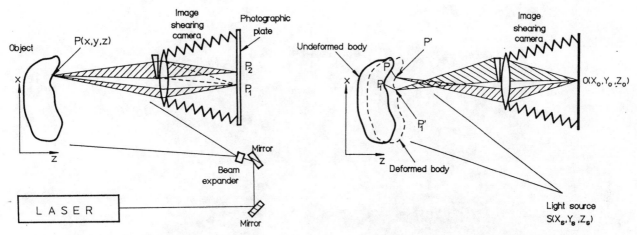

Fig. 1 : Schematic diagram of shearography

Fig. 2 : Change in optical path caused by deformation

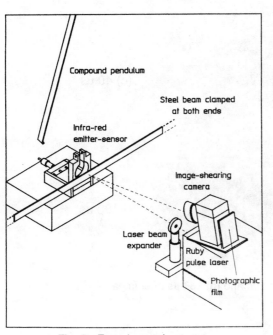

Fig. 3 : Experimental set-up

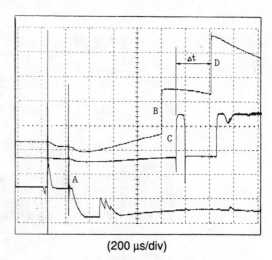

(200 µs/div)

Fig. 4 : Oscilloscope trace of event sequence

A - interruption of sensor ; B - first pulse ;

C - Impact ; D - second pulse ;

Δt - time after impact

683

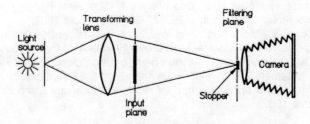

Fig. 5 : Fourier filtering arrangement for fringe observation

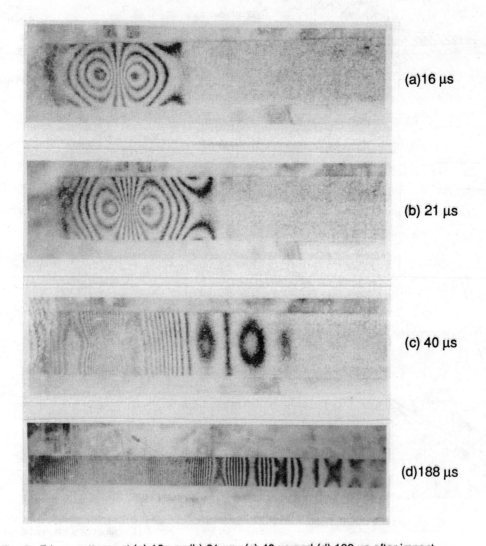

(a) 16 µs

(b) 21 µs

(c) 40 µs

(d) 188 µs

Fig. 6 : Fringe patterns at (a) 16 µs ; (b) 21 µs ; (c) 40 µs and (d) 188 µs after impact

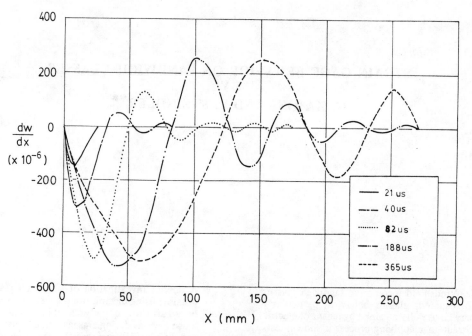

Fig. 7 : Displacement derivatives for right half of bar

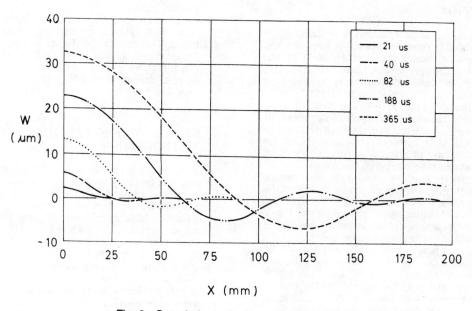

Fig. 8 : Out-of-plane displacement for right half of bar

STRAIN GAGE BEHAVIOR ON SANDWICH GLASSES
BY
G. KAJON* AND R. STEINDLER**

ABSTRACT: Windshield locomotive sandwich glasses properties are resumed; glasses behavior, particularly during tests, may be usefully obtained by means of electric strain gages. Strain gage applying process is shown; tests on sandwich glasses and on other materials (commercial glass, invar, carbon steel), with strain gages from the same group applied on, are related. Test results, i.e. thermal expansion coefficients, thermal hysteresis, thermal drift, mechanical hysteresis and creep, are shown and discussed.

INTRODUCTION

Locomotive windshields are structural components which are heavily stressed in various conditions. A stone or a bird that hit a locomotive running at a speed of about 300 km/h, may cause serious damages (cracks, failures) to windshield glasses. Moreover those accidents may happen at a temperature lower than 0°C or higher than 30÷35°C.

Windshield glass properties may be improved by using sandwich glasses, i.e. sandwiches made of two sheets of tempered glass with a polymer plate between them. These sandwich couple glass stiffness (glass is tempered for safety reasons in case of crashes) to polymer elasticity (polymer resilience compensates glass brittleness).

Due to the heavy working conditions, locomotive windshield glasses must be severly tested in order to be approved [1]. Among the tests one has to do, there are crash resistance and balistic trials: for example one fires a one kilogram bullet against a glass sample at a speed of up to 360 km/h, both at room temperature and at -8°C.

The need to find a new type of sandwich glass, for the European railways, has led us to investigate with care sandwich behavior particullary during tests. These new sandwiches are made by two glass sheets with a polycarbonate plate between them. Two polyvinyl butyral (PVB) sheets join the polycarbonate plate to the glass sheets.

* G. Kajon is research manager, Istituto Sperimentale Ferrovie dello Stato, Piazza Ippolito Nievo 46, 00153 ROMA, ITALY.

** R. Steindler is full professor, Dipartimento di Meccanica e Aeronautica, Università di Roma "LA SAPIENZA", Via Eudossiana 18, 00184 ROMA, ITALY.

A deeper investigation of sandwich glasses behavior is possible using electric strain gages. In fact strain gages, not only can show quickly changing strains and stresses, as those one has during crashes, but can also give the absolute and differential linear thermal expansion coefficients [2].

The aim of this paper is to verify strain gage application to materials such as glasses, whose surfaces can not be roughened before the application. By using strain gages, one can study not only locomotive windshield sandwich glass behavior during the tests, but also the behavior of other types of glasses (bullet-proof glasses, shock resistent glasses, etc.).

Up to our knowledge, except for some small technical notes, no report on strain gage application to glasses can be found. Therefore, a specific technology has been set up. Tanking into consideration specif recommendations [3], [4], [5], strain gage behavior has been studied in a large range of temperature (-25°C, +75°C) including locomotive windshields temperature working range.

STRAIN GAGE APPLICATION AND TEST METHODOLOGY

First of all it has been investigated the most suitable adhesive for applying strain gages to sandwich glasses. The temperature range (-25°C, +75°C) has suggested the use of a rapid adhesive; therefore a cyanide acrylate and an epoxy adhesive have been tested. 6 mm grid strain gages, autocompensated for carbon steel (HBM 6/120 LY 41), have been used. A set of strain gages of this type (all coming from the same lot) have been applied to a sandwich glass of 300 x 300 mm² formed by two 4 mm thick glass sheet and a 12 mm thick policarbonate plate; the strain gages have been also applied to a commercial 10 mm thick glass sheet of 200 x 200 mm² area. After the application, preliminary tests have been made at -25°C and +75°C.

The cyanide-acrylate adhesive (HBM Z 70) is solvent - free and is recommended for metallic and synthetic surfaces, but has not given satisfactory results. In fact we have had problems to locate strain gages due to adhesive viscosity; there have been slippings between gages and materials during preliminary tests.

The epoxy adhesive (HBM X 60) is composed by two phases, a powder component (pure resine) plus a liquid component (catalyst). It is recommended for metallic and non metallic surfaces, as concrete, plastic and glass surfaces. This adhesive has given better results: after surface cleaning with acetone there have not been slipping problems. However, at -25°C, some malfunctions have appeared, due to ice formation between the strain gage base and the glass surface. So before applying strain gages, glass surfaces have been cleaned with freon, to remove the present moisture completely, and the powder component has been increased with respect to the liquid component. In such a way no further malfunctions have been noticed. As the strain gage behavior at +75°C is satisfactory, the epoxy adhesive has been adopted and strain gages have been applied on the glass surfaces, after cleaning them with freon, with this kind of adhesive suitably proportioned.

In such a way strain gages have been applied on the surfaces of a 300 x 300 mm² sandwich glass plate and on the sides of the policarbonate (Fig. 1). For a better evaluation of the results of the tests (see Tab. II and III), strain gages of the same type have been applied on a 200 x 200 mm² commercial glass surface and on invar and carbon steel parallelepiped samples.

First of all we have measured the *strain gages apparent strains* from room temperature (+25°C) to "cold conditions" (0°C and -25°C) and to "hot conditions" (+50°C and +75°C). From the apparent strains ε_{appX}, we can calculate the thermal expansion coefficients β_X of the materials with the gages applied on. Infact we have:

$$\varepsilon_{appX}(t) = [\alpha_G/F + (\beta_X - \beta_G)] \, (t - t_{room}) \qquad (1)$$

where α_G and β_G are the temperature coefficient and the thermal expansion coefficient of the strain gage grid respectively, and F is its gage factor.

Fig. 1 - Strain gages applied on the glass and on the policarbonate of a sandwich.

Equation (1) tells us how the apparent strain of a gage of a definite lot depends on temperature t with respect to room temperature t_{room}. From equation (1) it is easy to get:

$$\beta_X = \beta_E + (\varepsilon_{appX} - \varepsilon_{appE})/(t - t_{room}) \qquad (2)$$

which tells us how β_X depends on the measured apparent strain ε_{appX} and on the apparent strain ε_{appE} of a strain gage applied on a material with thermal expansion coefficient β_E (In this case β_E is thermal expansion coefficient of carbon steel, for which the gage is autocompensated, and $\varepsilon_{appE}(t)$ is given by the manufacturer).

Thermal tests have been performed in order to measure strain gage thermal hysteresis and thermal drift. As regards to the *thermal hysteresis* we have considered both cold cycles and hot cycles. Plates and samples on which strain gages were applied have been first cooled from room temperature to -25°C and then heated again to room temperature; during these cold cycles we have stopped at 0°C. Plates and samples have been then heated from room temperature to +75°C and then cooled again to room temperature; during these hot cycles we have stopped at +50°C. Hysteresis have been calculated by measuring the strains during these thermal cycles.

To study the *thermal drift* of the strain gages, the same plates and samples have been cooled and kept for 72 hours at -25°C and then heated and kept for 72 hours at +75°C. The drifts are obtained measuring the changes of strains at these temperature.

The above mentioned recommendations [3], [4], [5], fix also the *mechanical tests*. Therefore a facility has been built (see further) to apply some established loads to sandwich glass plates for bending it. By loading and unloading the plate and measuring the strains at the same load values, it is possible to calculate the strain gage *mechanical hysteresis*. Keeping the sandwich glass plate at an extablished load and measuring the changes of the strains it is possible to calculate the *creep*.

The mechanical hysteresis tests have been performed at room temperature (+25°C), in cold conditions (0° and -25°C) and in hot conditions (+50°C and +75°C); the creep tests, lasting one month, have been made only at room temperature. The sandwich plate has been loaded and unloaded taking care not to exceed a glass stress egual to one forth of the failure stress.

FACILITIES

The *thermal tests* have been performed by applying four strain gages on the sandwich glass surface and two strain gages on the policarbonate side. For comparison three strain gages have been applied on the commercial glass surface and one strain gage has been applied on the invar and carbon steel samples. The thermal tests have been repeated three times.

Plates and samples have been cooled in a freezer with a thermostat, and have been heated in an air furnace, with a thermostat too; both in the freezer and in the furnace the thermostats keep the required temperature with the precision of 1°C degree. Plate and sample temperatures have been checked by foil Chromel- Alumel thermocouples applied on the glass surfaces with the same technology used to apply strain gages.

Fig. 2 - Facility used during mechanical tests of the strain
gages applied on the sandwich glasses.

The *mechanical tests,* repeated three times as the thermal
ones, have been performed applying four strain gages on
the glass surfaces of the sandwich plate: two of the strain
gages have been applied on the stretched sheet, and two on
the compressed sheet. A couple of strain gages, one
opposite to the other, is put in the centre of the plate, while
the other couple is put in its edge (the application of the
strain gages on the policarbonate side would not be
significant from a mechanical point of view). To perform
mechanical tests, a brass facility that can be housed both in
the freezer and in the furnace has been designed and built
(fig. 2). The facility is formed by a frame to include the
plate and by a stand pointed to the frame; a brass calibrated
screw, on the stand, loads the plate in its centre. The screw
is internally drilled, and two T strain gages (two
perpendicular grids) have been applied on its lateral surface,
so that the applied loads have been measured. The
sensitivity of the calibrated screw is 1.07 μm/m/N.
During the thermal and the mechanical tests, the strains
have been measured by a digital strain meter HBM DMD 20
A, with sensitivity 1 μm/m. A quarter-bridge circuit with
three-wire connection has been used.

TEST RESULTS

Tab. I gives the values of the *thermal expansion coefficients*
of the sandwich materials (glass and policarbonate) and of
the commercial glasses as obtained from equation (2).
Let us notice that the sandwich glass expansion coefficient
gradually decreases with temperature (except in the range
$t_{room} \rightarrow 75°C$) while the policarbonate coefficient increases
with temperature. As the sandwich material coefficients are
higher than those of the glass ($9 \div 10 \times 10^{-6} °C^{-1}$) and lower
than those of the policarbonate ($65 \times 10^{-6} °C^{-1}$) [6], then one

can make the hyphotesis that there is a gradual decreasing
trend of the adhesion of the sandwich materials with
temperature. A deeper analysis of the experimental results
has shown that when $t < -5°C$ the glass thermal expansion
coefficient is $15 \times 10^{-6} °C^{-1}$, while when $t > -5°C$ it is
$10.5 \times 10^{-6} °C^{-1}$. This may be explained by considering the
PVB sheet stiffening at -5°C temperature, which is the PVB
transition temperature.

The commercial glass expansion thermal coefficient values
agree with those given by the handbooks [6], i.e.
$10 \times 10^{-6} °C^{-1}$ at low temperature and at room temperature,
while are some higher at higher temperature.

Tab. I - Thermal expansion coefficents β (t) of different materials ($°C^{-1} \times 10^{-6}$)			
Temperature range	Sandwich		Commercial glass
	Glass	Policarb.	
-25°C → t_{room}	11.4±0.7	43.4±0.6	9.9±0.2
0°C → t_{room}	10.9±0.8	45.7±1.1	10.0±1.0
t_{room} → 50°C	10.5±0.9	50.2±2.1	10.1±0.1
t_{room} → 75°C	10.8±0.9	56.2±2.0	10.7±0.4

Tab. II gives the absolute values of the *thermal hysteresis*
of the strain gages applied to the sandwich materials,
commercial glass, invar and carbon steel. the value of the
hysteresis are very small, but not wholly negligeable at low
temperature; on the contrary, at temperature higher than
room temperature, the hysteresis is negligeable. However,
let us notice that the thermal hysteresis magnitude is the
same for glass and for metals, also in the cold cycle.

Therefore the very small value of the hysteresis is not typical of the particular application of the strain gages studied in this paper.

Tab. II - Thermal hysteresis of the strain gages applied on different materials (μ m/m)

Temper. (°C)	Sandwich		Commercial glass	Invar	Carbon steel
	Glass	Policarb.			
COLD CYCLE (t_{room} → 0°C → -25°C → 0°C → t_{room})					
t_{room}	12±6	13±5	13±4	7±3	8±2
0°C	7±4	20±2	4±2	5±2	4±2
-25°C	/	/	/	/	/
HOT CYCLE (t_{room} → 50°C → 75°C → 50°C → t_{room})					
t_{room}	2±1	5±3	10±2	2±1	3±1
+50°C	2±1	5±1	10±3	2±1	2±1
+75°C	/	/	/	/	/

Tab. III contains the *thermal drift* values of the strain gages applied to the various materials. The values have been taken, both in cold and hot conditions, after 72 hours.
Let us notice that the drift values are always very small, both in cold and hot conditions. Expressing the drift values in μm/m/h, as suggested by the above mentioned reccomandations [4], [5], we would obtain no thermal drift. Therefore the strain gage behavior, particularly on sandwich materials, is very good. To confirm this result, in one test, sandwich plate has been kept 400 hours longer at -25°C. In such a situation the measured strains have not exceded 5 μm/m in the case of glass surfaces and 10 μm/m in the case of on policarbonate side.

Tab.III - Thermal drift in cold an hot conditions of the strain gages applied on different materials (μ m/m) after 72 hours

Temp. (°C)	Sandwich		Commercial glass	Invar	Carbon steel
	Glass	Policarb.			
-25°C	5±2	15±2	3±1	2±1	2±1
+75°C	3±1	2±1	3±1	3±1	2±1

The *mechanical hysteresis* tests have been performed loading the sandwich plate at first to 700 N then after 24 hours to 1400 N and finally to 2100 N. Afterwards the plate has been unloaded, again step by step. At the maximum load the strain values measured the centre of the

plate have been about ±600 μm/m. This value corresponds to a stress of one forth of the glass failure. The strain values at the edge of the plate have been about ±300 μm/m.
During the tests we have noticed a material creep,; as indicated by the calibrated screw; therefore the load has been restored every hour in the first three hours and then after 24 hours.

Table IV contains the algebrical values of the *mechanical hysteresis* of the applied strain gages at different temperature: the strains heve been measured at the end of the step that is 24 hours after the load was applied and after it was restored.
First of all, let us notice that the calculated hysteresis are high, particullary at temperature higher than room temperature. At low temperatures the measured strains are equal to the strains measured at room temperature, at temperature superior to room temperature higher strains have been measured (±800 μm/m at sandwich center with maximum load applied).

Tab.IV - Mechanical hysteresis of the strain gages applied on sandwich surfaces (μ m/m)

Temp. (°C)	Load (N)	Centre strain gage (Inferior glass)	Centre strain gage (Superior glass)	Edge strain gage (Inferior glass)	Edge strain gage (Superior glass)
-25	0	20±2	-25±5	15±2	-15±5
	700	20±4	-15±2	12±2	-10±2
	1400	16±2	-12±2	12±2	-8±3
	2100	/	/	/	/
0	0	40±5	-20±5	30±8	-20±6
	700	30±5	-20±2	30±5	-10±2
	1400	30±5	-15±3	20±2	-10±2
	2100	/	/	/	/
Room	0	40±10	-20±8	10±3	-8±2
	700	50±15	-30±10	10±5	-10±2
	1400	15±2	-15±2	8±2	-6±1
	2100	/	/	/	/
50	0	50±5	-30±4	40±5	-30±2
	700	50±5	-30±2	30±10	-30±5
	1400	30±3	-20±5	30±5	-15±6
	2100	/	/	/	/
+75	0	100±10	-200±20	50±5	-60±15
	700	100±15	-150±20	40±10	-40±10
	1400	80±10	-100±15	30±5	-20±10
	2100	/	/	/	/

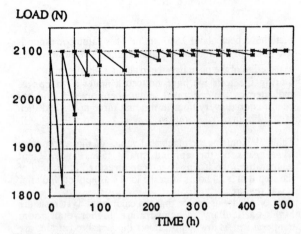

LOAD (N)

Fig. 3 - Creep test at room temperature: load trend, with load restorations every 24 hours.

Besides let us notice that the hysteresis of the strain gages applied on apposite faces of the sandwich at different loads and temperatures always show almost the same magnitude but opposite signs (compare the values of columns 1 and 2 and columns 3 and 4 in tab. IV). Therefore the hysteresis are not due to the strain gages themselves, but to the sandwich; it is probable that residual stesses take place in the sandwich structure.Moreover the increasing values of the strains and mechanical hysteresis with temperature may be due to a decreasing adhesion between the sandwich materials. In fact during the tests performed at 75°C the creep has prevented from easily restoring the load.

Creep tests have been performed restoring the load (2100 N) every 24 hours by means of the calibrated screw. Only after 20 days the load has no longer changed in a meaningful way. Fig. 3 shows the load trend during the second test. The following figures (4→7) show the different strain trends during the same test. The measured creeps with load applied are high but they become constant when load does not change longer in a meanigful way.

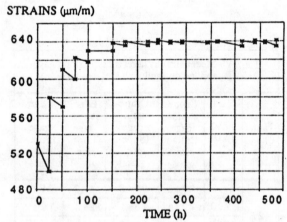

STRAINS (μm/m)

Fig. 4 - Creep test at room temperature: strain trend of the strain gage applied on the centre of the inferior glass.

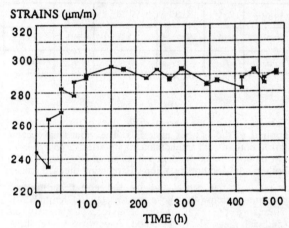

STRAINS (μm/m)

Fig. 6 - Creep test at room temperature: strain trend of the strain gage applied on the edge of the inferior glass.

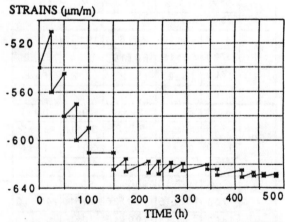

STRAINS (μm/m)

Fig. 5 - Creep test at room temperature: strain trend of the strain gage applied on the centre of the superior glass.

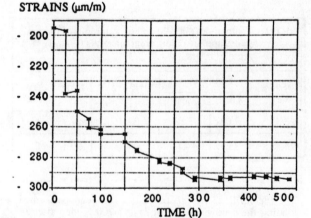

STRAINS (μm/m)

Fig. 7 - Creep test at room temperature: strain trend of the strain gage applied on the edge of the superior glass.

Moreover as for mechanical hysteresis, the values of the strain gages applied on opposite sandwich surfaces are of the same magnitude and of opposite sign (compare fig. 4 to fig. 5 and compare fig.6 to fig. 7). We may deduce that the creep is due to the sandwich and not to the applied strain gages. After the sandwich has been unloaded, there have been residual strains of about $\pm 10\mu m/m$.

The two other tests have given results similar to the related one, both with respect to the load trend and to the strain trend.

CONCLUSION

The performed tests show a really satisfactory behavior of the strain gages applied on the sandwich glasses. The expansion thermal coefficients coming from the apparent strains are reliable in the investigated temperature ranges. Thermal drift is pratically not present, while the thermal hysteresis is nearly negligeable. The mechanical hysteresis and creep are due to the sandwich materials.

Therefore the electric resistance strain gages, applied according to the test methodology given before, are a useful mean to study the behavior of new locomotive sandwich glasses during the tests as well as the behavior of other kind of glasses.

REFERENCES

[1] Specifica tecnica per la fornitura di vetri di sicurezza per rotabili ferroviari.
Specifica tecnica F.S. S.MB/A.03/ST 115.1, 1988.

[2] Steindler R.: "High temperature strain gage behavior on carbon materials", Experimental Mechanics, pagg. 241-248, September 1988.

[3] VDI/VDE 2635: "Dehnungsmesstreifen mit metallischgen Messgitter, Kenngrossen und Prufbedingungen", 1979.

[4] BSI: "Methods for calibration of bonded electric resistance strain gauges", 1972.

[5] NAS 942: "Strain gages, bonded resistance", 1963.

[6] "Handbook of thermophisical properties of Materials", Oxford, Pergamon Press, 1961-63.

ZERO-SHIFT EVALUATION OF AUTOMATIC STRAIN GAGE SYSTEMS

BASED ON DIRECT AND REVERSE-CURRENT METHOD

P.CAPPA - Z.DEL PRETE
University of Rome "La Sapienza"
Dept. Mechanics and Aeronautics
Via Eudossiana, 18 00184 Roma (Italy)

K.C.McCONNELL - L.W.ZACHARY
Iowa State University
Dept. Aerospace Eng.& Eng.Mechanics
Ames, IA 50011 USA

ABSTRACT

Solid-state digital-multimeter are being used in multichannel automatic data acquisition systems to determine strain values from strain gage resistance evaluation rather than using conventional Wheatstone bridge. Both the direct resistance method and the reverse current one are examined in two tests each one lasted for two weeks. Unrelevant differences were observed between the two methods in spite of the adopted general-purpose low-cost switch control unit.

INTRODUCTION

The effects of advances in technology on digital multimeter caused, as is well known, a sensible increase of metrological performances as accuracy and precision also in long-term measurements. The previous observation determined in 1983 [1] the proposal of a non traditional system to measure electrical strain gage outputs collected with a digital ohmmeter; the method is simply based on the direct measurements, carried out by a 4-wire connections, of the transducer resistance values. Moreover, the lead wire length is theoretically unimportant and the intrinsic limitation that is the zeroing the instrumentation at the gage location can be removed shortening, with a resistance very small compared to circuit resistance, at the instrument [2].

The strain system is then significantly simplified; in fact, from a comparative examination of the direct resistance system with the traditional one based on the Wheatstone bridge configuration, emerges that on the first system are not utilized a constant voltage supply unit, precision resistors to complete the bridge, to balance and to calibrate the bridge output. However, the intrinsic simplicity of the direct resistance method implies the unpossibility to compensate the effects caused by test area temperature variations as, on the contrary, it is possible, as is well known, utilizing 1/2 bridge and full bridge configurations.

Moreover, the development of intelligent instrumentations, that can listen from a computer different set-up configurations and send it data via a digital bus, makes possible sequential multichannel automatic strain gage systems simply based on a computer, a digital ohmmeter and a switch unit.

In previous papers [3,4] the limits of stability of automatic sequential systems based on the 4-wire direct resistance method were experimentally examined. It was decided to test the effectiveness of the method when general-purpose low-cost mechanical switches are utilized. The zero-drift values observed in 6-day static tests were always in ranges of + 10 to - 30 μm/m. in test area temperature variations of 24° to 50°C.

Successive experimental tests [5] on the utilization of high speed digital multimeter (100 000 readings/s) showed significant inaccuracy ($\pm$ 200 μm/m) that can be reduced adopting specific averaging scheme, to a value of $\pm$ 50 μm/m. Therefore, the direct resistance method seems to have some effectiveness only in quasi-static measurements.

However, the direct resistance method does not cancel factors such as thermoelectric and electro-chemical effects that can change measurements accuracy. To overcome these limitations the reverse current method was proposed and experimentally validated in preliminary tests [6] conducted on a single channel configuration. The results showed that the reverse current method is superior in holding the zero gage resistance reading at the cost of using several meters (reversible current source, digital ammeter, digital voltmeter).

This paper will comparatively examine the limits of stability of two sequential multichannel automated systems that use a 4-wire connection wiring scheme, one based on the direct resistance method the latter based on the reverse current method.

EXPERIMENTAL TEST SETUP AND PROCEDURE

To evaluate the metrological performances of automatic system in long term data acquisitions based either on the direct resistance method (DRM) and on the reverse current method (RCM), two electrical resistance strain gages were applied on a cantilever.

It was decided to utilize general-purpose strain gages (constantan foil in combination with polymide backing) and a 2-element rosette was chosen for this work (gage length: 1.5 mm; grid width: 1.6 mm; nominal resistance: 120 Ω). The rosette was applied to the cantilever in accordance with the manufacturer's recommendations, by means of a methyl-2-cyanoacrylate adhesive that is generally suggested for routine experimental analysis applications (long term operating temperature range: -32 to 65°C).

The gages installations were checked before and after the tests by measuring the resistance between the gages and the ground. The values observed, always higher than 20 000 MΩ, assured good mechanical properties of the adhesive layers. The observed behavior of the 2-element rosette installation is judged acceptable.

Two different lead wires were chosen in the two tests that were conducted: a 4-conductor flat cable (diameter of 0.4 mm) a 4-conductor twisted cable brieded shielded (diameter of 0.25 mm).

The adopted experimental tests set up are schematized in Fig.1. A low-cost general-purpose switch-control-unit was utilized; the switches have low thermal offset (< 3 μV at the end of their life) but this source of error is not compensated. To measure the current injected and the voltage drop developed over the strain gages a digital ammeter and a digital voltmeter were adopted; the metrological

performances of the chosen devices are reported in Tab.1. The reversible dc-current source, used to drive current through the switches, the lead wires and the gage resistances is characterized, for the selected current values, by the metrological characteristics reported also in Tab.1.

To monitor the environmental temperature variations, two chromel alumel thermocouples, test A, and one chromel alumel thermocouple, test B, were utilized. The thermocouple outputs were measured by a digital voltmeter via a multiplexer capable to complete the thermocouple circuits with a cold junction and to automatically compensate the cold junction temperature differences from 0°C (reference junction compensation accuracy of ± 0.1°C).

The devices are interfaced by means of the IEEE-488 Bus. The experimental data, gathered by a microcomputer are reduced and stored on a hard disc.

In the DRM analysis the current source is set to drive, through the gages, four current values equal to 500 μA, 1 mA, 5 mA and 10 mA; the developed voltage drops are measured by the digital voltmeter. By means of the adopted procedure, the four wire resistance measurement available in digital multimeter are simulated. However, it is necessary to observe that in the commercially available digital ohmmeter is possible to drive only one current value that is generally $\cong$ 1 mA. The DRM tests were conducted gathering the voltage drops, and calculating the resistance values by means of the selected nominal values. Hence, the resistance value $R_{n,1}$ at the generic n^{th} acquisition and for the ith current value selected, is obtained from:

$$R_{n,1} = \frac{V_{n,1}}{I_1} \qquad (1)$$

where $V_{n,1}$ is the generic voltage drop measured for the ith current value selected.

         I_1 is the nominal current value injected by the current source.

The first resistance values, relative to the two examined gages, are used as the reference readings. The zero shift values $\varepsilon_{zs,n,1}$ for the nth reading and for the ith current value is then calculated from the relationship:

$$\varepsilon_{zs,n,1} = \frac{R_{n,1} - R_{1,1}}{F \cdot R_{1,1}} \qquad (2)$$

where $R_{n,1}$ is the generic resistance value relative to one of the four current values selected

$R_{1,1}$ is the first resistance value relative to one of the four current values selected

F is the gage factor

The RCM has the metrological advantage of cancelling the effects of any dc-offset voltage that occurs because of wire-connection thermocouple effects. In the chosen experimental procedure the current source is set to drive a selected current value through the switches, the lead wires and the gages in both the directions. In the RCM analysis both the current injected and the voltage drops are measured by the digital ammeter and the digital voltmeter. The voltage-current relationships for the strain gage resistance R_g are given by:

$$V_p = I_p \cdot R_g + \Delta V_p \qquad (3)$$

$$V_n = I_n \cdot R_g + \Delta V_n \qquad (4)$$

where : V_p is the positive voltage reading
I_p is the positive current reading
ΔV_p is the positive current error voltage
V_n is the negative voltage reading
I_n is the negative current reading
ΔV_n is the negative current error voltage

Subtracting Eq.(4) from Eq.(3) gives:

$$R_g = \frac{V_p - V_n}{I_p - I_n} + \Delta R \qquad (5)$$

where ΔR is the error induced by $\Delta V_p - \Delta V_n$.

If the thermoelectric effects can be assumed to be the same for both positive and negative currents, then ΔR should be nearly zero. Thus the RCM appears to be able to reduce this source of error. In RCM analysis a complete set of data for strain gage resistance evaluation consists of positive and negative voltage and current values. The RCM metrological performances were tested with the same current values chosen in the DRM analysis, i.e. 500 μA, 1 mA, 5 mA, 10 mA. Finally the $\varepsilon_{zs,n,1}$ values are calculated utilizing Eq.(2).

Both the DRM and the RCM were examined by conducting two test; in the first test, test A, the 2-element rosette is connected to the switch control unit by shielded wire leads approximately 10 m long. To smooth the gage installation temperature variations the 2-element rosette installation was placed in a oven chamber. One of the two thermocouple was utilized to measure T_{oven} inside the oven near the gages, the latter T_{lab} to monitor the temperature outside the oven. In the second test, test B, the gages were connected to the switch control unit by unshielded wires approximately 1m long. The gage installations followed the laboratory temperature T_{lab} variations and only one thermocouple was used and placed at the strain gage locations. Both tests A and B lasted for two weeks and each data row, summarized in Tab.2 was collected every twenty minutes and the current values were forced only for the interval of time necessary for the controller to read the current and the voltage drop developed ($\leq$ 0.5 s).

TEST RESULTS

The experimental results relative to DRM analysis are reported in Fig.2A and Fig.2B for test A and test B respectively.

From an examination of Fig.2A a similar behavior of the two examined channels emerges, as a tendency. The same observation is not confirmed for test B, see Fig.2B. In fact, in test B it seems to be confirmed the high dependence of zero shift values, $\varepsilon_{zs,n,1}$, on the first resistance readings, $R_{1,1}$, accordingly with Eq.(2). If $R_{1,1}$ indeed is significantly different from the mean value of the all successive $R_{n,1}$ values, a relevant zero-shift obviously appears; this behavior is more evident for low current supply values, i.e. 500 μA. The current values chosen and the adopted experimental procedure do not cause appreciable heating effects of the two gages.

The environmental temperature variations, showed in Fig.3 for test A and in Fig.4 for test B, seems to cause relevant effects on $\varepsilon_{zs,n,1}$ values. From a comparative examination of Fig.2A with Fig.3 the dependence of $\varepsilon_{zs,n,1}$ on laboratory temperature variations emerges; in fact the five temperature "spikes" of $\cong 5°C$ cause a $\varepsilon_{zs,n,l}$ variation of $\cong 15 \, \mu m/m$. This observed "temperature induced apparent strain" seems to be mainly caused by the temperature coefficients of the devices, see Tab.1. The dependence of $\varepsilon_{zs,n,l}$ on T_{lab} is not denied by a comparative examination of Fig.2B with Fig.4; in this case two observed spikes of $2°-3°C$ determine an apparent strain of $\cong 5 \, \mu m/m$. Moreover in test B clearly appears that a positive T_{lab} trend causes a negative $e_{zs,n,l}$ trend. However, variations in the range of $18°-24°C$ observed in test A determine a zero-shift always in the range of -15 to $+20 \, \mu m/m$, while in test B a temperature range of $27°-30°C$ determines differences between the maximum and the minimum of $\varepsilon_{zs,n,l}$ values always less than $28 \, \mu m/m$.

The results relative to RCM are reported in Fig.5A and Fig.5B for test A and B respectively. Unsignificant differences emerges both in test A and test B, from the obtained zero-shift values of the two examined channels; in fact the $\varepsilon_{zs,n,l}$ is always in the ranges of -18 to $+17 \, \mu m/m$ for test A and of -7 to $+7 \, \mu m/m$ for test B, with the exception of the current value of $500 \, \mu A$ which shows a non repetitive scatter, probably caused for the same reasons ($R_{1,1}$ readings) previously indicated for DRM tests.

The obtained experimental results indicates that, as far as the examined system, the RCM do not improve metrological performances as accuracy and precision with respect to the DRM in spite of the adopted general-purpose low-cost mechanical switch control unit.

CONCLUSIONS

The results relative to a multichannel automatic system based on the direct resistance method indicate unrelevant zero-shift values in tests conducted over two weeks with a temperature variation ranging from $18°C$ to $24°C$ and from $27°C$ to $30°C$ and confirm the effectiveness of this simple method also in system based on low-cost switch control unit.

Almost identical zero-shift trends and ranges of variations were observed adopting the reverse current method, then, relatively to the examined experimental setup, this method seems to not confirm the superiority in maintaining the zero-gage resistance readings for long term data acquisition.

REFERENCES

1. Nelson E.J., Sikorra C.D., Howard J.L. "Measuring strain gages directly without signal conditioning", Experimental Techniques, v 7, n 9, pp 26-28, 1983.

2. Zachary L.W., McConnell K.C., Younis N.T."Accounting for lead wire resistance changes and loss of zero in long-term strain measurements" SEM Spring Conference on Experimental Mechanics, Albuquerque NM, June 4-6, pp 201-204, 1990.

3. Cappa P. "A comparative examination of automatic sequential direct systems for strain-gage data readings based on a low-cost switch-control unit", Experimental Techniques, pag. 13-15, Settembre, 1989.

4. Cappa P. "An experimental analysis of the zero-shift values of automatic and inexpensive strain gage instrumentation systems", Experimental Mechanics, March, pag. 88-92, 1991.

5. Cappa P., Del Prete Z. "An experimental analysis of accuracy and precision of a high speed strain gage system based on the direct resistance method", SEM Spring Conference on Experimental Mechanics, Milwaukee WI, June 10-13, pp 810-817, 1991.

6. Cappa P., McConnell K.G., Zachary L.W. "Zero-shift values of automatic and inexpensive strain gage instrumentation systems", Experimental Mechanics, v 31, n 1, pp 88-92, 1991.

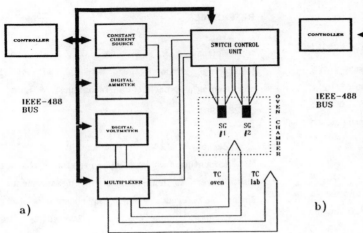

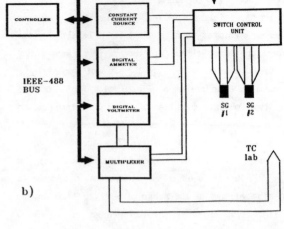

Fig.1   Scheme of the experimental arrangement;
         a) test A,
         b) test B.

Fig.2   Direct resistance method: zero-shift versus time;
         a) test A,
         b) test B.

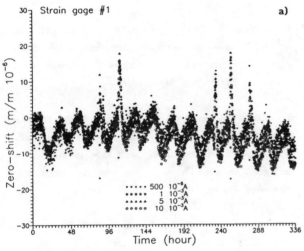

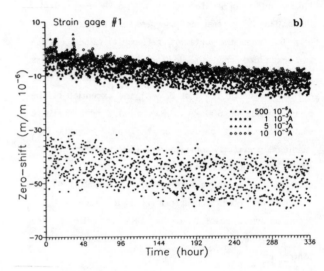

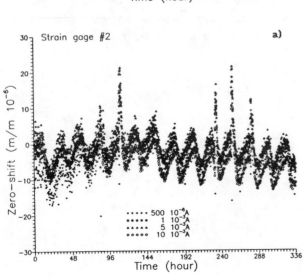

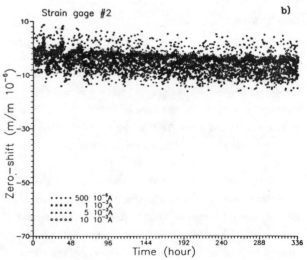

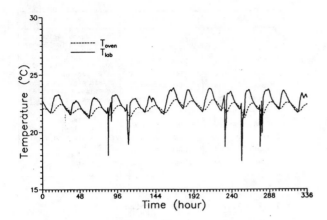

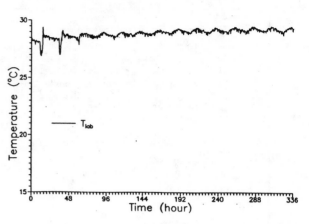

Fig.3

Temperature variations as a function of time; test A.

Fig.4

Temperature variations as a function of time; test B.

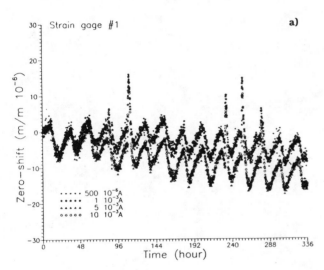

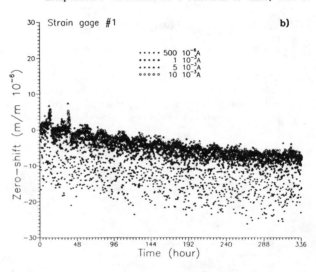

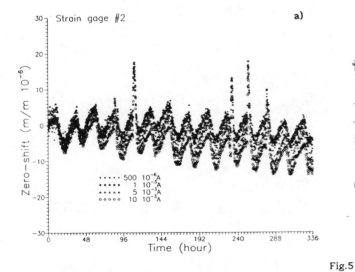

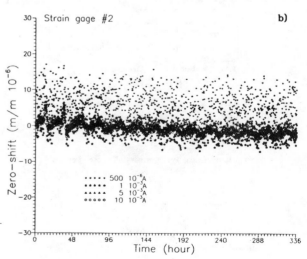

Fig.5   Reverse current method: zero-shift versus time;

a) test A,

b) test B.

Current Source

Accuracy: ±(% of programmed output + amps)

Range	Max. Res.	24 Hour (Tcal±1°C)	90 Day (Tcal±5°C)
1 mA	1 nA	0.001%+9.5nA	0.0052%+20nA
10 mA	10 nA	0.0031%+98nA	0.0074%+220nA

Tcal is the temperature of of calibration

Temperat. Coeff.
±(% of programmed output + amps)/°C

1 mA	0.00036%+1.2nA
10 mA	0.00036%+14nA

Noise & spurious responses (to 250kHz)

peak-to-peak	rms
0.02% of range + 0.7µA	0.003% of range + 70nA

Digital ammeter

Accuracy: (ppm of readings + ppm of Range)

Range	Max. Res.	24 Hour	90 Day
1 mA	100 pA	10+3	15+5
10 mA	1 nA	10+3	15+5

Temperat. Coeff.
(ppm of readings + ppm of Range/°C)

1 mA	2+1
10 mA	2+1

Digital Integrating voltmeter + Relay Multiplexer

Accuracy: ±(% of readings + volts)

Range	Max. Res.	90 Day 18°to28°C, NPLC≥1
300 mV	100 nV	0.008%+8µV
3 V	1 µA	0.008%+10µV

NPLC = Number of Power Line Cycles
(integration time)

Temperat. Coeff. = No additional accuracy error occurs
when operating inside 18° to 28°C.

Tab.1 – Metrological Performances of chosen Devices

DRM		RCM		Remarks
CH. 1	CH. 2	CH. 1	CH. 2	Data row collected: every 20min for 2 weeks
+500µA	+500µA	±500µA	±500µA	**Test A**
+1mA	+1mA	±1mA	±1mA	10m shielded twisted wires from devices to
+5mA	+5mA	±5mA	±5mA	strain gages into the oven; 2 thermocouple
+10mA	+10mA	±10mA	±10mA	measurements T_{lab} & T_{oven}
+500µA	+500µA	±500µA	±500µA	**Test B**
+1mA	+1mA	±1mA	±1mA	1m unshielded wires from devices to strain
+5mA	+5mA	±5mA	±5mA	gages in laboratory enviroment; 1 thermocoup.
+10mA	+10mA	±10mA	±10mA	measurements T_{lab}

Tab.2 – Tests Experimental Procedure

DISCRETE AVERAGING EFFECTS OF A STRAIN GAGE
NEAR A CIRCULAR HOLE

by

Nashwan Younis
Assistant Professor
Department of Engineering
Purdue University at Fort Wayne

Loren W. Zachary
Professor
Department of Aerospace Engineering and
Engineering Mechanics
Iowa State University

ABSTRACT

The discrete averaging effects of a strain gage along the gage filaments are taken into account in the assessment of the errors due to placement of the gage, gage length, gage width, and number of filaments. The gage is placed near the edge of a hole in an infinite plate subjected uniaxial tension.

INTRODUCTION

The averaging effect of a strain gage is a familiar source of error in typical stress concentration problems. Pople[1] lists many human dependent error sources that an engineer must take into account when designing and analyzing a strain gage experiment. Among the sources of errors listed is the placement of the gage. The effect of the strain gradients parallel and transverse to the gage measurement axis is a significant cause of measurement error. An excellent graphical representation of this problem is shown by Perry[2]. He presents a plot of the stress distribution in the near field of a circular hole in a large plate subjected to uniaxial load. When the gage is on the outer surface of the plate near the hole, the strain gage underestimates the maximum strain at the hole. If at all possible, more accurate strains are obtained by placing the gage on the inside of the hole surface. If such a gage placement is not possible, you must choose a small gage and place it as close to the hole as is possible.

The traditional method of examining the strain averaging is to use the average strain over the area of the entire strain gage grid. The gage filament covers only a portion of this area, and this fact needs to be accounted for in an analysis of errors due to strain gage placement. The average strain over the gage filaments is not the same as the average strain over the gage grid area.

A classical plate with a circular hole subjected to uniaxial loading is used as a vehicle for examining the effects of gage length, gage width, number of filaments, and gage misplacement on the average strain experienced by the gage. In this paper it is assumed that no shear lag occurs across the adhesive line, thus the strain experienced by each gage filament is the same as the strain in the plate directly below it. The strain is averaged over each filament length. It is also assumed that the strain does not vary across the individual filament and the strains at the axial midline of the filaments are used in the averaging process.

THEORY

The classical Kirsch[3] solution for the stresses around a hole in a large plate with normal stresses σ_0 applied in the y direction at infinity is, see Fig. 1,

$$\sigma_{rr} = \frac{\sigma_o}{2}\left[(1 - a^2/r^2)(1 + (3a^2/r^2 - 1)\cos 2\theta)\right]$$

$$\sigma_{\theta\theta} = \frac{\sigma_o}{2}\left[(1 + a^2/r^2) + (1 + 3a^4/r^4)\cos 2\theta\right]$$

$$\tau_{r\theta} = \frac{\sigma_o}{2}\left[(1 + 3a^2/r^2)(1 - a^2/r^2)\sin 2\theta\right]$$

In the end, the strain averaging of the gage is modeled by integrating the strains along the filaments. Thus, the strain in the y direction is needed along each filament. The next step is to convert the stresses in the r-θ system to stresses in the x-y coordinate system. The coordinates of point P are x and y and the corresponding coordinates are

$$r = (x^2 + y^2)^{1/2}$$

and

$$\theta_g = \mathrm{Tan}^{-1} y/x$$

The sign of θ_g is not a problem since it will always be in the first or fourth quadrant for this analysis and is positive measured ccw from the x axis. At this point the stresses in the r-θ system are calculated. Now the stresses need to be transformed to the x-y coordinate system using standard stress transformation equations. Only σ_x and σ_y are needed for the final calculation of the strain ε_y.

$$\sigma_x = \sigma_{rr}\cos^2\theta_g + \sigma_{\theta\theta}\sin^2\theta_g - 2\tau_{r\theta}\sin\theta_g\cos\theta_g$$

and

$$\sigma_y = \sigma_{\theta\theta}\cos^2\theta_g + \sigma_{rr}\sin^2\theta_g + 2\tau_{r\theta}\sin\theta_g\cos\theta_g$$

The culmination of these steps gives

$$\sigma_x = \frac{\sigma_o}{2}\left[\frac{a^2}{r^2} - 3\frac{a^4}{r^4} + 6\frac{a^2}{r^4}\left(2\frac{a^2}{r^2} - 1\right)x^2 + \frac{a^2}{r^6}\left(8 - 12\frac{a^2}{r^2}\right)x^4 + \frac{a^2}{r^6}\left(\frac{12a^2}{r^2} - 8\right)x^2y^2\right]$$

and

$$\sigma_y = \frac{\sigma_o}{2}\left[2 - 4\frac{a^2}{r^4}y^2 + 3\frac{a^4}{r^4} - \frac{a^2}{r^2} + 2\frac{a^2}{r^4}\left(1 - 6\frac{a^2}{r^2}\right)x^2 + 12\frac{a^4}{r^8}x^4 + \frac{a^2}{r^6}\left(16 - 12\frac{a^2}{r^2}\right)x^2y^2\right]$$

The last step is to convert the stresses to the strain along the filament using

$$\varepsilon_y = \frac{E}{1 - \nu^2}\left[\sigma_y - \nu\sigma_x\right]$$

The average strain experienced by the n filaments is

$$\varepsilon_{avg} = \frac{1}{nL_g}\sum_{i=1}^{n}\int_{L_g}\varepsilon_{yi}dy$$

where L_g is the gage length and ε_{yi} is the strain in the ith filament.

In the data presented it is assumed that the edge of the gage is at distance x_c from the edge of the hole and the center of the gage is displaced from the lateral axis of the hole by y_c. The width of the gage is w and the filaments are evenly spaced across the width. The average strain is a function of these variables and is written in terms of the non dimensional pi terms

$$\varepsilon_{avg} = g\left[\frac{w}{a}, \frac{L_g}{a}, n, \frac{x_c}{a}, \frac{y_c}{a}\right]$$

RESULTS

The last equation provides a setting for evaluating the influences of each of the parameters. One of the pi terms will be varied while the remaining are held constant. A few such examples will be used to illustrate the magnitude of errors that are possible. The per cent error is with respect to the maximum normal strain that exists at x=a and y=0. The values for Young's modulus and Poisson's ratio are, respectively, 29000 ksi (200 GPa) and 0.3.

The first case, Fig. 2, has a properly aligned gage ($x_c = y_c = 0$) and the gage length of 1/2 of the radius ($L_g/a = 0.5$). Note that increasing the number of filaments increases the

percent error at all w/a ratios. Additional filaments further away from the hole increases the error for a given width gage. A single filament at the hole's edge gives an error of 7.2%. Fig.'s 3 and 4 are for the case of $L_g/a = 0.5$, w/a = 0.5 and $y_c/a = 0$. The lateral distance from the hole is varied. Again there are significant errors encountered as both the number of filaments are increased and the distance from the hole is increased.

Case 3, Fig.'s 5 and 6, again have a properly aligned gage ($x_c = y_c = 0$) and a fixed width of w/a = 0.5. The difference in error between a single filament and two filaments is large for the same L_g/a ratios. The multiple filaments tend to the same line for large L_g/a ratios. Case 4, Fig.'s 7 and 8, show the effects of vertical misplacement. x_c is zero, $L_g/a = 0.5$, and w/a = 0.5. The predominate factor again is the number of filaments. For instance for n = 5 the percent error increases slightly going from $y_c/a = 0$ to 0.2. The fact that multiple filaments are used swamps the error increase do to y_c misplacement.

In general, the number of filaments has a large influence on the error. Secondly, the lateral and vertical misplacements of the gage, Fig.'s 4 and 7, give dramatic increases in error. The usual idea of keeping the gage short and narrow for this strain field case is apparent. An even better situation is obtained if the gage is placed on the inside of the hole surface. The results do show how integrating the strains over the gage filaments gives a good way of assesing the errors due to gage placement, gage size, and number of gage filaments.

ACKNOWLEDGMENTS

Dr. Younis wishes to acknowledge the support he received through a Purdue Research Foundation XLgrant.

REFERENCES

1. Pople, J. "Errors in Strain Measurement--the Human Factor (or How much Do I Contribute?)," Experimental Techniques, V8(9), pp. 34-38, Sept. 1984.
2. Perry, C.C., "The Resistance Strain Gage Revisited," Experimental Mechanics, V24(4), pp. 286-299, Dec. 1984.
3. Kirsch, G. "Die Theorie der Elasticitat und die Bedurfnisse der Festigkeitlehre," Z. Ver. deut. Ing., V32, pp. 797-807, 1898.

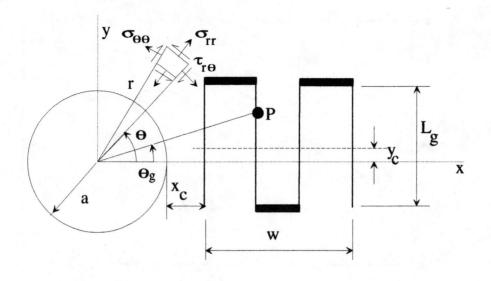

Fig. 1. Definition of Gage and
Stress Parameters

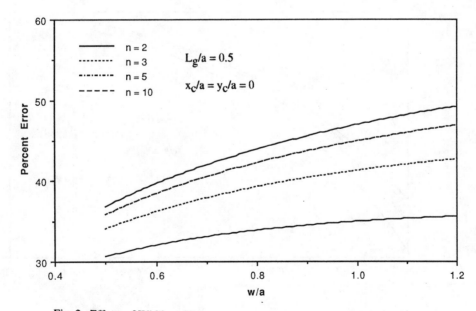

Fig. 2 Effects of Width on Error

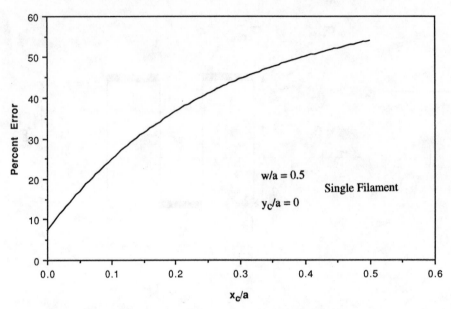

Fig. 3 Effects of Lateral Alignment on Error for a Single Filament

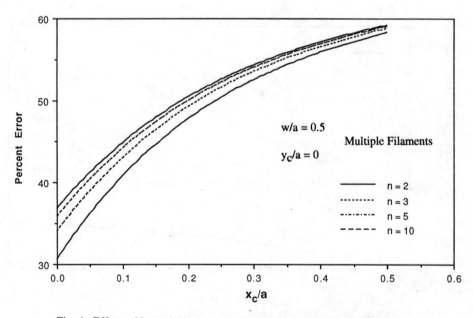

Fig. 4 Effects of Lateral Alignment on Error for Multiple Filaments

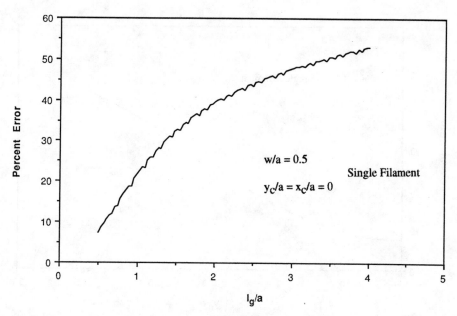

Fig. 5 Effects of Gage Length on Error for Single Filament

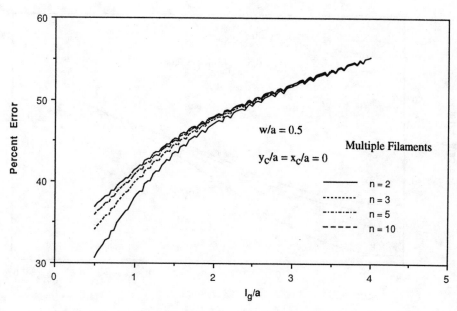

Fig. 6 Effects of Gage Length on Error for Multiple Filaments

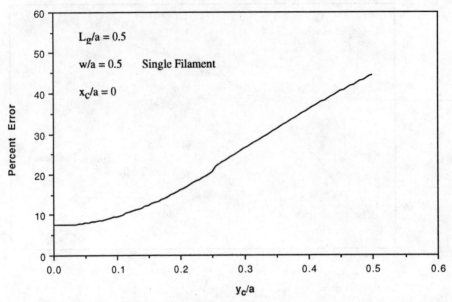

Fig. 7 Effects of Vertical Alignment on Error for Single Filament

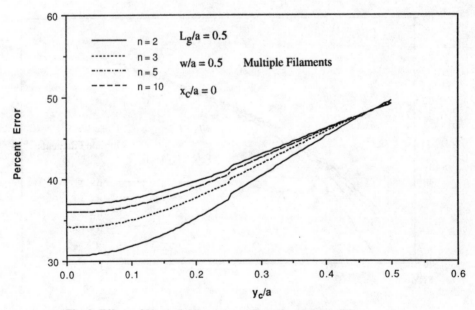

Fig. 8 Effects of Vertical Alignment on Error for Multiple Filaments

PIEZORESISTIVE STRESS SENSORS ON (110) SILICON WAFERS

Y. L. Kang
J. C. Suhling
Department of Mechanical Engineering, and
Alabama Microelectronics Science and Technology Center
Auburn University
Auburn, AL 36849-5341

R. C. Jaeger
Department of Electrical Engineering, and
Alabama Microelectronics Science and Technology Center
Auburn University
Auburn, AL 36849-5201

ABSTRACT

Structural reliability of electronic packages has become an increasing concern for a variety of reasons including the advent of higher integrated circuit densities, power density levels, and operating temperatures. A powerful method for experimental evaluation of die stress distributions is the use of test chips incorporating integral piezoresistive sensors. In this paper, the basic equations needed for the design of stress sensors fabricated on the surface of (110) oriented silicon wafers have been presented. Several sensor rosette configurations have been explored including the familiar three element 0-45-90 rosette. Rosette designs have been found which minimize the necessary calibration procedures and permit more stress components to be measured. It has been established that stress sensors on the surface of (110) test chips are sensitive to four out of the six stress components at a point.

INTRODUCTION

Stresses in electronic packages can cause premature mechanical failures due to such causes as fracture of the die, severing of connections, die bond failure, solder fatigue, and encapsulant cracking. These stresses often are thermally-induced and result from uneven expansions and contractions of the various assembly materials due to mismatches in the coefficients of thermal expansion (CTE's). Stresses also are caused by the presence of non-uniform temperature distributions across the device (thermal gradients) and various mechanical loads transmitted to the package. Structural failure of a component can occur due to excessively high static stresses at a particular temperature extreme or due to fatigue failure from time dependent (cyclic) temperature distributions which cause cyclic stress states. These material and structural reliability problems are of ever increasing concern as larger scale chips and higher temperature applications are considered.

Piezoresistive stress sensors (semiconductor strain gages) are a powerful tool for experimental structural analysis of electronic packages. They are conveniently fabricated into the surface of the die as part of the normal processing procedure. In addition, they are capable of providing non-intrusive measurements of surface stress states on a chip even within encapsulated packages. If the piezoresistive sensors are calibrated over a wide temperature range, thermally-induced stresses can be measured. Finally, a full-field mapping of the stress distribution over a die's surface can be obtained using specially designed test chips which incorporate an array of sensor rosettes and multiplexing circuitry.

In recent studies [1-2], the authors and their co-workers have reviewed and expanded on the general theory of piezoresistivity, and have derived the primary equations needed for designing silicon test chip stress sensors. The results in reference [1] were for fixed temperature conditions. In reference [2], emphasis was placed on including the influence of temperature in all of the theoretical developments. Conduction equations with the most general possible stress and temperature dependencies were first explored, and then later simplified to an applicable form by introducing suitable engineering assumptions. Expressions have been obtained for the resistance changes experienced by arbitrarily oriented filamentary resistors which are subjected to general temperature changes and three-dimensional stress states.

In the current microelectronics industry, it is most common for silicon devices to be fabricated using (100) silicon wafers. The other customarily utilized wafer orientation is (111). Ingots grown along this orientation benefit from higher crystallographic quality, and (111) wafers have been primarily used in semiconductor applications such as alloy junction devices and bipolar transistors. Sensors fabricated using these two most common wafer orientations were discussed in detail in reference [1]. Although not as popular, other wafer orientations such as (110) and (115) have also found application [3]. Some advantages of using (110) technology have been discussed in the literature. Silicon diode arrays used as photosensitive targets in vidicon tubes have been obtained with improved blooming control [4]. It has also been found that some transistors on (110) planes can achieve higher peak mobilities than those on (100) planes, as well as hole and electron mobilities that are nearly equal [5].

In this work, the theories developed by the authors have been applied to the special case of sensing resistors fabricated using (110) silicon wafers. General expressions for the resistance changes experienced by resistors which lie in the (110) plane have been derived. In particular, the normalized resistance change for an in-plane resistor at an arbitrary orientation has been expressed as a function of the stress components and the three piezoresistive coefficients. Several sensor rosette configurations have been explored including the familiar three element 0-45-90 rosette. Rosette designs have been found which minimize the necessary calibration procedures and permit more stress components to be measured. These configurations include the use of optimal resistor orientations, and the incorporation of both n-type and p-type resistors. The ability of sensors fabricated on (110) silicon to measure out-of-plane normal stresses has been studied.

APPLICATIONS USING (110) SILICON WAFERS

General Equations for Sensors on (110) Wafers

An arbitrarily oriented silicon filamentary conductor is shown in Figure 1. The unprimed axes $x_1 = [100]$, $x_2 = [010]$, and $x_3 = [001]$ are the principal crystallographic directions of the cubic (m3m) silicon crystal. The primed coordinate system is arbitrarily rotated with respect this unprimed crystallographic system. For this conductor, the normalized change in resistance can be expressed in terms of the off-axis (primed) stress components using [1]

$$\frac{\Delta R}{R} = (\pi_{1\alpha}' \sigma_\alpha')l'^2 + (\pi_{2\alpha}' \sigma_\alpha')m'^2 + (\pi_{3\alpha}' \sigma_\alpha')n'^2$$
$$+ 2(\pi_{4\alpha}' \sigma_\alpha')l'n' + 2(\pi_{5\alpha}' \sigma_\alpha')m'n' + 2(\pi_{6\alpha}' \sigma_\alpha')l'm' \qquad (1)$$

where $\pi_{\alpha\beta}'$ ($\alpha, \beta = 1, 2, ..., 6$) are the off-axis piezoresistive coefficients, and l', m', n' are the direction cosines of the conductor orientation with

respect to the x_1', x_2', x_3' axes, respectively. In eq. (1), the summation convention is implied for repeated indices, and reduced index notation has been used for the stress components

$$\sigma_1' = \sigma_{11}', \ \sigma_2' = \sigma_{22}', \ \sigma_3' = \sigma_{33}'$$
$$\sigma_4' = \sigma_{13}', \ \sigma_5' = \sigma_{23}', \ \sigma_6' = \sigma_{12}' \qquad (2)$$

The 36 off-axis piezoresistive coefficients in eq. (1) are related to the three unique on-axis piezoresistive coefficients $\pi_{11}, \pi_{12}, \pi_{44}$ (evaluated in the unprimed coordinate system aligned with the crystallographic axes) using the transformation [1]

$$\pi_{\alpha\beta}' = T_{\alpha\gamma} \pi_{\gamma\delta} T_{\delta\beta}^{-1} \qquad (3)$$

where

$$[\pi_{ij}] = \begin{bmatrix} \pi_{11} & \pi_{12} & \pi_{12} & 0 & 0 & 0 \\ \pi_{12} & \pi_{11} & \pi_{12} & 0 & 0 & 0 \\ \pi_{12} & \pi_{12} & \pi_{11} & 0 & 0 & 0 \\ 0 & 0 & 0 & \pi_{44} & 0 & 0 \\ 0 & 0 & 0 & 0 & \pi_{44} & 0 \\ 0 & 0 & 0 & 0 & 0 & \pi_{44} \end{bmatrix} \qquad (4)$$

and

$$[T_{\alpha\beta}] = \begin{bmatrix} l_1^2 & m_1^2 & n_1^2 & 2l_1 n_1 & 2m_1 n_1 & 2l_1 m_1 \\ l_2^2 & m_2^2 & n_2^2 & 2l_2 n_2 & 2m_2 n_2 & 2l_2 m_2 \\ l_3^2 & m_3^2 & n_3^2 & 2l_3 n_3 & 2m_3 n_3 & 2l_3 m_3 \\ l_1 l_3 & m_1 m_3 & n_1 n_3 & l_1 n_3 + l_3 n_1 & m_1 n_3 + m_3 n_1 & l_1 m_3 + l_3 m_1 \\ l_2 l_3 & m_2 m_3 & n_2 n_3 & l_2 n_3 + l_3 n_2 & m_2 n_3 + m_3 n_2 & l_2 m_3 + l_3 m_2 \\ l_1 l_2 & m_1 m_2 & n_1 n_2 & l_1 n_2 + l_2 n_1 & m_1 n_2 + m_2 n_1 & l_1 m_2 + l_2 m_1 \end{bmatrix} \qquad (5)$$

are elements of a six by six transformation matrix related to the direction cosines for the unprimed and primed coordinate systems. In eq. (5), the direction cosines for the two coordinate systems are given by

$$[a_{ij}] = \begin{bmatrix} a_{11} & a_{12} & a_{13} \\ a_{21} & a_{22} & a_{23} \\ a_{31} & a_{32} & a_{33} \end{bmatrix} = \begin{bmatrix} l_1 & m_1 & n_1 \\ l_2 & m_2 & n_2 \\ l_3 & m_3 & n_3 \end{bmatrix} \qquad (6)$$

where

$$a_{ij} = \cos(x_i', x_j) \qquad (7)$$

A general (110) silicon wafer is shown in Figure 2. The surface of the wafer is a (110) plane, and the [110] direction is normal to the wafer plane. The principal crystallographic axes $x_1 = [100]$ and $x_2 = [010]$ do not lie in the wafer plane and have not been indicated. For analysis, it is convenient to work in an off-axis primed coordinate system where the axes

x_1', x_2' are parallel and perpendicular to the primary wafer flat. Using eq. (1), the resistance change of an arbitrarily oriented in-plane sensor can be expressed in terms of the stress components resolved in this natural wafer coordinate system. The off-axis piezoresistive coefficients in the primed coordinate system must be first evaluated by substituting the unprimed values in eq. (4) and the appropriate direction cosines into the transformation relations given in eq. (3). For the primed coordinate system indicated in Figure 2, the direction cosines are

$$[a_{ij}] = \begin{bmatrix} -\dfrac{1}{\sqrt{2}} & \dfrac{1}{\sqrt{2}} & 0 \\ 0 & 0 & 1 \\ \dfrac{1}{\sqrt{2}} & \dfrac{1}{\sqrt{2}} & 0 \end{bmatrix} \qquad (8)$$

Substitution of the off-axis piezoresistive coefficients, calculated in the manner described above, into eq. (1) yields

$$\frac{\Delta R}{R} = \left[\left(\frac{\pi_{11} + \pi_{12} + \pi_{44}}{2} \right) \sigma_{11}' + \pi_{12} \sigma_{22}' + \left(\frac{\pi_{11} + \pi_{12} - \pi_{44}}{2} \right) \sigma_{33}' \right] l'^2 \qquad (9)$$
$$+ \left[\pi_{12} \sigma_{11}' + \pi_{11} \sigma_{22}' + \pi_{12} \sigma_{33}' \right] m'^2 + 2\pi_{44} \sigma_{12}' l' m'$$

where

$$l' = \cos\theta \qquad m' = \sin\theta \qquad (10)$$

are the direction cosines of the resistor orientation with respect to the x_1', x_2' axes, and θ is the angle between the x_1'-axis and the resistor orientation. Equation (9) indicates that the out-of-plane shear stresses σ_{13}' and σ_{23}' do not influence the resistances of stress sensors fabricated on (110) silicon wafers. This means that a sensor rosette on (110) silicon can at best measure four of the six unique components of the stress tensor at a point.

Three Element 0-45-90 Rosette

A three element rosette suitable for evaluating plane stress states on the surface of a die fabricated using (110) silicon is shown in Figure 3. The sensing elements make angles of 0°, 45°, and 90° from the x_1'-axis. Repeated application of eq. (9) to each of the piezoresistive sensing elements leads to the following expressions for the stress-induced resistance changes:

$$\frac{\Delta R_1}{R_1} = \left(\frac{\pi_{11} + \pi_{12} + \pi_{44}}{2} \right) \sigma_{11}' + \pi_{12} \sigma_{22}' + \left(\frac{\pi_{11} + \pi_{12} - \pi_{44}}{2} \right) \sigma_{33}'$$

$$\frac{\Delta R_2}{R_2} = \left(\frac{\pi_{11} + 3\pi_{12} + \pi_{44}}{4} \right) \sigma_{11}' + \left(\frac{\pi_{11} + \pi_{12}}{2} \right) \sigma_{22}'$$
$$+ \left(\frac{\pi_{11} + 3\pi_{12} - \pi_{44}}{4} \right) \sigma_{33}' + \pi_{44} \sigma_{12}' \qquad (11)$$

$$\frac{\Delta R_3}{R_3} = \pi_{12} \sigma_{11}' + \pi_{11} \sigma_{22}' + \pi_{12} \sigma_{33}'$$

For plane stress situations ($\sigma_{33}' = 0$), these equations can be inverted to solve for the in-plane normal stress components in terms of the measured resistance changes

$$\sigma_{11}' = \frac{2\pi_{11}\left[\dfrac{\Delta R_1}{R_1} \right] - 2\pi_{12}\left[\dfrac{\Delta R_3}{R_3} \right]}{\pi_{11}(\pi_{11} + \pi_{12} + \pi_{44}) - 2\pi_{12}^2}$$

$$\sigma_{22}' = \frac{(\pi_{11} + \pi_{12} + \pi_{44})\left[\dfrac{\Delta R_3}{R_3} \right] - 2\pi_{12}\left[\dfrac{\Delta R_1}{R_1} \right]}{\pi_{11}(\pi_{11} + \pi_{12} + \pi_{44}) - 2\pi_{12}^2} \qquad (12)$$

$$\sigma_{12}' = \left[\frac{1}{\pi_{44}} \right] \left[\frac{\Delta R_2}{R_2} - \frac{1}{2}\left(\frac{\Delta R_1}{R_1} + \frac{\Delta R_3}{R_3} \right) \right]$$

Values for all three of the piezoresistive coefficients must be found to utilize the expressions in eq. (12). These constants can be measured using uniaxial loading and hydrostatic pressure calibration procedures. If the wafer is cut into specimen strips as indicated in Figure 3, and a known uniaxial stress $\sigma_{11}' = \sigma$ is applied in the x_1'-direction, the expressions in eq. (11) reduce to

$$\frac{\Delta R_1}{R_1} = \left(\frac{\pi_{11} + \pi_{12} + \pi_{44}}{2} \right) \sigma$$

$$\frac{\Delta R_2}{R_2} = \left(\frac{\pi_{11} + 3\pi_{12} + \pi_{44}}{4} \right) \sigma \qquad (13)$$

$$\frac{\Delta R_3}{R_3} = \pi_{12} \sigma$$

With a controlled application of uniaxial stress, the relations in eq. (13) can be manipulated to determine the values of π_{12} and $(\pi_{11} + \pi_{44})$. Application of an additional state of stress is required to complete the calibration procedure. If this stress state is chosen to be a hydrostatic pressure ($\sigma_{11}' = \sigma_{22}' = \sigma_{33}' = -p$), the expressions in eq. (11) become

$$\frac{\Delta R_1}{R_1} = \frac{\Delta R_2}{R_2} = \frac{\Delta R_3}{R_3} = -[\pi_{11} + 2\pi_{12}]p \qquad (14)$$

With a controlled application of a hydrostatic loading,

eq. (14) can be used to determine the value of $(\pi_{11} + 2\pi_{12})$. The individual values of π_{11}, π_{12}, π_{44} can then be obtained by algebraic manipulation of the combined piezoresistive parameters obtained with the uniaxial loading and hydrostatic pressure calibration procedures.

Rotated Three Element 0-45-90 Rosette

The three element rosette presented above could not be calibrated with a single uniaxial loading test when the wafer was cut into strips as indicated in Figure 3. Analysis of the expressions in eq. (11) has indicated that a single uniaxial tension calibration procedure cannot yield all three of the needed piezoresistive coefficients when the wafer is cut into strips along either of the primed coordinate directions shown in Figure 3. Only uniaxial testing at an odd orientation (e.g. $\theta = 38°$) will provide an easy one step calibration of this sensor rosette. Such a procedure will require slicing the wafer into strips at the odd orientation. Therefore, the three element sensor rosette will not line up conveniently with the edges of the rectangular test chips eventually cut from these odd angle wafer strips.

Although not a major inconvenience, the difficulties discussed above can be avoided if an off-axis three element sensor rosette is utilized, and the wafer strips are cut parallel and perpendicular to the resistors in the rosette. Such a sensor rosette is shown in Figure 4, where the x_1'', x_2'' axes are rotated by 45° from the wafer coordinate axes x_1', x_2'. The sensing elements now make angles of 0°, 45°, and 90° from the x_1''-direction.

The direction cosines for the double primed coordinate system shown in Figure 4 are

$$[a_{ij}] = \begin{bmatrix} -\dfrac{1}{2} & \dfrac{1}{2} & \dfrac{1}{\sqrt{2}} \\[2mm] \dfrac{1}{2} & -\dfrac{1}{2} & \dfrac{1}{\sqrt{2}} \\[2mm] \dfrac{1}{\sqrt{2}} & \dfrac{1}{\sqrt{2}} & 0 \end{bmatrix} \tag{15}$$

Substitution of the off-axis piezoresistive coefficients, calculated using eq. (3), into eq. (1) yields

$$\frac{\Delta R}{R} = \left[C_1 \sigma_{11}'' + C_2 \sigma_{22}'' + \left(\frac{2C_2 - C_3}{2} \right) \sigma_{33}'' + C_3 \sigma_{12}'' \right] l''^2$$
$$+ \left[C_2 \sigma_{11}'' + C_1 \sigma_{22}'' + \left(\frac{2C_2 - C_3}{2} \right) \sigma_{33}'' + C_3 \sigma_{12}'' \right] m''^2 \tag{16}$$
$$+ \left[C_3 \left(\sigma_{11}'' + \sigma_{22}'' \right) - 2C_3 \sigma_{33}'' + 2 \left(C_1 - C_2 + 3C_3 \right) \sigma_{12}'' \right] l'' m''$$

where

$$l'' = \cos\phi \qquad m'' = \sin\phi \tag{17}$$

and

$$C_1 = \frac{3\pi_{11} + 5\pi_{12} + 5\pi_{44}}{8}$$

$$C_2 = \frac{3\pi_{11} + 5\pi_{12} - 3\pi_{44}}{8} \tag{18}$$

$$C_3 = \frac{\pi_{11} - \pi_{12} - \pi_{44}}{4}$$

are a set of linearly independent combined piezoresistive parameters.

Repeated application of eq. (16) to each of the piezoresistive sensing elements leads to the following expressions for the stress-induced resistance changes:

$$\frac{\Delta R_1}{R_1} = C_1 \sigma_{11}'' + C_2 \sigma_{22}'' + \left(\frac{2C_2 - C_3}{2} \right) \sigma_{33}'' + C_3 \sigma_{12}''$$

$$\frac{\Delta R_2}{R_2} = \left[\frac{C_1 + C_2 + C_3}{2} \right] \left(\sigma_{11}'' + \sigma_{22}'' \right)$$
$$+ \left[\frac{2C_2 - 3C_3}{2} \right] \sigma_{33}'' + \left[C_1 - C_2 + 4C_3 \right] \sigma_{12}'' \tag{19}$$

$$\frac{\Delta R_3}{R_3} = C_2 \sigma_{11}'' + C_1 \sigma_{22}'' + \left(\frac{2C_2 - C_3}{2} \right) \sigma_{33}'' + C_3 \sigma_{12}''$$

For plane stress situations ($\sigma_{33}'' = 0$), these equations can be inverted to solve for the in-plane normal stress components in terms of the measured resistance changes

$$\sigma_{11}'' = \frac{C_1 \left[\dfrac{\Delta R_1}{R_1} \right] - C_2 \left[\dfrac{\Delta R_3}{R_3} \right]}{C_1^2 - C_2^2}$$

$$+ \frac{2C_3(C_1 + C_2)\left[\dfrac{\Delta R_2}{R_2} \right] - C_3(C_1 + C_2 + C_3)\left[\dfrac{\Delta R_1}{R_1} + \dfrac{\Delta R_3}{R_3} \right]}{2(C_1 + C_2)\left(C_2^2 + C_3^2 - C_1^2 - 3C_1 C_3 - 3C_2 C_3 \right)}$$

$$\sigma_{22}'' = \frac{C_2 \left[\dfrac{\Delta R_1}{R_1} \right] - C_1 \left[\dfrac{\Delta R_3}{R_3} \right]}{\left(C_2^2 - C_1^2 \right)} \tag{20}$$

$$+ \frac{2C_3(C_1 + C_2)\left[\dfrac{\Delta R_2}{R_2} \right] - C_3(C_1 + C_2 + C_3)\left[\dfrac{\Delta R_1}{R_1} + \dfrac{\Delta R_3}{R_3} \right]}{2(C_1 + C_2)\left(C_2^2 + C_3^2 - C_1^2 - 3C_1 C_3 - 3C_2 C_3 \right)}$$

$$\sigma_{12}'' = \frac{(C_1 + C_2 + C_3)\left[\frac{\Delta R_1}{R_1} + \frac{\Delta R_3}{R_3}\right] - 2(C_1 + C_2)\left[\frac{\Delta R_2}{R_2}\right]}{2\left(C_2^2 + C_3^2 - C_1^2 - 3C_1C_3 - 3C_2C_3\right)} \qquad (20)$$

Values for all three of the piezoresistive coefficients must be found to utilize the expressions in eq. (20). These constants can be measured using a single uniaxial loading calibration procedure. When a known uniaxial stress $\sigma_{11}'' = \sigma$ is applied in the x_1''-direction, the expressions in eq. (19) reduce to

$$\frac{\Delta R_1}{R_1} = C_1 \sigma$$

$$\frac{\Delta R_2}{R_2} = \left\{\frac{C_1 + C_2 + C_3}{2}\right\}\sigma \qquad (21)$$

$$\frac{\Delta R_3}{R_3} = C_2 \sigma$$

With a controlled application of uniaxial stress, the relations in eq. (21) can be used to determine the three linearly independent combined piezoresistive parameters C_1, C_2, C_3. These parameters can then be algebraically manipulated to find the individual values of π_{11}, π_{12}, π_{44}.

Rosettes Capable of Measuring Four Stress Components

From eq. (9), it is seen that the resistance change of an in-plane sensor fabricated on (110) silicon depends on four stress components (σ_{11}', σ_{22}', σ_{33}', σ_{12}'). The rosettes discussed above have not been able to measure the out-of-plane normal stress σ_{33}'. It seems natural to assume that the potential exists to design a four element rosette capable of measuring four stress components. However, it can be easily shown using procedures similar to those in reference [1], that no four element rosette in the (110) plane can be found which is capable of measuring all four stress components.

The above discussion pertains to rosettes formed with identically doped sensing resistors. A four element sensor rosette which contains two n-type resistors and two p-type resistors has been designed by Miura, et al. [6] for (100) silicon. The configuration of the sensing elements for a conceptually similar rosette used with (110) silicon is illustrated in Figure 5. This sensor rosette is capable of measuring four stress components because the piezoresistive coefficients of the n-type and p-type resistors are different.

Repeated application of eq. (9) to each of the rosette elements in Figure 5 leads to the following expressions for the stress-induced resistance changes:

$$\frac{\Delta R_1}{R_1} = \left(\frac{\pi_{11}^n + \pi_{12}^n + \pi_{44}^n}{2}\right)\sigma_{11}' + \pi_{12}^n \sigma_{22}' + \left(\frac{\pi_{11}^n + \pi_{12}^n - \pi_{44}^n}{2}\right)\sigma_{33}'$$

$$\frac{\Delta R_2}{R_2} = \pi_{12}^n \sigma_{11}' + \pi_{11}^n \sigma_{22}' + \pi_{12}^n \sigma_{33}'$$

$$\frac{\Delta R_3}{R_3} = \left(\frac{\pi_{11}^p + \pi_{12}^p + \pi_{44}^p}{2}\right)\sigma_{11}' + \pi_{12}^p \sigma_{22}' + \left(\frac{\pi_{11}^p + \pi_{12}^p - \pi_{44}^p}{2}\right)\sigma_{33}'$$

$$\frac{\Delta R_4}{R_4} = \left(\frac{\pi_{11}^p + 3\pi_{12}^p + \pi_{44}^p}{4}\right)\sigma_{11}' + \left(\frac{\pi_{11}^p + \pi_{12}^p}{2}\right)\sigma_{22}'$$

$$+ \left(\frac{\pi_{11}^p + 3\pi_{12}^p - \pi_{44}^p}{4}\right)\sigma_{33}' + \pi_{44}^p \sigma_{12}'$$

(22)

The n and p superscripts on the piezoresistive coefficients in eq. (22) denote n-type and p-type resistors, respectively. These equations can be inverted to solve for the three in-plane stress components and the out-of-plane normal stress component. This calculation gives

$$\sigma_{11}' = \left(\frac{\pi_{11}^n D_2^p - \pi_{12}^n \pi_{12}^p}{\Delta}\right)\left[\frac{\Delta R_1}{R_1}\right] + \left(\frac{\pi_{12}^n D_2^p - \pi_{12}^n D_2^n}{\Delta}\right)\left[\frac{\Delta R_2}{R_2}\right]$$

$$+ \left(\frac{\left(\pi_{12}^n\right)^2 - \pi_{11}^n D_2^n}{\Delta}\right)\left[\frac{\Delta R_3}{R_3}\right]$$

$$\sigma_{22}' = \left(\frac{\pi_{12}^n \pi_{44}^p}{\Delta}\right)\left[\frac{\Delta R_1}{R_1}\right] + \left(\frac{D_2^p D_1^n - D_1^p D_2^n}{\Delta}\right)\left[\frac{\Delta R_2}{R_2}\right]$$

$$- \left(\frac{\pi_{12}^n \pi_{44}^p}{\Delta}\right)\left[\frac{\Delta R_3}{R_3}\right] \qquad (23)$$

$$\sigma_{33}' = \left(\frac{\pi_{12}^n \pi_{12}^p - \pi_{11}^n D_1^p}{\Delta}\right)\left[\frac{\Delta R_1}{R_1}\right] + \left(\frac{\pi_{12}^n D_1^p - D_1^n \pi_{12}^p}{\Delta}\right)\left[\frac{\Delta R_2}{R_2}\right]$$

$$+ \left(\frac{\pi_{11}^n D_1^p - \left(\pi_{12}^n\right)^2}{\Delta}\right)\left[\frac{\Delta R_3}{R_3}\right]$$

$$\sigma_{12}' = \left(\frac{1}{\pi_{44}^p}\right)\left[\frac{\Delta R_4}{R_4}\right] - \frac{D_3^p \sigma_{11}' + D_4^p \sigma_{22}' + D_5^p \sigma_{33}'}{\pi_{44}^p}$$

where

$$\Delta = D_1^n\left[\pi_{11}^n D_2^p - \pi_{12}^n \pi_{12}^p\right] + \pi_{44}^p\left(\pi_{12}^n\right)^2 + D_2^n\left[\pi_{12}^n \pi_{12}^p - \pi_{11}^n D_1^p\right] \qquad (24)$$

and

$$D_1 = \frac{\pi_{11} + \pi_{12} + \pi_{44}}{2}$$

$$D_2 = \frac{\pi_{11} + \pi_{12} - \pi_{44}}{2} \qquad (25)$$

$$D_3 = \frac{\pi_{11} + 3\pi_{12} + \pi_{44}}{4}$$

$$D_4 = \frac{\pi_{11} + \pi_{12}}{2} \qquad (25)$$

$$D_5 = \frac{\pi_{11} + 3\pi_{12} - \pi_{44}}{4}$$

have been introduced in eq. (23) to reduce the length of the formulas.

The expressions in eq. (23) require accurate values for six piezoresistive coefficients $(\pi_{11}^{n}, \pi_{12}^{n}, \pi_{44}^{n}, \pi_{11}^{p}, \pi_{12}^{p}, \pi_{44}^{p})$. These constants can be obtained using uniaxial loading and hydrostatic pressure calibration procedures. If the wafer is cut into specimen strips as indicated in Figure 5 and a known uniaxial stress $\sigma_{11}' = \sigma$ is applied in the x_1'-direction, the expressions in eq. (22) reduce to

$$\frac{\Delta R_1}{R_1} = \left[\frac{\pi_{11}^{n} + \pi_{12}^{n} + \pi_{44}^{n}}{2} \right] \sigma$$

$$\frac{\Delta R_2}{R_2} = \pi_{12}^{n} \sigma$$

$$\frac{\Delta R_3}{R_3} = \left[\frac{\pi_{11}^{p} + \pi_{12}^{p} + \pi_{44}^{p}}{2} \right] \sigma \qquad (26)$$

$$\frac{\Delta R_4}{R_4} = \left[\frac{\pi_{11}^{p} + 3\pi_{12}^{p} + \pi_{44}^{p}}{4} \right] \sigma$$

With a controlled application of uniaxial stress, the relations in eq. (26) can be manipulated to determine the values of $(\pi_{11}^{n} + \pi_{12}^{n} + \pi_{44}^{n})$, π_{12}^{n}, $(\pi_{11}^{p} + \pi_{12}^{p} + \pi_{44}^{p})$, and $(\pi_{11}^{p} + 3\pi_{12}^{p} + \pi_{44}^{p})$. Application of an additional state of stress is required to complete the calibration procedure. If this stress state is chosen to be a hydrostatic pressure $(\sigma_{11}' = \sigma_{22}' = \sigma_{33}' = -p)$, the expressions in eq. (19) become

$$\frac{\Delta R_1}{R_1} = \frac{\Delta R_2}{R_2} = -[\pi_{11}^{n} + 2\pi_{12}^{n}]p$$

$$\frac{\Delta R_3}{R_3} = \frac{\Delta R_4}{R_4} = -[\pi_{11}^{p} + 2\pi_{12}^{p}]p \qquad (27)$$

With a controlled application of a hydrostatic loading, eq. (23) can be used to determine the values of $(\pi_{11}^{n} + 2\pi_{12}^{n})$ and $(\pi_{11}^{p} + 2\pi_{12}^{p})$. The individual values of the six needed piezoresistive coefficients can be obtained by manipulating the combined parameters obtained using the uniaxial loading and hydrostatic pressure calibration procedures.

SUMMARY AND CONCLUSIONS

In this paper, the basic equations needed for the design of stress sensors fabricated on the surface of (110) oriented silicon wafers have been presented. Several sensor rosette configurations have been explored including the familiar three element 0-45-90 rosette. Rosette designs have been found which minimize the necessary calibration procedures and permit more stress components to be measured. It has been established that stress sensors on the surface of (110) test chips are sensitive to four out of the six stress components at a point.

ACKNOWLEDGEMENTS

This research was supported by the Alabama Microelectronics Science and Technology Center, and the Center for Commercial Development of Space Power with funds from NASA (Account NAGW-1192-CCDS-AL), Auburn University, and the Center's industrial partners.

REFERENCES

1. Bittle, D. A., Suhling, J. C., Beaty, R. E., Jaeger, R. C. and Johnson, R. W., "Piezoresistive Stress Sensors for Structural Analysis of Electronic Packages," Journal of Electronic Packaging, Vol 113(3), pp. 203-215, 1991.

2. Suhling, J. C., Beaty, R. E., Jaeger, R. C. and Johnson, R. W., "Piezoresistive Sensors for Measurement of Thermally-Induced Stresses in Microelectronics," Proceedings of the 1991 SEM Spring Conference on Experimental Mechanics, pp. 683-694, Milwaukee, WI, June 9-12, 1991.

3. Shimura, F., Semiconductor Silicon Device Technology, Academic Press, 1989.

4. Bean, K. E. and Lawson, J. R., "Application of Silicon Crystal Orientation and Anisotropic Effects to the Control of Charge Spreading in Devices," IEEE Journal of Solid-State Circuits, Vol. Sc-9(3), pp. 111-117, 1974.

5. Aoki, M., Yano, K., Masuhara, T. and Shimohigashi, K., "Fully Symmetric Cooled CMOS on (110) Plane," IEEE Transactions on Electron Devices, Vol. 36(8), pp. 1429-1433, 1989.

6. Miura, H., Nishimura, A., Kawai, S. and Nishi, K., "Development and Application of the Stress Sensing Test Chip for IC Plastic Packages," Proceedings of the 64th Annual Meeting of the Japanese Society of Mechanical Engineers, pp. 1826-1832, 1987.

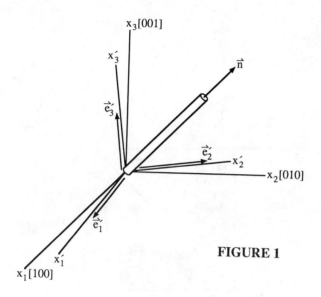

x₃[001]

x′₃

$\vec{e}_3'$

$\vec{n}$

$\vec{e}_2'$

x′₂

x₂[010]

$\vec{e}_1'$

x′₁

x₁[100]

FIGURE 1

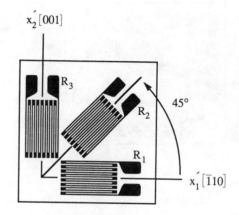

x′₂[001]

R₃

R₂

45°

R₁

x′₁[Ī10]

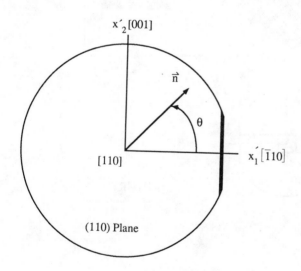

x′₂[001]

$\vec{n}$

θ

[110]

x′₁[Ī10]

(110) Plane

FIGURE 2

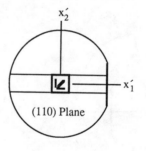

x′₂

x′₁

(110) Plane

FIGURE 3

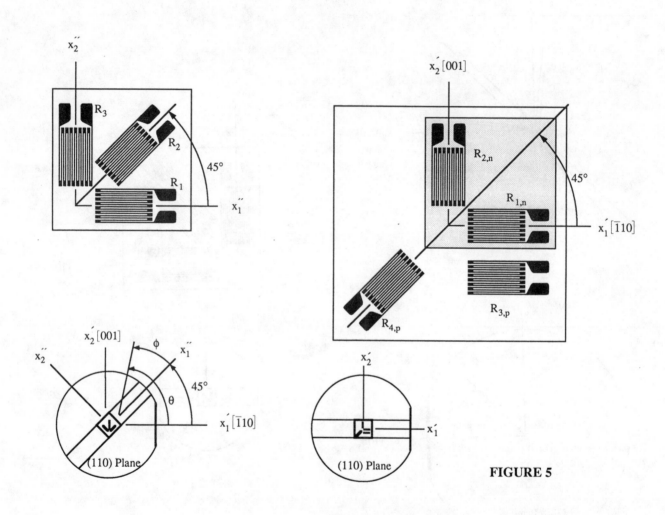

FIGURE 4

FIGURE 5

COMPARATIVE PERFORMANCE EVALUATION OF VARIOUS IMAGE PROCESSING
ALGORITHMS IN PHOTOMECHANICS

K. Ramesh

ABSTRACT

In the recent years several algorithms have been reported for automating the fringe data collection using the technique of Digital Image Processing (DIP). Fringe thinning is a very crucial step in any fringe processing application. In this paper the various DIP algorithms for fringe thinning are surveyed and a comparative performance evaluation of these are discussed.

INTRODUCTION

Ever since, the works of Müller and Saackel[1] and Seguchi et.al.[2] several investigators [3-9] have proposed various Digital Image Processing (DIP) algorithms for extracting quantitative data from fringe patterns observed in photomechanics. In any fringe processing application, one needs to do fringe thinning (since the fringes in general appear as broad bands), fringe ordering and collection of positional co-ordinates and corresponding fringe orders for further processing. Fringe thinning is a crucial step and the algorithm must be capable of extracting continuous fringe skeletons free of noise.

The various DIP algorithms reported in literature can be classified into two categories. In one, the fringe field is identified as a binary image and the fringe skeletons are obtained using algorithms that were primarily developed for optical character recognition [10]. The algorithms of Müller and Saackel [1], Seguchi et.al. [2] and the recent one of Chen and Taylor [7] come under this category.

In the other category, intensity variation within a fringe is used in one way or the other in devising algorithms for fringe skeleton determination. The algorithms of Yatagai et.al. [3], Gillies [5], Umezaki et.al. [6], and Ramesh and Pramod [9] come under this category. Though Voloshin and Burger [4] also used gray level variation within the fringe for fringe processing, Burger and his co-workers were essentially interested in using DIP as a tool for fringe multiplication [11] than for fringe sharpening (thinning) and hence not taken up for comparison in the present work.

In the following paragraphs the performance of the above mentioned algorithms are compared with the new thinning algorithm proposed by Ramesh and Pramod [9]. For the sake of completeness, the algorithms proposed by the various investigators are also summarized and the differences in the computational effort is also brought out.

ALGORITHMS BASED ON CONSIDERING THE FRINGE PATTERNS AS A BINARY IMAGE

Müller and Saackel determined the fringe center lines by fitting circles of various diameters in such a way that they touch the fringe edges; the centers of the circles are joined to form the fringe center lines. Seguchi et.al.[2] extracted the center lines of the fringes by progressively thinning the fringes through removing the outer layer of points until only the fringe center line is left. Though Müller and Saackel and Seguchi et.al. were the pioneers in applying DIP to Photoelasticity, the unsuitability of their algorithms for accurate extraction of fringes is noted by Umezaki et.al.[6]. Chen and Taylor [7] reported another iterative approach to thin fringes in photomechanics. They showed that though the fringe thinning algorithm could be identical for processing fringes obtained from different experimental techniques, the pre-processing steps required for the images is a function of the experimental technique.

Iterative approach to fringe thinning by Chen and Taylor [7]

In this approach the image is scanned left to right, right to left, top to bottom and bottom to top sequentially to eliminate border pixels forming the fringe band. During each such scan for every pixel with a gray level value below the threshold (a point on a fringe) they considered a 3x3 pixel matrix (Fig. 1(a)) to eliminate the border pixel. For example when the image is scanned from left to right, it is checked whether the point P(0,0) is an edge point. This is so when P(-1,0) is not a fringe point and P(1,0) is a fringe point. If P(0,0) is an edge point then in a 3x3 mask there can be four combinations of
_____

K. Ramesh is Assistant Professor in the Department of Mechanical Engineering, Indian Institute of Technology, Kanpur, 208016,INDIA.

pixels above and below it. The four combinations are (1) P(0,1) and P(0,-1) are both fringe points, (2) P(0,1) is a fringe point and P(0,-1) is not a fringe point, (3) P(0,1) is not a fringe point and P(0,-1) is a fringe point or (4) Both P(0,1) and P(0,-1) are not fringe points. The point P(0,0) is eliminated if any of the first three conditions are satisfied. The fourth condition indicates that the point P(0,0) forms a skeleton point in the horizontal direction and hence retained.

The eliminative conditions are pictorially shown in Fig. 1(b). Similarly the conditions for border pixel elimination for other directions are also shown in Fig. 1(b). In Fig. 1(b), the solid dots are fringe pixels, the circles are non-fringe pixels, and the solid triangle at the center is the pixel that is eliminated.

The elimination (as a fringe point) of each border pixel makes the fringe a little bit thinner. This process is continued until no more fringes are eligible for elimination.

ALGORITHMS BASED ON INTENSITY VARIATION WITHIN AN IMAGE

Utilisation of intensity variation within a fringe to detect fringe skeleton was first reported by Yatagai et.al. [3]. They were essentially concerned with the detection of fringe maxima to identify fringe skeletons. Gillies [5] reported a "differential zero crossing" algorithm for processing photoelastic fringes. He reported the problem of occurrence of spurious fringes while applying his algorithm and also suggested remedies to minimise them. He also reported a quantitative comparison of a few DIP algorithms. Umezaki et.al. [6] reported another algorithm for fringe skeleton detection using fringe minima as a criterion.

Ramesh et.al. [8] showed for the first time that fringe edge detection followed by fringe skeleton identification using a minimum intensity criterion greatly minimises the noise reported in other algorithms. However, the algorithm is limited to processing either horizontal or vertical fringes. Ramesh and Pramod [9] improved the earlier algorithm of Ramesh et.al. to process fringes of any orientation.

Skeletonisation algorithm of Yatagai et. al. [3]

The original algorithm proposed by Yatagai et.al. was to identify maxima. Since, in the analysis of isochromatics one is interested in identifying minima, the algorithm reported here is suitably modified to detect minima. The skeletonisation routine attempts to pick out the minima directly from the image and highlight them, giving a direct representation of the fringes. The algorithm detects minima in a two dimensional sense locally (i.e.) within a 5x5 pixel matrix as shown in Fig. 2(a). With respect to the four directions shown in Fig. 2(b), the minima conditions are defined for two typical directions 1 and 3 respectively as,

$$P_{00} + P_{0-1} + P_{01} < P_{-21} + P_{-20} + P_{-2-1} \text{ and } P_{00} + P_{0-1} + P_{01} < P_{21} + P_{20} + P_{2-1} \qquad (1)$$

$$P_{00} + P_{-11} + P_{1-1} < P_{22} + P_{21} + P_{12} \text{ and } P_{00} + P_{-11} + P_{1-1} < P_{-2-2} + P_{-2-1} + P_{-1-2} \qquad (2)$$

Figure 2(c) shows the pixels involved for each scan direction and similar to Eqs. (1) and (2) minima conditions can be easily written for directions 2 and 4.

When the minima conditions are satisfied for any of the two or more directions, the object point P(0,0) is recognized as a point on the fringe skeleton. Yatagai et.al. noted that the fringe skeleton thus obtained is not of one pixel width and in order to thin it further, they represented the skeleton obtained as a binary image and used Hilditch [12] algorithm to iteratively determine the fringe skeleton.

Differential - Zero - Crossing algorithm of Gillies [5]

Gillies investigated the performance of two edge detection operators namely Wilson's difference of Gaussian (DOG) implementation of Laplacian operator and Cosine Gabor function. He finally selected that DOG function is superior to the cosine Gabor function and used a 9x9 mask for detecting edges. The DOG function itself is complex which requires the evaluation of standard deviation of the pixels involved and further the mask size is much higher and hence this approach is computationally disadvantageous.

The first stage of the differential zero crossing algorithm is conventional zero crossing detection namely the fringe edge is identified. Once a zero crossing is detected, the pixel involved is labeled "dn" where the crossing occurs. The pixel opposite dn in a 3x3 square is labeled "opp-dn". The values of the pixels labeled dn and opp-dn are compared, and a positive gradient (dn opp-dn) in gray level values is taken as an indication of the forward edge of a fringe. If a forward edge is found, the algorithm increments the position of the central pixel in the direction "dn opp-dn" until a minimum is found, corresponding to the center of the fringe, as shown in Fig. 3. Scanning within a fringe is judged by selecting 'opp-dn' and this should include all possible combinations. However, the original reference does not clearly specify how this is done.

Iterative Algorithm considered for comparison by Gillies [5]

This algorithm uses a thinning technique to change the profile of the fringes while leaving the turning points, i.e.,the minima (and maxima), intact. The algorithm works in two perpendicular directions. The turning points in the gray levels are evaluated and left intact. The gradients around the remaining points are evaluated. If a point is not a turning point, the value of the pixel under consideration is set to the maximum value of the adjacent pixels. This process is repeated in two dimensions for each pixel found not to be a turning point. The net effect is to flatten the maxima and sharpen the minima in the gray levels, accentuating the fringes. The algorithm is essentially iterative in nature.

Algorithm of Umezaki et.al. [6]

Their approach is similar but more exhaustive than that of Yatagai et.al. [3]. They also considered a 5x5 pixel matrix (Fig. 2(a)) and used in all eight scans locally as shown in Fig. 4(a). In this scheme, the intensity distribution for the eight directions are obtained. For directions 1, 2, 3 and 4 this is nothing but the gray level values of the individual pixels in these directions. For directions 5, 6, 7 and 8 the average of neighboring pixel values has to be computed and for a typical direction 5 it is,

$$(P_{-2-1}, (P_{-10} + P_{-1-1})/2, P_{00}, (P_{11} + P_{10})/2, P_{21}) \qquad (3)$$

Point P(0,0) is selected as fringe point if it is a point of minimum intensity for atleast two or more of the scan directions. To decide whether the point P(0,0) is of minimum intensity for a particular scan direction, they checked whether it satisfies any one of the five conditions shown in Fig. 4(b).

Algorithm of Ramesh and Pramod [9] and its Computational Simplicity

In this algorithm, fringe edges are detected first and any further detailed computation is done only within the fringe band. It is shown in reference [8] that very simple method of global thresholding or dynamic thresholding is sufficient to detect fringe edges.

Once, the edges are determined the image is scanned row-wise (0 deg. scan), diagonal-wise (45 deg. scan), column-wise (90 deg. scan) and cross-diagonal-wise (135 deg. scan). For each scan direction, the pixel having minimum intensity between the edges is selected as skeleton point. There may be situations wherein more than one pixel may have the same minimum intensity. In such a case the center pixel is selected as skeleton point. Thus at the end of initial processing one gets four images of fringe skeletons corresponding to each scan direction. It is to be noted that these scans are done globally and are not for each individual pixels as it is done by Yatagai et.al. and Umezaki et.al.. The computations necessary for identifying the pixel having minimum intensity is done only once between the fringe edges. This approach reduces the number of computations by an order of magnitude. For example if a fringe has ten pixels width, along scan direction say 1 (Fig.2(a)), the algorithm of Yatagai and umezaki have to do the computation atleast ten times for this scan direction alone to identify the minimum intensity point. Further these algorithms do not recognise fringe areas initially and all the operations have to be done for the entire image irrespective of fringe density. Since the computations are done only within the fringe edges by Ramesh and Pramod [9] the computational effort is proportional to fringe density. Thus enormous amount of saving is achieved.

A novel approach with definite steps to retain which of the detected minimum intensity points as fringe points along a scan direction is reported by Ramesh and Pramod [9] and the scheme is shown in Fig. 5. The scheme involves logical operations globally and computational effort is minimal for this. Thus it is clear that the algorithm of Ramesh and Pramod is much superior computationally. With the development of the method of tiles [9], the algorithm also provides greater flexibility for processing.

PERFORMANCE EVALUATION OF VARIOUS ALGORITHMS

The best way to assess the performance is that all these algorithms must be made available on one image processing system and be used to extract the fringe skeleton of the same image. The other approach could be to study the performance of these algorithms by studying the results obtained by various investigators on similar images. All the algorithms mentioned above have been used to extract fringe skeletons of isochromatics for a circular disc under diametral compression obtained by photoelastic technique.

Usually photoelastic images have high contrast and good quality images can be obtained with little care on the part of the investigator. Hence, it can be assumed that to start with all the investigators have had almost similar images for analysis.

Fringe skeleton obtained by Chen and Taylor [7] is shown in Fig. 6(a). The figure clearly shows that extra lines are present (noise) apart from the fringe skeleton. Further, fringe areas close to the load application points are not detected. Gillies [5] had used the same image for comparing the performance of his algorithm with that of Yatagai et.al. and another iterative approach to fringe thinning. Figure 6(b) shows the fringe skeleton obtained by performing 9x9 convolution of DOG followed by differential zero crossing algorithm of Gillies. One can see fringe discontinuity and also random noise present in the processed image. Random noise is primarily introduced by the DOG operator. Fringe discontinuity indicates that all possible combination for fringe minimum intensity detection is not carried out. Figure 7(a) shows the fringe pattern obtained after three stages of iteration of the algorithm taken for comparison by Gillies. The image obtained by this method is not of one pixel width and further fringe areas in zone of stress concentration are not detected. Figure 7(b) shows the skeleton extracted by skeletonisation algorithm of Yatagai et. al. Gillies [5] while comparing Yatagai's approach used three minima as the criterion to produce better resolution than the two minima criteria as reported by Yatagai. The fringe skeleton thus obtained is comparatively very good. However, as noted by Yatagai et.al. themselves, fringe skeleton is not of one pixel width and one requires further processing by Hilditch algorithm for fringe skeleton extraction.

Figure 8 shows the fringe skeleton obtained by Umezaki et.al. for a circular disc under diametral compression. Figure 9(a) shows the isochromatic image used by Ramesh and Pramod [9] with the fringe skeleton superimposed on it and Fig.9(b) shows the improvements in the stress concentration zone obtained by the method of tiles [9]. It is clear that these two algorithm are the best for extracting fringe skeleton. However, the algorithm of Ramesh and Pramod is far superior computationally. Umezaki et.al. uses eight scan directions locally for each pixel in the entire image. Ramesh and Pramod uses only the first four scan directions of Umezaki et.al., globally and the detailed computations are done only within the fringe band. Good quality fringe patterns are obtained with the development of a novel scheme for removing discontinuities and noise in the fringe skeleton. Further, Ramesh and Pramod [13] have shown that their algorithm can be extended to process images obtained from other techniques and established appropriate pre-processing steps for images obtained by photoelasticity and moire.

CONCLUSIONS

Among the various DIP algorithms it is shown that the algorithm proposed by Ramesh and Pramod [9] guarantees, fringe skeleton free of noise and discontinuities and also provides better resolution in zones of stress concentration. Further, the algorithm is computationally much superior and is applicable to process fringe patterns obtained from any experimental technique provided appropriate pre-processing steps are developed. Hence, the algorithm of Ramesh and Pramod [9] is recommended for use in any application involving fringe thinning.

ACKNOWLEDGEMENTS

The research work reported in this paper is in part supported by Aeronautical Research and Development Board, Structures panel (Project No. 540), Government of India. The author thanks Mr. Vijay Pankhawala for processing Fig.9 in this paper. The author also wishes to thank Prof. K. Rajaiah and Prof. N. S. Venkataraman for their interest in the work.

REFERENCES

1. R. K. Müller and L. R. Saackel, "Complete automatic analysis of Photoelastic fringes," Expt. Mech. 19, 245-252 (1979).
2. Y. Seguchi, T. Tomita and M. Watanabe,"Computer aided fringe pattern analyser - A case of photoelastic fringe," Expt. Mech. 19, 362-370 (1979).
3. T. Yatagai, S. Nakadate, M. Idesawa and H. Saito, "Automatic fringe analysis using digital image processing techniques," Opt. Engg. 21, 432-435 (1982).
4. A. S. Voloshin and C. P. Burger,"Half fringe photoelasticity - A new approach to whole field stress analysis," Expt.Mech. 23, 304-314 (1985).
5. A. C. Gillies,"Image processing approach to fringe patterns," Opt.Eng. 27(10), 861-866 (1988).
6. E. Umezaki, T. Tamaki and S. Takahashi, "Automatic Stress Analysis of Photoelastic Experiment by Use of Image Processing and Numerical Analysis", Proc. of VI Int. Conf. on Exp. Mech.,Oregon, USA, pp 1227-1232, June 6-10 (1988).
7. T. Y. Chen and C. E. Taylor, "Computerised fringe analysis in photomechanics," Expt. Mech. 29, 323-329 (1989).
8. K. Ramesh, V. R. Ganesan and S. K. Mullick, "Digital image processing of photoelastic fringes - A new approach," Experimental Techniques, 15, 5, 41-46 (1991).
9. K. Ramesh and B. R. Pramod, "A new Fringe Thinning Algorithm in Photomechanics ", in Proc. of VII Int. Conf. on Expt. Stress Analysis, Las Vegas, USA, 8-11 June (1992).
10. R. W. Smith, "Computer processing of line images : A survey," Pattern Recognition 20, 7-15 (1987).
11. C. P. Burger,"New Approaches to Optical Methods in Experimental Solid Mechanics through Digital Image Processing", Proc. of VI Int. Conf. on Exp. Mech., Oregon, USA, pp 655-660, June 6-10, 1988.
12. C. J. Hilditch, Machine Intelligence 6, B. Melter and D. Michic (eds.), p 403, University Press, Edinburgh (1969).
13. K. Ramesh and B. R. Pramod, "Digital Image Processing of Fringe Patterns in Photomechanics", Opt. Engg. (in press).

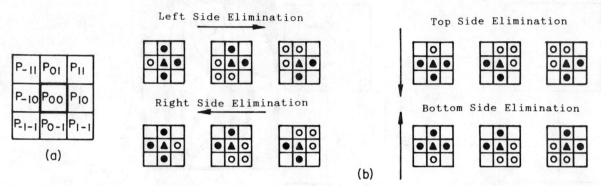

Fig. 1. (a) Pixel Matrix of 3x3. (b) Eliminative conditions for the thinning process. The arrows show the scan directions.

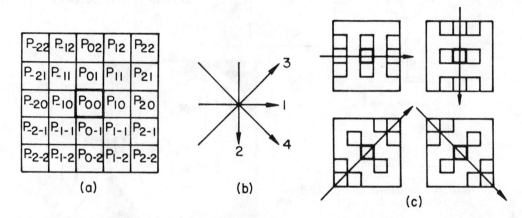

Fig. 2. (a) Pixel Matrix of 5x5. (b) Scan directions for fringe minima detection. (c) Pixels involved in each scan direction.

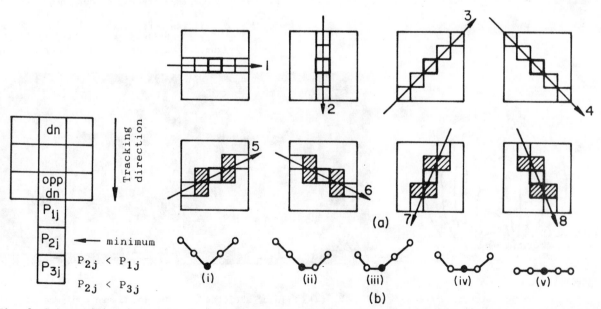

Fig. 3. Fringe minima detection procedure by Gillies.

Fig. 4. (a) Eight scan directions used by Umezaki et.al. and the pixels involved in each scan direction. (b) The object point is noted ('●' in the figure) as a point of minimum intensity if it satisfies any of the five intensity distributions shown.

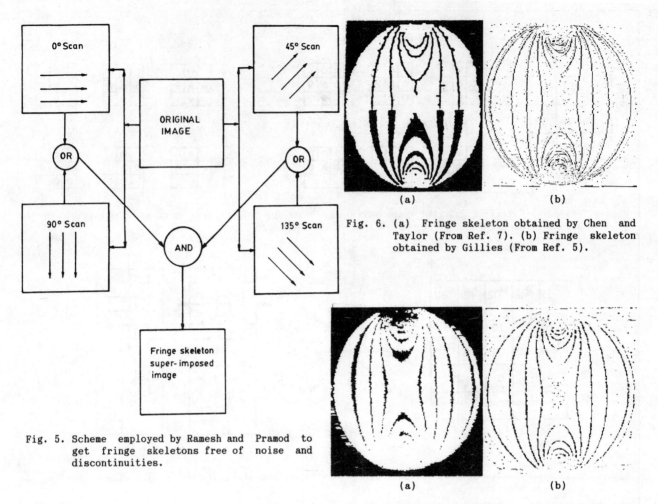

Fig. 5. Scheme employed by Ramesh and Pramod to get fringe skeletons free of noise and discontinuities.

Fig. 6. (a) Fringe skeleton obtained by Chen and Taylor (From Ref. 7). (b) Fringe skeleton obtained by Gillies (From Ref. 5).

Fig. 7. (a) Fringe skeleton obtained by the iterative algorithm taken for comparison by Gillies (From Ref. 5). (b) Fringe skeleton obtained by the skeletonisation algorithm of Yatagai et.al. (From Ref. 5).

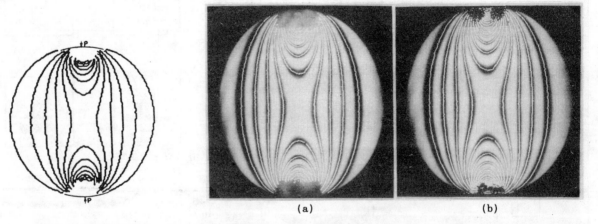

Fig. 8. Fringe skeleton obtained by Umezaki et.al.(from Ref.6).

Fig. 9. (a) Fringe skeleton obtained by Ramesh and Pramod. (b) Improvements achieved at the zones of stress concentration with the method of Tiles. In both the cases fringe skeleton is made white and superimposed on the original image for comparison.

DETERMINATION OF DEFORMATIONS ON THE SURFACE AND THE INTERIOR OF TRANSPARENT OBJECTS USING HOLOGRAPHIC INTERFEROMETRY

G.C.H. Winkenwerder and J.F. Cardenas-Garcia
Optomechanics Research Laboratory
Department of Mechanical Engineering
Texas Tech University
Lubbock, TX 79409-1021

ABSTRACT

Spatial deformations of diffuse reflecting surface and interior planes may be determined simultaneously, using holographic interferometry. The interferogram evaluations are made according to the 'mirror method', the 'translucence method', and the 'combined mirror and translucence method.' These experimental techniques developed by Schoenebeck are based on the 'ellipsoid method' formulated by Abramson. This paper demonstrates the application of these techniques for a statically loaded structure.

INTRODUCTION

In 1969, Abramson [1] first introduced the 'ellipsoid method,' a promising procedure to make and evaluate holograms. This method uses a coordinate system in the form of a set of ellipse/ellipsoid shells with the point of illumination and the point of observation as focal points. Object deformations and/or displacements perpendicular to the ellipses/ellipsoid shells are evaluated according to the interference patterns caused by differences in the light path length. This method allows the determination of only one component of the spatial displacement vector, except when the direction of deformation is known. Later work by Abramson [2,3,4,5,6,7] further defined the procedures needed to evaluate holograms. In 1979, Schoenebeck [8] reported that numerous existing studies related to methods for analyzing and understanding interferometric patterns obtained on holographic images, but these were not practical due to either their complexity, lack of precision, and/or limited applicability. To improve this state of affairs, he developed the 'mirror method' [8]. The 'mirror method' is a recording and evaluation technique which uses three different points of illumination and/or three different points of observation. With only one holographic setup and one holographic plate it is possible to simultaneously determine the three components of the spatial displacement vector. Further experimentation by Schoenebeck [9] led to the 'translucence method', which is another procedure whose development also relies on the 'ellipsoid method' of Abramson. The 'translucence method' is useful for determining deformations and displacements of diffuse-reflecting, but still translucent, surface or interior planes of transparent objects which lie in the bisector between the points of illumination and observation. This allows the determination of "in-plane" deformations/displacements according to the 'ellipsoid method.' Additionally, it is possible to have a 'combined mirror and translucence method' by performing a coordinate projection using the law of refraction. This permits the direct determination of spatial deformations of diffuse reflecting interior planes of transparent objects, independently of whether or not deformation occurs in this plane.

Thus, the objective of this paper is to review the 'ellipsoid', 'mirror', 'translucence', and 'combined mirror and translucence' methods, and to apply them to the analysis of a statically loaded structure.

THE ELLIPSOID METHOD

The fundamental idea behind the use and application of the 'ellipsoid method' is the choice of a generalized coordinate system for the holographic setup. Figure 1 shows the point of illumination (PI) located at the beam splitter, and the point of observation (PO) located behind the holographic plate, which serve as fixed coordinate system base points. An infinite set of point coordinates on the object surface, which define the object topography, are referenced to these base points.

Let us consider what happens to an arbitrary point as an object deforms due to the action of a force. Figure 1 shows an arbitrary point (PS) on the illuminated object surface before and after displacement ($PS_{undisplaced}$ and $PS_{displaced}$, respectively). It is easy to show that the change in path length of the light originating at PI, travelling to PS on the object surface, and on to PO, is a measure of displacement of the chosen arbitrary point. The geometry of an ellipse or ellipsoid with PI and PO as focal points is described for all other points whose overall object beam path length does not change ($|l1| + |l2|$ = constant). The connecting line between focal points defines the rotational axis of the ellipsoid. Using Figure 1 let us consider three additional cases of interest. Case 1 shows that point $PS_{undisplaced}$ on the object surface is displaced to $PS_{displaced}$ (both points lie on the same ellipse/ellipsoid shell) with no change in object beam path length. Cases 2 and 3 show an existing object beam path length difference which indicates that points $PS_{undisplaced}$ and $PS_{displaced}$ are located on different ellipse/ellipsoid shells. This difference in the sum of path lengths **l1** and **l2** may be one or more times the wavelength λ of the laser light. Therefore, the ellipses/ellipsoid shells may be interpreted as geometrical locations of interference surfaces. Each ellipse/ellipsoid represents the geometrical location of a specific interference surface, caused by a specific difference in path length due to displacement of the surface point with respect to its undisplaced location. Therefore, they are a direct measure of the displacements of the object surface.

Since a hologram does not remember which wave front (undisplaced or displaced object surface) was recorded first, only relative changes of surface points may be evaluated. Practically, the direction of displacement is often inferred from the holographic setup and the direction of the applied forces on the object. Quantitative evaluations of displacements are generally not concerned with their direction. Although, if necessary, displacement directions may be determined using real-time holography or strain gages, as alternative methods. In general, the direction of the displacement vector **D** from surface point $PS_{undisplaced}$ to $PS_{displaced}$ is unknown. The macro interference pattern only provides the order N of the interference fringes, which may be determined simply by counting fringes.

To make a determination of surface displacements, reference needs to be made to Figure 2. Figure 2 establishes the geometrical relationship needed to determine the change $|\Delta n|$ of the normal $|n|$, which bisects the angle α formed between rays **l1** and **l2**, at any point on the ellipse/ellipsoid shell. The displacement of surface point PS determines the change $|\Delta n|$ of the normal. Ellipses E_1 and E_1^* share the same focal points and are assumed to be spaced so that if point PS is displaced to an adjacent ellipse, a path length difference of one wavelength λ arises. The length changes of rays **l1** and **l2** due to this surface point displacement are $|\Delta l1|$ and $|\Delta l2|$, respectively. The following equation expresses the required relationship,

$$|\Delta l1| + |\Delta l2| = \lambda \quad ...for\ N = 1 . \quad (1)$$

The geometry of Figure 2 further dictates that the ray length changes be equal, which requires that Eq. 1 be written as

$$|\Delta l1| = |\Delta l2| = \frac{\lambda}{2} \quad ...for\ N = 1 . \quad (2)$$

Thus Eq. 2 describes the magnitude of the displacement component in the illumination and observation directions. In practical applications, the path length difference is very small with respect to the original path length ($|\Delta l1| << |l1|$ and $|\Delta l2| << |l2|$). This allows the approximation of the ellipse by a tangent to it,

and the ellipsoid by a tangential plane at the points of interest, respectively.

The displacement component normal to the ellipse/ellipsoid may be obtained from Fig. 2,

$$|\Delta n| = \frac{|\Delta l1|}{\cos\frac{\alpha}{2}} = \frac{|\Delta l2|}{\cos\frac{\alpha}{2}} \quad ...for\ N = 1 . \quad (3)$$

Since $|\Delta l1| = |\Delta l2| = \lambda/2$, Eq. 3 may be written as,

$$|\Delta n| = \frac{\lambda}{2} \cdot \frac{1}{\cos\frac{\alpha}{2}} \quad ...for\ N = 1 . \quad (4)$$

For path length differences which are some multiple N of λ, Eq. 4 may be rewritten as

$$|n| = |\Delta n| \cdot N = \frac{\lambda}{2} \cdot \frac{1}{\cos\frac{\alpha}{2}} \cdot N \quad (5)$$

for any arbitrary point on the object surface. Vector $|\Delta n|$ determines the magnitude of the displacement vector **D** normal to the ellipses/ellipsoids. This last equation is the fundamental equation used in the evaluation of holograms. The order of the macro interference pattern N may be obtained from the reconstructed virtual image of the object, and the displacement component normal to the ellipses/ellipsoids may be obtained from Eq. 5 for every arbitrary point on the object surface. The direction and magnitude of the displacement vector **D** can not be determined with the fundamental equation alone. In general, the displacement components normal and parallel to the ellipses/ellipsoids are described as out-of-plane and in-plane displacements, respectively.

THE MIRROR METHOD

The 'mirror method' is an extension of the 'ellipsoid method' and is used to determine the endpoints $PS_{undisplaced}$ and $PS_{displaced}$ of the displacement vector **D**. For the 2D case, i.e., for a planar displacement vector in the x-y plane, a second pair/set of ellipses with the focal points PI_2 and PO_2 is introduced as shown in Fig. 3. The endpoints of the displacement vector are also assumed and shown to lie on the ellipses E_2 and E_2^*. This determines that the intersection of the ellipses E_1-E_2 and $E_1^*-E_2^*$ are the endpoints $PS_{undisplaced}$ and $PS_{displaced}$, respectively, of the displacement vector **D**. The distance between the two points of intersection determine the magnitude of the displacement. For the 3D case, the ellipses are replaced by ellipsoid shells and a third pair/set of ellipsoid shells with the focal points PI_3 and PO_3 is introduced. The end points of the displacement vector D are now the intersections of the ellipsoid shells $E_1-E_2-E_3$ and $E_1^*-E_2^*-E_3^*$, respectively. Therefore, the magnitude of the displacement vector is also the relative distance between the points of intersection of the ellipsoid shells.

By replacing the ellipses/ellipsoid shells by their tangents/ tangential planes at the points of interest, other possible points of intersection are eliminated, since two lines (or three planes) may intersect only at one point. The objective is to determine the direction (unit) vectors n^o_η of the respective tangential planes T_η, which then allows to exactly define the [point of intersection of these tangential lines or planes. Once this intersection is known the displacement vector D is fully defined by three linear equations with three unknowns, the three components of the spatial displacement vector. These expressions take the following vectorial form:

$$\overline{n^o_\eta} \cdot \overline{D} = |\overline{n_\eta}| \qquad \ldots \eta = 1,2,3 \qquad (6)$$

or in coordinate form,

$$\begin{pmatrix} n^o_{1,x} \cdot x + n^o_{1,y} \cdot y + n^o_{1,z} \cdot z = |\overline{n_1}| \\ n^o_{2,x} \cdot x + n^o_{2,y} \cdot y + n^o_{2,z} \cdot z = |\overline{n_2}| \\ n^o_{3,x} \cdot x + n^o_{3,y} \cdot y + n^o_{3,z} \cdot z = |\overline{n_3}| \end{pmatrix} \quad . \qquad (7)$$

The coordinates for the points PI_η, PO_η, and $PS_{undisplaced}$ are used to determine the cosines of the resulting angles in the coordinate system. This makes this method not very sensitive to small errors (of a few mm) in the coordinate determination. The angles $\alpha_\eta/2$ in Eq. 5 should preferably be small, so that their cosines approach 1. This increases the sensitivity of the experimental setup for displacement measurement.

To record the spatial displacement components which correspond to Eq. 6, an appropriately configured holographic setup is required. One consideration is that the point of intersection between three tangential planes may be determined very precisely if they are oriented perpendicular to each other. For a holographic configuration where at least two of the planes are parallel to each other, no common point of intersection exists. In other words, the holographic setup geometry must allow large angles (~90°) between the three unit vectors n^o_η along the bisector directions.

In a holographic setup it is possible to use three points of illumination and three holographic plates for the recording of one arbitrary point on the object surface. It is also possible to use one real point of illumination and to create two virtual points of illumination by placing mirrors close to the object, so that the same surface point is illuminated from three different directions. This setup also uses three holographic plates which are necessary to obtain three different points of observation. The illumination via mirrors may cause additional interference on the object surface because of path length differences between the illuminating beams. To simplify the experimental procedure, only one holographic setup and only one holographic plate are used. Therefore the points of illumination are $PI_1 = PI_2 = PI_3$. Additional mirrors are placed close to the object. This allows the necessary different number of observation points (PO_η) for the same surface point.

A schematic showing the positioning of an additional mirror for evaluating two-dimensional (planar) displacement components using one holographic plate is shown in Fig. 4. The mirror has the effect of moving the points of observation PO_1 and PO_2 away from each other. The virtual point of illumination PO_2 appears behind the mirror, while the real points of observation PO_1 and PO_2' still fall together behind the holographic plate. The light beam originates at $PI_1 = PI_2$ and strikes the object surface from where it is diffuse-reflected towards the holographic plate directly and via the additional mirror. After making the holographic recording, the object surface may be observed, at the same time, directly and as a reflection in the mirror, from different directions of observation. The real point of observation behind the holographic plate may be assumed to be identical with the aperture of the photographic device which is used for the lasting recording of holographic images.

This means that to obtain three different directions of observation so as to be able to evaluate the spatial displacement components, only two additional mirrors are required, assuming the object can be observed directly through the holographic plate. If, for example, no displacement occurs in one direction (planar displacement), only one additional mirror is required. Since the object geometry is in general three-dimensional, a three-dimensional displacement evaluation, using Eq. 6, has to be performed. The value of N_η is set equal to zero along any direction with no displacement.

The definition of a coordinate system for a holographic setup is very important. The center point of the object surface facing the holographic plate may be designated and defined as the coordinate origin OO. The coordinate origin OO should be approximately at the center of the holographic plate, when observing the object through it. The axis from the coordinate origin to the center of the holographic plate may be defined as the x-axis. Furthermore, the coordinates of the points of illumination PI_η, the points of observation PO_η, and the points of interest on the object surface $PS_{undisplaced}$ are to be determined with respect to the defined coordinate system. In addition, the angles α_η, between the respective illumination and observation beams, need to be determined.

After the holographic recording is performed, the plate is developed and processed. A lasting picture of the reconstructed hologram is obtained using photography or an image processing system. For double exposure holography, the order of the macro interference fringe pattern is determined directly from the reconstructed images. Beginning from a defined reference point with the order 0, the fringes are counted along a defined line on the object surface. The bright fringes determine the whole-fringe orders (1, 2, 3, ...), while the dark fringes belong to the half-fringe orders (0.5, 1.5, 2.5, ...). Image processing systems may be used to simplify the counting process and to increase the precision of the analysis, especially for higher fringe orders. The fringe orders have to be determined for each direction of observation along the same defined line on the object surface. To increase the precision in determining fringe orders for the specified object point PS along the defined line, it is helpful to interpolate between fringe orders. This may be done graphically. Therefore, the fringe orders along the same defined line on the object surface are evaluated for each direction of observation and plotted over the relative coordinate ξ/l (with values from 0 to 1) of the respective line. ξ is the distance from the reference point to the surface point of interest along the defined line, while l is the overall length of the line. The plotted curves describe the fringe orders N_η as a function of the relative coordinate ξ/l. A perpendicular line has to be drawn at the location of the point of interest on the ξ/l-axis. This perpendicular line intersects the plotted curves for each direction of observation, respectively. The respective points of intersection determine the precise fringe orders which may be substituted into Eq. 6.

THE TRANSLUCENCE METHOD

In the past, interferometric analysis using holography has been applied only to object surfaces. Based on the 'ellipsoid method,' Schoenebeck [9] developed the 'translucence method' with the objective of applying holographic methods to determine deformations on the surface and the interior of transparent objects, simultaneously.

The 'translucence method' is suitable for application to transparent objects where the surface or plane of interest in the interior of the object is made diffuse-reflecting but still translucent. This allows a diffuse-reflecting plane in the interior of the object to be treated like a surface plane. The object is illuminated from the back, while it is observed from the front as shown in Fig. 5. The diffuse reflecting plane of interest inside the object has to lie in the bisector of angle α between the illumination and observation beams. Displacement components are measured in this plane which is perpendicular to the ellipses/ellipsoids which may be defined. Also, the illumination beam from the back has an exact angle of $\alpha/2$ with the plane of interest. Possible effects of refraction of the light beams passing through the transparent material need to be considered and, if necessary, corrected in the holographic setup. This correction may be performed according to the law of refraction or Snell's Law [10], given by the equation

$$\frac{\sin \epsilon}{\sin \epsilon'} = \frac{n}{n'} \tag{8}$$

where ϵ and ϵ' are the angles between the light beam and the line normal to the surface, when entering from material 1 into material 2, respectively. n and n' are the respective indices of refraction of material 1 and material 2. The index of refraction is defined as the partial fraction of the speeds of light in vacuum (air) and in the material being considered.

The 'translucence method' allows "in plane" displacements to be measured in the reflecting but still translucent plane of interest. By application of the 'translucence method' together with the 'mirror method' it is possible to determine the deflection perpendicular to the object surface and the "in-plane" deformations of the interior plane, simultaneously. Objects with irregularly shaped surfaces need to be placed in an appropriate immersion fluid, to overcome surface reflections. The immersion fluid has to have an equivalent index of refraction as the transparent object.

It is possible to combine the 'mirror' and the 'translucence method' to determine the spatial displacements of object points of a diffuse reflecting interior plane independently of whether or not the displacements occur in this plane. To do this, it is necessary to perform a coordinate projection for the points of illumination and observation according to the law of refraction. The projected coordinates may then be substituted and an evaluation performed according to the 'mirror method'. Fig. 6 shows the basis for this coordinate projection. The projected coordinates of the points of illumination and observation may be obtained from

$$\overline{PI_{proj.}} = (\overline{u} \cdot (|\overline{U}| + |\overline{Q}|)) + \overline{PS} \tag{9}$$

or in coordinate form

$$\begin{cases} PI_{proj.,x} = \left(\dfrac{P_x - PS_x}{|\overline{U}|} \cdot (|\overline{U}| + |\overline{Q}|) \right) + PS_x \\[2mm] PI_{proj.,y} = \left(\dfrac{P_y - PS_y}{|\overline{U}|} \cdot (|\overline{U}| + |\overline{Q}|) \right) + PS_y \\[2mm] PI_{proj.,z} = \left(\dfrac{P_z - PS_z}{|\overline{U}|} \cdot (|\overline{U}| + |\overline{Q}|) \right) + PS_z \end{cases} \tag{10}$$

According to the law of refraction, the speed of light changes inversely proportional to the index of refraction, when entering into a media with a different optical density. Since the frequency ν of the laser is constant the speed of light C and the wavelength λ change according to

$$\nu = \frac{C}{\lambda} \tag{11a}$$

with

$$\frac{\sin \epsilon}{\sin \epsilon'} = \frac{C}{C'} = \frac{n'}{n} \tag{11b}$$

it becomes

$$C' = \frac{n}{n'} \cdot n \; , \tag{11c}$$

and

$$\lambda' = \frac{C'}{\nu} = \frac{n}{n'} \cdot \lambda \; . \tag{11d}$$

EXPERIMENTAL RESULTS OF
THE STATIC LOADING OF A BEAM

To show the applicability of the previously described experimental procedures a PMMA beam model was built. A schematic showing some of the beam construction details is shown in Fig. 7, where the location of the diffuse-reflecting surface and interior plane are indicated. The beam is loaded along its top surface in the direction shown, the main deformation occurs in x-direction. The intent in holographically recording and evaluating this experiment using the 'mirror' and the 'combined mirror and translucence method,' is to determine the deflection of the bar perpendicular to the diffuse reflecting interior plane simultaneously with the deformation of the interior plane. Also, another independent evaluation is to be made, using the 'translucence method', to determine the "in-plane" deformation of the interior plane. The beam displacement curves along the surface and interior plane of the beam are determined holographically and compared with the theoretical values.

The experimental setup is shown in Fig. 8. The PMMA beam is mounted so that its free length is 300 mm. A load of 1.517 N is applied at the top of the beam in the positive x-direction using a string and a weight. Two mirrors are placed surrounding the beam, so that enough points on the surface and interior plane may be seen from three points of view, allowing an analysis to be made. Fig. 9 shows the placement of the object with the additional mirrors in the holographic setup as seen through the holographic plate. A double exposure hologram, of the unloaded and loaded beam, is made by using a ruby laser with a wavelength of 694.3 nm. Fig. 10 shows the reconstruction of the hologram. The macro interference fringes on the surface and interior plane, are a measure of the deflection and deformation due to the loading of the beam. The half-fringe orders versus the relative coordinate ξ/l along the defined lines on the surface and interior plane for the three images are determined from Fig. 10. The elastic bending curve of the prismatic beam with a load at its free end is calculated according to Gieck [11]:

$$D_{(\xi)} = \frac{F \cdot l^3}{6 \cdot E \cdot I} \cdot \left(2 - 3 \cdot \frac{\xi}{l} + \frac{\xi^3}{l^3}\right) \quad (12)$$

where E = 2900 N/mm², I = 480443.12 mm⁴, and ξ = 0 at the free end of the beam.

The displacements obtained in the object surface of interest are determined three-dimensionally by using the 'mirror method'. For the determination of displacements of object points in the interior plane, the necessary coordinate projection for the points of illumination and observation is performed and the 'combined mirror and translucence method' is applied. The theoretically and experimentally determined bending curves are plotted in Fig. 11. Fig. 12 shows these same results in a 3D plot. Additionally, an evaluation performed using the 'translucence method' is made to determine the "in-plane" deformations of object points in the interior plane. These values are graphically shown in Fig. 13.

DISCUSSION

These results show that the 'mirror method' and the 'combined mirror and translucence method' may be applied together to determine the deflection of the bar perpendicular to the diffuse reflecting interior plane. The deformation of the interior plane may also be simultaneously determined. The independent application of the 'combined mirror and translucence method,' and the 'translucence method' to the determination of the "in-plane" deformation of the interior plane, yields the same results. The 'combined mirror and translucence method' allows the determination of the spatial deformation of a diffuse reflecting plane in the interior of transparent objects, independently of whether or not the deformation occurs in this plane. The independent application of the 'translucence method' does require that deformation occurs in this plane. The theoretical accuracy of the experimental methods is limited by the accuracy of the defined coordinate system, which is mainly influenced by how well defined are the angles making up the coordinate system.

CONCLUSIONS

The purpose of this paper has been to present the theory and conduct experimentation related to the simultaneous determination of the spatial deformations of diffuse reflecting surface and interior planes of transparent objects, using holographic interferometry. The interferogram evaluations are made according to the 'mirror method', the 'translucence method', and the 'combined mirror and translucence method.' The results obtained show good agreement between theoretically and experimentally obtained results related to the simple loading of a cantilever beam.

BIBLIOGRAPHY

1. N. Abramson, "The Holo-Diagram: A Practical Device for Making and Evaluating Holograms," Applied Optics, Vol.8, No.6, pp. 1235- , 1969.
2. N. Abramson, "The Holo-Diagram II: A Practical Device for Information Retrieval in Hologram Interferometry," Applied Optics, Vol.9, No.1, pp. 97- , 1970.
3. N. Abramson, "The Holo-Diagram III: A Practical Device for Predicting Fringe Patterns in Hologram Interferometry," Applied Optics, Vol.9, No.10, pp. 2311- , 1970.
4. N. Abramson, "The Holo-Diagram IV: A Practical Device for Simulating Fringe Patterns in Hologram Interferometry, Applied Optics, Vol.10, No.9, pp. 2155- , 1971.
5. N. Abramson, "The Holo-Diagram V: A Device for Practical Interpreting of Hologram Interference Fringes," Applied Optics, Vol.11, No.5, pp. 1143- , 1972.

6. N. Abramson, "The Holo–Diagram VI: Practical Device in Coherent Optics," _Applied Optics_, Vol.11, No.11, pp. 562– , 1972.

7. N. Abramson, <u>The Making and Evaluation of Holograms</u>, Academic Press Inc., New York, N.Y., 1981.

8. G. Schoenebeck, "Eine Allgemeine Holographische Methode zur Bestimmung Raeumlicher Verschiebungen," Dr.–Ing. Dissertation, Technische Universitaet Muenchen, 1979.

9. G. Schoenebeck, "Die holographische Messung von Dehnungen auf Oberflaechen und im Inneren von Bauteilen. Grosse Deformationen und das Durchscheinverfahren (Translucence–Method)," in W. Waidelich (Editor) Optoelectronics in Engineering, Proceedings of the 9th international Congress Laser'89, Springer–Verlag 1990.

10. G. Schroeder, <u>Technische Optik</u>, 6te Auflage, Vogel Buchverlag Wuerzburg, 1987.

11. K. Gieck, <u>Technische Formelsammlung</u>, 27te Auflage, Gieck Verlag, Heilbronn, 1981.

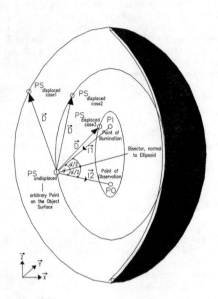

Figure 1 – The 'Ellipsoid Method'

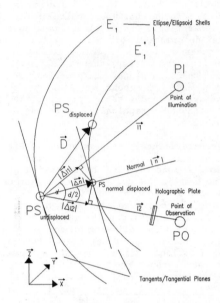

Figure 2 – Derivation of the Fundamental Equation for Evaluating Holograms

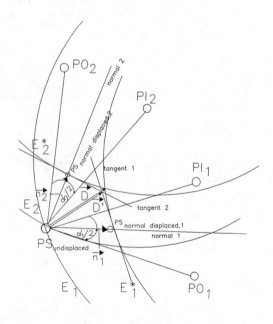

Figure 3 – Extension of the 'Ellipsoid Method'

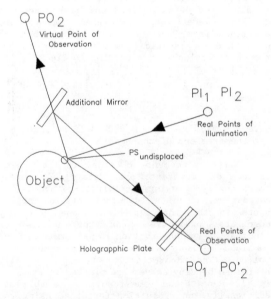

Figure 4 – The Principle of the 'Mirror Method'

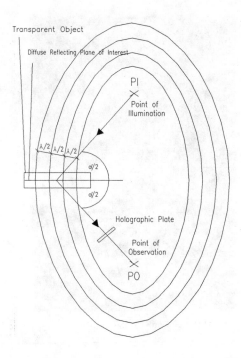

Figure 5 – Schematic of the 'Translucence Method'

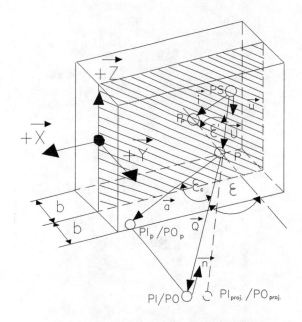

Figure 6 – Coordinate Projection for the 'Combined Mirror and Translucence Method'

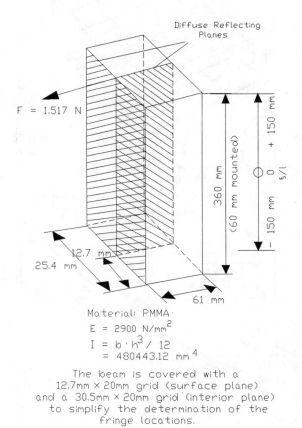

Material: PMMA
$E = 2900 \text{ N/mm}^2$
$I = b \cdot h^3 / 12$
$= 480443.12 \text{ mm}^4$

The beam is covered with a 12.7mm × 20mm grid (surface plane) and a 30.5mm × 20mm grid (interior plane) to simplify the determination of the fringe locations.

Figure 7 – Experimental Object – PMMA BEAM

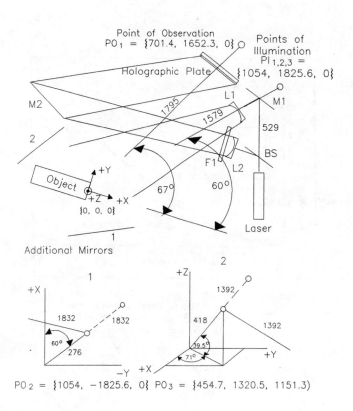

Figure 8 – Holographic Setup

Figure 9 – Placement of Object and
Additional Mirrors

Figure 10 – Double Exposure Hologram

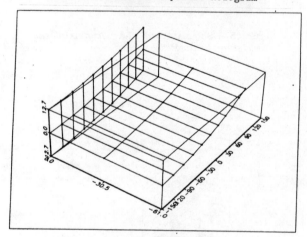

Figure 12 – Three Dimensional Deflection
and Deformation

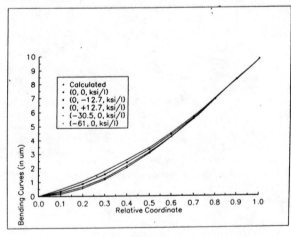

Figure 11 – Bending Curves vs. Relative
Coordinate Obtained with the
'Mirror' and the 'Combined
Mirror and Translucence Method'

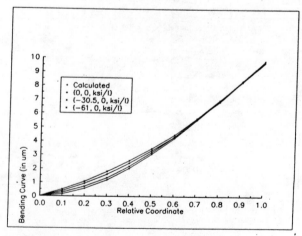

Figure 13 – Bending Curves vs. Relative
Coordinate Obtained with the
'Translucence Method'

726

High-Temperature Moire Interferometry Using Zero-Thickness Grating

F.X. Wang[1], P. Ifju[2] and B.S.-J. Kang[3]

ABSTRACT

The application of moire interferometry in elevated temperature environments hinges on the development of high-temperature resistant moire specimen grating [1]. Recently, Ifju and Post developed a procedure for producing zero-thickness specimen gratings [2] which have potential for use in high temperature moire interferometry (HTMI) applications. In this investigation, using the newly developed specimen grating transfer procedure [2], 500 lines/mm zero-thickness specimen grating was produced on a round fused quartz specimen. HTMI test was then conducted to evaluate the performance of the specimen grating under elevated temperatures. The quartz specimen was heated to 1,003 °C and moire fringes associated with material free thermal expansion were recorded from room to the final tested temperatures. Although the high temperature test was conducted in air, the moire fringes were remarkably stable and good moire fringe quality was observed to maintain well throughout the testing temperatures despite the presence of surface oxide effect on the gold strips. Preliminary test results are presented and experimental considerations related to HTMI tests are also discussed.

INTRODUCTION

Moire interferometry is a useful experimental technique capable of high sensitivity full-field surface deformation measurement. For a typical moire interferometry test, a grating (called specimen grating) is required to bond onto the specimen surface to assume the same surface deformation of the specimen. The application of moire interferometry in elevated temperature environments is thus hinged on the development of high-temperature resistant moire specimen grating [1].

Recently, Ifju and Post developed a procedure for producing zero-thickness specimen gratings [2]

1,3: Visiting Scientist and Assistant Professor, respectively, Mechanical and Aerospace Engineering Department, West Virginia University, Morgantown, WV 26506

2: Graduate Research Assistant, Department of Engineering Science and Mechanics, Virginia Polytechnic Institute and State University, Blacksburg, VA 24061

which have potential for use in high temperature moire interferometry (HTMI) applications. In this investigation, using the newly developed specimen grating transfer procedure [2], 500 lines/mm zero-thickness specimen grating was produced on a round fused quartz specimen. HTMI test was then conducted to evaluate the performance of the specimen grating under elevated temperatures. In the following, we first introduce the HTMI test optical setup, followed by procedure for producing the zero-thickness specimen grating, and finally, present preliminary evaluation results of the zero-thickness grating under elevated temperatures. Also, experimental observations and the effect of windows in the optical setup that are related to HTMI tests are discussed.

EXPERIMENTAL PROGRAM

Test Optical Setup

Fig.1 shows the optical setup for conducting HTMI test, which consists of a furnace, a four-beam u-v moire interferometry unit [3] that allows for adjustment of the u and v virtual reference gratings, collimating optics, laser and optical table. The incident wavefronts from the four-beam moire unit pass through the pyrex window and interfered with the specimen grating to generate the u and v moire fringes. Note that narrow-band filter was not used in this investigation. Detailed HTMI testing procedure can be found in Ref.1.

Zero-Thickness Specimen Grating

The processes for forming a diffraction grating on the specimen were basically the same as those outlined in the work conducted by Ifju and Post [2]. In summary, a zero-thickness grating capable of withstanding high temperature was developed using photoresist, gold, and the process of dry ion etching. The steps for producing the specimen grating are illustrated in Fig. 2.

(1) A highly adherent film of gold was vacuum-deposited on the polished surface of the specimen. Gold was chosen for this application since it has a relatively high melting point and has good reflectivity.

(2) A uniform layer of photoresist was applied on top of the gold layer. This was done by using a spinning process to insure that the photoresist

thickness was uniform. The layer was dried and baked to increase its hardness.

(3) The photoresist was exposed to a virtual grating formed by the interference of two intersecting beams of coherent light from a krypton laser (λ = 413 nm). After development, the photoresist has a corrugated surface with frequency (f), as shown schematically in the Fig. 2. Both linear and crossed-line grating can be produced by using step (3).

(4) Dry ion etching was then used to uniformly erode the photoresist. Subsequently, the reflective layer of gold was eroded. Where it was desired the gold layer was also etched to produce a grating directly embossed onto the specimen surface.

Using the above grating transfer procedure, we have successfully produced zero-thickness gratings on fused quartz, Zerodur^{TM}, silicon, and silicon nitride (Si_3N_4) specimens. However, as this is still an on-going research, only preliminary test results of a quartz specimen are presented in this paper.

Free Thermal Expansion Measurement

We conducted a preliminary evaluation of the performance of the zero-thickness specimen grating at high temperatures. 500 lines/mm zero-thickness specimen grating was produced on a round fused quartz specimen (diameter: 1 inch; thickness: 0.25 inch) and free thermal expansion measurement was conducted using HTMI. The quartz specimen was heated to 1,003 $^{\circ}$C and moire fringes corresponding to material free thermal expansion were recorded from room to the final tested temperatures, as shown in Fig. 3. It should be noted that although the high temperature test was conducted in air, the moire fringes were remarkably stable and good moire fringe quality was observed to maintain well throughout the testing temperatures despite the presence of surface oxide effect on the gold strips. Fig. 4 shows plot of measured thermal expansion versus temperature. As shown in Fig. 4, test results indicate that, from room to 650 $^{\circ}$C, the measured coefficient of thermal expansion (CTE) agrees with that of the gold strips, and above 650 $^{\circ}$C, the measured CTE value agrees with that of the the fused quartz specimen. This discrepancy may be due the imperfect dry ion etching of the quartz specimen (procedure 4 in Fig. 2). Furthermore, during the test we noted that, at around 600 $^{\circ}$C, the gold strips started to disappear gradually and was completely evaporated at about 650 $^{\circ}$C. This phenomenon is evidenced in Fig. 5 which includes enlarged views of moire fringes from 600 $^{\circ}$C to 700 $^{\circ}$C and shows that around 700 $^{\circ}$C, coarse fringes started to show up on, superimposed onto the fine moire fringes. These coarse fringes are caused by the interference of the laser light that passes through the front surface and hits the back surface of the specimen; they represent thickness variation of the quartz specimen. It is also noticed that the fine moire fringes still exist even after the gold strips were evaporated (Figs.3 and 5). And as shown in Fig. 4, after 700 $^{\circ}$C, the measured CTE value agrees well with that of the quartz material. It should be emphasized that the results shown in this paper are preliminary findings. We plan to conduct additional HTMI tests using zero-thickness specimen gratings to further investigate any incongruity related to the applications of the zero-thickness gratings for HTMI tests.

DISCUSSION

Effect of Window

As shown in Fig.6, in HTMI test, windows have to be placed (or inserted) in the optical paths. Questions have been raised, however, regarding the effect of window on moire fringe formation, especially in the presence of increasing furnace temperature. On the other hand, of the many HTMI tests we have conducted so far, we observe no evidence of any interference of the window to the moire fringe formation (after initial null-field adjustment). In the following, a simple optical analysis is presented to provide theoretical background that may explain the reason why the windows in the HTMI optical setup have little effect to the moire fringe formation.

In general, the two surfaces of the window are not parallel with each other and may be characterized by the two small tilt angles, α_1 and α_2, as shown in Fig. 6. A light wave travels through the window will alter its amplitude and phase. Following Fig. 6, the phase difference along the y-axis is

$$\phi(y) = (t + \Delta t) \, n \, 2\pi/\lambda$$

where n is the refractive index of the window and $\Delta t = (L-y) \, \alpha_2$. Then

$$\phi(y) = n \, t \, 2\pi/\lambda + n \, 2\pi \, (L-y) \, \alpha_2 \, / \, \lambda$$
$$= n \, (\, t + L \, \alpha_2) \, 2\pi/\lambda - n \, \alpha_2 \, y \, 2\pi/\lambda$$
$$= \phi_o - n \, \alpha_2 \, y \, 2\pi/\lambda$$

Neglect the constant term (ϕ_o) which does not alter the phase of the incident wave and therefore has no effect to moire fringe formation, the transmittance function of the window can be expressed as

$$T(y) = \exp \, (-i \, n \, \alpha_2 \, y \, 2\pi/\lambda)$$

If considering both x- and y-direction,

$$T(x,y) = \exp \, [-i \, n(\alpha_1 x + \alpha_2 y) \, 2\pi/\lambda]$$

Before hitting the window, the complex amplitude of a plane wave can be expressed as

$$U_1(x,y) = A(x,y) \, \exp[ik \, (\sin\theta_x x + \sin\theta_y y)]$$

where k is the propagation vector with amplitude of $2\pi/\lambda$, and $\theta_x = 90^{\circ} - l_x$ and $\theta_y = 90^{\circ} - l_y$, where l_x and l_y are directional cosines of the propagation vector k. After the wave travels through the window, the complex amplitude and phase of the wave is then

$$U_o = U_1(x,y) \, T(x,y)$$
$$= A(x,y) \, \exp\{ik[(\sin\theta_x - n \, \alpha_1)x + (\sin\theta_y - n \, \alpha_2)y]\}$$

From the above equation, one notes that the phase terms in the equation are still linear with deviations of $n\alpha_1$ along x-direction and $n\alpha_2$ along y-direction. The incident planar wavefronts remain planar and, if one adjusts the initial null-field to correct the effect of $n\alpha_1$ and $n\alpha_2$, then the windows will have no effect to moire fringe formation thereafter.

CONCLUSION

In this investigation, using the newly developed specimen grating transfer procedure [2], 500 lines/mm zero-thickness specimen grating was produced on a round fused quartz specimen. HTMI test was then conducted to evaluate the performance of the specimen grating under elevated temperatures. The quartz specimen was heated to 1003 °C and moire fringes associated with material free thermal expansion were recorded from room to the final tested temperatures. Although the high temperature test was conducted in air, the moire fringes were remarkably stable and good moire fringe quality was observed to maintain well throughout the testing temperatures despite the presence of surface oxide effect of the gold strips. Our preliminary results indicate that, from room to 650 °C, the measured CTE value agrees with that of the gold strips, and above 650 °C, the measured CTE value agrees with that of the quartz specimen. This discrepancy may be due the imperfect dry ion etching of quartz specimen. Finally, we present a theoretical argument to prove that the windows used in HTMI tests have little effect to the moire fringe formation.

ACKNOWLEDGEMENT

We are very grateful to the technical support and discussions provided by Dr. D. Post at V.P.I. His encouragement and kind support to allow the zero-thickness gratings be produced in his lab. is greatly appreciated.

REFERENCE

1. B.S.-J. Kang, F.X. Wang, and Q.-K. Liu, "High Temperature Moire Interferometry for use to 550 °C," 1990 SEM Fall Conference on Hologram Interferometry and Speckle Metrology, Baltimore, MD, pp.457-464, November (1990).

2. P. Ifju and D. Post, "Zero-Thickness Specimen Gratings for Moire Interferometry," Experimental Techniques, 15(2), pp.45-47, March/April (1991).

3. F.X. Wang, B.S.-J. Kang and K.Y. Lin, "Full-field Displacements by Four-beam Moire Interferometry," 1991 SEM Spring Conference on Experimental Mechanics, Milwaukee, WI, June 10-13, (1991).

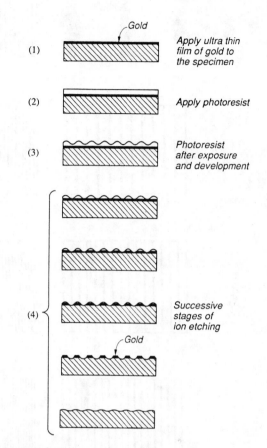

(1) — Apply ultra thin film of gold to the specimen

(2) — Apply photoresist

(3) — Photoresist after exposure and development

(4) — Successive stages of ion etching

Fig.2 Grating transfer procedure to produce zero-thickness specimen grating.

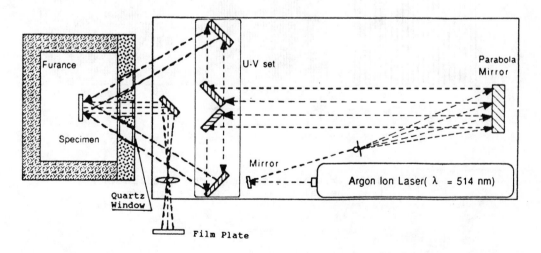

Fig.1 Optical setup for high temperature moire interferometry test.

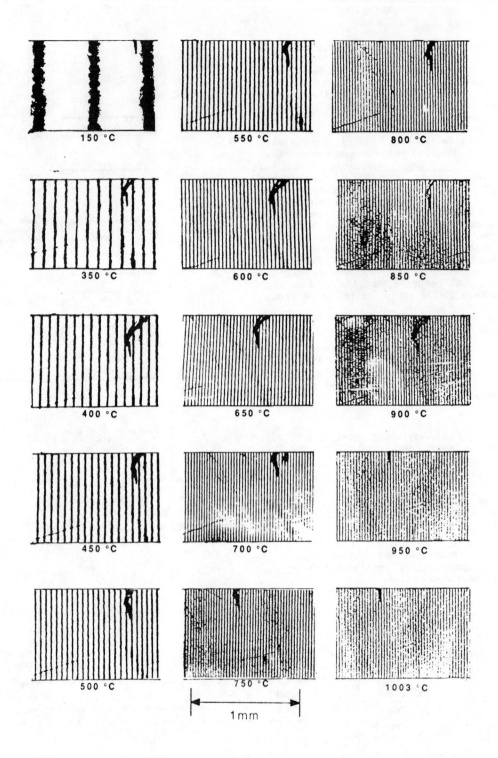

Fig.3 Moire fringes of fused quartz specimen under
free thermal expansion, f=1000 lines/mm.

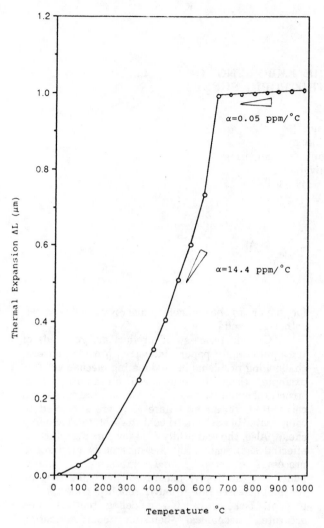

Fig.4 Measured thermal expansion of
the fused quartz specimen.

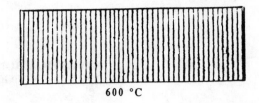

600 °C

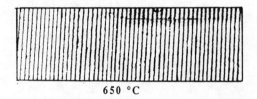

650 °C

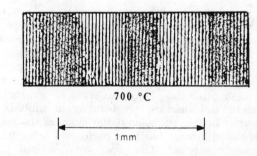

700 °C

|←————— 1mm —————→|

Fig.5 Breakdown of the gold strips.

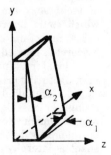

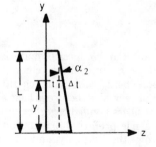

Fig.6 Schematic drawings of a typical window.

INVESTIGATION ON THE EMBOSSING OF
THIN NONLINEAR ORTHOTROPIC SHEETS

S. Liang
J. C. Suhling
Department of Mechanical Engineering
Auburn University
Auburn, AL 36849-5341
U.S.A.

ABSTRACT

In a paper embossing process, a metal punch called an embossing element is used to form a paper sheet into a certain permanent shape. A rubber layer is usually used underneath the paper to provide a flexible support. Embossing processes are designed to change the mechanical behavior and other properties of paper products. They also serve to add surface texture and increase ply bonding in multi-layer papers. In this study, an initial study of the paper embossing process has been performed using finite element analysis. The paper was modeled as a nonlinear orthotropic solid and the rubber was taken to be an incompressible hyperelastic material. Interface elements were introduced to simulate the behavior of the contact surfaces. Since the measured mechanical properties of the paper under consideration were highly dependent on moisture content, analyses were performed at relative humidity levels of 50% and 90%. The changes in the mechanical behavior of the paperboard after embossing were predicted.

INTRODUCTION

Unlike fiber-reinforced composite materials, paper or paperboard is a multiphase composite composed of moisture, fibers, voids, and chemical additives. Its three-dimensional structure is basically an assembly of discrete fibers bonded together into a complex network. A single preferred orientation of the fibers results from the hydrodynamic forces present in the papermaking machine. This orientation is called the machine direction (MD). The in-plane direction perpendicular to the preferred direction is called the cross-machine direction (CD). These in-plane directions of material symmetry allow for paper to be modeled macroscopically as an orthotropic solid.

Current process and product design needs of the pulp and paper industry provide several challenging problems in engineering mechanics. For example, these materials are often utilized in structural applications such as cones, spiral tubes, and corrugated containers where they are subjected to complicated biaxial and triaxial stress states, including shear. Also, the end utility of many paper products is affected significantly by the inherently mechanical processes of creping and embossing. Finally, laminated (multi-ply) papers will curl and develop residual stresses due to environmental changes. At present, lack of reliable modeling methods and accurate mechanical behavior characterization hampers analysis of such problems. Hence, it has been common practice in the paper industry to use trial and error, and empirical approaches for optimizing the designs of manufacturing processes and converted products. Such haphazard approaches will often lead to undesirable product characteristics or unexpected structural failures. Also, the current lack of technology limits creative design improvements which could improve product sales and curtail the excess use of materials and energy. Therefore, more research is needed within the pulp and paper industry to develop fundamental understandings of manufacturing processes and paper material behavior.

A simplified embossing configuration containing a single embossing element is shown in Figure 1. The metal punch (embossing element) is used to permanently deform the paper sheet. The thin paper sheet is laterally pressed by the embossing element into a relatively thick elastic rubber layer of low stiffness. The maximum embossing element penetration depth is chosen to cause inelastic deformation of the paper sheet. After this depth has been reached, the embossing element is retracted, and a non-flat textured sheet remains. Typically, this operation is performed continuously by taking paper off a roll and feeding it between a pair of stainless steel rolls. The first roll is called the embossing roll and contains a raised pattern of raised embossing elements. The second roll has an outside layer of rubber and is called the backing roll. Embossing processes are designed to change the mechanical behavior and other properties of paper products. They also serve to add surface texture and increase ply bonding in multi-layer papers.

The embossing process is a material forming process in which multibody contact is involved. The study of contact problems in elasticity using analytical methods has been reviewed by Lubkin [1]. Early finite element models of material contact were presented by Kikuchi [2], and Kikuchi and Oden [3]. These authors have also published a detailed monograph on the subject [4]. A large volume of work has recently appeared on the study of metal forming problems using finite element methods employing contact with friction. For example, Holzner and Mannl [5], and Sih, et al. [6] have used the finite element method to model elastic-plastic materials with nonlinear hardening which were subjected to axisymmetric sheet metal forming processes.

In this study, an initial study of the paper embossing process has been performed using finite element analysis. The objective of this investigation was to begin the formulation of a fundamental understanding of the mechanical behavior of paper during a typical embossing process. Several numerical simulations have been performed using the finite element method. The finite element models included large deformations (geometric nonlinearity), anisotropic nonlinear inelastic material behavior (material nonlinearity), and interface elements to describe contact surfaces (boundary nonlinearity). The computer codes calculated the permanent deformations, and residual stresses and strains in embossed paper sheets. Both loading and unloading of the material system have been considered. Changes in the stress-strain behavior and material properties of paper sheets due to embossing have been predicted by calculating the uniaxial tension response of the embossed sheets. Extensive experimental material characterization data have been used as input to the finite element models. These data included results of uniaxial, shear, and biaxial testing under different relative humidity levels where the nonlinear and inelastic mechanical behavior of the paper under consideration were measured.

FINITE ELEMENT MODELS

General Discussion

Numerical modeling in this work was performed using an iterative nonlinear finite element approach incorporating nonlinear material behavior and plasticity, large deformations, and contact stresses. All calculations were performed using commercially available computer programs. The finite element software package ABAQUS was chosen because of its ability to perform sophisticated nonlinear analyses. It allows for modeling of three-dimensional structures with general user-specified material nonlinearities. Also, it has special functions designed to accommodate large deformations (kinematic nonlinearities) and contact of multiple bodies. All preprocessing (mesh generation and model construction) and postprocessing (data analysis using color graphics) of the finite element models in this work were accomplished using the program PATRAN. The majority of the calculations in this work were performed on Sun SparcStations available on the College of Engineering Computer Network at Auburn University. In addition, ABAQUS calculations were also performed on the Cray X-MP/24 supercomputer operated by the Alabama Supercomputer Network.

Geometry and Loading

Precise modeling of the embossing of paper sheets is extremely difficult due to the complicated nature of the geometry and nonlinear material behavior, and the existence of material contact. Therefore, in this initial investigation only the idealized single element embossing configuration shown in Figure 1 was considered. In addition, only two-dimensional plane stress analyses of this geometry were performed. The analyzed planar configuration is illustrated in Figure 2. Because of symmetry, only the right half of the geometry in Figure 1 was modeled using a finite element mesh since the deformations are symmetric about the center line. The materials from top to bottom are the steel embossing element (considered rigid), paper sheet, and rubber (surface of backing roll). The executed two-dimensional simulations have served as test vehicles on which the performance of the iterative nonlinear finite element models could be evaluated.

As illustrated schematically in Figure 2, the center line of the embossing element was constrained to move vertically. The top edge of the embossing element was subjected to a prescribed downward displacement, and then this deformation was released. The right edge of the combined material system was constrained to move vertically. Since only the right half of the geometry in Figure 1 was meshed, the centerline of the combined material system was also constrained to move vertically. In the final boundary condition, the bottom edge of the rubber from the backing roll was fully constrained. This condition was chosen since the steel core of the backing roll was considered rigid and perfect bonding was assumed between the rubber and steel.

Finite element meshes for the two-dimensional embossing models were generated using the previously mentioned PATRAN software. The embossing element itself was described using the rigid surface definition procedure available in ABAQUS. Quadrilateral planar elements were then utilized to mesh the paper/rubber material system which is compressed by the embossing element. These elements used linear basis functions with four integration points. Also, elements incorporating general finite deformation formulations were chosen. As discussed in more detail below, the stress-strain relations for the rubber and paper materials were specified using built-in ABAQUS formulations and the results of material characterization experiments.

Two different embossing element cross-sectional shapes were considered in this study. These included a rounded rectangular element and a rounded circular element. Figures 3 and 4 show the chosen cross-sectional dimensions for the two embossing elements, and Figures 5 and 6 show the finite element meshes for the complete two-dimensional embossing models incorporating these elements. In Figures 5 and 6, the top four layers of elements represent the paper material and the bottom 15 layers represent the rubber material. The thickness (vertical dimension) of the paper layer was .254 mm and the thickness of the rubber layer was 2.032 mm. Both layers had a length (horizonal dimension) of 7.620 mm.

The embossing analyses were carried out in three loading steps. In the first step, an embossing element penetration of 1 mm was applied through a prescribed displacement of the embossing element. In the second step, the embossing element was retracted, and the residual stresses and permanent deformations in the paper sheet were calculated. In the final step, the embossing element, rubber layer, and all the interface elements were removed from the model. Uniaxial tension analyses for loading along the horizontal direction were then performed to monitor the changes in the mechanical response of the paper due to embossing.

Material Contact and Interface Elements

Material contact in the developed finite element models for the embossing process was modeled with the aid of interface elements. These elements were used to connect pairs of points from two materials which contact each other in a manner such that relative sliding can occur. In the embossing simulations, interface finite elements were used between the embossing element and the paper sheet, and also between the paper sheet and the rubber from the backing roll. Type IRS21 rigid surface interface elements were used between the rigid embossing element and the paper sheet. Such interface elements allow sliding over a finite distance along the rigid surface. Between the paper sheet and the rubber layer, type INTER2 interface elements were used to simulate the contact of the two deformable layers. At each integration point of the interface elements, a measure of relative displacement was used to determine whether or not there was contact. In the case of contact, a Lagrange multiplier was introduced at the integration point to impose the constraint that the surfaces cannot interfere. The sign of the Lagrange multiplier was monitored to detect any separation of the surface at that point.

The formulation used for the interface elements in ABAQUS requires them to be characterized by several parameters. These included the initial clearance, the coefficient of friction, the "stiffness of stick", and three so-called interface control parameters. The coefficients of friction were arbitrarily chosen to differ by an order of magnitude: $\mu = .02$ between the rigid embossing element and the paper sheet, and $\mu = .2$ between the paper sheet and the rubber layer. The "stiffness of stick" is an elastic stiffness which transmits shear forces across the interface as long as they are below the friction limit. This stiffness is applied using a penalty method procedure. Specification of higher values gives more assurance that no relative motion will occur between contacting surfaces until slip occurs. However, the convergence of the iterative finite element solution procedure will be more rapid when this stiffness is chosen to be smaller. The three interface control parameters allow the user to specify various tolerances which mandate how close various interface conditions are required to be satisfied. In this work, the calculated results from the numerical simulations were found to be very sensitive to the specified values of the "stiffness of stick" and the interface control parameters. It was found that convergence of the iterative finite element simulations to reasonable solutions occurred only when a tedious trial and error process was used to find the optimum values of these parameters.

Material Behavior - Rubber

In this work, the stress-strain behavior of the rubber was modeled using a hyperelastic (nonlinear elastic) formulation based upon using a strain energy density function. The strain energy density function was chosen so that the hyperelastic model was equivalent to the incompressible two parameter Mooney-Rivlin model for rubber elasticity. The strain energy function for this case is [7,8]

$$U = C_1 (I_1 - 3) + C_2 (I_2 - 3) \qquad (1)$$

where I_1 and I_2 are the first and second invariants of a general large deformation strain tensor, and C_1 and C_2 are material constants. Values of $C_1 = .550$ MPa and $C_2 = .138$ MPa were chosen based on experimental results for natural rubber. The stress-strain relations can be obtained from the strain energy density function using the general large deformation constitutive equation for hyperelastic materials [7,9]. For the material constants chosen in this work, the constitutive formulation for rubber yielded the uniaxial stress-strain curve illustrated in Figure 7.

Material Behavior - Paper

As surveyed by Perkins [10] and Suhling [11], paper and paperboard have been modeled macroscopically using elastic, viscoelastic, and inelastic formulations. Several continuum theories have been established for a paper sheet or laminate viewed as a three-dimensional orthotropic solid medium. The theory of linear orthotropic elasticity has been most often utilized to model the macroscopic behavior of papers. Since the mechanical behavior of most papers is highly nonlinear even at low strains, a linear elastic approach is especially unsuitable in the analysis of the embossing process, where high strains and permanent (inelastic) deformations take place.

There have been only a limited number of studies which have considered nonlinear elastic models [12-14] for the stress-strain behavior of paper. Even fewer have utilized elastic-plastic constitutive models [15-16]. In the work of Ramasubramanian and Ko [15], a nonlinear finite element analysis (using ABAQUS) of the spherical ball penetration test for paper was performed. In their study, an elastic-plastic constitutive model for paper was incorporated which included strain hardening patterned after measured uniaxial stress-strain data. Perkins, et al. [16] have proposed a new continuum elastic-plastic constitutive model for paper. Their theory is based on applying the minimum deformation work concepts introduced by Tate [17].

In this initial investigation on the embossing of paper, a incremental metal plasticity model with isotropic hardening was chosen to model the mechanical behavior of the paper material [7,9]. The paper was considered to be orthotropic linear elastic until onset of inelastic behavior. The stress-strain relations before yielding then have the form

$$\varepsilon_x = \frac{1}{E_1}\left[\sigma_x - \nu_{12}\sigma_y - \nu_{13}\sigma_z\right] \qquad \gamma_{xz} = \frac{\tau_{xz}}{G_{13}}$$

$$\varepsilon_y = \frac{1}{E_2}\left[\sigma_y - \nu_{21}\sigma_x - \nu_{23}\sigma_z\right] \qquad \gamma_{yz} = \frac{\tau_{yz}}{G_{23}} \qquad (2)$$

$$\varepsilon_z = \frac{1}{E_3}\left[\sigma_z - \nu_{31}\sigma_x - \nu_{32}\sigma_y\right] \qquad \gamma_{xy} = \frac{\tau_{xy}}{G_{12}}$$

where E_1, E_2, E_3 are the elastic moduli, ν_{12}, ν_{21}, ν_{13}, ν_{31}, ν_{23}, ν_{32} are the Poisson's ratios, G_{13}, G_{23}, G_{12} are the shear moduli, and the (x,y,z) coordinate system has been aligned with the material symmetry directions of the paper (x = MD, y = CD). The Poisson's ratios in eq. (2) are related through the formula

$$\frac{\nu_{ij}}{E_i} = \frac{\nu_{ji}}{E_j} \qquad (i, j = 1, 2, 3) \qquad (3)$$

Onset of plastic deformations was predicted using the anisotropic failure criterion of Hill [18,19]. This criterion is an anisotropic extension of the Von Mises theory for isotropic materials. In terms of the stress components in the (x,y,z) coordinate system aligned with the directions of material symmetry, this criterion predicts that inelastic behavior initiates when

$$A(\sigma_x - \sigma_y)^2 + B(\sigma_x - \sigma_z)^2 + C(\sigma_y - \sigma_z)^2$$
$$+ D\tau_{xz}^2 + E\tau_{yx}^2 + F\tau_{xy}^2 = 1 \qquad (4)$$

Quantities A, B, C, D, E, F in eq. (4) are material dependent strength parameters evaluated using

$$A = \frac{1}{2}\left[\frac{1}{X^2} + \frac{1}{Y^2} - \frac{1}{Z^2}\right] \qquad D = \frac{1}{Q^2}$$

$$B = \frac{1}{2}\left[\frac{1}{X^2} + \frac{1}{Z^2} - \frac{1}{Y^2}\right] \qquad E = \frac{1}{R^2} \qquad (5)$$

$$C = \frac{1}{2}\left[\frac{1}{Y^2} + \frac{1}{Z^2} - \frac{1}{X^2}\right] \qquad F = \frac{1}{S^2}$$

where X, Y, Z are the measured uniaxial "yield" stresses in the x, y, z directions, respectively, and Q, R, S are the measured pure shear "yield" stresses.

After the onset of inelastic behavior at a point, plastic material behavior was predicted using an isotropic hardening formulation [7]. The hardening curve was obtained from the shape of the x-direction (MD) stress-strain curve after yielding. Reduced material stiffnesses were then obtained from the instantaneous slope of the hardening curve. When unloaded, the stiffnesses were changed back to their elastic (initial) values. Such behavior is common in metals subjected to loading and unloading in uniaxial tension, and is also exhibited by paper.

Extensive experimental material characterization data have been used as input to the constitutive and failure models for paper discussed above. The paper considered in this study was machine made 100% Lakes States softwood unbleached Kraft paper (basis weight 205 g/m², mass density 670 kg/m³). Since the characteristic mechanical response of paper is highly affected by its moisture content, material property data obtained at two different relative humidity levels were considered. Experimental data were measured in a specially constructed environmental chamber at relative humidity levels of 50% and 90%. Details of the experimental procedure and the obtained results are contained in a separate publication by one of the authors [20]. Figures 8 and 9 show uniaxial tensile stress-strain curves obtained in the x = MD and y = CD testing orientations at relative humidity levels of 50% and 90%, respectively. From these data, several of the linear elastic material properties and uniaxial "yield strengths" were obtained. Also, the isotropic hardening curves at each moisture level were obtained from the MD stress-strain curves. The measured parameters obtained from the results in reference [20] are tabulated in Figure 10. To complete the formulation, several educated guesses were made for the remaining material parameters. These best estimate values are tabulated in Figure 11.

It is realized that the utilized inelastic constitutive model for the stress-strain behavior of the paper sheet is at best approximate. However, it has served as a test case on which to evaluate the effectiveness of the iterative nonlinear finite element technique for modeling the embossing process. In subsequent work, it is planned to put emphasis on further refinement of the paper constitutive and failure formulations used within the ABAQUS modeling procedure.

RESULTS AND DISCUSSION

The finite element meshes in Figures 5 and 6 were analyzed for the case of plane stress using the loading and boundary conditions discussed earlier. For each embossing element, the maximum penetration was chosen to be 1 mm, and the calculations were performed with paper material properties at relative humidity levels of 50% and 90%. Figures 12 and 13 show the predicted deformations at the point of maximum penetration at 50% and 90% RH for the rounded rectangular and rounded circular embossing elements, respectively. Figures 14 and 15 show the associated predicted deformations after the embossing element has been retracted and no longer contacts the paper sheet. The deformations in the paper sheet in these illustrations are permanent as a result of the inelastic stresses and strains experienced by the sheet during the penetration step. The embossing element and rubber layer returned to exactly the same shapes as before loading since these materials were modeled as either rigid or elastic.

It is noted that the calculated permanent deformations differed significantly for the two different embossing elements. Crimping occurred in the region of the paper which contacted the corner of the rounded rectangular embossing element. Also, the thickness of the sheet became noticeably more thin in that region after embossing. The rounded circular element created a much smoother permanent deformed shape for the paper sheet. As expected, it was found that the paper sheets were more easily formed at the higher moisture content where their stiffnesses and strengths were greatly reduced.

In addition to deformations, the finite element analyses calculated the stresses experienced in the paper sheet during the embossing process. For example, Figure 16 shows contour maps of the horizontal normal stress σ_x in the paper (RH = 50%) predicted at the positions of maximum embossing element penetration and after element retraction for the rounded rectangular element. Figure 17 illustrates the corresponding plots for the paper sheet embossed by the rounded circular element. It is interesting to note that for both elements, the stresses at many points change signs between the two configurations. This is due to the plastic strains in the sheet which prevent it from returning to its original flat configuration. A similar behavior is seen in metallic beams in bending which are plastically deformed [21].

It is expected that both the permanent deformations and residual stress distributions have an important influence on the increased flexibility and compressibility of embossed papers. The changes in the stress-strain behavior and material properties of the paper sheets due to embossing have been predicted by calculating the uniaxial tension response of the embossed sheets. The embossing element, rubber layer, and all the interface elements were first removed from the finite element model. The permanently deformed sheets were then subjected to prescribed axial deformations in the x-direction (MD), and the axial loads at the boundary were calculated. The predicted axial load versus deformation data were transformed to stress-strain data using the original cross-sectional area and length of the paper sheet. Figure 18 shows the deformed shapes of the paper sheet embossed by the rounded rectangular element (RH = 50%) at various stages of the uniaxial tension analysis. Figure 19 illustrates corresponding plots for the paper sheet embossed by the rounded circular element. It is noted that the sheets are returned to nearly flat configurations during the uniaxial tension loading process.

The stress-strain curves for the embossed sheets have been compared to those for the non-embossed paper. The results for both elements are shown in Figures 20-21 for relative humidities of 50% and 90%, respectively. As expected, the paper sheets had significantly reduced stiffness after embossing, especially when the loadings were small. This is due to the permanent deformations in the embossed sheets which are removed during the uniaxial loading. As the curvature of the embossed sheets was reduced and they became flat, the stress-strain curves approached those of the non-embossed sheet. It was also noticed that the sheets embossed by the rounded circular embossing element exhibited stiffer mechanical response than those embossed by the rounded rectangular embossing element.

SUMMARY AND CONCLUSIONS

A study on the paper embossing process has been performed using two-dimensional plane stress finite element analyses. The iterative nonlinear finite element models incorporated nonlinear material behavior and plasticity, large deformations, and contact stresses. The residual stresses and permanent deformations in the embossed paper sheets were calculated. Also, the changes in the mechanical behavior of the paper after embossing were predicted.

The analyses showed that the shape of the embossing element and the moisture content of the paper play a very important role in the embossing process. Although the considered two-dimensional cases do not represent the true geometry exactly, they have served as test vehicles on which the performance of the iterative nonlinear finite element models can be evaluated. The execution times for the two-dimensional calculations are expected to be several orders of magnitude less than the corresponding three-dimensional calculations to be performed in future investigations. Further experimental and analytical work is also needed to improve the models used for the paper constitutive behavior.

ACKNOWLEDGEMENTS

This research is based upon work supported by the Auburn University Pulp and Paper Research and Education Center.

REFERENCES

1. Lubkin, J. L., "Contact Problems," in Handbook of Engineering Mechanics, Edited by W. Flugge, Chapter 42, pp. 1-12, McGraw-Hill, 1962.

2. Kikuchi, N., "Seepage Flow Problems Using Variational Inequalities," International Journal of Numerical and Analytical Methods in Geomechanics, Vol. 1, pp. 283-297, 1977.

3. Kikuchi, N. and Oden, J. T., "Contact Problems in Elasticity," Texas Institute of Computational Mechanics (TICOM) Report 79-8, University of Texas, 1979.

4. Kikuchi, N. and Oden, J. T., Contact Problems in Elasticity: A Study of Variational Inequalities and Finite Element Methods, Society for Industrial and Applied Mathematics (SIAM), 1988.

5. Holzner, M. and Mannl, V., "Mechanics of Drawing with Rubber Pads," Proceedings of the Second International Conference on Technology of Plasticity, Edited by K. Lange, pp. 1151-1157, Stuttgart, Germany, August 24-28, 1987.

6. Sih, G. C., Chao, C. K., Lui, C. H. and Lin S. Y., "Deep Drawing of Plastically and Incrementally Deformed Circular Cylindrical Cup," Theoretical and Applied Fracture Mechanics, Vol. 15(1), pp. 35-62, 1991.

7. ABAQUS User's Manual, Version 4-8, Hibbitt, Karlsson, and Sorensen, Incorporated.

8. Green, A. E. and Zerna, W., Theoretical Elasticity, Second Edition, Oxford University Press, 1968.

9. Malvern, L. E., Introduction to the Mechanics of a Continuous Medium, Prentice-Hall, 1969.

10. Perkins, R. W., "Models for Describing the Elastic, Viscoelastic, and Inelastic Mechanical Behavior of Paper and Board," in Handbook of Physical and Mechanical Testing of Paper and Paperboard, Edited by R. E. Mark, Marcel Dekker, pp. 23-75, 1983.

11. Suhling J. C., "Continuum Models for the Mechanical Response of Paper and Paper Composites: Past, Present, and Future," in Material Interactions Relevant to the Pulp, Paper, and Wood Industries, MRS Vol. 197, Edited by D. F. Caulfield, J. D. Passaretti, and S. F. Sobczynski, Materials Research Society, pp. 245-255, 1990.

12. Thorpe, J. L., "Paper as an Orthotropic Thin Plate," TAPPI, Vol. 64(3), pp. 119-121, 1981.

13. Suhling, J. C., Johnson, M. W., Rowlands, R. E. and Gunderson, D. E., "Nonlinear Elastic Constitutive Relations for Cellulosic Materials," in Mechanics of Cellulosic and Polymeric Materials, Edited by R. W. Perkins, ASME, AMD-Vol. 99, pp. 1-13, 1989.

14. Paetow, R. and Gottsching, L., "The Two-Dimensional Nonlinear Elastic Material Law for Paper," Presented at the 1990 Progress in Paper Physics Seminar, Kalamazoo, MI, September 30 - October 3, 1990.

15. Ramasubramanian, M. K. and Ko, Y. C., "Relationship Between the In-Plane Paper Properties and the Ball Burst Strength," in Mechanics of Cellulosic and Polymeric Materials, Edited by R. W. Perkins, ASME, AMD-Vol. 99, pp. 105-111, 1989.

16. Perkins, R. W., Sinha, S. and Mark, R. E., "Micromechanics and Continuum Models for Paper Materials of Medium to High Density," in Proceedings of the 1991 International Paper Physics Conference, pp. 413-435, Kona, Hawaii, September 22-26, 1991.

17. Tate, A., "A New Approach to the Theory of Plastic Deformation," International Journal of Solids and Structures, Vol. 14, pp. 475-497, 1978.

18. Hill, R., Mathematical Theory of Plasticity, Oxford University Press, 1950.

19. Rowlands, R. E., "Strength (Failure) Theories and Their Experimental Correlation," in Handbook of Composites, Vol. 3, Edited by G. C. Sih and A. M. Skudra, pp. 71-125, Elsevier, 1985.

20. Yeh, K. C., Considine, J. M. and Suhling, J. C., "The Influence of Moisture Content on the Nonlinear Constitutive Behavior of Cellulosic Materials," in Proceedings of the 1991 International Paper Physics Conference, pp. 695-711, Kona, Hawaii, September 22-26, 1991.

21. Kachanov, L. M., Fundamentals of the Theory of Plasticity, Mir Publishers, 1974.

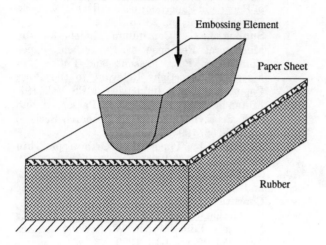

Figure 1 - Simplified Embossing Configuration

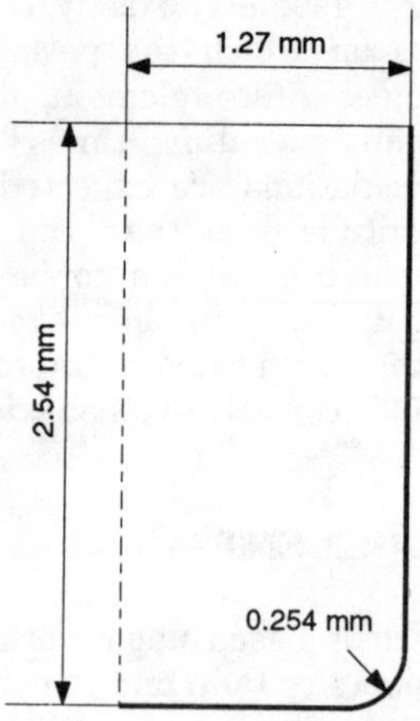

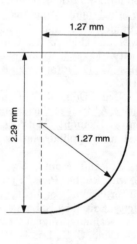

Figure 3 - Rounded Rectangular Embossing Element

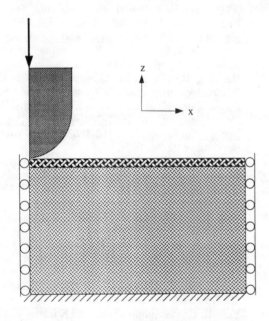

Figure 2 - Planar Embossing Model

Figure 4 - Rounded Circular Embossing Element

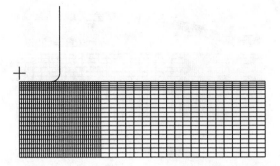

Figure 5 - Finite Element Mesh for Rounded
Rectangular Embossing Element

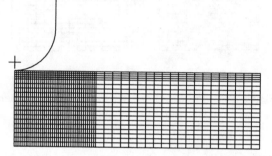

Figure 6 - Finite Element Mesh for Rounded
Circular Embossing Element

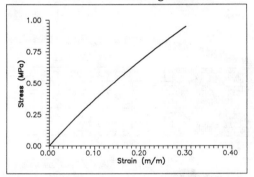

Figure 7 - Rubber Uniaxial Stress-Strain Curve

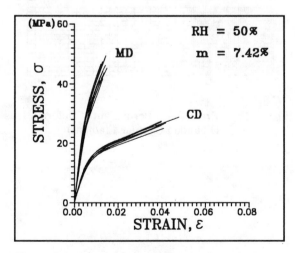

Figure 8 - Uniaxial Stress-Strain Curves for Paper

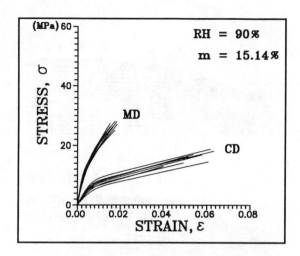

Figure 9 - Uniaxial Stress-Strain Curves for Paper

$\underline{RH = 50\%}$
$E_{11} = 6660$ MPa $X = 6.66$ MPa
$E_{22} = 2739$ MPa $Y = 4.66$ MPa
$\nu_{12} = 0.385$
$G_{12} = 1734$ MPa

$\underline{RH = 90\%}$
$E_{11} = 3973$ MPa $X = 2.98$ MPa
$E_{22} = 1259$ MPa $Y = 2.09$ MPa
$\nu_{12} = 0.4$
$G_{12} = 671$ MPa

Figure 10 - Measured Material Parameters

$\underline{RH = 50\%}$
$E_{33} = 6660$ MPa $Z = 10.00$ MPa
$\nu_{13} = 0.3$ $Q = 3.85$ MPa
$\nu_{23} = 0.1$ $R = 3.46$ MPa
$G_{13} = 1734$ MPa $S = 3.85$ MPa
$G_{23} = 1734$ MPa

$\underline{RH = 90\%}$
$E_{33} = 4500$ MPa $Z = 4.47$ MPa
$\nu_{13} = 0.3$ $Q = 1.72$ MPa
$\nu_{23} = 0.1$ $R = 1.55$ MPa
$G_{13} = 671$ MPa $S = 1.72$ MPa
$G_{23} = 671$ MPa

Figure 11 - Estimated Material Parameters

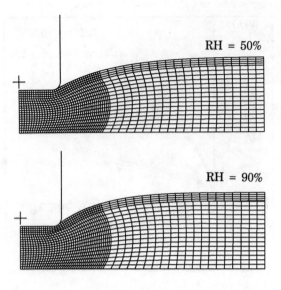

Figure 12 - Predicted Deformations at the Point of Maximum Penetration (Rounded Rectangular Element)

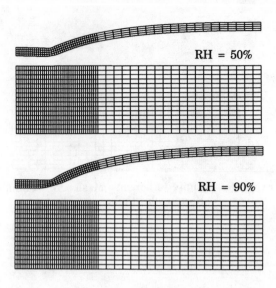

Figure 14 - Predicted Permanent Deformations (Rounded Rectangular Element)

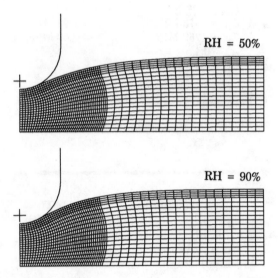

Figure 13 - Predicted Deformations at the Point of Maximum Penetration (Rounded Circular Element)

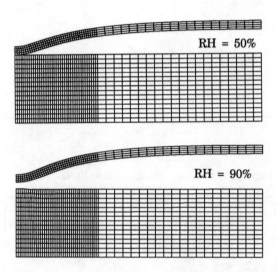

Figure 15 - Predicted Permanent Deformations (Rounded Circular Element)

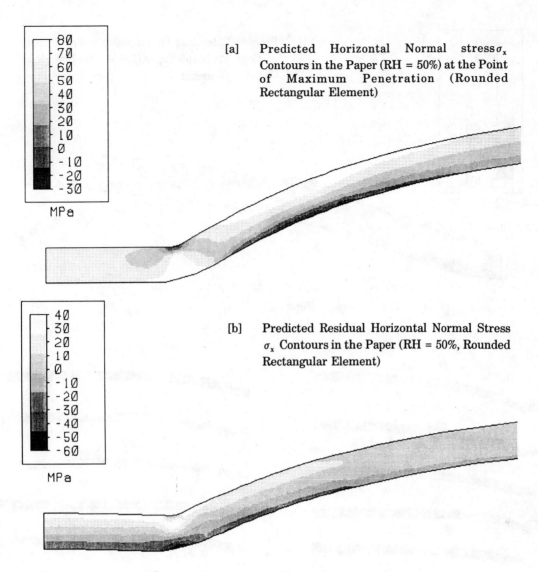

[a]   Predicted Horizontal Normal stress σ_x Contours in the Paper (RH = 50%) at the Point of Maximum Penetration (Rounded Rectangular Element)

[b]   Predicted Residual Horizontal Normal Stress σ_x Contours in the Paper (RH = 50%, Rounded Rectangular Element)

Figure 16

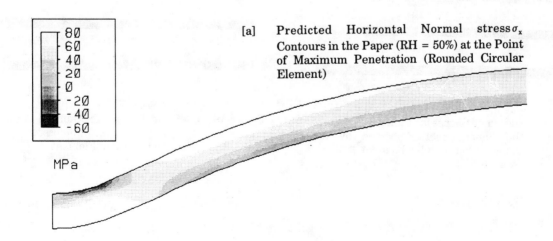

[a]   Predicted Horizontal Normal stress σ_x Contours in the Paper (RH = 50%) at the Point of Maximum Penetration (Rounded Circular Element)

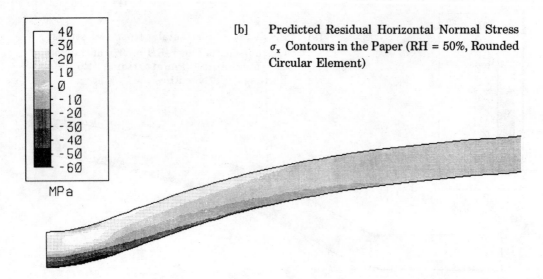

[b]   Predicted Residual Horizontal Normal Stress
σ_x Contours in the Paper (RH = 50%, Rounded
Circular Element)

Figure 17

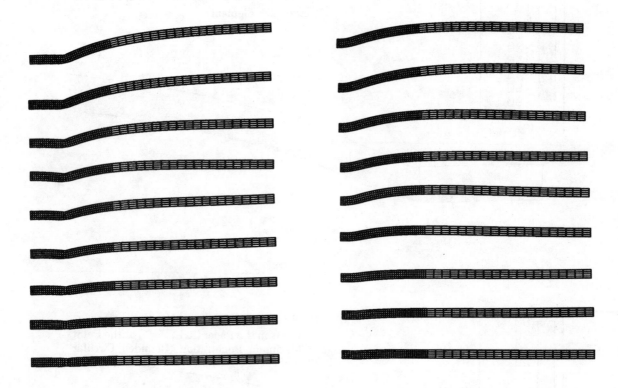

Figure 18 -   Deformed Shapes for Uniaxial Tension of
the Paper Sheet Embossed by the
Rounded Rectangular Element

Figure 19 -   Deformed Shapes for Uniaxial Tension of
the Paper Sheet Embossed by the
Rounded Circular Element

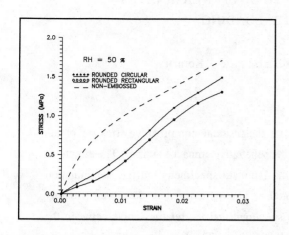

Figure 20 -   Stress-Strain Curves for the Embossed
Sheets at RH = 50%

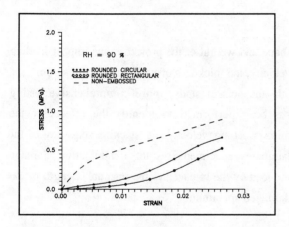

Figure 21 -   Stress-Strain Curves for the Embossed
Sheets at RH = 90%

RESIDUAL COMPRESSIVE STRENGTH OF CFRP LAMINATES
DAMAGED BY IMPACT LOADING

H.Ishikawa, T.Natsumura, Y.Tanaka and T.Koimai

ABSTRACT

An experimental investigation was conducted to estimate the residual compressive strength of the laminates of carbon fiber reinforced epoxy, damaged by the penetrative impact loading. The effects of the impact loading velocity and stacking sequency of the laminate specimens on the delamination damage and the compressive strength were investigated. The experimental data were mainly discussed by the delamination area, its total value of the specimen and the relative angle between the fiber orientations of the laminas of both sides of the delamination. The laminate with the stacking sequence of $[+30° \ a/-30° \ a/0° \ a]s$ is comparatively recommended for the delamination area and the residual compressive strength.

INTRODUCTION

Carbon-fiber reinforced epoxy (CFRP) laminates are being used in stiffness-critical structural components. In addition to the application, because of the demand for reduced structural mass, CFRP laminates are tried to be used for some strength critical applications. Strength critical componenets operate at high strain levels and their sensitivity to damage can affect their inservice conditions. Recent investigations [1-10] indicate that some of problems of the strength of CFRP laminates were the reductions of the compressive strength by the damage of the impact loading of the projectile. There are many factors on the strength reduction, such as the stacking sequency of the laminates, the shape and weight of the projectile, the impact loading velocity, the thickness of each lamina and so on.

In the present study, more comprehensive testing has been performed to identify the effects of the impact loading velocity and stacking sequency of the laminates specimens on the delamination damage induced by the impact and the residual strength of the damaged specimen.

TESTING METHOD

The test specimens were damaged by the projectiles with a steel sphere propelled normally to the center of the specimen. In order to discuss the effect of the projectile velocity on the characteristics of the impact damage, three velocity levels are

H.Ishikawa is Professor of Mechanical Engineering and T.Koimai a graduate student in the Department of Mechanical and Control Engineering, University of Electro-Communications, 1-5-1, Chofugaoka, Chofu, Tokyo 182, Japan

T.Natsumura and Y.Tanaka are Engineers of Mechanical Engineering in the Research and Development Department, Aero-Engine and Space Operations, Ishikawajima-Harima Heavy Industry Co.,Ltd, 3-5-1, Mukaidai, Tanashi, Tokyo 188, Japan.

realized, that is, low velocity (3.45 m/s) realized by the reaction force of coil spring, middle velocity (30~75 m/s) by the air pressure of compressor and high velocity (80~250 m/s) by the explosion of gunpowder. The shape and weight of the projectiles are shown in Table 1. The projectile velocity was measured by the signals from two photo-sensors located just ahead of the surface of the specimen. The kinetic energy of the projectile was calculated from its velocity and mass, and the value of the velocity is also shown in Table 1.

The filamentary material used in this investigation was a commercially-available, continuos-filament graphite, T300. The resin material was an epoxy, #2500. Test specimens were rectangular flat laminates, shown in Fig. 1. In order to charactrize the effect of the stacking sequency of the laminate on the impact damage, five kinds of the stacking sequency were used, shown in Table 2. Each stacking sequency has core laminas with $0°$ orientation fiber. Except for laminate 5 in Table 2, all of the laminates have in-plane symmetry of the fiber orientations with respect to $0°$ direction.

Testing procedure is as follows; at first the penetrative impact test by the projectile was performed. After the impact, each specimen was inspected ultrasonically, and the area of the interlaminar delamination was measured. Finally, the residual compressive strength of each damaged specimen was obtained by the static compression testing. The experimental data were mainly discussed by the delamination area, its total value and the relative angle between the fiber orientations of the laminas of both sides of the delamination.

EXPERIMENTAL RESULTS

Delamination Area

Typical test results of the ultrasonic inspection of the damaged specimen are shown in Fig. 2. The symbol H in three figures at upper portion, and symbol L in two figures at lower portion in Fig.2, and symbol M used in the subsequent section show the results on the specimens damaged by the high, low and middle velocities of the projectile, respectively. From the results, it is found that the shape of the interlaminar delamination is assumed to be an ellipse with major axis which coincides the fiber orientation of the back-side lamina of the delamination. From the assumption of the shape, we obtained the ellipsoidal area, An (n=1,2,3,4). As a typical example, the effect of the projectile velocity on An of the specimens damaged by the high velocity projectile is shown in Fig.3. The number (1~4) beside each symbol in the figure and the subscript n of An are the same meanings and they show the location of the interlaminar delamination, which can be refered to the schematically showed figure in Fig.3. At a constant velocity of the projectile, the backward interlaminar delamination of the specimen has a larger area, An. An of each interlamina is increased with the increase of the projectile velocity, and the increasing rate is greater for the backward interlamina.

Total area, A, of the delamination for each laminate specimen is defined as

$$A = \Sigma An \quad (n=1, 2, 3, 4)$$

Then, by using the area, A, we can discuss the effect of the stacking sequence of the laminate on the delamination damage. For the case of high projectile velocity (126 m/s, the projectile kinetic energy ,E, is 29.3 J), the value of A is ordered for the stacking sequence as

H5(100) > H3(96) > H2(69) > H4(64) > H1(34)

For the case of low projectile velocity (3.45 m/s, E is 30.6 J), the value of A is also ordered as

L5(100) > L4(84) > L3(80) > L1(68)

The number in the parentheses means the comparative value of the area A, when the maximum value of A is set to 100. There is a difference between these two cases that for the case of the low velocity the delamination area A of the stacking sequence L3 is less than that of L4.

In order to discuss the effect of the stacking sequence on the delamination damage, the relative angle between the fiber orientations of the laminas of both sides of the delamination is considered. The relationship between the relative angle (θ_i (i=1,2,3,4)) and the delamination angle, An, is shown in Fig.4. The subscript i means the location of the interlaminar delamination, shown in Fig. 4. There is less effect of θ_1 on the delamination area for all conditions of the projectile velocity. At the interlaminas between secon and third lamina and between fourth and fifth lamina from the impact side, the delamination areas are increased with the increase of θ_2 and θ_3. The effect of θ_4 on the delamination area is different at each impact velocity. For the conditions of the middle and high velocity of the projectile, the delamination area at θ_4=60° (the delamination between laminas of ±30° and ±60°) is less of about 50 % than it at θ_4=90° (the delamination between laminas of ±45°). Then, the stacking sequence of laminate 1 in Table 2 may be more preferable than that of lamina 2 that is commonly used.

The relatinship betwen the total delamination area and the summation of the relative angles of the fiber orientation in each lamina is expressed in Fig.5. For the cases of middle and high velocity of the projectile, the relationship is linear. The data (△ in Fig.5) of laminate 5 in Table 2 for the high velocity is deviated from the relation. This is probably caused by the anti-symmetry of the fiber orientation in the specimen. Because of the linearity, for example, for the high velocity, the total delamination area of laminate 1 where the summation angle is 180° is decreased by 70 % from that of laminate 3 where the summation angle is 360°. In the case of the low velocity, the linear relationship cannot be found, and the reason for this is not clear.

Residual Compressive Strength

Compressive strength, σ_s, is defined as

$$\sigma_s = P_{max} / lt$$

where P is the absolute value of the load of the compression test, and P_{max} is its maximum value. l and t are dimensions of the specimen, shown in Fig.1. The residual compressive strength, σ_s, of the damaged specimen is shown in Fig.6. The horizontal axis is the impact energy which is the kinetic energy of the projectile at the penetrative impact. The experimental data at the impact energy of 10 J. mean the strength, σ_s, of the non-damaged specimen. For the strength, σ_s, of the non-damaged specimen, there are differences between the values at the low/middle and high velocity. This is due to the dimensions of each specimen. The decreasing rate of the strength, σ_s, is maximum for a case of L3. The effect of the stacking sequence on the decreasing rate is expressed as

$$L3 > L1 > L2 > L4$$

for any impact velocity. Namely, laminate 3 has the greatest decreasing rate. However, as mentioned in the previous section, the total delaminationn area for laminate 3 is not necessarily great. Fig.4 shows that in the case of laminate 3, the delamination areas at θ_2 and θ_3 of 90° that are the neighboring interlaminas to 0° ply that withstands mainly the compressive load are fairly large. Thus, the maximum decreasing rate of the strength, σ_s, is caused by the large delamination areas at θ_2 and θ_3 of 90°.

In the case of laminate 4, the decreasing rate is smallest, though the total delamination area ia not necessarily small. In the laminate, the main delamination is initiated at θ_4 of 60° that is different from the loading direction (0°). This yields the smallest decreasing rate. In the case of laminate 5, the decreasing rate of σ_s is fairly small, though the total delamination area is largest. The reason for this phenominon is not clear, but is probably caused by the stacking sequence without in-plane symmetry of the fiber-orientations with respect to direction.0 °.

In the case of laminate 1, for any projectile velocity, σ_s of the non-damaged specimen is comparatively high and the decreasing rate of σ_s by the impact loading is low. Then, this laminate is preferable for the compressive loading.

CONCLUDING REMARKS

An experimental investigation was conducted to estimate the residual compressive strength of the CFRP laminates damaged by the penetrative impact loading. The effects of the impact loading velocity and stacking sequence of the laminate specimens on the delamination damage and the compression strength were investigated. From the experimental results, the following conclusions were obtained.

(1)The delamination damage of the laminate with the stacking sequence of [+30° a/-30° a/0° a]s is smallest, though that of the laminate with the stacking sequence of [45° a/-90° a/0° a]s is greatest.

(2)In cases of the middle and high velocity of impact loading, a linear relationship between the total delamination area and the summation of the relative angles of the fiber orientation in each lamina is found. Thus, there is a possibility that we can take the summation of the relative angle as an essential parameter to estimate the delamination damage.

(3)When the laminate specimenn has the delamination in the interlamina between the lamina with fiber orientation of 0 ° which coincides with the compressive strength loading direction and the other lamina, the decreasing rate of the residual comptressive strength of the damaged specimen from that of the specimen with no damage is great.

(4)In case of the high velocity of impact loading, the laminate with the stacking sequence of [+30° a/-30° a/0° a]s has a comparatively high compressive strength and a low rate of the decreasing of the strength by the impact damage.

REDERENCES

1. Waltere, R.W., Johnson, R.W., June, R.R. and Maccarty,J.E., Fatigue of Filametary Composite Materials, ASTM STP 636 (1977),228.

2. Rosenfeld, M.S. and Gauss, L.W., Fatigue of filamentary Composite Materials, ASTM STP 723 (1981),174.

3. Stellbrink, K.K. and Aoki, R.M., Proc. of 4th Int. Conf. Composite Materials, Tokyo, 1 (1982), 853.

4. Ramkumar, R.L., Long-Term Behahavior of Composites, ASTM STP 813(1983), 116.

5. Dorey, G., Proc. of Int. Conf. Structural Impact and Crashworthiness, London, 1 (1984), 155.

6. Bay, Y. and Harding, J., Proc. of Int. Conf. Structural Impact and Crashworthiness, London, 2 (1984), 482.

7. Rhodes, M.D., Williams, J.G. and Starnes, Jr. J.H., Polymer Composites,2(1981),36.

8. Williams, J.G. and Rhodes, M.D., Composite Materials: Testing and Design, ASTM STP 787 (1982),450.

9. Ishikawa, H. and Murakami, K., Zairyo (J. of the society of Materials Science, JAPAN), 36 (1987), 236 (in Japanese).

10.Ishikawa, H. and Murakami, K., J. of JSME, 56 (1991), 1343 (in Japanese).

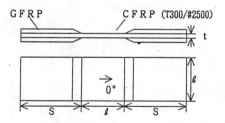

Dimensions (mm)	l	s	t
Low velocity type	40	50	2.9
Middle velocity type	40	50	2.9
High velocity type	80	40	3.9

Fig.1 Specimen geometry.

Table 1 Impact loading conditions.

	Low velocity	Middle velocity	High velocity
Method for impact	Coil spring	Air pressure	Gunpowder
Velocity (m/s)	3.45	30~75	80~250
Projectile	Steel sphere (φ10mm) with steel rod	Steel sphere (φ5mm) with aluminum hollow cylinder	Steel sphere (φ5mm)
Weight (g)	525	1.2	0.51
Impact energy (J)	30.6	5.29~33.1	16~156

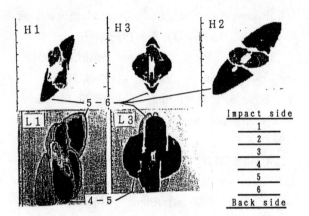

Fig.2 Ultrasonically inspection results.

Table 2 Stacking sequency of laminates.

Laminate No	Stacking sequency
1	[30° a／−30° a／0° a] s
2	[45° a／−45° a／0° a] s
3	[0° a／90° a／0° a] s
4	[60° a／−60° a／0° a] s
5	[45° a／90° a／0° a] s

Low velocity type: a=3
Middle velocity type: a=3
High velocity type: a=4

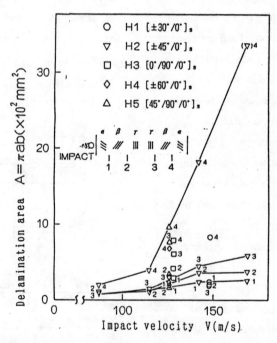

Fig.3 Relationship between the delamination area and the impact velocity for the high velocity of the projectile.

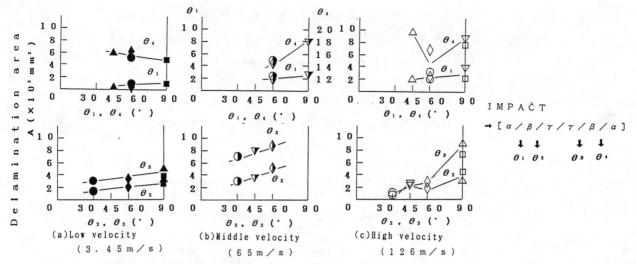

Fig.4 Relationship between the delamination area and the relative angle of
fiber orientations of each lamina.

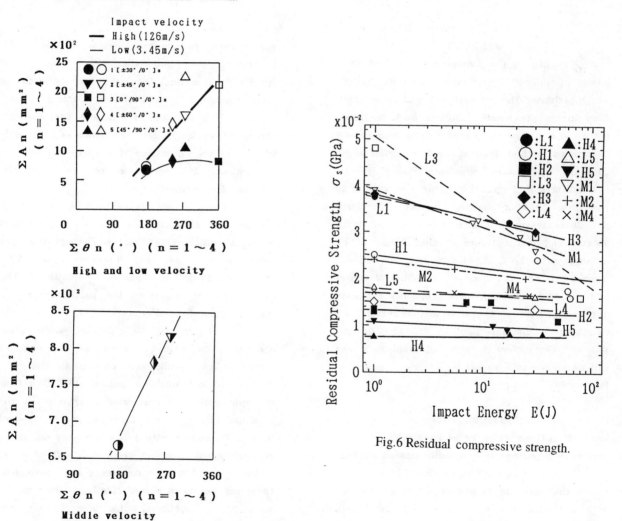

Fig.5 Relationship between the total delamination area and
the total value of relative angle of fiber orientations of each lamina.

Fig.6 Residual compressive strength.

An Improved Calculation of Residual Stress of Multilayer Thin Films with Finite Element Method

Ching-An Shao[‡], Hong-Jueng King[‡‡], Bor-Ming Lee[‡],

Fu-Pen Chiang[‡‡‡]

* Dept. of Civil Engineering, Chung-Cheng Institute of Technology, Ta-Hsi, Taoyuan, Taiwan, R.O.C.

** Dept. of Applied Physics, Chung-Cheng Institute of Technology.

*** Dept. of Mechanical Engineering, State University of New York, at Stony Brook, Stony Brook, New York, U.S.A.

ABSTRACT

Considering the poorly demonstrated calculation in Ennos'[1] summation average method which estimated the residual stress of optical thin films under previously designed multi-layers, we set up in our experiment a Michelson type reflective moire method to measure the partial slope contours of deformed substrate caused by the residual stress of optical thin films. According to the plate bending theory, the two-diemnsional principal stress at the nodal points of both single- and multi- layers of thin films can be obtained with the finite element method(FEM). By summing up the two-dimensional principal stress at nodal points method, we successfully got good approaches between the experimental results and estimated calculations. Combine ZnS with Ge and SiO with Ge, different slopes of residual stress will be shown with report to different sequent layers.

INTRODUCTION

Thin film optical filters have played a more and more important role in sophisticated electro-optical systems [2-6]. When a thin film is grown up to the stage of nucleation, either by CVD or PVD method, it (as well as a substrate) will introduce more or less the internal stress which comes from the accumulated effect of grain boundary model and recrystallization model [7-8]. Inproper design and fabrication of an optical filter will cause bucklings and cracks due to the large tensile and compressive residual stress. Ennos [1] had tried to estimate the residual stress of optical thin films composed of multilayers of the summation of average method. But the outcome is very poor compared with the results of experiment.

Unlike the average methods [4], we set up a whole-field reflective moire measurement method to measure the residual stress. The moire fringes can be seen in real time. However, Ligtenberg's method needs double exposure technique [9]. The moire patterns repersent the partial slope con tours of the deformed substrate [10,11]. From the plate bending theory [10] and the smooth spline algorithm, the principal stress of the bending substrate can be obtained. To estimate the residual stress of multilayer optical thin films from the information of correlated single layer, the principal stress of the single- or multi- layer of Ge and SiO and Ge with ZnS which were deposited respectively on Corning glass with a fixed deposition rate and vacuum conditions (as possible as they may be) is measured firstly. Owing to the variation of principal directions in an un-uniformed distribution of residual stress, a scheme of finite element method is employed to calculate the combined residual stress. Unlike the average summation method, the accumulating nodal principal stress for multilayers can be a combination of Ge and SiO or Ge and ZnS alternatively. Therefore, to estimate the outcoming residual stress is possible at the design stage. In our experiments, we found that for different coating materials will show different slopes of residual stress with respect to layer stacks. Experiments showed satisfactory in the estimated and the demonstrated data.

OPTICAL SET-UP

We set up a Michelson type, reflective moire arrangement as shown in Fig.1. Two crossed Ronchi gratings, T, were used as targets (spatial frequencies were 5 line pairs per mm (lpmm) and 12 lpmm respectively). The gratings were allowed to be interchangable, at will, for the requirement of sensitivity. The grating was illuminated by a diffused light source, L. Two optical reflective flats (with flatness of $\lambda/15$), A and B, were put at the two arms of the interferemeter. The gratings could be viewed from a camera through a high quality dielectric beam splittr (abbr.B.S.). The distances from the grating to the two optical flats were aligned to be equal. If they were not equal, a linear mismatch would occur. Two optical flats were also adjusted to the right angle by micro-screw stages, otherwise, rotational mismatch would occur. A deformed substrate, caused by the coated reflective thin films, was put at the top of the optical flat B. The moire fringes beaten from the reference grating which was reflected from the optical component A via the deformed grating mirrored from the deformed substrate. The moire fringes could be seen at the image plane of the camera in real time. These moire fringes represent the absolute partial slope contours of the bent subsbrate [10,11]. Ourset-up can also be applied to dielectric films by replacing the optical flat B with another ARC transparent optical flat C. Because the reflectance of the dielectric thin films is poor, another neutral density filter must be put in front of the component A to take proper intensity ratio.

EXPERIMENTAL DETAILS

(a.)Sample preparation

The Corning glass 0211 with diameter 1" and thickness 0.15 mm was chosen to be the substrate. Its Young's modulus and Poisson's ratio are $7.5*10^{10}$ N/m² and 0.22 [12] respectively. The coating plant was LH1100 equiped with thermal resistance and electron-beam gun sources. Coating materials were ZnS, SiO (acted as low index materials) and Ge (as high index material). Before running the coating process, the substrate should be carefully cleaned. Residual gas analyzer, optical thickness and deposition rate monitors were necessary instruments to monitor the fixed parameters (as possible as we could). Table (I) summarizes the sample sequents and vacuum parameters.

When the coating process for each sample is finished, the sample took the moire pattern from the optical set-up as in Fig.1. The two dimensional moire pattern is then separated by optical spatial filtering technique to get partial slope contours in X- and Y-dimension.

(b.)Computer simulation algorithms.

Most conventional average methods for measuring residual stress are based on the cantilever beam, that is, assuming the residual stress is homogeneous and isotropic. Judging from the different thermal expansion coefficients between the substrate and the thin films, and the different boundary conditions in the coating process, the distribution of residual stress should be in a two dimentional state.

After we have the two-dimensional partial slope contours ($\partial w/\partial x$ and $\partial w/\partial y$), we can get the curvature of the deformed substrate and the principal stress with the smooth spline algorithm and the plate bending theorem [10]. The nodal principal stress can be claculated by means of the finite element method. Then we can try to find the correlated mean values of each $\hat{H}$, H', $\hat{L}$ and L' layer (^ means it is a sandwich layer, ' means it is the outmost layer). The residual stress of the multilayer can be estimated by summing up the residual stress at nodal points of every single correlated mean values, $\hat{H}$, H', $\hat{L}$ and L'. The flow-chart of this simulation is listed in Fig.2.

EXPERIMENTAL RESULTS and DISCUSSION

In applying the above technique, the two-dimensional partial slope contours of different sequent layers are shown in Fig 3 to Fig 5. The equal spacing fringes represent a constant residual stress distribution. Some of the moire patterns clearly show the unequal spacing distribution, that means the residual stress is neither homogeneous nor isotropic.

Fig 6 to Fig 8 are the comparison between theoretical estimated curves and experimental results. An interested phenomenon is indicatied in these figures: the slope of the residual stress with respect to the sequent layers is almost constant but will depends on the coating materials.

CONCLUSIONS

A two-dimensional, whole-field reflective moire method is proposed to see moire fringes in real time. The residual stress of optical thin films at nodal points can be calculated by the plate bending theorem and the finite element method.

From the experimental results in this paper, it is hopeful to estimate the residual stress of multilayer optical thin film. The only tough job is we need a large experimental data base to hold the correlated residual stress of every single layer.A summation of the nodal principal stress will be errorless compared with the average summation method. Coating materials under fixed vacuum conditions seem to make constant slopes with respect to different combined layer stacks.

ACKNOWLEDGEMENT

The author would like to thank Dr. Philip Wu and Mr.Yuh Chang Chen for their kind suggestions and support. Finacial support provided by National Science Council of the Republic of China through contract NCS-0210-D-014-08 is also greatly appreciated.

REFERENCES

1.A.E.Ennos,"Stress developed in optical film coatings," A.O.5(1), p.p.51-61, 1966.

2.R.W.Hoffman,"The mechanical properties of non-metallic thin films," Physics of nonmetallic thin films, Ed. by C.H.S.Dupuy, A.Cachard, Plenum Press, N.Y. p.p.273-353, 1976.

3.R.W.Hoffman,"The mechanical properties of thin condensed films,"Physics of thin films, Vol.3, Ed.by G.Hass, R.E.Thun, Academic Press, N.Y.1976.

4.D.S.Campbell,"Mechanical properties of thin films," Handbook of Thin Film Technology, Ed. by L.I.Maissel, R.Gland, Chap.12, McGraw-Hill, N.Y. 1970.

5.H.K.Pulker,"Mechanical properties of optical films,"Thin Solid Films, 89, p.p.191-204, 1982

6.J.A.Thorton,D.W.Hoffman,"Stress-related effects in thin films," Thin Solid Films, 171, p.p.5-31, 1989

7.R.W.Hoffman,"Stress in thin films:the relevance of grain boundaries and impurities", Thin Solid Films, 34, p.p.185-190, 1976.

8.E.Klokholm,B.S.Berry,"Intrinsic stress in evaporated metal films", J.Electrochem. Soc., 115, p.p.823, 1968.

9.F.K.Ligtenberg,"The moire method:a new experimental method for the determination of moments in small slab models,"Proc.SESA X2(2),p83-98,1954

10.F.P.Chiang,"A whole-field method for the measurement of two-dimensional state of stress in thin films,"Exp.Mechs.,12(8),p.p.377-380,1972

11.R.P.Khetan,K.C.Jain,"Whole-field residual stress measurements in silicon wafer during integrated circuit fabrication,"SPIE Vol.955, p.p.2-13,1988.

12.G.C.Stony,Proc.Roy.Soc.London,A32,p172,1909

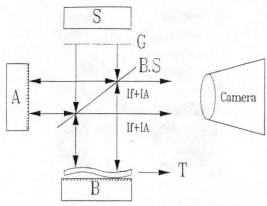

Fig. 1　Experimental setup---S: extend diffused light, G: crossed grating, A and B: reflective optical flats (λ/15), B.S.: beam splitter, T: thin film substrate.

Coating Material	Parameters	Vacuum Condition			
	Layer Structure	Starting Pressure	Optical Thickness	Substrate Temp	Deposition Rate
Case I L:SiO H:Ge	sub/L/air sub/L/H/air sub/L/H/L/air sub/L/H/L/H/air sub/L/H/L/H/L/air sub/L/H/L/H/L/H/air	1≑10⁻⁸ torr	L: λ/4 H: λ/4	150°C	L: 90 sec H:120 sec in λ/4 Time
Case II L:ZnS H:Ge	sub/L/air sub/L/H/air sub/L/H/L/air sub/L/H/L/H/air sub/L/H/L/H/L/air sub/L/H/L/H/L/H/air	1≑10⁻⁸ torr	L: λ/4 H: λ/4	150°C	L: 90 sec H:120 sec in λ/4 Time
Case III H:Ge L:SiO	sub/H/air sub/H/L/air sub/H/L/H/air sub/H/L/H/L/air sub/H/L/H/L/H/air sub/H/L/H/L/H/L/air	1≑10⁻⁸ torr	L: λ/4 H: λ/4	150°C	L: 90 sec H:120 sec in λ/4 Time

Table 1 Layer sequents and deposition parameters

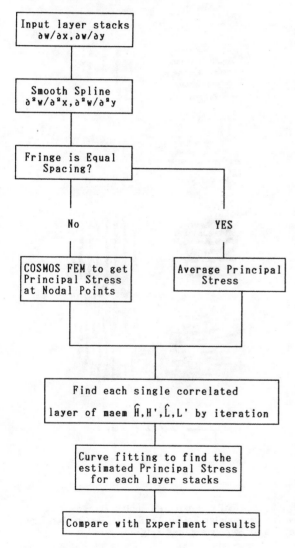

Fig. 2　Computer simulation flowchart (in which w is the deflection of the deformed substrate)

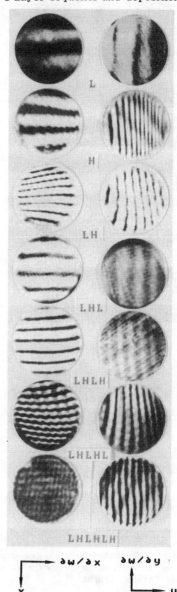

Fig. 3　Optically separated moire fringes due to coating materials: L: SiO, H: Ge of $\partial w/\partial x$ families (left) and $\partial w/\partial y$ families (right)

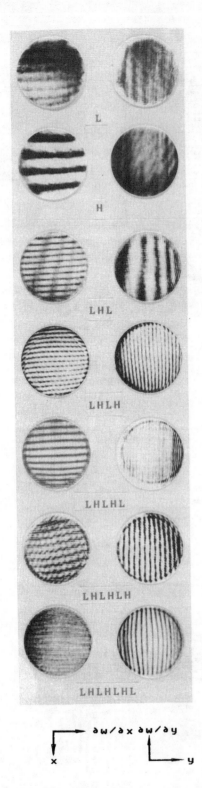

L

H

LHL

LHLH

LHLHL

LHLHLH

LHLHLHL

Fig. 4 Optically separated moire fringes due to coating materials: L: ZnS, H: Ge of $\partial w/\partial x$ families (left) and $\partial w/\partial y$ families (right)

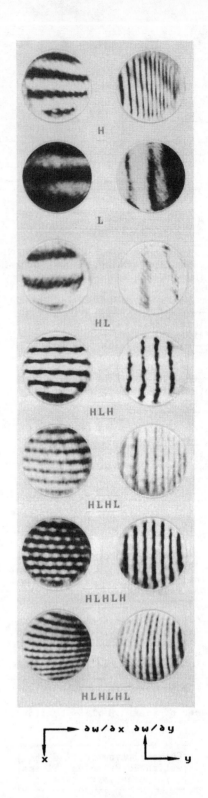

H

L

HL

HLH

HLHL

HLHLH

HLHLHL

Fig. 5 Optically separated moire fringes due to coating materials: H: Ge L: SiO of $\partial w/\partial x$ families (left) and $\partial w/\partial y$ families (right)

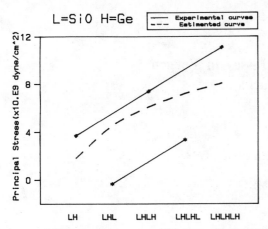

Fig. 6 Estimated curve compare with experimental results of SiO and Ge combinations as in case I

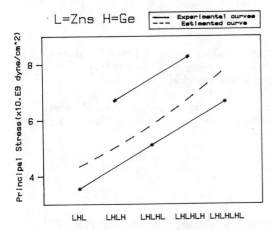

Fig. 7 Estimated curve compare with experimental results of ZnS and Ge combinations as in case II

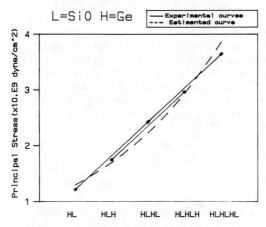

Fig. 8 Estimated curve compare with experimental results of Ge and SiO combinations as in case III

Quenching-Induced Residual Stresses in Forged
7150-Aluminum Blocks

J. Rasty, and J. Hashemi - Texas Tech University [1]
D.E. Hunter-Alcoa[2]
G. Roy, and D. Kiff- CANMET[3]

ABSTRACT

7150-Aluminum blocks measuring 15.88 cm(L) x 15.88 cm(W) x 8.26 cm(H) (6.25"x6.25"x3.25") were forged at 477°C (890° F) and subsequently quenched in 21° C (70° F) water. The purpose of this paper is to present the results of a joint research effort conducted by researchers at Texas Tech University, Alcoa Technical Center, and CANMET for determining the magnitude and distribution of residual stresses induced by quenching of forged aluminum blocks. Specifically, the "Treuting-Read" and "hole-drilling" techniques were utilized. Experimental procedures along with residual stress values on all surfaces of the block as well as stress distributions through the thickness of the block are presented.

INTRODUCTION

Residual or internal stresses are commonly defined as a system of self-equilibrating stresses which exist in an elastic body in the absence of external forces, moments and temperature gradients. It is important to distinguish between *macro residual stresses* and *micro-stresses*. Macro residual stresses vary continuously through the volume of the body and act over regions which are large compared with atomic dimensions. Microstresses, also known as textural stresses, act over dimensions of few atomic radius. In the material presented in this paper, the term "residual stress" refers to *macro-stresses* only.

Although the sources of residual stresses may vary from one component to another, the common mechanism responsible for existence of residual stresses is a dimensional incompatibility among different regions of the component. In cold metal forming operations, such as extrusion, forging, rolling, drawing, etc., this dimensional incompatibility is induced by nonuniform plastic deformation through the thickness of the material, i.e.; metal fibers which are in immediate contact with the die/tool area, flow at a slower rate (due to friction) than the fibers away from the die/tool area (J. Rasty and C.S. Hartley, 1990, 1991). The result is a nonhomogeneous deformation pattern with a corresponding residual stress distribution as depicted in Figure 1.

---

1) Jahan Rasty and Javad Hashemi are assistant professors at the Department of Mechanical Engineering at Texas Tech University, Lubbock, Texas 79409.
2) Daniel E. Hunter is staff engineer at Alcoa Technical Center, Alcoa Center, Pennsylvania 15069.
3) George Roy and D. Kiff are Research Scientist and Technologist, respectively, at Canada Center for Minerals and Energy Technology, Metals Technology Laboratories (CANMET/MTL), Ottawa, Ontario, K1A 061, Canada.

The evolution of residual stresses induced by quenching operations is a rather interesting one. Consider the case of residual stresses induced by quenching of the material used in this study. 7150-aluminum blocks were forged and water-quenched from a temperature of 477° C by immersing the blocks in 21° C water. Initially, the hot surface fibers cool at a faster rate than the center fibers. The large thermal contraction of the surface fibers, as compared to small contraction of the center fibers, produces a strain mismatch which places the surface fibers under tensile stress while the center fibers sustain a compressive stress as shown in Figure 2(b). Due to the lower yield stress of the hot center fibers, the compressive stress acting at the center of the block causes the center fibers to yield and shrink further to relieve some of the stress as shown in Figure 2(c). Once the equilibrium temperature has been reached and the center fibers have cooled, the total contraction will be greater for the center fibers than the surface ones, since the center fibers contract by both the cooling process as well as the plastic deformation induced by the initial compressive stresses at the center. The center fibers will then be in residual tension while the surface fibers will remain in residual compression as shown in Figure 2(d).

There are a number of destructive, semi destructive and nondestructive techniques available for the experimental measurement of residual stresses. Nondestructive techniques, although more popular in the industry for their ease of implementation, are not capable of providing through thickness data. Destructive techniques have been used quite successfully for the measurement of residual stresses in rods, tubes, and sheet materials (Rasty, 1986, 1987, 1989.) Although destructive techniques are different in their approach to the measurement of residual stresses, they are all based on the principal of removing part of the stressed material and recording the response of the remaining material as it adjusts its shape in order to maintain the equilibrium of the internal forces.

Residual stresses in 7150-aluminum blocks were measured by employing the "Treuting-Read" and "Hole Drilling" methods. The following sections, will present the experimental and theoretical procedures used in the application of these techniques to the measurement of residual stresses.

RESIDUAL STRESS MEASUREMENTS

I) Treuting-Read Method

Theoretical Background

Also known as the "Layer Removal" technique, this method was developed by Treuting and Read (1951) for determining the biaxial residual stress state in materials behaving in an elastically homogeneous manner. This method assumes that the stresses only vary through the thickness of the material. This assumption is quite valid for the case of quenched aluminum blocks considered in this study since the source of residual stresses is a temperature gradient which only varies through the thickness of the material.

In applying this method, thin layers of material are removed from the surface of the block. Removal of part of the stressed material disturbs the equilibrium of the forces thereby forcing the remaining material to change its shape in order to maintain the equilibrium of internal forces. This change of shape can be measured by observing the curvature of the material and later used to calculate the stresses in the removed material.

Figure 3. shows the schematic diagram of the aluminum blocks considered in this study with the xy plane in the initial midsurface of the block, and the x and y axis in the direction of principal stresses. The initial upper and lower surfaces of the specimen are the planes $z = z_0$ and $z = -z_0$. The variable upper surface is the plane $z = z_0$. As mentioned earlier, we can assume that the stress distribution is constant in the x and y directions and the only nonvanishing components are $\sigma_x(z)$ and $\sigma_y(z)$. Assuming that a uniformly thick layer of material is removed from the upper surface, as shown by the shaded area in Figure 3, the new upper surface is located at $z = z_0$. Denoting the resulting components of the curvature in the x and y directions as $\phi_x = \phi_x(z_1)$, and $\phi_y = \phi_y(z_1)$ respectively, the explicit expression for $\sigma_x(z_1)$ is given by

$$\sigma_x(z_1) = \frac{-E}{6(1-v^2)} \left\{ (z_0 + z_1)^2 \left[\frac{d\phi_x(z_1)}{dz_1} + v\frac{d\phi_y(z_1)}{dz_1} \right] \right.$$

$$\left. + 4(z_0 + z_1)\left[\phi_x(z_1) + v\phi_y(z_1) \right] - 2\int_{z_1}^{z_0} \left[\phi_x(z_1) + v\phi_y(z_1) \right] dz \right\} \qquad (1)$$

Where the derivatives and the integral can be obtained graphically as the slope and the areas of their corresponding curves. It should be mentioned that the blocks are assumed to be perfectly flat before the removal of the first layer, i.e.;
$\phi_x(z_0) = \phi_y(z_0) = 0$.

Should the specimens have an initial curvature, it must be subtracted from subsequent values to obtain ϕ_x and ϕ_y. The expression for $\sigma_y(z)$ is similar to equation (1) with the subscripts x and y interchanged.

The change in curvatures ϕ_x and ϕ_y can be calculated directly from change in surface strain values measured by a strain gage. Figure 4 shows an exaggerated diagram of a bent strip due to removal of a layer of stressed material. Denoting the lengths of the top surface, bottom surface, and center length of the strip by L_T, L_B, L_0 respectively, one can write

$$\varepsilon = \frac{L_T - L_o}{L_o} = \frac{(R_T - R_o)\theta}{L_o} \tag{2}$$

Denoting the thickness of the remaining material by t, equation (2) can be rewritten as

$$\varepsilon = \frac{L_T - L_0}{L_0} = \frac{(R_0 + \dfrac{t}{2} - R_0)\theta}{R_0\theta} \tag{3}$$

or,

$$\frac{1}{R_0} = \frac{2\varepsilon}{t} \tag{4}$$

where $\dfrac{1}{R_0}$ represents the curvature of the remaining strip of thickness, t, under a strain of ε.

Experimental Procedure

7150-Aluminum blocks measuring 15.88 cm(L) x 15.88 cm(W) x 8.26 cm(H) (6.25"x6.25"x3.25") were forged at 477° C (890° F) and subsequently quenched in 21° C (70° F) water. The experimental procedure for the determination of residual stresses involved the measurement of strains developed on one surface of a block while measuring the developed strains on the opposite side. The measured strains were then converted to curvature changes through equation (4) which were subsequently utilized in equation (1) to calculate the residual stress magnitude and distribution.

The strain gages used to obtain the strain data were bi-element gages of the type EA-06- 250TA-120 obtained from Micro-Measurements. As shown in Figure 5, three gages were attached at three different locations on the top side of the block, namely, at the center, at the middle of an edge, and at the corner. A shaper machine was employed for removal of material from the opposite (bottom) side of the block. In order to minimize the machining stresses, thin layers of 0.5 mm (0.02 in.) wide and 0.5 mm deep were made across the entire width of the block. The developed strains at each of the six locations were recorded after the thickness of the material was reduced by 1 mm (0.04 in.) This procedure was repeated until the thickness of the block was reduced by approximately 75%. It was assumed that the residual stress distribution due to quenching was symmetrical about the midplane of the block. This assumption was verified by observing the similarity of the data obtained at *midplane+20%* to those obtained at *midplane-20%* of the total thickness.

II) Hole-Drilling Technique
Theory and Experimental Procedure

The hole drilling method consists of machining a blind hole in incremental steps in a specimen and measuring the resulting change of strain in the vicinity of the hole (G. Roy, 1990). Three locations were selected for hole drilling, each one in the center of the top, bottom, and side surfaces, denoted H1, H2, and H3, respectively, as shown in Figure6. Measurements of strain in three different directions G_1, G_2, and G_3 of a rosette (Figure 7) provide the necessary data from which principal components of the original residual stress state σ_p and σ_q (normal to the hole surface) at the hole location can be calculated (Figure 8.)

To determine the stresses induced into the material during hole drilling, five coupons of dimensions, length and width 25.4 mm, and height 12.7 mm were from the block. The coupons were stress-annealed by heating them to 413° C (775° F) and holding them at this temperature for one hour. Next, the temperature was reduced to 232° C (450° F) at the rate of 30° C/hour. The coupons were soaked for two hours followed by air-cooling to room temperature. The hole drilling method was applied to one coupon by performing the hole drilling in nine increments of 0.13 mm, to a total depth of 1.00 mm at each location.

To interpret the strains, a relaxation matrix, referred to as R-matrix, was developed to relate the measured surface strains and the principal stresses at depths h_i, $\sigma_p(h_i)$, $\sigma_q(h_i)$, i=1,2,.....,N, where N indicates the number of subsurface layers identified during the incremental hole drilling. The method of strain interpretation by R-matrices is called the Relaxation Matrix Method (G.Roy,1990)

$$
\begin{bmatrix}
\varepsilon^1 \\
\varepsilon^2 \\
\cdot \\
\varepsilon^i \\
\cdot \\
\varepsilon^N
\end{bmatrix}
=
\begin{bmatrix}
R^{11} & 0 & \cdot & \cdot & \cdot & 0 & \cdot & 0 \\
R^{21} & R^{22} & 0 & \cdot & \cdot & 0 & \cdot & 0 \\
\cdot & \cdot & \cdot & \cdot & & & & \\
R^{i1} & R^{i2} & \cdot & \cdot & R^{ii} & 0 & \cdot & 0 \\
\cdot & \cdot & & & & & & \\
R^{N1} & R^{N2} & \cdot & \cdot & R^{Ni} & \cdot & \cdot & R^{NN}
\end{bmatrix}
\begin{bmatrix}
\sigma^1 \\
\sigma^2 \\
\cdot \\
\sigma^i \\
\cdot \\
\sigma^N
\end{bmatrix}
\tag{5a}
$$

where

$$
\varepsilon^i = \begin{bmatrix} \varepsilon_b^i \\ \varepsilon_s^i \end{bmatrix}, \quad
R^{ij} = \begin{bmatrix} R_{11}^{ij} & 0 \\ 0 & R_{22}^{ij} \end{bmatrix}, and \quad
\sigma^i = \begin{bmatrix} \sigma_b^i \\ \sigma_s^i \end{bmatrix}
\tag{5b}
$$

ε_b^i and ε_s^i are the biaxial and shear components of surface strain (h=0) around a hole of depth h_i. σ_b^i and σ_s^i are biaxial and shear components of the traction components $\sigma_p(h_i)$, and $\sigma_q(h_i)$. $R_{kk}{}^{ij}$, k=1,2, are called relaxation R-functions, and are elements of the relaxation submatrices R^{ij}; $R_{kk}{}^{ij}$=0 for j>i. The R-matrix is used to relate the relaxed surface strains to the stresses at the respective depths.

We can represent the R-functions as

$$
R_{11}^{ij} = \frac{1+\upsilon}{E} \frac{2E}{1+\upsilon} A^i(h_j), \quad and \quad R_{22}^{ij} = \frac{1}{E} 2EB^i(h_j)
\tag{5c}
$$

where the constants $A^i(h_j)$ and $B^i(h_j)$ depend on the depths h_j.

Let

$$A^{ij} = \frac{2E}{1+\upsilon} A^i(h_j) \quad \text{, and} \quad B^{ij} = 2EB^i(h_j) \tag{5d}$$

Then

$$R_{11}^{ij} = \frac{1+\upsilon}{E} A^{ij}, \quad \text{and} \quad R_{22}^{ij} = \frac{1}{E} B^{ij} \tag{6}$$

$A^i(h_j)$ and $B^i(h_j)$ are called partial relaxation constants and were determined numerically by the finite element method. The constants A^{ij} and B^{ij} are for large variations of Young's modulus and Poisson's ratio.

RESULTS AND DISCUSSION

I) Treuting-Read Method

Figures 9 through 14 show the residual stress distribution through the thickness of 7150 aluminum blocks at gage locations 1 through 6 (Figure 5) respectively. In all of above figures, the horizontal axis denotes the percentage of the thickness *remaining* upon the removal of a uniform layer from the bottom surface (strain gages were installed on the top surface.) Therefore, 100% thickness remaining (no material was removed) refers to a location at the bottom surface, while 0% thickness remaining (all of the material was removed) refers to a location at the top surface. Experiments were conducted until nearly 75% of the material's thickness was removed.

The assumption of residual stress symmetry about the block's midplane can be verified by noting the similarity in magnitude and distribution of the stresses in the 30-50% thickness region of figures 9-14, to those in the 50-70% region. The discontinuity in the stress distribution data is due to the fact that material removal and collection of data was only conducted up to 75% thickness mark. At this point, the block had become too thin to proceed without the addition of the effect of machining stresses, gripping stresses and other nuisance effects in the strain gage data. Therefore, the remaining part of the stress distribution (from 30% to 0% thickness) was obtained by utilizing the data from 70% to 100% thickness due to symmetry of the stress distribution.

The residual stresses calculated at each gage location (figures 9-14), indicate that the quenching process, as expected, results in a state of compressive stress near the exterior surfaces of the block (first 25% of thickness) and a state of tensile stress around the midplane of the block (from 25% to 75% of thickness.) The compressive stress zone assumes its maximum value of -81 Mpa (-11,800 psi) at the exterior surface, while the tensile region reaches its maximum magnitude of 44 Mpa (6,400 psi) at the midplane of the block. The similarity of the stress magnitude and distribution at gage locations 1-2, 3-4, and 5-6 indicate that the stresses are in an equal-biaxial state.

As one can observe from figures 9-14, the magnitude of the residual stress distributions decreases from the center of the block (gage locations 1-2) to its edge (gage location 3-4), and further decreases to the corner of the block (gage locations 5-6.) This behavior can be explained by observing that the material fibers at the edge of the block have a greater degree of flexibility (less restriction by the surrounding fibers) compared to the material fibers at the blocks center. Similarly, the material fibers at the block's corner have a greater degree of flexibility (less restriction from the surrounding material) compared to the material fibers at the edge and the center of block.

Due to the self equilibrating nature of residual stresses, one should expect that the sum of compressive and tensile forces resulting from a given stress distribution to be equal to zero. In the case of the stress distribution through the thickness of a block, this condition requires that the areas under the compressive and tensile regions to be equal. As shown in figures 9-14, the compressive and tensile stress region are quite equal in size (+/- 5%) which verifies the validity of the results.

II)   Hole-Drilling Technique

The results of the hole-drilling experiments are presented in figures 15 (a)-(c). The surface strain readings were used to calculate principal stresses in subsurface layers by the Relaxation Matrix Method. The induced stresses were averaged and subtracted from the stresses in locations H1, H2, and H3. The differences represent the principal stresses determined by the hole drilling method. The results indicate that similar stress states developed below the surfaces, like a double S, and equal-biaxial. Their magnitudes differ, but the stresses are compressive and decrease at high gradients from approximately -75 (10,885 psi) at the surface layers to -325 MPa (47,170 psi) at the depth of 0.2 mm. In the middle of the hole depths, 0.6 mm below the surfaces the stresses reach local maxima, -50 and -200 MPa, respectively, and at the depth of 1.2 mm, the stresses vary around-50 MPa.

SUMMARY AND CONCLUSIONS

The "Treuting-Read" and "Hole-Drilling" techniques were utilized in the measurement of residual stresses in 7150 aluminum blocks subjected to a water quench from 477° C. Both methods identified a compressive residual stress region at the exterior surface of the block. The residual stress magnitudes at the surface agreed quite well between the Treuting-Read (-81 Mpa) and the Hole-Drilling (-75 Mpa) techniques. Considering the fact that the room temperature yield stress of 7150 aluminum is approximately 200 Mpa, the magnitude of the residual stresses at the surface reaches nearly 40% of the yield stress of the material. The interpretation of strains measured during hole drilling is based on the theory of linear elasticity. Therefore, the method should be applied to the cases where hole drilling does not cause plastic deformation. The calculated stress states may be classified between uniaxial- and equal-biaxial compression. For such states, if the calculations indicate that the stresses are equal to 50% to 120% of the yield strength, then the accuracy varies from 5% to 20%. In such cases, much more complex numerical analysis is required to achieve better accuracy. The results indicate that hole were drilled under conditions of almost 50% of the yield stress. Therefore, the assumption of linear elasticity was not maintained in the analysis for the layers below the first one. The results were then affected by the first measurement. This explains the high value of residual stresses (-350 Mpa) at the subsurface layers. Additional analysis is required to account for the plasticity effect. The problem of plastically deformed regions around holes has been studied (Li, et al.) for non-incremental hole drilling.

It should be noted that only the Treuting-Read technique was used to obtain the residual stress distribution through the thickness of the block due to the limitation of hole-drilling technique in providing data beyond depths equal to the hole diameter (1.2 mm.) Results indicate a tensile residual stress with a maximum value of 44 Mpa (6,400 psi) at the midplane of the block. The assumption of symmetry of residual stresses about the midplane was verified by comparing the distribution of the data in the 30-50% of thickness region to that in the 50-70% of thickness region.

REFERENCES

Li, G.D., Liu, B.L., and Li, B.Y., "Influence of the Hole-Side Plastic Deformation as a Result of the Stress Concentration on the Accuracy of Residual Welding Stress Measurement by Small Blind Hole Relaxation Method and Its Modificatio," Report-Dalian Institute of Technology, Dalian, China.

Rasty, J. and Hartley, C.S., 1991, "Effect of Various Degrees of Cold Working on the Residual Stress Patterns of Drawn OFHC Copper Tubes," *Proceedings of the Society for Experimental Mechanics,* Spring Conference, June 9-13, 1991, Milwaukee, Wisconsin, pp. 392-404.

Rasty, J. and Hartley, C. S., 1990, "A Parametric Study of the Tube Drawing Process Utilizing the Finite Element Method," *Proceedings of the 1990 Pacific Conference on Manufacturing,* December 17-21, 1990, Sydney and Melbourne, Australia.

Rasty, J. and Hartley, C. S., 1989, "Determination of Residual Stresses in Drawn OFHC Copper Tubes Using Electrochemical Machining (ECM)," *Proceedings of the Society for Experimental Mechanics,* Spring Conference, May 28-June 1, 1989, Cambridge, Massachusetts, pp. 893-900.

Rasty, J. 1987, "Experimental and Finite Element Analysis of Residual Stresses in Zircaloy-4(R) Nuclear-Fuel Cladding, and OFHC Copper Tubes" Ph.D. Dissertation, Louisiana State University, Baton Rouge, Louisiana.

Rasty, J. and Hartley C. S., 1986, "Experimental Measurement of Residual Stresses in Nuclear-Fuel Cladding," *Proceedings of the Society for Experimental Mechanics, Spring Conference,* June 19-23, 1986, New Orleans, Louisiana.

Roy, G., 1984, "Measurement of Linearly Varying Applied Stresses by the Hole Drilling Stresses", 5th International Congress on Experimental Mechanics".

Roy, G., 1990, "Residual Stress Determination by the Hole Drilling Method: Theory and Applications", MTL Report 90-43(OP,J), submitted for publication to Experimental Mechanics.

Treuting, R.G., and Read, W.T., 1951, "A Mechanical Determination of Biaxial Residual Stress in Sheet Materials," Journal of Applied Physics, Vol. 22, pp. 130-134.

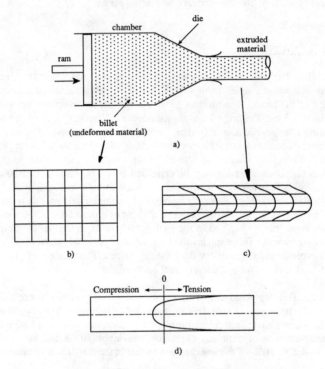

**Figure 1. Residual Stress Pattern due to Nonhomogeneous
Deformation Encountered in the Extrusion Process.**

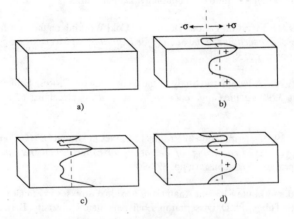

**Figure 2.   Evolution of Quenching-Induced
Residual Stresses.**

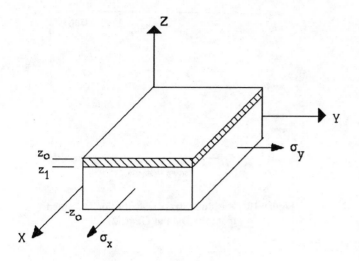

Figure 3.   Initial Block and the Layer to be Removed.

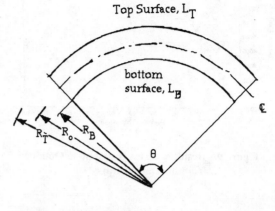

Figure 4.   Exaggerated Schematic of the bending of a Block due to the Removal of a Layer of Stressed Material.

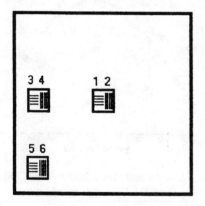

Figure 5.   Strain Gage Locations on Top Surface of the Block.

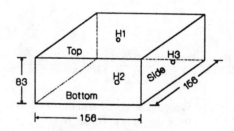

Figure 6.   Geometry of the Block and Locations Selected for Hole Drilling.

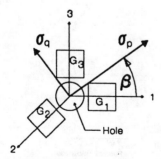

Figure 7.   Strain Gage Layout and the Orientation of the Principal Stresses with Respect to the Rosette.

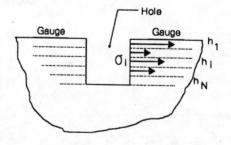

Figure 8.   Schematic Representation of Hole-Drilling and the Variation of the Principal Stresses Below the Surface, Averaged at h_i.

763

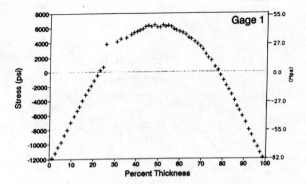

Figure 9. Residual Stress Distribution Obtained from the Data at Gage (1).

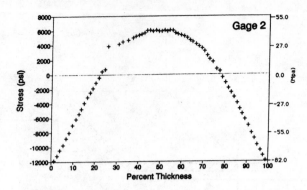

Figure 10. Residual Stress Distribution Obtained from the Data at Gage (2).

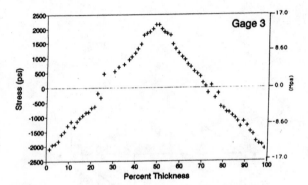

Figure 11. Residual Stress Distribution Obtained from the Data at Gage (3).

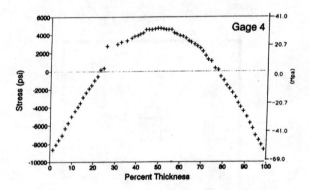

Figure 12. Residual Stress Distribution Obtained from the Data at Gage (4).

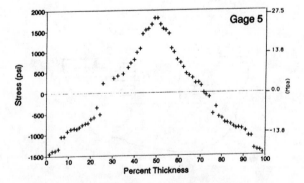

Figure 13. Residual Stress Distribution Obtained from the Data at Gage (5).

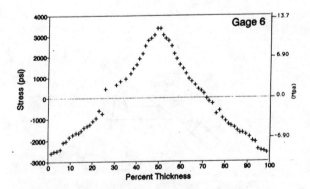

Figure 14. Residual Stress Distribution Obtained from the Data at Gage (6).

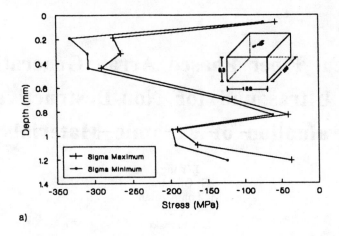

a)

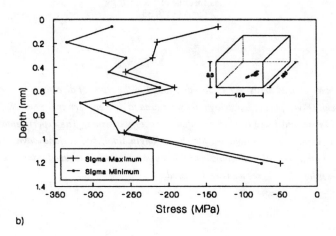

b)

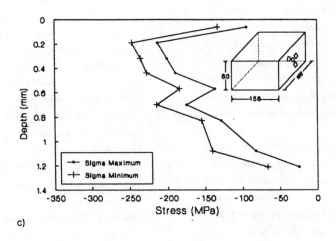

c)

Figure 15. Variation of the Principal Residual Stresses at the Depths h_i, at the
a) Top, b) Bottom, and c) Side Surfaces.

Optical Fiber Phased Array Generation of Ultrasound for Non-Destructive Evaluation of Ceramic Materials

J. Yang
G. Graham
M. Timmerman
C. Ume
J. Jarzynski

George W. Woodruff School of Mechanical Engineering
Georgia Institute of Technology
Atlanta GA 30332

The laser phased array technique was applied to the study of directivity patterns in ceramic blocks. Five optical fiber delay lines were used to deliver laser energy to CS-3 type ceramic blocks manufactured by Carborundum refractory division. The experimental and analytical directivity patterns obtained for shear, longitudinal, and surface waves will be presented. The theoretical predictions did not agree well with measured data. Several potential causes for the disagreement are discussed.

1. Introduction

Ultrasonic sensing techniques have a long and useful history for nondestructive testing of materials [J. Krautkramer and H. Krautkramer]. Research at Georgia Tech has focused on the use of lasers as ultrasound sources for materials evaluation in many areas of metallic and non-metallic materials [Umeagukwu et al.] [Yang et al.] [Berthelot and Jarzynski] [Berthelot]. One major ultimate goal of this research is to use laser generated ultrasound as a nondestructive probe for evaluation of materials and processes.

NDE of ceramics has an extensive history in the open literature [Akimov]. Already in commercial use are SLAM (Scanning Laser Acoustic Microscopes) and SAM (Scanning Acoustic Microscopes) for various ceramic applications such as the inspection of ceramic aircraft components [Sturges]. These technologies though very promising have fundamental limitations in depth of exploration, field of view, and large amounts of required computing time for even small samples.

A principle problem of ultrasonic nondestructive evaluation is the difficulty of correctly interpreting a signal spread out through a large area of the sample under test. One possible and extremely promising solution to this problem of hard-to-interpret sound patterns is the use of directed sound patterns generated by phased arrays [Ing]. The method developed at Georgia Tech is a synthesis of many individual techniques developed and investigated by others. The main source for the laser light is a large Nd:YAG laser used in pulsed mode to generate discrete packets of sound waves [Wagner] [Wagner and Deaton]. The light from the laser is introduced into a fiber-optic system that splits the light into separate channels [Vogel et al.] [Westervelt and Larson] [Addison]. Different fiber lengths in each channel introduce phase differences between the pulsed signals. When the pulsed signals impinge on the sample under test, thermoacoustic sound waves are generated. These waves are of a precise and known type and can be directed at will throughout the sample by meticulous control of the fiber spacing. The purpose of this paper is to present the results obtained by using the laser array to generate longitudinal, shear, and surface waves in ceramic blocks. The CS-3 ceramic samples were supplied by Carborundum refractory division. The directivity patterns of the experimental results are compared with the theoretical results. This paper also discusses the design and construction of the array setup.

2. Theoretical Sound Patterns

The sound waves generated by the laser are caused by slight expansions of the surface of the material. The generation and classification of these phenomena is complex but basically waves are either confined to the surface (Raleigh waves) or confined to the interior of the specimen (longitudinal and shear waves) [Hutchins] [Scruby]. Longitudinal and shear waves are differentiated as to the relative direction of the material displacement with respect to the travel direction of the wave. The use of various special techniques is described in the literature for the generation of any particular wave, such as oil surfaces, retraining surfaces, impedance matching exciters etc. [Krautkramer] [Scruby] [Hutchins].

The calculation of such wave patterns is summarized in the literature [Scruby]. This investigation concentrates on interior waves. The directivity patterns for single sources of longitudinal and shear waves are given in the literature as follows:

$$(2.1) \quad U_r(\phi_1) =$$

$$\frac{[2A_1 \sin(2\phi_1)\sin(\phi)(k^2 - \sin^2(\phi_1))]}{[(k^2 - 2\sin^2\phi_1)^2 + 4\sin^2(\phi_1)\sqrt{(1-\sin^2(\phi_1))}^2 \sqrt{k^2 - \sin^2(\phi_1)}]}$$

$$(2.2) \quad U_\phi(\phi_2) =$$

$$\frac{-kA_1 \sin(4\phi_2)}{[k(1-2\sin^2(\phi_2))^2 + 4\sin^2(\phi_2)\sqrt{(1-\sin^2(\phi_2))}^2 \sqrt{1-k^2\sin^2(\phi_2)}]}$$

U_r = longitudinal intensity

U_ϕ = shear intensity

$\phi_{1;2}$ = geometrical parameters; angles to surface

normal

A_1 = nominal field strength

$c_{1;2}$ = longitudinal and shear wave sound speeds

$k = \dfrac{c_1}{c_2}$ = ratio of sound speeds

These equations may also be expressed as graphs (Figure 2.1). These graphs represent intensities in an area of cylindrical symmetry perpendicular to a normal through a single point source into a semi-infinite solid.

Combining several point sources is the purpose of the phased array technique under development at Georgia Tech. Two major advantages may be gained by this technique. First, laser light is spread out over a larger area than a point source so a stronger acoustic signal can be generated without damaging the specimen under test. Second, the use of different phase relationships allows for "steering." Steering refers to the process of aiming the sound pattern in a desired direction. Figure 2.2 presents a simplified view of the geometry under investigation. The final wave pattern generated by the phased array is the product of the individual array intensities and a quantity derived from the array parameters known as the array factor [Vogel]:

$$(2.3) \quad I(\theta,\phi) = U_{single\ source}(\theta)\ I_{array}(\theta,\phi)$$

$$(2.4) \quad I_{array}(\theta,\phi) = \left\{ \frac{\sin(Nq)}{N\sin(q)} \right\}^2$$

$$(2.5) \quad q = (\pi d/\lambda)(\sin\theta - \sin\phi)$$

N = number of array elements

f = frequency

d = geometric parameter as per Figure 2.2

λ = wavelength

More detailed examples will be presented in the experimental results section [DeRidder] [Vogel]. The number of sources used in the array and the exact phase relationships between those sources is varied from experiment to experiment. Figure 2.2 should be viewed as a generalized simplified diagram for illustration purposes.

3. Experimental Setup

Table 3.1 gives a detailed description of each of the components used in the experimental setup. Figure 3.1 presents a schematic diagram of the apparatus used. This setup is used in a phased array mode where five optical fibers carry light to the sample under test . All the mechanical components of the set up are rigidly mounted to an optical bench for stability.

A brief descriptive overview of the setup begins with the primary light source, a large Nd-YAG laser. This laser is used in the pulse mode with a peak power of 1 kwatt but an average power of only 1 watt. The laser pulses every 100 μseconds. To focus this beam into the optical fiber an objective lens is used. The positioning of the lens with respect to the laser is achieved by a three-axis positioner. This alignment is critical as the numerical aperture of the lens is .4, but the numerical aperture of the fiber is .29, thus the half angle acceptance is only 16.85°. Next a star coupler splits the laser beam in the fiber into several separate beams. Each beam is contained in a fiber integral to the star coupler. A custom made spacer accurately positions each of the beams to form a phased array. The phased array impinges the laser light onto a custom made Carborundum ceramic prism target. Nine different blocks with varying lead angles were constructed.

Figure 2.2 shows the relationship between the targets and the phased array. The laser phased array beams create acoustical phenomena in the block that are detected by a PZT transducer. A special joining compound supplied with the transducer is required for good acoustical coupling. Finally the acoustical signal from the transducer is sent through a pre-amplifier for low pass filtering. This allows improvement of the signal-to-noise ratio in the range of interest. The filtered signal is captured by a digital storage scope. The oscilloscope is triggered by the reflected light pulse from one of the input fibers from the star coupler. This fiber drives a special circuit containing a infrared Si photodiode, an Analog Devices AD9686 fast level detector and a two stage high pass filter based on AD847 op-amps. Finally data from the oscilloscope is analyzed in digital form on a PC using MATLAB and other standard and custom software packages. For calibration and setup purposes, a laser power meter was used.

767

4. Experimental Procedures and Results

4.1.1 Laser Phased Array Generation of the Shear Wave

Preferential generation of certain wave types requires a technique more advanced than single source generation of ultrasound. In this research the authors used laser phased array to preferentially generate shear wave. The laser phased array is able to control the beam width and direction, and to effectively focus the beam provided the beam path lengths are sufficiently long.

The array setup is shown in Figure 3.1. The inter-element spacing controls the type and direction of the wave generated. A microscope objective lens is used to couple pulsed laser light to one of the five receiving fibers of the star coupler. Note that light reflected back into one of the receiving fibers is used for the photodiode trigger circuit thus allowing all of the transmitting fibers to be used in the array. The five transmitting fibers have increasing lengths with 60m difference between each resulting in an interelement phase lag of 0.292 μs. The five fibers are focused onto the surface of each of the ceramic blocks with block angles varying from 7.5^O to 75°. A 1 MHz shear wave transducer (PZT) is used to measure the transmitted ultrasound. The first peak-to-peak amplitude (millivolts) of the the received signals after averaging 256 cycles is used as a measure of sound pressure due to its relatively high signal to noise ratio. These amplitudes represent data points shown on the directivity plots.

The array spacing is determined based on the beam steering angle desired. The array spacing, d, is related to the steering angle, ϕ, by the following equation:

$$(4.1) \qquad d = \frac{\tau \, Cm}{\sin (\phi)}$$

where τ is the array delay time and Cm is the sound speed in the medium.

The directivity plots are obtained by focusing the array on the surface of blocks with angle θ while using the same array spacing, d. Typical shear wave signals obtained with a five fiber array are shown in the following figures. The directivity patterns are superimposed onto the theoretical results for comparison.

4.1.2 Discussion of the Results

The experimental directivity patterns for the shear wave are shown compared to the theoretical results in figure 4.1 for $\phi=30^O$ and in figure 4.2 for $\phi=45^O$ where the magnitude is a normalized voltage output. While more test blocks would increase the resolution of the experimental results, it is evident that the experimental results do not agree with the theoretical results. It is determined that the governing equations, developed for elastic, isotropic, and homogeneous materials such as metals, need some modification before being applied to composite materials such as ceramics; however, focusing the array at a certain angle does cause signal

apparatus	maker	description
Nd-YAG Laser	General Photonics	Two-45 model 1.064μm wavelength .4 Å line width/10Ghz Zenon arc lamp excitation .5 to 10 hz 5 mm beam width with .7 millirad divergence
Objective lense	Newport	M-20X model microscope achromatic 8.3 mm focal length NA=.40
Positioner	Line Tool Co.	3 axis type
Star Coupler	Canstar	5 x 5 type with integrated fiber optic leads
Spacer	custom made	6 positions, made of shim stock mounted on .813 mm steel plate
Targets	custom made	large Carborundum prisms from Carborundum Refractory Division
PZT transducer SWC mounting compound	Panametrics	1 Mhz shear wave transducer with 1.27 cm diameter
Oscilloscope	Tektronix	2430A digital storage scope 100 Mhz bandwidth GPIB interface
Preamp	Metrotek	MR101A model 1 to 63 db gain .5 to 4 Mhz bandwidth
Photodiode	EGG Vactec	Si photodiode 'SRP' family type
Power meter	Coherent	C25 model pyroelectric joule meter

Table 3.1 Details of Experimental Apparatus

enhancement at that angle. The signal strength was highest for the block angles, $\theta=37.5^O$ when $\phi=30^O$ and $\theta=45^O$ when $\phi=45^O$.

4.2.1 Laser Phased Array Generation of the Longitudinal Wave

Longitudinal waves are generated by the same technique as shear waves. A 1 MHz longitudinal wave transducer (PZT) is used instead of the shear wave transducer. Typical longitudinal wave signals are shown in the following figures superimposed on theoretical results for comparison.

4.2.2 Discussion of the Results

The experimental directivity patterns for the longitudinal wave are shown compared to the theoretical results in figure 4.3 for $\phi=30^O$, in figure 4.4 for $\phi=45^O$, and in figure 4.5 for $\phi=52.5^O$. As in the shear wave experiment, more test blocks would have been desirable. While the experimental results do not agree with the theoretical results at $\phi=30^O$ the agreement improves as the steering angle increases. The results at $\phi=52.5^O$ correlate well with the theoretical results. The signal strength was highest at 42.5^O for $\phi=30^O$, and at 75° for both $\phi=45^O$ and $\phi=52.5^O$.

4.3.1 Laser Phased Array Generation of the Surface Wave

The setup for measuring the directivity patterns for the surface wave is different from that of the shear and longitudinal wave. The experimental setup is shown in Figure 3.2. This setup consists of a single test specimen, an angle probe wedge receiver assembly, and a five element optical fiber array. The receiving assembly was placed on the same surface as the array source.

The assignment of directivity angles follows a different convention. The angle θ corresponds to the rotation of the test specimen with respect to the central axis of the array source. Also the beam steering angle of the surface wave represents the orientation of the array with universal coordinates. The direction of this steering angle is along the center line of the array which goes from the shortest array element towards the longest array element.

The choice of the phase lag for the surface wave experiments was based on the beam steering equation above and on preliminary experiments. Given this beam steering equation and the sound velocity of surface waves, the minimum required array phase lag is on the order of the 0.292 μs used in the shear and longitudinal wave experiments.

4.3.2 Discussion of the Results

The experimental directivity pattern for the surface wave is shown in figure 4.6. The figure shows that the sound field for the surface wave array is uniquely directional towards the beam steering angle, $\phi=90^O$. This trend supports the theory that the array can be used for beam steering.

An interesting result of the theoretical predictions is that the face of the major lobe forms a wide front with 15° of the beam steering angle, essentially becoming a plane wave of uniform strength in the far field. In ultrasonic testing applications, this wide wave front could be used to scan a

wide path along the material surface. An important point to notice is that the surface wave directivity patterns only represent half of the symmetric sound field in the positive scan direction. Therefore, the actual width of the wave front discussed here would cover an arc of 30° centered about the beam steering angle. No consideration was given to surface wave directivity in the negative scan direction.

According to Vogel, et. al., the broad spectrum of ultrasonic frequencies generated by laser excitation tends to suppress the effects of grating lobes. Therefore, the phase cancellation is less than that predicted by the theoretical model. Vogel points out that the amount of suppression is related to the number of array elements and the off-axis sensitivity of these elements. The experimental data does not indicate the grating lobes predicted. In addition, experimental error due to algebraic averaging over the surface of the transducer might also have contributed to these results.

5. Conclusions

The results for the shear wave directivity patterns are mixed but do indicate that, for inspection purposes, the receiving transducer should be placed at an angle between 37.5^O and 45°. The results of the longitudinal wave are less well behaved indicating that the receiving transducer should be placed at 37.5^O for lower steering angles and at 75° for higher steering angles. The results of the surface wave, which are very well behaved, produced results which agreed with the theoretical results near the steering angle but did not indicate a grating lobe at lower angles. Overall these experimental results did not agree with the theoretical results perfectly. This was expected, however, due to the fact that ceramics are a nonhomogeneous material.

The major sources of error in this experiment include the finite surface area of the PZT transducer (1.27 cm or 1/2") and surface and subsurface defects in the ceramic material. The surface area of the PZT caused the incident signals to be averaged which may have caused some signal cancellation. The defects, primarily air bubbles, in the ceramic material caused acoustic wave scattering which reduced the received signal to noise ratio.

In conclusion, while the experimental results do not agree totally with the theoretical results, the experimental results indicate that the array enhances the generation of ultrasound and, also, that laser phased array generation of ultrasound is capable of being used for nondestructive evaluation of ceramic materials.

6. Acknowledgements

The authors would like to acknowledge the support of the Manufacturing Machines and Equipment program of the NSF which provided funding for this research under grant No. DDM-9001733. They would also like to thank the SME Foundation for providing the seed money to purchase the equipment for this project under grant No. 588-1170.

7. References Cited

Addison, R. C. et al. "Synthesis of an Ultrasonic Array using Laser Based Techniques," in **IEEE 1987 Ultrasonics Symposium Proceedings**, vol. 2., (1987), pp 1109-13.

Akimov, A. Y. "Methods of Nondestructive Control of Ceramics (Review)," in **Glasses and Ceramics**, vol. 47, no. 5-6., (May-June, 1990), pp.213-7.

Berthelot, Y. and J. Jarzynski, "Directional Laser generation and Detection of Ultrasounds with Arrays of Optical Fibers," in **Journal of Nondestructive Evaluation**, vol. 9., no. 4, (December, 1990), pp. 271-279.

Berthelot, Y. "Thermoacoustic Generation of Narrowband Signals with High Repetition Rate Pulsed Lasers," in **Journal of the Acoustical Society of America**, (March, 1989), pp. 1173-81.

Deaton, J. B. and J. W. Wagner. "Modified Nd:YAG Laser Source for Generation of Narrowband Ultrasonic Signals," in **1988 Laser Electro Optics Annual Meeting**, (1988), p. 310-311.

DeRidder, N. "Analysis of Non-contact Laser-Fiber Optic Array for Generation of Ultrasound," a thesis. (Atlanta:Georgia Tech, 1990)

Hutchins, D. A. **Ultrasonic Generation by Pulsed Lasers**. (Ontario: Academic, 1988).

Ing, R. et al. "Focusing and Beamsteering of Laser Generated Ultrasound," in **IEEE 1989 Ultrasonics Symposium**, vol. 1, (1989), pp. 539-44.

Krautkramer J. and H.. Krautkramer. **Ultrasonic Testing of Materials**. (New York: Springer Verlag, 1983).

Scruby, C. B. et al. "Laser generation of Ultrasound in Metals,: **Research Techniques in Non-destructive [sic] Testing**, vol. 5, (1982), pp. 281-327.

Sturges, D. "Sounding out Ceramic Quality," in **Advanced Materials and Processes**, vol. 139., no. 4, (April, 1991), pp. 35-8.

Umeagukwu, C. and J. Jarzynski, "Laser Phased Array Generation of Ultrasound with Application to On-Line Nondestrudtive Weld Quality Control," NSF Design and Manufacturing Systems Grantees Conference, University of Texas, Austin, Texas, January 1991.

Umeagukwu, C., N. DeRidder, J. Yang, and J. Jarzynski, "Study of the Directivity Patterns of Laser-Optical Fiber Generated Ultrasound," Invited Paper, 121st Meeting of the JASA, Vol. 89, No. 4, Pt. 2, Baltimore, Maryland, April 1991.

Vogel, J. A. et al. "Beam Steering of Laser Generated Ultrasounds," in **Ultrasonics International 1987 Conference Proceedings**, pp. 141-52.

Wagner, J. et al. "Modulated Laser Array Sources for Generation of Narrowband and Directed Ultrasound," in **Journal of Nondestructive Evaluation**, vol. 9., no. 4, (December, 1990), pp. 263-70.

Westervelt, P. J. and R. S. Larson. "Laser Excited Broadside Array," in **Journal of the Acoustical Society of America**, vol. 54, (1973), pp. 121-2.

Yang, J., N. DeRidder, C. Ume, and J. Jarzynski, "Noncontact Optical Fiber Phased Array Generation of Ultrasound for Nondestructive Evaluation of Materials and Processes," submitted, **Ultrasonics**, 1991.

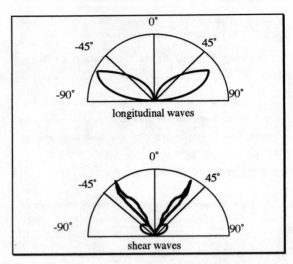

Figure 2.1 Shear and Longitudinal Patterns [Vogel]

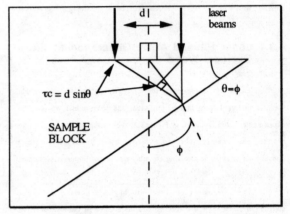

Figure 2.2 Geometry for relations 2.3 to 2.5 [DeRidder]

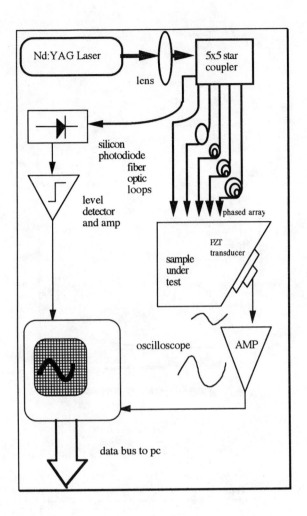

Figure 3.1 Experimental Setup

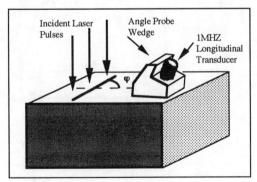

Figure 3.2 Surface Wave Setup

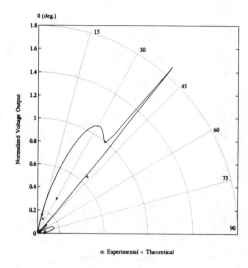

α: Experimental -: Theoretical

Figure 4.1 - Shear Wave φ=30°

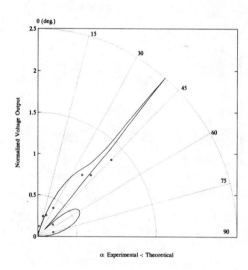

α: Experimental -: Theoretical

Figure 4.2 - Shear Wave φ=45°

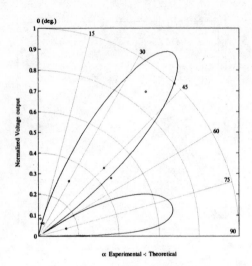

Figure 4.3 - Longitudinal Wave φ=30°

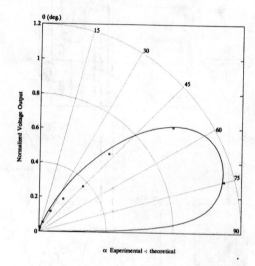

Figure 4.5 - Longitudinal Wave φ=52.5°

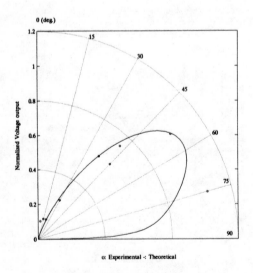

Figure 4.4 - Longitudinal Wave φ=45°

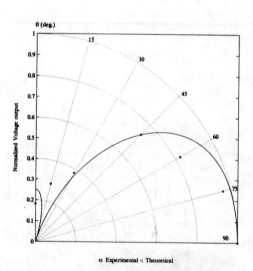

Figure 4.6 - Surface Wave φ=90°

STRUCTURAL PRODUCTS VERIFICATION TESTING

Donald F. Meinheit and Robert J. Krause†

ABSTRACT

During the construction of the Chicago O'Hare International Airport People Mover, variations in the planeness at the connection between the flange of a steel plate girder and an embedded plate in a precast-prestressed concrete crosstie caused cracking distress to occur in the anchorage plate region of the crosstie. As part of an installation procedure verification program to attach and hold the crossties down to the bridge girders, static and dynamic (fatigue) tests were performed on full-scale test specimens.

INTRODUCTION

Chicago O'Hare International Airport was built in the early 1960's and has been expanded several times. In 1987, a large new domestic terminal was built, and in 1993, a new international terminal will be open for operation.

Expanded airport facilities tend to increase passenger traffic and create a need to improve vehicular traffic in the terminal areas of the airport. Since the domestic and international terminals are separated at O'Hare by a considerable distance, additional inter-terminal vehicular traffic was not desired. Remote long-term parking and auto rental agencies are also located about three miles from the terminals. These latter areas are currently (1992) served by buses.

The People Mover System

To improve movement of passengers to and from long-term parking, car rental agencies and the international terminal, the O'Hare Automated Guideway Transit System (The O'Hare People Mover) is under construction.

The O'Hare People Mover is a 5.15 km (3.2 mi) long system consisting of unmanned, rubber-tired vehicles riding on a guideway of steel running rails. The running rails are supported directly on precast/prestressed concrete ties. The ties are either supported by steel girder bridges or a concrete cast-in-place slab-on-grade.

Objective

This paper describes some of the verification testing that was done to solve problems during the track work construction of the people mover. Prior to the start of construction, the prototype precast tie was extensively tested statically and under fatigue loadings. However, not all variations in details were investigated. Only the gross behavior of the tie was verified.

BACKGROUND FOR TESTING

Installation Conditions

During the final bolting of the precast ties to the elevated support structure, a steel plate girder, the concrete in the vicinity of the tie anchor plate was observed to crack and spall. Typical spalling concrete is shown in Fig. 1. Cracking and spalling of the tie only occurred in the elevated portion of the system; that is, the ties supported on the slab-on-grade did not experience any anchor plate region cracking of the concrete. Each tie has an anchor plate cast into the bottom of the tie like that shown in Fig. 2.

After aligning and leveling the running rail and shimming beneath the tie, the final step in installing the tie was to tighten high strength bolts connecting the flange of the plate girder and the anchor plate in the tie. The typical installation torque for the bolts was about 540 N-m (400 ft-lbs). At about one-half the installation torque, cracks formed adjacent to the anchor plate, as shown in Fig. 3. Further tightening generally propagated the crack into a spall. Because this condition could occur above vehicular and/or pedestrian traffic, a remedy to alleviate the formation of the crack was needed.

Cracking Cause

When the high strength bolts are tightened, the plate embedded in the tie deforms more than the flange of the supporting steel girder. Fabrication welding of the plate girder and its bearing stiffeners caused the top flange of the girder to warp due to thermally induced stresses. The condition, greatly exaggerated, is depicted in Fig. 4.

From a preliminary field investigation, the anchor plate of the tie tries to deform when of the bolt clamping forces are applied. The more flexible anchor plate tries to conform to the stiffer plate girder flange and induces pressures on a thin layer of concrete the thickness of the up-turned leg of the angle. See Fig. 4 for a sketch of this cracking scenario. Fabrication for flange of the plate girder, the anchor plate, and positioning of the anchor plate in the tie were all verified as being within tolerance.

†Senior Consultant and Consultant, respectively, Wiss, Janney, Elstner Associates, Northbrook, Illinois

Revised Tie Shimming Procedure

By trial and error testing, the cracking and spalling were eliminated using a special shimming procedure. The original shimming procedure used flat sheets of steel to provide a uniform bearing between the tie and girder. Because of the out-of-planeness, shimming could not be done tightly enough to approach the intended uniform bearing condition. A slightly modified shimming procedure, using the materials already purchase and a typical circular bolt washer within the shim stack, was found to eliminate the tie cracking.

TEST MATERIALS AND SETUP

Testing Objectives

When the prototype original tie testing was done, the bearing beneath the tie anchor plate was uniform like that used in the slab-on-grade ties; that is, the space between the tie and its support was grouted before the bolts were tightened. The revised special shimming procedure does not produce a uniform bearing, but all the load is concentrated at the bolt locations. This created the possibility of higher stresses in the cantilevered portion of the anchor plate and higher stress in anchor plate welds that may now possibly be fatigue sensitive.

The objective of conducting full scale laboratory tests, both static and fatigue, was to determine the magnitude of the stresses in the anchor plate and check the fatigue sensitivity of the revised support details for the tie. These tests were conducted prior to operation of the O'Hare People Mover, but after all the ties had been installed in the aerial portions of the system. These tests were critical in avoiding delaying the completion of the track work portion of the project.

Test Tie Details

A typical production crosstie was used for both the static and fatigue test. The photograph in Fig. 8 shows one of the types of ties tested. At the ends of the tie, cast-in inserts are used to attach the power/guidance rail and running rail anchorage hardware. Inserts also are cast-in in the center of the tie for the negative return rail.

Dimensions of the typical tie are given in Fig. 6. The tie cross section, through the tie anchor plate, is shown in Fig. 6.

Design Loads on Tie

The typical tie was designed for three dimensional loads; vertical, transverse and longitudinal. There are six points of load application to the tie, as shown in Table 1. Because of the considerable increase in testing expense, some of the three-dimensional loads for the static test were omitted. The test loads applied are indicated in Table 1. Loads were omitted or modified because their magnitudes were low or it was very difficult to synchronize the multi-axes loads during the fatigue cycling. The load magnitudes shown include impact and a load factor of about 1.5 times the service load and impact values.

Instrumentation

Loads applied to the tie, strains in the steel anchor plate and deflections of the tie in the anchor plate region were measured during the static test. In the fatigue test, only the applied load was monitored. Strain gages were located on lines 76.3 mm (3 in.) from the edge of the plate, resulting in the gages being located directly beneath the fillet weld used to attach the angle to the anchor plate. Only one of the anchor plates was instrumented.

Loads applied to the tie during test were measured using calibrated strain-sensing load cells.

Deflections of the anchor plate and the relative deflection of the tie and the anchor plate were observed during the static test. All deflections were monitored using dial indicating gages.

Figure 8 summarizes the locations of strain gages and deflection instruments relative to the load points. The direction of load application for the transverse and longitudinal loads is also shown in Fig. 8.

Loading Setup

For both the static and fatigue tests, the tie was supported on a simulated steel girder flange. Shims and shim washers were identical to those used in the field installation. The method of installation of the tie shims and the bolts connecting the tie to the girder were according to the approved written installation procedure.

Vertical, longitudinal and transverse loads for the static load test were applied with the framework shown in Fig. 9. The small vertical loads were applied using lead ingots. Other loads were applied using hydraulic rams reacting against reaction beams above and to the side of the tie.

An overall view of the fatigue load test setup is shown in Fig. 10. The two running rail loads were not equal as shown in Table 1. An off-centered load on a spreader beam was used to apply the desired load ratio. Other smaller loads were applied statically and held at their maximum magnitude for the two million cycle duration of the fatigue test.

TEST RESULTS

Static Tests

The loading sequence was specified by the tie designer. All vertical loads were applied first followed by the designated transverse load. To simulate acceleration and braking actions of the transit car, the longitudinal loads were applied last.

Each load type was applied incrementally, and at the end of the increment, instrumentation was read and recorded. This condition was defined as a load stage.

Cracking - Structural cracking of the tie was observed during the application of the transverse load to Point 4. This load represented the transverse load on the power/guidance rail post that steers the transit vehicle. Cracking of the prestress tie was anticipated when the full magnitude of the transverse load was applied. No extension or increase in the crack width was observed for the duration of the static test. Figure 11 shows the point when cracking occurred relative to the other applied loads to the tie.

Strains - Strain gages attached to the bottom of one of the anchor plates were monitored at each load stage. Strains were converted to stresses by multiplying by the modulus of elasticity of steel. A plot of the stress data for the static is shown in Fig. 11. Strains in the anchor plate due to bolt tightening have been removed by using the strains at the start of the load application portion of the test as a zero.

Plate stresses are seen to increase significantly as the vertical loads were applied to the running rail seats. The average bending stress in the anchor plate, as a result of the vertical load application, is about 110 MPa (16 ksi). Since the static test applied loads about 1.5 times the service load magnitudes, the stress range measured would likely cause a fatigue sensitive detail to initial and propagate a crack in the steel.

The application of the longitudinal loads also caused the stresses in the anchor plate to change. Longitudinal loadings should increase the stress on the bottom of the plate on one side of the tie and decrease the stress on the opposite side. The measured change in stress due to the longitudinal load was about 55 MPa (8 ksi) or about one-half the influence of the vertical load. Other applied loads did not significantly affect the magnitude of the stresses in the anchor plate.

Deflections - The concrete tie was essentially uncracked, with exception to one flexural crack, during this test. Because of the rigidity of the tie and the short cantilever span of the anchor plate, defections measurements were very small and mostly insignificant. The maximum deflection of the anchor plate cantilever was only about 0.64 mm (0.025in).

Visuals observations - After subjecting the test tie to the specified overload conditions, the tie was inspected for cracking and/or other structural related implications of distress. Cracking of the tie was minimal and no cracking occurred due to the revised shimming and bolt tightening procedure. Cracks that did appear were in locations that were anticipated.

Fatigue Test

The fatigue test applied 2 million repetitions of load to the running rail seats of the test tie. The tie used for the static test was also used for the fatigue test. Although the applied vertical load magnitude for the fatigue test was only about 75 percent of the maximum static vertical load, the stress range produced should have been significant enough for any fatigue sensitive detail to develop cracking within the 2 million cycle test. Additionally, the applied fatigue loads were 60 percent greater than the anticipated service load design level.

Two million load repetitions of the fatigue load caused no cracking to occur in the anchor plate steel or its weldments. Further, the tie did not exhibit any concrete cracking distress in the vicinity of the anchor plate nor did any earlier observed cracks from the static test extend or become wider. When all load was removed from the tie, the crack on the top surface of the tie closed and was only visible under magnification. No cracks could be found in the steel anchor plate after inspecting the plate and welds nondestructively.

CONCLUSIONS

Acceptibility of Anchor Plate Shimming Procedure

The static test clearly showed that the new bolt installation and tie shimming procedure used to connect the precast concrete crosstie tie to a steel plate girder eliminated the cracking and spalling created as a result of an earlier attachment procedure. No unusual and different characteristics of the tie behavior were observed as a result of the revised attachment procedure.

A fatigue test on a tie using the new shimming detail showed that the tie could withstand at least two million load repetitions without causing any cracking of the concrete in the tie or initiating cracks in the steel anchor plate details. The fatigue test applied vertical loads 60 percent greater than the design service loads.

These tests verified that the proposed shimming and bolt attachment procedures were acceptable and did not change the behavior of the precast/prestressed tie. The tests were important since they showed that no extraordinary measures had to be taken to correct a problem discovered when this track work structure was fully erected.

TABLE 1 - LOAD APPLICATION POINTS

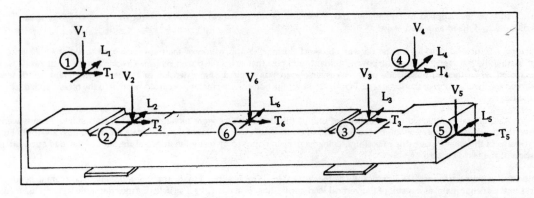

Load Point	Component	Static Load Magnitude, KN (Kips)		Fatigue Load Magnitude, KN (Kips)	
1	V_1	1.69	(0.38)	1.33	(0.30)
	T_1	1.73	(0.39)*	-	-
	L_1	11.12	(2.50)	-	-
2	V_2	85.85	(19.30)	82.29 to -15.57	(18.50 to -3.50)
	T_2	0.71	(0.16)*	-	-
	L_2	58.27	(13.10)	-	-
3	V_3	164.58	(37.00)	99.64 to -18.64	(22.4 to -4.19)
	T_3	0,71	(0.16)*	-	-
	L_3	60.05	(13.50)	-	-
4	V_4	9.34	(2.10)	-	-
	T_4	80.78	(18.16)	5.56 to -0.58	(1.25 to -0.13)***
	L_4	11.12	(2.50)	-	-
5	V_5	7.52	(1.69)*	6.01	(1.35)
	T_5	3.51	(0.79)*	-	-
	L_5	-	-	1.11	(0.25)
6	V_6	1.33	(0.30)	-	-
	T_6	-	-	-	-
	L_6	27.80	(6.25)	-	-

*   Load deleted from static test
**   Positive directions of loads shown
*** Maximum variable load applied statically for duration of test

Fig. 1 - Spalling of precast tie in anchor plate region

Spall

Anchor plate with
headed studs

Fig. 2 - View of typical tie anchor plate

Cracking caused by
tightening bolts

Figure 3 - Nature of cracking at anchor plate

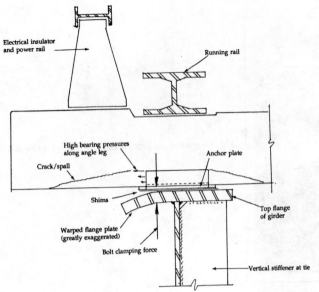

Fig. 4 - Conditions causing cracks/spalls at tie anchorage

Fig. 5 - View of precast tie supported on plate girder

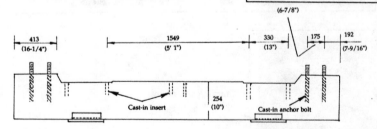

Fig. 6 - Dimensions of typical tie

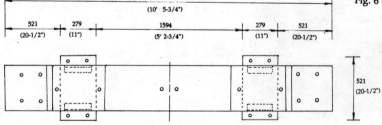

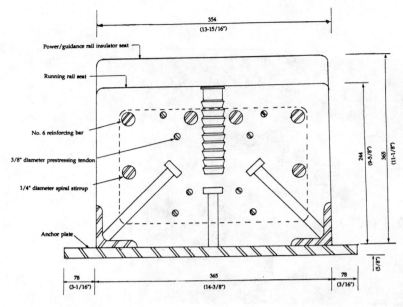

354
(13-15/16")

Power/guidance rail insulator seat

Running rail seat

No. 6 reinforcing bar

3/8" diameter prestressing tendon

1/4" diameter spiral stirrup

Anchor plate

244
(9-5/8")

365
(11-1/8")

(5/8")

78
(3-1/16")

365
(14-3/8")

78
(3/16")

Fig. 7 - Cross section of tie through anchor plate

1 strain gage on anchor plate

• Dial Gage measuring deflection

⊕ Load point on top tie surface

Fig. 8 - Deflection, strain and load point instrumentation on tie

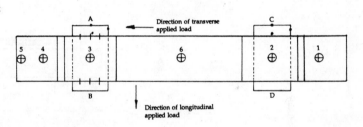

A

Direction of transverse applied load

C

5   4   3   6   2   1

B

Direction of longitudinal applied load

D

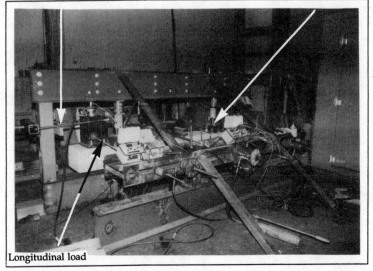

Transverse load

Vertical load

Longitudinal load

Fig. 9 - Static loading test setup

Fig. 10 - Fatigue loading test setup

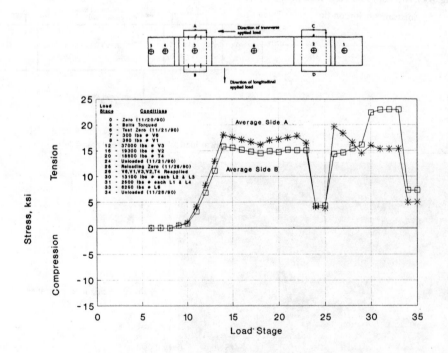

Fig. 11 - Average stress in anchor plate during static test

High Temperature Creep Deformation Fields around A Bicrystal Interface Crack

X. M. Li and F. P. Chiang

Laboratory for Experimental Mechanics Research
State University of New York at Stony Brook
Stony Brook, NY 11794-2300, U.S.A.

ABSTRACT

High temperature creep deformation fields near the tip of a bicrystal interface crack are quantitatively measured by applying the in-plane high temperature moiré technique. Tensile specimen made of pure aluminum bicrystal plate has a single edge crack along grain boundary. The interface is a twin boundary specified by crack on (041) plane and its tip along $[0\bar{1}4]$ direction for crystal 1, and on $(01\bar{6})$ plane and along [061] direction for crystal 2. The specimen is tested under high temperature with a constant applied load. The strain field and the strain rate field near the crack tip are evaluated from moiré fringe patterns recorded at different times. An analytical solution for this problem is constructed and compared with the experimental observation. Excellent agreement is found, in which the rate of creep strain has the singularity of the form $\dot{\epsilon}_\alpha \propto (r)^{-\frac{n_\alpha}{n_\alpha+1}}$, where $\alpha = 1,2$ are referred to crystals 1 and 2 respectively.

1 Introduction

Creep crack growth is considered as time-dependent extension of a macroscopic crack at elevated temperature under more or less constant load. Research in this subject has become more intensive in recent years. The problem of creep crack growth has been treated in two aspects; namely, the continuum-mechanical deformation fields in a cracked body and the micromechanisms of crack growth (grain boundary cavitation near crack tip and/or corrosive processes at crack tip). Based on the continuum-mechanics formulation, studies on creep crack growth in homogeneous, isotropic materials have been reported by many researchers, e.g. Barnby[1], Nicholson and Formby[2], Barnby and Nicholson[3], Bassani and McClintock[4], Hui and Riedel[5], Saxena, Ernst and Landes[6], Hui[7], Hawk and Bassani[8], Bassani and Hawk[9], Harper and Ellison[10], Moyer and Liebowitz[11], Riedel[12], Riedel and Detampel[13], and Kang, Zhuang and Liu[14] among others. Different forms of singularity in stress and deformation fields were proposed assuming power law creep behavior (Barnby[1], Barnby and Nicholson[3], Hui and Riedel[5], Hui[7], and Moyer and Liebowitz[11] etc.). Correlations between the rate of the creep crack growth, $\mathrm{d}a/\mathrm{d}t$, and the proposed fracture criterion, such as J-integral, C^*, elastic stress intensity factor K, net section

stress, and critical local strain, have been established in different situations (Barnby[1], Barnby and Nicholson[3], Saxena, Ernst and Landes[6], Harper and Ellison[10], and Hui[7], etc.).

For a situation in which an interface crack between anisotropic solids is considered, similar to those for homogeneous, isotropic materials, the nature of the linear elastic solution becomes important when constructing solution for steady state creep. Within the context of linear elasticity, Clements[15] found solutions for general two-dimensional problem of interface crack in anisotropic materials using Stroh's sextic formulation. Willis[16] obtained solutions for isolated dislocations and crack lying along the interface between anisotropic media. Ting[17,18] and Wu[19,20] studied the asymptotic stress fields near an interface crack in an bimaterial also using Stroh's sextic formalism. Two of the most important features of these solutions are the mixed fracture modes and the oscillatory crack tip singularity. Qu and Bassani[21] and Bassani and Qu[22] have further derived the condition for non-oscillatory crack tip singularity in anisotropic solids. Particularly for bicrystal interface crack if the grain boundary is a tilt boundary and the anti-plane deformation and in-plane deformation are decoupled, their solution shows that the stress intensity factors are real and the fracture modes are separable at crack tip, and the stress singularities at crack tip are no longer oscillatory. In a recent paper, Ting[23] has analyzed in detail the existence of oscillation in the solution of interface crack between anisotropic materials. More complete solutions are summarized in a paper given by Suo[24].

In studying high temperature creep crack growth of a bicrystal interface crack, it is important to quantify experimentally the high temperature deformation fields near the crack tip and pursue a solution which describes the nature of the problem. In this study, a tensile specimen made of aluminum bicrystal with an edge crack along grain boundary was tested at 400^0 C and under a constant applied load. In-plane creep deformation fields near the crack tip were mapped through moiré fringe patterns at different times. The strain field and the strain rate field near the crack tip were evaluated from corresponding moiré fringe patterns. Assuming the isotropic power law creep behavior, an analytical solution for near tip stress and strain rate fields is constructed and compared with the experimental observation. Excellent agreement is found in terms of stress and strain rate singularities.

2 Theoretical analysis

It is assumed that at the beginning of the creep process, $t = 0$, a lower level of load is suddenly applied and kept constant thereafter. As the load is applied, the material is under elastic deformation instantaneously. The distributions of the elastic stress and strain in the absence of creep can be described by the linear elastic solution for interface crack between anisotropic materials (Suo[24]). For f.c.c. single crystals, Hook's law can be written in the following form

$$\epsilon_i = \sum_{j=1}^{6} s_{ij}\sigma_j \qquad (1)$$

where
$\{\epsilon_i\} = [\epsilon_{11}, \epsilon_{22}, \epsilon_{33}, 2\epsilon_{23}, 2\epsilon_{31}, 2\epsilon_{12}]^T$, and
$\{\sigma_j\} = [\sigma_{11}, \sigma_{22}, \sigma_{33}, \sigma_{23}, \sigma_{31}, \sigma_{12}]^T$.
The superscript T denotes the transpose. The 6×6 matrix s is the compliance matrix.

Under the condition of plane stress ($\sigma_{33} = \sigma_{13} = \sigma_{23} = 0$), the elastic field can be represented in terms of holomorphic functions with its argument being complex variables defined in the following

$$\begin{cases} z_1 = r(\cos\theta + \mu_1\sin\theta) \\ z_2 = r(\cos\theta + \mu_2\sin\theta) \end{cases} \qquad (2)$$

where r and θ are polar coordinates defined in Fig.1; and μ_1 and μ_2 are two distinct roots, with positive imaginary part, of the characteristic equation

$$s_{11}\mu^4 - (2s_{12} + s_{66})\mu^2 + s_{22} = 0 \qquad (3)$$

The elastic stress components given in the coordinate system shown in Fig.3 are

$$\sigma_{11}^{(1)} = Re\left[\frac{ie^{\pi\epsilon}K z_1^{i\epsilon}\mu_1}{2\sqrt{2\pi z_1}\cosh(\pi\epsilon)} + \frac{ie^{-\pi\epsilon}\overline{K}z_2^{-i\epsilon}\mu_2}{2\sqrt{2\pi z_2}\cosh(\pi\epsilon)}\right]_{(1)}$$

$$\sigma_{12}^{(1)} = -Re\left[\frac{ie^{\pi\epsilon}K z_1^{i\epsilon}}{2\sqrt{2\pi z_1}\cosh(\pi\epsilon)} + \frac{ie^{-\pi\epsilon}\overline{K}z_2^{-i\epsilon}}{2\sqrt{2\pi z_2}\cosh(\pi\epsilon)}\right]_{(1)}$$

$$\qquad (4)$$

$$\sigma_{22}^{(1)} = Re\left[\frac{e^{\pi\epsilon}K z_1^{i\epsilon}\sqrt{H_{11}/H_{22}}}{2\sqrt{2\pi z_1}\cosh(\pi\epsilon)} + \frac{e^{-\pi\epsilon}\overline{K}z_2^{-i\epsilon}\sqrt{H_{11}/H_{22}}}{2\sqrt{2\pi z_2}\cosh(\pi\epsilon)}\right]_{(1)}$$

for single crystal 1, and

$$\sigma_{11}^{(2)} = Re\left[\frac{ie^{-\pi\epsilon}K z_1^{i\epsilon}\mu_1}{2\sqrt{2\pi z_1}\cosh(\pi\epsilon)} + \frac{ie^{\pi\epsilon}\overline{K}z_2^{-i\epsilon}\mu_2}{2\sqrt{2\pi z_2}\cosh(\pi\epsilon)}\right]_{(2)}$$

$$\sigma_{12}^{(2)} = -Re\left[\frac{ie^{-\pi\epsilon}K z_1^{i\epsilon}}{2\sqrt{2\pi z_1}\cosh(\pi\epsilon)} + \frac{ie^{\pi\epsilon}\overline{K}z_2^{-i\epsilon}}{2\sqrt{2\pi z_2}\cosh(\pi\epsilon)}\right]_{(2)}$$

$$\qquad (5)$$

$$\sigma_{22}^{(2)} = Re\left[\frac{e^{-\pi\epsilon}K z_1^{i\epsilon}\sqrt{H_{11}/H_{22}}}{2\sqrt{2\pi z_1}\cosh(\pi\epsilon)} + \frac{e^{\pi\epsilon}\overline{K}z_2^{-i\epsilon}\sqrt{H_{11}/H_{22}}}{2\sqrt{2\pi z_2}\cosh(\pi\epsilon)}\right]_{(2)}$$

for single crystal 2.

where K is the complex elastic stress intensity factor; and ϵ is the oscillatory index given by

$$\epsilon = (2\pi)^{-1}\ln\left(\frac{1-\beta}{1+\beta}\right) \qquad (6)$$

and

$$\beta = \frac{[(s_{11}s_{22})^{\frac{1}{2}} + s_{12}]_{(2)} - [(s_{11}s_{22})^{\frac{1}{2}} + s_{12}]_{(1)}}{(H_{11}H_{22})^{\frac{1}{2}}}$$

$$H_{11} = \left[2\left(\frac{1+\rho}{2}\right)^{\frac{1}{2}}\left(\frac{s_{11}}{s_{22}}\right)^{\frac{1}{4}}(s_{11}s_{22})^{\frac{1}{2}}\right]_{(1)} + \left[2\left(\frac{1+\rho}{2}\right)^{\frac{1}{2}}\left(\frac{s_{11}}{s_{22}}\right)^{\frac{1}{4}}(s_{11}s_{22})^{\frac{1}{2}}\right]_{(2)}$$

$$H_{22} = \left[2\left(\frac{1+\rho}{2}\right)^{\frac{1}{2}}\left(\frac{s_{11}}{s_{22}}\right)^{-\frac{1}{4}}(s_{11}s_{22})^{\frac{1}{2}}\right]_{(1)} + \left[2\left(\frac{1+\rho}{2}\right)^{\frac{1}{2}}\left(\frac{s_{11}}{s_{22}}\right)^{-\frac{1}{4}}(s_{11}s_{22})^{\frac{1}{2}}\right]_{(2)}$$

$$\rho = \frac{1}{2}(2s_{12} + s_{66})(s_{11}s_{22})^{-\frac{1}{2}}$$

For the problem under consideration, we have an aluminum bicrystal with crystal orientations shown in Fig.2, i.e. interface crack is on (041) plane and its tip along [0$\bar{1}$4] direction for crystal 1, and on (01$\bar{6}$) plane and its tip along [061] direction for crystal 2. Grain boundary (interface) in this case is a twin boundary with misorientation being 94.574⁰. Elastic constants for aluminum single crystals are[1] $s_{11} = 1.596 \times 10^{-11}$ (m^2/N), $s_{12} = -0.580 \times 10^{-11}$ (m^2/N), $s_{44} = 3.525 \times 10^{-11}$ (m^2/N). Matrices of conventional compliance for crystals 1 and 2, after transformation of coordinate systems, are tabulated in tables 1 and 2.

The oscillatory index in Eqs.(4)&(5) is calculated using Eq.(6), and found to be very small, i.e. $\epsilon = 0.0047$. Therefore in the region away from the crack tip we have $z^{i\epsilon} = 1 + \Delta$, and $|\Delta| \leq 10^{-3}$ for $h \leq r \leq 10h$, where h is the thickness of the specimen. Under the condition of

[1]source: F. Seitz and T. A. Read, "Theory of the plastic properties of solids", J. Appl. Phys., Vol.12, 1941, pp.100.

far field tensile loading, the oscillatory stress singularities can be neglected within this region; and Eqs.(4)&(5) become

$$
\begin{cases}
\sigma_{11}^{(\alpha)} = F_{11}^{(\alpha)}(\theta)(r)^{-\frac{1}{2}} \\[2mm]
\sigma_{12}^{(\alpha)} = F_{12}^{(\alpha)}(\theta)(r)^{-\frac{1}{2}} \\[2mm]
\sigma_{22}^{(\alpha)} = F_{22}^{(\alpha)}(\theta)(r)^{-\frac{1}{2}}
\end{cases}
\tag{7}
$$

where $\alpha = 1,2$ are referred to crystals 1 and 2 respectively; and functions $F_{ij}^{(\alpha)}$ are given as follows

$$
F_{11}^{(\alpha)} = Re\left[\frac{ie^{q\epsilon}K\mu_1^{(\alpha)}}{2\sqrt{2\pi(\cos\theta+\mu_1^{(\alpha)}\sin\theta)}\cosh(\pi\epsilon)} + \frac{ie^{-q\epsilon}\overline{K}\mu_2^{(\alpha)}}{2\sqrt{2\pi(\cos\theta+\mu_2^{(\alpha)}\sin\theta)}\cosh(\pi\epsilon)}\right]
$$

$$
F_{12}^{(\alpha)} = -Re\left[\frac{ie^{q\epsilon}K}{2\sqrt{2\pi(\cos\theta+\mu_1^{(\alpha)}\sin\theta)}\cosh(\pi\epsilon)} - \frac{ie^{-q\epsilon}\overline{K}}{2\sqrt{2\pi(\cos\theta+\mu_2^{(\alpha)}\sin\theta)}\cosh(\pi\epsilon)}\right]
\tag{8}
$$

$$
F_{22}^{(\alpha)} = Re\left[\frac{e^{q\epsilon}K\sqrt{H_{11}^{(\alpha)}/H_{22}^{(\alpha)}}}{2\sqrt{2\pi(\cos\theta+\mu_1^{(\alpha)}\sin\theta)}\cosh(\pi\epsilon)} + \frac{e^{-q\epsilon}\overline{K}\sqrt{H_{11}^{(\alpha)}/H_{22}^{(\alpha)}}}{2\sqrt{2\pi(\cos\theta+\mu_2^{(\alpha)}\sin\theta)}\cosh(\pi\epsilon)}\right]
$$

and

$$
q = \begin{cases} \pi & \text{if } \alpha = 1 \\ -\pi & \text{if } \alpha = 2 \end{cases}
$$

The elastic strain components are determined from Eq.(1)

$$
\begin{cases}
\epsilon_{11}^{(\alpha)} = (s_{11}^{(\alpha)}F_{11}^{(\alpha)} + s_{12}^{(\alpha)}F_{22}^{(\alpha)})(r)^{-\frac{1}{2}} \\[2mm]
\epsilon_{22}^{(\alpha)} = (s_{21}^{(\alpha)}F_{11}^{(\alpha)} + s_{22}^{(\alpha)}F_{22}^{(\alpha)})(r)^{-\frac{1}{2}} \\[2mm]
\epsilon_{33}^{(\alpha)} = (s_{31}^{(\alpha)}F_{11}^{(\alpha)} + s_{32}^{(\alpha)}F_{22}^{(\alpha)})(r)^{-\frac{1}{2}} \\[2mm]
2\epsilon_{23}^{(\alpha)} = (s_{41}^{(\alpha)}F_{11}^{(\alpha)} + s_{42}^{(\alpha)}F_{22}^{(\alpha)})(r)^{-\frac{1}{2}} \\[2mm]
2\epsilon_{12}^{(\alpha)} = (s_{66}^{(\alpha)}F_{12}^{(\alpha)})(r)^{-\frac{1}{2}}
\end{cases}
\tag{9}
$$

Assuming the isotropic power law creep behavior, the creep strain rate component under steady state creep is given by

$$
\frac{d\epsilon_{ij}^{ss}}{dt} = \frac{3}{2}\left(\frac{\sigma_e^{ss}}{\sigma_c}\right)^{n-1}\frac{S_{ij}^{ss}}{\sigma_c}
\tag{10}
$$

or equivalent creep strain rate under steady state creep

$$
\frac{d\epsilon_e^{ss}}{dt} = A(\sigma_e^{ss})^n
\tag{11}
$$

where ϵ_{ij}^{ss} is the strain component under steady state creep, S_{ij}^{ss} is the deviatoric stress component under steady state creep, σ_e^{ss} is the effective stress under steady state creep, ϵ_e^{ss} is the equivalent strain under steady state creep, σ_c is a material property, A is a constant, and n is the material hardening index.

As we mentioned earlier, the load is suddenly applied and then kept constant throughout the creep process. During the initial stage of the creep process, a transition from elasticity to power law creep will take place. This transition is known to be rapid (Nicholson and Formby[23]), and through which linear elastic stress distribution is replaced by a steady state creep stress distribution. By using the Hoff's[25] analogy argument, we have non-linear creep law $d\epsilon/dt = A\sigma^n$ and its analogy $\epsilon = A\sigma^n$ in non-linear elasticity. We adopt here the Neuber's[26] rule in analyzing the local elastic stress relaxation by creep flow. As shown in Fig.4, relaxation occurs, following the hyperbola $\sigma\epsilon = Q^2$, from the hypothetical linear elastic value down to the intersection with the power law plasticity $\epsilon = A(\sigma_e^{ss})^n$, which is the analogy of $d\epsilon/dt = A(\sigma_e^{ss})^n$. Thus the state of creep stress and strain approached at the end of the transition can be represented through hypothetical linear elastic stress and strain by means of a hyperbola, and the following relation should hold

$$
\sigma_e^E \epsilon_e^E = \sigma_e^{ss}\epsilon_e^{ss}
\tag{12}
$$

The hypothetical linear elastic stress and strain components are given by Eqs.(7)&(9). The elastic value of the effective stress and the equivalent strain can then be written as

$$
\sigma_e^E\Big|_{(\alpha)} = G_1^{(\alpha)}(r)^{-\frac{1}{2}}
\tag{13}
$$

$$
\epsilon_e^E\Big|_{(\alpha)} = G_2^{(\alpha)}(r)^{-\frac{1}{2}}
\tag{14}
$$

where

$$
G_1^{(\alpha)} = \left(\frac{3}{2}\right)^{\frac{1}{2}}[(F_{11}^{(\alpha)}-F_{22}^{(\alpha)})^2+(F_{11}^{(\alpha)})^2+(F_{22}^{(\alpha)})^2+6(F_{12}^{(\alpha)})^2]^{\frac{1}{2}}
$$

$$
G_2^{(\alpha)} = \frac{\sqrt{2}}{2(1+\nu)}(SF_1^{(\alpha)}+SF_2^{(\alpha)}+SF_3^{(\alpha)}+SF_4^{(\alpha)})^{\frac{1}{2}}
$$

783

and

$$
\left\{
\begin{aligned}
SF_1^{(\alpha)} &= [(s_{11}^{(\alpha)} - s_{21}^{(\alpha)})F_{11}^{(\alpha)} + (s_{12}^{(\alpha)} - s_{22}^{(\alpha)})F_{22}^{(\alpha)}]^2 \\
SF_2^{(\alpha)} &= [(s_{11}^{(\alpha)} - s_{31}^{(\alpha)})F_{11}^{(\alpha)} + (s_{12}^{(\alpha)} - s_{32}^{(\alpha)})F_{22}^{(\alpha)}]^2 \\
SF_3^{(\alpha)} &= [(s_{21}^{(\alpha)} - s_{31}^{(\alpha)})F_{11}^{(\alpha)} + (s_{22}^{(\alpha)} - s_{32}^{(\alpha)})F_{22}^{(\alpha)}]^2 \\
SF_4^{(\alpha)} &= \tfrac{3}{2}(s_{66}^{(\alpha)}F_{12}^{(\alpha)})^2 + \tfrac{3}{2}(s_{41}^{(\alpha)}F_{11}^{(\alpha)} + s_{42}^{(\alpha)}F_{22}^{(\alpha)})^2
\end{aligned}
\right.
$$

Substitute Eq.(13) and Eq.(14) into Eq.(12), note that $\epsilon_e^{ss} = A(\sigma_e^{ss})^n$, we have the steady state stress distribution as follows

$$
\sigma_e^{ss}\big|_{(\alpha)} = \left(\frac{G_1^{(\alpha)} G_2^{(\alpha)}}{A} \right)^{\frac{1}{n_\alpha + 1}} (r)^{-\frac{1}{n_\alpha + 1}} \tag{15}
$$

and the steady state strain rate distribution as

$$
\frac{d\epsilon_e^{ss}}{dt}\bigg|_{(\alpha)} = A^{\frac{1}{n_\alpha+1}} (G_1^{(\alpha)} G_2^{(\alpha)})^{\frac{n_\alpha}{n_\alpha+1}} (r)^{-\frac{n_\alpha}{n_\alpha+1}} \tag{16}
$$

Taking the logarithm on both side of Eq.(16), we have the following relation

$$
\log \left(\frac{d\epsilon_e^{ss}}{dt} \right)\bigg|_{(\alpha)} = C - \frac{n_\alpha}{n_\alpha + 1} \log r \tag{17}
$$

where

$$
C = \log \left[A^{\frac{1}{n_\alpha+1}} (G_1^{(\alpha)} G_2^{(\alpha)})^{\frac{n_\alpha}{n_\alpha+1}} \right]
$$

In the solution for bicrystal interface crack tip fields under steady state creep given by Eqs.(15)&(16), the complex constant K in Eq.(8) is replaced by K' and determined from boundary value problems.

3 Experiment

3.1 Specimen

A tensile specimen made of aluminum bicrystal plate was used in this study. The specimen had a thickness of $h = 2.5$ mm, and its in-plane geometries shown in Fig.1. An edge crack with finite radius of about 0.1 mm was machine cut along the grain boundary (interface), and followed by annealing at 150^0 C for 5 hours to eliminate the possible residual stress induced during machining process. The crystal orientations were determined by using the X-ray diffraction technique. As shown in Figs.1&2, the plane of deformation was defined as $x_1 - x_2$ plane with x_1 along [001] direction for both crystals, and x_2 along [041] direction for crystal 1 and [01$\bar{6}$] direction for crystal 2 respectively. The bicrystal

in this case had a twin boundary. The boundary misorientation was 94.571^0. The specimen surface was then polished and chemically etched. The material calibration was performed through simple tension tests with aluminum single crystals having the same crystal orientations as that of the crystals 1 and 2 respectively. The resulting stress-strain curves for two single crystals are shown in Fig.3. The Ramberg-Osgoog relation written in piece-wise formulation was used to fit the curves, i.e.

$$
\frac{\epsilon}{\epsilon_0} = \begin{cases} \sigma/\sigma_0 & \sigma \le \sigma_0 \\ a(\sigma/\sigma_0)^n & \sigma > \sigma_0 \end{cases} \tag{18}
$$

where σ_0 is the yield stress, ϵ_0 is the yield strain, n is the material hardening index, and a is a material constant.

The calibrated material properties are indicated in Fig.3.

3.2 Experiment

The in-plane moiré method (Chiang[27]) was used to quantitatively study the high temperature creep deformation fields near a bicrystal interface crack. Moiré fringes are the result of interference between two gratings. A cross grating of 500 line/inch (dot pattern) was photoprinted onto the specimen surface with its principal directions parallel to the in-plane coordinate axes x_1 and x_2. In order to sustain high temperature, the Kodak Photo Resist used to print gratings was mixed with T_iO_2 powder to a proper composition. The displacements represented by the moiré fringes are governed by the following equations,

$$
u_i = N_i p_i \qquad i = 1, 2 \tag{19}
$$

where N_1 and N_2 are fringe orders of u_1-field and u_2-field moiré fringe patterns respectively, and p_1 and p_2 are the pitches of cross grating in x_1-direction and x_2-direction, respectively.

To separate u_1 and u_2 an optical filtering technique (Chiang[28]) is used. The Eulerian descriptions of finite strain are used in the evaluations of the in-plane strain components.

The specimen with a bicrystal interface crack was tested at 400^0 C and under a constant applied load $\sigma_\infty = 0.12\sigma_0$, where σ_0 was the smaller yield stress of the two single crystals and σ_∞ was averaged over the uncracked ligament. As the creep deformation took place, a series of deformed specimen gratings were recorded at different times. The corresponding creep deformation fields at each time was constructed through techniques described in the previous section. These moiré fringe patterns were digitized and numerically differentiated with respect to the spatial coordinates x_1 and x_2 using a smoothed cubic spline approximation (Berghuaus and Cannon[29]). The in-plane strain components were calculated using the The Eulerian descriptions of finite strain, and the equivalent strain ϵ_e was obtained, under the assumption of incompressibility, from the following relation (neglect the elastic deformation near the crack tip):

$$\epsilon_e = \frac{\sqrt{2}}{3}\left[(\epsilon_{11} - \epsilon_{22})^2 + (\epsilon_{22} - \epsilon_{33})^2 + (\epsilon_{33} - \epsilon_{11})^2 + 6\epsilon_{12}^2\right]^{\frac{1}{2}}$$

(20)

where

$$\epsilon_{33} = -(\epsilon_{11} + \epsilon_{22})$$

Typical moiré fringe patterns recorded at different stages of creep are shown in Fig.5, and the corresponding equivalent creep strain were plotted and depicted in Fig.6&7, against radial distance, r, normalized by the specimen thickness, h. The equivalent creep strain rate was also evaluated from creep strain fields obtained as a function of time. Fig.8 show the equivalent creep strain rate, $d\epsilon_e/dt$, versus normalized radial distance, r/h. The complex constant K' in Eq.(8), and in turn the pre-exponentials in Eqs.(15)&(16), are undetermined. In order to compare the experimental result with the theoretical prediction given in Eq.(17), the rate of equivalent creep strain was again plotted in a double logarithmic coordinate system (shown as in Fig.11). The straight solid line in Fig.11 has the slope equal to $-n_\alpha/(n_\alpha+1)$, which is the slope in the linear relation of $\log \epsilon_e$ and $\log r$ predicted in Eq.(17). Thus from Figs.11 an excellent agreement between the experimental observations and the theoretical solution in terms of singularity field is obtained.

4   Conclusions and discussion

An analytical solution for the stress and the strain rate fields near a bicrystal interface crack under steady state creep condition is derived. The creep strain rate has a singularity of the form $-n_\alpha/(n_\alpha+1)$. The solution is valid in a small region surrounding the crack tip, i.e. $h \leq r \leq 10h$. Experimental observations (Fig.11) provide clear evidence for the correctness of this solution in terms of the strength of the singularities.

In the region very near the crack tip, no analytical solution is provided partly due to the difficulties involved with the oscillatory features inherited from the linear elastic solution, and partly due to the lack of information from experimental observations. It was observed from the experiments that extensive localized necking had developed within a small region around the crack tip (approximately the size of the specimen thickness). As a result, moiré fringes were lost within this region. Creep stress and creep deformation fields very near crack tip are of considerable interest especially when the mechanism of crack advance is concerned, and further work on this is needed.

Analytical solution as shown in Eqs.(15)&(16) are given in terms of effective stress and equivalent strain rate. According to Hoff[25], the initial linear elastic stress distribution near a bicrystal interface crack is rapidly re-placed by a steady state stress distribution, which is identical to the stress distribution derived from its non-linear elastic analogue. In other words, if a non-linear elastic solution for bicrystal interface crack does exist, the stress distribution so obtained can be used to approximate the steady state stress distribution in case of the steady state creep provided that the appropriate boundary conditions are satisfied. Consequently the strain rate components can be obtained from Eq.(10). The pre-exponentials in Eqs.(15)&(16) are controlled by a complex number K' which is determined from boundary value problems. It is not clear that to what fracture criterion this complex constant is associated with. Unlike the case of homogeneous, isotropic material, this can only be solved if the complete solution in terms of the stress and the strain rate components are provided. These problems remain to be further investigated.

Based on continuum crystal plasticity, Mohan et al [30] have recently reported a numerical analysis on a bicrystal interface crack with a symmetric tilt boundary. Their work was collaborated by Wang's[31] experiments. However these studies did not give an explicit non-linear elastic solution.

Acknowledgements

This work is financially supported by the Office of Naval Research, Mechanics Division, and through grant No. N0001491J1380 (Scientific Officer, Dr. Yapa D. S. Rajapakse)

References

[1] J. T. Barnby, Engineering Fracture Mechanics, 7, (1975), 299-304.

[2] R. D. Nicholson and C. L. Formby, International Journal of Fracture, 11, (1975), 595-604.

[3] J. T. Barnby and R. D. Nicholson, 'Local stress and strain during crack growth by steady state creep', Journal of Materials Science, 12, (1977), 2099-2108.

[4] J. C. Bassani and F. A. McClintock, International Journal of Solids and Structure, 17, (1981), 478-492.

[5] C. Y. Hui and H. Riedel, International Journal of Fracture, 17, (1981), 409-425.

[6] A. Saxena, H. A. Ernst and J. D. Landes, International Journal of Fracture, 23, (1983), 245-257.

[7] C. Y. Hui, International Journal of Solids and Structures, 22, (1986), 357-372.

[8] D. E. Hawk and J. L. Bassani, Journal of The Mechanics and Physics of Solids, 34, (1986), 191-212.

[9] J. L. Bassani and D. E. Hawk, International Journal of Fracture, 42, (1990), 157-172.

[10] M. P. Harper and E. G. Ellison, *Journal of Strain Analysis*, 12, (1977). 167-179.

[11] E. T. Moyer and H. Liebowitz, *Engineering Fracture Mechanics*, 28, (1987), 601-621.

[12] H. Riedel, *International Journal of Fracture*, 42, (1990), 173-188.

[13] H. Riedel and V. Detampel, *International Journal of Fracture*, 33, (1987), 239-262.

[14] B. S. J. Kang, Y. N. Zhuang and Q. K. Liu, *Proceedings of SEM Spring Conference on Experimental Mechanics*, (1991), 752-761.

[15] D. L. Clements, *International Journal of Engineering Science*, 9, (1971), 257-265.

[16] J. R. Willis, *Journal of The Mechanics and Physics of Solids*, 19, (1971), 353-368.

[17] T. C. Ting, *International Journal of Solids and Structures*, 22, (1986), 965-983.

[18] T. C. Ting and C. Hwu, *International Journal of Solids and Structures*, 24, (1988), 65-76.

[19] K. C. Wu, *Journal of Applied Mechanics*, 57, (1990), 882-886.

[20] K. C. Wu, *International Journal of Solids and Structures*, 27, (1991), 455-466.

[21] J. Qu and J. L. Bassani, *Journal of The Mechanics and Physics of Solids*, 37, (1989), 417-433.

[22] J. L. Bassani and J. Qu, *Journal of The Mechanics and Physics of Solids*, 37, (1989), 435-453.

[23] T. C. Ting, *Journal of The Mechanics and Physics of Solids*, 38, (1990), 505-513.

[24] Z. Suo, *Proceedings of The Royal Society*, (London), A427, (1990), 331-358.

[25] N. J. Hoff, *Quarterly Applied Mathematics*, 12, (1954), 49-55.

[26] H. Neuber, *Transactions of The American Society of Mechanical Engineers*, 83, (1961), 544-550.

[27] F. P. Chiang, in *Manual on Experimental Stress Analysis*, (ed. J. F. Doyle), The Society for Experimental Mechanics, Bethel, Connecticut, (1979), Chapter 6.

[28] F. P. Chiang, *Experimental Mechanics*, 9, (1969), 523-526.

[29] D. G. Berghuaus and J. P. Cannon, *Experimental Mechanics*, 13, (1973), 23-26.

[30] R. Mohan, M. Ortiz and C. F. Shih, *Journal of Applied Mechanics*, (1990), (to appear).

[31] J. S. Wang, *Acta Metallurgica*, (1990), (to appear).

$s_{ij}^{(1)}$	$j = 1$	$j = 2$	$j = 3$	$j = 4$	$j = 5$	$j = 6$
$i = 1$	2.2970	-0.8350	-0.8350	0.0000	0.0000	0.0000
$i = 2$	-0.0491	3.0741	-1.6121	1.4570	0.0000	0.0000
$i = 3$	-0.7859	-1.6121	3.0741	-1.4570	0.0000	0.0000
$i = 4$	-0.1965	1.4570	-1.4570	4.2979	0.0000	0.0000
$i = 5$	0.0000	0.0000	0.0000	0.0000	5.0750	0.0000
$i = 6$	0.0000	0.0000	0.0000	0.0000	0.0000	5.0750

Table 1: Elastic constants for crystal 1 ($\times 10^{-11}$ m^2/N).

$s_{ij}^{(2)}$	$j = 1$	$j = 2$	$j = 3$	$j = 4$	$j = 5$	$j = 6$
$i = 1$	2.2970	-0.8350	-0.8350	0.0000	0.0000	0.0000
$i = 2$	-0.8124	2.6661	-1.2041	2.1531	0.0000	0.0000
$i = 3$	-0.0226	-1.2041	2.6661	-2.1531	0.0000	0.0000
$i = 4$	0.2708	2.1531	-2.1531	18.8236	0.0000	0.0000
$i = 5$	0.0000	0.0000	0.0000	0.0000	20.3000	0.0000
$i = 6$	0.0000	0.0000	0.0000	0.0000	0.0000	20.3000

Table 2: Elastic constants for crystal 2 ($\times 10^{-11}$ m^2/N).

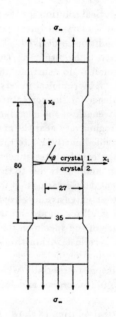

Fig.1 Specimen geometry (unit = mm).

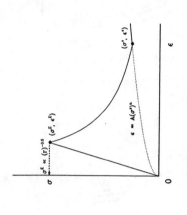

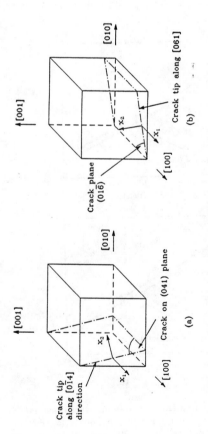

Fig. 2 Crystal orientation for aluminum single crystal under consideration.
(a) Crystal 1: Crack on (041) plane and its tip along $[0\bar{1}4]$ direction.
(b) Crystal 2: Crack on $(01\bar{6})$ plane ane its tip along [061] direction.

Fig.4 Relaxation of elastic stress by plastic deformation according to Neuber.

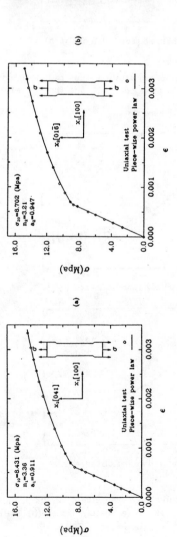

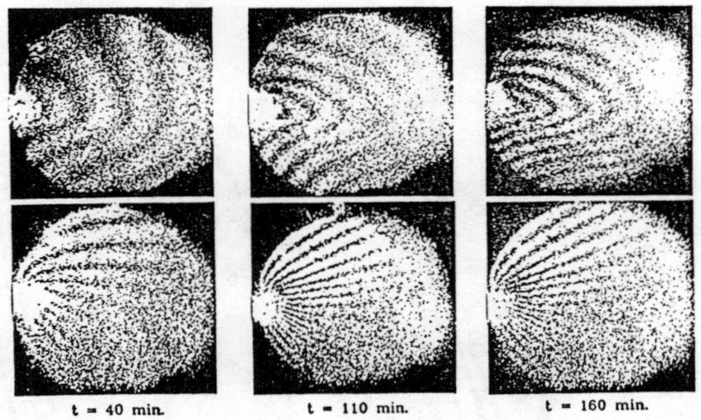

Fig.5 Moire fringe patterns of u-field (top) and v-field (bottom) obtained under steady state creep condition (T = 400° c, $\sigma_\infty = 0.12\sigma_0$)

Fig.3 Stress—Strain relation of aluminum single crystals under consideration. (a) crystal 1. (b) crystal 2.

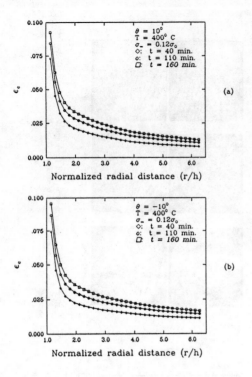

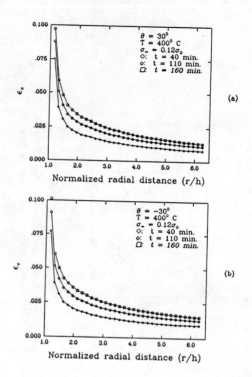

Fig.6 Equivalent creep strain versus radial distance from crack tip at (a) $\theta = 10^0$, and (b) $\theta = -10^0$.

Fig.7 Equivalent creep strain versus radial distance from crack tip at (a) $\theta = 30^0$, and (b) $\theta = -30^0$.

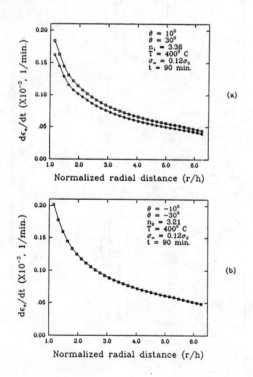

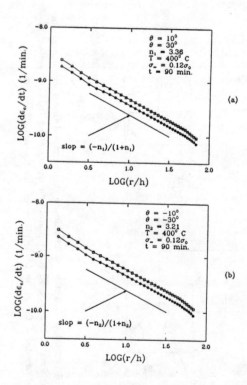

Fig.8 Rate of equivalent creep strain versus radial distance from crack tip (a) $\theta=10^0,30^0$ and (b) $\theta=-10^0.,-30^0$

Fig.9 Rate of equivalent creep strain versus radial distance from crack tip plotted in double logarithmic coordinate system. (a) $\theta=10^0$, 30^0, and (b) $\theta=-10^0.,-30^0$

A CALIBRATION METHOD FOR DETERMINING K_I USING THE METHOD OF CAUSTICS

I. Miskioglu, Assistant Professor
Mechanical Engineering-Engineering Mechanics Department
Michigan Technological University
Houghton, MI 49931

N. T. Younis, Assistant Professor
Engineering Department
Purdue University at Fort Wayne
Fort Wayne, IN 46805

S. E. Egleston, Research Assistant
Mechanical Engineering-Engineering Mechanics Department
Michigan Technological University
Houghton, MI 49931

ABSTRACT

The uncertainty in selecting the length parameter, the maximum diameter, of the caustic image is investigated. A simple calibration method is used to determine mode one, K_I, stress intensity factor at a crack tip. The accuracy is further improved by using white light. The effect of the pinhole size upon the determination of K_I is investigated. The accuracy of the proposed measurement location is demonstrated by comparing experimental results to theory.

INTRODUCTION

The method of caustics has been used for the last twenty years to determine mode I stress intensity factor (SIF) at a stationary crack tip. It inherently provides information close to the crack tip where the theory of elasticity near-field solution is valid. The crack caustic image has the shape of a generalized epicycloid.

According to the method, mode I SIF is a function of the experimental setup, model thickness, stress-optical constant of the material, and the maximum transverse diameter of the caustic image, D_{tmax}. D_{tmax} is the most sensitive parameter because it is raised to the power of 5/2. However, due to the diffraction effects, the caustic band has a finite width and herein lies the measurement problem.

Currently, the literature is inconclusive regarding the measurement of D_{tmax}. There are four proposals for measuring D_{tmax}. They are:
1. At the transition from the inner dark space to the bright rim, D_1 [1].
2. The points with the maximum light intensity, D_2 [2].
3. The intermediate diameter D_3, which is the mean distance between D_1 and D_2 [3].
4. The outer diameter of the caustic image D_4 [4].

In order to clarify this situation, the calibration technique to measure the stress-optical constant outlined in [5] together with a Mode I fracture specimen is utilized in this study. According to this calibration technique, the caustic image resulting from the light transmitted through a circular hole in a stressed plate has the shape of a nephroid. The stress optical constant value depends on the experimental setup, model thickness, the hole size, and the maximum longitudinal diameter of the caustic image. Again the caustic band has a finite width. Three different stress-optical constants are determined based on D_1, D_2, and D_4. Mode I SIF is calculated by using the stress-optical constant corresponding to where the maximum transverse diameter of the cracked caustic is measured.

Thin plexiglas specimens with a double edge crack are considered. The cracked and the calibration specimens are taken from the same plexiglas (PMMA) sheet. Traditionally, the stress-optical constant used for plexiglas is 1.08×10^{-10} m^2/N. By using this value, the difference between the four K_I values is significant. However, with the calibration technique, the difference is decreased. The transmitted caustic is considered in this study.

Data for the optical property (stress optical constant) of PMMA can be looked up in a handbook, but one has to be particularly careful in selecting and using data for the properties of PMMA. Plexiglas made by one manufacturer may be very different from plexiglas made by another. In part, because all polymers contain a spectrum of molecular lengths and any slight change in processing will change the spectrum. The difference is also due to the details of the polymerization, additives properties, and the properties can be further changed by mechanical processing. For all these reasons, data from a handbook, are at best approximate. For accurate stress optical constant, one has to conduct tests on the specific sheets of PMMA used.

The rest of the paper is organized in the following manner. First, a brief theory of the cracked and circular hole caustics is presented. Next, we discuss the experimental procedure that was followed to obtain the data used in this paper. After that, we summarize important results and discuss them. Finally, we evaluate the results obtained and appraise the usefulness of the technique being proposed.

THEORY

With the method of caustics, the stress singularity of the elastic field is transformed to an optical singularity represented by the caustic.

Consider an elastic plate under conditions of generalized plane stress with a crack under the opening mode of deformation. Due to the high stress concentration in the region surrounding the crack tip, both the thickness and the refractive index of the material will change. As a consequence, the area surrounding the crack tip acts much like a divergent lens. The light rays transmitted through the lens are deflected outward, which form the caustic surface. When the caustic surface is projected on a screen a singular curve, called the caustic, is formed. However, the caustic image has a finite width which is problematic. Theoretically, the transmitted crack caustic equations are:

$$x_c = r_{oc}(\cos\ \theta + 2/3 \cos 3\ \theta/2) \qquad (1a)$$

$$y_c = r_{oc}(\sin\ \theta + 2/3 \sin 3\ \theta/2) \qquad (1b)$$

where r_{oc} is the initial curve radius, $-\pi < \theta < \pi$. Mode I stress intensity factor, K_I, effect the size of the caustic image which has the shape of generalized epicycloid as shown in Fig. 1. Experimentally, K_I can be calculated from

$$K_I = \frac{0.09339\ D_{maxc}^{5/2}}{z_o cd\ \lambda^{3/2}} \qquad (2)$$

where z_o is the distance from the model to the screen, c is the stress optical constant of the material, d is the model thickness, λ is the magnification factor, and D_{maxc} is the maximum transverse diameter of the caustic image. It is obvious that K_I depends on the model stress optical constant. Therefore, the stress optical constant should be determined experimentally.

The stress optical constant can be determined by the method of caustics as outlined in [5]. According to this method, the transmitted caustic through the plate with a small circular hole subjected to uniaxial tensile load will give the stress optical constant. Theoretically, the transmitted caustic equations for the hole are:

$$x_h = r_{oh}\ (\cos\ \theta + 1/3 \cos 3\ \theta) \qquad (3a)$$

$$y_h = r_{oh}\ (\sin\ \theta + 1/3 \sin 3\ \theta) \qquad (3b)$$

where r_{oh} is the hole initial curve radius. The shape of the caustic image is a nephroid as shown in Fig. 2. The stress optical constant can be determined experimentally from

$$c = \frac{0.001648\ D_{maxh}^4}{z_o d\sigma a^2\ \lambda^3} \qquad (4)$$

where D_{maxh} is the maximum longitudinal diameter, a is the radius of the hole, and σ is the applied stress.

By measuring the maximum longitudinal diameter of the hole caustic, we can determine the stress optical constant of the specimen c. Hence, Mode I stress intensity factor can be calculated from (2) by using the calibrated c and measuring the maximum transverse diameter of the crack caustic. However, there is more than one diameter to be considered from the caustic image.

EXPERIMENTAL PROCEDURE

In this section, we discuss the models used, light sources that are used in the experiments, and the steps in achieving the results. The results will be presented in the next section.

An optically isotropic material PMMA was used for the experiments. The cracked and central hole models were taken from the same plexiglass sheet.

Double edge crack specimens were considered for the determination of mode I stress intensity factor. The geometry of the crack and the calibration specimens are shown in Figs. 3 and 4, respectively. The size of the hole was taken as recommended by [5].

Two light sources were used in this study. First, the traditional caustic light source, a monochromatic light beam emitted from a He-Ne laser is considered. Difficulties were encountered in locating the caustic inner diameter. Second, to reduce the diffraction effects, a white light with a small pinhole was used which resulted in accurately locating the caustic inner diameter. Pinhole sizes of 0.343 mm and 0.793 mm are used and the effect of the pin hole size is investigated.

All models were loaded in tension. The caustic image was photographed with 35 mm camera and then analyzed with an image processor to measure the maximum diameter.

First, using the laser light source, the experimental crack and calibration caustics are shown in Figs. 5 and 6, respectively. Theoretically the relevant caustic line should be defined by the transition from the dark inner region to the bright rim of the caustic pattern. But, due to the light diffraction effects, the caustic rim will have a band shape rather than a fine line. Three different diameters were located for each caustic image. They are: the outer diameter D_o, the diameter based on the maximum light intensity within the bright rim D_m, and the inner diameter D_i. Therefore, three values for mode one stress intensity factor were calculated from eq. (2) by using the corresponding value of the stress optical constant obtained from eq. (4). The best results obtained are the ones based on the inside diameter which will be shown in the results section. However, locating the caustics inner diameters for both the cracked and calibration specimens are sometimes problematic. This is due to the fact that the transition from the dark region to the bright rim is inconclusive. The characteristic inner diameter is the distance between two points on the caustic curve. Looking at Figs. 5 and 6, one can argue about which characteristic points should be considered. Hence, the inner caustics diameters can not be located with high accuracy.

Second, a white light source was used to increase the accuracy in locating the inner diameters. The experimental crack caustic is shown in Fig. 7 and the calibration caustic image is shown in Fig. 8. It is clear that the transition from dark region to the bright rim is more definite. Furthermore, points which do not lie on the caustic curve are eliminated. Three stress intensity factors were determined using the same procedure outlined using a laser light source.

RESULTS AND DISCUSSION

In this section, two sets of results are presented. First, the results obtained using a laser light source are presented and the disadvantages of this technique are discussed. Second, white light results are evaluated and the effect of the pinhole size is investigated.

With the laser light, the calibration specimen was subjected to three different loads and three diameters are measured. They are the inside diameter, the maximum light intensity, and the outside diameter. The applied loads and the resulting stress optical constants are shown in Table 1. The double edge crack specimen was subjected to four different loads and mode one stress intensity factors are calculated by using three diameters for each case. K_I was determined based on the corresponding calibration stress optical value. $K_I/\sigma(\pi a)^{1/2}$ results calculated from inside, maximum light intensity, and outside diameters are listed in Table 2, 3 and 4, respectively. σ is the applied stress and a is the crack length. The percentage difference between the experimental values and the theoretical value of 1.127 [6] is also listed in Tables 2-4. It is clear that K_I values based on the inner caustics diameters are the most accurate ones. However, the location of the inner diameter is inconclusive. Therefore, a white light was used to enhance the accuracy of measurements.

With the white light, the calibration specimen was subjected to three different loads and with each load the experiment was repeated three times. Three diameters were considered, the profile (digital image analysis) inside diameter, the maximum light intensity diameter, and the outside caustic diameter. The average stress optical value for each load is listed in Table 5. The crack specimen was subjected to five loads and each experiment was repeated three times. The resulting $K_I/\sigma(\pi a)^{1/2}$ values, using the calibration values, and the percentage difference is shown in Tables 6-8. Again, accurate K_I values are obtained by considering the inside diameter.

According to the method of caustics, the light source must have the essential features of a point source. The results listed in Tables 5-8 are obtained by using a 0.343 mm pinhole size. It is important to mention that when a pinhole size 0.793 mm was used, accuracy of K_I values suffered as shown in Tables 9-11.

CONCLUSIONS

In this study, experimental results for the determination of mode one stress intensity factor using the experimental method of transmitted caustic were presented. The paper discussed the importance of calibration and a new light source is proposed.

Diffraction effects in the vicinity of the caustic lead to ambiguities in locating the caustic maximum diameter. The optical property (stress optical constant) of plexiglas require special attention. It is essential that the stress optical constant must be determined experimentally and then used in K_I calculation.

Calculating K_I based on different diameters and the corresponding stress optical constant enhance the accuracy of the optical method of caustics. The results obtained in this study lead to the following conclusions.

1. Accurate K_I results can be obtained if the inside edge of the caustic is taken as the maximum transverse diameter regardless of the light source that is used as shown in Figs 9 and 10.
2. It is advantageous to use a white light for two reasons. First, the edge of the caustic can be located accurately. Second, although the underestimated laser source error is less than 6%, white light results represent the largest values.
3. Regardless of the light source being used, a large underestimate of K_I results are obtained if the maximum light intensity or the outside caustic diameter are considered.
4. It is essential to use a small pinhole size. In this study, the effect of the pinhole size was investigated. The results from a pinhole size of 0.793 mm indicate that K_I is underestimated, sometimes more than 10%.

REFERENCES

1. Nigam, H. and Shukla, A., "Comparison of the Techniques of Transmitted Caustics and Photoelasticity as Applied to Fracture," Experimental Mechanics, 28 (2), 123-131 (1988).

2. Beinert, J. and Kalthoff, J.F., "Experimental Determination of Dynamic Stress Intensity Factors by Shadow Patterns," Mechanics of Fracture, VIII, ed. G.C. Sih, Martinus Nijhoff Publishers, The Hague, The Netherlands (1981).

3. Kamath, S.M. and Kim, K.S., "Coherent-Light Shadow Spot of a Crack Under Mode I Loading: Theory and Experiment," Experimental Mechanics, 26 (4), 386-393 (1986).

4. Kalthoff, J.F., "Shadow Optical Method of Caustics" Handbook on Experimental Mechanics, ed. A.S. Kobayashi, Prentice-Hall, Englewood Cliffs, New Jersey (1987).

5. Younis, N.T. and Zachary, L.W., "A New Technique for the Determination of Stress-Optical Constants Using the Shadow Spot Method," Experimental Mechanics, 29 (1), 75-79 (1989).

6. Hellan, K., Introduction to Fracture Mechanics, McGraw-Hill, New York (1984).

Table 1- Stress Optical Constant Using Laser

Load N	c_1 $10^{-10}m^2/N$	c_2 $10^{-10}m^2/N$	c_3 $10^{-10}m^2/N$
596	1.119	1.783	2.409
796	1.252	1.584	1.937
996	1.038	1.428	1.810

c_1 based on inside diameter
c_2 based on points with maximum light intensity
c_3 based on outside diameter

Table 2- Laser Inside Diameter Mode One SIF Results

Load N	$K_I/\sigma(\pi a)^{1/2}$ Experimental	% Difference from Theoretical
398	1.160	2.9
597	1.095	-2.8
796	1.061	-5.9
896	1.097	-2.7

Table 3- Laser Maximum Light Intensity Diameter Mode One SIF Results

Load N	$K_I/\sigma(\pi a)^{1/2}$ Experimental	% Difference from Theoretical
398	0.810	-28.1
597	0.904	-19.8
796	0.899	-20.2
896	0.893	-20.8

Table 4- Laser Outside Diameter Mode One SIF Results

Load N	$K_I/\sigma(\pi a)^{1/2}$ Experimental	% Difference from Theoretical
398	0.854	-24.12
597	0.797	-29.30
796	0.790	-29.90
896	0.740	-34.30

Table 5- Stress Optical Constant Using White Light

Load N	c_1 $10^{-10}m^2/N$	c_2 $10^{-10}m^2/N$	c_3 $10^{-10}m^2/N$
592	0.612	1.622	2.078
796	0.607	1.456	1.844
961	0.603	1.355	1.724

c_1 based on profile inside diameter
c_2 based on points with maximum light intensity
c_3 based on outside diameter

Table 6- Profile Inside Diameter Mode One SIF Results, Pinhole Size=0.343 mm

Load N	$K_I/\sigma(\pi a)^{1/2}$ Experimental	% Difference from Theoretical
409	1.096	-2.9
614	1.169	3.5
725	1.165	3.2
836	1.170	3.6
898	1.207	6.9

Table 7- Maximum Light Intensity Diameter Mode One SIF Results, Pinhole Size=0.343 mm

Load N	$K_I/\sigma(\pi a)^{1/2}$ Experimental	% Difference from Theoretical
409	0.862	-23.6
614	0.817	-27.6
725	0.806	-28.6
836	0.782	-30.7
898	0.785	-30.5

Table 8- Outside Diameter Mode One SIF Results, Pinhole Size=0.343 mm

Load N	$K_I/\sigma(\pi a)^{1/2}$ Experimental	% Difference from Theoretical
409	0.829	-26.6
614	0.768	-32.0
725	0.751	-33.5
836	0.709	-37.2
898	0.715	-36.7

Table 9- Profile Inside Diameter Mode One SIF Results, Pinhole Size=0.793 mm

Load N	$K_I/\sigma(\pi a)^{1/2}$ Experimental	% Difference from Theoretical
427	1.000	-11.4
618	1.145	1.4
734	1.108	-1.9
840	1.003	-11.2
938	1.116	-1.2

Table 10-Maximum Light Intensity Diameter Mode One SIF Results, Pinhole Size=0.793 mm

Load N	$K_I/\sigma(\pi a)^{1/2}$ Experimental	% Difference from Theoretical
427	1.143	1.2
618	1.094	-3.1
734	1.011	-10.5
840	1.018	-9.8
938	1.044	-7.5

Table 11- Outside Diameter Mode One SIF Results, Pinhole Size=0.793 mm

Load N	$K_I/\sigma(\pi a)^{1/2}$ Experimental	% Difference from Theoretical
427	1.198	6.1
618	1.070	-5.2
734	1.037	-8.1
840	0.988	-12.5
938	1.003	-11.2

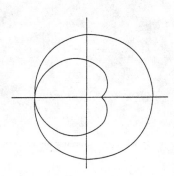

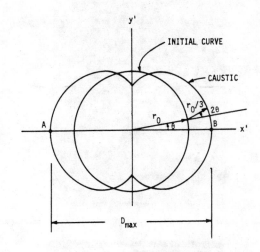

Fig. 1: Theoretical form of the caustic at a crack tip.

Fig. 2: Theoretical form of the caustic around a central hole.

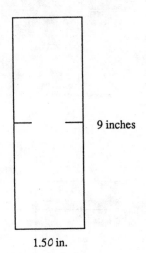

9 inches

1.50 in.

Crack length = 0.25 in.

Thickness = 0.130 in.

Fig. 3: Double edge crack specimen geometry.

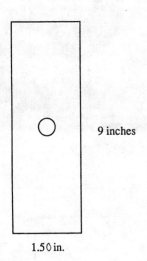

9 inches

1.50 in.

Hole diameter = 5/64 in.

Thickness = 0.130 in.

Fig. 4: Calibration specimen geometry.

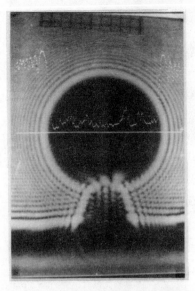

Fig. 5: Laser light intensity distribution of crack caustic.

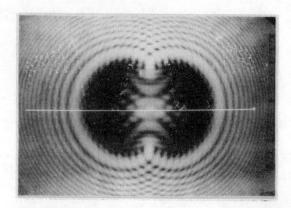

Fig. 6: Laser light intensity distribution of central hole caustic.

Fig. 7: White light intensity distribution of crack caustic.

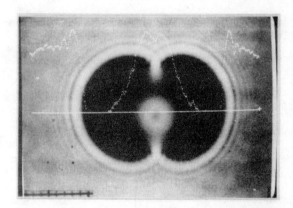

Fig. 8: White light intensity distribution of central hole caustic.

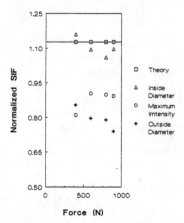

Fig. 9: Laser source SIF results.

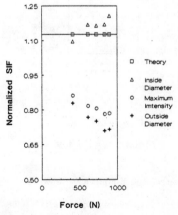

Fig. 10: Small pinhole SIF results.

THE STATE OF STRESS AT A CRACK TIP STUDIED BY CAUSTICS

M. Konsta-Gdoutos, E.E. Gdoutos and E.I. Meletis

ABSTRACT

The objective of the present work is to study the triaxial character of the stress field in the neighborhood of a crack tip. Experiments performed on 2090 Al alloy precracked double cantilever beam specimens are reported. The specimens were illuminated by a laser light beam and caustics were obtained from the light rays reflected from the front face of the specimens. The specimen dimensions, the applied loads and the geometrical characteristics of the optical set up were adjusted so that caustics created from a host of initial curves of various radii were obtained. An empirical triaxiality factor k related to the triaxial character of the stress field in the vicinity of the crack tip was introduced. Values of k at various distances from the crack tip were obtained by comparing experimental and theoretical caustics. The results of the investigation lead to the determination of the limits of applicability of plane stress caustics as a function of specimen thickness.

INTRODUCTION

Determination of stress intensity factors by the method of caustics is based on the assumption that conditions of plane stress prevail in the vicinity of the crack tip. This, however, is not the case since in the immediate vicinity of the tip a region exists that is under strong plane strain influence and further away from the tip the stress field is three-dimensional. The three-dimensionality of the state of stress dies out at a critical distance from the tip giving rise to conditions of plane stress. The changing state of stress in the neighborhood of the tip complicates the experimental determination of stress intensity factors since the values of the stress-optical constants entering into the evaluation equations change drastically when the stress state changes from plane strain to plane stress.

The problem of stress state in the neighborhood of the crack tip was first addressed by Levi et al[1]. By performing a finite element analysis of the problem of a finite width plate with a straight crack they found that the principal stress normal to the plane of the plate approaches zero at a distance from the crack tip equal to half specimen thickness. This result indicates that conditions of plane stress dominate at distances from the crack tip larger than half the specimen thickness. Rosakis and Ravi-Chandar[2] determined the extent of the region of three-dimensionality of the stress field

in the neighborhood of the crack tip using the method of caustics and came to the conclusion that the state of stress approaches that of plane stress at distances from the crack tip greater than half the specimen thickness. Meletis et al[3] established the size of the three-dimensional region around a crack tip as it is influenced by specimen dimensions and applied loading. In a recent publication[4] the first two authors discussed the potential applications and limitations of caustics as applied to determine the mode-I crack tip stress intensity factor. Furthermore,[5,6] they established the limits of applicability of the method and showed that precautions should be taken with regard to selection of material, load level, specimen size and the optical arrangement, the combination of which could have adverse effects on the character of the caustics or the end results. They determined the bounds of optical arrangement and applied loads for correct evaluation of transmitted or reflected caustics and provided simple guidelines for the correct application of the method.

In the present work the triaxial character of the state of stress in the neighborhood of a crack tip was investigated using the method of caustics. A triaxiality factor was introduced and determined as a function of the distance from the crack tip. These results help to establish the limits of applicability of the method of caustics under conditions of plane stress in crack problems.

STRESS-OPTICAL RELATIONS

The state of stress in the neighborhood of the crack tip is three-dimensional. It changes from plane strain at the tip to plane stress at a critical distance further away from the tip through an intermediate region in which a three-dimensional stress state dominates. The out-of-plane normal stress σ_z for the extreme cases of plane stress and plane strain is equal to zero and $v(\sigma_x+\sigma_y)$, respectively, where σ_x and σ_y are the normal in-plane stresses and v is Poisson's ratio. For the characterization of the three-dimensionality of the stress field in the neighborhood of the crack tip an empirical triaxiality factor k is introduced such that

$$\sigma_z = k v (\sigma_x + \sigma_y) , \quad 0 \le k \le 1 \qquad (1)$$

k takes the values of 0 and 1 for plane stress ($\sigma_z=0$) and plane strain ($\sigma_z=v(\sigma_x+\sigma_y)$), respectively. For three-dimensional stress states its value can be used as a measure of the three-dimensionality of the stress state.

Based on equation (1) and using the Neumann-Maxwell stress-optical law we obtain for the variation of the optical path $\Delta s_{t1,2}$ of a light ray traversing the specimen along the directions of principal stresses σ_1 and σ_2

M. Konsta-Gdoutos is graduate student, E.E. Gdoutos (SEM member) is Professor, Democritus University of Thrace GR-671 00 Xanthi, Greece. E.I. Meletis is Associate Professor, Department of Mechanical Engineering, Louisiana State University, Baton Rouge, LA 70803-6413.

$$\Delta s_{t_{1,2}} = (\alpha_t \sigma_{1,2} + \beta_t \sigma_{2,1}) t \qquad (2)$$

where t is the thickness of the plate. The stress-optical constants α_t and β_t are given by

$$\alpha_t = \frac{1}{E} [(1 - k v^2) b_1 - v [2 - \kappa (1 - v)] b_2 + (n - n_0) v (k - 1)] \qquad (3a)$$

$$\beta_t = \frac{1}{E} [- v (1 + kv) b_1 + (1 - v) (1 + vk) b_2 + (n - n_0) v (k - 1)] \qquad (3b)$$

where E is the modulus of elasticity n and n_0 are the indices of refraction of the specimen and the surrounding medium, respectively, and $b_{1,2}$ are constants entering into the Neumann-Maxwell stress-optical law

$$\Delta n_{1,2} = b_1 \varepsilon_{1,2} + b_2 (\varepsilon_{2,1} + \varepsilon_3) \qquad (4)$$

In the above equation $\Delta n_{1,2}$ expresses the variation of the index of refraction along the directions of the in-plane principal strains ε_1 and ε_2.

Equation (3) for k=0 gives the values of the stress-optical constants α_t and β_t for conditions of plane stress

$$\alpha_t = \frac{1}{E} [b_1 - 2 v b_2 - v (n - n_0)] \qquad (5a)$$

$$\beta_t = \frac{1}{E} [b_2 - v (b_1 + b_2) - v (n - n_0)] \qquad (5b)$$

while for k=1 it gives the values of the stress-optical constants α_t and β_t for conditions of plane strain

$$\alpha_t = \frac{1}{E} [(1 - v^2) b_1 - v (1 + v) b_2] \qquad (6a)$$

$$\beta_t = \frac{1}{E} [- v (1 + v) b_1 + (1 - v^2) b_2] \qquad (6b)$$

For the light rays reflected from the rear face of a transparent specimen the variation of the optical path $\Delta s_{r_{1,2}}$ along the directions of principal stresses σ_1 and σ_2 is given by

$$\Delta s_{r_{1,2}} = 2 (\alpha_r \sigma_{1,2} + \beta_r \sigma_{2,1}) t \qquad (7)$$

where the stress-optical constants α_r and β_r are obtained from equation (3) by replacing n_0 by $n_0/2$.

Finally, the variation of the optical path Δs_f of a light ray reflected from the front face of the specimen is given by

$$\Delta s_f = c_f (\sigma_1 + \sigma_2) t \qquad (8)$$

where

$$c_f = - \frac{v}{E} (1 - k) \qquad (9)$$

Equation (9) for k=0 and k=1 gives the values of $c_f = -v/E$ and $c_f = 0$ for conditions of plane stress and plane strain, respectively.

EXPERIMENTAL PROCEDURE

A series of experiments were performed on 2090 Al double cantilever beam (DCB) specimens (Fig.1). Four specimen thicknesses were tested, t=3.0, 5.5, 8.0 and 12.5 mm, producing different loading conditions ranging from plane strain to plane stress. The specimens were first fatigue-precracked up to the final crack length, which was a=54.0, 35.8, 59.8 and 47.5 mm for the 3.0, 5.5, 8.0 and 12.5 mm thick specimens, respectively. Then, mirror-like specimen surfaces were produced by polishing down to 1μm finish in order to obtain high quality reflected caustics. Subsequently the specimens were loaded to various levels and caustic curves were obtained from several initial curves for each loading level.

The optical arrangement used is shown in Fig. 2. A coherent parallel light beam emanating from a 5 mW Ne-He laser was used to illuminate the specimens. When the specimen was loaded a virtual caustic was formed on a reference plane at a distance z_0 behind the specimen. The image of the caustic was focused onto a reference screen by lens L_2 and was photographed by a camera. The distance z_0 can be accurately determined from the values of b,c and the focal length f of lens L_2 by using the relationship [7]:

$$z_0 = \frac{cf}{c - f} - b. \qquad (10)$$

The magnification from the reference plane at distance z_0 behind the specimen to the real screen is

$$m = \frac{c}{z_0 + b} = \frac{c - f}{f}. \qquad (11)$$

To obtain different values of the radius of the initial curve two lenses (L_2) of focal length 1 m and 2 m were used and the distance c between lens L_2 and the real screen was varied. The distance b between the specimen and the lens L_2 was kept constant at 0.75 m.

DETERMINATION OF TRIAXIALITY FACTOR k

In the optical method of caustics a specimen is illuminated by a parallel, convergent or divergent light beam and the reflected and/or transmitted rays undergo an optical path change dictated by the stress field. The change of the optical path is caused by the variation of the thickness and refractive index as the specimen is subjected to loading. Under stress gradients resulting around geometrical disconti-nuities, the reflected or transmitted rays generate an envelope in the form of a highly illuminated three-dimensional surface in space. When this surface is intersected by a reference screen, a bright curve, the so-called caustic curve, is formed. In the case of transparent materials three caustics are formed. They are created by the light rays reflected from the front and rear surfaces and by the rays that are transmitted through the specimen. In the case of opaque materials only one caustic is formed by the light rays as they are reflected by the specimen surface. The dimensions of the caustic are quantitatively related to the state of affairs near the geometrical discontinuity and they can therefore be used for the determination of the stress concentration or stress intensity factor.

For the case of a through crack in an opaque plate subjected to mode-I loading the stress intensity factor K_{Iopt} is given by[2,3]

$$K_{Iopt} = \frac{E D^{5/2}}{10.71 (1 - k) z_0 v t} \qquad (12)$$

798

where D is the maximum transverse caustic diameter formed by the reflected rays and z_0 is the distance between the specimen and the viewing screen where the caustic is formed. The triaxiality factor k was defined in equation (1).

The caustic is created from the light rays reflected from the points of the circumference of a circle (called the initial curve) which surrounds the crack tip. The radius r_0 of the initial curve is given by [2,3]

$$r_0 = \left[\frac{(1-k)v|z_0|K_I}{1.671 E} \right]^{2/5} = 0.316 D \qquad (13)$$

Equation (13) indicates that the radius r_0 of the initial curve, which actually is the generatrix curve of the caustic, depends on material properties (Poisson's ratio and modulus of elasticity), the thickness of the specimen, the distance between the specimen and the viewing screen on which the caustic is formed, the applied load and crack length as they are expressed by the stress intensity factor and the triaxiality factor k. The radius of the initial curve can be changed by changing any one of the above parameters.

In order to study the extent of the three-dimensional region around the crack tip, caustics were created from different initial curves. The size of the initial curve can be adjusted by providing specific values to the parameters in eq. (2). For a given specimen geometry, material and load, the size of the initial curve depends only on the distance z_0 between the specimen and the viewing screen. By varying z_0 the radius r_0 of the initial curve can be varied accordingly. Furthermore, r_0 can be varied by varying the specimen thickness, load and crack length. To prevent the influence of plastic deformation on the obtained caustics, r_0 should be kept significantly larger than the plastic zone. This can be verified by checking the geometrical dimensions of the caustic. Caustics generated from the elastic region have a characteristic epicycloid form [2,3]. On the other hand, deviations from the epicycloid are detected when the caustic is formed from the region inside the plastic zone. By measuring the transverse diameter of the caustic obtained for different values of the radius of the initial curve and using eq. (12) the opening mode stress intensity factor (K_{Iopt}) is found in terms of the triaxiality factor k. On the other hand the theoretical value of the stress intensity factor K_{Ith} for the double cantilever beam specimen is calculated by [8]

$$K_{Ith} = \frac{2\sqrt{3}P}{t\sqrt{h}}(a/h + 0.64) \qquad (14)$$

where P is the applied concentrated load and h=12.5 mm is half height of the specimen. The triaxiality factor k is then determined from the condition

$$K_{Iopt} = K_{Ith} \qquad (15)$$

RESULTS

Figures 3-6 present the variation of the triaxiality factor k versus t_0/t for four different thicknesses t=3.0, 5.5, 8.0 and 12.5 mm of the double cantilever beam specimens studied in the present work. For all specimens the triaxiality factor k decreases from a value close to one as the crack tip is approached to zero at a critical distance r_c from the tip. This means that the state of stress changes from plane strain at the tip to plane stress at a distance r_c. Between these two extreme conditions the state of stress is three-dimensional. The critical distance r_c at which the three-dimensional state of stress smooths out to plane stress changes with the

specimen thickness. Thus, at a specimen thickness t=3 mm $r_c \approx 0.7t$, at t=5.5 mm $r_c \approx 0.65t$, at t=8.0 mm $r_c \approx 0.5t$ and t=12.5 mm $r_c \approx 0.37t$. These results further refine the general conclusion of Rosakis and Ravi-Chandar[2] according to which "plane strain conditions prevail at distances from the crack tip which are larger than half of the specimen thickness" ($r_0/t > 0.5$). According to the results of this investigation plane stress conditions dominate at distances from the crack tip greater than half the specimen thickness for thin specimens and smaller than half the specimen thickness for thick specimens.

These findings indicate that special care should be taken when the method of caustics which is usually based on the condition of plane stress is used to determine stress intensity factors in crack problems. For the correct evaluation of the caustics the generatrix curve of the caustics, the so-called initial curve, should lie in the region where plane stress conditions dominate. This has an implication on the selection of the material and dimensions of the specimen, the applied load and the geometry of the optical arrangement. It can be shown that the condition the initial curve to lie in the plane stress region is not satisfied and the interpretation of caustics is not correct for large specimen thicknesses, small applied loads, small distances between the specimen and the reference screen and large magnification factors of the optical arrangement. On the contrary, the applied load should be high enough, the specimen thickness small, the distance between the specimen and the reference screen large and the magnification factor of the optical arrangement small. The experimentalist should properly select all these factors to correctly apply the method of caustics in crack problems.

CONCLUSIONS

The three-dimensionality of the stress field in the neighborhood of the tip of a through crack in a plate was studied by the method of caustics. The main results of the present study may be summarized as follows:

1. The state of stress in the neighborhood of the crack tip changes from plane strain at the tip to plane stress at a critical distance r_c from the tip. Between these two extreme stress conditions the state of stress is three-dimensional.

2. An empirical triaxiality factor k related to the triaxial character of the stress field in the vicinity of the crack tip was introduced. The variation of k along the crack front was determined for various specimen thicknesses.

3. The critical distance from the crack tip r_c at which plane stress conditions dominate depends on the thickness of the plate. For thicknesses from 3 mm to 12.5 mm studied in the present investigation r_c varies between 0.70 and 0.37 times plate thickness.

4. When applying the method of caustics to determine stress intensity factors in crack problems special care should taken to ensure that the initial curve lies in the region where conditions of plane stress dominate.

5. The last conditions has an implication on the selection of the material and dimensions of the specimen, the applied load and the geometry of the optical arrangement. Generally speaking for the initial curve to lie in the plane stress region the applied load should be high enough, the specimen thickness small, the distance between the specimen and the

reference screen large and the magnification factor of the optical arrangement small.

REFERENCES

1. Levy, N., Marcal, P.V. and Rice, J.R., "Progress in three-dimensional elastic-plastic stress analysis for fracture mechanics". Nuclear Engng. Design, 17, 64-75, 1971.
2. Rosakis, A.J. and Ravi-Chandar, K., "On crack tip stress state: An experimental evaluation of three dimensional effects". Int. J. Solids Structures, 22, 121-134, 1986.
3. Meletis, E.I., Huang Weiji and Gdoutos, E.E., "A study of the three-dimensional region at crack tips by the method of caustics". Engng Fracture Mech., 39, 875-885, 1991.
4. Konsta-Gdoutos, M. and Gdoutos, E.E., "Some remarks on caustics in mode I stress intensity factor evaluation". Theor. Appl. Fracture Mech. (to appear).
5. Konsta-Gdoutos, M. and Gdoutos, E.E., "Limits of applicability of the method of caustics in crack problems". Engng Fracture Mech. (to appear).
6. Konsta-Gdoutos, M. and Gdoutos, E.E., "Guidelines for applying the method of caustics in crack problems". Experimental Techniques, 16,26-28, 1992.
7. Rosakis, A.J., Zehnder, A.T. and Narasimhan, R., "Caustics by reflection and their application to elastic-plastic and dynamic fracture mechanics. Optical Engng, 27, 596-610, 1988.
8. Kanninen, M.F., "An augmented double cantilever beam model for studying crack propagation and arrest". Int. J. Fracture, 9, 83-91, 1973.

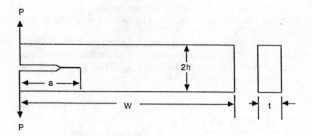

Fig. 1 Double cantilever beam specimen.

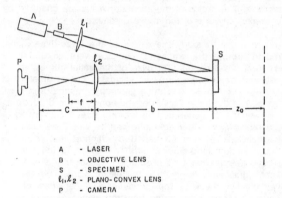

A - LASER
B - OBJECTIVE LENS
S - SPECIMEN
ℓ_1, ℓ_2 - PLANO-CONVEX LENS
P - CAMERA

Fig. 2 Optical arrangement for caustics.

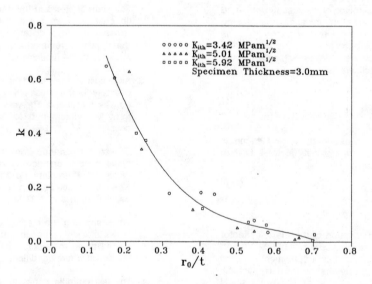

Fig. 3 Triaxiality factor k versus r_0/t for t=3.0 mm.

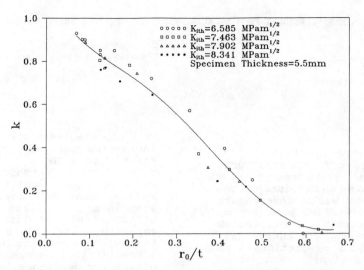

Fig. 4 Triaxiality factor k versus r_0/t for t=5.5 mm.

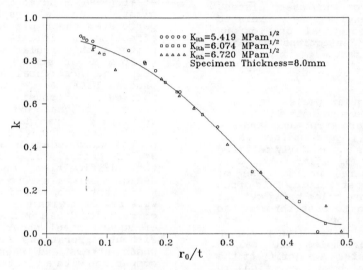

Fig. 5 Triaxiality factor k versus r_0/t for t=8.0 mm.

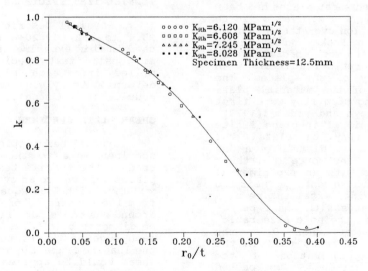

Fig. 6 Triaxiality factor k versus r_0/t for t=12.5 mm

EXPERIMENTAL RESULTS FROM BUCKLING BEHAVIOR OF STEEL SHEAR PLATES

P.Smith Neto
Departamento de Eng. Mecânica
U.F.U. – Uberlândia
38.400 – Uberlândia, MG, Brazil

S.F. Stiemer
Department of Civil Engineering
U.B.C. – Vancouver
V6T 1W5 – Vancouver, B.C, Canada.

ABSTRACT

Shear walls of large offshore structures are weakened by holes cut in them to allow the passage of services and equipment. The object of this project was to investigate experimentally the buckling behavior of steel square plates with circular holes in order to provide data for the verification of theoretical predictions. A finite element analysis had been previously performed to predict the ultimate load carrying capacity and buckling behaviour of such shear plates. The experimental results were correlated well with the theoretical predictions regarding lateral deflections and the critical buckling loads.

INTRODUCTION

Flat rectangular plates are very common structural component in modern buildings and offshore structures and are often subjected to a pure uniform shear stress. These plates are normally referred to as shear plates or shear webs. Cost effectiveness requires optimal use of space and weight of a structure. This often results in one or more holes being cut out of pipes or ducting to pass through the web and reduce the overall structural weight. These shear plates with plain or reinforced circular holes are called perforated shear plates. A majority of the work in this area has been theoretical in nature. Elastic in-plane stress analysis of square perforated shear plates has been done by Wang(1945), who applied a finite Airy's stress function over the domain of the plate. Studies by Rockey, Anderson and Cheung(1969) were the most informative as they combined theoretical analysis with experimental study of the plates. The combined effects of the material plasticity and buckling stability were first dealt with by Uenoya and Redwood(1978). Using a two dimensional in-plane finite element program they calculated the elastic-plastic stress distribution due to shear loading. They correlated their analytical results with an experimental study carried out concurrently. Their two part solution provided excellent results for perforated plates with small perforation. However, as the hole size ratio, D/b, became greater than 0.7, the restricted number of terms used in the Fourier series approximation of the deflected shape produced unexpected results.

For the clamped plate they found that by increasing the hole size, the ultimate elastic buckling capacity is increased rather than decreased, as had been expected. The results from Uenoya and Redwood shows that any circular perforation in a shear plate has a significant effect on the stability and ultimate load capacity of the plate. They also noted that with increasing hole size there is a considerable increase in the amount of plasticity developed in the plate before the ultimate capacity is reached. Martin et al.(1988) studied the ultimate elastic plastic buckling capacity of square perforated shear plates. The parameters affecting the ultimate capacity of square plates with circular perforations under uniform shear stress were investigated using the incremental structural analysis program NISA 83. In the present paper, particular emphasis was placed on the design of adequate experimental apparatus required for examination of the buckling and collapse behavior of square shear plates which contain openings. Outlines are the criteria of such an apparatus and the difficulties encountered during design. In the second part, experiments using that recommended testing procedures were realized with the purpose to generate correlation data for the buckling behavior of square steel shear plates (with and without perforations) subjected to uniform shear stress and thereby to enable a comparison with a finite element analysis.

TENSILE TEST SPECIMENS

Physical Description. 750mm x750mm x3.4 mm CSA G40.20-M steel plates were used in this experiments. Four 25 mm x 330 mm tensile test specimens were cut and milled from each plate in order to determine the yield strength and elastic modulus of the steel.

SHEAR PLATE SPECIMEN

Physical Description. The shear plate specimens were from the same material being used in the tensile test experiment. The plates were cut to an overall size of 650mm x 650 mm, with four square notches removed from the corners to provide a 75 mm strip around the edges for clamping. Eleven 12.7 mm diameter bolt holes were drilled along each edge of the plates for mounting in the loading frame(figure 1). Once clamped, shear would be applied on a 500 mm x500 mm test area of the plate.

The loading frame through which the shear was applied is shown in figures 4 and 5. In total, four specimens were tested, one without a hole and three with a hole. Plate#1 was a non-perforated plate, while plates #2, #3 and #4 had a 100 mm circular perforation located on the compression diagonal, on the tension diagonal, and at the center of the plate, respectively.

Instrumentation. The amount of instrumentation varied from plate to plate. Plate #1 had six rosette strain gauges placed along one of the loaded edges to determine whether uniform shear stress was being obtained in the plate. In addition, two rosette strain gauges were placed at the center of the plate, one on each side. Lateral deflections of the plate were monitored by three Linear Voltage Displacement Transducer (LVDTs) located on the compression diagonal, the tension diagonal, and at the center of the hole. The locations and numbering of the strain rosettes and LVDTs are shown in figure 3. Plates #2 and #3 had two rosette strain gauges located at the centers of the plate, one on each side as shown in figure 2. Furthermore, three strain gauges were placed around the inside of the holes. Three LVDTs were located at the same points on the plates as on Plate #1(figure6).

Steel Plate Design. During the planning of the test specimen and frame assembly, a variety of parameters had to be considered, which will be outlined below. In designing the test specimen, the first consideration taken into account was its size. Requirements included sufficient area to allow cutting of the corners, drilling of bolt holes, placement of deflection gauges and adequate working area. A large plate was desired to reduce the scaling effect involved when scaling results up to actual circumstances. It was also necessary, though, to keep the plate small enough to be easy to handle and work with. The plate thickness had to allow for sufficient deformation, yet not buckle prematurely. The result was a plate of 650mm x 650mm x 4mm. Also considered, was the necessity for the plate to be made of high strength steel so as to reduce the possibility of local yield before failure. Considerations dealt with the specimen design. During design of the specimen and the framing apparatus, a number of options were considered. In coming up with final plan, many calculations were needed. The first step in the design process involved the examination of the apparatus used by Rockey, Anderson and Cheng(1969), and that proposed by Jackson(1984). Upon analysis, based on material strength, a simple design, similar to that of Rockey, was considered. This analysis including finding the theoretical forces and determining the ability of the frame to

be a mechanism which would produce pure shear forces on the plate. The used criterion was that the clamping device had a rigidity of approximately 10 times that of the shear plate. This was to ensure that the boundaries remain rigid while the specimen buckled. Calculations, based on bending and torsional rigidities were made to ensure that this was achieved. To ensure that no compressional or tensile forces were transferred to the plate, the center of the pins had to be positioned directly over the corner of the testing area of the plate. These forces would result from the angular displacements, up to 15 degrees, that would accompany the plate deformations during loading. It was in this respect that fault was found with Rockey's design and necessitated the use of fillers to raise the boundary clamps as per Jackson's proposal. To allow for the expected angular displacements, the corners of the specimen were cut and the pins moved directly over these new corners. The next concern was to ensure that the plate areas near the pin were properly traced. This was prevented material from being pulled out or pushed in under the pins at the corners during deformation. It was required the bolts be positioned as close as possible to the corner without interfering with the angular displacement of the plate and the hinge. This problem was satisfied lifting the boundary clamps and countersinking holes for the bolts in the "B" filler. The stability at the corners of the assembly was also questioned. To improve the stability and help maintain alignment of the assembly during testing, it was decided that one continuous pin should be used rather than two separate plugs. The pin was designed to withstand double shear above and below the reduced section. Also spacing and edge distance requirements allowed a maximum of eleven bolts. The final point of interest was that of gripping by the machine onto the mounting arms. Calculations concerning this possibility using wedge clamps were carried out assuming that friction was negligible and the distributions of stresses was even. The maximum forces on the arm were found for both shear and compression. An element from the smaller dimension side of the arm was analyzed using Tresca failure criterion. The arm was found to have adequate factored bearing and shear resistance. Specific instructions include drilling for the holes through the plate while in arranged position to ensure alignment and that holes be drilled with adequate diameter for one-half inch bolts. Extensive study was done to ensure that the assembly provided adequate strength, stability and rotational mobility.

ANALYSIS

The mean value of the elastic modulus was determined to be 185.36 GPa, with a coefficient of variation of 3.25%. The rather high coefficient of variation substantiates the anisotropic characteristic of the elastic modulus, since the four tensile test specimens from each plate were cut parallel to one edge of the plate. The mean value for the yield stress was found to be 364.11 MPa with a coefficient of variation of 2.26%.

Lateral Plate Deflections. Under continuous loading, lateral plate deflections eventually increased to an order of magnitude of the plate thickness. At this level of post buckling, both bending and stretching of the middle surface of the plate must be considered in the analysis of the plate. For lateral deflections larger than the plate thickness, tensile stresses in the middle of the plate have the benefitial effect of stiffening the plate. This behavior is observed in figure 7 and figure 8 for non-perforated and perforated plates, respectively.

Figure 7 compares lateral deflections at the center of a non-perforated plate between the test specimen and the ideal plate. The ideal plate is the result of a finite element analysis using the same material properties as the test specimen. The variations between the curves are mainly due to the geometrical imperfections in the specimen. Small geometrical imperfections in the test specimen caused deflections to develop from the commencement of loading and hence caused non linearities as the critical load was approached. However, the beneficial effects of in-plane stiffening were retained in the presence of imperfections. This is illustrated in figure 8 where the experimental results extended above the 270 kN elastic buckling load to approximately 420 kN, at which point the limit of the testing apparatus was reached. Figure 8 shows the lateral deflection curves for the three perforated plates. As all plates had equals holes diameters, the variation in strength was due to the hole locations. After buckling had began, all the load was carried by a tension field in the plate. The largest reduction of capacity was expected to take place in the plate with the hole located in this area. This was observed with plates #3 and #4. Plate #2, with the unsymmetric hole location (15 degrees off the tensile axis) was the strongest. Plate #4, with the hole at the center, was the weakest. All three plates displayed similar load deformation behavior. Figure 8 shows three distinct regions of buckling behavior: elastic, elasto-plastic and plastic. The elastic buckling range ended at approximately 2mm

of lateral deflection and 210 kN of applied tensile force. Beyond deflections of 2mm, the slope of the curves decreased until approximately 8mm of deflection. This increase in lateral deflection per unit load indicated the elasto-plastic range. After deflections of 8mm, the slopes of the curves were almost horizontal. This indicated the plastic range in which the deformations increased dramatically with only a minor increase in load.

The presence of perforations in the plates cause larger lateral deflections at any applied load, as witnessed by comparing deflections of non-perforated and perforated plates in figure 8. This observation is anticipated due to the imperfections in metallic crystal created by the perforations. The imperfections (line defects) are significant when the metallic crystals are plastically deformed under shear stresses. These line defects cause the metal crystals to be more ductile than would be possible in their absence. Compared to the non-perforated plate, the larger deflections and lower ultimate shear stresses for the perforated plates are similar to the findings of a computer analysis of a simply supported plate by Martin et allie (1988). The analytical simply supported plate and the clamped test specimen both reveal that when the lateral displacement are small, the material behaves elastically. Also, above the critical load, the displacements continue to increase very rapidly with only a small increase in applied load. Figure 8 indicates that the plate stiffens after initial buckling and can still carry more load. The results of the elastic-plastic buckling capacity are shown in figure 10. The capacities are normalized to the concentrically perforated plate's elastic-plastic capacity. The values of shear stresses for the normalization process are not the ultimate capacities, but are shear stress values taken at an arbitrary lateral deflection of 12 mm where the load deflection curves are essentially constant. Figure 10 reveals that the concentrically perforated plate provides a lower bound for the capacity of a plate with a hole in any of the three locations indicated. It can be seen that these results resemble the results obtained from Martin's finite element analysis(1988). The finite element results are reproduced on figure 10 for comparison. The three different experimental hole locations reveal that the elastic-plastic buckling load was increased if the hole was moved from the plate tension diagonal to the compression diagonal. The largest load increase was obtained for Plate #2 (hole at 105 degrees from horizontal) with a 17.5% increase over the plate with the concentric hole. Furthermore, the concentric hole provides the lowest elastic-plastic buckling capacity of the three perforated plates. From Figure 10 it is observed that the non-perforated plate exhibits the upper limit of the load capacities when compared to the perforated plates. Based on figure 9, a similar plot of perforated plate capacities can be obtained, where the shear stress values of the perforated plates are normalized to the shear stress of the non-perforated plate. It is interesting to note that the perforated plate with the concentric hole has 76.5% of the capacity of a non-perforated plate.

Shear Stress. The results of the measurements made by the six strain rosettes are shown in figure 9. It shows the ratio of the maximum shear stress measured at a strain rosette location to the applied shear stress plotted as a function of the applied tensile load.

It can be seen that the maximum shear stress is approximately equal to the applied shear stress (ie.ratio approximately equal to one) up to a load of approximately 400 kN. At around 400 kN, the ratio starts to increase very rapidly and depending on the rosette location, the maximum shear stress increases up to twelve times the applied shear stress. Since the maximum shear stress depends on the measured strains, a large increase in the maximum shear stress, therefore, implies a large increase in the strains at the rosette location. Furthermore, the increase in the maximum shear stress occurs over a small load interval. Thus, the plate edge undergoes large increase in strains with only small increases in load, indicating that yielding of the plate edge is occurring.

CONCLUSIONS

The following conclusions may be drawn from these results:
1. The non-perforated plate exhibits the upper limit of the load capacities when compared to the perforated plates.
2. The elastic-plastic buckling capacities increase away from the tension diagonal. This representation allows the designer to determine the loss in capacity of the shear plate once a perforation is introduced.
3. The perforated plate with concentric hole has 76.5% of the capacity of a non-perforated plate. The theoretical analysis for this project modelled the plates subject to uniform shear stress along the edges. The loading mechanism was designed to produce the same conditions. The results indicate that the loading mechanism produced relatively uniform shear stress. The values of maximum shear stress obtained from Rosettes#1-#5 were approximately equal, within +/- 12%. Only values from Rosette #6 were significantly different. However, Rosette #6 was located

close to an imperfection,consisting of overlapping bolt holes. Larger amounts of deformations were observed at this bolt location in the tested specimens than at other bolt holes. The localized slip would account for the lower shear stress. The maximum shear strain increased linearly for all six locations until the plate was subject to approximately 270 kN. At this load, inelastic buckling started and shear strains increased non-linearly. Rosettes #1 and #2, located close to the center on both sides of plate, measured uniform shear strains until inelastic buckling began. The differences in shear stress on either side of the plate were due to initial imperfections. The shear strains were monitored until the gauges delaminated at approximately >400 kN due to large buckling deformations.It can be seen that these experimental results resemble the results obtained from finite element analysis. The three different experimental hole locations reveal that the elastic-plastic buckling load was increased if the hole was moved from the plate tension diagonal to the compression diagonal.

ACKNOWLEDGEMENTS

The financial support received from the National Science & Engineering Research Council of Canada and CAPES-Coordenação de Aperfeiçoamento de Pessoal de Nivel Superior of Brazil is acknowledged.

REFERENCES

* Martin,A.,Stiemer,S.F. And Osterrieder P.,"Ultimate Load Capacity of Square Shear Plates with Circular Perforations", Canadian Journal of Civil Engineering,Volume 15,Number3, 1988.
* Rockey,K.C.,Anderson,R.G.,and Cheng,Y.K."The Behavior of Square Shear Webs Having a Circular Hole", Symp. On Thin Walled Steel Structures, University College of Swansea,Crosby Lockwood and Sons Ltd.1969,pp.148-169.
* Uenoya.M. And Redwood,R.G."Elasto-Plastic Shear Buckling of Square Plates with Circular Holes",Computers and Structures,Vol.8,pp.291-300,Pergamon Press Ltd.,1978.
* Wang,Chu-Kia."Theoretical Analysis of Perforated Shear Webs",presented at a meeting of the ASME Cincinnati Section-,Cincinnati, Ohio Oct.2-3,1945.
* Jackson,D.A.,"Testing Apparatus Proposal",University of British Columbia,Vancouver,B.C,1988.
* VanVlack, L.H., "Elements of Materials Science and Engineering",University of Michigan,Michigan,1959.

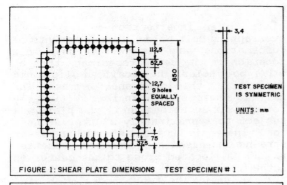

FIGURE 1: SHEAR PLATE DIMENSIONS   TEST SPECIMEN # 1

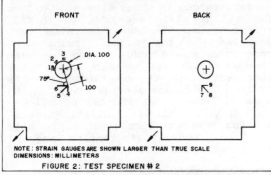

FIGURE 2: TEST SPECIMEN # 2

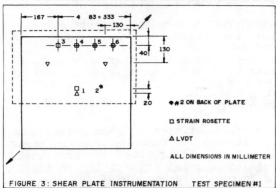

FIGURE 3: SHEAR PLATE INSTRUMENTATION   TEST SPECIMEN #1

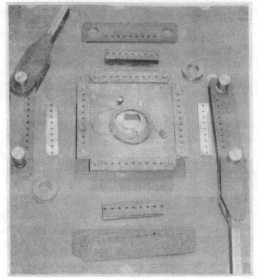

FIGURE 4: TEST APPARATUS AND SHEAR PLATE SPECIMEN.

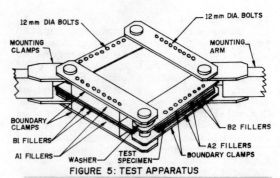

FIGURE 5: TEST APPARATUS

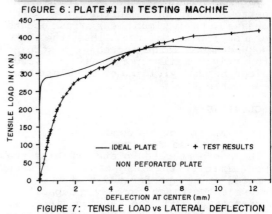

FIGURE 6: PLATE#1 IN TESTING MACHINE

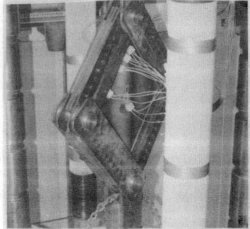

FIGURE 7: TENSILE LOAD vs LATERAL DEFLECTION

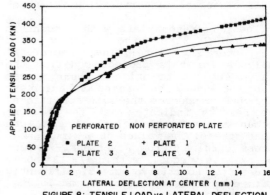

FIGURE 8: TENSILE LOAD vs LATERAL DEFLECTION

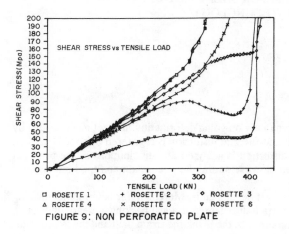

FIGURE 9: NON PERFORATED PLATE

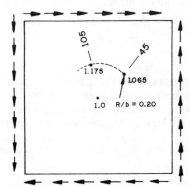

ELASTIC-PLASTIC CAPACITY FOR VARIOUS HOLE LOCATIONS NORMALIZED
TO CONCENTRIC HOLE'S ELASTIC-PLASTIC BUCKLING CAPACITY
EXPERIMENTAL RESULT

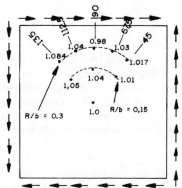

ULTIMATE ELASTIC-PLASTIC CAPACITY FOR VARIOUS HOLE
LOCATIONS NORMALIZES TO THE CONCENTRIC HOLE ULTI-
MATE ELASTIC-PLASTIC BUCKLING CAPACITY.

FIGURE 10: ELASTIC-PLASTIC BUCKLING
CAPACITY

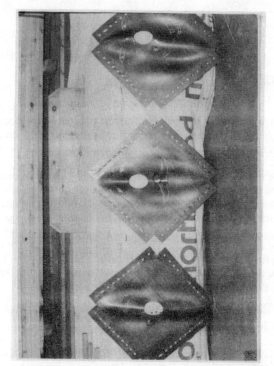

FIGURE 11: PLATE #2, #3 AND #4 AFTER TENSILE
TEXT

AN AUTOMATED DATA ACQUISITION SYSTEM FOR SHEET METAL TESTING USING IMAGE PROCESSING TECHNOLOGY

J. H. Kim and N. Bay

ABSTRACT

An automatic, on-line system has been developed registering the continuously on-going deformation in sheet metal testing by image processing technology. The test surface is provided with a grid and the grid distortion is registered by a CCD camera applying a frame grabber and a personal computer. The registered distortion is analysed and distributions of the principal strains in size and direction are calculated as well as the accumulated effective strain, the strain path and the limit strains.

The system is applied to tensile testing and the double blank stretching test developed by Marciniak for determining forming limit diagrams. In tensile testing the typical shift from a ho-mogenous strain distribution to local necking is clearly indicated. In the double blank stretching test performed with different initial geometries of the blank the strain path and the limit strains are determined and the deviations from a linear strain path discovered.

The system works on an AT-type personal computer with a rather small storage capacity and calculation speed thereby limiting the test velocity and range. However, today access to more powerful personal computers is already easy and cheap to obtain thereby making it possible to overcome these problems. Specifications on the necessary demands for a more operative system are given.

INTRODUCTION

Analyses of sheet metal formability estimating the forming limit diagrams imply detailed studies of the strain distribution in the testpiece during deformation. Such analyses require a large amount of data to be measured and processed. The conventional way to handle this problem is by providing the test surface with a grid, stepwise deform the workpiece, photograph the deformed grid after each step and measure the deformed grid in a measuring microscope [1,2]. Manual operation of these routines is very timeconsuming and therefore restricted to local, rather small regions and in a limited number of steps. It may, furthermore, cause introduction of errors. Development of an image processing technique would make it possible to carry out more detailed analyses with less risk of mistakes.

Recent development and applications of image processing technology for studies of strain distributions in metal forming has shown the good potentials of this technique. At the Institute of Manufacturing Engineering, Technical University of Denmark, Glibbery [3] has developed an automated method for the analysis of geometry, flow and strain distribution in true 3-D model experiments. Others [4-6] have developed image processing systems for the study of sheet metal forming after deformation has been carried out. The present paper describes the development and application of an image processing system applicable for analysing the on-going deformation in sheet metal testing.

DEVELOPMENT OF SYSTEM

Grid

In order to study the local deformation the workpiece was provided with a grid consisting of circular spots ø 1.7 mm arranged in a square grid with 5.0 mm spacing, Fig. 1. The grid was applied manually by painting using a sheet template provided with holes drilled in it. The template was placed on top of the test specimen and the grid was painted on the workpiece surface with a water-proof color pencil. As seen in Fig. 1 the position and contour is not very accurate adopting this method and a better solution would be to apply electrochemical or photochemical etching techniques but accuracy of the position of the points is not of large importance using the image processing technique since the actual position of each spot and its movements in time is registered.

Dr. J. H. Kim is assistant professor at Dept. of Die and Mould Design, Seoul National Polytechnic University, 172 Kongnung-Dong, Nowon-Gu, Seoul 139-242, Korea and Dr. N. Bay is associate professor at the Inst. of Manuf. Engn., Bldg. 425, Technical University of Denmark, 2800 Lyngby, Denmark.

The present research work was carried out at the Technical University of Denmark during Dr. J. H. Kim's stay there as post-doctoral researcher 1990-91.

Image processing system

Before and during deformation images of the grid are captured by a CCD video camera. These images are digitized by a frame grabber installed in a personal computer (IBM compatible type AT). Focal length of the camera is approximately 500 mm and the resolution is 604×576 pixels. The frame grabber has a spatial resolution of 512×512 pixels with an intensity resolution of 256 grey tones. The digitized image is represented on a 13" color monitor with the same resolution 512×512 pixels. Fig. 2 shows the set-up for double blank stretching tests.

After each frame is grabbed, the threshold value separating the black spots from the background of the image is determined. In the computer vision system applied each pixel occupies an 8-bit byte which can store 256 grey levels. In this case the computer needs a memory size of 512×512 = 262.144 bytes for storing the entire screen image. In the planned multistage operations accumulating the results determined in each step the amount of data is too comprehensive to handle on an AT-type personal computer without data compression during operation.

When each frame has been grabbed the image is therefore operated on by shrink and expand algorithms to eliminate noise after which the centroids of the deformed spots are calculated as representative nodal points in the grid. The coordinates of the nodal points are stored for further processing and the system is now ready to grab the next image calculating the strains after the whole deformation procedure has been carried out. The various programmes developed for these operations are all programmed in C-language. The described procedure makes stepwise analysis possible without requiring a large memory capacity in the computer.

Fig. 3 shows an example of the estimated nodal points indicated with crosses in the centroids of the spots. This image is presented with pseudo color overlays on the monitor.

Calculation of strains

Calculation of the size and direction of the principal strains are carried out both stepwise and linearly (assuming a co-axial strain path) for comparison of the two methods. The calculations are based on the coefficient method developed by Bredendick[7]. This method utilizes the coordinates of a quadrilateral element in the analysis in order to eliminate the effect of element rotation and has proven to give better results than the commonly adopted circle grid technique[8].

APPLICATION OF SYSTEM

The system has been applied to two types of sheet metal tests, i.e. uniaxial tensile testing and the double blank stretching test. The results of these investigations are described below.

Test material

The test material was 1.0 mm deep drawing steel DIN St1403m. The mechanical properties of the material was measured by tensile testing performed on specimens cut out 0°, 45° and 90° with respect to the rolling direction. An average expression for the stress strain curve was estimated as:

$$\sigma_0 = 552.8 \times (0.0028 + \epsilon)^{0.21} \quad [N/mm^2]$$

The normal and plane anisotropies were estimated to be:

$$R = 1.305$$

$$\Delta R = 0.593$$

The geometry of the specimens for the two series of experiments is shown in Fig. 4.

Tensile test

The system was first tested in a simple well-known test, the uniaxial tensile test. An example of a grid pattern before and after deformation is shown in Fig. 1. Workpieces of dimensions 300×80×1.0 mm were provided with a grid array of 13×11 circular spots, covering a test area of 60×50 mm in the initial state. Placing the CCD camera in a distance of 400 mm from the workpiece surface allowed registration of the whole test area during the entire test. An image with 107 and 149 pixels per 30 mm surface length was obtained in the x- and y-direction respectively. This corresponds to a spatial resolution of 0.28 and 0.20 mm per pixel respectively.

The execution time calculating the coordinates of the nodal points by the image analysis developed was approximately 30 secs. in each step. The total time per deformation step to accomplish an image of the deformed grid including image grabbing, thresholding, freezing, selecting image boundaries, shrinking and expanding for image enhancement and finally calculating the nodal point positions and storing these data was 45 secs. The test speed, 5 mm/min, was chosen as slow as possible thereby enabling capture and processing of 6-8 images in each test, the limitation being set by the time needed for the analysis between each step of image grabbing.

Fig. 5 shows the grid before deformation and at two different steps of deformation, just before and just after the onset of necking. The accumulated effective strain of each element is indicated too. The homogeneous strain distribution below the point of instability is clearly noticed and so is the highly inhomogeneous deformation after necking has occurred. Maximum strain is seen to be localized in the center of the neck as to be expected. The strain is here larger than 0.80 whereas the instability strain is seen to be in the range 0.24-0.38 (the strain outside the local necking).

Fig. 6 shows in the left hand part the strain path and the measured limit strain of the element having maximum effective strain in the tensile test. The right hand part shows the accumulated effective strain adopting a linear and an incremental method of calculation. The linear method of calculation based on the assumption of a co-axial strain path uses only the initial and final position of the nodal points whereas the incremental method calculates the accumulated strain by a stepwise procedure summing up the incremental strain in each deformation step in order to obtain the total strain. It is noticed that the strain calculated by the linear method results in slightly lower values than by the incremental method. The difference is however very small in this case where the material is deformed monotonically along an almost linear strain path.

Double blank stretching test

The double blank stretching test is developed by Marciniak[1]. It is a general test for determining the Forming Limit Diagrams (FLD) for sheet material. Two blanks are used in each experiment, a test blank and a dummy blank, the latter provided with a central hole, Fig. 4. The test blank is placed on top of the dummy and both are securely clamped along their edges, see Fig. 7. When the ringformed punch is moved upwards the central part of the test plate is stretched. The hole in the dummy is essential to facilitate stretching of the central part of the test blank over the punch thereby suppressing a circumferential fracture which would otherwise occur at the punch periphery at an early stage of the process. The dummy is therefore often referred to as the driving blank.

The circular punch of Fig. 7 will produce equi-biaxial deformation but the double blank stretch testing technique has been extended to cover strain ratios in the range $0 < \varepsilon_{min}/\varepsilon_{max} \leq 1$ by application of elliptical punches and similarly shaped dies with different aspect ratios[9]. Another approach which has proven useful is that of using only one circular punch to determine the entire forming limit curve, $-\frac{1}{2} \leq \varepsilon_{min}/\varepsilon_{max} \leq 1$ [10-14]. In this case straining conditions with strain ratios less than 1 are produced using blanks with outcuts on the two sides, $W < 250$ mm in Fig. 4. This approach was adopted in the present experiments using tools developed by Rasmussen[13].

A main advantage of the double blank stretching test is that the testpiece remains flat during stretching resulting in true in-plane deformation. Filming of the deforming surface during testing is possible and the result will be an undistorted image of the actual deformations. Fig. 8 shows test samples after deformation till fracture has occurred. In order to obtain different strain paths tests were carried out with the following width of the test blank: W = 90, 150, 190, 210 and 250 mm, Fig. 4. The specimen of width 250 mm has the shape of a regular octagon and is stretched equi-biaxially.

The test blanks were provided with a grid array of 6×6 spots covering a test area of 25×25 mm in the initial state. During testing this area is expanding. Placing the CCD camera in a distance of 200 mm from the workpiece surface allowed registration of the whole test area during the entire test. An image with a spatial resolution of 0.107 and 0.148 mm per pixel in the x- and y-direction respectively was obtained. The speed of the punch was chosen to be 5 mm/min enabling 6-8 images to be grabbed and processed during testing as in the tensile test experiments.

Fig. 9 shows the principal strains as they develop during deformation determined according to the two different basic calculation methods, i.e. the linear and the incremental method. The discrepancy between the two curves are due to the non-linear strain path which is especially pronounced in case of large strain ratios. This is due to increasing amount of rotation of the principal strain direction during deformation. Table 1 shows the angle of rotation registered on the maximum strained element for the five different aspect ratios of the test blanks applied. The reason for the increased amount of rotation with increasing strain ratio is the decreasing amount of constraint dictated by the specimen geometry leaving possibilities for the deformation to adjust to anisotropy and local inhomogenities. In biaxial stretching the geometry forces no constraint, in uniaxial tension the specimen geometry forces maximum constraint on the deformation behaviour. From Fig. 9 it is noticed that the ratio between minor and major strain is changing considerably when the initial ratio is about 0 (W = 190 mm) indicating a non-linear strain path.

width length [mm]	90 250	150 250	190 250	210 250	250 250
angle of rotation [degs.]	2.7	3.4	9.8	31.3	54.5

Table 1: Relationship between specimen geometry (deformation path) and angle of rotation of principal directions during deformation.

Neither of the two methods of strain calculation adopted are correct but may be applied as approximate solutions. In the following the linear method is applied when calculating the principal strains. As regards to calculation of the accumulated effective strains the stepwise incremental method is allowed. The difference between the two methods are, however, small in this case, see Fig. 10.

Figs. 11a and b show the strain path of a number of neighbouring elements in a biaxial stretching experiment (W = 250 mm). Four elements were selected in longitudinal and in transverse direction and among these the element of maximum strain. The relationship between the two principal strains of the different elements appear rather uniform for all elements with small scatter. Similar results were obtained for other strain paths[15].

The limit strains were determined as the principal strains in the maximum deformed element when local necking or fracture had occurred. They can be read from Fig. 9 as the end points of the solid curves. Fig. 12 shows the limit strains for the five different strain paths analysed in the present study. Two of them are coinciding. For comparison the forming limit diagrams obtained by Kleemola and Kumpulainen[11] and Rasmussen[14] are shown for similar material adopting the same test method. Some discrepancy is found between the three investigations. This may be due to deviations in material properties and uncertainties connected with the determination of the limit strains. In order to ensure a reliable FLD-curve it should be based on more experiments and a refined grid providing a better resolution.

DISCUSSIONS AND CONCLUSIONS

The system has proven to work satisfactory giving reliable data on grid distortion, strain distributions and limit strains. However, limitations were set by the limited calculation speed and storage capacity of the computer, an IBM compatible type AT. The latter made it necessary to process each image determining the representative nodal points before grabbing the next image. The time necessary to grab an image and store it on the hard disk of the AT type computer applied was approximately 1 sec. and 4 secs. respectively, i.e. 5 secs. all in all, whereas it took 45 secs. to grab an image, compress and process the data and store the nodal point coordinates of the 13×11 grid applied in the tensile test. This explains the low test speed adopted (5mm/min.).

A more powerful computer with a larger storage capacity would make it possible to store all images as grabbed and carry out the data processing after deformation. A grabbed image of 512×512 pixels requires about 260 kbytes. In the present study the compressed and processed data representing the coordinates of the nodal points required about 3.5 kbytes per image of the 13×11 grid applied in the tensile test and 0.8 kbytes per image of the 6×6 grid applied in the double blank stretching test. The total memory size necessary if all images should be grabbed before processing would be N×260 kbytes where N is the number of images grabbed in each test. Modern personal computers with a 386 or a 486 processor and a larger memory capacity (40 Mbytes or more) would be suitable for this procedure. This would allow for storage of all the images as grabbed, not processing until after the test had been carried out.

The faster PC-processor would furthermore make it possible to run the test with a higher, more realistic deformation speed. In the double blank stretching test the punch travel was of the order of 50 mm. A realistic speed of the punch comparable to normal industrial conditions would be at least 1 mm/sec. With 5 secs. all in all for grabbing and storing an image this would allow grabbing of 10 images which is somewhat less than appropriate for a good formability test where 15 images would be more convenient. A personal computer with a 386 or 486 processor would however easily manage to grab and store 15 images in 50 secs.

The grid chosen in the present analysis was noticed to be rather large limiting the accuracy in strain estimation. This is especially important when estimating the limit strains since the strain gradients near local necking and cracks are large and the chosen grid size will heavily influence the limit strain estimation. For the present investigations a grid size of ø 0.8-1.0 mm spots in a 2.5-3.0 mm square grid array would be more appropriate than the one applied which had ø 1.7 mm spots in a 5×5 mm grid. An improved spatial resolution of the image analyzer of 2-4 times would also be desirable.

ACKNOWLEDGEMENT

The authors would like to acknowledge Dr. Stephen Glibbery for his help during development of the software and Mr. Søren Lassen for his help in the experimental work.

REFERENCES

1. Marciniak,Z. and Kuczynski, K. "Limit strains in the processes of stretch-forming sheet metal". Int. J. Mech. Sci., 9, 609-620, 1967.
2. Tadros, A. and Mellor, P.B. "An experimental study of the in-plane stretching of sheet metal". Int. J. Mech. Sci., 20, 121-134, 1978.
3. Glibbery, S. "3-D strain determination using model material and image processing techniques". Proc. 9th Int. Conf. on Experimental Mechanics, Copenhagen, Aug. 1990, 198-207.
4. Fujimori, N. "Microcomputer-aided analytic method for VTR images of two dimensional plastic deformation". Proc. 1st. Int. Conf. on Technology of Plasticity: "Adv. Technol. of Plasticity", Tokyo, Sept. 1984, 1, 327-332.
5. Schedin, E. and Melander, A. "The evaluation of large strains from industrial sheet metal stampings with a square grid method". J. Applied Metalworking, 4, no. 2, 143-156, 1986.
6. Vogel, J.H. and Lee, D. "An automated two-view method for determining strain distributions on deformed surfaces". J. Materials Shaping Technology, 6, no. 4, 205-216, 1989.
7. Bredendick, F. "Visioplastische Deformations- und Spannungsermittlung". Die Technik, 24, 247-251, 1969.
8. Danckert, J. and Wanheim, T. "The use of a square grid as an alternative to a circular grid in the determination of strains". J. Mech. Work. Techn., 3, 5-15, 1979.
9. Marciniak, Z., Kuczynski, K and Pokora, K. "Influence of the plastic properties of a material on the forming limit diagram for sheet metal in tension". Int. J. Mech. Sci., 15, 789-805, 1973.
10. Hecker, S.S. "Sheet stretching experiments". Paper in: Armen, H. and Jones, R.F. Jr. (ed.): ASME Ann. Winter Meet. San Francisco, Dec. 1978, 85-94.
11. Kleemola, H.J. and Kumpulainen, J.O. "Factors influencing the forming limit diagram: Part I - The experimental determination of the forming limits of sheet steel". J. Mech. Work. Techn., 3, 289-302, 1980.
12. Gronostajski, J. and Dolny, A. Determination of forming limit curves by means of Marciniak punch". Memoires Scientifiques Revue Metallurgie, 1980, 570-578.
13. Rasmussen, S. Nytoft "Limit strains in sheet metal forming". M.Sc.-thesis, Techn. Univ. Denmark, Jan. 1981, Rep. No. MM-81.02.
14. Rasmussen, S.Nytoft "Theoretical prediction of strainpath dependence of limit strains in sheet materials". Ann. CIRP, 30, No. 1, 179-184, 1981.
15. Kim, J.H. "Development of an automated system for sheet metal testing using image processing technique". Rep. No. MM91.18, Techn. Univ. Denmark, Aug. 1991.

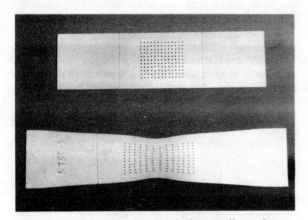

Fig. 1:   Specimen before and after tensile testing.

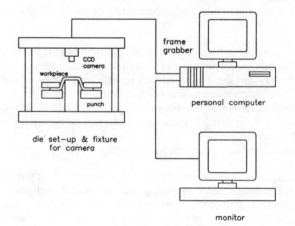

Fig. 2:   Experimental set-up for double blank stretching test.

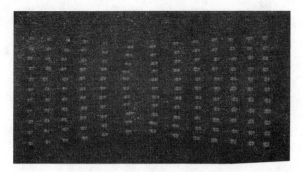

Fig. 3: Image on monitor showing the estimated nodal points.

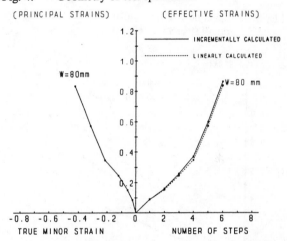

TEST	SPECIMENS	W or a * b (mm)
double blank stretching test	Ø 53 250 250 W	90 150 190 210 250
tensile test	b a	300 * 80 400 * 20

Fig. 4: Geometry of test specimens.

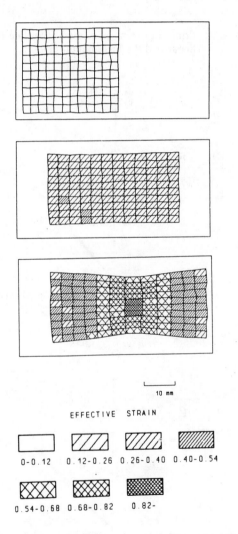

EFFECTIVE STRAIN

0-0.12	0.12-0.26	0.26-0.40	0.40-0.54

0.54-0.68	0.68-0.82	0.82-

Fig. 5: Deformed grid and strain distribution in tensile testing. a: no deformation, b: just below insta-bility, c: above instability.

(PRINCIPAL STRAINS)   (EFFECTIVE STRAINS)

INCREMENTALLY CALCULATED
LINEARLY CALCULATED

W=80mm   W=80 mm

TRUE MINOR STRAIN   NUMBER OF STEPS

Fig. 6: Strain path, limit strain and comparison of effective strains calculated linearly and incrementally.

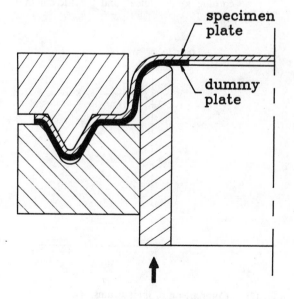

specimen plate

dummy plate

Fig. 7: Working principle of the double blank stretching test.

813

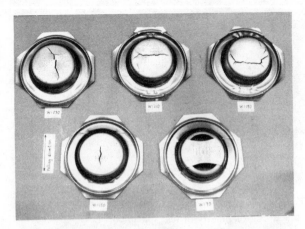

Fig. 8: Specimens after deformation in the double blank stretching test.

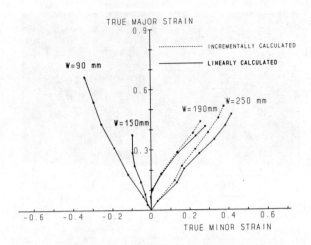

Fig. 9: Principal strains calculated according to the linear and the incremental method.

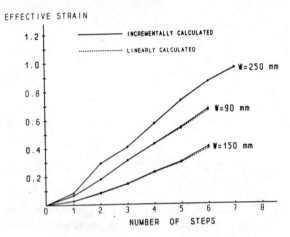

Fig. 10: Accumulated effective strains calculated according to the linear and the incremental method.

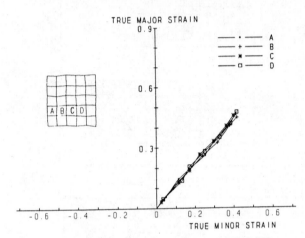

STRAIN HISTORY OF EACH ELEMENT ALONG THE ROW

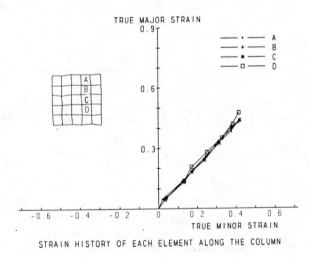

STRAIN HISTORY OF EACH ELEMENT ALONG THE COLUMN

Fig. 11: Strain paths of four neighbouring elements in longitudinal and transverse direction.

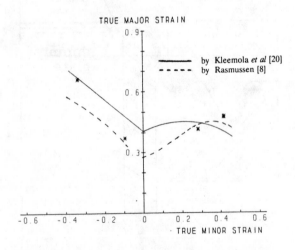

Fig. 12: Comparison of limit strains.

A Two-Dimensional Stress Analysis and Strength Evaluation of Band Adhesive Butt Joints Subjected to External Bending Moments

Toshiyuki SAWA ,Katsuhiro TEMMA and Tohru NISHIGAYA

ABSTRACT

The stresses and strength of band adhesive butt joints, in which the interfaces were bonded partially, were examined, when the joints of dissimilar adherends were subjected to external bending moments. Bending tests were performed. The joint strength were evaluated analytically. Analytical results were consistent with the experimental ones.

1. INTRODUCTION

Recently, due to the improvement in the properties of adhesive bonds adhesive joints have become increasingly used in mechanical structures. Adhesive joints have some advantages over mechanical joints in such areas as bolting and riveting, but structures which consist of adhesive joints have previously been designed empirically. It is a problem how to evaluate adhesive joint strength because of a large deviation in the joint strength. However, data is now available for the establishment of an optimal design method. In establishing such a design method for adhesive joints, it is necessary to know a relationship between the stress distribution in joints and the joint strength. Up to now, some investigations have been carried out on butt, scarf and lap adhesive joints using the finite element method[1]-[4], the photoelastic[5] experiments and the theory of elasticity[6]-[9]. But the stress distributions of band adhesive joints, in which the adhesive efficiently resists external loads by bonding partially at the interface in comparison to the usual butt joints in which the adhesive is bonded completely at the interface, have yet been fully elucidated, expect for some investigations[11]. It is important to examine a relationship between the stress distribution and the joint strength in band adhesive joints.

The purpose of this study is to analyze the stress distribution in a band adhesive joint and to examine a relationship between the stress distribution and the joint strength, when the joint is subjected to an external bending moment. Four-point bending tests were performed 30 times in order to examine the joint strength. A statistic procedure is applied to the experimental results and the joint strength is determined experimentally. The stress distribution of the joints is analyzed using the two-dimensional theory of elasticity by replacing dissimilar adherends and an adhesive with finite strips. The effects of the ratio of Young's modulus of adherends to that of an adhesive, the thickness of the adhesive and the bonding area on the stress distributions at the interfaces between the adhesive and the adherends are clarified by numerical calculations. Experiments were performed concerning the strains of adherends. The numerical results are compared with the experimental ones. Moreover, a relationship between the joint strength and the stress distribution is discussed.

2. EXPERIMENTAL PROCEDURE

Four-point bending tests were performed 30 times for each band adhesive joint in order to examine the joint strength as shown in Fig.1. Figure 2(a) shows the dimensions of the specimens used in the experiments concerning the joints strength. In the interface of the specimen steps were manufactured the depth of 1mm in order to make a disbonded area, and two bonded areas were made. The dimensions of joint specimens in which the adhesives are bonded completely are the same of the band joint specimens. The specimens were manufactured from steel for structural use (S45C,JIS) and aluminum (A2017P,JIS). Six kinds of specimens (St-St, Al-Al, and St-Al) for band adhesive joints and butt adhesive joints (of which the interface was bonded completely) were prepared. After bonding and solidifying six kinds of specimens by epoxide bond (SUMITOMO 3M Co.,Ltd., Scotch-weld 1838) at room temperature, a bending moment was applied. Then, the joint strength was measured. In addition, experiments were performed concerning the strains produced on adherends. Figure 2 (b) shows the specimen used in the experiments concerning the strains on adherends. The specimens were manufactured from steel for structural use (S45C,JIS) and aluminum (A1080P,JIS), and strain gauges were attached to the position of 3mm from the interface. After bonding and solidifying a pair of dissimilar specimens by using an epoxide bond at room temperature, a bending moment was applied. Then, the strains of the adherends were measured.

3.THEORETICAL ANALYSIS

Figure 3 shows a band adhesive joint, in which two dissimilar finite strips are bonded partially at the interface in the region of $c-l_2 \leq x_1 \leq c+l_2$, and subjected to an external bending moment. In order to analyze the stress distributions at the interface between the adhesive and the adherends, two adherends are replaced with finite strips [I] and [III], and the adhesive with finite strip [II]. The length of finite strips [I] and [III] are designated by $2l_1$, their height by $2h_1$ and $2h_3$, their Young's modulus by E_1 and E_3, and their Poisson's ratio by ν_1 and ν_3, respectively. The characteristics of strip [II] are designated by $2l_2$, $2h_2$, E_2 and ν_2,respectively. It is assumed that the external bending

---

T.SAWA is Associate Professor in the department of mechanical engineering of Yamanashi University(4-3-11,Takeda,Kofu,Yamanashi,400 Japan). K. TEMMA is Associate Professor of Kisarazu National College of Technology. T. NISHIGAYA is a graduate student of Yamanashi University.

moments acting on the upper and the lower ends of the joints are replaced with symmetrically distributed stresses $F(x_1)$ and $G(x_3)$ with respect to the y_1 and y_3 axes in the range $x_1 \leq e_1$ on the upper surface of the strip[I] and $x_3 \leq e_3$ on the lower surface of the strip [III]. Expanding the distributions $F(x_1)$ and $G(x_3)$ into the Fourier series, the boundary conditions shown in Fig. 3, where the displacement in the x-direction is denoted by u, the displacement in the y-direction by v, and upper suffixes I, II and III correspond to finite strips [I], [II] and [III], respectively, are expressed as follows;

(i) on finite strip [I] (adherend)   (ii) on finite strip [II] (adhesive)

$$\left.\begin{array}{l} x_1 = \pm l_1 \ ; \ \sigma_x{}^{\mathrm{I}} = \tau_{xy}{}^{\mathrm{I}} = 0 \\[4pt] y_1 = h_1 \ \ ; \ \sigma_y{}^{\mathrm{I}} = F(x_1) = \sum\limits_{s=1}^{\infty} b_s{}^{\mathrm{I}} \sin\left(\dfrac{2s-1}{2l_1}\pi x_1\right) \\[4pt] \qquad \tau_{xy}{}^{\mathrm{I}} = 0 \\[4pt] y_1 = -h_1 \ ; \ \sigma_x{}^{\mathrm{I}} = \tau_{xy}{}^{\mathrm{I}} = 0 \ \ (|x_1| \leq -l_2 + c) \end{array}\right\}(1)$$

$$\left.\begin{array}{l} x_2 = \pm l_2 \ ; \ \sigma_x{}^{\mathrm{II}} = 0 \\[4pt] \qquad\qquad \tau_{xy}{}^{\mathrm{II}} = 0 \end{array}\right\}(2)$$

(iii) on finite strip [III] (adherend)   (iv) at the interface between finite strips [I] and [II]

$$\left.\begin{array}{l} x_3 = \pm l_3 \ ; \ \sigma_x{}^{\mathrm{III}} = \tau_{xy}{}^{\mathrm{III}} = 0 \\[4pt] y_3 = -h_3 \ ; \ \sigma_y{}^{\mathrm{III}} = G(x_3) = \sum\limits_{s=1}^{\infty} b_s{}^{\mathrm{III}} \sin\left(\dfrac{2s-1}{2l_1}\pi x_3\right) \\[4pt] \qquad \tau_{xy}{}^{\mathrm{III}} = 0 \\[4pt] y_3 = h_3 \ \ ; \ \sigma_x{}^{\mathrm{III}} = \tau_{xy}{}^{\mathrm{III}} = 0 \ \ (|x_3| \leq -l_2 + c) \end{array}\right\}(3)$$

$$\left.\begin{array}{l} (\sigma_y{}^{\mathrm{I}})_{y_1=-h_1} = (\sigma_y{}^{\mathrm{II}})_{y_2=h_2} \\[4pt] (\tau_{xy}{}^{\mathrm{I}})_{y_1=-h_1} = (\tau_{xy}{}^{\mathrm{II}})_{y_2=h_2} \\[4pt] \left(\dfrac{\partial u^{\mathrm{I}}}{\partial x_1}\right)_{y_1=-h_1} = \left(\dfrac{\partial u^{\mathrm{II}}}{\partial x_2}\right)_{y_2=h_2} \\[4pt] (v^{\mathrm{I}})_{y_1=-h_1} = (v^{\mathrm{II}})_{y_2=h_2} \\[4pt] (-l_2+c \leq |x_1| \leq l_2+c \ , \ |x_2| \leq l_2) \end{array}\right\}(4)$$

(v) at the interface between finite strips [II] and [III]   ,where

$$\left.\begin{array}{l} (\sigma_y{}^{\mathrm{II}})_{y_2=-h_2} = (\sigma_y{}^{\mathrm{III}})_{y_3=h_3} \\[4pt] (\tau_{xy}{}^{\mathrm{II}})_{y_2=-h_2} = (\tau_{xy}{}^{\mathrm{III}})_{y_3=h_3} \\[4pt] \left(\dfrac{\partial u^{\mathrm{II}}}{\partial x_2}\right)_{y_2=-h_2} = \left(\dfrac{\partial u^{\mathrm{III}}}{\partial x_3}\right)_{y_3=h_3} \\[4pt] (v^{\mathrm{II}})_{y_2=-h_2} = (v^{\mathrm{III}})_{y_3=h_3} \\[4pt] (-l_2+c \leq |x_3| \leq l_2+c \ , \ |x_2| \leq l_2) \end{array}\right\}(5)$$

$$b_s{}^{\mathrm{I}} = \frac{1}{l_1}\int_{-e_1}^{e_1} F(x_1)\sin\left(\frac{2s-1}{l_1}\pi x_1\right)dx_1$$

$$b_s{}^{\mathrm{III}} = \frac{1}{l_3}\int_{-e_3}^{e_3} G(x_3)\sin\left(\frac{2s-1}{l_1}\pi x_3\right)dx_3$$

$$(s = 1, 2, 3, \cdots\cdots)$$

$$M = \int_{-e_1}^{e_1} F(x_1)\cdot x_1\,dx_1 = \int_{-e_3}^{e_3} G(x_3)\cdot x_3\,dx_3$$

Each finite strip is analyzed as a three-body contact problem using Airy's stress functions which are selected from solutions for the method of variables.

4. ANALYTICAL RESULTS AND COMPARISONS BETWEEN EXPERIMENTAL AND ANALYTICAL RESULTS

4.1 Analytical Results

In the numerical calculations, stress singularity is caused at the edges of the interfaces ($y_2=\pm h_2$, $x_2=\pm l_2$). The number of terms in the series was taken as 50, so that a satisfactory convergence was expected. Each stress was obtained until the points of 0.4% inside the bonded parts. Figure 4 shows the effect of Young's modulus on the maximum principal stress distribution at the interfaces $y_2=+h_2$ and $y_2=-h_2$, where the ratio E_1/E_3 was held constant at 3 and the ratio E_1/E_2 was varied as 5, 10 and 60. The abscissa is the ratio of the distance x_1 to the half length l_1 of the adherend and the ordinate is the ratio of the maximum principal stress σ_1 to the maximum value P of $F(x_1)$. In Fig.4, it was assumed that the bending moments act linearly on the upper($y_1=h_1$) and the lower($y_3=-h_3$) surfaces in the region $x_1 \leq l_1$ ($F(x_1)=G(x_3)$) and the bonded regions are put as $l_2=0.2l_1$, $c=0.8l_1$. From the results, it is seen that singular stresses occur at the edges of the interfaces and that the maximum principal stress σ_1 increases near the edge of the interface with an increase of the ratio E_1/E_2. Figure 5 shows the effect of the ratio E_1/E_3 of Young's modulus of adherends. The ratio E_1/E_2 was held constant at 60 and the ratio E_1/E_3 was varied as 1, 3 and 10. The ratio $E_1/E_3=1$ means the case where adherends are similar material. The maximum principal stress near the point $x_1/l_1=1.0$ at the interface ($y_2=h_2$) increases with an increase of the E_1/E_3 and near the point $x_1/l_1=1.0$ at the interface $y_2=-h_2$ it increases with a decrease of the ratio E_1/E_3. From the results, it is predicted that the joint's fracture occurs at the interface of which Young's modulus of the adherend is larger and that the joint strength in the case where adherends are dissimilar is smaller than that in the case where adherends are similar. Figure 6 shows the effect of the thickness $2h_2$ of the adhesive layer, where $h_1=h_3$, the ratio h_1/h_2 was varied as 50, 100 and 200, and E_1/E_3 was 3 and $E_1/E_2=60$. The stress singularity at the edge of the interface increases with an increase of the ratio h_1/h_2. Figure 7 shows the effect of the bonding areas. In the figure, the ordinate is the ratio σ_1/P of the maximum principal stress σ_1 to the maximum value P of $F(x_1)$. The value of c is put as $c=l_1-l_2$ and the ratio of $2l_2/l_1$ is put as 1.0 (bonded completely at the interface), 0.6 and 0.4. From the results, it is seen that the stress distribution in the case where the value of $2l_2/l_1$ is 0.6 is similar to the case where the value of $2l_2/l_1$ is 1.0 (bonding completely at the interface). Thus, it is expected that a band adhesive joint in which the interface is bonded partially efficiently resists external loads in comparison to the case where the interface is bonded completely.

4.2 Comparison of the numerical results with the experimental ones

Figure 8 shows a comparison of the numerical results with the experimental ones with respect to the strains on the adherend in the y-direction produced at the positions (y_1=-4.5mm, y_3=4.5mm) situated 3mm from the interface. The ordinate is the strain of the specimen in the y_1-direction and the y_3-direction, and the abscissa is the distance x_1 from the center of the specimen. A solid line represents the numerical results and the mark O represents the experimental results. In the numerical calculations, the material constants E_1 and ν_1 were put as 206GPa, and 0.3 (steel), E_3 and ν_3 as 68.7GPa and 0.3 (aluminum), respectively. Those of the adhesive layer were put as 3.6GPa and 0.38 and $2h_2$ was measured as 0.0055mm. It is seen that the analytical results are fairly consistent with the experimental ones.

4.3 Joint strength

Table 1 shows a comparison between the analytical and the experimental results concerning the joint strength. The experiments were performed 30 times using the specimens shown in Fig.2. Figure 9 shows the normal probability distributions of the joint strength in the case where the adherends are dissimilar. The ordinate is cumulative probability and the abscissa is a bending moment (the joint strength). The joint strength was determined when 5% of the specimens subjected to bending moments were ruptured, that is, 95% of the specimens were not ruptured. In order to predict the joint strength theoretically, experiments concerning the adhesive strength were performed using hollow cylinder specimens[12]. From the experiments, the adhesive strength σ_a was 47.4 MPa in the case where adherends were St and St, 43.9 MPa in the case where adherends are Al and Al ,and 41.2 MPa in the case where adherends were St and Al. In this study, it is assumed that joint fracture occurs when the maximum principal stress near the edges of interfaces (0.4% inside the bonded parts) becomes to equal the adhesive strength. The maximum principal stress theory and the maximum distortion energy theory (Mises's criterion) were used in order to evaluate the joint strength. From Table 1, it is seen that the analytical results due to the maximum principal stress theory were consistent with the experimental ones and the evaluation by Mises were larger than the experimental results. It is expected that the strength of a band adhesive joint in which the interface is bonded partially is approximately the same of a butt adhesive joint in which the interface is bonded completely.

5.CONCLUSIONS

This paper dealt with a stress analysis and an evaluation of joint strength in band adhesive butt joints of dissimilar thin plates subjected to bending moments. The following results were obtained.
(1) Experiments concerning the strains on adherends and four-point bending tests were carried out. A statistic procedure was applied to the experimental results and the joint strength was determined.
(2) Replacing adherends and an adhesive with finite strips, the stress distributions at the interface were analyzed using the two-dimensional theory of elasticity (plane strain).
(3) The effects of the ratios of Young's moduli among adherends and an adhesive and the thickness of the adhesive layer on the stress distributions at the interfaces were shown by the numerical calculations using the method mentioned (2). As a result, it was seen that with an increase of the ratio E_1/E_2 and the ratio h_1/h_2, the stress increased at the edge of the interface.
(4)The joint strength was evaluated based on the maximum principal stress theory and Mises's criterion using the stress distributions obtained by the analysis. It was demonstrated that the evaluations by the maximum principal stress theory were consistent with the experimental results.
(5) It was seen that when a bonding area was determined taking into account an external load distribution, it might be possible that the band adhesive joint had the same strength as the case where the interface was bonded completely. In addition, it was seen that the joint strength in the case where adherends were dissimilar was smaller than that in the case where adherends were similar.

REFERENCES

(1) Baker,R.M. and Hatt,f., AIAA J., Vol.11, No.12(1973), p.1650.
(2) Sen,J.K. and Jones,R.M.,AIAA J., VOl.18, No.11(1980), p.1376.
(3) Adams,R.D., Harris,J.A., Int. J. Adhesion and adhesives, vol.7, No.2(1987), p.69.
(4) Suzuki,Y., Bull. of the JSME, VOl.27, No.231(1984), p.1836.
(5) Chow,C.L.,Woo, Int. Cong. Exp. Mech., (1984), p.256.
(6) Erdogan,F. and Ratwani,M., J.composite Materials, 5(1971), p.378.
(7) Wah,T., Int. J. Mech. Soci., 18(1976), p.223.
(8) Renton,W.J., J.adhesion, 10(1979), p.1.
(9) Sawa,T., Nakano,Y., Temma,K., J.adhesion, 24(1987), p.1.
(10) Sawa,T., Iwata,A. and Ishikawa,H., Bull. JSME, Vol.29, No.258(1986), p.4030.
(11) J.Pirvics, J.Adhesion, 6(1974), p.207.
(12) Sawa,T. and Kobayashi,T., Int. Cong. Exp. Mech., (1988), p.630.

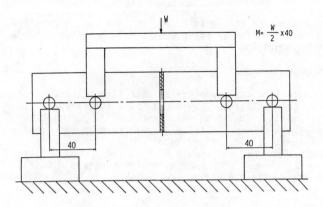

$M = \dfrac{W}{2} \times 40$

Fig.1 Setup of experimental apparatus

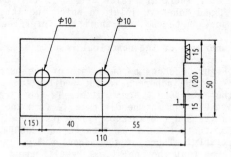

(a) A specimen used in experiment concerning joint strength

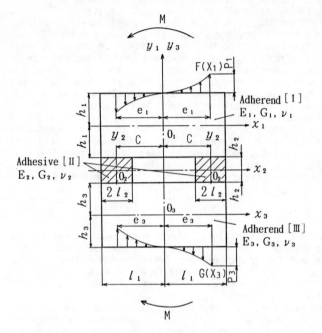

Fig.3 A band adhesive butt joint subjected to a bending moment

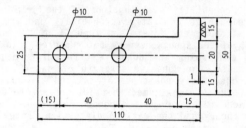

(b) A specimen used in experiment concerning strains

Fig.2 Dimensions of specimens used in experiments

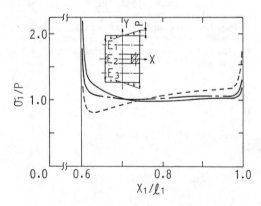

(a) maximum principal stress ($y_2 = h_2$)

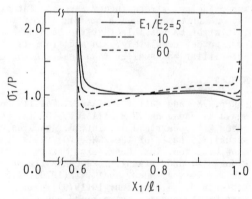

(b) maximum principal stress ($y_2 = -h_2$)

Fig.4 Effect of ratio of Young's modulus among adherends and an adhesive on stress distribution ($E_1/E_3 = 3$)

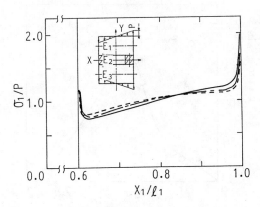

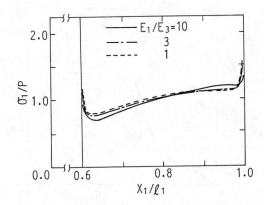

(a) maximum principal stress
$(y_2=h_2)$

(b) maximum principal stress
$(y_2=-h_2)$

Fig.5 Effect of ratio of Young's modulus of adherends
on stress distribution $(E_1/E_2=60)$

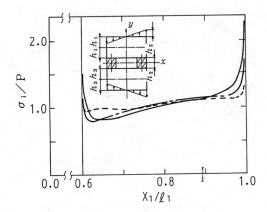

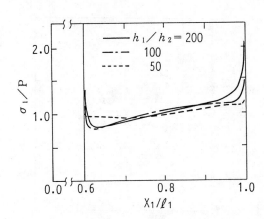

(a) maximum principal stress
$(y_2=h_2)$

(b) maximum principal stress
$(y_2=-h_2)$

Fig.6 Effect of the thickness of adhesive on
maximum principal stress distribution

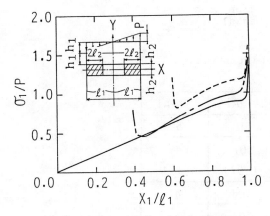

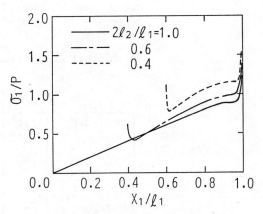

(a) maximum principal stress
$(y_2=h_2)$

(b) maximum principal stress
$(y_2=-h_2)$

Fig.7 Effect of the bonding areas on maximum
stress distribution at the interface

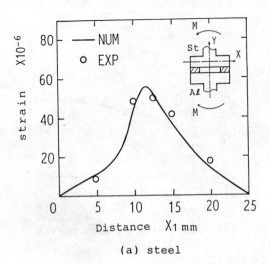

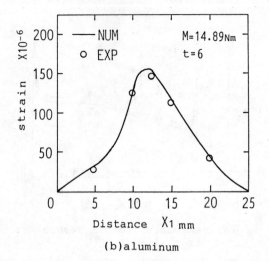

(a) steel

(b)aluminum

Fig.8 Comparisons between analytical and
experimental results

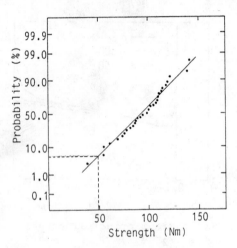

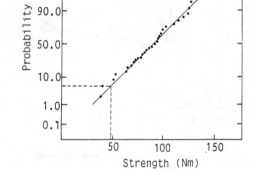

(a) butt adhesive joint
(interface is bonded completely)

(b) band adhesive joint

Fig.9 Normal probability distribution concerning
the joint strength (experiments)

Table.1 Comparisons of the joint strength

(Nm)

		St-St	Al-Al	St-Al
completed adhesion $(2l_2/l_1=1.0)$	EXP	123	110	50
	NUM	118 (329)	107 (297)	48 (134)
Band Adhesion $(2l_2/l_1=0.6)$	EXP	120	108	47
	NUM	116 (299)	104 (269)	44 (119)

(   ) is the value by Mises's criterion